The Beer-Taster's Log

A *World Guide to more than 6000 Beers*

by James D. Robertson
Foreword by Fred Eckhardt

A Storey Publishing Book

STOREY

Storey Communications, Inc.
Schoolhouse Road
Pownal, Vermont 05261

The mission of Storey Communications is to serve our customers by publishing practical information that encourages personal independence in harmony with the environment.

Edited by Elizabeth McHale and Nancy Ringer
Cover design by Randy Mosher
Text design and production by Greg Imhoff and Therese G. Lenz
Production assistance by Cindy McFarland, Allison Cranmer, and Susan Bernier

Much of the material in this book previously appeared in an annual directory entitled *The Beer Log,* Bosak Publications, 1992, 1993, 1994, and 1995.

Printed in the United States by R. R. Donnelley
10 9 8 7 6 5 4 3 2 1

Library of Congress Cataloging-in-Publication Data

Robertson, James Donald, 1935–
    The beer-taster's log : a world guide to more than 6000 beers / by
James D. Robertson : foreword by Fred Eckhardt.
        p.   cm.
    "A Storey Publishing book."
    Includes index.
    ISBN 0-88266-939-7 (pbk : alk. paper)
    1. Beer.   I. Title
TP577.R578   1996
641.2'3 --dc20   96-15284
                                                                    CIP

Contents

Foreword

I first met Jim Robertson in 1993 at a homebrewers' festival in Temecula, California, where he was promoting his newest book, *A Beer Drinker's Guide to Southern Germany.* For many years I had been familiar with his work, from the *Great American Beer Book* in 1978 through several incarnations of *The Connoisseur's Guide to Beer,* beginning in 1982. These were especially helpful in my own research, particularly for their listings of the addresses of many of the world's breweries. His career working for the U.S. government in Europe had given him wide latitude to travel and experience the wonder of Europe, which is at least as much gastronomic as it is scenic, architectural, and historical. An old proverb tells us: "If you can't eat it or drink it, don't buy it." On his travels, Jim seems to have done much eating and drinking, and, oddly, never to have gained so much as a pound, something I envy him for. As for us, Robertson offers readers so much information (over 6000 brews in this book), we may find it hard to digest. Nevertheless, let me urge you to make the attempt.

A Brief History of Beer

Early peoples first made beer using only grains, which are composed mostly of starch. They developed a system of steeping grains in cold water to start the sprouting process and then stopping it by heating the grains to dry them. This process, called malting, produces enzymes which allow grains to convert their starches into fermentable sugars. It was found that these partially converted grains could be steeped in warm water to reactivate the conversion process and the resultant "wort" would (if allowed) ferment to make beer. These methods originated in the ancient middle eastern empires of Mesopotamia, Babylon, and Egypt.

The Revolution

The Europeans found this system flawed in many ways, most importantly because if the beer were to be stored over any long period it would sour, unless it were made very strong. Strong beer was dangerous but weak beer soured early, and those who drank only water tended to die young. Experiments using various herbs showed that some of them were effective in slowing the souring process, but it wasn't until the ninth century that hops began to be used for this purpose. The addition of hops, the first true revolution in brewing, became more and more popular, so that by the fifteenth century English brewers were starting to use them and by the eighteenth century most European beer was made using hops. The beers of this time were bitter and often heavy. In the sixteenth century, authorities had begun to assert control over brewing methods. The Reinheitsgebot purity law of 1516 discouraged the use of wheat in brewing, and while this was only partially successful, barley emerged as the dominant ingredient in beer. Temperature control was instituted in the malting process, allowing the production of comparatively pale beers, especially pale ale. Improved production methods brought about increased clarity in the finished product, and the so-called **India Pale Ale** (IPA) became the hallmark of this era.

The Smooth Revolution

In the eighth or ninth century, Bavarian monastic brewers began storing their excess winter beer in naturally cool caves for consumption during the summer months. Before long they found that this cool-aged beer improved significantly in drinkability and mellowness. Soon they were packing their storage caves with ice harvested from surrounding lakes to further improve the product. Such cold-aged beer was called **lager** beer from the German word *lagern,* to store.

By the early nineteenth century, this system had been institutionalized by some brewers. The yeast they used came to be called "bottom-fermenting" or "cold-fermenting" yeast, because it worked through the body of the fermenting beer and then settled to the bottom of the vessel, where it could be harvested. At such cold temperatures, this bottom fermentation worked much more slowly, taking longer for the yeast to react, with the result that the finished beer was smoother, needed fewer hops, and could be brewed to a lower alcohol content. This made for a very mellow product, a variety greatly appreciated for its smooth drinkability and less bitter taste. These brewers became famous, and their brewing systems were copied widely across Europe and North America.

Most notable among them were the brewers at Plzen in what was then Bohemia (now the Czech Republic), a part of the old Austro-Hungarian Empire. A number of Plzen brewers formed a company to create an entirely new method of brewing resulting in a truly revolutionary product. First, it was brewed from very pale malts, much paler than those used in the English IPA type of brew; second, it was cold-fermented in the new Bavarian style with a lower alcohol and hop content; and third, it was served up in the new and beautiful glassware just then being popularized in Bohemia. The result was **Plzen Urquel** (Pilsner Original), a stunning success. Within 50 years the Pilsner-style beer had become the most imitated beer style on the planet. Brewers competed to make paler, mellower, and less hoppy beers, which spawned even paler, more mellow, nearly hop-free beers. The Pils style, as it came to be called, was the first **world** beer style.

More importantly, the proliferation of these new bottom- and cold-fermented lager beers reduced the variety of beers available to much of the world market. By the end of the nineteenth century, beers had come to be categorized by their style, such as Pilsner, porter, stout, Munchner, Dortmunder, pale ale, and others.

By 1950, the American version of the Pilsner type beer, brewed with additional grains (called adjuncts) such as corn or rice had become dominant around the world. The brewers of Canada, Australia, Mexico, South America, Asia, and much of Europe, including some in England and Germany, brewed their beer with grain adjuncts, along the American model. In the United States, the old styles were disappearing. There remained only the American version of lager beer and a few ales. Beer was either dark or light colored, and it was all bland. Moreover, brewers began to hire marketing people, who concluded that Americans didn't like beer and, therefore, less taste would be better for the product. They invented malt liquor (less taste, more alcohol), light beer (less taste, lower calories), and followed with dry beer (less taste and aftertaste). There was even color-free beer.

As early as 1934, it was useless to categorize most beer on the market in the United States, by any particular style. People began to search for beer using the country of origin as a style definition. Thus we looked to Canada, Australia, England, Germany, and Mexico if we wished to find beer with more taste or a different style. Unfortunately, the brewers of these countries were busy copying American brewers. It only seemed like their beer was different.

The Great Beer Counter-Revolution

By 1972, some British beer enthusiasts had become alarmed at the Americanization of their beer, and they formed an organization called CAMRA (**Cam**paign for **R**eal **A**le) in an effort to stop the mongrelization of their favorite beverage. Some Americans were alarmed, as well. San Francisco's Anchor Brewery, the last steam brewery in the world and America's smallest small brewery, had been rescued from bankruptcy in 1965 by Fritz Maytag, who set about brewing a purist's version of traditional steam beer. Maytag soon proved that small could be successful, and others took up the challenge.

In 1976, CAMRA member Michael Jackson, a British journalist, published his *World Guide to Beer,* based on the great beer styles of the world. It was a stunningly impressive book, with beautiful color photographs, maps, and labels. The book was an introduction and guide for brewers, wholesalers, importers, and most particularly for beer enthusiasts in the United States. This book generated an incredible surge of interest in all of the beers described. This development led an American importer, Charles Finkel, and his Merchant du Vin

Company of Seattle, Washington, to become the first American entrepreneur to import beer by its style. People no longer searched to find beer from obscure countries; rather, they sought obscure beer **styles**.

Small brewers, calling themselves microbrewers, began to appear. The brewpub phenomenon, consisting of pubs, restaurants, and taverns, with their own breweries, was revived. These new craft brewers were successful because they brewed in greater variety, adopting beer styles of old Europe and adding their own variations, in effect inventing their own beer styles.

In 1976 there remained only 48 brewers in the United States, and they all brewed pretty much the same product. Predictions were made that fewer than ten breweries would remain by the year 2000. Now, in 1996, there are about 850 breweries and brewpubs in operation, and by the year 2000, according to Jim Robertson, there may be about 2,000 breweries on these golden shores. He may be right, for we've come a long way in the last 24 years. We are presently leading the world in this endeavor, not only in the preservation of imperiled beer styles but also in the invention of new beer types.

Even more important is the fact that others around the globe are beginning to follow this example and are starting their own small breweries and brewpubs. To bring this to full fruition, we will soon have to search for beer once again "by-the-country," because before long we'll have Mexican stouts, German stouts, Bulgarian stouts, and Japanese stouts, as we already have American stouts, Canadian stouts, Australian stouts, African stouts, Malaysian and Caribbean stouts, not to mention chocolate stouts, coffee stouts, raspberry stouts, and bourbon stouts.

Thus, this book is organized by continent and country, rather than the soon-to-be-outmoded beer-by-style system. However, let us explore the wonderful world of beer-by-the-style, to provide you the reader with some background information.

Lager Beer

We are at the beginning of an era, where for the first time in history almost all of the world's brewers have access to the information and ingredients necessary to produce any, or all, of the world's beer styles. Large American brewing companies are starting to make some beers from their own past. A good example of this is Anheuser-Busch. Not only have they bought an interest in a major U.S. microbrewery (actually ex-microbrewery), Red Hook of Seattle, but they are delving into their own files to re-create some of their late nineteenth-century successes. They are currently marketing a porter, a Munich dark, and a marvelous re-creation of a late nineteenth-century amber lager with at least three times the hop content of Budweiser itself.

An understanding of beer styles stems from knowledge of the characteristics of individual brews. Taste and color tell us much of what we need to know to identify or define a beer's style, but we also want to know its ingredients, strength, hop content, and production method. Most of these beers in this book are actually brewed to styles we call "American" or "European" lager. These are all descendants of Pilsner Urquel, the original beer of Plzen. Until just a few years ago, that beer had maintained its production integrity very much as it was brewed in the late nineteenth century. It was a bottom-fermented, cold-aged lager beer brewed from very pale, malted, two-row Continental barley. This is very special barley that has only two rows

of grain on its stem, whereas in the United States our most popular barley is an easily cultivated six-row variety that has much greater starch conversion enzyme power and more protein than its two-row counterpart. It was discovered early on that this greater protein content caused problems in brewing brilliantly clear beer such as that from Bohemia. However, since six-row barley has extra enzyme power, it was found that other cheaper grains could be substituted for it in part with relatively small impact on the finished product. These additional grains (corn and rice were the most popular) were used sparingly (20%) before prohibition. More recently American lager has strayed further and further from its European roots and has come to be brewed with large amounts (over 45%) of these adjuncts.

Pilsner Urquel is brewed to an original gravity (the density of the beer wort before the addition of yeast) of 12 Plato. Original gravity is usually expressed in "degrees Plato," a percent value showing the fermentable sugar content of that wort that is available for conversion to alcohol by the yeast. Original gravity (OG), then, is a factor of the beer's strength, a glimpse of what may be possible. In some countries this is expressed as specific gravity (SG), a measure of the weight of a liquid in comparison to the weight of an equal volume of water. Beer is heavier than water, which has a specific gravity of 1.000, and thus has a higher specific gravity. The amount by which the SG of beer is greater than the SG of water can be estimated as one one-thousandth of its 1:4 relationship with original gravity; the SG of beer is one plus one one-thousandth of its original gravity multiplied by four. This may sound complicated, but really it's quite simple: specific gravity = 1 + ([degrees Plato x 4]/1000). Thus, the specific gravity of Pilsner Urquel is 1 + (.004 x 12) = 1.048; any amount of Pilsner Urquel weighs 1.048 times as much as an equal amount of water.

The ingredients in beer often have different fermentation capabilities, and therefore they have a salient effect on the most important strength quantifier, the beer's alcohol content. The strength of Pilsner Urquel is 3.5% alcohol by weight (abw) or 4.3% alcohol by volume (abv). Why are two figures used to express the same thing? The difference is based on the fact that the specific gravity of water is 1.000, while that of alcohol is 0.796. This means that alcohol weighs only 79.6% as much as water and is therefore, lighter than water. The percentage of alcohol content by weight is thus less than the percentage of alcohol content by volume; the abw of a beer is equal to 79.6% of its abv. In the case of Pilsner Urquel, .796 x .043(abv) = .035, or 3.5% abw.

Another factor in the study of a particular beer is its hop quotient. Hops add a piquant effect to the beer. Their aroma gives the beer much of its character and their bittering elements add another dimension to its taste. The aromatic elements in beer are not readily quantified, but we can gain information about what to expect by knowing the variety of hops used. In the case of Pilsner Urquel, this is a hop variety, called Saaz. The bitterness level gained from these hops, however, can be measured. Bitterness is measured in International Bitterness Units (IBU), units of weight equal to one part per million (ppm) of an alpha acid called isohumulone, the bittering agent in hops, in the finished beer. Different varieties of hops can contain and/or release into the wort varying levels of isohumulone. For example, 43 ppm iso-alpha acid has been incorporated into Pilsner Urquel, expressed simply as 43 IBU.

Another element in the study of individual beers is color. Color can be analyzed and measured, but it is much simpler to record the color as ranging from light, pale, and dark straw; light, pale, dark, and very dark amber; and "black" (actually very dark brown) beer. Pilsner Urquel's brilliant straw color is a result of a particular grain malting system, which dries the malted grains at relatively low temperatures. Darker beers use, in addition to pale malts, a portion of malts that have been roasted or dried at very high temperatures .

To summarize: Pilsner Urquel is a straw colored beer with 12 Plato or 1.048 original gravity, 4.3% abv and 43 IBU. The fact that there is only 4.3% alcohol content by volume tells us that there is a modest amount of unfermentable goods in the beer, and that is indeed the case. These unfermentables, called extract, are mostly complex sugars, or dextrins; they give the beer its great taste and a somewhat full mouth-feel, called body. If the quantity of extract were greater, the beer might taste too sweet and be weaker in alcohol content. If it were smaller, it might taste dry (less sweet) and be stronger in alcohol content.

Modern American Lager

As we have already noted, American lager was copied from the original Pilsner Urquel and modified through the years. Today, most American lager is based on the most successful beer in the world: **Budweiser**. In the beginning Budweiser was patterned after **Budweiss**, a Bohemian brew from Budvar in what is now the Czech Republic. This original Budweiss had an original gravity of 11.3 P (1.045), 4.4% abv, and about 35 IBU (our guess, since they couldn't measure bitterness in those early days). Budweiss was brewed by methods similar to those employed to make Pilsner Urquel. Anheuser-Busch's Budweiser, as it is today, has an original gravity of 11 P (1.044), 4.7% abv, and 8–10 IBU, making it considerably less bitter, a bit drier in taste, and a little paler in color than its progenitor. In addition, Budweiser uses about 35% rice in its makeup, a blend of American hops with some imported Saaz, and a mixture of two- and six-row American barley. Most modern American lagers differ little from this recipe except in small details such as adjuncts used, malt-to-adjunct ratios, hops, and, of course, price. Many of America's large brewers have shamelessly copied this one beer type, following the guidelines set forth in 1977 by the Master Brewers Association of the Americas (MBAA): original gravity 10.7–12.1 P (1.043–1.048), 3.9–4.9% abv, and 10–23 IBU. Most of the world's brewers make their beer within these parameters. Those who don't (mostly European brewers) depart from them only in their bitterness levels, which range from about 18–35 IBU for the most part. These beers are sometimes called **Pils**, **Continental Lagers**, or **International Lagers**. A few brewers attempt to make authentic 100% malt (all-malt) lagers by shunning adjuncts, but they continue to follow the parameters outlined above, differing only in specific malt and hop combinations.

Malt Liquor, Light Beer, Dry Beer, and Ice Beer

These beer styles have the American lager in their roots. Many states have laws limiting the alcohol content of beer — they don't allow a beer with more than 5% abv to be called beer. The brewer then has to find another name for his product. The most popular name used is **Malt Liquor**. Malt liquors are lagers too, but they are stronger than their American lager cousins because: (1) they start at a higher gravity; (2) the beer is fermented more thoroughly, sometimes by the addition of special enzymes, to convert more of the extract to alcohol; and (3) these beers usually have a lower hop content, with bitterness less than 8 IBU. The net result is usually a pale, straw-colored insipid brew. Occasionally a good European beer is imported into the United States; since these brews often have alcohol levels of just over 5% abv, they too must be classified as "malt liquor." Such labels are the kiss-of-death to a good beer, so most European brewers simply add water to the beers they send to the United States. This has the effect of lowering the alcohol to less than 5% abv, diluting the color, and reducing the hop levels a bit. In this way they become more acceptable to the U.S. market.

Light Beer, or low-calorie beer, is brewed to have fewer calories. Since there are 7.1 calories for each gram of alcohol, it is the major calorie contributor in beer. Brewers add water to light beer to reduce the alcohol content somewhat, nearer to 4% than 5% abv, or employ a special enzyme to change the unfermentable dextrins to fermentable sugars, thus allowing the addition of even more water. The conversion of dextrins leaves these beers with very little taste.

Dry Beer, invented by the Japanese, is similar to light beer. The intent was to limit the aftertaste, a factor of the dextrin content of beer. In dry beer, dextrins are also converted to fermentable sugars, but it is higher in alcohol content than light beer because no water is added. Brewers need fewer ingredients to make this beer as strong as regular beer.

Ice Beer was invented by the Canadians. The theory is that if one slightly freezes beer and then removes the ice crystals, the flavor and alcohol content will be concentrated. Original ice beer was Eisbock, a strong European beer that had an immensely concentrated flavor and alcohol content. Ice beer found in the marketplace today has less flavor because it originates from the relatively bland American lager.

Great Lager Styles of Central Europe

Many other great lager styles began in Central Europe. Dortmund, a great brewing city in north Germany, originated a pale lager style, which became famous as the **Dortmund Lager** in the later part of the last century, but its popularity had faded by the end of World War II. This style is currently being revived by many craft lager brewers. Dortmund beer (called "export" in Europe) is a bit heavier than Pils (12.5–14.9 P; 1.050–61 SG), slightly less hoppy at 24–37 IBU, and a bit drier from a more complete ferment than Pils or American. This beer is also a little darker because Dortmund malt has a slightly higher drying temperature than Pils malt.

The original dark lager was the **Munich** (or **Bavarian) style**. Munich lagers are very flavorful, rich in maltiness, modest in alcohol content (4.8–6.3% abv), mellow in hoppiness (18–25 IBU), and dark to very dark amber colored from the use of Munich malt, which has a higher drying temperature than Pils malt. While dark beers have only recently again become very popular in the United States, the Munich lager style has been copied across the world.

American dark lagers are very similar to the American Pils–style described above. They are not as dark as Munich beers in color, not quite as hoppy, and are sometimes brewed as regular pale lagers with brewer's caramel coloring added, instead of dark malts, to darken their color. In a similar vein, **bock beer** (a dark, bottom-fermented beer originating from Einbeck, Germany in the mid-thirteenth century, which according to German standards has 1.064 SG, 16 P, and 6% abv) in the United States is often the brewery's regular lager with the addition of caramel color. These days, craft brewers are brewing their bock beers to the more traditional higher German standards.

Other beer styles similar to the Bavarian are the closely related **Kulmbach** and **Einbeck types**, slightly darker and heavier lagers than the classic Munich style.

Between the two world wars, Munich and Bavarian brewers began experimenting with pale beers similar to those becoming popular in the rest of the world at that time. The resulting Munich style was very pale in color but otherwise similar in makeup to regular Munich darks. This Munich brew has overtaken its precursor and dominates the modern Bavarian market to the extent that today one has trouble finding a good Munich dark in that city.

Another popular nineteenth-century lager beer style is the recently revived **amber lager**, a beer type originating from Vienna that is a bit stronger than Pils or Munich. It is an amber beer made with malt that has been kiln dried at temperatures lower than those used for Munich malt yet higher than those used in Plzen and Dortmund. Generic amber lager is usually brewed at regular beer strengths, while the **Vienna lager** itself is a bit stronger at about 13.5 P (1.055) OG, with 5% abv, and 32–40 IBU. Many of the world's seasonal beers are made as Vienna lagers, particularly **Oktoberfest** and holiday fest-beers.

Ale Is Beer, Too

As noted earlier most of the beers described in this book are American or European lager types, but the old ways are returning. Ale is making a comeback, and a good thing too, because without ale the new brewing revolution would have been delayed for another ten years or so, or might never have happened at all. Let me explain: a lager brewer needs about three or four times as much beer storage space as an ale brewer, plus good temperature control. This translates into at least twice the cost and twice the space needed for the brewery. Many of our most successful microbrewers could not have been started, never mind become successful, if they had brewed only lager beer. That means there would have been no New Albion (Sonoma, CA), the first true microbrewery in the United States, which, although failing itself, showed others the idea was sound. (There would have been no Sierra Nevada, no Red Hook, no Full Sail, and no Widmer.) Numerous immensely successful craft ale brewers started on a shoestring (production less than 1,800 U.S. beer barrels their first years) and probably never would have managed it without brewing ale-beer instead of lager-beer. Ale-beer is the cornerstone of modern new craft brewing.

So just what constitutes an ale, anyway? Well, in its present-day incarnation, ale is warm, top-fermented (meaning yeast rises to the top of the fermenting mixture to be skimmed) beer, sometimes aged, and sometimes not aged at all. Using modern brewing methods, ale brewers can formulate their beer from ingredients similar to those used in lager production, allowing them to attain the same advantages that brought nineteenth-century lager brewers such huge success. Today's ales can be very pale in color, modestly hopped, and reasonably low in alcohol content. The advantage of these new ales is that, because of their fast brewing cycles, they have more assertive taste elements. You know you are drinking beer when you taste an ale, and after nearly a century of lager beer degradation, taste is a welcome element in new craft brews.

Golden Ale

The most popular of the new ale types is golden or blond ale, similar in taste and construction to American and European lagers. Golden and blond ales (sometimes called American ales or American pale ales) are regular strength beers (10–12.5 P, 1.040–1.050 SG, 3.5–5% abv, and usually less than 20 IBU). Almost all American craft brewers shun adjuncts in these ales and brew 100% all-malt brews.

Pale Ale

The next most popular group of imports and new craft beers is a direct contribution from the British. These are pale ales, regular strength beers that are darker in color (pale to dark amber or copper) and usually hoppier (20–50 IBU). Pale ales are brewed with pale malt (usually two-row), often imported from England, plus a variety of dark malts (high-temperature kiln-dried malts), such as amber malt and brown malt (frequently called "chocolate" malt). Occasionally a bit of roast malt is added as well. English pale ales are frequently hopped with English style hops, such as East Kent Goldings, Fuggles, and Bullions, but American variants use Cascades, Willamettes, and other American specialty hops or even Continental hops. The best pale ales are brewed with very hard water. Substyles of pale ale are often labeled **bitter**, **best bitter**, and **extra special bitter** (ESB); comparable brews are also called **amber ale**, **red ale**, or **Irish ale**. **Scottish ales** are similar to pale ales but differ by being a little darker in color and having more maltiness from dark caramel or crystal malt, an occasional hint of butterscotch flavor, and less bitterness. They are often a bit higher in extract, giving them a tad more sweetness in their makeup. Some Scottish ales are weaker in alcohol content as well.

Brown Ales

Brown ale is very dark amber beer brewed with pale malt (the major ingredient in almost all beers, light or dark), some roast malts, and caramel (crystal) malt.

English mild ales, rarely found in the United States, are brown ales (OG 7–9 P, 1.028–36, 3–4% abv, and 14–20 IBU) with great taste (particularly when compared with tasteless U.S. low-calorie brews). Only one U.S. craft brewer brews a mild ale with wide distribution: **Grant's Celtic Ale** from Washington State.

What has come to be called **English brown ale** is similar to mild ale but slightly stronger (OG 10–12 P, 1.040–48, 4–5% abv, and 15–25 IBU). There is occasionally a touch of diacetyl (butterscotch) in its taste. **American brown ales** are stronger (10–14 P, 1.040–55; 4–5.5% abv), hoppier (25–60 IBU), and sometimes darker from more roast malt, but never do they contain any diacetyl. Beers called **dark ales**, **red ales**, and **Irish ales** may be closely related to these or to the English brown ale group.

Porter

Another ale beer is porter, a black beer first created in 1732 in London. These beers have OG 10–15 P (1.040–60), 4–6% abv, with a wide-ranging bitterness of 20–50 IBU. There are also lager porters, which are not as dark or hoppy as ale porters. Porters tend to be brewed with black malt and can have some molasses or licorice in their makeup.

Stout

Dry Stout is an ale type that covers a wide range of gravities, strengths, and tastes. Stout evolved from porter in the nineteenth century when Guinness first produced a stout-porter. Its strength ranges from OG 9–13 P, 1.036–52 up to OG 18 P, 1.074 for **Foreign Extra Stout** or **Double Stout**, with 30 to 100 IBU, and in color they are very dark brown, almost black. Stouts often use roast barley rather than the black malts called for in porter. Other popular stout styles include **sweet stout**, **milk stout** (sweetened with lactose, an unfermentable sugar), **lager stout** (sometimes called cream stout), and **oatmeal stout** (brewed with a small amount of flaked oats). There is also the closely related **Deutsche Porter**, a strong (17 P) lager porter brewed in Eastern European countries. Stout also takes kindly to flavoring elements such as coffee, raspberry, and chocolate.

Belgian Yeast

All beer yeasts have unique character. In the nineteenth century when yeasts began to be identified and classified, it was discovered that most ale beers were actually the result of a ferment of a group of ale yeasts. In contrast, lager brewers were developing, isolating, and using single strains — pure yeast strains. During prohibition in the United States (1919–1933), American brewers put their yeast in yeast banks where they were preserved for future use. This process produced pure yeast strains for all branches of brewing. U.S. beers in the post-prohibition period were considered more sterile or "clean." British and German brewers "cleaned up" their yeasts during and after World War II, but the Belgians resisted this trend. To this day, Belgian beers have a very unique taste, exacerbated by the use of more than one yeast — sometimes as many as three different yeasts: one for the major ferment, one for the aging cycle, and another in the bottle (for bottle-conditioned beers). Belgian top-fermenting yeast strains often impart startlingly different flavor profiles to their beers. If you were tasting your first

Belgian ale, you might think there was a flaw in the beer.

Belgian ales are lower in bitterness (15–35 IBU) than British and American ales and employ different blends of English, German, Czech, Yugoslavian, and Belgian hops. Belgian brewers sometimes add special brewing sugars that impart their own unique flavor. Some of the brown and red ales, especially those from Flanders, are particularly special with a tart sweet-sour finish. There is also a special Belgian type called **Saison**, a regular strength ale spring-brewed for winter consumption, ranging from golden amber to copper in color.

Hybrid Ferment Beers

In addition to top- and bottom-fermented beers, there are hybrid styles composed of elements from both brewing systems. Most of the hybrid styles are the result of brewers attempting to brew lager beers using top-fermenting yeasts and equipment. In many ways they are more ale than lager in concept.

The first of these types was originally called **sparkling lager ale**, and later came to be popularly known as **cream ale**. Cream ale was created by American ale brewers who, lacking storage facilities to brew lager beer, began to brew beer similar to Pils but from top-fermenting ale yeast. Such beers were also called **American** or **Canadian Ales**. These are regular strength beers (OG 11–14 P, 1.044–56, 10–22 IBU) from a hybrid ferment that uses both warm fermentation (with either ale or lager yeast) and cold aging (lager style). They taste quite similar to American lagers and serve the same market. When these lager ales were brewed using bottom-fermenting yeast at warmer ale-type temperatures, the result was called "bastard ale" by the nineteenth-century brewing establishment.

Modern lager breweries have developed many so-called ales in this fashion. Most noteworthy is Coors-brewed **George Killian's Irish Red**, which is widely copied by many lager brewers as bottom-fermented red ales or Irish ales.

American brewers in California developed another hybrid style that was called **Steam Beer** and later **California Common Beer**. California Common Beer was brewed in the ale style (warm-fermented with little or no aging) with bottom-fermenting yeast. The style was developed during and after the California gold rush. This is a regular strength beer that is dark in color, similar to the hues of Vienna or Munich. Modern common or steam beer is usually lager-aged at 55°F/13°C, rather than the 33°F/0.5°C for normal lagers. Today, steam beer is a trademarked name that may be used only by San Francisco's Anchor brewery.

A third hybrid style was developed in Germany, where brewers clung to their old top-fermenting yeasts but aged their dark copper-colored ales in the new lager style. These were called **alt-bier** (old beer). Alt-bier is brewed with Munich and Vienna malts, mixed with up to 40% wheat malt, and has OG 11–12 P, 1.044–48; 4.5–5% abv, 28–40 IBU, and a dark amber or copper color.

Closely related to alt-bier is **Kölsch-bier**, developed in Koln (Cologne), Germany and brewed by similar methods but colored as pale as the new lager beers becoming popular in that mid-nineteenth-century era. Kölsch-bier parameters are defined by German law: OG 11.2–11.8 P, 1.045–47; dark straw to light amber in color, using pale malt and Vienna malt with up to 20% wheat malt; 16–34 IBU from Hallertauer, Perle, or Spalt hops; and with fermentation and aging taking place within a particular temperature range.

Hybridization is becoming more mainstream among brewers as they mix and match mashing, brewing, fermenting, and aging styles to conform with their own situation and equipment availability. A good example of this is the way many English and American ale brewers cold-condition their ales before bottling to enhance stability and shelf-life.

Wheat and Rye Beers

As a readily available ingredient, wheat has often been a major element of beer. Wheat is a mellowing ingredient, but it is difficult to use in brewing because its excess protein causes problems in clarification. By the late nineteenth and early twentieth century, after the lager revolution had made clarification a major concern in brewing, wheat beer production became limited, and only recently has it made a comeback. There are four major wheat beer traditions: Belgian, Bavarian, North German, and American.

Belgian Wit (White) Beers have a mixture of wheat, raw and malted barley, and even some raw oats. They are brewed by a long and complex mashing process and (in addition to limited hops) often include herbs and spices such as coriander and Curacao orange peels in their makeup. They are on the low side of regular beer in strength (OG 10.5–11 P, 1.042–44). Wit beers have that distinct Belgian flavor about them even when they are copied by new American brewers.

Bavarian Weizen (White) Beers are brewed with 40–75% wheat malt plus pale malt to gravities of 12–15 P, 1.048–61 with low bitterness levels of 13–17 IBU. They are usually pale, ranging in color from dark straw to light amber, although dark wheats, called **dunkel weizen**, are common, as are strong **weizenbocks**. The distinctive feature of Bavarian white beer is its yeast strain, which imparts a very unique clove/banana-like taste. This beer style, which had almost disappeared, began to make a comeback in the 1970s and 1980s. In the 1980s the unfiltered or yeasted versions (**hefe-weizen**) gained popularity, eventually surpassing the kristalklar filtered versions.

North German Weisse (White) Beer survives as the ever popular **Berliner Weisse** from that city. Berliner Weisse is brewed only in Berlin and is very tart from a lactobacillus yeast strain. This beer is brewed to OG 7–10 P, 1.028–40 with 30–75% wheat, alcohol at 5% abv and 5–15 IBU.

American wheat beer has gained in popularity. Some American wheats are brewed in the above three styles in a rather conscious effort to maintain authenticity, but most American wheat beers are made simply by using 50% wheat to augment the usual barley ferment. These wheat beers may contain up to 75% wheat and are often unfiltered, in which case they may be labeled hefe-weizen even though they use standard ale yeasts and lack the Bavarian clove taste on the finish.

Rye Beer

More recently rye beers have begun to appear in the United States and in Europe. Rye malt is even more difficult to filter than wheat, so a lesser portion in the malt (10–30%) is the usual practice, although there is a German **Roggenbier** (rye beer) of 100% rye malt. We may expect to see more hefe-rye beer now that a few brewers are experimenting with this style.

Spontaneous Ferment Brewing

Originally, beer was the result of a wild or spontaneous ferment. During the nineteenth century, Louis Pasteur, Emil Hansen, and others isolated and identified various yeast strains in Europe. Most brewers took to using these specific yeasts for their brewing needs, but in the Senne River valley southwest of Brussels some brewers continued to use wild yeast strains. These beers are called **Lambic beers**, named after a small town nearby. The yeast strains found in each of them are various and diverse, so much so that Lambic beers are rarely copied in other regions, as the composite yeast mix is quite difficult to culture.

Lambic beer is one of the planet's strangest beer types. At its best it is tart and fruity, almost like a white wine. The most popular Lambic is **Gueuze Lambic**, a careful blend of one-third young (one-year-old) and two-thirds old (two-years-old) Lambic; the addition of young Lambic to old Lambic causes a second ferment in the bottle. The Gueuze Lambics have an original gravity of 12.9–13.5 P and 6.3% abv, with an acidic finish of about 1% lactic acid. The grain mix is composed of two parts pale malt and one part raw wheat. The beer is hopped with aged one– to three-year-old hops during a long wort boil.

Belgian Fruit Lambics may be the most popular variation of this spontaneous ferment ale type. The brewer uses the Lambic beer as a base for the addition of various fruits. Originally, these were Schaarbeek kriek sour black cherries, dried on the tree and added to eighteen-month-old Lambic beer to steep for about six months. The result was beer with a champagne-like dry and fruity taste. Later, raspberries and different fruits were utilized. The beers sold in the United States are sweetened, yielding a soft sweet-sour finish more popular with Americans.

Fruit Ales

As Belgian fruit Lambics became popular on the American scene, American craft brewers began to experiment with fruit ales. Among the earliest was McMenamin's Hillsdale Brew Pub in Portland, Oregon, with a draft raspberry ale called **Ruby**. Ruby was an unremarkable, lightly flavored beer, but it remains one of their bestsellers to this day with OG 9.8 P, 1.039, 3.8% abv, and 20 IBU. There are many American fruit ales on the market today. They are usually in the regular beer range (10–11 P, 1.040–44) and brewed mostly with pale two-row malt and/or wheat malt, with an addition of various fruits including raspberries, blackberries, strawberries, blueberries, lemons, and many other fruits and berries. The bitterness is kept rather low (10–15 IBU for the most part).

Smoked Beers

Rauchbier is brewed from malt that has been fire-dried, a throw-back to the old days when all malt was thus kilned and all beer must have had at least a hint of smoky flavor. Today, rauchbier is a bottom- and cold-fermented lager beer made only in Bamberg in Bavaria, Germany, but copied elsewhere. Whereas there are some 150 breweries within 25 miles of Bamberg, only a few brew rauchbier. It is regular strength beer that has OG 12–13 P, 1.048–52, 4.3–4.8 abv, 20–30 IBU, and a dark amber color.

Peat Smoked Beers, pale amber lagers with a slightly sweet finish, are popular in Europe. They are brewed with Scotch whisky malt and regular pale malt with minimal bitterness.

American Smoked Porter is one of several American smoke styles becoming popular in the United States. Smoke rides well in a Porter. The wood is usually fruit wood, or alder on the West Coast.

Heavy Beers

Strong beers (over OG 12.5 P, 1.050) are great favorites of beer lovers everywhere. With the exception of the insipid American malt liquors, they have stronger and more aggressive taste elements. Strong beers are brewed from all brewing systems and are in four classes: special beer, strong beer, double beer, and barleywine/triple beer. Strong beers must be consumed with great respect, as they can pack a stern wallop.

Special or Seasonal Beers and Ales have OG 12.5–14.9 P, 1.050–61, 5–6% abv, and 20–40 IBU. Through 1976 almost no breweries bothered with seasonal brews, and San Francisco's Anchor brewery was the first in the new wave of craft brewers to honor this old tradition with their **Our Special Ale**, a Christmas brew in the India Pale Ale (IPA) style. Since then many brewers have brewed special seasonal beers for many occasions. Indeed, craft brewers have used the seasonal nature of beer as a cornerstone of their marketing strategy. Most popular of these seasonals are the fall harvest and spring brews sometimes called **Oktoberfest** and **Märzen** beers. These latter are usually cold-fermented lager beers in the Vienna lager style, but a bit stronger. Oktoberfest and Märzen beers are also made by ale brewers, along similar lines, but are top-fermented as ales and sometimes cold-lagered in the alt-bier style.

Strong beer or **ale** has OG 15–17.9 P, 1.062–73, 6–7.5% abv, and 20–40 IBU. This is a very popular beer strength. Malt liquors fit here, and some old friends such as **Danish Carlsberg Elephant** come to mind. Traditional among these strong beers are **bock beers** (and stronger **double bocks**), a late winter seasonal lager type. Bock beers are usually dark with original gravity of 16 P (1.066), 6.6% abv, and a usually modest bitterness of 20–35 IBU. Double bocks are similar to these, but at 18 P (1.074) and 7.5% abv. There are, additionally, also pale bock beers and ale-brewed bocks.

India Pale Ales (OG 12.5–17.5 P, 1.050–70 SG, 5–7.5% abv, and 40–60 IBU) are another strong revivalist style gaining popularity. Originally brewed for the British in India, it became very popular during the last century. They are strong and hoppy light to pale amber ales.

Belgian Abbey Dubbel (OG 15–17 P and 1.063–70 SG) is a strong brown ale type with a Belgian taste, pale to dark amber in color, lightly hopped at 18–25 IBU, and quite popular in Belgium. **Belgian Trappist beers** are good examples of this beer type.

Belgian Golden Ale (15 P, 1.062 and 6.5% abv) is a strong, dark, straw-colored beer with about 30 IBU and great Belgian flavor. The original of this type, **Duvel** (devil), is copied both in Belgium and in the United States.

French Bière de Garde and **Bière de Paris** (OG 14.6–18.5 P, 1.060–70, 6.5–8.5% abv, and 25–30 IBU) are pale beers (pale amber or gold to reddish brown) usually unfiltered and bottle-conditioned. These beers are similar to Belgian beers and are brewed with similar yeast combinations.

Double or Triple beer, Ale or Barleywine has OG 18 P, 1.074, above 7% abv, and 20–40 (or more) IBU. What are now called barleywine style ales were once **strong ales**, **Burton ales**, **old ales**, and **Scotch ales**. They are still called that in England, but the stronger varieties (20 P and up) are also called barleywines. Lager brewers brew extra strong **double bocks** (18 P and up), **Eisbocks**, and the rare really strong beers such as **Swiss Samichlaus**, (OG 28.7 P, 1.123, 14.3% abv, 17 IBU), brewed annually in December for release the following December. These heavy lagers are mostly dark brews (pale amber to black in color), but pale strong lagers are not unknown.

Imperial Stout is barleywine strength stout, originally brewed to be sent to old imperial Russia from the end of the eighteenth century until World War I. Imperial Stouts expect to have about OG 24 P, 1.100, 8.5–10.5% abv, over 50 IBU, and will usually be very dark in color. American craft brewers abuse this style regularly by incorrectly labeling some of their stronger stouts as "Imperial" when the gravity labors at a mere 15–18 P, 1.062–74.

Cataloging Beer Styles

As I listed in *Essentials of Beer Style,* all beer may be categorized into five groups. The laws of many countries, including Canada and Germany, codify these or similar categories into their alcohol management rules:

1. Small or "light" beer, usually under 10 P (1.040) OG, 4.2% abv, and 8–20 IBU.

2. Regular beer, 10–12.5 P (1.040–1.050) OG, 3.8–5.5% abv, and 12–40 IBU. Most beers of the world fit into this category.

3. Special or seasonal beer, ale, or malt liquor, 12.5–14.9 P (1.050–1061) OG, 5–6% abv, and 20–40 IBU.

4. Strong beer or ale, 15–17.9 P (1.062–73) OG, 6–7.5% abv, and 20–40 IBU.

5. Double or Triple beer, ale, or barleywine, 18 P (1.074) and over OG, above 7% abv, and 20–40 (or more) IBU.

———————■———————

In using *The Beer-Taster's Log,* you will no doubt run into all of these groups and styles as detailed above. As you work your way around the world, beer by beer, I hope this information helps you to taste and enjoy for years to come.

To Your Health!
Fred Eckhardt

Introduction

It is the combination of carefully selected malt, hops, and yeast that makes any given beer unique. The malt and hops give it character, and the yeast gives it a distinctive style. Throughout the processes of brewing, fermenting, bottling, shipping, and storing, innumerable other factors can also influence the characteristics that a given beer displays — which makes the work of a taste panel challenging, to say the least. The panel that evaluated the beers described in this book judged each sample on the basis of visual appearance, aromatic features, sensations to the palate, and aftertaste.

When I first started assembling panels of taste testers for evaluating beers, most of the panel members were experienced wine tasters. Being competent at tasting in general, they were able to adapt quite readily to judging beers. Gradually, though, the composition of the taste panel changed to include experienced beer drinkers as well — with little effect on the results. Since 1976, when the beer tastings became increasingly serious, over 200 individuals have participated in the evaluations. Very few were actually involved in the trade; most were seasoned world travelers who had experience drinking the world's great beers in their countries of origin.

At present, roughly half the panel members are homebrewers. One panel member is in the process of establishing a microbrewery; at least two others have previous beer judging experience. All are valued for their knowledge of and ability to identify beer types and styles, malt and hop varieties, and — most important — brewing faults and problems.

Procedure

When tasting beer, it is important to know what foods will not interfere with the palate. Salty and oily foods should be avoided, as they directly affect the palate's sensitivity to certain features of the brew. Of course, this eliminates virtually all the foods traditionally associated with enjoying beer: pretzels, sausages, chips, salted or plain nuts, and so on. We have found that plain, lightly salted, unbuttered popcorn is the most effective in "clearing the palate" between brews and does little to blunt the taster's ability.

The effects of food on palate sensitivity were noticeable early in the tasting efforts, but it took longer to assess the effect on the palate of tasting the beer itself. We assumed that the effect of the alcohol would be appreciable. After all, wine tasters regularly spit out taste samples rather than swallow and undergo impairment of the senses. Nonetheless, the alcohol is absorbed by the mucous membrane of the mouth, and some exhilaration of spirit and reduction of tasting skills may occur. Over the span of 19 years of tasting experience, we have found that people vary greatly in terms of tolerance and palate ability with regard to beer. Some are able to judge relatively fine points of difference among brews after tasting over 30 samples, whereas others have difficulty making judgments after tasting only a dozen or so. In fact, because the taste sample size is small and tastings are spread out over an extended period of time, we believe that the relatively low alcohol content of most beers represents less of a factor in palate sensitivity than does the individual tester's innate ability.

In designing tastings, some thought must be given to pairings and order of presentation. Beers are always served in pairs unless there is a sample whose properties are so unique as to defy comparison. To minimize preconceptions, only one of the tasters knows what beers are being evaluated. A tasting session generally consists of nine "flights" of two beers each. The lightest and palest beers are served early, with a gradual increase in color, flavor, and intensity, ending with porters, stouts, and barleywines. The stronger beers tend to stun the palate and can impair the tasters' ability to judge a weaker beer served subsequently.

The taste panel is served the beer samples in a French Pilsener glass, an inexpensive style of stemware with a medium-size bowl that closes in slightly at the top. This has two advantages. One, the closed-in top allows the aroma and bouquet to be captured within (aroma is the aspect of the "nose" derived from the ingredients, and bouquet is the aspect that results from the process of fermentation). Two, the bowl affords the opportunity to warm the brew slightly with the heat of the palms to bring out any qualities that might be masked by coldness.

Beer should be tasted as one would taste a fine wine. First, the taster looks at the color. It may range from palest white or gold to deep dark amber and opaque brown. It may be brilliantly clear, hazy, or cloudy depending on style. Next, the taster smells the beer. In fact, in tasting beer the best tool is the nose. One's ability to taste depends very much on one's ability to smell. Our sense of taste alone can only distinguish four primary tastes: sweet, sour, bitter, and salty. However, our sense of smell — with over 5 million smell-sensing cells recognizing some 10,000 odors — forewarns the brain about the taste that is about to be experienced. Only after letting their nose receptors do their work will the tasters take a sip.

Initially the taster takes a small sip, letting the liquid roll around in the mouth and exposing it to the sweet, sour, and bitter detectors. The sip should slide down the sides and under the tongue. Then the taster takes a larger sip and tries to aspirate it (that is, suck in some air so it bubbles through the beverage in the mouth). This increases the taster's sensitivity to the brew. There may be a single palate sensation; one notable taste or flavor; or complexities involving the front of the palate (the initial taste — as on the front of the tongue), the mid-palate (taste experienced on the middle or sides of the tongue), and the finish (taste experienced at the point of swallowing). Finally the taster swallows some of the beer in order to appreciate the finish and the aftertaste (sensations remaining in the mouth after swallowing).

Sensory Perception

The aroma and flavor of malt are easy to recognize, especially if it has been roasted or smoked. Even if not, the malt in beer is not so different from the malted milk and candy we knew in our childhood. The distinctive aroma and flavor of hops used for bittering are also familiar to beer drinkers. Less familiar are the complex odors and flavors resulting from the use of aromatic hops. Most of the pleasant herbaceous, complex, and fragrant components come from these hops.

Unpleasantness in beer often has a complex or obscure origin and can be traced to raw materials, contamination in the brewing process, improper handling in shipment or storage (as in exposure to temperature extremes, vibration, or light), or excessive elapsed time from production to consumption. The more commonly encountered odors and flavors are described below, together with clues to their origin. Some of these off flavors can occur in combination.

Winelike Qualities. Indicates presence of esters, an organic compound formed by the reaction of an acid and an alcohol. Considered an advantage in an ale, but considered a flaw in a pilsner.

Leather, Paper, Cardboard, Woodiness. Indicates exposure of the beer to oxygen.

Soapiness. Indicates presence of octanoic acid (or caprylic acid), a fatty acid that can also take on a rancid character.

Cheese. Indicates presence of isovaleric acid resulting from the oxidation of isopentyl alcohol (also known as isoamyl alcohol or simply amyl alcohol).

Banana. Indicates presence of isoamyl acetate, an acetic ester of amyl alcohol from fusel oil, also called amyl acetate, banana oil, or pear oil.

Milk. Indicates formation of lactic acid resulting from bacterial fermentation of starch, molasses, or sugar.

Green Apple. Indicates presence of acetylaldehyde or dehydrogenated alcohol, a reactive organic compound intermediate in the state of oxidation.

Medicinal. Indicates presence of a phenolic, soluble acidic compound derived from actions of a phenol with an aldehyde.

Corn. Indicates presence of dimethyl sulfide, a compound containing two methyl groups in the molecule.

Butter, Butterscotch. Indicates presence of diacetyl (or biacetyl), a diketone with a buttery aroma or flavor (diacetyl is the flavor in butter, a contributing flavor in tobacco and coffee, and is used to synthetically flavor margarine).

Rubber, Skunk. Indicates presence of mercaptan, a compound analogous to alcohols and phenols, but containing sulfur in place of oxygen.

Acetone. Indicates bacterial infection in the fermentation of corn mash.

Rancid, Rancid Butter. Indicates the presence of butyric acid as a result of oxidation of normal butyl alcohol or butyl aldehyde or by fermentation of molasses; may also be caused by the action of anaerobic bacteria on lactic acid.

Technical Data

In compiling *The Beer-Taster's Log,* I included technical data on specific beers wherever it was available. The information came from brewers who use various methods to quantify their brews. In all cases, the technical data is given exactly as it was provided by the brewer.

Alcohol content is listed by volume (abv) or by weight (abw). The abw measurement cites the weight of alcohol as a percentage of the total weight of the beer. A 5% abw means that there are 5 grams of alcohol dissolved in every 100 grams of beer. The abv measurement cites the volume of alcohol present in a given volume of fluid, so a 5% abv means that 5% of the volume in a 12-oz. bottle of beer is alcohol, or there is 0.6 oz. of alcohol in that bottle of beer.

Another beer classifier is "strength" or "density." Density is the amount of sugar dissolved into solution in the wort. Original gravity measures the difference between wort density and water density as a percentage: Water has a gravity of 1.000; wort will have a gravity higher than 1.000 because there are fermentable and unfermentable sugars and other solids dissolved in it. Brewers often drop the decimal point (especially in Britain), listing the gravity as a four-digit number, such as 1050.

The brewing industry is sometimes more likely to use a measure of the percentage of dissolved solids expressed in degrees Plato (named after its originator). The relationship between gravity and degrees (or percentage) Plato is about 4 gravity points to each 1% or degree Plato. The higher the number, the greater the density and potential for alcohol generation (but this is no guarantee of high alcohol content).

There are standards for quantifying hop bitterness, color, and carbonation. Bitterness is measured in international bitterness units (IBU) — the higher the number, the greater the bitterness.

Two color scales are commonly used in brewing: Standard Reference Method (SRM) and Lovibond. Brewers tend to use degrees Lovibond to measure the color of their malts, but generally measure the color of finished beers in SRM.

Terminology

abv	alcohol by volume
abw	alcohol by weight
IBU	International Bitterness Units
°L	degrees Lovibond; measures color of malt
SRM	Standard Reference Method; measures color of beer

Rating and Scoring

The beers were judged on (1) how well they fit the manufacturer's definition (according to the label), and (2) how pleasing they were to the tasters. Over 90% of the beers rated in this book were evaluated by a taste panel of six or more tasters. Each beer was rated on visual appearance, aromatic features, sensations to the palate, and aftertaste.

From the outset I thought it important to devise a numerical scoring/rating system. After all, people who rate beer, wine, and other things feel most comfortable when they can score numerically on an agreed-upon scale. People who read about beer generally prefer numerical scores over rating systems that use symbols such as stars or mugs. I had spent many years tasting and judging wine, and I felt that a similar system could be devised as long as it was fairly objective. Tasting beer involves an essentially subjective analysis. Individual preference, experience, and taste preclude much objectivity; so I attempted to construct a reasonably objective rating scale.

Tasters were asked to rate each beer on a 15-point scale. When the beer was essentially true to type, they rated it 0 to 3 if they did not wish to taste it again; 4 to 6 if it was fair; 7 to 9 if it was good and worthy of consideration for everyday use; 10 to 12 if it was very good and worth paying a premium for or seeking out; and 13 to 15 if it was excellent and worth both paying a premium for and going out of the way to find.

Because the most common number of tasters at any given tasting session was 6, a maximum score of 90 was used (6 x 15). However, readers recently pressured me to go to a 100-point scale. If more or fewer tasters are involved in an evaluation session, simple mathematics is used to arrive at the final score. To eliminate unusual bias, the highest and lowest scores are discarded. (This is common practice in evaluating test results.)

Whenever there was an opportunity to

retaste a beer that had performed below an average standard of acceptability, it was submitted to the taste panel again. In all cases, the best performance is reported and the best score listed.

The following descriptions characterize the beers that received ratings in that range.

0–20. Poor. Atypical of type. Has unpleasant features, flawed aroma or taste or both. Badly mishandled, gone off with age. Improperly made. Unforgivable faults. Undrinkable, or tastes like carbonated water or soda pop. A beer you would not purchase again.

21–40. Fair. May not be true to type. Noticeable faults, but not overwhelming. Poorly balanced. May have some good features (e.g., may be thirst quenching), but inferior to most other beers or lacking what other readily available beers offer. Not a beer you would prefer to purchase again.

41–60. Good. Typical of type. Faults are small and forgivable. Good balance. Pleasant and enjoyable. Good serviceable beer for thirst quenching and regular enjoyment, if obtainable at a good price.

61–80. Very Good. True to type. No significant faults or offensive features. Well balanced. Aroma, flavor, and aftertaste all present to the appropriate degree, but short of excellent. A beer you would be willing to pay some premium to purchase or to go out of your way to obtain.

81–100. Excellent. Characteristic of the best of type. No faults or offensive features. All components of aroma and taste in harmony. Aroma, flavor, and aftertaste very much present and appropriate. A beer that deserves a premium price and one that you would go out of your way to obtain.

Key to Taste Panel Ratings

Each rating is made up of two parts: a letter indicating the beer style a particular beer most closely resembles; and the numeric rating it received from the taste panel. For example, a beer may have a rating of [S, 90]. This means it was judged as most resembling a Stout and that it earned a combined numeric rating of 90 (out of 100 possible points), indicating that it was "excellent" as a Stout.

Beer Style Designation

A	Top-fermented ale
B	Bottom-fermented beer
BK	Bock
BW	Barleywine
D	Dry
F	Faro
IPA	India Pale Ale
K	Kölsch
L	Lambic / Gueuze
LO	Low-Calorie
MB	Malt beverage / Malta
ML	Malt liquor
NA	Non-alcoholic beer
P	Porter
RA	Reduced alcohol
S	Stout
ST	Steam beer
W	Wheat / Weizen
WBK	Weizenbock
NR	[No rating]

Numeric Rating

0–20	Poor
21–40	Fair
41–60	Good
61–80	Very good
81–100	Excellent

Note: Some of the beers listed in *The Beer-Taster's Log* may no longer be available or may only be available at certain times of the year. Breweries change their venue from time to time — for example, they often brew special seasonal styles for various holidays or they may only be able to brew with certain ingredients when those ingredients, such as raspberries, pumpkin, or winter wheat, are in season. In addition, it is not uncommon for microbreweries to change their offerings when a new brewmaster joins the brewery.

Canary Islands

Sical, S.A.
Brewery in Las Palmas

TROPICAL EXPORT PILS
BEER — bright gold, hop aroma,
all hop palate, sour finish and aftertaste. [B, 29]

Congo

SCBK (Congo Brewing)
Brewery in Pointe Noir

N'GOK IMPORTED BEER —
gold, hop nose, almost skunky, high
carbonation, light hop flavor, dry
hop aftertaste. [B, 32]

Ethiopia

Asmara Brewery
Brewery in Asmara

ASMARA LAGER BEER —
deep bright gold, big malt nose,
good body, big malt flavor, long
dry hop aftertaste. [B, 56]

Ethiopian Beverage Co.
Brewery in Harar

HARAR BEER — pale gold,
slightly toasted malt aroma and

Notes

flavor; burnt malt appears in the fairly long aftertaste. [B, 41]

Gambia

Banjul Breweries, Ltd.
Brewery in Banjul

JULBREW LAGER — yellow-gold, caramel-malt aroma; malt flavor reflects some of the caramel; medium to good body, light off-dry malt aftertaste. [B, 33]

Ivory Coast

Solibra Abidjan
Brewery in Abidjan

MAMBA MALT LIQUOR — bright gold, fine carbonation, beautiful malt nose, pleasant tasting complex malt flavor, big body, long off-sweet malt aftertaste. [ML, 63]

Kenya

Kenya Breweries, Ltd.
Brewery in Nairobi

TUSKER MALT LAGER — pale gold, dry malt nose, lightly sweet malt flavor, candy and hop finish, strong dry and bitter hop aftertaste. [B, 26]

Liberia

Monrovia Breweries, Inc.
Brewery in Monrovia

MONROVIA CLUB BEER — bright deep gold, hop nose, vegetal malt flavor; improves to just plain malt at the finish; dry hop aftertaste has a sour component. [B, 21]

Malta

Simonds Farsons Cisk, Ltd.
Brewery on Malta

FARSONS SHANDY — bright gold, cointreau-like nose, light fruit flavor, really no beer taste at all, light body; pleasant, but not really like a shandy which is fruit juice (like lemonade) added to beer. The beer taste should still come through. [B, 27]

Morocco

Brasseries du Maroc
Brewery in Casablanca

FLAG EXPORT BEER — gold, hop aroma a bit obscured by a papery oxidation; some hops and malt show but the beer was oxidized; dry finish and aftertaste. Found in Florida. [B, 27]

Nigeria

Nigerian Breweries, Ltd.
Brewery in Lagos

GULDER LAGER BEER — gold, grape soda nose, grapey hop flavor and aftertaste, a very strange beer with a chemical background in the aftertaste. [B, 9]

STAR LAGER BEER — hazy gold, skunky hop nose and taste, long aftertaste like the flavor. [B, 6]

South Africa

South African Breweries, Ltd.
Brewery in Johannesburg

ROGUE LONG BREW BEER — gold, apple-malt nose, highly carbonated, faint malt flavor, faint short hop aftertaste. [B, 35]

CASTLE LAGER — deep gold, bright hop nose and pronounced hop flavor; finely carbonated with small bubbles; straightforward hop palate lacks complexity; slightly bitter dry hop aftertaste. [B, 36]

HANSA PILSENER — pale gold, lovely malt and hop aroma, lots of carbonation; good balance between the hops and the malt on the palate but the flavor is marred by excessive carbonation; finishes quite tasty though, and the aftertaste is long and good with both malt and hops; excellent except for the CO^2. [B, 49]

LION LAGER — pale amber, pleasant lightly malted nose, faint off-dry fruitlike flavor, little complexity, medium length off-dry malt aftertaste; very drinkable, but it has little zest. [B, 40]

AMSTEL LAGER — bright medium deep gold, balanced malt-hop aroma, good dry malt palate in front; becomes a little sweeter at the finish but is pleasant; some bitter hops appear in the aftertaste, which is long and good, excellent except for being too highly carbonated. [B, 41]

LION LAGER — deep gold, grainy aroma shows a little hops; grainy malt and light hop flavor, medium to good body, hop finish, long dry hop aftertaste; good refreshing semi-dry malt taste is quite attractive, very drinkable, 5% abv. The trade boycott with South Africa lasted over ten years. This is a fresh sample tasted in late 1995. [B, 55]

Swaziland

Swaziland Brewers, Ltd.
Brewery in Mbabane

SIMBA IMPORTED LAGER — pale yellow-gold, nose like Concord grapes, fairly sweet grape flavor, highly carbonated, grape aftertaste, like a New York wine cooler. [B, 24]

Togo

B.B. Brewery
Brewery in Lome, Kara

NGOMA TOGO PILS — hazy gold; hop nose that in some samples has a skunky edge; big hop flavor, smooth and balanced (despite the poor nose), dry hop finish and aftertaste. [B, 50]

NGOMA AWOOYO SPECIAL — amber; malt nose is lightly toasted but has a dank component; off-dry malt flavor has a touch of sour that is more noticeable in the finish and in the back of the long dry hop aftertaste; seems to have high alcohol as it is a bit winelike. [B, 53]

NGOMA LOME LAGER — gold, skunky hop nose, creamy texture, flavor of hops and malt, medium body, dry hop finish; fairly long aftertaste shows some malt with the dry hops. [B, 40]

Zaire

SBK Brewery
Brewery in Kinshasa

NGOMA CASTEL BEER — hazy yellow-gold, fruity malt aroma; palate has an off-dry malt front, dry middle, and an off-dry malt finish; medium body, short dry malt aftertaste. [B, 42]

China

Beijing Brewery
Brewery in Chaoyang District, Beijing (Peking)

TIENTAN BEER — hazy yellow-gold, strong hop nose, big hop flavor, off-dry malt in finish, dry bitter hop aftertaste, could use more malt for better balance. This has been seen labeled as Tiantan and means "Temple of Heaven." Brewery on label given as Tiantan Brewery. [B, 29]

Beijing Wuxing Brewery / Shen Ho Shing Brewery
Brewery in Beijing (Peking)

MON-LEI BEER — gold, off-dry malt nose and flavor, fairly dry hop finish, long dry aftertaste, good balance, good body. [B, 40]

FIVE STAR BEER — pale gold, off-dry malt nose, toasted (a bit burnt) malt flavor and long aftertaste. Also has been seen as "Specially Brewed Five Star Beer." Most recently (1996) seen with label citing Shen Ho Shing Brewery as brewery of origin. [B, 52]

NINE STAR PREMIUM BEER — gold, hop nose, good malt and hop flavor, good body, some complexity, off-dry finish, long dry hop aftertaste. Brewery named as Five Star Brewery. [B, 46]

Chu Jiang Brewery
Brewery in Guangzhou City (Canton), Guangdong

CHU SING BEER — pale gold, light off-dry grainy malt aroma, off-dry malt flavor has a papery finish, long dull malt and sour hop aftertaste. [B, 39]

Feng Shon Brewery
Brewery in Beijing (Peking)

PEKING BEER — pale gold, clean malt aroma, fruity malt

flavor, hop finish, off-dry malt aftertaste, pleasant but without much complexity. [B, 31]

Guangzhou Brewery
Brewery in Guangzhou City (Canton), Guangdong Province. Labels also mention Pijiuchang Brewery, Pearl River Brewery.

DOUBLE HAPPINESS GUANGZHOU BEER — pale gold, hop nose is almost skunky; high carbonation, light malt flavor in front, hops develop in the middle to finish, light body, dry hop aftertaste. [B, 34]

SONG HAY DOUBLE HAPPINESS BEER — gold, beautiful malt nose, mild dry malt flavor, faintly buttery in back, short dry malt aftertaste. [B, 27]

HUA NAN BEER — yellow-gold, pleasant malt nose; malt flavor has hops in back; hop finish and aftertaste, fairly refreshing. [B, 43]

BAIYUN BEER — hazy yellow, off-dry malt nose and front palate, sour hop finish and aftertaste. [B, 28]

CANTON LAGER BEER — gold, faint malt nose, malt flavor, big body, long malt aftertaste. [B, 24]

SWEET CHINA — yellow-gold, pineapple nose and flavor, smooth and round, faint finish and aftertaste; seems a bit artificial, but is flavored with real pineapple. [B, 24]

Hangzhou Brewery
Brewery in Hangzhou City, Zhejiang Province

EMPERORS GOLD BEER — gold, malt nose, faintly oxidized and slightly sour malt flavor, dry finish; off-dry malt aftertaste reminds you of molasses. Known in China as West Lake Beer, made with Zhejiang barley. [B, 36]

Hua Du Brewery
Brewery in Beijing

LONGXIANG BEER — pale gold, hoppy nose is almost skunky; light hop flavor has malt in back and is drinkable and refreshing; light body, dry hop finish and fairly long aftertaste. [B, 61]

Huaguang Brewery
Brewery in Shanghai

PANDA BEER — bright tawny-gold, malt and light hop nose; sharp malt flavor that turns somewhat sour at the finish, this continues into the aftertaste. [B, 29]

Jiangshan Brewery
Brewery in Jiangshan, Zhejiang Province

CHUNG HUA BEER — pale gold, faint malt and hop nose; hops start off the palate yielding soon to off-dry malt with a spicy background; the finish and aftertaste are almost too sweet malt. Brewery named is Cian Jiang Brewery of Zhe Jiang. I feel there may be something amiss with the spelling. [B, 41]

Jinan Brewery
Brewery in Jinan, Shandong Province

BAOTU QUAN BEER — pale gold, lovely malty aroma with good hops in back, big flavor like the nose, tasty and balanced, good body, very long dry hop aftertaste; well-made brew that should not be chilled to enjoy its flavor. [B, 60]

Qingdao (Tsing-Tao) Brewery
Brewery in Tsing-Tao, Shandong Province

TSING-TAO BEER — tawny-yellow, malt nose, malt and hop flavor, good body, medium dry malt finish and aftertaste with plenty of hop backing; 3.5% abv. [B, 40]

CHINA CLIPPER BEER — pale gold, malt aroma with a hop background, dry malt flavor, hop middle, malt finish and aftertaste, pleasant and balanced. [B, 40]

JINDAO BEER — deep gold, fruity malty nose; flavor is mostly malt but there are hops in back; medium body, medium dry malt finish and aftertaste. [B, 12]

Shansui Brewery / Guang Dong Brewery
Brewery in Xinan, Sanshui County, Guangdong Province

CHANGLEE BEER — brilliant medium deep gold, faint off-dry malt nose, light body, light malt flavor, brief malt aftertaste. [B, 40]

Shenyang Brewery
Brewery in Tiexi District, Shenyang City, Liaoning Province

CHINA GOLD BEER — bright deep gold, hoppy ale-like nose, bright hop and malt flavor, good balance, low carbonation, some hop bite in the finish and long malt aftertaste. [B, 68]

SNOWFLAKE BEER — gold, light malt and hop nose, malt and hop flavor, medium body; malt finish drops off to nothing, virtually no aftertaste. In China, this can be found as Xuehua Beer (which means "snowflakes"). [B, 16]

SHENYANG EXPORT SPECIAL BEER — deep gold, malt nose; lightly toasted off-dry malt flavor; light body, long off-dry malt aftertaste. [B, 40]

Taiwan Tobacco & Wine Monopoly Bureau
Brewery in Taipei, Taiwan

DYNASTY TAIWAN BEER — deep yellow-gold, rich appetizing malt aroma; clean malt flavor is lightly toasted; long clean malt aftertaste, pleasant drinkable brew when fresh. [B, 69]

DYNASTY PREMIUM DRY BEER — pale gold, pleasant malt nose with good hops, good tasting off-dry malt flavor, light body, pleasant butterscotch and honeyed finish, clean long malt aftertaste. [D, 52]

CHINA BEER — hazy pale amber, toasted malt aroma, good toasted malt flavor, finish, and aftertaste, fairly well-balanced. From Chien-Kuo Brewery. [B, 49]

TAIWAN DRAFT BEER — gold, hop aroma, big hop flavor, style of an English bitter, austere, long dry hop aftertaste. [B, 49]

Tianjin Beer Brewery
Brewery in Nankai District, Tianjin City

GREAT WALL BEER — deep gold, toasted caramel malt nose, light body; good hop and malt flavor up front, but finish is bitter and burnt. Label says Tientsin Brewery, Tientsin. [B, 39]

Yantai Brewery of Shandong Province
Brewery in Yantai City, Shandong Province

TSING-TAO PORTER — deep brown with a big roasted malt flavor and a hop finish; big body; long roasted malt and hop aftertaste. In China this is labeled Qingdao Black Beer and runs 17.8–18.2 P and over 5% abv. [P, 42]

Zhujiang Brewery
Brewery in Zhujiang (Shanghai)

YI KING CHINESE BEER — medium gold, malt nose, off-dry malt front palate, hop middle and finish, good body, dry hop aftertaste. [B, 50]

GOLDEN DRAGON BEER — pale gold, light fruity-malt aroma, off-dry light malt flavor, almost no hops, off-dry malt aftertaste. [B, 47]

ZHU JIANG BEER — pale gold, faint malt aroma, clean crisp pleasant dry malt flavor, light to medium. [B, 52]

Fiji

Carlton Brewery (Fiji), Ltd.
Brewery in Suva

FIJI BITTER BEER — tawny, faint apple and malt nose, malt flavor with a candy background, woody middle, grainy finish and aftertaste. [B, 37]

Hong Kong

Hong Kong Brewery, Ltd.
Brewery in Hong Kong

MON-LEI BEER — pale bright yellow, malt aroma and flavor, some sour hops in the finish and aftertaste. [B, 25]

SUN-LIK BEER — bright yellow-gold, faint malt nose, malt and hop flavor, dry hop finish, light dry hop aftertaste. [B, 53]

India / Pakistan

Associated Breweries & Distilleries
Brewery in Bombay, India

MAHARAJA LAGER BEER — gold malt nose with a trace of chocolate, dull malt flavor, medium body, light malt finish and aftertaste, dry and short. [B, 9]

High Range Breweries, Ltd.
Breweries in Voranad and Kerala, India

KINGFISHER LAGER BEER — brilliant pale gold, big aromatic hop nose with plenty of malt, sprightly malt and hop flavor, short sour malt aftertaste. [B, 30]

Hindustan Breweries & Bottling, Ltd.
Brewery in Thana, India

BOMBAY BEER — clear tawny-gold, faint malt nose, light body, off-dry and vegetal malt palate, dull malt finish and aftertaste. [B, 15]

Kalyani Breweries, Ltd.
Brewery in Calcutta, India

TAJ MAHAL LAGER BEER — deep gold, highly carbonated, pleasant malt palate, medium body, pleasant malt aftertaste of medium length. [B, 37]

TAJ MAHAL PREMIUM LAGER BEER — gold, skunky/soapy nose, dull malt flavor, dry short malt aftertaste. Brewed and bottled in England for UB Ltd., Bangalore, India. [B, 39]

Khoday Brewing & Distilling Industries Private, Ltd.
Brewery in Bangalore, India

SOVEREIGN LAGER BEER — tawny-gold, aroma of ferruginous springwater and toasted malt, watery body, flavor like the nose; finishes good toasted malt, but there is little aftertaste. [B, 42]

Mohan Meakin Breweries, Ltd.
Mohan Nagar Brewery in Ghaziabad, India

GOLDEN EAGLE LAGER BEER — deep gold, pleasant off-dry malt aroma; smoky-salty malt flavor that is not unpleasant, short dry malt aftertaste; hops are faint at best. [B, 50]

Mohan Rocky Springwater Breweries, Ltd.
Brewery in Khopoli, India

EAGLE LAGER BEER — brilliant amber-gold, dank toasted malt nose, weak toasted malt flavor, watery body, brief malt aftertaste. [B, 12]

Murree Brewery Co., Ltd.
Brewery in Rawalpindi, Pakistan

MURREE EXPORT LAGER — pale yellow-gold, off-dry malt nose, dry sour malt flavor, long dry and bitter hop aftertaste. [B, 16]

Sheeba Breweries (P.V.) Ltd.
Breweries in India

INDIAN GURU LAGER BEER — bright gold; aroma is almost skunky, but not quite, instead is hops and banana; hop flavor with malt in back and good complexity, long dry hop and malt aftertaste. Brewed and bottled in England for Sheeba Breweries. [B, 42]

UB Ltd.
Brewery in Bangalore, India

FLYING HORSE ROYAL LAGER BEER — gold; aroma has hops but is mostly malt; buttery malt flavor, ashy finish and aftertaste. [B, 13]

Indonesia

Pt. Delta
Brewery at Djakarta (affiliated with Breda Breweries of Holland)

ANKER BEER — deep gold; off-dry malt nose has hops in back; malt flavor has a faint hop background; good body, very well-balanced, dry malt finish and long dry malt aftertaste. [B, 46]

ANKER EXTRA STOUT — deep brown, very thick brown head, rich malt aroma, rich sweet malt flavor, big body, long dry malt aftertaste. [S, 48]

CARLSBERG BEER — gold, hop aroma and flavor, good body, slightly sour hop finish, dry and slightly sour hop aftertaste. [B, 42]

Pt. Multi Bintang
Brewery in Tangerang

BINTANG PILSENER BEER — gold, fragrant hop nose, light dry hop flavor, light to medium body, light dry hop finish and aftertaste, medium duration. [B, 40]

GUINNESS FOREIGN EXTRA STOUT — opaque brown, big thick tan head, rich malt nose, complex rich dry off-dry malt flavor, quite clean, good body; finishes lighter and drier than the flavor; light dry malt aftertaste has only fair length. [S, 67]

GREEN SANDS SHANDY — gold; dominant aroma and flavor is light lime; there is a faint maltiness in behind, but it is more like a soft drink with a malt base, and 1% alcohol; there is also a noticeable apple component. [ML, 14]

P.T. San Miguel Brewery
Brewery in Tambun, Bekasi, West Java. One of the San Miguel, Manila breweries.

SAN MIGUEL BEER — gold, hop aroma with malt backing, good hop and malt flavor, well-balanced, good body, long dry hop aftertaste, good satisfying serious brew. [B, 67]

SAN MIGUEL DARK BEER — deep red-brown, rich off-dry toasted malt nose, complex toasted malt and licorice flavor, pleasant long malt aftertaste. [B, 84]

Japan

Kirin Brewery Co., Ltd.
Twelve breweries in Japan, including Tokyo and Kyobashi

KIRIN BEER — pale yellow-gold, off-dry malt nose; flavor has more hops than malt; hop finish and aftertaste are light and long; medium body, clean tasting. [B, 67]

KIRIN LIGHT BEER — bright gold, faint off-dry malt and hop nose, very light hop and malt flavor, light dry malt finish, brief dry malt aftertaste. [LO, 28]

KIRIN DRAFT BEER — bright gold, faint malt aroma and flavor, faint dry hop finish and aftertaste. [B, 13]

KIRIN FINE MALT — deep gold, big hop and malt nose, good body; flavor is malt in front, hops in back, medium dry long malt aftertaste. [B, 54]

KIRIN ICHIBAN — hazy gold, grainy malt nose, malt flavor, hop finish, medium length. Called Ichiban Shibori in Japan. [B, 43]

KIRIN DRY DRAFT BEER — brilliant gold, light perfumy malt nose, very dry malt flavor, finish, and aftertaste. [D, 36]

BUDWEISER BEER — pale yellow-gold, almost no aroma at all, light body, very dry malt fla-vor with hops in back, brief faint malt aftertaste. [B, 45]

HEINEKEN BEER — bright gold, faint malt nose, malt flavor with hops faintly in back, hop finish, brief dry hop aftertaste. [B, 26]

CIPANGO BEER — gold, pleas-ant light malt and hop aroma, very light flavor like the nose, hops more noticeable in the dry finish and aftertaste. [B, 19]

KIRIN AKI AJI — gold; big malt aroma is very nice; dull dry malt flavor, dry malt aftertaste. [B, 40]

KIRIN PREMIUM BEER — gold; big fruity enticing malt aroma; slightly toasted malt fla-vor, light body, good character, long dry malt aftertaste. [B, 53]

KIRIN KANSAI TASTE — gold, slightly stinky malt nose, off-dry fruity malt flavor like a malt liquor, good body; cuts off abruptly at the finish. [B, 26]

KIRIN RICH TYPE — hazy gold, malt nose with faint hops; carbon-ation sting rides a good malt and hop flavor; good balance and body, long dry aftertaste. [B, 54]

KIRIN GOLDEN BITTER — hazy gold, malt and hop aroma, very dry hop flavor; highly car-bonated to extent it interferes with the flavor; good body, long dry aftertaste. [B, 39]

KIRIN BLACK BEER — deep ruby brown, burnt malt aroma; burnt malt flavor has a bite and a licorice background; tastes like "more"; short aftertaste. [B, 58]

KIRIN LAGER — gold, ample hop aroma; dry hop flavor is a bit sour, especially at the finish; dry hop aftertaste. [B, 35]

Sapporo Breweries, Ltd.
Brewery in Tokyo

SAPPORO LAGER BEER — medium gold, mellow hoppy nose; pleasant hop flavor has good malt in support; brief dry hop aftertaste. [B, 23]

SAPPORO DRAFT BEER — hazy gold, fruity malt and apple peel nose, plenty of malt throughout pal-ate, dry hop aftertaste. [B, 14]

SAPPORO BLACK BEER — opaque red-brown, heavy malt aroma with a tang in back, flavor like the nose, medium body, creamy texture, faintly sour malt aftertaste. [B, 49]

NEXT ONE LIGHT AND TASTY DRAFT BEER — pale gold, sour hop nose, high carbonation, light body, faint malt and hop palate, faint dry hop aftertaste. [B, 26]

YEBISU DRAFT BEER — deep gold, good beery nose with plenty of hops; zesty dry flavor has more hops than malt, additional malt would help the balance; hop finish, long dry hop aftertaste. [B, 47]

YEBISU PREMIUM DRAFT BEER — deep hazy gold, big malt and hop nose, big body, hefty malt flavor, long long dry malt and hop aftertaste. [B, 55]

SAPPORO DRAFT DRY — brilliant gold, very light perfumy malt aroma, very dry malt flavor, dry malt finish and aftertaste, not much to it. [D, 31]

SAPPORO DRAFT THE WINTER'S TALE 1991 — gold, dank malt nose; crisp dry malt flavor tastes better as you continue to drink it; dry malt finish and aftertaste. [B, 43]

SAPPORO THE WINTER'S TALE 1992 — gold, hop and vegetal malt nose, hop and sour malt flavor, medium body, long dry hop aftertaste. [B, 43]

YEBISU DRAFT STOUT — deep gold, pleasant malt nose, alcoholic malt flavor, medium body, smooth, dry malt aftertaste. [S, 5]

SAPPORO SPECIAL CLEAN MALT DRAFT BEER — gold, hop nose, medium dry malt flavor, dry hop finish and aftertaste, good length. "Clean" means made with hulled malt. [B, 50]

SAPPORO MALT 100 ALL MALT BEER — medium deep gold, big grainy malt and hop nose, good body, clean malt flavor, long malt aftertaste with hops faintly in back. [B, 63]

SAPPORO GINJIKOMI SPECIAL CLEAN MALT — gold, beautiful fresh malt and hop nose is appetizing; pleasant malt flavor is faintly oxidized; medium dry malt and light hop aftertaste. Made with hulled malt. [B, 45]

SAPPORO HI-LAGER — hazy gold, pleasant fruity malt aroma and flavor, fairly light, good body, dry and fairly long malt aftertaste. All barley malt used. [B, 47]

HOKKAIDA NAMA — gold, faint malt aroma, malt and hop flavor, highly carbonated, dry hop finish and aftertaste. [B, 38]

SAPPORO HAIZEN (ROASTED) DRAFT — amber, dry malt nose and taste, faintly oxidized, dull dry malt finish, short dry malt aftertaste. [B, 28]

SAPPORO ORIGINAL DRAFT BEER — tawny-gold, big hop nose, bright hop flavor, good body, dry hop finish and aftertaste, fairly long. [B, 50]

SAPPORO STOUT DRAFT — pale gold, perfumy malt nose; flavor is malty and drier than the aroma; dry malt finish and aftertaste, medium to light body, good with food. [B, 22]

Asahi Breweries
Brewery in Tokyo

ASAHI LAGER BEER — very pale gold, clean fresh springwater and malt nose, flavor like the nose, very light and inoffensive, little aftertaste. [B, 54]

ASAHI DRAFT BEER — bright gold, light hop and malt aroma, light grape hop flavor, dry hop finish and aftertaste. [B, 32]

ASAHI SUPER DRY — light gold, faint apple malt nose, light body, weak malt flavor, short weak dull malt aftertaste. [D, 25]

Notes

ASAHI "Z" DRAFT BEER — deep gold, hop and malt nose, light malt flavor, dry hop finish, long dry hop aftertaste. [B, 41]

COORS BEER — light gold, clean light grainy nose, pleasant off-dry malt flavor, light body, long pleasant malt aftertaste. [B, 48]

ASAHI ORIGINAL ALE 6 — gold, light fruity malt aroma and flavor, big body, very long fruity malt aftertaste; it is off-dry and reminds me of Champale, except that it is not grape. [A, 40]

ASAHI WILD BEAT — hazy gold; dry lightly toasted malt and hop nose; slightly toasted malt flavor, pleasant, dry hop and malt finish and aftertaste, good length. [B, 58]

ASAHI HORO NIGAI BEER — gold, lovely malt and hop nose, highly carbonated, light malt flavor, touch of oxidation, dry malt and hop finish, short aftertaste. [B, 29]

DER LOWENBRAU DRAFT BEER — gold, malt and hop aroma and flavor, slightly oxidized, dull malt and hop finish, short aftertaste; tends to sweetness at end. [B, 30]

ASAHI EDOMAE DRAFT BEER — gold, flowery hop and malt aroma; refreshing dry hop flavor has malt in back; medium body, dry hop finish and aftertaste. [B, 56]

Orion Breweries
Brewery in Nago, Okinawa

ORION LAGER BEER — deep yellow-gold, malt aroma and flavor, light hops in the finish and aftertaste. [B, 10]

ORION DRAFT BEER — gold, good hop and malt nose, bright hop and malt flavor, highly carbonated, light body, dry malt finish and aftertaste, quite short. [B, 48]

Suntory, Ltd.
Breweries in Osaka and Tokyo

SUNTORY REAL DRAFT BEER — gold, faint malt aroma, medium body; carbonation dominates the flavor which is malt and apple peel; dull dry malt finish and aftertaste. [B, 34]

SUNTORY BEER — bright pale gold; dull faintly hopped nose is a little stinky; flavor is dull malt and hops; dry hop finish, and the aftertaste is dry sour hops. [B, 36]

SUNTORY MALT'S ALL MALT BEER — very deep gold, big grainy malt nose, good body, slightly off malt flavor, long dry hop aftertaste. [B, 39]

SUNTORY LIGHT'S — pale gold, dusty malt nose; dull malt flavor tends toward off-dry; sort of creamy, dry malt finish and aftertaste. [LO, 31]

Korea

Chosun Brewery Co., Ltd.
Brewery in Seoul

CROWN LAGER BEER — pale gold, faint malt and hop nose, faint sweetness way in back; flavor is off-dry malt with hops; medium body, fair duration. [B, 52]

CROWN DRY — gold, faint malt and hop nose, light weak malt flavor, light body, short dry aftertaste. [D, 52]

HITE BEER — hazy pale gold, light malt and hop nose, light dry faint hop flavor, some faint sweetness in the finish, light body, faint dry malt aftertaste. [B, 25]

Jinro Coors Brewing Co., Ltd.
Brewery in Seoul

CASS FRESH BEER — pale gold, very finely carbonated (small bubbles), hop aroma, light dry hop flavor, light to medium body, dry hop finish and aftertaste, not long but very refreshing. [B, 54]

Oriental Brewery Co., Ltd.
Brewery in Seoul

ORIENTAL OB LAGER BEER — pale gold, light malt and apple peel aroma and flavor, mostly a dry malt finish and aftertaste. [B, 24]

OB DRY BEER — bright gold, hop nose; palate is sweet malt up front; watery hop finish, light short dry hop aftertaste. [D, 39]

NEX BEER — bright deep gold, faint malty aroma, very malty taste, slightly sweet, sweeter in the finish and aftertaste, light body. [B, 23]

Malaya

Malayan Breweries Pte., Ltd.
Brewery in Singapore. Archipelago Brewery Co. (1947), Ltd.

ANCHOR PILSENER BEER — deep gold, hop and malt nose, slightly roasted malt flavor, malt-hop finish, decent balance, good body, long malt and hop aftertaste. [B, 39]

TIGER GOLD MEDAL LAGER BEER — gold, good malt and hop nose, light malt flavor with apple peel in finish, dull malt and hop aftertaste. [B, 32]

ABC EXTRA STOUT — opaque brown, brown head, off-dry malt and hop nose; palate is complex; herbal roasted malt is off-dry until the finish which is dry and faintly burnt; long off-dry malt aftertaste with some licorice and molasses, an interesting stout. [S, 59]

New Guinea

Papua New Guinea Pty, Ltd.
Brewery in Port Moresby, New Guinea is one of the San Miguel, Manila, owned breweries.

SAN MIGUEL PILSNER BEER — medium gold, malt nose, woody malt flavor, faint dry hop aftertaste. [B, 12]

SAN MIGUEL NEGRA DARK BEER — pale red-brown, dry roasted malt nose and similar but drier flavor, dry hop finish and aftertaste. [B, 49]

SP Brewery, Ltd.
Brewery in Papua

SOUTH PACIFIC SPECIAL EXPORT LAGER — pale gold, pleasant malt aroma with hops in back; palate is off-dry malt in front, dry in the middle and finish; off-dry malt aftertaste. [B, 49]

Philippines

Asia Brewery, Inc.
Brewery in Manila

MANILA GOLD PALE PILSEN BEER — pale bright gold, sweet fruitlike aroma, very dry hop flavor, finish, and aftertaste. [B, 25]

San Miguel Brewery
Brewery in Manila is one of three in the Philippines.

SAN MIGUEL BEER — pale yellow-gold, complex malt and strong hop nose, creamy and fresh tasting, excellent balance, good fresh malt and hop flavor, long refreshing dry hop aftertaste. [B, 67]

SAN MIGUEL PALE PILSEN — pale straw yellow; malt nose is a bit grainy; malt flavor with light hop background, medium body, light dry hop aftertaste. [B, 29]

SAN MIGUEL DARK BEER — deep red-brown, light rich toasted malt aroma, well-balanced rich malt and hop flavor, toffee-mint finish, long refreshing malt and hop aftertaste; marvelous big bodied brew is very satisfying. [B, 86]

RED HORSE MALT LIQUOR — pale gold, faint wine malt nose; fruity malt flavor is refreshing but not complex; slight hop tang in the aftertaste. [B, 34]

Samoa

Western Samoa Breweries, Ltd.
Brewery in Apia

RAINMAKER IMPORTED PREMIUM BEER — tawny-gold, faintly skunky hop nose; complex flavor is hops at first, then light off-dry malt, long off-dry malt aftertaste. [B, 34]

Tahiti

Brasserie de Tahiti
Brewery in Papeete

HINANO TAHITI LAGER BEER — pale gold, malt aroma with good hops, clean bright hop and off-dry malt flavor, light body, dry light hop finish and aftertaste. [B, 34]

Thailand

Boon Rawd Brewery Co., Ltd.
Brewery in Bangkok

SINGHA LAGER BEER — brilliant gold, pleasant malt nose with good hop character, strong and bitter hop flavor, lingering hop aftertaste. [B, 40]

SINGHA LAGER STOUT — deep gold; sour grainy nose and taste with a large dose of hops that hang on into the long aftertaste; big body, strong brew. [B, 16]

SINGHA GOLD LIGHT BEER — gold, hop aroma, thin very dry hop flavor, high carbonation; fades fast; leaves dry sour hop aftertaste. [B, 27]

Thai Amarit Brewery, Ltd.
Brewery in Bangkok

SIAM ALE — pale gold; skunky hop nose overwhelms any malt; off-dry malt front palate, hop finish, long strong hop aftertaste. [A, 14]

AMARIT LAGER BEER — pale gold, clean malt aroma with hops in back, too high carbonation; balanced malt and hop flavor; bitter hop aftertaste. [B, 34]

PAYAK LAGER BEER — medium pale gold, hop nose, dry hop and malt flavor, not balanced, dry hop finish and aftertaste. [B, 32]

BANGKOK BEER — pale gold; skunky nose at first but it yields to faint malt; faint malt flavor is very short. [B, 14]

Vietnam

Hue Brewery
Brewery in Hue City

HUE BEER — pale gold; slightly perfumy malt aroma has a light hop backing; dry hop flavor seems a little sour at first but quickly takes on a light grape character; medium body, grape finish, dry hop aftertaste, creamy refreshing brew. [B, 54]

Saigon Beer Co.
Brewery in Ho Chi Minh City

SAIGON EXPORT — pale gold; dull malty aroma is faint and a little grape; dull off-dry malt flavor, medium to light body, dry malt finish and aftertaste. [B, 29]

AUSTRALIA

Ltd. / Coopers Brewery Ltd.
Breweries in Upper Kensington, Burnside, and Leabrook

BIG BARREL AUSTRALIAN LAGER — deep gold, faint malt aroma, light hop flavor, dry hop aftertaste, fairly dull and short. [B, 24]

THOS. COOPER ADELAIDE LAGER — medium bright gold, light malt and hop nose, malt flavor, fresh and zesty up front and in finish, weak in the middle, light body, off-dry malt and hop finish and aftertaste, fairly short. The description of this beer exactly matches my notes for Copper Gold Crown Beer tasted here in the 1970s and early 1980s, and must be a new label for that product. [B, 34–45]

COOPER'S SPARKLING ALE — draft version, cloudy gold, bright hop aroma, tangy big hop flavor, malt finish; bright long aftertaste has both malt and hops; a very nice zesty brew. [A, 61]

COOPER'S ORIGINAL PALE ALE — golden amber, hop nose, dry hop palate, light body, light dry hop finish and aftertaste, medium length. [A, 53]

COOPER'S LIGHT — deep gold, fresh hop aroma, bright but light hop and malt flavor, light body, dry hop finish and aftertaste, not much length. [LO, 38]

Notes

COOPER'S GENUINE DRAFT — hazy gold, malt aroma and flavor, good body; finishes dry malt leading into a long dry malt aftertaste. [B, 56]

COOPER'S REAL ALE — cloudy gold, distinctive malt aroma, bright tangy English-style ale flavor, good malt and a lot of hops; stays dry while giving up lots of flavor for the palate; heavy body, great complexity and duration. [A, 53]

COOPER BEST EXTRA STOUT — dark brown, spicy malt aroma, rich roasted malt flavor, medium to good body, complex yet clean, long malt aftertaste. [S, 67]

COOPERS BLACK CROW — deep gold, wet cloth and malt nose, dry sour malt flavor, medium body, dull sour malt aftertaste, very dry at the end. [B, 20]

South Australia Brewing Co.
Breweries in Adelaide and Thebarton (So. Australia)

BROKEN HILL LAGER BEER — pale gold, faint malty cider nose, hop flavor, dry hop aftertaste with little length. [B, 53]

BROKEN HILL OLD STOUT — deep reddish-brown, off-dry complex roasted malt nose with some chocolate and black malt; big roasted malt flavor is not as sweet as the nose with enough harshness from the roasting to balance the sweetness; finish is drier still; medium body, long dry roasted malt aftertaste, an excellent stout. [S, 74]

OLD AUSTRALIA STOUT — opaque brown, fruity-winey complex toasted malt nose, dry toasted malt flavor, off-dry malt finish, long dry malt aftertaste with concentration. [S, 71]

SOUTHWARK PREMIUM LAGER BEER — deep gold, off-dry apple peel and malt aroma, off-dry malt palate, some roasted malt in back. dry malt aftertaste, very little discernible hop character. [B, 43]

SOUTHWARK EXPORT PILSENER — gold, pleasant aroma of malt and hops; flavor is malt with hop backing; sour hop finish, very little aftertaste. [B, 60]

SOUTHWARK BITTER BEER — gold, hop nose, big hop flavor, good body, harshly bitter up front; smoother toward the finish and aftertaste but stays hoppy. [B, 32]

WEST END EXPORT BEER — gold, big hop nose; slightly roasted malt and hop flavor; dry hop finish and aftertaste, good length, good flavor. [B, 50]

WEST END XXX BITTER BEER — yellow-gold, hop nose, bitter hop flavor; enough malt to provide some balance; finishes softer, long smooth dry hop and malt aftertaste. [B, 47]

SOUTHWARK GOLD LAGER BEER — gold, dusty buttery malt nose with a faint sense of vinegar in back, high carbonation, off chemical taste, bad, bad, bad. [B, 37]

WEST END EAGLE BLUE — pale amber, big malt aroma, grainy malt flavor, light body, light malt finish and short dry malt aftertaste. [B, 35]

WEST END SUPER — amber-gold, good hop and malt aroma, somewhat grape malt taste, off-dry for the most part, good body, off-dry malt finish and aftertaste, good duration. [B, 38]

WEST END DRAUGHT — tawny-gold, good hop aroma; malty flavor has good hop backing; good body, balanced long dry hop aftertaste, pleasant and drinkable and rated at 4.5% abv. [B, 53]

BROKEN HILL REAL ALE — gold, big hop nose, big bitter dry hop flavor, bitter hop aftertaste, medium to good body, very long, no character beyond the bitterness. [A, 56]

The Brisbane Brewery Pty., Ltd.
Brewery in Brisbane

AUSTRALIA PREMIUM LAGER — deep gold, lovely

beery malt nose, fruity malt and tart hop flavor, good body, short malt and hop aftertaste. [B, 35]

Carlton & United Breweries, Ltd.

Operates ten breweries in Australia, including Brisbane, Melbourne, Carlton, and Sydney. Products exported to the U.S.A. cite brewery of production being in Melbourne. Tooth labels (including Reschs) are designated as being from Sydney.

FOSTER'S LAGER — gold, fresh light hop and malt aroma, light body, fresh well-hopped flavor, pleasantly balanced, good finish, long dry hop aftertaste. Available on draft in the U.S.A., but that Foster's is made in Canada (see Molson). [B, 67]

FOSTER'S LIGHT LAGER — bright gold, light dry malt aroma; flavor is weak malt and carbonation; light body; faint malt aftertaste is short. [LO, 17]

FOSTER'S SPECIAL BITTER — tawny-gold, pleasant hop aroma, very light dry hop flavor, light body, more dry than bitter, very long very dry hop aftertaste, somewhat low alcohol (2.8%). [B, 36]

VICTORIA BITTER ALE — yellow-gold, pungent hop nose, big hop flavor well-backed with malt, big body, long dry hop aftertaste, a big hoppy brew. [A, 49]

ABBOTS LAGER — yellow-gold, apple-malt nose, light malt flavor, light body; finishes slightly sour; short malt aftertaste. [B, 29]

MELBOURNE BITTER — amber-gold, malt nose, light bitter hop flavor, light body, very sharp hop finish and aftertaste. [A, 40]

RESCHS SPECIAL EXPORT PILSENER — pale gold, light fresh light malt and hop aroma; good flavor is off-dry malt at first, then clean dry hops, short dry hop aftertaste. Has been labeled Reschs Premium Lager. [B, 37]

RESCHS REAL BITTER BEER — amber-gold, slightly stinky hop nose, faintly sour hop palate, medium body, long dry hop aftertaste. [B, 27]

TOOTHS KB LAGER — pale gold, faint malt nose, light body, light malt flavor, light dry hop finish and aftertaste. [B, 29]

SHEAF STOUT — deep dark brown, almost opaque, toffee-coffee nose, big smoky coffee flavor, medium body, long pleasant coffee-malt aftertaste. Was previously labeled Tooth Sheaf Stout before C&U took over Tooth. [S, 74]

NQ LAGER — deep gold, light hop aroma with some malt; flavor starts out hops but malt quickly joins in and there is lots of it; big body, a very hefty brew, good balance; very long aftertaste has rich malt and dry hops. [B, 58]

CAIRNS DRAUGHT — deep gold, light hop nose, big hop and malt flavor, good body; finishes

with complex malt and dry hops; long medium dry hop and malt aftertaste; aftertaste gets more hoppy as it goes; a long bright and complex beer with dry hops and off-dry malt. [B, 56]

N.T. DRAUGHT BEER — deep amber-gold, big vegetal malt and hop aroma; lusty malt and hop flavor is a bit on the sour side; big body, hop finish, long dry hop aftertaste has a malty background. N.T. Brewery Pty., Ltd. Darwin. Version from a 2-liter Darwin "Stubby." [B, 56]

N.T. DRAUGHT BEER — gold, big malty nose and taste, good body, long off-dry malt aftertaste. Draft version. [B, 58]

KENT OLD BROWN — amber-brown, light malt aroma and flavor, very good balance, smooth and delicious, dry malt finish and aftertaste, light, dry, and easy to drink. [B, 40]

CARLTON D-ALE — bright gold, grape malt aroma, very grape malt flavor, off-dry malt finish, long off-dry malt aftertaste. [A, 38]

CARLTON CROWN LAGER — gold, big hop and malt aroma, pleasant malty flavor with good hop support, good body, dry hop finish; long dry hop aftertaste still shows plenty malt flavor. [B, 61]

CARLTON GENUINE DRAUGHT — deep gold, light malt and hop nose; some complexity in the flavor which is balanced malt and hops; good body, malt and dry hop finish; long dry hop aftertaste does show continuation of the malt of the flavor. [B, 54]

Castlemaine Perkins Ltd.
Brewery in Milton (Queensland)

CASTLEMAINE SPECIAL DRY BEER — deep gold, sort of a sour hop nose, very good crisp hop and malt flavor, good body, very long dry hop and malt aftertaste. [D, 58]

CASTLEMAINE XXXX BITTER ALE — gold, light malt and hop aroma, zesty well-hopped palate with fine balance, dry hop finish, long dry hop aftertaste well-backed with malt, good tasting brew. [A, 70]

CASTLEMAINE XXXX LIGHT BITTER — gold, faint hop and malt nose, very dry hop flavor; some malt joins in at the finish and stays for the aftertaste; light body, short light dry hop aftertaste. [B, 27]

CASTLEMAINE XXXX GOLD LAGER — deep gold, light hop

and malt aroma, dry hop flavor, medium body, light dry hop finish and aftertaste. [B, 42]

CASTLEMAINE XXXX EXPORT LAGER — light gold, spicy malt aroma, big hop flavor with a spicy background, dry hop finish and aftertaste. [B, 20]

CASTLEMAINE XXXX DRAUGHT — deep gold, likable hop and malt aroma, bright hop flavor; malt shows in the finish; long balanced hop and malt aftertaste. [B, 20]

CARBINE STOUT — tawny-brown, big toasty malt nose, dry roasted malt flavor, balanced, good body, complex toasted malt finish and aftertaste. [S, 50]

Eumundi Brewing Co. Pty., Ltd.
Microbrewery in Eumundi (Queensland)

EUMUNDI LAGER — pale amber, complex malt aroma, very smooth malt flavor, not much hops, good body, pleasant, drinkable; finishes dry malt; fairly long dry malt aftertaste. [B, 55]

Frontier Brewery / Top End Frontier Hotel Brewery Bar
Brewpub in Darwin (Northern Territory)

FRONTIER GOLD ALE — pale gold, light malt aroma, lactic background to a light malt palate, pretty good of type, long faintly spicy aftertaste. When I talked to brewmaster Dieter Streke, he said the beer is made with a 40% wheat malt and should not have the lactic bite. To make the point he served up some of the same batch that he had bottled from cask directly (without going through the lines to the taps) and it was clean and bright without any lactic acid. [W, 54]

KAKADU LAGER — gold, faint hop aroma, hefty bold hop flavor, dry hop finish, light body; at finish flavor drops off fast to a light long dry hop aftertaste. [B, 55]

MATILDAY SPARKLING ALE — gold, malt aroma; big malt flavor has plenty of hop bite; this beer too has a faint lactic background from the taps which the brewmaster assures me came from insufficient cleaning of the lines; long dry hop and malt aftertaste. [A, 47]

OLD BUFFALO BITTER — amber, malt aroma; big bold flavor has much hops and malt; good body; long dry hop aftertaste has plenty of malt backing; a big full-flavored brew that is very enjoyable. [A, 63]

Geelong Breweries Co. Pty., Ltd.
Microbrewery in Moolap (Victoria)

VAN DIEMENS LAGER BEER — gold, malty-apple nose, cidery malt flavor, finely carbonated; faintly oxidized but not to point of being harmed; medium body; ends

sweeter than it starts but remains pleasant throughout. [B, 52]

COOK'S EXPORT LAGER — pale gold; malty aroma and flavor shows a background of hops; medium to good body, dry hop finish and aftertaste, 4.9% abv. [B, 60]

GEELONG LAGER — pale gold; malt aroma and flavor has a good hop support; medium to good body, dry hop finish and aftertaste, very similar to Cook's Export Lager, also 4.9% abv. [B, 60]

GEELONG BITTER — amber-gold, bright hop nose, crisp well-hopped flavor, medium to good body, dry hop finish and aftertaste, 4.9% abv. [B, 55]

GEELONG LIGHT — pale gold, light malt and hop aroma, light hop and malt flavor, light body, light dry hop finish and aftertaste, 3.3% abv. [LO, 38]

DOUBLE GOLD — pale gold, faint grain and hop aroma, somewhat grainy flavor, very light body; light dry hop aftertaste is short; 2.5% abv. [LO, 27]

GEELONG DRAUGHT — gold, hop aroma, crisp hop flavor, medium to good body, good balance, dry hop finish and aftertaste, 4.9% abv. [B, 62]

JAMES SQUIRES AUSTRALIAN TABLE BEER — amber-gold; appetizing malt aroma has some hops; flavor is first hops, mostly malt, and then hops again at the finish; medium to light body, long dry hop aftertaste, fairly ordinary; brewed and

Notes

bottled for Breweries of Australia Pty., Ltd. [B, 54]

Grand Ridge Brewing Co. Pty., Ltd.
Microbrewery in Mirboo North (Victoria)

MOON LIGHT — amber, good malt aroma, big malty flavor, well-bodied, dry hop finish, long very hoppy aftertaste, a pleasant easy drinking beer. [LO, 38]

BREWER'S PILSENER — gold, malt aroma, malty flavor, good body, smooth and balanced, malt finish and aftertaste shows very little hops. [B, 47]

Hahn Brewing Co.
Microbrewery in Camperdown (New South Wales)

HAHN PREMIUM LAGER — gold, fruity malt aroma and flavor, good body, slightly off-dry malt aftertaste, medium length. [B, 40]

HAHN PREMIUM LIGHT — pale gold, light malt aroma and flavor, light body, clean light medium dry malt aftertaste with a faint hop background. [LO, 36]

HAHN SYDNEY BITTER — amber-gold, sour malt aroma and flavor, good body, dry malt finish and aftertaste. [A, 47]

Lederberger Brewing Co. Ltd.
Microbrewery in Tatura (Victoria)

LEDERBERGER DRAUGHT BEER — bright gold, hop nose, big hop flavor, big body, long dry hop aftertaste, a big brew. [B, 60]

LEDERBERGER LAGER BEER — gold, light hop aroma, dry hop flavor, good body; dry hop aftertaste is fairly brief. [B, 38]

The Lord Nelson Brewery Hotel
Brewpub in the Rocks section of Sydney

OLD ADMIRAL — deep amber, big malt aroma, rich smooth malt flavor with some hops, big body, big taste; long rich aftertaste is a continuation of the palate; 6.7% alcohol helps the flavor rather than mars it; a beautiful ale. [A, 69]

VICTORY BITTER — copper-amber, bright well-hopped nose, big hop flavor, good body, dry hop finish and long dry hop aftertaste, a typical English-style bitter. [A, 60]

QUAYLE ALE — pale yellow; light wheaty aroma (it is a wheat beer); pleasant light dry wheaty flavor, very smooth, light body, light dry malt finish and aftertaste, brief. [W, 56]

TRAFALGAR PALE ALE — gold; interesting fruity hop nose (uses Australian Pride of Ringwood hops); bright bitter ale flavor has good hop balance; good body, dry hop finish, medium long dry hop aftertaste; a nicely made beer with good character. [A, 79]

THREE SHEETS — golden amber, big complex hop and malt aroma; complex flavor shows an abundance of malt and hops; big body, stays smooth throughout, a very interesting beer unique in its style, long complex hop and malt aftertaste; perhaps it is the Tasmanian Hallertau hops that make it so interesting; a good likable brew. [A, 89]

Matilda Bay Brewing Co. Ltd.
Brewery in Fremantle, Perth. Red Back Brewpubs in Melbourne and Perth.

RED BACK MALTED WHEAT BEER — bright gold, big head, fruity malt aroma; off-dry malt flavor with a sharp and spicy component that continues on into the aftertaste; light body. [W, 37]

DOGBOLTER SPECIAL DARK LAGER — dark brown, chocolate malt and roasted barley aroma; smooth flavor reflects the nose; very malty, big body, dry roasted malt finish and aftertaste, not much length. Made and bottled in Perth. [B, 53]

DOGBOLTER SPECIAL DARK LAGER — amber, big dry malt aroma and flavor, good body, faint roasted malt character but more dry than toasty, dry malt finish and aftertaste, very good with food. Draft version made in Melbourne. [B, 74]

RED BACK LIGHT — pale gold, light slightly grainy malt aroma and flavor, light body, dry malt finish and aftertaste, short. Seen only on draft. [LO, 38]

BRASS MONKEY STOUT — deep brown, tan head, clean malt aroma, rich roasted barley flavor, good body, not big, dry malt finish and long dry malt aftertaste. Seen only on draft. [S, 54]

IRONBREW — very deep amber, fruity aroma; rich fruity malt flavor is a knockout; medium dry malt finish, long dry malt aftertaste; has 7.1% alcohol, but it is not all that noticeable; an excellent brew. [B, 83]

OKTOBERFEST — fairly deep golden color, light malt nose and taste, medium body, dry hop finish, very long dry hop aftertaste. [B, 58]

RED BACK HEFE-WEIZEN — cloudy gold, bright wheat malt nose, big malt flavor with a great spicy character but no acidity, long clean aftertaste, a very nicely made beer. [W, 63]

RED BACK CRYSTAL — bright clear gold, clean malt aroma and flavor, very smooth, very bright, especially at the finish, long dry malt aftertaste, another nicely made brew. [W, 58]

MATILDA BAY PILS — pale gold, light hop aroma and flavor, medium to good body; dry malt finish and aftertaste is only lightly hopped. [B, 47]

PORT MELBOURNE PALE ALE — amber-gold, fresh malt and hop nose; very bright flavor offers both malt and hops; excellent balance, good body, complex and delicious, long dry hop aftertaste, another winner. [A, 81]

Mildura Brewery, Ltd.
Brewery in Mildura

DOWN UNDER LAGER BEER — tawny-gold, vegetal malt nose, wine malt flavor up front, bitter hop finish, dull malt aftertaste. [B, 14]

Northern Breweries Pty., Ltd.
Brewery in Mildura

KANGAROO BEER — bright gold, grainy malt nose, off-dry malt flavor up front; hop middle is quite bitter; dry hop finish and aftertaste. [B, 28]

Powers Brewing Co., Ltd.
Brewery at Yatala (Queensland)

POWER'S LIGHT BEER — deep gold, faint hop nose, light dry hop flavor, very faint malt way in back, light to medium body, short dry hop aftertaste. [LO, 32]

Notes

POWER'S BITTER — deep gold, faint hop nose, big hop flavor, fairly dry, certainly bitter, dry hop finish and aftertaste, good length. [B, 47]

POWER'S BIG RED — gold, malty nose; big malty flavor does have some background hops; big body, malt finish, long dry malt aftertaste. [B, 55]

POWER'S PREMIUM DRY — amber-gold; malt and hop aroma is a bit vegetal; light hop flavor tends to the dry side; light body, dry hop finish and aftertaste. [D, 38]

GENUINE BITTER QUEENSLAND DRAUGHT — gold, light hop nose, pleasant balanced malt and hop flavor, good body, long dry hop aftertaste. [B, 41]

Pump House Brewery & Tavern / Tankstream Brewing Co.
Brewpub at Darling Harbour (Sydney)

BREWER'S DRAUGHT — gold, mild malt aroma, bright dry hop flavor, good malt backing, long dry hop aftertaste. [A, 53]

PUMPHOUSE EXTRA — gold, mild malt aroma, very malty flavor, good body, dry malt aftertaste. [B, 46]

GOLDEN WHEAT — pale gold, faint wheaty-malt nose, light body, light malt flavor, dry malt finish, short dry malt aftertaste. [W, 47]

THUNDERBOLT ALE — amber-gold, hop nose, bright hop and malt ale flavor, good body, dry hop finish; long dry aftertaste has plenty of both hops and malt. [A, 60]

BULLSHEAD BITTER — amber, really nice hop aroma, bright hop flavor, plenty of malt for good balance, big body, faintly soapy but still very good, dry hop finish and aftertaste, good long aftertaste too. [A, 56]

FEDERATION ALE — deep amber, malt nose, big dry malt flavor, big body, a slightly roasted character to the malt, long dry malt aftertaste, very enjoyable. [A, 55]

Riverside Agencies, Pty., Ltd.
Contractor at Alice Springs (Northern Territory)

RED CENTRE LAGER BEER — pale gold, hop nose, caramelized malt flavor; hops come in at the finish for the aftertaste, but unfortunately clash with the malt. Contract brewer not presently known. [B, 60]

Sanctuary Cove Brewing Co.
Microbrewery in Southport (Queensland)

CANE TOAD BEER — deep gold; smooth aroma has hops, malt, and alcohol (7%); huge malt flavor well-backed with hops, enormous body, malt finish, long malt aftertaste, an excellent bock-style beer. [B, 79]

Swan Brewery Co., Ltd.
Brewery in Canning Vale, Perth (Western Australia)

SWAN EXPORT LAGER — deep gold, hop nose, brisk hop palate with plenty of malt, good body and balance, dry hop finish, fairly long dry hop aftertaste, good tasting brew. [B, 54]

SWAN GOLD LAGER — gold, fresh fruity malt and dry hop aroma, smooth light dry malt and hop flavor, medium body, light dry hop aftertaste with little duration. [B, 45]

SWAN PREMIUM LAGER — pale gold, apple-malt nose; palate starts out hops but ends up being largely malt; clean and refreshing, somewhat assertive because of the hops up front, dry finish and aftertaste, good length. [B, 64]

SWAN LIGHT LOW ALCOHOL BEER — bright gold, vegetal malt nose, light body, slightly grainy malt palate, light grainy malt finish, short aftertaste. [LA, 24]

EMU EXPORT — gold, malt nose and flavor, dry malt finish and aftertaste, ordinary. [B, 27]

Tasmanian Breweries, Pty., Ltd.
Breweries in Hobart and Launceston. Also known as Cascade Brewery Co., Ltd. The Launceston brewery was Boags Brewery Pty., Ltd. and the

Boags name is used on exports to the U.S.A. while the Cascade and Boags name is used in Australia. The Two Dog logo appears on the Boags products in the U.S.A. and on Cascade products in Australia.

BOAG'S LAGER — pale gold, light malt and perfumy hop nose, good body, light malt flavor, hop finish, short dry hop aftertaste. Originally introduced in the U.S.A. as Cascade Lager, encountered a trade name conflict, reintroduced as Tasmanian Lager Beer, later introduced as Boag's. [B, 36]

BOAGS DRAUGHT BEER — bright gold, faint apple nose, very little beer flavor, just some faint apple and malt fizzy water with a trace of hops in the finish, long faint dry hop aftertaste. [B, 27]

BOAGS XXX ALE — pale yellow, light malt nose, light off-dry malt flavor, light hop finish, short dry light hop aftertaste. [A, 34]

BOAGS PREMIUM LAGER — deep gold, hop nose; flavor is malt first, then hops; light body, short dry hop aftertaste. [B, 19]

BOAGS PREMIUM LIGHT — bright gold, nice beery grainy malt nose, light body, light malt flavor with a slight vegetal character, light malt finish and aftertaste. [LO, 21]

RAZOR'S EDGE LAGER BEER — gold, faint malt nose, high carbonation, hop flavor, finish, and aftertaste; ends well but could use more flavor up front. [B, 40]

CASCADE LAGER — gold, bright hop nose, dry hop flavor, plenty of malt in there as well, very good balance, dry hop finish and aftertaste, a delightful refreshing brew. [B, 71]

CASCADE SPARKLING PALE ALE — gold, big hoppy nose, flavor, finish, and aftertaste, a good strongly hopped bitter brew; wakes up your senses. [A, 56]

CASCADE SPARKLING BITTER BEER — gold, minty hop aroma, big hop flavor; dry hop finish and aftertaste are a bit softer. [A, 49]

CASCADE DRAUGHT — deep gold, a well-hopped malt nose; complex flavor has plenty of both malt and hops but the hops eventually win out as they carry better into the bitter hop finish and long dry hop aftertaste. [B, 32]

CASCADE SPECIAL STOUT — deep brown, rich malt aroma and flavor of chocolate malt and roasted barley, caraway spice background to palate, long dry and rich roasted malt aftertaste, very good of type. [S, 70]

JAMES BOAGS PREMIUM LAGER — deep gold, highly carbonated, sour vegetal hop aroma, light dry hop flavor, finish, and aftertaste. [B, 46]

Notes

Toohey's Ltd.
Breweries at Lidcombe (Sydney), Grafton, and Cardiff

TOOHEY'S LAGER BEER — deep gold; malt nose has some good hops in back; complex balanced flavor that develops both the hops and malt on the palate; stays dry throughout; finishes dry malt and hops, fairly long. [B, 59]

TOOHEY'S LITE LAGER BEER — tawny-gold, faint malt nose, grainy malt flavor, light body, light dry grainy malt aftertaste, short. [LO, 23]

TOOHEY'S DRY — gold, malt nose, malt flavor, light body, dry malt finish and aftertaste, little length. [D, 25]

TOOHEY'S CLASSIC BITTER — gold, light hop aroma and flavor, medium body, light dry hop aftertaste, medium length. [B, 49]

TOOHEY'S DRAUGHT BEER — gold, light hop aroma, light hop and malt flavor, medium body, medium dry hop aftertaste, fair length. [B, 49]

TOOHEY'S OLD BLACK ALE — deep amber brown, malt nose, light roasted barley taste, medium body, reasonably smooth and well-knit, dry toasted malt finish; aftertaste is light but long; very drinkable; goes down easily. [A, 61]

TOOHEY'S RED BITTER BEER — deep gold, big hop nose, big bitter hop flavor, huge body; finishes hops like it starts; very long and flavorful dry hop aftertaste, pretty good beer for everyday use. [B, 59]

TOOHEY'S BLUE LABEL LIGHT BITTER — brownish amber, light hop nose, good light hop flavor with some malt, medium to light body, dry and slightly sour hop aftertaste, good length. [B, 34]

THE CARIBBEAN

Bahamas

Commonwealth Brewery Ltd.
Brewery in the Bahamas

KALIK — pale gold, light hop aroma, light hop flavor, light hop finish and aftertaste. [B, 42]

KALIK GOLD LIMITED EDITION EXTRA STRENGTH — gold, malty nose, big rich malty flavor with a honeyed alcohol nature, rich long and creamy, big body; high alcohol is a bit off-putting and I wouldn't find this refreshing on a warm day. [B, 56]

Barbados

Banks Barbados Breweries, Ltd.
Breweries in Bridgetown, St. Michael, and Wildey

BANKS LAGER BEER — pale gold, delicate perfumy hop and sweet malt nose, flavor like the nose fades across the palate, smooth, medium body, weak malt finish and a short malt aftertaste. [B, 30]

Notes

EBONY SUPER STRENGTH — deep brown, strong caramel, molasses, and roasted malt aroma; strong alcoholic component to the roasted malt flavor giving it a Port-like quality; long and strong off-dry roast malt aftertaste. [B, 29]

Dominican Republic

Cerveceria Bohemia, S.A.
Brewery in Ciudad Trujillo

BOHEMIA CERVEZA — hazy pale amber-gold, light malt nose and flavor with some hops in back; cuts off quickly; brief aftertaste. [B, 37]

Cerveceria Nacional Dominicana, C.X.A.
Brewery in Santo Domingo

PRESIDENTE CERVEZA PILSENER TYPE BEER — bright gold, hop aroma, grainy flavor, dry malt and hop finish, short dry aftertaste, smooth but brief. Export version. [B, 53]

PRESIDENTE CERVEZA TIPO PILSENER — hazy gold, hop nose; dry malt flavor with hops coming in at the finish; good balance, dry malt aftertaste has a bit of oxidation. [B, 52]

Cerveceria Vegana, S.A.
Brewery in Ciudad Trujillo

CERVEZA QUISQUEYA — bright gold, off-dry buttery nose, off-dry fruity-malt palate; high carbonation tends to balance the sweetness; buttery finish and aftertaste. Export version. [B, 62]

CERVEZA QUISQUEYA TIPO PILSENER — hazy gold, pleasant malt aroma, good tasting malt flavor with good hop support, creamy, balanced, long dry malt and hop aftertaste. Domestic version. [B, 62]

Grenada

Grenada Breweries, Ltd.
Brewery in Georgetown

CARIB LAGER — gold; pleasant light flowery hop and fruity malt aroma that is a bit off-dry; fresh tasting fairly dry palate similar to the nose, very drinkable, light body, dry finish and aftertaste, not much length. [B, 41]

Jamaica

Desnoes & Geddes, Ltd.
Brewery in Kingston

RED STRIPE LAGER BEER — pale tawny-gold, good bright hop and malt nose, full-flavored dry malt and hop palate, hops dominate, pleasant and very drinkable, long dry hop aftertaste. [B, 49]

DRAGON STOUT — opaque, brown head, rich off-dry malt nose, big body, lightly sweet malt palate, very tasty, long dry malt aftertaste. [S, 79]

Puerto Rico

Brew Master's Corp.
Brewery in San Juan

BREW MASTER'S LAGER BEER — medium deep gold, off-dry malt aroma, off-dry fruity malt and cardboard flavor, dry malt finish and aftertaste. [B, 25]

Cerveceria Corona, Inc.
Breweries in San Juan and Santurce

CORONA BEER — pale golden yellow, good hop nose; malt flavor is mostly carbonation; light dry malt aftertaste. Export version. [B, 37]

CORONA CERVEZA — pale gold, hop nose, light body, light dry malt flavor, light dry malt aftertaste. [B, 23]

MEDALLA LIGHT CERVEZA — gold, light off-dry malt aroma, high carbonation, light dry malt flavor, light body, short faint dry malt aftertaste. Packed for Medalla Co., San Juan. [B, 21]

Cerveceria India, Inc.
Brewery in Mayaguez

INDIA BEER — pale yellow, fresh malt aroma; clean malt flavor but it is a little dull; lacking balance and complexity, short uninteresting aftertaste. Export version. [B, 50]

INDIA LA CERVEZA DE PUERTO RICO — pale gold, pleasant malt nose, creamy texture, off-dry grainy malt flavor; light dry malt aftertaste has good length; light but pleasant. Domestic version. [B, 50]

Trinidad

Caribe Development Co.
Brewery in Port-of-Spain

ROYAL EXTRA STOUT — deep brown, sweet malt nose and flavor, creamy, like a malt, big body; seems to dry a bit in the aftertaste and as you sip it; long with plenty of alcohol (6.6% abv). [S, 46]

CARIBE LAGER — pale yellow-gold, lovely hop and fruity malt aroma, light body, light fairly dry malt flavor, short off-dry malt aftertaste. [B, 46]

CARIBE — pale gold, lovely hop aroma; dry light flavor doesn't show much of either hops or malt; no aftertaste beyond a faint sensation of dryness. [B, 35]

CARIB SHANDY — pale gold, faint ginger aroma, light gingery flavor, medium dry ginger finish and aftertaste, good body. [B, 16]

Notes

CENTRAL AMERICA

Belize

Belize Brewing Co.
Brewery in Ladyville

BELIKIN BEER — bright gold, large bubble carbonation, good malt aroma with light hops, dry malt flavor, straightforward without complexity, dry malt aftertaste with fair duration, pleasant. [B, 50]

BELIKIN STOUT — deep brown, sweet malt nose, sweet complex winelike palate, heavy body, high alcohol, faintly bitter dry hop aftertaste. [S, 36]

Costa Rica

Cerveceria Costa Rica, S.A.
Brewery in San José

BAVARIA GOLD BEER — medium deep gold, faint off-dry fruity malt aroma with a cardboard background, light sour malt flavor, hop finish and aftertaste, not well-balanced and some off flavors in back. [B, 26]

El Salvador

Cerveceria la Constancia, S.A.
Brewery in San Salvador

PILSENER OF EL SALVADOR EXPORT BEER — pale tawny-gold, light off-dry hop aroma, light body, off-dry straightforward malt and hop flavor, dry hop finish and aftertaste, not much length, but pleasant and refreshing. [B, 38]

SUPREMA SPECIAL BEER — gold, big fragrant hop aroma; zesty well-hopped flavor has plenty of malt in back to balance; slight grape background, big body; long hop aftertaste still has enough malt in reserve to keep it from going dry until the very end. [B, 56]

REGIA EXTRA — pale gold; hop nose is almost skunky; very light hop taste, light body, light dry hop finish and aftertaste, medium length. [B, 37]

NOCHE BUENA SPECIAL DARK LAGER — dark amber, lightly toasted malt aroma, flavor to match, medium body, a little dankness in back, very slightly off-dry toasted malt aftertaste, medium long. [B, 56]

Guatemala

Cerveceria Centroamericana, S.A.
Brewery in Guatemala City

MONTE CARLO LAGER BEER — pale yellow, slightly skunky hop nose, bright hop flavor, nice hop finish, light body, short dry hop aftertaste, refreshing but very short. [B, 41]

MEDALLA DE ORO — pale gold, skunky hop nose, high carbonation, big hop flavor, dull malt finish and aftertaste. [B, 31]

MOZA BOCK BEER — amber, faint fruity nose, light off-dry malt palate, faint hops way in the back, long off-dry malt aftertaste. [BK, 28]

FAMOSA IMPORTED LAGER BEER — gold; nose is more malt than hops but there is plenty of

both; dry hop flavor, very dry hop aftertaste, medium length. [B, 48]

CABRO EXTRA — pale gold, light malt and hop nose, gassy, medium body; flavor almost completely masked by the carbonation until the finish which is hops and malt; medium long dry malt and hop aftertaste; probably pretty good if there were less carbonation. Cerveceria Nacional, S.A., Guatemala City. [B, 34]

Honduras

Cerveceria Hondureña, S.A.
Brewery in San Pedro Sula

PORT ROYAL EXPORT — medium gold, faintly skunky hop nose; elusive malt and hop palate that is slightly fruity at the finish; high carbonation, light body, soapy aftertaste. [B, 24]

SALVA VIDA — gold, skunky nose evolves to hops and malt with a little time; flavor is very slightly oxidized malt; medium to light body, dry malt finish and aftertaste, medium length. [B, 46]

Panama

Cerveceria Panama, S.A.
Brewery in Panama City

CERVEZA SOBERANA — pale gold, faint dry malt aroma, papery malt flavor, metallic aftertaste, light body, low carbonation. [B, 18]

GUINNESS EXTRA STOUT — opaque brown, brown head, big malt and hop nose, dry and bitter hop and malt flavor, not much character, long dry and bitter aftertaste. (Brewed under license.) [S, 41]

Cerveceria del Baru, S.A.
Brewery in David and Chiriqui

CERVEZA CRISTAL — pale gold, fruity off-dry malt nose with some cardboard in back, light body; cardboard reflects into the flavor; fairly long neutral malt aftertaste. [B, 33]

CERVEZA PANAMA LAGER ALEMANIA STYLE — bright gold, light malt nose, slightly sweet malt flavor, medium length dry malt aftertaste; lightly done but pleasant and refreshing. [B, 41]

Cerveceria Nacional, S.A.
Brewery in Panama City

HB CERVEZA NEGRA — bright brown, light dry malt nose and taste, dry finish, little aftertaste, overall a pleasant dark beer. [B, 30]

CERVEZA BALBOA — medium gold, off-dry banana fruit nose, light body, light banana flavor with a sense of acetone, long sour metallic banana aftertaste. [B, 15]

ATLAS CERVEZA LAGER — bright gold, pleasant malt aroma, good malt and hop flavor, nicely balanced, light body, not much of an aftertaste, but a refreshing hot weather brew. [B, 45]

EUROPE

Austria

Adambräu Gesellschaft, M.B.H.
Brewery at Innsbruck

TIROL EXPORT LAGER — amber, off-dry roasted malt and caramel nose, lightly roasted malt palate, hops from middle-on, long hop aftertaste. [B, 57]

ADAM CLASSIC — gold, hop nose, malt flavor, high carbonation, hop finish, dry hop aftertaste. [B, 48]

ADAM HELLES EXPORT — gold; grainy nose seems a bit oatlike; malt flavor with hops in back, dull malt finish, long dry hop and malt aftertaste. [B, 27]

ADAM DUNKEL — brown, dry malt nose, off-dry malt flavor, medium body, off-dry malt finish, fairly dry malt aftertaste; reminds you of a malta (malz bier). [B, 37]

ADAM FESTBIER — brown color, big roasted malt nose, dry roasted malt flavor, finish and aftertaste like the flavor, smooth, balanced, and tasty. [B, 83]

Notes

Brauerei Eggenberg
Brewery in Vorchdorf

EGGENBERGER
SCHLOSSPILS BEER — bright
gold, light hop nose, malt flavor,
light hop and malt aftertaste, little
duration. [B, 17]

EGGENBERGER URBOCK 17 —
medium deep bright gold, good malt
and hop nose, big hop flavor with
plenty of malt, big body, complex;
malt really develops well at the finish and into the long aftertaste. A
very good bock. [BK, 73]

EGGENBERGER URBOCK 23 —
brilliant deep gold, creamy, lovely
slightly roasted big malt nose, huge
body, high alcohol, great malt flavor, smooth and rich; concentrated
malt really fills your mouth and
senses; smooth despite its size,
touch of honey at the finish, very
long malt aftertaste. A great sipping
beer, but it is filling. [BK, 87]

MacQUEENS NESSIE WHIS-
KEY MALT RED BEER — bril-
liant deep gold, excellent lightly
toasted but big malt nose, huge
malt flavor, very heavy body, a
little hop bite at the finish; all malt
and very very long, can't call it
dry but it is not at all sweet despite
the large amount of malt, 7.5%
abv and a 170 density. In the
U.S.A., it is labeled MacQueens
Nessie Original Red Ale. [B, 75]

Privatbrauerei Fritz Egger
Brewery in Unterradlberg

EGGER PILS — yellow-gold,
roasted malt nose and taste, long
roasted malt flavor. [B, 56]

EGGER NATUR-BRÄU — gold,
hop nose with plenty of off-dry
malt, big off-dry toasted malt and
hop flavor, a very good tasting
flavor, high carbonation, off-dry
malt and hop finish; aftertaste is a
bit too sweet. Gravity 12.2 P,
5.2% abv. [B, 47]

Brauerei Fohrenburg
Brewery in Bludenz

FOHRENBURGER
BLONDES — gold; hop nose
does have some malt in back;
flavor is slightly sour malt; malt
finish and aftertaste with hops at
the end. [B, 34]

FOHRENBURGER
JUBILÄUM — gold, toasted
malt nose and taste, off-dry malt
finish; malt aftertaste is a bit
drier; good body, gravity 13.2 P,
5.6% abv. [B, 49]

FOHRENBURGER PILS — gold,
big head, pleasant malt and hop
aroma and taste, finishes dry, long
dry good tasting complex malt and
hop aftertaste; medium to good
body. [B, 75]

FOHRENBURGER
CHARAKTER — gold, some particulate matter in solution, rich malt
nose and taste, very good malt flavor, good body, rich malt finish and

aftertaste, a classical Märzen,
gravity 13.3 P, 5.6% abv. [B, 67]

Gösser Brauerei A.G.
Brewery in Loeben-Göss (Affiliated with Steirische Brauindustrie, A.G.)

GÖSSER GOLDEN ROCK
FAMOUS AUSTRIAN BEER —
gold, light malt and hop aroma,
malt and hop flavor, hop finish,
dry hop aftertaste. [B, 23]

GÖSSER BEER — pale gold,
malt nose with hops in back,
smooth malt and hop flavor, dry
hop finish and aftertaste. [B, 53]

GÖSSER EXPORT BEER — deep
bright gold, big hop aroma, smooth
hop flavor; aftertaste is hops and
malt; medium body. [B, 52]

GÖSSER STIFTSBRAU —
extremely deep red-brown, slightly
toasted malt nose, off-dry roasted
malt flavor, medium to good body,
malt finish and aftertaste; could
use a little more hops for better
balance and complexity. [B, 27]

GÖSSER HELLER BOCK —
medium deep gold, light hop and
malt aroma, balanced hop and
malt flavor, more hops than malt,
however, medium length hop
aftertaste. Very big and good
tasting brew. [BK, 67]

GÖSSER MÄRZEN — gold, pleasant malt nose, big malt and hop flavor on the sour side, dry sour malt
and hop aftertaste. [B, 27]

GÖSSER EXPORT DARK
BEER — deep brown, malt

aroma; off-dry malt flavor shows some chocolate malt; good body; finishes a bit drier than the flavor but retains all of the malty quality and is definitely on the sweet side; long off-dry malt aftertaste. It is too sweet to drink with food, being better after a meal like a dessert (or with dessert). [B, 53]

Harmer K.G. / Ottakringer Brauerei
Brewery in Vienna

OTTAKRINGER FASSL GOLD EXPORT LAGER BEER — brilliant gold, lovely hop aroma, finely balanced hop and malt flavor, good body, clean bright taste throughout, pleasant hop finish, long appetizing hop aftertaste; a very good beer. [B, 91]

OTTAKRINGER GOLD FASSL PILS — pale bright gold, faint hop and malt aroma, hop flavor, finish, and aftertaste. [B, 29]

OTTAKRINGER BOCK — tawny gold, beautiful complex hop and malt nose, big malt flavor with a lot of hop character; big body, richly flavored, lingering aftertaste like the flavor. [BK, 69]

OTTAKRINGER HELLES BIER — gold, huge hop nose; flavor is mostly malt; hop finish, dry light hop aftertaste. [B, 37]

Brauerei Hirt
Brewery in Remlen

HIRTER PRIVAT PILS — gold, malt aroma and flavor, good body,

dry malt finish and aftertaste, gravity 12.3 P, 5.2% abv. [B, 50]

Hofer K.G.
Brewery in Sattledt

MONCH'S GOLD MÄRZEN BIER — gold, dull malt nose, dry malt and hop flavor, medium to good body, dry malt finish and aftertaste, gravity 12.2 P, 5.2% abv. [B, 50]

Brauerei Hofstetten
Brewery at St. Martin

STEINBOCK 17° — tawny-gold, huge toasted malt nose, intense malt flavor like the nose, chewy big body and long malt aftertaste, 7.7% alcohol. [BK, 97]

Burgerbräu Kaiser
Brewery in Innsbruck

INNSBRUCK IMPORTED LAGER BEER — bright gold, big hop nose; flavor is hops and only hops all the way through to the long hop aftertaste. Not especially bitter, just hops and nothing but hops. [B, 26]

KAISER MÄRZEN FASSTYP — gold, big complex malt nose; malt flavor is on the dry side, dry malt aftertaste; lacks richness but otherwise is good; long, nicely balanced, gravity 12.1 P, 5.2% abv. [B, 56]

KAISER KUR PILS — gold, hop nose and flavor, dry hop aftertaste. [B, 27]

Notes

KAISER DOPPEL MALZ FASSTYP — deep brown, roasted malt and caramel nose; big sweet caramel malt flavor is like a malta and is too sweet; big body, long off-dry malt finish and aftertaste, gravity 13.3 P, 4.7% abv. [B, 60]

KAISER PREMIUM — gold, bright hop nose, good malt and hop flavor; piquant-spicy-tangy nature, balanced and smooth, finishes malt, dry hop aftertaste, an interesting complex beer. [B, 67]

Brauerei Kapsreiter
Brewery at Scharding/Inn

KAPSREITER LANDBIER HELL — pale gold, bright hoppy-malt nose, taste like the aroma, balanced and smooth, big body; dry hop aftertaste is long; gravity 12.8 P, 5.3% abv. [B, 63]

KAPSREITER LANDBIER GOLDBRAUN — deep amber-brown, big malt nose, good rich malt flavor, good body, ends dry malt; has a breadlike quality; excellent with food; gravity 12.8 P, 4.4% abv. [B, 53]

KAPSREITER MÄRZEN — gold, hop nose, malt and hop flavor, good body, balanced; big, fairly rich, dry malt aftertaste is a bit dull, but aroma and front palate are very good; gravity 12.2 P, 5.1% abv. [B, 61]

Vereinigte Kärtner Brauereien A.G.
Brewery in Villach

VILLACHER GOLD EXPORT BEER — gold, good malt aroma with light hops, light body; hop flavor is best up front, flattens and weakens to the finish; light dry hop aftertaste. [B, 47]

Österreichische Brauerei A.G.
Breweries in Linz, Weiselburg, Kaltenhausen (Salzburg), et al.

AUSTRIAN GOLD LAGER BEER — gold, rising hop nose with an off-dry malt background, medium dry hop flavor, dull dry hop and malt aftertaste. [B, 37]

ADLER BRAU EXPORT — amber, light toasted malt nose, hop flavor, bitter hop aftertaste. [B, 49]

EDELWEISS HEFETRUB-WEIZENBIER — hazy gold, very sweet malt nose, good tasting bright malt flavor with a spicy background, toasted malt and spicy clove finish and long clean aftertaste, very refreshing weizenbier. From Hofbrau Kaltenhausen. [W, 62]

EDELWEISS KRISTALLKLAR WEIZENBIER — hazy gold, fruity estery nose (possibly banana), refreshing light spicy flavor, zesty and bright, fairly long aftertaste. From Hofbrau Kaltenhausen. [W, 26]

EDELWEISS WEIZENBIER DUNKEL — hazy amber, fruity-berry aroma, with a faint estery character (possibly banana); this time the banana quality is in with the wheat and a spicy bite in the flavor; long spicy hop and malt aftertaste. From Hofbrau Kaltenhausen. [W, 25]

Brauerei Schwechat A.G.
Brewery in Vienna

STEFFL EXPORT — gold, malt nose and taste, hop finish, dry hop aftertaste. [B, 23]

VIENNA LAGER BEER — gold, lovely malt and hop nose, highly hopped palate, hop finish, long dry hop aftertaste, medium body, little complexity. [B, 27]

Privatbrauerei Josef Sigl
Brewery in Obertrum am See

WEIZEN GOLD DUNKELES HEFEWEIZEN — hazy amber, foamy, malt nose with a lactic acid background like cloves, off-dry malt front palate, spicy middle and finish, good body; too much carbonation as it interferes with the flavors that are otherwise balanced; long spicy malt aftertaste. [W, 35]

WEIZEN GOLD HEFEWEIZENBIER — slightly hazy gold, spicy complex clove nose and big spicy flavor, creamy, lively, tasty, a sprightly dry malt finish with the spiciness in back, long aftertaste like the finish. [W, 80]

WEIZEN GOLD CHAMPAGNER WEIZENBIER — pale gold, malt nose; spice is there but it is very faint; more a dry sparkling malt flavor, dry malt finish and aftertaste; Champagne-like. [W, 72]

Vertrieb Fa. Tigast Handelges. m.b.H.
Brewery in Wörgel

SIXTUS BRÄU PILS — gold, hop nose, bright hop taste, lots of malt backing, very drinkable and refreshing, dry hop finish, long dry hop aftertaste, gravity 12 P, 5% abv. [B, 57]

Steirische Brauindustrie, A.G. / Br. Puntigam / Bruder Reininghaus Brauerei A.G.
Breweries in Graz and Puntigam

PUNTIGAMER PANTHER GENUINE DRAFT BEER — gold, malt nose, malt and bitter hop flavor and finish, long bitter aftertaste. [B, 60]

PUNTIGAMER PANTHER DARK MALT BEER — deep brown, big malt nose, rich dark malt flavors, some chocolate and coffee notes, medium body, long dry malt aftertaste, good rich malt all the way across the palate, good balance, drinkable. [B, 60]

PUNTIGAM EXPORT BEER — deep gold, dry hop nose; flavor is dry hops in front, malt at the finish; long dry malt and hop aftertaste. [B, 50]

PUNTIGAMER MÄRZENBIER — gold, big malt nose, very dry malt flavor and aftertaste. [B, 47]

Brauerei Stiegl
Brewery in Salzburg

STIEGL GOLDBRAU — deep golden amber; big malt nose, big malt front palate, vanishes in the middle, dull malt finish and long dull malt aftertaste. [B, 43]

STIEGL WEIHNACHTSBOCK — deep gold, faint off-dry malt nose, huge malt flavor, heavy body, rich and full flavored, complex, rich malt finish; feels good in your mouth, long malt aftertaste holds the richness of the flavor; very satisfying, a marvelous brew. [BK, 83]

COLUMBUS MÄRZEN — amber-gold, light clean hop and malt nose; flavor is strong hops at first, smooths out a bit, malt comes in at the middle and stays through the finish and into the aftertaste; good complexity, good balance. [B, 59]

Notes

Mc CHOUFFE®

BIERE FORTE D'ARDENNE
ARDENNE STRONG BEER

8,5% alc./vol.

COLUMBUS GOLDEN
BOCK — bright deep gold,
toasted malt and hop nose; hops
dominate front palate; lacks a
middle; malt at the finish and
aftertaste, not much complexity,
so-so balance. [BK, 45]

COLUMBUS FESTIVAL
DARK — deep ruby color, roast
malt aroma and flavor, off-dry malt
finish, medium body, long sweet
malt aftertaste. It is luscious but
heavy and filling; one would probably be enough. [B, 45]

STIEGL COLUMBUS PILS —
deep gold, light hop aroma, bold
complex hop flavor, big body;
dry hop finish has good malt
backing, long dry hop aftertaste.
[B, 59]

Brauerei Wieselburger
Brewery in Wieselburg

WIESELBURGER BIER DAS
STAMMBRÄU — pale gold, light
hop nose, malty flavor, big body,
long dry malt aftertaste, gravity
12.6 P, 5.4% abv. [B, 52]

Brauerei Wurmhöringer
Brewery in Altheim

WURMHÖRINGER SPEZIAL
BIER — gold, roasted malt aroma
with good balancing hops (a very
appetizing nose), smooth roasted
malt and hop flavor, excellent balance, good body, long dry hop
aftertaste, a marvelous beer,
gravity 12.3 P, 5% abv. [B, 85]

WURMHÖRINGER MÄRZEN
BIER — gold, big malt and hop
nose and taste; good balance, good
body, very tasty, long malt and hop
aftertaste, a delectable brew. [B, 86]

Brauhaus Zillertal / Simon Strasser
Brewery at Zell a Ziller

ZILLERTAL EDEL MÄRZEN —
gold, big strong malt nose, big
malt taste, good body; long malt
aftertaste is a bit sweet; gravity
12.2 P, 4.9% abv. [B, 58]

Zipfer Bräu / Brauerei Zipf
Breweries in Zipf on export labels and Rezpt on domestic labels (Older labels state affiliation with Österreichische Bräu A.G., and use the name Brauerei Zipf Vorm Wm. Schaup)

ZIPFER URTYP LAGER BEER —
pale gold, bright hop nose, big hop
flavor, overdone hops, bitter hop
finish and aftertaste. [B, 50]

ZIPFER BIER IMPORTED
LAGER BEER — gold; lovely hop
nose that showed a lot of malt given
some time, good hop flavor, especially in the middle, long bitter hop
aftertaste, better balance than the
beer above. [B, 34]

ZIPFER MÄRZEN — pale gold,
mild hop nose, high carbonation;
pleasant, lightly hopped flavor with
some malt, short hop and sour malt
aftertaste. This was found in the
U.S.A.; the version found in Austria
had a malt nose, hefty malt flavor,
medium body, dry malt finish and
aftertaste, gravity 12.1 P, 5.2% abv.
Not any better than the export version, but definitely more of a
märzen in style. [B, 53]

ZIPFER JOSEFI BOCK — gold,
big malt nose; hops are in back,
huge malt flavor goes on and on;
alcoholic, powerful, yet stays balanced; a really great brew at 7.1%
abv and a density of 16.20. [BK, 90]

Azores

S. Miguel
Brewery in Azores

ESPECIAL — orange-gold color,
off-dry slightly dank malt aroma,
off-dry almost too sweet malt flavor,
soft finish, slightly sweet malt aftertaste; no discernible hops. [B, 34]

Belgium

Brasserie d'Achouffe
Brewery in Achouffe

LA CHOUFFE BELGIAN ALE — cloudy gold, big head, fruity-spicy nose, complex sweet and tart flavor, delicious and creamy, bright and finely carbonated, big body; stays strong and lasts long; beautifully balanced, excellent. [A, 93]

Mc CHOUFFE ARDENNE STRONG ALE — cloudy orange-amber, fruity ale nose, very creamy, very malty, huge intense flavor of concentrated malt; big body, great length, long and strong with plenty of alcohol and a great flavor, excellent balance, great taste, another excellent brew, 8.5% abv. [A, 94]

Alken-Maes Brewery
Brewery in Kontich (Ownership is shared by Kronenbourg of France and Maes of Belgium)

RUBENS GOLD — beautiful brilliant golden amber; complex hop and malt nose has a little tang to it; big zesty ale flavor, slightly acidic, big body, dry hop finish and aftertaste, long complex and interesting, real excitement for the palate. Bottle-conditioned, this fine ale is made for Br. Corsendonk; OG 1043, 4.5% abv. [A, 83]

MAES PILS — brilliant deep gold; highly carbonated with a large bubble head, lots of malt and hops in the aroma; good body, big hop flavor well backed with malt; tends to fade in the middle; dry hop finish and aftertaste. [B, 51]

Brie de l'Ancre / Brij Het Anker
Brewery in Mechelen

GOUDEN CAROLUS (CAROLUS D'OR) — deep red-brown, big clean roasted malt aroma, great complexity, sweet and delicious sipping beer, marvelous for dessert; 7.5% alcohol. [A, 76]

TOISON D'OR — hazy gold, tart ale nose, zesty ale flavor, plenty of hops, big body, long malt and hop aftertaste, balanced and sprightly, good brew. [A, 65]

TRIPLE TOISON D'OR — hazy yellow, great complex citrus hop nose, big strong flavor with lots of both hops and malt, big body, vinous, sour licorice aftertaste, very good brew with considerable alcohol (7%). [A, 65]

Bierbrouwerijen Arcense
Brewery in Arcense

MAGNUS — cloudy brown, light malt aroma, heavy body, winey, alcoholic (7%), creamy, tasty malt flavor; long on the palate and very good. [A, 69]

Brouwerijen Artois Brasseries
Brewery in ten cities of Belgium (including Leuven/Louvain)

STELLA ARTOIS — gold, sour malt aroma with good hops, big hop flavor and finish; clean dry hop aftertaste with good length. [B, 51]

LOBURG BIERE LUXE — yellow-gold, well-hopped malt nose, big hop flavor, bitter hop aftertaste, reasonably good balance and length. [B, 34]

KETJE PALE ALE — pretty tawny-gold, huge fluffy long-lasting head, very faint malt aroma, zesty pale ale style well-hopped flavor, malt finish, long slightly sour hop aftertaste. [A, 51]

S.A. Bass Sales N.V.
Brewery in Mechelen

MAC EWANS SCOTCH ALE — almost opaque red-brown, tan head, sweet malt and hop palate, very pleasant, high alcohol (7.2%), less sweet at the finish, good balance; off-dry malt and hop aftertaste is quite long. Brewed under license by Scottish and Newcastle Breweries of Edinburgh, Scotland. [A, 65]

BASS OLD BARLEY STOUT — opaque brown, brown head, off-dry malt nose, rich malt palate, nicely balanced, dry malt finish and aftertaste. [S, 62]

LAMOT PILSOR BEER — yellow-gold, more hops than malt in the nose, strong hop flavor with a sour malt background, aftertaste like the flavor. [B, 25]

Bavik-De Brabandere
Brewery in Bavikhove

PETRUS OUD BRUIN — deep rosy-brown, tight tan head; rich heavy malt aroma that is sort of bready; palate starts out sweet malt, then goes to neutral at the middle, takes on a bready nature at the finish, and ends up with a malt aftertaste; no acid and if there are hops they are too well buried to be detected under the malt. This is a Tripel. [A, 48]

P.H. Vandenstock, S.A., Brasserie Belle-Vue
Brewery in Brussels

GUEZE BELLE-VUE — cloudy amber, sour summer sausage nose, strong sweet malt flavor, strong lambic background, long aftertaste like the flavor. [L, 45]

BELLE-VUE CREAM BEER — deep gold, good smooth lambic nose of grain, fruity wheat, and faint lactic acid; good citruslike flavor and long aftertaste. [L, 40]

BELLE-VUE KRIEK BEER — cherry red, foamy, cherry-lambic nose with good cherry candy up front, good tart cherry flavor but more sweet than tart; very clean and long; dry, and tart on the palate like a liqueur; quite good of the type. [L, 83]

BELLE-VUE FRAMBOISE RASPBERRY ALE — pinkish amber, tart raspberry nose, creamy and rich with excellent carbonation for a great mouthfeel, bright tart rich raspberry flavor, medium body, long dry raspberry aftertaste; very refreshing, a lip-smacker; a raspberry lambic matured three years in oak barrels. [L, 82]

Brasserie La Binchoise
Brewery in Binche

FAKIR — cloudy gold with particulate matter in solution, finely carbonated, spicy perfumy nose with a lactic-lemony background, lemony acidic flavor and aftertaste, not unpleasant but light and not complex, 6.8% abv. [A, 41]

LA BINCHOISE SPECIALE NOEL — hazy amber, big head, delicate subtle complex spicy-soapy-resinous aroma, creamy texture, spicy creamy soft nutmeg flavor; good body, high alcohol, malty finish and long delicately spiced malty aftertaste; very nicely done. Made with two strains of top-fermenting yeast, pale, Munich, and caramel malts, Slovenie and Kent-

Goldings hops, and spices (cloves, coriander, etc.). [A, 88]

Bry de Block
Brewery in Merchtem/ Peizegem

SATAN ALE — hazy amber, big head, lemony nose, strong sweet and sour palate, lots of lemony-lactic bite, long aftertaste. [A, 35]

KAASTAR — hazy amber, rich malt nose, very rich malt flavor, hop finish, big body, long malt and hop aftertaste, a powerful brew. [A, 60]

Brouwerij Bockor
Brewery in Grimbergen

JACOBINS KRIEK LAMBIC — cherry-red color, clean fresh spicy cherry aroma, low carbonation, short aftertaste, sweet black cherry soda with a little bite. [L, 38]

GUEZE LAMBIC JACOBINS — brilliant amber, no nose, sour, sweet, and bitter flavor, finish, and aftertaste; no balance and no style. [L, 48]

Brie du BOCQ
Brewery in Purnode-Yvoir

SAISON REGAL CHRISTMAS CUVEE 1982 — medium amber, light malt nose, full body, sweet malt palate, overly so from front to the middle; finish is slightly drier, excellent fresh malt aftertaste, high alcohol (8%). [A, 59]

SAISON REGAL — medium amber, slightly hazy, beautiful long-lasting fluffy white head, clean perfumy malt aroma, malt flavor with some acid at mid-palate; good balance, malt finish with acid in back, acidic hop aftertaste with surprisingly little malt showing, fairly high density (13°). [A, 67]

LA GAULOISE — medium to deep amber, beautiful fluffy white head, perfumy malt and faint acid nose, much like the Saison Regal above but sweeter, less acidic, and more malty, big wine malt flavor, big body; some acid comes in at the finish and stays behind the malt through the long aftertaste; the acid never dominates like it did in the Saison Regal; a very high density brew rated at 20°. [A, 73]

RUBENS RED — orange color, finely carbonated with a big head, sweet citrus malt aroma, sweet malt and tangy hop flavor, more sweet malt than anything else, light body, off-dry malt finish, long off-dry malt aftertaste. Bottle-conditioned, made for Bierbrouwerij Corsendonk; OG 1043, 4% abv. [A, 60]

Brouwerij Boon
Brewery in Lembeek

PERTOTALE FARO ALE — amber, vinegar and spice aroma, very complex light spicy fruity vinegar flavor, light body, bright and refreshing; not unlike Raspberry Shrub or raspberry vinegar, a drink that was popular with Colonial Americans. [F, 51]

KRIEK BOON — rosy amber, faint cherry aroma; bright flavor that is sweet cherry up front but which soon balances with the lactic acid of the lambic; smooth sharp and clean, somewhat winelike, long tart cherry aftertaste; an excellent kriek. [L, 75]

FRAMBOISE BOON — amber, raspberry nose, light raspberry flavor; sharp and clean as the sweetness of the raspberries is balanced by the tartness of the lambic; unfortunately the body is thin and the palate is brief. [L, 49]

GUEUZE BOON — brilliant gold; thick head that stays to the bottom of the glass; clean spicy lambic nose, smooth spicy-fruity-acidic flavor; long fruity aftertaste is like fermented apple cider. [L, 75]

BOON MARITAGE PARFAIT 1986 VINTAGE FRAMBOISE — pink, raspberry lambic nose, very smooth lightly sweet yet tart raspberry flavor; tartness fades before the finish leaving a delicate raspberry with some faint yeasty or fermentation flavors. This framboise is made from blending only casks of the 1986 Boon Framboise instead of that from several different vintages. [L, 85]

GUEZE F. BOON MARITAGE PARFAIT 1986 VINTAGE — gold, bright tangy lightly lactic nose, smooth bright refreshing, smooth lightly lemony lactic taste, medium body, nicely balanced, mellow flavor, dry lemony finish and aftertaste, good length. [L, 80]

Bernardijner Bier / Abbaye de Bornem
Abbey brewery at Bornem

ABBAYE DE BORNEM DOUBLE — rosy brown, malt aroma with a faint wintergreen background and a trace of acid, fresh piquant malt flavor; acid is more noticeable in the long complex malt aftertaste, but never becomes obtrusive; in fact, it grows on you. A very complex brew. [A, 61]

Bosteels Family Brewery
Brewery in Buggenhout

PAUWEL KWAK — garnet, delicate and slightly sweet complex malt, licorice, and coffee bean nose, good concentrated tangy malt flavor, plenty of alcohol, big body, tangy malt finish, long dry malt aftertaste. [A, 57]

CUPIDO NATURAL ALE — bright deep amber, malt and fruity ester nose, thin body, weak flavor, faint lactic-salty malt palate, short aftertaste. [A, 19]

Abbaye de Brogne
Abbey brewery at Defosse St. Gerard

ABBAYE DE BROGNE CHRISTMAS — brilliant red, rich sweet malt nose; rich wine malt palate is not quite so sweet as the nose, piquant finish, winelike aftertaste. [A, 72]

Brasserie Cantillion
Brewery in Bruxelles

CANTILLION KRIEK LAMBIC — red, sour and sharp nose; strong sour cherry flavor is sharp and assertive; medium body, long fruity sharp aftertaste. [L, 20]

CANTILLION FRAMBOISE ROSÉ DE CAMBRINUS — rosy-orange, sour dry raspberry nose and taste, sharp to the point of being offensive, sour dry raspberry aftertaste. [L, 27]

GUEUZE CANTILLION — hazy gold, sour lambic acidic nose; very sour lemony palate, so sour that it chills you down your spine; bilious dry aftertaste, too sour. [L, 26]

Brasserie Centrale S.A.
Brewery in Marbaix-la-Tour

SAISON REGAL BIERE LUXE — pale amber, foamy; nose starts out off-dry malt but builds in sweetness as it goes until it begins to clash with the hops; the flavor is strong and sweet, very long aftertaste like the flavor. [A, 67]

Br. Clarysse N.V.
Brewery in Krekelput-Oudenaarde

ST. HERMES ABDIJBIER ABBEY ALE — bright gold, grainy aroma (possibly rye), grainy taste, big body, dry grainy aftertaste, medium length; alcohol is not obtrusive, top-fermented, 7.5% abv. [A, 73]

Brouwerij Corsendonk
Brewery at Oud Turnhout

CORSENDONK AGNUS — deep gold, complex beautiful aroma with fruit, anise, and herbs; big flavor of roasted malt with an anise background, interesting, complex, and zesty; really lasts a long time; fine sipping beer. [A, 69]

CORSENDONK PATER NOSTER — cloudy amber, malt nose, foamy; big palate starts out fruity malt, finishes spicy, long hop aftertaste; complex and very long, very likable; has plenty of alcohol (7%), but it is barely noticeable. [A, 76]

CORSENDONK MONK'S PALE ALE — hazy gold, fruity malt nose, big strong malt flavor, noticeable alcohol, good spicy hop character in back and in the finish, long hop and malt aftertaste; a sensational sipping beer that will knock your socks off. [A, 83]

CORSENDONK MONK'S BROWN ALE — cloudy brown, big malt nose, complex big malt flavor, big body, subtle and balanced, very long lasting; easy to drink. [A, 78]

De Dolle Brouwers
Brewery in Esen

ARA BIER — hazy gold, finely carbonated; malty-alcoholic nose doesn't warn you of the power of the palate; creamy mouth feel, good body, delicious big malt flavor, lemony finish and aftertaste, very long and very good. [A, 90]

STILLE NACHT — clear orange-amber, finely carbonated creamy appearance, spicy steak-sauce aroma; caramel-sweet malt palate is a bit sharp at first, but smoothes out and softens as it goes if you stick with it; very strong with lots of alcohol, intense, apple butter in finish and aftertaste; as you sip it the sharpness abates layer by layer. [A, 68]

OER BIER — hazy amber, huge concentrated malt and lactic acid aroma, big sweet lactic-malt flavor, huge body, balanced, complex, steak-sauce aftertaste, very interesting. [A,72]

BOS KEUN SPECIALE PAASBIER — hazy gold; great rich complex aroma that was sweet and dry at the same time; creamy textured, a huge flavor with all kinds of good things going on, extraordinarily complex, 1,000 delights, long and rich, a great beer. On testing the aroma, there's no way to predict what your nose may pick up and bring into your head. For me, the first whiff brought to mind a platter of fresh fried clams — a wonderful scent of a fond memory. Other tasters experienced similar (and different) reactions. [A, 99]

Notes

Brasserie de Kluis
Brewery in Hoegaarden

HOEGAARDEN WHITE ALE — cloudy yellow-white, foamy, tutti-frutti nose, sharp puckery taste; finish is softer, but the flavor lasts throughout and into the long aftertaste. [W, 26]

HOEGAARDEN GRAND CRU TRIPLE — hazy pale amber, lovely fruity-apple aroma; big complex grainy flavor is fruitlike in front, slightly acidic in the middle; grainy finish, strong and long, dry aftertaste, very interesting and very good, high alcohol (8.7%). [A, 78]

DIESTER'S BEER — fairly deep copper-red, creamy head, light fruity-malt nose, off-dry toasted malt flavor, smooth creamy texture, big body, winelike and alcoholic (8%), very long aftertaste, off-dry to sweet malt throughout. [A, 49]

HOEGAARDEN GRAND CRU ALE — hazy gold, big foamy head; complex malt aroma with an almost citruslike tang, big complex citrus, anise, malt, hops, alcohol, cherries, pine needles, fruit, and berry flavor, incredibly complex; the flavor really flows; balanced and very long, fascinating well-made brew; one of the most interesting beers I have ever tasted. [A, 83]

OUD HOEGAARDS BIER — hazy pale yellow, pleasant fruity-citrus nose, off-dry lemony palate, sour finish and aftertaste. [W, 52]

De Koninck Brewery
Brewery in Antwerp

DE KONINCK — bright copper, toasted malt nose, faint lactic in back; dry hop flavor is astringent on the palate; long long dry hop aftertaste. [A, 47]

De Smedt Brewery
Brewery in Opwijk

AFFLIGEM TRIPLE ABBEY BEER — hazy golden-amber, tangy hop and sweet fruity malt nose, finely carbonated; big fruity hop flavor is also spicy; huge body, great complexity, noticeable alcohol; finish is sweet and spicy and hot with alcohol; very long and very good. [A, 93]

AFFLIGEM DOBBEL — amber, off-dry malt aroma, crisp malt flavor, very complex with both sweet and dry aspects, somewhat winelike, finely carbonated, fairly dry for a double (but not dry); has noticeable alcohol; great with food, just marvelous by itself. [A, 83]

ABBAYE d'AULNE 8% — deep amber, toasted malt aroma, strong toasted malt flavor with a carbonation bite, high alcohol, smooth, winelike, finishes big, very long malt and alcohol aftertaste. [A, 70]

ABBAYE d'AULNE 10% — deep amber, big toasted malt aroma, very strong toasted malt flavor, no carbonation bite, very high alcohol component on the palate, also very smooth, winelike; finishes lighter and drier, but then the alcohol is more noticeable; long and alcoholic. [A, 70]

AFFLIGEM NÖEL — deep amber, highly carbonated with a big thick head, faintly sweet malt and big spicy hop nose, creamy; plenty of sweet malt on the palate but the strong hops dominate; there is a balance, however, among the malt, hops, alcohol, fruit, lactic acid, and the licorice that is ever present in the background; goes dry at the very end; a good sipping beer that will be even better given more time. [A, 91]

Brasserie De Troch
Small family-owned and operated brewery in Wambeek

DE TROCH GUEUZE LAMBIC — hazy gold, lightly spiced aroma, lightly spiced acidic flavor, very smooth light acidic-hop aftertaste, pleasant of the type. Bottle-conditioned like all the De Troch beers. [L, 61]

DE TROCH EXOTIC LAMBIC — gold, light sour lemon-spicy aroma; flavor is like a spicy sour pineapple candy; spicy sour pineapple aftertaste is very long. [L, 50]

DE TROCH FARO LAMBIC — hazy gold; spicy nose has an underlying sweetness; sweet and sour flavor is on the acidic side; long sour aftertaste has a background sweetness. [L, 56]

DE TROCH TROPICAL LAMBIC — gold, sour and somewhat sharp banana nose, sharp banana oil flavor with a sour background, long sharp banana aftertaste. [L, 47]

DE TROCH KRIEK LAMBIC — rosy color, sharp sour black cherry aroma and flavor; the cherry part is fairly faint for a kriek; sour cherry aftertaste is long. [L, 53]

DE TROCH FRAMBOISE LAMBIC — rosy, sour raspberry nose, sharp sweet and sour raspberry flavor and aftertaste. [L, 53]

DE TROCH FRAISE LAMBIC — gold with a faint rosy cast; sour berry nose that I first thought was black currants; fruity berry flavor with a sharp acidic background, long sour fruit aftertaste. [L, 60]

DE TROCH MIRABELLE LAMBIC — pale amber, plumlike aroma with a sharpness, medium sharp plumlike flavor, less sharp than most fruit lambic, fruity aftertaste with a sour background. [L, 53]

DE TROCH PECHE LAMBIC — peachy-gold, light peach and lambic nose, fruity peach flavor with a sour background, pleasant bright peachy-acidic aftertaste. [L, 50]

S.A. Brasserie Demarche
Brewery at Ciney

CUVEE DE CINEY SPECIALE DE CHEVTOGNE — deep amber, beautiful malty-soapy nose; palate starts off light malt but quickly gains intensity to a big complex off-sweet malt middle and finish, long rich off-sweet malt aftertaste. [A, 61]

CUVEE DE CINEY BLONDE — amber, malt aroma, acidic malt palate, very acidic finish and aftertaste; the malt fades but the acid lingers. [A, 25]

CINEY 10 SPECIALE — amber, very faint fruity malt nose, big malt and alcohol flavor; lacks balancing hops; long malt aftertaste. [A, 65]

Brasserie / Brouwerijen Dilbeek
Brewery in Itterbeek (Export labels say Timmerman's Breweries)

TIMMERMAN'S PECHE LAMBIC — hazy gold, sour peach nose, complex peach flavor with a lambic tang, very tasty, fairly dry medium long aftertaste, nicely done. [L, 71]

TIMMERMAN'S FRAMBOISE LAMBIC — hazy red-brown, raspberry nose, raspberry-lambic flavor, tasty, medium length aftertaste like the flavor; nicely done as well. [L, 70]

TIMMERMAN'S KRIEK LAMBIC — cloudy orange-brown, sharp citrus-sweet cherry nose, intense sharp acidic and sweet cherry flavor, off-sweet finish, faint malt aftertaste. [L, 52]

TIMMERMAN'S GUEUZE LAMBIC — pale hazy amber-gold; spicy clean malt nose has sherry and vermouth tones; lightly sweet and fruity flavor, medium body, spicy apple finish and aftertaste, very little acid anywhere. [L, 72]

Brie Dubuisson Freres
Breweries in Pipaix and Tournai

BUSH BEER STRONG ALE — pale amber, off-dry candy fruit nose, heavy body; concentrated flavor is off-dry malt up front, hoppy in the middle, faintly hoppy and alcoholic at the end; high alcohol (9.5–10%), great length, a fascinatingly complex sipping beer, bold, powerful, and delicious. When exported to the U.S.A., it was labeled "Scaldis" to avoid incurring the wrath of Anheuser-Busch. [A, 93]

SCALDIS BELGIAN SPECIAL ALE — golden amber, strong malt and hop aroma, intense but smooth malt palate, rich and alcoholic, very mouth filling, very long, a blockbuster of a brew. [A, 93]

SCALDIS NÖEL SPECIAL BELGIAN ALE 1993 —amber, complex hop and concentrated malt aroma, big strong flavor of complex malt, hops, and alcohol, a marvel on the palate; big body, strong and very long, beautiful balance and smooth despite its strength; a well-matured high extract brew that should last for years and years. [A, 87]

SCALDIS NÖEL 1994 — cloudy amber, complex estery malt and hop nose, big fruity creamy delicious alcoholic flavor, big body, long well-hopped aftertaste, a great brew. [A, 100]

Brasserie Dupont / Abbaye de la Moinette
Brewery in Tourpes

SAISON DUPONT — hazy yellow, huge head, finely carbonated; big vegetal-malt aroma, sweet and spicy (possibly coriander), big spicy flavor (nutmeg, cloves, etc.); big body, strong alcohol, creamy yet chewy, extremely complex; refreshing despite its size, a marvelous saison, a great example of the style. [A, 74]

MOINETTE BELGIAN ALE — gold, big tight long-lasting head; big rich hop flavor has a tart acidity that starts early and stays; plenty of malt in back, good body, big and long and strong. [A, 56]

FORET BOTTLE CONDITIONED SAISON ALE — hazy gold, big tight head, mild lactic aroma and flavor, lots of complex fruity esters, very refreshing, creamy, good body, long fruity and mildly lactic aftertaste. [A, 73]

DUPONT AVEC LES BON VOUEX — hazy gold, big tight head; spicy nose has a fruity backing; spicy-fruity complex flavor, medium body; ends dry and aftertaste is long. [A, 70]

Flanders Family Brewers
Brewery in Geel

FLANDERS FARMERS ALE — hazy rose color, light chocolate malt nose, soft yet richly flavored, smooth chocolate malt flavor, big body, long malt aftertaste. If there are hops, I can't detect them. [A, 73]

FLANDERS GRAND CRU TRIPLE — hazy pale amber; strong spicy complex nose was thought at first to be chemical-banana oil-odd whatever, but as time passed it was realized that it was the senses that were being overwhelmed and it was complex malt, spice, honey, hops, alcohol, and almost anything that you could think up; the palate was complex toasted malt, spice, and in the back of the palate, salty; high alcohol is ever-present, right into the long dry malt aftertaste, a very interesting sipping beer. [A, 79]

Brasserie Friart / Abbaye Le Roeulx
Abbey brewery at Le Roeulx

ST. FEUILLIEN CHRISTMAS — deep rosy-amber, off-sweet malt nose, semi-dry malt palate, brief finish, very little aftertaste. [A, 83]

ST. FEUILLIEN BELGIAN SPECIAL BLONDE ALE — gold, big tight head, zesty spicy malt aroma, tangy spicy flavor; touch of lactic acid only makes it more interesting; well made, refreshing, and long. [A, 73]

Brasserie / Brouwerij de Gouden Boom
Brewery in Bruges

WHITE OF BRUGES — cloudy yellow-white, light ephemeral citrus nose, complex fruity flavor, dry finish, full body, off-dry malt aftertaste. [W, 42]

BLANC DE BRUGES — very pale yellow; off-dry malt aroma is lemony; sweet malt flavor with an acidic background; somewhat sweet finish continues in a long off-dry malt aftertaste. Probably the same beer as above but with a new label. [W, 39]

BRUGSE TRIPEL — hazy amber, big head, nose of well-fruited spicy malt with an acetone background, big body, smooth, balanced; spicy palate is complex; very good mouthfeel; like the Steenbrugge, but more refined, sweeter, and less creamy. Another sample tasted in March 1995 was similar but highly alcoholic, showing all of the 9.5% abv. [A, 81]

STEENBRUGGE TRIPEL BLONDE D'ABBAYE — hazy gold, big head, aroma of complex spice, malt, and honey, etc.; creamy big complex flavor with acetone and alcohol, spice, and fruit; long complex aftertaste continues the flavor for a long time; very interesting beer, 9% abv. [A, 71]

STEENBRUGGE DUBBEL BRUIN — cloudy brown, acetone; alcohol and malt vie for dominance in the aroma; flavor is complex malt with chocolate tones and shows little of the acetone; very foamy (most of contents fled the bottle on opening), medium dry; some acetone returns for the aftertaste but it is mostly malt; fairly long and stays strong, 6.5% abv. [A, 39]

Gouden Carolus
Brewery in Mechelen

GOUDEN CAROLUS BELGIAN ALE — deep amber, faint off-dry malt nose; complex malt flavor is strong and off-dry in the middle and finish; dry malt aftertaste. [A, 76]

Grimbergen Abbey (Watou Prior)
Abbey brewery at Grimbergen, Belgium. Labels indicate other secular breweries which may have made the brews under license, a common practice by Belgian abbeys. Examples seen are Brasserie Maes in Waarloos and Brasserie L'Union in Jumet.

GRIMBERGEN DOUBLE — deep ruby-amber, big malt aroma, big complex roasted malt and hop flavor; off-dry soft rich roasted malt finish; drops off quickly, however, to a light fresh clean malt aftertaste. [A, 93]

GRIMBERGEN TRIPLE — deep gold, light fruity-malt and lychee nut aroma, big strong hop and malt flavor, alcoholic (9%), off-dry malt and hop finish and aftertaste, long and delicious, a huge delicious brew. [A, 98]

HET KAPPITEL — cloudy-brown, mild malt aroma, intense sweet fruity-coffee flavor, big body, tangy yet smooth, complex, dry malt finish and long aftertaste. [A, 59]

N.V. Br. Haacht, S.A.
Brewery in Boortmeerbeek

ADLER PREMIUM LUXUS BIER — pale tawny-gold, fairly good head, malt aroma, light malt and hop palate, faint off-dry malt aftertaste, overall light and brief. [B, 42]

PRIMUS HAACHT PILS — bright yellow, big head, but short lived, light malt and hop nose, dry hop flavor, little aftertaste. [B, 38]

HAACHT DRAFT — bright gold, low head, smooth light hop and malt nose, off-dry malt palate, light hop aftertaste. Also called Star Pils Excelsior. [B, 50]

VERY DIEST — medium deep rosy-brown, grainy malt nose, weak body, watery, off-dry clean malt flavor, short malt aftertaste, low-alcohol beer. [NA, 38]

ADLER BIER — bright gold, good creamy head, clean pilsener aroma with plenty of malt and hops; front palate is all hops, malt joins the hops in the middle and stays to the finish; mild hop aftertaste is fairly long. [B, 53]

Brasserie Halle
Brewery in Halle

FRAMBOISE VANDER LINDEN — reddish-amber, fine creamy head, raspberry nose, raspberry-malt flavor; off-sweet but tending toward sour at the finish; long long raspberry aftertaste. [L, 53]

Huyghe Brewery
Brewery in Melle/Ghent

ARTEVELDE GRAND CRU — amber, big head, faint tangy citrus light malt nose, smooth likable malt flavor, tasty and refreshing; a malty brew for the most part but there are plenty of hops from the middle on. [A, 72]

BLANC DES NEIGES — hazy gold, perfumy lemon-grapefruit soda nose, light body, dry and sour malt flavor with a pine background, fairly long aftertaste like the flavor. [A, 27]

MATEEN TRIPLE — gold, big head, big fruity-malt aroma, quite lemony, huge rich malt flavor,

heavy body; hops emerge at the finish but they were in back all along; long delicately spiced malt aftertaste, great sipping beer. [A, 93]

DELERIUM TREMENS BELGIAN ALE — hazy gold, very complex fruity-citrus-fennel-birch beer nose, beautiful complex fruity spicy citrus malt and hop flavor, big body, very long and fairly strong, a delicious bright taste. [A, 90]

S.A. Interbrew N.V.
Brewing Co. in Bruxelles

CAMPBELL'S CHRISTMAS (1991) — deep rosy-amber, huge nose of alcohol, hops, and malt; flavor is mostly malt on the sweet side, more rich than sweet; very big in flavor and body, long rich malt aftertaste; alcohol shows all the way through (8.1%). This could be either made by Whitbread in England or made in Belgium under license from Whitbread. [A, 90]

CAMPBELL'S CHRISTMAS 1992 — very deep dark amber, smooth rich malt aroma, big malt flavor, high alcohol, very classy brew, finely carbonated, very long and smooth, wants for nothing. Made under the supervision of Whitbread PLC London, England. [A, 89]

BERGEN BRÄU IMPORTED PREMIUM LAGER BEER — gold, dull European hop nose; dank sour malt flavor is musty and papery; thin body; papery malt aftertaste shows an oxidized beer. Found in a can in California. [B, 34]

N.V. De Keersmaeker S.A.
Brewery in Kobbegem

MORT SUBITE KRIEK LAMBIC — cherry-red, lightly carbonated, delicate off-sweet cherry aroma, tart cherry flavor, sweet and sharp at the same time, light body, good balance; lightly finished and little aftertaste. [L, 58]

MORT SUBITE CASSIS LAMBIC — orange, big cassis nose; flavor is ripe tart cassis and raspberry with a sense of caraway; complex tart berry aftertaste. [L, 68]

MORT SUBITE PECHE LAMBIC — gold, peach juice nose, nice clean peachy flavor, medium body, dry peachy finish and aftertaste, excellent balance; the sourness of the lambic never reveals itself other than to balance off the sweetness of the peach juice; delightful. [L, 81]

Brasserie Lefebvre / Abbaye de Floreffe
Abbey Brewery at Quenast

ABBAYE DE FLOREFFE LA MEILLEURE — deep rosy amber, sweet malt nose and flavor, good body, good clean malt finish and aftertaste, quite long and tasty. [A, 62]

ABBAYE DE FLOREFFE DOUBLE — deep amber, big dense head; bright tangy nose shows plenty of hops and malt; big tangy

acidic hop flavor, very smooth, long malty aftertaste. [A, 69]

ABBAYE DE BONNE ESPERANCE STRONG ALE — hazy gold, lactic malt nose, big strong sweet malt palate, creamy with fine carbonation; fills your mouth with good flavors and the creaminess; noticeable alcohol (7.5% abv); malty finish and aftertaste is dry at the end and long. [A, 68]

Brasserie de Abbaye de Leffe
Abbey brewery in Dinant (Other Abbaye de Leffe brews are made by Brasserie St. Guibert; label may say S.A. Abbaye de Leffe)

ABBEY DE LEFFE BIERE LUXE — deep reddish orange-brown, good malt nose, off-dry malt flavor, clean and bright, not flabby or cloying, long sour malt aftertaste. [B, 32]

ABBEY OF LEFFE BLOND — pale amber, faint malt aroma, thin malt flavor, a bit weak, medium body, dry malt finish, some off-dry malt in the aftertaste. [A, 38]

Notes

_____
_____
_____
_____
_____
_____
_____
_____
_____
_____
_____
_____
_____
_____
_____
_____
_____
_____
_____
_____
_____
_____
_____
_____
_____
_____
_____
_____
_____
_____
_____
_____
_____
_____
_____

Liefmans Brewery
Brewery in Oudenaarde

LIEFMAN'S GOUDENBAND — hazy mahogany; a complex rich aroma that includes herbs, strong citrus, prunes, Worcestershire sauce, and black cherry flavor (though it is not a kriek beer) that gradually becomes malty; acidic background; seems a bit winelike; long acidic malt aftertaste. [A, 69]

LIEFMAN'S KRIEK BIER — opaque reddish-brown; fruity cherry aroma is both sweet and sharp; zesty semi-dry cherry flavor like an aperitif, finishes more malty, long and interesting, an ale with cherries, a very good kriek. [L, 63]

LIEFMAN'S FRAMBOZENBIER/BIERE DE FRAMBOISES — red-brown color, almost opaque, raspberry nose, raspberry flavor together with hops and malt, long surprisingly dry aftertaste, a very interesting, likable, and very good brew of type. [L, 83]

Lindeman's Farm Brewery
Brewery in Viezenbeck

LINDEMAN'S GUEZE LAMBIC BEER — cloudy peach color, strong lemony aroma, strong complex flavor with citrus, cloves, honey, malt, and hops; extremely long aftertaste like the flavor, typical gueze. [L, 42]

LINDEMAN'S KRIEK LAMBIC BEER — pale pink color; aroma like faint cherries laid on a gueze; complex cherry, cinnamon, and citrus flavor; the cherries mitigate the intensity of the sour lambic flavors; light body, surprisingly dry finish and aftertaste, considerable length. [L, 42]

FARO LAMBIC BELGIAN ALE — medium to pale copper color, lactic nose, intense sweet malt and sour lactic flavor, medium body, long tenacious sweet malt aftertaste. Faro is a lambic sweetened with candy sugar, and that's just what it tastes like. [F, 45]

GUEZE LAMBIC BELGIAN ALE — cloudy-orange, fruity-lactic nose, big head, dry tangy acidic taste, dry tangy aftertaste; overall the brew is quite dry. [L, 48]

LINDEMAN FRAMBOISE — rosy-orange, nose like Chambord with a lambic background; the raspberries show well; sour green apple and raspberry flavor, complex; the beer (malt and hops) shows up in the finish and aftertaste. Very interesting and quite pleasant. [L, 65]

LINDEMAN'S PECHE LAMBIC — amber-gold, clean peach nose, bright clean peach flavor; lambic tang is in the background; very tasty and pleasant, medium length. I suspect that they toned down the lambic character for the American market. [L, 62]

CUVÉE RÉNÉ GUEUZE — hazy gold, lemony-spicy acidic aroma and palate, good balance, medium body, bright and refreshing, sour-fruity aftertaste, long and very good of type. [L, 86]

Brasserie Maes
Brewery in Waarloos (Maes is in partnership with Kronenbourg of France)

MAES PILS — brilliant deep gold, highly carbonated with a large bubble head, lots of malt and hops in the aroma, good body, big hop flavor well backed with malt; tends to fade in the middle; dry hop finish and aftertaste. [B, 51]

Martens Brewery
Brewery in Bocholt

BOCHOLTER KWIK PILS PREMIUM BEER — pale golden amber, complex hop and faint off-dry malt aroma, complex hop flavor and finish, good body, bitter hop aftertaste. [B, 49]

SEZOENS BOCHOLT BELGIAN ALE — pale golden amber, complex hop and malt nose with some charcoal and lactic acid in back; flavor is more malt than hops; the charcoal and lactic acid reappear in the finish; dry malt aftertaste. [A, 38]

N.V. Br. Martinas S.A. / John Martin N.V.

Brewery in Merchtem, affiliated with S.A. Interview. Some of the John Martin beers are brewed and bottled in Great Britain, others are brewed at facilities in England or Scotland and shipped to Belgium where they are bottled.

GINDER ALE — deep tawny-gold, huge thick head, small bubbles and long lasting, toasted malt nose, good body, toasted malt flavor, a little background acid, soft malt aftertaste with good duration. [A, 57]

GORDON FINEST GOLD BLOND ALE — gold; sweet malt aroma shows a great deal of alcohol; big malt and alcohol flavor, big body, very alcoholic and malty throughout, surprisingly little duration. Brewed in Edinburgh by Scottish & Newcastle, bottled by John Martin in Antwerp. [A, 73]

GORDON HIGHLAND SCOTCH ALE — deep rose-brown, extremely dense small bubble long-lasting brown head, well-balanced rich roasted malt and hop aroma and flavor, full body, high density, high alcohol (8%), extremely long rich malt aftertaste. Brewed by Scottish Brewers Ltd. and bottled by John Martin of Antwerp, Belgium. [A, 85]

GORDON DOUGLAS SCOTCH BRAND ALE — deep amber, light dry malt aroma, concentrated malt flavor, big body; aftertaste is briefly off-dry malt but quickly goes and stays dry; a big brew that feels good in your mouth. Made for John Martin of Antwerp, Belgium. Some are bottled in Belgium. [A, 73]

MARTIN'S PALE ALE — amber, big head, complex pine needle and citrus aroma, big hop and malt flavor, very zesty; pine needles in back at the finish and goes with the malt into the aftertaste; very big body, rich off-dry flavor, very pleasant long malt aftertaste. Made by Courage for John Martin N.V. of Antwerp, Belgium. Brewed in the U.K., bottled in Belgium. [A, 63]

Moortgat Breweries
Breweries in Breendonk and Puurs

DUVEL BELGIAN BEER — creamy copper-gold, sweet clean malty aroma; huge complex flavor that is candy and toasted malt in front, smoky in the middle, and finishes clean bright malt; long malt aftertaste, a strongly flavored brew at 8% alcohol; this is a great sipping beer. [A, 83]

DUVEL BELGIAN ALE — cloudy gold, big off-dry malt aroma, huge body; big complex flavor that appears intensely sweet at first, but quickly takes on a sharp hop character; long tart aftertaste; a very big flavorful brew that shows a lot of both malt and hops. [A, 58]

MAREDSOUS 8% — deep amber, lovely roasted malt nose, big rich off-dry roasted malt flavor, long aftertaste like the flavor, big body, long off-dry malt aftertaste, delicious. [A, 75]

MAREDSOUS 9% — cream color, creamy head; complex citrus, berry, and nutty flavor (reminds me of a rum-topf); rich dry complex flavor that is mostly roasted malt; very mouth-filling and very long. [A, 75]

MAREDSOUS 6% — cloudy orange-brown, huge head, tangy-spicy ale aroma, zesty fruity malt, hop, and citrus flavor, assertive but not offensive, complex, extremely long aftertaste like the flavor, a dynamite brew. The Maredsous brews are an abbey beer produced under license from Brasserie de Maredsous, Denee, Belgium. [A, 59]

STEENDONK BRABANT WHITE ALE — pale whitish-gold, off-dry grapefruit nose, finely carbonated, lemony-grapefruit flavor, lemon finish and aftertaste. [W, 31]

BEL PILS — very pale gold, European hop aroma and crisp hop flavor, medium body, good carbonation level, good creamy mouthfeel, tasty, dry hop finish and aftertaste. [B, 55]

SILVER PILS — pale gold, fine head, toasted malt and hop aroma, slightly sweet malt and hop taste, malt in front, malt and hops in the middle, hop finish; long aftertaste starts out malty but ends up mostly hops; plenty of body, quite complex, and has character throughout. Contract beer made for Delhaize Le Lion supermarkets. [B, 56]

Brasserie Neve
Brewery in Schepdaal

GUEZE DE NEVE — amber, big head, aroma of sardines in olive oil with an acidic background; palate is briefly malt then acid; little aftertaste. [L, 25]

Brasserie d'Orval
Abbey brewery in Villers-Devant-Orval

ORVAL ABBEY'S ALE BIERE LUXE — deep foamy orange, soapy-sweet malt aroma; intense aromatic flavor fills the senses; alcoholic, resinous, hoppy, tangy, long aftertaste like the flavor, a very tasty brew with great complexity. [A, 60]

ORVAL TRAPPISTE ALE — pale orange, sharp hop nose, intense hop flavor, pungent sweet hop finish, long hop aftertaste, big and

powerful, a real mouthful of good brew. [A, 60]

Brasserie Palm
Brewery in Londerzeel

PALM ALE — amber, lovely malt aroma, zesty dry hop flavor, big body, malt finish, long dry hop aftertaste, excellent balance, a good tasting even natured brew. [A, 63]

SPECIALE AERTS — bright copper, roasted malt aroma, rich off-dry malt flavor, dry hop aftertaste. Brasserie Aerts, Brussels. [B, 69]

AERTS 1900 — amber, big head, tangy malt aroma and flavor; the tang softens as it goes and leaves a smooth malt finish and aftertaste; good body, very good flavor with great malt character. [A, 76]

PALM BOCK PILS — bright tawny-gold, bright hop nose and palate, off-dry malt at finish, long smooth dry hop aftertaste. [BK, 52]

S.A. Brasserie Piedboeuf N.V.
Brewery in Jupile

PIEDBOEUF BLONDE — pale tawny-gold, pleasant hop nose, light body, low carbonation, light malt flavor, dry brief malt and hop aftertaste. This is labeled a "table beer." In Belgium, it costs about 23–25 cents. [A, 51]

PIEDBOEUF TRIPLE — pale gold, dry malt and hop aroma, slightly off-dry malt flavor, hop and malt middle and finish, hop aftertaste, fairly long and also fairly dry, light body, but pretty good for under 30 cents. [A, 53]

JUPILER — bright gold, medium head, malt and hop aroma, off-dry malt palate, hop finish, dry malt aftertaste. [B, 50]

HORSE ALE — amber, faint malt and hop nose; big flavor has both hops and malt; very complex, malt finish; aftertaste starts out malt but there is considerable hop character at the very end. [A, 50]

Brewery Riva
Brewery in Dentergem

RIVA 2000 LAGER BEER — brilliant gold, well-carbonated, off-dry malt aroma with hops and toasted malt in back, complex flavor, bitter hop finish, long malt and dry hop aftertaste. [B, 62]

VONDEL TRIPLE — copper, piquant candy-citrus aroma, intense off-dry malt and tangy hop palate, long aftertaste like the flavor. [A, 60]

WITTEKOP BIERE BLANCHE — cloudy yellow, delicate fruity aroma with an acidic backtaste; lemony palate is forthright but delicate; interesting, pleasant, well balanced, winelike, and very long. [W, 60]

LUCIFER ALE — gold, big foamy head, perfumy winelike fruity aroma, big strong zesty hop palate, good tasting, big body, lots of alcohol, off-dry malt finish with a mild licorice background, extremely long malt aftertaste, big and very good. [A, 75]

DENTERGEMS WHITE ALE — hazy yellow, huge head, soapy nose, wheaty-malt flavor, smooth, medium body, cuts off abruptly, little or no aftertaste. [W, 56]

RIVA CHRISTMAS 1983 — medium deep amber, big tan head, clean malt aroma, big refreshing clean malt flavor, full body, very satisfying, long straightforward rich malt aftertaste. [B, 67]

RIVA BLANCHE DENTERGEMS BELGIAN ALE — cloudy yellow, tart spicy complex malt aroma, low carbonation, light body; flavor is first faintly sweet for a brief moment, thence light dry malt with a faint lactic acid bite; medium long dry malt aftertaste has a spicy component, but overall comes off as being surprisingly bland and light for a white beer. [W, 32]

Brasserie Rodenbach
Brewery in Roselare

RODENBACH BELGIUM BEER — deep copper-red, strong roasted malt aroma with a sour background, very strong off-dry malt with an acidic background, long strong aftertaste like the flavor. [A, 50]

ALEXANDER RODENBACH — hazy amber, powerful acidic hop nose, complex malt and hop flavor with an acidic background, very strong with a lemony-cherry backtaste, fairly sweet malt finish and aftertaste with none of the acidity showing. [A, 64]

Notes

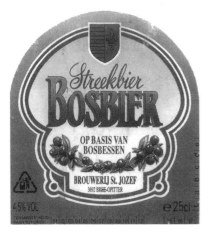

RODENBACH GRAND CRU — deep ruby, strong winelike estery aroma, tangy, fruity-berry, complex, rich, alcoholic, and lovable to the inured; big fermented fruit palate seems strong or harsh at first, but soon softens as the complex character develops; the flavor reflects much of the aroma; there is acid, alcohol, rich fruit (seemingly mostly cherry-like), great complexity, gets better and better as you sip it; big mouth feel, long and strong; dries somewhat into the aftertaste, to some an acquired taste, to others pure nectar. [A, 79]

Roman N.V.
Brewery at Oudenaard

ROMAN SPECIALE MATER — red, lovely malt aroma, smooth off-sweet malt flavor, lovely long malt aftertaste, a very very drinkable beer. [A, 75]

ROMAN DOBBELEN BRUINEN ALE — dark amber, big bright malt aroma and flavor, very big body, long off-dry malt aftertaste. [A, 73]

ROMAN SLOEBER GOLDEN ALE — gold, rich malt aroma and flavor, very richly flavored, big body, off-dry malt finish and aftertaste. [A, 69]

ENAME DUBBEL ABBEY ALE — amber, huge malt nose, equally big malt flavor with a great richness and strength, big body, long and strong malt aftertaste. [A, 83]

ENAME TRIPEL ABBEY ALE — deep gold, fresh well-malted nose, off-dry malt flavor, malty finish and aftertaste; never gets dry; also there is plenty of alcohol throughout (9% abv). [A, 58]

St. Bernardus Bry
Brewery in Wajou

ST. SIXTUS ABDY BIER — deep copper, sweet apple malt aroma, very sweet and very complex malt palate, finishes better than it starts, extremely pleasant malt aftertaste, huge body, great length; needs time to develop as this beer is meant to ferment in the bottle for five or more years. In Belgium this brew is labeled St. Sixtus Abt and is rated at 8.5% abv. [A, 61]

ST. SIXTUS PRIOR — deep hazy-brown, faint malt aroma, slightly perfumy, big body, palate of malt, candy, and acid in a somewhat confused state; all three flavors go into the aftertaste, but the acid is the most noticeable. This brew is rated at 7.5% abv. [A, 46]

ST. SIXTUS PATER — lightly hazy medium deep brown, light sweet malt nose, palate of off-dry malt, acid, hops, with a candy sweetness in back; complex aftertaste of all components has a questionable balance. This brew contains 6% abv. [A, 47]

Brasserie St. Guibert S.A. NV
Abbey brewery in Mont St. Guibert

VIEUX TEMPS — medium to deep amber, dense amber head, malt aroma and palate, touch of acid in back, malt finish and aftertaste; the acid background is there all the way through. [A, 48]

TONGERLO NORBERTIJNERBIER — nearly opaque reddish-brown, fine creamy head, malt nose, slightly acidic malt palate; the acid fades as you go; medium body; long malt aftertaste has only the faintest trace of the acid. [A, 54]

ABBAYE DE LEFFE BLONDE ALE — deep gold, highly carbonated, light hop aroma, good hoppy ale-like flavor, long hop aftertaste. [A, 83]

LEFFE RADIEUSE BELGIAN ALE — deep copper, hop nose, complex hop palate with bitter and off-dry tones, very long hop aftertaste. [A, 56]

LEFFE BELGIAN DARK ALE — dark copper, good malt and hop aroma, fine malt flavor with hops in back, well-balanced, long aftertaste; pleasant to drink. [A, 81]

LEFFE BLONDE ABBEY ALE — hazy gold, finely carbonated, very faint aroma of malt with herbs and honey; herbal-honey flavor is light but interesting; creamy, dry herbal aftertaste has an underlying sweetness, but overall the palate is dry. [A, 83]

Brouwerij St. Jozef
Brewery in Bree-Opitter

BOSBIER STREEKBIER OP BASIS VAN BOSBESSEN — red, faint barley-Cassis aroma, light fruity-berry Cassis aperitif palate, pleasant, medium body, semi-sweet taste, finishes fruity malt; fruity-berry aftertaste has long length. [A, 54]

Abbaye St. Remy
Abbey brewery at Rochefort

BIERE DES TRAPPISTES ROCHEFORT 10° — deep red-brown, fairly clear, tan head, sweet clean malt nose with some cherry fruit tones, big sweet clean malt flavor; a very big strong flavor with lots of hops and malt and complexities like anise, coffee, and various fruits; big body, highly carbonated; the first thing you notice is the carbonation, then the hops, and lastly the malt, but the overall impression is more malt than anything else, a very long complex aftertaste. This is a beautiful beer. It is balanced, strong but smooth, and very very long. [A, 89]

BIERE DES TRAPPISTES ROCHEFORT 8° — deep red-brown, a bit hazy, fluffy tan head, zesty malt aroma, good body, big malt and hop flavor, excellent balance, very big and very tasty, medium long complex aftertaste, crisp and bright throughout, real sipping beer. [A, 78]

BIERE DES TRAPPISTES ROCHEFORT 6° — deep amber, slightly hazy, big eggshell colored head, light malt nose, good tasting light malt and hop flavor, medium body, fine balance; refreshing and drinkable, good drinking beer, especially with food. [A, 75]

Abbaye de Scourmont
Abbey brewery at Scourmont, Chimay

CHIMAY RED CAP ALE — hazy deep brown, big head, chocolate and fruity malt and hop aroma with a faint lactic background, rich complex zesty roasted malt flavor; excellent balance, good body, smooth, long tasty aftertaste like the flavor. This bottle had a red capsule which denotes 7% alcohol. A white capsule denotes 8% and a blue capsule is 9%. [A, 85]

CHIMAY BLUE CAP SPECIAL — deep orange-brown, huge tan head, faint malt nose, big rich sweet and sharp flavor, plenty of both malt and hops, very long aftertaste like the flavor; good but not as complex as the red cap above. As found in Belgium. [A, 63]

CHIMAY ALE GRANDE RESERVE — deep orange-brown, big head, complex malt and citrus nose; assertive malty ale flavor is sweet, spicy, and fruity; smooth and well balanced, very complex; spiciness is most pronounced in the finish, very long aftertaste. [A, 83]

CHIMAY CINQ CENTS ALE — faintly hazy-amber, highly carbonated, light lactic nose with malt in back; big malt flavor that is very complex with lactic acid, spice, pine needles, and fruit; big long aftertaste, a big pleasureful brew. [A, 78]

CHIMAY WHITE CAP — hazy gold, faint citrus malt nose, big strong hop flavor, sharp spicy and complex, yet creamy, big body, very well balanced; ends dry hops; long dry hop aftertaste, some alcohol noticeable. [A, 92]

CHIMAY BLUE CAP — deep amber-brown, huge beige tight head, beautiful spicy nose, big rich very spicy flavor, big body, bright dry well-spiced and very long aftertaste; complex and quite alcoholic, great mouthfeel, creamy and fills all the corners of your mouth with flavor. This "blue cap" has 9% abv, while the red cap is 7% and the white cap is 8%. As found in U.S.A. [A, 80]

Brouwerij Sefir / Dendria
Brewery in Aalst

DB URTYP EUROPABIER — pale gold, fine head, lightly hopped malt nose, well-hopped flavor, sour hop finish and aftertaste. This was a much advertised brew, supposedly made in Germany for Belgian tastes. [B, 53]

Brasserie de Silly
Brewery in Silly

SAISON SPECIALE ARTISANAL BELGIAN ALE — hazy orange, ephemeral lightly fruited nose; sweet complex powerful (startling considering the lack of warning from the nose) flavor, much like a sparkling Cognac and Grand Marnier combination; big body, long aftertaste like the flavor. [A, 60]

DOUBLE ENGHEIN BRUNE — orange, fruity malt nose, finely carbonated and with a creamy texture, very sweet malt palate; hop bite and alcohol warmth shows in the finish; complex long aftertaste shows some almonds, 8% abv. [A, 75]

ENGHEIN SAISON DOUBLE — light amber, big head, light toasted barley and wheat malt nose with an acidic background, light body, cereal-like brief palate, faintly sour malt aftertaste, like a light saison. Naturally fermented in the bottle according to the label and made by R.C.M. 12313 H.R.B. [A, 43]

Brouwerij Slaghmuydler
Brewery in Ninove

WITKAP PATER ABBEY SINGEL ALE — gold, pleasant bright fruity malt aroma, finely carbonated, a pleasant wheat beer flavor; lots of fruitiness and a little acid to balance off the sweetness; refreshing, good creamy mouthfeel, medium body, spicy finish, delicate long spicy aftertaste. [W, 87]

Brasserie / Bierbrouwerijen Sterkens
Brewery in Meer

STER ALE — medium amber, pleasant roasted malt aroma, a trace of dry mustard in back, dry malt flavor, creamy, medium body, fairly long malt aftertaste, pleasant drinking. [A, 40]

ORIGINAL ST. SEBASTIAAN CROCKALE — amber-brown, big rich malt aroma, big dry complex malt flavor, big and beautiful, off-dry malt finish, long rich malt aftertaste. [A, 73]

ST. SEBASTIAAN GOLDEN BELGIAN ALE — hazy gold, big toasted malt nose, big malt flavor, medium body, high alcohol, tangy cider-like bite at the finish, long hop aftertaste. [A, 73]

ST. SEBASTIAAN DARK BELGIAN ALE — deep ruby-amber, big complex nose with hops, malt, alcohol, lactic acid, and maybe even acetone, off-dry lightly acidic flavor, alcohol noticeable on the palate, spicy complex finish and aftertaste, very long; keeps changing as you drink it and becomes more drinkable; has to be served at room temperature to get the full effect, which is quite good. [A, 70]

ST. PAUL DOUBLE — hazy amber, malt and alcohol nose, strong malt flavor, alcohol on the palate, but well-balanced, big body, long malt aftertaste. [A, 62]

ST. PAUL TRIPLE — hazy gold, fruity-banana malt nose, big strong malt and lactic flavor, piney background, high alcohol, big body, extremely long aftertaste like the flavor, very good complex flavor. [A, 75]

FLANDERS FARMERS ALE — amber, big malt nose, excellent malt flavor, smooth and delicious, no detectable hops. Made for Flanders Family Brewers of Geel. [A, 73]

BOKRYKS KRIUKENBIER BELGIAN ALE — golden amber, good head, honeyed acidic lambic aroma, big acidic flavor, complex and balanced, plenty of hops and malt, sour finish and aftertaste; starts out big with plenty of hops and malt; rich and long. Bottled in a stoneware crock (kruik). [A, 82]

HOOGSTRATEN POORTER — deep amber, big tight head, huge outgoing complex aroma of malt, hops, and lactic acid, good body; smooth creamy rich flavor starts out roasted dry nutty and a little burnt, goes then into a lovely lightly burnt malt, hops and malt balance into the finish; aftertaste is similar but drier, gets better as you go with all kinds of complexities weaving in and out; good creamy mouthfeel obtains throughout and the aftertaste is best part of the palate so it leaves you very pleased. [P, 82]

ST. PAUL BLOND — brilliant gold, fragrant hop aroma; bright hop flavor has plenty of malt support and a tart lactic background, especially noticeable in the finish and aftertaste; medium body, very long dry hop aftertaste. [A, 73]

Brewery Strubbe
Microbrewery in Ichtegem

ICHTEGEM'S ALE — an "old brown" ale; this has a red-brown color, light lactic aroma, light lactic flavor softened by some sweet malt; medium body, complex lightly sweet berrylike finish and aftertaste; the lactic sour-tart taste is very soft at the end and the brew is quite refreshing, 5% abv. [A, 79]

VIAS KOP (FLAX HEAD) — hazy gold, lemony spicy aroma, tight head, bright spicy-lemony flavor; a white beer but not brewed from wheat; long dry spicy aftertaste, top-fermented, 5.3% abv. [A, 71]

HOUTEN KOP (WOODEN HEAD) — amber-gold, faint fruity-grainy-herbal nose; dry tart flavor shows some coriander; good body, dry medium long herbal aftertaste, top-fermented, 6.5% abv. [A, 73]

Brasserie Union S.A.
Brewery in Jumet

CUVEE DE L'HERMITAGE — tawny-amber, rich malt aroma, off dry toasted malt and bitter hop flavor, big winelike body, strong malt flavor, big hop finish, smooth hop aftertaste with plenty of malt, a fine sipping beer with 8% abv. [B, 57]

CUVEE DE L'HERMITAGE CHRISTMAS — deep amber, big complex rich tangy candy caramel malt aroma, concentrated malt and hop flavor, long hop and malt aftertaste, big body, fairly strong flavor, high alcohol (7.5%), strong stuff. This was the 1987 issue. [A, 61]

GRIMBERGEN DOUBLE — deep ruby-amber, big malt aroma, big malt and hop flavor, very complex, off-dry roasted malt finish; drops off fast to a surprisingly weak aftertaste. [A, 93]

GRIMBERGEN TRIPLE — deep gold, light fruity litchi nut nose, big strong malt and hop flavor, lots of alcohol, particularly at the finish and in the aftertaste; very long rich malt aftertaste has a touch of sweetness; a huge delicious beer. [A, 98]

Brouwerij Van Honsebrouck
Brewery in Ingelmunster

BRIGAND BELGIAN ALE — hazy amber-gold, big head, strong off-dry lactic nose and flavor, complex, in some ways like a mead, high alcohol (9%); powerful in that you feel it in your nose from its volatile nature when you are sipping; long aftertaste like the flavor; strong sipping beer that is good of type. [A, 80]

GUEZE ST. LOUIS — pale amber, aroma like fruit, herbs, and sausage; a definite gueze palate, fruity and lactic, smooth and creamy, nothing offensive; medium long aftertaste like the flavor, a very good gueze. [L, 70]

KASTEEL BIER/BIERE DU CHATEAU — cloudy amber, off-dry roasted malt nose, high alcohol, interesting and complex, strong sweet malt flavor, sweet malt finish, long dry malt aftertaste. [B, 63]

Brewery Van Hougaerde
Brewery in Leuven/Louvain

LEOPOLD THREE STARS PILS — pale gold, good malt and hop nose with a fruity backtaste, sour malt finish, long sour hop aftertaste. [B, 14]

Van Steenberge Brewery
Brewery in Ertvelde (The corporate name Brasserie Bios is still used on some labels.)

AUGUSTIJN — amber, tangy-soapy aroma, grain and bitter hop flavor, tangy sweet finish, long off-dry hop aftertaste, very complex, very big and assertive, very long. [A, 40]

BIOS COPPER ALE — medium deep cloudy red-brown, sharp yeasty sweet spicy nose, sweet and sour lactic palate, tenacious long hop aftertaste. [A, 37]

GULDEN DRAAK — hazy amber; hefty malt aroma shows lots of the 11.5% alcohol; huge alcoholic malt flavor is off-dry in the mouth, really fills your mouth and senses; long dry malt aftertaste. In the United States it is labeled Golden Gragon and comes in small bottles with 10.5% abv and large bottles with 11.5% abv like the European bottling. The sample of this beer tasted in the U.S.A. in early 1995 was deep amber, had a huge alcoholic-malt aroma and palate, big bodied, very long, and very complex. It is well-balanced, though somewhat on the sweet and vinous side. It ages well in the bottle. Another sample tasted in a more benign setting, showed a trace of isovaleric acid and epoxides (oxidized hop oils which give a faint geranium smell, which could come from the use of aged hops, a Belgian brewing technique intended to reduce the hop bitterness). [A, 67]

PIRAAT ALE — deep gold, big complex lactic-fruity-spicy malt aroma; creamy palate has great mouthfeel and a spicy-malty flavor with plenty of alcohol; huge body, complex throughout, very long and tasty, on the vinous side because of the high alcohol (10.5% abv). Tasted in early 1995, this is to be marketed as Pirate Ale in the U.S. It ages well in the bottle. Bottle cap says Br. Bios, label says Van Steenberge. [A. 98]

BORNEM DOUBLE — amber, tan head, lactic aroma; lactic acid is first thing noticeable in the flavor, but this subsides with time and eventually disappears into the grain and spiciness; complex creamy palate, big body, medium dry and spicy at the finish; plenty of alcohol (8% abv) but it is not obtrusive; nicely balanced. [A, 80]

Brouwerij Van Zulte
Brewery in Zulte

ZULTE — medium deep red-brown, rich malt aroma and palate, medium body; touch of sourness in back of the palate develops and comes forward in the long malt aftertaste. (Note: I have also seen this brew labeled as having been made by NV Alken-Maes S.A.) [A, 49]

Westmalle Abbey
Cistercian Trappiste Abbey Brewery in Westmalle

WESTMALLE TRIPLE ABBEY BEER 8% — bright gold, fine bitter hop aroma and bright hop flavor, full-bodied, good balance, dry hop and malt finish, long dry hop aftertaste, high alcohol (8%), delicious brew. [A, 72]

WESTMALLE TRIPLE 9% — hazy amber, honeyed fruity malt nose, big sweet malt flavor, very smooth and very long. [A, 68]

WESTMALLE DUBBEL ABBEY BEER — fairly deep cloudy orange-brown, delicious complex off-dry malt nose, rich and full bodied; big roasted malt flavor is quite complex and seems to change as it goes; very long aftertaste like the flavor, a truly great Trappiste brew. [A, 91]

Brasserie Wiel
Brewery just outside Bruxelles

WIEL'S — pale tawny-gold, fine head, beautifully hopped nose (Saaz hops), medium body, good hop flavor well-backed with malt, fairly dry, smooth long dry hop aftertaste. [B, 60]

Brasserie Wieze
Brewery in Van Roy

WIEZE LAGER BEER — brilliant gold, medium hop nose with good malt, good clean malt-hop flavor with springwater background, slight metallic finish, good balance, very drinkable. [B, 75]

Notes

Bosnia

Banjalucka Pivara
Brewery in Banja Luka

NEKTAR BEER — pale amber, malt aroma with an off-dry fruity-apple background; palate like the nose, but there are some hops; long faintly sour dry hop after-taste. [B, 27]

Bulgaria

Brewery Haskowo
Brewery in Haskowo

ASTICA — bright gold; sweet nose is like a banana popsicle with a malt, pear, and lactic back-ground; lactic-malt flavor, loses the lactic and gains malt as it goes, aftertaste is almost all malt; not unlikable, but a little rough. [B, 47]

Brewery Zagorka
Brewery Stara Zagora

ZAGORKA IMPORTED PRE-MIUM LAGER — bright gold, faint malt and hop nose, good body, weak dry hop flavor, dry hop finish and short dry hop after-taste. [B, 42]

Czechoslovakia

Pivovary Bohemia
Brewery in Prague (Praha)

OLD BOHEMIA HELLES BEER — gold, dry malt and hop aroma and flavor, good balance, bright taste, very smooth, dry finish and aftertaste, good length, 5% abv. [B, 49]

OLD BOHEMIA DUNKLES BEER — brown, dry malty aroma and flavor, smooth tasty flavor, good body, dry malt finish and after-taste, very good with food. [B, 67]

Budvar Brewery
Brewery in Ceske Budejovice

BUDVAR BUDWEISER — bright tawny-gold, lively hop aroma; flavor is bright hops, there is malt but it is in the background; the hops are strongest at the finish, for the aftertaste is long light hops. Well-made well-balanced likable brew. On draft, the hops seem less pronounced; the malt shows better, and this results in an improved balance and a more deli-cate hop aftertaste, making a good beer even better. This is the 12° density version, the most well-known Budvar and the one exported to most of the world. [B, 61]

BUDVAR BUDWEISER — tawny-gold, off-dry malt aroma with hops in back, creamy off-dry malt flavor with the hops well in back; finish has more hops and a slight salty nature; long aftertaste is once again malty like the flavor. This is the 10° density version, available locally. [B, 54]

Chebski Starovar
Brewery in Cheb/Eger

EGER URBIER — gold, good malt nose with hops, smooth malt flavor, light and dry, good body, fairly long dry malt aftertaste. [B, 36]

Crystal Pivovare / Samson Brewery
Brewery in Cescké Budejovice

CRYSTAL LAGER BEER — bright deep gold, big bubble loosely knit head, European hop nose; Euro-hop and carbonation palate has some roasted-burned malt in back; medium body, rich malt and hop finish, nutty hop aftertaste, long and dry. [B, 36]

CRYSTAL DIPLOMAT DARK BEER — deep amber, fairly rich dry malt aroma, rich dry malt flavor, medium body, very slightly off-dry at finish, medium long rich malty aftertaste. [B, 63]

Czech Pilsner Group
Brewing Group in Czech Republic

KAREL IV PREMIUM LAGER — gold, light malt nose; malty flavor has just the faintest trace of oxida-tion; medium body, light dry malty finish and aftertaste. [B, 51]

Pivovar Herold Breznice
Brewery at Sladovny-Vyzkum a Sluzby-Praha

HEROLD SVETLY LEZAK — deep gold, bright hop nose, good body, excellent dry hop flavor, very long dry hop aftertaste, well-made good tasting beer. [B, 80]

HEROLD TMAVE PIVO — brown, big malty aroma and flavor, good body, rich dry malty finish and aftertaste; stays dry all the way across the palate yet has a richness that is very attractive. [B, 73]

Brewery Hradec Kralove
Brewery in Hradec Kralove

HRADECKY LEV BLACK LION — light brown, fresh malt nose, moderately rich malt flavor, medium to light body; light malt aftertaste is a bit off-dry (and sweeter than the flavor) and fades quickly. [B, 40]

HRADECKY LEV LION — gold; malt aroma shows a trace of oxidation; light malt flavor, light body, dry malt finish and aftertaste; the flavor fades quickly but the dryness stays. [B, 24]

HRADECKY LEV DOUBLE BOCK — gold, off-dry malt nose, off-dry malt flavor, good body, big malt finish; dry malt and hop aftertaste is long; does not show the alcohol or body requisite for a double bock. [B, 34]

Jihoceske Pivovare K.P. / Crystal Pivovare
Samson Brewery in Ceské Budejovice

SAMSON 10° — bright gold, good head, pleasant balanced hop and malt aroma, sharp hops on front of palate, off-dry malt middle, crisp hop finish, very long dry and slightly sour hop aftertaste, also a faint trace of oxidation. [B, 34]

SAMSON 11° — tawny-gold, flowery hop aroma, moderately sweet hop flavor; malt shows well in the middle and finish; light nutty aftertaste shows both hops and malt; quite pleasant. There was also a trace of oxidation here, but it showed only in the nose. [B, 49]

Pivovar Karlovy Vary
Brewery in Carlsbad (Karlovy Vary)

KAREL SVELTE — brilliant deep tawny-gold, dense head, rich fruity aromatic slightly sweet nose, some background of pineapple; pleasant flavor is a bit too sweet up front, it dries toward the finish, and ends with a dry hop aftertaste. [B, 30]

Pivovare Krusovické
Brewery in Krusovické

KRUSOVICKÉ PIVO — dark amber, faint chocolate malt nose, medium body, light off-dry chocolate malt flavor, low carbonation, dull slightly sweet malt finish and aftertaste; could use more carbonation to pick up the malt flavor and balance off the sweetness. [B, 40]

KRUSOVICÉ BOHEMIAN LAGER — gold, very attractive Czech hop nose, big bright hop flavor, medium to good body, dry hop finish and aftertaste, balanced and bright, aged 70 days, made with Zatec hops. [B, 64]

Brewery Litovel, Moravkoslezs ké Pivovary
Brewery in Litovel

LITOVEL PREMIUM BEER — gold, lovely nose and taste of bright hops and good tasting malt, very bright and refreshing, dry malt and hop finish and aftertaste, balanced and long, gravity 12 P, 5% abv. [B, 80]

Náchod Brewery Ltd.
Brewery in Náchod

PRIMATOR URTYP DUNKEL — deep brown, dry very malty aroma, smooth balanced clean dry malty flavor; tastes nourishing; good body, dry malt finish and aftertaste, good length. [B, 76]

Pivovare Nosovice
Brewery at Dageb Solna

RADHOST — golden amber, hop nose, malt palate, smooth and fairly rich, long malt and hop aftertaste. [B, 59]

Nová Paka Brewery
Brewery in Nová Paka

KUMBURAK — deep gold, straightforward malt nose; big malty flavor has a bitter hop background, quickly makes a transformation to a dry bitter finish showing little or no malt; long dry bitter hop aftertaste, seems a bit offish at first but it grows on you. [B, 57]

Praske Pivovare
Brewery in Zavod Smichov

SMICHOVSKY STAROPRAMEN — bright tawny-gold, big head, soapy nose, off-dry malt and light hop palate, touch of oxidation in front, long sour hop aftertaste. [B, 19]

STAROPRAMEN — brilliant gold, big European hop aroma and taste, excellent of the style, dry hop finish and long dry hop aftertaste, really fine beer for hop lovers. Found in California in early 1994 as being from the Staropramen Brewery of Prague. [B, 73]

Prerov Brewery
Brewery in Prerov

ZUBR PREMIUM BEER — gold; pleasant malty aroma has a good hop backing; good tasting malt and hop flavor; medium body, good balance, dry malt and hop finish and aftertaste, gravity 12 P, 5% abv. [B, 73]

Radegast Brewery
Brewery in Nosovice

RADEGAST CZECHOSLOVA-KIAN BEER — bright gold, big hop nose, big but ordinary dry hop flavor, good body; seems a bit tired crossing the palate; faint trace of oxidation in back; finishes just like it starts; medium to brief dry hop aftertaste; lacks complexity. Version found in the U.S.A. [B, 34]

RADEGAST PREMIUM LIGHT — gold, malt aroma; palate is first dry hops then switches to dry malt; medium body, dry malt finish and aftertaste, good length, 4.75% abv. Tasted in Europe. [B, 47]

RADEGAST PREMIUM DARK — brown, light dry malt aroma and flavor; some off-dry malt in back shows better at the finish and aftertaste; fairly long, and with good body. [B, 50]

Severoceske Pivovare
Brewery in Velke Brezno

BREZNAK SVETLY LEZAK — tawny-gold, slightly hazy, very little head, hop aroma; malt palate is sweetest in the middle; hops show in the finish as an edge, brief aftertaste is hops but not as pronounced as the finish. [B, 40]

Starobrno Brewery
Brewery in Brno, Moravia

STAROBRNO EXPORT LAGER BEER — deep gold, bright hop nose, very large hop flavor with plenty of malt in support, big body, strong hop finish, and long hop aftertaste, bold, rich, and long. [B, 61]

U Fleku
Brewpub/Restaurant in Prague

FLEKOVSKY LEZAK — opaque brown; huge dense head that lasts to the bottom of the mug; slightly sweet dark and caramel malt palate, slightly underhopped, chewy rich flavor throughout; not complex, but rich and satisfying, very drinkable; high extract, low alcohol, very long malt aftertaste; a great deal of unfermented malt in solution, and fairly high density (13°). [B, 89]

U SV. TOMASE
Brewpub and restaurant in Letenska (Prague)

SPECIAL BRANIK — tawny-gold with a creamy head, well-hopped Hallertau (Zatek) nose; very dry bright and bitter palate that increases at the finish leading into a very long strong dry hop aftertaste; has a nutty quality that makes you feel like you had been eating peanuts with your beer. [B, 79]

TOMASOVSKY LEZAK — deep red-brown, light large bubble short-lived head, scorched malt aroma with hops in behind, pleasant fresh malt palate, low carbonation, long slightly off-sweet refreshing aftertaste with the hops on the sides of the tongue, very chewy and satisfying dark lager. [B, 57]

Urquell Brewery
Brewery in Pilsen. Facilities are shared with the Gambrinus Brewery.

PILSNER URQUELL — bright tawny-gold, good head, appetizing hop aroma, smooth well-balanced malt and hop flavor, refreshing and satisfying, long smooth dry hop aftertaste, excellent classic Pilsener beer. In Czechoslovakia it is called Prazdroj. Freshly bottled, it is almost indistinguishable from the fresh draft except for the thickness of the head, which is very dense on draft. [B, 79]

GAMBRINUS PILSEN — deep gold, appetizing hop nose, bright hop flavor with plenty of malt in support; malt emerges well at the finish, and stays to balance a long dry hop aftertaste. Gambrinus Brewery, Pilsen. [B, 47]

WENZEL'S BRÄU — bright gold, roasted malt and hop aroma; palate has an off-dry front, but this quickly becomes big hops; some malt rejoins the hops at the finish, but the long aftertaste is dry hops backed with faintly sour malt. This is a pleasant lovely tasting brew when fresh. Gambrinus Brewery. [B, 40]

Notes

DIA PIVO — bright gold, low and short-lived head, sour malt aroma, light body, light malt flavor with noticeable carbonation; some tannin appears in the throat; short dry aftertaste. A low density (8°) beer made for diabetics with 3.5% alcohol. From Západoceske Pivorary, a Gambrinus affiliate. [B, 35]

SVETOVAR PUVODNI LEZAK — pale amber, thick head, grainy aroma, off-dry grainy palate; hops appear in the finish; light dry hop aftertaste with a nutty quality, 3.1% alcohol. Also from Zápoadoceske Brewery. [B, 37]

Pivovar Velke Popovice
Brewery in Velke Popovice (suburb of Prague)

VELKE POPOVICKY KOZEL SVETLY LEZAK — gold, fruity cereal grain nose, light fruity malt flavor, light body, sweet malt finish, long malt aftertaste. [B, 43]

VELKE POPOVICKY KOZEL HELLES — deep gold, light dry hop aroma; bright hop flavor is very tasty; medium to light body, bright dry hop finish and aftertaste. Found in Europe. [B, 69]

VELKE POPOVICKY KOZEL DUNKEL — deep brown, semi-rich malt aroma and flavor, a tasty likable malt, medium body, long off-dry malt finish and aftertaste. Found in Europe. [B, 53]

KOZEL PREMIUM BEER — deep gold, European hop aroma; pleasant balanced malt and hop flavor; medium body, very European style, dry hop finish and aftertaste, a very tasty brightly hopped beer. Version appearing in the U.S.A. [B, 69]

Pivovar Vratislavice
Brewery in Vratislav

VRATISLAV PREMIUM BEER — gold, big European hop nose, dry hop flavor, medium body, dry hop finish, long dry hop aftertaste. [B, 43]

VRATISLAV DARK BEER — deep amber, dry malt aroma; some faint fruity esters are present; light fairly dry malt flavor; finish is slightly sweet malt as is the medium long aftertaste; pleasant but little complexity. [B, 38]

VRATISLAV PREMIER PIVO — gold, dry Euro hop aroma and flavor, medium body, long dry hop aftertaste; tasted in Europe; probably the domestic version equivalent of the Premium. [B, 50]

VRATISLAV BOHEMISCHE DUNKEL LAGER — brown, dry malty nose and taste, medium body, very pleasant dry malty flavor, long dry malt aftertaste, the European version of the dark; seems to be very much like the exported brew. [B, 65]

Vysoky Chlumec Brewery
Brewery in Vysoky Chlumec

LOBKOWICZ PREMIUM LAGER BEER — deep gold, lovely European hop aroma, bright malt and hop flavor, good balance, good body, a trace of oxidation in the back; dry hop aftertaste has good duration; good enough to taste good even with the touch of oxidation. [B, 69]

Dalmatia

Jadranska Pivovare
Brewery in Split

JADRAN BEER — cloudy yellow; faint fruity malt aroma has some oxidation; highly carbonated; flavor is mostly malt, but there are hops in there as well; medium body, hop finish; dry malt aftertaste has little length. [B, 34]

Denmark

Albani Breweries, Ltd.
Brewery in Odense

ALBANI EXPORT BEER — yellow-gold, light malt nose with light hops in back, pleasant flavor with a good mix of hops and malt, malt finish, light dry malt and hop aftertaste. [B, 46]

ALBANI PILSNER — gold, medium hop nose, good hop and malt pils flavor, good balance, pleasant but not complex or long. [B, 46]

GIRAF MALT LIQUOR — fairly deep amber-gold, lovely malt and hop nose; bitter hops briefly on front of palate, but big off-dry malt comes quickly in for an overall malt flavor; hops reappear in the finish; long off-dry malt and hop aftertaste, complex, good body, good tasting. [ML, 65]

ALBANI PORTER — deep molasses brown color, smooth light malt aroma, big rich malt flavor with a touch of sour malt in back, extended rich malt aftertaste, good body, smooth and delicious, extremely complex; tone of coffee, licorice, and chocolate weave in and out; balanced, delightful. This is one of my top ten all-time favorites. I recently tasted a bottle that was eight years old, and it received top scores in a blind tasting from everyone present. [P, 100]

ALBANI PÂSKEBRYG — deep pale amber, malt nose with slight hops, big malt and hop flavor, long malt-hop aftertaste, very drinkable. (Paske is Danish for Easter and bryg is beer.) [B, 60]

ALBANI JULE BRYG — medium amber, malt and light hop nose, big hop and malt flavor; palate is first malt then hops develop across it to dominate the finish; decent balance, long big dry hop aftertaste. [B, 62]

Ceres Breweries, Ltd.
Brewery in Aarhus, Horsens

CERES BEER — gold, faint apple-malt nose, light off-dry malt flavor, brief dry hop aftertaste. [B, 27]

RED ERIC MALT LIQUOR — yellow-gold, aroma of hops and off-dry toffee-malt, hops and toffee palate, good body, lots of character, long dry hop and malt aftertaste. [ML, 37]

CERES STRONG ALE — gold, malt nose; very strong malt flavor shows the alcohol as well (7.7%); well hopped in back, very strong and very long, a real mouthful. [A, 78]

CERES ROYAL EXPORT — gold, sweet apple aroma, sweet malt flavor, big body; there is a sense of alcohol but it's not excessive; sweet malt finish, long off-dry malt aftertaste. [B, 38]

CERES STOUT — dark brown, fairly rich nutty malt aroma, dry nutty malt flavor, good body, dry nutty aftertaste, short, 7.7% abv. [S, 53]

Faxe Bryggeri A/S
Brewery in Faxe

FAXE PREMIUM DANISH EXPORT BEER — gold, big head, soapy malty nose, grapelike soapy taste, medium body, dull malty finish and aftertaste. [B, 26]

Harboes Brewery
Brewery in Skaelskor

HARBOE BEAR BEER — pale bright gold, fresh malt aroma; off-dry malt flavor in front, but by the finish it is all bitter hops; long dry and bitter hop aftertaste. [ML, 47]

HARBOE GOLD EXPORT BEER — deep clear gold, light malt and hop aroma; light dry flavor at the start but the finish is off-dry malt; the aftertaste is good dry malt and hops; the balance stays good throughout. [B, 41]

Lolland-Falsters Bryghus
Brewery at Nykobing, Falsters Island

LOLLAND-FALSTERS EXPORT DANISH BEER — bright gold, clean malt nose; flavor is lightly toasted malt up front, bitter hops at the finish; complex, good body, long lightly hopped dry aftertaste with a smoked background. [B, 26]

DANISH DYNAMITE — hazy gold, light hop and malt nose, a trifle skunky at first; big rich malt flavor has a lot of hops in back and finishes "hot"; big body, long bitter-dry hop aftertaste. [B, 61]

Thor Breweries
Brewery at Randers

THOR BEER — pale gold, light off-dry malt nose, malt-hop flavor, medium body, fair balance, medium to long dry hop aftertaste. [B, 41]

DANISH GOLD — pale bright gold, malt nose, strong hop flavor, dry hop aftertaste, medium body, fair length. [B, 18]

BUUR BEER DE LUXE — deep gold, fresh and clean malt-hop aroma, huge sweet hop flavor, big body, slightly soapy finish, long hop aftertaste, a wonderful brew with great taste. [B, 69]

The United Breweries, Ltd.
United Breweries is an amalgamation of Carlsberg Breweries and the Tuborg and Royal Breweries in Copenhagen, Elsinore, and Silkeborg.

CARLSBERG ROYAL LAGER BEER — deep gold, light pleasant and clean malt aroma; hops are in back; light dry good hop flavor, good balance, light off-dry malt aftertaste. [B, 60]

CARLSBERG ELEPHANT MALT LIQUOR — deep gold, light fruity malt aroma with some hops and apple peel, big pungent flavor with lots of character; almost a sense of menthol there is so much volatility; big strong malt aftertaste with hops to support and give balance. [ML, 25]

CARLSBERG SPECIAL DARK BEER — deep amber, light balanced malt and hop aroma, light body; light flavor with hops not arriving until the finish, short medium dry aftertaste. [B, 51]

TUBORG BEER — pale gold, pleasant malt nose with some hop character, big sharp hop flavor, touch of sour in the finish, strong and long dry hop aftertaste. [B, 30]

CARLSBERG BEER — bright gold, big hop nose, lovely bright hop flavor, good long dry hop aftertaste, balanced and fairly complex. [B, 47]

CARLSBERG LIGHT — bright gold, faintly skunky nose, off-dry malt and sour dry hop flavor; aftertaste like the flavor has medium length. [LO, 26]

TUBORG ROYAL DANISH EXTRA STRONG BEER — brilliant deep gold, hop and malt nose, strong wine off-dry malt palate, long malt aftertaste; definitely strong flavored as promised and likely has high alcohol as well (around 8%). [B, 43]

TUBORG PORTER DOUBLE STOUT — opaque, brown head, strong malt nose, slightly bitter, rich complex malt flavor, balanced and even stronger than the nose, big hops at the finish; long aftertaste has both hops and malt aplenty. [P, 83]

CARLSBERG SPECIAL BREW EXTRA STRONG EXPORT LAGER — bright gold; beautifully balanced big malt and hop aroma; a big mouthful of flavor with both malt and hops, big body, noticeable alcohol, long balanced malt and hop aftertaste, 8% abv. [B, 51]

IMPERIAL STOUT — almost opaque-black; rich complex stout aroma hinting of all kinds of good things; luxurious malt flavor, good body, fairly dry, very long dry malt aftertaste. Wiibroes Brewery, Elsinore. [S, 67]

NEPTUN DANISH PILSNER — brilliant pale gold, malt nose, malt flavor, light hops in the finish, light dry hop aftertaste. Neptun Brewery, Silkeborg. [B, 47]

NEPTUN GOLDEN BROWN — brilliant gold, earthy hop nose, big hop and off-dry malt flavor, good body, doubtful balance, off-dry malt and bitter hop finish, long bitter and dry hop aftertaste. [B, 18]

NEPTUN PAASKE BRYG — gold, light malt and hop nose, strong hop flavor with too little malt in support, long dry bitter hop aftertaste. An Easter festival beer which is supposed to be a bock-style brew. [B, 58]

NEPTUN PINSE BRYG — bright lime green (colored green intentionally), malt and big hop aroma, very well-hopped flavor with just a little (too little) malt for balance, long dry bitter hop aftertaste, not unlike the Easter beer above. Pinse is Danish for Whitsuntide or Pentecost, a religious festival for the seventh Sunday after Easter. [B, 58]

GREEN ROOSTER MALT LIQUOR — another bright lime green beer, delicious aromatic clover hop aroma, complex hop flavor, full-bodied, balanced, malt finish, long dry hop and malt aftertaste, a delicious well-hopped brew. This is a fantastic brew. Don't let the color put you off. [ML, 64]

TUBORG GOLD LABEL BEER — pale gold; smooth hop aroma is well backed with malt; smooth dry hop flavor, finely carbonated and quite creamy, good body; plenty of malt to back the prevailing hop character that lasts throughout; refreshing, dry hop finish and aftertaste, medium to good length. Originally found in Canada, arrived in U.S.A. in early 1994. [B, 63]

CARLSBERG PORTER IMPERIAL STOUT — dark brown; light malty nose shows a lot of alcohol (7.8% abv); tastes like it smells (malty and alcoholic); starts out like it is going to be rich but it is not; heavy thick body, finishes dry and alcoholic, smooth dry malty aftertaste. [P/S, 69]

Notes

Estonia

Saku Ölletehas
Brewery in Eesti

SAKU ORIGINAL BEER — gold; light malty aroma shows some European hops; dry malt and hop flavor, a decent but ordinary Pils, medium body, medium long dry hop aftertaste, just a touch of oxidation at the end; no faults stick out, but it is average at best. [B, 36]

SAKU ESTONIAN PORTER — amber; fruity estery nose is a bit buttery and sweet; big complex roasted malt flavor is also a bit buttery; some sweetness in back that never quite emerges; medium body, long lightly roasted malt aftertaste. [P, 55]

Finland

Hartwell Co., Inc.
Breweries in Kaarina, Turku, Vaasa, and Karelia

KARJALA EXPORT BEER — deep tawny gold, fine hop aroma, sprightly hop flavor, big body, spicy finish, long dry hop aftertaste, a satisfying and filling beer. [B, 60]

Osakeyhtio Mallasjuoma, Inc.
Breweries in Lahti, Heinola, Oulo

FINLANDIA GOLD BEER — gold, lovely malt aroma, pleasant malt flavor with plenty of hop character, excellent balance, long dry hop aftertaste, fairly complex and very drinkable. [B, 83]

FINLANDIA LIGHT BEER — bright tawny-gold, mild hop aroma; hop palate is shallow and not well-balanced; malt aftertaste is a bit sour. [B, 29]

ERIKOIS EXPORT OLUT IVA LAHDEN — tawny gold, roasted malt, toffee, and molasses nose, toasted grainy malt flavor; very pleasant to sip; long dry malt aftertaste. [B, 56]

Sinebrychoff Brewery
Brewery in Helsinki

KOFF FINNISH BEER — bright gold, zesty hop nose, big hop flavor, fairly well balanced, long hop aftertaste, no shortage of hops. [B, 47]

KOFF IMPERIAL STOUT — deep brown, caramel and hop aroma, dry rich malt and hop flavor, plenty of both, bitter and dry hop aftertaste with a herbaceous background. [S, 53]

France

Brasserie Amos
Brewery in Metz

AMOS IMPORTED FRENCH BEER — yellow-gold; malt nose is big at first but fades; pleasant off-dry malt flavor, heavy body, a bit winelike, off-dry malt finish and aftertaste; lacks complexity. [B, 31]

Brasserie Benifontaine / Yves Castelaine-Artisan Brasseur
Brewery in Nord Pas de Calais

CASTELAIN BLOND BIÈRE DE GARDE — deep gold, fruity malt aroma, big earthy malt flavor, winelike, complex, medium long dry malt aftertaste, very flavorful and smooth. [B, 68]

ST. AMAND FRENCH COUNTRY ALE — brilliant reddish amber, earthy fruity malt aroma, earthy malt flavor, good body, nice balance, most winelike in the finish, long dry malt aftertaste. Although labeled a bière de garde, it doesn't have the expected body, depth of flavor, or winelike character, and would appear to be ready to drink without additional bottle aging. Label says Brasserie Castelaine, Benifontaine, France. [A, 67]

JADE FRENCH COUNTRY ALE — hazy gold, lacy head, finely carbonated, big hop nose, spritzy well-hopped flavor, good body; uniformly hopped through the flavor, finish, and the aftertaste; not complex but very nice. [A, 53]

CH'TI BLOND BIÈRE DE GARDE — gold, big malty nose; sweet malt flavor shows some alcohol; tasty, long sweet malt aftertaste. [A, 40]

CH'TI AMBRÉE — amber, big malty nose, hefty long medium off-dry malt flavor and aftertaste; alcohol is there but not in the way of anything, like a big malt wine. [A, 76]

Brasserie Duyck
Brewery in Jenlain

JENLAIN FRENCH COUNTRY ALE — bright pale amber, fresh malt nose, finely carbonated, bright malt flavor like a delicate barley wine, fairly dry malt throughout, especially in the long aftertaste, very good with food. [A, 52]

LE MADELON FRENCH COUNTRY BEER — deep amber, roasted malt nose with a Kir-like background, winelike dry roasted malt flavor, complex, soft, and smooth; a bit like a porter but not enough to be named one; few hops, if any. [B, 27]

TRADER JOE'S RESERVE BROWN HOLIDAY ALE 1992 — brilliant amber, sour spicy nose; nutmeg, clove, and ginger flavor, but malt still shows; good balance, very nicely done, medium length. [A, 65]

TRADER JOE'S RESERVE BROWN HOLIDAY ALE 1993 — hazy amber, spicy tart aroma; flavor is spicy but has a malty sweetness as well, finely carbonated; short aftertaste shows some of the sweetness; different from the 1992 version, but complex and refreshing. [A, 84]

TRADER JOE'S RESERVE BROWN HOLIDAY ALE 1994 — hazy dark amber, spicy aroma; flavor is spicy but has a malty sweetness as well; finely carbonated, good body; rich malty aftertaste shows some of the sweetness; complex and refreshing. [A, 68]

JENLAIN ORIGINAL FRENCH BLONDE ALE — hazy gold, European-style hop nose, big sweet wine/grape flavor, creamy, light to medium body, drinkable and refreshing, short dry malt aftertaste. [A, 65]

JENLAIN ORIGINAL FRENCH ALE — hazy amber, light sweet malt nose; honeyed malt flavor is winelike with high alcohol; medium to good body, dry malt finish and long aftertaste. [A, 58]

JENLAIN ORIGINAL AMBER ALE — amber, smooth malt aroma and flavor, medium body, smooth, fairly dry in the finish and aftertaste. [A, 61]

Brasserie Enfants de Gayant S.A.
Small brewery in Douai. The abbey ales are brewed under contract for Abbey Crespin.

ST. LANDELIN BLONDE ABBEY ALE — gold; aroma and palate are bright malt without noticeable alcohol (5.9% abv); there is also a faint spicy character that adds interest; good body, fairly smooth and balanced from 9 months of aging, long malty aftertaste. [A, 65]

ST. LANDELIN AMBER ABBEY ALE — golden amber, very big malt aroma and flavor with a spiciness and noticeable alcohol (6.8% abv), big body, long complex aftertaste. [A, 72]

ST. LANDELIN BROWN ABBEY ALE — deep amber, big malt aroma, big body, very tasty malt flavor, 6.2% abv, long rich malt aftertaste. [A, 74]

Societé Européene de Brasseries
Brewery in Sevres

SKANSEN SPECIAL LAGER — pale amber, roasted malt nose, off-dry toasted malt flavor, spicy hot component to the malt aftertaste. [B, 27]

KANTERBRAU GOLD BIÈRE SPECIALE — yellow-gold, malt nose; bit of an ale-like hop bite on the front of the palate, then roasted malt emerges and pushes the bitter hops to the background;

long hop and roasted malt aftertaste; balance is a bit off. [B, 50]

Brasserie Facon
Brewery in Pont de Briques

ALE DE GARDE DE SAINT ARNOULD — cloudy gold, fruity melon and malt nose, strong malt flavor, noticeable alcohol, long malt aftertaste. [A, 30]

Le Grands Chais de France
Brewery in Schiltigheim

CHIC ALSACE BEER — pale gold, light sweet hop and malt nose, light body, hop flavor, sour hop aftertaste; lacks body and complexity. [B, 39]

CHIC LITE ALSACE BEER — very pale gold, dank malt nose, grainy carbonated water flavor, somewhat gassy, metallic malt finish and aftertaste, little character. [LO, 14]

Brasseries Kronenbourg, S.A.
Brewery in Strasbourg

KRONENBOURG 1664 IMPORTED BEER — medium gold; light malt aroma is almost fruity; vinous malt flavor, medium long dry hop aftertaste. [B, 38]

KRONENBOURG 1664 DARK BEER — deep copper color, extremely light malt aroma, malt

flavor, light body, dull dry malt aftertaste. [B, 28]

KRONENBOURG 1664 MALT LIQUOR — bright amber-gold, good sour malt aroma; carbonation competes with the malt flavor; heavy body, long smooth malt aftertaste. [ML, 43]

TOURTEL DE-ALCOHOLIZED BEER — gold; hop aroma is slightly skunky; grainy hop flavor, light body, short off-dry malt aftertaste. [NA, 32]

Brasserie La Choulette S.A.
Small brewery in Hordain

LA CHOULETTE BLONDE — gold; bright nose shows both hops and malt; big drinkable flavor shows a bit more malt than hops, but is balanced; good body, long malty aftertaste with a background spiciness. [A, 71]

LA CHOULETTE AMBRÉE — amber, big malt aroma and flavor, big bodied and very rich; long malt aftertaste retains the caramel richness of the flavor. [A, 83]

LA CHOULETTE AMBRÉE AMBER ALE — amber, toasted malt nose, rich toasted malt flavor, big body; has a honeyed chocolate nature; long, smooth, and rich malt. Version found in U.S.A. in 1995. [A, 83]

LA CHOULETTE BIÈRE DES SANS CULOTTES — gold, rising malt aroma, big bright malt flavor, good body, very drinkable; malty aftertaste is not long, but there is noticeable alcohol (7% abv). [A, 65]

Brasseurs de Paris / Brasserie Nouvelle de Lutèce
Brewery B.N.L. Port Autonome de Paris, Bonneiul

BIÈRE DE PARIS — beautiful brilliant pale amber, light fragrant toasted malt aroma with a tang, light body, delicate toasted malt flavor with a caramel background, balanced hop finish, long dry hop aftertaste. It is a barley of great delicacy and finesse. It is excellent with food. In France it is labeled Lutèce Bière de Paris. [A, 80]

Haag-Metzger & Cie., S.A. / Brasserie Meteor
Brewery in Hochfelden

METEOR PILS BIER DE LUXE — pale yellow-gold, faint pils-style nose with more hops than malt, crisp hop flavor, long clean dry hop aftertaste. [B, 32]

La Grande Brasserie Moderne
Brewery in Roubaix

SEPTANTE ROUGE — pale amber, strong aromatic nose with hops and malt; interesting palate that is first off-dry malt; hops join the malt at mid-palate, then a long dry aftertaste of hops and malt; medium body, complex, clean, long, and flavorful. [A, 54]

SEPTANTE 5 — pale copper-amber, off-dry malt aroma, strong dry malt flavor, big body, malt finish, pleasant malt aftertaste, well-balanced, somewhat winelike, noticeable alcohol, well made. [ML, 81]

SEPTANTE VERTE — medium deep gold, weak hop and malt aroma, good big hop flavor with plenty of malt, faintly sour background to the long malt aftertaste, a good beer with food. [A, 54]

SUPER 49 GRANDE BIÈRE DE LUXE — hazy gold, pleasant hop and malt nose, sour malt palate, metallic background; long sour hop aftertaste with some fruity malt hiding somewhere. [B, 26]

TERKEN BRUNE — deep amber-brown, lightly toasted big malt nose, good body, good and big toasted malt flavor, long dry malt aftertaste, hops not noticeable if there; has complexity, however, and is a well-made malt brew with a good level of intensity. [B, 83]

TERKEN BIÈRE DE LUXE — deep gold, light malt nose, light and smooth malt flavor, good body, some noticeable alcohol, soft texture, tasty. [B, 52]

TRADER JOE'S SPECIAL DARK HOLIDAY ALE — deep amber, malt nose, big toasted malt flavor; finish has a scorched component; long toasted malt aftertaste is also a bit burnt. [A, 65]

Notes

BREUG LAGER BEER — hazy pale yellow; hop nose is strong and very European; slightly oxidized malt flavor is faintly like cardboard; weak body, almost watery, dry hop aftertaste. [B, 26]

L'Alsacienne de Brasseries, S.A.
Brewery in Schiltigheim. Some labels identify brews as being made by Heineken in Schiltigheim.

MÜTZIG EXPORT BEER — pale gold, strong perfumy pine needle nose, hop and malt flavor, light body, dry malt aftertaste. [B, 7]

MÜTZIG — pale gold, hop nose, complex malt and hop flavor, hop finish and faint sour hop aftertaste. [B, 7]

Brasserie Mattiere du Pêcheur, S.A.
Breweries in Schiltigheim and Strasbourg

FISCHER BEER — pale gold, pleasant off-dry malt and hop nose, light body, pleasant slightly off-dry malt flavor; aftertaste is drier than the flavor and is still mostly malt; fairly short. [B, 55]

FISCHER ALE — pale gold; pleasant off-dry malt and hop nose is sweeter than above, but the malt flavor is nicely dry with the hops in back; good balance, long dry aftertaste like the flavor. [A, 54]

FISCHER D'ALSACE — bright gold, hop aroma; hop flavor has the malt sliding in from mid-palate on; very good balance, malt finish, good body, long dry malt and hop aftertaste, well-made beer. [B, 69]

FISCHER D'ALSACE BITTER — pale amber, hop nose; fairly bitter hop flavor that extends into a long dry aftertaste. [B, 9]

FISCHER D'ALSACE AMBER — light amber, aroma with plenty of off-dry malt and bright hops; flavor starts out with the malt, hops come in the middle and stay for the finish and long aftertaste; good hefty body, some complexity, a good very drinkable brew. [B, 63]

FISCHER LA BELLE STRASBOURGEOISE — deep gold, grainy malt nose; malt flavor seems to gain strength as it crosses the palate; hops join the malt at the finish, leading into a good long aftertaste with both components in harmony. [B, 47]

FISCHER PILS — pale gold, light malt nose; malt flavor gets hops as it approaches the finish; long fairly dry hop aftertaste. [B, 46]

FISCHER GOLD — gold, off-dry fruity malt aroma, strong vinous malt flavor, long malt aftertaste, heavy body. [B, 53]

36.15 PECHEUR LA BIÈRE AMOREUSE — bright gold; flowery, fruity, herbal, complex aroma (has added myrrh, ginger, cardamom, ginseng, cola, cinnamon, mango, licorice, myrtle, and eleutherococque); fruity herbal flavor, almost cherry-like, good body, medium length, not beerlike. [ML, 17]

ADELSHOFFEN BIÈRE SPECIALE D'ALSACE — deep yellow, off-dry fruity malt aroma with a touch of hops, very complex flavor of fruit and faint hops, a bit winelike, not dry, long roasted malt aftertaste. [B, 27]

MÜNSTERHOF FRENCH BEER — deep gold, malt nose, light malt and hop flavor, sour malt finish and aftertaste. [B, 26]

ADELSHOFFEN TRADITION — medium deep gold, very pleasant fruity aroma, light body, pleasant slightly burnt fruity malt flavor, little depth, pleasant malt finish and short aftertaste. [B, 27]

ADELSCOTT SMOKED MALT LIQUOR — bright orange, butterscotch and smoky barbecue nose, smoky sweet malt palate, light body, some alcohol noticeable, very pleasant and very drinkable. [ML, 53]

ADELSHOFFEN EXPORT — hazy tawny-gold, faint fruity malt nose, strange fruity malt flavor, light body, dull dry malt aftertaste. [B, 19]

ZELE — deep gold, lime aroma, light body, light lime flavor, not beerlike, probably flavored like the Canadian Zélé, light and brief. [ML, 26]

Brasseries Pelforth, S.A.
Brewery in Lille. Also uses corporate name Brasseries Pelican on some labels.

PELFORTH PALE ALE — deep gold, good malt nose; pleasant tasting malt and hop flavor; excellent balance, good body, off-dry malt aftertaste. Labeled also La Bière Blonde De France. [B, 60]

GEORGE KILLIAN'S BIÈRE ROUSSE (RED ALE) — reddish brown, big nose with lots of hops and molasses-caramel malt; flavor starts out big hops and finishes dry roasted malt; good balance, big body, long clean dry malt aftertaste. [A, 85]

PELICAN EXPORT BEER — gold, fresh fruity-malt nose, papery malt flavor, medium body, dull hop finish and aftertaste. [B, 44]

Brasserie St. Leonard
Brewery in St. Leonard / St. Martin, Boulogne

BRASSIN DE GARDE DE SAINT LEONARD — bright amber-peach, very faint toasted malt flavor, touch of hops in the finish; is winelike without being wine; long dry hop aftertaste still shows good malt, a very nice brew, especially good with food. [A, 67]

Brasserie de Saint Sylvestre
Brewery in St. Sylvestre

3 MONTS FLANDERS GOLDEN ALE — amber, malt nose with a citrus background, rich complex malt flavor, high alcohol, full bodied, long malt aftertaste. [A, 56]

ST. SYLVESTRE'S CHRISTMAS ALE 1992 — deep amber, concentrated malt aroma, strong flavor of concentrated malt well backed with hops, creamy, even and potent, vinous, good mouth feel, rich yet dry, plenty of alcohol, big body; stays constant right through the finish and long aftertaste. [A, 64]

ST. SYLVESTER'S FLANDERS WINTER ALE 1993 — deep amber; big head but finely carbonated; strong hop and off-dry malt aroma, big flavor of hops, malt, and alcohol, big body, smooth and balanced; sweet malt hangs right in there with the hops all the way across the palate; very long aftertaste like the flavor but drier. [A, 86]

ST. SYLVESTRE'S FLANDERS WINTER ALE 1995 — amber, sweet fruity nose, saccharin-sweet and oxidized taste, out-of-balance, likely spoiled. [NR]

Notes

Brasserie Schutzenberger, S.A.
Brewery in Schiltigheim

SANT'OR MALT BEVERAGE — very pale bright gold, faint hop nose, vegetal malt flavor, weak body, malt finish and aftertaste like the flavor. [NA, 26]

SCHUTZ PILS LUXE BIERE D'ALSACE — tawny-gold, good hop and malt nose, good hop flavor up front, good malt in the middle; aftertaste has an unpleasant overly sour component that is not in the flavor. [B, 17]

SCHUTZENBERGER JUBILATOR FRENCH BEER — yellow-gold, good hop nose with off-dry malt in back; palate is mostly sharp bitter hops except for some malt at the very beginning and some off-dry malt in the finish; complex flavor, long dry aftertaste shows both hops and malt. [B, 28]

SCHLOSS JOSEF ALSATIAN MALT BEVERAGE — gold, stinky hop nose; palate is faintly malty, but is impaired with oxidation. [NA, 7]

Union de Brasseries
France's largest brewery with five brew-plants in Paris. There are other breweries at other locations such as St. Amand-les-eaux.

"33" EXPORT BEER — deep bright gold, clean bright malt aroma with good hops and some yeast, big hop flavor in front, malt in back, good body, sour malt finish, good balance, long dry well-hopped aftertaste; a lively tasty brew that wakes up your palate. [B, 69]

"33" EXTRA DRY BEER BLONDE SPECIALE — amber-gold, bright well-hopped aroma, big flavor with lots of hops and off-dry roasted malt, complex, good body, good balance, long dry aftertaste like the flavor. [B, 83]

"33" RECORD BEER — deep yellow-gold, clean off-dry malt aroma with some hops, big rich off-dry malt flavor with good hop support, pleasant dry hop finish and aftertaste. [B, 69]

SLAVIA EXTRA DRY — deep tawny-gold, off-dry fruitlike malt aroma with a spicy background of something resembling woodruff, big toasted malt and hop flavor; long dry hop aftertaste with malt holding well in the background. [B, 52]

ROEMER PILS — deep yellow-gold, hop nose, tart and sour palate; long aftertaste like the flavor, but the more unpleasant aspects mar the effect. [B, 40]

PORTER 39 — deep red-brown, clean sweet fruity-toasted malt aroma, roasted malt flavor, lingering aftertaste like the flavor, a good porter. [P, 58]

PANTHER MALT BEVERAGE — bright amber, nice malt nose; tastes like cereal grain soda pop; hop bite in the short aftertaste. [NA, 27]

PANACH' BEER — tawny-gold, off tuna salad aroma, citrus soda pop flavor; reminds you of a French citron pressé; not much of a beer; this product is flavored. [B, 12]

Germany

Brauerei Aktien
Brewery in Kaufbeuren

AKTIEN EDEL AUSSTICH — bright gold, complex clean appetizing hop nose, smooth malt flavor with good hop support, good body and balance, long dry malt and hop aftertaste. [B, 52]

AKTIEN JUBILAUMS PILS — bright gold, complex and appetizing hop nose, nice hop flavor well backed with malt, good tasting, clean, balanced, and quite long. [B, 43]

STEINGADENER WEISSE DUNKEL — cloudy orange, grainy nose, malt and carbonation palate, dull and short. [W, 14]

AKTIEN FRUNDSBERG EXPORT DUNKEL — deep amber, nice malt nose, straightforward malt flavor, one dimensional, no character, no complexity, fairly brief malt aftertaste. [B, 29]

AKTIEN ST. MARTIN DUNKLER DOPPELBOCK — deep orange-amber, off-dry grainy malt aroma, off-dry malt flavor, good body, hop finish, long dry malt aftertaste. [BK, 67]

AKTIEN TÄNZELFEST-BIER — brilliant gold, complex malt and hop aroma, fairly rich malt flavor, medium body, dry malt finish and aftertaste. [B, 50]

AKTIEN HELL — gold, big malt and hop nose, big malt and dry hop flavor, light to medium body, long dry malt and hop aftertaste. [B, 55]

AKTIEN OKTOBERFEST — gold, malt nose, light malt flavor, hops way in back, light dry malt finish and aftertaste. [B, 40]

AKTIEN WEIZEN — gold, clove nose, spicy flavor, light body, dry finish, light dry lightly spicy aftertaste, good hot weather beer. [W, 56]

AKTIEN HEFEWEIZEN (WEIZEN MIT SEINER HEFE) — hazy gold; aroma is faintly and briefly sweet, but soon turns to spicy malt; tangy spiced malt taste, medium body, dry spicy finish; short dry aftertaste has a bitterness in back; the taste just doesn't come together. [W, 47]

HOLZHAUSENER LANDBIER — gold, off-dry light malt nose, light medium dry malt flavor with a honeyed background, dry malt finish, medium body, short dry malt aftertaste. [B, 45]

AKTIEN GOLD PREMIUM LAGER — bright gold, zesty European hop nose; dry hop flavor has good malt backing, good balance and body; dry malt finish; long dry and bitter aftertaste shows both malt and hops but has less balance than the flavor. [B, 62]

Brauerei Albquell
Brewery-Gasthof in Trochtefingen

ALBQUELL PILSNER — gold, big hop nose, bright sour hop flavor, dry hop finish, good body, long dry slightly sour hop aftertaste; nicely made classical Pils. [B, 65]

ALBQUELL URTRUNK — hazy gold, hop nose, big sour hop flavor, dry hop finish, good body, long dry hop aftertaste; a tad less sour than the Pils, but very similar and a little more balanced. [B, 68]

ALBQUELL EDELBIER EXPORT — gold, hop nose, big malt and hop flavor, good body, excellent balance, long dry hop aftertaste. [B, 71]

Brauerei Aldersbach / Frhr v. Aretin, K.G.
Brewery in Aldersbach

ALDERSBACHER KLOSTER HELL — gold, malt and hop aroma, very light malt flavor and finish, weak malt aftertaste. [B, 24]

ALDERSBACHER DUNKEL HEFE-WEIZEN — deep amber-brown, nice spicy hop and malt nose, bright fruity-spicy malt flavor, long dry malt aftertaste with the fruit and spice way in back, a tangy, tasty, drinkable beer. [W, 80]

Notes

Allgäuer Brauhaus
Brewery in Kempten

ALT KEMPTENER WEISSE DUNKEL — deep cloudy brown, terrific appetizing wheat and barley malt nose; zesty tangy flavor is smooth and drinkable; good body, great character, long long malt aftertaste. [W, 91]

ALLGÄUER BRAUHAUS URTYP EXPORT — gold, faint hop and malt nose, dull dry malt flavor; dry hop aftertaste has a little sweetness in back; medium length; clean tasting but not exciting; 5% abv. [B, 53]

ALLGÄUER BRAUHAUS DAS HELLE — gold, very faint hop nose, hop and malt flavor, not in balance, dry hop aftertaste, medium length. [B, 32]

ALLGÄUER BRAUHAUS FÜRSTADT WEIZEN — cloudy gold, big bright spicy nose, creamy, good malt and clove flavor, balanced; the malt softens the spicy nature; long aftertaste like the flavor. [W, 80]

ALLGÄUER BRAUHAUS EDELBRÄU — gold, big malt nose, strong malt flavor, tasty lip-smacking sipping beer, big body, long dry malt aftertaste, excellent balance, excellent beer. [B, 87]

TEUTSCH PILS — gold, malt and light hop nose; flavor is malt first, thence big hops to the finish; long dry hop aftertaste. [B, 56]

ALT KEMPTENER HEFE WEISSE — cloudy brownish-amber, big tight head, smooth spicy aroma, big rich spicy-malty flavor, nicely balanced, good body; head stays right to the bottom of the glass; malty spicy aftertaste is very long and very good; 5% abv. [W, 91]

FÜRSTABT WEIZEN HEFETRUB — cloudy gold, big thick head, light spicy nose, spicy malt flavor, balanced, good body, dry spicy malt finish and aftertaste, good duration; 5% abv. [W, 74]

Altenburger Brauerei Gmbh.
Brewery in Altenburg

ALTENBURGER BRAUNBIER — clear amber-brown, faint malt nose, dry malt flavor, medium body, dry malt finish and aftertaste, pleasant and likable, good with food; gravity 11 P, 4.7% abv. [B, 70]

Brauhaus Altenmünster-Weissenbrunn / Brauhaus Marktoberdorf
Brewery in Altenmünster

ALTENMÜNSTER HOPFIG HERB — gold complex malt and hop aroma, dry hop and malt flavor, good body, dry long bitter hop aftertaste; gravity 11 P, 4.8% abv. [B, 37]

ALTENMÜNSTER BRAUER BEER — deep gold, complex hop aroma, big hop flavor, creamy texture, slightly sour hop finish and aftertaste; pretty good except that it could use a bit more malt, especially in the finish. [B, 62]

ALTENMÜNSTER MAI-BOCK — beautiful deep gold, light toasted malt nose, pleasant big off-dry toasted malt flavor, rich and delicious, very smooth, big body, some alcohol noticeable; really feels good while it is in your mouth; short dry malt aftertaste. [BK, 86]

Altes Brauhaus Gmbh.
Brewery in Lippstadt

WESTFALEN PILS — gold, slightly toasted malt and hop aroma, pleasant bright hop flavor, lightly carbonated, slightly sour hop finish and aftertaste. [B, 46]

Privatbrauerei Hellbräu Altöttinger
Brewery in Altötting

ALTÖTTINGER FEIN HERB HELL-BRÄU — gold, malt aroma, pleasant malty flavor, lightly hopped, dry malt and light hop aftertaste. [B, 57]

ALTÖTTINGER BAYRISCH DUNKEL — deep brown, big off-dry grainy malt nose; rich malt flavor is also grainy; big body, good balance, delicious, off-dry malt finish, long dry malt aftertaste, good complexity and very drinkable, excellent dark pils. [B, 91]

ALTÖTTINGER
DULT-MÄRZEN — hazy-gold
with particles, sudsy carbonic
sweet nose; strange sweet flavor
stays sweet throughout, right
through the aftertaste; good body,
long length. [B, 37]

Klosterbrauerei Andechs
Kloster Brewery in Erling-Andechs

ANDECHS SPEZIAL HELL —
pale gold, complex off-dry malt and
hop aroma, bright complex zesty
very malty flavor, full bodied, big,
rich, clean, and strong malt finish
and fairly long aftertaste; gravity
13.3 P, 5.8% abv. [B, 74]

ANDECHS ANDECHSER
HELL — pale gold, hop aroma
and flavor, very smooth, light
body, very easy to drink, medium
long dry hop aftertaste; gravity
11.3 P, 4.8% abv. [B, 72]

ANDECHS EXPORT
DUNKEL — deep amber-brown,
lovely toasted malt nose, good dry
toasted malt flavor; complex with
lots of underlying other flavors
like fruit, spices, aromatics, etc.;
medium body, dry malt finish,
long lightly burnt malt aftertaste;
gravity 12.8 P. [B, 43]

ANDECHS BERGBOCK
HELL — brilliant deep gold; lovely
nose is mostly hops but is well
backed with malt; big malt and hop
flavor, really smooth, creamy,
vinous, very long malt aftertaste;
gravity 16.3 P. [BK, 81]

ANDECHS DOPPELBOCK
DUNKEL — deep amber-brown;
extremely rich malt nose is very
complex with all kinds of earthy
notes; a very complex flavor that
seems to flip back and forth from
dry to off-dry, again with all kinds
of flavors weaving in and out; some
would say it had an earthiness, I like
the word funky; very long dry malt
aftertaste; gravity 18.3 P, 7% abv. I
believe this to be my favorite beer
in all the world. [BK, 100]

ANDECHSER HEFETRUB
WEISSBIER — hazy deep
brownish-gold, lightly spiced
nose, mellow spiced flavor, very
nice and creamy, well bodied,
long dry malt and spice aftertaste;
gravity 13 P, 5.1% abv. [W, 77]

C.H. Andreas Westfälische Pils Brauerei
Brewery in Hagen

ANDREAS PILS — tawny-gold,
clean aromatic hop nose with an
off-dry malt background, bright hop
flavor with an off-dry malt backing,
burnt malt aftertaste. [B, 36]

Arcobräu, Grafliches Brauhaus
Brewery in Moos

ARCOBRÄU MOOSER
HELL — brilliant clear gold, big
hop nose, balanced hop and malt
flavor, good body, dry malt finish
and aftertaste. [B, 59]

Notes

ARCOBRÄU PILSENER — pale gold, clean hop nose, big hop flavor in front, malt in middle, dry hop finish, long dry hop aftertaste, good body, fairly complex, good balance. [B, 67]

ARCOBRÄU URWEISSE — hazy gold, bright hop nose, big spicy clove, hop and malt flavor, very smooth, good body, light spicy finish, long spicy malt aftertaste. [W, 47]

GRAF ARCO GRAFEN HELL — gold, lovely malt and hop nose, zesty fresh flavor, big malt finish, long malt aftertaste with plenty of good hop support. Grafliches Brauereien Arco, Adldorf. [B, 67]

COUNT ARCO'S BAVARIAN WEISSBIER WITH YEAST — gold, spicy lactic nose, pleasant spicy flavor with off-dry wheat in back, good mouthfeel, short dry spicy malt aftertaste. [W, 61]

COUNT ARCO'S BAVARIAN FESTBIER — gold, beautiful fresh rising malt aroma, fresh creamy medium dry malt flavor, good body, very drinkable, long medium dry lightly toasted malt aftertaste. [B, 72]

Brauerei Arnold
Brewery in Lauf

ARNOLD PILSENER — medium to deep gold, low carbonation, light roasted malt nose and flavor, medium length dry roasted malt aftertaste, pleasant but lacks complexity. [B, 51]

ARNOLD BAVARIAN DARK BEER — deep copper-brown, beautiful roasted malt nose, tasty malt flavor, light body; pleasant but lacks depth and length. [B, 45]

BARON VON FUNK PREMIUM BEER COOLER — cloudy gold, malty-citrus flavor like a shandy, but with more fruit than beer, sweet and light, sticky-sweet finish, almost no aftertaste. [ML, 47]

Auerbräu A.G.
Brewery in Rosenheim

AUERBRÄU PILS — gold, faint hop aroma, dull off-dry malt flavor, medium body, dull malt finish and aftertaste, some sourness at the end. [B, 40]

AUERBRÄU HELL — gold, light hop nose, dry malt flavor, good body, dry malt finish and aftertaste. [B, 49]

AUERBRÄU ROSENHEIMER HELLES — gold, very faint hop nose; malty flavor is slightly sweet; sweetness is most noticeable in the aftertaste, good body, good length. [B, 53]

AUERBRÄU EXPORT — gold, dense head, light hop nose, light bright dry hop taste, good body, good dry hop finish and aftertaste, long and fairly strong, 5.5% abv. [B, 78]

AUERBRÄU ROSENHEIMER HEFE-WEISSBIER NATURTRUB — hazy light amber, huge head, highly carbonated, spicy nose, bright spicy-sweet flavor with a touch of roasted malt, especially toasty at the finish, complex spicy sweet aftertaste; gravity 12.6 P, 5.5% abv. [W, 69]

AUERBRÄU ROSENHEIMER HEFE-WEISSBIER — hazy amber-gold, huge head, spicy nose, sweet spicy flavor, good body; very sweet malty spicy aftertaste is long; gravity 12.6 P, 5.5% abv. [W, 43]

BIERBICHLER WEISSBIER — hazy amber-gold, huge head, caramel nose, sweet caramel malt and faint spice flavor, medium body, off-dry malt finish and aftertaste, good length; gravity 12 P, 5% abv. [W, 50]

Augusta-Bräu
Brewery in Augsburg

BAYRISCH HELL VOLLBIER — deep gold; light aroma is mostly hops with faint malt in back; light malt and hop flavor, medium body, medium to short light dry malt and hop aftertaste. [B, 34]

Augustiner Brauerei, A.G.
Brewery in Munich

AUGUSTINER BRÄU MUNICH EXPORT LIGHT BEER — beautiful bright gold, clean but very light aroma, slightly off-dry malt flavor with delicate hop background, clean light malt and hop finish, long mild dry hop aftertaste, very smooth and tasty. [B, 38]

AUGUSTINER BRÄU MUNICH MAXIMATOR DARK EXPORT BEER — pale brown with copper tones, strong malt and hop nose, rich complex malt flavor with plenty of zest and character, slightly bitter and dry hop finish and aftertaste, a lovely double bock with lots of gusto. [BK, 80]

AUGUSTINER BRÄU MÜNCHEN OKTOBERFEST BIER — bright gold, slightly off-dry malt aroma, very well-balanced malt and hop flavor, big body; alcohol seems high; very long slightly sour hop aftertaste, smooth and flavorful beer with good balance. [B, 53]

AUGUSTINER BRÄU EDELSTOFF EXPORT — pale gold, aroma and flavor like a packaged dry chicken noodle soup; had to be a bad bottle. [B, 22]

AUGUSTINER WEISSBIER — hazy gold, huge head, smooth bright spicy nose, sweet spicy malt flavor, fairly dry, medium body; fairly dry spicy malt aftertaste is medium long; 5.4% abv. [W, 47]

Schlossbrauerei Autenried
Brewery at Autenried

AUTENRIEDER WEIZEN — hazy gold, big thick head, clean malt aroma, smooth malt flavor, very refreshing; faint trace of cloves is way in back of nose and palate; good body, good balance, long dry malt aftertaste. [W, 78]

AUTENRIEDER PILSNER — gold, fragrant hop nose, good hop flavor; long dry hop aftertaste has a bit of sourness at the end. [B, 58]

AUTENRIEDER URTYP HELL — deep gold, light malt aroma, malt flavor, hops in back, dry malt aftertaste. [B, 57]

AUTENRIEDER URTYP DUNKEL — brown, off vegetal (garbage) nose; taste to match the bad aroma; dull dry malt aftertaste. [B, 45]

Brauerei Bavaria-St. Pauli
Brewery in Hamburg

GRENZQUELL GERMAN PILSNER — gold, good hop nose, bright well-hopped flavor well backed with malt, good body, lots of hop character, long dry hop aftertaste, a big tasty brew. [B, 45]

ASTRA EXCLUSIVE — bright gold, dry faintly toasted malt nose, lightly sour and bitter hop flavor, one dimensional (hops) taste, short dry hop aftertaste. [B, 45]

GRENZQUELL GERMAN DARK PILSNER — deep copper, good hop and roasted malt aroma and flavor, thin body, some molasses in the finish, virtually no aftertaste. [B, 53]

JEVER PILSENER — bright tawny-gold; aroma is more malt than hops; big body; flavor starts out malt but gradually turns to hops; building bitterness as it goes until it finishes quite bitter, lingering bitter hop aftertaste. [B, 24]

ASTRA ALE — pale amber, good malt nose; pleasant malt flavor, but is too sweet and it becomes cloying after a while; long too sweet malt aftertaste. [A, 53]

ASTRA MEISTER BOCK — medium gold, good hop and malt aroma, light body, light malt flavor; faint molasses aftertaste has little length. [BK, 34]

ASTRA PILSENER — gold, skunky hop nose, dry hop flavor, good body, good carbonation level; stays dry throughout, only a little malt showing; dry hop finish, long dry hop aftertaste. [B, 45]

Brauerei Bayer
Brewpub in Viereth

BAYER MÄRZEN — deep amber-brown, strong malt nose with a fruity character, big fruity-malt flavor, long aftertaste like the flavor; would be better more dry as the fruit is sort of candylike. [B, 50]

Bayerische Brauerei, A.G.
Brewery in Kaiserslautern

BARBAROSSA KAISER BIER — gold, very foamy, fruity malt nose; flavor is off-dry malt and sharp hops with a faint acidic background; complex and interesting, short dry aftertaste. [B, 53]

BARBAROSSA GOLD EXPORT — gold, complex toasted malt nose; malt palate briefly up front, then drops off to nothing immediately; wood and corn are behind the light malt aftertaste. [B, 27]

BBK PILS — pale bright gold, light hop nose; palate is mostly hops but there is some malt; fair balance but short and dull. [B, 27]

Brauerei Beck & Co.
Brewery in Bremen

BECK'S BEER — pale gold, mild malt nose, light body, pleasant light hop flavor, fine balance, light dry hop finish and aftertaste. [B, 61]

BECK'S DARK BEER — medium deep amber-brown, hop nose, big hop flavor, finish, and bitter hop aftertaste, plenty of hops for everyone. [B, 59]

ROLAND LIGHT LOW-CALORIE BEER — pale gold, light but good hop nose, weak body, hop and grainy malt palate, sour hop aftertaste. [LO, 18]

DRIBECK'S LIGHT BEER — deep gold, grainy malt aroma, light body, good hop and malt flavor, hop finish, fairly long dry hop aftertaste. [LO, 36]

HAAKE BECK NON-ALCOHOLIC MALT BEVERAGE — bright gold, malt aroma; flavor starts out dry malt, becomes big hops; grainy malt finish, sour hop aftertaste, some complexity and fairly interesting. [NA, 46]

BECK'S OKTOBERFEST BIER 1993 — amber, austere hop nose, dull off-dry malt flavor, medium body, aftertaste like the flavor, drinkable but not interesting. [B, 40]

BECK'S OKTOBERFEST BIER 1994 — brilliant amber, malt nose; lightly toasted dry malt flavor is very good, flavor drops off fast; good body; malt fades away replaced with some dry hops for the aftertaste; better than the 1993 version. [B, 60]

Privatbrauerei Beck / Beck-Bräu OHG
Brewery in Trabelsdorf, 8602 (near Würzburg)

BECK UNSER DUNKLES — brown, toasted malt nose, light toasted malt flavor, medium body, dry toasted malt finish and aftertaste, not long. [B, 39]

Privatbrauerei Becker
Brewery in St. Ingbert

BECKER'S JUBILÄUMSBOCK — deep brown, big malt nose and taste, nice balance; has a chocolate character; fairly complex, good body, very long malt aftertaste, nice drinkable brew. [B, 74]

BECKER'S EXPORT — brilliant medium deep gold, faint hop nose, high carbonation, light body, light malt and hop flavor, pleasant, good balance, faint hop finish, and faint dry hop aftertaste. [B, 31]

BECKER'S PILS — pale yellow-gold, ample hop aroma, strong bitter hop flavor, sour hop finish and long sour-bitter hop aftertaste. [B, 34]

BECKER'S EXTRA HERB PREMIUM PILS — bright gold, beautiful hop aroma, strong bitter hop palate, long sour bitter metallic hop aftertaste. [B, 30]

Brauerei Max Bender
Brewery in Arnstein

ARNSTEINER PILSNER — gold, big head, light hop nose, austere dry hop flavor, light body; dry hop aftertaste has good length; gravity 11 P, 4.9% abv. [B, 47]

Hofbrauhaus Berchesgaden
Brewery in Berchesgaden

BERCHESGADENER BIER — gold, pleasant malt and hop nose, big flavorful dry malt and hop taste, good body and balance, long dry hop and malt aftertaste. [B, 82]

BERCHESGADENER WEIZEN — hazy gold, nice clean spicy-fruity malt nose, tangy zesty clove and malt palate, long clean satisfying aftertaste like the flavor; feels good in your mouth; very tasty and refreshing. [W, 67]

Exportbierbrauerei Berliner Bürgerbräu
Brewery in Berlin

BERLINER PILS EXPORT — deep tawny-gold, big hop nose, bitter hop palate, medium body, long sour hop aftertaste. [B, 34]

TÜRMER GERMAN BEER — gold, fresh malt nose, medium body, fruity-malt flavor, sour malt and hop aftertaste. [B, 29]

Berliner Brewery
Brewery in Berlin

SCHUTER'S RED STAR SELECT — tawny-gold, faint malt aroma, sour hop flavor, dry hop finish, dry hop aftertaste with a sour background. [B, 14]

Burger Bräu Bernkastel
Brewery in Bernkastel-Kues

BERNKASTELER PILS — pale gold, strong sweet hop aroma; malt starts the flavor but it is dominated and finished with hops; long dry hop aftertaste; the hops and malt cross but seem to come together. [B, 49]

Notes

Binding Brauerei, A.G.
Brewery in Frankfurt

STEINHAUSER BEER — bright gold, light hop nose with good malt support, light body, smooth hop flavor and finish, good balance, long dry hop aftertaste. [B, 47]

RÖMER PILS — yellow-gold, sweet hop nose, brief off-dry malt flavor, light body, light medium dry malt aftertaste with hops in back. [B, 36]

CLAUSTHALER HERBFRISCHES SCHANKBIER — deep gold, grainy hop aroma, high carbonation, grainy hop and CO_2 flavor, long dry hop aftertaste. Version tasted in Europe. [NA, 56]

CLAUSTHALER BIER — bright gold, fragrant honeyed malt aroma, off-dry malt palate; long off-dry malt aftertaste goes bitter at the end. Export version to the U.S.A. [NA, 53]

CAROLUS DER STARKE DOPPELBOCK — very deep ruby-brown color, big rich sweet chocolatey malt aroma with an unusual fruit-like component, big body, huge powerful complex dry malt, hop, and alcohol flavor, complex, high alcohol (7.5%), medium long dry malt aftertaste, very drinkable brew, very delicious; gravity 18 P. [BK, 100]

BINDING EXPORT — tawny-gold, sweaty sock and malt nose; tasty dry malt flavor shows none of the offishness of the aroma; slightly sour hop and malt after-taste; good flavor but the nose is a spoiler. [B, 37]

Bischoff-Bräu
Brewery in Munchberg

BISCHOFF-BRÄU DOPPELBOCK — deep gold, hop and malt aroma, big complex bright hop and rich malt flavor, warmth from alcohol (8% abv), balanced, ends dry malt and hops, very long rich aftertaste; gravity 18 P. [BK, 98]

BISCHOFF-BRÄU LEICHT — pale gold, lovely malt and hop aroma; good hop flavor is pleas-ant and drinkable; light body, long dry hop aftertaste, a very good light beer; gravity 7 P, 2.8% abv. [LO, 60]

BISCHOFF-BRÄU PILSNER — gold, nice tight head; lovely aroma shows both hops and malt; bright hop flavor, well backed with malt, good body, tasty and drinkable, long dry hop aftertaste; gravity 11 P, 5% abv. [B, 66]

BISCHOFF-BRÄU VOLLBIER — gold, malt and hop aroma, dry malt flavor with the hops in back; malty finish is a bit sweet; dry hop after-taste, medium body, good balance, satisfying beer; gravity 11 P, 4.7% abv. [B, 57]

BISCHOFF-BRÄU EXPORT — deep gold, big tight head, malt nose, good malt flavor; has rich-ness; very smooth, drinkable, good body, good taste and very good mouthfeel, dry malt finish and aftertaste, good duration; gravity 12 P, 5.1% abv. [B, 72]

Brauerei Bischoff
Brewery in Winnweiler

BISCHOFF PREMIUM EXPORT BEER — gold, toasted malt nose, off-sweet toasted malt flavor, dull finish and aftertaste, not interest-ing. [B, 32]

BISCHOFF PILS — bright gold, light off-dry hop and malt aroma, off-sweet malt flavor, little finish, faint sour fruity apple aftertaste. [B, 59]

Brauerei Bischofshof
Brewery in Regensburg

BISCHOFSHOF URHELL — gold, hop nose, pleasant bright hop flavor, good body, dry hop finish and long dry hop aftertaste. [B, 56]

BISCHOFSHOF HEFE-WEISSBIER HELL — hazy gold, big spicy clove and malt aroma, creamy and refreshing, good body, spicy malt finish; long aftertaste is dry malt. [W, 70]

Bitburger Brauerei Thomas Simon
Brewery in Bitburg

BITBURGER PREMIUM PILS — gold, big hop nose, bright hop flavor, medium body, hop finish, long hop aftertaste. A nice straightforward pils. [B, 39]

BITBURGER DRIVE ALKOHOLFREI — gold, faint malt nose, complex malt flavor, dry malt finish, short dry malt aftertaste. [NA, 30]

Schlossbrauerei Braunfels
Brewery in Braunfels

BRAUNFELS PILS — gold, tangy hop nose and taste, short dry hop aftertaste. [B, 31]

BRAUNFELSER 1868 — gold, hop nose and taste, some oxidation, long sour hop aftertaste. [B, 27]

Bräuwastl
Brewery in Weilheim

BRÄUWASTL KRISTALLWEIZEN — slightly hazy amber, big head; complex malt aroma was relatively dry; barley malt and wheat about 50–50 on the palate, nice balance, very smooth, brief malt aftertaste, but a good tasting brew. [W, 60]

Privatbrauerei Franz Britsch / Adler Bräu Moosebeuren
Brewery in Moosebeuren

ADLER BRÄU MOOSEBEUREN WEIZEN — hazy-cloudy deep gold, some particulate matter, clove aroma; big spicy flavor has some sweetness; medium body; some honeyed sweetness is out of balance with the spiciness, this carries into the finish and aftertaste; 5.2% abv. [W, 47]

ADLER BRÄU MOOSEBEUREN SPEZIAL HELLES EXPORTBIER — brilliant gold; malt aroma has hops in back; complex big malt flavor has concentrated malt and noticeable hops; medium body, dry malt finish and aftertaste; 5.1% abv. [B, 60]

ADLER BRÄU MOOSEBEUREN PILS — brilliant pale gold, big head, bright hoppy nose, good hop flavor, very slightly sweet malt finish, medium body, dry hop aftertaste with good length, a classic pils; 4.9% abv. [B, 64]

ADLER BRÄU MOOSEBEUREN UR-GUT — gold, big hop nose; dull flavor is more malt than hops; good body, dull dry malt finish and aftertaste; gravity 12.7 P, 5.1% abv. [B, 39]

Brauerei Brombach, Erdinger Weissbräu / Privatbrauerei Erdinger Weissbräu Werner Brombach Gmbh.
Brewery in Erding

ERDINGER WEISSBIER (HEFE) — cloudy gold, foamy, piquant fruity-grainy nose, clean balanced wheaty flavor with a delicate clove background, pleasantly off-dry and lightly hopped at the finish, long slightly off-dry malt aftertaste, smooth and mellow brew, very pleasant. [W, 73]

Notes

ERDINGER PIKANTUS STARKE WEISSBIER — reddish-brown, roasted malt and wheat grain aroma, off-dry complex malt flavor, highly carbonated, very long and likable; seems more like a weizenbock. Also export to U.S.A. as Pikantus — dark amber, big head, tangy wheat beer nose with a light lactic-spice touch, tangy wheat-malt-lactic flavor, very light acid, adds rather than detracts, very tasty and quite long. [BK, 80]

PREMINGER ALKOHOLFREI WEISSBIER — bright gold, grainy nose, light grainy flavor, touch of honey in the brief aftertaste. [NA, 14]

ERDINGER WEISSBIER KRISTALLKLAR — gold, nice toasted malt nose; malt flavor has just a faint trace of spice; light body, light dry malt finish and aftertaste, very refreshing. [W, 64]

ERDINGER WEISSBIER DUNKEL — deep amber, faint malt aroma, light malt flavor with faint spice in back, light body, light and dry malt finish and aftertaste. As found in Germany. [W, 60]

ERDINGER DARK WEISSBIER (HEFE) DUNKEL — deep amber, big head, malt aroma; spicy clove flavor is overly sour and clashes with the malt; short dry malt aftertaste. As found in the U.S.A. [W, 24]

PIKANTUS DUNKLES WEIZENBOCK — dark amber, big tight head, tangy wheat beer nose with a light spicy touch, tangy wheat-malt-lactic flavor;

very light acid, adds rather than detracts; very tasty and quite long, finishes with a lightly sweet malt background. Labeled in Germany Erdinger Pikantus Starke Weissbier. [WBK, 65]

Privatbrauerei Ambros Brütting
Brewery in Staffelstein

HOFLIEFERANT BAYRISCH HELL — gold, malt nose, high carbonation; flavor has only light malt and hops; dull malt finish; faint hops join the malt in the brief aftertaste. [B, 27]

HOFLIEFERANT BOCK BIER — amber-gold, big rich hop and toasted malt nose, huge rich roasted malt flavor; long rich aftertaste is a continuation of the flavor; high alcohol (7%) is not noticeable in the rich malt flavor; a finely balanced excellent bock. [BK, 96]

HOFLIEFERANT EXPORT EXQUISIT — tawny-gold, big toasted malt nose and flavor, dry malt finish, long dry malt and hop aftertaste, good body and good balance. [B, 88]

KLOSTERBIER ALTBIER — brown, sour yeasty hop aroma; smooth malty flavor is dry; light body, dry malt finish and aftertaste; gravity 11 P, 4.8% abv. [A, 50]

AMBROS BRÜTTING PILSNER — gold, stinky hop nose, sour hop flavor, finish, and aftertaste, ends dry; 5.2% abv. [B, 38]

Brauerei Bucher Gmbh.
Brewery in Gundelfingen

BUCHER OKO-BIER PILS — gold, malt aroma and flavor, medium body, off-dry malt finish and aftertaste. [B, 53]

BUCHER HEFE-WEIZEN — hazy brown, malty nose and taste, medium body, dry malt aftertaste, very little spiciness shows anywhere; gravity 12 P, 5% abv. [W, 45]

BUCHER URDEUTSCH DUNKEL — brown, malt aroma and flavor, fairly rich malt, bright and tasty, medium body, dry malt finish; long dry malt aftertaste is very nice; gravity 12 P, 5% abv. [B, 67]

Radbrauerei Gebr. Bucher
Brewery in Günzburg

GÜNZBURGER HEFE-WEIZEN — hazy gold, faint spicy nose, good well-spiced clove and malt flavor, high carbonation; flavor is on the light side and the carbonation interferes; smooth, light to medium body, light brief spicy aftertaste. [W, 47]

Produktions und Vertriebs Gmbh. / Burg Krone
Brewery in Bad Blankenburg

BURG KRONE PILS — gold, malt and hop aroma and taste, a

bit oxidized, light body, dry malt finish and aftertaste; gravity 11 P, 4.8% abv. [B, 36]

Burger & Engelbrau A.G.
Brewery in Memmingen

BURGER & ENGELBRAU VOLLBIER HELL — pale gold, rich malt nose, beautifully balanced smooth flavor, more malt than hops, quite dry, a bit light, but fairly long and very drinkable. [B, 30]

MEMMINGER GOLD EXPORT — gold; faint malt aroma has a bready-yeasty background; malt flavor, light to medium body, dry malt finish and aftertaste, clean but not interesting; gravity 11.5 P, 5% abv. [B, 50]

Bürgerliches Brauhaus A.G.
Brewery in Ingolstadt

HERRN BRÄU AROMATOR DOPPELBOCK — pale brown, sour malt aroma and flavor, big body; long malt aftertaste is drier and less sour than the flavor. [BK, 57]

HERRN BRÄU LEICHTES WEIZEN — cloudy gold, light spicy nose, spicy flavor, light body, smooth mellow but dull dry lightly spiced aftertaste, brief; main flavor is good but that is all there is; 1.5% abv. [W, 36]

Bürger Bräu
Brewery in Hof

BÜRGER BRÄU EDEL PILSNER — gold, big head, hop nose, hop and malt flavor, medium body, malty aftertaste, not intere sting, 4.8% abv. [B, 46]

Brauerei Büttner
Farm brewery in Untergreuth (near Bamberg)

BÜTTNER VOLLBIER HELL — golden amber; huge head takes up most of the carbonation leaving little for the palate; dry hop aroma, rich hop and malt flavor, very smooth, refreshing; alcohol is detectable; dry hop aftertaste is long. This beer is available only on draft at the brewery restaurant. [B, 77]

Brauerei Cluss A.G.
Brewery in Heilbronn

CLUSS BOCK DUNKEL — brilliant copper, big malt Ovaltine nose, very complex, a great nose; rich malt flavor but lighter than promised by the aroma; light to medium body, long dry light malt aftertaste. [BK, 50]

CLUSS PILSENER — gold, malt nose; palate is mostly malt but there is high carbonation as well and some hops in back; there is plenty of both hops and malt at the finish leading into a long dry hop aftertaste. [B, 73]

CLUSS RATSHOF PILS — gold, hop and malt nose, pleasant light dry hop and malt flavor, hop finish, long dry hop aftertaste, very pleasant. [B, 58]

CLUSS EXPORT — gold, faint malt nose, fairly big malt flavor with plenty of hops in support; malt dominates the flavor especially as it crosses the palate, then the hops are alone in the fairly long aftertaste. [B, 55]

CLUSS KELLER PILS — hazy gold; big nose is mostly hops with malt in back; flavor and aftertaste are like the nose without the malt and hops ever coming together. [B, 38]

DUTTENBERGER ENGELBRÄU URTYP — gold, malt and hop aroma; big flavor is mostly malt; touch of soapiness; some hops appear in the finish; medium long dry hop aftertaste. [B, 56]

CLUSS FESTBIER — bright gold; malt and alcohol are in the nose; sweet malt and alcohol taste; sweet malt finish and aftertaste with hops coming in to dry the ending; 5.6% abv. [B, 60]

Brauerei Convikt
Brewery in Dillengen am Donau

CONVIKT EGAUER ZWICK'L DUNKLES KELLERBIER — bright copper-amber, light roasted malt nose, faintly sweet and grainy malt flavor, quite pleasant, finely carbonated, good balance, medium body; finishes even better than it

starts with a good long medium dry roasted malt aftertaste. [B, 77]

Cramer K.G. / Brauerei Warsteiner GEBR
Brewery in Warstein

WARSTEINER PREMIUM VERUM — bright pale gold, very good complex hop aroma, bright complex malt and hop flavor, excellent balance, big hop finish, long dry hop aftertaste, a very fine pilsener. [B, 63]

WARSTEINER LIGHT — brilliant gold, light hop aroma, good dry hop flavor, light body, fairly good balance, light dry hop finish and aftertaste, medium length, a decent low-calorie brew. [LO, 41]

WARSTEINER ALKOHOLFREI — pale gold; big malty nose has some hops in back; finely carbonated; very good malt flavor starts out off-dry, but finishes dry; fairly long dry malt and hop aftertaste; one of the better low-alcohol beers, though I would hardly agree with the label Der Traum von einem Bier (a dream of a beer). [NA, 41]

Dortmunder Actien Brauerei / Dortmunder Hansa Brauerei
Merged breweries in Dortmund

DORTMUNDER HANSA EXPORT — deep gold, strongly hopped nose, heavy body, big hop flavor and finish, long dry hop after-

taste. Has reached the U.S.A. as Dortmunder Hansa Imported German Beer. [B, 50]

ALT SEIDELBRÄU — deep gold, big hop nose with a sour malt background, big bitter hop flavor, big body; very well hopped to the point of being harsh; long dry hop aftertaste. [B, 15]

DAB MEISTER PILS — gold, clean malt aroma, fresh hop and malt flavor, good tasting, good body; has zest and character; long dry hop aftertaste. [B, 85]

DAB EXPORT — medium deep gold, lightly hopped nose, heavy body, big flavor with plenty of hops and malt, good balance, stays off-dry throughout, including the finish and early aftertaste; bitterness arrives at the very end and almost clashes with the sweet character. [B, 53]

DAB KRAFT-PERLE CEREAL BEVERAGE — dark reddish-brown, burnt sugar aroma; tastes like fermented maple sugar and butter, a bit too sweet. Non-alcoholic. [NA, 9]

DORTMUNDER ACTIEN ALT — deep amber, dry roasted malt nose, tangy malt flavor, light body, brief finish, faint aftertaste. [A, 31]

DAB ORIGINAL SPECIAL RESERVE BEER — bright gold, lovely hop aroma, lively hop flavor, medium body, tasty and long. [B, 53]

DAB TRADITIONAL DARK — brilliant amber, yeasty sour malt

nose, dry malt flavor, light dry malt finish and long aftertaste. [B, 56]

DAB LIGHT — brilliant pale gold, hop and grain nose; hop palate shows little, if any, malt; fairly long sour hop aftertaste. [LO, 13]

Dachsbräu
Brewery in Weilheim

DACHS WEIZEN — hazy brown, pleasant spicy malt aroma and flavor, long dry malt and spice aftertaste. [W, 62]

Weizenbrauerei Deggendorf
Brewery in Deggendorf

BAYER WEIZEN — hazy amber, big spicy-fruity malt nose and flavor, dry malt finish; fruit and spice return for the long aftertaste; good tasting brew. [W, 61]

Deininger Kronenbräu A.G.
Brewery in Hof

EKU HEFE-WEIZEN — bright gold, big head, spicy lactic and wheat nose, flavor to match, good complexity, long and tasty. [W, 29]

EKU WEIZENBOCK DUNKEL — medium deep amber-brown, toasted wheat nose; flavor has a lactic bite but it is overall a big malt taste; a candy sen-sen like aftertaste, very complex and very long, noticeable alcohol. [W, 57]

EKU HEFE WEISSBIER HELL — bright gold, lovely clean spicy clove nose, pert clean and smooth flavor like the nose, medium body, bright and tasty throughout, very refreshing, a very good hefe-weisen. [W, 78]

EKU HEFE WEISSBIER DUNKEL — brown, faintly spicy clove and caramel nose, very smooth and drinkable but not big flavored, light and refreshing, delightful. [W, 61]

DEININGER PILS — bright pale gold, hop nose and big hop flavor, creamy texture, dusty background, long zesty hop aftertaste. [B, 60]

DEININGER EXPORT — bright deep gold, malt and hop nose, malt palate, smooth and balanced, brief dry hop aftertaste. [B, 59]

DEININGER KRISTALL WEIZEN — bright gold, big head, refreshing lactic clove nose, spicy with a clean fruit background, flavor like the nose, complex and balanced; long aftertaste is a continuation of the flavor, leaves your mouth clean and refreshed. [W, 71]

EKU WEIZEN KRISTALL-KLAR — bright gold, big head, fruity lactic nose, light flavor like the nose, medium length clean fruity-spicy aftertaste. [W, 79]

DEININGER HELL — brilliant gold, bright hop and malt aroma, clean appetizing hop flavor, dry malt and hop finish and aftertaste. [B, 61]

DEININGER HOFQUELL — brilliant pale gold, appetizing malt and hop nose, clean hop flavor, soapy hop finish and aftertaste. [B, 55]

DEININGER FESTBIER — medium bright gold, good malt and hop nose, pleasant malt flavor, good body, malt finish, medium long dry malt aftertaste. [B, 60]

DEININGER HEFE-WEISSBIER — hazy gold, spicy clove nose, spicy zesty malt flavor, smooth and refreshing, good balance between the spice and the malt, cream, richly flavored, long medium dry spicy malt aftertaste, excellent wheat beer. [W, 87]

Privatbrauerei Diebel
Brewery in Issum/Wiederrhein

DIEBEL'S ALT — brown, tangy ale-like nose, smooth zesty malt flavor with good hops in back, dry malt finish and long dry malt aftertaste; there is a spicy ale-like tang in the background all the way across the palate and through the aftertaste as well. [A, 69]

Dillinger Brauhaus, Gmbh.
Brewery in Dillingen

CONVIKT MEISTER-SCHUTZ — gold, light malt nose, malt flavor, medium to short dry malt aftertaste; nice malt brew but lacks zest. [B, 50]

Dinkelacker Wülle, A.G.
Brewery in Stuttgart

DINKELACKER PRIVAT LIGHT BEER — gold, complex malt and hop aroma, great heft and plenty of zest, good body, plenty of character, good bright hop flavor, well balanced, long dry hop aftertaste. [B, 68]

DINKELACKER BLACK FOREST LIGHT BEER — cloudy gold, blueberry malt aroma, off-dry malt flavor, dank finish and aftertaste. [B, 50]

DINKELACKER BOCK C.D. EXTRA — dark brown, big malt aroma and flavor, big body, rich malt flavor, long dry malt aftertaste. [BK, 89]

DINKELACKER DARK IMPORT PRIVAT — brown, big malt nose, rich malt flavor with a yeasty nature, sour malt finish, long dry malt aftertaste; also seen labeled as Dinkelacker Dark C.D. Extra. [B, 68]

DINKELACKER WEIZEN-KRONE — yellow, huge head, pleasant light malt aroma, highly carbonated, sour malt finish, dry malt aftertaste. [W, 24]

DINKELACKER DARK BREW — amber-brown, big roasted malt nose and flavor, sour malt finish, long dry malt and hop aftertaste, good balance, drinkable. [B, 58]

PRO NON-ALCOHOLIC BEER — bright gold, hops first in the aroma then grainy malt, bright hop and off-dry malt flavor, slightly sour malt aftertaste. [NA, 43]

DINKELACKER CD PILS — brilliant gold, faintly sweet hop nose; a little malty sweetness starts the flavor, but it is soon dry hops from mid-palate on; dry hop finish and aftertaste. [B, 57]

DINKELACKER WEIHNACHTSBIER SPEZIAL — deep gold, very nice light hop and toasted malt nose, beautifully balanced dry malt and hop flavor, good body, creamy and smooth; long malt aftertaste ends dry hops very late; a delicious complex and satisfying beer; 5.5% abv. [B, 81]

DINKELACKER VOLKSFESTBIER — brilliant gold, big dense head, huge hop nose, good body, big appetizing malt and hop flavor, clean and dry, long dry hop aftertaste; this seems to be available only at the Bad Canstatter Volksfest near Stuttgart. [B, 82]

DINKELACKER OKTOBERFEST PREMIUM GERMAN BEER — gold, stinky chemical aroma, dry metallic taste, out of balance, sour metallic aftertaste; all samples found were off. [B, 42]

SANWALD WEIZEN DUNKEL HEFETRUB — tawny-amber, big head, clean wheaty-malt nose; bright clean flavor is mostly wheat and malt with just a touch of lactic character; taste is just a little bit sweet; good balance between the sweetness and the lactic bite, long dry aftertaste. [W, 55]

SANWALD WEIZEN KRONE KRISTALLKLAR — bright gold, big head; faint wheaty-malt nose is on the sweet side; light flavor is also slightly sweet like the nose; acid is way in back, almost unnoticeable; light body; long off-dry malt aftertaste with lactic spice appearing at the end; drinkable but not much offered. [W, 26]

SANWALD HEFE WEISSE — bright gold, huge head, faint fruity-tart nose, light dry malt flavor with very little acidic tang, pleasant but brief. [W, 43]

SANWALD WEIZEN PERLSTARK — bright gold, clean weizen (wheat-malt-lactic) nose, not much lactic spice, smooth, well balanced, slightly sour aftertaste. [W, 47]

Brauerei Distelhäuser
Brewery in Tauber Bischofsheim-Distelhausen, 6972 (near Würzburg)

DISTELHÄUSER PREMIUM PILS — gold, hop nose and flavor, long dry hop aftertaste, good body, but just hops. [B, 50]

DISTELHÄUSER EXPORT — gold, malt nose and flavor, good body, dry hop finish, long dry hop aftertaste. [B, 56]

DISTELHÄUSER MÄRZEN — gold, malt nose, strong sweet malt flavor, good balance, good body,

long dry hop and malt aftertaste; gravity 13 P, 5.4% abv. [B, 62]

Dom Brauerei
Brewery in Köln

DOM KÖLSCH — deep gold, big hop nose backed with roasted malt, light body, tasty hop and roasted malt flavor, slightly bitter hop finish and aftertaste, highly carbonated and a bit too light, but tasty nevertheless. [K, 45]

Dortmunder Union Schultheiss
Brewing Conglomerate with breweries in Dortmund and Berlin. Includes Dortmunder Union Brauerei A.G.; Dortmunder Ritterbrauerei, A.G.; and The Schultheiss Brauerei, A.G. of Berlin.

DORTMUNDER UNION SIEGEL PILS — pale yellow-gold, good sour malt aroma with hops in back, fine malt and hop flavor, a very good pilsener-style beer, long dry hop aftertaste. [B, 75]

DORTMUNDER UNION PILSENER — tawny-gold, toasted malt aroma, pleasant toasted malt flavor, good balance, light body; a little sour malt in back but it doesn't mar the taste; toasted malt carries through the palate into the finish and aftertaste; light and not complex. [B, 34]

BERLINER WEISS SCHULTHEISS — pale cloudy white, foamy, yeasty nose and flavor, medium long semi-dry yeasty-malt aftertaste. [W, 42]

BERLINER UR-BOCK — hazy deep amber-gold, toasted malt nose and flavor, somewhat uninteresting dry malt aftertaste, lacks zest. [BK, 38]

GERMANIA PREMIUM MALT BEVERAGE — yellow-gold, off-dry grainy malt nose; grainy palate is off-dry in front, dry in the middle-on; dry malt aftertaste has little duration; tastes like a light beer, which is good for a non-alcoholic brew. [MB, 18]

DORTMUNDER UNION BEER — deep bright gold, toasted malt aroma and flavor, medium body, good flavor but not enough of it, fairly short dry malt aftertaste, lacks complexity and depth. [B, 43]

DORTMUNDER UNION MALT LIQUOR — bright tawny-gold, lovely rich roasted malt aroma; big malt flavor is especially good up front on the palate; finish is sour hops and this becomes the aftertaste; good length. [ML, 34]

DORTMUNDER UNION SPECIAL — pale gold, intense and complex malt aroma; good malt flavor is strongly accented with hops; balanced, straightforward well-hopped beer, long dry hop aftertaste, an excellent pilsener. [B, 80]

DORTMUNDER UNION ORIGINAL — brilliant almost colorless pale yellow-gold, hop nose;

bitter dry hop flavor has malt backing; good body, long dry hop aftertaste. [B, 65]

DORTMUNDER UNION LIGHT BEER — bright gold, big hop nose, light body; flavor is carbonation and faintly sour malt; brief light dry aftertaste. [B, 25]

DORTMUNDER UNION DARK BEER — medium deep amber-brown, outstanding rich malt and hop aroma, medium body, finely carbonated, rich dark malt flavor; hops come in at the finish; pleasant dry malt and hop aftertaste; an excellent dark pilsener that goes very well with salamis and other cold wursts. [B, 57]

DORTMUNDER RITTER BRÄU LIGHT BEER — deep yellow, big hop and malt nose, huge hop flavor, big body, long sharp and dry hop aftertaste, a robust well-hopped brew. [B, 71]

DORTMUNDER RITTER PILS — gold, big hop nose; big hop flavor has a sour component in back; plenty of malt in back, good body, finishes dry hops without the bitterness, long dry hop aftertaste, a hearty brew, a good pils. [B, 60]

DORTMUNDER RITTER BRÄU BOCK — deep gold, beautiful toasted malt and hop aroma, very complex, delicious, rich toasted malt flavor, excellent balance, a blockbuster, long long rich malt and hop aftertaste. [BK, 85]

DORTMUNDER RITTER DARK — medium deep brown, heavy malt nose with complex vegetal components (like celery seed

and sage); hops join in for the flavor but the malt holds dominance and is somewhat sour, the sourness does get in the way; long dry and slightly sour malt aftertaste. [B, 50]

DORTMUNDER RITTER EXPORT — deep gold, malt and hop nose, vegetal malt flavor; short dry malt aftertaste has a sourness in back. [B, 32]

GASTHAUS SPECIAL — medium gold, creamy texture, pleasant mild hop nose, good body, bright hop flavor, very short dry hop aftertaste. [B, 42]

DORTMUNDER WESTFÄLIA SPECIAL — gold, faint malt and hop nose, sour malt flavor; hops seem out of balance; sharp hop finish and aftertaste. [B, 32]

DORTMUNDER WESTFÄLIA EXPORT BEER — bright pale gold, light hop nose, off-dry malt flavor, bitter hop finish and aftertaste. [B, 32]

BRINKHOFF'S NO. 1 — bright gold, extremely fresh hop aroma; palate is slightly bitter hops but there is enough malt for good balance; good body, very smooth, long malt aftertaste. [B, 56]

SCHULTHEISS GERMAN PILSENER — pale gold, melonlike malt aroma at first, then malt only, dry malt flavor, hop finish, dry malt aftertaste. [B, 39]

MAXI MALZ — dark brown, malt nose, dry malt flavor, very drinkable, good body, lightly hopped, dry malt finish, short dry malt aftertaste; a non-alcoholic "malta" attributed to Dortmunder Ritterbrauerei. [MB, 29]

DORTMUNDER RITTER KRAFTBORN CEREAL BEVERAGE — dark ruby-brown; malt extract aroma is much like Postum, sweet malt cereal flavor; light to medium body, clean, short aftertaste. [MB, 27]

RITTER FIRST PREMIUM PILS — pale gold, very nice European hop and grain aroma, grainy malt and hop flavor, decent balance, medium body, dry hop and grainy malt aftertaste. [B, 53]

Dortmunder Stifts Brewery
Brewery in Dortmund

DORTMUNDER STIFTS PREMIUM GERMAN PILSNER — bright gold, light sour hop aroma, sour well-hopped flavor, highly carbonated, finishes bitter hops; long dry hop aftertaste is more pleasant not being as bitter as the flavor. [B, 29]

Brauerei Drei Kronen
Brewery in Zapfendorf

DREI KRONEN BRÄU ZAPFENDORF PILS — gold, grainy hop nose, sweet grainy malt flavor; light grainy malt finish and aftertaste stays on the sweet side; medium body. [B, 46]

DREI KRONEN BRÄU ZAPFENDORF VOLLBIER — gold, grassy-cheesy hop nose, off-dry malt flavor, medium body; slightly sweet aftertaste has medium length. [B, 27]

Brauerei Düll
Brewery-Gasthof in Gnodstadt

DÜLL BOCK — golden amber, very complex malt and hop nose, wonderfully appetizing, big strong malt flavor, big hops as well, high alcohol (6.8%), long and strong aftertaste like the flavor. [BK, 82]

DÜLL PILS — gold, malt nose, malt flavor starts off-dry, finishes dry leading into a dry malt aftertaste, some hop sourness at the very end. [B, 34]

DÜLL MÄRZEN — gold, malt nose, dry malt flavor; long dry malt aftertaste has some tones of vegetable, herbs, and honey. [B, 37]

Ebelsbacher Klosterbräu
Brewery in Ebelsbach

EBELSBACHER KLOSTERBRÄU DUNKEL — brown, big head, light malt aroma, big medium dry malt flavor, not sweet, just very malty, good body, very drinkable; dry malt aftertaste has good length. [B, 72]

EBELSBACHER KLOSTERBRÄU KLOSTERHELL — deep gold, hop nose, plenty of malt support, big malt flavor, dry malt and hop aftertaste. [B, 50]

EBELSBACHER KLOSTERBRÄU KLOSTER-PILS — deep gold, hop nose, good hop and malt flavor, a bright taste, good body and balance, long dry hop and malt aftertaste, a likable brew and easy to drink. [B, 63]

Privater Brauhaus Ebensfeld
Brewery in Ebensfeld

SCHWANNEN BRÄU PIL-SNER — gold, malt aroma, semi-sweet malt flavor, medium body, sweet malt finish and aftertaste; 4.9% abv. [B, 47]

SCHWANNEN BRÄU FRÄNKISCHES LANDBIER — gold, malty nose, big dry malty flavor, good body; dry malt finish and aftertaste with the hops staying in back; 4.9% abv. [B, 47]

SCHWANNEN BRÄU BAYERISCH DUNKEL — brown, dry malt aroma and taste; finish and aftertaste are clean faintly sweet malt; smooth and drinkable; leaves a good malt taste

in your mouth; good body, good length; 5.2% abv. [B, 61]

SCHWANNEN BRÄU SPEZIAL EXPORT — gold, dull malty nose, dull dry malt flavor, medium body, dull dry malt finish and aftertaste, an uninteresting beer; 5.3% abv. [B, 38]

ADAM RIESE URTRUNK — dark brown, rich sweet malt aroma, alcoholic rich malt flavor, medium body; dry malt aftertaste makes it go well with food; 5.6% abv. [B, 70]

Privaterbrauereigasthof Eck
Brewery Gasthof in Böbrach-Eck

ECKER BRÄU WILDERER DUNKEL — brown, light roasted malt nose, off-dry malt front palate, dry malt middle and finish, good body, good balance, long dry malt aftertaste, smooth, drinkable, and has zest. [B, 77]

ECKER BRÄU EDEL PILS — deep gold, fragrant hop aroma, complex rich hop and malt flavor, good body, complex dry hop and malt finish and aftertaste, long and very good, an excellent brew. [B, 90]

ECKER BRÄU FAHNDERL-WEISSE HEFE-WEISSBIER — clear gold, lovely light clove aroma, light clove and malt flavor, balanced, smooth, clean, dry malt finish and aftertaste. [W, 70]

ECKER BRÄU VOLLBIER HELL — brilliant gold, roasted caramel malt nose, smooth light

roasted malt flavor, medium to long dry malt aftertaste, very likable beer. [B, 78]

Privatbrauerei Eder
Brewery in Grossostheim

EDER PILS — hazy yellow, light hop nose, big hop flavor up front, sour malt in back, fair balance, long dry hop aftertaste. [B, 43]

BAVARIA BAYERISCH WEIZEN — gold, lactic spicy malt nose, clean wheat taste with only the faintest lactic spice, clean wheat and malt finish and aftertaste. [W, 47]

EDER PRIVAT EXPORT — hazy gold, grainy molasses nose, big body, big malt flavor, long and rich, ends dry malt. [B, 60]

EDER DOPPELBOCK DUNKEL — deep ruby-brown, big toasted malt nose, big creamy rich malt flavor, finely carbonated, huge body, very long and very satisfying. [BK, 94]

BAVARIA DUNKLER STARKBIER — deep amber, lovely toasted malt nose, big malt flavor, rich and delicious, a heavy malt beer with lots of alcohol; long malt aftertaste continues to show the alcohol. [B, 78]

BAVARIA BAYERISCH MÄRZEN DUNKEL — deep amber-gold, lovely malt nose, big dry roasted malt flavor, very drinkable; dry malt aftertaste has a caramel nature, but is quite dry. [B, 46]

EDER PRIVAT ALT — amber-gold, malt and hop aroma, fairly sharp ale-like malt flavor, medium body, dry malt finish and aftertaste, overall a bit sharp on the palate; 5% abv. [A, 47]

EDER'S EXPORT — gold, big head, light dry malt aroma with hops faintly in back, off-dry malt flavor, good body; can sense more than taste the alcohol; has richness and length; 5.5% abv. [B, 60]

BAVARIA DUNKLES HEFE-WEIZEN — hazy amber-gold, big head, spicy aroma and flavor, fairly dry; dry lightly spiced aftertaste is short; 5.3% abv. [W, 53]

BAVARIA HEFE-WEIZEN — gold, huge tight head, spicy nose, big spicy flavor, balanced, medium body, long spicy aftertaste; 5.3% abv. [W, 77]

Privatbrauerei Ehnle
Brewery in Lauterbach

LAUTERBACHER HEFEWEIZEN — hazy gold, faint complex nose includes pine and cloves, very light spicy clove flavor, finish and aftertaste, medium to light body, pleasant and refreshing but brief. [W, 48]

LAUTERBACHER SCHLANKE WEISSE — hazy gold, faint spicy aroma, light spicy clove flavor, very light body, brief light spicy malt aftertaste. [W, 47]

LAUTERBACH BROTZEITBIER — deep gold, big hop and roasted malt nose,

delicious flavor like the aroma, very good balance, good body, very drinkable tasty brew, an excellent beer for food or just plain sipping. [B, 89]

LAUTERBACHER URHELL — gold, stinky malt nose, very dry malt palate, long dry sour hop and malt aftertaste. [B, 45]

LAUTERBACHER URTYP HELLES VOLLBIER — gold, sweat-sock aroma, odd malt flavor, medium body, dry malt finish and aftertaste; 4.8% abv. [B, 20]

Eichbaum Brauerei, A.G.
Brewery in Mannheim

EICHBAUM FESTBIER — pale amber, faint malt and hop nose, faintly sweet malt palate; some hops arrive for the finish; slightly sour and bitter long hop aftertaste. [B, 30]

EICHBAUM APOSTULATOR — brilliant pale ruby-brown; big toasted malt nose has a brief puff of cherry at the beginning; big complex fruity malt flavor, long malt aftertaste seems a bit smoky, a real lip-smacking brew. [BK, 84]

EICHBAUM EXPORT ALTGOLD — bright gold, good malt and hop aroma and flavor, fine balance, smooth and mellow, medium body, medium long aftertaste like the flavor. [B, 59]

Notes

EICHBAUM PILSENER EICHKRONE — bright pale gold, good well-hopped aroma, bright hop flavor, long complex aftertaste with both hops and malt. [B, 52]

EICHBAUM MAIBOCK — pale amber-gold, big toasted malt aroma, sense of alcohol as well (6.6%), rich malt flavor, great balance with the hops, good body, long off-dry malt and hop aftertaste. [BK, 85]

EICHBAUM KRISTALL WEIZEN — bright gold, spicy lactic nose, fresh clove taste, clean and refreshing, medium length, a bit on the weak side. [W, 60]

EICHBAUM HEFE WEIZEN — cloudy yellow-gold, slightly yeasty and spicy nose; complex flavor has some of the yeast; fairly smooth, definitely mellow; good carbonation level to give it balance; fairly long. [W, 68]

EICHBAUM DUNKLES WEIZEN — hazy amber, light lactic-spice nose, light malt and spice flavor, light body, pleasant and drinkable; finishes quite well and has a long malt and clove aftertaste. [W, 72]

EICHBAUM UREICH PILS — gold; big hop aroma fills the room; assertive hop flavor, tiny touch of malty sweetness in back, dry hop finish and aftertaste, a big hoppy beer; 4.8% abv. [B, 59]

Einbecker Brauhaus, A.G.
Brewery in Einbeck

EINBECKER UR-BOCK STARKBIER — amber-gold, sour hop nose, pleasant hop palate up front; sour hop finish that goes into a long sour hop aftertaste. [BK, 45]

EINBECKER UR-BOCK — pale amber-gold, roasted malt and hop aroma; pleasant malt and hop flavor has licorice and caramel in back; big body; a pervasive saltiness comes in at the finish and stays through the aftertaste and is detrimental to the flavors. [BK, 45]

EINBECKER MAI-UR-BOCK — amber, mild complex malt aroma, big complex malt and hop flavor, noticeable alcohol (6.5%), long dry malt and hop aftertaste, big body. [BK, 77]

EINBECKER UR-BOCK DUNKEL — brown, low head, dry roasted malt aroma, big dry lightly roasted malt flavor, a bit off-dry, good body, dry malt finish and aftertaste; palate is a bit alcoholic (6.5% abv). [BK, 80]

Erste Kulmbacher Actienbrauerei, A.G.
Brewery in Kulmbach

EKU BAVARIA SPECIAL RESERVE — bright gold, complex malt and hop nose, more hops than malt, medium body, good long dry malt finish, little aftertaste. [B, 42]

EKU KULMINATOR URTYP HELL 28 — brilliant deep amber, strong and complex malt aroma; big intense concentrated malt flavor, more than enough malt and alcohol; some hops but the flavor is mostly malt, very winelike, long long off-dry malt aftertaste; almost overwhelming, but actually is just a fantastically good monster brew. [BK, 91]

EKU KULMINATOR DUNKLER DOPPELBOCK — bright deep amber, complex sweet toasted malt and licorice nose; malt is like Ovaltine, big grainy malt flavor; very heavy and filling, but very good and very long. [BK, 61]

EKU BAVARIA DARK RESERVE — deep copper-brown, faint vegetal malt aroma, dull dry malt flavor, finish, and short aftertaste. [B, 31]

EKU JUBILÄUMSBIER — bright tawny-gold; appetizing malt and hop aroma that fills a room; marvelous malt and hop flavor starts out off-dry and finishes with bright hops; long dry hop aftertaste has a hint of roasted malt in back; good balance, wonderful festbier. [B, 80]

EKU KULMBACHER EXPORT — brilliant gold, big head, absolutely beautiful apple-malt aroma; faint off-dry fruity malt flavor is masked with excessive carbonation; complex finish and long dry malt aftertaste; balance is hurt by the CO_2. [B, 58]

EKU PILS — medium deep gold, pleasant fruity-malt aroma,

bitter hop palate, poor balance, medium long dry bitter hop aftertaste. [B, 29]

EKU KULMBACHER HELLER MAIBOCK — bright deep gold, creamy head, off-dry malt and hop nose, huge body; complex and big malt flavor that is generally dry; hops appear in the finish; long fairly dry hop aftertaste, very good balance. [BK, 91]

EKU ALT BAYERISCHES HEFE-WEIZEN DUNKEL — cloudy light brown, very foamy, huge head, aroma like fermented wheat, a bit off-dry but mostly just grainy on the palate, too much carbonation for the flavor, long dry malt aftertaste, reasonably pleasant and refreshing overall despite the carbonation. [W, 61]

EKU HEFE-WEISSBIER DUNKEL — deep hazy amber, faint malt nose, clean and crisp malt flavor; dry but has a richness; long dry malt aftertaste. [W, 61]

EKU OKTOBERFEST — bright gold, good hop and malt aroma, not big but pleasant, light complex malt and hop flavor, dry hop finish and aftertaste with a touch of sour malt at the end. [B, 49]

EKU EDELBOCK — deep gold, flowery fruity off-dry malt and hop aroma, very appetizing; palate is big off-dry malt in front and middle, finishes caramel sweet; hops appear in the aftertaste behind the caramel, but way behind; long long full and rich malt aftertaste, a little light on the hops, but very delicious. [BK, 38]

EKU RUBIN DARK — dark amber-brown, very malty toasted aroma, very dry toasted malt flavor, light body; hops come in at the finish and stay into a long complex dry aftertaste; overall it is dry and malty, also it is a bit confused. [B, 64]

HOFBRÄU LIGHT RESERVE — tawny-gold, big malt-hop aroma and flavor; a bit clumsy as there is far too much hops for the malt; long dry hop aftertaste, lacking in balance and finesse. [B, 50]

HOFBRÄU BAVARIA DARK RESERVE — deep brownish-orange, light malt aroma, strong malt taste, finishes smoothly, however, leading into a fairly long dry malt aftertaste. [B, 51]

EKU FESTBIER — gold, big head, malt nose; rich malt flavor is fairly dry; a bit alcoholic, big body, strong dry malt aftertaste; gravity 13.5 P (1053 OG), 5.8% abv. [B, 73]

EKU KRISTALL WEISSBLIER KLAR — gold, lightly spiced-citrus-clove aroma, creamy mouthfeel, refreshing and smooth, very pleasant, long slightly off-dry and spicy aftertaste. [W, 79]

Brauerei C. Endriss
Brewery in Plochingen

PLOCHINGER EDEL TYP PREMIUM LAGER — gold, lovely hop nose, big complex malt and hop flavor, medium body, dry hop finish and aftertaste; 5.4% abv. [B, 70]

Crailsheim Engel-Bräu
Brewery in Crailsheim

HORAFFIA PILS — bright gold, dry hop aroma, very dry well-hopped flavor, medium body, dry hop finish and aftertaste. [B, 60]

ENGEL EXPORT — gold, malt aroma and flavor, medium body, dry malt aftertaste. [B, 61]

ALT CRAILSHEIMER DUNKEL — brown, dry malt nose, very dry malt flavor, medium body, dry malt aftertaste, good with food. [B, 60]

WEIHNACHTSENGEL EXCLUSIV FESTBIER — gold, lovely complex dry malty aroma and taste, good body, dry malt finish and aftertaste; 5.4% abv. [B, 80]

ENGEL BOCK — gold, dry malt and light hop nose, complex malt and hop palate; there is alcohol (7% abv) but it doesn't step forward; dry malt and hop aftertaste is long; there is richness especially in the aftertaste. [BK, 84]

Engel Brauerei
Brewery at Schwäbische Gmund

TYROLIAN BRÄU BEER — bright gold, good malt and hop nose; malt and hop flavor up front, goes to slightly sweet malt in mid-palate, finishes dry malt; long dry malt and hop aftertaste. [B, 43]

ST. BERNARD BRÄU BEER — bright gold, light malt aroma with faint hops, balanced malt and hop flavor, long dry hop aftertaste. [B, 43]

ANGEL BREW BEER — gold, big toasted malt aroma, rich malt and hop flavor; really feels good in your mouth; big body; long dry hop aftertaste has good malt support; a delicious and beautiful beer. [B, 87]

TROMPE LA MORT DOUBLEBOCK — deep gold with an amber tinge, rich malt aroma, very rich malt flavor, big body, huge, very strong and very long dry malt aftertaste. [BK, 72]

BIERE DES DRUIDES — hazy yellow, toasted malt nose and flavor, malt finish and aftertaste; good while it is in your mouth, but it quits as soon as you swallow it. [B, 30]

Brauerei Erharting
Microbrewery-brewpub in Neuperlach section of Munich

ERHARTING HELL EXPORT — gold, big head, beautiful appetizing hop and malt nose; bright hop flavor is well backed with malt; good body, long dry complex aftertaste. [B, 79]

ERHARTING DUNKLE RITTER WEISSE — brown, spicy-coffee nose; spicy flavor is clean, bright, and refreshing; good body, good mouthfeel, long dry malt aftertaste; 5.3% abv. [W, 72]

Landbrauerei Ludwig Erl
Brewery in Geiselhöring

ERL-HELL HELLES EXPORT BIER — gold, big somewhat stinky hop nose, big hop flavor, good body, sour hop and off-dry malt aftertaste, poorly balanced. [B, 30]

Erste Bayerische Exportbierbrauerei
Brewery in Fortschendorf

LEINER EDEL PILS — gold, big head, faint hop nose, bright hop flavor, light body, dry hop finish; long dry hop aftertaste has some malt at the end; gravity 11 P, 4.7% abv. [B, 61]

Erzquell Brauerei
Brewery in Erzquell

ERZQUELL EDELBRAU BEER — deep copper-brown, light malt nose, pleasant off-dry malt palate in front, flat in the middle, flabby malt finish; off-dry malt aftertaste has little length or character. [B, 30]

Privatbrauerei Eschenbacher-Wagner Bräu
Brewery in Eschenbach

ESCHENBACHER EDEL MÄRZEN — hazy amber, roasted malt and dry hop aroma, complex palate exactly like the nose, excellent balance, very drinkable, full bodied and full flavored, long and satisfying. [B, 89]

Klosterbrauerei Ettal Gmbh.
Monastery brewery at Ettal

ETTALER KLOSTER DUNKEL — deep tawny-amber, light malt aroma; flavor is mostly malt except for a good hop finish; some complexity, good balance, long dry malt and hop aftertaste, very drinkable brew. [B, 51]

ETTALER CURATOR DUNKLER DOPPELBOCK — deep rosy-amber, rich off-dry malt nose (almost sweet) and flavor, good body, high alcohol, rich long slightly sour malt aftertaste. [BK, 70]

ETTALER KLOSTER WEISSBIER — hazy gold, faint malt nose; delicate refreshing flavor of wheat, malt, and cloves; very good up front; softens a bit at the middle, but stays good; fairly long aftertaste like the flavor. [W, 57]

ETTALER KLOSTER WEISSBIER DUNKEL — medium deep amber, faint lightly spiced wheat beer nose, light clove and malt flavor, light body, spicy finish, fairly long aftertaste like the flavor but quite light. [W, 48]

Ettl Bräu
Brewery in Teisnach

ETTL-HELL — gold, malt nose and flavor, somewhat flabby, medium long malt aftertaste, malt all the way through. [B, 21]

Privatbrauerei Euler, Gebr.
Brewery in Wetzlar

STRASSBRÄU PILSENER SPEZIAL HESSENLAND BIER — pale gold, yeast and malt aroma; flavor is mostly hops, complex but not well balanced; a burnt malt taste shows up in the finish and dominates the long aftertaste. [B, 53]

EULER LANDPILS — pale gold, lovely hop and malt aroma, big hop flavor, good body, sour hop finish, sharp bitter hop aftertaste. [B, 38]

KLOSTER ALTENBERG KLOSTER BIER — bright gold, smoky toasted and sour malt aroma; slightly sour malt flavor has plenty of hops; medium body, short hop aftertaste. [B, 27]

Notes

MAXIMILIAN TYP MUNCHEN HELLER BOCK — medium deep tawny-gold, beautiful complex apple aroma, delicious strong malt flavor, complex, a little on the sweet side, but still well balanced, long medium dry malt aftertaste. Also seen labeled more simply as Maximilian Heller Bock. [BK, 64]

ALT WETZLAR DARK BEER — deep copper, light toasted malt nose, light body; palate is first malt, then bitter hops at the finish; sour, bitter and dry hop aftertaste. [B, 34]

Brauerei Falter
Brewery in Hof

FALTER PILS — gold, big head, fairly rich malt nose, rich malt flavor; seems to show a touch of alcohol; medium body, rich long malt aftertaste; 4.9% abv. [B, 47]

Edelweissbrauerei Farny
Brewery in Dürren

FARNY HEFE-WEISSE WEIZENQUELL — hazy gold, light spicy nose; bright spicy taste has a sweet finish, medium body; aftertaste starts out off-dry malt then dries; 5.2% abv. [W, 71]

FARNY WEIZEN — pale bright gold, faint malt aroma, dry malty flavor without spiciness, highly carbonated, carbonic feel and taste on the tongue, dry malt finish and aftertaste, not interesting, a kristallklar weizen; 5.2%. [W, 43]

Privatbrauerei Fässla
Brewpub in Bamberg

FÄSSLA GOLD PILS — gold, very nice appetizing hop nose, plenty of malt in back, big malt and hop flavor, dry and delicious, big bodied; long dry hop aftertaste still has plenty of malt in support for good balance; good brew. [B, 75]

FÄSSLA HELL LAGER BIER — pale amber, light malt nose and flavor, medium body, medium long dry hop aftertaste. [B, 47]

ECHTES BAMBERGER ZWERGLA — brown, roasted malt nose, strong heavily roasted malt flavor, good body; extremely long roasted malt aftertaste (strongest flavored aftertaste I've experienced); fairly pleasant despite its almost overwhelming strength across the palate. [B, 67]

Brauerei Faust
Brewery in Millenberg am Main

JOHANN GOTTRIED FORST PILS — yellow-gold, toasted malt nose and taste with a sharp hop background, finishes a bit sour, long dry hop aftertaste borders on bitter. [B, 39]

FORST HEFE-WEISSBIER — amber, sharp tangy aroma like ginger ale, smoky flavor with a lactic acid-spice background, some off-dry malt in the middle and in the aftertaste; balance is a bit shaky. [W, 52]

Brauerei Felsenkeller
Brewery in Herford

HERFORDER PILSNER — deep tawny-gold, bright hop nose, big sour hop palate; finish is harshly bitter; long bitter hop aftertaste. [B, 25]

HERFORDER PILS PREMIUM BEER — pale gold, faint malt and hop aroma with a trace of skunk, light hop palate, slightly bitter long dry hop aftertaste. [B, 29]

Privatbrauerei Felsenkeller
Brewery in Beerfelden

MÜMLINGTHALER SCHANKBIER — pale bright gold, dank fruity nose, dry fruity malt taste, some sourness in the finish, long dry aftertaste. [LO, 18]

BEERFELDER FELSENBOCK — amber; light malt nose has a chemical-like component; malt flavor is tasty but lacks zest; medium body, medium length malt aftertaste. [BK, 59]

BEERFELDER BOCK — amber-gold, big alcoholic malt nose (7% abv); huge malty flavor shows no alcohol; extremely smooth and silky, big body, delicious, malty finish and aftertaste, a fine bock. [BK, 93]

Felsenkeller Brauerei
Brewery in Monschau

ZWICKELBIER HEFETRUB-DUNKEL — hazy amber, pleasant malt aroma, very dry malt flavor, light body, short dry malt aftertaste. [B, 41]

Fiedler Gmbh.
Brewery in Koblenz

FIEDLERS BOCK — deep gold, faint fruity-sour malt nose, like cherry Kool-Aid, strong malt flavor with the hops in back, heavy body, noticeable alcohol, extremely long dry hop aftertaste. [BK, 53]

FIEDLERS PILS IM STEIN — bright gold, toasted malt and hop nose, light smooth malt flavor, dry malt and hop finish and aftertaste. [B, 59]

Forschung's Brauerei
Microbrewery in Munich with a biergarten from May to October

ST. JAKOBUS BLONDER BOCK — amber-gold, big head, luscious appetizing malt and alcohol nose, big chewy concentrated malt and alcohol flavor, almost like a bierbrand, huge body, very

rich, delicious, long rich malty aftertaste; 7.5% abv. [BK, 89]

St. Martin Brauerei Fohr OHG.
Brewery in Lahnstein/ Rhein

SCHNEE BOCK — deep amber, both hops and malt in nose, strong malt and hop flavor, good balance, plenty of alcohol as well (7.5%), long malt aftertaste, good tasting bock. [BK, 77]

LAHNSTEINER JÄGER-BOCK — amber, very complex nose with hops, banana fruit, and malt, strong malt flavor, very intense, big body; lots of alcohol (you can feel it in your mouth, nose, and sinuses); very long strong malt aftertaste, a blockbuster bock. [BK, 93]

Privatbrauerei Frank
Brewery in Neunburg

NEUNBURGER WEIZEN HEFETRÜB — hazy gold, lightly spiced malt aroma, good bright spicy malt flavor, finish, and light aftertaste. [W, 67]

Franken Brauerei
Brewery in Mitwitz

FRANKEN BRÄU PILSENER PREMIUM — gold, big hop nose and flavor, plenty of malt in support, very big body, solid flavor, very well balanced, big long malt and hop aftertaste. [B, 84]

FRANKEN BRÄU KELLER
GOLD DUNKEL — brown, rich
roast malt aroma and flavor, no
harshness, very smooth, good
body and balance, long dry
roasted malt aftertaste, a delicious
brew. [B, 90]

FRANKEN BRÄU FEST
BIER — gold, good hop and malt
aroma, very appetizing nose; big
flavor has hops but is mostly malt;
very fine balance, rich tasting,
good body, dry hop finish; long
dry aftertaste has plenty of both
hops and malt. [B, 65]

FRANKEN BRÄU BOCK
BIER — pale gold, barely any
aroma at all; flavor is faint malt
but mostly is alcohol; big body,
off-dry malt finish and aftertaste,
plenty of alcohol showing (7.2%);
big concentrated malt palate has to
be sipped slowly and then it tastes
better. [BK, 80]

Frankenthaler
Brauhaus A.G.
Brewery in Frankenthal

PFÄLZER GOLD EXPORT
HELL — gold, malt and hop
aroma; hops stay in back; palate
up front is dry malt; off-dry in
back, medium body; dry malt
aftertaste has good hop support;
gravity 12 P, 4.9% abv. [B, 47]

FRANKENTHALER
FESTBIER — amber, malt nose,
big malt flavor; has some caramel in
back; good and clean, good body,
long clean malty aftertaste; gravity
13 P, 5.3% abv. [B, 67]

Brauerei Franz
Brewery in Rastatt

TURKENLOUIS BOCKBIER —
pale amber, rich malt nose, big
rich malt flavor, very full-bodied,
some hops but mostly malt, very
satisfying, filling brew, very long
malt aftertaste. [BK, 73]

Brauerei Fuch
Brewery in Windesheim

FUCH'S FEST BOCK — amber,
toasted malt nose, palate to
match, medium body, very long
toasted malt aftertaste, good balance between the malt and the
hops. [BK, 65]

Carl Funke, A.G.
Stern Brewery in Essen

GERMAN STAR NON-
ALCOHOLIC MALT
BEVERAGE — bright gold,
sweet grainy malt nose, cereal-like
grainy flavor, weak body, grainy-
tinny aftertaste with little length.
[MB, 14]

STERN PREMIUM LAGER —
bright gold, nice light malt and
hop aroma, slightly toasted malt
flavor, good balance; hops come
in for the finish but it stays more
malty; good body, long dry malt
and hop aftertaste. [B, 67]

Fürstlich
Fürstenbergische
Brauerei, K.G.
Brewery in
Donauschingen

FÜRSTENBERG PILSENER —
bright gold, malt aroma with hops
in back, big hop flavor, nicely balanced; hops ease off a bit at the
finish and the long aftertaste is
smooth light dry hops; a nicely-
made very serviceable clean tasting pilsener. [B, 61]

FÜRSTENBERG IMPORTED
GERMAN BEER — deep bright
gold, smooth hop aroma with a little
roasted malt in back; palate is
mostly malt but there is good hop
support; very good balance, complex and interesting, long dry hop
aftertaste. [B, 49]

FÜRSTENBERG FESTBIER —
amber, faint malt nose; nice malty
flavor is a tad too sweet; good
body; finish and aftertaste are still
malty but drier; gravity 12 P, 5.3%
abv. [B, 60]

Klosterlichen
Brauhaus Furth
Klosterbrewery in Furth

FURTHER KLOSTERBIER
URSTOFF HELL — gold, malt
aroma and light faintly malt flavor, light body, not much intensity
of flavor, almost no aftertaste;
gravity 11 P, 4.8% abv. [B, 34]

FURTHER KLOSTERBIER
EDEL WEISSE — cloudy gold,
big tight head, faintly spicy

aroma, smooth mellow spicy taste, good body, rich and satisfying; dry malt aftertaste has a good mouthfeel and flavor; gravity 13 P, 4.7% abv. [W, 60]

FURTHER DUNKEL EXPORT — amber-brown, rich malt aroma, rich dry malt flavor, smooth and mellow, very tasty, good body, very satisfying; good tasting dry rich malt aftertaste is long; gravity 13 P, 4.7% abv. [B, 77]

Brauhaus Füssen
Brewery in Füssen

FÜSSENER EDEL PILS — brilliant deep gold, light hop nose, bright crisp hop flavor, malt finish, long pleasing aftertaste, well balanced. [B, 72]

FÜSSENER FEST BOCK — medium deep brown color, malt nose and very rich malt flavor, big body, smooth, long rich malt aftertaste, very delicious and alcoholic (7.25%). [BK, 72]

FÜSSENER EXPORT — tawny-gold, light malt and hop aroma; palate has plenty of hops in front, gets more malty from middle on; good balance, good body, long malt aftertaste; good but lacks the crispness of the Pils. [B, 61]

Privatbrauerei Gaffel
Brewery in Köln

GAFFEL KÖLSCH — light amber-gold, bright ale-like nose, light body, big dry hop palate, medium to light body, dry hop finish, long dry hop aftertaste, quite bitter but not unpleasant, like an aperitif. [K, 60]

Privatbrauerei Gambrinus Nagold
Brewery in Hamburg

BÖLK STOFF — gold, tangy hop and malt aroma, strong malt and big bright hop flavor, zesty and mouth-filling, complex and strong, very long dry hop and malt aftertaste, good strong sipping beer that lasts and lasts. [B, 80]

Brauerei Gampert
Brewery in Weissenbrunn/Kronach

GAMPERTBRÄU FÖRSTER PILS — gold, unusual complex malt and carbonation nose, hop and off-dry malt flavor, long dry malt aftertaste. [B, 40]

Privatbrauerei Ganter
Brewery in Freiburg

GANTER EXPORT — deep gold, light malt nose, big malt flavor, very pleasant; light dry hop aftertaste has odd sour features. [B, 53]

Brauerei Gatzweilers
Brewery in Dusseldorf

GATZWEILERS ALT — medium brown, sour hop nose and front palate, dry hop middle and finish, dry hop aftertaste with some sour malt in back, medium body, medium length. [A, 36]

Notes

Brauerei H. Geismann
Brewery in Fürth

HUMBSER PILS — gold, malt and hop aroma, dry hop finish and aftertaste, a bit sour on the end, plenty of hops throughout; 4.9% abv. [B, 40]

Privatbrauerei Geussen-Bräu E. Knorr
Brewery in Neustadt

GEUSSEN PILS — pale gold, light hop nose, big hop flavor, well backed with malt, light body, very dry malt and hop aftertaste, good length; gravity 11 P, 4.9% abv. [B, 59]

Gilden Brauerei
Brewery in Köln

GILDEN KÖLSCH — gold, light hop and malt aroma and flavor, smooth and balanced, light body, long aftertaste like the flavor. [A, 40]

Alpirsbacher Klosterbrauerei / C. Glauner
Brewery at Alpirsbach

ALPIRSBACHER KLOSTER DUNKEL — deep amber-brown, faint malt nose, medium body, very dry malt flavor, no complexity, light brief dry malt aftertaste. [B, 47]

ALPIRSBACHER KLOSTER HEFE WEIZEN — hazy tawny-gold, off-dry wheaty malt aroma, off-dry wheat and barley malt flavor, no spicy tang, very long aftertaste like the flavor but a bit more dry, fresh and clean in the mouth, very pleasant and refreshing. [W, 67]

ALPIRSBACHER KLOSTER KRISTALLKLAR WEIZEN — bright gold; faint slightly sweet malt aroma that is very clean; full body, rich malt flavor, well balanced, refreshing, long off-dry fairly delicate aftertaste. [W, 60]

ALPIRSBACHER KLOSTER SPEZIAL — bright tawny-gold, slightly sweet hop aroma; palate is off-dry malt up front; dry in the middle with a faint vegetal nature, finishes with both hops and malt leading into a long dry hop aftertaste with a faint sour vegetal malt background. [B, 53]

ALPIRSBACHER KLOSTER PILS — bright tawny-gold, creamy head, faintly off-dry malt aroma with a hop backing, slightly sour malt front palate, very dry middle, sour malt and dry hop aftertaste. [B, 56]

Adlerbrauerei Göggingen
Brewery in Göggingen

GÖGGINGER EXPORT — bright gold, hop aroma, sweet malt and dry hop flavor, very tasty, good body, long well-hopped aftertaste, balanced; 5.2% abv. [B, 78]

GÖGGINGER PILS — gold, hop nose, bright hop flavor, medium body; there is a malty sweetness that develops for the finish; long off-dry malty aftertaste; 4.9% abv. [B, 58]

Gold Ochsen, Gmbh.
Brewery in Ulm

GOLD OCHSEN PREMIUM BEER — gold, roasted malt and hop nose, tasty roasted malt flavor, lovely up front but weak at the finish, short dry roasted malt aftertaste. [B, 50]

GOLD OCHSEN HEFE WEIZEN — deep gold, lovely lightly toasted dry malt aroma, creamy head, pleasant slightly sweet smooth malt flavor with a wheaty background, virtually no spice or acid, very good duration and balance, lots of character, very refreshing. [W, 63]

GOLD OCHSEN KRISTALL WEIZEN — gold, big head, clean wheat and hop aroma with faint lactic spice; flavor is quite lactic with lots of cloves overriding the malt; very good front palate, but it doesn't last for long. [W, 39]

Privatbrauerei Göller
Brewery in Zeil am Main

GÖLLER ZUR ALTEN FREYUNG PILSNER — gold, light hop aroma and flavor; big malt backing from mid-palate to the finish; dry hop aftertaste has malt in back; medium body, good length; 5% abv. [B, 50]

GÖLLER ZUR ALTEN FREYUNG DUNKEL — brown, great malty nose, rich big medium dry malty flavor with the hops in back, good body, dry hop and malt finish and aftertaste; gravity 12 P, 4.9% abv. [B, 61]

GÖLLER WEIZENBOCK — hazy amber, nose of spicy candy and fresh tar, big spicy caramel alcohol flavor, big body, smooth and spicy, not crisp but like a dessert, very different and very interesting; 7% abv. [BK, 63]

Brauerei Götx
Brewery in Geislingen/ Altenstadt

DIE DUNKLE BARTELSTEINER WEISSE — hazy amber, light clove nose, spicy clove flavor; very dry finish and it sort of dies at that point, leaving only some faint sourness as an aftertaste. [W, 40]

Brauerei Götz
Brewery in Geislingen and Scheer/Donau

GÖTZ ADLER PILS — fairly deep gold, pleasant hop nose, big dry hop flavor, medium body, lots of taste, dry hop finish and aftertaste. Tasted on draft at Scheer. [B, 60]

GÖTZ ADLER EXPORT — bright gold, smooth light malt nose, smooth malt flavor, good body, light medium dry malt finish and aftertaste. Tasted on draft at Scheer. [B, 63]

GÖTZ WEIZEN KRISTALL — gold, bright spicy aroma and flavor, very clean and refreshing, medium body, light spicy hop and dry malt finish and aftertaste, zesty throughout. Tasted on draft at Scheer. [W, 67]

GÖTZ GUTSHOF WEIZEN HEFE HELL — hazy gold, light clove aroma, clean bright spicy flavor, creamy and good bodied, dry hop finish and aftertaste, refreshing with some complexity. Tasted on draft at Scheer. [W, 70]

BARTELSTEINER WEISSE DIE DUNKLE — hazy brownish gold, faint spicy nose, big bright spicy flavor, good body, good mouthfeel, dry spicy finish and aftertaste. Tasted on draft at Scheer. [W, 80]

Privatbrauerei Graf-Eder Gmbh. & Co., K.G.
Graf Brewery in Oberndorf

OBERNDORFER PRIVAT — gold, mild hop and malt nose, malt palate; light hops appear in the finish, dry wimpy hop aftertaste. [B, 50]

OBERNDORFER PILSENER — gold, big head; highly carbonated (you can even taste it); creamy, light malt and hop nose, dry malt flavor with a dry hop finish, medium long dry hop aftertaste. [B, 50]

Notes

Privater Brauereigasthof Greifenklau
Brewery-Gasthof in Bamberg

GREIFENKLAU EXPORT — amber-gold, good appetizing malt and hop aroma, delicately smoked malt flavor, long dry slightly smoked malt aftertaste, nicely done and very likable. [B, 67]

Brauerei Grohe
Brewery in Darmstadt

GROHE BOCK — amber, lovely fresh fruity malt aroma, beautiful off-dry malt and hop flavor, excellent balance, medium to light body, dry hop finish, long off-dry malt aftertaste, a very pleasant easy-to-drink brew. [BK, 75]

GROHE MÄRZEN — amber, fruity-malt nose, flowery fruit-like off-dry malt flavor, touch of banana, light to medium body, medium to long off-dry malt aftertaste. [B, 43]

Brauerei H. Grosch
Brewery in Rödenthal

GROSCH'N PILSNER — gold, dank grassy nose, grassy hop flavor, sour malt aftertaste, light body; gravity 11 P, 4.9% abv. [B, 37]

Grüner Bräu
Brewery in Bad Tölz

GRÜNER BIER DUNKEL — dark brown, light malt aroma and taste, very little hop character, medium body, short malt aftertaste. [B, 67]

GRÜNER EXPORT — deep gold, light malt aroma, medium body, light malt flavor, smooth and drinkable, medium long malt aftertaste. [B, 45]

TÖLZER EDEL WEIZEN — hazy brown, light slightly lactic nose and flavor, very smooth and drinkable, medium body; medium length malt aftertaste with a trace of the lactic spice which is more pronounced at the end. [W, 56]

TÖLZER WEISSE — bright gold, very light smooth malt nose and taste, only a trace of arctic-weizen character, very mild, medium body; mild malt aftertaste has medium length and little spiciness; pleasant enough but a bit weak for those who like their weizen to have zest. [W, 52]

BAD TÖLZER TRADITIONSBIER HELL — pale gold, particles in suspension, dull hop aroma and taste; finish and aftertaste are sweet and sour malt; more dull and unbalanced than offensive, medium body; 5.2% abv. [B, 30]

GRÜNER KELLER BIER — gold, malt nose, smooth malty flavor, good body, dry malt finish and aftertaste. [B, 80]

GRÜNER HELLER BOCK — gold, toasted malt aroma and flavor, good body, smooth malty finish and aftertaste has good hop support, a good bock with lots of character. [BK, 73]

GRÜNER DUNKEL BOCK — brown, malty nose, off-dry rich malt flavor, good body, long rich malt aftertaste. [BK, 67]

Hirschbrauerei Gunzburg
Brewery in Gunzburg

GUNZBURG HIRSCH-BRÄU HELL — gold, very nice (but different) malt and hop nose; dry malt palate has some kind of hop background not familiar to me; dry hop finish and aftertaste, medium body; aroma is better than the flavor; 4.8% abv. [B, 63]

Burgerliches Brauhaus Zum Habereckl PBH
Brewery in Mannheim

HABERECKL MÄRZEN — hazy amber, big head, off-sweet faintly acidic fading nose, crisp malt flavor with no acidity, some yeast in the finish, short malt aftertaste. [B, 62]

HABERECKL FEUERIO TROPFEN JAHRGANG 1988

STARKBIER — deep ruby-brown, rich malt aroma; huge (no, enormous) rich malt flavor that lasts and lasts and lasts; one of the best examples found to prove what can be done with malt alone. [B, 93]

Hacker-Pschorr, A.G.
Brewery in Munich

HACKER EDELHELL EXPORT — gold, medium hop aroma, bright hop flavor with an off-dry malt background, good body, excellent balance, plenty of character, long dry hop aftertaste with a hint of malt in back, very nicely done. [B, 61]

HACKERBRÄU EDELHELL — gold, dry malt and lightly hopped aroma; big straightforward malt flavor shows little or no hops; big body, malt finish, medium long dry malt aftertaste. [B, 40]

HACKER-PSCHORR ORIGINAL OKTOBERFEST BIER BRÄUROSL-MÄRZEN — deep amber, big malty nose and taste; a beer to chew on; big in every way, but expertly balanced; long rich dry malt aftertaste, not to be missed. [B, 80]

HACKER-PSCHORR OKTOBERFEST MÄRZEN — pale amber, light malt aroma, bright malt-hop flavor, well balanced, tasty complex malt and hop finish and aftertaste. [B, 68]

HACKER-PSCHORR LIGHT BEER — pale gold, beautiful clean malt and hop aroma, big malt and hop flavor, very good balance; more hops appear at the finish and stay for the aftertaste; stays clean and good throughout. [B, 74]

HACKER-PSCHORR DARK BEER — medium dark amber-brown, malt-hop aroma with molasses in back, good tasting toasted malt flavor, medium body; finish is a bit weak, but the medium long toasted malt aftertaste is excellent. [B, 53]

HACKER-PSCHORR WEISS BIER — foamy pale yellow-gold, yeasty nose, medium body; grainy dry flavor has a yeasty-spicy-smoky pine resin background; fairly bright, extremely complex, very pleasant and interesting, finish and aftertaste like the flavor but more dry, good duration. [W, 63]

PSCHORR-BRÄU WEISSE (WEISSBIER WITH YEAST) — cloudy gold, spicy clove nose, flavor starts tart and spicy, finishes a bit sweeter, good carbonation, medium body, fairly long off-dry malt aftertaste. [W, 48]

PSCHORR-BRÄU WEISSE DARK (WITH YEAST) — hazy amber-brown, bright spicy nose; big spicy flavor that gets better as it goes; rich and strong; has hops in back throughout; long spicy malt aftertaste. [W, 69]

HACKER-PSCHORR MAIBOCK — brilliant deep tawny-gold, big smooth hop and malt aroma, good off-dry malt and hop flavor, extremely fine balance, very tasty; finish is off-dry malt and hops, and there is a long complex hop and malt aftertaste. [BK, 82]

PSCHORR MUNICH — bright copper, caramel nose, light carbonation, winelike malt flavor, heavy body; some hops show lightly in the finish and aftertaste, but they have trouble getting through the winelike malt. [B, 15]

HACKER-PSCHORR FEST BEER — pale amber-gold, roasted malt and hop aroma; good hop and malt palate, but there is a faint sourness that carries through and does mar the aftertaste. [B, 28]

HACKER-PSCHORR BRAUMEISTER PILS — bright gold, toasted malt and hop nose, pleasant hop and toasted malt flavor, good body; finish is mostly malt; good long dry hop aftertaste. [B, 67]

HACKER-PSCHORR ANIMATOR DUNKLER DOPPELBOCK — deep ruby-amber-brown, rich malt aroma; fruity-malt flavor has a rich backtaste; complex, balanced, very satisfying, long long dry and rich malt aftertaste. [BK, 87]

HACKER-PSCHORR HUBERTUS BOCK — deep gold, huge off-dry malt nose, big, rich, smooth, balanced clean malt flavor, high alcohol (6.8%), finely carbonated, very drinkable despite its heft, long rich malt aftertaste, super beer. [BK, 93]

Kloster Brauerei Hamm Gmbh.
Brewery in Hamm

KLOSTER PILSENER — tawny-gold, slightly smoky hop nose, somewhat sour hop and malt flavor, long dry and slightly sour malt aftertaste. [B, 34]

Hannen Brauerei, Gmbh.
Brewery in Mönchengladbach

HANNEN ALT — amber-brown, dull dry malt nose and taste, thin body; dull aftertaste shows a sense of toffee-coffee rather than the taste of it. [A, 46]

Hansa Bier-Vertriebs Gmbh.
Brewery in Bad Sassendorf

HANSA EXPORT — bright gold, low head, light hop nose; small flavor has some hops and malt, but not much; light body, slightly dull dry hop finish and aftertaste. [B, 50]

Traditionsbrauerei Harklberg
Brewery in Passau

HARKLBERG HOCHFÜRST PILSENER — gold, fresh hop nose; hop flavor is a little sour, especially at the finish; dull aftertaste. [B, 30]

HARKLBERG URHELL — gold, stinky hop nose, zesty hop and malt flavor, flabby finish, dull aftertaste. [B, 27]

HARKLBERG JAKOBI WEIZEN — cloudy gold, malt nose, light slightly fruity-spicy malt flavor; long dull dry malt aftertaste has cloves way in back; medium body, not balanced. [W, 27]

HARKLBERG JAKOBI DUNKLE WEISSE — hazy brown, huge dense head like a fass (draft) beer, smooth spicy malt nose, fresh lightly spiced malty-fruity flavor, good body, slightly spicy malt finish, long dry malt and hop aftertaste, good tasting satisfying brew. [W, 63]

BRAUEREI HARKLBERG JUBILÄUMSBIER — gold, malt aroma and taste, big body, dry malt finish and aftertaste, sort of ordinary; gravity 12.7 P, 5.2% abv. [B, 53]

BAYERWALD BROTZEITBIER — gold, big head, nice hop nose, dry hop flavor, medium body, dry hop finish and aftertaste; 4.7% abv. [B, 47]

Familienbrauerei Hartmann
Brewery in Würgau

HARTMANN EDEL PILS — pale gold, malt and hop nose; big flavor is mostly malt; light body, dry malt finish and aftertaste; gravity 11 P, 4.9% abv. [B, 49]

HARTMANN FELSENTRUNK — brownish amber-gold, malt aroma; flavor has a smoky character that is not in the nose, smoke is very light but dominates the taste; medium body; aftertaste is dry malt with only the very faintest trace of the smoky flavor; gravity 12 P, 5.2% abv. [B, 60]

Schlossbrauerei Haselbach / Josef Stockbauers Erben
Brewery in Haselbach, 8391 (just north of Passau)

D'WIRTSDIRN SCHWARZE DUNKLES HEFEWEISSBIER — brown, big thick head; malt aroma has a spicy background; flavor is more roasted malt than spice (which is way in back); big tasty flavor, very smooth long malt aftertaste, with the spiciness still hiding far in back. [W, 50]

Hasen-Brau A.G.
Brewery in Augsburg

HASEN-BRÄU AUGSBURGER EXPORT — bright gold, malt aroma and flavor, well balanced and smooth, medium long dry malt aftertaste, pleasant but not exciting. [B, 53]

HASEN-BRÄU DOPPELBOCK DUNKEL — brown, rich earthy malt aroma, rich full-flavored malt palate, very satisfying, sense of high alcohol, long rich malt aftertaste, real sipping beer. [BK, 83]

HASEN-BRÄU EXTRA — gold, hop nose, faint dull off-dry malt and hop flavor, medium body,

even fainter aftertaste like the flavor. [B, 27]

HASEN-BRÄU HELL — gold, light soapy hop nose, good malt and hop flavor, balanced, dry hop aftertaste with the malt laid back in behind. [B, 37]

BUNST BIER VOLLBIER HELL — gold, slightly soapy hop nose, soapy flavor, hop finish, medium length slightly dry hop aftertaste. [B, 27]

HASEN-BRÄU AUGSBURGER MÄRZEN — gold, zesty hop and malt nose, big balanced malt and hop flavor, perky and alcoholic (5.7%), richly malted, long dry hop aftertaste, more like a heller bock than a Märzen. [B, 85]

Hofbrauhaus Hatz
Brewery in Rastatt

BERNHARDUS BOCK — bright gold, visibly dense, viscous, beautiful hop nose, humongous body, very high density, great balance, high alcohol (6.9%), big malt flavor, clean hop finish; malt rolls back in to dominate the long aftertaste that is also well balanced and the overall impression is just great strength, neither the sweetness of the malt nor the bitterness of the hops; a magnificent brew. [BK, 93]

AUGUST HATZ PRIVAT — gold, delightful hop aroma, very good hop and malt flavor, sour hop finish, long dry and faintly sour hop aftertaste, excellent balance, a really good tasting brew. [B, 80]

Gdbr. Hausmann
Brewery in Ramstein

RAMSTEINER EXCLUSIV PREMIUM PILSENER — gold, some particulate matter in suspension, lovely light flowery aromatic hop nose, big hop flavor, plenty of body, lots of malt in back, slightly oxidized, long dry hop aftertaste, very drinkable and very good with food. [B, 60]

RAMSTEINER EXCLUSIV PREMIUM DUNKEL — amber, big toasted malt aroma; malty flavor is off-dry in front, dry by the finish; good body, loads of flavor, long dry malt aftertaste; has a rich quality; feels good in your mouth. [B, 78]

Heidelberger Schlossquell Brauerei, A.G.
Brewery in Heidelberg

VALENTINS KLARES WEIZENBIER — bright gold, big head, clean grainy malt aroma with a touch of refreshing clove-lactic spice; clean fresh bright flavor is like the nose but better; lingering wheat and malt aftertaste; delicious and refreshing, very drinkable. [W, 90]

HEIDELBERGER SCHLOSSQUELL PILS — gold, complex hop and malt nose, zesty hop and malt flavor, long dry hop aftertaste. [B, 59]

Brauerei Heller
Brewery in Bamberg

AECHT SCHLENKERLA RAUCHBIER MÄRZEN — brown, appetizing smoked malt nose, a bit like a fine summer sausage but more like the delicate smoking used with salmon, light fresh smoked flavor, good body, long smooth and delicious, hop finish; dry malt aftertaste has the smoke in behind; very nicely done, the perfect classical rauchbier; gravity 13 P, 4.8% abv. [B, 93]

Henninger Brauerei KGuA
Brewery in Frankfurt

HENNINGER INTERNATIONAL — gold, faint sweet malt aroma, highly carbonated, light off-dry malt flavor, little hop character, light off-dry malt aftertaste, needs more hops. [B, 19]

HENNINGER BIER — deep gold, clean hop aroma with a touch of roasted malt in back, good dry hop flavor, big body, good balance, excellent finish and dry hop aftertaste, fresh tasting and refreshing. [B, 68]

HENNINGER DARK BIER — rosy-amber; dry roasted malt nose yields some hops when swirled; good malt and hop flavor, complex, balanced, long roasted malt and hop aftertaste, good beer with lots of character. More recently labeled Christian Henninger Dark Beer. [B, 80]

HENNINGER KAISER PILSENER — deep gold, appetizing hop aroma, excellent malt and hop flavor, extremely dry, pleasant dry finish and long dry hop aftertaste, finely balanced, bright and refreshing. [B, 60]

HENNINGER KAISER EXPORT — tawny-gold, balanced hop and malt nose and taste, hops in front, malt middle, hop finish and aftertaste. [B, 50]

GERSTEL BRÄU NON-ALCOHOLIC BEER — bright deep gold, rich grainy malt nose, pleasant grainy flavor, good but short; some hops appear in the aftertaste. [NA, 40]

CHRISTIAN HENNINGER BEER — medium gold, soapy hop nose, bright hop flavor, good balance; good long dry hop aftertaste, but there is not much complexity. [B, 51]

KARAMALZ ALKOHOLFREIES MALZGETRÄNK — deep red, light smoky-sweet malt nose, slightly smoky sweet malt flavor, long sweet malt aftertaste. [M, 27]

HENNINGER HELLER BOCK — gold, lovely malt and hop aroma, big balanced malt and hop flavor, a tasty lip-smacking brew, very smooth, long malt aftertaste, beautifully made. BK, 97]

HENNINGER DUNKEL — deep brown, rich malt nose and taste, dry malt finish and long dry malt aftertaste, excellent balance, very well-made beer. [B, 87]

HENNINGER DOPPELBOCK DUNKLER BOCK — reddish-amber; aroma of hops, licorice, molasses, and roasted malt; big palate is mostly malt; quite complex, delicious, well balanced, drinkable and satisfying, a smooth double bock; 8.1% abv. [BK, 98]

HENNINGER DOPPELBOCK — deep brown, big dry roasted malt aroma, very complex; huge flavor is dry rich malt; finishes big with off-dry malt, long dry malt aftertaste; so much flavor you don't even notice the 8.1% alcohol; an almost perfect double bock. [BK, 100]

HENNINGER DARK MALT LIQUOR — dark red-brown, big complex malt aroma; roasted malt flavor has a sweetness; at mid-palate the roasted malt takes on a burnt nature that clashes with the sweetness; at the finish the burnt character is most pronounced and the balance is at its worst; the sweet-ness reasserts itself in the aftertaste as the burnt quality fades to more of a normal roasted malt style; good

body, good length. [B, 77]

GERMANIA PREMIUM BEER — gold, faint malt nose, somewhat tired grainy malt flavor, a little oxi-dation in back, medium body, light malt finish and aftertaste; despite faults it is very good with salad and bread and butter. [B, 47]

Brauerei Herrenhausen
Brewery in Hannover

HERRENHAUSEN EXPORT LAGER BEER — medium gold, sharp hop and malt nose; flavor is malt in front, hops in the middle and finish; long malt aftertaste, good balance and good flavor. [B, 50]

HORSY DEUTSCHES QUALITÄTSBIER — bright tawny-gold, big hop aroma with a perfumy malt background, com-plex malt and hop palate, more malt than hops, complex and well balanced, good hop finish, long malt aftertaste. [B, 77]

Brauerei Herrnbräu
Brewery in Ingolstadt

MÖNCHSHOF KAPUZINER WEISSE HEFETRÜB — cloudy amber, huge head, wheat and lactic acid nose, complex creamy off-sweet malt palate with lactic over-tones; doesn't come off well at all; long acidic malt aftertaste. [W, 27]

Heylands Brauerei Gmbh.
Brewery in Aschaffenburg

HEYLANDS FESTBOCK — brilliant deep gold, lovely sweet creamy roasted malt nose and taste; richness is maintained throughout; off-dry front, dry middle, sweet finish; long dry malt aftertaste, finely carbonated, a beautifully made delicious brew. [BK, 72]

SEPPLS URBRÄU PREMIUM DUNKEL — medium deep amber, complex rich malt aroma, light malt flavor, medium body, medium long light dry malt aftertaste. [B, 55]

HEYLANDS SEPPL-BOCK DUNKEL — brown, dry toasted malt nose, flavor to match, very smooth, long dry malt aftertaste, richly flavored; 7% alcohol is barely noticeable amid all that malt. [BK, 89]

SEPPLS URBRÄU DUNKEL — medium deep brown, good toasted malt nose, dry malt flavor, medium body, faintly sour dry malt aftertaste. [B, 45]

ANNO 1792 — fairly deep gold; dry malt nose is a bit soapy; big dry malt flavor, good body, dry malt finish and aftertaste; 5.2% abv. [B, 53]

Brauerei Hiernickel OHG (Hiernickel Bräu A.G.)
Brewery at Hassfurt am Main

HIERNICKEL PILS — gold, hop nose, big hop and malt flavor, smooth and drinkable, light body, dry malt and hop finish and aftertaste; gravity 11 P, 5% abv. [B, 52]

HIERNICKEL SPEZIAL MÄRZEN — gold; malt aroma and taste is a bit on the sweet side without enough hops to balance the sweetness; big body, off-dry malt finish and aftertaste; gravity 13 P, 5.3% abv. [B, 48]

Privatbrauerei Hildebrand Gmbh. & Co., K.G.
Pfungstädter Brauerei, Brewery in Pfungstädt

PFUNGSTÄDTER — pale yellow-gold, hop and sour malt aroma; good flavor with a touch of roasted malt to give it richness; good tasting finish, good balance, long malt aftertaste. [B, 49]

BOCKALE PREMIUM CLASS — pale gold, faint hop and roasted malt aroma, highly carbonated, big hop flavor, and long hop aftertaste; could use more malt for a better balance. [B, 42]

ST. NIKOLAUS DUNKLES STARKBIER — copper-amber, caramel and roasted malt nose, delicious and appetizing; palate is big malt right from the start and it stays; a little smoky-toasty; faint sour hops join the malt in the long aftertaste; very attractive Christmas beer. [B, 65]

PFUNGSTÄDTER MAIBOCK — pale amber, lovely malt nose, hop flavor, well balanced with malt, long dry hop aftertaste, a very nice appetizing May Bock. [BK, 61]

PFUNGSTÄDTER EDEL PILS — very pale yellow-gold; big nose shows plenty of hops and malt; medium body, hop finish, dry hop aftertaste, quite long. [B, 47]

Privatbrauerei Karl Hintz
Brewery in Marne i Holstein

DITHSMARSCHER MAIBOCK — copper-amber, rich malt nose and zesty malt flavor, big body, long malt aftertaste, very rich and very good. [BK, 74]

DITHSMARSCHER UR-BOCK — deep bright reddish copper, light malt aroma, big malt flavor, plenty of hops for balance, rich and big bodied, very long malt and hop aftertaste. [BK, 73]

Hirsch Brauerei Honer
Brewery in Wurmlingen

HIRSCH HONER PILS — light gold, pleasant hop nose, smooth lightly hopped flavor, light body, light dry hop aftertaste, light everything. [B, 40]

HIRSCH GOLD EXPORT — pale gold, faint malt nose, pleasant light malt flavor, almost no hops at all; dry malt aftertaste has good length, but the brew simply needs more hop character. [B, 47]

JAEGERHOF PILS — gold, hop nose, very little flavor on the front of the palate, not much anywhere, dry hop finish and aftertaste, very short. [B, 46]

Privatbrauerei Hoepfner
Brewery in Karlsruhe

HOEPFNER PILSNER — gold, beautiful hop nose, big bright dry hop flavor, medium body, dry hop finish and aftertaste, good length. [B, 58]

HOEPFNER EXPORT — gold, hop and malt both in the aroma; flavor is dry malt and hops; medium body, nicely balanced, dry malt finish and aftertaste. [B, 60]

Hofbrauhaus Freising
Brewery in Freising

GUTSTETTER DUNKLE WEISSE — brilliant amber, complex spicy roasted malt nose, off-dry roasted malt spicy flavor; roasted malt dominates the spice; big roasted malt finish and aftertaste, good body, a good brew but a very different kind of weisse; gravity 12.6 P, 5.4% abv. [W, 61]

Hofbräuhaus Munich
Brewery in Munich

HOFBRÄU OKTOBERFEST BEER — amber, big hop nose with plenty of malt, big chewy palate with lots of hops and malt, big body, good balance, long dry malt and hop aftertaste. [B, 53]

HOFBRÄU MÜNCHEN DUNKELER MAI-BOCK — medium amber, light fruity malt and hop aroma, flavor like the nose, excellent balance, marvelous flavor, very mellow and very long, delightful, alcohol 6.4%, density 17.4 P. [BK, 84]

HOFBRÄU MÜNCHEN ROYAL EXPORT HELL — bright gold, fragrant roasted malt and hop aroma, delicious and complex malt and hop flavor, excellent balance, long and dry, good body, a brightly flavored good tasting brew. [B, 71]

HOFBRÄUHAUS MÜNCHEN DELICATOR — deep amber, light malt aroma, big dry malt flavor, big body, long dry malt aftertaste, a solid doublebock. [BK, 84]

HOFBRÄUHAUS MÜNCHEN BOCK HELL — gold, great malt-hop aroma, huge hop and malt flavor; malt is a bit toasted; great balance, huge body, high density

(16.3°), high alcohol (6.7%), delicious, long dry malt and hop aftertaste much like the flavor. [BK, 95]

HOFBRÄUHAUS MÜNCHEN HELL — gold, marvelous hop and malt aroma, flavor to match, big and bright, complex and very well balanced, long medium dry hop aftertaste, very drinkable and great with food. [B, 87]

HOFBRÄUHAUS MÜNCHEN DUNKEL — dark amber-brown, rich lightly toasted malt nose, flavor to match the nose, good body, fine balance, very drinkable; long dry malt aftertaste with the hops way in back but contributing to the balance; very good with German wursts. [B, 87]

MUNCHENER KINDL WEISSBIER — hazy gold, lots of fruity esters in the nose but no spice; flavor somewhat like a weizenbier but there is little spiciness; medium body; not a clean taste, seems to be a little infected; dry aftertaste. As found in the U.S.A. [W, 29]

MUNCHENER FESTBIER — gold; malty aroma is complex and shows alcohol (5.7% abv); smooth malt flavor, good body, soft off-dry malt finish and aftertaste; gravity 13.6 P. [B, 53]

Hofer Bierbrauerei
Brewery in Hof

FRÄNKISCH FEST BIER — deep gold, papery malt nose, big malt flavor, dull malt finish and aftertaste, a bit off-dry and somewhat flabby. Made for Marco Getränktmarkts of the Nürnberg-Kulmbach area. [B, 30]

Hofmark Spezialitäten Brauerei
Brewery in Cham

HOFMARK HERRENPILS — pale yellow-gold, beautiful hop and roasted malt aroma, complex interesting dry malt flavor, brief malt finish, medium long dry malt aftertaste. [B, 51]

DAS FEINE HOFMARK LAGER BEER — hazy gold, faint off-dry malt aroma, light malt flavor, not exciting or long. [B, 56]

HOFMARK GOLD — gold, sour hop nose; hop flavor turns malty as it crosses the palate; good body, good complexity, long dry malt aftertaste. [B, 59]

DAS FEINE HOFMARK WÜRZIG HERB — gold; toasted malt nose has faint fruitiness and a tang; big hop flavor, big body; some off-dry malt appears at the finish and carries into the long aftertaste to lurk behind the hops; good balance, good beer. [B, 67]

DAS FEINE HOFMARK WÜRZIG MILD — gold, apple-malt nose, much like cider and hops, good flavor like the nose but more dry, highly carbonated, excellent balanced mid-palate and finish, long dry malt and hop aftertaste, very appetizing brew. [B, 52]

Schlossbrauerei Hohenkammer
Brewery in Hohenkamm

HOHENKAMMER WEISSE — hazy gold, pleasant complex spicy-berry peach fruit nose, complex flavor with malt, spice, and fruit, creamy, light body; sags a bit at the finish; fruity aftertaste. [W, 69]

HOHENKAMMER SCHLOSSBIER SCHLOSS-BRÄU HELL — very deep gold, hop nose, good hop and malt flavor, highly carbonated, dry malt finish and aftertaste. [B, 39]

Holsten Brauerei
Brewery in Hamburg

SENATOR URBOCK MAIBOCK — pale amber, smoky caramel nose and taste, heavy body, long roasted malt aftertaste. [BK, 17]

HOLSTEN LAGER — yellow-gold; hop nose has a little malt in back; big hop flavor, too much for the malt and balance, long strong dry bitter hop aftertaste. [B, 34]

HOLSTEN PILS — gold, complex dry hop and faint malt nose, big flavor with plenty of hops and light malt, good body, long dry hop aftertaste, a classical north German pils. [B, 40]

HOLSTEN CERVEZA TIGRE — light gold, malt nose, sour and bitter hop palate, finishes quite sour, poor balance, long slightly sour hop aftertaste. [B, 36]

HOLSTEN EXPORT — bright gold, big roasted malt aroma, some hops in the back of the nose; lots of hops in the flavor, but they are neither sharp nor unpleasant; good toasted malt appears at the finish and there is a pleasant long dry roasted malt aftertaste. [B, 72]

HOLSTEN DRY BIER — bright gold, rising malt aroma, dry malt flavor, dull dry hop finish and aftertaste. [D, 34]

HOLSTEN PREMIUM BEER — bright gold, vegetal malt nose, dry hop flavor, long dry hop aftertaste. [B, 32]

EXTRACTO DE MALTA HAMBURG MALT BEVERAGE — deep brown, lightly carbonated, malty cereal aroma, molasses-malt flavor, very heavy body, thick and chewy, sweet but not cloying; some hops creep in for the finish and aftertaste, but overall it stays malty; very long sweet malt aftertaste. [MB, 45]

DRESSLER EXPORT BEER — yellow-gold, hop nose, strong bitter hop flavor, long dry and bitter hop aftertaste, very austere. [B, 12]

HOLSTEN PILSENER KRÄFTIG-HERB — bright tawny-gold, fine malt and hop aroma; palate is more malt than hops; slightly sour hop aftertaste. [B, 38]

HOLSTEN LIGHT — gold, malt nose, unbalanced malt and hop flavor, weak body, light dry hop finish and aftertaste. [LO, 21]

HOLSTEN MAIBOCK HELLES BOCKBIER — deep gold, rich malt nose; big flavor has both malt and hops; big body, finishes with plenty of both malt and hops, smooth straightforward full flavored beer; long malty aftertaste has a good hop background. [BK, 78]

HOLSTEN FESTBOCK PREMIUM — brown; malt nose is light but has a complex herbal quality; flavor has herbs and rich roasted malt; medium to light body, creamy texture, dry spicy roasted malt aftertaste. [BK, 57]

Weissbierbrauerei Hans Hopf
Brewery in Miesbach

HOPF WEISSE EXPORT — clear gold, light spicy malt aroma (not the usual cloves), fruity background like apple and banana, sweet malt and faint lactic acid palate; a bit too sweet and not enough balancing factors to mitigate the sweetness; good body, long too sweet malt aftertaste. [W, 34]

HOPF DUNKLE SPEZIAL
DUNKLES HEFEWEISSBIER —
clean deep amber-brown, big head,
hefty malt aroma; strong malt flavor
but there is no follow-through; weak
off-dry malt aftertaste. [W, 36]

Privatbrauerei Hösl
Brewery in Mitterteich

HÖSL'S PREMIUM
WEIHNACHTSBIER — bright
gold, hop aroma, big hop flavor,
fairly strong, good body, big and
bold, smooth and balanced; dry
hop aftertaste is long and delicious; 5.5% abv. [B, 80]

RESI HELLES WEISSBIER —
hazy gold, huge head, bright spicy
aroma and off-dry malty flavor,
medium body; dry spicy aftertaste
has good length; gravity 11 P,
4.9% abv. [W, 79]

ABT ANDREAS
KLOSTERTRUNK — deep rosy-
brown, big caramel nose, mocha
taste with a caramel background,
medium body; caramel finish and

aftertaste are medium dry; very
long and very good of the type;
5.3% abv. [B, 80]

M. Hubauer
Gmbh. & Co.
Brewery in Gräfelfing

BAYERN HALBE
VOLLBIER — bright gold, faint
hop aroma, light dull dry malt and
hop flavor, medium body, dull dry
malt aftertaste; 4.7% abv. [B, 39]

Hübsch & Koch
Brewery in
Bohlendamm, Hannover

PUPASCH DUNKEL — amber,
pleasant malt and hop nose, light
toasted malt flavor, tasty and pleasant, light dry malt aftertaste, a flavorful easy drinking beer. [B, 62]

Brauerei Hümmer
Brewery in Dingolhausen

HÜMMER GERMAN EXPORT
BEER — tawny-gold, mild hop
and malt nose, smoky malt flavor;
hops in the finish but well buried
under the smoked flavor; long
smoky aftertaste. [B, 29]

Hersteller
Hürner Bräu
Brewery in Ansbach

HIRSCHEN HELL — gold,
skunky nose, light hop flavor,
medium body, dull dry hop finish
and aftertaste; 4.7% abv. [B, 40]

Privatbrauerei Ibel
Brewery in Kappel

IBEL-BRÄU BOCK — gold, malt
nose, big malty alcoholic taste, a
huge complex brew, enormous
body, rich and delicious, long complex malt and alcohol aftertaste;
gravity 17 P, 7.4% abv. [BK, 90]

IBEL-BRÄU LAGERBIER —
pale amber-brown, dry malt
aroma, dry malt flavor, medium
body, dry malt finish; long dry
malt aftertaste has some hops;
goes well with food. [B, 52]

IBEL-BRÄU PILS — gold, malt
aroma; big dry malt flavor has
plenty of hop support; medium to
light body, dry malt finish and
aftertaste, very long and balanced;
gravity 11 P, 5.1% abv. [B, 63]

IBEL-BRÄU WEIZENBIER —
hazy amber, big head, spicy
aroma; big spicy flavor has an
estery malt character as well; good
body, long spicy malt aftertaste, a
very good hefe-weizen; gravity
12 P, 5.3% abv. [W, 80]

IBEL-BRÄU VOLLBIER —
gold, lovely complex malt and
hop aroma, big rich malty flavor,
light body, dry hop finish, long
dry hop aftertaste; gravity 11 P,
4.7% abv. [B, 82]

Ingobräu
Brewery in Ingolstadt

TILLY BRÄU HELL — gold, light
hop nose and flavor, smooth with
good malt backing, medium body,

light hop finish, dry hop aftertaste, not likable; 4.6% abv. [B, 56]

Privatbrauerei Franz Inselkammer
Brewery in Aying

CELEBRATOR DOPPELBOCK — deep red-brown, good caramel and toasted malt aroma, some sweetness in back, big body, complex off-dry toasted malt flavor; hop finish that gradually becomes dry; long dry hop aftertaste, good balance, especially in the middle, low carbonation. [BK, 63]

AYINGER MAIBOCK — medium pale gold, good hop and toasted malt nose, complex hop flavor; plenty of malt backing most of which doesn't appear until mid-palate; big body, off-dry malt finish, long dry malt and hop aftertaste, very complex throughout, and delicious. [BK, 82]

AYINGER FEST-MÄERZEN — tawny-copper, toasted malt nose; huge hop and toasted malt flavor is short-lived; light body, faint roasted malt finish and aftertaste; very nice but just doesn't last long enough. [B, 42]

AYINGER JAHRHUNDERT BIER — pale gold, faint malt aroma, good hop and malt flavor up front, becomes simple off-dry malt at the finish, long faint hop aftertaste. [B, 29]

AYINGER ALTBAYERISCHE DUNKEL — deep red-brown, rich toasted malt nose, off-dry roasted malt flavor, enough hop backing for good balance, medium body, long pleasant dry malt aftertaste. Also labeled Ayinger Altbairisch Dunkel. [B, 87]

AYINGER WEIHNACHTSBOCK — dark brown, lovely slightly toasted malt nose, pleasant dry malt flavor; fades a bit at the finish; very little aftertaste. [BK, 62]

AYINGER OKTOBER FEST-MÄERZEN — brilliant amber, pleasant malt nose, caramel malt flavor well backed with hops, dry hop finish and aftertaste, very pleasant and drinkable. [B, 72]

Schlossbrauerei Irlbach
Brewery in Irlbach, 8444 (between Regensburg, Amberg, and Nürnberg)

IRLBACHER VOLLBIER HELL — gold, pleasant malt and hop nose, smooth balanced flavor, long dry hop aftertaste, a good long refreshing brew. [B, 78]

IRLBACHER PILS — gold, nice hop and malt nose, balanced mostly hop flavor, long dry hop aftertaste, good body. [B, 46]

IRLBACHER SCHLOSSHERRN WEISSE — deep brown, thick head, light lactic-malt nose, flavor to match, medium long dry malt aftertaste, very drinkable. [W, 47]

Notes

IRLBACHER ECHT
BAYERISCHES HEFE-
WEIZEN — hazy gold, light
spicy malt nose and taste, good
balance, dry malt finish and
aftertaste. [W, 59]

Irseer Klosterbrauerei
Brewery at Irseer

IRSEER KLOSTER
STARKBIER — brownish amber,
toasted malt nose, dry malt flavor,
richer at the end than at the start;
off-dry rich malt aftertaste is very
long; excellent balance, a big
beautiful strong brew. [B, 87]

Isar Bräu
*Brewpub at
Grosshesselohe, Isartal
Bahnhof, suburb of
Munich*

ISAR BRÄU WEISS BRÄU —
cloudy amber, spicy nose; spicy
sweet malt flavor is bright and refreshing; medium body, off-dry malt
and spicy clove finish and aftertaste,
like a dark hefe-weizen. [W, 77]

Brauerei
Isenbeck, A.G.
Brewery in Hamm

ISENBECK EXPORT DELUXE —
gold, pleasant off-dry malt aroma,
off-dry malt and hop flavor, long
dry hop aftertaste. [B, 34]

ISENBECK EXTRA DRY —
gold, mild beautiful smoky hop
nose, big hop flavor, hop finish,
long dry hop aftertaste. [B, 69]

ISI 08 SPECIAL BEER — pale
gold, faint malt aroma, light malt
and hop flavor, light body, cereal
grain aftertaste, little length, a very
low alcohol malt beverage. [NA, 24]

Brauerei Jacob
Brewery in Bodenwöhr

BODENWÖRHER JACOB
ALTBAYERISCH HELL — gold,
malt nose, good body, dry malt flavor, finish, and aftertaste. [B, 35]

Jahns Bräu
Brewery in Ludwigstadt

FALKENSTEINER PREMIUM
HEFE-WEIZEN — hazy gold,
very nice spicy aroma, good
body, bright spicy malt flavor,
long dry spicy malt aftertaste,
stays bright throughout. [W, 80]

Privater Brauerei
Gasthof Deutscher
Rhein / Jankåbräu
BRD
*Brewery-Gasthof in
Zwiesel*

JANKÅBRÄU BÖHMISCHES
BOHEME — gold, smooth pleasant hop nose and taste, plenty of
supporting malt, long dry malt and
hop aftertaste, a good tasting
refreshing pils. [B, 80]

JANKÅBRÄU BÖHMISCHES
KUPFER SPEZIAL — brown, light
malt nose and flavor good body,
long dry malt aftertaste. [B, 63]

JANKÅBRÄU BÖHMISCHES
SCHWARZESWEIZEN — dark
brown, big tan head, typical rich
spicy malt aroma and taste, good
body, good balance, flavorful,
long malt aftertaste. [W, 57]

Jhring-Melchior K.G. /
Licher Privatbrauerei
Brewery in Lich

LICHER PILSNER PREMIUM —
bright gold, pleasant light hop
aroma, zesty hop flavor with plenty
of malt in back; a little soapiness in
the long malt aftertaste but not
enough to be bothersome. [B, 56]

LICHER DOPPELBOCK
PREMIUM — deep amber, big
malt nose, chewy malt flavor, big
and bold, very rich, full bodied,
very long malt aftertaste, a clean
and complex brew with lots of
character. [BK, 90]

Privatbrauerei Kaiserbräu
Brewery in Bamberg

BAMBERGER KRONEN PREMIUM PILSENER BEER — bright gold, beautiful hop nose, strong hop flavor, long dry hop aftertaste borders on being bitter. [B, 25]

Brauerei Kaiser (W. Kumpf)
Brewery in Geislingen/Steige

KAISER WEISSBIER — hazy yellow, big head, faintly lactic wheat nose and flavor; fades almost immediately upon swallowing. [W, 63]

GEISLINGER KAISER IMPORTED GERMAN BEER — bright pale gold, nice zesty hop nose, complex and aromatic, bright hop flavor; smooth faint papaya way in back, but it never comes forward; long dry hop aftertaste. [B, 55]

Kaiser Brauerei
Brewery in Neuhaus

KAISER BAVARIA LIGHT BEER — medium gold, light austere hop aroma, dry and well-hopped palate, good body, long dry hop aftertaste. [B, 69]

NEUHAUS KAISER PILS — bright greenish-gold, hop nose and big hop flavor, dry hop finish and medium long dry hop aftertaste. [B, 48]

ECHT VELDENSTEINER LANDBIER — deep amber, toasted chocolate malt nose and flavor, good carbonation level; flavor is better than the aroma; tasty and very drinkable; seems to be a little smokiness in back; light body, fairly brief dry malt aftertaste. [B, 53]

KAISER WEISSE (WEIZENBIER MIT SEINER HEFE) — hazy gold, huge dense head, malt aroma, fruity malt flavor with no lactic spice, good body; very long malt aftertaste shows only the faintest trace of cloves at the end. [W, 63]

VELDENSTEIN KAISER PILS — gold, faint oxidized nose, dry and bitter hop flavor, finish and aftertaste, very long aftertaste but faulted with a metallic background, probably too old a sample although found shortly after it appeared on New Jersey shelves. [B, 74]

KAISER RITTER PILSENER — gold, nice malty aroma and flavor, light clean smooth off-dry malt finish and aftertaste, light body, good length; 5.2% abv. [B, 53]

Privatbrauerei Kaiserhofbräu
Brewery in Märkstetter Marktredwitz

FRÄNKISCH WEIZEN HEFE DUNKEL — amber-brown, faint spicy malt nose, off-chemical taste of banana and phenolic, sweet malt aftertaste with odd components. Brewed under contract for Marco Getränktmarkt of Kulmbach. [W, 14]

KAISERHOF FESTBIER — deep gold, lactic hop and malt aroma, smoked malt flavor, dry smooth smoked malt aftertaste. [B, 40]

KLOSTER-LANDBIER — dark brown; roasted malt nose with a little smoke, even more smoke flavor is almost burnt; long lightly smoked malt aftertaste. [B, 47]

Sclossbrauerei Kaltenberg / Irmingard Prinzessin von Bayern Gmbh.
Brewery at Schloss Kaltenberg

KÖNIG LUDWIG DUNKEL — deep red-brown, light off-dry malt nose, smoky malt flavor; smokiness becomes overdone in the aftertaste. [B, 67]

KALTENBERG HELL — gold, malt nose, high carbonation, vegetal malt flavor with hops in back, medium body, brief dull malt aftertaste. [B, 37]

PRINZREGENT LUITPOLD KÖNIGSLICHES DUNKLES

WEISSBIER — very slightly hazy brown, pleasant spicy clove nose, well-spiced flavor; finishes malty with the cloves removing to a supporting position; fairly short malt and spice aftertaste. [W, 45]

PRINZREGENT LUITPOLD HEFE-WEISSBIER — hazy gold, faintly spicy malt nose; rich alcoholic malt flavor with the spiciness taking a backseat; long dry malt and clove aftertaste. [W, 63]

KALTENBERG ERNTEDANK FEST BIER — hazy gold, big alcoholic malt nose; strong malt flavor is a bit on the sweet side and a bit alcoholic (5.6% abv); big body; sweet malt finish and aftertaste has a lasting alcoholic tang; a bit like a bierbrand (beer brandy) in its effect on the palate; gravity 13.5 P. [B, 58]

KALTENBERG PILS — deep gold; light hop aroma shows some malt; big malty aroma and flavor, good body; finish and aftertaste are malty and more or less dry; a little malty sweetness appears at the beginning of the aftertaste but fades quickly. This is the pils served at the Kaltenberg Braustürbl. [B, 67]

Brauerei Karg
Brewery in Murnau am Staffelsee

KARG WEISSBIER — hazy gold, fresh spicy nose and taste, creamy, finishes malt, spicy malt aftertaste, long, clean, and refreshing. [W, 70]

SCHWARZER WOIPERLINGER DUNKLES HEFE-WEISSBIER — cloudy brown, spicy nose; spicy malt flavor is smooth and creamy; fine balance, long dry spicy malt aftertaste, good body; excellent beer with rich foods, and a marvelous beer just by itself. [W, 89]

Karlsberg Brauerei
Brewery in Homburg

KARLSBRÄU GERMAN LAGER — deep golden amber, faint hop and malt aroma, flavor of yeast and malt, mild hop background, sour hop finish and aftertaste. [B, 43]

WALSHEIM BEER — gold, beautiful malt and hop nose; flavor starts out on the sweet side, finishes dry and slightly sour hops; long dry hop aftertaste. [B, 41]

KARLSBRÄU MANNLICH — bright yellow-gold, nice hop nose, good balance, off-dry malt and hop palate, hop finish, medium long dry hop aftertaste, good tasting satisfying brew. [B, 71]

KARLSBERG BOCK — deep rose-amber, faint malt aroma, light to medium body, light dry malt flavor, pleasant long dry malt aftertaste. [BK, 56]

Karmelitan Brauerei
Brewery at Straubing

KARMELITAN KLOSTER DUNKEL — deep amber, lovely off-dry toasted malt nose, medium dry toasted smoky malt flavor, medium body, dry malt finish, long dry malt aftertaste, not much complexity but very drinkable. [B, 72]

Brauerei Kauzen
Brewery in Ochsenfurt am Main

KAUZEN DUNKELER KAUZ DUNKLES HEFE WEISSBIER — deep hazy amber, big head, rich wheat-malt nose, very complex with tobacco and chocolate, carbonation, grains, sour malt, faint spices; good while it lasts but it cuts off quickly once swallowed. [W, 39]

KAUZEN HEFE-WEISSBIER — cloudy gold, lightly spiced soapy malt nose, pleasantly spiced malt flavor, medium body, somewhat dull dry malt aftertaste. [W, 47]

KAUZEN FESTBIER — gold; nice malt, hop, and alcohol aroma; malt and alcohol flavor, medium body, off-dry malt finish and aftertaste, very pleasant and long; 5.8% abv. [B, 63]

KAUZEN PREMIUM PILS — gold, faint hop nose, sweet malt flavor, medium body, off-dry malt finish and aftertaste; 4.9% abv. [B, 47]

KAUZEN BOCK — gold, beautiful malty aroma, big balanced malt and hop flavor, big body; smooth mid-palate is mostly malt but shows some alcohol as well; dry malt finish and aftertaste, excellent big flavored heller bock; 7.2% abv. [BK, 89]

Privatbrauerei Kesselring
Brewery in Marksteft am Main

MARUHN PILS — bright gold, good hop aroma, medium dry hopped malt flavor, highly carbonated, slight papery mid-palate, dry finish and short dry hop aftertaste. Made for B. Maruhn of Die Grosste Biermarkt in Welt of Pfungstadt. [B, 36]

UR FRÄNKISCHES LANDBIER — amber, toasted malt nose, malt palate, no complexity, malt finish, short malt aftertaste. [B, 46]

KESSELRING PILS — gold, bright hop nose with malt in back, very bright flavor like the nose; malt rolls in at mid-palate and stays into the long rich malt aftertaste; good body, bright zesty brew; one of the better Pilseners encountered. [B, 88]

SCHLEMMER WEISSBIER MIT HEFE — hazy gold, dry malt nose, faintly spicy malt flavor; long dry malt aftertaste has no spicy component; very drinkable and refreshing. [W, 50]

URFRÄNKISCHES LANDBIER — brown, dry hop nose, big dry hop flavor, medium body; dry hop aftertaste with malt showing in back; 5.1% abv. [B, 47]

Brauerei Kiesel
Brewery in Traunstein

KIESEL HEFE-WEISSBIER EXPORT — bright amber, pleasant chocolate, almond and toasted wheat-malt aroma, toasted malt and hop flavor, very long on the palate, refreshing, long, very good of type. [W, 52]

KIESEL PILS — gold, beautiful off-dry malt nose with good hop balance, touch of apple in back; big complex hop flavor well backed with malt; rich and full, long complex dry malt and hop aftertaste. [B, 79]

KIESEL MÄRZEN — medium deep dull gold, lightly carbonated, pleasant malt aroma, light grainy flavor, some hop character but not much, short dry malt aftertaste. [B, 37]

KIESEL EXPORT HELL — pale yellow, pleasant malt and hop aroma, medium body, good flavored malt and hop palate, well balanced; long dry hop aftertaste keeps the good flavor in your mouth. [B, 57]

KIESEL FESTBIER — pale yellow, good hop aroma, medium body; bright hop flavor has plenty of malt in support; good balance, good body, long dry malt and hop aftertaste, a tasty brew from start to finish. [B, 70]

KIESEL PERL-BOCK DOPPELBOCK — medium yellow, malt aroma, heavy body, all-malt flavor, big and complex, winelike with high alcohol, long off-dry malt aftertaste; good but could use more hops. [BK, 63]

KIESEL WEISSBIER EXPORT — bright gold, foamy, off-dry malt nose and taste with hops in back; there's a little lactic-like bite on the sides of the tongue, but there is no lactic flavor; pleasant and refreshing, fairly short dry malt aftertaste. [W, 49]

Kronenbrauerei Otto Kimer Söhne
Brewery in Tuttlingen/ Möhringen

KRONEN PILS — gold, hop nose with plenty of supporting malt; slightly sour hop flavor well backed with malt; long dry sour hop aftertaste. [B, 57]

KRONEN GOLD EXPORT — gold, light malt and hop nose, off-dry malt flavor, dry hop finish, long hop and malt aftertaste. [B, 60]

KRONEN BRÄU VOLLBIER — gold, faint hop nose, fairly rich malt flavor, finishes dry hops like the Pils, long dry sour hop aftertaste. [B, 63]

KRONEN WEIZEN EXPORT — gold, big head, fresh clove aroma, clean and bright spicy clove and malt flavor, balanced, refreshing; feels good in your mouth; long dry spicy aftertaste, an excellent and very drinkable weizen. [W, 84]

KIRNER'S AECHT BADENER — gold, nice hop nose, some complexity, rather ordinary malt palate; smooth and only lightly hopped; not much of an aftertaste. [B, 45]

Berliner Kindl Brauerei, A.G.
Brewery in Berlin

BERLINER KINDL PILS GERMAN BEER — pale gold, malt and hop aroma, medium body, some complexity; malt palate until the finish when the hops come in; dry bitter hop aftertaste. [B, 34]

BERLINER KINDL WEISSE — yellow-gold, foamy, very complex yeast-bread-wheat-malt aroma, very aromatic; flavor like the nose at first, but the finish tends toward sour; long aftertaste is decidedly sour. [W, 42]

Privatbrauerei Kitzmann K.G.
Brewery in Erlangen

KITZMANN JUBILAUMS ERLANGER — gold, complex malt and hop aroma, slightly sweet rich clean malt taste, medium body, long clean malt aftertaste; 5.7% abv. [B, 87]

KITZMANN EDEL PILS — gold, light bright hop aroma and flavor, medium body, dry refreshing light malt aftertaste with the hops solidly in back. [B, 70]

KITZMANN WEISSBIER MIT HEFE — hazy gold, off-dry malt and spicy flavor, medium body, pleasant and refreshing off-dry malt and clove flavor, medium dry malt aftertaste. [W, 67]

Alte Klosterbrauerei Vierzehnheiligen
Brewery in Vierzehnheiligen

ROTHELSER BIER PILS — gold; odd hop nose is barely perceptible; dry hop flavor with a malt backing, medium body, sour and dry hop finish and aftertaste, good length; gravity 11.9 P, 4.7% abv. [B, 32]

Klosterbrauerei Gmbh.
Brewery in Metzingen (Metzingen Bräustätte Stuttgart)

BRLÄUCHLE HELLER BOCK — pale golden amber, attractive lightly toasted malt aroma, big malt flavor; nicely carbonated and this balances the malt more than hops; big body, very long aftertaste. [BK, 80]

SIGEL KLOSTER KRISTALL-WEIZEN — brilliant gold, big head; sweet nose with a clove background, also seemed to be a faint sense of acetone; flavor is somewhat candylike with the lactic acid (cloves) in competition rather than

balanced; finish is a bit sweet with citrus in behind; fairly short aftertaste has some banana. [W, 24]

SIGEL KLOSTER HEFE-WEIZEN — hazy amber, big head, dry malt aroma; dry malt flavor shows some cloves as well; fair to good body, complex, medium long dry aftertaste of malt and faint cloves. [W, 60]

SIGEL KLOSTER HEFE-WEISSBIER — gold, big hop nose, malt flavor, a bit dull, light dry malt aftertaste with medium length. [W, 60]

SIGEL KLOSTER PILSENER — gold, dull malt aroma and flavor, medium body, aftertaste like the flavor, not interesting. [B, 48]

Privatbrauerei Koller-Fleischmann A.G. / Landshuter Brauhaus
Brewery in Landshut

LANDSHUTER BRAUHAUS KOLLERBRÄU-HELL — gold, hop and toasted malt aroma, toasted malt flavor, smooth and tasty, medium body; dry toasted malt aftertaste is brief; 4.5% abv. [B, 65]

König Brauerei, K.G.
Brewery in Duisberg

KÖNIG PILSENER — brilliant gold, good hop aroma; big hop flavor is smooth and well balanced with malt; finishes malty, long dry hop aftertaste. [B, 40]

Königsbacher Brauerei, A.G.
Brewery in Koblenz

KÖNIGSBACHER PILS — gold, big vegetal malt nose, off-dry vegetal malt flavor, long pleasant off-dry malt aftertaste. [B, 49]

KÖNIGSBACHER ALT — deep copper, heavy roasted malt nose, big malt flavor with plenty of hops, medium body, lots of character, good malt finish, brief malt aftertaste. [A, 51]

KÖNIGSBACHER UR-BOCK — tawny gold, rich roasted malt nose, big beautiful roasted malt flavor, magnificent balance, huge and long; they don't get any better than this; a perfect score. [BK, 100]

KÖNIGSBACHER MALZ — reddish-brown color, sweet malt nose, very sweet malt flavor; only bite is from carbonation; very long sweet malt aftertaste. [M, 27]

Köstritzer Schwarzbierbrauerei
Brewery in Bad Köstritz

KÖSTRITZER — opaque brown, brown head, big malt aroma, pure malt flavor like a finely carbonated malta, very sweet, big body, long strong malt aftertaste; it is drinkable, but too sweet. Tasted as found in Germany. [B, 67]

KÖSTRITZER SCHWARZBIER — very deep dark amber, dry malt aroma, big dry malt flavor, medium to good body; grows on you as you sip it and your opinion of the dry maltiness grows as well; smooth, dry malt finish and aftertaste, good length. Tasted in U.S.A. in 1994 in both bottles (CA and NJ) and on draft (FL). [B, 67]

Privatbrauerei Gebr. Krauss
Brewery in Riedbach

FRANKEN BRÄU SPEZIAL — gold, malt and spicy hop aroma, off-dry malt and spicy hop flavor, so-so balance, good body, off-dry malt aftertaste. [B, 40]

FRANKEN BRÄU PILS — gold, nice hop nose; palate is big bright hops; medium to good body, only fair balance, long sour hop aftertaste. [B, 45]

Privatbrauerei Krautheim-Volkach, Frederick Düll OHG
Brewery in Krautheim

KRAUTHEIMER PILSNER — gold, light hop nose, dull malt and hop flavor, medium body; malty

aftertaste is on the dull side; 5% abv. [B, 40]

Privatbrauerei Krombacher
Brewery in Krombach

KROMBACHER PILS — brilliant deep gold, toasted malt aroma and flavor, creamy but lightly carbonated, good strong flavor with a fine hop finish; complex hop and malt aftertaste is long and fairly dry; good balance, likable beer. [B, 53]

Kronenbrauhaus Lüneberg
Brewery in Lüneberg

MORAVIA BEER — bright pale gold, good fragrant aromatic hop nose, big hop flavor, medium length dry hop aftertaste. [B, 46]

MORAVIA DARK BEER — tawny-brown, hop nose, roasted malt flavor with only faint hops, long dry malt aftertaste; some off flavors persist throughout and mar the palate. [B, 20]

Privatbrauerei A. Kropf
Brewery in Kassel

KROPF EDEL PILS — bright medium deep gold, faint malt nose, dull dry hop flavor, fairly light body, weak dull dry hop finish and aftertaste. [B, 32]

MEISTER PILS — pale gold, toasted malt nose, good toasted

malt flavor, medium body, long pleasant dry toasted malt aftertaste. [B, 63]

KROPF GENUINE GERMAN DRAFT — bright gold, beautiful roasted malt nose, good hop palate well backed with malt, good tasting, good body, short dry hop aftertaste. [B, 57]

KROPF DARK GERMAN BEER — brown, faint malt aroma, dry malt flavor, burnt finish, good balance but little zest, fair length. [B, 41]

KROPF GENUINE GERMAN LIGHT — pale gold, pleasant malt nose, sour hop flavor, light body, metallic finish, long bitter hop aftertaste. [LO, 42]

KROPF MAI-BOCK — deep gold, rich malt nose, big malt flavor, rich and full-bodied, long malt aftertaste. [BK, 87]

KROPF MARTINATOR DOPPELBOCK — deep rosy-amber, malt nose, huge off-dry malt flavor, big body, complex throughout; very long malt aftertaste is a bit drier than the flavor; very good tasting brew. [BK, 95]

Brauerei Krug
Brewery in Ebelsbach/Main

KRUG EDEL HELL — gold, sour hop nose and taste, good body, long aftertaste like the flavor. [B, 40]

KRUG GOLDEN PILS — gold, malt and hop nose, hop and malt flavor, good balance; dry hop finish is soften by a good level of malt; long dry hop and malt aftertaste. [B, 51]

KRUG ALT FRÄNKISCH — deep amber, roasted malt nose and taste, creamy, dry but rich, slightly toasted dry malt finish and long dry malt aftertaste. [B, 74]

KRUG HEILIG LÄNDER — golden amber, big malt nose and taste, malt finish, dry malt aftertaste; seems to be some faint hops in the aftertaste, but largely this is a malt only beer. [B, 47]

KRUG WEISSE — hazy gold, big spicy lactic nose, light spicy flavor, creamy; dry malt aftertaste has some length. [W, 61]

Brauerei zum Kuchlbauer Gmbh.
Brewery in Abensberg

KUCHLBAUER WEISSE — hazy deep gold, highly carbonated, big tight head, bright spicy nose, big sweet spicy taste, light body; off-dry malt aftertaste is nice and very long; gravity 11 P, 5.2% abv. [W, 69]

Notes

Kulmbacher Schweizerhofbrau
Brewery in Kulmbach

KULMBACHER SCHWEIZERHOFBRAU — bright gold, magnificent hop aroma; flavor starts out bitter hops, malt comes in at mid-palate, and it finishes off-dry malt; balance is very good; good body, long dry malt and hop aftertaste. [B, 42]

KULMBACHER SCHWEIZERHOFBRAU BOCK — brilliant gold, lush hop aroma, good body, rich malt and hop flavor, extremely complex, marvelous balance, long well-hopped aftertaste, a delicious gem of a beer. [BK, 96]

KULMBACHER SCHWEIZERHOFBRAU HELLER — deep golden amber, beautiful hop nose, big body; big rich flavor of hops well backed with malt; good balance, very long on the palate; loaded with flavor. [B, 42]

Kuppers Kölsch, A.G.
Brewery in Köln

KUPPERS KÖBES KÖLSCH — deep gold, beautiful aromatic hop nose, off-dry hop flavor, perfumy finish; long delicious aftertaste that ends up bittering hops; a good long complex brew. [K, 62]

Brauerei Kurfürsten
Brewery in Köln

KURFÜRSTEN KÖLSCH — tawny-gold, dry hop nose; flavor is first hops, then sour malt; long dry hop and sour malt aftertaste. [K, 38]

Brauerei Ladenburger
Brewery in Neuler

MEISTERBRÄU EXPORT — gold, faint malt nose, light malt flavor, touch of malty sweetness in the finish, short off-dry malt aftertaste. [B, 27]

Privatbrauerei Lamm Bräu Rolf Goetz
Brewery-Gasthof in Bingen (near Sigmaringen)

LAMM BRÄU PILSENER — beautiful gold, hop and malt nose; good bright hop flavor well balanced with malt; some complexity, medium long dry hop aftertaste. [B, 63]

LAMM BRÄU EDEL HELL — gold, pleasant hop nose, big hop flavor with plenty of malt in support, very malty in mid-palate, dry hop finish, long dry hop and malt aftertaste, nicely done brew. [B, 73]

Neumarkter Lammsbräu
Brewery in Neumarkt

NEUMARKTER LAMMSBRÄU ÖKO DUNKEL — amber-brown like a port wine, rich malty aroma;

malt flavor is light and dry rather than rich like the nose; light to medium body; light dry malt aftertaste is brief; gravity 11.5 P, 4.8% abv. [B, 50]

Lamm Brauerei
Brewery in Sindelfingen

LAMM BRÄU PILS — brilliant gold, beautiful hop nose, bright hop flavor, bitter hop finish, long bitter hop aftertaste; a very good serviceable beer, especially with food. [B, 60]

LAMM BRÄU EXPORT — brilliant amber, balanced hop-malt aroma and taste, smooth, appetizing; malt dominant in mid-palate, hops in lead in front and at finish; long dry hop and malt aftertaste, another good beer with food. [B, 56]

WURTTEMBERG'S NATURTRUBE LAMM BRÄU — gold, highly carbonated, no nose, complex rich dry malt and hop flavor, dry hop finish, medium long dry malt aftertaste. [B, 70]

Privatbrauerei Gasthof Landwehrbräu Fam. Wörner
Brewery-Gasthof in Reichelshofen

ROTHENBURGER LANDWEHR PILSNER — pale gold, great malt-hop nose, big hop flavor, well backed with malt, dry hop finish and aftertaste, very long. This is the draft version served at the brewery. [B, 67]

ALT FRÄNKISCH-DUNKEL —
deep amber-brown, malt aroma,
big malt flavor, heavy body but
smooth on the palate, dry malt
finish and aftertaste, very little
hops in the aftertaste, a solid full-
flavored malt brew. This is the
draft version served at the brewery. [B, 93]

ROTHENBURGER
LANDWEHR SCHANKBIER —
pale gold, stinky hop nose, light
body, very delicate malt and hop
palate; light malt aftertaste has a
faint hop background. [LO, 20]

ROTHENBURGER LANDWEHR-
BIER PILSNER — gold, malt nose,
pleasant hop flavor, good malt backing, dry hop finish, very long dry
hop aftertaste. This is the bottled
version of the Pilsner described
above. [B, 84]

ROTHENBURGER EXPORT
EDELHELL — gold, malt aroma,
hop and malt flavor; dry hop aftertaste has a sour component in behind the hops. [B, 47]

ROTHENBURGER
LANDWEHR ALTFRÄNKISCH
DUNKEL — beautiful deep
amber-brown, pleasant faintly
toasted malt aroma, mild dry malt
flavor, some complexity at the finish, long dry malt aftertaste, very
drinkable, excellent with food.
This is the bottled version of the
brew. [B, 60]

Brauerei Lang
Brewery in
Schwäbische Gmünd

LA BIERE DE LA GRANDE
ARMÉE — hazy yellow-gold, luscious malt aroma with some toasted
quality and dry smoked sausage,
creamy texture with small bubble
carbonation, rich toasted malt flavor; long aftertaste like the flavor,
but attenuated. [B, 42]

Lederer Bräu
Brewery in Nürnberg

LEDERER EXPORT — amber,
good hop nose with malt and yeast
in back; big flavor of molasses,
hops, and salt (each flavor separate
and distinct); big body, long dry hop
aftertaste. [B, 37]

LEDERER EXPORT LIGHT —
pale yellow-gold, low carbonation, faint malt nose, thin body,
light dull malt palate, short dry
malt aftertaste. [B, 28]

LEDERER PILS — bright pale
gold, dry hop aroma and flavor,
malty backing, medium body, dry
hop finish and aftertaste; palate
stays dry; good with food. [B, 60]

Brauerei Robert
Leicht, A.G.
Brewery in Vahingen/
Stuttgart

SCHWABEN BRÄU GERMAN
PILSNER BEER — yellow-gold,
light malt nose with some hops,
dull malt flavor, bitter hop aftertaste. [B, 24]

SCHWABEN BRÄU
PILSENER — gold, hop nose and taste, long dry hop aftertaste. [B, 32]

SCHWABEN BRÄU MEISTER PILS — bright gold, hop nose; pronounced hop flavor; hop finish, long dry hop aftertaste. [B, 32]

SCHWABEN BRÄU EXPORT — bright tawny-gold, balanced hop and malt nose and flavor, good body, fairly smooth, appetizing, long dry malt and hop aftertaste. [B, 39]

DAS ECHTE SCHWABEN BRÄU — tawny-gold, big hop nose, heavy body, big hop flavor, plenty of malt in support, long dry hop aftertaste. [B, 61]

SCHWABEN BRÄU URTYP 1878 — gold, dry hop nose and flavor; fairly long dry aftertaste features neither hops nor malt, just dry. [B, 32]

DAS ECHTE SCHWABEN BRÄU MÄRZEN — gold, dull malty aroma; strong dry malt flavor has a vegetal and straw background; good body, dull dry malt finish and aftertaste; gravity 13 P, 5.5% abv. [B, 47]

SCHWABEN BRÄU WEIHNACHTS BIER — gold, dry malt and hop aroma, dull dry malt flavor, medium body, dry malt finish and aftertaste; gravity 12 P, 5.5% abv. [B, 45]

SCHWABEN BRÄU VOLKFEST BIER — gold, malt and hop aroma, big dry malt flavor with hops in back, huge body; palate shows some alcohol (5.5% abv); pleasant big malt finish and aftertaste like a märzen bier; gravity 13 P. [B, 69]

Brauerei Leikeim
Brewery in Altenkunstadt

LEIKEIM DAS ORIGINAL — gold, complex malt nose; tangy malt flavor is very hefty and well backed with strong hops; big body; long aftertaste has plenty of both malt and hops; the malt dominates throughout this big-flavored brew, yet there is harmony among the components; a lusty brew. [B, 77]

LEIKEIM WEISSE (MIT SEINER HEFE) — hazy gold, huge thick head, fruity-spicy malt nose, smooth creamy fruity-spicy malt flavor, dry malt aftertaste, good body and balance, very drinkable. [W, 84]

ALT KUNESTATER URSTOFF — amber-brown, malt nose, big dry roasted malt flavor, good body, long off-dry malt aftertaste. [B, 59]

LEIKEIM KUNATOR DER DUNKELER DOPPELBOCK — amber, light fruity malt and alcohol nose, big body, huge strong malt palate, creamy, smooth, balanced, full and rich, quite alcoholic throughout, very long rich malt aftertaste; gravity 21 P, 8.2% abv. [BK, 98]

LEIKEIM PREMIUM EXPORT — gold, malty aroma and flavor, medium body, dry hop finish and aftertaste. [B, 47]

Lindener Gilde-Bräu, A.G.
Gilde brewery in Hannover

GILDE RATSKELLER PILS-BEER — bright gold, well-hopped nose; hops dominate the flavor; some off-dry malt appears at the finish; aftertaste is out-of-balance hops and off-dry malt. [B, 23]

GILDE EDEL EXPORT — deep gold, good hop aroma, big body, big hop flavor; hops fade at the finish but are replaced with malt; excellent balance; a marvelous tasting brew with a long dry malt and hop aftertaste. [B, 90]

GILDE PILSENER — gold, hop nose, big hop flavor, big body, very long dry hop aftertaste. [B, 49]

BROYHAN PREMIUM BEER — gold, hop aroma and strong hop flavor, long dry and somewhat bitter hop aftertaste. [B, 46]

Familienbrauerei Link
Link brewery in Tuttlingen-Möhringen

MÖHRINGEN HERRENHAUS PILS — gold, big hop nose, big lusty flavor with an abundance of both hops and malt, rich long malt aftertaste, excellent balance, a super beer. [B, 87]

 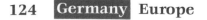

Werner Lippert Gmbh. & Co. K.G.
Brewery in Hof

LIPPERT'S PILS — gold, hop nose, malt and sour hop flavor, medium body, malt and hop finish and aftertaste; 4.7% abv. [B, 47]

Privatbrauerei Löwenbräu Bamberg K.G.
Brewery in Bamberg

ST. STEPHANUS FEST BIER — amber, fruity malt aroma, pleasant malt and hop flavor, fairly dry, good balance, medium body, brief length. [B, 59]

BAMBERGER LÖWENBRÄU FRÄNKISCHES URBIER — deep amber, sweet clean malt nose, off-dry malt and hop flavor, plenty of alcohol, medium body; long malt aftertaste stays off-dry. [B, 50]

BAMBERGER LÖWENBRÄU EXPORT — deep gold, rich malt nose and flavor, complex and tasty, good body, long dry malt aftertaste, very good with food or by itself, one of Germany's best export-style beers. [B, 86]

Löwenbrauerei Hall / Fr. Erhart Gmbh. & Co.
Brewery in Schwabisch Hall

HALLER LÖWENBRÄU MEISTER GOLD — gold, stinky hop nose, big hop flavor, medium body, sour hop finish and aftertaste; 4.9% abv. [B, 34]

Löwenbräu Meckatz-Benedikt Weiss K.G.
Brewery in Meckatz

MECKATZER WEISS GOLD — brilliant gold; hop nose is a bit strange at first with some malodorous character, then it becomes grassy, but like it went through a cow; dull strange vegetal-malt flavor; has to be a bad bottle, nobody would intentionally make this commercially. [W, 34]

Brauerei Löwenbräu
Brewery in Munich

MUNICH OKTOBERFEST BEER — amber, beautiful hop aroma with a touch of caramel, big body; big hop flavor is well equipped with toasted malt; long rich and dry malt aftertaste. [B, 50]

LÖWENBRÄU MUNICH LIGHT SPECIAL — gold, lovely hop nose, marvelous complex hop and malt flavor, big body, chewy, very well balanced, long dry hop aftertaste. [B, 60]

LÖWENBRÄU MUNICH DARK SPECIAL — deep brown with an amber tinge, very clean malt aroma with some hops; strong flavor starts out malt, finishes hops; long dry hop aftertaste has a little sour malt in back, gives it an earthy quality. [B, 40]

Notes

LÖWENBRÄU
OKTOBERFEST — brilliant deep
gold; dense head lasts all the way to
the bottom of the glass; big body;
balanced rich malt and hop nose;
delicious rich malt flavor well
backed with hops; long delicious
dry hop aftertaste. This is the brew
served at the festhalle. [B, 89]

LÖWENBRÄU
OKTOBERFEST — deep amber,
lovely dry hop nose, quality clean
hop nose, smooth balanced hop and
rich malt palate, very drinkable, fairly
long on the palate; gravity 13.7 P,
5.8% abv. Bottled version. [B, 89]

DER LÖWENBRÄU PREMIUM
PILSENER — pale gold, nice
thick head, clean hop nose, big
fresh hop and malt flavor; high
carbonation is more noticeable to
the eye than the palate; creamy
texture, delicious complex long
dry hop aftertaste, excellent balance throughout. [B, 60]

LÖWEN WEISSE KLARES
WEIZENBIER — bright clear
gold, big head, pleasant clean off-
dry malt nose, pleasant slightly
sweet malt flavor with just a little
lactic tang, really good balance;

long pleasing aftertaste like the
flavor. [W, 67]

TRIUMPHATOR DUNKLER
DOPPELBOCK — deep red-
brown; roasted malt aroma is complex and rich; big rich malt flavor
is on the sweet side in front, dries
at the middle; long medium dry
malt aftertaste, very complex and
very good; gravity 18.3 P, 7.7%
abv. [BK, 78]

LÖWENBRÄU HELLER
BOCK — brilliant gold, beautiful
hop nose, big bright malt flavor;
strong, rich, and complex; full body,
finely carbonated; long malt and
hop aftertaste with hops coming on
strongly at the very end. [BK, 87]

LÖWENBRÄU
SCHWARZEWEISSE DUNKLES
HEFE-WEIZEN — slightly hazy
deep copper-amber; wheat and malt
aroma has a faint lactic acid character like clove spice; palate to match,
nicely balanced, smooth, well made,
very drinkable. [W, 56]

LÖWENBRÄU BOCKBIER
HELL — deep gold, fragrant hop
nose, big hop and malt flavor, big
body, finishes dry hops; aftertaste
is dry hops and malt; this is a beer
with plenty of everything including an excellent balance. [BK, 84]

Löwenbrauerei
Passau A.G.
Brewery in Passau

LÖWENBRAUEREI-PASSAU
URTYP HELL — gold, bright hop
nose, malty Ovaltine flavor, very
straightforward and very clean,

light body, light medium dry malt
aftertaste, very clean throughout;
gravity 11 P, 4.8% abv. [B, 62]

Löwenbräu Trier J.
Mendgen
Brewery in Trier

PETRISBERGER PILSENER
FEINER ART — pale yellow-gold,
light hop nose, bright hop flavor,
long dry hop aftertaste; some sour
hops at the very end that linger on
for quite a time. [B, 58]

TRIERER LÖWENBRÄU
EDELPILS — gold, light malt
aroma, light hop and malt flavor,
hop finish, long dry hop aftertaste.
[B, 56]

TRIERER LÖWENBRÄU
KURFURST EXPORT — pale
gold, malt nose, malt front palate,
dry hop finish, long hop aftertaste,
very drinkable. [B, 53]

TREUERER ALT — brown, malt
nose and big malt flavor, a bit
sweet up front, drier at the middle
and finish, long dry malt aftertaste. [A, 59]

Privatbrauerei Gebr.
Michel / Mahr's Bräu
Brewery in Bamberg

MAHR'S BRÄU PILSENER —
pale gold, spicy hop nose, dry
spicy hop flavor, medium body;
spicy hop aftertaste is very dry
and very long; 4.9% abv. [B, 53]

MAHR'S WEISSE — hazy gold,
big head, spicy malt aroma and

flavor, good body, off-dry spicy malt aftertaste, very long; gravity 12.3 P, 5.2% abv. [W, 51]

Brauerei Maisach / J. Sedllmayr
Brewery in Maisach

MAISACH RÄUBER-KNEISSL — copper-brown, dry malt aroma and palate; despite being dry it is quite rich; big body, long dry malt aftertaste, very satisfying and great with food. [B, 67]

MAISACH HELLER BOCK — deep tawny-gold; beautiful complex malt and hop aroma, so good it sends a shiver down your spine; big body, delicious long complex flavor of balanced hops and malt; wonderful long aftertaste is a continuation of the flavor gradually becoming more dry as it goes; this is about as good as a pale lager can get. [BK, 91]

MAISACH BRAUEREI PILS — bright gold, well-hopped aroma, beautiful hop flavor, long dry hop aftertaste, good body, excellent balance, a classic pils. [B, 68]

MAISACHER HELLES EXPORT — gold, nice malt and hop aroma; balanced big clean flavor is mostly hops; medium body, dry hop finish and aftertaste. [B, 68]

MAISACHER SEDLMAYR-WEIZEN — hazy gold, lightly spiced malt aroma, big spicy flavor, good body, long slightly off-dry malt aftertaste. [W, 91]

Privatbrauerei Gebr. Maisel
Brewery in Bayreuth

HERRENBRÄU GERMAN PILSNER — gold, nice malt aroma with a touch of hops, good malt-hop balance, bitter finish, long strong hop aftertaste. [B, 42]

HERRENBRÄU GERMAN WEIZEN — pale gold, dense head, pleasant smoky wheat aroma, sweet and sour wheat beer flavor (fruity-spicy), clean off-dry long malt aftertaste. [W, 14]

HERRENBRÄU GERMAN LIGHT   deep bright gold, fine hop and roasted malt aroma, very appetizing, sharp hop flavor with the malt in back, hop finish, long bitter hop aftertaste. [LO, 34]

MAISEL FEST BIER — bright amber, beautiful well-hopped roasted malt aroma, delicious smooth brew with plenty of hops and malt, excellent balance, clean, good body, long roasted malt aftertaste, a really fine beer. [B, 92]

MAISEL BAYRISCH — deep bright gold, foamy, complex hop nose and flavor, malt finish, brief dry malt aftertaste. [B, 47]

MAISEL DAMPFBIER — bright amber, faint off-dry malt aroma, palate starts out sweet malt; goes a little sour in the middle and dry hops come in for the finish and long aftertaste. [B, 31]

Notes

MAISEL'S PILSNER — pale gold, light pleasant malt and hop aroma, bright malt and hop flavor, good balance, good body, off-dry malt finish, long dry hop aftertaste; not complex but very pleasant all the way through. [B, 52]

MAISEL MALT LIQUOR EXPORT — pale gold, light hop aroma, bright hop flavor, good body and balance, long dry hop aftertaste, very much like the Maisel Pilsner. [B, 50]

MAISEL'S KRISTALLKLAR WEIZEN — deep bright gold, big head, tart nose; lactic acid and cloves start the flavor, softens as it goes, smooth light dry malt aftertaste; nicely balanced and very drinkable. [W, 32]

MAISEL'S HEFE-WEISSBIER — pale cloudy amber, light pleasant malt aroma, sour banana flavor; long malt aftertaste retains much of the banana. [W, 42]

MAISEL HEFE WEISSE — hazy amber, big head, light lactic-malt aroma, big clove flavor, zesty and bright, hefty body, refreshing and dry, dry malt finish and aftertaste. [W, 70]

MAISEL BRÄU SPEZIAL — pale copper-gold, malt nose with an artificially sweet quality, palate similar but more noticeable, complex but strange and unbalanced, highly carbonated; pleasant malt and hop aftertaste has good length. [B, 27]

MAISEL TRADITIONAL — pale apricot color, light toasted malt aroma, flavor like the nose, sweet malt in the finish; slightly sour hop aftertaste that loses most of its sourness as you continue to drink the beer. [B, 43]

MAISEL ORIGINAL 1887 HELLES EXPORT BIER — bright gold; pleasant aroma is mostly malt; good refreshing light hop flavor, malt finish, smooth and very drinkable, long dry malt aftertaste. [B, 80]

MAISEL DUNKEL — deep orange-brown, dry malt nose, dull dry malt flavor, long faintly sour malt aftertaste. [B, 25]

MAISEL'S WEIZEN BOCK — cloudy brown; has sediment; very foamy, fruity wheat grain and apple peel aroma; initially some lactic acid on the palate, but it didn't last; promises sweetness but stays dry; full but not heavy; high carbonation balances complex flavors rather than intrudes; long on the palate; feels good in your mouth; very good of type. [W, 57]

FORST HEFE-WEISSBIER — tawny-gold, slightly sharp wheat nose, complex and full bodied, big grainy palate, long complex malt aftertaste. [W, 52]

FORST WEISSBIER — bright gold, huge head, grainy wheat aroma, clean light pleasant grainy palate, medium to long dry malt aftertaste, very good tasting. [W, 40]

JOHANN GOTTFRIED FORST PILS — slightly cloudy yellow-gold, toasted malt aroma and taste, good hop tang but a bit on the sour side, long dry hop aftertaste. Faust Brauerei, Miltenberg. [B, 40]

JOHANN GOTTFRIED FORST DUNKEL — medium deep copper, roasted malt nose, good head, creamy roasted malt flavor, light body; lacks depth and is a bit dull; medium long dry malt aftertaste. [B, 38]

KRITZENTHALER ALKOHOLFRIES PILSNER — deep gold, grainy malt nose, big malty flavor, light body, short grainy malt aftertaste. [NA, 32]

BENEDIKTINER DUNKEL — dark brown, pleasant malty-chocolate nose; big rich malt flavor is off-dry at first, but is dry by the finish; there are dry coffee-like tones in the aftertaste; light body; no length, but is very pleasant and easy to drink; gravity 11 P, 4.4% abv. [B, 67]

Privatbrauerei Mall
Brewery in Meckesheim

MALL-BRÄU EXPORT — gold, pleasant hop and malt aroma, very tasty big malt and bright hop flavor, good body; rich dry malt aftertaste retains the malty character and good hop taste of the flavor; 5.1% abv. [B, 70]

Klosterbrauerei Mallersdorf
Kloster brewery in Mallersdorf

KLOSTERBRAUEREI MALLERSDORF VOLLBIER HELL — gold, light dry hop nose; bright malty flavor has some hops; medium body, off-dry malt finish and aftertaste; only real sweetness is at the end; gravity 12 P, 5% abv. [B, 67]

Marburger Brauerei Otto Beyer
Brewery in Marburg

ALT MARBURGER DUNKEL — brilliant amber, dry malt nose and flavor; aftertaste is a continuation of the flavor as well and is only medium in duration; there is a touch of sourness at the very end; so-so beer, but it does grow on you if you keep drinking it. [B, 51]

Brauerei Märkelsteiner
Brewery in Marktredwitz

BRAUMEISTER HELL — deep gold, hop nose, light off-dry malt flavor, hops in back; long malt aftertaste is a little more dry. [B, 41]

Mauritius Brauerei
Brewery in Zwickau, Sachsen

MAURITIUS BOCK DUNKEL — deep brown, dry malt nose, big malt flavor, big body, dry malt finish and aftertaste, plenty of malt; 6.9% abv doesn't seem to show. [BK, 86]

Mauth-Bräu Gmbh.
Brewery in Mühlbühl

SECHSÄMTER LANDBIER — deep gold, light hop and malt nose, big rich toasted malt flavor, medium body, excellent dry toasted malt aftertaste; 5.4% abv. [B, 70]

Privatbrauerei Wilhelm Mayer
Brewery in Rottweil

ORIGINAL ROTTWEILER SCHWARZBIER — deep rosy-brown, pleasant dry lightly toasted malt nose; burnt nature on the palate gives the malt more complexity; faint dry malt aftertaste; dies immediately as it is swallowed leaving little after; also the balance is questionable. [B, 38]

Privatbrauerei Mittenwalder
Brewery in Mittenwald

MITTENWALDER DUNKEL — medium deep ruby-brown, lovely malt nose and flavor, magnificent balance, long malt aftertaste, very pleasant and satisfying. [B, 80]

Notes

MITTENWALDER WEIHNACHTSBOCK HELL — gold, perfumy malt nose, sour malt palate, short malt aftertaste. [B, 40]

MITTENWALDER JOSEFI BOCK DUNKEL — deep ruby-brown, rich malt nose, rich off-dry malt flavor, long malt aftertaste, good drinkable brew. [BK, 52]

MITTENWALDER VOLLBIER HELL — gold, malt and faint hop aroma; malt flavor is off-dry and a little vegetal at first and becomes drier toward the finish; light dry malt aftertaste, somewhat dull. [B, 40]

Privatbrauerei Modscheidler K.G.
Brewery at Buttenheim

ST. GEORGEN BRÄU DUNKELER DOPPELBOCK — brown, excellent dry malt nose with good hops in support, big malt flavor again with plenty of hop backing, big body, complex, long long dry malt aftertaste with the hops dropping out early. [BK, 82]

Brauerei Moninger
Brewery in Karlsruhe

MONINGER BERTHOLD BOCK DUNKEL — brown, lovely rich and roasted dry malt nose, good carbonation level, rich dry malt flavor; hops join with the carbonation to balance the richness of the malt; long rich malt aftertaste, excellent brew. [BK, 91]

MONINGER WEIHNACHTS BIER — gold; malty aroma has a good hop background; soft dull malty flavor, good body, dry malt and hop finish and aftertaste; gravity 12 P, 5.6% abv. [B, 50]

MONINGER EXPORT — gold, malt nose, dry malt flavor; touch of hops and some malty sweetness join in for the aftertaste; medium body; 5.2% abv. [B, 47]

Mönchshof Brauerei Gmbh.
Brewery in Kulmbach

KULMBACHER MONKSHOF KLOSTER SCHWARZ BIER — deep copper-brown, light toasted malt aroma, mellow and smooth, lovely malt flavor, beautiful balance, long dry malt aftertaste, a lovely brew. [B, 84]

KULMBACHER MONKSHOF AMBER LIGHT BEER — gold, fragrant roasted malt and hop aroma, big body, big roasted malt and hop flavor, excellent balance, an excellent beer. [B, 80]

KULMBACHER MÖNCHSHOF FESTBIER — bright gold, subdued malt and hop aroma; smooth malt flavor has good hop backing; good balance, heavy body, long and delicious hop and malt aftertaste. [B, 85]

KULMBACHER MÖNCHSHOF PILSENER — bright pale gold, malt nose and flavor, medium to light body; dry hop finish and long hop aftertaste which is a tad sour. [B, 37]

GREGORIUS WIESENFESTBIER — bright gold; delicious toasted malt nose is really malty (like malted milk-malty); delicious appetizing palate is first malt, then hops; all stays in balance right into the long complex malt and hop aftertaste; a very very nice drinkable brew. [B, 84]

MÖNCHSHOF URSTOFF DARK SPEZIAL STARKBIER — reddish brown, malt nose, huge strong smooth malt flavor, enormous body; you can taste the alcohol; very long pleasant strong malt aftertaste; a pleasure to sip. [B, 73]

MÖNCHSHOF URSTOFF SPEZIAL STARKBIER — deep amber, huge malt nose, concentrated malt palate, medium body; long dry malt aftertaste is like dry molasses. [B, 80]

KULMBACHER MONKSHOF DRY LIGHT BEER — pale gold, good malt nose with hops in back; a little toasted malt barely found in the nose is the good flavor; medium body; hops appear at the finish; long dry roasted malt aftertaste. [B, 65]

KULMBACHER MONKSHOF KLOSTERBOCK BEER — rosy-amber, fragrant roasted malt, caramel, and hop aroma, big body; front palate is off-dry roasted malt; finishes dry malt and hops; long pleasant malt and hop aftertaste leaves your mouth feeling good. [BK, 84]

KULMBACHER MONKSHOF DARK BEER — tawny-brown, rich toasted malt aroma with hops in back, rich full toasted malt flavor, good balance; malty-molasses middle and finish, but the long aftertaste is tasty dry malt and the lasting memory is that dry malt rather than the sweeter malt earlier. [B, 77]

KULMBACHER MÖNCHSHOF OKTOBERBIER — brilliant gold, big toasted malt aroma with hops in back, light body, light flavor of hops and toasted malt, long dry hop aftertaste, not big but very drinkable. [B, 82]

KULMBACHER MONKSHOF HELLER BOCK — medium gold, rising toasted malt and hop aroma, big body; rich dark malt flavor has powerful hops in back trying to break through; strong, complex, and excellently balanced; very long complex dry hop and malt aftertaste. [BK, 75]

KAPUZINER SCHWARZE HEFE-WEIZEN — amber-brown, big head, malt nose and fresh malt flavor, medium body, smooth rather than zesty, pleasant long dry malt aftertaste. [W, 53]

MÖNCHSHOF KLOSTER BOCK HELL — gold, good light malt and hop nose; big complex flavor has malt, hops, and alcohol (7%); good balance, very big with plenty of everything, long complex malt and hop aftertaste, a marvelous brew. [BK, 95]

Hofbrauhaus Moy
Brewery in Freising

HOFBRAUHAUS MOY JÄGERBIER — bright gold, light off-sweet nose with hops in back, good smooth delicate malt and hop flavor, finely balanced, slightly sweet malt aftertaste, a nice silky smooth brew. [B, 60]

HOFBRAUHAUS MOY REGENT — bright gold, dry complex malt nose with a little ale-like tartness, good smooth delicate taste similar to above but with more hops in front, long dry hop aftertaste. [B, 63]

HOFBRAUHAUS MOY EDELWEIZEN KRISTALLKLAR — bright gold, big head, clean wheat nose, zesty clean wheat and malt flavor, tastes good, good body, slightly sweet finish and aftertaste, medium to short. [W, 56]

Klosterbrauerei Münnerstadt
Brewery in Münnerstadt

KLOSTER PILS — gold, nice malt and hop nose; malty flavor has hops in back; dry malt and hop aftertaste has a very dry ending with lots of hops; gravity 11 P, 4.7% abv. [B, 56]

KLOSTER URSTOFF SPEZIAL MÄRZEN — amber-brown, lovely malt nose, dry malt flavor, big body; aftertaste is mostly dry malt with an off-dry malt backing, but it does have a bright hoppy ending; gravity 13.6 P, 5.4% abv. [B, 50]

Notes

Privatbrauerei Burgerbräu Naila (Wohns)
Brewery in Naila

WOHN HELLER BOCK — gold, lovely fruity malt and hop aroma, sweet malt and flowery hop taste; touch of alcohol gives it warmth; very smooth silky brew with a long complex aftertaste; gravity 16 P, 7.1% abv. [BK, 89]

WOHN PILSNER — gold, mild hop nose; flavor is good hops and malt; medium body, creamy mouthfeel, light dry hop aftertaste; gravity 11 P, 4.9% abv. [B, 65]

WOHN ALT NAILAER DUNKEL — deep amber, hint of toasted malt in the aroma, light toasted malt flavor, medium body, light dry malt finish and aftertaste; gravity 11 P, 4.8% abv. [B, 43]

WOHN FESTBIER — gold, complex malt nose, rich complex malt flavor, big body, dry malt finish and aftertaste; very tasty and shows some alcohol; gravity 13 P, 5.6% abv. [B, 78]

WOHN MÄRZEN — deep gold, malty aroma and flavor, spicy hops balance the sweetness of the malt, fairly dry malt and hop finish and aftertaste; more hops than most märzens and it really grows on you; gravity 13 P, 5.6% abv. [B, 69]

WOHN LAGER HELL — gold, light dry hop aroma and flavor, good malty background, light to medium body, dry hop finish and aftertaste; gravity 11 P, 4.7% abv. [B, 48]

Nordbräu Gmbh.
Brewery in Ingolstadt

POPPER MALT BEVERAGE — medium deep yellow-gold, grainy malt nose, light grain and hop palate, clean tasting, medium length aftertaste like the flavor. [NA, 40]

NORDBRÄU EDEL-WEISSES HEFE-WEIZEN — hazy gold, lightly spiced nose, smooth lightly spiced palate, medium body, light dry spiced malt aftertaste; 5.6% abv. [HW, 73]

NORDBRÄU PILS — bright gold, pleasant hop and malt aroma and flavor, balanced, good body, dry hop finish and aftertaste, a very bright tasting refreshing brew; 5.2% abv. [B, 50]

NORDBRÄU SCHANZER WEISS DUNKEL HEFE-WEIZEN — hazy brown, big head, malty aroma, malty lightly spiced flavor, medium body, dry malt finish and aftertaste; a faint trace of spiciness is still there at the end; 5.4% abv. [W, 53]

Privatbrauerei Oberäu Wochinger K.G.
Brewery in Holzkirchen

HOLZKIRCHNER OBERÄU PILS — gold, hop nose, big hop flavor, well backed with malt, highly carbonated, good body, long dry malt and hop aftertaste. [B, 46]

HOLZKIRCHNER OBERÄU EDEL EXPORT — very deep gold, faint malt nose, fairly big malt flavor, big body, long malt aftertaste. [B, 40]

HOCHLAND HELL — gold, malt-hop nose and flavor, off-dry malt finish, long drier malt aftertaste. [B, 40]

HOLZKIRCHNER OBERÄU URTYP HELL — gold, malt and light hop aroma; flavor is mostly big malt with some hops in back; dry malt-hop finish and long dry hop aftertaste; gravity 11.9 P, 5% abv. [B, 50]

HOLZKIRCHNER WEISSE DUNKEL — deep amber-brown, citrus lemony-grapefruit malt nose, creamy, light spicy clove and malt flavor, dry malt finish; long dry malt aftertaste shows little of the spiciness. [W, 52]

HOLZKIRCHNER WEISSE BAYERISCHES HEFEWEIZEN — hazy gold, faint lactic spice in behind a malt aroma, mild spicy flavor, medium body, long mild spice and malt aftertaste. [W, 53]

HOLZKIRCHNER LAURENZI EXPORT DUNKEL — good deep brown, roasted malt nose, rich roasted malt flavor, finishes dry, long dry malt aftertaste, medium body, good balance. [BK, 70]

HOLZKIRCHENER GOLD EXPORT HELL — gold, malt aroma and flavor, good body, medium dry malt aftertaste, ordinary beer; 5.5% abv. [B, 50]

Brauerei D. Oechsner
Brewery in Ochsenfurt

OECHSNER PREMIUM PILS —
deep gold, delightful hop nose,
zesty malt and hop flavor, mostly
hops but with great supporting
malt, medium body, excellent balance, rich and smooth, very refreshing; long dry hop aftertaste
retains the malt as well; this is a
perfect Pilsener; gravity 11 P,
4.9% abv. [B, 80]

OECHSNER WEISSBIER —
cloudy golden-amber, dry spicy
aroma and flavor, medium body, dry
spicy finish and aftertaste, more
hoppy than most wheat beers; gravity 12 P, 5.2% abv. [W, 49]

OECHSNER MÄRZEN
EXPORT — gold, big bright hop
and malt aroma, very tasty rich hop
and malt flavor; feels great in your
mouth; good body, rich and very
long hop and malt aftertaste, an ab-
solute treasure, and perhaps the best
Märzen in my experience. [B, 94]

OECHSNER HELLER BOCK —
deep gold, extremely complex
huge hop aroma, intense hop and
malt flavor, expert balance; a lip-
smacking big complex brew that
offers an abundance of everything
but doesn't assault the palate;
incredible brew, extremely long
fine aftertaste much like the flavor. [BK, 100]

Brauhaus Oettinger Gmbh.
Brewery in Oettingen

ORIGINAL OETTINGER
DUNKLES HEFEWEIZEN —
amber-brown, big head like a fass
(draft) beer, light lactic nose, good
malt-wheat-clove flavor, medium
dry malt aftertaste. [W, 60]

ORIGINAL OETTINGER
PILS — gold, big strong hop nose
and flavor, dry hop finish, very
long strong hop aftertaste; hops,
hops, and more hops. [B, 63]

ORIGINAL OETTINGER
EXPORT — gold, dry malt aroma,
sour dry hop finish and aftertaste,
highly carbonated. [B, 57]

ORIGINAL OETTINGER
HEFEWEISSSBIER — hazy
gold, faint clove and malt aroma,
pleasant spicy malt flavor, light
body, lightly flavored, dry malt aftertaste of medium duration. [W, 40]

OETTINGER HELL — gold,
stinky hop nose, light dry hop
flavor, medium body, dry malt
finish and aftertaste, a bit dull;
4.7% abv. [B, 40]

Privatbrauerei Karl Olpp
Brewery at Bad Urach

URACHER OLPP HELL — bright
gold, hop and grain nose and taste,
very drinkable and refreshing, medium body, short duration, not done
in a German style. [B, 56]

BAD URACH OLPP DOPPELBOCK — copper-brown, sweet malt nose, big malt and hop flavor, balanced, delicious, smooth, long malt and hop aftertaste, very likable; 8.1% alcohol not at all obtrusive. [BK, 95]

BAD URACH OLPP MAIBOCK — brilliant gold, big rich dry malt aroma, excellent balance, great dry malt and hop flavor, unbelievably smooth; alcohol not really noticeable although 8.1%, just seems to smooth it off even more; long dry malt and hop aftertaste, a big winner. [BK, 98]

Osnabrücker Aktien-Brauerei
Brewery in Osnabrück

WÖLFBRÄU IMPORTED GERMAN BEER — medium deep gold, dry hop and grainy malt nose with an off-dry malt component in the background, dry hop palate, some sour malt in the finish, brief dry and sour aftertaste. [B, 42]

Bierbrauerei Ott
Brewery in Bad Schussenried

OTT URTYP — gold, good hop nose, malt-hop flavor, medium dry hop finish and aftertaste, not interesting. [B, 50]

SCHUSSENRIEDER PILSENER — gold, hop nose, pleasant hop flavor, dry hop finish and aftertaste. [B, 55]

OTT SPEZIAL — gold, pleasant hop and malt nose, plenty of both in the flavor, good body, good tasting, long dry hop and malt aftertaste, good brew. [B, 70]

Brauerei Ottweiler
Brewery in Ottweil

KARLSKRONE EDEL PILS — gold, hop nose, dull malt flavor, long dry malt aftertaste. [B, 50]

Paderborner Brauerei Gmbh.
Brewery in Paderborn

PADERBORNER LIGHT BEER — pale gold, light malt nose, sour hop flavor, medium long dry hop aftertaste. [LO, 3]

PADERBORNER REGULAR BEER — deep gold, hop aroma, yeasty cereal and malt flavor, malt finish and short malt aftertaste. [B, 39]

PADERBORNER GERMAN PILSENER — deep bright gold, mild malt and hop nose, bright hop flavor, sour metallic finish; short dry hop aftertaste keeps some of the metallic nature of the finish. [B, 20]

Palmbräu Zorn Söhne
Brewery in Eppingen

PALMBRÄU PILSENER — gold, sour hop nose; bright hop flavor well balanced with malt, hop finish and very long dry hop aftertaste. [B, 56]

PALMBRÄU KRAICHGAU EXPORT — gold, faint malt nose and taste, short weak dry malt aftertaste. [B, 24]

PALMBRÄU SCHWARZER ZORNICKEL DUNKLES BOCKBIER — deep brown, tan head, roasted malt malt nose, rich balanced roasted malt flavor, big body, smooth, creamy and complex; ends dry stays rich; very long; slides down easily; 7% abv. [BK, 90]

PALMBRÄU ZORNICKEL STARKBIER — amber-gold, rich dry malt aroma; rich malt flavor has a touch of caramel but is mostly dry; some alcohol shows; dry malt finish and aftertaste; gravity 17 P, 7% abv. [BK, 94]

Parkbrauerei A.G.
Breweries in Pirmasens and Zweibrücken

PARKBRÄU EXPORT — pale gold, light but very good hop aroma well backed with malt, good body, creamy texture, bright tangy hop flavor and long dry hop aftertaste, good tasting refreshing brew. [B, 65]

PARKBRÄU PILS — medium gold, zesty hop and lightly toasted malt nose, well-balanced lively hop and toasted malt flavor, good body, lightly bitter dry hop finish and aftertaste, straightforward well-made brew. [B, 68]

PARKBRÄU PIRMINATOR — deep bright gold, toasted malt nose, big bright rich malt flavor, high alcohol, big body, huge but very well balanced; long dry hop aftertaste has plenty of malt backing. [BK, 84]

Patrizier-Bräu, A.G.
Brewery in Nürnberg

PATRIZIER EXPORT — deep amber, light hop nose, medium body, good malt flavor with the hops in back, long dry malt aftertaste. [B, 50]

PATRIZIER EDELHELL EXPORT — bright gold, nice complex hop aroma, big hop flavor up front; malt shows through in the finish; good balance, very good taste, complex; softens and gets better as you sip; pleasant long malt aftertaste. [B, 60]

PATRIZIER PILS — bright deep gold, toasted malt and hop aroma, light malt and hop palate; not exciting; brief malt aftertaste. [B, 32]

BAMBERGER HOFBRAU BEER — tawny-gold, slightly off-dry malt and grain aroma, grainy slightly toasted palate, very light body, virtually no finish or aftertaste. [B, 31]

PATRIZIER ZERO NON-ALCOHOLIC MALT BEVERAGE — amber-gold, grainy malt aroma like Grape-Nuts, light off-dry grainy flavor, brief dry malt aftertaste. [NA, 17]

PATRIZIER POCULATOR — pale brown, toasted malt aroma, intense dry malt flavor, big body; only medium duration but the feel of the strong flavor lasts in your mouth. [BK, 82]

PATRIZIER BRÄU KUPFESTUBE — medium deep brilliant amber, toasted malt aroma and flavor, some smoke in the backtaste and in the finish, long toasted smoky malt aftertaste, very dry and very drinkable. [B, 69]

PATRIZIER BEER — hazy golden amber, toasted malt nose, low carbonation; huge malty flavor needs more hops and/or carbonation for balance, still it is pleasant; good body; finishes like it starts; short malty aftertaste. [B, 34]

Paulaner Salvator Thomasbräu, A.G.
Brewery in Munich

PAULANER SALVATOR — deep brown, complex hop and malt aroma, huge fresh malt flavor, big body, very rich, clean and complex, extremely long dry malt aftertaste, noticeable alcohol (7.5%), a great double bock. [BK, 94]

PAULANER HELL URTYP EXPORT — gold, rich malt aroma, strong hop flavor, sour malt and dry hop finish and aftertaste, good long palate. [B, 58]

PAULANER ALTBAYERISCHES HEFE WEISSBIER — bright gold, clean wheat nose with only the faintest trace of yeast, bright perky dry spicy flavor, big body, fresh, long dry hop aftertaste; this one is best served with the twist of lemon. [W, 58]

PAULANER OKTOBERFEST BIER — bright deep gold, well-balanced hop and toasted malt aroma, complex toasted malt flavor, hop backing, good balance, good tasting, long pleasing rich and dry malt and hop aftertaste. [B, 74]

PAULANER URTYP 1634 — deep gold, toasted malt aroma, medium body; flavor is mostly malt but there are enough hops for good balance; slightly sour hop finish, medium long dry hop aftertaste; lacks the depth and character normally found with a Paulaner beer. [B, 40]

PAULANER MÜNCHENER MÄRZEN — copper-gold, toasted malt aroma, creamy texture, rich toasted malt flavor; hops are there but well in back; decent balance, good tasting flavor and finish, long refreshing dry malt aftertaste. [B, 64]

PAULANER ALT MÜNCHENER DUNKEL — deep reddish brown, very faint malt aroma; lovely malty flavor is a bit light; full bodied, light malt finish, lighter and brief malt aftertaste. [B, 47]

PAULANER FEST-BIER — bright gold, pleasant hop nose and flavor, good body, good feeling in the mouth, very long pleasant dry hop aftertaste. [B, 69]

PAULANER WIES'N-MÄRZEN — amber, delicate roasted malt aroma, pleasant toasted malt flavor; not much depth or character, but it is pleasant; dry malt finish and aftertaste. [W, 50]

PAULANER GERMAN PILS — yellow-gold, beautiful hop nose, delicious big hop flavor, long slightly sour dry hop aftertaste. [B, 34]

PAULANER MÜNCHENER UR-BOCK HELL — amber-gold, toasted malt and hop aroma, medium body, good tasting toasted malt and hop flavor, bright and hoppy up front, rich toasted malt at the finish, complex, balanced, long toasted malt aftertaste. [BK, 96]

PAULANER MAIBOCK — bright tawny-gold, light roasted malt nose, light body; flavor is mostly hops, but there is malt and carbonation showing as well; bitter and dry hop finish and aftertaste. [BK, 31]

PAULANER WEISSBIER ALTBAYERISCHES BRAUART — bright gold, foamy, clove-apple-wheat-citrus aroma; spicy-sweet palate is mostly cloves; malt finish and aftertaste shows little of the spiciness and is quite long. [W, 59]

PAULANER ORIGINAL MÜNCHENER HELL — pale

gold, smooth malt and hop nose; hefty flavor has both malt and hops aplenty; very straightforward hop character, good balance, dry hop finish and long aftertaste. [B, 57]

PAULANER HEFE-WEIZEN — hazy gold, big head, off-dry tangy spicy nose with a caramel background; bright zesty flavor has good balance between the spice and the sweetness of the malt; good body, refreshing, good length; the touch of cloves in the nose and taste is just right for the balance. [W, 43]

PAULANER MÜNCHEN NR. 1 EXTRA PREMIUM LAGER — bright gold, hop nose and flavor, good body, long dry hop aftertaste; an excellent well-balanced brew that is most satisfying. [B, 72]

PAULANER OKTOBERFEST — amber, big malt nose, big toasted malt flavor, smooth and dry, long dry hop aftertaste, an excellent beer with food. [B, 74]

PAULANER UR-BOCK HELL — tawny-gold, strong aroma with plenty of both hops and lightly toasted malt; high alcohol (6.8%) adds to a rising nose; flavor is big malt and light hops; huge malt aftertaste is on the dry side, certainly drier than the flavor. [BK, 62]

THOMAS BRÄU NON-ALCOHOLIC BREW — deep gold, appetizing hop aroma, light to medium body; pleasant malt and hop flavor is somewhat grainy but less so than most of the type; finishes bigger than it starts (more hop development); fairly long dry hop aftertaste, although light; contains less than 0.5% abv. [NA, 41]

Brauerei Emil Petersen Gmbh. & Co., K.G.
Brewery in Flensburg

FLENSBURGER PILSENER — pale gold, pleasant light fresh malt aroma; malt palate with a flash of bitter hops in the middle that stay into a long dry bitter hop aftertaste. [B, 69]

Dampfbierbrauerei Zwiesel — W. Pfeffer
Brewpub in Zwiesel

PFEFFERBRÄU ZWIESEL SPEZIAL PILSENER — gold, big hop nose, very aromatic, smooth malt flavor, finishes weakly, pleasant dry malt aftertaste. [B, 57]

PFFERBRÄU MÄRZENBIER — amber, hop and malt aroma, spicy hop and malt flavor (more herbal than spice actually), low carbonation, dry spicy finish and aftertaste. [B, 52]

Brauerei Pinkus Müller
Brewery in Münster

PINKUS WEIZEN — pale gold, faint wheat nose, clean wheat flavor, brief citrus finish; light wheat-malt aftertaste has little duration; good balance, very pleasant drinking beer. [W, 65]

PINKUS PILS — bright gold, pleasant hop aroma; good hop flavor has plenty of malt and carbonation in back; highly hopped finish and long aftertaste. [B, 26]

PINKUS MALZ BIER — dark brown, roasted malt aroma, light body, off-dry roasted malt flavor, brief sweet malt finish, short malt aftertaste, nonalcoholic. [MB, 7]

PINKUS ALT — deep tawny-gold, strong hop and roasted malt flavor with an acidic background, medium body, a high acid and very malty brew. [A, 12]

PINKUS HOME BREW UR PILS — gold, good but austere nose, good body, refreshing and pleasant well-hopped flavor, very drinkable, slightly bitter dry hop aftertaste. [B, 73]

Brauerei Plank Gmbh.
Brewery in Wiefelsdorf

JURA WEISSE DUNKLES HEFE-WEIZEN — cloudy brown; dry malty nose has a touch of spice; dry spicy malt flavor is smooth and mellow; medium body, dry malt aftertaste; 5% abv. [W, 80]

JURA WEIZEN MIT SEINER HEFE — gold, beautiful spicy aroma, smooth refreshing tasty spicy malt flavor, medium body; light spicy aftertaste is medium long; 5% abv. [W, 67]

Notes

Brauerei Pöllinger
Brewery in Pfeffenhausen

PÖLLINGER EXPORT — gold, toasted malt aroma and flavor, medium body, dry malt finish and aftertaste, a bit dull overall; gravity 12 P, 5.2% abv. [B, 45]

PÖLLINGER WEIZENPERLE — hazy gold, big head, light spicy nose, big spicy flavor, medium body, long spicy dry aftertaste; gravity 12 P, 5.5% abv. [W, 70]

PÖLLINGER HELL — gold, malt aroma and taste, light to medium body, some sourness in finish and aftertaste; gravity 11 P, 4.9% abv. [B, 50]

Postbrauerei Karl Meyer
Brewery in Nesselwang with hotel and restaurant

DER POSTILLION HEFE-WEIZEN — cloudy brown, malty aroma, very faint spicy malt flavor, very pleasant, medium body; spiciness is best at the finish; short dry malt aftertaste; 5.25% abv. [W, 57]

POSTBRAUEREI EDEL EXPORT — bright gold, light hop nose, pleasant hop and malt flavor, tasty and drinkable, medium body, dry hop finish and aftertaste; 5% abv. [B, 64]

POSTBRAUEREI LAGER HELL — gold, hop nose, dry hop flavor with good malt support, medium body, dry hop finish and aftertaste, medium length, pleasant but ordinary; 4.5% abv. [B, 56]

POSTBRAUEREI EDEL PILSENER — brilliant gold, hop nose, big malt and hop taste, good body, long dry malt and hop aftertaste, very long and very nice ending; 4.8% abv. [B, 61]

POSTWIRT'S DUNKEL — brown, tight head, malt nose, quite dry malt flavor, long dry malt finish and aftertaste; 5.25% abv. [B, 69]

POSTBRAUEREI URBRAU HELL — gold, big head, pleasant hop and malt aroma, balanced hop and malt flavor, good body, good taste; medium to dry malt and hop aftertaste is long; 4.75% abv. [B, 65]

POSTBRAUEREI POSTHORN GOLD — gold, big head, hop nose; hop flavor has big malt support; big body, very good balance, finishes with plenty of both hops and malt, long complex well-balanced aftertaste; 5.25% abv. [B, 90]

POSTBRAUEREI KIRCHWEIHBIER — clear deep gold, hop nose; flavor is mostly rich malt but there is hop backing; pleasant taste, big body, dry hop finish and aftertaste; gravity 13 P, 5.45% abv. [B, 71]

POSTBRAUEREI TRADITIONSBOCK — deep gold, huge malt nose, very good tasting malt flavor with lots of caramel, very big bodied, rich dry caramel malt finish and aftertaste, long and tasty, a great malty bock; gravity 16 P, 6.4% abv. [BK, 96]

Privatbrauereigasthof Prässlbräu
Brewery-Gasthof in Adlersberg

PRÖSSLBRÄU ADLERSBERG PALMATOR — dark reddish-brown; chocolate malt nose is smooth; a little smoky and faintly buttery, very rich chocolate malt flavor, extremely rich yet dry, very complex, big body, long dry roasted malt aftertaste; 6.3% alcohol is absorbed easily by the strength of the flavor and not even noticeable; this is a great beer. [BK, 97]

PRÖSSLBRÄU ADLERSBERG VOLLBIER DUNKEL — deep red-brown, malt nose, very smooth rich dry malt flavor, good body, long dry malt aftertaste. [B, 89]

PRÖSSLBRÄU ADLERSBERG KLOSTER-PILS — gold, pleasant strong hop nose, big hop flavor, long dry hop aftertaste. [B, 60]

Püls-Bräu
Brewery in Weismain

PÜLS-BRÄU KRONE PILS — gold, big hop nose, zesty malt and hop flavor; as you sip it the hops gradually take a more and more prominent position on the palate; big body, long dry hop aftertaste. [B, 55]

PÜLS-BRÄU SPEZIAL — gold, malty nose, light dry hop taste, medium body, dry hop finish and aftertaste; gravity 13 P, 5.4% abv. [B, 50]

ABT KNAUER BOCK — gold, malt and alcohol aroma; huge flavor shows plenty of both hops and malt; big body; dry hop and alcohol aftertaste is long; 7.5% abv. [BK, 88]

PÜLS-BRÄU ALTFRÄNKISCHER KELLERTRUNK — deep amber, low head, very malty aroma, big toasted malt flavor, very tasty, good body, malt finish; malt aftertaste starts out sweet but dries by the end; gravity 12 P, 5.2% abv. [B, 71]

Quenzer-Bräu Gmbh.
Brewery in Bad Urach

QUENZER SPEZIAL EXPORT — tawny-gold, beautiful hop nose, smooth malt flavor with a mild hop finish, long dry hop aftertaste. [B, 61]

Radeberger Exportbrauerei
Brewery in Berlin

RADEBERGER PILSENER — bright gold, medium hop nose with some malt in back, bright hop flavor, finish, and aftertaste; fairly long but lacks complexity. [B, 31]

RADEBERGER GERMAN PILSENER — tawny-gold, aromatic ester and soapy nose, hop flavor up front, soapy malt finish, good body, long dry malt and hop aftertaste. [B, 31]

LANDSKRON PILS — pale yellow, light sour hop nose, hop flavor, sour hop finish, medium long dry and slightly sour hop aftertaste; so-so balance as there is little malt showing. [B, 26]

Rauchenfels Steinbrauerei
Brewery in Neustadt

RAUCHENFELS STEINBIERE STONE BREWED BEER — tea color, smoky malt aroma, light body, pleasant smoky malt flavor, good tasting, fine finish, fairly long smoked malt aftertaste. [W, 71]

Reichelbrauerei Kulmbach
Brewery in Kulmbach

KULMBACHER REICHELBRÄU HELL EXPORT DE LUXE — bright tawny-gold; big hop nose has some malt in back; big hop flavor; malt shows well in the finish and stays through the long dry aftertaste. [B, 51]

KULMBACHER REICHELBRÄU FRANKISCHES URBIER — brilliant amber, pleasant toasted malt and hop nose, big body; big malt flavor has a coffee-like background, good balance, long dry malt and hop aftertaste. [B, 69]

KULMBACHER REICHELBRÄU EDELHERB PILS — bright deep gold, lovely flowery hop nose, bright hop palate, good balance and complexity, malt finish, medium body, long dry hop and malt aftertaste. [B, 75]

Notes

KULMBACHER REICHELBRÄU BAVARIAN DARK BEER — deep amber-brown, complex toasted malt aroma, medium body, lightly flavored dry toasted malt and hop taste, long dry malt aftertaste. [B, 50]

KULMBACHER REICHELBRÄU EISBOCK 24 — deep brown, rich complex off-dry aromatic malt nose; body so huge it seems thick; very rich heavy malt flavor, like a smooth malt tonic; very complex malt flavors, high alcohol, long concentrated malt aftertaste, an extraordinary beer. [BK, 89]

KULMBACHER REICHELBRÄU PRINZENTRUNK FESTBIER — gold, hardly any aroma at all; flavor is light malt but there is too little of it; good body, dry malt finish and aftertaste, no length, no intensity; gravity 13.2 P, 5.5% abv. [B, 50]

Privatbrauerei Heinrich Reissdorf
Brewery in Köln

REISSDORF KÖLSCH — medium to deep gold, faint but very clean malt aroma; palate is zesty hops in front, malt in middle and finish; good balance, long dry malt and hop aftertaste, a very good Kölsch. [K, 73]

Bierbrauerei Wilhelm Remmer
Brewery in Bremen

BREMER DOM BRÄU — pale yellow, vegetal malt nose, strong hop palate, long dry hop aftertaste. [B, 16]

Klosterbrauerei Reutberg
Kloster Brewery in Sachsenkam

REUTBERGER KLOSTER-WEISSE — cloudy gold, big head, spicy aroma and flavor, big body; spicy aftertaste has a "hot" hoppy background in the throat as you swallow; gravity 11 P, 4.9% abv. [W, 56]

REUTBERGER EXPORT HELL — gold, hop aroma, malt flavor; hops in the nose of this beer are like that hotness in the throat in the beer above; medium body, dry malt and hop aftertaste; gravity 12 P, 5.1% abv. [B, 47]

REUTBERGER EXPORT DUNKEL — amber-brown, malt and hop aroma; curious house flavor (as mentioned in the brews above) is in the back of the palate and clashes with the sweetness of the malt; otherwise an off-dry malt flavor with a drier malt aftertaste; gravity 12 P, 5.2% abv. [B, 38]

Rhanerbräu
Brewery in Rhan b. Rötz (between Cham and Schönthal)

RHANER EXPORT HELL — gold, hop nose, malt flavor, good balance and body, off-dry malt finish and aftertaste. [B, 65]

Riedenburger Brauhaus Michael Krieger K.G.
Brewery in Riedenburg

RIEDENBURGER WEIZEN — clear amber-gold, light spicy malt nose, clean creamy spicy malt flavor, dry malt finish, faintly spicy long malt aftertaste. [W, 65]

REIDENBURGER WEISSE EXPORT — hazy gold, lightly spiced malt aroma, light bright spicy flavor with a touch of cloves, good body, refreshing and drinkable, long lightly spiced dry malt aftertaste; gravity 12 P, 5.2% abv. [W, 63]

Brauerei Riegeler
Brewery in Riegel/ Kaiserstuhl

RIEGELER FELSEN PILS — gold, big hop nose and taste, good body, good flavor; hop finish and long dry hop aftertaste has a spiciness that would appear to be Tettnanger hops. [B, 90]

RIEGELER SPEZIAL EXPORT — gold, hop and malt nose, malt flavor, short dry malt aftertaste. [B, 67]

Privatbrauerei Johann Röck K.G.
Brewery in Nesselwang

BÄREN PILS — gold, hop aroma, mild dry malt-hop flavor, good body, very good balance, refreshing, complex, long dry hop aftertaste, a superb Pils. [B, 87]

BÄREN GOLD — deep gold, light malt nose and flavor, well balanced, dry hop finish and long aftertaste, medium to good body, balanced and smooth, a delicate brew with great finesse. [B, 67]

BÄREN BRÄU ALTBAYRISCH DUNKEL — brown, nice malt aroma, dry rich clean malt flavor, medium long dry malt aftertaste. [B, 72]

BÄREN BRÄU ALPEN BOCK — dark amber-brown; rich concentrated malt nose has great complexity and earthiness; extremely big rich roasted malt flavor; has a nut-like quality; quite complex; long dry roasted malt aftertaste continues the nutty taste; a most satisfying bock and one of the best found. [BK, 98]

BÄREN WEIZEN HEFETRUB — hazy gold, clean zesty nose, nice mild malt taste, very drinkable, medium body, good balance; dies at the finish; very little aftertaste. [W, 60]

Privatbrauerei Röhrl
Brewery in Frontenhausen

RÖHRL EXPORT BEER — gold, hop nose, hop flavor with plenty of malt, long bright malt aftertaste, balanced and bright, good tasting brew. [B, 60]

RÖHRL VILSTALER DUNKLES HEFE-WEIZEN — deep brown, very clear with all the yeast in the bottom, big malt nose, delicate spicy malt flavor, smooth and tasty, rich malt finish, long dry malt aftertaste, an excellent hefe-weizen. [W, 89]

RÖHRL SYMPATHIKUS WEIZENDOPPELBOCK MIT SEINE HEFE — hazy amber, tight long-lasting head, big concentrated malt flavor with a faint touch of spiciness, big body; complex long aftertaste shows malt, hops, spice, and alcohol; 7% abv. [BK, 94]

Brauerei Gebr. Röhrl
Brewery in Straubing

STRAUBINGER WEISSE BERNSTEIN-WEIZEN — dark hazy amber, mild spicy nose, light spice flavor, good body, lightly spiced and caramel finish; short aftertaste is more malty than spicy; pleasant and good tasting; gravity 12.8 P, 5.3% abv. [W, 50]

Rother Bräu
Brewery in Roth

RÖTHER BRÄU URTRUNK — gold with particulate matter in solution, big head, faintly herbal malt nose, dry hop flavor, medium body, dry hop finish and aftertaste; 4.7% abv. [B, 50]

Notes

Badische Staatsbrauerei Rothaus A.G.
Brewery at Rothaus, Hochschwarzwald

ROTHAUS DUNKEL EXPORT — deep amber, roasted malt aroma and big roasted malt flavor, not complex but very tasty, good body; tastes better as you continue to drink it; touch of sour malt at the finish, long malt aftertaste. [B, 80]

ROTHAUS MÄRZEN — bright gold, medium rich malt nose, extremely smooth pleasant malt flavor, some complexity, very drinkable, long malt aftertaste. [B, 86]

ROTHAUS PILS TANNEN ZÄPFLE — brilliant yellow-gold; big hop nose has plenty of malt in back; finely carbonated, good body, smooth dry malt flavor, creamy texture, hop finish, long dry hop aftertaste. [B, 82]

STAATSBRAUEREI ROTHAUS PILS — gold, pleasant malt nose, good malt flavor, very tasty, good body, fine balance, very clean and refreshing, long dry malt aftertaste. [B, 70]

Rotochsen Brauereigasthof Hermann Veit
Brewery Gasthof in Ellwangen

ROTOCHSEN EDEL EXPORT — deep gold, malt nose; smooth malt flavor has dry hops in back; good balance, long dry hop aftertaste. [B, 61]

ROTOCHSEN STIFTSHERREN PILS — pale gold, light dry hop aroma, dry hoppy flavor, long dry hop aftertaste, good body, good balance, very good with food. [B, 67]

ELLWANGER ROTOCHSEN TRADITIONSBOCK — deep gold, rich toasted malt nose, big rich creamy toasted malt flavor, big body, strong and long dry malt aftertaste, a real lip smacker; high alcohol (6.6%) is not obtrusive, actually it is just another component of the rich complex flavor. [BK, 95]

ELLWANGER ROTOCHSEN KRISTALL-WEIZEN — clear gold, large bubble head; aroma is malt and faint cloves; lightly spiced malt flavor, medium body; aftertaste is a continuation of the flavor. [W, 55]

ELLWANGER ROTOCHSEN HEFE-WEIZEN — slightly hazy gold, light clove and malt nose, big well-spiced flavor, big body, long dry malt aftertaste with the cloves way in back. [W, 61]

ELLWANGER ROTOCHSEN DUNKLES HEFE-WEIZEN — hazy amber, big spicy clove and malt nose and taste, creamy texture, very complex, good body; complexity increases across the palate; the aftertaste is dry malt and the cloves stay all the way through. [W, 77]

Pflugbrauerei Rottweil
Brewery in Rottweil

SCHWARZWÄLDER URTYP-EXPORT — gold, very faint malt nose, faint malt flavor, brief malt aftertaste. [B, 24]

Privatbrauerei W. Rummel
Brewery in Darmstadt

DARMSTÄDTER UR BOCK DOPPELBOCK — amber, light malt nose, good malt flavor, finely carbonated; there is some complexity contributed by background hops; good body; hops show best in the finish and aftertaste; very well balanced, long long dry hop and malt aftertaste. [BK, 85]

DARMSTÄDTER PILSNER — brilliant gold, dense head, beautiful clean hop nose; bright hop flavor has good malt support; balanced, creamy, long dry hop aftertaste. Tasted on draft. [B, 77]

Privatbrauerei W. Rummel Gmbh. & Co., K.G.
Brewery in Darmstadt

DARMSTÄDTER PILSNER — brilliant gold, dense head, beautiful clean hop nose; bright hop flavor has good malt support; balanced, creamy, long dry hop aftertaste. Tasted on draft. [B, 77]

DARMSTÄDTER WEISSBIER KRISTALLKLAR — brilliant clear deep gold, spicy nose; good tasting flavor has malt and spice; pleasant and refreshing; slight sweetness gradually replaces the spiciness in the aftertaste; 4.8% abv. [W, 72]

DARMSTÄDTER WEISSBIER HEFE-HELL — very slightly hazy-gold, light spicy nose, bright spicy malt taste, pleasant and refreshing, smooth and balanced; like the kristallklar, but without the sweetness in the aftertaste; 4.8% abv. [W, 74]

DARMSTÄDTER MÄRZEN DUNKEL — amber, malt aroma and flavor; taste is a very nice malt, a bit toasted and caramelized; big body, dry caramelized malt finish and aftertaste; 5.6% abv. [B, 80]

Brauerei Franz Josef Sailer
Brewery in Marktoberdorf

SAILER PILS — pale gold, complex hop and toasted malt nose, light body, toasted malt front palate, tangy hop finish, long dry hop aftertaste. [B, 40]

SAILER WEISSE WITH YEAST — pale cloudy amber, huge head, good grainy nose; gives the sense of being smoky but isn't; sharp grainy flavor, fairly long grainy aftertaste with a bit of spice in back. [W, 46]

SAILER WEISSE — pale golden amber, foamy; lovely aroma is grainy; slightly sweet and piquant, complex smoky-malty flavor, slightly sweet malt finish; balance is good; long off-dry malt aftertaste, pleasant and refreshing. [W, 63]

OBERDORFER WEISSE WITH YEAST — hazy gold, foamy, wheat nose, creamy texture, frothy, pleasant and refreshing dry barley malt and wheat palate, grainy finish and aftertaste, good balance, a finely made wheat beer. [W, 60]

OBERDORFER DUNKLES HEFEWEIZENBIER — hazy deep amber, big head, light lactic and fruity wheat-malt aroma, good body; good complex flavor of cloves, wheat, malt, and hops; rich and satisfying, long pleasant malt aftertaste. [W, 64]

OBERDORFER WEISSE — brilliant gold, foamy, spicy-lactic nose; palate has only the faintest trace of lactic acid and is instead quite malty; pleasant and refreshing, very long malt aftertaste; has good zest. [W, 60]

CHRISTKINDLBIER WEIHNACHTEN 1987 — deep gold, huge malt nose with some lactic spice, lactic acid and malt palate; flavor has an aromatic quality; very long sour hop and lactic malt aftertaste; interesting but there are better weizens. [W, 16]

FRANZ JOSEPH JUBELBIER — deep gold, dense head, charcoal nose; smoky-charcoal malt and lactic acid taste, acid eases toward the finish; long weizen aftertaste, a kristallklar. [B, 25]

URGÄUER WEIZEN — gold, spicy nose, bright clove spice and malt nose and flavor; fades a bit at the finish; very refreshing, medium dry wheat malt aftertaste. [W, 64]

ALTENMUNSTER BRAUER BIER PREMIUM BAVARIAN BEER — pale gold, big hop nose, dry hop palate with some toasted malt in back, good flavor, good body, dry hop finish and long dry hop aftertaste. [B, 62]

RAUCHENFELS STEINBRAU — amber, interesting complex hop and malt aroma, smooth peppery malt flavor, medium body; has great style; appetizing and attractive, smooth and balanced, long faintly off-dry malt aftertaste. [B, 68]

RAUCHENFELS STEINWEISS — red-amber, light smooth smoky nose like a fine smoked cheese; big smoky flavor starts out boldly, but diminishes in its smokiness as it crosses the palate and finishes dry and lightly smoked; very dry aftertaste has only a little smoke; a very interesting smoked dunkel hefe-weizen; very attractive. [W, 71]

Schlossbrauerei zu Sandersdorf
Brewery in Sandersdorf

BARON DE BASSUS DUNKLES — deep amber-brown, rich toasty nose, big malty flavor, medium body, dry molasses-like finish and aftertaste, very long and good; 4.9% abv. [B, 77]

Sandlerbrauerei
Brewery in Kulmbach

KULMBACHER SANDLERBRÄU PILS — pale gold, toasted malt aroma, mild hop flavor, sour malt finish and long aftertaste. [B, 24]

Privatbrauerei Rudolf Schäff / Schäffbräu
Brewery in Treuchtlingen

ALTMÜHLTALER PILSENER — pale gold, big hop nose, hefty body, strong hop and malt flavor; dry hop aftertaste has a sourness that causes it to end poorly. [B, 47]

ALTMÜHLTALER SCHLOSSBRAUEREI URTYP HELL — gold, big strong hop nose, dull hop flavor, off-dry soft dry hop aftertaste. [B, 29]

SCHÄFF FEUERFEST EDEL BIER — tawny port color, beautiful roasted malt aroma, extremely heavy body, almost syrupy, intense roasted smoked malt flavor, sweet sipping beer, very long smoky roasted malt aftertaste, no carbonation, a very long-lived beer, almost impervious to mishandling. [B, 65]

SCHÄFF PILSENER — pale yellow-gold, light sour hop aroma, highly carbonated; palate starts off as strong hops, softens toward middle where some malt joins in to set the balance; malt finish, long sour malt and hop aftertaste. [B, 46]

SCHÄFFBIER — medium pale yellow-gold, lovely well-hopped aroma with a touch of roasted malt, good body; complex flavor is mostly hops; malt finish, good balance, long pleasant malt and hop aftertaste. [B, 63]

Brauerei Schaffer
Brewery in Schnaittach/Bayern

SCHAFFER BOCK BIER — deep gold; big malt and hop aroma shows some alcohol; big malty flavor, quite smooth and balanced, touch of alcohol for warmth; long tasty aftertaste has both malt and hops. [BK, 79]

Privatbrauerei Schaller-Bräu
Brewery in Bonstetten

SCHALLER HEFE-WEIZEN DUNKEL — hazy brown, light spicy nose, light spicy malt flavor, a bit off-dry; tastes good; good body, long off-dry spicy malt aftertaste; gravity 12.8 P, 5.2% abv. [W, 71]

SCHALLER HEFE-WEIZEN HELL — hazy gold, big head, light spicy nose, bright spicy taste, dry spicy aftertaste, good body, good length, a pleasant bright tasting brew; gravity 12.7 P, 5.1% abv. [W, 69]

 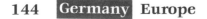

Privatbrauerei Scheidmantel
Brewery in Coburg

SCHEIDMANTEL COBURG PILS — pretty gold, malty-hop nose, big flavor with plenty of malt and hops, creamy mouthfeel, smooth and drinkable, dry malt and hop finish and aftertaste; gravity 11 P, 5.1% abv. As found in Germany. [B, 71]

SCHEIDMANTEL CORTENDORFER DUNKEL — hazy amber-brown, malt aroma and flavor, touch of sour vegetable in back, dull dry malt finish and aftertaste. [B, 40]

COBURG PILS — pale gold, grainy malt aroma and flavor, medium body, not bright but refreshing, dry hop finish and aftertaste. As found in the U.S.A. [B, 56]

SILBER BOCK — gold, pure malt aroma; palate starts out as grainy malt, goes to sweet malt in the middle, stays sweet into a long malty aftertaste; mostly malt and alcohol with hops coming in lightly at the finish; a good very malty sipping beer. [BK, 83]

SCHEIDMANTEL HEFE-WEISSE — hazy gold, yeasty-spicy-lactic aroma; flavor is overly lactic and lacks the banana-clove taste expected of a hefeweizen; finishes sour and is not likable. [W, 16]

Privatbrauerei Scherdel
Brewery in Hof

SCHERDEL PILSNER PREMIUM — gold, complex malt and hop nose, big complex flavor like the aroma, spruce or pine in the finish, long dry malt aftertaste. [B, 41]

Klosterbrauerei Scheyern
Brewery at Scheyern

KLOSTERBRAUEREI SCHEYERN DUNKLER KLOSTERBOCK — deep amber-brown, light dry malt aroma, dry malt flavor, long pleasant off-dry malt aftertaste which gets a bit sweeter at the end; medium duration, very drinkable. [BK, 67]

KLOSTERBRAUEREI SCHEYERN KLOSTER-DOPPELBOCK DUNKEL — deep brown, somewhat stinky-earthy roasted malt aroma, big dry roasted malt flavor, extremely rich and yet surprisingly dry, lush yet smooth, very long dry malt aftertaste; has great subtlety; a marvelous brew despite the offish start; 7.3% alcohol is barely noticeable. [BK, 92]

KLOSTERBRAUEREI SCHEYERN KLOSTER-GOLD — gold, fragrant hop nose, sweet hop flavor, good body, fair balance, long dry hop aftertaste. [B, 53]

Notes

KLOSTERBRAUEREI
SCHEYERN KLOSTER-WEISSE
HELL — hazy gold, big head,
grapefruit-like aroma, vegetal-
grapefruit flavor, long dry malt
aftertaste. [W, 27]

KLOSTERBRAUEREI
SCHEYERN KLOSTER-WEISSE
DUNKEL — hazy brown; nose of
cloves, candy, and fruit; strong
spicy-candy flavor, very assertive;
flavor carries into the long aftertaste. [W, 40]

Brauerei Schimpfle
Brewery in Gessertshausen

LINDENBRÄU EXPORT — pale
gold, toasted malt nose, very little
head, pleasant toasted malt flavor,
smooth and delicious; medium
long dry malt aftertaste has a bit
of the toastiness; good body, very
pleasant with a nice mouthfeel;
not complex but is wholesome and
malty; 5.5% abv. [B, 72]

Brauhaus Schinner
Brewery in Bayreuth

SCHINNER MEISTERSINGER
KLASSIC PILS — gold, malt and
hop aroma and flavor, balanced,
light body; dry hop finish and aftertaste has some malt too; gravity
11 P, 4.8% abv. [B, 51]

SCHINNER ALTFRANKEN
DUNKEL BRAUNBIER — amber,
big head, big clean malty nose,
clean crisp malt flavor, just the
slightest bit sweet, simple not complex, tasty, very nice of type, very
drinkable, light body; malty aftertaste is long and clean; gravity 11 P,
4.8% abv. [B, 63]

Schlossbrauerei am Hallertau
Brewery in Hallertau

BLACK JACK BAYERNS PRE-
MIUM PILSENER — gold, hop
nose, bright hop taste, medium
body, bright dry hop aftertaste; has
length; gravity 11.9 P, 4.9% abv.
[B, 60]

Schlossbräu / Private Spezialbierbrauerei Helmut & Sophia Prinzing
Brewery in Mickhausen

SCHLOSSBRÄU HELL — gold,
short-lived head, big hop aroma,
malt and hop flavor, dry hop finish, long slightly vegetal malt aftertaste; 4.8% abv. [B, 42]

SCHLOSSBRÄU HEFE-
WEISSBIER — hazy gold;
malty aroma has a faint spicy
background; lightly spiced dry
malt flavor, medium to light
body; dry malt aftertaste has a
touch of spice; gravity 11 P, 4.9%
abv. [W, 60]

SCHLOSSBRÄU PRIVAT EX-
PORT DUNKEL — brown, dry
malty roasty aroma and flavor,
medium body, dry malt finish and
aftertaste; 4.5% abv. [B, 60]

SCHLOSSBRÄU MÄRZEN —
bright deep gold, dry malt aroma
and very dry malt flavor, medium
to good body, extremely dry malt
aftertaste; 5.6% abv. [B, 60]

SCHLOSSBRÄU FESTBIER —
gold, bright hop and malt nose;
malty flavor has the hops coming in
at the finish; dry malt and hop aftertaste has good length; medium
body; pleasant, tasty, and balanced;
5.2% abv. [B, 59]

SCHLOSSBRÄU URHELL —
gold; dry malt nose has a dank
background; dry malt flavor, good
body, dry malt finish and aftertaste;
4.9% abv. [B, 46]

Schloss Bräu
Brewery in Stamsried

HERZOG PILSENER — gold,
hop nose with a meaty background, big malt and hop flavor,
finishes weakly, medium length
dry hop aftertaste. [B, 37]

Brauerei Schlässer
Brewery in Dusseldorf

SCHLÖSSER ALT — deep brownish amber, bright hoppy nose; dry hop flavor has an ale-like tang; dry hop aftertaste is long and keeps the tangy ale background throughout. [A, 60]

Privatbrauerei Gasthof Schmid / Brauerei Biberach
Brewery-Gasthof in Biberach-Roggenburg

BIBERACHER UR-DUNKEL — dark brown, lovely malt nose, light body, smooth malt flavor, pleasant dry malt aftertaste. [B, 70]

BIBERACHER MÄRZEN — deep gold, hop nose with a faint yeasty-bready nature (but pleasantly so), good malt and hop flavor, balanced, rich tasting, good body, dry malt-hop finish and aftertaste, very good with German country wursts and pâtés. Draft version at the Gasthof. [B, 91]

BIBERACHER MÄRZEN — amber, light malt aroma and flavor, very little hops, low carbonation, pleasant and smooth, light short malt aftertaste. Bottled version. [B, 91]

Privatbrauerei Adolf Schmid
Brewery in Usterbach üb Augsburg, 8901

REISCHENAU GOLD HELLES EXPORT — gold, hop nose, malt flavor with fine hops in back; finish and long aftertaste are more malt than hops; good body, good balance, a fine beer. [B, 70]

USTERBACHER PILSNER — gold, hop nose, big hop flavor with plenty of support from the malt, dry hop finish, very well balanced, long dry malt and hop aftertaste. [B, 58]

USTERBACHER BAYERISCH HEFE-WEIZEN — cloudy gold, big spicy malt nose and taste, plenty of cloves and cinnamon; good finish like the flavor leading into a long dry malt and hop aftertaste with a spicy background. [W, 67]

USTERBACH URHELL — bright gold, hop nose, malt and hop flavor, medium body, dry hop finish and aftertaste with a malty sweetness in back; 4.9% abv. [B, 49]

USTERBACH DUNKLE WEISSE — hazy deep amber; nose is very faintly spiced; smooth spicy rich flavor, medium body, off-dry spicy malt finish, aftertaste like the finish but a tad drier; 5.3% abv. [W, 80]

USTERBACH EDEL EXPORT — pale gold, malt aroma and flavor of off-dry malt, pleasant slightly sweet malt finish and aftertaste; hops come in late but stay in back; good body, good length; gravity 12.6 P, 5.5% abv. [B, 52]

Privatbrauerei Schmitt
Brewery in Schesslitz

SCHMITT-BRÄU EDEL
PILS — gold, low carbonation, bright hop aroma and flavor, medium body, dry hop finish and aftertaste; 5.1% abv. [B, 47]

SCHMITT-BRÄU JURA
HELL — gold, dry malt aroma and taste, medium body, dry malt finish and aftertaste; there are some hops, and they are most noticeable in the aftertaste; 5.3% abv. [B, 45]

Privatbrauerei Schmucker
Brewery at Mossautal

SCHMUCKER DOPPEL-BOCK
DUNKEL — deep amber-brown, rich dry malt nose, perfect balance, delicious dry roast malt palate, very long with great depth of flavor, excellent double bock. [BK, 92]

SCHMUCKER HEFE-
WEIZEN — hazy gold, big tight head, complex spicy cinnamon and clove, creamy big complex spicy flavor, good body, lots of spice throughout; marvelous aftertaste is long and like the main palate; 5% abv. [W, 90]

SCHMUCKER KRISTALL
WEIZEN — gold, faint malt nose, dry malt flavor, good body, short dull malt finish and aftertaste; 5% abv. [W, 39]

SCHMUCKER HEFE-WEIZEN
DUNKEL PREMIUM — hazy amber; aroma is more caramel than spice; big spicy palate is softened by the caramel; good body, dry malt finish, long dry malt aftertaste; 5% abv. [W, 53]

SCHMUCKER SCHWARZ BIER
PREMIUM — deep amber-brown, faint malt aroma, good big dry malt flavor, good body, dry malt finish and aftertaste; has a harsh edge in the end of the palate; 4.8% abv. [B, 67]

Privater Brauereigasthof Schneider
Brewery-Gasthof in Essing

JOS. SCHNEIDER MAIBOCK — deep gold, hop nose, big hop taste with the malt in back, dry hop finish, long dry hop aftertaste, really good clean and bright flavor, good body and balance, very enjoyable. [BK, 81]

JOS. SCHNEIDER MÄRZEN — pale amber, hop nose, big hop and malt flavor, finishes dry, long dry hop and malt aftertaste, excellent balance, good body, a very fine brew. [B, 80]

JOS. SCHNEIDER DUNKEL — brown, malt aroma, rich straightforward malt palate, dry malt finish and long dry malt aftertaste, good body and balance, well-made beer. [B, 77]

G. Schneider & Sohn K.G. / Brauerei Kelheim
Brewery in Munich

SCHNEIDER WEISSE HEFE-
WEIZENBIER — hazy amber, slight lactic nose but mostly a pleasant malt, mellow and smooth flavor, good balance; sour finish shows the lactic acid and spice promised by the nose; long faintly sour aftertaste. [W, 36]

AVENTIUS
WEIZENSTARKBIER — hazy deep copper color, huge dense head, delightful appetizing malt-wheat-lightly lactic nose, big off-dry malt and lactic acid/spicy flavor, high alcohol, frothy, big body, heavy flavor, extremely tasty and balanced, very long complex aftertaste like the flavor; a dandy weizenbier, perhaps the best I ever tasted from a bottle. [W, 90]

L. Schönberger Sohne
Brewery at Gross-Bieberau

SCHÖNBERGER FEST BOCK — deep amber-brown, big roasted malt aroma, complex rich malt flavor up front on the palate; pungent hops in back that show best in the finish; good balance, medium to long malt and hop aftertaste, a marvelous tasting brew. [B, 89]

SCHÖNBERGER UR-BOCK — copper-amber, huge roasted malt aroma and flavor; flavor is drier than the nose and has many subtle nuances; long complex malt aftertaste, 6% alcohol. Excellent brew. [BK, 92]

SCHÖNBERGER ODENWALDER LANDBIER — gold, hop nose; palate has more malt than hops but the balance is very good; good body; long dry malt aftertaste has hops showing well at the very end. [B, 63]

Schwannen-Brauerei A.G. & Co., K.G.
Brewery in Schwetzingen

SCHÖFFERHOFER WEIZEN — pale yellow-gold, dusty clove and malt aroma, sweet malt and clove flavor, good body, spicy malt finish and aftertaste drier than the flavor. [W, 50]

SCHÖFFERHOFER HEFEWEIZEN — hazy gold, bright spicy hop nose, zesty spicy hop and malt flavor, creamy and smooth, long dry spicy malt aftertaste. [W, 61]

Schwarzbrauerei Zusmarshausen
Brewery in Zusmarshausen

SCHWARZBRÄU FEINES HELLES — gold with particles, tight head, light hop nose, big hop flavor, medium body, dry hop finish and aftertaste; 4.9% abv. [B, 59]

SCHWARZBRÄU PILSENER — gold, hop nose, big hop flavor, good body and balance, very long good dry hop aftertaste. [B, 79]

SCHWARZBRÄU EXQUISIT SPEZIALBIER — gold, malt and hop nose, big malt flavor with a hop finish; dry hop aftertaste is very dry and very long; huge body, a big mouthful of flavor. [B, 81]

SCHWARZBRÄU DUNKLES EXPORT WEIZEN — hazy brown, head like a fass (draft) beer, clean spicy nose, very pleasant fruity-spicy flavor, nicely balanced, good body, long dry malt aftertaste. [W, 93]

Brauerei zum Schwarze Adler
Brewery in Wassertrüdlingen

SCHWARZE ADLER PRIVAT WEIZEN HEFE-WEIZEN — cloudy gold, faint sour hop and malt aroma, some soapiness in back, light spicy malt and hop flavor, light to medium body, short aftertaste like the flavor. [W, 40]

Notes

SCHWARZE ADLER PRIVAT PILS — gold, dull dry hop nose and taste, dry sour hop finish and aftertaste, medium body; 4.7% abv. [B, 47]

Privatbrauerei Schweiger
Brewery in Markt Schwaben bei München

SCHWEIGER HELLES EXPORT — gold, malt nose, malt flavor with good hop support, off-dry hop finish, good body, good balance; hop aftertaste is similar to finish but drier; fairly long. [B, 56]

SCHWEIGER SCHMANKERL WEISSE — very slightly hazy gold, faint spicy nose, bright clove flavor, finish, and aftertaste; short, but good while it lasts. [W, 57]

SCHWEIGER SPORT WEISSE LEICHTE WEISS — hazy gold, dull aroma dull lightly spice malt flavor, light body, dry malt aftertaste; 2.9% abv. [W, 29]

Brauhaus Schweinfurt
Brewery in Schweinfurt

SCHWEINFURTER FRANKEN GOLD EXPORT — gold, malt nose, lightly toasted malt and sour hop taste, medium to good body; off-dry malt finish and aftertaste shows little or no hop presence until the end and then they are on the sour side; long and mostly sweet; gravity 12 P, 5.4% abv. [B, 51]

SCHWEINFURTER WEISSBIER MIT HEFE — cloudy deep gold, faint spicy aroma, light spicy-malt flavor, mostly sweet, sweet spicy malt finish and aftertaste, pleasant, more fruity-citrus than spicy, medium body; gravity 12 P, 5.2% abv. [W, 47]

ALT SCHWEINFURTER DUNKEL — brown, caramel malt aroma, chocolate-caramel flavor, good body; dryness of malty aftertaste comes as a surprise considering the sweetness of the palate; gravity 12 P, 5.2% abv. [B, 77]

SCHWEINFURTER PILSNER — gold, hop nose, malt flavor, off-dry malt finish and aftertaste, sour hops at the very end, light body, medium duration; gravity 11 P, 5.1% abv. [B, 40]

Privatbrauerei Sester
Brewery in Köln

SESTER KÖLSCH REIN OBERGÄRIG HELL — yellow-gold, light hop nose, dry hop flavor, bitter hop finish, sour aftertaste. [K, 23]

Brauerei K. Silbernagel A.G.
Brewery in Bellheim

BELLHEIMER SILBER BOCK — gold, sweet malt and hop nose, malt palate with light hops, strong but not powerful, long medium dry malt aftertaste; stays very drinkable. [B, 67]

BELLHEIMER LORD — gold, big hop nose, dry hop flavor, medium body, dry hop finish and aftertaste, fair length; 4.9% abv. [B, 47]

BELLHEIMER DOPPEL-BOCK — dark brown, big malty nose; very rich malt flavor shows a lot of alcohol (7% abv); delicious rich malt aftertaste is on the sweet side. [BK, 94]

Schlossbrauerei Soldenau
Brewery in Soldenau

ORIGINAL ALT BAYERISCHE UR WEISSE — deep amber, big head, big aroma of malt with faint lactic-clove spice way in back, light piquant clove flavor, some soapiness in the finish, light body, dull soapy malt aftertaste. Bottled for Privatbrauerei Will, Motten. [W, 37]

SOLDENAUER SCHLOSS DUNKLES WEISSBIER — very slightly hazy amber-brown; aroma is mostly malt but there is some faint spicy clove in back; flavor is largely spicy malt; a dry malt finish and aftertaste; the spice is up front and doesn't leave; an interesting brew; 5% abv. [W, 39]

Spaten Franziskaner-Bräu KgaA
Brewery in Munich

SPATEN CLUB WEISS BIER — bright gold, big head; fresh clean fruity malt nose has only the faintest wheat component; very fresh slightly grainy flavor with a pleasant spicy tang, good balance; fairly short malt aftertaste and very little spicy-lactic character, but good and refreshing. [W, 70]

SPATEN OPTIMATOR DOPPELSPATEN — deep orange-brown, dry toast and malt aroma, very appetizing, heavy body, medium dry molasses and roasted malt flavor with a hop tang in back, good tasting sour malt finish and long aftertaste, excellent balance; a wonderful smooth and rich dark doublebock that makes your mouth feel good. In Germany, may also be labeled a Frühjahrstarkbier. [BK, 78]

SPATEN MUNICH LIGHT — deep gold, toffee malt aroma, heavy body, big hop and malt flavor; the hops are bitter and the malt is off-dry, the balance is excellent; long bright hop aftertaste, a heavy-handed brew and a wonderful mouthful of beer. [B, 53]

SPATEN URMÄRZEN OKTOBERFEST BEER — copper-gold, good hop and roasted malt aroma, smooth well-balanced malt and hop flavor, flavorful and complex, long dry hop and malt aftertaste, rich satisfying brew. [B, 72]

SPATEN PILS — deep gold, good hop nose and flavor, sharp hop finish, long good hop aftertaste, a good appetizing brew; goes very well with food. [B, 40]

SPATEN FRANZISKUS HELLER BOCK — tawny-gold; toasted malt and hop aroma is very slightly on the off-dry side; big body, flavor like the nose, complex and balanced, slightly off-dry malt and bright hop finish; long malt and hop aftertaste is drier than the flavor; a very satisfying brew that also goes well with food. [B, 85]

SPATEN GOLD — bright gold, light malt and hop nose; good flavor throughout has both hops and malt; well balanced, good complexity, long dry hop and malt aftertaste. [B, 40]

FRANZISKANER HEFE-WEISSBIER — cloudy gold, light wheat aroma, smooth light grainy palate; a touch of lactic acid is immediately noticeable on the front of the palate and again appears in the finish, otherwise it is not there; medium long aftertaste like the finish. [W, 56]

FRANZISKANER DARK WEISSBIER (HEFE) DUNKEL — cloudy amber, big head, spicy nose, big spicy flavor; finish shows a toasted malt that outlasts the spiciness; dry malt aftertaste. [W, 72]

SPATEN DUNKEL — deep brown, malt aroma and flavor, good body, smooth and delicious, long malt aftertaste, very drinkable. [B, 58]

SPATEN PREMIUM LAGER — gold, malt aroma, bright malt flavor, good body, subtle hop finish, long dry hop aftertaste. [B, 72]

SPATEN PREMIUM BOCK — tawny-gold, pleasant smooth nutty malt and bright hop aroma; smooth hop and malt flavor is a little off-dry but has good balance; big body, chewy, some noticeable alcohol, smooth, rich, refreshing, very drinkable; malt carries through; some sour hops appear in the long aftertaste; a well-made classical German bock that is very smooth. [BK, 87]

FRANZISKANER DARK WEISSBIER (HEFE) DUNKEL — cloudy amber, big head, spicy nose, big spicy flavor; finish shows a toasted malt that outlasts the spiciness; dry malt aftertaste. [W, 72]

LUDWIG THOMA DUNKEL — deep amber, big malty Ovaltine nose, huge dry malty flavor, big and rich, not complex, dry malt finish and long dry malt aftertaste; 5.5% abv. [B, 78]

Spath Bräu
Brewery in Lohberg am Ossen

OSSER HELL — gold hop nose, big malt flavor, malt finish, long dry malt aftertaste, good body and balance. [B, 57]

OSSER GOLD — deep gold, malt aroma and big malt flavor, long malt aftertaste; hops very light throughout, but a nicely made pleasant tasting brew. [B, 60]

OSSER WEISSE (MIT SEINER HEFE) — clear gold, light aroma of hops and spicy cloves, zesty clove flavor, very sparkly and creamy, refreshing; finishes with the spice leading the flavor into a lightly spiced malt aftertaste with good duration. [W, 77]

Burgerliches Brauhaus Spessart
Brewery in Wiesen

WIESENER RÄUBER BOCK — amber, big very rich malt nose, huge malt flavor, big body, rich, strong, smooth, and very long. [BK, 88]

Brauerei Spezial
Brewpub in Bamberg

SPEZIAL RAUCHBIER LAGER — amber, meaty smoked malt nose, very dry smoked malt flavor; dry malt finish and aftertaste has the smoke but it gradually sets in far to the back. [B, 48]

SPEZIAL RAUCHBIER MÄRZEN — deep amber, meaty smoked malt aroma, big flavor like the nose, smooth, very tasty and very drinkable; there's a hidden sweetness in there also; complex and interesting, medium dry long malt aftertaste with a faint smoky background. Now I see why the Bambergers like rauch bier. [B, 74]

St. Pauli Brauerei
Brewery in Bremen

ST. PAULI GIRL BEER — pale gold, faint malt and hop aroma, mild pleasant hop flavor with good balance between the malt and the hops, slightly hopped finish, mild dry hop aftertaste, a smooth brew. [B, 62]

ST. PAULI GIRL DARK BEER — deep brown, hops more than malt in the nose; taste is heavy malt and light hops; fairly good balance, appetizing finish and medium long aftertaste like the flavor. [B, 69]

ST. PAULI N.A. BREW — gold, pleasant malt nose with some background hops, light dry hop flavor with some malt in back, long dry hop aftertaste. [NA, 42]

Privatbrauerei Jacob Stauder
Brewery in Essen

STAUDER BEER — bright tawny gold, faint roasted malt nose and taste, light body, brief dry malt aftertaste. [B, 27]

STAUDER PILS — deep gold, hop aroma, slightly sour hop flavor with plenty of malt backing, good body, decent balance; long dry hop aftertaste is a bit sour. [B, 57]

Privatbrauerei Franz Steegmüller / Flötzinger Bräu
Brewery in Rosenheim

FLÖTZINGER BRÄU ROSENHEIM PILS — faintly hazy gold, malt and hop aroma; malt and hop flavor is faintly sweet; medium body, dull off-dry malt aftertaste; 4.8% abv. [B, 40]

FLÖTZINGER BRÄU ROSENHEIM HELL — pale gold; malt aroma is faintly grape (like Concord grape juice); grape malt flavor, medium body, dry malt finish and aftertaste; 4.8% abv. [B, 45]

FLÖTZINGER BRÄU ALTBAYERISCHES HEFE-WEIZEN — hazy gold, light spicy malt nose, big sweet and spicy flavor, medium body, sweet spicy finish and aftertaste, very long and clean tasting; 4.8% abv. [W, 63]

FLÖTZINGER BRÄU ALTBAYERISCHES HEFE-WEIZEN DUNKEL — hazy amber-gold, big head, faint spicy nose and taste, caramel malt backtaste; finish and aftertaste are malt, and caramel without any spiciness; 4.8% abv. [W, 47]

FLÖTZINGER BRÄU EXPORT DUNKEL — amber-brown, sour malt aroma and taste, bad phenolic flavor, bad bottle. [B, 25]

FLÖTZINGER BRÄU MÄRZEN — deep gold, low head, good malt aroma; big malt and hop flavor is very complex; good body; finish is dry malt, so is the long aftertaste that is a bit sweet on the end. [B, 58]

Brauerei Stempfhuber
Brewery in Horneck

HORNECKER HEFE-WEIZEN EXPORT — hazy gold, light complex citrus spice aroma, lemony-spicy flavor, medium to good body; lightly dry spicy finish and aftertaste keeps the lemony character; gravity 12 P, 5.2% abv. [W, 37]

HORNECKER EDEL HELL — gold, malty aroma and flavor, medium to good body, off-dry malt finish and aftertaste; gravity 12 P, 5% abv. [B, 57]

Stiftungsbrauerei
Brewery in Erding

DIE SCHWARZE DUNKLES WEISSBIER — brown, malt nose with a lactic-spice background, flavor like the nose but even spicier, dry malt finish and aftertaste. [W, 40]

Brauerei Storchenbräu Hans Roth
Brewery in Pfaffenhausen

STORCHEN BRÄU BAYRISCH HELL — pale gold, hop nose, dry hop flavor, off-dry malt comes in late, medium body, dry hop and sweet malt finish, dry hop aftertaste; 4.8% abv. [B, 56]

STORCHEN BRÄU SPEZIAL HELL — gold, hop and malt aroma, malty flavor, medium body, dry hop finish, dry hop aftertaste; 5.2% abv. [B, 60]

Notes

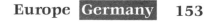

Privatbrauerei Stöttner
Brewery in Pfaffenberg

STÖTTNER-BIER PILS — gold, hop aroma; hop flavor is ordinary and lacks character, mostly just bitterness; medium body, dry hop finish and aftertaste; 4.8% abv. [B, 43]

STÖTTNER-BIER HELL — gold, malt aroma and flavor, pleasant but not exciting, medium body, dry malt finish and aftertaste; 4.7% abv. [B, 50]

STÖTTNER-BIER EXPORT HELL — gold, malt aroma, malt and hop flavor, medium body; dry finish and aftertaste has both malt and hops; 5% abv. [B, 57]

STÖTTNER-BIER PFAFFENGOLD — gold, malt aroma, sweet malt flavor, medium body, off-dry dull malt finish and aftertaste; 5.5% abv. [B, 45]

PFAFFENBERGER WEISSE — hazy gold, spicy nose, big bright spicy flavor of off-dry malt and cloves to balance, medium body, long off-dry malt and spicy aftertaste, extremely nice tasting, especially the aftertaste, a good classical hefe-weizen; 5.5% abv. [W, 72]

STÖTTNER RADLER-HALBE — very pale gold, lemony aroma, clean lemony flavor, light body, refreshing real lemon taste, malt and lemon aftertaste, a typical radler blend of lemonade and beer; 2.5% abv. [LO, 50]

Privat Landbrauerei Strössner
Brewery in Ahornberg

AHORNBERGER MAIBOCK — bright gold, malt nose, big rich malt flavor, slightly bitter hop finish, long light malt aftertaste, very pleasant. [BK, 40]

AHORNBERGER WÜRZIG LANDBIER — bright gold; smooth hoppy aroma and flavor has good malt support; good body, good length, smooth dry hop aftertaste; 4.6% abv. [B, 53]

BAHRENTRUNK DUNKELBIER — brown, big malt aroma, big bright malty flavor, medium to good body, somewhat dry malt finish, long dry malt aftertaste. [B, 57]

Brauerei Stumpf
Brewery in Lohr

BAVARIAN ABBEY LIGHT LAGER NON-ALCOHOLIC MALT BEVERAGE — gold, dull malt nose, light grainy very malty flavor, straight malt finish and aftertaste. [NA, 28]

KEILER WEISSBIER DUNKEL — amber; light wheat beer nose (some malt, some wheat, some cloves); light spicy clove flavor, very mild, highly carbonated, light body, fairly long aftertaste like the flavor. [W, 41]

ORIGINAL 1878 LOHRER BEER — golden amber, pleasant roasted malt and hop aroma, light off-dry roasted malt flavor; hops show well in the finish; long caramel malt and dry bitter hop aftertaste has good length and complexity. [B, 42]

BAVARIAN ABBEY LAGER — pale amber, light roasted malt nose and taste, very light on the hops, brief malt aftertaste; lacks zest without enough hops to balance. [B, 46]

LOHRER BÖCKLE — amber-gold, aroma of malt, hops, and alcohol (7% abv), strong malt and alcohol flavor, very assertive taste; has to be sipped gently for enjoyment; sweet malt and alcohol aftertaste. [BK, 79]

Erste Coburger Exportbrauerei Anton Sturm
Brewery in Coburg

STURMS PILSNER — gold, big head, hop and malt aroma; big bright hop flavor has both hops and malt; medium body, dry hop finish and aftertaste; 4.9% abv. [B, 72]

Stuttgarter Hofbrau
Brewery in Stuttgart

STUTTGARTER HOFBRAU HERRN PILS — bright gold, aroma of wet wool, hop flavor, plenty of supporting malt, slightly sour hop finish, long dry hop aftertaste. [B, 32]

STUTTGARTER HOFBRAU PILSNER — slightly tawny-gold; good hop nose is sort of sweet; austere dry hop palate, good body, long dry hop aftertaste. [B, 47]

STUTTGARTER HOFBRAU WEIHNACHTS-BIER — pale gold, malt nose, malt flavor with hops and some alcohol in back, medium body, medium long aftertaste like the flavor; 5.7% abv. [B, 53]

Stuttgarter Lokalbrauerei
Brewpub in Stuttgart

CALWER-ECK-BRÄU NATURTRUB — cloudy gold, yeasty hop aroma, good flavor of yeast, malt, and hops, interesting, good body; smooth, not rough or coarse in any way; a little off-dry in front, but dry by the finish; long dry malt and hop aftertaste. [B, 80]

FLORIANO MAIBOCK — cloudy brown, thick brown head, very little nose; smooth malty flavor starts out off-dry and dries toward the finish; medium long dry malt aftertaste. [BK, 65]

Herzoglich Bayerisches Brauhaus Tegernsee
Brewery in Tegernsee

QUIRINUS DUNKELER DOPPELBOCK — light brown, rich soft malt nose, velvety sweet malt in the mouth; sweetest at the finish, yet has a dry malt aftertaste that fades very slowly; a very tasty brew. Bottled version. [BK, 87]

QUIRINUS DUNKELER DOPPEL-BOCK — brown, lightly toasted malt nose and flavor, on the sweet side but very complex and earthy, dry malt finish, off-dry malt aftertaste, big body, excellent balance, absolutely delicious and very drinkable. Draft version at the Brauhaus Tegernsee. [BK, 71]

DER BLAU PAGE HELLER BOCK — hazy yellow-gold, lovely off-dry malt aroma; huge malt flavor is drier than the nose; very big body, honeyed texture, long dry malt aftertaste, well-made brew; good balance, but the hops aren't quite enough for the malt. [BK, 75]

TEGERNSEE HELLER BOCK — hazy amber-gold, pleasant toasted malt nose, rich toasted malt and hop flavor, complex, very good balance, rich, delicious, and very long. Bottled version. [BK, 90]

TEGERNSEE HELLER BOCK — bright gold, hop nose, big hop and malt flavor; balanced and rich; complex malt and hop finish leads into a long dry malt aftertaste. Draft version at the Brauhaus Tegernsee. [BK, 90]

TEGERNSEE DUNKEL EXPORT — dark amber-brown, pleasant malt aroma, lovely roasted malt flavor, refreshing and drinkable, good body, good balance, very satisfying, medium long dry malt aftertaste. [B, 85]

BRAUHAUS TEGERNSEE DUNKLER DOPPELBOCK — deep amber-brown, malt aroma and flavor; palate is sweet in front, off-dry in the middle, and stays off-dry thereafter; good body, very good of the type, long off-dry malt aftertaste; quite enjoyable, but not one of the blockbusters. [BK, 84]

TEGERNSEE SPEZIAL — gold, hop aroma, excellent balanced hop and malt flavor, long dry hop aftertaste; good body, and about as good a balance as you can imagine; this is the best in a German export style that I have tasted. [B, 84]

TEGERNSEER HELL — gold, lovely hop aroma, good hop and malt flavor, excellent balance, good body, long dry hop and malt aftertaste; a really good beer superbly balanced. [B, 87]

TEGERNSEER HELLES — bright gold, tight head, good appetizing malt and hop aroma, big hop and malt flavor, good body, tastes good, long dry hop finish and aftertaste, probably a newer label of the Hell above. [B, 80]

Postbrauerei Thannhausen
Brewery in Thannhausen

POSTBRÄU BERNHARDI GOLD SPEZIAL MÄRZEN — gold, big hop aroma; malt flavor has plenty of hop support; big body; richness goes all the way through the palate into the aftertaste; long rich malt aftertaste goes dry at the end. [B, 90]

POSTBRÄU HEFE-WEIZEN — hazy gold, odd dull malt aroma, pleasant bright and clean spicy clove and malt palate, medium body, short dry malt aftertaste. [W, 57]

Privatbrauerei Thier
Brewery in Dortmund

DORTMUNDER IMPERIAL IMPORTED BEER — deep gold, beautiful well-hopped aroma with a touch of roasted malt; nicely balanced; palate starts with the malt but quickly goes to hops; finishes toasted malt with a slightly sour

background; lingering pleasant dry hop aftertaste; a good complex appetizing brew. [B, 62]

DORTMUNDER IMPERIAL OKTOBERFEST BIER — orange-brown, very faint roasted malt aroma, toasted malt flavor with little or no hops, pleasant and malty without complexity, fairly long dry malt aftertaste. [B, 58]

DORTMUNDER IMPERIAL ALT BEER — deep copper, soft toasted malt nose, well-hopped flavor; balance seems a bit off; some toasted malt at the finish, but too little and too late for balancing the flavor; lacks depth as well; faint dry hop aftertaste. [A, 36]

HÖVELS ORIGINAL BITTER BIER — amber, highly carbonated, big head, big hop nose, bitter and bright hop flavor with plenty of malt backing, big body, delicious and complex, long dry hop aftertaste; 5.5% abv. Made for Hövels Hausbrauerei, Dortmund. [B, 86]

Fürstliche Brauerei Thurn und Taxis
Brewery in Regensburg

THURN U TAXIS HEFEWEIZEN — cloudy amber, sweet wheaty weizen nose, much sweeter than usual for a wheat beer, spicy-fruity palate, complex, long off-dry malt aftertaste with only the faintest hint of cloves. [W, 60]

THURN U TAXIS POSTMEISTER DOPPELBOCK — medium brown, big malt nose, strong malt flavor but very smooth, excellent balance, well rounded, quite long and very delicious. [BK, 88]

SCHIERLINGEN ROGGEN OBERGÄRIG HEFETRUBE — hazy deep amber, big head, sweet and sour lactic-rye nose with a buttery background; buttery malt taste up front, lactic spice finish and aftertaste. Made for A.D. Laber Fürstliches Specialtätes-Brauhaus zu Schierling. [W, 65]

THURN U TAXIS DAS FURSTLICHE PILSENER — gold, hop nose; hop flavor balanced well with malt; good body; long and strong dry hop aftertaste shows no malt whatever. [B, 57]

THURN U TAXIS EXPORT — gold, hop nose, good hefty hop and malt flavor, nicely balanced, big body, long malt aftertaste. [B, 62]

THURN U TAXIS DAS FÜRSTLICHE WEIZEN MIT HEFE — very slightly hazy gold; huge head is thick and long lasting; spicy aroma, dry spicy flavor, dry spicy finish and long dry aftertaste; very refreshing; leaves your mouth feeling very clean; a lot of yeast in the bottom of the bottle; 5.3% abv. [B, 57]

THURN U TAXIS FÜRST CLASS PILSENER — gold, big head; very hoppy aroma is almost skunky (but not quite); big hop flavor is more aromatic than bitter; plenty of malt to balance; big body, long dry hop aftertaste, a classic pils; 4.9% abv. [B, 67]

THURN U TAXIS ST. WOLFGANG DUNKEL EXPORT — dark amber-brown, big malty nose, medium body, smooth and dry malty flavor, dry malt finish and aftertaste; 4.8% abv. [B, 69]

THURN U TAXIS HELL — bright gold, big head, light dry malt and hop aroma, light dry malt and hop flavor, medium body, touch of sweet malt in the aftertaste; 4.5% abv. [B, 42]

THURN U TAXIS FÜRSTEN GOLD MÄRZEN — deep coppery gold, malty aroma and rich malty flavor; a little too sweet but tastes good; smooth off-dry malt finish and aftertaste; gravity 13 P, 5.3% abv. [B, 62]

Tochterfirma Weissbräu Gmbh.
Brewery in Traunstein

AYINGER EXPORT-WEISSBIER — clear bright gold, foamy, pleasant wheat nose, bright grainy flavor with a bit of clove spice in back from the lactic acid, quite tasty and fairly long. [W, 55]

AYINGER HEFE-WEISSBIER — slightly cloudy gold, foamy, slightly sour malt nose; big acidic spicy flavor overwhelms the malt; long spicy aftertaste. [W, 28]

AYINGER UR-WEIZEN — hazy copper, wheaty malt nose, creamy, toasted malt and wheat palate, pleasant and straightforward, short dry toasted malt aftertaste. [W, 48]

Brauhaus Torgau Gmbh.
Brewery in Torgau

TORGAUER RITTER DUNKEL — deep amber-brown, tan head, faint malt nose, concentrated big rich and dry malt flavor, good body, big alcohol-rich malt middle, dry malt finish, long dry malt aftertaste; very finely carbonated; 6.5% abv. [B, 89]

Hofbrauhaus Traunstein
Brewery in Traunstein

HOFBRAUHAUS TRAUNSTEIN FÜRSTEN QUELL — gold, hop nose, dull malt flavor, dry malt and hop finish and aftertaste, uninteresting. [B, 34]

HOFBRAUHAUS TRAUNSTEIN ALBAIRISCH DUNKEL — deep amber-brown, pleasant toasted malt aroma, creamy roasted malt flavor, dull dry malt finish and aftertaste. [B, 50]

HOFBRAUHAUS TRAUNSTEIN ALTBAIRISCH UR-WEIZEN — deep amber-brown, faint malt nose, big spicy malt flavor, medium long malt aftertaste with a clove background; pleasant but lacks depth and strength. [W, 70]

HOFBRAUHAUS TRAUNSTEIN HOFBRÄU WEISSE — cloudy gold, clean faintly spicy malt nose, big clove and malt flavor, lemony finish, good body, fine balance, very complex and delicious, long fresh cinnamon and clove aftertaste, very interesting and very good sipping beer. [W, 92]

Brauerei Treiber
Brewery in Treibe

FESTBRÄU IMPORTED GERMAN PILSENER BEER — brilliant gold, hop and sour malt nose, big hop flavor; sags a bit in the middle, ends in a long soapy hop aftertaste. [B, 28]

Tucher Bräu A.G.
Brewery in Nürnberg

TUCHER UBERSEE EXPORT BEER — tawny-gold, malt aroma, medium body, very lightly dry toasted malt and hop flavor, dry slightly sour hop finish, light dry hop and toasted malt aftertaste. Also Tucher Ubersee Export (domestic version), same as foregoing except that there is no toasted nature to the malt and the hops are not sour, giving a smoother and cleaner taste. [B, 47]

BRÄUHAUS ROTHENBURG GERMAN PILSENER — gold, light hop nose, harsh bitter hop flavor, sour metallic finish and aftertaste. [B, 30]

TUCHER GERMAN PILSENER — bright gold, nice hop nose with some malt support, big hop flavor, long dry and bitter hop aftertaste. Tucher Pilsener (the domestic version) is identical except for the name on the label. [B, 37]

TUCHER WEIZEN — bright deep gold, foamy, beautiful malt nose; zesty piquant flavor up front, dry very fresh and crisp wheaty middle, long clean off-dry malt finish and medium long aftertaste; a very fine brew that is a pleasure to drink. [W, 69]

TUCHER HEFE WEIZEN — brilliant deep gold, foamy, good malt aroma with some wheat and yeast in back; piquant spicy flavor starts up front and stays throughout; a bit yeasty in the middle, slightly off-dry raspberry malt finish; medium long dry malt aftertaste keeps much of the piquancy of the flavor, very nicely done. [W, 77]

TUCHER HEFE-WEIZEN DUNKLES — amber, malt nose, high carbonation; hop, spice, and malt flavor (in that order); refreshing and drinkable, fairly light-handed, short malt aftertaste. [W, 46]

TUCHER IMPORTED GERMAN BEER LIGHT — medium deep gold, hop and faintly roasted malt aroma, a complex palate of hops and dry roasted malt, roasted malt finish, long slightly sour malt aftertaste. [B, 67]

TUCHER IMPORTED GERMAN BEER DARK — pale copper, faint toasted malt nose and flavor, weak body, faintly sweet short malt aftertaste. [B, 31]

TUCHER LORENZI BOCK HELL — bright gold, malt and corn nose, toasted malt and corn flavor, finishes cleaner and better with just the malt, long dry malt aftertaste. [BK, 40]

TUCHER ALT FRANKEN EXPORT DUNKEL — deep amber, pleasant malt aroma, good tasting light malt flavor, light body, almost nothing at the finish, faint brief malt aftertaste. [B, 56]

TUCHER MAIBOCK HELL — deep gold, lovely toasted malt nose, big zesty hop and toasted malt flavor, fairly intense, very long aftertaste like the flavor, an excellent beer. [BK, 88]

TUCHER FESTBIER MÄRZEN — tawny-gold, pleasant toasted malt aroma; highly carbonated; good toasted malt flavor, sour hop aftertaste. [B, 52]

TUCHER BAJUVATOR DOPPELBOCK — deep red-amber, roasted malt nose and taste; delicious, rich, and clean; long roasted malt aftertaste is medium dry; very drinkable. As found in Germany. [BK, 90]

TUCHER SEBALDUS FEST — pale gold, big bright hop and malt aroma, soft malty flavor, medium to good body, fresh and balanced, long medium dry malt and hop aftertaste, a tasty likable brew available in the U.S.A. as of early 1995 in the half-liter bottle. [B, 80]

TUCHER BAJUVATOR DOPPELBOCK — amber-brown, beautiful rich malt aroma; rich malty flavor is on the sweet side; big body; long rich malty aftertaste shows some roasted character; available in the U.S.A. in early 1995 in the half-liter bottle. [BK, 90]

TUCHER BAYERISCHES WEISSBIER HEFE-WEIZEN — tawny, faint citrus nose; spicy lactic flavor on front of the palate, medium dry malt in the middle, and a touch of lactic with the malt in the finish; medium body, very brief dry malt aftertaste with no spice at all at the end. [W, 49]

SEBALDUS WEIZENBOCK DUNKEL — rich brown color, big creamy head and creamy texture, bright spicy clove aroma, zesty spicy rich malt flavor, complex and refreshing, long bright aftertaste like the flavor. [BK, 87]

TUCHER FESTBIER — deep gold, malt aroma, smooth malt flavor, lightly hopped, good body, complex malt aftertaste, good length. [B, 61]

TUCHER URFRÄNKISCH DUNKEL — dark brown; odd aroma shows tobacco; flavor is chocolate, caramel, coffee, and toffee; very sweet like a dessert, good body; long aftertaste is much drier than the flavor; 4.4% abv. [B, 67]

Ulmer Münster Brauerei
Brewery in Ulm

MÜNSTER WEIHNACHTS BIER — deep gold, rich toasted malt aroma, full rich malt flavor, very complex and smooth; finely balanced; creamy, fairly long dry malt aftertaste. [B, 67]

ULMER MÜNSTER ZUNFTMEISTER SPEZIAL DUNKEL — medium pale amber, nice toasted malt nose; palate has a big malt front, smooth middle making the transition to a hop finish; delicious, long complex dry hop and malt aftertaste, good body, good beer. [B, 78]

ULMER MÜNSTERKANZLERGOLD HELLES STARKBIER — faintly hazy amber-gold; complex malt nose with chocolate, Ovaltine, Postum features; equally complex malt flavor, pleasant and very long malt aftertaste. [B, 78]

SCHLOSSHERR PILS — gold, malt and hop nose; dry malt flavor, finish, and aftertaste; good hop support, pleasant and refreshing; seems to be virtually identical to Rats Krone Pils below. [B, 74]

RATS KRONE HELL — gold, good, malt-hop nose, smooth malt flavor with the hops in back, good dry malt finish, long dry malt and hop aftertaste. [B, 74]

RATS KRONE PILS — gold, beautiful hop nose, good flavor with plenty of both malt and hops, long dry malt and hop aftertaste, good tasting beer. [B, 81]

LÖWENBRÄU NEU-ULM WEIZEN — gold, bright big spicy nose, creamy, big sparkle on the tongue; clean flavor feels good and is refreshing; plenty of spice and zest, long bright spicy aftertaste, a delightful beer. [W, 91]

HIRSCH BIER URHELL — medium deep gold, vegetal-malt nose, malt flavor, dry malt finish and aftertaste; not much offered. [B, 47]

SCHLOSS EXPORT — medium deep gold, light hop nose, very light hop and malt flavor, high carbonation, light to medium body, short dry hop aftertaste. [B, 48]

WAPPEN EXPORT — gold, big head, light hop nose; flavor mostly hops but there is background malt; balanced palate, medium body, dry hop and malt finish and aftertaste; 5.5% abv. [B, 60]

WAPPEN PILS — gold, big malt nose and flavor, hardly any hops except in the aftertaste, pleasant but not exciting, brief aftertaste. [B, 45]

Bergbrauerei-Ulrich Zimmerman
Brewery in Ehingen-Berg

ULRICHS HEFE-WEIZEN — hazy amber-gold, slightly spicy nose; good spicy flavor, finish, and aftertaste; lightly spiced and nicely made; very drinkable and refreshing; made with Tettnanger and Hallertau hops; 5% abv. [W, 80]

ULRICHSBIER-LA SPEZIAL — amber-gold, faint hop nose, straightforward malt flavor, clean but a little sweet, dry malt finish and aftertaste, not exciting; 5% abv. [B, 50]

Klosterbrauerei Ursberg
Kloster brewery in Ursberg

URSBERGER ALOISIUS HELLER DOPPELBOCK — gold, rich clean big malt nose, and flavor, extremely creamy; shows some alcohol (7.8% abv); big body, long rich malt aftertaste. [BK, 85]

URSBERGER PILS — gold, lovely mild hop aroma, very appetizing; flavor is balanced hops and malt; good body, long complex dry malt and hop aftertaste, a very tasty pils; 4.8% abv. [B, 91]

URSBERGER HELL — bright deep gold, big tight head, malty aroma, pleasant off-dry malt flavor, good body, off-dry malt finish and aftertaste, nice but a bit too sweet; 4.8% abv. [B, 50]

URSBERG MÄRZEN — gold, complex appetizing rich malt nose, excellent dry malt flavor, very tasty, dry very malty finish and aftertaste, very complex, very good; long and keeps the richness right to the end; 5.5% abv. [B, 94]

V. Koch'sche Brauerei
Brewery in Gottsmannsgrün

GOTTSMANNSGRÜNER PILS — gold, bright malt and hop aroma, big malt flavor with good hop support, medium body; hops fade at the finish leaving only the malt; dry malt aftertaste; 4.7% abv. [B, 52]

GOTTSMANNSGRÜNER DUNKEL — brown, dry malt aroma, pleasant straightforward big dry malt flavor, good body; touch of sweet malt in the finish and aftertaste, otherwise quite dry; 5% abv. [B, 61]

Brauhaus Vetter
Brewpub (Hausbrauerei) in Heidelberg

VETTER BRAUHAUS PILS — hazy gold, malty nose, fresh malt taste with a dry hop background, dry hop finish, long dry hop aftertaste, very fresh and drinkable, good hoppy flavor. [B, 90]

VETTER ALT HEIDELBERGER DUNKEL — hazy amber, dry malt aroma and flavor; pleasant

dry malt has character; good body; smooth, dry malt finish; long dry malt aftertaste. [A, 78]

VETTER 33 — cloudy amber; concentrated malt nose; huge and very rich clean malt; there is high alcohol (11% abv) but it is not all that noticeable amongst the concentration of malt; huge body, big mouthfeel, delicious very long sweet malt aftertaste; does a number on your senses; gravity 33 P. [B, 95]

Fürstlicher Brauerei Schloss Wächtersbacher
Brewery in Wächtersbach, 6480, Hessen

WÄCHTERSBACHER JUBILAUMSBIER 400 PREMIUM — tawny-gold, roasted malt nose, malt flavor, nutty candy finish, long somewhat dull malt aftertaste; lacks zest. [B, 37]

WÄCHTERSBACHER FÜRSTEN PILS CLASSIC — pale gold, faint malt nose, dry malt palate, bone dry finish, fairly long dry malt aftertaste. [B, 43]

Brauerei Wagner
Brewery in Kemmern

WAGNER BRÄU MÄRZEN — deep tawny-gold, very faint malt aroma, big hop flavor up front, sour hop finish and aftertaste; not well balanced. [B, 23]

WAGNER BRÄU BOCK —
medium deep orange-brown, faint
malt aroma, big creamy head, good
texture, smoked coffee flavor, bitter
hop finish and long aftertaste; not
balanced. [BK, 42]

Privatbrauerei Wagner/ Weiss Rössl Bräu
Brewery in Eltmann-Rosstadt

WEISS RÖSSL LEONARDI
BOCK — brown, lovely lightly
toasted malt nose, big malt flavor, excellent balance, good
body; good tasting long malt
aftertaste. [BK, 85]

WEISS RÖSSL RATSHERREN
DUNKEL — brown, cereal malt
aroma and flavor, good body, long
dry malt aftertaste. [B, 48]

WEISS RÖSSL FESTBIER —
deep gold, pleasant malt aroma,
good dry malt flavor, medium long
very dry malt aftertaste, good hop
balance. [B, 67]

WEISS RÖSSL MÄRZEN —
deep gold, toasted malt nose, very
nice; lovely toasted malt flavor
finishes richly; smooth dry medium long malt aftertaste. [B, 86]

WEISS RÖSSL FRANKEN
RAUCHBIER — deep amber,
aroma like smoked bacon, smoked
salty meat flavor; fades a bit at the
finish but remains on the palate
for a very long time. [B, 53]

WEISS RÖSSL URSTOFF —
pale gold, complex malt aroma,
pleasant straightforward malt

flavor, light body, pleasant and
very drinkable, medium long dry
malt aftertaste. [B, 51]

KARLSKRONE — gold, hop and
toasted malt aroma, flavor to
match, sour hop finish and long
dry sour hop aftertaste. Made for
Aldi, Mulheim A.D., Ruhr. [B, 57]

WEISS RÖSSL KELLERBIER —
brown, dry concentrated malt
aroma and flavor, rich rather than
sweet, medium body; good flavor
goes very well with game or rich
sauces; very long rich malt aftertaste. [B, 84]

TRUNSTADTER SCHLOSS-
BRÄU PILS — gold, very
perfumy malty aroma; flavor is
sweet malt, finally goes to dry
hops at the aftertaste; medium
body, long aftertaste; 4.7% abv.
Made by Hersteller Wagner,
Rosstadt. [B, 56]

Brauerei Waldschlössen
Brewery in Dresden

EDEL WEISS MALT
LIQUOR — deep tawny-gold,
faint sweet malt nose, dry hop
palate, big body, high extract,
long malt aftertaste, noticeable
alcohol, not much middle palate.
[ML, 34]

Bayerische Staatsbrauerei Weihenstephan
Brewery, school, and yeast manufacturing facility in Freising

VITUS WEIZENBOCK — pale
amber, pleasant malt-wheat nose,
faint trace of lactic spice, good flavor much like the aroma with a hint
of sweetness, balanced, complex,
pleasant and refreshing; medium
long aftertaste like the flavor, but
drier. [W, 80]

WEIHENSTEPHAN
KORBINIAN DUNKLES
STARKBIER — amber-brown,
malt nose, good body, rich malt
flavor, dry hop finish, very good
balance, long dry hop aftertaste,
very satisfying. [B, 85]

WEIHENSTEPHAN
WEIZENBIER KRISTALL
EXPORT — bright gold, big head,
fresh grainy wheat and barley malt
aroma, quite fresh and zesty, very
little acid in the malt flavor but
enough for character, long malt
aftertaste, bright, pleasant, refreshing, and very drinkable. Presently
in U.S.A., this brew is labeled
Weihenstephan Weizenbier Crystal Clear. [W, 60]

WEIHENSTEPHAN HEFE-
WEISSBIER — hazy gold, lactic
spicy clove nose, flavorful zesty
clove flavor; spice strong in front,
eases off in mid-palate enough for
smooth slightly off-dry malt to
rise up; finish and aftertaste are
off-dry malt, with the spicy cloves

coming again very late in the long aftertaste. [W, 53]

WEIHENSTEPHAN HEFE WEISSBIER DUNKEL — hazy medium deep amber, big fairly tight tan head; zesty spicy nose has a definite clove-like character; lightly spiced clove and malt flavor, light to medium body, some complexity; finishes with a lighter spicy clove nature, but the cloves stay right through the long aftertaste; tangy and refreshing. [B, 70]

STEPHANSQUELL HELLES STARKBIER — medium deep gold, very rich malt aroma, huge malty flavor (like malted milk powder), a bit winelike but has a good balance, long dry malt aftertaste. On U.S. market this brew has been called Weihenstephan Original [B, 48], but has recently been seen with the Stephansquell label. [B, 87]

WEIHENSTEPHAN EDEL-PILS — gold, good appetizing European hop nose, dry and bitter hop flavor, dry hop finish and aftertaste, very long and very dry. [B, 56]

WEIHENSTEPHAN EXPORT DUNKEL — light amber-brown, lightly toasted malt aroma; flavor is lightly toasted malt but there is a hop background; the toasted malt has a slight burnt nature that shows up in the finish; medium body; very long dry aftertaste is like the flavor. [B, 61]

Weissbrauerei Unertl
Brewery in Haag

UNERTL WEISSBIER — hazy gold, sediment in bottom of glass, huge head, spicy nose, spicy flavor; unbalanced with the sweets and sours clashing in your mouth; long spicy aftertaste; gravity 11.2 P, 4.8% abv. [W, 43]

Brauhaus Weissenbrunn
Brewery in Weissenbrunn

ORIGINAL BAVARIAN OKTOBER BIER — tawny-gold, good malt and hop nose with roasted malt in back, good flavor with plenty of hops, long hop aftertaste. [B, 47]

ADLER BRÄU — gold, beautiful hop nose, pleasant well-balanced hop flavor, plenty of malt backing, malt finish, faintly bitter dry hop aftertaste. [B, 58]

Privatbrauerei Weissenfelser Felsbräu
Brewery in Weissenfelsen

WEISSENFELSER FELSBRÄU PILS — gold, complex toasted malt nose, rich toasted malt flavor, good body, toasted malt finish and aftertaste; long and malty with the hops to dry the palate; good balance; 4.9% abv. [B, 75]

WEISSENFELSER FELSBRÄU DOPPELBOCK — deep brown, rich toasted malt toffee-like nose, rich yet dry malty flavor, huge body, dry malt finish and aftertaste; gravity 18 P, 6.8% abv. [BK, 90]

Klosterbrauerei Weltenburg Gmbh.
Monastery brewery at Weltenburg

WELTENBURGER KLOSTER SPEZIAL DUNKEL — amberbrown, big malt nose, rich malt flavor, light body, very little hops (if any), no complexity, medium to short aftertaste of malt with a bit of sour at the end. [B, 51]

WELTENBURGER KLOSTER ASAM-BOCK — deep rubybrown, excellent earthy toasted malt nose; very complex palate of chocolate, acid, malt, and hops; rich, big, and interesting; gets better as it goes; long medium dry malt aftertaste is interesting in itself considering the way the palate starts out; an absolutely delicious experience. [BK, 95]

WELTENBURGER KLOSTER BAROCK DUNKEL — deep rich amber-brown, light toasted malt nose, smooth rich toasted malt flavor, good body, medium intensity, long light and dry malt aftertaste; leaves a very good taste in the mouth; gravity 12 P, 4.5% abv. [B, 68]

WELTENBURGER KLOSTER HEFE-WEISSBIER DUNKEL — deep amber, huge dense head, lactic clove spice nose, light clove and malt flavor, light body, medium long light dry aftertaste like the flavor; overall seems a bit puny, at least compared to other Weltenburger brews. [B, 56]

Privatbrauerei Heinrich Wenker / Dortmunder Kronen
Krone am Markt brewery in Dortmund

DORTMUNDER KRONEN CLASSIC — medium deep gold, big hop nose, good hop and grainy malt flavor, slightly off-dry malt finish, medium body; complex and well balanced; long fairly dry hop aftertaste, delightful. [B, 77]

DORTMUNDER KRONEN PILSKRONE — amber, toasted malt aroma; toasted malt flavor has hops in back; sour hop aftertaste detracts from what is otherwise a very nice brew. [B, 38]

DORTMUNDER KRONEN CLASSIC ALT DARK — medium deep copper, nice toasted malt aroma, grainy toasted malt flavor, short dry malt and hop aftertaste. [A, 29]

Privatbrauerei Herbert Werner
Brewery in Tuzenhausen

DACHSER FRANZ DUNKEL — amber; faint malt aroma is lightly roasted; slightly roasted dry malt flavor, light body, medium long dry malt aftertaste; gravity 11 P, 5.1% abv. [B, 58]

Werner-Bräu
Brewery in Poppenhausen

WERNER PILSENER — gold, malt and hop aroma and flavor, quite tasty, excellent balance, long dry hop and malt aftertaste. [B, 67]

Brauerei Wernesgrüner
Brewery in Wernesgrün

WERNESGRÜNER PILSENER — pale gold, dry hop aroma and bitter hop taste, medium body, bright dry hop finish and aftertaste, long; 4.9% abv. [B, 58]

Privatbrauerei Gasthof Wichert
Brewery-Gasthof in Lichtenfels

WICHERT PILSENER — gold, aromatic hop nose, hop and malt flavor, dry hop finish, long dry hop aftertaste. [B, 57]

WICHERT DUNKLES — brown, malt aroma, lightly smoked malt flavor, long and dry malt aftertaste, a pleasant good tasting brew. [B, 63]

Privatbrauerei Franz Josef Wicküler
Brewery in Wuppertal

WICKÜLER PILSENER BEER — gold, big hop aroma; finely carbonated; big hop flavor with fine malt backing, excellent example of a pils style from central Germany, good body; malt shows well in the finish and aftertaste, but the hops dominate; good duration. [B, 69]

C. Wiederholt's Brauerei Gmbh.
Brewery in Noerten-Hardenberg

CASSEL SCHLOSS PREMIUM BEER — gold, big hop nose, big hop flavor, plenty of malt backing; finishes hops with the malt showing very well at the end; good balance, refreshing, complex, long complex hop and malt aftertaste. [B, 71]

Privatbrauerei M.C. Wieninger
Brewery in Telsendorf

WIENINGER HELLER BOCK — gold, touch of citrus in the malt aroma, big rich and alcoholic malt flavor, low carbonation, very smooth; rich aftertaste shows a lot of malt, some hops, and some alcohol; gravity 16.4 P, 7.3% abv. [B, 59]

WIENINGER IMPULSATOR — deep amber, big roasted malt nose; rich malty flavor is neither dry nor sweet, but is definitely rich with a vinous quality; big body; long rich aftertaste is more dry than the flavor; gravity 18.4 P, 7.1% abv. [BK, 100]

Aachener Burgerbrauerei / Peter Wiertz Gmbh.
Brewery in Aachen

BURGERBRÄU PILS — gold, faint malt and hop aroma, dull malt flavor with some hops in back, dull malt finish, short dry malt aftertaste. [B, 40]

Wildbräu
Brewery in Grafing

LANDPILS NACH ALTER BRÄUHERRN ART — pale gold, light hop aroma, mild hop flavor, long dry sour hop aftertaste. [B, 29]

Brauhaus Wilhermsdorf
Brewery in Wilhermsdorf

ALT WILHERMSDORFER DUNKEL — very deep amber, smooth dry malt aroma, dry malt palate, finishes off-dry malt; there is a back taste of alcohol although the alcohol rating is not high (4.1%); soft texture, long malt aftertaste; it has a good flavor and it grows on you. [B, 80]

Privatbrauerei Will
Brewery in Motten

WEIHNACHTS BOCK — gold, light hop nose, rich malty alcoholic flavor, full body; balanced with plenty of both malt and hops; very very long rich aftertaste; gravity 16 P, 6.5% abv. [BK, 84]

ORIGINAL BAYERISCHES HEFE-WEIZEN — hazy gold, nice bright very spicy aroma, big bright spicy flavor, good body, long medium dry spicy aftertaste. [W, 84]

WILL BRÄU PILSNER — bright gold, light dry hop aroma and flavor, medium body, light dry hop finish and aftertaste; 4.7% abv. [B, 49]

WILL PILS DE LUXE — gold, very bright hoppy aroma and flavor, good body, good complexity; long dry hop aftertaste stays big and complex; 4.9% abv. [B, 59]

E. Winkels K.G.
Brewery in Karlsruhe

WINKELS MEISTER BRÄU PILSENER — gold; big hop nose that was extremely fragrant, you could smell it a good foot away; lusty malt flavor well balanced with hops; long bitter hop aftertaste; best described as a big rough and tumble brew. [B, 52]

WINKELS MEISTER BRÄU EXPORT — gold, big malt and hop nose, finely carbonated, balanced malt and hop flavor, smooth and delicious, long bright hop aftertaste. [B, 56]

WINKELS MEISTER BRÄU HEFE WEIZEN — hazy gold, medium head, pleasant malt nose with a tartness in back, zesty malt and clove flavor; good balance set between the sweetness of the malt and the tartness of the lactic acid; complex and refreshing; long aftertaste follows the flavor in kind. [W, 59]

Brauhaus Winter
Brewery in Köln

RICHMODIS KÖLSCH — cloudy yellow, sweet light ale-like nose, some amyl acetate, unbalanced sour taste, long sour aftertaste. [K, 14]

Spezialitäten Bierbrauerei C. Wittman OHG
Brewery in Landshut

WITTMAN URHELL — gold, malt nose, dry malt flavor, medium body, dry malt finish and aftertaste, good length; 4.9% abv. [B, 52]

WITTMAN PREMIUM EXTRA PILS — gold, pleasant likable hop aroma; bright hop flavor shows some malt; medium body, dry hop and malt finish and aftertaste, long; gravity 11 P, 4.8% abv. [B, 63]

WITTMAN FESTBIER — gold, big head; aroma is mostly malt but there are big hops and alcohol there as well; rich malty flavor, good body, very smooth, dry and rich malt finish and aftertaste, a good brew, no warts whatever; 5.5% abv. [B, 78]

Privatbrauerei Oberäu Wochinger K.G.
Brewery in Holzkirchen

HOLZKIRCHNER OBERÄU PILS — gold, hop nose, big hop flavor; well backed with malt; highly carbonated, good body, long dry malt and hop aftertaste. [B, 46]

HOLZKIRCHNER OBERÄU EDEL EXPORT — very deep gold, faint malt nose, fairly big malt flavor, big body, long malt aftertaste. [B, 40]

HOCHLAND HELL — gold, malt-hop nose and flavor, off-dry malt finish, long drier malt aftertaste. [B, 40]

HOLZKIRCHNER OBERÄU URTYP HELL — gold, malt and hop aroma; flavor is mostly malt with some hops in back; dry malt-hop finish, long dry hop aftertaste. [B, 46]

HOLZKIRCHNER WEISSE DUNKEL — deep amber-brown, citrus lemony-grapefruit malt nose, creamy, light spicy clove

and malt flavor, dry malt finish; long dry malt aftertaste shows little of the spiciness. [W, 52]

HOLZKIRCHNER WEISSE BAYERISCHES HEFEWEIZEN — hazy gold, faint lactic spice in behind a malt aroma, mild spicy flavor, medium body, long mild spice and malt aftertaste. [W, 53]

HOLZKIRCHNER LAURENZI EXPORT DUNKEL — good deep brown, roasted malt nose, rich roasted malt flavor, finishes dry, long dry malt aftertaste, medium body, good balance. [BK, 70]

Woinemer Hausbrauerei
Brewpub in Weinheim

WOINEMER HELL — hazy amber, hop nose, bright hop flavor; excellent balance with the malt that takes the lead in the long aftertaste; a delightful bright beer that goes very well with food or can stand by itself. [B, 82]

WOINEMER MAI BOCK — hazy amber, faint malt and hop nose, huge malt flavor with plenty of hops for balance and complexity, big body, long dry malt and hop aftertaste. [BK, 75]

WOINEMER DUNKEL — deep amber-brown, soft malt nose and flavor, medium body, brief medium dry malt aftertaste. [B, 53]

Privatbrauerei Georg Wolf
Brewery in Fuchsstadt

WOLF PILS — gold, light hop nose, strong dry hop flavor, light body; big dry hop aftertaste is long and dry; gravity 11 P, 4.9% abv. [B, 52]

Wolfstetter Bräu George Huber
Brewery in Vilshofen

WOLFERSTETTER VOLLBIER HELL — gold, sour hop nose, very sour hop taste, dry hop finish and aftertaste. [B, 30]

WOLFSTETTER HERREN PILS — gold, zesty hop nose, malt flavor with a hop finish, long dry hop aftertaste. [B, 53]

WOLFSTETTER EXPORT HEFE-WEIZEN — hazy gold, pleasant spicy malt nose, big spicy malt flavor, huge palate, big body; has to be taken in small sips, no guzzling this one; spicy malt finish and aftertaste, a brute of a beer. [W, 56]

WOLFSTETTER RATSHERREN WEISSBIER — brown, pleasant spicy malt aroma, creamy malt and spicy cloves on the palate, fairly big, good body, smooth and creamy, dry malt finish and aftertaste. [W, 47]

Brauerei Wolters
Brewery in Brunswick

WOLTERS PILSENER — deep gold, nice hop nose with good hop backing; flavor starts out as malt but quickly turns hoppy and the hops stay on to give an overall dry and bitter flavor; long hop aftertaste is especially bitter. [B, 50]

J. Wörner & Sohne K.G. Erbacher Brauhaus
Brewery at Erbach

ERBACHER PRÄDIKATOR DOPPELBOCK — deep amber-brown, delightful rich sweet malt nose, big rich malt with a sour background, excellent background, medium dry long malt, a delicious brew. [B, 86]

ERBACHER PREMIUM GERMAN LAGER — pale gold, pleasant complex malt and hop nose, bright hop and malt flavor, creamy, well balanced, very enjoyable, dry finish and aftertaste. [B, 65]

Privatbrauerei Burgerbräu Wörner OHG
Brewery in Bamberg

KAISERDOM PILSENER — brilliant deep gold, roasted malt aroma with good hops and a touch of caramel; good roasted malt flavor with hops showing up in the middle for a beautiful balance; long roasted malt aftertaste. [B, 75]

KAISERDOM RAUCHBIER — deep copper-brown, rich smoked malt nose; reminds you of smoked cheese, meat, pepperoni; very tasty; smoke overrides the hops and malt flavors, but it is still pleasant; interesting brew, long smoky aftertaste. [B, 64]

BURGERBRÄU BAMBERG PILS — medium gold, off-dry malt and hop nose; big hop flavor with the malt showing in the finish and aftertaste; medium long appetizing malt and hop aftertaste. [B, 28]

SIMPATICO BEER — bright gold; faint sweet hop aroma that turns toward sour shortly; unbalanced sour hop flavor, brief dry and sour hop aftertaste. [B, 34]

DOMFÜRSTEN BIER — medium pale gold, toasted malt and hop aroma; toasted malt up front on the palate, balanced hop and malt middle, long sour aftertaste. [B, 27]

PROSTEL HERBFRISCHES SCHANKBIER — pale gold, stinky grainy aroma, woody-grain flavor, tinny finish and aftertaste. [NA, 18]

KAISERDOM UR-BOCK STARKBIER — medium deep amber, mellow toasted malt nose, soft and smooth toasted malt palate, good intensity, no faults, long aftertaste like the flavor. [BK, 85]

KAISERDOM HEFE WEISSBIER — hazy amber, faint clove and wheat aroma; refreshing spicy clove, yeast, and wheat flavor; light and smooth, pleasant finish, medium long clean dry aftertaste like the flavor. [W, 56]

KAISERDOM EXTRA DRY — pale gold, rising malt nose, hops in back; sour hop flavor, especially so in the finish; bitter dry hop aftertaste, lots of bite and lots of character. [D, 27]

BAUNACHER BRAUHAUS PILS — gold, dull malt aroma and flavor with some hops, light body; hops show better in the aftertaste; good length; gravity 11.4 P, 4.7% abv. [B, 37]

KAIERDOM PILS VOM FASS — gold, peachy aroma and flavor, pleasant, tasty, smooth, very drinkable; there is some malty sweetness from mid-palate on; this is the Kaiserdom Pils on draft. [B, 74]

BAMBERGER KAIERDOM WEIZEN KRISTALLKLAR — bright gold, big head, lightly spiced carbonic nose, smooth slightly spicy taste with a carbonic bite, medium body, short dry malt aftertaste; has a bright and refreshing quality but needs to be well chilled to mitigate the effect of the carbon dioxide on the palate; 5.3%

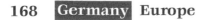

abv. Found in Florida in half-liter German "stubbies" with overprinted domestic labels. [W, 59]

ALT BAMBERG DUNKEL — amber-brown, roasted malt aroma, dry roasted and caramel malt palate, medium to good body, long dry roasted malt aftertaste; 5.2% abv. Also found in Florida as above. [B, 72]

Brauerei Adolf Wurm OHG
Brewery in Werneck

WERNECKER PREMIUM PILS — gold, hop nose; flavor is both hops and malt; light body; aftertaste is hops and malt with some sweetness, but is dry hops at the end; gravity 11 P, 4.9% abv. [B, 47]

WERNECKER MÄRZEN GOLD — amber-gold, rich malt aroma, rich malt flavor and plenty of it, good body; hops are in there but there is not enough to balance the sweetness of the malt; long off-dry malt aftertaste; gravity 13 P, 5.4% abv. [B, 56]

Würzburger Hofbrau, A.G.
Brewery in Würzburg

WÜRZBURGER HOFBRAU LIGHT BEER — gold, marvelous balanced malty hop aroma, bright sour malt and hop flavor, lingering malt aftertaste, a satisfying bright pilsener beer. [B, 80]

WÜRZBURGER HOFBRAU BAVARIAN DARK BEER — deep amber-brown, heavy malt nose, hearty rich malt flavor, more mellow than zesty, sour malt finish, long malt aftertaste. [B, 65]

WÜRZBURGER OKTOBERFEST BEER — medium amber-brown color, faint hop aroma, delicious roasted malt flavor with a caramel background, excellent balance, soft and mellow, rich lingering malt aftertaste. [B, 80]

WÜRZBURGER BOCK BEER — deep dark brown, subdued burnt malt nose with plenty of hop support, roasted malt flavor, distinctive and with great character, long roasted malt aftertaste. [BK, 65]

WÜRZBURGER HOFBRAU MAY BOCK — pale copper-gold, hop aroma, tangy big hop flavor, very complex, big body, very long on the palate; really wakes up your tongue. [BK, 78]

WÜRZBURGER HOFBRAU ALCOHOL FREE LIGHT MALT BEVERAGE — amber, slightly sweet grainy aroma, watery, dry grainy flavor and aftertaste, not much length. [NA, 18]

WÜRZBURGER HOFBRAU PILSNER — pale yellow-gold, lovely malt nose; flavor is malt in front, hops at the finish, a little weak in the middle as it makes the transition; sour hop aftertaste. [B, 31]

Notes

BOLD GOLD MALT LIQUOR — pale gold, slight grape-soap nose, lightly sweet malt flavor, soft and delicate; faint hops appear in the long malt aftertaste. [ML, 31]

JULIUS ECHTER HEFE-WEISSBIER — brilliant amber, big head, zesty flowery honeyed malt aroma, bright spicy palate; wheat comes in nicely at the finish; refreshing and well balanced, wheat grain and faint clove aftertaste, good length, lots of character, an excellent beer of the style. [W, 74]

WÜRZBURGER HOFBRAU BAVARIAN HOLIDAY BEER — deep copper-brown, rich roasted malt aroma, big rich and beautiful toasted toffee-malt flavor, dry finish, excellent balance, long rich malt aftertaste, some sense of alcohol; very drinkable and feels good in your mouth; a great brew. [B, 95]

WÜRZBURGER HOFBRAU FESTBIER — amber, flowery hop nose, big off-dry malt and hop flavor, mild, smooth and balanced, good body, dry hop finish and

aftertaste, excellent beer; gravity 13 P, 5.5% abv. [B, 90]

WÜRZBURGER HOFBRAU SYMPATOR DOPPELBOCK — amber, malty nose, rich balanced complex concentrated malt flavor; alcohol is high (7.9% abv) but not obtrusive; big body, magnificent taste, just delicious and very long on the palate; sipping beer as it is too strong to quaff; gravity 18 P. [BK, 100]

WÜRZBURGER BÜRGERBRÄU PILS — gold, dry hop aroma and flavor well backed with malt, medium body, dry malt and hop finish and aftertaste, a little sourness at the end, fairly long; gravity 11 P, 5% abv. [B, 42]

WÜRZBURGER HOFBRÄU PILS VOM FASS — gold, bright hop nose, good body balanced malt and hop flavor; delicious and has character; long dry hop aftertaste; this is the beer as found on draft in Germany. [B, 82]

WÜRZBURGER HOFBRAU FALLFEST BEER — deep dark amber; flowery malt nose shows some hops; big off-dry malt and hop flavor; mild, smooth, and balanced; good body; dry malt finish and aftertaste shows good balancing hops; good duration, excellent beer; gravity 13 P, 5.5% abv. Bottled as export to the U.S.A. [B, 69]

Zeltbräu Hof
Brewery in Hof

ZELTBRÄU BAYRISCH GOLD — deep gold, light malt

nose, malt flavor on the dry side, medium body, dry malt finish and aftertaste; gravity 13.2 P, 5.5% abv. [B, 53]

SCHMIDTS HEINER DUNKLE WEISSE — deep hazy brown, tan head; spicy aroma has a bit of ashtray; spicy malt flavor, good body, light spicy finish, dry aftertaste; gravity 12.8 P, 5% abv. [W, 37]

ZELTBRÄU HOFER GASSENHAUER DUNKEL — brown, nice big fresh Ovaltine malt nose; dry malty flavor has an inherent richness; good body; dry malty aftertaste is long and faintly honeyed; subtle and complex, big and balanced, elegant, a beauty; gravity 13.2 P, 5.3% abv. [B, 92]

Brauerei Zoller-Hof
Brewery in Sigmaringen

ZOLLER BRENZKOFER DUNKEL — amber, light hop nose, medium body, dry malt flavor, short dry malt aftertaste. [B, 64]

ZOLLER FURSTEN HEFE-WEIZEN — hazy gold like grapefruit juice appearance, spicy clove nose, creamy feel in the mouth, clean light clove and malt flavor, refreshing and balanced, long clean fruity-malty aftertaste; a pleasure to drink. [W, 90]

ZOLLER FURSTEN KRISTALL WEIZEN — pale gold, light malt aroma and flavor; smooth, light, and refreshing; light body, medium long light dry malt aftertaste, excellent wheaty malt character throughout and no spiciness. [W, 80]

ZOLLER FURSTEN PILS — pale gold, big head, light hop nose, dry hop flavor, long dry hop aftertaste. [B, 77]

ZOLLER SPEZIAL-EXPORT — gold, dense head, clean hop nose, smooth hop flavor with a touch of malty sweetness, off-dry malt finish, long slightly off-dry malt and hop aftertaste. [B, 77]

ZOLLER BÖCKLE DUNKLES BOCK BIER — deep amber, thick tan head, faint malt nose, rich dry malt flavor, big body, very long rich dry malt aftertaste with some hops at the end, a delicious bock. [BK, 73]

ZOLLER FIDELIS WEIZEN — cloudy brown, fresh spicy malt nose, very rich flavor of malt and cloves, creamy texture, good body; long aftertaste like the flavor except the lactic acid is more noticeable. [W, 84]

ZOLLER FRISCH & LEICHT — pale gold, light hop aroma, pleasant light dry hop flavor with a good malty background, refreshing, light body, tasty, balanced, dry hop finish and aftertaste, a nicely made light beer; 2.7% abv. [LO, 60]

ZOLLER HOF WEISSBIER — gold, big tight head, very nice spice and malt aroma, fresh spicy-malt flavor; smooth, balanced, and creamy; long spicy malt aftertaste; 4.8% abv. [W, 87]

Herbert Zötler Gmbh. Adlerbrauerei Rettenberg
Brewery in Rettenberg

ZÖTLER PRIVAT PILS — pale gold, tight head, very nice hop and malt nose, complex spicy hop and sweet malt flavor, medium body, long dry hop aftertaste with sweet malt in behind; 4.7% abv. [B, 59]

ZÖTLER GOLD — gold, big head, light hop nose, light off-dry malt flavor, medium body, dull malty aftertaste; 5.3% abv. [B, 52]

ZÖTLER BAYERISCH HELL — pale gold, hop nose, dull dry malt flavor, medium body, dry malt finish and aftertaste; 4.7% abv. [B, 45]

ZÖTLER HEFE-WEIZEN — slightly hazy deep gold; faint malt nose is a bit brothy; good slightly spicy flavor; spice vanishes at finish leaving a long dry malt aftertaste; 5.2% abv. [W, 53]

Brauerei Zunstherrn
Brewery in Weitnau

ZUNSTHERRN HEFE-WEIZEN — hazy gold, big head, pleasant light spicy nose, medium big spicy flavor, smooth, good body, lightly spiced medium dry malt aftertaste; 4.9% abv. [W, 67]

ZUNSTHERRN EXPORT — brilliant medium gold, malt aroma and flavor, medium body, dry hop finish and aftertaste, ordinary brew; 5% abv. [B, 50]

Notes

Zwiefalter Klosterbrauerei
Brewery at Zwiefalt

ZWIEFALTER KLOSTERBRÄU PILSNER EDELTYP — gold, faintly roasted malt aroma, malt flavor with good hop support, a big lusty flavor, good body, long dry malt and hop aftertaste. [B, 67]

ZWIEFALTER KLOSTERBRÄU HEFE-WEIZEN — hazy gold, cereal and faint malt nose, malty flavor, medium body, dry malt finish and aftertaste; 4.7% abv. [W, 40]

ZWIEFALTER KLOSTERBRÄU PRIVAT — gold, hop nose; dull slightly oxidized malt taste; medium body, dull malt finish and aftertaste; 4.7% abv. [B, 38]

Great Britain

Abington Brewery Co., Ltd.
Brewery in Bedford

MISTRAL LAGER — gold, dank malt nose, dull malt flavor, dull malt aftertaste, short. [B, 16]

Adnams Sole Bay Brewery
Brewery in Southwold, Suffolk

ADNAMS BROADSIDE STRONG PALE ALE — amber, spicy nose, fruity ale flavor, high alcohol content (6.3%), creamy, smooth, balanced, quite malty throughout, long dry malt and hop aftertaste. [A, 79]

Allied Breweries (U.K.), Ltd.
Breweries include Ind Coope, Tetley-Walker, Lorimer, Beskins, Warrington & Ansells with locations in Burton-on-Trent and Leeds, England; Edinburgh, Scotland, et al.

DOUBLE DIAMOND ORIGINAL BURTON ALE — deep amber, beautiful rich off-dry roasted malt nose, dry bitter palate up front, off-dry malt finish; long very dry hop aftertaste that borders on bitter; excellent balance, medium body; has a sense of high alcohol; delicious. [A, 53]

DOUBLE DIAMOND PILSENER BEER — amber, big pungent hop aroma, big dry hop flavor, creamy, finely carbonated, long dry hop aftertaste; flavor could use more malt. [B, 57]

TETLEY BITTER — pale amber, nice hop aroma, finely carbonated, tart ale flavor with lots of hop character, fruity malt finish, long dry hop aftertaste. From Joseph Tetley & Son, Leeds. [B, 56]

TETLEY SPECIAL PALE ALE — medium amber, toasted malt aroma; flavor starts out like the nose, but the hop intensity increases across the palate to a sharp bitter hop aftertaste, with the roasted malt sliding into the background. [A, 30]

LORIMER'S TRADITIONAL SCOTCH ALE — golden amber; beautiful roasted malt aroma with good hops and a beneficial touch of sour malt that gives balance; intense roasted malt flavor, lingering dry malt aftertaste; big and powerful brew that has plenty of alcohol (7.2% abv). From Lorimer's Breweries, Ltd. of Edinburgh. [A, 67]

LORIMER'S SCOTTISH BEER — golden amber, big hop nose, huge mouth-filling malt and hop flavor, good balance; dry hop aftertaste has a touch of sour malt. From Lorimer's Breweries, Ltd. of Edinburgh. [B, 47]

ST. CHRISTOPHER NON-ALCOHOLIC BEER — amber, slightly sweet grainy aroma, watery; dry flavor that shows neither malt nor hops; odd dry aftertaste. [NA, 14]

JOHN BULL BEER — tawny-gold, bright hop and malt aroma; zesty big hop flavor well-backed with malt; full-bodied, good balance, long dry hop aftertaste. [B, 31]

CHESTER GOLDEN ALE — amber, malt nose and flavor, some off-dry malt at the finish, dull dry malt aftertaste. The Cheshire, Chester, and Mitchell brews were previously made by Greenall Whitley Co., Ltd. in Warrington, Cheshire, England. [A, 38]

CHESHIRE ENGLISH PUB BEER — deep amber, light

roasted malt nose with an apricot background, big body, off-dry malt flavor, finishes dry malt, long dry faintly hopped malt aftertaste. [A, 56]

MITCHELL'S CENTENARY ALE — deep copper-amber, complex malt aroma with a tangy hop background, tangy off-dry complex malt and hop flavor, good body, balanced sipping beer, dry middle and finish, excellent lightly sweet long malt aftertaste. [A, 86]

MITCHELL'S BITTER — amber, light hop and malt nose, light hop and malt flavor, weak middle, light sour hop finish and aftertaste. [A, 27]

MITCHELL'S BROWN ALE — ruby-brown; complex toasted malt nose has scents of licorice and bread as well; weak flavor is only faint malt; medium body, little or no aftertaste. [A, 32]

Alpine Ayingerbrau (U.K.), Ltd.
Brewery in Tadcaster, England

ALPINE AYINGERBRAU LAGER — gold, sour hop nose, flavor, and aftertaste. [B, 25]

Bass Charrington, Ltd.
A conglomerate of breweries comprised of the Bass, Worthington, Tennent Caledonian, Mitchells & Butler, and Charrington United. Breweries are in Burton-on-Trent, Birmingham, Sheffield, Tadcaster, and Runcorn, England; Belfast, No. Ireland; and Glasgow and Edinburgh, Scotland.

PIPER EXPORT ALE — deep amber color, roasted mash aroma, burnt toffee-apple flavor, sour in back; assertive at the beginning with the scorched malt and this mars the pleasant aspects; long dry off aftertaste. [A, 28]

BARBICAN NON-ALCOHOLIC MALT BEVERAGE — deep bright gold, dull toasted grainy nose, very light body, light grainy flavor, tartness in mid-palate, brief dry hop aftertaste. [NA, 16]

BASS NO. 1 BARLEY WINE — amber, tart citrus-cherry-licorice nose; palate is sweet malt in front, briny middle, and cuts off quickly at the finish; very complex but surprisingly brief, also the saltiness doesn't go well with the other flavors. [A, 31]

CHARRINGTON BARLEY WINE — very deep red-brown, rich complex nose of malt, coffee, and licorice; complex and rich malt flavor is a little too sweet in the middle; heavy body, off-sweet finish and aftertaste, very long duration; a complex malt sipping beer with hops faintly in the background. [BW, 56]

BASS PALE ALE — brilliant copper color, big malt and hop aroma, full rich malty flavor, excellent balance, marvelous long rich and dry aftertaste. Draft version. [A, 86]

BASS PALE ALE I.P.A. — brilliant copper, pleasant malt aroma, good malt flavor with plenty of hop support, well-bodied, excellent balance, long dry hop aftertaste. Bottled version. [A, 84]

WORTHINGTON E BRITISH BEER — pale amber, toasted malt nose, smoky well-hopped roasted malt flavor, complex and long, good flavor but a bit shallow. [B, 51]

WORTHINGTON'S ORIGINAL PALE ALE (WHITE SHIELD) — yellow-gold, yeasty aroma, delicate and complex malt and hop flavor, some yeast in the background, smooth and rich, long dry hop aftertaste. [A, 72]

TENNENT'S LAGER BEER — tawny-gold, creamy, clean malty aroma and malt flavor, faintly soapy backtaste, clean fresh malt finish, long dry malt aftertaste. [B, 83]

TENNENT'S EXTRA — deep gold, mild very good malt and hop aroma, good hop flavor with enough malt for balance, good body, malt finish, long satisfying dry hop aftertaste. [B, 49]

TENNENT'S MILK STOUT — opaque brown, rich malt nose with a smoky-burnt background, rich off-sweet malt flavor, medium body, pleasant long dry malt aftertaste. [S, 47]

TENNENT'S STOUT — deep brown, fragrant malty nose, very sweet flabby malt flavor, off-dry malt aftertaste. [S, 45]

George Bateman & Son
Brewery in Wainfleet

BATEMAN'S VICTORY ALE — amber-brown; malt nose is a bit winelike; big flavor starts out dry malt but finishes with a touch of caramel, concentrated taste with a hint of licorice, full bodied, long malt aftertaste like the flavor; the hops stay in back but are there; very tasty and very drinkable. [A, 65]

BATEMAN'S XXXB ALE — amber, fruity malt and alcohol aroma, flavor like the aroma, malt finish; long malt aftertaste shows some alcohol; complex, very warming and enjoyable. [A, 62]

Belhaven Brewery, Ltd.
Brewery in Dunbar, Scotland

BELHAVEN SCOTTISH ALE — copper-amber, toasted malt and hop aroma, hop flavor up front; malt in the middle, smoother and cleaner toward the finish; medium long dry hop aftertaste; good flavor for the most part. [A, 68]

TRAQUAIR HOUSE ALE — bright copper, lovely roasted malt aroma, intense roasted malt and sweet ale flavor, real sipping beer, great finish, long strong medium dry malt aftertaste. [A, 90]

BELHAVEN SCOTTISH PREMIUM LAGER — slightly hazy gold; malt nose that is both sweet and tart; very dry hop flavor with some dull malt in back, dry hop finish and long dry hop aftertaste. [B, 25]

ST. ANDREWS ALE — amber, toasted malt and European hop aroma, toasted malt and dry hop flavor, good body; malt takes on some caramelized character; flavor begins to develop a honeyed roasted malt background, but all this lets down at the end after showing some nice development. [A, 56]

Boddinton's Breweries, Ltd.
Brewery in Manchester

BODDINGTON'S BITTER BEER — deep bright gold, strong roasted malt aroma, pleasant roasted malt flavor, light body, very light dry hop aftertaste. [B, 29]

BODDINGTON'S DRAUGHT PUB ALE — hazy gold, big creamy head, faint lemony-fruity nose, bitter hop taste, tart finish, dry hop aftertaste, low carbonation, medium body, 4.8% abv. [A, 51]

S.A. Brain & Co., Ltd.
Brewery in Cardiff, Wales

BRAIN'S RED DRAGON IPA — copper-amber, nice delicate toasted malt nose, tangy complex malt and hop flavor, medium body, excellent balance, long good dry complex malt and hop aftertaste, very drinkable. [A, 83]

Broughton Brewery, Ltd.
Brewery in Broughton, Peeblesshire

SCOTTISH OATMEAL STOUT — deep brown, nose of malt extract like an unmalted barley, flavor like the nose but with some rolled oats, light on alcohol (3.8% abv), medium to light body; easy to drink; dry malt finish and aftertaste. [S, 61]

GREENMANTLE ALE — amber, light dry malt aroma, light dry dull malt flavor, no complexity, dry malt aftertaste, not long, 3.9% abv. [A, 34]

Matthew Brown P.L.C.
Lion Brewery in Blackburn

JOHN PEEL EXPORT BEER — tawny-gold, off-dry malt nose, big pleasant balanced malt palate, assertive, complex, and very long, a very good brew. [B, 72]

Caledonia Brewing Co., Ltd.
Brewery in Edinburgh, Scotland

MacANDREW'S SCOTCH ALE — bright copper, strong aromatic hop and toasted malt nose with a spruce-pine resin background, very complex flavor with smoky malt (like Scotch's whiskey), licorice, and peat, long rich aftertaste, a very good sipping beer. [A, 73]

GOLDEN PROMISE ALE — pale amber, big malt aroma; thin malt flavor is disappointing and surprising considering the strength of the nose; light body, dry malt finish and aftertaste. [A, 43]

Notes

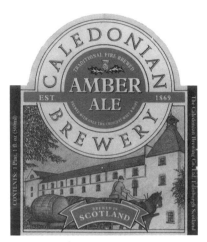

CALEDONIAN DOUBLE DARK ALE — deep amber, big dry nutty malt and alcohol nose, very dry malt flavor with roasted malt, medium body, a little smoky in the finish; light dry malt aftertaste is not long. [A, 63]

CALEDONIAN AMBER ALE — pale orange-amber, slightly hazy, toasted barley nose, roasted barley flavor, good body, slightly burnt finish, very long dry malt aftertaste. [A, 47]

CALEDONIAN GOLDEN PALE ALE — hazy gold, big hop aroma with plenty of malt support; big dry hop flavor is more like a pilsener than a pale ale; good supporting malt throughout, good body, long dry hop aftertaste. [A, 53]

Carlsberg Brewery
Brewery in Northampton

CARLSBERG SPECIAL BREW — bright amber-gold, big malt and malt aroma, big mouthful of flavor, lots of both malt and hops, big body, winelike and alcoholic (8%), complex and balanced; extremely long malt aftertaste has some hops in back for balance; nicely made beer. [B, 81]

Castle St. Brewery, Ltd.
Brewery in Sunderland

HERITAGE ENGLISH ALE — bright amber, appetizing toasted malt aroma; complex sharp hop flavor has a sweet malt component as well as licorice, orange peel, etc.; sour hop aftertaste, big body, good balance, high alcohol (7.2% abv), a good barleywine-style ale. [A, 86]

Cornish Brewery Co., Ltd.
Brewery in Redruth

CHURCHILL AMBER BEER — amber, toasted malt nose and flavor, medium to light body, long scorched malt flavor, toasted malt finish, long toasted malt aftertaste. [B, 31]

CHURCHILL LAGER — hazy gold, damp hay and malt nose, dry malt palate, dry hop finish, long dry hop aftertaste. [B, 35]

CHURCHILL DRY BEER — bright gold, faint malt nose, pleasant malt-hop flavor, hop finish, medium body, faintly sour long dry hop aftertaste. [D, 32]

Courage, Ltd.
Breweries in London, Reading, Plymouth, and Bristol

COURAGE LAGER EXPORT BEER — yellow-gold, high carbonation; hops dominate the nose and taste; long sour hop aftertaste. [B, 27]

JOHN COURAGE EXPORT — tawny-gold, foamy, off-dry malt nose, bitter hop flavor, doubtful balance, slightly off-dry malt aftertaste. [B, 31]

BULLDOG PALE ALE — pale yellow, hop nose, dull hop flavor up front, light hop finish, very brief dry hop aftertaste, almost none at all. [A, 29]

BULLDOG LAGER BEER — bright pale gold, intense fruity-malt aroma, big body, lots of hops in the flavor all the way through, long dry hop aftertaste, very good brew. [B, 60]

JOHN COURAGE AMBER LAGER — amber, light toasted malt nose, toasted malt flavor, smooth, medium body, long dry malt aftertaste. [B, 49]

IMPERIAL RUSSIAN STOUT 1983 — opaque brown, buttery roasted malt aroma; palate starts dry malt, gets intensely sweet in the middle, finishes sour, and this sourness carries into the long malt aftertaste. [S, 14]

1993 IMPERIAL RUSSIAN STOUT — deep brown, alcoholic port-like aroma, complex semi-sweet malt flavor, low carbonation, very smooth, big body, pleasant and satisfying, long malty port-like alcoholic aftertaste. The OG is a hefty 1098 and there is 10% abv. [S, 83]

MARTIN'S PALE ALE — amber, big head, complex pine needle and citrus aroma, big hop and malt flavor, very zesty; pine needles in back at the finish that go with the malt into the aftertaste; very big body, rich off-dry flavor, very pleasant long malt aftertaste. Made by Courage for John Martin N.V. of Antwerp, Belgium. Brewed in the U.K., bottled in Belgium. [A, 67]

HOFMEISTER SPECIAL VERY STRONG LAGER — golden amber, honeyed malt nose, strong alcoholic malt flavor, hops and alcohol aftertaste, strong and long, 9% abv. Made under agreement with Henninger Brau A.G. of Frankfurt, Germany. [B, 70]

Cumbrian Brewery Co., Ltd.
Brewery in Warrington

BEAVER EXPORT LAGER BEER — tawny-yellow, off-dry malt aroma, sharp hop flavor, dry hop aftertaste. [B, 16]

BURKE'S IRISH BRIGADE EXPORT STOUT — deep brown, roasted malt nose, good body, mellow flavor, well-balanced, pleasant long dry hop aftertaste with a trace of anise in back. [S, 52]

Davenport Brewery, Ltd.
Brewery in Birmingham

DAVENPORT'S HARVEST BREW — medium amber, tangy-fruity citrus-ale nose, dry malt palate with a faint sour hop component in back, pleasant and very drinkable; some sweet malt appears in the finish; good balance throughout, long complex malt and hop aftertaste, good sipping beer. [A, 86]

Edwin Cheshire Ltd.
Brewery in Stansted

KINROSS SCOTCH ALE — bright copper, off-dry caramelized malt nose and taste, not too sweet, consistent across the palate, good balance, long dry malt aftertaste, pleasant sipping beer. [A, 62]

Edwin Holden, Ltd.
Burton Bridge
Brewery in Dudley

BURTON BRIDGE BURTON FESTIVAL ALE — copper-amber, toasted malt nose, huge malt flavor, big body; hops are present but only in back; fruity off-dry apple-like finish, lightly hopped malt aftertaste. [A, 72]

BURTON BRIDGE BITTER ALE — hazy amber, complex hop and malt aroma; finely carbonated; light body, flavorful malt-hop palate, good balance; long smooth aftertaste has a cider-like quality. [A, 61]

BURTON BRIDGE XL BITTER — amber, complex nose of cantaloupe, melon, shellac, and cider; flavor is off-dry malt at first then linseed and woody oxidation; bad sample. [A, 30]

BURTON BRIDGE BURTON PORTER — tawny-brown, light off-dry malt nose, zesty hop and malt flavor, light but balanced, dry hop finish, long dry hop aftertaste. [P, 58]

Elgood & Sons Ltd.
North Brink Brewery in Wisbech, Cambridgeshire

NORVIG ALE — hazy gold, faint malty apple-like nose, chemical-apple taste; odd off-dry aftertaste is faintly apple-like. [A, 9]

FLAG PORTER — amber-brown, off-dry malty aroma, creamy texture; light off-dry malt palate is weak for a porter; pleasant off-dry malt finish and aftertaste, a bit wishy-washy. [P, 53]

Everard's Brewery, Ltd. / Tiger Brewery
Brewery at Burton-upon-Trent

EVERARD'S TIGER BEST BITTER — orange, extremely faint malt nose, light malt flavor, thin body; there is a little complexity but overall it is on the dull side; dry hop finish and aftertaste, 4.2% abv. [A, 37]

Felinfoel Brewing Co., Ltd.
Brewery in Llanelli, Wales

DRAGON ALE — amber; fairly strong hop nose is a little stinky; light body, thin hop flavor, malt finish; light malt and hop aftertaste is medium to long. [A, 38]

DOUBLE DRAGON ALE — very deep amber, zesty hop nose, big sweet hop flavor, good body, zesty hop finish, long spicy hop aftertaste; tastes like a good brewpub ale. Subsequently labeled Hercules Ale and, most recently, Welsh Ale. [A, 61]

JOHN BROWN ALE — copper-brown, faint malt aroma and flavor, short dry malt aftertaste. [A, 37]

FELINFOEL BITTER ALE — gold, hop nose, sharp hops up front on the palate; the flavor gradually softens until it is weak sour hops at the finish; thin body, weak watery aftertaste; just a quick burst of hops and that's that. [A, 35]

FELINFOEL CREAM STOUT — almost opaque red-brown, faint burnt licorice and malt nose, bitter and dry licorice flavor, finish, and aftertaste. [S, 20]

ST. DAVID'S PORTER — deep red-brown, faint malt aroma, malt flavor with a licorice finish, dry licorice aftertaste. Later labeled Princess Porter and then Welsh Porter. [P, 12]

HERCULES ALE — copper, candy nose, sweet licorice flavor, complex and alcoholic but overwhelmingly sweet right through the aftertaste, 7–8% abv. Same as Double Dragon and Welsh Ale. [A, 3]

WELSH ALE — deep amber, nose a bit off at first, then exotic spicy hops; very strong almost overwhelming malt and hop flavor; sweet then tart then sweet again, finishes sweet leading into a long off-dry aftertaste. Most recent label for Double Dragon and Hercules Ale. [A, 72]

FELINFOEL HERITAGE ALE — deep bright copper, light candy sweet nose, tart candy flavor, sour hop finish, good body, long dry hop aftertaste. [A, 32]

PRINCESS PORTER — deep ruby-amber, chicken coop aroma, dull watery malt flavor, mercifully brief. First imported as St. David's Porter and now called Welsh Porter. [P, 2]

FELINFOEL FESTIVE ALE — hazy amber, faintly acetone aroma, a big malt flavor, noticeable alcohol, very strong and very long. This is the 1991 issue. The 1993 version had less acetone, but was very strong and alcoholic. It did not go well with food, and was a little harsh. [A, 60]

WELSH BITTER ALE — deep amber; malt aroma has a fruitiness in back; big malt flavor, pleasant and on the dry side, medium body; finishes drier than it starts; medium long dry malt aftertaste. Previously labeled Dragon Ale. [A, 50]

Fuller, Smith & Turner, Ltd.
Brewery in Chiswick

FULLERS PALE ALE — tawny, toasted malt aroma, toasted malt flavor up front, bitter middle and finish, thin and watery, short dry hop aftertaste. [A, 27]

FULLERS LONDON PRIDE TRADITIONAL ENGLISH ALE — pale amber, lightly toasted malt nose, big hop flavor with the malt in back, dry hop finish and aftertaste with a touch of sour malt in back. [A, 34]

FULLERS ESB (EXTRA SPECIAL BITTER) EXPORT ALE — copper-amber; delicate off-dry toasted malt aroma, off-dry front palate, middle is rich hops, big dry hop finish; long dry hop aftertaste, fine carbonation, excellent body; hops dominate but the malt never gets shoved into the background; a super brew. On draft, it is similar but a lot smoother and even more drink-able. This is an excellent beer. I have even had badly mistreated samples that tasted great. [A, 89]

FULLERS 1845 BOTTLE CON-DITIONED STRONG ALE — deep amber, bright hoppy aroma and flavor, smooth and balanced, medium body, dry hop finish and aftertaste; the British amber malt and Goldings hops give it a bright British character. [A, 66]

FULLER'S OLD WINTER ALE 1995 — amber, rich malty nose; soft and smooth well-aged malty flavor tastes like a cask-conditioned brew; rich, smooth, and delicious; long faintly sweet malt aftertaste is a bit caramel-like; good for slow sipping enjoyment. [A, 80]

George Gale & Co., Ltd.
Brewery in Horndean

ANGEL STEAM BREWED BEER — bright copper, sweet roasted malt aroma, high carbon-ation, roasted malt and sharp hop flavor; complex but not attrac-tive with the hops and malt clashing at times; long dry hop aftertaste. [B, 36]

Notes

ANGEL STEAM BREWED ALE — amber, good roasted malt nose with some background hops, fine hop and roasted malt flavor, light body, pleasant finish, nicely balanced, long pleasing dry hop and malt aftertaste, very tasty and very good with food. [A, 51]

GEORGE GALE & CO. HSB BITTER — deep amber, funky malt nose, huge toasted malt flavor, big body, light hop finish, long dry malt aftertaste. [A, 84]

TUDOR HORNDEAN PALE ALE — deep amber, light malt aroma with good background hops, medium body, good bright malt flavor, malt finish, very drinkable; long off-dry malt aftertaste with hops coming in brightly at the very end. [A, 83]

PRIZE OLD ALE — cloudy deep brown, complex fruity-ale nose, somewhat like a hard cider, but more malty, assertive; strong barleywine-style flavor is complex off-dry malt; winelike, alcoholic; extremely long malt aftertaste, like almost a half hour later you can still taste it; a humongous sipping beer. [A, 60]

Gibbs Mews, PLC.
Brewery in Salisbury

OLD THUMPER EXTRA SPECIAL ALE — medium amber, marvelous smooth complex slightly sweet hop aroma, bright smooth complex roasted malt and hop flavor, good body and balance, finishes off-dry malt, extremely long malt aftertaste, very drinkable. Made for Ringwood Brewery, Ringwood. [A, 86]

FORTY-NINER FINEST ALE — pale amber, beautiful hop nose, complex with good malt support, good zesty malt and hop flavor; malt stays through the finish, but mostly the palate is hops; long dry hop aftertaste. Made for Ringwood Brewery. [A, 58]

THE BISHOP'S TIPPLE — deep amber, beautiful complex sweet berries and hop nose, well balanced with malt, good body, big smooth creamy rich malt flavor, off-dry in front, dry at finish, very long medium dry malt sort of sherry-like aftertaste (perhaps because it is 6.5% alcohol), excellent balance, very likable. [A, 95]

FARMER'S VELVET STOUT — extremely deep opaque brown, brown head, dry smoky-coffee nose, light body for a stout, dry smoky malt flavor and aftertaste. Brewed by the Old Brewery, Oakhill, Somerset, bottled by Gibbs Mews of Salisbury. [S, 52]

FARMER'S ALE — hazy pale amber, big fruity malt aroma, dry malt flavor with a burnt component, bitter hop finish, short dry hop aftertaste, medium body; faint citrus background is present throughout. Also brewed by Old Brewery and bottled by Gibbs Mews. [A, 34]

SARUM SPECIAL FINE PALE ALE — hazy dark amber, fruity malt nose, sweet malt front palate, dry middle, bitter finish, light body, faintly sweet malt aftertaste; doesn't quite come together. [A, 34]

Greenall Whitley Co., Ltd.
Brewery in Warrington, Cheshire

CHESTER GOLDEN ALE — amber, malt nose and flavor, some off-dry malt at the finish, dull dry malt aftertaste. [A, 38]

MITCHELL'S CENTENARY ALE — deep copper-amber, complex malt aroma with a tangy hop background, tangy off-dry complex malt and hop flavor, good body, balanced sipping beer, dry middle and finish, excellent lightly sweet long malt aftertaste. [A, 86]

Greene King, Ltd.
Breweries in Bury St. Edmunds and Biggleswade

GREENE KING ALE — bright amber, faint sour malt nose, light body, light bitter hop flavor, weak slightly sour malt and hop aftertaste. [A, 12]

ABBOT ALE — pale amber, apple-malt aroma, bitter hop flavor, long dry and bitter hop aftertaste. Another sample had a distinct pine character instead of the apple. It too lacked balance. [A, 25]

ST. EDMUND SPECIAL PALE ALE — fairly deep tawny-gold, candylike ale nose, sweet with a resiny background, sharp tangy hop-ale flavor, heavy body; big malt finish and aftertaste but there are unlikable components. [A, 20]

SUFFOLK DARK ENGLISH ALE — deep red-brown, big ale aroma with an off-dry, berry-like background, very complex malt and hop flavor with an acidic finish and aftertaste. [A, 45]

ABBOT DRAUGHT PUB ALE — brilliant amber; huge head was on two levels (the top one white, the lower one tan); malty aroma, creamy texture, soft malty flavor, soft and dry malt finish and aftertaste, medium long. Packaged in a can supposed to contain an element that creates the style of draught beer. It did give the beer a huge head and a creamy draught-like texture, but the second half of the can did not give this effect when poured. I guess it has to be all poured at once. [A, 66]

Brewers Guinness PLC
Brewery in London, English affiliate of Arthur Guinness of Ireland

GUINNESS DRAFT BITTER — amber, big thick head, faintly fruity malt aroma, malt flavor, weak body, lightly carbonated, weak dry and harsh malt aftertaste. This is packaged in a can. [A, 24]

PUB DRAUGHT GUINNESS — deep brown, pleasant hop and malt aroma, very dry mild hop flavor, medium body, dry hop finish, long dry hop aftertaste; packaged in a can this seems to be a lot lighter than the bottled or draft versions. [S, 19]

Hall & Woodhouse, Ltd.
Brewery in Blandford Forum

BROCK LAGER — hazy yellow, malt nose, light body; malt flavor is faintly salty and sour in the finish; medium dry malt aftertaste. [B, 16]

BADGER LIGHT ALE — pale sherry color, faint toffee-like nose, light body, molasses-flavored; pleasant molasses finish and aftertaste, but the weak body is off-putting. [A, 49]

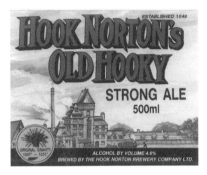

Harvey & Son (Lewes) Ltd.
Bridge Wharf Brewery in Lewes

HARVEY'S ELIZABETHAN ALE — hazy amber, big bubble head, toasted malt nose, strong sweet-ale palate; complex but has balance problems with many flavors coming at you from many directions; noticeable alcohol (over 8%), sour licorice aftertaste. [A, 36]

W.H. Brakspear
Brewer at Henley-on-Thames

HENLEY ALE — pale amber, nose shows a lot of malt; strong sweet malty flavor shows alcohol; big body, long off-dry malt finish; aftertaste starts off-dry, ends dry malt. [A, 56]

Hook Norton Brewery Co. Ltd.
Brewery in Banbury, Oxfordshire

OLD HOOKY STRONG ALE — pale amber, strong caramel nose, malty flavor, soft and too sweet, little complexity, just lots of caramel; shows some alcohol in the fairly long aftertaste. OG is 1047–1051, and there is 4.6% abv. [A, 34]

King & Barnes, Ltd.
Brewery in Horsham

KING & BARNES SUSSEX BITTER PALE LIGHT ALE — pale amber, light apple-malt nose, watery, light ale palate, little finish and aftertaste, not much to it. [A, 46]

KING & BARNES FESTIVE ALE — deep amber, light faintly soapy malt nose, watery, weak ale flavor, smoky finish, short sour malt aftertaste. [A, 44]

KING & BARNES FINEST OLD BROWN ALE — deep reddish-brown, slightly smoky malt nose, weak malt flavor with light hops in the finish, faint smoky malt aftertaste, questionable balance. [A, 48]

KING & BARNES 1994 CHRISTMAS ALE — amber, concentrated malt nose, big concentrated malt and alcohol taste, smooth, vinous, warming, rich long malty aftertaste, bottle-conditioned, 8% abv, brewed and bottled for King & Barnes. [A, 75]

Maclay & Co., Ltd.
Thistle Brewery at Alloa, Scotland

FRAOCH HEATHER ALE — gold, bright hoppy aroma, zesty dry complex hop flavor; a very smooth silky palate that is sort of slick; good body, long dry hop aftertaste. [A, 62]

Mansfield Brewery, Ltd.
Brewery in Mansfield

MARKSMAN IMPORTED ENGLISH LAGER BEER — hazy gold, light hop nose, light body, not much flavor beyond the carbonation, just some faint malt and hops, dry hop finish, very little aftertaste. [B, 32]

KINGPIN ENGLISH LAGER BEER — hazy amber, nice toasted malt nose; good malt flavor but it is a bit too light; faintly sour short malt aftertaste. [B, 46]

MANSFIELD BEST BITTER — brilliant amber, faint complex burnt vegetal-butter nose; burnt malt and bitter hop palate, malt finish, and a long malt aftertaste has hops arriving at the end. Sounds worse than it is, and it actually grows on you as you drink it. [A, 43]

OLD BAILY STRONG BITTER — deep amber, flat, well-hopped toasted malt flavor, long dry toasted malt aftertaste; needs the missing carbonation. [B, 36]

Marston, Thompson, and Evershed Ltd.
Brewery in Burton-upon-Trent

MARSTON'S PEDIGREE BITTER — gold, faint lemony hop aroma, lightly bitter English hop taste, low carbonation, dry hop finish and aftertaste, OG 1.043, 4.5% abv. Tasted in a small bottle (11 oz.) found in England. Another sample in a larger bottle (20 oz.) was deep gold; had a tangy ale-like hop nose; dry hop flavor that was quite austere; dry hop finish, long very dry aftertaste. [A, 63]

McMullen & Son Ltd.
Brewery in Hertford

CASTLE SPECIAL PALE ALE — medium amber, light complex off-dry hop aroma with interesting fruity notes like papaya and citrus, light body, light off-dry hop flavor, complex middle and finish, long light medium dry hop aftertaste. [A, 37]

Nethergate Brewery
Brewery in Suffolk

OLD GROWLER ALE — brilliant amber, caramel melony malt and hop aroma, dry toasted malt flavor, big body; there is a little burned malt that contributes some unwanted astringency, but the complexity grows on you despite that harshness; big dry finish, long well-hopped aftertaste, 4.1% abv. [A, 39]

OLD GROWLER PORTER — brown, big rich roasted malt aroma, concentrated malt flavor, medium to good body; long rich roasted malt aftertaste has some chocolate character. [P, 51]

Norwich Brewery Co.
Brewing Co. in Norwich

ANGLICAN STRONG ALE — hazy amber, big bubble head, crisp off-dry and citrus-ale nose; crisp tart flavor is strong hops in front, medium dry hops in the middle and finish; lots of bite on the sides of your tongue, dry hop aftertaste. Made in Manchester for Norwich. [A, 38]

Orkney Brewery
Brewery in Quoyloo, Sandwick, Orkney Islands, Scotland

DRAGONHEAD ORKNEY STOUT — deep brown, brown head; reich dry malt nose seems to have an oatmeal character; good body, dry malt flavor, finish, and aftertaste retains the oaty nature. 4.0% abv. [S, 67]

ORKNEY DARK ISLAND — deep amber, complex malt nose, luscious rich dry malt flavor, heavy body, smooth, balanced; stays rich but never gets sweet; very long rich dry malt aftertaste. 4.6% abv. [B, 83]

Notes

James Paine Brewery, Ltd.
Brewery in St. Noets

PAINE'S PALE ALE — tawny-gold, good hop aroma, light body, light watery malt and hop flavor, dull bready aftertaste. [A, 17]

Pitfield Brewery
Brewpub in London

DARK STAR NATURAL BEER — deep amber, off-dry slightly toasted malt nose, toasted malt palate with a slight chocolate background; finishes dry malt but there is only a short aftertaste of dry malt; pleasant but little length. [B, 67]

Eldridge Pope & Co., Ltd.
Brewery in Dorchester

THOMAS HARDY'S OLD ALE — bright reddish persimmon color, intense hop nose, very heavy body; robust malty-herbal hop flavor that carries through to a rich finish; long strong malt and hop aftertaste, a concentrated ale, luxuriously flavored. This is the description of the 1979 bottling. [A, 84]

THOMAS HARDY'S ALE 1982 — deep cherry-amber, strong fruity-malt nose with melon, papaya, and acid, heavy body; intensely sweet malt flavor is a little salty at first; extremely long malt and hop aftertaste, quite different from the 1979. [A, 83]

THOMAS HARDY'S ALE 1989 — hazy amber, beautiful roasted malt aroma with a definite sense of alcohol; taste is extremely rich malt heavily flavored with alcohol, but the very long aftertaste is dry malt; big bodied, aging very well, and has an excellent balance. [A, 85]

THOMAS HARDY'S ALE 1991 — cloudy amber, most appetizing rich malt nose with little apparent alcohol; body is huge; flavor is strong rich malt, particularly good on the front of the palate, but a bit coarse at the finish; aftertaste is already becoming dry but its strength is as yet unabated. [A, 83]

THOMAS HARDY'S ALE 1986 — dark amber and hazy; aroma transcends normal bounds with herbs, spices, flowers, smoke, leather, and tobacco, even scents normally found in fine old Bugundies and Barolos; the palate is like the nose but the features are greatly attenuated and underlie the malt; body is medium and there is a delicacy of flavors that is not there in younger samples; finish is very much like fine sweet sherry, almost like Pedro Ximenez grapes after they have been dried to raisins in the hot Spanish sun. [A, 94]

THOMAS HARDY ALE 1984 — paler than the 1986 (more like the 1989) and, by the aroma, the development of the brew is troubled. There is an acidic sparkle that masks most of the subtle complexities, all but the malt, herbs, and spices. On the palate, the same effect obtains, but the brew is bright and tasty with the spicy lightly acidic tang. Body is only medium, but the brew is very good to sip and ends with a smooth semi-dry spicy malt aftertaste. [A, 68]

THOMAS HARDY'S ALE 1988 — deep hazy amber, concentrated malt nose, flavor like a malt syrup, very low carbonation; at the finish there is a salty-sweet feeling on the palate as the flavor seems to flip around in confusion (or because the flavors are so strong the palate flips around in confusion), big long malt aftertaste. [A, 24]

POPE'S '1880' BEER — bright amber, complex roasted off-dry malt, orange peel, and hop aroma, complex creamy licorice, molasses, and toasted malt flavor, very dry and very long malt aftertaste. This is the bottled Pope's Dorset India Pale Ale. [A, 75]

ROYAL OAK PALE ALE — brilliant deep amber; complex rich off-dry malt and hop ale nose that favors the malt; big delicious malt flavor, fairly intense but still smooth, big body, finishes gently, long slightly off-dry mild malt aftertaste, not a whole lot of complexity but very well balanced, and a very very drinkable ale. [A, 67]

THOMAS HARDY COUNTRY BITTER — hazy amber, big bright hop nose; flavor has plenty of both hops and malt; well balanced, good body, smooth dry hop finish and aftertaste; fairly long, and in good condition even though tasted eight months after its "pull" date; a bottle-conditioned ale with 4.2% abv. [A, 73]

T.D. Ridley & Sons, Ltd.
Brewery in Chelmsford

BISHOPS ALE — amber, very big zesty hop and malt aroma, big head, roasted malt flavor, hop finish, long dry aftertaste with plenty of both hops and malt, a good well-balanced beer. [A, 83]

Robinwood Breweries & Vintners
Microbrewery in Todmorden

OLD FART — dark amber, very foamy, lactic nose and harsh acidic taste. [A, 8]

G. Ruddle & Co., Ltd.
Brewery in Oakham, Rutland

RUDDLE'S COUNTRY ALE — medium tawny-brown, pungent malt nose, sour malt flavor with a bitter hop finish, long dry bitter hop aftertaste. [A, 27]

RUDDLES COUNTY TRADITIONAL ENGLISH BEER — bright medium copper, tea, malt, and hop aroma, complex off-dry malt flavor, medium body, somewhat sweet finish with pine in the back of the tongue, dry hop aftertaste, interesting and fairly likable. [A, 40]

RUDDLE'S BITTER ENGLISH BEER — brilliant amber, light toasted malt nose, good hop and malt flavor, very light body, short dry hop aftertaste. [A, 26]

The Old Brewery
Samuel Smith's Brewery in Tadcaster

SAMUEL SMITH'S OLD BREWERY GOLDEN BROWN ALE — medium deep amber, burnt malt aroma with a trace of something like orange oil, smooth fruity-toffee malt flavor, well balanced and mellow, pleasant and appetizing dry malt aftertaste. [A, 72]

SAMUEL SMITH'S OLD BREWERY PALE ALE — pale amber, pale copper head, lovely roasted malt and molasses aroma, big hop flavor with plenty of roasted malt in support, big body, finely carbonated, long dry hop and roasted malt aftertaste, another lovely ale. [A, 85]

SAMUEL SMITH'S NUT BROWN ALE — red-brown, complex off-dry toasted malt nose with an apple backing, medium body, big complex ale flavor, slightly sweet finish, very long dry malt aftertaste. [A, 38]

SAMUEL SMITH'S OATMEAL STOUT — deep ruby-brown, almost opaque, complex fruity-malt aroma; palate is dry malt in fruit, off-dry malt at the finish; rich and full-bodied, soft and smooth, no bite whatever, long fairly dry malt aftertaste. [S, 78]

Notes

TADDY PORTER — brilliant deep red-brown, generous brown head, complex dry coffee bean aroma; dry rich clean malt and hop flavor has a mocha background; delicious and satisfying, long long clean dry malt aftertaste, a beautiful brew. [P, 93]

SAMUEL SMITH'S IMPERIAL STOUT — deep brown, intensely sweet malt nose, big sweet malt flavor but not cloying, good flavor, good body, good balance, dry malt aftertaste, well-made brew. [S, 68]

SAMUEL SMITH'S PURE BREWED LAGER BEER — hazy gold, hop nose; dry hop flavor has good malt backing; good balance, high carbonation, medium long dry hop aftertaste. [B, 51]

SAMUEL SMITH'S WINTER WELCOME ALE 1990–1991 — hazy gold, faintly skunky nose, big hop flavor, big body; malt

rolls in at mid-palate and is there in quantity; alcoholic finish, long dry malt aftertaste. [A, 59]

SAMUEL SMITH'S WINTER WELCOME ALE 1991–1992 — peach color; strong hop nose is almost skunky; finely carbonated, strong hop flavor, assertive and alcoholic, dull malt and sour hop aftertaste. [A, 75]

SAMUEL SMITH'S WINTER WELCOME ALE 1992–1993 — hazy amber, well-hopped alelike aroma, slightly toasted, big rich toasted malt flavor, big body, very long and rich toasted malt aftertaste. [A, 80]

SAMUEL SMITH'S WINTER WELCOME ALE 1993–1994 — brilliant copper-amber, smooth Fuggles hop aroma, big bright and zesty; delicious flavor that is equally hops and malt; creamy texture and a little on the sweet side, very good balance, dry malt finish; long dry aftertaste shows both the hops and malt. [A, 62]

SAMUEL SMITH WINTER WELCOME ALE 1994–1995 — deep amber; big hop nose seems to be slightly "light struck," but the big flavor is complex bitter hops; good body, long bitter aftertaste; a very good ale that is brightly hopped. [A, 62]

Scottish and Newcastle Breweries, Ltd.

Conglomerate comprised of MacEwan's, Younger's, and Newcastle Breweries in Edinburgh, Scotland, Newcastle-on-Tyne, England, et al.

MacEWAN'S SCOTCH ALE — deep amber, creamy, big piquant malt nose, big body, distinctive meal and malt flavor with good bittering hops in back, long dry hop and malt aftertaste. [A, 78]

MacEWAN'S TARTAN ALE — dark brown with reddish hues, creamy texture, strong off-dry malt taste, licorice and malt finish and aftertaste, quite long and very good. [A, 80]

MacEWAN'S EDINBURGH ALE — deep brown, creamy, rich very complex malt nose, beautiful rich roasted-smoky malt flavor, long smoky aftertaste, easily the best of the MacEwan ales. [A, 91]

MacEWAN'S STRONG ALE — deep amber-gold, clean delicate malt nose, rich full-flavored off-dry malt taste, very heavy body, long malt aftertaste. [A, 79]

MacEWAN'S MALT LIQUOR — extremely deep brown color, almost opaque, light toffee aroma, heavy body, rich very sweet malt flavor, bitter hop finish, long dry coffee aftertaste, high alcohol (7.8%). [ML, 50]

MacEWAN'S STRONG MALT LIQUOR — deep dark brown, slightly sweet roasted malt aroma, sweet caramel and toasted malt flavor with a touch of licorice, big body, balanced, lingering malt aftertaste. [A, 50]

MacEWAN'S EXPORT — amber, off-dry malt nose with some odd background, malt flavor, light body, brief dry malt aftertaste with some sweetness at the end. [A, 27]

NEWCASTLE BROWN ALE — dark amber-brown, nutty malt aroma, smooth and mellow malt flavor, some bitter hops at the finish, long dry hop and malt aftertaste, a delightful brew. A bottle received fresh from a London shop in early 1994 was very dull and uninteresting, but draft Newcastle Brown served in American pubs has continued as described before. [A, 72]

NEWCASTLE LIGHT ALE — medium copper-gold, off-dry malt nose, slightly sweet malt flavor; softens and fades at the finish; very little aftertaste. [A, 40]

YOUNGER'S TARTAN BITTER — amber, strange off nose with malt hidden beneath, sort of like burnt candy, bitter hop flavor, dry bitter hop aftertaste with little length. [A, 6]

YOUNGER'S KESTREL LAGER — bright amber-gold, good hop and malt aroma, strong bitter hop flavor up front; hops fade a bit and are replaced by malt in the mid-palate; medium body, soft and pleasant malt finish, medium length dry malt and light hop aftertaste, very drinkable. [B, 47]

YOUNGER'S KESTREL SUPER STRENGTH VERY STRONG LAGER — gold, stinky strong hop nose, winelike with noticeable alcohol (9.5%), strong and sweet (strong hops and sweet malt), heavy body, long off-dry hop and malt aftertaste; gets better as you continue to drink it; very much like drinking a malt whiskey. [B, 74]

GORDON HIGHLAND SCOTCH ALE — deep rose-brown, extremely dense small bubble long-lasting brown head, well-balanced rich roasted malt and hop aroma and flavor, full body, high density, high alcohol (8%), extremely long rich malt aftertaste. Brewed by Scottish Brewers Ltd. and bottled by John Martin of Antwerp, Belgium. [A, 85]

GORDON DOUGLAS SCOTCH BRAND ALE — deep amber, light dry malt aroma, concentrated malt flavor, big body; aftertaste is briefly off-dry malt but quickly goes and stays dry; a big brew that feels good in your mouth. Made for John Martin of Antwerp, Belgium. [A, 73]

THEAKSTON OLD PECULIER YORKSHIRE ALE — brown, aroma of canned brown bread, dry malty-molasses flavor, malt finish, light malt aftertaste; tastes a whole lot better than it sounds. Theakston brews were previously made by T & R Theakston, Ltd. with breweries at Masham and Carlisle, England. [A, 51]

Notes

THEAKSTON BEST BITTER
ALE — tawny-gold, fragrant hop
aroma with a touch of apple cider,
light carbonation, good tasting
malt and hop flavor, good balance,
bitter hop finish, long dry hop
aftertaste. [A, 49]

DOUGLAS SCOTCH BRAND
ALE — deep amber, sherry-like
malt aroma; rich concentrated cof-
fee-sherry is one of the many flavors that continue to rise up as it
warms; big body; aftertaste is
briefly off-dry malt but quickly goes
and stays dry with warming alcohol;
a big brew that feels good in your
mouth. Made for John Martin of
Antwerp, Belgium. [A, 93]

GORDON FINEST GOLD
BLOND ALE — gold; sweet malt
aroma shows a great deal of alcohol; big malt and alcohol flavor,
big body, very alcoholic and malty
throughout, surprisingly little duration. Brewed in Edinburgh by
Scottish & Newcastle, bottled by
John Martin in Antwerp. [A, 73]

YOUNGER'S TARTAN SPE-
CIAL — dark amber, malt nose; dry
malty flavor is a bit toasty; medium
body; palate stays dry throughout;
long dry malty aftertaste. [A, 67]

Shepherd Neame Ltd.
Canterbury Brewery in Faversham

CANTERBURY HOP PICKER'S
PALE ALE — copper-amber, dry
complex ale aroma with a buttery
component, dry sour hop flavor
and aftertaste. [A, 39]

CANTERBURY PREMIUM
ALE — amber, light hop and malt
aroma (with a faint background of
paint thinner); flavor starts out with
hops, but a chemical taste develops
and the hops turn sour; must be bad
sample. [A, 19]

CANTERBURY REGIMENTAL
DINNER ALE — amber, aroma of
sweet malt, hops, apple, and cardboard; strong hop flavor has plenty
of supporting malt, but the balance
is questionable; hops go from bitter
to salty then sour. [A, 42]

KINGFISHER LIGHT
PREMIUM LAGER BEER —
pale hazy gold, big hop nose, big
dry hop flavor, light body; flavor
cuts off as soon as you swallow.
Made under license/for UB Ltd.,
Bangalore, India for distribution
in U.S.A. [LO, 36]

KINGFISHER PREMIUM
LAGER BEER — brilliant pale
gold, big hop nose plenty of
malt; flavor is mostly hops but
there is plenty of supporting
malt; short sour hop aftertaste.
Again, made for UB Ltd. [B, 42]

MASTER BREW PREMIUM
ALE — pale amber, malt nose
with hops in back, good malt presence; hops stay back until finish
and then roll out forcefully, and
dominate the aftertaste; like the
Bishop's Finger, but not as big or
as balanced; pleasant and very
drinkable. [A, 63]

BISHOP'S FINGER KENTISH
ALE — amber, malt nose with
hops in back; big assertive flavor
has strong malt presence; plenty

of hop support; hits every corner
of your mouth; big body; hops
emerge at the finish and dominate
thereafter; a round brew very balanced yet powered throughout,
very long hoppy-ale-like aftertaste. [A, 81]

SPITFIRE PREMIUM ALE —
amber, roasted malt aroma;
toasted malt flavor is a bit dull;
medium to light body, dry hop
aftertaste. [A, 35]

T & R Theakston, Ltd.
Breweries at Masham and Carlisle

THEAKSTON OLD PECULIER
YORKSHIRE ALE — brown,
aroma of canned brown bread, dry
malty-molasses flavor, malt finish,
light malt aftertaste; tastes a whole
lot better than it sounds. [A, 51]

THEAKSTON BEST BITTER
ALE — tawny-gold, fragrant hop
aroma with a touch of apple cider,
light carbonation, good tasting
malt and hop flavor, good balance,
bitter hop finish, long dry hop
aftertaste. [A, 49]

Daniel Thwaites & Co., Ltd.
Brewery in Blackburn

BIG BEN ENGLISH BEER —
tawny-gold, clean malt and hop
aroma with a roasted malt background; pleasant and clean roasted
malt flavor, but there is little
depth; slightly salty finish, medium long dry roasted malt aftertaste. [B, 46]

Tollemache & Cobbold Breweries Ltd.
Brewery in Ipswich

TOLLY ORIGINAL PREMIUM ALE — bright pale copper, toasted malt aroma, strong toasted malt flavor, medium body; finish is like the flavor but less intense; long sharp and sour hop aftertaste, overall seems a bit coarse. [A, 42]

Vaux Brewery
Brewery in Sunderland and Sheffield, England. Includes subsidiary S.H. Ward & Co., Ltd.

VAUX DOUBLE MAXIM SUNDERLAND BROWN ALE — amber, mild hop and strong malt nose; flavor starts out as sour malt, but quickly becomes bright hops; sour malt returns for the aftertaste; weak body for a brown ale, and not much duration. [A, 34]

WARD'S ENGLISH ALE — amber, finely carbonated, mild off-dry ale nose, lots of good malt and hop flavor, but light bodied; pleasant flavor is best at the finish; slightly off-dry malt aftertaste has only fair length, and overall the brew lacks depth. [A, 46]

WARD'S GOLDEN ALE — bright amber, faint hop nose with an off-dry malt background, good body, mild slightly sweet malty-ale flavor, very pleasant mild medium long malt aftertaste, no raves but quite pleasant. [A, 65]

Watney-Mann & Truman Brewers, Ltd.
Brewing Co. comprised of nine regional companies: Watney, Combe & Reid, Truman, Usher, Bryborough, Wilson, Webster, Phoenix, Norwich, and Mann. Breweries in Norwich, Mortlake, London, Edinburgh, Halifax, Manchester, and Trowbridge.

WATNEY'S RED BARREL — bright amber, tangy malt nose, zesty malt and hop flavor, bright and well balanced, tangy in front, off-dry malt in the middle, dry at the finish, complex and long. This beer has also been labeled Watney's Traditional Beer in the U.S.A. Widely available on draft. [A, 75]

WATNEY'S STINGO DARK ALE — opaque brown, all-malt treacle nose with a faint sourness in back, taste of heavy malty-molasses, tenacious long sweet malt aftertaste, despite all that sweet malt; the balance is fairly good; an interesting barley-wine style with 7% abv. [A, 34]

WATNEY'S STINGO CREAM STOUT — opaque brown, off-dry concentrated malt nose, big smoky (very much burnt) malt flavor, big body, pleasant, decent balance, overall fairly dry, not filling, long dry malt aftertaste. [S, 59]

Notes

WATNEY'S CREAM STOUT — deep brown, tan head; malty nose doesn't yield expected roasted barley or chocolate malt, but the roast barley is there on the palate; very smooth and soft, but not long. [A, 36]

MANN'S THE ORIGINAL BROWN ALE — brown, good rich coffee aroma with a charcoal background, finely carbonated, full all-malt flavor, no hops noticeable, smooth and mellow, good balance, lightly sweet long malt aftertaste, a delightful 'mild.' [A, 61]

USHER'S WINTER ALE — medium brown, light malt nose; dry and robust malt flavor, you can really sink your teeth into it; long flavored dry malt aftertaste, marvelous sipping beer. [A, 92]

TRUMAN'S CHRISTMAS ALE — medium deep amber; beautiful complex citrus-ale nose that reminds you of margarita mix; malt and hop flavor with an ale-like character, excellent balance, complex, long, and satisfying. [B, 85]

SCOTTISH PRIDE LIGHT BEER — deep tawny-gold, malt nose with a sourness in back, light dry malt flavor, light body, very little aftertaste. From Drybrough & Co., Ltd., Edinburgh. [B, 27]

LONDON LIGHT LAGER BEER — bright gold, malt nose, weak malt flavor, thin body, weak brief malt aftertaste. [LO, 34]

WATNEY'S LIGHT — deep gold, lovely malt nose with good hop backing, light body; light malt flavor is faintly sour; short dull malt

aftertaste. From Watney, Combe, Reid & Co., Ltd. [LO, 20]

WATNEY'S LIGHT BEER — hazy gold, slightly stinky soapy hop aroma; strange light sour vegetal malt flavor, reminds you of cabbage; short sour malt aftertaste. From Watney-Truman, Ltd. [LO, 20]

Charles Wells, Ltd.
Brewery in Bedford

GOLD EAGLE BITTER — tawny-gold, beautiful hop and malt aroma, good balance, bitter hop flavor with a caramel aftertaste. [A, 57]

CHARLES WELLS LIGHT ALE — tawny-gold; hop nose has a pine and barnyard background; hop flavor but there is unpleasantness in behind; long aftertaste like the flavor. [A, 17]

CHARLES WELLS BOMBADIER ALE — amber, complex elusive nose of flowers and hops, toasted malt flavor with little depth, light body, slightly bitter hop aftertaste with little duration. [A, 38]

OLD BEDFORD ALE — deep brilliant amber, mild toasted malt aroma with a sour background; strong hop flavor has good supporting malt for balance; sweet ale mid-palate, strong finish, long off-dry malt and hop aftertaste, big body, huge flavor; a big bright sipping beer that is not for the weak of spirit. [A, 63]

CHARLES WELLS DRAGOON PALE ALE — amber; oxidized aroma and flavor (despite the sample being freshly arrived in country); just wet cardboard for taste, dry slightly oxidized finish and aftertaste. [A, 13]

Whitbread & Co., Ltd.
A large brewing conglomerate with breweries in Cheltenham, Leeds, Liverpool, Luton, Faversham, Durham, Salford, Sheffield, Samlesbury, Marlow, Portsmouth, Tiverton, Wateringbury, and Romsey, England

WHITBREAD TANKARD LONDON ALE — tawny-brown, caramel and yeast nose, good malty flavor, good balance, short dry malt aftertaste. [A, 69]

WHITBREAD ALE — deep tawny-brown; beautiful rich and smooth caramel-malt aroma has a substantial hop background; big hop and caramel malt taste, very appetizing, finely balanced, long well-hopped and malted aftertaste, a very enjoyable brew. [A, 78]

WHITBREAD BREWMASTER — brownish gold, highly carbonated, malt aroma and flavor, dry malt finish and medium aftertaste, not well balanced. [B, 34]

MACKESON STOUT — very deep dark brown, almost opaque, rich malt aroma, heavy body, syruplike, rich coffee-malt flavor, excellent stout and a worthy rival of Guinness, perhaps not as dry but in some respects a bit richer. [S, 89]

GOLD LABEL NO. 1 SPARKLING BARLEY WINE — rosy-orange, sweet candy-apple nose, assertive aroma and flavor much like some of the strongly flavored fruity cough medicines, but not medicinal; strong hops really bite the corners of your mouth and back of the tongue; long bitter hop aftertaste, a powerfully strong sipping beer. [BW, 20]

MACKESON TRIPLE STOUT — extremely deep opaque brown, roasted malt aroma, off-dry malt flavor, very rich and very big, long rich off-dry malt aftertaste, quite drinkable for a heavy brew. [S, 58]

CAMPBELL'S CHRISTMAS — deep copper, big sweet rising malt nose, rich, complex, intensely flavored malt, big bodied, long off-dry malt aftertaste, an incredible beer made for the Belgian market, a must try for any serious beer drinker. [A, 91]

CAMPBELL'S SCOTCH ALE — very deep amber-brown, fresh and tangy ale nose, big malt and hop flavor, very insistent, almost overwhelming, complex, strong, aftertaste like the flavor but a bit less intense and drier, very long. Also made for the Belgian market. [A, 84]

CAMPBELL'S GOLD LABEL — deep amber, huge head, light complex toasted malt and hop aroma, big malt and hop flavor, excellent balance, big body, long delicious complex malt and hop aftertaste, a

huge brew, winelike and alcoholic (10%), great sipping beer. Made for the Belgian market. [A, 83]

BODDINGTON'S BITTER BEER — deep bright gold, strong roasted malt aroma, pleasant roasted malt flavor, light body, very light dry hop aftertaste. This brew was previously made by Boddinton's Breweries, Ltd. in Manchester, England. [B, 29]

Wrexham Lager Beer Co., Ltd.
Brewery in Wrexham, Wales

WREXHAM LAGER BEER — medium to deep gold, skunky hop nose, high carbonation, complex malt and hop flavor, light body, sour malt finish and aftertaste. [B, 34]

Young & Co. Brewery, PLC.
Brewery in London

YOUNG'S SPECIAL LONDON ALE — amber, soapy tangy citrus-ale nose like hard cider, big tangy zesty strong ale flavor, complex, a real mouthful of ale, good and powerful, extremely long complex dry hop aftertaste, a classy ale with no coarseness. [A, 84]

YOUNG'S RAM ROD SPECIAL ALE — amber, light ale nose, light salty ale flavor, kind of ordinary, light dry hop aftertaste with medium duration. [A, 47]

Notes

OLD NICK BARLEY WINE STYLE ALE — deep copper-red, light citrus and fruity malt aroma, tart malt and hop palate, dry hop finish, beautiful flavor transition in the mid-palate, excellent balance, long complex medium dry malt and hop aftertaste. [A, 62]

YOUNG'S WINTER ALE 1988 — very deep amber, faint malt nose, light burnt dry malt flavor, complex dry malt finish, long pleasant dry malt aftertaste; leaves your mouth clean and dry. [A, 58]

YOUNG'S WINTER ALE 1990–1991 — deep amber, light malt aroma, smooth malt flavor; faint buttery background detracts from the enjoyment; sour malt finish, short dry malt aftertaste, lacks zest. [A, 48]

YOUNG'S WINTER ALE 1995 — deep amber, bright concentrated malt aroma, rich malt flavor, medium to good body, long rich concentrated malt aftertaste. [A, 79]

YOUNG'S ORIGINAL LONDON PORTER — deep ruby-amber, very faint dry malt nose, very dry and faintly sour malt flavor; long malt aftertaste ends bitter hops; not really very interesting. [P, 30]

YOUNG'S OATMEAL STOUT — deep ruby-brown, faint malt nose, dry malt flavor, touch of smoke in the finish; dry malt aftertaste has good length. [S, 47]

Greece

Atalanti Brewery / Henninger Hellas S.A.
Brewery in Athens

AEGEAN HELLAS BEER — gold, malt aroma with just a touch of hops, malt flavor with little complexity, light body, sour malt aftertaste. [B, 45]

SPARTAN LAGER EXPORT — bright yellow-gold, pleasant malt nose with good hop background, dull off-dry malt flavor, dry and bitter hop aftertaste. [B, 43]

AEGEAN LAGER BEER — gold, dull malt aroma, dull malt flavor, slightly oxidized, sour hop finish, dry sour hop aftertaste, may be new label of Aegean Hellas, but certainly not a very fresh sample. [B, 24]

Hellenic Brewery and Winery, S.A.
Brewery in Athens.
Also uses names Athenian Brewery, S.A. and Karolos Fix, S.A.

ATLAS GREEK BEER — medium to pale gold, faint malt and hop nose, dull malt flavor and aftertaste. [B, 37]

FIX BEER — gold, malt and hop nose, off-dry malt flavor, finish, and aftertaste. [B, 50]

ATHENIAN GREEK BEER — yellow-gold, creamy head, light pilsener-type nose, slightly bitter hop flavor, very faint and short dry hop aftertaste. [B, 50]

MARATHON GREEK BEER — yellow-gold, faint malt nose; light hop flavor is on the bitter side; very faint dry hop aftertaste. [B, 50]

FIX 1864 SPEZIAL — bright gold, lovely malt and hop aroma, off-dry malt palate up front, sharp hop finish, short dry hop aftertaste, not much character. [B, 24]

Holland

Bavaria Breweries / Swinkel's Holland BV
Brewery in Lieshout

BAVARIA LAGER — pale yellow, vegetal malt nose, malt and hop flavor, dry hop finish and aftertaste. [B, 31]

SWINKEL'S EXPORT BEER — medium gold, highly carbonated, pleasant beery malt and hop aroma, good hop and malt flavor, well-balanced, dry hop finish and aftertaste, clean and refreshing. [B, 36]

SWINKEL'S IMPORTED BEER — pale gold, very faint malt nose, light body, light off-dry malt palate, highly carbonated, faint malt aftertaste. [B, 27]

SWINKEL'S LIGHT IMPORTED BEER — bright gold, grainy malt nose; flavor starts as grainy malt and dies out quickly; no finish or aftertaste. [LO, 17]

GUILDER IMPORTED BEER — pale gold, grainy barley nose, high carbonation, dull malt flavor, dry malt finish, short dry malt after- taste. [B, 34]

BAVARIA MALT BIER — bright gold, faint malt nose, weak and wa- tery, pleasant light malt flavor, short malt aftertaste. They claim very low alcohol (less than .09%). [M, 34]

SWINKELS BROWN ALE — amber-brown, rich malt aroma when swirled, rich malty flavor, chewy and complex, smooth and balanced; changes across the pal- ate; sometimes a bit sweet, some- times a bit dry; dries at the long malty aftertaste. [B, 86]

Royal Brand Brewery
Brewery in Wijlre. Some labels spell the town name Wyrle.

BRAND HOLLAND BEER — pale gold, pleasant hop nose, bright hop well-balanced flavor, good hop finish, long dry hop aftertaste, brisk and refreshing. Also has been labeled Brand Lager Beer. [B, 64]

BRAND BEER — pale gold, light hop aroma; hop palate is balanced very well with malt; smooth with some complexity, long dry hop aftertaste. [B, 64]

Bierbrowerij de Drie Hoefijzers
Brewery in Breda is affiliated with Skol, International and owned by Allied Breweries (U.K.), Ltd.
Also uses Posthoorn Brewery name.

BREDA ROYAL HOLLAND BEER — gold, strong hop nose, dull malt and hop flavor, dull malt aftertaste. [B, 29]

ROYAL DUTCH — yellow- gold, medium hop nose, dull hop flavor, bitter hop finish and aftertaste. [B, 14]

ROYAL DUTCH KOSHER HOLLAND BEER — deep gold, hop nose with a skunky back- ground; hop palate has some malt in back; dry almost bitter hop aftertaste. [B, 16]

SKOL LAGER BEER — tawny-gold, finely carbonated, malt and hop nose, light hop flavor, finish, and dry hop aftertaste. [B, 25]

THREE HORSES BRAND PILSENER LAGER BEER — gold, sharp hop nose; flavor is sour malt with a bitter hop background; strong bitter hop aftertaste. [B, 32]

Bierbrowerij St. Christoffel
Brewery in Roermond, Limburg

CHRISTOFFEL BIER — hazy gold, big head but light carbonation on the palate, grainy malt nose, very dry hop flavor, big body, solid strong long dry hop aftertaste; a very dry well-hopped beer but it carries it off very well and it is super with food. More recently imported with a St. Christoffel Blond label. [B, 73]

ST. CHRISTOFFEL ROBERTUS — golden amber, good malt aroma, bright and rich malt flavor, good body, long smooth malty aftertaste, 5.5% abv. A second sample, tasted in early 1995, was hazy amber; had a tangy ale-like aroma; big bright assertive hop-ale flavor, good body, long dry hop aftertaste. [B, 63]

Brouwerij de Dissel
Brewery in Breda

REMBRANDT MASTERPIECE BEER — gold; European hop nose is almost skunky; dry hop flavor, good body; finish shows a trace of oxidation; medium dry hop and malt aftertaste. [B, 34]

Grolsche Bierbrowerij
Brewery in Enschede

GROLSCH NATURAL HOLLAND BEER — amber, tart hop nose, rich sour malt flavor with plenty of good hops, long dry hop aftertaste, good complex brew. [B, 48]

GROLSCH LAGER BEER — bright gold, beautiful malt and hop aroma; flavor starts out bright and hoppy but smoothly makes the transition to a dry malt finish; good body, very good balance; long dry aftertaste has both hops and malt; good very drinkable brew. [B, 56]

GROLSCH PREMIUM DRY DRAFT BEER — deep gold, pleasant malt aroma, soapy hop flavor, brief dry hop finish; long faintly dry hop aftertaste comes in quite a while after you swallow. [B, 20]

GROLSCH DARK BEER — deep amber; faintly skunky nose at first but this can be swirled away to be replaced with hops and malt; big hop flavor is too much hops and too little malt for balance; further, the skunk tries to return, long dry hop aftertaste can barely keep the skunk at bay. [B, 47]

GROLSCH AUTUMN AMBER — amber, European hops and caramel malt aroma, light malt front palate; hops join in right away and stay; medium body, long dry hop aftertaste. [B, 38]

GROLSCH MEI BOCK — very deep gold; skunky nose that slowly shows more hops than polecat; hop flavor is better than the smell; dry hop finish, long dry hop aftertaste; never gets around to tasting good. [B, 32]

GROLSCH AMBER BEER — deep amber, light roasted malt aroma, dry roasted malt flavor, medium body, very dry uninteresting finish and aftertaste; no complexity but is thirst quenching; nothing offensive about it. [B, 40]

GROLSCH BOK — reddish amber, dry malty nose, big off-dry malty flavor, good body; finish and aftertaste still quite sweet and very malty, although drier than the main palate. [BK, 60]

NAVIGATOR MALT LIQUOR — gold, malty alcoholic aroma and flavor, big body; flavor is sweet and winelike; good with spicy food but the alcohol is too forward; 10% abv. [ML, 44]

B.V. Gulpener Bierbrowerij
Brewery in Gulpen

X-PERT HOLLAND BEER — amber-gold, hop nose, thin hop flavor, weak body, watery, bitter hop and sour malt finish, faintly bitter long dry hop aftertaste. [B, 31]

GULPENER HOLLAND PILSENER BEER — tawny-gold, malty-grainy aroma; palate is hops in front, roasted malt in the middle, sour hops at the finish; long dry hop aftertaste, good balance, pleasant drinking beer locally known as Limburg Bitter. [B, 57]

Heineken Brouwerjen
Three breweries in Holland at Amsterdam, Rotterdam, and Hertogenbosch. The Rotterdam brewery supplies all the export lager.

HEINEKEN LAGER BEER — medium gold; nose is smooth hops and malt; flavor is dry and well-hopped; well-balanced, good body, long dry hop aftertaste. On draft it is very similar except that there is less hop intensity in the aftertaste. [B, 72]

HEINEKEN SPECIAL DARK BEER — copper-gold, pleasant rich malt aroma and taste, fine balance, long pleasing medium dry malt aftertaste. [B, 75]

AMSTEL LIGHT — pale gold, faint malt aroma, dull dry malt flavor, brief aftertaste. [LO, 20]

BUCKLER NON-ALCOHOLIC BREW — gold, grainy hop nose and taste, light body, thin even, medium length faint aftertaste like the flavor. The local version (in the Netherlands) is a little better equipped with malt and hops, both in the aroma and flavor, is less grainy and more malty. According to the ratings of my taste panel, about 20% better. [NA, 35]

HEINEKEN TARWEBOK — deep brilliant amber, big dry toasted malt nose, strong malty taste, good body, off-dry malt finish and aftertaste, good length; has noticeable alcohol; good concentration of malt. [BK, 63]

La Trappe
A Trappiste brewery located at Abbaye de Koningshoeven (Abdij Van Koningshoeven), Schaapskool in Terberg/Tilburg

LA TRAPPE ENKEL — gold; stinky grassy nose at first but the malt rises through the badness; a bright taste has a light lactic flavor over the malt; dry malt finish and aftertaste; the malt lasts quite long in the mouth and the spiciness stays as well blending nicely with the hops that emerge in the aftertaste. This ale is described as being a "single." [A, 58]

LA TRAPPE DUBBEL — amber, big malty nose with a spiciness, very bright big malt flavor with a spicy background, full bodied; a touch of hops join the spicy malt in the aftertaste; 6.5% abv. [A, 80]

LA TRAPPE TRIPEL — gold, big head, highly carbonated, spicy aroma; bright spicy hoppy flavor shows plenty of malt, hops, and 8% abv; tingles in your mouth, on the sweet side in front, but dries toward the end. [A, 71]

LA TRAPPE QUADRUPLE — deep copper-amber; light malt aroma is faintly spicy; concentrated malt flavor is quite sweet and slightly spicy; the sweetness goes into the aftertaste as does a bit of the spiciness but they are not really balanced; some odd esters in the aftertaste and it is a bit winey (10% abv), but is still a very tasty abbey ale. OG is 1084–1088. [A, 52]

LA TRAPPE ALE — amber-gold, faint fruity alcoholic nose, strong spicy clove palate with noticeable alcohol, long spicy aftertaste. Made for John Martin of Antwerp, Belgium. Strangely, it is labeled as a product of Belgium. [A, 69]

Bierbrowerij dee Leeuw
Brewery in Valkenburg

LEEUW HOLLAND PILSENER — gold, good toasted malt and hop aroma; malt palate shows best at the finish; very tasty, long dry malt and hop aftertaste. [B, 40]

Bierbrowerijen Lindeboom B.V.
Brewery in Meer

LINDEBOOM HOLLAND PILSENER BEER — dull gold, big head, big and bright hop nose; palate starts out off-dry malt, hops come roaring in at mid-palate and stay, malt returns at the finish for balance; aftertaste is long and complex; high carbonation intrudes on the good flavor. [B, 37]

Oranjeboom Breweries
Breweries in Rotterdam. Affiliated with Skol, International and owned by Allied Breweries (U.K.), Ltd.

ORANJEBOOM HOLLAND PILSENER DE LUXE — yellow-gold, strong vegetal malt and wild-flower hop aroma, tart hop flavor with slightly sour malt way in back; weak mid-palate, but finishes well with dry hops; dry hop aftertaste with good duration. [B, 45]

Bierbrouwerij Schinnen
Brewery in Schinnen. Also uses Meens Brewery and Alfa Brewery corporate names.

ALFA FRESH HOLLAND BEER — bright gold, off-dry apple peel and malt aroma, sweet candy apple and caramel flavor, light body, fairly shallow, faint off-dry malt aftertaste. [B, 56]

JOSEPH MEENS HOLLAND PREMIUM BEER — gold, pleasant hop and malt nose, hop palate with the malt in back, a bit coarse and certainly strong flavored, dull sour malt aftertaste. [B, 37]

ALFA EDEL PILS — brilliant gold, finely carbonated, good head, lightly toasted malt aroma, big malt flavor, off-dry malt finish, long dry hop aftertaste. [B, 57]

ALFA SUPER DORTMUNDER — bright gold, beautiful faintly fruity apple nose, marvelous slightly sweet apple-like malt flavor, big body, high alcohol, a big but elegant brew, long dry aftertaste. [B, 79]

United Dutch Breweries
Breweries in Amsterdam. Also includes Union Export Brewery, Amersfoort.

JAEGER BEER — gold, big apple and hop aroma, complex malt and hop flavor, but not balanced, hard bitter hop aftertaste. [B, 16]

PETER'S BRAND HOLLAND PILSENER BEER — pale yellow; nose is a bit skunky briefly at first, then light malt and hops come in like a typical Pils style; hop flavor is also briefly skunky but quickly develops into a good light hops with plenty of complexity and character; long dry hop aftertaste. [B, 60]

Hungary

Borsod Brewery
Brewery in Bocs

BORSOD PREMIUM — gold light malt and hop aroma, very dry malt and hop flavor, almost too dry, long dry hop aftertaste. [B, 40]

Iceland

Brewery Egill Skallagrimsson Ltd.
Brewery at Reykjavik

POLAR BEER — pale amber-gold, toasted malt nose, light body, pleasant toasted malt flavor; hops come in at the finish; long dry hop aftertaste, good balance. [B, 59]

Ireland

Beamish & Crawford, Ltd.
Brewery in Cork

BEAMISH IRISH STOUT — deep ruby-brown; big thick head that really stands up; very little nose, only some faint malt, light body, thin bitter coffee flavor, finish, and aftertaste; disappointing. [S, 20]

Dempsey's Brewery, Ltd.
Brewery in Inchicore, Dublin

DEMPSEY'S BEER — pale copper, light toasted malt aroma, tangy smoky ale flavor, dry finish, long sour hop aftertaste; starts out good, ends poorly; lacks good balance. [A, 20]

Arthur Guinness Son & Co., Ltd.
St. James's Gate Brewery in Dublin, Dundalk, et al. Also some beers (like Extra Stout) are brewed in Scotland, England, and in many countries throughout the world for local markets.

GUINNESS EXTRA STOUT — opaque red-brown color, creamy tawny head, very full-bodied, dense and thick, complex Worcestershire sauce nose, dry coffee-toffee flavor with a chocolate finish, long dry complex malt aftertaste; excellent stout — the baseline description of the classic stout. On draft, it seems to be darker in color, less carbonated, more spicy, and smoother than the bottled version. It is very mellow, excellently balanced, and the head stays on right to the bottom of the glass. [S, 74]

Notes

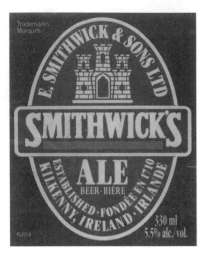

GUINNESS CREAM STOUT — extremely deep brown, low carbonation, strong scorched malt flavor, bitter and flat, harsh long hop aftertaste. [S, 18]

HARP LAGER — deep gold, pungent hop nose, bitter hop flavor, long bitter hop aftertaste, great for true hop-heads. Version exported to the U.S.A. [B, 42]

HARP LAGER BEER — pale gold, lovely well-hopped aroma, finely carbonated, bright strong hop flavor, good balance, more hops than malt but done right. This is the version shipped to Canada; it is higher in alcohol, has better balance, and I find it much tastier than the version above. [B, 60]

GUINNESS GOLD LAGER BEER — pale gold, good well-balanced hop and malt nose, good crisp hop flavor, good balance, clean dry hop finish, long dry hop aftertaste, very drinkable and re-freshing. [B, 60]

KALIBER ALL NATURAL NON-ALCOHOLIC BEER — tawny-gold, grainy sweet malt nose, sour grainy palate; slightly roasted character, gets stronger at the finish; very long tenacious dry roasted malt aftertaste. [NA, 48]

PUB DRAUGHT GUINNESS — the so-called draft version in a can; deep brown, pleasant hop and malt aroma, very dry mild hop flavor; medium body, dry hop fin-ish, long dry hop aftertaste; seems to be a lot lighter than the bottled or draft versions. [S, 19]

KILKENNY IRISH BEER — deep amber, big bright hop aroma, big hop flavor, very big bodied, hefty and very long dry hop after-taste; very well hopped through-out, but there is no lack of malt either; fairly good balance, big and brightly flavored brew. Smithwick & Sons Ltd., Kilkenny, St. Francis Abbey Brewery from Guinness. [B, 72]

GUINNESS FOREIGN EXTRA STOUT — deep brown, very dry malt aroma; austere dry malt fla-vor has a sour component; more dry than bitter, good body, made for West Indies. [S, 69]

James J. Murphy & Co., Ltd.
Lady's Well Brewery in Cork

MURPHY EXPORT STOUT — opaque black, red shows when held to strong light; faint sweet-ness behind a generally sour and dry malt nose; flavor is dry malt up front, sour at the finish, long dry malt aftertaste; balance seems off. [S, 26]

MURPHY'S IRISH STOUT GENUINE PUB DRAUGHT — almost opaque ruby-brown, big creamy head, faint burnt malt nose, overall dry but some malt sweetness in back, light body, roasted malt flavor with virtually no hops, light dry roasted malt aftertaste, burnt at the end and watery as well. [S, 46]

E. Smithwick & Sons, Ltd.
Brewery in Kilkenny affiliated with Guinness

SMITHWICK'S ALE —amber, strong malty nose, big malt flavor; alcohol is noticeable even though only 5.5% abv; bold, big bodied, long malty aftertaste. Tasted in bottle. On draft, in Canada, it was lighter and smoother. [A, 60]

SMITHWICK'S DRAUGHT — brilliant amber, big long-lasting head; dry hop and malt flavor is very smooth and drinkable; dry malt finish and aftertaste, not big bodied, fairly long. Tasted on draft in Canada. [A, 61]

SMITHWICK'S BITTER — deep amber, bright hoppy nose with plenty of malt backing; big flavor has lots of hops and malt both; long hoppy aftertaste seems to approach dryness but can't quite get there because of the concentration of malt which is inherently sweet; good body and good length. Tasted on draft in Canada. [A, 57]

Italy

Birra Moretti S.p.A.
Brewery in Udine. Also Castello Brewery in San Giorgio di Nogaro.

MORETTI PILSENER — deep gold, clean malt and hop aroma and taste, excellent balance, light body, long aftertaste like the flavor, very tasty and very drinkable. [B, 57]

SCHLOSS-BIER EXPORT LAGER — gold, creamy, nice hop and malt aroma, faint malt flavor and aftertaste, medium to light body. [B, 24]

MORETTI EXPORT BEER (BIRE FURLANE) RESERVA CASTELLO — brilliant gold, pleasant malt and hop aroma, off-dry apple and malt flavor; palate drops off rapidly after a good start; short faint dry malt aftertaste. [B, 39]

MORETTI BIRRA FRIULANA — bright gold, grainy aroma, grainy malt flavor with a good hop background, long dry malt aftertaste. [B, 36]

CASTELLO BEER — pale bright gold, off-dry fruity malt and apple nose, pleasant light malt flavor, light fruity malt finish, dry malt aftertaste. [B, 39]

SAN SOUCI DOUBLE MALT — pale gold, light beery nose, fresh malt flavor with good hop balance, long dry hop aftertaste, very drinkable. [B, 57]

MORETTI LA ROSSA DOUBLE MALT BEER — rosy amber, big toasted malt nose, huge rich and complex toasted malt flavor with plenty of hop support, good body, alcoholic, long aftertaste like the flavor; a little clumsy, but there is a lot to it. [B, 89]

MORETTI DOUBLE MALT DARK (BIRRA DOPPIO MALTO BRUNA) — deep reddish amber, big sweet malt aroma, buttery brown sugar flavor, light body; long malt aftertaste is a bit flabby. [B, 34]

OLD VENICE ITALIAN PILSENER — yellow-gold, pleasant malt aroma, sour malt and hop palate, bitter hop finish, light body, short dry hop aftertaste. [B, 27]

Birra Dreher S.p.A.
Breweries in Milano, Pedavena, and Massafra

DREHER FORTE EXPORT LAGER BEER — deep yellow-amber, dank malt nose; off-dry front palate, middle gets some bitter hops, finish is bitter hops and faintly sour malt which comes off better than it sounds; long dry hop aftertaste, fairly good tasting brew with a good balance. [B, 65]

DREHER EXPORT BEER — pale gold, faint malt aroma, weak body, dry malt flavor, medium dry malt finish and long malt aftertaste. [B, 37]

DREHER PILSENER — bright gold, high carbonation on the tongue, slightly dank malt aroma; flavor is lightly malt at first and hops show in the middle and finish; there isn't much malt to show; long dry hop aftertaste. [B, 25]

Birra Forst S.p.A.
Brewery in Merano

FORST EXPORT — bright gold, perfumy hop aroma, medium body, bitter hops in both finish and aftertaste, too much carbonation. [B, 58]

LBF
Flavored malt beverage producer in Canelli

VERDI SPARKLING ITALIAN — almost clear faint greenish-yellow; this sparkling beverage is described as being a malt beverage with natural flavors; aroma of apples, sparkling apple juice flavor, light body, refreshing, pleasant sweet apple finish, brief sweet apple aftertaste; definitely not beerlike in any way as there is no malt for the palate, and cannot be rated as a beer. [ML, NR]

Birra Menabrea
Brewery in Biella

MENABREA BEER — pale gold, flowery hop nose; bright hoppy taste is astringent; very dry hoppy aftertaste, good duration. [B, 53]

Birra Messina S.p.A.
Breweries in Milano and Messina

MESSINA BEER — bright gold, nice beery malt and hop nose; palate is off-dry fruity malt and hops; hops most notable in mid-palate; off-dry malt takes over again in the finish, and stays for the long dry aftertaste. [B, 50]

MESSINA ITALIAN BEER — deep gold, hop nose, big hop flavor, dry hop finish and short dry hop aftertaste. [B, 50]

Pedavena
Brewery in Pedavena

PEDAVENA PILS CLASSICA — pale gold, European hop nose; puckery dry hop flavor has just a little malt; medium body, highly carbonated, dry hop finish, short dry hop aftertaste; tastes similar to a north German pils. [B, 40]

Birra Peroni S.p.A.
Breweries in Naples, Rome, and Padova

PERONI PREMIUM BEER — amber-brown; zesty hop and malt nose and taste dominated by the hops; strongly flavored, big bodied, long aftertaste similar to the flavor. [B, 80]

PERONI BEER — bright pale gold, lovely hop and malt aroma; big good tasting flavor that is more hops up front; malt is there but shows best in the middle; good body, hop finish; malt is most noticeable in the long balanced aftertaste; good brew. [B, 83]

PERONI BIRRA — gold, faint apple peel and malt nose, big body; big hop flavor softens a bit at the finish; pleasant long dry hop aftertaste. [B, 37]

NASTRO AZZURRO EXPORT LAGER — pale gold, faint hop nose with a little malt and yeast, big body; complex flavor is mostly hops; long hop aftertaste has a little sour malt far in back. [B, 29]

ITALA PILSEN — pale gold; hop and malt nose has a skunky component; highly carbonated, good hop and malt flavor, smooth, well-balanced, good body, long dry hop aftertaste, very drinkable. [B, 73]

ITALA PILSEN EXPORT BEER — deep amber-gold, big head but not creamy, light hop and malt aroma, big body, complex malt and hop flavor, noticeable

alcohol, decent balance, strong dry hop aftertaste, overall a pretty good effort. [B, 85]

RAFFO BEER — brilliant pale tawny-gold, toasted caramel nose, malt and bitter hop flavor, slightly sour malt finish and aftertaste. [B, 14]

Birra Poretti S.p.A.
Breweries in Induno and Olona

PORETTI ORO BEER — tawny-gold, vegetal malt aroma with some hops in back; flavor is much like the nose; light body, short dry aftertaste. [B, 17]

SPLÜGEN ORO — deep gold, creamy head, faintly sour malt nose, slightly sour malt flavor, big body, aftertaste like the flavor. [B, 27]

SPLÜGEN BOCK — creamy tawny-gold, clean fruit-like malt aroma with the hops in back; complex flavor shows a good balance between the hops and the malt with off-dry malt coming in at the finish; long good dry malt and hop aftertaste, an almost perfect brew. [BK, 93]

SPLÜGEN DRY — hazy gold, hop nose, hint of strawberry; front palate is hops, sour malt finish; short dry aftertaste has more metal than merit. [B, 24]

BIRRA D'AQUINO ITALIAN BEER — pale gold, light malt aroma, dry malt and hop taste, dry hop finish; fairly long dry aftertaste shows the hops and malt. [B, 37]

Prinz Bräu Carisio S.p.A.
Brewery in Carisio

PRINZ EXPORT — deep gold, beautiful hop aroma with a trace of smoky malt; medium hop flavor has little depth or complexity; dull slightly sour aftertaste. [B, 34]

Birra Wührer S.p.A.
Brewery in Brescia

CRYSTALL WÜHRER BEER — yellow-brown, lovely malt and hop aroma; bitter hop flavor has a soapy background; clean dry hop finish and aftertaste; actually tastes better than its description. [B, 56]

SIMPLON BRÄU SPECIAL EXPORT — deep gold, beautiful medium hop nose, harsh hop flavor; hops dominate the finish and aftertaste and are a bit softer there, but the flavor is just too much bitter hops. [B, 49]

Wünster S.p.A.
Brewery in Bergamo

WÜNSTER EXPORT 14 — gold, beautiful hop nose, big hop flavor with underlying off-dry malt, very good balance; malt rises to the finish; long medium dry malt aftertaste, big bodied good tasting brew. [B, 57]

WÜNSTER SUPER 18 DOPPIO MALTA SCURA — this double malt dark bock is deeply saturated red-brown; has a toasted malt aroma; big body, soft and smooth tasty malt flavor, toffee finish with a touch of licorice, long toffee aftertaste, well-balanced full flavored brew. [B, 90]

Latvia

Aldaris Brewery
Brewery in Aldaris

ALDARA LUKSUSA ALUS — gold, light fruity hop nose, creamy, light hop flavor, medium body, short light hop aftertaste, 5.2% abv. Brewed in cooperation with the Pripps (Sweden) and Hartwell (Finland) breweries and with permission of the St. Karinas Brewery. [B, 41]

Luxembourg

Brasserie Diekirch Brauerei
Brewery in city of Luxembourg

DIEKIRCH PILS — gold, good malt aroma, classic pils flavor, dry hop aftertaste, well-made, well-balanced brew. [B, 68]

DIEKIRCH MALT LIQUOR — deep gold, hop nose with a touch of smoky malt, strong hop and roasted malt flavor; finish is like the flavor but weaker; short faint dry aftertaste. [ML, 53]

DIEKIRCH MALT LIQUOR EXCLUSIVE — never found a sample good enough to taste. [ML, 29]

Brasseries Reunies de Luxembourg S.A.
Breweries at Mousel and Clausen

MOUSEL BEER — bright gold, dull malt aroma; malt palate has some hops in back; short dry aftertaste. [B, 34]

ALTMUNSTER — medium gold, good malt and hop aroma; flavor is malt at first, hops come in at the middle and stay; good body, long dry hop aftertaste. [B, 71]

Macedonia

Skopska Pivara
Brewery in Skopje

SKOPSKO LAGER BEER — brilliant gold, very strong hop nose and taste; flavor eases off from mid-palate on; good body; finish is hops joined by malt; fairly long dry malt and hop aftertaste. [B, 47]

Montenegro

Niksicko Pivovare
Brewery in Niksic

NIKSICKO PIVO — gold, malt aroma with a celery-like background, flavor like the nose, salty molasses finish, dry malt aftertaste. [B, 18]

Norway

Ringnes Brewery
Brewery in Oslo

RINGNES SPECIAL BEER — tawny-gold, strong hop nose and big hop flavor, lots of hops and malt and loaded with character, good malt finish and aftertaste, long and delicious. [B, 73]

RINGNES MALT LIQUOR — deep gold, off-dry malt nose, very sweet malty taste and aftertaste, sharp hop bitterness at the very end. [ML, 20]

RINGNES EXPORT — gold, aroma of hops and caramel; really good hop and malt flavor up front, but it sags in the middle, and finishes poorly of sour celery; short dry offish aftertaste. [B, 61]

RINGNES SPECIAL BOCK BEER — dark red-brown, strong roasted malt, molasses and prune nose, very heavy body; good molasses-treacle flavor that is delightful; long rich malt aftertaste, excellent. [BK, 62]

RINGNES LOW — bright gold; slightly skunky nose at first, this evolved into hops and tuna salad; very light slightly malty flavor, light body, grainy finish and aftertaste. [LO, 18]

RINGNES ZERO PLUS — bright gold; skunky nose at first but the malt soon fights its way through; high carbonation, grainy malt flavor, little body, dry malt finish and aftertaste, medium length. [NA, 37]

RINGNES DARK — bright redbrown, sweet malt aroma, light body, pleasant off-dry malt flavor, long off-dry malt aftertaste; nice but could use more heft. [B, 47]

RINGNES SPECIAL CHRISTMAS ALE — deep amber; faintly smoky malt aroma, there is some sweetness in behind; zesty smooth pleasant malt flavor, good balance throughout, medium body, touch of caramel in back, long dry malt aftertaste; didn't find any hops to mention. [A, 69]

NORSK NON-ALCOHOLIC MALT BEVERAGE — pale yellow-gold, faint malt nose, faint grainy malt and CO_2 palate, sour light metallic aftertaste. [B, 36]

RINGNES ALE SPECIAL JUBILEE — bright amber, toasted malt nose; good off-dry malt flavor is like brown sugar; finish and aftertaste are drier malt than the flavor; mellow and long. [A, 68]

RINGNES PILSENER ØL — pale gold, big hop aroma and flavor, good body, very long dry hop aftertaste. [B, 42]

Aass Brewery
Brewery in Drammen

AASS BOK BEER — very deep copper color, complex yeasty malt aroma, big body, full rich roasted malt flavor, good long rich malt aftertaste, a delicious brew. [BK, 50]

AASS NORWEGIAN BEER — light amber-gold, light hop aroma, medium hop flavor with a slightly sour finish, a little unbalanced, medium dry hop aftertaste. [B, 37]

AASS EXPORT NORWEGIAN BEER — amber-gold, big hop nose, big hop and toasted malt flavor, slightly sour hop finish, good balance; long dry hop aftertaste still retains some of the roasted malt character; a good tasting beer. [B, 63]

AASS JULE ØL — bright caramel-copper color, lovely light malt and hop aroma, delicious toasted malt flavor, off-dry malt finish with a touch of hops, good appetizing dry malt and hop aftertaste. [A, 69]

AASS PILSNER — amber-gold, flowery complex off-dry melony-malt aroma, very complex malt and hop flavor, fine hop finish, big body, long dry hop aftertaste; malt hangs in there all the way through keeping up an excellent balance. [B, 72]

AASS WINTER — amber, nice straightforward malt and hop nose, honeyed malt front palate, dry middle and finish, very long off-dry malt aftertaste, hops at the very end, some complexity, very drinkable. [B, 78]

Notes

AASS AMBER — medium amber, faintly toasted malt nose, big malt flavor with hops in back, good body; tastes very good; not complex but very drinkable, good balance; hops are in there all the way but never come to the foreground; good balance, dry malt aftertaste. [B, 60]

E.C. Dahl's Bryggeri A/S
Brewery in Trondheim

DAHL'S PILS — pale gold, good hop and malt nose, smooth, well-balanced hop and malt flavor, medium body; long dry hop aftertaste is also sour and bitter. [B, 53]

DAHL'S EXPORT — tawny-gold; beautiful hop and malt nose is more like a Pils than the Pils above; high carbonation, big hop flavor, good balance, dry hop finish, and brief dry hop aftertaste. [B, 67]

Frydenlund Bryggerie
Brewery in Oslo

FRYDENLUND'S EXPORT III PILSENER BEER — gold, hop nose, bitter hop taste throughout broken only with some off-dry malt in front and a saltiness in the finish, long dry hop aftertaste. [B, 34]

FRYDENLUND NORWEGIAN PILSENER BEER — bright pale gold, skunky nose, thin hop flavor, light body, dry hop finish and short dry hop aftertaste. [B, 31]

NORSK BEER — medium yellow; a briefly skunky nose soon became good malt and hops; hoppy flavor up front, sour malt in the back; this sourness becomes the finish and aftertaste; overall poorly balanced. [B, 36]

SKI BEER — medium gold, very light hop and malt aroma, nice well-hopped flavor, thin body, sour malt finish and aftertaste, highly carbonated and not balanced. [B, 27]

Hansa Bryggeri
Brewery in Bergen

HANSA FJORD NORWEGIAN PILSENER BEER — pale hazy yellow-green color, beautiful malt and hop aroma, off-dry malt flavor with excellent hop balance, luscious and full-flavored, big body, complex, refreshing, long dry hop aftertaste. Most recently seen labeled Hansa Beer From Norway. [B, 91]

HANSA EXPORT ØL — bright tawny-gold, salty malt cereal aroma, flavor to match, mild salty finish, dry salty hop aftertaste. [B, 39]

HANSA PILSNER ØL — pale gold, faint apple-like aroma with hops in back; taste is all up front and is all hops; quick hop finish, virtually no aftertaste. [B, 42]

HANSA PILS — gold, big hop nose, sharp hop flavor, long dry hop aftertaste; a beautiful beer for those who love hops. [B, 47]

HANSA DARK — bright copper color, lovely malt nose with some small amount of hops, pleasant but weak flavor, brief dry malt and hop aftertaste. [B, 38]

L. Mack's Ølbryggerie
Brewery in Tromsø

MACK POLAR BEER — hazy amber, dusty malt nose, light body; malt flavor is very slightly papery; dull malt finish and aftertaste. [B, 19]

Schous Brewery
Brewery in Oslo

SCHOUS NORWEGIAN PILSNER — gold; skunky aroma that really hangs in there; smoked charcoal flavor shows nothing of the skunk; some hops, a little malt, but is unbalanced and watery; a dull brief brew. [B, 18]

Poland

Okocim Brewery
Brewery in Okocim

OKOCIM FULL LIGHT BEER — yellow-gold, malt aroma and flavor, soapy background, dry hop aftertaste. [B, 47]

OKOCIM PORTER — dark brown, roasted caramel malt nose and flavor, huge complex off-dry malt flavor, good balance; off-dry malt finish with some hops starting to appear; long off-dry malt aftertaste, very nice. [P, 93]

Pivovare Pardubice
Brewery in Pardubice

PARDUBICKY PORTER/ PERNSTEIN PORTER — dark brown, rich malt aroma, off-dry malt flavor, big body; shows some alcohol; long and sweet, gravity 19 P, 6.8% abv. [P, 60]

Zywiec Brewery
Brewery in Zywiec

KRAKUS LIGHT BEER — gold, faint off-dry malt nose, creamy texture, big yeasty barley-malt flavor, fairly long dry malt aftertaste. [LO, 44]

KRAKUS PREMIUM BEER — gold, delicate malt aroma with finely balanced hop backing, subtle malt and hop flavor, smooth and light, short dry hop aftertaste. [B, 58]

ZYWIEC FULL LIGHT BEER — deep gold, complex off-dry malt and hop aroma, good body; pleasant flavor has more malt than hops; hop finish, long dry hop aftertaste. [B, 57]

ZYWIEC FULL LIGHT PIAST — very faint malt aroma, sour malt flavor and finish; dry hop aftertaste still has some of the sourness. [B, 35]

ZYWIEC BEER — tawny-gold; malt aroma has a brackish background; good hop flavor but there is still a salty nature; light body, quick dry hop finish and short dry hop aftertaste. [B, 41]

ZYWIEC POLISH LAGER BEER — tawny-gold, good rising malt and hop nose, good body, malt flavor, good hop balance, smooth dry hop finish, pleasant long dry hop aftertaste. [B, 56]

Portugal

Companhia União Fabril Portuense, Unicer-União Cervejeria
Breweries in Oporto and Leca do Balio

CRISTAL BEER — deep yellow-gold, faint malt aroma, very lightly hopped clean dry flavor, medium body, crisp clean finish, tasty dry malt aftertaste. [B, 40]

UNICER SUPER BOCK — bright gold; European hop nose is a bit stinky at first but this goes off shortly; big hop flavor with plenty of malt; hops dominate the front palate and malt takes over near finish; balanced, big body, finely carbonated, long dry hop aftertaste. [B, 63]

Empresa de Cervejas de Madeira
Brewery in Funchal, Madeira

CORAL BEER — gold, faint malt and hop nose; flavor is mostly carbonation with some faint hops and malt; dry hop finish, short dry hop aftertaste. [B, 26]

Sociedad Central de Cervejas
Breweries in Lisbon, Vialonga, and Coimbra

CERVEJA SAGRES — pale yellow; skunky vegetal nose yielded to hops and malt after a few minutes; malt flavor showed some oxidation; bitter hop aftertaste. [B, 38]

SAGRES DARK BEER — very dark brown, strong malt aroma, heavy body, big molasses-like flavor with a bitter background, sweet molasses finish and aftertaste, a very filling beer. [B, 51]

CERVEJA TOPAZIO — medium to deep gold; nose starts out briefly skunky then turns to malt; palate starts as off-dry malt and dries at the finish with the carbonation dominating the middle; sweetness reappears in the long aftertaste. [B, 17]

EUROPA BEER — gold; European hop nose is almost (but not quite) skunky; big hop pils-style flavor with a sweet malt backdrop, full body, creamy texture, hop finish; long hop aftertaste has malt support. [B, 47]

Russia

Russian Breweries
The situation of Russian breweries is still in a confused state so I have lumped them together under a single heading with any identification included with the write-up.

ALDARA ALUS — hazy gold, sour creamy malt nose, sour malt palate with a hop bite in back, rough hop aftertaste, not a pleasant brew. No brewery cited but a brewery origin date of 1865 given. Alus means ale. [A, 12]

PORTERIS — hazy amber-brown, off-dry roasted malt nose, lovely big roasted malt flavor, rich, delicious, and very long, an excellent porter (porteris). Label says 20%, which I presume to be 20° density. Porteris is labeled almost identically to Aldara so it is further presumed they are from the same brewery. [P, 80]

RUSSKOYE PREMIUM RUSSIAN LAGER BEER — bright deep gold, soapy malt nose, dry malt flavor, hop finish; soapy malt aftertaste has good length. From Obolon Brewery, Kiev. [B, 30]

MOSCOVA BEER OF RUSSIA — hazy gold, very fruity malt and European hop nose, pleasant fruity malt flavor and finish, lightly hopped, good body, long dry malt aftertaste, bigger in the front than at the finish. Moscow Brewery, Moscow—since 1863. [B, 53]

RUSKI IMPORTED RUSSIAN BEER — gold, mango-papaya tropical fruit aroma and flavor; finish is even more fruit-like; dry malt aftertaste. From Oboken Brewery, Kiev. [B, 32]

TROIKA ORIGINAL RUSSIAN BEER — gold; dank aroma is mostly cardboard with faint hop and malt background; dank malt flavor, sour finish, short aftertaste. From the Moscow Brewery. [B, 18]

Serbia

BIP Pivovare
Brewery in Belgrade

MARCUS BEER — deep yellow, pleasant light malt aroma and flavor, dull malt aftertaste. [B, 25]

BELGRADE GOLD BEER — hazy gold, off-dry malt nose, big malt and hop flavor, expertly balanced, dry malt-hop finish and after-taste, good body, very much to-gether and very drinkable. [B, 91]

Slovakia

Pivovare a Sladovne Martin, Brewery Martin / Turciansky Pivovar
Brewery at Banska Bystrica

URPIN — deep gold, hop nose, malt flavor, medium to light body, medium long dry malt and hop aftertaste. [B, 52]

MARTINSKY ZDROJ — brilliant gold, finely carbonated, delicious hop and malt aroma, big body, full flavored malt palate with good hop support, malt finish and long malt aftertaste. [B,71]

MARTINER PREMIUM LAGER BEER — deep gold; pleasant malt aroma has some faint hops in back; roasted malt flavor is a little on the sweet side; dry malt finish, medium long dry malt aftertaste. [B, 37]

Topvar Brewery
Brewery in Topol'cany

TOPVAR LIGHT BEER — gold, finely carbonated, light malt aroma, dull dry malt palate, dry malt finish and aftertaste, medium long; 3.5% abv. [B, 37]

Zlaty Bazant A.S.
Brewery in Hurbanovo

GOLDEN PHEASANT BEER — gold, pleasant malt aroma and flavor; finishes a bit sweet, but is pleasant and has a richness; full bodied, creamy and malty taste, dry hop finish and aftertaste; 4.4% abv. [B, 57]

Slovenia

Pivovarna Lasko
Brewery in Lasko

GOLDEN HORN EXPORT SPECIAL — deep golden amber, grainy malt nose, good hop flavor, medium length grainy aftertaste. [B, 46]

GOLDHORN CLUB — hazy gold, buttery malt nose with sweet hops in back, malt flavor with a hop finish, dry hop aftertaste with return of the buttery malt in the back. [B, 34]

Union Pivovare
Breweries in Triglav, Ljubijana

UNION SVETLO PIVO — gold, vegetal malt nose, strong hop flavor, malt well in back, long dry hop aftertaste, very much a German Pils style. [B, 38]

Notes

UNION EXPORT BEER — medium gold, apple cider and malt nose, big well-balanced hop flavor, hop finish, brief sour hop aftertaste, highly carbonated, too much so. [B, 50]

UNION EXPORT STOUT — very deep brown color, austere pine needle and celery seed aroma, light body, good roasted-smoky malt flavor, slightly sour brief aftertaste; the flavor is quite pleasing. [S, 46]

UNION PREMIUM BEER — gold; fragrant malt nose has a soapy background; flavor has big hops in front, but soon the malt takes over; big body, long and strong dry hop aftertaste. [B, 50]

UNI NON-ALCOHOLIC BREW — gold, grainy malt nose and taste, medium to light body, dry malt finish and aftertaste. [NA, 23]

RED BREW-STER — gold, fragrant flowery malt aroma, pleasant bright malt and hop flavor, medium to good body, dry hop finish, long dry hop aftertaste. [B, 47]

Zagrebacke Pivovare / Karlovacka Pivovara
Brewery in Karlovac

ZAGREBACKE KARLOVACKO SVIJETLO PIVO LIGHT BEER — pale yellow, sour Pils nose, sour-bitter hop flavor, short aftertaste like the flavor. [B, 17]

KARLOVACKO SPECIAL BEER — amber-yellow; faint

wine aroma that is sweet and fruity; watery body, low carbonation, full off-dry malt flavor with a touch of oxidation, slight roasted malt aftertaste. [B, 27]

KARLOVACKO LIGHT BEER — amber-yellow, fruity-malt aroma, fruity sour malt palate, very long sweet-sour aftertaste. [B, 17]

KARLSBEER — deep gold, fragrant malt and hop nose, big dry malt front palate, dry hop finish, long dry hop aftertaste. [B, 75]

Spain

Sociedad Anonima Damm
Breweries in seven locations in Spain, including Barcelona

ESTRELLA DORADA CERVEZA ESPECIAL PILSEN — tawny-gold, winelike aroma with hops and toasted malt, good malt flavor up front, some complexity including nuts and apples, light body, malt aftertaste. [B, 56]

YOLL DAMM EXTRA CERVEZA ESPECIAL — tawny-gold, pleasant malt nose with just a touch of hops, creamy big hop flavor, harsh bitter hop aftertaste. [B, 31]

DAMM BEER — deep gold, faint grainy aroma and taste; front is off-dry, finish is dry, short dry aftertaste. [B, 30]

CERVEZA AGUILA DORADA — tawny-gold, faint malt nose, malt flavor with a nutty background, brief malt aftertaste. Aguila Breweries, S.A. [B, 21]

AGUILA IMPERIAL — bright gold, malt nose, lightly toasted crisp and dry malt flavor, balanced, good body, long malt aftertaste. [B, 73]

San Miguel Fabricas De Cerveja y Malta, S.A.
Breweries in Lerida, Malaga, and Burgos

SAN MIGUEL LAGER BEER — hazy yellow-gold, sour malt nose and taste, dry malt aftertaste with some hops in back and at very end. [B, 36]

SAN MIGUEL SELECTA — amber-gold, off-dry toasted malt nose and flavor; palate is fairly strong and gets some hops at the finish; good body, a bit winey, long malt aftertaste. [B, 67]

SAN MIGUEL PILSENER — pale gold, faint malt nose with even fainter hops, light body, neutral malt flavor, very light hops, medium length dry malt aftertaste. [B, 36]

Cervejeria San Martin
Brewery in Orense

SAN MARTIN CERVEJA ESPECIAL — pale amber-gold, faint malt aroma, malt-hop flavor with a salty background, medium length dry malt and hop aftertaste, a little metallic at the end. [B, 15]

La Zaragozana, S.A.
Brewery in Zaragoza

AMBAR SPECIAL BEER — deep gold, big malt nose is off-dry, malt flavor like the nose except there are faint hops at the finish, good balance, fair body, dry hop aftertaste, 5.2% abv, 13 P. [B, 47]

Sweden

Åbro Brewery
Brewery in Vimmerby

VIKING LAGER BEER — brilliant pale gold, floral, spice, and fruit aroma, complex flavor but light, weak malt palate, sour hop finish and aftertaste. [B, 17]

Falcon Brewery
Brewery in Falkenberg

FALCON EXPORT III BEER — gold, light malt aroma, bitter hop flavor, light malt finish and aftertaste, some oxidation. [B, 27]

Grängesbergs Breweries, Ltd.
Breweries in Grängesberg

GRÄNGES BEER III — light gold, pleasant and balanced malt-hop aroma, flavor mostly hops, bitter hop finish and aftertaste. [B, 50]

GRÄNGES SWEDISH BLONDE BEER — tawny-yellow, dry roasted malt aroma, good dry roasted malt flavor, light body; long roasted malt aftertaste gradually fades without losing any of its character. [B, 60]

Mariestads Bryggerie Aktiebolag
Brewery in Grängesberg

MARIESTADS FESTIVAL BEER — deep yellow-gold, faint hop and malt aroma, weak body, almost watery, little flavor beyond the carbonation, bitter hop aftertaste. [B, 37]

Pripp Bryggerie
Breweries in Stockholm and Gothenberg et al.

PRIPPS EXPORT III SWEDISH BEER — deep tawny-gold; hops dominate the nose and taste; malt shows well in the finish; long malt and apple aftertaste, very good beer. [B, 75]

THREE TOWNS — tawny-gold, beautiful off-dry winelike malt nose; big hop flavor and hops dominate the palate throughout; long dry hop aftertaste. [B, 51]

PRIPPS 150 JUBILEE EXPORT BEER — deep gold, classical Pilsener aroma of dry slightly vegetal malt and bright hops, big clean hop flavor, good balance; fades at the finish and there is little aftertaste, but it is good while it is there. [B, 62]

DART MÖRKT STARKÖL —
copper-red, beautifully balanced
hop and malt aroma, mild harmo-
nious hop and malt flavor, long
complex dry aftertaste, very good
and very drinkable. [B, 63]

KALBACK LAGER — bright
pale gold, low carbonation, pungent hop aroma; soft smooth palate shows little of the hops in the
nose; light body, dry, clean, but
without zest or length. [B, 34]

NORDICK WÖLF LIGHT —
medium to pale gold, light hop
nose, light body, light hop flavor,
brief hop aftertaste, no complexity. [LO, 24]

PRIPPS LAGER — bright medium
pale yellow-gold, hop nose, high
carbonation, hop flavor and finish,
brief hop aftertaste; pleasant while it
is in your mouth. [B, 50]

Switzerland

Cardinal, S.A. / Feldschlossen, S.A.
Breweries in Fribourg, Sibra, Frankendorf, Rheinfelden, and Waedenswil

CARDINAL LAGER BEER —
tawny-gold, smooth malt aroma
with good hop backing, finely balanced flavor with good hops and
malt, long dry aftertaste, very well-
made beer. [B, 83]

FELDSCHLOSSEN
HOPENPERLE — amber, malty
Tirolean-style aroma, good malt
and well-hopped flavor, excellent
balance, bright malt finish, long
dry hop aftertaste, well-made beer.
Previously seen as Feldschlossen
Bier Special and Spezial Hell (the
latter in Europe). [B, 75]

MOUSSY ALCOHOL-FREE
LIGHT MALT BEVERAGE —
deep clear bright gold, grainy malt
aroma and flavor, medium body,
little zest, grainy aftertaste. [NA, 39]

EX BIER — bright tawny-gold,
malty molasses aroma, flat malt
flavor; little zest, but there is a
long dry malt aftertaste. [NA, 16]

ELAN-THE SWISS BREW —
bright gold; grainy nose is off-dry;
grainy malt flavor is a tiny bit
drier; medium length dry malt
aftertaste, not bad for a non-
alcoholic brew. [NA, 49]

CARDINAL AMBER LIGHT —
brassy amber, honeyed malt nose,
dull dry malt flavor, medium to
short malt aftertaste. [LO, 23]

Brauerei Erlen
Brewery in Glarus

GLARNER BEER — bright gold,
nice hop nose well backed with
malt, good hoppy flavor, pleasant
and balanced, very tasty, quick
finish, very little aftertaste. [B, 53]

Brauerei A. Hürlimann, A.G.
Brewery in Zurich

HÜRLIMANN STERN BRÄU/
SPEZIAL BIER — amber, big off-
dry malt aroma with good hops;
enormous malt and hop flavor is
very assertive; sour hop finish,
long dry hop aftertaste, a good
tasting balanced brew with lots of
power. This is not the same beer
as Hürlimann Export Lager
shipped to the U.S.A. in the
1970s. [B, 51]

BIRELL MALT BEVERAGE —
gold, hop and malt nose, light hop
flavor, thin body, dry hop finish
and aftertaste; seems to get more
hops as it goes; very beerlike for a
nonalcoholic beer. [NA, 47]

HÜRLIMANN DARK SWISS
LAGER — reddish-brown, malt
nose, low carbonation, off-dry
malt flavor, light body, brief medium dry malt aftertaste. [B, 37]

SAMICHLAUS PALE BEER —
brilliant deep amber, complex dry

toasted malt nose, huge intensely sweet palate, very complex, powerful sipping beer, long licorice aftertaste, a beauty. Notes are from 1986 brew. The 1987 was very much the same except the alcohol seemed to be a bit more noticeable. This beer has been discontinued, only the Dark is still made. [A, 87–95]

SAMICHLAUS DARK BIER — very deep bright amber-brown, rich Grape-Nuts and smoky malt nose, very complex; big rich malt flavor is on the sweet side; finishes semi-dry, long dry malt aftertaste; doesn't quite have the complexity of the Samichlaus Pale, but is a good sipping beer for the winter. Notes are for the 1986 brew. The 1987 seemed to be more complex, had a slightly more burnt nature, and was a bit more strongly flavored. The 1988 was not tasted. The 1989 was extremely complex adding chocolate tones and at times seemed to have a sherry quality much like Bristol Milk; some tasters thought it overwhelming, a fantastic sipping beer. The 1990 was very alcoholic, winey, much like a sherry and tasters once again mentioned the Bristol Milk, and the aftertaste seemed sweeter than usual. The 1991 was very much like the 1990 except the nose was a bit bready and the aftertaste was a little short and somewhat more dry. The 1993 is amber-brown, has a big complex nose which isn't enough to warn you about the powerful flavor to follow, the palate is very strong roasted barley, seems

smoky and even a little burnt, rich and alcoholic, almost too strong when first released but several months later was coming into "flower" although still intense, needs some time to come together, extremely long, this is an excellent example of a beer to be "laid down" for the future like a fine young red wine. It is labeled Samichlaus Brown. A year in the bottle did little to reduce its strength, but the balance improved with the components of flavor coming together. With the big malt and alcohol, there has developed an added "sense" of anise (but not a licorice taste). The 1994, labeled again Samichlaus Dark Bier, is amber, equipped with a big roasted malt and alcohol nose, has a strong flavor that shows malt, hops, alcohol, and other complex spice and herbal notes, but everything is separate and needs time to knit together. [A, 60–95]

HEXENBRÄU SWISS DUNKEL — amber-brown, rich faintly burned roasted malt aroma; roasted malt flavor tastes a little chocolatey; straightforward dark lager with little complexity, medium body, pleasant and drinkable; stays dry; good with food. [B, 53]

Brauerei Löwenbräu
Brewery in Zurich

LÖWENBRÄU SWISS BEER SPECIAL EXPORT LIGHT — amber, creamy, apple and malt nose, strong malt flavor, bitter hop finish and aftertaste. [B, 42]

LÖWENBRÄU ZURICH EXPORT LIGHT — pale gold, apple peel and malt aroma, good malt and hop flavor, good balance; long dry hop aftertaste has a little unneeded sourness. [LO, 51]

LÖWENBRÄU ZURICH EXPORT DARK — deep amber-brown, faint vegetal aroma, dry and dull flavor, sour finish, brief weak malt aftertaste. [B, 31]

LÖWENBRÄU ZURICH LIGHT — pale gold, weak malt aroma, light hop and malt flavor, dry in front, sweet in the finish, light body, brief dry hop aftertaste. [LO, 51]

LIBERO NON-ALCOHOLIC MALT BEVERAGE — pale gold, yeasty bready aroma with a faint touch of molasses, watery body, dull malt flavor, quick finish, no aftertaste. [NA, 20]

Warteck Brewery
Brewery in Basel

WARTECK NON-ALCOHOLIC MALT BEVERAGE — bright deep gold; malty aroma has a skunk for company; sour malt flavor, long dry and sour malt aftertaste. [NA, 29]

WARTECK LIGHT BEER — bright gold, faint malt aroma, very light malt flavor, some hop tang in the finish, long dry hop aftertaste. [LO, 27]

WARTECK LAGER BEER — hazy gold, lovely malt and hop nose, good malt flavor backed with hops, good balance, finishes with dry hops, long dry hop aftertaste. [B, 53]

Ziegelhof Brewery
Brewery in Liestal

ALPENSTEIN NON-ALCOHOLIC MALT BEVERAGE — medium gold, lovely well-hopped aroma, good tasting sour hop flavor, good balance, long dry hop aftertaste. [NA, 47]

THE MIDDLE EAST

Cyprus

Cyprus, Keo, Ltd.
Brewery in Cyprus

KEO PILSENER — cloudy yellow; tart malty aroma, rhubarb-like; malt flavor, low carbonation, short malt aftertaste. [B, 21]

Israel

National Breweries, Ltd.
Breweries in Tel Aviv, Bat Yam, and Netanya

MACCABEE PREMIUM BEER — gold, creamy head, soft malt nose; crisp malt and hop flavor fairly dry at finish; high carbonation, pleasant dry brief malt and hop aftertaste. Tempo Beer Industries. [B, 45]

GOLD STAR — amber; big off-dry malt nose at first, quickly fades; flavor off-dry, but dries at the middle; dry malt finish, medium body, medium to long dry malt aftertaste. Tempo Beer Industries. [B, 45]

BEERSHEBA PREMIUM — gold, hop nose, sour hop flavor, high carbonation, medium body, light malt aftertaste with little duration. [B, 16]

Notes

MALT STAR NON-ALCOHOLIC BEER — deep ruby-brown, off-dry grainy aroma, lightly sweet malt flavor (lists sugar and caramel as ingredients); finish is a bit drier; light short off-dry grainy aftertaste, less than 0.5% abv. Tempo Beer Industries. [NA, 23]

Lebanon

Almaza Brewery
Brewery in Almaza

ALMAZA PILSENER — gold; a little skunky first, but this soon cleared to a malt and hop nose; light body, light malt and hop flavor, dull malty aftertaste. [B, 37]

Turkey

Efes Breweries
Brewery in Istanbul

EPHESUS TURKISH PILSNER BEER — pale gold, off-dry malt aroma with the hops in back, light body, light malt flavor, light malt finish and aftertaste. [B, 39]

EFES PILS — deep gold, toasted malt and hop aroma, good balance, flavor like the nose, fairly complex, medium long dry malt-hop aftertaste. [B, 69]

EFES PILSEN — pale gold, light malt nose and taste, refreshing, long dry malt aftertaste; hops stay well in the back but are there. [B, 47]

NEW ZEALAND

Brewer's Arms

Brewpubs in Merivale and Ferrymead areas of Christchurch. Affiliated with McCashin's Brewery & Malthouse of Nelson.

MERIVALE LAGER — gold, mild malt aroma and flavor, lightly hopped, smooth fresh dry brew, medium body, light dry hop finish and aftertaste. I believe this is named Ferrymead Lager at the Ferrymead Brewer's Arms. [B, 54]

CANTERBURY ALE — amber, mild malt aroma and flavor, smooth with just a touch of roasted barley, light body, dry malt finish and aftertaste. [A, 54]

CLASSIC DARK — deep brown, faint malt aroma and flavor, fairly dry, fairly light, light dry malt aftertaste with little duration. [B, 35]

Dominion Breweries, Ltd.

Breweries in Auckland, Mangatainoka, and Timaru

DB EXPORT BEER — medium gold, dry but fruity malt nose; winey malt palate has a berrylike nature; hops come in at the finish; dry hop aftertaste. [B, 37]

DB EXPORT LAGER — gold; aroma has both malt and hops; flavor is dominated by the malt with the hops holding back but evident enough for good balance; plenty of body, long dry malt aftertaste. [B, 50]

DB EXPORT DRY LAGER — brilliant gold, big malt and light hop aroma, smooth light malt flavor, light body, dry malt finish, medium length dry malt aftertaste. [D, 50]

DB DRAUGHT BITTER BEER — amber-gold, hop aroma, big hop flavor, plenty of malt in back, very good body; finishes dry hops; long dry hop aftertaste still shows enough malt for balance. [B, 57]

DB BITTER BEER — amber-gold, light malt nose, pleasant malt flavor, medium to good body; light malt finish and aftertaste has some malt showing but it is in back. [B, 57]

DOUBLE BROWN BEER — amber-gold, faint malt aroma, fruity malt flavor; finishes malty as well, leading into a fairly long medium dry malt aftertaste. [B, 40]

DOUBLE VITA-STOUT — opaque brown, brown head, chocolate malt and roasted barley aroma, rich clean chocolate malt and roasted barley flavor, good body but not big; ends fairly dry and has a very long pleasant aftertaste like the flavor; pleasing and surprisingly drinkable. [S, 56]

KIWI LAGER — bright gold, perfumy clean hop nose, bright hop flavor with good malt backing, big body, big taste, clean hop aftertaste with good duration. [B, 57]

WAITEMATA SPARKLING PALE ALE — amber, light malt nose, dry malt and hop flavor, medium body, light dry malt and hop finish, dry mostly malt aftertaste; not much hops showing throughout, certainly not bittering hops. [A, 47]

TUI EAST INDIA PALE ALE — deep gold, very pleasant malt aroma; bright flavor starts out hops and ends malty; big body, long malt aftertaste. Made at Mangatainoka by DB Central Brewery Ltd. [A, 62]

JOSEPH KUHTZE LAGER BEER — gold, hop aroma, big spicy hop flavor with plenty of supporting malt, very good body; good carbonation level gives a very fine mouth feel; long complex malt aftertaste retains some of the spicy character; a very tasty brew. [B, 72]

JK DRY LAGER — gold, malt and hop aroma; hops are first on the palate, thence malt; smooth dry malt finish and aftertaste; a brief aftertaste but the beer has a lot of flavor for a dry. Joseph Kuhtze Brewing Co., Ltd., Auckland. [B, 49]

KUHTZE LIGHT LAGER — gold; light malt nose has some hops in back; light hop flavor has malt in back; a little grainy to my taste, light body, light dry hop aftertaste, not much length. [LO, 30]

Dux DeLux
Brewpub in Christchurch

DE LUXE LAGER — pale gold, malt aroma, bright hop flavor, light and dry, very refreshing, good balance; malt shows best in the long aftertaste; pleasant and drinkable. [B, 61]

HEREFORD BITTER — amber, big malt nose, roasted barley flavor, medium body, dry hop and roasted malt finish, short dry hop aftertaste, smooth and likable. [B, 47]

NOR'WESTER STRONG PALE ALE — hazy gold, zesty hop-ale aroma and flavor, very brightly flavored, off-dry malt finish and long aftertaste. [A, 55]

BLUE DUCK DRAUGHT — gold, strong malt aroma, dry malt flavor, medium body, smooth and tasty, but very light, short dry malt aftertaste. [B, 45]

SO'WESTER DARK STRONG STOUT — dark brown, brown head, roasted barley and chocolate malt aroma, smooth dry malty flavor, good body but not big, extremely long dry malt aftertaste. [S, 60]

Harrington's Olde Brewery Inn
Brewpub in Christchurch

HARRINGTON'S DRAUGHT — deep gold, lovely hop and malt aroma and flavor, smooth and balanced, good body, zesty, long dry malt and hop aftertaste. [B, 60]

HARRINGTON'S RAZOR BACK BITTER — deep gold; bright hop aroma has malt in back; big hoppy flavor similarly supported by the malt; good balance, good body, long dry hop aftertaste. [B, 55]

HARRINGTON'S LAGER BEER — gold, light hop nose and taste, balanced, quite dry; has zest yet is smooth and drinkable; dry hop finish and aftertaste. [B, 47]

HARRINGTON'S DARK BEER — dark brown, roasted malt aroma and flavor, good body, dry malt finish; long dry malt aftertaste has a toasted background quality. [B, 55]

BIG JOHN — deep amber, malt nose, big malt flavor; high alcohol is noticeable (6.5%) but not obtrusive; big body, very smooth, long off-dry malt aftertaste. [B, 57]

HARRINGTON'S WHEAT BEER — pale gold, clean wheaty nose and taste, no spiciness, light body, no aftertaste beyond a sense of dryness. [W, 45]

NGAHERE GOLD SPECIAL LAGER — gold, big alcoholic malt nose and taste, big body; lots of tangy flavor but there is too much alcohol (7.2%) and it interferes with the flavor; long malt aftertaste has hops in back. [B, 42]

Independent Breweries, Ltd.
Brewery in Auckland

NEW ZEALAND PREMIUM LAGER BEER — hazy gold, light malt nose; light malt flavor is a bit off-dry; seems to get sweeter in the finish and aftertaste. [B, 43]

NEW ZEALAND DRAUGHT PREMIUM BEER — deep gold, malt and hop aroma; malt flavor has some hops way in back; good body, fairly dry throughout, dry malt finish; long dry aftertaste shows more hops than was on the palate earlier. [B, 50]

NIGHTHAWK DARK ALE — amber-brown, good roasted malt aroma, light roasted malt flavor, medium body, dry finish and aftertaste like the flavor, but a bit spicy, dry, long and quite good. [A, 57]

PANTHER PREMIUM LAGER — deep gold, fruity malt aroma; malt flavor is dry but maintains fruitiness like the nose; good body, light dry malt aftertaste. [B, 54]

BIGHORN BLUE — amber-gold, malt aroma, light grainy malt flavor, light body, light malt finish, very little aftertaste. [B, 36]

BIGHORN NEW ZEALAND BEER — deep gold, light malt nose, faint malt flavor, medium body, almost no aftertaste. [B, 37]

BOK LAGER — gold, clean malt and hop nose, light malt flavor, medium body, light dry hop finish, short dry hop aftertaste. [B, 36]

The Loaded Hog / Plains Brewing Co.
Brewpubs in Christchurch, Wellington, and Timaru

PORT NICK LAGER — gold, hop aroma; big hop flavor that is more dry than bitter; plenty of malt in support for good balance, smooth and long. This brew was called Plains Lager at Timaru. [B, 60]

RED DOG DRAUGHT — amber-gold, light malt and hop aroma and flavor, bright and zesty, a faint toasted quality, good body, very long dry malt aftertaste. [B, 64]

HOGS HEAD DARK ALE — deep brown, light roasted malt aroma, roasted barley flavor, medium body, light, smooth, dry, and pleasant, dry

roasted barley aftertaste; stays dry and very drinkable. [A, 59]

WEISSBIER WHEAT BEER — pale gold; clean fresh nose is very wheatlike (100% wheat malt); flavor bright and hoppy (the most well-hopped brew at the pub, surprisingly enough), clean and long dry hop aftertaste. Claims to have been made with a wild yeast, but I couldn't tell. [W, 57]

Marlborough Brewing Co., Ltd.
Microbrewery in Marlborough

MARLBOROUGH DRAUGHT — deep amber, malt nose, malt flavor, light body; dry malt aftertaste is light and not long. [B, 32]

McCashin's Brewery & Malthouse
Brewery in Stoke, Nelson

McCASHIN'S SOUTHERN LIGHT LAGER — gold, faint malt nose, grainy malt flavor, very faint grainy malt finish, only a sense of dryness for an aftertaste, a low-alcohol brew. [B, 27]

MAC'S GOLD ALL MALT LAGER — gold, hop nose, very dry hop flavor, dry hop finish; some malt joins the hops in the aftertaste. [B, 41]

MAC'S ALE — amber, hop nose; dry hop flavor has some ale-like tang for character; dry hop finish

and aftertaste, fairly long and very dry. [A, 49]

BLACK MAC TRADITIONAL DARK MALT ALE — very deep brown, light malt nose, big malt flavor is more dry than rich, very nicely balanced, dry malt finish, long dry malt aftertaste shows some background hops, an excellent beer. [B, 7]

MAC'S REAL ALE — fairly deep amber, fruity tea-like aroma, big malt flavor with hops in back, medium body; dry malt aftertaste has some hops in support; good length, good beer. [A, 60]

New Zealand Breweries Ltd.
Breweries in Auckland, Wellington, Dunedin, Hastings, and Christchurch. Previously identified as Lion Breweries, Ltd.

STEINLAGER NEW ZEALAND LAGER BEER — pale gold; lovely aroma is more hops than malt; good hop flavor up front; off-dry malt develops in the mid-palate; dry hop aftertaste with that malt in the background, good balance, good tasting, lots of character and very drinkable. [B, 60]

STEINLAGER BLUE LAGER BEER — gold, light hop aroma, medium body, malt flavor; dry malt aftertaste has a light hop background. [B, 50]

STEINLAGER DRY BEER — gold, good hop and malt aroma,

pleasant dry hop and malt flavor, medium body, medium long dry aftertaste. [D, 42]

RHEINECK LAGER BEER — gold, smooth malt and hop aroma, big malt flavor; some hops in the finish and aftertaste but it is largely a malt beer, medium dry at best. [B, 50]

RHEINECK DRY BEER — gold, very malty aroma, dry malt flavor; if there are hops I can't taste them; dry malt finish, very short dry malt aftertaste. [D, 38]

LION BROWN DRAUGHT BEER — deep amber-gold, light malt aroma and flavor, medium body, light malt finish, short dry malt aftertaste. [B, 47]

LION RED BEER — deep gold, faint malt nose, bright malt and hop flavor, good body, finishes malty, medium to short dry malt aftertaste. [B, 48]

WAIKATO DRAUGHT BITTER BEER — amber, pleasant light malt and hop aroma; smooth malt flavor is bright and tasty; medium body, dry malt finish, long dry malt aftertaste, a nice drinking beer. [B, 56]

RED BAND EXPORT BEER — amber-gold, malt aroma and flavor, big body, malt finish and long dry malt aftertaste, plenty of malt for the palate all the way through. [B, 55]

SPEIGHT'S EXTRA GOLD — gold; malt nose has a spiciness about it; malt flavor has plenty of hop backing; good body, dry malt finish; fairly long dry malt after-taste gets a nice infusion of hops at the end; a lot of beer for your money. [B, 61]

SPEIGHT'S GOLD MEDAL ALE — deep gold, fruity malt and hop aroma and flavor, medium to good body, medium dry malt fin-ish, fairly long dry malt aftertaste; a decent brew that is very popular on the South Island. [B, 60]

HAWKES BAY LEOPARD DRAUGHT BEER — amber, dry malt aroma and flavor, medium body, only a faint dry malt after-taste. This is the only "Leopard" product I could find in New Zealand after Leopard Breweries, Ltd. of Hastings was absorbed by NZB. The others listed below were exported to the U.S.A. at various times. [B, 40]

LEOPARD LAGER — gold; sweet fruity malt nose reminds you of pineapple; off-dry malt fla-vor has hops in back; light body; flavor doesn't develop and ends weakly with carbonation and dry hops. [B, 19]

LEOPARD EXPORT LAGER BEER — pale gold; malt nose has a pine needle and sour back-ground; fruity malt flavor, sour hop finish; dry sour hop aftertaste has an apple background. [B, 16]

LEOPARD STRONG BEER — tawny gold, sour fruity malt aroma; malt flavor has some applelike tones; light sour malt aftertaste. [B, 29]

WARDS CANTERBURY DRAUGHT BEER — deep gold, malt and hop aroma, big well-hopped malt flavor, good body; very long aftertaste shows plenty of both malt and hops; a good beer with lots of character made from Canterbury (NZ) malted barley and Nelson hops. [B, 73]

TENNENT'S LOW ALCOHOL LAGER BEER — gold, soapy nose; grainy flavor is faintly cheesy; light grainy flavor, very brief dry malt aftertaste. [B, 15]

Newbegin Brewery Ltd.
Microbrewery in Auckland

SILVER FERN NATURAL LAGER — gold, big hop nose, highly hopped malt flavor, malt finish, long dry hop and malt aftertaste, big body, a big tasty well-flavored brew. [B, 59]

Settlers Brewing Co.
Brewery in Henderson

STOCKAN DRAUGHT ALE — amber-brown, big roasted barley aroma and flavor, medium body, spicy finish, long roasted malt aftertaste. [B, 59]

STOCKAN MUNICH LAGER — deep gold, spicy malt aroma and taste, dry hop finish, long dry hop aftertaste; a definite spicy background character pervades the entire sensation. [B, 55]

Shakespeare Tavern & Brewery
Brewpub in Auckland

FALSTAFF'S REAL ALE — amber, dry hop aroma and flavor, very dry, bright, and well-hopped flavor like an English Bitter, smooth and quaffable, dry hop finish and aftertaste, good length. [A, 60]

MacBETH'S RED ALE — deep amber, smooth malt aroma and flavor like a Scottish ale, good body, light dry malt finish, very drinkable, long dry malt aftertaste. [A, 56]

BARRACLOUGH LAGER — pale gold, hop aroma and light bitter hop flavor, smooth and balanced, medium body, hop finish, long dry hop aftertaste. [B, 57]

KING LEAR OLD ALE — deep brown; big malt nose shows some of the alcohol (7.5%); very rich malt flavor has plenty of hops for a good balance; fruity nature overall, big body, very rich and very long. [A, 80]

WILLPOWER STOUT — deep brown, brown head, smooth medium dry roasted malt nose, only lightly bittered (more like an English style than Irish), good body (not big), smooth and mellow, long medium dry malt aftertaste, a pleasant sipping beer. [S, 54]

Westland Breweries Ltd.
Brewery in Greymouth

MONTEITH'S EXTRA BITTER BROWN BEER — deep amber, malt aroma, bright malt flavor, fairly rich and quite smooth; finish is dry malt but still stays rich; long malt aftertaste. [B, 59]

NORTH AMERICA

Canada

Algonquin Brewing Co.

Brewery in Formosa Springs (Ontario). Some labels say Northern Algonquin British Columbia.

FORMOSA SPRINGS COLD-FILTERED DRAFT — gold, faint malt and hop nose; estery malt flavor is grapelike; finish and aftertaste are like the flavor but have a more grainy, short dry aftertaste. [B, 41]

ALGONQUIN LIGHT BEER — pale gold, malt and hop aroma, good body, creamy, malt palate with some hops, pleasant finish and aftertaste. [LO, 30]

ALGONQUIN COUNTRY LAGER — gold, malt nose, weak malt flavor, light body, dull dry malt aftertaste. [B, 32]

ALGONQUIN SPECIAL RESERVE ALE — pale amber, faint malt nose, high carbonation, tart hop and buttery malt flavor, medium body, short dry malt aftertaste. [A, 26]

Notes

ALGONQUIN CANADIAN LIGHT — pale gold, clean malt and hop nose, light body, hop finish, metallic flavors in the aftertaste. [LO, 28]

NORTHERN GOOSE SUPER LIGHT BREW NON-ALCOHOLIC MALT BEVERAGE — gold, off-dry grainy nose, carbonation and grainy malt flavor, little follow-through except for a sour grainy sensation. [NA, 14]

ROYAL AMBER LAGER — amber-gold, faint malt nose, dull malt flavor, sour vegetal malt finish and aftertaste, not likable. Made with barley and wheat malt. [B, 17]

FORMOSA SPRINGS LIGHT — gold, faint malt and hop aroma; flavor is mostly carbonation with faint hops in back; faint malt finish, short dry aftertaste, 4% abv. [LO, 26]

FORMOSA SPRINGS BAVARIAN STYLE BOCK BEER — pale amber, faintly fruity nose; malty flavor has an interesting faintly acidic background; some of the 6% abv shows; the faint

acidity balances the sweetness; long malty aftertaste; the beer grows on you. [B, 61]

HUNT CLUB CREAM LAGER — hazy gold, malt aroma, dry malt flavor, fairly refreshing; carbonation keeps it bright; dry malt aftertaste has a touch of sweetness; good length, 5% abv. [B, 50]

MARCONI'S EUROPEAN LAGER — gold, weak malt nose, pleasant soft malty flavor, medium body, dry hop finish and aftertaste, medium length, 5% abv, made for Marconi's Restaurant & Brewery of Etobicoke, Ontario. This was a bottled sample. [B, 39]

ALGONQUIN BLACK & TAN — amber-brown, malt aroma, smooth malt flavor, medium body, dry malt finish and aftertaste; easy drinking brew, but is not well-balanced needing some more hop bite; also there is a coarseness in the aftertaste; 5% abv. [B, 42]

Amsterdam Brasserie & Brewpub
Microbrewery in Toronto (Ontario). Original location and brewpub closed in late 1994; now colocated with Rotterdam Brewing facilities upstairs from Rotterdam pub.

AMSTERDAM OKTOBERFEST — amber-brown, faint malt aroma; big smoky malt flavor is a surprise when warned only by the very light scent; good body, dry

smoked malt finish and aftertaste, great with German cuisine. [B, 61]

Big Rock Brewery
Brewery in Calgary (Alberta)

ROYAL COACHMAN DRY ALE — gold; toasted malt aroma reminds you of Grape-Nuts cereal; tasty toasted malt flavor, light body, toasted malt aftertaste with medium length. [A, 55]

BUZZARD BREATH ALE — tawny-gold, light dry toasted malt aroma; dry malt flavor is slightly toasted; medium body, dry malt finish and aftertaste, medium length. [A, 48]

COLD COCK WINTER PORTER — very deep amber-brown, complex rich malt aroma; dry malt palate but there are complex hop flavors; light hop background shows best in the finish and aftertaste; interesting and fairly long dry malt aftertaste. [P, 67]

COCK O' THE ROCK PORTER — deep ruby-brown, complex chocolate malt and hop nose, surprisingly dry palate; flavor is big, lots of hops and malt but the malt dominates; very long, a big pushy brew. [P, 67]

TRADITIONAL ALE — light copper-amber, malt nose, pleasant malt flavor, medium long malt aftertaste. [A, 28]

BIG ROCK PALE ALE — deep gold, toasted chocolate malt nose, delicious light malt flavor, pleasant but brief. [A, 43]

BIG ROCK BITTER PALE
ALE — pale amber, bright citrus-ale nose, zesty well-hopped flavor, good body, very flavorful, nice balance, big but not overdone, some complexity, good hop finish, long hop aftertaste. [A, 67]

McNALLY'S EXTRA PURE MALT IRISH STYLE ALE — deep bright amber; good toasted malt nose really comes at you; rich malt flavor is delicious; faint hop finish, long malt aftertaste with hints of caramel and butter. [A, 62]

SPRINGBOK ALE — deep gold, light chocolate malt aroma, big bright creamy malt and hop flavor, smooth, balanced, tasty, good body, long dry malt aftertaste. [BK, 69]

ZEB O'BREENS IRISH ALE — amber, dry malt and hop nose, flavor, finish, and aftertaste, very well-balanced, smooth, and dry, medium body, fairly long. Contract brew for the Goat Hill Tavern of Costa Mesa, CA. [A, 47]

ALBINO RHINO — amber-gold, dry malt and hop aroma, very dry hop flavor, driest at finish; long dry hop aftertaste goes more bitter at the end. Contract brew for Goat Hill Tavern of Costa Mesa, CA and Whistler Brewing Co. of Whistler (British Columbia). [A, 20]

PIG TAIL ALE — amber, very faint malt nose, very dry malt and light hop flavor, good body; aftertaste is just dryness. Made for Pig's Ear Pub of San Bernardino, CA. [A, 47]

WARTHOG ALE — amber, big appetizing malt aroma, bold hop

palate, good body; hops continue with strength into the finish and aftertaste which is very long; a very satisfying brew, 5.25% abv. [A, 61]

ALBINO ALE — amber-gold, vegetable soup and malt aroma; tastes like it smells; medium body, brief aftertaste. [A, 20]

GRASSHÖPPER WHEAT ALE — hazy deep gold, malty nose, sort of a honeyed malt flavor, medium body, very smooth, dry hop finish, medium long but very light dry hop aftertaste, a bit on the dull side. [W, 49]

Brasscrie Brasal Brewery Inc. / Brasserie Allemande Inc.
Microbrewery in LaSalle (Quebec)

BRASAL BOCK MALT LIQUOR — brilliant amber-brown, complex slightly sweet roasted malt nose, big strong roasted malt and alcohol flavor, quite rich; hops arrive for the finish, then a long dry roasted malt and hop aftertaste; 7.8% abv, a very good bock. [BK, 88]

BRASAL HOPPS BRAU — gold, hop nose; dry hop flavor has plenty of malt backing; smooth and balanced, dry hop finish and aftertaste, long and likable. [B, 62]

Notes

BRASAL SPECIAL AMBER LAGER — deep gold, toasted grainy malt aroma, big complex toasted malt flavor, rich and long, likable and satisfying, smooth with nothing overpowering; the 6.1% abv is only noticeable in the aftertaste. [B, 75]

Brick Brewing Co., Ltd.
Brewery in Waterloo (Ontario)

BRICK PREMIUM LAGER BEER — gold, off-dry malty aroma, dry malt flavor, dry hop finish, long dry malt and hop aftertaste, good balance. [B, 53]

RED BARON BEER — pale gold, light malt and hop nose, light malt flavor with good hop backing, dry hop finish and aftertaste. [B, 48]

BRICK AMBER DRY BEER — deep gold, malt nose, slightly buttery malt palate, creamy, smooth, pleasant, dry malt finish and aftertaste. [D, 38]

ORIGINAL RED CAP ALE — gold, fruity-spicy aroma, big bright hop flavor, medium body, dry hop finish and aftertaste, good length. [A, 39]

C'Est What
Brewpub in Toronto (Ontario). The wort is prepared at Brew Perfect, a brewery in Oakville (Ontario), and fermented at C'Est What

C'EST WHAT MILD BROWN ALE — deep amber, light malty aroma, mild dry malt flavor, dry malt finish and aftertaste, short, 3.5% abv. [A, 56]

C'EST WHAT COFFEE PORTER — dark brown, slight roasted malt nose, big bodied, smooth, dry roasted malt flavor; long dry malt aftertaste is not as roasted as the main flavor but does show a touch of the coffee. Made with two-row carastan, black, and chocolate malt with some rolled oats. 5.3% abv. [P, 72]

C'EST WHAT HENRI III (STRONG HENRY) — amber-gold, spicy aroma shows ginger, coriander, and a touch of orange, flavor matches nose, strong taste, long spicy-malty aftertaste. [A, 54]

Canadian National Breweries
Brewery in Markham (Ontario)

CANADIAN GOLD COLD FILTERED DRAFT BEER — gold, very beautiful malt and hop aroma, very light fresh malt and hop flavor, good balance, light body, brief light dry malt and hop aftertaste. [B, 43]

CC's Brewpub
Brewpub in Mississaugua (Ontario)

CC'S MILLCREEK LAGER — gold, pleasant off-dry malt nose, highly carbonated, light bright refreshing malt palate, slight dry hop finish and aftertaste, not long. [B, 59]

CC'S MILLCREEK DARK LAGER — dark brown, faint malt nose, almost no flavor (very faint dry malt); ends quite dry, little aftertaste. [B, 41]

Canadian Heritage Brewing Co.
Brewery in Richmond (British Columbia)

STEVESTON HERITAGE OLD COUNTRY PREMIUM PILSNER — amber-gold, off-dry fruity melon and citrus nose, fruity malt flavor, dry hop finish and aftertaste. [B, 49]

Charley's Tavern
Brewpub in Windsor (Ontario)

TIMEOUT LAGER — gold, light dry hop aroma and flavor, medium body, very smooth, finishes dry, very drinkable, even quaffable, about 5% abv. [B, 45]

TIMEOUT ALE — deep gold, fairly big dry hop flavor, good carbonation level, good body, dry smooth light hop flavor, ends dry, light and dry hop aftertaste, very drinkable, 5% abv. [A, 50]

College St. Bar
Brewpub in Toronto (Ontario). The wort is brewed and provided by the Select Brewery of Toronto with fermentation being accomplished on premises.

CSB SELECT PILSNER — deep bright gold, pleasant malt and hop nose, likable dry malty flavor; dry malt finish and aftertaste shows some graininess. [B, 60]

CSB SELECT STICKLE STOUT — very dark brown, big tan head, aroma of toasted and chocolate malt, big dry roasty flavor; finish shows enhanced roasted malt, almost smoky; medium long dry roasted malt aftertaste, a good long dry stout; 4.5% abv. [S, 67]

CSB SELECT BITTER — amber; hop nose has a soapy background; dry hop flavor has an underlying sweetness; medium long dry hop aftertaste, 4.5% abv. [A, 61]

Conners Brewing Co.
Conners Brewing Enterprises, Ltd. Brewery on earlier labels listed as Don Valley Brewing Co. in Mississauga (Ontario); now listed as Toronto (Ontario); brewery is in St. Catherines (Ontario).

CONNERS BREWERY ALE — amber, light malt aroma; hops dominate the flavor but there is still plenty of malt; big body, hop finish, short dry hop aftertaste. [A, 52]

CONNERS SPECIAL DRAFT — amber-gold, faint malt aroma, bitter and dry hop flavor, high carbonation, long dry bitter aftertaste, a straight plain bitter brew. [A, 33]

CONNERS BEST BITTER — orange-amber, low carbonation, hoppy aroma; big bright well-hopped flavor has plenty of malt; hefty dry hop finish and aftertaste, very long on the palate. [A, 57]

CONNERS PREMIUM LAGER — gold, big strongly hopped aroma, big hop flavor, good body, dry hop aftertaste. [B, 45]

CONNERS DARK ALE — brilliant amber, light northwest hop nose, nice good tasting northwest hop flavor, a little sweet but balanced, creamy finish, big fairly dry hop aftertaste. [A, 78]

CONNERS IMPERIAL STOUT — very dark brown, rich malt nose of chocolate malt and roasted barley, rich flavor like the aroma, big body, very long malty aftertaste; stays both rich and dry. [S, 91]

Notes

MOVENPICK PILSNER — gold, beautiful aroma of malt and European hops, a little sweet malt and hop flavor; complex and has balance; good body, off-dry malt and hop finish and aftertaste. Made for Movenpick restaurants. [B, 54]

Creemore Springs Brewery, Ltd.
Brewery in Creemore (Ontario)

CREEMORE SPRINGS PREMIUM LAGER — pale amber, faint caramel nose, big malt flavor, touch of bitter hops at the finish, good body, dry hop aftertaste. [B, 46]

Denison's Brewing Co. / Growlers Bar / Conchy Joe's Oyster Bar
Brewpub in Toronto (Ontario)

ROYAL DUNKEL — hazy golden amber; complex grainy aroma that is faintly spicy (like cinnamon); dry malt finish, long dry malt aftertaste. Specific gravity 1053, 4.9% abv. Supposed to be patterned after König Ludwig Dunkel of Germany. [B, 69]

GROWLER'S LAGER UNFILTERED — amber, dry malt aroma and flavor, dry malt finish and aftertaste, medium length, medium body. Specific gravity 1047, 4.7% abv. [B, 56]

GROWLER'S WEIZEN — hazy gold; clean spicy malt aroma is faintly cloves; bright spicy malt flavor, balanced and smooth, clean bright and refreshing, long spicy aftertaste, specific gravity 1050, 5.6% abv. [W, 67]

GROWLER'S OKTOBERFEST FILTERED — gold, light malty nose; faint caramel flavor is on the dry side; very dry malt finish and aftertaste, fairly long, specific gravity 1053, 5.4% abv. [B, 60]

GROWLER'S MÄRZEN — gold, fresh malt aroma; fairly rich malty flavor is surprisingly dry; good body, dry malt finish and aftertaste, specific gravity 1054, 5.4% abv. [B, 60]

Drummond Brewing Co., Ltd.
Brewery in Red Deer (Alberta). Calgary and Edmonton mentioned on early labels.

DRUMMOND DRY — hazy gold, very nice hop and malt aroma and flavor, medium body, good balance; finishes just like the flavor and this stays into a medium length aftertaste. [D, 35]

DRUMMOND BEER — pale gold, dry malt nose, dry hop and malt flavor, balanced, hop finish and aftertaste. [B, 43]

DRUMMOND LIGHT — pale gold, slightly stinky sour hop nose; dull sour malt and hop palate has little length. [LO, 20]

Eurobeer Corp.
Brewery in Windsor (Ontario)

ST. STEPHEN LAGER — gold, faintly malty fruity nose, sweet in back; flavor is the same including the background sweetness; medium dry finish and aftertaste still the same in back, driest at the end. [B, 38]

Granite Brewery
Brewpubs in Halifax (once named Ginger's Tavern) and Toronto

BEST BITTER REAL ALE — deep amber, appetizing dry hop nose; big hop flavor has a sweetness up front, dry middle, off-dry malt finish; big body; long complex hop aftertaste gets drier as it goes. This is a well-made likable ale made with Ringwood yeast and Yakima Fuggles hops, having a density of 1046 and 4.5% abw. This seems to have been named Ginger's Best Bitter when the Halifax pub opened. It is regularly available at both locations. At Toronto, it is cask-conditioned and dry hopped giving it a smoother and more balanced character. [A, 72]

KEEFE'S IRISH STOUT — dark brown, virtually no aroma; dry hoppy flavor is not strong; medium body, finishes lightly dry and only slightly bitter; light dry aftertaste has little length. This is a top-fermented unpasteurized unfiltered black bitter stout with a density of 1042 and 4% abw. It is regularly available at both locations. [S, 53]

PECULIAR STRONG ALE — dark brownish-amber, light malt aroma with a slight hop background; malty flavor is very slightly sweet, very smooth, good body; malty aftertaste is more dry than the flavor, but the operative descriptor for this brew is smooth. Peculiar has a density of 1056, 5.6% abw, and is designed to emulate Old Peculier from the Theakston Brewery of England. It is regularly available at both locations. [A, 72]

GRANITE SUMMER ALE — golden amber, light hop aroma, light but bright hop flavor, good mouthfeel, medium body, very drinkable, dry hop finish and aftertaste, not long but very quaffable. Density of 1042 and 4.5% abw, this is one of Granite's seasonal brews. [A, 67]

Granville Island Brewing Co.
Brewery in Vancouver (British Columbia)

ISLAND LAGER TRADITIONAL BEER — bright gold,

toasted malt aroma, big body, complex well-hopped flavor, bitter hop finish, long complex dry hop and toasted malt aftertaste. [B, 29]

ISLAND BOCK — amber, rich malt nose, big toasted malt and bright hop flavor, perfect balance, delicious and very long aftertaste like the flavor. Can't think of a thing to improve on this brew; one of Canada's finest. [BK, 90]

Great Lakes Brewing Co.
Brewery in Brampton (Ontario)

GREAT LAKES LAGER — pale amber, slightly scorched fruity malt nose with a little tang, lightly scorched hard candy malt flavor, light body, malt aftertaste with medium duration. [B, 34]

UNICORN ALE — deep amber; pleasant malt nose is a bit sweet; caramel malt front palate; hops come in at the finish and clash; light body, complex, long, but there is an imbalance. [A, 43]

Great Western Brewing Co., Ltd.
Brewery in Saskatoon (Saskatchewan)

GREAT WESTERN LAGER BEER — hazy gold, very foamy, faint hop and malt nose, malt flavor, big body, long off-dry malt aftertaste. Made for Connoisseur Beverage International Inc. of Minneapolis, MN. [B, 40]

Notes

GREAT WESTERN LIGHT BEER — gold, hop nose, light hop flavor, light body, faint dry hop finish and aftertaste, very little aftertaste, and no complexity. Contract brew as above. [LO, 32]

LISTWIN'S KODIAK MILD DRAFT LAGER BEER — deep gold, hop aroma, very malty flavor with good hop support, sour hop finish; very end is dry hops; overall appearance (package is a large plastic bottle) cries out to malt liquor fans. [ML, 40]

Hart Breweries, Ltd.
Microbrewery in Carleton Place (Ontario)

HART CREAM ALE — hazy gold, sweet fruity grape-bubble gum aroma, creamy cantaloupe and hop flavor, feels good in the mouth, dry sour aftertaste; strange but it grows on you; interesting and, given time, likable. [A, 49]

HART AMBER ALE — golden amber; big well-hopped aroma followed by a flavor that is mostly hops but which has a hefty malt background that keeps it from becoming dry; the hops take more assertive role from the middle on, but it never loses the malty sweetness. This is a very flavorful big-bodied ale that keeps its balance even though highly hopped and heavily malted. This sample was freshly delivered from the brewery. A sample found earlier (that may not have been as fresh) was hazy amber; had a dry malty nose; toasted malt and hop flavor (Briess malt) with the hops strongest in the finish, and with a very dry harsh aftertaste. [A, 61]

Old Heidelberg House
Old Heidelberg Brewery and Restaurant in Heidelberg (Ontario). It is a malt extract brewery.

HEIDELBERG O-B BREW — amber, dry malt and hop nose, very dry hop flavor, light body, dry short bitter hop aftertaste. [B, 27]

Heuther Hotel / The Lion Brewery & Museum
Brewpub and hotel in Waterloo (Ontario)

LION LIGHT LAGER — gold, light dry malt nose and flavor, hop finish, medium to short dry hop aftertaste, clean and refreshing. [B, 50]

LION DRY — pale bright gold, little aroma, bright malt flavor, dry malt-hop finish and aftertaste. [D, 47]

HEUTHER'S PREMIUM LAGER — medium deep gold, good big malt aroma and taste, good body, long clean malt and hop aftertaste, excellent balance, noticeable alcohol, Heuther's best brew. [B, 90]

LION LAGER — gold, light malt aroma, good malt flavor with hops in back, similar to the Lion Light but bigger, bright refreshing malt flavor, dry hop finish and aftertaste, good and long. [B, 59]

ENGLISH ALE — deep dark amber, malt aroma, very dry strong malt flavor, a touch winey from the alcohol, austere dry malt finish and aftertaste, almost like a stout but with a good rather than heavy body, nicely made and enjoyable. [A, 69]

ADLY'S ALE — amber, malt nose, strong dry malt flavor, big body, a bit winy from the alcohol, dry malt finish, short dry aftertaste, very drinkable. [A, 52]

Horseshoe Bay Brewing Co.
Microbrewery in Horseshoe Bay, Vancouver (British Columbia)

BAY ALE —amber, malt nose, very little carbonation, slightly sour malt flavor, dry finish and aftertaste, very brief. [A, 4]

James Gate
Brewpub in Toronto. The beers are brewed at the Marquée brewpub in

Mississauga, not open to the public.

GATE ALE — amber, good malt and hop aroma, pleasant dry malt and hop flavor, medium body, long dry malt aftertaste. [A, 67]

GATE GOLD LAGER — amber, dry malt and hop aroma and flavor, smooth and pleasant, light to medium body, long dry malt and hop aftertaste; the recipe is undergoing continuing gradual alterations to improve the hop character. [B, 67]

Labatt Brewing Co., Ltd.

Breweries in St. John's, Newfoundland; Halifax, Nova Scotia; West St. John, New Brunswick; La Salle, Quebec; Waterloo, London, and Weston Ontario; Winnipeg, Manitoba; Saskatoon, Saskatchewan; Edmonton, Alberta; Vancouver, Creston, and New Westminster, British Columbia. Corporate headquarters are in London, Ontario.

LABATT'S 50 ALE — medium deep bright gold, light hop nose, medium body, bright zesty hop flavor, quite tasty, long hop aftertaste with some slightly sour malt background. Export to the U.S.A. is labeled Labatt's 50 Canadian Ale. [A, 52]

LABATT'S PILSENER BEER — bright gold, dry hop nose, dry malt and hop flavor, medium body, finish and long aftertaste like the flavor, good clean serviceable pilsener. Long known as Labatt's Blue in Canada and more recently labeled as such. [B, 56]

GOLD KEG BEER — deep tawny-gold, big malt and hop aroma, good hop flavor, tasty; pleasant sour hop aftertaste is long. [B, 64]

COOL SPRING LIGHT BEER — bright gold, virtually no nose, light body; faint off-dry malt flavor fades as it crosses the palate; brief dull malt aftertaste. [LO, 30]

CERVOISE ALE — pale gold, good malt aroma; bright malt flavor that fades across the palate; short dull malt aftertaste. [A, 33]

LABATT'S CRYSTAL LAGER BEER — gold, malt and hop nose, high carbonation, complex malt and hop flavor, long dry hop aftertaste, a pleasant very drinkable beer. [B, 57]

LABATT'S DRY LIGHT BEER — pale yellow, faint malt nose; palate is faint malt and carbonation; very short dry malt aftertaste. [D, 20]

LABATT'S DRY — bright gold, light malt and hop aroma, smooth, light bodied, well-balanced, very faint brief malt aftertaste. [D, 34]

LABATT EXTRA DRY BEER — pale gold, faint malt nose, malt palate, dry hop finish and aftertaste. [D, 28]

Notes

LABATT'S IPA — gold, malt nose, big off-dry malt flavor; high CO_2 but it is needed to balance the malt; dry malt finish and short aftertaste, better than average malty brew. [IPA, 46]

LABATT'S VELVET CREAM PORTER — brown, light malt nose; light malt flavor is off-dry up front, medium body, dry malt finish, long dry malt aftertaste, very drinkable. [P, 27]

JOHN LABATT'S EXTRA STOCK MALT LIQUOR — deep bright gold, fragrant complex malt and hop aroma, big body, huge complex malt flavor, excellent hop balance, dry malt finish and long aftertaste, a big beautiful brew. [ML, 76]

LABATT'S EXTRA STOCK MALT LIQUOR — gold, straightforward malt flavor, good body, hefty malt flavor, finish and aftertaste like the flavor. I thought this would be the same as above exported to the U.S.A., but it doesn't have the heft or the complexity. [ML, 76]

KOOTENAY PALE ALE — medium to deep gold, lovely zesty hop nose; clean and bright at the start, flattens out at the finish, and has a slightly dull malt aftertaste; still a pleasant beer. [A, 53]

KOKANEE PILSENER BEER — medium gold, light hop nose, pleasant and smooth malt and hop flavor, dry malt aftertaste, pleasant but a bit light. [B, 43]

JOCKEY CLUB BEER — deep gold, pleasant malt-hop aroma, tasty malt and hop flavor, long dry hop aftertaste. [B, 64]

BLUE STAR — tawny gold, hop nose; flavor briefly is malt, quickly turns hop bitter; bitter finish, and long dry bitter hop aftertaste; very good of type. [B, 51]

GUINNESS EXTRA STOUT — opaque brown, roasted malt nose, heavy body, complex coffee-malt flavor; long dry malt aftertaste retains much of the richness of the flavor. [S, 63]

LABATT BLUE LIGHT — medium deep gold, bright hop and malt nose, light nondescript malt and hop flavor, light body, little aftertaste. [LO, 19]

JOHN LABATT CLASSIC BEER — bright deep gold color, off-dry hop nose, big dry malt and bitter hop flavor, dry hop finish and aftertaste, medium length. [B, 14]

JOHN LABATT'S CLASSIC LIGHT — bright gold, light hop nose, dull malt and hop flavor, mostly carbonation, brief malt-hop aftertaste. [LO, 16]

LABATT GENUINE COLD FILTERED DRAFT — gold, malt nose, malt and hop flavor, a touch of citrus in back, high carbonation, short dry malt and hop aftertaste. [B, 61]

LABATT .5 — pale gold, grainy malt and hop nose; also a trace of corn comes through; light body, dull malt flavor, weak grainy aftertaste, another uninteresting non-alcoholic malt beverage. [NA, 23]

OLAND EXPORT ALE — pale gold, pleasant malt and hop aroma, good mild clean taste, medium to light body, good balance, a little hop zest at the finish, dry clean hop aftertaste. Oland Breweries, Halifax, Nova Scotia, is the originating brewery and brewery of record. [A, 71]

OLAND'S OLD SCOTIA ALE — bright gold, light tangy ale nose with good hops, big ale flavor with plenty of hops and slightly off-dry malt, good body; sags a little at the middle to finish, but rebounds well in the long hop aftertaste; good brew. [A, 60]

OLAND'S LIGHT BEER — bright gold, nice hop nose, fairly complex lightly hopped flavor, light body, hop and faintly sour malt aftertaste. [LO, 40]

OLAND'S SCHOONER BEER — pale bright gold, good fresh malt and hop aroma, high carbonation, balanced malt and hop flavor, lovely malt finish, lingering dry hop aftertaste. [B, 52]

OLAND EXTRA STOUT — dark brown, light molasses aroma, light

body, medium sweet malt flavor, likable although light. [S, 64]

ALEXANDER KEITH'S INDIA PALE ALE — tawny-gold, fine malt aroma with good hop character; pleasant malt flavor that finishes with good hops; long dry hop aftertaste, good balance, and very drinkable. Oland Breweries, Ltd. [A, 60]

ALEXANDER KEITH'S LIGHT BEER — light tawny-gold, pleasant malt-hop aroma and flavor, light body, quick hop finish, light short dry hop aftertaste. [LO, 36]

KEITH'S SPECIAL DRY — pale gold, rising malt and hop nose, good body, big malt and light hop flavor, good balance, fairly long dry malt aftertaste, one of the better dry beers. [D, 41]

BUDWEISER LAGER BEER — pale gold, light malt and hop aroma, good balanced hop and malt flavor, very good body, good balance, dry hop finish, long dry hop aftertaste. A good Budweiser indeed, and one with 5% alcohol, which you don't find in the U.S.A. [B, 53]

BUD LIGHT — pale gold, pleasant light malt aroma, very light malt flavor, faint off-dry malt aftertaste with little length. [B, 16]

LABATT ICE BEER — gold, big bright beery hop and malt aroma, good balance; shows its alcohol (5.6%); big body; big flavor shows plenty of off-dry malt and bright hops, sweetest at the finish; aftertaste is slightly less off-dry and is long, good tasting summertime beer. [B, 47]

LABATT WILDCAT BEER — bright gold, lovely perfumy malt aroma, very fragrant and floral; there's malt and hops in the flavor and it is quite flowery as promised by the nose; good body, short malt aftertaste, 5% abv. [B, 46]

LABATT WILDCAT STRONG BEER — gold; very nice malt and hop nose also shows some alcohol; big dry flavor shows lots of malt and hops; hefty body; you can taste the alcohol (6.1% abv); dry hop finish and aftertaste has some malt in back. [B, 50]

LABATT MAXIMUM ICE STRONG BEER — gold, big malt nose, off-dry (almost sweet) malt flavor, quite alcoholic (7.1% abv), big body, short dry malt aftertaste. [B, 47]

JOHN LABATT CLASSIC WHEAT — brilliant deep gold, fresh malt nose; fresh grainy malt flavor is a bit off-dry; medium body, creamy in the mouth but thin on flavor, faintly honeyed, ends dry, not long. [W, 41]

ELEPHANT RED ALE — red-amber, malt nose, very well-balanced malt and hop flavor, good tasting, big body, long and smooth; made under supervision by Carlsberg Breweries. [A, 64]

LABATT'S COPPER AMBER LAGER — amber-gold, big European hop nose; fruity hop taste is a bit sweet; medium body, long dry faint European hop and malt aftertaste. [B, 52]

Notes

PRESIDENT'S CLUB LIGHT DRAFT — pale gold, light pleasant faint Saaz hop nose, light perfumy malt taste, weak body, light dry hoppy finish and aftertaste, 4% abv. Made under contract for grocery chains that carry President's Club line of store brands. [LO, 29]

PRESIDENT'S CLUB PREMIUM DRAFT — gold; light malt nose is a little perfumy and soapy; finely carbonated, malty flavor, medium body, light dry hop finish and aftertaste, 5% abv. Made under contract for grocery chains that carry President's Club line of store brands. [B, 23]

PRESIDENT'S CLUB STRONG DRAFT — gold, grapey vinous malty nose; hops start of a vinous malty taste; medium to big body; vinous alcoholic aftertaste comes off a bit bland; 5.9% abv. Made under contract for grocery chains that carry President's Club line of store brands. [B, 32]

LABATT TWIST — bright gold, lemony aroma like lemon peel or Fresca soft drink, lemon soda flavor, sweet and light, light weak body, low alcohol (2.3% abv), brief lemony aftertaste. [B, 22]

LABATT WILDCAT MOUNTAIN ALE — gold, light hop nose, light dry hop flavor, medium body; dry hop finish and aftertaste shows some sweet malt at the end; 5.2% abv. [A, 42]

PC (President's Club) ICE BREWED ULTIMATE DRY — pale gold, very light hop nose, medium body, hop flavor, high carbonation, dry hop finish and aftertaste, 5.5% abv. Made for various supermarket chains featuring PC generic brands. [L, 42]

Lakeport Brewing Co.
Brewery in E. Hamilton (Ontario). Formerly named Amstel Breweries.

PRIVATE SELECTION PREMIUM LIGHT BEER — fairly deep gold; big very fragrant nose shows both sour hops and sweet malt (but more malt than hops); very light body, grainy malt and light hop flavor, light dry aftertaste of short to medium duration. Made for Ralph's Grocery Co., Los Angeles, CA. [LO, 27]

PRIVATE SELECTION PREMIUM DRAFT BEER — fairly deep gold; big fragrant nose is similar to brew above but showing much more malt than hops; flavor is more malty and sweeter; light to medium body, light off-dry malt finish, medium dry light malt aftertaste, short to medium duration. Also made for Ralph's Grocery Co. [B, 33]

PC (President's Club) PREMIUM DRAFT — gold, aroma of both malt and hops, flavor to match; finishes dry hops but the malt is still there too; aftertaste like the finish, good duration, 5% abv. [B, 36]

PC (President's Club) PREMIUM LIGHT — pale gold; faint malt nose has some hops hiding in back; light malt and hop flavor, light body, brief aftertaste, 4% abv. [LO, 30]

PC (President's Club) PREMIUM STRONG DRAFT — deep gold; malty nose has good supporting hops, good body; alcohol does show slightly; fairly long aftertaste is mostly malt but the hops come in at the end; 5.9% abv. [B, 47]

PREMIUM ONTARIO LAGER — golden color; bright nose shows malt and some hops; smooth hop flavor has malt in behind; fairly long dry hop aftertaste, 5% abv. [B, 42]

PREMIUM ONTARIO LIGHT — pale gold, light malt nose, light hop flavor, light body, brief aftertaste, balanced but not exciting, 4% abv. [LO, 34]

LAKER PREMIUM LAGER — gold; aroma shows both malt and hops; light hop flavor with good malt backing, medium body, hop finish, long dry hop aftertaste, 5% abv, probably same as Laker Lager above with a new label. [B, 37]

LAKER PREMIUM LIGHT — pale gold, faint malt nose, very

light malt and hop flavor, light body, brief aftertaste. [LO, 30]

AROUND ONTARIO 7.3 STRONG BEER — deep gold; aroma is mostly malt and alcohol though there are some faint hops; big strong off-dry malt flavor is sweet and alcoholic; big body; hops are there but decidedly in third place; finish is smooth malt; long slightly off-dry malt aftertaste; this is a very smooth beer with 7.3% abv. [B, 72]

HENNINGER EXPORT BEER — bright gold, beautiful hop aroma, finely carbonated, bright hop flavor, good balance; finish is both hops and malt, as is the long aftertaste; good German-style brew. [B, 43]

HENNINGER MEISTER PILS PREMIUM PILSENER — pale gold, perfumy hop nose, finely carbonated, well-balanced hop and malt flavor, hops stronger than the malt, light hop finish, dry hop aftertaste with good length. [B, 33]

AMSTEL BEER — pale gold, light hop and malt aroma and flavor, good body, hop finish, short hop aftertaste. [B, 45]

AMSTEL LIGHT BEER — very pale gold, faint grainy sour hop nose, thin sour hop flavor, brief aftertaste. [LO, 27]

GRIZZLY BEER CANADIAN LAGER — bright gold, lovely hop nose, zesty hop flavor, good character, medium dry hop finish, long aftertaste; while the hops stay in the foreground throughout, there is a background of off-dry malt in back that comes in early and stays; all is harmoniously done; good brew of its type. [B, 59]

LAKER LAGER — gold, malt and hop aroma, light hop flavor with good malt backing, medium body, hop finish, long dry hop aftertaste. [B, 30]

LAKER LIGHT — pale gold, faint malt nose, light hop flavor, light body, brief aftertaste, like a little brother of Laker Lager. [LO, 23]

STEELER LAGER — bright gold, malt aroma; malt palate with hops coming in at the finish; medium long dry hop aftertaste. [B, 23]

BIRRA PERONI — brilliant deep gold, fragrant hop aroma, pleasant dry hop flavor, long dry hop aftertaste, a good reproduction of the well-known Italian beer. [B, 57]

DAVE'S DOPPELBOCK — pale gold, estery malt aroma; dull malty taste shows some of the 5.9% abv; medium body; ends drier and sharper; a bit on the odd side and not very attractive. [B, 19]

Marconi's Steak & Pasta House

Brewpub in restaurant in Etobicoke (Ontario, near Toronto airport)

MARCONI'S EUROPEAN LAGER — golden amber, dry bright malt aroma and taste, medium body, dry malt finish and aftertaste, little length. Tasted on draft at the pub, it is also produced in bottles by Algonquin under contract. [B, 53]

MARCONI'S LIGHT — golden amber, faint malt nose, light dry malty flavor, light body, dry finish and short aftertaste. [LO, 49]

MARCONI'S OKTOBERSTEIN — amber; grainy aroma and flavor is like unmalted barley grain; light body, dry finish and aftertaste, fairly brief, a very different taste for a beer. [B, 60]

MARCONI'S THICK ICE — deep amber-gold, malt aroma; malt flavor shows some alcohol; long malty aftertaste, very appetizing brew with 6.7% abv. [B, 61]

MARCONI'S STOUT — deep brown, rich malt nose; light malty flavor again shows the grainy taste of unmalted barley; medium body, very long dry malt aftertaste. [S, 59]

MARCONI'S CHAMPAGNE — gold; sweet nose is very much like a Canadian off-dry champagne from the Niagara Valley; flavor matches the nose and style; medium to good body, high alcohol (8.3% abv); long grapey aftertaste is dry at the end. A very good effort in creating a champagnelike brew. [B, 67]

MARCONI'S HARVEST — deep gold, malt nose; pumpkin and malt flavor has no spice; light body; short aftertaste dries as it goes. [B, 57]

The Master's Brasserie & Brew-pub
Brewpub and restaurant in Ottawa (Ontario)

MASTER'S LAGER — amber, bright malt and hop nose, dry hop flavor, finish, and aftertaste, balanced and bright. [B, 51]

MASTER'S ALE — amber, malt and hop nose, well-hopped flavor, dry hop finish and aftertaste, good length, similar to the Master's Lager but more complex. [A, 56]

McAusland Brewing Inc.
Brewery in St. Ambroise (Quebec)

ST. AMBROISE PALE ALE — amber, zesty ale nose with plenty of hops, strong hop flavor well-backed with malt, smooth, balanced, long, and very drinkable. OG 1049, 5% abv. [A, 76]

GRIFFON BROWN ALE — brilliant medium deep amber-brown; lightly roasted malt nose is faintly buttery (but not in a bad sense); very dry malt flavor has caramel in the finish; dry malt aftertaste, not complex but very pleasant to drink; OG 1048, 4.5% abv. [A, 56]

ST. AMBROISE OATMEAL STOUT — deep brown, chocolate malt and roasted barley nose, classic stout flavor, dry roasted, smooth, good body, roasted barley finish and aftertaste, long and dry. OG 1050, 5% abv. [S, 79]

GRIFFON BLONDE EXTRA PALE ALE — gold, bright hop nose, big dry hop flavor, good body, long and balanced, ends dry hops; OG 1050, 5% abv. [A, 53]

Molson O'Keefe Breweries / Molson Breweries of Canada, Ltd.
Breweries in St. John's, Newfoundland; Montreal, Quebec; Toronto, Rexdale, Willowdale and Barrie, Ontario; Edmonton, Lethbridge and Calgary, Alberta; Winnipeg, Manitoba; Regina, Saskatchewan; and Vancouver, British Columbia. Molson recently purchased Carling O'Keefe, one of the two other large national Canadian brewers.

MOLSON CANADIAN LAGER BEER — pale gold, off-dry malt aroma with hops in back, good malt flavor well-balanced with hops, good long dry malt and hop aftertaste, very smooth drinkable brew. [B, 75]

MOLSON CANADIAN LIGHT — gold, slightly skunk hop nose, hop flavor, high carbonation, dull malt finish and aftertaste. [LO, 21]

MOLSON EXPORT ALE — brilliant tawny-gold, clean malt and distinctive hop nose, good flavor with balanced hops and malt, a bright beer with good body, and a long and pleasant malt-hop aftertaste. [A, 70]

MOLSON GOLDEN — pale gold, light malt and hop aroma, light body, light off-dry malt flavor, hops way in back, light malt and hop finish, medium dry hop aftertaste with little length. [B, 36]

OLD STYLE PILSNER BEER — bright gold, aromatic hop and malt nose, highly carbonated, big well-balanced hop and malt flavor; finishes well and the aftertaste is pleasant and long. [B, 67]

MOLSON STOCK ALE — gold, off-dry malt nose, good malt and hop flavor, smooth, balanced, long dry hop aftertaste. [A, 56]

INDIA BEER — bright yellow-gold, off-dry malt aroma with a good hop backing, pleasant mild hop flavor, very good balance, dry malt finish, long dry hop aftertaste. [B, 64]

LAURENTIDE ALE — pale gold, fresh beery malt and hop nose, refreshing fruity malt flavor, medium dry malt finish; hop aftertaste that works at going dry as it goes. [A, 53]

MOLSON LIGHT — pale gold, pleasant well-hopped malt aroma, light body, faint malt flavor, light hop finish, short hop aftertaste. [LO, 30]

MOLSON PORTER — deep copper-brown, lovely roasted malt nose, roasted malt flavor; just enough hops to balance and retain the porter character; smooth, slightly dry hop aftertaste with good length. [P, 72]

MOLSON BRADOR MALT LIQUOR — bright gold, light off-dry malt aroma, heavy body, noticeable alcohol, pleasant sweet malt flavor, medium dry hop finish, dry hop aftertaste, nicely made beer, very good of type. [ML, 50]

MOLSON SPECIALE — bright gold, pleasant malt and hop nose, light malt flavor, light body; slight hop finish drops off quickly; short dry hop aftertaste. [B, 34]

MOLSON EXPORT LIGHT — medium gold, good malt and hop aroma, good malt flavor up front; hops come in nicely in the middle and finish; short dry hop aftertaste. [LO, 33]

MOLSON LITE — pale gold, slightly vegetal malt nose, light malt and hop flavor, light body, short slight hop aftertaste. [LO, 27]

MOLSON DIAMOND LAGER BEER — bright pale gold, austere malt nose, highly carbonated, bright well-hopped flavor, malt and hop finish, dull malt aftertaste. [B, 48]

MOLSON SPECIAL DRY — pale yellow-gold, hop nose, some noticeable alcohol, dry hop flavor, medium body, medium length dry hop aftertaste. [D, 24]

Notes

MOLSON DRY — pale gold, touch of skunk in a hop nose, good hop and malt flavor, good body, long dry hop aftertaste. [D, 57]

LOWENBRAU SPECIAL BEER — pale gold, light hop and malt aroma, mild hop and off-dry malt palate, more malty in the front, more dry hops in the middle and finish, pleasant long dry hop aftertaste. [B, 56]

MOLSON EXEL — pale gold; grainy hop nose reminds you of grape-nuts; grainy flavor, dry hop finish, short dry grain and sour hop aftertaste. [NA, 20]

MOLSON CLUB ALE — bright gold, fruity malt aroma with off tones in back (like a sweaty sock); hop flavor is a bit sour; dry hop aftertaste. [A, 18]

BENNETT'S DOMINION ALE — bright gold, hop aroma and flavor, finishes a bit sour, very long bitter hop aftertaste. [A, 52]

CARLING BLACK LABEL BEER — medium gold, tangy hop and malt aroma, good dry hop flavor, pleasant dry hop aftertaste. [B, 37]

BLACK HORSE BEER PREMIUM STOCK — yellow-gold, hop nose, big bitter hop flavor, full-bodied; good complex aftertaste that is on the bitter side. [B, 33]

MAGNUM ALE — deep gold, hop aroma with good malt background, malt and hops both vie for the lead on the palate, hop finish and aftertaste. [A, 46]

RALLYE ALE — gold, malt aroma and flavor, light body, light malt finish, little aftertaste. [A, 47]

O'KEEFE'S OLD VIENNA LAGER BEER — gold, malt and hop aroma and flavor, medium dry hop finish, dry hop aftertaste. [B, 58]

CALGARY AMBER LAGER BEER — amber, light toasted malt nose and taste, good balance, good body, smooth, dry malt finish; malt aftertaste has medium duration. [B, 37]

CINCI LAGER BEER — gold, well-hopped appetizing well-hopped malt aroma, dry balanced malt and hop flavor, dry hop finish and aftertaste, good length. [B, 59]

CINCI CREAM LAGER BEER — pale bright gold, beautiful beery nose with plenty of hops and malt, off-dry pleasant malt flavor, light body, short dry hop finish and aftertaste, pleasant tasty brew. [B, 59]

DOW CREAM PORTER — deep red brown, creamy, very faint malt aroma, slightly sweet malt flavor, but still pleasant, fair balance, smooth, dry light malt finish and aftertaste, tasty and drinkable. [P, 73]

TRILIGHT EXTRA LIGHT BEER — pale gold, very faint flowery hop nose, light very dry hop and malt flavor, very light body, very short dull aftertaste. [LO, 17]

COLT .45 BEER — medium bright gold, light malt aroma with faint hops, creamy inoffensive malt flavor, light grainy finish and short aftertaste. [B, 20]

CHAMPLAIN PORTER — deep red brown, faintly smoky and roasted malt aroma; overall malt is off-dry; perhaps a little too sweet, but still quite smooth and mellow; sweet finish and aftertaste. [P, 23]

O'KEEFE'S EXTRA OLD STOCK MALT LIQUOR — brilliant deep gold, beautiful clean sweet malt aroma, good off-dry hop and malt flavor, excellent balance, very long pleasant malt aftertaste. [ML, 56]

O'KEEFE ALE — gold, clean malt and bright hop nose, good balanced malt-hop flavor, pleasant hop finish and lingering aftertaste. Version shipped to the U.S.A. is called Canadian O'Keefe Ale and is identical to the domestic Canadian product. [A, 60]

O'KEEFE LIGHT — pale gold, light malt nose, light off-dry malt flavor, dry malt and hop aftertaste, medium length. [LO, 19]

O'KEEFE GOLDEN LIGHT CANADIAN BEER — medium yellow, sour malt aroma with some hops; complex flavor is sour malt in front and dry hops in the middle and finish; short dry hop aftertaste. [LO, 36]

MONTREAL EXPORT — deep gold, hop nose, off-dry front palate, dry hop middle and finish, dry hop aftertaste, medium length. Contract brew for Montreal Brewery, Inc. [B, 47]

TOBY ALE — amber-orange color, off-dry hoppy malt aroma; front palate is balanced hops and malt; flattens out a bit in the middle, finishes bitter hops and malt; balance is off. [A, 27]

BROWN'S ORIGINAL CANADIAN BEER — gold, faint apple-malt nose, dull malt and hop flavor, little aftertaste. Contract brew using Yukon B.C. corporate name, made for F&A Importers, Louisville, KY. [B, 46]

F&A IMPORTED CANADIAN BEER — bright gold, big head, pleasant malt-hop nose and flavor, good balance, short dry hop aftertaste. Contract brew for F&A Importers, Louisville, KY. [B, 53]

HEIDELBERG FINE QUALITY BEER — medium gold, faint hop nose, light body, light malt flavor, faint malt finish, dry aftertaste. [B, 36]

CANADIAN RED CAP CREAM ALE — deep yellow-gold, light hop nose with a fruity-malt background, off-dry and sharp ale-like flavor, plenty of malt and hops, dry hop finish, long dry hop aftertaste. [A, 41]

CARLSBERG BEER — bright pale gold, off-dry malt nose, balanced hops and malt flavor, dry hop and sour malt aftertaste, medium length. [B, 46]

CARLSBERG LIGHT BEER — tawny gold, light hop and malt aroma; carbonation dominates the flavor which is faint off-dry malt and hops; aftertaste like the flavor, medium length. [LO, 17]

MILLER HIGH LIFE — pale yellow gold, pleasant fragrant hop nose, dull malt and hop palate, pleasant dry hop finish, fairly dry hop aftertaste with good duration. [B, 17]

COORS LIGHT — pale gold, fresh beery nose, light off-dry malt flavor, very light hop finish, brief hop aftertaste. [LO, 30]

MILLER LITE — pale gold, malt and faint hop nose, very light body, faint malt and hop finish, no aftertaste. [LO, 25]

COORS BEER — very pale gold, light malt and hop nose; pleasant flavor is mostly off-dry malt; pleasant fairly long aftertaste shows both malt and hops. [B, 33]

FOSTER'S LAGER — deep gold, light off-dry malt nose, off-dry malt and hop palate, good body, dry hop finish; dry hop aftertaste fades quickly. [B, 36]

DUFFY'S ALE — amber, smooth malt and hop nose and taste, very good balance, long dry malt aftertaste. [A, 45]

OV BOCK BIER 1992 — golden amber, rich fruity malt aroma, good balanced malt and hop flavor, an abundance of malt, big body, sense of alcohol, long malt aftertaste, a full-flavored brew. [BK, 69]

BLACK ICE — gold, very Molson-like hop and light fruity malt aroma, complex off-dry malt and hop flavor, good body, hop finish, long off-dry malt and hop aftertaste, 5.5% alcohol. Label says Black Ice Filtrage Glacé (cold filtered). For domestic markets. [B, 35]

MOLSON ICE — deep gold; complex aroma has some malt but is mostly hops; bright well-hopped flavor, big body, 5.6% alcohol; really fills your mouth; very tasty and satisfying; very long dry hop aftertaste does show some supporting malt; a very good offering from Molson for American markets. [B, 43]

CARLING ICE BEER — gold, interesting hop nose with good malt backing; flavor is hops and alcohol; good body, long dry hop aftertaste, 5.5% alcohol, similar to Molson Ice above. [B, 34]

CARLING LIGHT BEER — gold, faint malt nose; fainter malt flavor is a bit off-dry; little body; good carbonation level but that is the best feature; faint and short dull dry malt aftertaste. [LO, 26]

CARLING DRAFT BEER — gold, fruity sweet nose (sort of like bug spray), off-dry malt flavor; sweetness lasts but the beer has little character. [B, 37]

MOLSON CANADIAN ICE FILTERED DRAFT BEER — gold; pleasant malt and hop nose that is a little sweet and flowery; bright and big refreshing malty flavor that stays on the sweet side; good body, dry hop finish; long

dry hop aftertaste takes on a malty twist at the end; 5.5% abv. [B, 49]

CARLING BEER — gold, very faint malt aroma, finely carbonated, light malt flavor with a faint vegetal background; ends light off-dry malt; short aftertaste, 5% abv. [B, 41]

MOLSON CREAM ALE — amber-gold; a fruity nose that seems not to be either malt or hops; biggest part of the flavor is carbonation; faintly oxidized malt flavor, dry at the end, short dry malty aftertaste, a member of the Molson Signature Series, 5.1% abv. [A, 20]

MOLSON AMBER LAGER — amber, light toasted malt aroma, highly carbonated, dry malt flavor, good body, dry malt finish and aftertaste, fairly short, no complexity, just straightforward dry malt, 5.3% abv, another of the Molson Signature Series. [B, 42]

MOLSON XXX STRONG ICE BREWED BEER — gold, perfumy malt nose; slightly off-dry malt flavor but it dries as it approaches the finish; big body, high alcohol (7.3% abv); good balance especially at the finish when the hops kick in; medium long dry malt aftertaste. [B, 59]

RED DOG ALT BEER — gold, faint malt and European hop nose, light dry hop flavor, medium body, dry hop finish, smooth dry hop aftertaste, 5.5% abv. [A, 43]

RICKARD'S RED — golden-amber, faint malt and hop nose; dry malty flavor is almost nondescript; dry malt finish and aftertaste has a

slight sweetness way in back. Tasted on draft in Toronto area. [B, 44]

CARLING STRONG — gold, very faint malt nose, not much flavor except for alcohol (6.1% abv); long aftertaste is almost solely alcohol. [B, 33]

Moosehead Breweries, Ltd.
Brewery in St. John (New Brunswick)

MOOSEHEAD CANADIAN LAGER BEER — pale gold, very good malt and hop nose, balanced slightly off-dry malt and hop flavor, smooth, very pleasant and quite drinkable, long malt aftertaste. [B, 56]

MOOSEHEAD LIGHT — pale gold, light malt nose, light off-dry malt flavor at first, then dry at the finish, brief malt aftertaste, on the dull side. [LO, 34]

MOOSEHEAD PALE ALE — pale gold; light off-dry aroma shows malt, yeast, and hops; off-dry malt and well-hopped flavor, dry hop-malt finish, medium dry hop-malt aftertaste. [A, 37]

MOOSEHEAD PREMIUM DRY — bright gold, light malt nose, zesty dry hop flavor, good body, excellent balance, crisp and refreshing, medium length dry hop aftertaste. [D, 60]

TEN-PENNY ALE — pale amber, light hop aroma and flavor, dry hop finish and aftertaste, a decent little Canadian ale. [A, 47]

MOOSEHEAD EXPORT ALE — pale amber-gold, off-dry malt and bitter hop nose, flavor like the nose, great complexity, good hop finish, long hop aftertaste, one of Moosehead's better efforts. [A, 60]

ALPINE LAGER BEER — pale gold, malt aroma and taste with hops in back, pleasant tasting and very drinkable, light body, light malt finish and aftertaste; the carbonation is high and the hops stay in back. [B, 40]

ALPINE LITE BEER — pale yellow-gold, malt and hop aroma, pleasant light malt and hop flavor, finely carbonated, medium long light malt and hop aftertaste. [LO, 27]

ALPINE GENUINE COLD FILTERED BEER — gold, faint malt nose; malt flavor has a faint citrus background; highly carbonated, medium body, short and light dry malt and hop aftertaste. [B, 25]

MOOSEHEAD'S GOLDEN LIGHT BEER — pale gold, lovely fragrant hop nose, pleasant malt flavor, light body, medium long malt aftertaste, well-made and good for a low-calorie beer. [LO, 47]

MOOSEHEAD LONDON STOUT — very deep brown, almost opaque, molasses and malt flavor, quite sweet, very long aftertaste like the flavor, definitely a dessert beer. [S, 58]

JAMES READY ORIGINAL LAGER BEER — bright gold, light aromatic off-dry clover, hop, and grain nose, light hop and malt flavor, faint malt finish, light body, short malt aftertaste. [B, 34]

CLANCY'S AMBER ALE — brilliant pale golden-amber, pleasant faint hop nose, bright hop flavor with plenty of supporting malt, good body, light dry hop finish and long tasty aftertaste. [A, 51]

MOOSEHEAD CANADIAN ICE BEER — pale gold, bright hop nose, faint dry hop flavor with some sweet malt in back, medium body, faint dry hop finish and aftertaste. [B, 36]

MOOSEHEAD PREMIUM DRY ICE — bright gold; very fragrant malt and hop nose is on the sweet side; flavor is like the nose, very pleasant and drinkable; finish is semi-dry hops, big body, 6% abv; aftertaste is slightly drier hops, but is only medium long. [B, 52]

MARINER ALE — brilliant pale gold, tight head, pleasant but light hop and off-dry malty nose, bright hop and lightly sweet malty flavor, medium body, pleasant but not very interesting, medium long dry hop and malt aftertaste, good hot weather beer. [A, 45]

Niagara Falls Brewing Co., Ltd.
Brewery in Niagara Falls (Ontario)

GRITSTONE PREMIUM ALE — deep amber, faint sour malt nose, ephemeral malt flavor, long dry malt aftertaste; there are hops but there is not a good balance between those hops and the malt. [B, 30]

Notes

OLDE JACK BITTER STRONG ALE — amber, very malty aroma and flavor, straightforward big dry chocolatey flavor (but not chocolate malt), big body; medium dry malt finish retains some of the chocolate character, and a long light malt aftertaste; 7.2% abv is noticeable. [A, 73]

MAPLE WHEAT — amber, low carbonation, dry malty-wheat nose with a touch of maple sugar; big flavorful brew with the maple coming on boldly in the mid-palate; strongest in the finish and aftertaste, but the hops and malt hang in there as well, so does the alcohol (at 8.5% abv); a big rich, strong, and sweet beer, excellent of type. This is the version tasted in Ontario and definitely worth finding. Imported into the U.S.A. in late 1995, it was different. There was not as much maple character up front; much dryer overall; still well-balanced, but not as attractive for those who would like a pronounced maple taste, and perhaps not quite so alcoholic. [Domestic W, 67; Export W, 66]

BROCK'S EXTRA STOUT — opaque brown, concentrated sweet chocolate malt and roasted barley nose; flavor is malt that is a bit sweet at first, then more dry; medium body, dry malt finish and aftertaste, 5.8% abv. [S, 78]

NIAGARA TRAPPER COLD FILTERED DRAFT BEER — deep gold, grapey nose, grapey-guava taste, thin, short. [B, 5]

EISBOCK '93–'94 — hazy amber, toasty perfumy malt with noticeable alcohol in the aroma; big flavor like the nose, huge but not harsh, very warming, great mouthfeel; complex malt and hops throughout with spices, citrus, fruit, and all kinds of flavors and sensations, there's even a little chocolate in the very long aftertaste; 8% abv. This brew has been repeated for the 1994–1995 season showing up in Ontario outlets in mid-October. [BK, 91]

NIAGARA FALLS KRIEK — hazy orange-amber, aroma of cherries and malt, flavor of dry cherries and grainy malt; malty aftertaste has the dry cherries fading into the background; medium body, more interesting than good. This is supposed to be Olde Jack with an infusion of black cherries, 6.5% abv. [L, 53]

NIAGARA FALLS APPLE ALE — slightly hazy gold, creamy texture, clean green apple aroma like fresh cut fruit, taste like an apple candy; apple peel finish has a tinge of tartness, medium dry clean apple aftertaste, good length and stays clean throughout; nicely made and very attractive to the palate, made using apple concentrate. [A, 60]

Northern Breweries Ltd.
Breweries in Sudbury, Sault Ste. Marie, Timmins, and Thunder Bay (Ontario)

NORTHERN LIGHT BEER — gold, faint sour hop nose, hop flavor, light body, faint malt finish, short dry hop aftertaste. [LO, 25]

NORTHERN ALE — bright yellow, light hop nose, sour hop flavor, medium body, light malt finish and aftertaste. [A, 20]

NORTHERN SUPERIOR LAGER BEER — hazy gold, light hop nose, high carbonation, light body; flavor has light hops and malt but is mostly carbonation; brief aftertaste with little or no flavors. [B, 28]

NORTHERN EXTRA LIGHT BEER — pale gold, very faint pleasant malt aroma, light malt flavor, thin body, brief malt aftertaste, light flavored and light bodied, ephemeral and dull, 2.4% abv. [LO, 25]

EDELBRAU BEER — hazy gold, light hop nose, high carbonation, very light malt and hop flavor, brief malt aftertaste. [B, 48]

THUNDER BAY CANADIAN LAGER BEER — gold, sour hop nose, light malty flavor, light body, smooth; fairly good flavor as it grows on you; good malt and hop balance, medium long but with little complexity. [B, 40]

O'Toole's
Brewpub in Toronto (Ontario). Brewing is done at the Select Brewery, right around the corner in Toronto. The wort is then transferred to O'Toole's for the fermentation. All are brewed from extract.

ULTRA LIGHT LAGER — gold, faint malt aroma; equally faint malt flavor has a sweetness in back; medium to light body, off-dry malt finish and aftertaste, not much length. [LO, 50]

GERMAN LYNCHING LAGER — deep gold, hop nose, big dry and hoppy pils-style flavor, good body, plenty of malt backing, long complex hop and malt aftertaste. [B, 67]

SMITHWICK'S TYPE BITTER (a.k.a. DROP DEAD DARK) — fairly deep amber; ale-like well-hopped aroma also shows good malt; bright somewhat hoppy flavor has a hefty malt backing; long hoppy aftertaste isn't really as dry as it might be for there is a concentration of malt supporting the hops; good and long. [B, 57]

O'TOOLE'S IPA — gold, faint malt aroma, bright zesty malt and hop flavor, very long malt and hop aftertaste. [A, 58]

KILLER CREAM ALE — deep golden amber, off-dry malt aroma and flavor, big body, long malty aftertaste. [A, 56]

O'TOOLE'S RED ALE — reddish amber, light malt aroma, smooth malty flavor; malt finish and aftertaste has a faintly sweet background. [A, 50]

O'TOOLE'S WHEAT LAGER — deep gold, light malty nose, light dry malt flavor, smooth and pleasant, short dry malt aftertaste. [W, 53]

Okanagan Spring Brewery Ltd.
Brewery in Vernon (British Columbia)

SPRING PREMIUM LAGER — gold, malt nose, dry malt flavor, dry slightly buttery malt aftertaste. [B, 52]

OKANAGAN SPRING OLD MUNICH WHEAT BEER — cloudy brown, like old time cider, dry malt aroma with a brown sugar background, off-dry roasted malt flavor with a tart finish, roasted malt aftertaste. [W, 56]

Notes

OLD ENGLISH PORTER STYLE MALT LIQUOR — deep ruby brown; huge malt Ovaltine nose seems a bit scorched at first; big delicious roasted malt flavor softens as you drink it; good carbonation level, sort of earthy, lots of complexity, ample body, very smooth in the middle; the 8.5% abv is only slightly noticeable, lots of things going on in your mouth; dry malt finish, long dry malt aftertaste, an excellent classical porter. [P, 80]

SPRING EXTRA SPECIAL PALE ALE — hazy golden amber, malty Postum/Ovaltine nose, medium body; dry malt flavor offers little of interest, brief malt aftertaste; fine while it is your mouth, but there is no real character. [A, 43]

Old Credit Brewing Co.
Microbrewery in Port Credit (Ontario)

OLD CREDIT AMBER ALE — amber; light malt aroma shows a touch of infection, this is reflected in the taste which is acidic and

phenolic; low hopped dry malt finish and aftertaste. [A, 34]

Pacific Western Brewing Co., Ltd.
Brewery in Prince George (British Columbia). Some early labels also include a Vancouver origin. Zélé beers carry corporate identifier of Zélé Brewing Co., Prince George (British Columbia).

YUKON CANADIAN CREAM ALE — pale gold, hop nose, off-dry malt and hop flavor, off-dry malt finish and aftertaste, a bit dull overall. [A, 26]

PACIFIC REAL DRAFT — gold, fruity malt nose, fruity malt and carbonation palate, medium body, off-dry malt finish and short aftertaste. [B, 36]

BULLDOG CANADIAN LAGER BEER — tawny-gold, pleasant malt aroma, good hop flavor, light body, well-balanced, dry hop finish, virtually no aftertaste. [B, 40]

IRON HORSE MALT LIQUOR — bright gold, good malt and hop aroma, off-dry malt flavor, good balance, pleasant and long malt aftertaste. [ML, 41]

YUKON GOLD PREMIUM PILSNER — yellow, appetizing hop nose, off-dry malt and hop flavor, good balance, very tasty, long aftertaste like the flavor. [B, 51]

ROYAL CANADIAN PREMIUM BEER — tawny-gold, big malt and

hop aroma, bright hop flavor, dry hop finish, medium body, long off-dry malt and hop aftertaste. [B, 39]

ZéLé DRY LIGHT BEER — pale gold, persistent skunky nose; that the flavor is pleasant malt with a subtle hop background comes as a surprise; light body, short malt aftertaste. [LO, 18]

ZéLé DRY BEER — bright gold; pleasant malt aroma is not really dry, but the malt flavor goes dry quite suddenly, ending up very dry in the finish and aftertaste. [B, 47]

Pepperwood Bistro
Brewpub in Burlington (Ontario)

EMILY'S CREAM ALE — gold; very nice hop and malt aroma is appetizing; smooth dry hop flavor, very drinkable, medium body; dry hop finish shows some of the complexity of the palate; long dry hop aftertaste. [A, 60]

VICTORIA RED ALE — reddish amber, hop nose, dry malty flavor, good body, smooth dry malt aftertaste. [A, 54]

PEPPERWOOD UNFILTERED RED ALE — reddish amber, bright hop nose, good body, brisk dry malt and hop flavor; snappy dry hop finish and aftertaste with a faint sweetness coming in at the end. This cask-conditioned brew is also known as Morgan's Premium Ale. [A, 73]

PEPPERWOOD CELEBRATION ALE — brown, chocolate malt nose; chocolate malt palate is a bit sharp at first but overall is bright and tasty; good body, long dry aftertaste; there is a trace of a coffeelike nature that comes from the use of coffee beans in the brew. [A, 56]

Quinn's on the Danforth
Brewpub in Toronto (Ontario)

COUNTY CORK LAGER — gold, faint hop nose; front palate is big hops; malt in the middle and finish, good body, dry malt finish and aftertaste with a sense of a bigger malt background, medium length, very flavorful. [B, 56]

DUBLIN DARK — amber, malt nose, dry malt flavor, finish, and aftertaste, medium body, medium length. [B, 53]

Rotterdam Brewing Co.
Brewpub in Toronto (Ontario)

ROTTERDAM AMBER LAGER — golden amber, malt and hop aroma; bright malt flavor finishes very dry hops; good body, long very dry hop aftertaste, 5% abv. [B, 41]

ROTTERDAM NATURAL BLONDE — gold; light dry nose shows hops and malt; light dry flavor is balanced hops and malt; good body, dry hop finish and aftertaste, fair length, 5% abv. [B, 38]

ROTTERDAM NUT BROWN ALE — brownish-amber, light dry

malt aroma and flavor, medium body, pleasant and drinkable, dry malt finish and aftertaste, average duration, 5% abv. [A, 45]

ROTTERDAM FRAMBOISE — pink color with a bright pink head, beautiful raspberry aroma; raspberry flavor has a bite like a Belgian-style frambozenbier; medium body, long dry raspberry aftertaste, 6.5% abv. [A, 61]

ROTTERDAM SCOTCH ALE — dark reddish-amber, malt nose, smooth malty flavor, good body; has a rich quality and is good of style, long rich malt aftertaste dries at the very end; 5.5% abv. [A, 61]

Saxon Brewery
Brewery in Montreal (Quebec)

KEELE'S CANADIAN BEER — pale gold, very faint malt aroma, low carbonation, light body, light malt flavor, brief aftertaste. [B, 45]

Sleeman Brewing & Malting Co., Ltd.
Silver Creek Brewery in Guelph (Ontario)

TORONTO LIGHT — pale yellow-gold, fruity soda pop nose, light body, low carbonation, soft and flabby, light dry slightly sour hop flavor, dull hop finish and aftertaste. [LO, 27]

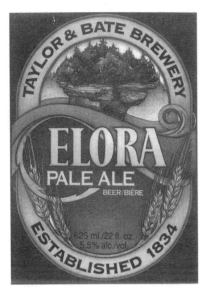

SLEEMAN SILVER CREEK LAGER — hazy gold, off-dry malt nose, fruity-malt front palate, balanced middle, hop finish, medium dry hop aftertaste. [B, 37]

SLEEMAN CREAM ALE — tawny-gold, off-dry malt aroma, zesty hop flavor, fruity malt and citrus backing, fruity malt finish, long malt aftertaste. [B, 42]

STROH'S FIRE BREWED BEER — pale gold, light fruity malt aroma, malt flavor, very little hops, malt finish, brief malt aftertaste. [B, 26]

SLEEMAN ORIGINAL DARK — amber, malt aroma with some background hops, dry malt flavor, some off-dry malt in the middle, finely carbonated, medium body, little complexity, very lightly hopped, short dry malt aftertaste, 5.5% abv. [B, 50]

ARCTIC WOLF BEER —gold, light malt aroma, light apple-melon off-dry malt flavor, light body, off-dry malt finish, almost no aftertaste, 5% abv. [B, 34]

Summit Brewery
Brewery at Prince George (British Columbia) and St. Catherines (Ontario)

W J MACKAY CLASSIC CANADIAN PILSNER — pale gold, faint malt aroma, light body, slightly off-dry malt flavor, malt finish and brief malt aftertaste. [B, 38]

Taylor & Bate Brewing Co.
Microbrewery in Elora (Ontario)

ELORA PALE ALE — amber, malty nose; smooth malty flavor is fairly gentle; faintly sweet and very quaffable; hops come in at mid-palate; medium body, dry smooth malt and hop finish and aftertaste, pleasant and drinkable. [A, 67]

Thornbury Brewing Co.
Brewery in Thornbury (Ontario)

BEAVER VALLEY AMBER — amber, malt aroma with a sour background, very light flavor like the nose, dull off-dry malt finish and aftertaste. [B, 43]

Tracks Brewpub
Brewpub in Brampton (Ontario)

OLD MILL LAGER — deep gold, malt nose, pleasant malt and hop flavor, dry malt finish and aftertaste, not big or long. [B, 47]

Trafalgar Brewing Co.
Microbrewery in Oakville (Ontario)

PORT SIDE AMBER PREMIUM ALE — gold, clean fresh malt aroma, taste to match, medium body, lightly hopped, smooth and drinkable, dry malt aftertaste. [A, 61]

OAKVILLE ABBEY BELGIAN STRONG ALE — amber; big malty nose is faintly alcoholic (6.5% abv); smooth slightly sweet and vinous flavor, good mouthfeel and big body, dry malt finish and aftertaste with a faint sweetness way in back with the alcohol, a Belgian white ale. [A, 72]

Unibroue Inc. / La Brasserie Broubec Inc.
Brewery in Chambly (Quebec), successor to the Massawippi Brewing Co.

MAUDITE — amber, strong hop nose with plenty of sour malt and alcohol (8%), finely carbonated; has a spicy lactic background to the nose and taste; huge body, plenty of malt and hops in the flavor well-backed with fruit, spice, and acid; the acidity is most noticeable at the finish; long spicy aftertaste, well-made brew refermented in the bottle. [A, 67]

Upper Canada Brewing Co., Ltd.
Brewery in Toronto (Ontario)

UPPER CANADA ALE — amber, complex hop aroma with smoky slightly off-dry malt in back; flavor is like the aroma; smoky hop finish, off-dry malt aftertaste; doesn't quite come together. [A, 39]

UPPER CANADA DARK ALE — deep amber, complex aromatic hop and malt aroma with a trace of sourness in back; flavor is much like the aroma except the sourness is more noticeable and there is a scorched malt background; big hop finish and aftertaste has plenty of malt in back, but it doesn't come together and the effect is harmed by the off features. [A, 47]

UPPER CANADA TRUE LIGHT — bright gold, light malt nose, very light malt flavor, weak body, very dry brief malt aftertaste. [LO, 27]

UPPER CANADA LAGER — bright gold, faint malt and hop aroma; dry hop flavor is too bitter for the amount of malt; bitter finish and aftertaste, poorly balanced. [B, 32]

UPPER CANADA REBELLION MALT LIQUOR — bright deep gold, very pleasant malt aroma, big fresh malt flavor, big body; lots of alcohol showing (6%) with some hops in the finish; very long malt, alcohol, and hop aftertaste, balanced, good feel in the mouth, very fine balance, excellent tasting brew. [A, 78]

UPPER CANADA NATURAL LIGHT LAGER — deep gold, fruity hop nose, sour hop flavor, light body, minty finish, short hop aftertaste. [LO, 25]

UPPER CANADA WHEAT BEER — tawny-gold, very nice complex but faint malt aroma, tangy sour malt flavor, light body, refreshing dry wheat finish, medium to short dry wheat and malt aftertaste. [W, 29]

PUBLICAN'S SPECIAL BITTER ALE — golden amber, malt nose, hop flavor, short dry hop aftertaste, questionable balance. [A, 42]

COLONIAL STOUT — ruby-brown, nice roasted barley and chocolate malt aroma; flavor starts out malty but fades as it crosses the palate, finishes light and dry malt, ends with a sour background. [S, 36]

UPPER CANADA POINT NINE — gold, light (faint) slightly grainy malt nose, light body, light malt flavor, refreshing but brief, a low alcohol beer (0.9% abv). [LO, 25]

UPPER CANADA TRUE BOCK — deep amber, light toasted and slightly fruity malt aroma, very malty flavor, light dry malt with some alcohol (6.5% abv); dry hops lightly join in at the finish; medium body, long dry malt and hop aftertaste, a good tasting enjoyable brew. [B, 67]

UPPER CANADA PALE ALE — copper-gold, toasted malt nose with some flowery hops, big good tasting hop flavor, good body, big hop finish and aftertaste, very flavorful beer, 4.8% abv. [A, 63]

Vancouver Island Brewing Co.
Microbrewery in Victoria (British Columbia)

PIPER'S PALE ALE — amber, toasted malt aroma; malt flavor has faint hops; finely carbonated, good body, very drinkable, pleas-

ant and interesting, long dry malt aftertaste. [A, 49]

Wellington County Brewery
Brewery in Guelph (Ontario)

WELLINGTON BLACK KNIGHT ESB — red brown, faint chocolate malt nose, light but complex malty flavor, very tasty and quite drinkable; hops kick in at the finish, stay for aftertaste and balance off the malt; leaves a light lingering roasted malt aftertaste, nicely done. [A, 86]

WELLINGTON LAGER BEER — tawny-gold, pleasant sweet malt and hop aroma; palate is sweet malt up front; dry hops in the middle, dry hop finish and aftertaste, finely balanced, good body, fairly long. [B, 67]

WELLINGTON ORIGINAL COUNTY ALE — copper-amber, pleasant malty nose on the sweet side, dry malt flavor, hops at the finish, long dry hop aftertaste, good body, very flavorful. [A, 64]

WELLINGTON ARKELL BEST BITTER — pale amber, toasted malt aroma; palate starts toasted malt, fades out by the finish; faint dry hop aftertaste is only on the sides of the tongue; 4% abv. [B, 43]

WELLINGTON SPECIAL PALE ALE — amber, lovely toasted malt aroma, zesty toasted malt and hop flavor, excellent balance, medium body, pleasant but short. [A, 51]

WELLINGTON IRON DUKE — deep amber, faint malt nose, big malty flavor; good hops in support, but they stay in back; good body, balanced, low carbonation, long balanced hop and malt aftertaste. [A, 69]

Whistler Brewing Co., Ltd.
Microbrewery in Whistler (British Columbia)

WHISTLER BLACK TUSK ALE — deep amber-brown; roasted malt nose shows some chocolate malt; dry roasted malt flavor has some chocolate and black patent malt; medium body, smooth and very drinkable, long dry malt aftertaste. [A, 66]

WHISTLER PREMIUM LAGER — bright deep gold; aroma on opening was delightful with malt and spicy hops; malty flavor is a tad sweet; finely carbonated, light dry hop finish; malt aftertaste has hops in back. [B, 50]

MOTHER'S PALE ALE — slightly hazy amber, malt and hop aroma; flavor is malt up front, then hops; medium body, good balance, pleasant taste, dry hop finish, long dry hop aftertaste. [A, 63]

York Brewing Co.
Brewery in Brampton (Ontario) I have heard that York (British Columbia) has recently ceased operations.

YORK PILSNER LAGER
BEER — gold malty-Ovaltine nose,
big malt flavor, hops at finish, long
dry hop and malt aftertaste. [B, 40]

Mexico

Cerveceria
Cruz Blanca, S.A.
Brewery in Ciudad Juarez

CRUZ BLANCA CERVEZA
FINA — pale gold, pleasant malt
aroma with a touch of hops; bitter
hops greet the palate, softening
slightly and changing to malt by
the finish; somewhat dull dry malt
and hop aftertaste. [B, 31]

CHIHUAHUA MEXICAN
BEER — pale gold, hop nose,
light hop flavor, short dry hop
aftertaste. [B, 27]

CERVEZA HOMBRE — gold,
slightly sweet fresh clean malt
nose, light malt flavor, almost no
aftertaste. [B, 16]

NUDE BEER — pale gold,
sweet grapey and grainy aroma,
highly carbonated; malt flavor is
sort of sweet in front, dull in the
middle, and dry in the aftertaste;
more of a label novelty than a
quality beer. [B, 19]

SIMPATICO BEER — pale gold,
sour hop aroma, little flavor on the
front of the palate, sour hop finish
and aftertaste, weak and dull.
There is also a Simpatico beer
made in Germany and several versions made in the U.S.A. [B, 23]

Cerveceria
Cuauhtemoc, S.A.
Breweries in Monterrey,
Toluca, Guadalajara,
Tecate, Mexico City,
Nogales, Culican, and
Ciudad Juarez

BOHEMIA ALE — pale gold, off-
dry malt aroma, fresh malt flavor,
dry malt and hop finish and aftertaste, good body; has complexity,
length, and interest; very pleasant
and refreshing. [A, 50]

TECATE CERVEZA — pale gold,
very nice malt and hop aroma,
very light and pleasant malt and
hop flavor, light body, good balance; light aftertaste is a continuation of the flavor; very nice but
just too light. [B, 57]

CERVEZA CARTA BLANCA —
pale gold, malt aroma and light
malt flavor, medium body, very
light dry hop aftertaste, good hot
weather quaffing beer. [B, 38]

CARTA BLANCA DARK
SPECIAL — bright rosy-amber,
sour hop nose; malt starts out the
flavor but only briefly; little mid-
palate and finish, light malt aftertaste. [B, 31]

INDIO CERVEZA OSCURA —
copper color, very faint caramel
malt nose, full faintly sweet malt
flavor, off-dry malt aftertaste, no
complexity. [B, 46]

BRISA CERVEZA LIGERA —
very pale gold, faint sour malt
aroma, weak body, very faint malt
flavor, no aftertaste. [LO, 20]

Notes

NAVIDAD CERVEZA COMMERATIVA — red-brown color, very faint dull malt aroma, mealy flavor with a tart-sweet background, weak body, off-dry malt aftertaste. A Christmas beer not seen recently. [B, 41]

TECATE LIGHT — pale yellow-gold, fruity malt aroma, light body; flavor starts as fruity malt, finishes thin hops; faint aftertaste is grainy, vegetal, and slightly sour. [LO, 20]

Cerveceria Moctezuma, S.A.
Breweries in Orizaba, Guadalajara, Mexico City, Monterrey

SUPERIOR LIGHT BEER — pale gold, light malt aroma, light body; light malt flavor has only a trace of hops; fairly long dry malt aftertaste. [B, 36]

DOS EQUIS XX AMBER BEER — deep mahogany, clean off-dry malt nose, big malty-molasses flavor with a fine hop finish; stays reasonably dry throughout; medium body, good balance, long dry malt aftertaste. [B, 60]

DOS EQUIS XX LIGHT BEER — bright gold, faint malt aroma and flavor, clean malt finish, long dry malt aftertaste. [LO, 37]

DOS EQUIS SPECIAL LAGER — bright gold, high carbonation, flowery malt aroma, off-dry malt palate, finishes sour malt, dry malt aftertaste. [B, 50]

SOL ESPECIAL — bright gold, perfumy hop nose, light body, dry hop flavor, pleasant dry hop and malt aftertaste. [B, 37]

TRES EQUIS XXX LIGHT BEER — very pale color, almost colorless, light malt aroma, very mild malt flavor and aftertaste. [B, 47]

TRES EQUIS XXX CERVEZA OSCURA — deep copper color, slightly sour malt nose, hop flavor with some herbal character; dry hop aftertaste still has the herbal nature. [B, 20]

NOCHE BUENA CERVEZA ESPECIAL — brilliant pretty red-brown color, soft malt nose with light background hops, big hop flavor up front, roasted malt finish, good balance, long dry malt aftertaste, good flavorful Christmas beer. [B, 83]

HUSSONG'S CERVEZA CLARA — bright pale gold, light hop nose, light grainy malt flavor, thin body, watery and weak; doesn't develop much and fades quickly. [B, 29]

NOCHE BUENA CERVEZA ESPECIAL — brilliant pretty red-brown color, soft malt nose with light background hops, big hop flavor up front, roasted malt finish, good balance, long dry malt aftertaste, good flavorful Christmas beer. This beer disappeared from U.S.A. stores for about 5–6 years, reappearing in December 1993. It was slightly different than that described above, being amber-gold, having a faint malt

aroma; big malt flavor but having very little roasted character; dry malt finish, medium long and very malty aftertaste. I liked the old version better. [B, 51]

Cerveceria Modelo, S.A.
Breweries in Mexico City, Torreon, Guadalajara, Ciudad Obregon, and Mazatlan

MODELO ESPECIAL — tawny-gold, malt aroma; faint malt flavor that gains in strength at the finish; fairly long dry malt aftertaste. [B, 16]

HATUEY BEER — tawny-gold, candy malt aroma, sweet malt flavor at first, dull middle, faint hop finish behind the malt, short dry malt and hop aftertaste. Label says Modelo Brewing Co., Auburndale, FL, bottled under authority and supervision of Bacardi & Co., Nassau, Bahamas. [B, 47]

CORONA EXTRA — bright gold, pleasant malt and hop nose, bright hop flavor, light body, dry hop finish and aftertaste, little strength and little length. [B, 46]

CORONA LIGHT — bright gold, light pleasant fruity-honey-malt nose, light dry hop flavor, light body, short sour hop aftertaste. [LO, 40]

NEGRA MODELO DARK BEER — medium brown, malt aroma, dry malt flavor, dry malt finish and aftertaste, good balance, good length. [B, 75]

Cerveceria del Pacifico, S.A.
Brewery at Mazatlan

CERVEZA PACIFICO CLARA — brilliant pale gold, complex and interesting off-dry flowery hop aroma, very dry hop and malt flavor, short dry aftertaste. [B, 34]

Cerveceria Yucateca, S.A.
Brewery in Merida

MONTEJO PREMIUM BEER — yellow-gold, clean malt aroma with a light hop background, slightly soapy hop flavor, dry sort of salty finish, short sour hop and malt aftertaste. [B, 32]

MONTEJO DARK BEER — deep copper, creamy, faint malt nose and taste, light body, short malt aftertaste. [B, 32]

United States

A1A Ale Works
Brewpub in St. Augustine, FL. Affiliated with Ragtime in Atlantic Beach, FL.

KING ST. WHEAT — hazy gold, dry wheaty-malty aroma and flavor, light body, dry and refreshing, not long. [W, 50]

MATANZAS BAY BERRY ALE — peach color; fruity berry aroma is not immediately recognizable as any particular fruit or berry; flavor is indistinct raspberry and a dry berry at that; dry fruity finish and aftertaste. [A, 47]

A1A HONEY ALE — gold, off-dry slightly honeyed malt aroma and flavor, medium dry malty flavor, medium body, off-dry malt finish; long aftertaste has a richness; the balance could be better but it is still pleasant. [A, 49]

RED BRICK BEER — amber, dry hoppy aroma and flavor, medium body, dry hop finish and aftertaste, very good with food. [A, 60]

BRIDGE OF LIONS BROWN ALE — deep amber, roasty malt nutty aroma, complex roasted nutty malt flavor, medium body; roasted character carries through the finish and stays for the aftertaste; good length. Brewmaster plans to increase the body in future batches. [A, 60]

ALEXANDER STRANGE STOUT — deep amber-brown, chocolate malt and roasted barley aroma, light to medium body; flavor like the aroma is good but of medium intensity; trace of phenol in the finish and aftertaste does not impair the flavor value. Again, the brewmaster intends to increase the body in future runs. [S, 55]

WOOD BUTCHER'S ALE — gold; very nice aroma shows malt and Saaz hops; grainy malt flavor has the Saaz hops as a background; good body, dry hop finish and aftertaste, long and interesting, dry and refreshing in a European style. [A, 66]

Notes

Abita Brewing Co.
Brewery in
Abita Springs, LA

ABITA GOLDEN LAGER — gold, malt nose; flavor starts out briefly as malt and immediately dry hops take over; good body, medium dry hop aftertaste, good refreshing beer. [B, 65]

ABITA AMBER LAGER — amber, fruity aroma, fruity malt flavor with a toasted malt background; fades to a brief dry hop aftertaste; pleasant and very good with food. Made with crystal malt. [B, 68]

ABITA FALL FEST BEER — brilliant amber, rich malt aroma with lots of hops, big hop flavor with plenty of roasted malt in back, very good balance and mouthfeel, pleasant hop finish, medium to light body, medium dry hop aftertaste, very drinkable, a good well-made beer. [F, 74]

ABITA TURBO DOG BEER — deep ruby-amber, light roasted malt aroma, roasted malt flavor, toast finish, finely carbonated, medium body, medium long dry malt aftertaste, very likable straightforward brew. This is a strong dark ale made from British pale, crystal, and chocolate malts using Chinook hops for bittering and Willamette as a dry finishing hop; specific gravity 1.060, 5% abw. [B, 65]

ABITA BOCK BEER — amber; big hop aroma shows malt as well; big complex flavor is mostly hops but there is enough malt to provide balance; big body, some sense of alcohol; finishes dry hops, but the very long aftertaste keeps the complexity and has an abundance of both hops and malt. This is Abita's Mardi Gras beer available from late January to May. [BK, 73]

ABITA ANDYGATOR — amber, great malty nose, big bright malt flavor backed with an abundance of hops, strongly flavored (with both the malt and hops), big body, plenty of hop bite, complex, sense of alcohol, long big dry hop aftertaste. This is Abita's 1992 Christmas beer, made with several malts, Golding and Kent hops, and a German alt yeast. It's a dandy. Made from only British pale malt and Mt. Hood hops; specific gravity 1.080, 7% abw. Tasted over two years later (late 1994); the aroma was more fruity, the flavor had become more complex with some chocolate tones in the finish, and was smoother and more delicious than before. [BK, 93]

ABITA ANDYGATOR — amber, complex fruity aroma, big malt flavor, very alcoholic, very long malt aftertaste. This is a special version of Andygator made on a trial basis for the brewery staff with extraordinary alcohol content (about 8% abw). It was not marketed. It was different from regular Andygator pretty much only by alcohol content and of about the same scoring value. [BK, 83]

LANDRY'S 1940 BEER — gold, pleasant malt aroma; flavor begins with malt but overall has to be described as dry and hoppy; good body, finishes dry hops, medium dry hop aftertaste. Made for Landry's Restaurant of Hammond, LA. [B, 54]

MULATE'S BEER — deep gold with amber tones, bright fruity malt aroma with a hop background, tasty hop flavor with plenty of malt in support, big body, dry hop finish, dry hop aftertaste with enough malt for good balance. Made for Chez Mulate's Restaurants of Louisiana (New Orleans, Breaux Bridge, and Baton Rouge). [B, 56]

ABITA PURPLE HAZE RASPBERRY WHEAT ALE — hazy amber-gold; sweet spicy nose is not instantly recognizable as raspberry; the flavor is more obvious as spicy raspberry-lactic acid; medium body, long dry spicy faintly fruity aftertaste. Tasted on draft at Brewpub on the Square in San Marcos, TX. [W, 50]

ABITA XXX-MAS ALE 1994 — fairly deep amber, very fruity malt nose; big strong roasted malt flavor has a fruitiness and a hop bite;

medium body; complex roasted malt-fruity hop aftertaste is long. [A, 78]

Alaskan Brewing & Bottling Co.
Brewery in Juneau, AK

ALASKAN AMBER BEER — tawny amber, zesty off-dry malty ale aroma, clean and fresh malt, finely carbonated, good tasting malt and citrus hop flavor with little or no hop bite, good body, very long smooth dry hop aftertaste, excellently balanced, clean, and very drinkable brew. Made with two-row barley malt, Cascade and Saaz hops. [B, 93]

ALASKAN PALE ALE — gold, bright ale aroma with a citrus background, zesty malt and hop flavor off-dry malt front, dry hop middle and finish, good body, good balance, smooth and mellow, long dry hop aftertaste. Made with two-row barley malt, Chinook, Willamette, and Tettnanger hops. [A, 75]

ALASKAN SEASONAL SMOKED PORTER 1989 — opaque brown, thick brown head, dry smoked coffee nose, very dry smoked malt flavor; although very smoky it is neither overpowering or unpleasant; very finely carbonated, very long smoked aftertaste, well-done smoked porter. Roasted malt is smoked over alder wood at a salmon smokehouse across the street from the brewery. [P, 67]

ALASKAN 1989 AUTUMN ALE — deep amber, complex toasted malt aroma, big dry toasted malt flavor, finely carbonated, not complex, very long dry malt aftertaste, satisfying and drinkable. [A, 73]

ALASKAN 1990 WINTER STOCK ALE — bright amber-gold, zesty citrus-malt aroma, huge malt and hop flavor, excellent balance, long dry hop aftertaste, all the superlative descriptions apply, an excellent almost perfect brew. One of the ten best beers on my list, done in the style of an IPA. [A, 96]

ALASKAN 1990 WHEAT BEER — hazy-gold, clean fresh light malt aroma, highly carbonated, bright malt flavor on the fruity side, medium body; finishes well but the light short dry malt aftertaste is somewhat disappointing. [W, 48]

ALASKAN SPRING WHEAT — gold, wheaty malt aroma; off-dry malt palate has a wheat-like background; finishes like the flavor leading into a fairly clean but brief malt aftertaste that is a little drier than the flavor. Made from a blend of 50% wheat and 50% barley malt lightly spiced with Tettnanger and Hallertau Mittelfruh hops. [W, 48]

ALASKAN SEASONAL BREAKUP BOCK — amber, big malt nose, rich and dry malt flavor, very smooth, creamy, big body, high alcohol, drinkable, long dry malt aftertaste. Brewed with wheat, pale malts, and dark specialty malts, using an ale yeast at cold "altbier"-style fermentation with Cascade and Tettnanger hops. [BK, 70]

Notes

ALASKAN ARTIC ALE — brown, big malt and hop aroma, complex and big malt-hop flavor, very smooth, big bodied, dry finish and aftertaste. Made from pale, caramel, Munich, and chocolate malts with Chinook and Willamette hops. [A, 63]

Allagash Brewing Co.
Microbrewery in Portland, ME

ALLAGASH WHITE — very pale gold, faint malty nose, light off-dry malt front palate, dry middle and finish, long dry malt aftertaste, very long and very drinkable, a most likable brew. [A, 82]

American River Brewing Co.
Brewery in Auburn, CA

AMERICAN RIVER OATMEAL STOUT — brown, chocolate malt and roasted barley nose; a harshness in the flavor from too much chocolate malt, smooths out by the finish and aftertaste but there is too much bite up front; medium body, good length. [S, 55]

AMERICAN RIVER AMBER LAGER — amber, beautiful

roasted malt and hop nose, big flavor like the nose, good body, balanced; dry hops come forward a bit in the finish and aftertaste; long and tasty, very likable. [B, 75]

Anchor Brewing Co.
Brewery in San Francisco, CA

ANCHOR STEAM BEER — bright copper color, foamy, finely carbonated, rich malt aroma with plenty of hops; creamy malt flavor picks up hops as it crosses the palate; full bodied, complex, long, and very satisfying. Made from two-row malt, whole hops, and bottom-fermenting yeast at high temperatures (60–70°F), conditioned at 50–55°F, and kraeusened. [ST, 63]

ANCHOR PORTER — deep brown, light malt aroma, big creamy malt flavor; extremely complex with hints of molasses, licorice, and different kinds of malt; big bodied, rich, and very long. Made from two-row barley malt, black malt, roasted barley, whole hops, and bottom-fermenting yeast. [P, 92]

ANCHOR WHEAT — bright gold, pleasant aroma just like freshly milled malt, light malt flavor much like the nose, smooth and pleasant, refreshing and mellow, light dry malt finish and aftertaste; slides down easily. This brew was found on draft as recently as early 1992 and makes occasional brief periodic appearances in bottles. The recipe calls for over 70% wheat malt, several

varieties of hops, and is top-fermented. [W, 53]

OLD FOGHORN BARLEYWINE STYLE ALE — reddish-amber, strong roasted malt, caramel, and molasses aroma; rich and intense malt flavor with hops, citrus and caramel tones, definitely on the sweet side, but complex; well-balanced, and very long. A great sipping beer. [A, 77]

LIBERTY ALE — deep amber, lush hop and malt aroma; complex palate with several kinds of malt, hops, spices, citrus, and apricot; very flavorful and very long. This was a specialty ale first made in 1975 and put into production in 1983. It is made from malted barley, whole hops from the Yakima Valley, top-fermenting yeast, and is dry hopped. [A, 86]

OUR SPECIAL ALE — deep amber, complex and subtle spice aroma; there is both malt and hops, but the spice somewhat overwhelms them; short aftertaste. This is a brew that appears each year as Christmas approaches and which has been spiced since 1987. They are not exactly the same each year, but since they have been spiced, the variation is minor. The 1990 was a bit less spiced and smoother than the 1989. The 1991 is more subtly spiced and you can taste the malt. Since Anchor started producing a Wassail for Christmas, the 1991 is the most likable O.S.A. they have offered. The 1992 ranks well also as it has a very complex spicy aroma and a good dry spicy flavor with a lot of cinnamon. The 1993

O.S.A. is dark ruby-amber, has a complex spiced aroma with cinnamon, nutmeg, ginger, but they aren't as easily identified as usual and the malt is evident; flavor is smooth and lightly spiced and a little on the sweet side; good body, good balance, long spicy aftertaste. The 1994 is dark amber, has a spicy aroma like mince meat, good body, dry spicy aftertaste. On draft, it was different, not like mince meat, but more like the 1993, with the spices more separately identifiable, and much more softly spiced. In 1995, the beer was dark brown, had a nutmeg and ginger aroma, a flavor that seemed mostly ginger, with the ale components not showing until the aftertaste, still the class act of the flavored style of ale. [1990 A, 84; 1991 A, 72; 1992 A, 67; 1993 A, 63; 1994 A, 62; 1995 A, 64]

POTRERO COMMONS ALE — cloudy amber, big malt aroma, complex chocolate malt flavor, chewy with a ale bite in back, big bodied, creamy and smooth, balanced and long. A complex brown ale. [A, 89]

ANCHOR SPRUCE BEER — hazy gold, delicate spruce aroma, resiny spruce flavor, aftertaste like spruce gum. [B, 48]

Anderson Valley Brewing Co.
Brewery and brewpub in Boonville, CA

DEEP ENDERS DARK PORTER — very deep brown, complex aromatic smoky roasted malt and hop aroma, dry roasted smoked malt flavor, medium body, long dry roasted malt aftertaste with a faint citrus background; gravity 12.75 P, 3.6% abw. [P, 53]

POLEEKO GOLD LIGHT ALE — hazy gold, pleasant grapefruit nose, grapefruit-ale flavor, long dry hop aftertaste with some of the grapefruit sourness still there. Made with Pacific-Northwest hops; specific gravity 1.052, 4.0% abw. [A, 31]

BOONT AMBER ALE — hazy peachy-amber; fresh citrus ale aroma is a tad soapy; high carbonation, fresh tangy-spicy mildly citrus ale flavor, long off-dry malt and hop aftertaste. Flavor created by use of crystal and caramel malts and a 16-hour mash; specific gravity 1.054, 4.1% abw. [A, 65]

HIGH ROLLERS WHEAT BEER — hazy yellow, peach and melon aroma, finely carbonated; off-dry palate but isn't malty; pleasant sweetish aftertaste. Made with 50% wheat malt; specific gravity 1.050, 4.0% abw. [W, 67]

BARNEY FLATS OATMEAL STOUT — deep red-brown color, complex smoky nose, dry smoked malt and coffee flavor, off-dry malt finish, long smoked malt aftertaste, pleasant of type. Another sample had none of the smokiness, but rather a toasted malt aroma, strong off-dry malt flavor, noticeable alcohol, considerable complexity, and a long toasted malt aftertaste. Made from pale, caramel, chocolate malts; blended with oats; specific gravity 1.062, 5.1% abw. [S, 86]

Notes

BELKS BITTER ALE (ESB) —
hazy deep gold, hop aroma, big
dry hop flavor, very long dry and
bitter hop aftertaste; great if you
really like hops, plenty of hop
character and it blends nicely with
the malt for good balance; specific
gravity 1.063, 5.2% abw. [A, 68]

RASPBERRY WHEAT — faintly
pink, distinct aroma and flavor of
raspberries all the way through,
good body; also has length, but is
more or less sweet raspberry to the
end. Made with 1 pound of raspberries per gallon of brew; specific gravity 1.056, 4.6% abw.
[WA, 46]

WINTER SOLSTICE ALE —
pale amber; nose shows cinnamon
and malt with vanilla faintly in
behind; medium body, flavor
lightly spiced, hops barely noticeable, light spicy finish and aftertaste, medium duration. Does
have vanilla and cinnamon added;
specific gravity 1.061. The
bottled version, Winter Solstice
1993 Select Ale, seemed to have a
more complex and stronger flavor
that some thought to be more
gingerlike and others thought to be
more like a spruce beer. [A, 56]

WINTER SOLSTICE 1994
SELECT ALE — amber, spicy
malt nose, dry spicy malt flavor,
medium body; dry spicy hop aftertaste has limited length. [A, 47]

HORN OF THE BEER BARLEY
WINE — deep copper color, big
alcoholic malt nose, flavored like
the aroma, huge body, very long
and strong malt aftertaste, almost
too much flavor and strength for

casual drinking. Made using ale
yeast followed by four months on
a champagne yeast; specific gravity 1.092, 8.1% abw. [BW, 73]

WHAMBER — amber; tangy
complex nose that is malty sweet
yet has an almost acidic bite; it
balances well however, and lasts
well. This is a wheat ale, finished
with Mt. Hood hops, and given a
16-hour mash like the Boont
Amber above; specific gravity
1.064, 5.0% abw. [A, 57]

Andrew's Brewing Co.
*Microbrewery in
Lincolnville, ME*

ANDREW'S OLD ENGLISH
PALE ALE — golden amber,
bright appetizing hop nose
(Hallertau, Willamette, Cascade),
big hop flavor like the nose, huge
body, bright hop finish, long hop
aftertaste, a beautiful well-made
pale ale. [A, 83]

ANDREW'S OLD ENGLISH
PORTER — deep reddish brown,
tan head, light hop nose; smooth
flavor is first malt then hops; excellent balance between the
chocolate, crystal, and pale malts;
a lovely dry mild porter with great
complexity, a pleasure to drink,
great length. [P, 83]

ANDREW'S OLD ENGLISH
BROWN ALE — brown, malt
aroma; crisp dry hop flavor shows
more of the Hallertau, Willamette,
and Cascade hops and none of the
chocolate malt; not really roasted
but there is a little smokiness show-

ing; medium body, light hop finish,
a mild dry hop aftertaste. [A, 69]

Anheuser-Busch, Inc.
*World's largest brewer
with breweries in St.
Louis, MO; Newark, NJ;
Los Angeles, CA; Tampa,
FL; Houston, TX; Colum-
bus, OH; Jacksonville, FL;
Merrimack, NH;
Williamsburg, VA;
Fairfield, CA;
Baldwinsville, NY; Fort
Collins, CO.*

BUDWEISER LAGER BEER —
pale gold, light but good hop and
malt nose, balanced, dry malt and
hop finish, and a fairly long aftertaste. Made with two-row and
six-row barley malt. First brewed
in 1876. [B, 63]

BUDWEISER LIGHT BEER
(BUD LIGHT) — brilliant pale
gold, pleasant malt aroma, good
balance malt and hop flavor, light
but tasty, slight malt and hop finish,
brief aftertaste. Made with two-row
and six-row barley malt. [LO, 36]

BUDWEISER DRY BEER (BUD
DRY) — bright gold, beautiful malt
aroma with hops in back; dry malt
flavor is pleasant but brief. [D, 45]

BUDWEISER ICE DRAFT COLD
FILTERED BEER — gold; aroma
has a lot of hops and some malt;
flavor is like the nose but not as big;
medium body, hop finish, short hop
aftertaste. Beer rests at 28°F for
several days before being cold
filtered. [B, 43]

MICHELOB BEER — gold, hop aroma, very good balance between the hops and malt, good body, pleasant fresh and dry malt and hop flavor, medium long aftertaste with slight hop character. Made with a high percentage of two-row barley malt and imported hops. [B, 74]

MICHELOB LIGHT — pale gold, fragrant malt aroma, highly carbonated, good but light malt flavor, light hop finish, medium length aftertaste, good character for a light beer. Made with a high percentage of two-row barley malt and imported hops. [LO, 52]

MICHELOB DRY — pale bright gold, dry malt nose, dry malt flavor, good balance, but little aftertaste. [D, 30]

MICHELOB GOLDEN DRAFT — bright gold, pleasant hop and malt aroma; mild pleasant flavor showing both hops and malt; medium body, innocuous, nice tasting, with a dry aftertaste. [B, 39]

MICHELOB GOLDEN DRAFT LIGHT — pale gold; hop nose that is almost skunky; light flavor starts out mostly hops, finishes mostly malt; dry malt aftertaste with little duration, light body. [LO, 25]

MICHELOB CLASSIC DARK BEER — medium deep copper-brown; faintly roasted light malt aroma and flavor, very lightly flavored; carbonation dominates the taste; light body, short slightly off-dry faint malt aftertaste. Made like Michelob but with addition of roasted barley malt. [B, 27]

BUSCH PREMIUM BEER — pale yellow, faintly off-dry malt aroma, highly carbonated; smooth malt and hop flavor is all up front; light and refreshing; fades quickly at the finish, slight hop aftertaste. [B, 36]

BUSCH LIGHT DRAFT — pale gold, light malt aroma, light malt aroma, good tasting malt flavor, good body, dry finish and aftertaste. Brewed with a blend of two-row and six-row barley malt together with cereal grains. [LO, 43]

ANHEUSER NATURAL LIGHT — pale gold, grainy malt aroma, dry and refreshing malt flavor, well balanced; long on the palate and good to drink. Made with a blend of two-row and six-row barley malt. [LO, 45]

ANHEUSER NATURAL PILSNER — pale gold, faint malt aroma and flavor, noticeable carbonation, hops almost not there at all, brief dry malt aftertaste. [B, 34]

ANHEUSER MAERZEN BEER — amber-gold, terrific malt nose, delicious toasted malt flavor, complex, long hop aftertaste. [B, 69]

KING COBRA PREMIUM MALT LIQUOR — bright gold, appetizing sweet malt aroma, highly carbonated, good malt flavor but definitely on the sweet side, soft and smooth, pleasantly finished and with a good long malt aftertaste. It is made with six-row barley malt; 4.5% abw. [ML, 53]

Notes

O'DOULS NON-ALCOHOLIC BREW — bright gold, wet cereal grain aroma, light grainy flavor, dry finish, dull aftertaste of medium duration. It has less than 0.5% abv. and 70 calories per 12-oz. portion. [NA, 24]

JAGUAR PREMIUM MALT LIQUOR — bright gold, light malt aroma, off-dry malt flavor, sweetest in middle, good body, medium length, dry at very end. [ML, 47]

BUDWEISER ICE DRAFT COLD FILTERED LIGHT BEER — gold; aroma has a lot of hops and some malt; flavor is like the nose but not as big; light to medium body, hop finish, short hop aftertaste. Beer rests at 28°F for several days before being cold filtered. It is similar to Budweiser Ice Draft Cold Filtered above, except it has 96-calories per 12-oz. portion. [LO, 47]

BUDWEISER ICE DRAFT LIGHT BEER — pale gold, very faint non-descript nose, carbonation and some faint malt for a flavor, light body, no finish, no aftertaste, scarcely a beer at all. Only 96-calories per 12-oz. portion. [LO, 7]

ELK MOUNTAIN AMBER ALE — amber; malt nose shows some background hops; bright well-hopped flavor has a little malty sweetness in back; this sweetness shows more in the finish, dry hop and malt aftertaste, a very pleasant and bright tasting beer. Tasted on draft during test market period and again once released in bottle. Made with 100% barley malt, whole cone hops, and English ale yeast; specific gravity 1.056, 4.1% abw, 30 IBU. [A, 75]

ELK MOUNTAIN RED LAGER — reddish-amber, smooth malt and hop nose; smooth dry malt and hop flavor shows neither the hops or malt to advantage; balanced; faint fruity character stays in back; dry malt and hop finish and aftertaste, medium body, medium long, nothing stands out, made with Hallertau hops at the Specialty Brewing Group at Merrimack, NH. [B, 53]

RED WOLF LAGER BEER — amber, very faint toasted malt nose, dull dry malt flavor, medium body, medium long dull dry malt aftertaste. [B, 32]

BUSCH NA — gold, very faint malt nose, watery; faint carbonic taste is all there is for a flavor; little more taste than bottled water, nothing in the aftertaste. [NA, 8]

BUD ICE ALE — gold, malty aroma; malty flavor is quite sweet; medium to big body; some hops appear faintly in the finish and aftertaste but it is mostly off-dry

malt; fairly long sweet malt aftertaste; this is different from Bud Ice Draft, 5.5% abv. Note: The word "ale" on the label is very small and there probably only because the sample was for the California market and had alcohol higher than 5% abv. It is most certainly a lager beer. [B, 45]

BUD ICE LIGHT BEER — gold, malt and light hop aroma and flavor, bright carbonic taste, refreshing and dry, little duration, but definitely good hot weather refreshment. This is different from Bud Ice Draft Light. [LO, 47]

ZIEGEN BOCK AMBER — pretty amber, good attractive malty nose, rich malt flavor, good body, smooth, long dry malty aftertaste. Made by Anheuser-Busch at their Houston brewery for the greater Houston market, supposedly to compete with the Shiner Bock, which is popular in the area. [BK, 59]

CROSS ROADS BEER — hazy gold, spicy aroma, big spicy clovelike flavor, creamy mouth-feel, medium body; easy to drink, first sip is best; bright, refreshing, but brief. [W, 38]

ANHEUSER LIGHT — pale gold, faint malty water aroma, faint car-bonated malt water flavor, light body, faint dry malt finish and after-taste has a metallic-tinny back-ground, a 75-calorie light beer with little character. [LO, 7]

MICHELOB AMBER BOCK — brilliant deep amber, very faint malt aroma, faint dry malt flavor, dry malt finish and aftertaste; made with roasted barley and rice; it's most prominent feature is its deep rich color. [B, 19]

CHRISTMAS BREW BEER 1995 — amber; aroma shows some malt; some alcohol and carbonation; malt is sweetened with alcohol on the palate and joined by some hops in the middle, but the hops don't develop until the finish and then extend into the aftertaste; medium body; smooth but packs punch expected of a winter holiday brew. [B, 40]

ANHEUSER-BUSCH BLACK & TAN PORTER — dark amber, toasted malt aroma; smooth dry toasted malt flavor shows some black patent malt and some ashtray character; roasted flavor is missing the center; dry roasted malt finish and aftertaste. [P, 46]

Appleton Brewing Co. / Adler Brau

Microbrewery in Appleton, WI adjacent to two restaurants to which the beer is piped directly, giving it additional status as a brewpub

ADLER BRAU LIGHT — gold, hop nose, light malt flavor, very light body, not much of an aftertaste. Made with Saaz hops; gravity 9.5 P, 3.4% abw. [LO, 27]

ADLER BRAU LAGER — gold, light hop aroma and flavor, medium body, dry hop finish and aftertaste. The brew is finished with Cascade hops; gravity 11 P, 3.8% abw. [B, 47]

ADLER BRAU AMBER — amber, dry malt and hop aroma, smooth dry malt and hop flavor, medium to good body, long dry malt and hop aftertaste; specific gravity 1.054, 4.5% abw (5.5% abv). [B, 46]

ADLER BRAU OKTOBERFEST — gold, hop nose, big malty taste with the hops in back, good body, medium dry malt finish and aftertaste; specific gravity 1.065, 5.0% abw. [B, 54]

ADLER BRAU PILSNER — gold, big hop nose (Saaz hops, it seems), medium body, dry hop flavor, finish, and aftertaste; gravity 13.0 P, 4.5% abw. [B, 53]

ADLER BRAU WEISS — gold, malt aroma, smooth wheat and barley malt flavor, no spice; soft, smooth, and refreshing; light body, medium dry malt aftertaste. Recipe calls for 45% wheat malt; gravity 14.75 P, 4.9% abw. [W, 49]

ERICH'S WEISS BIER — amber-gold, very interesting fruity nose; bright clove-citrus-banana-hop flavor, but the banana overrides everything right through the aftertaste; made with 50% wheat malt, 45% two-row pale, and 5% Munich malt, and hopped with Northern Brewer, Hallertau, and Cascade hops; OG 1054, FG 1.014, 5.9% abv, 15 IBU. [W, 46]

ADLER BRAU PUMPKIN
SPICE — gold, spicy nose and
taste, an appetizing pumpkin pie
flavor, good body, long aftertaste
like the flavor; not made with
pumpkin, just the pumpkin pie
spices; specific gravity 1.045,
4.1% abw. [B, 52]

ADLER BRAU BOCK — golden
amber, pleasant hop and malt
aroma, taste to match, pleasant,
dry, appetizing, light body, light
hop and malt aftertaste. Made
with a high percentage of black
and caramel malt; gravity 12.5 P,
4.3% abw. [BK, 48]

ADLER BRAU PORTER —
brown, dry malt aroma and flavor,
good body, good balance, dry
roasted malt aftertaste; specific
gravity 1.060, 4.8% abw. [P, 48]

ADLER BRAU OATMEAL
STOUT — brown, dry roasted barley and chocolate malt nose; flavor
is like the nose but a bit more dry;
good body, dry malt finish and aftertaste. Made with roasted barley and
oatmeal; specific gravity 1.054,
3.8% abw. [S, 62]

ADLER BRAU PALE ALE —
gold, big hop aroma, flavor to
match, good body, good balance,
dry hop finish and aftertaste, fairly
long and quite tasty; gravity 13.1 P,
4.5% abw. [A, 67]

ADLER BRAU
DOPPELBOCK — amber, big
malt and hop nose; big rich malt
and hop flavor, bigger even than
promised by the aroma; big body,
finishes strongly, long complex
aftertaste, good hefty brew finely
balanced despite its size; gravity
17.1 P, 5.7% abw. [BK, 72]

DR. BRAU GINSENG — amber,
spicy-peppery nose and taste,
medium to good body, interesting,
dry peppery aftertaste. Pale lager
made with ginseng root; gravity
13.0 P, 4.7% abw. [B, 53]

Arrowhead Brewing Co.
Brewery in Chambersburg, PA

RED FEATHER PALE ALE —
pale amber, big ale-like hop and
malt aroma with some citrus, zesty
hop flavor, malt in back, full body,
big and balanced; long dry hop
aftertaste has a subtle malt component in back; an excellent beer.
Made with two-row British pale,
crystal, and chocolate malts, Cascade, Willamette, and Northern
Brewer hops, fire-brewed, and
top-fermented; gravity 11.75 P
(OG 1047, FG 1.011), 3.8% abw
(4.6% abv). [A, 74]

LIGHT FEATHER GOLDEN
ALE — hazy gold, pleasant malt
and hop aroma, bright well-
hopped flavor, dry hop finish and
aftertaste, very good for a light
beer. [A, 62]

THE SHIPYARD EXPORT
ALE — hazy amber, big malty
aroma with some background hops,
big malty flavor with plenty of
northwest hops, big body, good balance but only moderately complex,
big malt finish; medium dry malt
aftertaste has good length. Made
for Kennebunkport B.C. [A, 56]

HOBOKEN SPECIAL RESERVE
ALE — hazy pale amber, tangerine nose, finely carbonated, big
fruity tangerine flavor, a bit dull,
light body, dull dry malt finish and
aftertaste. Made for Gold Coast
Brewing of Hoboken, NJ. [A, 47]

ARROWHEAD BROWN ALE —
amber, faint malty aroma, light
fruity malt taste, medium body,
light fruity malt finish and aftertaste, medium length. [A, 56]

SHANGHAI PALE ALE —
amber, bright hop and toasted malt
aroma, big toasted malt flavor,
medium body, bright hop finish
and aftertaste, rich, complex, and
long. [A, 78]

Assets Grille and Brewing Co.
Brewpub in Albuquerque, NM

SANDIA STOUT — brown;
malty aroma has a light toasty
quality; chocolate malt flavor with
coffeelike character; smooth and
dry, good body; finish shows the

roasted barley but with no obtrusive bite; long dry malt aftertaste has hops faintly appearing near the end to balance nicely; pleasant satisfying brew. Made with roasted barley, chocolate malt, and Chinook hops; specific gravity 1.410, 4.5% abw. Tasted at the 1993 GABF and at the pub with same results. [S, 67]

ROADRUNNER ALE — deep golden, dry malt and hop aroma; dry malt flavor shows the hops as well; light body; hops show best in the finish and aftertaste; not long on the palate. Made like an English bitter and finished with Fuggles hops; OG 1050, 4.2% abw. Tasted first at the 1993 GABF, then at the pub at which time this ale was not only light bodied, but almost watery. [A, 61]

DUKE CITY AMBER — deep amber, rich malt and light hop aroma, pleasant big rich malt flavor, very smooth, good body, smooth dry hop finish and long light dry hop aftertaste, smooth and likable. This ale is made with crystal malt, Northern Brewer, Cascade and Fuggles hops; specific gravity 1.050, 4.2% abw. It is my choice for the best brew at Assets. [A,74]

CURLEY'S KÖLSCH — gold, light malt aroma, light hop flavor, light body, clean tasting, short dry hop aftertaste. Made from pale malts and malted wheat with Hallertau and Cascade hops; 3.2% abw. This version was tasted at the 1993 GABF in Denver, CO. [K, 54]

KAKTUS KÖLSCH — very pale gold, faint malt and hop aroma,

light dry hop flavor, finishes even drier, light body, very dry hop aftertaste. At Assets, I was told that this was the same recipe as Curley's Kölsch, renamed for the pub menu (I guess "Curley" had his 15 minutes of fame.) At the 1994 GABF, the recipe states that it is made with Vienna malt, balanced with Mt. Hood hops; specific gravity 1.044, 3.7% abw. It seemed similar except that the hop character appeared to be different (less of the Cascade and Hallertau style that I happen to like). [K, 50]

ASSETS RASPBERRY ALE — gold, big raspberry nose; light raspberry flavor is a bit sweet, finish is drier; medium long dry aftertaste still tastes of the raspberry. [A, 42]

S.S. RIO GRANDE COPPER ALE — pale copper-amber, complex hop and malt aroma, malt flavor, medium body, smooth malty finish and dry hop aftertaste. Decent brew made with Northern Brewers hops. [A, 61]

Atlantic Brewing Co.
Microbrewery and The Lompoc Cafe and Brewery (Brewpub) in Bar Harbor, ME

BAR HARBOR REAL ALE — deep amber (almost brown), big malt and hop aroma and flavor, slightly toasted, big body, balanced, smooth, finishes dry, medium long dry hop aftertaste, very drinkable. Made with pale two-row English, crystal, and black patent malts; gravity 12 P (OG 1048), 4.4% abw. [A, 69]

ACADIA PALE ALE — deep gold, pleasant malt and hop aroma, zesty hop flavor, good body, very drinkable, long dry hop aftertaste with plenty of malt in back. Made with pale two-row English and Munich malts; gravity 12 P, 4.4% abw. [A, 71]

ACADIA AMBER ALE — dark amber, light malt and hop nose, good body, very smooth malt flavor, long dry aftertaste. [A, 62]

COAL PORTER — brown, big chocolate malt and hop nose, smooth but big dry malt and hop flavor, dry malt finish and aftertaste, a big attractive fairly strong porter. Made with two-row English pale, chocolate and black malts; gravity 12.5 P (OG 1050), 5.2% abw. [P, 64]

GINGER WHEAT — deep gold, dry gingery nose and palate; ginger stays back and never takes over; bright flavor with pizzazz, dry gingery-malt finish, medium long dry aftertaste. Made with 60% barley and 40% wheat malt and fresh ginger. [W, 67]

BAR HARBOR BLUEBERRY ALE — deep amber; fruity blueberry aroma is not easily identified unless you expect blueberries; tart-soapy-malty blueberry flavor has a real beery background, you know that the base is good beer; good body; dry hop aftertaste has good length; OG 1050. [A, 52]

Atlantic Coast Brewing, Ltd.
Microbrewery in Boston, MA (Charlestown section)

TREMONT ALE — amber, dry hop aroma and flavor, dry hop finish and aftertaste, medium duration, well balanced; made with Fuggles and Kent-Goldings hops; specific gravity 1.049, 4% abw. [A, 47]

TREMONT BEST BITTER — gold, dry hop aroma and flavor, medium body, dry hop finish and aftertaste, medium length, well-balanced, cask-conditioned; made with Fuggles and Kent-Goldings hops; specific gravity 1.049. [A, 48]

TREMONT PORTER — deep brown, good malty aroma, bright crisp malt flavor, good carbonation level, medium body; long dry crisp malt aftertaste has plenty of hops for balance; refreshing and very drinkable; OG 1056. [P, 83]

Avery Brewing Co.
Microbrewery in Boulder, CO

ELLE'S BROWN ALE — deep red-brown, chocolate malt nose, smooth dry malty taste, medium body, dry malt finish and aftertaste, medium length. Made with chocolate and Munich malts and three different hops; specific gravity 1.062, 4.5% abw. [A, 67]

OUT OF BOUNDS STOUT — dark opaque brown, chocolate malt and deep roasted barley nose, dry perfumy roasted malt flavor, long dry malt aftertaste. Made with Bullion and Willamette hops, a high percentage of specialty malts; specific gravity 1.070, 4.5% abw. [S, 77]

RAZZY WHEAT ALE — reddish gold, bright raspberry nose, dry raspberry flavor, dry raspberry and malt aftertaste. [A, 49]

REDPOINT ALE — amber, bright well-hopped aroma and flavor, good body, dry hop finish and aftertaste. Made with lots of Cascade hops; specific gravity 1.056, 4.8% abw. [A, 67]

RASPBERRY TRUFFALE — dark amber, raspberry aroma; raspberry flavor has a chocolatey background; light body, interesting raspberry-chocolate truffle aftertaste, medium duration, a very interesting brew; they accomplished what they set out to create — a raspberry truffle ale. [A, 79]

Brewed and Baked in Telluride
Brewpub in Telluride, CO

SNOW WHEAT — amber, big spicy nose, tangy well-spiced palate, a hefe-weizen style, good body, well spiced into the finish and the long aftertaste. Made with 60% wheat and 40% barley malt and unfiltered; gravity 9.5 P, 3.9% abw. [W, 61]

RUNNER'S HIGH — amber-brown, hop nose and palate, good body, medium dry malt and hop finish and aftertaste. An unfiltered lager; specific gravity 1.056 (gravity 13.5 P), 4.7% abw. [B, 57]

PANDORA PORTER — brown, dry grainy and chocolate malt nose and flavor, drier finish, long dry malt aftertaste continues to be dominated by chocolate malt; specific gravity 1.052 (gravity 14 P), 4.5% abw. [P, 53]

STORMY STOUT — dark brown, roasted barley and chocolate malt aroma, bright chocolate malt flavor, good body, decent balance, medium length; a little acidic bite in the back of the aftertaste mars the effect. Made with Briess Dark extract, roasted barley, and chocolate malt; gravity 1.60 P, 5.5% abw. [S, 54]

Baltimore Brewing Co.
Brewpub in Baltimore, MD

DE GROEN'S LAGER — bright amber, light hop and malt nose, creamy smooth light hop flavor, plenty of supporting malt, dry hop finish, long dry hop aftertaste. [B, 65]

DE GROEN'S AMBER — deep amber, faint malt nose, hop and toasted malt flavor, dry hop finish, medium length, dry hop aftertaste. [B, 64]

DE GROEN'S PILS — golden amber, fresh hop nose with lots of malt, big dry hop European-style flavor, long dry hop aftertaste. Step infusion mash of 100% pale two-row pale malt, highly hopped with domestic Nugget hops and finished with Czech Saaz hops; specific gravity 1.051, 4.55% abw. [B, 62]

DE GROEN'S WEIZEN — gold, light malt aroma, spicy clove flavor, medium body, dry spicy finish and aftertaste, medium length; done with a delicate hand, but very pleasant and refreshing; 53% wheat malt in step infusion mash with pale malt and a small quantity of two-row Munich malt; Bavarian weizen yeast used in primary fermentation, cold secondary fermentation with lager beer as kraeusen, made with domestic Cluster, Nugget, and Tettnanger hops; specific gravity 1.048, 3.94% abw. [W, 60]

DE GROEN'S MÄRZEN — amber-gold, big malt nose, strong malt flavor; some hops show in the middle and finish, but this is a malty brew first and foremost; drier at the finish than at the start, interesting but doesn't quite come together in some batches, but does so in others. Step infusion mash of two-row German Caramunich malt, two-row Munich malt, and two-row pale malt, hopped with domestic Nugget and Tettnanger, and German Hallertau Hersbrucker; specific gravity 1.051, 4.55% abw. [B, 41]

DE GROEN'S
WEIZENBOCK — cloudy amber-brown, big head; zesty spicy nose has lots of malt; flavor matches the nose but is even bigger than expected; good body, long lightly spiced malt aftertaste, a good drinking brew. Wheat malt in step infusion mash with pale, caramelized, and Caramunich malts, using Bavarian weizen yeast in the primary fermentation, secondary fermentation in cold storage with lager beer kraeusen, and with domestic Cluster, Nugget, and Tettnanger hops; specific gravity 1.064, 5.3% abw. [WBK, 70]

DE GROEN'S MAI BOCK — deep golden amber, smooth malt and hop aroma and taste, nicely balanced with the hops in back; smooth dry hop mid-palate, finish, and aftertaste; good body, medium alcohol, overall dry with fruity fresh malt and hops appearing in the aftertaste, a good classical bock. [BK, 66]

DE GROEN'S WEIZEN BIER — hazy gold; banana aroma and flavor has a light spiciness in back; medium to light body; long and dry keeping the banana nature. [W, 65]

Bandersnatch Brewing Co.
Brewpub in Tempe, AZ

BIGHORN PREMIUM ALE — brilliant clear amber, light hop nose; complex hop flavor shows plenty of malt; medium body, good northwest hop character;

stays hoppy throughout but doesn't lack for malt; long dry hop aftertaste, a good English bitter-style ale. [A, 74]

CARDINAL PALE ALE — bright gold, light hop nose, creamy, light and bright dry hop flavor, light to medium body, dry hop finish and long dry hop aftertaste, again the northwest hop character but lighter and refreshing. [A, 67]

BANDERSNATCH MILK STOUT — opaque brown, huge tan head, beef bouillon aroma, dry malt flavor, long dry malt aftertaste. This sample was bottled by the brewpub and shipped to me on the east coast. It was slightly harmed by the journey, but this showed up only in the aroma. A recent change in recipe has resulted in more of an Australian-style stout, much less dry than reported here. [S, 49]

EDINBREW — deep amber, aroma of dry hops and malt, a big flavor with plenty of both malt and hops, good balance, good body, long dry malt aftertaste; done like a Scottish ale, but with a northwest hop twist. [A, 71]

Bar Harbor Brewing Co.
Microbrewery in Bar Harbor, ME

HARBOR LIGHT PALE ALE — deep hazy amber, light malt and hop nose, bright tangy ale taste, hop front and malt back, good body; long dry malt and hop aftertaste is much like the flavor; some

complexity as the malt and hops vie for dominance and never clash. Made with extract and crystal malt, hopped with Cascade hops; OG 1043. [A, 65]

CADILLAC MTN. STOUT — opaque brown, brown head, malt nose with a complex citrus-yeast background, big dry malt palate; hops come in at the finish; long dry malt and hop aftertaste; definitely a dry stout style, and although your first thought is homebrew, it really grows on you. It is an imperial-style stout made with black malt extract and roasted barley; specific gravity 1.070. [S, 68]

THUNDER HOLE ALE — reddish brown, malt nose; malt flavor has hops in support and has some complexity; medium body, dry hop finish, long fairly dry hop and malt aftertaste. Made with malt extract, crystal and chocolate malts, and Willamette and Cascade hops. [A, 70]

Bardo Rodeo
Brewpub in Arlington, VA

BARDO GRAND CRUE — hazy gold, light spicy citrus aroma and flavor; a wit bier style made with coriander and orange peel; medium body, light spicy aftertaste; specific gravity 1.056, 5.0% abw. [W, 49]

BEAT MY WHEAT — pale hazy gold, light malt aroma, light dry malt flavor, an American-style wheat beer, light to medium body, dry malt finish and aftertaste; specific gravity 1.047, 4.2% abw. [W, 50]

CENTENNIAL IPA — amber, big hop aroma, strong hop flavor, good body, long and strong dry hop aftertaste; specific gravity 1.075, 5.1% abw. [A, 69]

DREMO TIBETAN BIG FOOT — amber, huge hop nose with plenty of malt in back; flavor is everything promised by the nose and more; a monster brew with more than enough hops and malt for the palate; long complex aftertaste shows some of the alcohol (6% abw); specific gravity 1.066. This is an excellent beer. [BW, 85]

EL JEFFE — cloudy gold, bright spicy classical hefe-weizen nose; good spicy flavor is as expected; medium body, long spicy aftertaste, a good example of the style; specific gravity 1.056, 4.9% abw. [W, 67]

OIL CAN PORTER — brown, chocolate malt aroma and flavor, rich and clean all the way across the palate, long tasty aftertaste; specific gravity 1.064, 4.5% abw. [P, 72]

SLANT SIX STRONG — amber-gold, hop aroma; big dry hop and malt flavor has plenty of bite and character; long dry hop aftertaste; specific gravity 1.070, 5.2% abw. [A, 79]

WHITE LIGHTNIN' — dark amber, big malty aroma; huge strong malt flavor is concentrated and quite alcoholic; huge body; long and strong malt aftertaste continues to yield alcohol; specific gravity 1.104, 9.0% abw. This is a huge brew, well worth sampling. [BW, 85]

Barley's Brewing Co.
Brewpub in Columbus, OH, called Ale House No. 1

BARLEY'S PILSNER MILD — gold, light Saaz hop aroma, big bright hop flavor, good body, long dry hop aftertaste, a very European-style beer. [B, 52]

IRISH ROGUE — amber-gold, complex Cascade and Hallertau hop aroma, smooth complex hop and malt flavor; very easy to drink; well-hopped finish and long dry hop aftertaste. It is dry hopped. [A, 69]

BARLEY'S PALE ALE — amber, mild hop aroma, very smooth big dry ale flavor, good body, fairly complex, long dry hop aftertaste. [A, 72]

IVAN PORTER — dark brown, mild chocolate malt and hop aroma; flavor is hops and dry complex malt showing less chocolate malt than the nose; well-hopped finish, long dry hop aftertaste, overall very smooth and drinkable. [P, 74]

Notes

Bayern Brewing Co.
*Microbrewery in
Missoula, MT*

BAYERN PILSENER — gold, touch of malt vinegar in the nose; malt flavor has a grassy component, like cut alfalfa or hemp; long grainy aftertaste, not likable; made with two-row Harrington and Munich malts, hopped with Hallertau Perle and Saaz hops; OG 1050, FG 1.010, 5% abv, 34 IBU. [B, 47]

Beach Brewing Co.
(Mill Bakery,
Eatery & Brewery)
*Brewpub and
microbrewery in Orlando,
FL. Brews for itself and
for Tallahassee and
Gainesville Mill Bakery,
Eatery & Brewery estab-
lishments. Affiliated with
other Mills in Winter
Park, FL; Baton Rouge,
LA; Charlotte, NC; and
others as planned.*

RED ROCK — amber, good malt and faint hop aroma; malt comes through much stronger on the palate with a caramel background; good body, creamy, balanced; finishes fairly dry leading into a long dry malt and hop aftertaste. Roasted barley malt and Cascade hops are used, but the roasted nature is not obvious. [B, 67]

HORNET'S TAIL — amber, big hop nose, big bright hop flavor has plenty of malt, big body, sense of alcohol, long strong hop and malt aftertaste, a real mouth full of taste, huge and good. [A, 69]

HONEY WHEAT LIGHT BEER — slightly hazy gold, pleasant malt nose; bright malt flavor has a tang in the finish, the honey is only apparent on the front palate, pleasant bite stays into aftertaste; light body; highly and finely carbonated, the carbonation definitely adds to the refreshing character, medium length; a very good American-style wheat beer, better than most. [W, 69]

HARVEST GOLD LIGHT — gold, faint malt and hop nose, light malt and hop flavor, light body, clean and pleasant, light dry short malt aftertaste; specific gravity 1.046, 3.7% abv. [LO, 45]

KNIGHT LIGHT — pale gold, aromatic hop nose, light hop flavor, light body, light medium long clean dry hop aftertaste. As tasted in Orlando. [LO, 42]

KNIGHT LIGHT — gold, grainy malt aroma and flavor, light body, little length. The Hallertau hops used barely show. As tasted in Winter Park. [LO, 42]

MAGIC BREW — deep ruby-amber, big hop nose; good hop and malt flavor shows the hops to good advantage; light body, good long dry malt aftertaste. As tasted in Orlando. [A, 63]

MAGIC BREW — ruby amber, malt aroma, creamy caramel flavor, good mouthfeel, decent balance; hops slowly come in at the finish; long dry malt and hop aftertaste. As tasted in Winter Park. [A, 63]

PALE ALE — golden amber, clean flowery hop and malt aroma, big hop palate; malt comes in at the middle; good body, long dry hop aftertaste, lots of character, an excellent bright and refreshing well-hopped brew. [A, 74]

COPPER CREEK ALE — gold, big bright hop aroma and flavor, good body, off-dry malt finish and aftertaste. This brew is made with Hallertau hops; gravity 11.25 P, 3.5% abv. As found in Charlotte. [A, 46]

RED OKTOBER — gold, big hop aroma and flavor, good body, dry hop finish and aftertaste, an American pale ale; specific gravity 1.056, 4.5% abv. Tasted in Charlotte. [A, 60]

49ER GOLD — gold, malt and hop aroma and flavor, medium body, dry hop finish and aftertaste; gravity 11.2 P, 3.7% abv. Tasted in Charlotte. [A, 50]

NUT BROWN ALE — amber, light malt aroma, very light malt flavor on the dry side, no discernible aftertaste. Tasted in Charlotte. [A, 45]

HARVEST TRAIL ALE — deep amber-gold, malt aroma and flavor, medium body, dry malt finish and aftertaste. English-style brown ale; 3.9% abv. Tasted in Charlotte. [A, 48]

HARVEST GOLD BARLEY — pale gold, malt nose, light dry malt flavor, finish, and aftertaste, not much duration on the palate. Tasted in Charlotte. [LO, 45]

McKNIGHT'S SPECIAL STOUT — dark brown, roasted barley and chocolate malt nose, dry flavor like the aroma, medium body, dry malt finish and aftertaste; specific gravity 1.056, 4.6% abw. Tasted in Charlotte. [S, 48]

MILL CHERRY STOUT — dark brown; faint berry aroma overrides the malt; tart cherry flavor, dry malt finish and aftertaste with the cherry in behind, good body, overall tart and dry; 4.9% abw. Tasted in Charlotte. [S, 47]

HORNET'S TAIL — amber, big hop nose; big bright hop flavor has plenty of malt; big body, sense of alcohol, long strong hop and malt aftertaste, a real mouthful of taste, huge and good, flavored with chocolate malt; specific gravity 1.047, 4% abw. Tasted in Charlotte. [A, 69]

HARVEST GOLD LIGHT — gold, faint malt and hop nose, light malt and hop flavor, light body, clean and pleasant, light dry short malt aftertaste; specific gravity 1.046, 3.7% abw. Tasted in Charlotte. [LO, 45]

Beaver Street Brewery & Whistle Stop Cafe
Brewpub in Flagstaff, AZ

BEAVER STREET PALE ALE — gold, beautiful appetizing Cascade hop nose, big bright hop taste, good body, wonderful long and complex dry hop aftertaste; one of the best American pale ales I have tasted, this is a beer made to my standard of perfection. At the 1994 GABF, this brew was named Derail Pale Ale and specified as being made with pale and Carastan malts; specific gravity 1.052, 5.2% abw. [A, 96]

BEAVER STREET RED ALE — deep gold, faint dry hop nose; flavor is very good, smooth dry hops and roasted malt; dry hop finish, and long dry hop aftertaste. [A, 69]

BEAVER STREET BITTER — deep amber, faint roasted malt nose, dry roast malt flavor with only a tad of chocolate malt showing, smooth and dry; finish shows a bit more of the chocolate malt; dry roasted malt finish and long dry aftertaste; made with a mix of chocolate and dark crystal Munich malts. [A, 74]

BEAVER STREET PILSENER — bright gold, dry light hop aroma and flavor, good body, dry hop finish and aftertaste, very long. Made with pale, carastan, and Munich malts and Saaz hops; specific gravity 1.050, 5.1% abw. [B, 68]

RAIL HEAD RED — golden amber, very lovely malt aroma, bright malt flavor, dry malt finish and aftertaste, good body, excellent flavor; specific gravity 1.054, 5.5% abw. [B, 75]

Notes

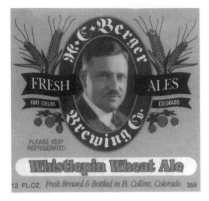

Belmont Brewing Co.
Brewpub in Long Beach, CA

TOP SAIL AMBER ALE — amber, little nose, dry hop flavor; medium body, dry malt and hop aftertaste with fair duration. Made with carastan, Munich, pale, and crystal malts; hopped with Cascade hops; gravity 14 P, 4% abw. [A, 48]

LONG BEACH CRUDE POR-TER — deep amber-brown, dry chocolate malt nose, very dry chocolate malt flavor, medium body, long aftertaste like the flavor, more like a stout than a porter; hopped with Cascades; gravity 14.5 P, 4.5% abw. [P, 65]

WHALE ALE — hazy gold, faint malt nose, dry soapy malt flavor, finishes very dry, short dry malt aftertaste. [A, 43]

MARATHON PALE ALE — gold, big ale nose; hefty hop flavor that drops off abruptly; light dry hop aftertaste. [A, 47]

STRAWBERRY BLONDE ALE — gold; faint strawberry nose riding in behind the malt, but in the mouth the strawberry is very noticeable up front, yields a bit to the malt and hops in mid-palate, but never fades completely; good body; strawberry takes a back seat at the finish but is still noticeably present, starts to dry at finish; long dry hop aftertaste with the strawberry sweetness in back, fairly interesting. [A, 56]

Note: The brewpub offers mixtures of some brews: Penny Fogger — a mix of the porter and amber that comes out malty and dry, and Black and Tan — a mix of the pale and porter that also comes out malty like the Penny Fogger, but lighter. It is now possible to find the Belmont brews in 22-oz. bottles.

Bend Brewing Co.
Microbrewery in Bend, OR

BEND STRONG ALE — cloudy amber, hop aroma, big bright hop flavor, fruity component in back, medium body, dry hop finish and aftertaste; made with two-row, English pale, carastan, and caramel malts; hopped to 38 IBU with Columbus, Northern Brewer, Willamette, and Kent-Goldings; OG 1072, FG 1.016, 5.8% abw. [A, 79]

H.C. Berger Brewing Co.
Microbrewery in Fort Collins, CO

INDEGO ALE — amber, complex hop aroma and taste, smooth and balanced, very drinkable, long dry hop aftertaste. This alt is made with eight malts and four varieties of hops. More recently labeled Indego Pale Ale. [A, 68]

INDIA PALE ALE — amber, light hop aroma, very dry hop flavor, smooth, balanced, very long dry hop aftertaste. [A, 53]

WHISTLEPIN WHEAT BEER — golden amber, big foamy head, fresh malt aroma and flavor, smooth, balanced, tasty, long dry malt aftertaste, a nice American-style wheat; made with 50% Red winter wheat from England and German hops. [W, 50]

RED BANSHEE ALE — deep amber, light toasted malt aroma; malt and hop flavor has the components clashing and there is some phenolic character; medium body, long aftertaste like the flavor. Made with toasted malts and German hops. This tasted on draft in Boulder in late 1993. In mid-1994, it was again tasted, but this time from a 22-oz. bottle. It was deep amber, had a rich malty aroma showing some chocolate malt; dry malt flavor with a dirty-earthy quality like it was starting to develop some phenolics; medium to light body, short dry malt aftertaste. [A, 45]

RED ASS ALE — gold, bright hop aroma, big dry hop flavor, plenty of malt support, medium body, long dry hop aftertaste, made for Red Ass Brewing Co. of Ft. Collins, CO. [A, 67]

Berghoff Brewery & Restaurant
Brewpub and restaurant in Chicago, IL

BERGHOFF LITE — pale gold, pleasant but light malt aroma, weak body, light hop flavor, medium long light hop aftertaste. [LO, 34]

BERGHOFF DORTMUNDER REGULAR — pale gold, pleasant malt nose with hops in back, bright hop flavor, excellent balance, long dry hop aftertaste, bright and refreshing. [B, 63]

BERGHOFF WEISSE — hazy gold, faint honeyed malt nose, honeyed malt flavor, light and refreshing, dry malt aftertaste of medium length, no spiciness. [W, 53]

BERGHOFF AMBER ALE — amber, pleasant tangy hop aroma, light hop flavor, long dry hop aftertaste. [A, 62]

BERGHOFF DORTMUNDER DARK — deep amber, zesty hop nose; big flavor is off-dry malt up front, dry hops in the middle, and off-dry malt in the finish and aftertaste; good length. The beer is a bit winelike in nature, but good. [B, 68]

Berkshire Brewing Co.
Microbrewery in South Deerfield, MA

STEEL RAIL EXTRA PALE ALE — hazy cloudy gold, dank malty aroma, dankish slightly sweet malty flavor, finish, and aftertaste. [A, 33]

BERKSHIRE ALE TRADITIONAL PALE ALE — hazy amber, aroma shows some malt and plenty of hops, big hop flavor with enough malt support for balance; shows a touch of northwest hops; dry hop finish and aftertaste, little malt left at the end. [A, 64]

Big Nose Brewing Co.
Microbrewery in Denver, CO

BIG NOSE RED ALE — deep gold, grainy malt aroma, dry malt flavor, medium body, dry malt finish and aftertaste; specific gravity 1.050, 4.3% abw, SRM 11.87; made with galena hops (MJ 23.5). [A, 65]

Big Time Brewing Co.
Brewpub in Seattle, WA

HEFERYZEN — hazy gold, rye bread aroma, fresh lightly spicy hop and malt flavor, dry hop finish, long dry hop and malt aftertaste, very nicely done. Made with 11% flaked rye; gravity 13.4 P, 3.7% abw. [A, 68]

Notes

ATLAS AMBER — hazy amber, hop nose with a hint of caramel, hop and malt flavor to the finish, thereafter just dry hops; an ESB northwest-style beer; specific gravity 1.054, 3.8% abw. [A, 47]

OLD RIP OATMEAL STOUT — deep brown, roast barley aroma and flavor, medium body, medium dry malt finish, dry malt aftertaste; gravity 17.8 P, 4.8% abw. [S, 49]

OLD WOOLY PORTER — dark brown, chocolate nose, chocolate malt flavor, dry malt aftertaste with some dry hops. This ale is cask-conditioned (cellared 6 months); gravity 24 P. [P, 57]

PRIME TIME PALE ALE — gold, big off-dry malt nose; flavor is malt also but a bit drier; good body, dry malt finish and aftertaste; specific gravity 1.048 (gravity 11.8 P), 3.2% abw. [A, 50]

BHAGWANS BEST IPA — amber, hop nose, big hop flavor, good body, long dry hop aftertaste; specific gravity 1.064, 4.5% abw. [A, 67]

BIG TIME HEFEWEIZEN — hazy gold; surprisingly big nose shows some hops as well as malt and wheat; fresh lightly spicy flavor, fairly good body, good length to the dry hop aftertaste; specific gravity 1.048, 3.6% abw. [W, 53]

COAL CREEK PORTER — dark brown, rich malt nose, big balanced malty flavor, good body, long malt aftertaste, ends up fairly dry. An ale made with Chinook and Centennial hops; specific gravity 1.057, 3.9% abw. [P, 72]

OLD WOOLLY BARLEY WINE — deep brown, rich malt and alcohol nose, big body, very bold malt flavor, high alcohol, long complex malt aftertaste, a big burly brew; specific gravity 1.096, 7.7% abw. [BW, 73]

DUBLIN STOUT — deep brown, classical roasted barley and chocolate malt aroma; smooth balanced flavor features the malt, this continues into the aftertaste; a very nice easy to drink medium weight stout; specific gravity 1.048, 3.3% abw. [S, 72]

BIG TIME OLD SPICE — amber, pumpkin pie spice nose and taste, typical of the style, medium to light body; spicy finish and aftertaste shows neither malt nor hops, but is long lasting; specific gravity 1.056, 3.7% abw. [B, 62]

RAINFEST ESB — amber, hop nose; delicious hop flavor shows much Cascade hop presence; good body, long dry hop finish and long aftertaste, complex and interesting, a marvelous tasty ale; as good an ESB as I have had; made with pale, 80L crystal, Munich, and light Carastan malts; bittered with Chinook hops and aggressively finished with Cascade and Centennial hops; OG 1062, 6.2% abv, 50 IBU. [A, 93]

Bird Creek Brewery
Microbrewery in Anchorage, AK

OLD 55 PALE ALE — amber gold, big hop aroma, big hop flavor, heavy body, long dry hop aftertaste, a good well-hopped brew. It is brewed from extract with Cascade and Chinook hops, kraeusened, and cask- and bottle-conditioned; specific gravity 1.048 (gravity 12 P), 3.6% abw. [A, 72]

DENALI STYLE ALE — copper-gold, big bright Northwest hop aroma, very well-hopped palate, medium body, dry hop finish and aftertaste. [A, 70]

Birkebeiner Brewing Co.
Brewpub in Spokane, WA

FATHER HAVERMALE ALE — gold, dry hop aroma, bright dry hop flavor, light body, smooth and balanced, very dry hop aftertaste; specific gravity 1.038, 3.2% abw. [A, 63]

BIRKEBEINER GOAT BEER — dark brown, tight tan head, big dry malty flavor, good body, dry malty aftertaste; very long and stays dry to the end; specific gravity 1.080, 6% abw. [B, 72]

SASQUATCH'S FAVORITE STOUT — very dark brown, chocolate malt and roasted barley aroma; classical stout flavor is dry chocolate malt with plenty of roasted character to the malt; medium body (light for a stout); dry aftertaste is a continuation of the flavor; specific gravity 1.055, 4.2% abw. [S, 79]

BIRKEBEINER SMOKED SCOTTISH ALE — amber, aroma of faintly smoked malt; flavor is more smoky than the nose and the long aftertaste seems even more so; medium body, long duration; specific gravity 1.040, 3.1% abw. [A, 63]

Birmingham Brewing Co.
Microbrewery in Birmingham, AL

RED MOUNTAIN GOLDEN LAGER — gold, big bright hop-malt aroma and flavor, medium body, dry hop finish and aftertaste. Made with two-row malt; specific gravity 1.046 (gravity 11.4 P), 4.2% abw. [B, 58]

RED MOUNTAIN GOLDEN ALE — gold, malt aroma and flavor, good body, dry malt finish and aftertaste. It is fermented and aged as a lager brewed with two-row pale malt and European hops; gravity 11.5 P. [A, 50]

RED MOUNTAIN RED ALE — amber, lightly toasted malt aroma; malt flavor also shows some roasted barley; hops are there but stay in back; medium body,

medium length dry malt aftertaste. Made with two-row pale and roasted malts with English and America hops; gravity 12.5 P, 4.9% abw. [A, 49]

RED MOUNTAIN WHEAT BEER — gold, dull malt aroma with a chemical background; some spicy-fruity esters come up if you swirl the beverage; tinny finish, dull dry malt aftertaste. Brewed with half wheat and half barley malt; specific gravity 1.042 (gravity 10.5 P), 3.9% abw. [W, 28]

Bison Brewery
Microbrewery/Brewpub in Berkeley, CA

LEMONGRASS WHEAT — gold; sweet malty-wheaty aroma and flavor with enough lemon grass that it can be detected (but not enough to taste like Thai soup); long faintly lemony (but still off-dry) aftertaste, a sour mashed wheat ale using 57% wheat malt, a blend of Wyeast 1007 and 3068 hopped with Centennial and Cascade hops, and spiced with a touch of lemon grass; specific gravity 1.054. [W, 68]

BISON SPRING BOCK — hazy amber, pleasant light northwest hop aroma, creamy with a good mouthfeel, big bright hop flavor, plenty of supporting malt, big body, quite chewy, dry malt and hop finish, long complex malt and hop aftertaste. [BK, 86]

Notes

BISON SMOKED SCOTCH ALE — hazy dark amber; smoked sausage nose turns fruity malt; big dry smoked malt flavor, rich and pleasant, medium dry smoked malt finish, medium long dry smoked malt aftertaste; OG 1066. [A, 67]

BISON PUMPERNICKEL ALE — deep amber-brown; faint chocolate malt nose seems a little bready but that may be influenced by the name; very complex malt flavor shows chocolate, black patent, and crystal malts, but there may be others; plenty of burnt roasted flavors and some coffee tones, creamy texture, good body, long dry malt aftertaste, good interesting beer. [A, 74]

BISON HONEY-BASIL ALE — cloudy amber-gold; aroma starts out like perfumed hand soap (like Cashmere Bouquet), gradually develops some citrus-northwest hops, then clearly evolves to basil which gets more pronounced with time; spicy herbal flavor becomes identifiable as basil after a few sips; medium body; spicy herbal quality of flavor is most pronounced in the finish and aftertaste; the honey never rises to compete with the basil; made with fresh basil and hopped with Centennial and Cascade hops; 10% orange honey added at secondary racking, fermented with Wyeast Whitbread yeast; specific gravity 1.051, 5.1% abv. Tasted in bottle 8 months after bottling. [A, 53]

BISON SPRING FEST ALE — hazy amber; very nice fruity hop nose is a mild citrus orange-pineapple; big hoppy fruity flavor is very tasty; creamy texture, dry hop finish and aftertaste, a bit short except for the hops; specific gravity 1.066. [A, 55]

CORIANDER RYE ALE — deep gold, fruity citrus Northwest hop and malt aroma, spicy coriander and Northwest hop flavor; use of rye malt is not noticeable; cool and refreshing dry palate, good mouthfeel, complex and interesting, medium body, long dry spicy aftertaste; has a lot going for it. [A, 83]

The Bitter End Bistro & Brewery
Brewpub in Austin, TX

UPTOWN BROWN ALE — brown, malty aroma, dry malt flavor, medium body, light dry malt aftertaste; specific gravity 1.045, 3.4% abw, 20 IBU. [A, 47–50]

AUSTIN PALE — golden amber, light hop and malt aroma, dry hop and malt flavor, dry hop finish and aftertaste; a smooth ale that is generally dry but for a touch of background sweetness most noticeable in the aftertaste; made with Cascade and Columbus hops; specific gravity 1.056, 4.2% abw, 35 IBU. [A, 64]

SLEDGEHAMMER STOUT — deep brown, faint chocolate malt and roasted barley aroma, light flavor like the nose, light body, no depth, light chocolate malt and roasted barley aftertaste. [S, 53]

BAT CITY LAGER — amber-gold, pleasant malt and hop nose, spicy hop flavor, medium body, dry hop finish, very dry hop aftertaste. [B, 66]

BITTER END IPA — deep gold, malty nose, big off-dry malt palate, big body, long hoppy aftertaste. [A, 66]

BITTER END BITTER — amber-gold, hop aroma; smooth hop flavor is not especially bitter; medium body, dry hop finish and aftertaste. The IPA is more bitter than the Bitter. [A, 66]

EZ WHEAT — pale gold, light malt nose, light dry malt palate, light body, dry wheaty finish and aftertaste, not long. [W, 56]

Black Mountain Brewing Co.
Brewery and restaurant (Satisfied Frog) in Cave Creek, AZ

CRAZY ED'S CAVE CREEK CHILI BEER — gold, bright jalapeño pepper nose, hot jalapeño pepper taste, finish, and aftertaste. Made in bottles at Cave Creek and by Evansville B.C. under contract for distribution in various major metropolitan areas. Some early samples were found without the chili pepper in the bottle, but more recent (1992–1993) ones do have the pepper. The recipe at Cave Creek calls for gravity 11.5–12 P, 3.7–3.9% abw (4.7–4.9% abv). See Evansville for the specs on the nationally distributed product. [B, 19]

CRAZY ED'S ARIZONA PILSNER BEER — gold, bright

hop and malt nose; hop flavor is good despite some unbalance in mid-palate; vegetal malt finish, dry hop aftertaste with good length. [B, 27]

ED'S ORIGINAL CAVE CREEK BEER — gold, bright hop and malt nose, hop flavor, malt finish, dry hop aftertaste with good length. Made with two-row malted barley and Saaz hops; gravity 11.5–12 P, 3.7–3.9% abw. [B, 47]

JUANDERFUL WHEAT — hazy pale gold, light malt nose, dry malty flavor, light body, dry malt finish and aftertaste, unfiltered; 5% abw. [W, 50]

MURPHY'S MILE HIGH LAGER — gold, light malt aroma; dry malt flavor is highly carbonated, medium body, dry malt finish and aftertaste; 4.7% abw. [B, 49]

PHANTOM AMBER — pale amber, light malt nose, medium dry malt flavor, medium body, dry malt finish and aftertaste; 4.7% abw. [B, 51]

SOUTH OF THE BORDER PORTER — light brown, light malt aroma; light medium dry malt flavor shows some alcohol (7% abw); medium body; long somewhat alcoholic medium dry malt aftertaste has a background malty sweetness. [P, 58]

CRAZY ED'S BLACK MOUNTAIN GOLD PREMIUM BEER — hazy gold, pronounced hop nose, sharp hop flavor but there is plenty of malt for balance; big body, hop finish and long dry hop aftertaste. [B, 69]

DEL RICO — hazy gold; jalapeño pepper nose which comes as no surprise since there is a small jalapeño pepper in the bottle; hot jalapeño pepper and malt taste, strange, hot, and long. The pepper had no flavor or heat left, it was all in the brew by the time I got to it. [ML, 29]

CAVE CREEK CHILI LIGHT BEER — pale gold, light attractive chili-pepper aroma, light body; good jalapeño chili flavor is blended nicely with the malt; aftertaste like the main palate; the chili is done with a light hand. [LO, 52]

Blind Pig Brewing Co.
Microbrewery in Temecula, CA

BLIND PIG PALE ALE — gold, appetizing dry malt and hop aroma and taste, very smooth and balanced; dry hop aftertaste has good length; made using Irish Northdown hops for bittering; specific gravity 1.053, 4.25% abw. [A, 78]

BUTTERFIELD CANYON AMBER — amber; complex toasted malt aroma makes me think of smoked chipotle chilis; delicate roasted malt and hop flavor, dry hop finish and aftertaste; made with roasted malt and Willamette hops; specific gravity 1.065, 4% abw. [A, 67]

BLIND PIG INDIA PALE ALE — deep gold; lovely hop aroma features Cascades, Centennial, and Chinook hops; very big hop flavor, big body, some alcohol (7% abw), long dry hop aftertaste; specific gravity 1.072. [A, 68]

Notes

BLIND PIG CREAM ALE — deep gold, lovely dry hop nose, big bright dry hop flavor, very refreshing and drinkable, medium body, long dry hop aftertaste, a good appetizing and satisfying beer. [A, 72]

BLIND PIG BARLEYWINE — deep amber, great very attractive malty nose; big malty flavor has a good hop balance, good body but not huge; fairly easy to drink; shows alcohol but is not overbearing; long rich malt aftertaste, a good tasting barleywine with considerable drinkability. [BW, 74]

OLD BLUE GRANITE — hazy amber; big concentrated malt nose has good hop support; concentrated rich malt flavor is on the sweet side; big body, rich malt finish and long malt aftertaste; gravity 24 P, 70 IBU. This seems to be the latest step in the evolution of Blind Pig's Barleywine-style ale, found in bottle in late 1995. [BW, 74]

BLIND PIG GOLDEN ALE — gold, hop nose and taste, good body; assertive hop character wakes up your palate; dry hop fin-

ish and aftertaste, good length, a bright interesting brew. [A, 66]

Blue Ridge Brewing Co.
Brewpub in Charlottesville, VA

HAWKSBILL GOLDEN LAGER — gold, smooth mild hop aroma, pleasant rich malt and dry hop flavor, good body, long dry hop aftertaste; 5% abv. [B, 64]

PINEY RIVER AMBER LAGER — amber-gold, very light hop nose, medium body, light hop (Northern Brewers) flavor, long dry hop aftertaste; 5% abv. [B, 61]

AFTON ALE — amber, light hop nose, bright tangy hop palate; again Northern Brewers hops, but this time dry hopped with Eroica hops; good body, long zesty dry hop aftertaste, nicely done, some of the 5.5% alcohol shows. [A, 72]

HUMPBACK STOUT — deep brown; nose shows lots of black malt and a touch of chocolate malt; medium body, smooth complex malt flavor, long dry malt aftertaste, more like a porter than a stout. [S, 64]

Bluegrass Brewing Co.
Brewpub in Louisville, KY

BLUEGRASS ALT — amber-gold, complex malt aroma; complex dry malt flavor is not exciting; medium body, dry malt and hop aftertaste; made from 11% wheat malt, two-row, Munich, caramel-60, and a

touch of chocolate malt, with Perle and Tettnanger hops; specific gravity 1.044, 3.5% abw, SRM 12, 22 IBU. [A, 42]

DANIEL BOONE PALE ALE — amber-gold, beautiful bright hop aroma and flavor, medium body, dry hop finish and aftertaste, a very good tasty flavor; aggressive bitterness comes from Chinook, Willamette, and B.C. Kent-Goldings hops; specific gravity 1.052, 4% abw, SRM 14, 30 IBU. [A, 82]

DARK STAR PORTER — brown, dry malt aroma and taste, medium body, dry hop finish and aftertaste, long duration. [P, 68]

F.P. PILS — gold, dry hop aroma and flavor, very tasty good drinking beer, dry hop finish, very dry and very long hop aftertaste; made from two-row, caramel-10, and Carapils malts, with Perle and Tettnanger hops, and finished with Saaz hops; specific gravity 1.048, 3.74% abw, SRM 3, 15 IBU. [B, 67]

LOUISVILLE KÖLSCH — gold, light malt nose, very dry malt flavor, medium to light body; dry malt aftertaste is not long; brewed with 5% wheat, two-row, Munich, and caramel-20 malts, Perle and Mt. Hood hops; specific gravity 1.042, 3.5% abw, SRM 4, 15 IBU. [K, 48]

PADDY WHACKER OATMEAL STOUT — dark brown, dry chocolate malt and roasted barley aroma and flavor, plenty of hops in support, smooth and balanced, long complex dry malt and hop aftertaste; brewed with 10% oat flakes, two-row, caramel-60, roasted barley, and chocolate malts, and not filtered; specific gravity 1.056, 4.3% abw, SRM 50, 35 IBU. [S, 72]

SOB'S ESB — amber, bright hop aroma and flavor, medium body, dry finish and long dry hop aftertaste, specific gravity 1.052, 4.2% abw, SRM 11, 35 IBU. [A, 67]

Bluewater Brewing Co.
Brewpub in Tahoe City, CA

BEAR CLAW BROWN ALE — brown, pleasant malt and light hop aroma, smooth dry malt flavor, medium body, dry malt aftertaste; made with pale, caramel, and chocolate malts; hopped with Perle, Cascades, and Willamette hops; specific gravity 1.052, 4.2% abw. [A, 67]

EAGLE ROCK RASPBERRY — pale amber, raspberry aroma, light dry raspberry flavor, light to medium body, dry raspberry finish and aftertaste, fairly long; specific gravity 1.052, 4.2% abw. [A, 50]

MISTY MOUNTAIN OATMEAL STOUT — dark brown, big bright complex malt aroma; big but smooth and balanced flavor shows some of the oats; long dry malt aftertaste. Made with roasted barley, chocolate malt, malted wheat, and oatmeal; hopped with Cascade and Mt. Hood hops; specific gravity 1.056, 4.5% abw. [S, 74]

Bohannon Brewing Co.
Brewery in Nashville, TN

MARKET STREET PILSENER DRAFT BEER — tawny-gold, off-dry malt and CO_2 nose, creamy, zesty fruity-malt flavor, medium long malt and hop aftertaste, clean, very pleasant, and very drinkable; specific gravity 1.050, 4.2% abw. [B, 70]

MARKET STREET OKTOBERFEST — amber, hop nose; big malt flavor has plenty of supporting hops; big body, balanced, long dry malt aftertaste; made with pale and dark malts; specific gravity 1.060, 4.7% abw. [B, 63]

MARKET STREET WHEAT BEER — gold; pleasant malt nose does show some faint hops; dry malt flavor, clean American-style wheat, very refreshing, light bodied, finishes dry malt, fairly long, very quaffable. Made with 40/60 wheat and barley malt; specific gravity 1.042, 3.4% abw. [W, 50]

MARKET STREET GOLDEN ALE — deep gold; bright northwest hop aroma shows some Cascades, but is not assertive; dry hop flavor shows little malt initially but it develops with time; good body and balance, very drinkable, dry hop finish, long dry hop aftertaste with good malt support. Made with 100% two-row pale malt, Irish stout yeast, and Northwest hops; an American pale ale; gravity 11.5 P, 4.4% abv. [A, 59]

Notes

Bootlegger's Brewing Co.
Brewpub in Bakersfield, CA

BOOTLEGGER'S BIG RED ALE — reddish-amber, faint malt aroma, good malt and hop flavor, big body, dry hop finish and aftertaste, very dry at the end and medium long. [A, 54]

BOOTLEGGER'S RASPBERRY ALE — hazy gold, big rising raspberry aroma, dry raspberry flavor; short dry aftertaste has very little raspberry remaining, mostly just dry hops. [A, 34]

VOLUPTUOUS BLONDE ALE — gold, malty nose; dry malty flavor has a sweetness in back that comes out more in the finish; medium length, light to medium body, very quaffable. There seems to be a connection to Frugatti's Voluptuous Blonde Ale from interior decorations showing that label and Frugatti's Big Red Ale labels made by Minnesota B.C. under contract. [A, 47]

BOOTLEGGER'S SUMMER WHEAT ALE — cloudy gold, faint malt aroma, extremely dry malty flavor, dry hop finish; dry aftertaste is almost bracing but has no specific hop character; short and very quaffable. [W, 40]

ST. PATRICK'S DAY IRISH RED ALE — copper-amber, light malty nose; tangy hop flavor up front, then goes very dry losing the bright hop character that started the palate; smooth, medium to good body, medium long very dry aftertaste, a good unfiltered ale. [A, 68]

34TH STREET PORTER — brown, light roasted-caramel nose, very dry roasted malt flavor, medium body, dry malty finish and aftertaste, quite short. [P, 50]

Boscos Pizza Kitchen & Brewery
Brewpub in Germantown, TN

TENNESSEE CREAM ALE — deep gold, malt aroma, dry malt flavor; hops stay in back, come out a bit in the finish and aftertaste; overall dry and malty, somewhat brief on the palate; made with pale, Munich, caramel, and carapils malts, with Perle and Tettnanger hops; specific gravity 1.042, 3.5% abw. [A, 53]

BLUFF CITY AMBER — amber, dry malt nose, dry malt flavor, good complex malt and hop character, medium to long dry hop (Cascades) aftertaste; specific gravity 1.056, 4.5% abw. [A, 68]

GERMANTOWN ALT — deep amber; crisp dry aroma and flavor shows both the malt and hops; long dry aftertaste is more malt than hops; specific gravity 1.048, 3.8% abw. [A, 62]

BOSCOS WHEAT BEER — gold, good malty aroma, light dry malt flavor, light body, good length to dry malt aftertaste; specific gravity 1.046, 3.7% abw. [W, 54]

Boston Beer Works
Brewpub in Boston, MA

BOSTON RED — amber, good dry well-hopped aroma; big hop and malt flavor is extremely complex; four malts (Vienna, wheat, black, and crystal) Yakima Northern Brewer and Hallertau hops, and alt yeast all contribute to that complexity; long dry malt aftertaste; specific gravity 1.050, 4.3% abw. [A, 82]

KENMORE KÖLSCH — medium gold, light malt nose; bright malt flavor shows some of the wheat (10% wheat malt); good body, very smooth, light long medium dry malt aftertaste. Made with alt yeast and American Hallertau hops; specific gravity 1.042, 3.1% abw. [K, 68]

ACME LIGHT — pale gold, clean malt nose, very dry hoppy flavor (Tettnanger), medium body, long dry hop aftertaste; specific gravity 1.036. [LO, 53]

RASPBERRY ALE — deep gold, light malt flavor with just a hint of raspberry; bright fruity malt flavor (would have trouble recognizing the raspberry on the palate); light body, finish is more fruity than raspberry, light dry malt aftertaste, very refreshing pleasant easy-to-drink beer; specific gravity 1.036. [A, 58]

BUCKEYE OATMEAL STOUT — opaque brown, rich complex malt nose, dry malt flavor (very dry), medium body, fairly short dry malt aftertaste.

Made with ale yeast, four types of malt (pale, wheat, chocolate, and roasted barley), and 20% flaked oatmeal; specific gravity 1.052, 4.4% abw. [S, 73]

BEANTOWN NUT BROWN ALE — ruby-brown, big malt nose and taste, similar to the stout, but no so dry; good body, fairly long dry malt aftertaste. Made with chocolate, crystal, and wheat malts; specific gravity 1.050, 3.7% abw. [A, 72]

BLUEBERRY ALE — deep gold, very much a berry nose, somewhat candylike, flavor like the nose, finishes dry; very long dry malt aftertaste, but the berry is in behind all the way through. The berries have been marinated in Hercules Strong Ale and the brew is hopped with American Hallertau. [A, 63]

FENWAY PARK PALE ALE — copper-gold, light malt and hop nose, big bright balanced malt and hop flavor, good body, very drinkable, smooth, mellow, dry, delicious; long dry hop aftertaste is a continuation of the good flavor; a beautiful brew. Made with three different malts and four varieties of hops, plus sugar in the kettle. It is then dry hopped with British Columbia Goldings hops; specific gravity 1.048, 4.0% abw. [A, 65]

HERCULES STRONG ALE — deep amber-gold, honeyed fruity malt aroma, some apricot in back, low carbonation, huge body, very complex enormous malt flavor, noticeable alcohol, almost viscous, extremely long and strong chocolate malt and hop aftertaste, great sipping brew; a blockbuster beer that I could get stuck on very easily. Considered a barleywine by the brewer, this ale is made with pale and Munich malt, sucrose, and Chinook hops, and is dry hopped; specific gravity 1.098, 7.6% abw. [BW, 93]

BACK BAY IPA — golden-amber, great malt-hop aroma and flavor, bright, complex, and zesty, big body, full flavored, very long dry hop aftertaste, a winner. Made with five malts (pale, wheat, Carapils, Vienna,and chocolate), Centennial hops, and dry hopped with Cascades; specific gravity 1.060, 6.5% abw. [A, 74]

GREAT PUMPKIN ALE — orange-amber, light pumpkin pie spice aroma and flavor, medium body, spicy off-dry pumpkin pie aftertaste. It is made using pumpkins with the spices added to the kettle; specific gravity 1.047, 3.6% abw. [A, 53]

CURLEY'S IRISH STOUT — deep brown, huge tight head, chocolate malt and roasted barley nose; big dry flavor also shows the components of the aroma; complex dry malty finish, long long aftertaste, absolutely delicious. Made with pale malt, roasted barley, flaked barley, and Golding hops; specific gravity 1.050, 5.5% abw. [S, 83]

CENTENNIAL ALT — amber, big hop and malt aroma, bright snappy malt and hop flavor, smooth and tasty, medium to good body, long dry hop finish and aftertaste. [A, 60]

BLUEBERRY ALE — deep gold, fruity aroma not immediately recognizable as blueberry, clearly blueberries on the palate, medium body, fairly dry berry finish and aftertaste, long with the berry taste staying throughout. [A, 63]

Boston Beer Co.
Brewery in Boston, MA. Facilities of Pittsburgh B.C., F.X. Matt B.C., and G. Heileman B.C. used for regional package production.

SAMUEL ADAMS BOSTON LAGER — golden amber, zesty malt and hop aroma, complex dry hop flavor, plenty of malt in the flavor and in the long aftertaste, good balance throughout, an excellent brew, probably the best of the nationally available brands. The brew is dry hopped with Hallertau-Mittelfrüh hops; starting gravity 13 P (1050), 3.6% abw. [B, 79]

BOSTON LIGHTSHIP — tawny-gold, big luscious off-dry malt nose, big dry malt flavor, dry hop finish, light body, long dry malt aftertaste, good thirst quencher, one of the most flavorful of the low-calorie beers. Made with Saaz, Hallertau-Mittelfrüh, and Tettnanger hops; 2.9% abw. [LO, 62]

SAMUEL ADAMS DOUBLE BOCK DARK LAGER — deep amber, big fruity toasted malt nose, huge body, big chocolate malt flavor, long and delicious, a chewy lip-smacker. Made with Saaz and Tettnanger hops; 8.5% abv. [BK, 87]

SAMUEL ADAMS 1989 WINTER LAGER — amber, rich malt nose, lovely toasted malt and hop flavor, terrific balance, good body, smooth, very tasty, long and delicious; ends surprisingly dry for a big malty brew. This is my favorite from Jim Koch's repetoire. [B, 80]

SAMUEL ADAMS WINTER LAGER 1990–1991 — amber, big toasted malt aroma, bold toasted malt and hop flavor, balanced, complex, very drinkable, and long ending with an extended dry malt aftertaste. [B, 84]

SAMUEL ADAMS WINTER LAGER 1991–1992 — amber, big complex aroma with plenty of malt and hops, huge malt and hop flavor, big body, noticeable alcohol, great complex hop finish and a long dry hop aftertaste. Although different each year, every one is a star. [B, 89]

SAMUEL ADAMS WINTER LAGER 1992–1993 — amber, interesting complex malt and hop aroma, very smooth, good body, easy to drink, dry hop finish, long dry hop aftertaste, excellent balance throughout. It is a dark wheat bock, brewed with extra barley malt. Kent-Goldings hops are added early and Saaz and Tettnanger are added late. [B, 76]

SAM ADAMS WINTER LAGER 1993–1994 — hazy amber, light fruity malt nose, interesting fruity malt and subtle hop flavor, complex, medium body; delicious aftertaste is complex fruity malt with a distinct hop character. Same recipe holds as above. [B, 73]

SAMUEL ADAMS WINTER LAGER 1994–1995 — amber, lovely malty aroma, complex malt flavor with plenty of hops, good flavor, good balance, beautiful stylish finish; leaves your mouth feeling good; long complex aftertaste, grows on you, no warts on this one. Same recipe holds as above. [B, 83]

SAMUEL ADAMS WINTER LAGER 1995–1996 — amber, complex malt and hop aroma features the malt; big complex flavor shows an abundance of both malt and hops; balanced, rich, and satisfying, nutty finish and long nutty aftertaste, nicely done. [B, 82]

SAMUEL ADAMS OCTOBERFEST SPECIAL BREW — hazy amber, zesty hop nose, tangy hop palate with good malt backing, very drinkable and very long dry hop aftertaste. Another lip-smacker, but a bit smaller than the double bock which makes it more drinkable and better with food. Extra roasted crystal malt gives it its color and character. [B, 72]

SAMUEL ADAMS BOSTON STOCK ALE — pale amber, complex toasted malt and hop nose; front palate is hops, middle is fruity malt; has dry and off-dry components present at the same time in a complex mix; extremely long malt aftertaste with a background hint of pine. Extremely interesting and pleasant brew that is fair competition to the Boston Lager where they are both available. This ale gets its earthy flavors from Fuggles and Goldings hops from Kent and its spicy bitterness and aroma from Saaz hops. [B, 81]

SAMUEL ADAMS WHEAT BREW — deep gold, zesty spicy clove aroma, medium spicy-lactic flavor, pleasant and refreshing, light body, fairly short aftertaste like the flavor; a German-style weizen but done with a light hand. Weihenstephan top-fermenting wheat beer yeast, a blend of wheat and barley malt, and Tettnanger and Saaz hops are used; 3.4% abw. [W, 47]

SAMUEL ADAMS CRANBERRY LAMBIC — amber, fruity aroma, fruity-berry tart flavor, long dry tart aftertaste. This brew is made with fruit, wheat and barley malt, and top-fermenting yeast. The wheat portion is fermented a second time with fresh cranberries and maple syrup is added to balance the tartness of the fruit; 3.4% abw. Tasted again as the 1993 issue, the color was peachy-amber, aroma was malt with hops in back showing no fruit; flavor is tart cranberry with a sweet-sour fruit background; dries at finish, short dry aftertaste. [L, 47]

SAMUEL ADAMS DUNKEL WEIZEN — brown, tangy hop aroma, zesty spicy flavor, spicy finish, and long well-spiced aftertaste, a real European-style weizenbier. Tasted on draft. Made with a special roasted wheat malt. [W, 62]

SAMUEL ADAMS CREAM STOUT — deep brown, dry roasted barley and chocolate malt nose and taste; malt is almost burnt; faint chocolate malt in back, medium body, smooth, dry malt finish, fairly long dry malt aftertaste. This is a top-fermented beer containing chocolate malt and roasted barley using Kent-Goldings hops only during the boil. It is long-conditioned. [S, 71]

SAMUEL ADAMS DARK WHEAT — amber, aroma of roasted barley, carbon dioxide, and soap, smooth roasted barley flavor with a little orange peel in the finish, medium to light body, lightly spiced aftertaste with dry roasted wheat at the end. This is the bottled version of the Dunkel Weizen, made with a Bavarian weizen yeast. [W, 43]

SAMUEL ADAMS BRIDAL ALE — brilliant deep gold; zesty spicy nose has an orange component; bright refreshing spicy malt flavor, medium to light body, very smooth and likable, light spicy orange-malt aftertaste, not long. This is a wheat beer flavored with coriander and orange, like a Wit or white beer. It does have some added spiciness from the fermentation that gives it clove and banana tones and more complexity. Tasted on draft. [A, 65]

**SAMUEL ADAMS BROWN
ALE** — light brown, malty aroma
and taste, medium to good body, dry
malt finish and aftertaste. Brewed
with pale, caramel, and chocolate
malts; hopped with Northern Brewers and Kent-Goldings; gravity 12 P,
3.5% abw. [A, 53]

**SAMUEL ADAMS TRIPLE
BOCK** — dark ruby-amber-
brown, legs on the glass like a
high gravity sherry (gravity
38–44 P), low to medium carbonation (varies from cask to cask),
complex port wine–Pedro
Ximinez sherry and
Worcestershire sauce aroma; huge
complex flavor is very sherrylike;
high in alcohol (over 11% abv),
huge body; definitely like a sherry
or a port wine; rich and very long.
Long aged (approx. four months)
on champagne yeast in old
wooden bourbon casks, this beer
is more winelike than any other
I've tasted. Actually would be
better if it were longer aged.
Tasted many times on draft and,
since late 1994, in bottle. [BK, 95]

**SAMUEL ADAMS HONEY
PORTER** — very deep amber,
slightly sweet faintly chocolate
malt aroma with a light honey and
toasted background, flavors follow
on from the nose and flow nicely
together, palate finishes sweeter
but more complex than the flavor,
good body; long long aftertaste
finally shows the hops; excellent
effort, very enjoyable brew. [P, 76]

**SAMUEL ADAMS
HEFEWEIZEN** — very cloudy
gold; aroma has a slightly stinky
component; spicy lactic flavor,
finishes very dry, lactic drops in
behind the malt at the end, light
body, fair length, representative of
style. Tasted on draft. [W, 57]

**SAMUEL ADAMS SUMMER
WHEAT BEER** — golden with a
touch of amber; zesty fruity off-
dry malt aroma is fairly big; tasty
malty flavor has a hop background
and stays dry despite indications
to the contrary from the nose; finishes dry hops leading into a long
smooth very dry hop aftertaste.
Found on draft. In bottle, it had a
delightfully fresh malt nose, dry
malt flavor, light body, dull dry
malt aftertaste. [W, 56]

**SAMUEL ADAMS SCOTCH
ALE** — dark amber (brilliant garnet); lovely malty aroma has a
touch of smokiness; smooth malty
flavor is like the nose but shows
more of the smoke and has a little
sweetness in back; very smooth
with a sense of alcohol, medium
body, lightly smoked off-dry malt
finish and aftertaste, excellent balance, should go well with food;

nicely done using Fuggles and
Goldings hops. [A, 73]

OLD FEZZIWIG ALE — brilliant
amber; faint aroma is mostly cinnamon and ginger; light spicy palate shows little beery quality;
medium length, light body, overall
a bit dull; supposed to be made
with chocolate and caramel malt
but they don't show. [A, 33]

**SAMUEL ADAMS CHERRY
WHEAT** — hazy amber-gold;
maraschino cherry aroma, reminds
you of a chocolate covered cherry;
dry cherry taste, dry finish and aftertaste shows some creamy malt;
well-made; if compelled to make a
cherry flavored beer for some rea-
son this would be about the best you
could expect. Made with cherries
and cherry juice. [W, 53]

Boulder Creek Brewing Co. / Boulder Creek Grill & Cafe
Microbrewery and brewpub in Boulder Creek, CA

ST. SEVERINS KÖLSCH — pale
gold, nice malt nose, dry hop flavor, finish, and aftertaste, pretty
good kölsch-style beer; gravity
11.75 P, 3.75% abw. [K, 52]

**OLD MACLUNKS SCOTTISH
ALE** — amber, hop nose and flavor,
plenty of malt but only in support of
the hops; malt more noticeable in
the finish and aftertaste where it
provides a good balance with the
dry hops, good length; gravity
12.5 P; 3.5% abw. [A, 51]

Boulevard Brewing Co.
Microbrewery in Kansas City, MO

BOULEVARD IRISH ALE — amber; aroma is similar to the pale ale but fainter and drier; big dry roasted malt flavor has complexity, collapses in the middle, but returns for a good finish. The aftertaste is somewhat dull. [A, 52]

BOULEVARD PALE ALE — hazy amber-gold, big fruity ale nose, a bit of orange peel in back, tangy light hop flavor, big body; a lot of extract showing but the flavor is on the light side; dry hop finish and aftertaste. Made with Harrington two-row, British Carastan (30L), and British Crystal (60L) malts using infusion mash; specific gravity 1.049, 3.8% abw. [A, 47]

BULLY! PORTER — dark brown, roasted barley and chocolate malt nose, burnt roasted barley flavor, medium body, dry finish, long dry faintly burnt aftertaste. Made with unmalted winter wheat; specific gravity 1.058, 4.31% abw. [P, 50]

BOULEVARD UNFILTERED WHEAT — gold, light malty aroma and taste, light body, very lightly hopped, smooth and dry, light dry malty aftertaste, medium length. Made with 28% unmalted winter wheat; specific gravity 1.046, 3.63% abw. [W, 41]

BOB'S '47 MUNICH STYLE LAGER — amber-gold; good dry and complex aroma and flavor shows both malt and hops but a tad more of the malt; dry hop fin-ish and aftertaste; uses low alpha hops Hersbrucker, Strisselspalt, and Cluster; specific gravity 1.054, 4.25% abw. [B, 65]

Brandon Brewing Co.
Microbrewery in Brandon, OR

BRANDON SCOTCH ALE — dark amber, pleasant malt and hop nose, malty flavor, medium body, some dry hops in the finish, dry malty aftertaste; made with English pale ale malt and roasted barley; hopped with Cascade and Saaz hops; lagered 4 months; OG 1071, FG 1.013, 28 IBU, 7% abv. [A, 61]

Brazos Brewing Co.
Brewpub in College Station, TX

NURSE SHARK WHEAT — gold, wheaty malt aroma, smooth and soft malty flavor, light to medium body; ends very dry but malty not hoppy; very long dry malt aftertaste; made with 40% wheat malt. [W, 59]

HARVEST MOON ALE — bright gold, lightly hopped Fuggles and malt aroma, light faint malt and dry hop flavor, medium body, long dry hop aftertaste. [A, 59]

TEXAS SUNSET AMBER ALE — amber, malt and faint Cascade hop nose; smooth mostly malty flavor has a light hop backing; medium body, dry hop and malt finish and aftertaste, good length. [A, 57]

BLACKWELDER'S IPA — medium deep gold, big hop nose, bright hop flavor, long spicy hop aftertaste, medium body, pronounced hop character throughout, dry hopped. [A, 76]

BRAZOS RIVERBOTTOM STOUT — deep amber-brown; roasted malt aroma has some chocolate malt, smooth roasted malt flavor; medium to good body; smooth and soft but has a richness as well; long dry roasted malt aftertaste. [S, 59]

Breckenridge Brewery
Brewpub in Breckenridge, CO

BRECKENRIDGE INDIA PALE ALE — hazy amber, creamy, soapy citrus malt nose, light malt flavor with a hop and citrus background, dry hop finish, very very long pleasant complex dry hop and malt aftertaste, well-made brew. Made with pale, Munich, and caramel malts; brewed with Washington Perle, Willamette, and British Columbia Bramling hops. It is dry hopped with Bramling and Czechoslovakian Saaz hops; gravity 14.0 P, 4.6–4.8% abw, SRM 7.5, 60 IBU. [A, 78]

BRECKENRIDGE MOUNTAIN WHEAT — pale hazy gold, lemony spicy malt aroma, spicy malt flavor, finish, and aftertaste. Made with 60% malted wheat and 40% two-row pale malt; hopped with Washington Hallertau and Czech Saaz hops; gravity 12.5 P, 4.2–4.4% abw, SRM 4.5, 17 IBU. [W, 47]

AVALANCHE ALE — gold, fruity malt nose and flavor, hops stay in back, dry malt finish and aftertaste. Some bottled versions had an acidic backtaste. Better samples had a concentrated malt nose with lots of esters, strong estery-alcohol flavor with a trace of acetone, and a long estery aftertaste that was noticeable right down into your throat. Made with pale, Munich, chocolate and caramel malts and has a blend of Chinook, Willamette, and Washington Tettnanger hops; brewed with Whitbread yeast; gravity 13.5 P, 4.5% abw, SRM 9.5, 18 IBU. [A, 62]

BRECKENRIDGE OATMEAL STOUT — deep brown, classic roasted barley and chocolate malt nose, good tasting flavor like the aroma, very dry and very long, a good stout. Brewed with caramel, chocolate, and black malts, 10% roasted barley, and 10% oatmeal, using Washington Chinook and Perle hops; gravity 13.0 P, 4.0% abw, SRM 11.0, 45 IBU. [S, 64]

BLUE RIVER BOCK — amber, hop and off-dry malt aroma; flavor is big bright hops well backed with an off-dry malt; finishes dry malt, and has more of a dry hop aftertaste; a very bright refreshing beer made with caramel malt; gravity 17.0 P, 6.0% abw, SRM 22, 20 IBU. [BK, 79]

BRECKENRIDGE MÄRZEN OKTOBERFEST — deep gold, big malt nose and taste, clean, fresh, and long. This brew is hopped with German Hallertau and Washington Tettnanger hops, and brewed with

caramel and chocolate malt; gravity 13 P. [B, 52]

BRECKENRIDGE HEFE-WEIZEN — hazy gold; light malt aroma and flavor is faintly spicy; light body, malty finish, medium long light dry malt aftertaste. [W, 54]

AUTUMN ALE OKTOBERFEST — amber, big hop aroma, smoked malt flavor, medium body, light smoked malt aftertaste, long dry smoky aftertaste. Brewed with chocolate and caramel malts, hopped with German Hallertau and Washington Tettnanger hops; gravity 15.3 P, 6.75% abw. [A, 36]

ASPEN SILVER CITY ALE — pale gold, malt nose, light malt and dry hop flavor; doesn't taste "clean"; medium body, short light dry aftertaste, not refreshing. Made for Aspen Beer Co., apparently replacing contract previously held by Rockies Brewing Co. (new name of Boulder B.C.). [A, 45]

BRECKENRIDGE CHRISTMAS ALE 1995 — dark amber, off-dry malty aroma, alcohol and sweet malt flavor; taste doesn't develop; medium body; sweet malt aftertaste still shows the alcohol. Found in full liter swing-top bottle. [A, 45]

Brew Moon
Brewpub in Boston, MA

MOONLIGHT ALE — gold, faint malt aroma; light malt flavor borders on the sweet side (without actually being sweet); light body (almost watery), light dry hop finish and aftertaste, medium length, and is sweetest at the end. Made with two-row pale malt and flaked maize; hopped with Hallertau, Tettnanger, Fuggles, Willamette, and Cascade hops. [A, 47]

BOSTON SPECIAL
RESERVE — pale gold, grainy light nose, light malt flavor, light body; ends dry but doesn't show much hopping anywhere. It is a light pilsener made entirely with two-row pale malt and hopped with Hallertau, Fuggles, and Tettnanger hops; gravity 14 P. [B, 43]

ORION'S RED ALE — reddish-amber, malty aroma and flavor, light to medium body, dry malt finish; hops show a bit in the brief aftertaste. It is not as robust as is touted on the descriptive beer menu, and is made using two-row pale, caramel-40, and Carapils malts; hopped with Cascades, Willamette, Hallertau, and Tettnanger hops. [A, 47]

GRASSHOPPER IPA — amber, bright malty aroma; big ale-like malt flavor shows some hopping; good body; hops gain at the finish but the flavor is best described as strong off-dry malt; bright hoppy aftertaste is drier than the palate and has some length; gravity 15 P. [A, 60]

ECLIPSE EXTRA STOUT — dark brown, chocolate malt and roasted barley aroma, smooth palate like the nose, medium body, light for a stout but good tasting; dry finish and aftertaste takes on a chocolate-coffee character with roasted chocolate at the end; good duration. Although the flavor is that of a stout, the body makes it seem more like a porter. It is made with 60% pale malt, with caramel-40, Carapils, and roasted barley hopped with Cascades; gravity 18 P. [S, 56]

DIRTY WATERS ALE — dark amber, dry malt nose; odd dry malt flavor seems a bit "dirty-earthy"; medium body, dry malt and light hop finish and aftertaste, medium length. [A, 40]

The Brewery at 34 Depot St.
Brewpub in Pittsfield, MA

IRONWORKS INDIA PALE ALE — deep amber-gold, light sweet hop aroma; bright hoppy flavor has a sweet malt backing; good body, long complex medium dry malt and hop aftertaste; made with Willamette and Cascade hops, finished with Kent-Goldings; OG 1058. [A, 79]

LENOX HALF STOCK RED ALE — dark amber; light dry hop aroma has a good malt backing; flavor like the nose, good balance, medium body, complex and tasty, medium dry long hop and malt aftertaste; an Irish-style red ale made with Fuggles and Willamette hops, finished with Kent-Goldings; OG 1052. [A, 74]

Brewmasters Pub Restaurant & Brewery
Brewpub in Kenosha, WI

KENOSHA GOLD — deep gold, hop aroma and clean hop taste, good body, smooth and light, very dry hop finish and aftertaste. Made with two-row American and Belgian specialty malts; specific gravity 1.046, 3.8% abw. [B, 63]

JOHNSON'S HONEY LAGER — gold, honeyed malt aroma and flavor, good body, dry malt finish and aftertaste. Made with two-row American malt, flaked maize, and honey; hopped with Centennial and Tettnanger hops; specific gravity 1.060, 5.3% abw. [B, 47]

AMBER VIENNA STYLE — golden amber, complex malt and hop aroma; bright hop flavor shows good malt; dry hop and malt finish goes very dry in the aftertaste. Made with American two-row and Belgian Munich malt, boiled with Centennial, and finished with Tettnanger hops; specific gravity 1.052, 4.5% abw. [B, 64]

OKTOBERFEST ALT — brown, big fruity malt aroma and taste, very complex, off-dry malt finish, dry malt aftertaste. Made with six-row and two-row malts and Saaz hops; gravity 15.5 P, 5.25% abw. [A, 57]

ROYAL DARK — amber-brown; malt aroma is a bit off-dry, slightly sweet malt palate, good body; there is a little hop bite in the finish, long slightly off-dry malt aftertaste. Made with American two-row and Belgian specialty malts; specific gravity 1.050, 4.5% abw. [B, 48]

PIKE CREEK AMBER — amber, hop aroma, light malt and hop flavor, medium to good body, soft and smooth, dry hop finish and aftertaste, a Vienna style made with Tettnanger hops; OG 1052. [B, 60]

Brewmeisters Brewpub and Grill
Brewpub in Palm Springs, CA

DESERT MIST PALE ALE — very pale gold, light hop aroma and flavor, dry hop finish and medium long dry hop aftertaste; nothing stands out and what is there is very light. [A, 45]

MOONLIGHT AMBER ALE — hazy amber, smooth dry hop aroma and flavor, medium body, very smooth, but fairly light flavored, long dry hop aftertaste, good with food. [A, 47]

BLACK WIDOW DARK ALE — deep amber, faint malt nose; malty flavor is very lightly hopped; dry malt finish and aftertaste, medium length. [A, 50]

CHOCOLATE COFFEE PORTER — deep brown, almost opaque; coffee is first evident to the nose then the chocolate malt; dry coffee-like flavor is pleasant and smooth; medium body, fairly long aftertaste is dry but retains the coffee-chocolate. [P, 62]

Brewpub / Café on the Square
Brewpub and café in San Marcos, TX

MOORE'S MILD ALE — brown, tan head, bright hoppy aroma; flavor starts out hoppy with a sweetness in back, this sweetness develops into a rich malty concentration by mid-palate, and a long off-dry smooth malty aftertaste; medium body, a typical English "mild." [A, 66]

Bricktown Brewery
Brewpub in Oklahoma City, OK

COPPERHEAD PREMIUM ALE — copper color, light malt and hop aroma; flavor is light malt and hops but has complexity; medium to light body, smooth and tasty, light hop finish, light dry hop aftertaste; specific gravity 1.042, 3.2% abw. [A, 65]

BISON WEIZEN — gold, malt aroma, light malt flavor with only a sense of hops, light body, fairly short light malt aftertaste; specific gravity 1.036, 3.0% abw. [W, 50]

LAND RUN LAGER — pale gold, light malt aroma and flavor, lightly hop finish, light body; light malt aftertaste has little duration. Made with Saaz hops; specific gravity 1.042, 3.2% abw. [B, 47]

RED BRICK ALE — amber, light roasted malt aroma and flavor, hop finish, lightly hopped off-dry malt aftertaste. Made with Chinook, Cluster, and Cascade hops; specific gravity 1.044, 3.2% abw. [A, 48]

BRICKTOWN STOUT — dark brown, chocolate malt and roasted barley nose, flavor like the nose, but very light, light body for a stout, complex but brief aftertaste. Made with six malts and three hop varieties; specific gravity 1.045, 3.2% abw. [S, 51]

Bridgeport Brewing Co.
Brewery and brewpub in Portland, OR

BRIDGEPORT BLUE HERON PALE ALE — amber, malt and faint citrus nose, off-dry lightly toasted malt flavor, good body, pleasant, good malt finish, long dry slightly smoked malt aftertaste with very dry hops at the end; complex, well-balanced brew. [A, 73]

BRIDGEPORT COHO PACIFIC LIGHT ALE — light amber, complex toasted malt and hop aroma, very dry flavor just like the nose, good body, dry hop finish and long dry hop aftertaste, well-made, very drinkable, and very good with food. [A, 73]

BRIDGEPORT PALE ALE — deep amber, big fruity and well-roasted malt aroma and flavor, round, rich, alcoholic, beautiful taste, good body, good balance, very drinkable; unfortunately it is brief on the palate. [A, 90]

BRIDGEPORT OLD KNUCKLEHEAD BARLEYWINE STYLE ALE — deep reddish amber, lovely toasted malt aroma, big rich complex off-dry malt flavor, some alcohol, strong and with lots of different tastes, big body; dry malt finish with hops coming in for balance; long dry malt aftertaste with plenty of hops, a wonderful beer of the barleywine style. [BW, 98]

BRIDGEPORT PINTAIL ESB ALE — hazy amber, fruity-estery-buttery nose; palate is mild hops up front, but is bittersweet and astringent at the finish; long bitter hop aftertaste, not really a pleasant brew even for those who prefer strong hops; harsh and unbalanced at the end. I've tried this in many bottled samples and on draft at the brewpub with the same results. [A, 49]

ST. JOHN'S GOLDEN ALE — amber-gold, bright hop aroma; zesty hop flavor has good malt support; complex, tasty, likable, long dry hop aftertaste; made from two-row pale, honey, and Munich malts; hopped with Czech Saaz and German Spalts hops; OG 1044, FG 1.012, 3.6% abv, 45 IBU. Tasted at Oregon Brewers Festival and at the pub on draft. [A, 80]

BRIDGEPORT NUT BROWN ALE — deep amber-red-brown (garnet), malty nose; smooth malty flavor, not strong, just pleasant and drinkable; roasted malt shows best in the aftertaste. Tasted in the pub on draft. [A, 65]

XX DUBLINER STOUT — very dark brown, brown head, chocolate malt and roasted barley nose, smooth rich roasted malt flavor, good body, dry roasted malt finish and aftertaste. Tasted in the pub on draft. [S, 74]

BLUE HERON PALE ALE (CASK CONDITIONED) — dark amber, carbonic malt and hop aroma, very smooth, medium body; good flavor shows both malt and hops in balance; ends with a dry malt and hop aftertaste. Tasted on draft at the pub. [A, 65]

BRIDGEPORT NUT BROWN ALE — dark amber, complex malt and hop aroma, delicious fresh malt and hop flavor, balanced, smooth, and dry, long nutty aftertaste, a most attractive and drinkable brew. [A, 52]

Bridger Brewing Co.
Microbrewery in Belgrade, MT

BRIDGER GOLD — amber, malt aroma, dry malt flavor, medium body, dry malt and hop aftertaste, a fairly complex altbier with an ale-like tang in the background of the palate; fermented warm with a German ale yeast, then aged cold; specific gravity 1.046, 4% abw. [A, 53]

BRIDGER HARVEST — cold, yeasty nose, dry malt palate, medium body, dry malt finish and aftertaste; made with wheat and barley, a lager yeast and aged cold; specific gravity 1.046, 4% abw. [W, 53]

Broad Ripple Brewing Co.
Brewpub in Indianapolis, IN

BROAD RIPPLE ESB — tawny gold, hop nose and taste, very dry, good body, dry hop finish, long dry hop aftertaste, smoothly hopped all across the palate; gravity 12.25 P (1.045). [A, 63]

BROAD RIPPLE IPA — gold, strong hop nose, big hop flavor, quite highly hopped, good body, dry hop finish and long dry hop aftertaste. Made with Pale and Crystal malts and Cluster and British Columbia Kent hops; gravity 15 P. [A, 80]

BROAD RIPPLE PORTER — brown, caramel malt aroma, dull malt flavor, short dry malt aftertaste; gravity 14.25 P (1.055). [P, 41]

BROAD RIPPLE KÖLSCH — tawny-gold, big malt and hop nose, huge dry hop flavor, good body; long dry hop aftertaste retains much of the strength of the flavor. Hopped with Hallertau and Saaz hops; starting gravity 11.5 P. [K, 53]

BROAD RIPPLE INDIA PALE ALE — deep gold, big bright hop nose, plenty of malt to balance; big flavor has both malt and hops with malt dominating at first then the hops come in to balance very nicely; big and bright, very big body, dry hoppy finish; big hop aftertaste is very long and good. This may be their best effort to date. [A, 80]

The Broadway Brewing Co.
Microbrewery in Denver, Co. Makes bottled beer for Crested Butte B.C. and Wynkoop B.C.

WHITE BUFFALO PEACE ALE — bright gold, faint fruity malt nose, light fruity malt flavor, light to medium body, dry light hop finish and aftertaste. See Crested Butte B.C. [A, 46]

RED LADY ALE — dark red-amber, light northwest hop aroma, light bright and refreshing hop flavor, good malt support, medium body, pleasant light dry hop finish and aftertaste, very drinkable. See Crested Butte B.C. [A, 62]

Brooker Creek Grille & Taproom
Brewpub in Palm Harbour, FL

HIGH SKY ALE — dark amber, roasted malt and Cascade hop nose, huge roasted malt and Cascade hop flavor, huge body, long rich malt and Cascade hop aftertaste; enormous full-flavored and full-bodied brew made using 50L crystal caramalt, English ale yeast, and plenty of Cascade hops. [A, 97]

NORTH BAY BAVARIAN WHEAT ALE — hazy gold, rich malty nose; a big lush flavor shows plenty of malt and hops; very big body (enormous for a wheat beer), long dry hop aftertaste, refreshing although big and bold; made with English pale malt and dextrin wheat fermented with Wyeast 305b. This is the heaviest bodied wheat ale I can ever recall tasting. [W, 88]

Buckhead Brewery
Brewpub in Tallahassee, FL

WILDERNESS WHEAT — hazy gold; dry malty aroma has a light faintly fruity background which may be from a dash of raspberry supposed to be in the recipe; light body, dry malt flavor shows none of the berry; dry malt finish and aftertaste; good length, but still no raspberry showing on the palate. [W, 58]

SOUTHERN BELLE ALE — pale gold, light malty aroma, light malt flavor with a hint of honey up front, medium body, attractive hop tang at the finish, dry hop aftertaste; palate is just a tad too sweet. [A, 52]

PANTHER PALE ALE — deep gold, light hop aroma; dry hop flavor is Northern Brewer and Willamette hops; medium body, dry hop finish and aftertaste. [A, 60]

RED HILLS AMBER — amber, malt nose, light dry hop flavor, medium to light body, dry malt finish and aftertaste, not long. [A, 49]

SEMINOLE STOUT — deep amber, smooth malty aroma and flavor; some of the rolled oats show on the palate; medium body; palate stays dry and has some light roasted character; very drinkable and well made with a fine balance. [S, 79]

Buffalo Brewing Co.
Microbrewery and Abbott Square brewpub in Lackawanna/Buffalo, NY

BUFFALO LAGER — tawny-gold, malt-hop nose, dry hop flavor and aftertaste, medium length; OG 1048, 3.8% abw. [B, 53]

BUFFALO PILS — tawny-gold, complex bright and pleasant hop and off-dry malt nose; front palate is big dry hops; malt comes in to support at mid-palate; good body, good complexity, long and very drinkable; specific gravity 1.056, 4.4% abw. [B, 64]

Notes

LIMERICK'S IRISH STYLE RED ALE — hazy amber, hoppy ale nose, bright and balanced malt and hop flavor, good body, long dry hop aftertaste with honeyed malt in support of and balancing the hops, extremely drinkable; OG 1050, 3.9% abw. [A, 68]

BLIZZARD BOCK BEER — hazy deep amber; bright hop aroma is first like lavender; tasty dry malt and hop flavor, good body, smooth, long dry hop aftertaste. Some samples had a faint grapefruit background to the aftertaste and little length. [BK, 62]

BUFFALO WEISSE — hazy gold, bright zesty clove aroma, taste like the nose, smooth, refreshing, balanced, very pleasant to drink, dry faintly spicy wheaty-malt aftertaste with very good length. Made with 54% wheat malt and two strains of yeast which are not filtered out, kraeusened; 3.8% abw. [W, 67]

CLARK'S ARMORY ALE — deep gold, light aromatic cascade hop aroma, light hop flavor, medium body; flavor tails off at the finish; short dry hop aftertaste. Made for Clark's Ale House of Syracuse, NY. [A, 47]

BUFFALO OKTOBERFEST BEER — golden amber, slightly buttery aroma, malty buttery flavor, dry malt aftertaste, diacetyl all the way through. Made with two different caramelized malts; 4.0% abw. [B, 14]

BUFFALO LIGHT BEER — tawny-gold, light malt-hop nose, light dry hop flavor and aftertaste,

light body, good tasting but not long; 2.5% abw. [LO, 46]

Buffalo Bill's Brewery
Brewpub in Hayward, CA

PUNKIN ALE — hazy pale orange, clean light off-dry fruity tangerine nose; palate is fruity malt first, then hoppy in middle and finish; fruity malt and bright hop aftertaste, medium body, good balance, interesting and very drinkable. [A, 73]

BUFFALO BILL'S PUMPKIN ALE 1992 — gold, pumpkin spice and eucalyptus aroma, big spicy cinnamon, nutmeg, etc. flavor; good body, long spicy aftertaste like the flavor, very good of the type. [A, 70]

BUFFALO BILL'S DOUBLE CREAM ALE — hazy gold, light fruity aroma (like melon and peaches), creamy texture; hops on front of the palate, fruity malt in the middle, dry hop finish and aftertaste; medium length. [A, 34]

RAUCH BEER SMOKED PORTER — amber, smoked sausage aroma, a bit peppery, harsh smoked flavor, dry smoked aftertaste with considerable length. [B, 15]

Buffalo Brewpub
Brewpub in Williamsville, NY

BUFFALO BITTER — amber, bright hop aroma, low carbonation, good malt and hop flavor,

quite tasty like an ESB, good body, fairly long dry hop aftertaste. Made with English malt and Chinook hops; specific gravity 1.065, 4.25% abw. [A, 53]

BUFFALO OATMEAL STOUT — dark brown, roasted barley nose, malt flavor; some hops in the finish but still mostly a malty brew; ample but not big, reasonably long malt aftertaste. Made with 25% rolled oats and roast barley mash-hopped with Tettnanger and Cascade hops; specific gravity 1.060, 4.0% abw. [S, 49]

Burkhardt Brewing Co.
Microbrewery in Uniontown, OH

BURKHARDT WHITE CLIFF — pale gold, bright hop aroma and flavor, good body, long dry hop aftertaste. Made with Whitbread yeast and flavored with Cascade and Northern Brewer hops; specific gravity 1.047, 3.6% abw. [A, 69]

ECLIPSE SCOTCH ALE — deep amber, malt nose; complex very dry malt flavor has an underlying sweetness and some roasted barley character; low carbonation, long malty aftertaste; made using crystal, chocolate, and extract dark malts with a short fermentation and long cold aging; hopped with Hallertau hops; specific gravity 1.041, 3.6% abw. [A, 64]

BURKHARDT MUG ALE — amber, light hop nose and taste, very smooth, good balance, medium dry and pleasant; finishes dry hops leading into a fairly long but light dry hop aftertaste. A nut brown ale short fermented and aged with crystal and dark extract malts and Northern Brewer hops; specific gravity 1.049, 4.2–4.4% abw. [A, 50]

NORTH STAR — deep gold, dry nose, slightly off-dry malt flavor; finishes lightly sweet, but aftertaste is a drier malt; low carbonation adds to the effect of sweetness. This is a light American-style ale made from extract, fast warm-fermented and long cold aged; specific gravity 1.043, 4.1% abw. [A, 53]

BURKHARDT'S HEFE-WEIZEN — hazy gold, light spicy malt aroma; flavor is complex with cloves, bananas, and checkerberry; pleasant and refreshing, medium body, light dry and short, made with wheat malt and German yeast; specific gravity 1.034, 3.1% abw. [W, 47]

BURKHARDT'S ENGLISH STYLE BITTER — deep gold, dry hop nose, dry bitter hop flavor, very dry, good body, long and dry aftertaste. Made with Belgian yeast and extract, having a faint lactic background. [A, 68]

Butterfield Brewing Co.
Brewpub and restaurant in Fresno, CA

TOWER DARK ALE — brown, overdone roast malt aroma, a bit burnt as well; roasted malt flavor lacks complexity and interest; dull malt aftertaste. Made from pale, caramel-40L, Carapils, chocolate, wheat, roast, and black malts; specific gravity 1.068, 5.5% abw. [A, 31]

MAIBOCK — gold, hop nose, smooth malt and hop flavor, has balance; malt shows best in the finish; dry malt and hop aftertaste. Brewed with two-row pale, Munich, wheat, Carapils, and chocolate malts; gravity 18.5 P, 6% abw. [BK, 63]

BUTTERFIELD MAXIMATOR — brown, rich malt aroma and flavor, big body; hops at the finish but this is mostly a high malt doublebock; malty aftertaste stays rich and full, but is not long; specific gravity 1.084, 6.5% abw doesn't really intrude. [BK, 72]

BUTTERFIELD OATMEAL STOUT — dark brown, dry malt nose; light dry malt flavor is mostly roasted barley, smoothed out by the oats; good body; fairly long malt aftertaste is on the dry side; specific gravity 1.060, 4.5% abw. [S, 73]

Notes

BUTTERFIELD BROWN
ALE — brown, malt aroma, dry
malt flavor, finish, and aftertaste,
big body, fairly long; specific
gravity 1.068, 4.5% abw. [A, 47]

BUTTERFIELD RASPBERRY
WHEAT ALE — pinkish gold,
raspberry nose; dry raspberry-
wheat flavor comes as a surprise
(that it is so dry); tasty and refreshing, light body; big alcohol
masked by the raspberry; long dry
raspberry-wheat aftertaste. Made
as a wheat beer with raspberry
puree substituting for finishing
hops; specific gravity 1.084, 6.5%
abw. [A, 47]

SAN JOAQUIN ALE — gold,
light hop aroma and flavor, fairly
dry, medium body, dry hop finish,
not much of an aftertaste. Made
with two-row pale caramel, wheat,
and roasted malt; gravity 12.5 P,
3.5% abw. [A, 43]

WILLAMETTE ALE — amber-
gold, hop aroma, light hop flavor,
dry hop finish and aftertaste.
Made with two-row pale, caramel-

10L/20L/90L, Munich, Carapils,
wheat, and roasted malt; gravity
14.5 P, 4% abw. [A, 43]

IMPERIAL STOUT — brown,
faint roasted malt aroma, light
roast barley malt flavor, finishes
dry malt, long dry malt aftertaste.
Made with two-row pale, Munich,
caramel-40L/90L, Carapils, wheat,
roast, chocolate, and black malts;
gravity 21 P, 7% abw. [S, 47]

BUTTERFIELD WEIZEN — gold,
light clean American-style wheat
nose, light dry wheat flavor, light
body, good flavor for refreshment,
very clean palate, fairly short light
dry wheat aftertaste. Made with
70% wheat malt; specific gravity
1.044, 4.0% abw. [W, 47]

BRIDALVEIL ALE — amber;
malt and hops show in the nose;
big well-hopped and malted flavor, big body; seems to be rich
tasting at first but the richness
doesn't last and a little metallic
offishness develops in the mouth
as you hold it, other than that it is
a good hoppy brew; made with
two-row pale, crystal, caramel-
40L, Munich, Carapils, chocolate,
and wheat malt, plus roasted barley balanced with Chinook, Northern Brewer, Willamette, and
Cascade hops; OG 1065, FG
1.024, 5.5% abv, 31 IBU. [A, 53]

Callahan's Pub &
Brewery
Brewpub in
North San Diego, CA

MESA PALE ALE — gold, pleasant malt and hop nose, very

refreshing malt and hop taste, light
body, very drinkable, very long
dry hop aftertaste. [A, 61]

CALLAHAN RED — amber, big
malty aroma and flavor, slightly off-
dry malt aftertaste; doesn't have the
zest of the Pale Ale. [A, 47]

NAMELESS NUT BROWN —
amber-brown, light malt aroma,
fairly light chocolate malt flavor,
dry malt finish and short dry malt
aftertaste. [A, 40]

Cambridge
Brewing Co.
Brewpub in
Cambridge, MA

REGATTA GOLDEN — hazy gold,
big malt and hop nose and flavor,
complex, good body, good balance,
dry hop finish, long dry hop and
malt aftertaste. [A, 62]

CAMBRIDGE AMBER —
medium pale amber, light malt and
hop nose, good body, dry malt
finish, long complex dry malt and
hop aftertaste. Made with a variety of roasted malts and a blend of
three hops, including Cascades;
specific gravity 1.048, 4.2% abw.
[A, 67]

CHARLES RIVER PORTER —
deep mahogany, big malt and hop
nose, smooth malt and hop flavor
with some roasted barley, good
balance, good body, long dry hop
aftertaste; specific gravity 1.064,
5.0% abw. [P, 66]

TALL TALE PALE ALE —
slightly hazy golden amber, rising

hop aroma, big very complex hop flavor, a little hop bite especially in the finish, very long dry hop aftertaste; hopped with Cascades; OG 1062. [A, 66]

HONEY GINGER ALE — a beer not a ginger ale at all, deep gold; honeyed ginger nose is fairly sweet, taste is drier than indicated by the aroma but not dry; dry gingery malt finish, short gingery aftertaste; OG 1048. [A, 52]

BANNATYNE'S SCOTCH ALE — amber, off-dry malt aroma and strong rich malt and alcoholic flavor, big body, long rich malt aftertaste; made with a variety of roasted malts and a touch of brown sugar and molasses; specific gravity 1.084, 6.4% abw. [A, 80]

WINTER WARMER — mahogany color, spicy over the malt in the nose, cinnamon-nutmeg off-dry malt flavor, medium body, long spicy aftertaste; enough malt to be tasted but for the most part the spices take center stage. [A, 64]

TRIPEL THREAT — gold, fruity nose, strong sweet peach fruity flavor, good body, long medium dry hop aftertaste, interesting; done in the Belgian style, flavored with coriander; gravity 21.25 P (1.084), 6.5% abw. [A, 70]

BELGIAN TRIPEL — amber; powerful but balanced somewhat sweet fruity aroma and flavor; not peachy like the Tripel Threat (which was the medal winner at the 1992 GABF); rich and alco-holic, big body, very long medium dry hop aftertaste; fairly true to the purported style. [A, 74]

CAMBRIDGE RYE — deep golden amber, dry somewhat grainy aroma; light dry malt flavor is also a bit grainy; medium body; dry light grainy finish and aftertaste with some hops showing at the end; fairly brief. [A, 49]

BLUNDERBUSS BARLEYWINE — deep brown, big malty nose, huge malt and hop flavor, powerful but balanced, very rich, huge body, very long complex strong balanced aftertaste. Made using a double mash process yielding a high gravity (OG 1109), 11% abv. [BW, 71]

TRIPLE J BIG MAN ALE — amber; hop nose has a malt backing; huge flavor with plenty of both hops and malt, big body; long hoppy aftertaste is well endowed with malt; a monster of an ale with plenty of alocohol as well (6.5% abv). [A, 79]

CAPITAL BREWING CO.
Brewery in Middleton, WI; uses bottling facilities of Stevens Point B.C. in Stevens Point, WI for packaging.

CAPITAL GARTEN BRÄU SPECIAL — amber, well-balanced malt and hop nose, fine malt palate with a light hop finish, medium body, good balance, long dry hop aftertaste; gravity 11.8 P, 3.9% abw, 32 IBU. [B, 76]

Notes

CAPITAL GARTEN BRÄU WILD RICE — amber-gold, malty aroma, fresh off-dry fruity malt flavor, heavy body, medium dry malt finish and aftertaste. [B, 31]

CAPITAL GARTEN BRÄU DARK — deep amber, malty-molasses nose, dry malty flavor with the molasses still in back, dry malt aftertaste of medium length; gravity 13.2 P, 4.2% abw. [B, 64]

CAPITAL MAIBOCK — amber-gold, huge complex malt aroma, rich and strong malt flavor, dry malt aftertaste, very tasty, very complex, and very long. [BK, 64]

CAPITAL GARTEN BRÄU OKTOBERFEST — medium amber-gold color, complex fragrant hop aroma; well-balanced dry hop and malt flavor that continues into a long dry aftertaste; smooth and tasty throughout; gravity 13.5 P, 4.5% abw. [B, 81]

CAPITAL GARTEN BRÄU BOCK — amber-brown, big malt nose, almost molasses-like, big slightly toasted malt flavor and finish, excellent long dry malt aftertaste, very drinkable. [BK, 67]

CAPITAL GARTEN BRÄU LAGER — pale amber, big hop and malt nose, big rich malt and hop flavor, good body and balance, long dry malt and hop aftertaste. [B, 67]

WISCONSIN AMBER — amber, hop aroma, good balanced hop and malt flavor, medium to good body; dry hop finish and aftertaste still has some malt. Made with 5 malts and Mt. Hood hops; gravity 12.8 P, 4.2% abw. [B, 47]

COUNTRY INN ALE — golden amber; fruity hop nose shows some litchi and kumquat, as well as a touch of roasted malt; the flavor is roasted malt alone; very complex and tasty, good body, long dry hop aftertaste, very drinkable. Made for Millrose B.C. of So. Barrington, IL. [A, 72]

MILLROSE DARK STAR LAGER — brilliant amber, roasted dry malt aroma and flavor, good body, creamy and finely carbonated, very smooth, dry malt finish and aftertaste. Made for Millrose B.C. [B, 75]

CAPITAL DOPPELBOCK — brilliant amber-brown, lovely roasted malt aroma, big rich alcoholic roasted malt flavor, big body, strong and delicious, smooth rich and complex; long aftertaste continues the flavor; a wonderful doppelbock. [BK, 98]

Capitol City Brewing Co.
Brewpub in Washington, DC

PALE ALE — amber, light dry hop aroma, medium body; dry hop flavor stays into fairly short aftertaste. [A, 47]

ALTBIER — amber, stinky hop nose, almost no flavor (very faint hops and malt), dry hop finish, short dry hop aftertaste. [A, 34]

BITTER — amber, light ale-like aroma (tangy hops); flavor slightly bitter hops at first, takes on a light honeyed sweetness in the middle,

acidic finish is too sour; medium sour hop aftertaste. [A, 52]

PORTER — deep brown, roasted malt aroma and flavor, very tasty, medium body, roasted malt finish and aftertaste, good duration. [P, 65]

ELEANOR'S AMBER — amber, lightly tangy hop nose with malt support, good ale taste with hops and malt; has complexity; medium body, dry hop finish and aftertaste. [A, 64]

Cardinal Brewing Co.
Microbrewery in Charleston, WV

SENECA RED — reddish amber; infected aroma and flavor like a gueuze that has gone off; a sweet background is all that remains of the intended flavor. [A, 1]

NEW RIVER ALE — hazy gold, huge head, tangy lightly acidic aroma and flavor, not attractive, likely infected or spoiled, dry lactic acid finish and aftertaste; not pasteurized or filtered and found in a store at warm temperature. [A, 33]

Carver's Bakery Cafe Brewery
Brewpub in Durango, CO

RASPBERRY WHEAT ALE — deep gold, malt aroma with no apparent berry, big malt and bitter hop flavor (again no raspberry), dry malt finish and aftertaste. Whole raspberries are added to a light wheat ale (40% wheat, 60% barley, Cascade and Willamette hops); specific gravity 1.044, 3.53% abw. [W, 50]

GOLDEN WHEAT HONEY ALE — gold, honey and wheat aroma; light flavor is off-dry wheat and honey up front, but finishes dry; light body; light short aftertaste is on dry side. Made with 20% wheat, pale malts, and a touch of honey; specific gravity 1.042, 3.33% abw. [A, 50]

OLD OAK AMBER ALE — pale amber, light malt aroma and flavor, medium body, dry malt finish and aftertaste. Aged on oak chips; specific gravity 1.048, 3.31% abw. [A, 50]

IRON HORSE STOUT — deep brown, faint aroma of roasted barley and chocolate malt; light smooth and dry palate shows the roasted and chocolate malt promised by the aroma; good body, plenty of malt but mildly bitter as well; long fairly complex dry aftertaste; specific gravity 1.062, 3.86% abw. [S, 65]

JAMES BROWN ALE — brown, dry malt aroma and flavor, light body, fairly short dry nutty malt aftertaste; specific gravity 1.048, 3.11% abw. [A, 45]

Cascade Lakes Brewing Co.
Microbrewery in Redmond, OR

BANDIT'S BEST BITTER — amber, beautiful complex spicy Northwest hop aroma; bright hop flavor has plenty of supporting malt

for good balance; low carbonation, medium to good body, big dry hop aftertaste lasts and lasts; made with two-row pale and 30L and 70L crystal malts, hopped with Columbus hops; OG 1044, FG 1.016, 3.67% abv, and 40 IBU. [A, 79]

Casco Bay Brewing Co.
Microbrewery in Portland, ME

KATAHDIN GOLDEN BEER — deep gold, bright hop and fruity malt aroma, a big enjoyable dry hop and malty ale-like flavor, good body; very long dry hop and malt aftertaste is big and rich; of the well-hopped Pilsener style this is a dandy leaving your mouth with a clean dry feeling. Tasted on draft at The Great Lost Bear in Portland, ME. Tasted a few months later in a 12-oz. bottle; it was similar but the hops clearly out distanced the malt. [B, 69]

KATAHDIN STOUT — very deep brown, chocolate malt and roasted barley nose, light fruity roasted malt flavor like the aroma; stays dry and remains rich throughout; good body, long rich dry roasted malt aftertaste, a classical oatmeal stout, very smooth and tasty. Tasted at Great Lost Bear on draft and in 22-oz. bottle. [S, 65]

Notes

KATAHDIN RED ALE — amber, smooth malty nose with a good hop background, smooth dry malt and hop flavor; starts out malty and the hops come in at the middle; good body, excellent balance, complex and delicious, extremely long; aftertaste is like the flavor; great with food. Tasted on draft at The Great Lost Bear. [B, 98]

Catamount Brewing Co.

Brewery in White River Junction, VT

CATAMOUNT GOLD — deep gold, big nose with lots of fruity malt and hops, bright hop palate, good body; long hop aftertaste supported with plenty of malt. A hefty well-made brew made with a blend of pale and lightly roasted malts and fresh Willamette hops; specific gravity 1.044, 3.5% abw. [B, 82]

CATAMOUNT AMBER — medium deep amber, subdued malt aroma, good tasting malt flavor, good body, good balance, long malt aftertaste, a satisfying, pleasant, very drinkable brew. This ale is made with six-row and crystal malts milled at the brewery seasoned with Galena and Willamette hops, top-fermented; specific gravity 1.048, 4% abw. [B, 62]

CATAMOUNT PORTER — deep mahogany, rich rising straightforward malt nose; big rich dry malt flavor with a lightly scorched backtaste that doesn't mar the effect; long dry malt aftertaste. This beer is made from dark and roasted malts blended with Galena and Cascade hops; specific gravity 1.052, 4.4% abw. [P, 62]

CATAMOUNT CHRISTMAS ALE 1990 — hazy amber, roasted malt aroma, big dry roasted malt flavor, big hop finish, noticeable alcohol, very long dry malt and hop aftertaste. A very very good Christmas ale. [A, 82]

CATAMOUNT CHRISTMAS ALE 1991 — amber, beautiful big hop aroma with plenty of malt in back, big strong flavor much like the nose, delicious, appetizing, expertly balanced, very long hop aftertaste. This is the best effort from Catamount to date. [A, 92]

CATAMOUNT CHRISTMAS ALE 1992 — deep amber, great spicy malt-hop aroma; big complex spicy palate loaded with both malt and hops, richly flavored,

excellent balance; very long dry hop aftertaste; like the 1991 — why change a good thing. [A, 92]

CATAMOUNT CHRISTMAS ALE 1993 — deep mahogany color, big bright hop aroma with lots of malt in support; complex hop and malt flavor has strength; lots of different flavors, big and balanced, very long and delicious, high alcohol, another winner. [A, 84]

CATAMOUNT CHRISTMAS ALE 1994 — amber, huge malt and hop nose with alcohol, huge hop and malt flavor, big body, very long complex malt and hop aftertaste, good balance, an annual winner. [A, 91]

CATAMOUNT CHRISTMAS ALE 1995 — deep amber; huge malt and hop aroma shows plenty of Cascade hops; huge well-hopped flavor like the nose has enough malt support for balance; big body, long complex malt and hop aftertaste. Tasted on draft and in bottle and as good as ever. [A, 91–95]

ETHAN ALLEN ALE — hazy gold, melony malt nose; carbonation sting is quite noticeable; malt dominates the flavor but the balance between the malt and hops is so-so; medium to light body, medium length dry malt aftertaste. [A, 31]

POST ROAD REAL ALE — amber, bright zesty hop nose with good malt, big complex hop flavor, big body, long dry hop aftertaste well supported with malt, very tasty ale indeed. Made for Old Marlborough B.C., Marlboro, MA, the beer is brewed with six-row, crystal, and Carapils malts and hopped with Willamette and Cascade hops. [A, 77]

LE GARDE — amber, light malt and hop aroma, big sweet malt flavor, winelike, big body, sweet malt finish and long off-dry malt aftertaste. A French country ale-style brew made for Dark Cloud Brewery, associated with Old Marlborough B.C. [A, 53]

NEWMAN'S SARATOGA BRAND LAGER BEER — hazy gold, bright fruity hop nose, flavor like the nose, good body, good balance, long dry hop aftertaste. This is a dortmunder-style beer hopped with Saaz, Hallertau, and Hersbrucker hops. Made for William S. Newman B.C., Albany, NY. [B, 49]

NEWMAN'S ALBANY AMBER — amber, big malt aroma, bright malt and hop flavor, high carbonation, good long malt finish and aftertaste. A Vienna-style lager, made for William S. Newman B.C., Albany, NY, brewed with roasted and black malts and hopped with German Hallertau and Yakima Cascade hops; specific gravity 12.6 P, 5.6% abw. [B, 62]

COMMONWEALTH BURTON ALE — amber, dank nose, dull malt flavor, short dry malt aftertaste. Made for Commonwealth B.C. of Boston. [A, 49]

CATAMOUNT 1992 OCTOBERFEST — amber-gold, spicy hop nose, marvelous dry hop and malt flavor, excellent mouthfeel, medium body; dry malt aftertaste has great length; very good with food. [B, 72]

CATAMOUNT 1993 OCTOBERFEST — deep amber-gold, beautiful appetizing malt and hop nose, highly carbonated; big flavor starts out with fruity malt, then dry hops join the malt in the middle; medium to good body, excellent balance, good mouthfeel; dry malt and hop aftertaste has great length. Very drinkable with a flavor that makes you want another glass. Made with two-row and caramel malts and hopped with Yakima, Hallertau, and Tettnanger varieties; specific gravity 1.052, 4.4% abw. [B, 80]

CATAMOUNT 1994 OCTOBERFEST — golden amber, bright complex malt and hop aroma; balanced flavor has rich malt and complex hops; style is pretty much southern German leaning to maltiness rather than the hops; rich yet dry long malt aftertaste has the hops in back; made with American two-row malt with Northern Brewer and Tettnanger hops; specific gravity 1.052, 4.4% abw. [B, 67]

CATAMOUNT 1995 OCTOBERFEST — deep amber-gold; bright zesty nose shows plenty of malt well backed with hops; rich balanced flavor is mostly rich malt but does have plenty of hops; long fairly rich (but not sweet) malt aftertaste has hops in back, much like the 1994. [B, 74]

Notes

PIKE PLACE PALE ALE — hazy amber, light malt nose, light toasted nutty malt flavor, burnt malt finish; long aftertaste shows faintly of the burnt malt. Made for Pike Place Brewery and Merchant du Vin for national distribution; uses Cluster and Northern Brewer hops. [A, 56]

CATAMOUNT BOCK — deep mahogany; complex funky aroma has citrus, roasted barley, butter, and oxidation; big hop and malt flavor is much better than the nose, but "off" components bother the flavor especially in the finish and long aftertaste. Bottled version in 1993. [BK, 45]

CATAMOUNT SPRING BOCK — dark amber, balanced malt and hop aroma; dry malt and hop flavor lacks the balance of the nose; dry hop finish, and long dry hop aftertaste. Draft version in spring of 1993. [BK, 68]

CATAMOUNT SPRING BOCK — dark amber; light pleasant malty nose has hops in back; flavor is hoppy up front and the malt is reluctant to emerge and stays back; medium to good body; very refreshing but unlike a spring or May bock because the malt stays back; dry hop finish and very long dry hop aftertaste. Draft version in spring of 1994. [BK, 68]

PLIMOTH ROCK ALE — slightly hazy amber; pleasant lightly toasted malt aroma has just a hint of hops; big hop and malt flavor; big body, very complex; flavor is strong; long aftertaste similar but greatly attenuated.

Made for Plymoth Plantation Inc., Plymouth, MA. [A, 74]

CATAMOUNT AMERICAN WHEAT — gold; hop nose has a fruity citrus background; light dry hop flavor, medium body, very dry finish and aftertaste, monolithic without any distinctive character; made with 50% wheat and 50% two-row malted barley, top-fermenting yeast, and Yakima Hallertau hops; specific gravity 1.043, 3.6% abw. [W, 27]

BASIL'S RED BANK ROCKET RED ALE — amber, pleasant appetizing hop aroma, bright dry hop flavor, good body, has complexity, dry hop finish and aftertaste, good length. Made for Basil T. Leaf restaurant in Red Bank, NJ. [A, 66]

Celis Brewery
Microbrewery in Austin, TX

CELIS WHITE — very pale cloudy yellow-gold, almost a white, attractive spicy-orange aroma and flavor, dry with plenty of hops and malt, medium body, dry malt aftertaste, a very nice typical Belgian white ale-style wheat brew. This top-fermented brew is made from 50% wheat and 50% barley malt, hopped with Willamette and Kent-Goldings hops, and flavored with coriander and curaçao; specific gravity 1.047 (gravity 12 P), 3.9% abw, 12–15 IBU. This is a true example of a Belgian white beer. [W, 76]

CELIS GOLDEN — pale gold, malt and flowery hop nose nose, big malt flavor, big body, malt finish and aftertaste; long with hops showing up at the end. This is a bottom-fermented brew made from 50% two-row and 50% six-row malts, using Czechoslovakian yeast and Saaz hops with cornflakes added for dryness; specific gravity 12.2, 3.9% abw, 20–25 IBU. [A, 53]

CELIS PALE BOCK — gold, complex fruity malt aroma that has peach and melon tones; malt flavor has the fruitiness in back; medium body, dry malt finish and aftertaste, not much length. This Belgian-style pale ale is brewed with equal parts two-row and six-row malts with some caramel malt for color. It is hopped with Willamette, Saaz, and Cascades; gravity 12.3 P, 3.9% abw, 20–25 IBU. [BK, 50]

CELIS GRAND CRU — pale yellow-gold; aroma is spicy cloves; clove and herb flavor, very smooth and nicely made, long spicy-herbal malt aftertaste. This ale is made with pale lager malts, hopped with Saaz and Cascade hops and flavored with curaçao and other spices; specific gravity 1.070 (gravity 19.8 P), 7% abw, 15–20 IBU. [A, 53]

CELIS RASPBERRY — pinkish color, clean raspberry nose, fairly dry raspberry flavor; the tartness of the ale mitigates the natural sweetness of the berry and there is no sweetness beyond the natural flavor of the berry; aftertaste is dry and not long, but the raspberry stays in your mouth for more than a half hour; medium body. [A, 73]

Centurion Brewing Co.
Microbrewery in Torrance, CA

CENTURION BOCK BEER — deep dark amber, rich dry malt nose; big rich flavor shows plenty of hops and malt; good body, dry hop finish, long dry hop and rich malt aftertaste; made with seven malts including pale, BRU malt from British Columbia, Munich 100, 20 Lovibond, and honey; hopped with Hallertau and Hersbrucker, creating a rich classical bock beer; 5.7% abw. [BK, 78]

Champion Brewing Co.
Brewpub in Denver, CO

RED LIGHT — reddish amber, hop aroma and flavor, medium body, dry hop finish and aftertaste. Made with caramel malt; gravity 8.5 P, 3.4% abw. [LO, 53]

HOME RUN ALE — deep amber, no discernible aroma, lightly roasted barley malt flavor, medium body, very dry malt finish and aftertaste, long long duration; gravity 12.5 P, 3.8% abw. [A, 67]

STOUT STREET STOUT — dark brown, light roasted barley and chocolate malt aroma; bright flavor but the body is a bit weak; medium long dry malt aftertaste; gravity 14.0 P, 4.1% abw. [S, 47]

BLACK FOREST — deep amber, black cherry nose, big black cherry flavor, like a tart maraschino; very long dry malt aftertaste with the cherry remaining faintly to the end. [B, 67]

CHAMPION BUCKWHEAT — pale gold; very faint aroma has a touch of a raspberry-like fruity ester, it is also in the flavor but only up front; no raspberry by the finish, medium body, dry malt finish and aftertaste, medium length; gravity 13.2 P, 4.2% abw. [W, 34]

NORM CLARKE'S SPORTS ALE — deep gold, light malt nose, light malt flavor, light body, light dry malt finish and aftertaste, not much length to it. This is an alt-style beer made with a touch of wheat; gravity 12.5 P, 4.0% abw. [A, 40]

CHAMPION IRISH RED ALE — reddish amber, faint hop nose, dry hop flavor, finish, and aftertaste, dry and refreshing, medium duration; gravity 12.5 P, 3.6% abw. The amber ale at Champion in 1994 was called Larimer Red Ale and seems to be the same ale. [A, 42]

Cherry Street Brewery
Brewpub and restaurant in Tulsa, OK

MAPLE RIDGE GOLDEN ALE — bright gold, dry light European hop (Saaz and Hallertau) aroma, fairly big dry hop flavor, good body; dry finish shows both malt and hops; complex dry hop aftertaste. [A, 67]

CHERRY STREET HEFE WEISSEN — hazy gold, faint malt nose, dry slightly spicy malt flavor, medium body, long spicy dry malt aftertaste, very refreshing and drinkable. Made with honey, wheat, domestic two-row barley, and finished with Tettnanger hops. [W, 68]

WEWOKA WHEAT — gold, faint malty nose, dry refreshing malt flavor, light body, medium dry malt finish and aftertaste; good American-style wheat made with honey, wheat and barley malt, and finished with Tettnanger hops. [W, 54]

PRAIRIE PALE ALE — deep gold, faint complex hop and malt aroma; big flavor shows a lot of malt; dry finish, long complex dry hop aftertaste; made with Nugget, Willamette, and Cascade hops. [A, 72]

RED BUD AMBER ALE — red amber, faint dry hop and malt nose; very dry flavor borders on austere; medium body; malt shows best at the finish; long dry hop aftertaste. [A, 60]

GOOD GUS STOUT — opaque, faint chocolate malt and roasted barley nose; big coffee-like flavor shows all the components promised by the aroma; hops are noticeable from mid-palate on but never get past that roasted coffee bean character; dry malt finish and aftertaste a good flavorful stout. [S, 73]

Other brews include Lincoln Lager and Skyline Porter.

Cherryland Brewery
Microbrewery in Sturgeon Bay, WI

GOLDEN RAIL — amber-gold, malt and hop nose and taste, medium body, dry malt and hop finish and aftertaste. Made with pale and crystal malt, hopped with Tettnangers; specific gravity 1.052, 4.0% abw. [A, 45]

SILVER RAIL — gold, hop aroma and flavor, medium body, fairly dry hop finish and aftertaste. Made with pale malt, Hallertau and Cascade hops; specific gravity 1.045, alcohol 3.7% abw. [A, 47]

CHERRY RAIL — gold, maraschino cherry nose and taste, light body, very little follow-through, short cherry aftertaste. Made with pale malt infused with cherries; specific gravity 1.048, 3.8% abw. [A, 42]

APPLE BACH — amber, off-dry malt aroma; apple-like malt flavor has a tartness in back; medium body; light long dry malt aftertaste keeps the apple. Made with pale

and caramel malts, Cascade and Tettnanger hops; specific gravity 1.056, 4.2% abw. [A, 43]

Chicago Brewing Co.
Brewery in Chicago, IL

LEGACY LAGER — an amber brew with an appetizing hop and malt aroma, finely carbonated, good well-hopped flavor, good body, balanced and long; gravity 12.5 P, 3.9% abw. [B, 83]

LEGACY RED ALE — amber color, tangy malt and hop aroma, big and clean well-hopped flavor, complex and tasty, dry hop finish, plenty of malt throughout, long dry aftertaste; gravity 12.5 P, 4.2% abw. [B, 75]

HEARTLAND WEISS — hazy gold, spicy malt aroma with a light lactic touch, light spicy malt flavor, very refreshing, smooth, good body, lightly spiced and dry malt aftertaste, a good German weissbier style; gravity 12.0 P, 3.9% abw. [W, 64]

BIG SHOULDERS PORTER — deep brown, big complex aroma with roasted and fruity notes, lots of roasted malt, dry malt and hop flavor, good body, a good tasting porter, long dry malt aftertaste; gravity 13.5 P, 5% abw. [P, 65]

Clement's Brewing Co.
Brewpub in Ithaca, NY

CLEMENT'S PILSENER SUPER PREMIUM LAGER — gold, hop nose and taste a little on the sour side, medium body, dry hop finish and lengthy aftertaste, good Germanic-style beer. [B, 49]

CLEMENT'S DARK DOUBLE BOCK — deep amber, big malt and hop nose, flavor like the nose, excellent balance, long dry hop finish and aftertaste, again very German. [BK, 53]

CLEMENT'S BLOND DOUBLE BOCK — hazy gold, big off-dry malt nose, big malt and hop flavor, richly flavored, heavy body; long off-dry malt and hop aftertaste that goes very dry hops at the end. [BK, 62]

CLEMENT'S AMBER — amber, good malt and hop aroma, creamy smooth complex malt flavor, dry malt finish, long dry malt aftertaste. Served as Old Bay Special Amber in the Old Bay Pub in New Brunswick, NJ. [B, 49]

CLEMENT'S OKTOBERFEST — amber, faint off-dry malt nose; big malt flavor is drier than the nose but not dry; good tasting, finely balanced, creamy texture, good body; very drinkable brew that kicks sweet but stays dry. [B, 78]

CLEMENT'S PORTER — deep ruby-brown, tan head; light dry malt aroma becomes roasted chocolate malt once it warms up; light dry roasted malt flavor, medium body, light dry roasted malt aftertaste with good length, good with food. Named Cole Porter in the brewpub. [P, 62]

Coeur D'Alene Brewing Co. / T.W. Fischer's Brewpub
Microbrewery and brewpub in Coeur D'Alene, ID

T.W. FISHER'S LIGHT — gold, dank nose; malt flavor has a cooked corn background; light body, brief light and dry malt aftertaste. Made with pale malt and Willamette hops; gravity 10.3 P, 2.8% abw. [LO, 36]

T.W. FISHER'S CENTENNIAL PALE ALE — gold, off-dry malt aroma, dry malt and light hop flavor, medium body, short dry malt aftertaste. Made with two-row pale and caramel malts with Cascade and Bullion hops; gravity 11.25 P, 3.7% abw. [A, 42]

T.W. FISHER'S FESTIVAL DARK ALE — deep amber, light malt nose, grainy malt flavor with hops in back, same for finish and aftertaste; uses two-row pale, crystal, dark Munich malts with a touch of roasted malt with Cascade and Willamette hops; specific gravity 1.044, 3.6% abw. [A, 47]

T.W. FISHER'S FULL MOON STOUT — dark brown, roasted malt nose with a very grainy background, same for the flavor, dull grainy aftertaste. Made with roasted barley and rolled oats; gravity 12 P, 4.2%. [S, 43]

Notes

T.W. FISHER'S LIGHT WHEAT BEER — pale gold, light grainy malt aroma; decent malt flavor although it is a bit grainy; dry malt finish is a bit weak; light dry malt aftertaste, Willamette hops barely noticeable; 2.8% abw. [W, 40]

T.W. FISHER'S NUT BROWN ALE — light brown, light dry malt nose, smooth dry malt palate, hopped with Willamette and Cascade hops, medium body, light dry malt finish and aftertaste; specific gravity 1.044, 3.7% abw. [A, 44]

T.W. FISHER'S RED OKTOBER — deep ruby-brown, dry malty aroma; flavor is mostly dry malt but there is some light hop character in back; dry malt finish and aftertaste; made with caramel and crystal malts, Willamette, Cascades, and Bullion hops; specific gravity 1.050, 4.0% abw. [B, 43]

Cold Spring Brewing Co.
Brewery in Cold Spring, MN

COLD SPRING BEER — pale gold, fragrant malt aroma, good clean malt and hop flavor, medium dry long aftertaste. [B, 42]

KEGLE BRAU — tawny-gold, lovely malt and hop aroma, good malt and hop flavor, very tasty, bright hop finish and long hop aftertaste. [B, 67]

COLD SPRING EXPORT — medium gold, complex hop aroma and flavor, dry hop finish, and long dry hop aftertaste, a well-made and complex brew. [B, 47]

NORTH STAR BEER — medium gold, clean rich malt nose, lightly hopped flavor, light body, clean light malt and hop finish, weak short aftertaste. [B, 35]

GEMEINDE BRAU — gold, malt aroma, malt and hop flavor, dry hop finish and aftertaste with only medium duration. Made for Gemeinde Brau, Inc., Amana, IA. [B, 32]

WESTERN PREMIUM BEER — pale gold, bright malt aroma, pleasant malt flavor, finish, and aftertaste, good length. [B, 50]

FOX DELUXE BEER — pale gold, pleasant malt nose, high carbonation, off-dry malt finish and aftertaste, medium length. [B, 29]

WHITE LABEL LIGHT BEER — medium gold, faint malt aroma, clean refreshing malt aroma, off-dry malt finish and aftertaste. [B, 43]

COLD BRAU PREMIUM BEER — pale gold, light fresh malt aroma, refreshing clean malt flavor, very light in hop character,

pleasant malt finish and aftertaste, fair length. [B, 45]

KARLSBRAU OLD TIME BEER — bright gold, sour malt nose, vegetal malt flavor and finish, long slightly sour malt aftertaste. [B, 23]

KOLONIE BRAU — pale gold, lovely complex malt and hop aroma, equally complex malt and hop flavor, good balance; more malt than hops, but the hops do show well in the finish and long aftertaste. Made for Gemeinde Brau, Inc., Amana, IA. [B, 50]

COLD SPRING SELECT STOCK PREMIUM BEER — gold, clean dry malt aroma, medium body, light dry malt flavor, brief dry malt aftertaste. [B, 24]

COLD SPRING PALE ALE — gold, dry malty nose and taste; there are hops in back and they come out late and the flavor ends dry; medium body, medium long dry malt aftertaste. [A, 45]

COLD SPRING EXPORT LAGER — gold, dry malty flavor has some hops in back; medium body, dry hop finish and aftertaste, medium duration. Similar to the Pale Ale and perhaps a little more complex and better flavored. [B, 47]

GOATS' BREATH BOCK — amber, caramel malt nose, big caramel flavor with alcohol, semi-dry caramel malt finish and aftertaste, made for Signature Beer Co. [BK, 54]

SAN RAFAEL AMBER ALE — amber, light hop and malt nose;

very dry palate has malt and hops but is mostly just dry; good body, malty finish, some sweetness in back. Made for J&L Brewing of San Rafael, CA. [A, 57]

RED ASS ALE — amber, smooth hop aroma, smooth big dry hop flavor; lots of hops and that's all; flavorful but the malt doesn't show until the finish and then it stays for the entire aftertaste; could use more malt and have it further to the front of the palate. Made for Red Ass Distributing of Ft. Collins, CO. Previously made for Red Ass by H.C. Berger. [A, 59]

NAKED ASPEN RASPBERRY WHEAT — brilliant clear gold, faint berry aroma, dry berry flavor, some notes of cedar and tobacco, medium body; berry taste is faint in the main palate but more noticeable and less dry in the long aftertaste. [W, 44]

NAKED ASPEN PALE ALE — hazy amber, bright hop aroma; hop flavor up front on palate, slides off from mid-palate on and fades out to a brief dry hop aftertaste with little of the intensity shown at the start; you have to keep sipping on it to keep the flavor in your mouth, but does taste good while it is there and is very drinkable. [A, 59]

NAKED ASPEN BROWN ALE — amber-brown, complex lightly toasted malt aroma also shows some hops; flavor like the nose but not as strong or as good; medium body, dry finish and aftertaste with some malty sweetness at the end, very long aftertaste. [A, 56]

COLD SPRING RIVER ROAD RED ALE — pale reddish-amber, faint malt and hop aroma; palate shows light hops and toasted malt, fades quickly; brief hop aftertaste, good hot weather refreshment. [A, 46]

WOLF PACK WHEAT ALE — amber-gold; off-dry fruity malt nose has a grainy component; grain and hop palate has high carbonation; creamy texture, medium long aftertaste. [W, 35]

PONDEROSA PALE ALE — brilliant amber, bright northwest hop aroma, taste like the nose, some caramel sweetness in the finish, dry hop aftertaste, interesting and likable. Made for Reno B.C. [A, 66]

CAVE CREEK CHILI LIGHT BEER — pale gold, light attractive chili-pepper aroma, light body; good jalapeño chili flavor is blended nicely with the malt; aftertaste like the main palate; the chili is done with a light hand. [LO, 52]

SAN RAFAEL AMBER ALE — fairly deep amber, malty nose, malt flavor is a bit toasty, medium body, rich malty aftertaste, good length. Made for J&L Brewing of San Rafael, CA. [A, 57]

SAN RAFAEL RED DIAMOND ALE — reddish orange-amber, bright hop aroma, well backed with malt, good hop and malt flavor, dry hop and malt finish and aftertaste, bright, zesty, refreshing, and flavorful. Made for J&L Brewing of San Rafael, CA. [A, 83]

Columbus Brewing Co.

Brewpub and attached restaurant in Columbus, OH. Has 12-oz. bottled beers made by F.X. Matt in Utica. There is some hand-bottling done at the brewery.

GIBBY'S GOLD — light gold, nice hop nose, light soapy malt flavor, dry hop aftertaste. [B, 49]

COLUMBUS PALE ALE — deep golden amber, light but complex fruity malt and hop nose, big malt flavor with good hops, smooth and bright, medium to good body, good balance, long dry hop aftertaste, a delicious brew. [A, 72]

NUT BROWN ALE — deep amber-brown, roasted malt aroma, big smooth dry malt flavor, medium to good body, long rich malt aftertaste, pleasant and drinkable. [A, 68]

PILSNER STYLE — gold, dry hop aroma, smooth and delicious dry hop flavor, long light dry hop aftertaste. [A, 70]

BLACK FOREST PORTER — deep brown, malt nose, sweet malt palate, big body, almost viscous, long malt finish and aftertaste with an acidic tang in back. [P, 47]

COLUMBUS PALE ALE — amber, pleasant malt and hop aroma and flavor, balanced, good body, dull dry malt finish and aftertaste. Brewed with a number of English and crystal malts; gravity 12 P, 4.25% abw. [A, 72]

COLUMBUS NUT BROWN ALE — brown, malt nose; off-dry malt flavor dries a bit at the finish; thin body, dry malt aftertaste; gravity 12.5 P, 4.5% abw. [A, 68]

COLUMBUS 1492 LAGER — amber-gold, hop nose well-backed with malt, bright and zesty, good hop and malt flavor, good long dry hop aftertaste. Made with Hallertau hops; gravity 12 P, 4.5% abw. [B, 67]

NEW ALBANY PILSENER — gold, light dry hop aroma, light and smooth dry hop flavor with malt faintly in back, long light dry hop aftertaste. Made for New Albany B.C., New Albany, OH, for sale at the New Albany Country Club. This brew is similar to the Pilsner Style above except that it is less malty, using more crystal malt than pale malt. [A, 65]

NEW ALBANY PALE ALE — amber-gold, fresh complex malt aroma shows a little chocolate malt and roasted barley; bright hop and malt flavor reflects the aroma but lightly; very smooth, medium to good body, dry hop aftertaste. Made for New Albany B.C. as above. [A, 70]

COLUMBUS NUT BROWN ENGLISH STYLE ALE — brown, roasted malt nose, balanced nutty sweet malt flavor, finishes dry, medium body, long dry malty aftertaste. [A, 68]

Commonwealth Brewing Co.

Brewpub in Boston, MA. Bottled beers are made under contract by F.X. Matt in Utica, NY and Catamount in White River Junction, VT.

STANLEY CUP STRONG ALE — hazy amber, spicy faint clove off-dry nose, medium body, soft, low carbonation, tangy off-dry spicy clove flavor, buttery finish, hop aftertaste. [A, 58]

GOLDEN ALE — pale gold, light hop aroma, medium body, light hop and malt flavor, low carbonation, dry hop aftertaste. Made with English pale malt and Cascade hops; gravity 10.4 P, 3.25% abw. [A, 50]

AMBER ALE — amber, light malt aroma, light body, light malt and hop flavor, dry hop finish. [A, 48]

COLD DRAUGHT BLOND ALE — tawny-gold, clean crisp hop nose, light clean dry malt flavor, dry malt finish and medium aftertaste; the 20% wheat malt wouldn't be noticed unless you knew. [W, 45]

BOSTON'S BEST BURTON BITTER — copper color, big malt and dry hop nose; flavor is more malt than hops; finish is off-dry malt, but goes dry at the end of the long aftertaste. Kent-Goldings and Cluster hops are used; gravity 12 P, 3.95% abw. [A, 67]

CLASSIC STOUT — very deep brown, light smooth malt aroma

with a touch of hops, classic stout nose, not big but pleasant, good dry malt and hop flavor, smooth finish and long aftertaste like the flavor, very drinkable. [S, 59]

GOLDEN ALE — pale gold, light hop aroma, medium body, light hop and malt flavor, low carbonation, dry hop aftertaste. Made with English pale malt and Cascade hops; gravity 10.4 P, 3.25% abw. [A, 50]

INDIA PALE ALE — amber, big hop nose, bright almost sweet hop palate, good body, quite complex and very good, long dry malt and hop aftertaste. Made from pale and crystal malts with Cluster, Fuggles and Goldings hops; gravity 14.5 P, 4.8% abw. [A, 73]

CooperSmith's Pub & Brewing
Brewpub in Fort Collins, CO

MOUNTAIN AVENUE WHEAT — hazy gold, fresh malt aroma, big spicy flavor, smooth, bright and tasty, finishes dry, a very well-made brew. [W, 61]

PEACH WHEAT — tawny-gold, clean fruity nose; very big spicy palate is excellent except that there is little follow-through; weak finish, dry aftertaste. [W, 50]

DUNKEL WEIZEN — brown, malt nose; light lactic flavor could use a bit more malt for balance; good body, smooth long dry malt aftertaste shows more malt and less spice than the flavor. 50/50 pale and wheat malt with a little

crystal and chocolate malt, lightly hopped with Mt. Hood hops; gravity 12.5 P, 3.8% abw. [W, 50]

PUNJABI PALE ALE — amber, malt aroma with some orange peel; flavor is all malt to mid-palate and then hops; doesn't quite come together; big body, sour hop finish, dry sour hop aftertaste. Made with pale and crystal malts with Cascade and Centennial hops, dry hopped as well; specific gravity 1.064, 5% abw. [A, 39]

ALBERT DAMM BITTER — amber, faint malt nose, thin body, low carbonation, light malt flavor, finish, and aftertaste, dry and dull. [A, 42]

COOPERSMITH'S NUT BROWN ALE — reddish-amber-brown, light chocolate malt aroma, light chocolate and black malt flavor, light body, pleasant, smooth, and short. Made with pale, crystal, amber, chocolate, and cara malts; lightly hopped with Willamette; specific gravity 1.044, 3.7% abw. In 1994 renamed Not Brown Ale. [A, 47]

HORSETOOTH STOUT — very dark brown, coffee and chocolate nose, light malt flavor, low carbonation, light body, short dry malt aftertaste. [S, 48]

DUNRAVEN ALE — amber, appetizing malt nose, tasty malt and hop flavor, light body, very smooth and drinkable; dry aftertaste doesn't give enough follow-through to the flavor. Crystal, amber, and a little wheat malt are used; gravity 11.5 P, 3.4% abw. [A, 51]

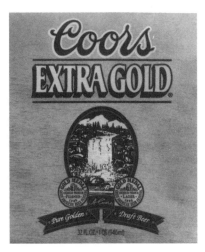

SIGDA'S GREEN CHILI
BEER — gold, light chili pepper
nose, almost like green bell peppers, flavor like the aroma, dry
and hot and very long. Made with
Anaheim chilis, pale ale malt,
cluster and Tettnanger hops, then
"dry chilied" with Serrano chilis
and not filtered; specific gravity
1.048, 3.8% abw. [B, 36]

Adolph Coors Co.
*Breweries in Golden, CO
and Memphis, TN with a
packaging plant in
Elkton, VA*

COORS BEER — pale gold,
lovely fresh clean malt aroma,
hops barely noticeable, light body,
slightly off-dry malt taste, very
light, very refreshing, very
quaffable, medium to short duration; gravity 10.4 P, 3.57% abw,
SRM 2.5, 11.5 IBU. [B, 65]

COORS LIGHT — very pale
yellow-gold, very clean malt aroma,
perky clean malt flavor, light and

brief; gravity 8.1 P, 3.28% abw,
SRM 2.2, 11 IBU. [LO, 29]

GEORGE KILLIAN'S IRISH RED
LAGER — pale copper-red, light
toasted malt aroma, light body,
clean fresh and balanced hop and
malt flavor, light but lingering malt
aftertaste; gravity 12.2 P, 3.90%
abw, SRM 14.5, 14.5 IBU. [B, 42]

COORS GOLDEN LAGER —
yellow-gold, clean malt nose, very
light malt flavor, a little hop bite
in back, light and short malt aftertaste. [B, 28]

COORS EXTRA GOLD — bright
yellow-gold, pleasant malt aroma,
pleasant off-dry malt and hop flavor, long off-dry malt aftertaste;
gravity 11.4 P, 3.90% abw, SRM
4.8, 13.5 IBU. [B, 51]

COORS EXTRA GOLD LIGHT —
gold, fresh perfumy malt nose on
the sweet side, light body, light malt
flavor, weak dry malt finish, brief
malt aftertaste. [LO, 30]

HERMAN JOSEPH'S
ORIGINAL LIGHT DRAFT
BEER — pale gold, nice beery malt
nose, highly carbonated, light body,
pleasant malt and hop flavor, good
balance, brief aftertaste. [LO, 41]

HERMAN JOSEPH'S ORIGINAL
DRAFT BEER — gold, pleasant
light fresh malt and hop nose, clean
flavor like the nose, zesty hop finish, short hop aftertaste, a very
pleasant little brew. [B, 62]

COORS WINTERFEST ALE
1995–1996 — deep amber, light
malty aroma; flavor is mostly malt
but there are supporting hops;

medium body, malty finish and aftertaste, smooth light and pleasant;
made from two-row pale, caramel,
and roasted malts with Saaz hops;
4.5% abv, 5.7% abv. [B, 51]

COORS WINTERFEST 1994–
1995 — deep amber, light malt
aroma; dry malt flavor has some
nuttiness; light body, dry malty
aftertaste, medium length; gravity
14.4 P, 5.7% abv, SRM 13, 20
IBU. [B, 45]

COORS WINTERFEST 1993–
1994 — medium deep brown,
light malt nose, big off-dry malty
flavor, medium body; dry malt
aftertaste is not long, very good
while you are drinking it, but it is
too brief. The recipe is different
each year; gravity 14.4 P, 4.5%
abw, SRM 13, 20 IBU. [B, 63]

COORS WINTERFEST 1992–
1993 — deep gold, light dry hop
nose; malt and dry hop flavor is a
bit rough but there is a lot of it; fair
to good balance, good body, light
short dry malt aftertaste. [B, 46]

COORS WINTERFEST 1991–
1992 — brilliant amber, plain malt
nose, big malt flavor, especially at
the finish, very tasty brew, long
hop aftertaste, best of the
Winterfests to date. [B, 70]

COORS WINTERFEST 1990–
1991 — amber, fruity-malt aroma,
malt flavor, an estery quality to
both the nose and taste, ends up
with an off-dry malt aftertaste,
still with that estery quality in
back. [B, 62]

COORS WINTERFEST 1989–
1990 — tawny-gold, faint fruity

malt aroma, off-dry malt flavor, soft and light with low carbonation, medium dry finish, light short malt aftertaste, a wimpy brew. [B, 41]

First tasted the 1987–1988 version which was similar to the 1989–1990, but had more hops.

COORS EXTRA GOLD DRAFT — bright gold, beautiful malt and hop aroma, slightly off-dry malt palate, very drinkable, medium body, long off-dry malt aftertaste. [B, 47]

KEYSTONE — light gold, light malt nose, malt flavor with a touch of apple, medium body, malt aftertaste of medium length; gravity 10 P, 3.82% abw, SRM 2.7, 12 IBU. [B, 30]

KEYSTONE LIGHT — light gold, very faint malt nose with a trace of apple, off-dry malt flavor, weak body, dry malt aftertaste, short to medium length; gravity 8.1 P, 3.81% abw, SRM 2.2, 5 IBU. [LO, 16]

KEYSTONE DRY — pale hazy gold, fruity malt nose, faint fruity malt flavor, light body, dull faintly fruity malt aftertaste; gravity 9.7 P, 3.90% abw, SRM 2.7, 7.1 IBU. [D, 26]

KEYSTONE ICE — pale gold, fresh malty nose, smooth malt flavor, some hops in back; malty sweetness at the finish, but aftertaste is dry; medium length; 5.2% abv. [B, 53]

COORS CUTTER NON-ALCOHOLIC BEER — pale gold, grainy malt nose, thin body, wet paper and malt flavor, dry malt finish, short malt aftertaste; gravity 5.6 P, less than 0.35% abw, SRM 2.1, 9.5 IBU. [NA, 45]

COORS PREMIUM DRY BEER — gold, pleasant fruity-malt nose, high carbonation, off-dry fruity malt front palate; middle and finish are dry malt; brief light dry malt aftertaste, light body. [D, 42]

ZIMA CLEAR MALT — clear colorless, citrus aroma, low carbonation, very light grapefruit-lemony flavor, little body, no sense of alcohol, very little and brief aftertaste. (Zima Beverage Co., Memphis, TN) [B, 13]

CASTLEMAINE XXXX EXPORT LAGER — gold, light malt nose; dry hop flavor with some malt support but it is vegetal in nature; highly carbonated, drinkable but no raves, good body, slight sweetness to the malt in the aftertaste. Made with Australian hops and under authority of Castlemaine Perkins of Australia by Unibev Ltd., Golden, CO. Not unlike the Australian version, but their big popular "Fourex" in the Northern Territories is the ale. [B, 45]

COORS EISBOCK — bright gold, faint malt nose, light malt flavor with good hops in back, medium to good body, dry finish, medium long dry malt aftertaste. Well-made brew, not highly hopped, but certainly enough to be considered risqué for a nationally distributed brand. [BK, 50]

Notes

SHULERS LAGER — very pale gold, faint malt nose, very light malt and hop flavor, light body, slightly off-dry weak malt aftertaste. Labeled Shulers B.C., Golden, CO; found in cans in a grocery store just outside Tulsa, OK. [B, 30]

COORS ARTIC ICE BEER — yes folks, that's how they spelled it; deep gold, malty nose, big body, ephemeral palate, very short; gravity 11.4 P, 5.4% abw. [B, 41]

COORS OKTOBERFEST MÄRZEN — deep golden amber, dry malt nose and flavor, good body, dry malt finish and aftertaste, hops barely noticeable, somewhat long; made with two-row Moravian and Carapils malts; hopped with Hersbucker and Saaz hops; gravity 13.7 P, 5.7% abw, 23 IBU. [B, 68]

COORS WEIZENBIER — gold, dry malty nose, dry malty flavor; a little touch of sweetness promised by the nose appears in the finish; dry malt aftertaste, light body; made with pale and caramel malts with malted spring wheat; gravity 12.8 P, 5.4% abw, 15 IBU. [W, 41]

COORS ARTIC ICE LIGHT BEER — brilliant gold; fruity malt nose is a bit pear-like; dry malt and light hop flavor, light body, dry hop finish; dry aftertaste has both hops and malt. [LO, 45]

COORS OKTOBERFEST MÄRZEN — copper-gold, lightly roasted malt aroma, off-dry malt flavor, medium body, medium dry malt finish and aftertaste, a commonplace beer. [B, 68]

GEORGE KILLIAN IRISH BROWN ALE — amber-brown, faint vegetal-malt nose; dry malt flavor is a bit monolithic; a little stringent in the corners of the mouth, perhaps from slightly scorched malt, this shows mostly in the finish and aftertaste. [A, 33]

ZIMA GOLD — fairly deep gold, curious gingery-cinnamon-nutmeg aroma, light ginger-ale like taste, light body, short sweet gingery finish and aftertaste. [B, 27]

COORS RED LIGHT BEER — golden-amber, sweet fruity nose with lots of estery qualities like melon and banana, light thin, even watery body, light slightly dry and lightly fruity flavor, very short aftertaste. [LO, 16]

Copper Tank Brewing Co.
Brewpub in Austin, TX

COPPER LIGHT — pale gold, light malt aroma, pleasant malt and hop flavor, medium to light body, dry malt and hop finish and aftertaste, good duration, very nice. [A, 66]

WHITE TAIL ALE — deep gold, dry hop aroma, smooth dry hop flavor, medium body, dry hop finish and aftertaste, a good tasting pale ale. [A, 66]

BIG DOG BROWN ALE — brown, light malt nose, very smooth light dry malt flavor, medium body, medium long light dry malt aftertaste, soft and smooth throughout. [A, 54]

RIVER CITY RASPBERRY ALE — pinkish-gold, light fruity raspberry nose, big tart raspberry flavor, medium body; dry hop finish and aftertaste has a tart raspberry background. [A, 53]

FIRE HOUSE STOUT — dark brown, chocolatey nose, chocolate malt and roasted barley flavor, medium to big body; long rich aftertaste shows roasted and chocolate malts; good mouthfeel, a well-made stout. [S, 80]

COPPER TANK SPECIAL PALE ALE — deep gold, big hop and malt aroma, big hop flavor, good body, long dry hop finish and aftertaste; a good tasting, drinkable ale meant to be an IPA but the hops were filtered out somewhat excessively by error, losing most of the intended hop character, still a good ale and excellent with food. [A, 73]

ILLBE BOCK — deep amber, good bright hop nose; rich malty flavor has plenty of hop support; good body, long dry malt and hop aftertaste; 6.2% abw. [BK, 73]

Coyote Springs Brewing Co. and Cafe
Brewpub in Phoenix, AZ; formerly named Barley's Brewpub

KOYOTE KÖLSCH — gold, malt nose, very bright malt and hop flavor, good body, dry malt and hop finish and aftertaste, a very tasty zesty brew; gravity 11.25 P, 3.9% abw. [K, 52]

NUTS TO YOU NUT BROWN ALE — brown, hoppy fruity aroma, a sense of lactic in back; flavor has even more (and clearly) lactic acid in behind the hops; medium body; acidity mars the flavor and aftertaste. Tasted at GABF in Denver in 1992, apparently a victim of some mistreatment on its journey. Made with caramel and chocolate malts, Northern Brewer hops; specific gravity 1.049, 4.2% abw. [A, 77]

BISON BROWN ENGLISH ALE — this nut brown ale is the successor to Nuts to You and was tasted at the 1993 GABF-brown; bright well-hopped and malted aroma, good nutty dry malt flavor has the hops in back; medium body, long dry nutty aftertaste. Made with five malts and Northern Brewer hops; specific gravity 1.049, 4.2% abw. [A, 72]

NUTZ — This is the version of the brewery's nut brown ale tasted at GABF in 1994, a good nutty brown ale with a soft smooth character identical to Bison Brown above; OG 1048, 5% abw. [A, 67]

TRICK PALE ALE — gold; big bright hop aroma has that lactic acid in behind, it is more pronounced on the palate but still in behind the hops, it stays well into the aftertaste. This was also tasted at GABF in 1993 and had suffered from mishandling; gravity 12.5 P, 4.2% abw. [A, 34]

PROSPECTOR PALE ALE — amber-gold; aroma shows both malt and hops; big hop flavor with plenty of malt for good balance; overall it is a dry flavor, especially at the finish; long dry hop aftertaste. [B,70]

COYOTE GOLD — gold, dry hop nose with some malt showing; very dry hop flavor, finish, and aftertaste; not much malt showing past the aroma, but enough for balance. An American cream ale-style lager, it is made with two-row Munich, Cara Pils, and caramel malts with Yakima Valley hops; specific gravity 1.048, 4.8% abw. [A, 62]

DRY GULCH STOUT — very deep brown color, roasted barley nose; dry roasted malt flavor makes you think of coffee; finish shows that it was dry hopped; long dry hop aftertaste, very pleasant and drinkable. At the 1994 GABF the offered stout was I'll Be Shocked which was the same as described here as Dry Gulch. It is an oatmeal stout with a distinct roasted coffee character; specific gravity 1.049, 5.2% abw. [S, 73]

FRONTIER BROWN — very deep amber-brown, light malt aroma, roasted barley malt flavor, very smooth, good body, malty and drinkable, light dry roasted malt finish and aftertaste, short duration. [B, 76]

COYOTE CHRISTMAS ALE — deep amber-gold; spicy nose made me think of ginger, but it is nutmeg, cloves, coriander, and cinnamon; spicy flavor (still made me think of ginger, but I had a head cold); long dry spicy aftertaste, a good wassail. [A, 67]

Notes

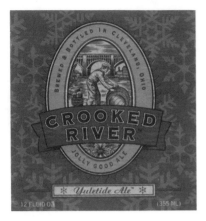

COYOTE LAGER — pale gold, bright hop aroma and flavor, light to medium body, dry hop finish and aftertaste. Tasted while still in second fermentation, so it was not finished. It does show good promise for a bright refreshing pilsener-style beer. [B, 62]

LOST DUTCHMAN LAGER — amber, good malt nose and taste, good body; hops stay in back as they should for the style. Made with German Pils malt, light and dark caramels malts; Perle and Tettnanger hops; specific gravity 1.052, 4% abw. [B, 63]

OATMEAL STOUT — very dark brown, roasted barley and chocolate malt aroma, dry roasted malt flavor, complex showing some chocolate and coffee, good balance; finishes very well leading into a long aftertaste like the flavor, but more dry. This too was tasted while still fermenting, but it was very near to being ready for release. [S, 68]

COYOTE SPRINGS EUROPEAN PILSNER — deep gold, big malt aroma, crisp dry malt flavor, dry hop finish and aftertaste. Uses American two-row and light caramel malts with Saaz hops; specific gravity 1.046, 3.6% abw. [B, 67]

BOCK AROUND THE CLOCK — amber, big hoppy aroma and flavor, big body, very flavorful; malt shows well in the finish and aftertaste; dry and long. They use Munich and dark caramel malts with Perle and Tettnanger hops in this lager; specific gravity 1.062, 5.2% abw. [BK, 63]

COYOTE SPRINGS INDIA PALE ALE — amber-gold, dry malt and hop aroma, zesty complex malt and hop flavor, medium body; complex finish and long aftertaste has a bite at the end; very drinkable. Made from five malts flavored with Galena and Perle hops, conditioned with some oak chips; specific gravity 1.062, 5% abw. [A, 73]

Crane River Brew Pub and Cafe
Brewpub in Lincoln, NE

SOD HOUSE ALTBIER — golden brown, dry spicy aroma and flavor, good body, dry hop finish and aftertaste; there's a little bitter bite on the end. Made from six malts including wheat, Munich, and Vienna and Hallertau hops; specific gravity 1.046, 3.8% abw. [A, 53]

SOLSTICE SPICE — light brown, spicy like pumpkin pie aroma, light spicy flavor shows mostly ginger; finish and aftertaste show a little malt, but the ginger dominates. English-style brown ale accented with ginger root; specific gravity 1.046, 3.4% abw. [A, 47]

Crescent City Brewhouse
Brewpub in New Orleans, LA

CRESCENT CITY PILSNER — gold, fresh and crisp hop nose, bright hop flavor, good body, dry hop finish and aftertaste, good length, very nice European-style pils. [B, 67]

RED STALLION — amber-gold; malt aroma immediately makes you think of a Vienna-style lager; slightly off-dry malt flavor has the hops in back, malt finish and long malt aftertaste. [B, 58]

BLACK FOREST — dark mahogany, complex chocolate malt nose; dry chocolate malt flavor is very attractive; good body; long aftertaste is an extension of the taste; very drinkable and satisfying. [B, 73]

CRESCENT CITY MARDI GRAS — dark amber, malt nose, light dry malt flavor, medium body, medium length. [B, 47]

Crested Butte Brewery & Pub, Idlespur, Inc.
Brewpub in Crested Butte, CO

RED LADY ALE — reddish amber, bright malt and hop nose,

mild malt and hop flavor, very drinkable, balanced, pleasant, long dry hop aftertaste. Made with pale, caramel, and chocolate malts; brewed with Northwestern hops and dry hopped as well; gravity 12.5 P, 4.07% abw. [A, 64]

BUCKS WHEAT — hazy gold, malt nose, malt flavor with good hop balance, medium body, dry hop finish and aftertaste; OG 1048, 3.86% abw, 4.83% abv. [W, 63]

3-PIN GRIN PORTER — brown, faint chocolate malt nose, dull malt flavor, medium body, light hop finish and a dry hop aftertaste. Made with chocolate malt and American hops; OG 1049, 3.91% abw, 4.89% abv. [P, 26]

RASPBERRY-OATMEAL STOUT — deep brown, great tart raspberry-malt nose, thin body; dull malt flavor shows little of the aroma; dull aftertaste. Made with oatmeal and raspberry puree; gravity 13 P, 3.9% abw, 45 IBU. [S, 62]

WHITE BUFFALO PEACE ALE — golden amber; bright hoppy aroma has plenty of malt backing; bright refreshing hop flavor is smooth and balanced with a sweetness in back that is strongest in the finish; good body, not very drinkable; long dry hoppy aftertaste has a little kick; specific gravity 1.052, 4.28% abw, 20 IBU. [A, 80]

RODEO STOUT — deep brown, big chocolate malt and roasted barley aroma; flavor reflects the aroma but not as good; medium body; good complexity showing notes of licorice, oatmeal, and malty sweetness; long light dry roasted malt aftertaste is a continuation of the palate; a little light for a stout, but a very good-tasting one made from pale, caramel, and chocolate malts roasted barley, oatmeal, black malt flour, licorice, with lactose added, balanced with Perle and Chinook hops; OG 1063, FG 1.023, 6.2% abv, 40 IBU. [S, 66]

Crooked River Brewing Co.
Microbrewery in Cleveland, OH

CROOKED RIVER SETTLERS ALE — hazy amber, bright fruity malt aroma; big strong flavor starts out with malt but soon powerful hops bounce in and the character of the brew becomes a huge flavorful ale; good body; the bold hop flavor continues in the dry hop aftertaste; a really good brew for "hopheads." [A, 86]

CROOKED RIVER YULETIDE ALE — amber, hop and toasted malt nose, big dry astringent hop palate; takes the juice right out of your tongue; very long and very dry hop aftertaste. [A, 53]

CROOKED RIVER YULETIDE ALE 1995 — dark amber; big spicy pumpkin pie aroma tends toward sweetness and alcohol; spicy flavor is a bit winey and shows little of the malt and hops; long sweet and spicy. [A, 64]

Notes

CROOKED RIVER BLACK
FOREST LAGER — deep gold;
malt nose is clean and sweet; soft
dry straightforward malt flavor
has a light hop support; good
body, soft and smooth, fairly dry
malt aftertaste. [B, 50]

CROOKED RIVER LIGHT-
HOUSE GOLD — gold; faint
malt aroma has an unpleasant
background component; dry malty
flavor, very mild, medium to light
body, creamy mouthfeel, dry light
malt finish and aftertaste. [B, 27]

CROOKED RIVER IRISH STYLE
RED — red-amber, English hop
aroma, a bit soapy; big soapy hop
flavor also has some vegetal malt;
medium body, dry hop finish and
aftertaste. [A, 42]

CROOKED RIVER
DOPPELBOCK — dark amber;
plenty of hops, malt, and alcohol
for the nose; big alcoholic-malt
flavor shows little of the hops
promised by the aroma; huge

body, rich alcoholic finish and
aftertaste; alcohol overrides
everything else. [BK, 86]

Crown City Brewery
Brewpub in Pasedena, CA

MT. WILSON WHEAT BEER —
gold, malty-wheat nose, refreshing
malt flavor with light hops, long
dry malt aftertaste. [W, 57]

ARROYO AMBER ALE — dark
amber, light hop aroma, bright
smooth hop and malt flavor with a
nice little bite, very tasty, light dry
malt aftertaste with medium duration. [A, 68]

BLACK CLOUD OATMEAL
STOUT — very dark brown,
brown head, dry coffee-malt
aroma and flavor, tart dry finish,
long dry malt aftertaste, quite
flavorful. [S, 74]

BLACK BEAR STOUT — dark
brown, tan head, chocolate malt and
roasted barley aroma and taste; the
finish cuts off abruptly in strength to
a light but long-lasting roast barley
aftertaste; medium body, smooth,
pleasant, drinkable; a lightweight as
a stout, but an easy drinking dark
flavorful beer. [S, 67]

*Note: They also serve a "Half &
Half," a mix of the Wheat and
whichever Stout is available.*

Dallas County
Brewing Co.
Microbrewery in Adel, IA

OLD DEPOT ALE — deep gold,
faint off-dry malt aroma, good

light off-dry malt flavor with a
light hop finish, medium body,
light dry hop aftertaste. Some
samples came with a fruity malt
nose that was of peaches, apples,
and melon with a fruity taste as
well; gravity 11.1 P, 3.6% abw,
SRM 8.0, 15.0 IBU. [A, 45]

OLD DEPOT PORTER — deep
brown, dry malt aroma and flavor;
some chocolate malt shows, finish
shows some smokiness; heavy
body; smokiness and chocolate
malt not in tune in some batches,
okay in others; roasted malt aftertaste, good mouthfeel; gravity
14.0 P, 4.20% abw, SRM 20.0,
35.0 IBU. [P, 63]

OLD DEPOT LAGER — gold,
dry hop aroma and taste, very
pleasant, medium body, refreshing
dry hop finish and aftertaste, good
length; gravity 11.8 P, 3.5% abw,
SRM 5.0, 12.0 IBU. [B, 60]

OLD DEPOT LIGHT BEER —
gold, dry hop aroma and flavor,
light body; short dry hop aftertaste
shows only a little buttery malt;
gravity 10.0 P, 3.5% abw, SRM
5.0, 18.0 IBU. [LO, 40]

Dempsey's Sonoma
Brewing Co.
Brewpub in Petaluma, CA

RED ROOSTER ALE — amber-
gold, lovely hop aroma and flavor,
great balance, good body, excellent mouthfeel, extremely long
flowery hop and dry malt aftertaste, a remarkably good tasting
ale; gravity 14.5 P, 4.5% abw.
More recent recipe cites gravity

12.8 P, 4.8% abw, but this has not been tasted. [A, 84]

RIVERSIDE WHEAT BEER — gold, light malt nose, light wheat malt flavor, wheat and dry hop finish and aftertaste, fairly light body and very short on the palate. Made with 40% wheat malt and Hallertau hops; 3.5% abw. [W, 40]

SONOMA IRISH ALE — amber, chocolate malt aroma and flavor, medium body, dry hop and roasted malt finish and aftertaste, excellent balance, very good flavor, another remarkably good brew; gravity 13.0 P, 4.2% abw. More recent recipe cites specific gravity 12.5 P, 4% abw, but that brew has not been tasted. [A, 83]

UGLY DOG STOUT — deep brown, chocolate malt and roasted barley aroma and flavor, big bodied yet very smooth, very good balance, noticeable alcohol (7% abw), finishes smoothly, long rich malt aftertaste; gravity 17 P. [S, 63]

PETALUMA STRONG ALE — amber; big hoppy aroma shows a lot of malt; flavor shows plenty of malt and hops; big body; long strong aftertaste is a continuation of the flavor; gravity 16 P, 6% abw. [A, 84]

Deschutes Brewery & Public House
Brewpub and microbrewery in Bend, OR

DESCHUTES BREWERY JUBEL ALE 1991 — deep amber, gorgeous rich malt nose, rich malt flavor, medium long, big bodied, fairly dry malt aftertaste; specific gravity 1.065, 5.6% abw. [A, 67]

DESCHUTES DUNKELWEIZEN — brown, complex malt and hop aroma, good body, off-dry malt flavor backed with hops; slightly drier malt aftertaste has more hop character. Made with 50% wheat; specific gravity 1.054, 4.6% abw. [W, 47]

CASCADE GOLDEN ALE — gold, malt aroma, light malt flavor, dry malt aftertaste. Finished with Cascade hops; specific gravity of 1.042, 3.3% abw. [A, 48]

BACHELOR BITTER — copper-amber, good big bitter hop flavor, good body, fairly big dry malt and bitter hop flavor, good body, and long dry hop aftertaste. Dry hopped with Kent Goldings; specific gravity 1.048, 4.1% abw. [A, 62]

BLACK BUTTE PORTER — dark ruby-brown, lightly fruity off-dry roasted and chocolate malt aroma; has lots of coffee showing; smooth roasted barley flavor, medium body; has good balance despite being sort of sweet because there are good hops in there as well as several kinds of malt; hops do stay in back throughout; malt finish and aftertaste seems almost smoky and is a little sweet in back; very long roasted malt aftertaste, a delicious, very pleasant and likable brew; specific gravity 1.054, 4.5% abw. [P, 76]

Notes

MIRROR POND PALE ALE —
amber-gold, fruity malt aroma,
good body, dry Cascade hop finish
and aftertaste; specific gravity
1.052, 4.2% abw. [A, 49]

FESTIVAL PILS — gold, big hop
aroma, big bright hoppy flavor,
very dry through to the long dry
hop aftertaste. Hopped with Saaz
hops; specific gravity 1.050, 4.2%
abw. [B, 53]

BOND STREET BROWN
ALE — brown, light dry roasted
malt aroma and flavor, touch of
chocolate also, good body, dry
malt finish and aftertaste; specific
gravity 1.051, 4.2% abw. [A, 67]

OBSIDIAN STOUT — dark
brown, roasted barley and chocolate
malt aroma and flavor, good balance, good body, dry malt finish and
aftertaste, a very drinkable brew.
Made with eight malts; specific
gravity 1.065, 5.6% abw. [A, 79]

WYCHICK WEIZEN — cloudy
amber, malt aroma, off-dry malt
flavor, no spice. Made with 40%
wheat malt; specific gravity 1.049,
4.1% abw. Also called Wychick
Wheat. [W, 41]

SOUTH SISTER SCOTCH
ALE — dark brown, sweet caramel malt aroma, dry malt flavor,
off-dry malt finish and aftertaste,
goes dry malt at the very end.
Made with six malts; specific
gravity 1.068, 4.1% abw. [A, 58]

DESCHUTES OREGON
BREWERS FESTIVAL IPA —
cloudy gold, fruity aroma, bright
fruity flavor, some citrus grapefruit/
pineapple; dry hop finish and aftertaste continues to show some fruit
in back; made with pale ale, American two-row, Carapils, and crystal
80L malts; hopped with Styrian
Goldings; OG 1065, FG 1.018,
6.2% abv, 70 IBU. [A, 79]

Detroit & Mackinac Brewery
Microbrewery in Detroit, MI

WEST CANFIELD ALE — gold,
buttery nose, thin malt and hop
flavor, short dry hop aftertaste;
gravity 12 P. [A, 25]

DETROIT & MACKINAC IPA —
gold, malt nose; flavor has more
hops than malt but is light to point
of seeming thin; light body, light
dry hop and malt aftertaste. Made
with Chinook, Willamette, and
Tettnanger hops; gravity 13.0 P.
[A, 45]

DETROIT & MACKINAC IRISH
RED ALE — amber, malt aroma,
caramel malt and faint hop flavor,
creamy, good body, dry malt aftertaste. Made using Willamette and
Tettnanger hops; gravity 12.3 P.
[A, 47]

MACKINAC GOLD — gold; dry
spicy malt aroma and flavor does
show some hops; medium body,
light dry malt and flowery hop
finish and aftertaste, smooth, fair
length. Made with Tettnanger
hops; gravity 12.0 P. [A, 61]

MACKINAC BLACK — dark
brown; light wheaty aroma has a
faint chocolate malt background;
light flavor like the nose, light
body, refreshing, light medium
length dry malt aftertaste. Made
with 40% wheat malt. [W, 47]

Devil Mountain-Bay Brewing Co.
*Brewery in Benicia, CA.
Formerly the Devil Moun-
tain Brewpub and brew-
ery in Walnut Creek, CA.
Some earlier labels said
beer was brewed and
bottled by Bay B.C.,
Benicia, CA, under the
trade name Devil Moun-
tain Brewery.*

RAILROAD ALE — hazy amber,
pleasant citrus hop ale nose; zesty
citrus hop flavor with hop strength
growing across the palate and
strongest at the finish; delicious
and balanced, medium dry malt
aftertaste. Brewed with Galena
and Cascade hops and English ale
yeast; gravity 15 P. [A, 84]

IRON HORSE ALE — hazy deep
amber, highly carbonated, foamy,
tangy citrus nose, good malt and
hop flavor with the citrus background, medium body, light malt
aftertaste, medium length. [A, 53]

GAYLE'S PALE ALE — hazy
gold, bright citrus nose (grapefruit
this time), lemon and grapefruit
background to the malt flavor,
medium body, refreshing but not
much like an ale. [A, 35]

DEVIL'S BREW PORTER —
deep brown, effervescent, smoky
chocolate malt aroma, very dry

smoky malt flavor, full flavored big body, good balance, long strong malt aftertaste, very drinkable, very good of type. Brewed with chocolate roasted malt and Cluster and Cascade hops; specific gravity 1.046, 3.5% abw. [P, 75]

DIABLO GOLDEN ALE — gold, finely carbonated, complex malt and hop aroma; hop flavor has malt in back; medium body, fairly brief dry hop aftertaste; made with pale and caramel malts; hopped with Mt. Hood and Hallertau hops. [A, 47]

Dilworth Brewing Co.
Brewpub in Charlotte, NC

REED'S GOLD — gold, hop aroma, sweet malt in back, cardboard and malt flavor, dry malt aftertaste; specific gravity 1.044, 3.8% abw. [A, 38]

ALBEMARLE ALE — dark amber, faint malt aroma and flavor, fairly brief dry malt aftertaste; made with pale, crystal, and Munich malts; specific gravity 1.048, 4% abw. [Λ, 45]

DILWORTH PORTER — dark brown, roasted barley aroma and flavor, good body, harsh malt and hop flavor, lacks balance. Made with pale, crystal, and roasted barley malts; gravity 13 P, 4.5% abw. [B, 36]

DILWORTH SCOTTISH ALE — deep gold, big malt nose and taste, good body; finish and aftertaste are slightly off-dry malt; 4.5% abw. [A, 65]

Dixie Brewing Co.
Brewery in New Orleans, LA

DIXIE LAGER — gold with a touch of amber, lightly hopped slightly sour malt aroma, light body, refreshing hop flavor, medium dry finish and aftertaste. Also seen labeled Dixie Beer, this beer is made with barley malt, rice, and Cluster and Cascade hops; specific gravity 1.044, 3.6% abw. [B, 52]

DIXIE LIGHT BEER — deep golden color, slightly sweet malt and apple aroma, light bodied, light "beery" (pleasant malt and hops) taste, malt finish, and brief aftertaste. [LO, 53]

DIXIE AMBER LIGHT — amber color, good malt and hop aroma, light malt flavor, too much carbonation, short aftertaste. [B, 42]

NEW ORLEANS BEST — pale gold, pleasant hop nose; palate is malt with a slight hop bite; light body, medium length. (Royal B.C.) [B, 27]

NEW ORLEANS BEST LIGHT — yellow-gold, light malt aroma, good carbonation level, pleasant malt flavor, medium length. (Royal B.C.) [LO, 39]

COY INTERNATIONAL PRIVATE RESERVE CASK 36 — gold, zesty ale-like aroma, clean tangy hop flavor, good body, malt aftertaste. (Royal B.C.) [B, 51]

Notes

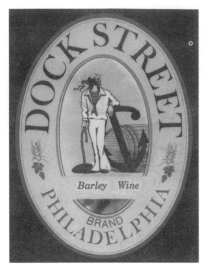

DIXIE BLACKENED VOO DOO LAGER — deep amber-rose color, pleasant malt and hop aroma; big dry toasted malt flavor with some hops in back but could use more; good body; more hops arrive in the finish but a bit late; dry hop aftertaste. This is an all-malt beer, made from five different malts and Mt. Hood and Cascade hops; specific gravity 1.052, 4.0% abw. [B, 63]

RATTLESNAKE BEER — pale gold, malt and hop aroma, malt flavor, light body, light hop and malt aftertaste. Made for Kershenstine Enterprises, Eupora, MS. Previously made by Spoetzl B.C. [B, 42]

DIXIE BASIN STREET PORTER — brown, malty nose, big dry malt flavor, finish, and aftertaste. Made with five malts and three varieties of hops, warm-fermented; 3.8% abw. [P, 68]

DIXIE BAYOU BOCK — amber, big hop and malt aroma and flavor, good body, long complex dry malt and hop aftertaste. Made with Mt. Hood and Hallertau hops; 5.7% abw. [BK, 69]

DIXIE HOLY SMOKE — deep gold, light smoked malt aroma and taste, medium body; good smoked flavor lasts into the finish and aftertaste, but does not overwhelm the malt and hop flavors; good length, nicely done. Made from pale and caramel malts gently smoked for 1 1/2 hours over beechwood; specific gravity 1.053, 3.7% abw. [B, 67]

DIXIE WHITE MOOSE — very pale yellow, real sweet chocolate aroma (not chocolate malt) and flavor, very clean and delicious, a chocolate freak's dream, not really a beer but very nice; specific gravity 1.045, 3.6% abw. [B, 67]

DIXIE BASIN STREET ALE — gold, dry hop nose; malt joins the hops on the palate for a nice well-balanced taste; hops strongest at the finish and into the long dry aftertaste; 4.0% abw. [A, 67]

DIXIE JAZZ AMBER LIGHT — pale amber, grainy malt nose, dry grainy malt flavor, light body, light dry malt aftertaste; specific gravity 1.030, 3.3% abw. [LO, 36]

DIXIE CRIMSON VOO DOO ALE — definitely red, grainy malt nose, very malty flavor, ends dry and bitter, almost no hops until the finish, medium body, a red ale but not exciting. [A, 44]

Dock Street Brewing Co.
Brewpub and restaurant in Philadelphia, PA

DOCK STREET WEISS BIER — hazy gold, light fresh malt aroma, bright malt flavor with plenty of hops; a lot of hops for a wheat beer but the balance is good; dry mostly hop finish, long dry hop aftertaste. Mix is 50% wheat. [W, 50]

DOCK STREET PALE ALE — tawny-gold, faint hop nose, bright hop flavor with plenty of malt, good body, dry hop finish, long dry hop aftertaste, excellent balance, complex, feels good in your mouth. [A, 75]

DOCK STREET IMPERIAL STOUT — opaque brown, tan head, malt aroma, concentrated malt flavor; burnt nature of the malt is most noticeable in the finish; long tapering malt aftertaste. [S, 50]

DOCK STREET BARLEY WINE 1991 — deep brown, big dry chocolate malt nose and taste; strong hops back the malt but can barely compete and stay in back except at the finish and aftertaste; big, complex, and very long, feels great in your mouth; have this at the end of your beer drinking, because if you have it first it is almost overwhelming and, for certain, you won't be able to taste anything else afterward. Made with six-and two-row malts; gravity 27.4 P, 9% abw. [BW, 90]

DOCK STREET BARLEY WINE 1993 — deep brown, even the

head is brown; big bright hop and malt aroma, huge body, great balance, strong and alcoholic, smooth despite its strength; shows some sherry-like features; extremely long and rich aftertaste, a luscious monster. Made from all two-row malts including English and chocolate malt and warm-aged on champagne yeast; gravity 27.4 P, 9% abw. [BW, 92]

DOCK STREET AMBER — pale amber, light malt nose, dry malt and hop flavor; long aftertaste has dry hops and malt with a touch of malt sweetness at the end; gravity 12.3 P, 4.2% abw. [B, 83]

DOCK STREET BOHEMIAN PILSNER — golden amber, beautiful hop nose and taste, very well balanced with malt, some complexity, dry hop finish and aftertaste, good duration. Made with Zatec and Hallertau hops; gravity 12.9 P, 4.1% abw. [B, 62]

DOCK STREET CREAM ALE — gold, somewhat sweet appetizing malt aroma, smooth and soft malt flavor, off-dry malt finish; aftertaste is soft dry malt but lacks length. Brewed with 25% dextrose; gravity 12.8 P, 4.2% abw. [A, 53]

DOCK STREET DORTMUNDER — amber-gold, hop nose, good dry hop flavor, well bodied, long dry hop aftertaste, made to style. Made with Vienna, caramel, and Munich malts, Hersbrucker and Tettnanger hops; gravity 14.1 P, 4.5% abw. [B, 49]

DOCK STREET OLD ALE — gold, big spicy hop aroma, big off-dry malt and complex hop flavor, big body, dry finish, long aftertaste. Made with English pale and crystal malts, dry hopped with Kent-Goldings and Fuggles hops, and aged with oak; gravity 18.1 P, 5.8% abw. [A, 67]

DOCK STREET PUMPKIN ALE — pale amber; light spicy aroma shows only spice; light spicy flavor shows cinnamon, nutmeg, and allspice, not much malt or hops evident; made with pumpkin, spices lightly done; very nice of type. [B, 50]

DOCK STREET DUNKLES — brown, dry roasted malt aroma and flavor, good and complex hop backing, good body, long bright aftertaste. Made with Munich malt and Tettnanger, Perle, and Hersbrucker hops; gravity 13.5 P, 4.3% abw. [B, 53]

DOCK STREET ENGLISH MILD — brown; light aroma and dry flavor shows mostly malt including some chocolate malt; hop background is English Fuggles giving a distinctive English character; medium body, dry malt finish and aftertaste. Recipe calls for mostly crystal malt; 3.15% abw. [A, 45]

DOCK STREET KÖLSCH — gold, light hop aroma, malt flavor, off-dry malt finish; hops come in again during the aftertaste. Made with 13% wheat malt, Tettnanger, Hallertau, and Saaz hops; 4.2% abw. [K, 53]

DOCK STREET HELLES — deep gold, bright hop nose and taste, hop finish and aftertaste, very long, very German; malt is there but barely noticeable; gravity 12.4 P, 3.8% abw. [B, 68]

DOCK STREET ILLUMINATOR — amber, very faint malt aroma; toasted malt flavor is fairly strong but has a scorched component in back; finishes as it starts; long toasted malt aftertaste, not particularly well-balanced and, except for the unwanted burnt nature has little to separate it from other similar brews; made with Tettnanger and Hallertau hops; gravity 16.7 P, 5.65% abw. [BK, 53]

DOCK STREET BELGIAN WHITE BEER — cloudy gold, big head; bright pungent well-hopped flavor has orange/citrus and coriander spice in back; the malt is strong enough to hold back the orange and coriander until the finish; medium body, spicy finish, long spicy-citrus aftertaste. Fairly good witbier. Tasted at another time and place, there was a faint malt aroma, the flavor was on the lemony side and there was no trace of the coriander; the finish was lemony but there was only malt in the aftertaste. [B, 67]

DOCK STREET TRIPEL — hazy golden-amber, lovely and big complex aroma, big rich malt flavor, long rich malty aftertaste with fruity esters throughout and with hops in the back, dry only at the very end, a juicy brew with lots of ale-like character. [A, 79]

Dubuque Brewing & Bottling Co.

Brewery in Dubuque, IA. This was the old Dubuque Star Brewery and has operated under a variety of corporate names, mostly Zele B.C., but also Dubuque Star B.C. and Simpatico Breweries. Most recently the corporate name of choice has been Dubuque Brewing & Bottling Co. The brewery is presently owned by Brandevor U.S.A., Inc.

ERLANGER MAERZEN BIER — amber, soapy malt aroma, clean malt flavor, good body, fairly long malt aftertaste with hops at the very end. [B, 43]

DARRYL'S ORIGINAL PREMIUM LAGER BEER — hazy gold, light malt aroma, touch of hops first then light malt for the palate, fresh malt finish and aftertaste, little depth or duration. Also called Darryl's Pig Pounder for Gilbert Robinson, Inc. Made with pale malt, Cluster, Cascade, and Hallertau hops; gravity 12.2 P, 3.95% abw. [B, 39]

DUBUQUE STAR BEER — pale gold, pleasant off-dry malt and hop aroma, light hop flavor, medium body, clean and refreshing, brief malt aftertaste. [B, 42]

CHAU TIEN EMPEROR BEER — gold, hop nose with good malt backing; fruity hop flavor has good hops and malt in the middle; high carbonation, good body, dry finish and long dry hop aftertaste, complex, clean, and long. [B, 70]

BULL SHOOTERS BEER — brilliant pale gold, malt aroma, highly carbonated, big rich malt flavor, hefty body, long pleasant medium dry malt aftertaste. Contract brew for Sporting Chance, Inc., Kirkland, WA. [B, 71]

WILD BOAR SPECIAL AMBER — golden amber, clean fruity-malt aroma, big fleshy malt flavor, hops appear at finish, balanced hop and malt aftertaste, big body, excellent balance. Made with two-row and caramel malt, Cascade and Tettnanger hops; gravity 12.8 P, 3.9% abw. Made for Georgia B.C. [B, 77]

WILD BOAR CLASSIC PILSNER — amber-gold, northwest hop aroma with carbonation and some malt; complex hop aroma reflects the nose; highly carbonated; a bright snappy flavor that works well; brewed with Carapils and pale malt with Saaz hops; gravity 12.3 P, 3.8% abw. Made for Georgia B.C. [B, 73]

WILD BOAR WINTER SPICED LAGER — amber, aroma of fresh cut pine; lightly spiced flavor with what seems to be a pine resin background; not exciting, very little of the spiciness; maybe best at the finish, certainly better in the aftertaste where it joins in with dry hops; medium body, medium length, overall a little dull for the type. Made for Georgia B.C. [B, 46]

PUBLICK HOUSE PALE ALE — gold, grainy malt aroma, off-dry grainy flavor, light to medium body; light dry malt aftertaste is medium long; borders on dull and really could use more barley malt. Made for a restaurant in Sturbridge, MA. [A, 31]

WILD WINTER — amber, spicy aroma and flavor, medium body; fairly long aftertaste shows some malt underlying the spice flavors. This is the 1995 version of Wild Boar spiced winter beer. [A, 31]

BEERGUY AT THE TOP — bright gold, dry malt aroma, creamy good medium dry malt flavor; hops come in the middle but stay far back; good malt finish, medium long dry malt aftertaste, good balance, very drinkable. Contract brew for American Beerguy, Berkeley, CA. [B, 49]

TRESTLES LAGER BEER — hazy gold, big hop nose leaps out at you (hops-malt-hops); flavor is malt-hops-malt, finishes dry malt, long dry malt aftertaste; good body, good balance, very drinkable brew. Contract brew for Beach Beer Inc., Newport Beach, CA. [B, 76]

SIMPATICO AMBER — hazy amber, malt nose, good malt and hop flavor, good body, creamy finish, long malt aftertaste, a very well-made beer; gravity 12.5 P, 4.3% abw. [B, 76]

SIMPATICO GOLDEN LAGER — gold, appetizing Cascade hop aroma, smooth light hop and malt flavor, light body, light

dry hop finish and aftertaste; gravity 11 P, 3.65% abw. [B, 60]

SIMPATICO GOLDEN RESERVE — gold, malt aroma, off-dry malt flavor, tart hop finish; malt finish and aftertaste has a buttery background. Made using Hallertau hops; gravity 12.3 P, 3.94% abw. [B, 63]

TGIF PREMIUM AMBER BEER — gold, malt and light hop nose and taste, medium body, dry hops at the finish and into the fairly long aftertaste; gravity 12.3 P, 3.9% abw. Made for Friday's Brewing Co. Called Friday's Amber at GABF in 1994. [B, 6]

TGIF AMBER LIGHT — gold, light malt nose and taste, light body, short dry malt aftertaste; specific gravity 7.9 P, 2.8% abw. Made for Friday's B.C. and the TGI Friday's restaurant chain. Called Friday's Amber Light at 1994 GABF. [LO, 22]

GOLDEN RAIL — hazy amber, malt nose, very bitter hop flavor, very dry hop aftertaste; specific gravity 1.052, 3.9% abw. Made for Cherryland B.C. of Sturgeon Bay, WI. [B, 46]

CHERRY RAIL — pinkish-gold, maraschino cherry aroma and flavor, light body, dry cherry aftertaste, has cherry flavor added; specific gravity 1.052, 4% abw. Made for Cherryland B.C. of Sturgeon Bay, WI. [B, 34]

CHAMPIONS CLUBHOUSE CLASSIC PREMIUM BEER — golden amber, attractive malt aroma, fairly big and rich malt flavor, good body, dry malt finish and aftertaste, very short on the palate. Claims to be microbrewed and to comply with German Purity Law of 1516; it is made with pale and caramel malts, Cascade, Tettnanger, and Hallertau hops; specific gravity 12.7 P, 4.1% abw. [B, 53]

RHOMBERG CLASSIC AMBER BEER — bright amber, zesty malt-hop nose and flavor, smooth, balanced, tasty, medium body, long dry hop aftertaste; 4.3% abw. Contract brew made for Rhomberg Brewing Co. of Davenport, IA, originally under the name Rhomberg All Malt Beer. Made with caramel and crystal malts. [B, 60]

RHOMBERG CLASSIC PALE BEER — bright deep gold, big malt aroma, heavy body; almost too much malt on the palate but it is balanced off not by hops but with carbonation; soft malt finish and long malt aftertaste, nicely done and very drinkable. Contract brew as above; originally labeled Rhomberg Classic All Malt Pale Beer. [B, 64]

PINK TRIANGLE PREMIUM LIGHT BEER — deep gold, good hoppy nose, big well-hopped dry taste, good body for a light beer, dry hop finish, short dry hop aftertaste, pretty good except for the length. Made for Pink Triangle Breweries, a portion of profits goes to local AIDS organizations and other gay and lesbian nonprofit groups. This is

the second gay-lesbian beer I have heard about, the other was Wilde's. [B, 61]

BUFFALO BREW — hazy gold, sweet malt nose, sweet malt flavor; tinny-salty component in the finish but this does not appear in the aftertaste, off-dry malt aftertaste; made with caramel malt, Cascade, Hallertau, and Tettnanger hops; gravity 12.2 P, 4% abw. Made for Buffalo Ranch Steak House. [B, 42]

SCRATCH BEER — deep gold; pleasant malty aroma is a tad off-dry; flavor is malty with some hops; finishes drier than it starts; medium dry aftertaste. This is a novelty package with a nude on the label covered with a material that can be scratched off. Made for Tidwell Enterprises of Blythe, CA. [B, 47]

BRAEMOUNT SELECT PREMIUM MALT LIQUOR — hazy gold, toasted malt nose, light toasted malt flavor, sort of monotonic, off-dry toasted malt finish and aftertaste, quite short. [ML, 45]

SIMPATICO HAND CRAFTED LAGER — hazy gold, hop nose; big malt and European hop flavor is a little sour but typically European pils in style; a little sweetness in the finish, but the aftertaste is dry malt and hops; medium body, decent balance. [B, 53]

SIMPATICO HAND CRAFTED AMBER — amber, northwest hop aroma is weak; big dry hop palate, medium body, long dry hop aftertaste. [B, 53]

HORNBLOWER OFFICER'S RESERVE — gold, malt aroma, grainy malt flavor, malt finish and aftertaste; needs some hops for better balance, but taste is pleasant. [B, 46]

MALLARD BAY RED ALE — amber, roasted malt nose; dry roasted malt flavor is a bit off-dry; good body, very pleasant, drinkable, driest at aftertaste, long dry malt, made by Hops & Barley B.C. [A, 72]

DUBUQUE STAR BIG MUDDY RED UNFILTERED ALE — hazy reddish amber; malty aroma seems a bit roasted; rich roasted malt flavor, medium body, dry lightly roasted malt aftertaste with good length. Made with roasted malt with Cascade and Willamette hops; gravity 13.5 P, 4.3% abw. [A, 66]

HOG'S BREATH LAGER — amber, pleasant hop and toasted malt aroma and taste, medium body, good flavor, dry hop finish and aftertaste. Made for the Providence Brewing Co. of Providence, RI. [B, 50]

OXFORD RASPBERRY WHEAT — pinkish amber, big raspberry nose, light dry raspberry flavor, like a dry raspberry soda, light body; dry raspberry finish and aftertaste is less obviously raspberry than the main flavor. An ale made for Oxford B.C. of Linthicum, MD. [A, 38]

APPLE BACH — amber, apple aroma, unlikable sweet-sour apple taste, dry apple finish, medium body, long strange apple aftertaste, not likable. Made for Cherryland Brewery of Sturgeon Point, WI. [B, 22]

WILD WHEAT — cloudy amber-gold, fruity aroma and flavor, a bit "pickly" up front with lambic-style acidity, medium to light body; flavor is long lasting; as you continue to drink it, there appears to be more wheat beer character developing. Made for Wild Boar B.C. [W, 56]

Durango Brewing Co.
Microbrewery in Durango, CO

DURANGO DARK — deep amber, malt aroma, light malt flavor, not much follow-through; gravity 12.5 P. [B, 43]

COLORFEST — pale gold, malt nose and taste, thin body, no follow-through; gravity 14.5 P. [B, 45]

Eddie McStiff's
Brewpub in Moab, UT

MCSTIFF'S AMBER ALE — amber, light hop nose and flavor, dry hop finish and aftertaste, very brief. Made with British Carastan malt; gravity 9.5 P, 3.2% abw. [A, 47]

McSTIFF'S RASPBERRY WHEAT — gold, raspberry nose, nice berry flavor, off-dry malt and fruit finish and aftertaste. Naturally reduced raspberries added late instead of finishing hops; specific gravity 1.040, 3.2% abw. [W, 56]

McSTIFF'S BLUEBERRY WHEAT — gold, faint berry aroma and flavor, light body; dry wheaty aftertaste has lost most of the berries. Probably the same wheat beer as above but with a change in fruit added; specific gravity 1.040, 3.2% abw. [W, 50]

McSTIFF'S SPRUCE BEER — gold, light spruce bough aroma and flavor, light body, very light spruce finish and aftertaste; medium length and very lightly done on the spruce throughout, leaves a very nice feeling in the mouth and is quite refreshing. Made with spruce root and bark, probably added to that same wheat beer; specific gravity 1.040, 3.2% abw. [B, 67]

CANYON CREAM ALE — gold, dry malt aroma and flavor, medium body, dry malt finish and aftertaste, not much length, made with top-fermenting yeast, but cold-fermented; specific gravity 1.042, 3.2% abw. [A, 53]

McSTIFF'S CHESTNUT BROWN — amber-brown, dry malt nose and taste, hops stay in back, medium body, dry malty finish and aftertaste with hops balancing in at the end; specific gravity 1.042, 3,2% abw. [A, 53]

Edgefield Brewery (McMenamins)
Brewery, winery, brewpub, vineyard, movie theater, and bed-and-breakfast in Troutdale, OR. Part of the McMenamins chain of brewpubs and breweries.

Notes

POWELL BUTTE BITTER — gold, light hop aroma, smooth light hop flavor, medium to light body, very smooth and easy to drink, good balance, light dry hop finish and aftertaste; made with 40L crystal and two-row pale malts; hopped with Nugget hops three times during the brewing process; OG 1040, FG 1.008, 3.2% abv, 17 IBU. [A, 76]

El Dorado Brewing Co.
Microbrewery in Mt. Aukum, CA

EL DORADO REAL MOUNTAIN ALE — amber; lovely complex flowery northwest hop aroma has lots of interesting components like grapefruit and pineapple; big hop flavor is very attractive up front and bitter in the middle and finish; medium body, good long bitter hop aftertaste. [A, 68]

El Toro Brewing Co.
Microbrewery in Morgan Hill, CA

EL TORO GOLDEN ALE — amber-gold, big bright hop nose, excellent very bright tasty hop flavor, medium body, dry hop finish and aftertaste, a very good tasting beer. [A, 82]

EL TORO AMBER ALE — amber, bright hop aroma and flavor, medium body; dry hop finish and aftertaste loses some of the brightness of the main palate, but it is still good. [A, 68]

EL TORO KICK ACE BARLEYWINE — amber, strong malty nose, big strong malt and alcohol (8.75% abv) flavor, big body, long strong malt and alcohol aftertaste, a good barleywine; OG 1090. [BW, 73]

Erie Brewing Co.
Microbrewery in Erie, PA

MAD ANTHONY'S RED — pale amber, faint malt nose, complex dry malt flavor, medium body, good balance, good taste, dry malt finish and aftertaste. [A, 73]

RAIL BENDER SCOTCH ALE — brilliant gold, light malt aroma and taste, medium body, dry malt finish and aftertaste, good length. [A, 66]

Eske's: A Brew Pub / Sangre de Cristo Brewery
Brewpub in Taos, NM

TAOS GREEN CHILI BEER — pale hazy gold, faint chili aroma; chili flavor is very much clean green chiles, not just a hot burning but rather the green chile taste; medium body, dry chile finish, and long aftertaste that continues the chili taste but which is slightly hotter than the palate sensation while the beer is in your mouth. Made with roasted green chiles; specific gravity 1.044, 3.58% abw. [B, 53]

ESKE'S SCOTTISH ALE — amber, big hop aroma; strong hops start the flavor, then it smooths out as the malt comes in to help balance the taste; big body; finishes balanced with both hops and malt showing the way into a long aftertaste. Made with caramel Munich and Carapils malts and Chinook and Cascade hops; specific gravity 1.068, 5.19% abw. [A, 67]

10,000 FOOT STOUT — dark, almost black; strong malt and hop aroma and flavor shows roasted barley and chocolate malts; very complex, heavy body; long rich aftertaste gives you as much malt and complexity as you could want; specific gravity 1.073, 5.99% abw. [S, 78]

ARTIST'S ALE — gold, assertive hop nose, huge dry hop flavor, medium body, big dry hop finish and aftertaste, quite long; specific gravity 1.047, 3.78% abw. [A, 62]

RIO REFRESCO WHEAT ALE — hazy gold, light hop nose; substantial palate shows both the hops and malt; good body, good taste, although not light like many American wheat beers, it is refreshing; very long malty aftertaste. Made with 10% wheat malt and Cascade hops. [A, 56]

MESA PALE ALE — deep gold, light malt nose; pleasant balanced flavor shows plenty of malt and hops; good body, fairly rich, long dry malt aftertaste, a very fine brew, perhaps Eske's best among regular offerings; specific gravity 1.060, 5.5% abw. [A, 74]

ESKE'S SPECIAL BITTER — deep amber, light malt aroma and flavor, good body, pleasant and tasty, dry finish and aftertaste; specific gravity 1.045, 4.5% abw. [A, 65]

OL' 43 BLONDE ALE — deep gold, malt nose, very malty slightly off-dry flavor, big body, malt finish, light short dry malt aftertaste. [A, 62]

SECO STOUT — opaque, brown head; dry malt nose shows some chocolate malt and roasted barley; light dry malt flavor is true to the aroma; good body, flavor biggest at the finish, very smooth and drinkable, lightly hopped, very long dry roasted barley and chocolate malt aftertaste; specific gravity 1.050, 4.5% abw. [S, 62]

BERT & ERNIE BARLEYWINE — amber, big alcohol and malt aroma keeps the hops suppressed; huge alcoholic (9% abv) flavor shows malt more than hops; enormous body, northwest hops (Cascade and Chinook) very evident at the finish giving the brew a citruslike character that shows more in bottled samples than it did when fresher and on draft; long complex aftertaste shows all the major components (alcohol, malt, and hops in that order). [BW, 72]

ESKE'S HOLIDAY CHEER — deep amber, aroma of ginger, cinnamon, and orange peel, medium to good body; flavor like the aroma but tends to being more citrus in the finish; very evident citrus backtaste in the aftertaste. Tasted in bottle in January 1994. This beer was made with orange zest in the boil and was finished with it as well. When fresh and on draft, the citrus nature was less pronounced. [A, 62]

Etna Brewing Co.
Brewery in Etna, CA

ETNA EXPORT LAGER BEER — hazy gold, fresh fruity malt nose, bright hop and malt flavor, light body, tasty, drinkable, short dry aftertaste. Brewed with pale, Carapils, and Munich malts using a single temperature infusion mash and lagered for 4 to 5 weeks before packaging; gravity 12.25 P, 3.5% abw. [B, 52]

ETNA ALE — deep golden amber, zesty light hop and fruity malt aroma, light malt and hop flavor, light body, brief light dry malt aftertaste. The brew is top-fermented and cold-lagered; gravity 12 P, 3.4% abw. [A, 50]

ETNA DARK LAGER BEER — deep amber-brown, big dark malt nose with a slightly smoked background, light body, flavor like the nose but not as strong nor as smoked, medium long dry malt aftertaste; gravity 12.5 P, 3.6% abw. [B, 54]

Notes

ETNA WEIZEN — pale gold, malt aroma, slightly spicy malt flavor, light wheaty finish and aftertaste. Brewed with 30% wheat, top-fermented, and cold-lagered; gravity 9.5 P, 2.76% abw. [W, 62]

Eugene City Brewery
Microbrewery located in the lower level of West Bros. Bar-B-Que restaurant in Eugene, OR. It is not associated with the interests that contracted for brews with Kessler using the corporate name Eugene City B.C.

CITY IPA — deep yellow, bright hop aroma, smooth malt and hop flavor; alcohol shows a bit; good body, good balance, dry finish and aftertaste. Made with two-row and caramel malts; specific gravity 1.062, 5.6% abw. [A, 69]

BREWERS EXTRA SPECIAL BITTER — copper, flowery hop nose, very dry hop flavor, good body, finishes quite hoppy, long dry bitter hop aftertaste; specific gravity 1.050, 3.6% abw. [A, 54]

BLACK HOLE STOUT — dark brown, big malt aroma, dry malt flavor, fairly rich and smooth, good body, dry hop finish, complex dry malt and hop aftertaste; specific gravity 1.071, 5.4% abw. [S, 64]

EUGENE CITY BITTER — amber-gold, light hop and malt aroma, light dry hop and malt flavor, medium body, dry hop finish and aftertaste, not much zest to the flavor, long and dry; made with two-row and caramel malt with Chinook and Cascade hops; specific gravity 1.046, 3.5% abw. [A, 54]

OLD CURMUDGEON BARLEY WINE — deep brown; malty aroma is touched with caramel, complex caramelized malt; high alcohol (6.9% abw) and hop flavor is a little out-of-balance; big body; the caramelized aftertaste is very pleasant and that saves the day; specific gravity is 1.090. [BW, 60]

ORCA PALE ALE — gold, dry hop aroma and taste, medium bodied, very smooth palate with good balance, long dry hop and malt aftertaste; specific gravity 1.054, FG 1.011, 5.5% abv, 30 IBU. [A, 61]

Evansville Brewing Co.
Brewery in Evansville, IN

FALLS CITY LIGHT BEER — pale gold, light malt aroma, light grainy-malt flavor, weak malt finish, short malt aftertaste. [LO, 27]

THE EAGLE PREMIUM MALT LIQUOR — gold, grainy malt nose with some background hops, clean refreshing bright off-dry malt and hop flavor, good body, medium long off-dry malt aftertaste; specific gravity 1.054, 5.0% abw. [ML, 42]

WIEDEMANN LIGHT — pale gold, light dry hop and malt nose and flavor, medium long dry hop aftertaste, very drinkable and refreshing. [LO, 47]

WIEDEMANN BEER — gold, light hop nose, good malt and hop flavor, fairly dry, drinkable, and refreshing, fairly long dry hop aftertaste. [B, 27]

BRIGADE PREMIUM BEER — gold, malt nose, light malt and hop flavor, light body, hop finish, dry hop aftertaste with little duration. [B, 34]

BRIGADE LIGHT PREMIUM BEER — gold; hop nose is first a bit overly fragrant with some off notes, malt soon comes to the rescue but only faintly; sour hop flavor, light body, sour hop finish; aftertaste is the same sour hops but drier and more attenuated, but long lasting. [LO, 26]

BRIGADE NA NON-ALCOHOLIC MALT BEVERAGE — gold, dank grainy malt nose, grainy flavor, light body, grainy finish and aftertaste, very brief. [NA, 26]

DOG POUND BREW — pale gold, faint dry hop aroma, creamy and refreshing but lightly flavored, very drinkable, medium long light dry hop aftertaste. Made for Great American Brew Co., Fairfax, VA. [B, 49]

CRAZY ED'S CAVE CREEK CHILI BEER — gold, bright jalapeño pepper nose, hot jalapeño pepper taste (pepper first then the heat), finish, and aftertaste. Lots of real jalapeño character. Made for Black Mountain Brewery of Cave Creek, AZ; specific gravity 1.046, 3.8% abw. [B, 19]

BIRELL NON-ALCOHOLIC MALT BEVERAGE — gold, hop aroma, good hop and malt flavor, good body, fairly long dry hop and malt aftertaste, good for a non-alcoholic brew; specific gravity 1.014, 0.35% abw. Previously made in U.S. by Jones B.C. [NA, 50]

BICYCLE FLAVORED BEER VERI BEERY — pinkish gold, big clean raspberry nose, clean raspberry flavor, tasty, light bodied, brief raspberry aftertaste, very drinkable. Made for Bicycle Beverage Corp. of Chicago. [B, 64]

BICYCLE FLAVORED BEER APRICOT STONE — golden-peach, slightly dry apricot nose, apricot and malt flavor, not overly sweet, pleasant, semi-dry apricot flavor, finish, and aftertaste, not long. Made for Bicycle Beverage Corp. of Chicago. [B, 63]

BICYCLE FLAVORED BEER MISTY LIME — color of lime juice, lime aroma, lime and malt flavor like a lager and lime as served in British pubs, very slightly sweet, good lager and lime, dry lime and malt finish and aftertaste. Made for Bicycle Beverage Corp. of Chicago. [B, 67]

JOHN GILBERT'S RIVERBOAT BRAND LAGER BEER — gold, canned corn nose, off-dry malt flavor, some toasted malt in back, dry toasty finish, light body, short dry malt aftertaste. [B, 36]

GERST AMBER LAGER BEER — amber, fruity malt nose, malt flavor, dull dry malt finish and aftertaste, short; specific gravity 1.046, 3.8% abw. [B, 19]

DRUMMOND BROS. PREFERRED BEER — pale gold, faint perfumy malt nose; flavor is mostly malt, hops are very light; pleasant very light flavor, slightly sweet finish, brief and a bit dull; specific gravity 1.042, 3.6% abw. [B, 43]

GRINGO LIGHT PILSNER — gold, fruity apple aroma, light weak malt flavor, light body, off-dry malt finish and aftertaste; made for Gringo B.C. of Santa Fe, NM. [B, 30]

GRINGO EXTRA BEER — cloudy gold; big caramel malt nose has some hops in back; very clean malty taste, semi-sweet malt aftertaste, medium body, very drinkable. Also made for Gringo B.C. [B, 51]

NEW FRONTIER AMBER LAGER — amber, light toasted malt aroma, toasted malt flavor, medium body; medium long dry malt aftertaste has a little malty sweetness in the background. [A, 47]

BRIGADE PREMIUM ICE BEER — gold, big head, very nice malt and hop nose, big malt flavor, medium body; malty aftertaste is not long; 5.5% abv. Made for Walgreen Drug Store chain. [B, 42]

BLUE RIDGE LAGER — amber, Bohemian hop aroma (possibly Saaz); big Euro-hop flavor has plenty of malt backing; good body, good balance, good Bohemian-style pils flavor, dry hop finish, long dry hop aftertaste; well-made pils that tastes very much like many eastern Bavarian beers. Comes in a cobalt blue glass painted bottle. Contract brew made for Rainbow Ridge B.C. [B, 67]

WHITE RIDGE WHEAT BEER — pale honey gold color, light toasted malt and hop aroma and flavor; light and dry lightly roasted malt flavor has some coffee tones; light to medium body, medium length. Contract brew made for Rainbow Ridge B.C. issued in a white painted clear bottle. [W, 22]

RED RIDGE ALE — honey gold color, light toasted malt nose, light toasted malt and hop flavor; malt is up front on the palate and the hops are in the finish, doesn't quite come together. Contract brew made for Rainbow Ridge B.C. issued in a red painted clear bottle. [A, 40]

1995 SANTA CLAUS CHRISTMAS ALE — deep gold; light malty aroma has a light hop background; flavor same as the nose, medium body, light dry malt and hop aftertaste. [B, 43]

Note: Evansville acquired several labels from G. Heileman (Drewry's Beer, Drewry's Light'n Dry Beer, Drummond Bros., Drummond Bros. Light, Cook's Goldblume Beer, Cook's Goldblume Premium Light Beer, Falls City Beer, Sterling Beer, and Sterling Light Beer) and the rights to sell Wiedemann Bohemian Special Beer and Wiedemann Bohemian Special Light Beer in five states. Wiedemann labels sold elsewhere are still produced by G. Heileman.

Fields Restaurant & Brewpub
Brewpub in Eugene, OR, originally (and still sometimes) named Oregon Fields B.C.

DUCKTAIL ALE IPA — deep golden amber; malt aroma has a vegetal component; malty flavor also is a bit vegetal; medium body,

slightly off-dry malty aftertaste, good length. [A, 56]

Firehouse Brewing Co.
Brewpub in Rapid City, SD

BUFFALO BITTER — amber, bright caramel malt aroma, light malt flavor like the aroma, light body, dry hop finish and long aftertaste; specific gravity 8.6, 3.0% abw. [A, 67]

RUSHMORE STOUT — brown, chocolate malt and alcoholic nose, big rich and full roasted barley flavor, dry malt finish and aftertaste; specific gravity 12.2, 3.8% abw. [S, 70]

BROWN COW ALE — brown, fruity malt nose and taste, off-dry malt finish, medium long dry malt aftertaste; specific gravity 10.7 P, 3.15% abw. [A, 50]

DITTOHEAD PORTER — dark brown, dry malt nose and taste, medium body, dry hop finish and aftertaste, not long on the palate; specific gravity 11.3, 3.5% abw. [P, 53]

ROUGH RIDER BARLEY WINE — deep amber, big sweet malt aroma, concentrated sweet malt flavor from extra sugars added to the fermentation, big body; high alcohol (8.4% abw) makes for a winey taste; long sweet malt aftertaste; specific gravity 22.6. [BW, 61]

Fish Brewing Co.
Microbrewery in Olympia, WA

FISH EYE IPA — amber-gold, big hop aroma, robust hop flavor, medium to good body, dry hop finish and aftertaste; made with generous amounts of Kent-Golding hops; specific gravity 1.062. [A, 69]

FISH TALE PALE ALE — deep amber, fairly complex malt and hop aroma, medium body; lightly sweet malt flavor is balanced with assertively bitter hops; quite smooth, well-hopped finish and aftertaste. [A, 67]

MUDSHARK DARK PORTER — light brown, malt nose; rich smooth malty flavor has a faint chocolate-like backing; medium to good body, starts to dry at the finish, dry hop aftertaste; specific gravity 1.060. [P, 63]

TROUT STOUT — deep brown, light dry malt and slight hop aroma, medium to good body; Chinook hops more noticeable in the finish and aftertaste, where they slowly emerge from under the roasted malt that dominates the main flavor; very long complex aftertaste shows both malt and hops; specific gravity 1.060. [S, 72]

LEVIATHAN BARLEYWINE — tawny amber like a tawny port, off-dry malty nose, semi dry malt taste, more bitter than hop flavored; doesn't come together and lacks character; good duration, made with British pale, crystal 17L, and chocolate malt, hopped with Chinook and Cascade hops; OG 1089, FG 1.025, 7.5% abv, 85–90 IBU. [BW, 53]

Flat Branch Pub & Brewing
Brewpub in Columbia, MO

FLAT BRANCH BROWN ALE — brown, malty nose, smooth malty flavor, light body, lightly hopped, long complex malty aftertaste. Made with two-row pale, crystal, Victory, and chocolate malts with flaked barley and Mt. Hood hops; specific gravity 11.3 P, 3.5% abw. [A, 63]

FLAT BRANCH GREEN CHILI BEER — gold, nice peppery nose; smooth lightly peppered flavor shows the malt and hops without overpowering them; smooth and balanced; long aftertaste shows a light pepper taste over the malt and hops; made with two-row pale malt and Bullion and Mt. Hood hops, with a generous amount of Anaheim chiles added to the fermenter and Serrano chilies in the conditioning tank; gravity 11.5 P, 3.7% abw. [B, 65]

Notes

FLAT BRANCH HEFE-WEIZEN — hazy gold, pleasant classical clove spice aroma, bright refreshing flavor, medium body, lovely balanced long spicy malt and hop aftertaste; made with 50% two-row pale malt and 50% malted wheat, a weizen yeast, and Cascade, Mt. Hood, and Hallertau hops; gravity 10.8 P, 3.6% abw. [W, 70]

FLAT BRANCH INDIA PALE ALE — gold, big bright well-hopped aroma and flavor, very tasty, plenty of hops, big body, long well-hopped complex dry aftertaste; made with two-row pale, crystal, and Carapils malts, Bullion, Cascade, and Centennial hops in the boil, and dry hopped with Centennial hops and oak chips; gravity 15.5 P, 4.9% abw. [A, 98]

MARKET SQUARE STOUT — brown; chocolate malt dominates the nose; rich dry complex malt flavor; plenty of roasted barley makes for a classical dry stout taste; very very smooth; long aftertaste is dry but still has a richness; made with twelve different grains, an abundance of roasted barley and flaked oats; gravity 14 P, 4,8% abw. [S, 73]

The Florida Brewery, Inc.
Brewery in Auburndale, FL

GROWLIN GATOR LAGER — pale yellow-gold, pleasant malt nose; refreshing malt flavor is good while it lasts (which is not for long); light body, fine for hot weather drinking. Recently, most samples of this beer seen have been made by August Schell B.C. of New Ulm, MN. [B, 41]

ABC BEER — gold, malt and light hop nose, flavor like the aroma, light hop finish; medium long aftertaste has some hops and malt, overall fairly dry. Made for ABC Liquors chain of Florida. [B, 47]

ABC ALE — deep gold, dry hop nose, tangy hop flavor; has some malt in back, dry hop finish and aftertaste; medium length. Also made for ABC Liquors. [B, 47]

ABC LIGHT — gold, attractive malt and hop nose, light malt flavor, light body, very faint and brief malt aftertaste. Another made for ABC Liquors. [LO, 29]

ABC MALT LIQUOR — deep gold, malt and hop nose; flavor is mostly malt but there are some hops in back; long off-dry malt aftertaste. Made for ABC Liquors chain of Florida. [ML, 47]

Flying Dog Brew Pub
Brewpub in Aspen, CO

AIREDALE PALE ALE — deep gold; lovely nose shows hops and malt, flavor nicely balanced between the malt and the hops, good body, long dry malt and hop aftertaste; a very pleasant easy to drink brew. Made with pale and caramel malts, and Fuggles and Kent-Goldings hops, including dry hopping; gravity 13 P. [A, 62]

WOLFHOUND IRISH STOUT — brown, roasted barley and chocolate malt nose and taste, very smooth and dry, medium to good body, long dry aftertaste like the flavor. Made from pale, caramel, and black malts plus black barley; gravity 12.5 P. [S, 60]

IRISH SETTER STOUT — dark brown, malt nose and taste, medium body, fairly long dry malt aftertaste; specific gravity 1.064. [S, 53]

SHEEPDOG STOUT — dark brown; soapy nose and taste, one taster felt it was like detergent, otherwise a smooth fairly rich oatmeal stout with fairly good duration. 12–15% oats are added on the mash; gravity 14.0 P. [S, 27]

RED WARLOCK RASPBERRY COOLER — pink, spicy nose and taste, dry finish and aftertaste, somewhat short; gravity 11 P. [A, 47]

BLOODHOUND RASPBERRY STOUT — almost black, certainly opaque, big raspberry nose, medium strength raspberry-malt flavor, finishes very dry, fairly long dry malt aftertaste; gravity 20 P. [S, 67]

RED DOG GINGER BEER — pale gold, ginger nose like a ginger snap cookie, light ginger flavor; dry finish and aftertaste is malt and hops, no ginger. This is not a soft drink, but rather a beer made with grated ginger root in the brew kettle with Cascade and Centennial hops; gravity 10 P. [A, 53]

GREYHOUND HONEY ALE —
pale gold, honey malt nose and
taste, very light finish, and less
aftertaste. Made from half malt
and half clover honey; gravity
11 P. [A, 50]

K-9 CLASSIC PALE ALE — gold,
malt nose and taste, very light flavor, light body, dry finish and aftertaste without much character. Made
with pale, wheat, and caramel malts
and Centennial and Cascade hops;
gravity 13 P. [A, 41]

DOG HOUSE WHEAT — gold,
cereal nose and grainy taste;
stays a little off-dry and is only
faintly spicy. It is a wheat ale
made with 50% wheat and
lightly hopped with Hallertau
hops; gravity 11.5 P. [W, 27]

OLD PAL — dark brown, malt
nose, dry malt palate, medium
body, short dry malt aftertaste. A
dark old ale made using caramel,
pale, and black malts; specific
gravity 1.060. [A, 47]

RIN TIN TAN BROWN ALE —
brown, very appetizing hop
aroma, big bright hop flavor with
plenty of malt, very drinkable,
good body, finishes dry hops, long
dry hop aftertaste. Made with
pale, caramel, and black malts,
Centennial and Cascade hops,
including dry hopping; specific
gravity 1.056. [A, 74]

BULLMASTIFF BROWN
ALE — brown, malty nose and
taste, good body but on the dull
side. Made from pale, caramel,
and black malts and Fuggles hops;
gravity 12.5 P. [A, 41]

DOGGIE STYLE PALE ALE —
amber, peachy fruity malt and
bright hop aroma, big hop flavor,
big body, complex and interesting,
long dry hop aftertaste, another
winner from the Dog. American
version of the classic English-style
pale ale, this is made with Chinook and Cascade hops, dry
hopped; specific gravity 1.048.
This is the only Flying Dog beer
found bottled. [A, 75]

ENGLISH SETTER BITTER —
amber-gold; hops dominate the
nose and the flavor; taste is very
big hops, yet the brew is complex
and well-balanced; finishes dry
hops leading into a long dry hop
aftertaste; one of the better made
English-bitter style ales made on
this continent. Made from pale
and caramel malts, with Fuggles
and Kent-Goldings hops; gravity
12.5 P. [A, 78]

SCOTTIE SCOTTISH EXPORT
ALE — deep amber, big hop nose,
big and bright hop palate, very
zesty, medium long dry hop aftertaste. Made with pale and caramel
malts, lightly hopped with
Fuggles; gravity 12.5 P. [A, 61]

OL' YELLER GOLDEN ALE —
gold, hop nose and taste, medium
body, dry hop finish and aftertaste.
Made with pale, wheat, and Munich
malts, and Hallertau and Saaz hops;
specific gravity 1.044. [A, 48]

Notes

HAIR OF THE DOG PORTER — brown, dry malt nose and flavor, medium body, smooth, dry and balanced, but short. Made with pale, caramel, and black malts, Chinook and Cascade hops; specific gravity 1.052. [P, 53]

FLYING MC DOG SCOTCH ALE — ruby-brown, buttery malt nose; caramel malt flavor has an alcohol and medicinal background; dry malt finish and aftertaste. Made with pale and caramel malts with Centennial hops; gravity 14 P. [S, 21]

BULLDOG IMPERIAL STOUT — dark brown, malt aroma and flavor, big body; seems a bit duller than other stouts from Flying Dog. An imperial-style stout; gravity 20 P. [S, 47]

BLITZEN'S GNARLY BARLEY WINE — amber, hop nose, huge hop flavor, big body, faint lactic bite in back, long long long hop aftertaste; gravity 24 P. [BW, 76]

Frankenmuth Brewery, Inc.
Brewery in Frankenmuth, MI

FRANKENMUTH GERMAN STYLE PILSENER — gold, good malt and hop nose, rich hop flavor; has plenty of malt; good body, long dry hop aftertaste; specific gravity 1.046, 4% abw, 20 IBU. [B, 84]

FRANKENMUTH GERMAN STYLE DARK — deep rosy-amber, off-dry malt aroma, straightforward dry malt flavor, long dry malt aftertaste, smooth and very drinkable; specific gravity 1.054, 4.15% abw, 25.5 IBU. [B, 83]

FRANKENMUTH GERMAN STYLE BOCK — brown, big malt nose, smooth complex roasted malt flavor, big body, balanced, richly flavored, long dry malt aftertaste; made from six different malts and aged twelve weeks; specific gravity 1.068 (16.6 P), 5.3% abw, 21 IBU. [BK, 84]

FRANKENMUTH WEISSE BEER — bright gold, melon-mango fruit and malt nose, finely carbonated, faint fruity-malt-wheat flavor, light body; faint spice joins malt in the finish; medium long spicy malt aftertaste. Top-fermented, this is a bottle-conditioned beer; specific gravity 1.050, 3.93% abw, 14 IBU. [W, 42]

FRANKENMUTH EXTRA LIGHT — pale gold; faint malt nose with a hop background that makes you suspect that it will go skunky when it gets over-the-hill; light body; weak malt flavor is mostly carbonation; light malt finish, brief malt aftertaste with a sour touch at the very end; specific gravity 1.046, 3.6% abw, 14 IBU. [LO, 20]

OLD DETROIT AMBER ALE — light amber, malt aroma, zesty dry hop flavor, creamy texture, dry hop finish, dry malt aftertaste; specific gravity 1.048, 3.6% abw, 25 IBU. [B, 47]

ISLAND GOLD BEER — deep gold, fruity malt aroma, dull malt flavor, thin body, weak short malt aftertaste. Contract brew for Bay B.C., Put-in-Bay, OH. [B, 10]

PERRY'S MAJESTIC LAGER BEER — amber-gold, faint off-dry malt aroma, dull medium-dry malt flavor, medium body, medium long slightly sour dry malt aftertaste. Touted as an all organic beer; specific gravity 1.048, 3.9% abw. Made for Riverosa Co., New York City. [B, 50]

FRANKENMUTH OKTOBERFEST — amber, fruity estery malt nose, dry malty flavor; there are hops in back, but overall the balance is not good; dry malt finish and aftertaste; specific gravity 1.046, 3.5% abw, 18 IBU. [B, 36]

BRIMSTONE AMBER ALE — brilliant amber, vey malty aroma, big malt flavor, big body, very drinkable, fairly dry finish and aftertaste, quite long. Made for Brimstone B.C. [B, 71]

OLD DETROIT RED LAGER — amber, fruity estery malt aroma, big fruity-malt flavor, off dry malt backtaste, good body, very drinkable, dry malt finish, short dry malt aftertaste; specific gravity 1.041, 3.4% abw, 18 IBU. [B, 58]

FRANKENMUTH YULETIDE PORTER 94 — brown; toasty dry malt nose has a touch of ashy background; finely carbonated, not creamy though; flavor is light lightly toasted dry malt; light body, faintly ashy dry malt aftertaste. [P, 47]

O'MALLEY'S LOST IRISH STYLE ALE — deep amber, good tight head, attractive medium rich malty aroma; malt flavor has a dry hop background that emerges at the finish; medium body, dry mostly malt aftertaste, overall dry, malty, and very drinkable. Made for The Fort Wayne B.C. of Indiana. [A, 61]

Frederick Brewing Co.
Microbrewery in Frederick, MD

BLUE RIDGE PORTER — deep amber; light malt aroma seems to have some chocolate malt in it; big strong malty flavor has a lot of character, there's hops in there too; good body, well-balanced some faint malty sweetness in behind the hops at the finish, long dry malty aftertaste with hops in back; made with Cascade and Chinook hops; this one is a winner; specific gravity 1.058, 4.1% abw. [P, 86]

BLUE RIDGE AMBER LAGER — amber, light toasted malt aroma and flavor, simple and straightforward, medium body, light dry malt finish and aftertaste; specific gravity 1.050, 3.95% abw. [B, 65]

BLUE RIDGE GOLDEN ALE — medium deep gold, nose of malt and northwest hops, good carbonation level, pleasant smooth balanced hop and malt flavor, creamy mouthfeel and drinkable, good body, finishes nicely with mostly

dry hops but with a malty sweetness in back to balance, pleasant long dry hop and malt aftertaste. Made with Willamette and Cascade hops; specific gravity 1.047, 3.65% abw. [A, 75]

BLUE RIDGE WHEAT BEER — pale gold, lightly spiced malt aroma, malt flavor with a spicy herbal background, light to medium body, spicy herbal malt aftertaste, made with 50% malted wheat; specific gravity 1.035, 3.1% abw. [W, 71]

BLUE RIDGE STEEPLE STOUT — dark brown, chocolate malt and roasted barley aroma and flavor, almost smoky, dry American style, big bodied; hops appear at the finish but don't make much of a contribution to the taste; a sipping beer. [S, 79]

BLUE RIDGE ESB RED ALE — copper-amber; lightly roasted malt aroma is a touch sour, also is a little buttery; dry toasted caramel malt flavor, sweet background, medium body; dry hops are there but stay behind the caramel and toasted malt. [A, 57]

BLUE RIDGE CRANBERRY NOEL — slightly hazy amber; faint fruity nose seems a bit skunky at first; tart fruity flavor is on the dry side; weak watery body, tart fruity dry aftertaste, a bit dull. [B, 25]

Notes

BLUE RIDGE HOPFEST BROWN ALE — hazy medium deep amber, good hop and malt nose; plenty of malt on the palate (especially up front) but the hops dominate; toasted malt takes over in the finish; long roasted malt aftertaste; hops and malt vie for position across the palate adding to interest. [A, 74]

Fredericksburg Brewing Co.
Brewpub in Fredericksburg, TX

FREDERICKSBURG ENGLISH BROWN ALE — amber-gold, pleasant light hop and malt nose, very smooth malt and hop flavor, good tasting, medium body, dry malt and hop finish; long dry hop aftertaste shows malt as well; excellent with food. [A, 72]

EDELWEISS UNFILTERED WHEAT ALE — gold, light malt aroma; flavor starts off with a bit of malty sweetness but is other-wise dry; light body, long dry wheat and malt aftertaste; an American-style wheat ale made with 40% malted wheat. [W, 55]

NOT SO DUMB BLONDE ALE — pale gold, faint malt and hop nose; slightly fruity malt flavor is mostly dry; although it is described as being highly hopped, the hops stay in the background, contributing more to the dryness than bitterness; long dry hop and fruity malt aftertaste. [A, 53]

ENCHANTED ROCK RED ALE — amber-red, pleasant malty nose, good dry complex malt and hop flavor, medium body, dry hop finish; long dry malty aftertaste has a hop background; made with four different malts. [A, 59]

Free State Brewing Co.
Brewpub in Lawrence, KS

AD ASTRA ALE — pale amber, hop aroma and flavor, medium body, big dry hop finish, long dry hop aftertaste. A Düsseldorf-style altbier brewed with pale, caramel, and Munich malts and Perle and Willamette hops; gravity 13 P, 4.1% abw. [A, 67]

COPPERHEAD PALE ALE — deep gold, bright hop aroma and flavor, medium body, dry hop finish, long dry hop aftertaste, decent balance. An IPA-style ale made with English malts and Cascade hops; gravity 14.5 P, 4.7% abw. [A, 72]

IRONMAN IMPERIAL STOUT — dark brown, chocolate malt and roasted barley aroma and flavor, complex and smooth, medium body, dry malt finish, long dry malt aftertaste, very drinkable if not big as expected of an imperial stout; made with ten malts and three hop varieties; gravity 19.0 P, 6.4% abw. [S, 69]

WHEAT STATE GOLDEN — gold, faint malt nose, dry light malt flavor, light body, refreshing and delicately hopped, little length to the dry malt and hop aftertaste. Made with 25% wheat and barley malt, German alt yeast, and flavored lightly with Hersbrucker hops; gravity 11 P, 4.2% abw. [K, 53]

JOHN BROWN ALE — pale brown, dry malt aroma, light dry malt flavor, medium to light body, brief dry malt aftertaste, smooth but light for a brown ale; gravity 12.5 P, 3.9% abw. [A, 45]

FREE STATE HEFE-WEIZEN — pale gold, light very dry malt nose and flavor; no spiciness so it is very much an American-style hefe; light body, light short dry malt aftertaste. Made with 50% wheat malt, not filtered; 3.5% abw. [W, 47]

MEADOWLARK ALE (KÖLSCH) — deep gold, hop nose, dry hop flavor, not much character to the hops; very little malt showing, mostly just dry; made from two-row, Munich, and biscuit malts; hopped with Cascades and Saaz, dry hopped with Saaz; OG 1043, FG 1.010, 3,6% abv, 20 IBU. [A, 42]

Fremont Brewing Co.
Brewpub in Fremont, CA

CALIFORNIA AMBER ALE — amber, dry malt and hop aroma and flavor, a good balanced flavor with the crystal malts in tune with the bitter cluster hops and floral Cascades, medium body, dry hop finish and aftertaste; specific gravity 1.056, 5.3% abw. [A, 68]

FREMONT E.S.B. — amber, dry hop aroma, complex balanced dry slightly roasted malt and bitter Chinook hop flavor, big body, dry hop finish and aftertaste; specific gravity 1.073, 6.2% abw. [A, 67]

MISSION WHEAT — gold, light dry malty aroma and flavor, no spiciness, refreshing and light; dry malt aftertaste has no hefeweizen character, and even though it is claimed that it is made in that style, it is more like a kristall-klar; specific gravity 1.048, 4.8% abw. [W, 50]

TROPICAL ALE — peachy-gold; fruity aroma shows some cherry, guava, and other tropical fruits, fruity flavor is like the nose, medium body, fruity aftertaste; specific gravity 1.058, 3.9% abw. [A, 45]

Frio Brewing Co.
Microbrewery in San Antonio, TX

FRIO LAGER BEER — deep gold, light malt aroma, dry hop and fruity-grainy malt flavor, medium to light body; grainy malt has become quite dry by the aftertaste, good length. [B, 53]

Full Sail Brewing Co. / Hood River Brewing Co. / McCormick & Schmick Restaurant
Brewery and brewpub in Hood River and Portland, OR

FULL SAIL GOLDEN ALE — faintly hazy amber-gold, pleasant and clean malt aroma, tasty malt and hop flavor, good balance, good body, lovely malt finish, long dry malt aftertaste, very very drinkable; made with two-row pale, crystal, and dextrin barley malts; hopped with Mt. Hood and Northwestern Tettnanger hops; 3.5% abw. [A, 76]

FULL SAIL AMBER ALE — amber, beautiful zesty hop aroma, big hop flavor with plenty of malt for support, medium body, very tasty, long dry hop aftertaste; very good tasting brew made with two-row pale, crystal, and chocolate barley malts; well hopped with Cascade and Mt. Hood hops. [A, 75]

WASSAIL WINTER ALE 1993 — deep amber-brown, complex appetizing chocolate aroma, big and bright malt and hop flavor, big body, off-dry malt aftertaste, good length; few hops to be found. This is a beer to be sipped and savored in cold weather, not quaffed in the summer. Brewer says it is highly hopped including a Spalt hop finish; gravity 17 P, 5.2% abw. [A, 65]

WASSAIL WINTER ALE
1994 — deep amber, malty nose, big spicy hop and roasted malt flavor; a good flavor that grows on you and goes dry at the end; long dry hop aftertaste. [A, 74]

WASSAIL WINTER ALE
1995 — brilliant deep amber; sweet malt aroma has a hop background; dry bitter hop flavor, medium body; aftertaste continues the dry bitter hops and also has noticeable alcohol. [A, 55]

FULL SAIL RED ALE (SHRED RED) — reddish amber-gold, hop aroma, big dry complex hop flavor, medium body, fairly smooth, long dry hop aftertaste. [A, 65]

FULL SAIL IPA — pale gold, attractive spicy hop nose, bright and tasty spicy hop flavor, good body, dry and complex, long dry hop aftertaste; made with four malts; hopped with Challenger and East Kent Goldings; OG 1064, FG 1.014, 5.4% abv, 56 IBU; a beauty. [A, 77]

McCORMICK & SCHMICK PILS — gold, hop nose, big dry and bitter hop flavor, medium to good body, very long dry hop aftertaste, a very good tasting well-hopped brew. [B, 75]

FULL SAIL NUT BROWN ALE — amber-brown, roasted malt aroma, dry roasted malt flavor, medium body; aftertaste is lighter than the flavor and of medium duration. [A, 54]

MAIN SAIL STOUT — deep amber-brown, light roasted malt

aroma and flavor, medium body, medium to short malty aftertaste, much like a stout light. [S, 45]

BOARD HEAD BARLEYWINE — amber, faint hop and malt aroma, bright off-dry malt flavor; a tasty brew but not strong or heavy as expected of a barleywine; fairly long tasty aftertaste. [BW, 55]

TOP SAIL IMPERIAL PORTER — brown, roasted malt aroma and flavor, mellow and very smooth, good body, good carbonation level for the style, tasty roasted malt finish and aftertaste, good length. [P, 58]

McCORMICK & SCMICK AMBER (C.C.) — amber, bright hoppy aroma, interesting complex spicy hop taste, smooth and mellow, good body, good flavor, light dry hop finish and aftertaste. [A, 65]

Fullerton Hofbrau / Whaler's Brew
Brewpub in Fullerton, CA

PRINCE'S PILSENER — hazy gold, hop nose, bright hop and dry malt flavor, crisp and complex, good body, long dry hop aftertaste, an excellent brew. [B, 58]

KING'S LAGER — gold, light hop nose, big dry malt and light hop flavor, good body; smooth, but lacks the complexity of the Pils; long dry malt and hop aftertaste. [B, 62]

EARL'S ALE — amber, big hop nose and taste, good body, smooth,

plenty of malt for good balance, long hop aftertaste. [A, 68]

DUKE'S BOCK — deep amber, chocolate malt aroma; huge malt flavor starts out a bit off-dry with the hops in behind; big body, smooth and rich; that touch of sweetness stays in the background disappearing at the finish; long rich dry malt and hop aftertaste. [BK, 64]

FULLERTON HOFBRAU RASPBERRY WEIZEN — hazy gold with a pinkish tinge in the head, raspberry aroma; big raspberry soda flavor tends toward sweetness; light body, off-dry raspberry finish and aftertaste; never does more than approach dryness as the raspberry really stays. [W, 42]

FULLERTON HOFBRAU WEIZEN — hazy gold, light fruity-citrus aroma; malty palate is drier than the nose; refreshing and smooth, light body, dry malt finish, light dry malt aftertaste. [W, 62]

FULLERTON HOFBRAU PALE BOCK — hazy gold; complex malt and hop aroma, big slightly off-dry malt flavor has enough hops to be zesty and bright; off-dry malt finish, fairly complex, dry aftertaste. [BK, 64]

Gambrinus Brewing Co.
Microbrewery in Columbus, OH

GAMBRINUS QUALITY PALE BEER — deep gold, bright well-hopped nose, big dry hop flavor, good body, long dry hop after-taste; well-made in that although highly hopped it has a smoothness and balance. [B, 68]

AUGUSTINER BEER — amber with a rosy tint; malty nose has a candy-like sweetness; tastes like the aroma with the candy sweetness up front and in the middle; finish is dry hops, dry hop aftertaste, medium duration. [B, 53]

CRANBERRY LAMBIC — amber, fruity almost medicinal aroma and taste, not attractive or pleasant, sour fruity finish and long sour fruity aftertaste. [L, 14]

D.L. Geary Brewing Co.
Brewery in Portland, ME

GEARY'S PALE ALE — deep bright golden amber, big citrus hop and fruity-malt nose; complex dry hop palate borders on bitter but comes off very good; dry hop finish; long dry hop aftertaste that is a bit tart at the end; a very well-made and likable brew. [A, 75]

HAMPSHIRE WINTER ALE 1989–1990 — cloudy amber, tart complex fruity-hop aroma, huge dry hop flavor with loads of malt in back, big body, extremely long dry hop aftertaste, a big sipping beer with very good balance. [A, 93]

HAMPSHIRE SPECIAL ALE 1990–1991 — bright amber, big toasted malt aroma, huge malt and hop flavor, rich and delicious, long dry hop aftertaste, great balance, good sipping beer. [A, 91]

HAMPSHIRE SPECIAL ALE 1991–1992 — hazy amber, citrus hop and malt aroma, big zesty complex hop ale flavor, rich malt backing, big long hop aftertaste, another delicious sipping beer. [A, 80]

HAMPSHIRE SPECIAL ALE 1992–1993 — hazy amber; smooth light citrus hop nose (some samples were faintly buttery); complex malt, hop, and alcohol palate; very rich and distinctive, an abundance of hops, malt, and alcohol throughout; big body, long tart hop aftertaste; perhaps a bit too much bite, but still good. [A, 71]

HAMPSHIRE SPECIAL ALE 1993–1994 — hazy amber, finely carbonated; big hop nose and taste has plenty of supporting malt; big body, creamy, rich and delicious flavor, very smooth; long big hop aftertaste, like lasting a half hour or so. [A, 92]

HAMPSHIRE SPECIAL ALE 1994–1995 — amber, big beautiful complex malt and hop aroma; big bright malt flavor is mostly hops but there is plenty of malt; big dry hop aftertaste is long and delicious. [A, 91]

HAMPSHIRE SPECIAL ALE 1995–1996 — amber, big well-hopped and heavily malted aroma has a stiff dose of alcohol to warm you; huge delicious full flavor like the nose, smooth and creamy despite its heft; the hops hang back to give the toasted malt full play; very long and continues to show alcohol right to the end. [A, 90]

Notes

GEARY'S LONDON
PORTER — deep brown, very attractive malty nose, bright dry malt flavor, good balance between the hops and the malt, medium body; highly carbonated (which further balances the sweetness of the malt and adds to the overall dry effect); long very dry malt and hop aftertaste, an excellent porter. [P, 78]

McDUFF'S BEST BITTER
ALE — amber-gold, light fruity-spicy malt nose, medium body, bright hop flavor, dry bright spicy hop finish and aftertaste. Made with Goldings hops, cask-conditioned; OG 1049. Brewed and bottled for Gritty McDuff's, a Portland brewpub. [A, 32]

Genesee Brewing Co.
Brewery in Rochester, NY

GENESEE BEER — gold, good malt aroma, pleasant malt flavor with a slight hop taste, good balance, good body, short dry hop aftertaste. [B, 52]

GENESEE CREAM ALE — gold, big malt nose with a slight hop backing, good balanced malt and hop flavor, finishes a bit weakly; medium length after-taste, what is there is pleasant; brewed with top-fermenting yeast and kraeusened; specific gravity 1.047, 3.7% abw. [A, 54]

GENESEE BOCK BEER — deep amber, malt aroma with lightly roasted malt character, fair body, good balance, pleasant long malt aftertaste. [BK, 62]

GENESEE OKTOBERFEST
BEER — deep amber nice malt aroma, very smooth malt flavor, lightly hopped, dry malt finish and aftertaste, medium duration. [B, 54]

GENESEE LIGHT — pale color, mild malt aroma with some yeast in back, light body, dry and light hop flavor, light finish and brief aftertaste. [LO, 29]

GENESEE NA
NON-ALCOHOLIC BREW — pale gold, dull malt nose, thin body, weak malt flavor, almost watery, high carbonation, little aftertaste; light but refreshing when you are very thirsty. [NA, 41]

GENESEE CREAM LIGHT
CREAM ALE — medium yellow-gold, light fruity malt and talcum powder nose, medium dry malt and hop flavor, hop finish; off-dry malt aftertaste has good length. [A, 47]

TWELVE HORSE ALE — bright gold, fresh malt aroma; bright malt flavor with the hops gradually coming in as it crosses the palate; dry hop finish and after-taste; lighter than I remember it from some years back, but still pleasant and refreshing. Brewed top-fermented with six-row malt and corn grits, with Yakima Valley hops; specific gravity 1.047, 3.8% abw. [A, 71]

KOCH'S GOLDEN ANNIVER-SARY BEER — bright gold, light malt aroma, malt flavor, medium body, fairly long malt aftertaste. Uses corporate name of Fred Koch Brewery from which brewery in Dunkirk, NY originated the brand. It is brewed with six-row malt and a blend of American hops. [B, 28]

KOCH'S GOLDEN ANNIVER-SARY LIGHT BEER — pale gold, pleasant hop and malt aroma, light body, weak malt flavor, thin body, brief aftertaste. [LO, 26]

BLACK HORSE PREMIUM
ALE — bright gold, nice hop and malt aroma, rich flavor with a malt front and hop middle and finish, good balance, quite zesty; long aftertaste shows both hops and malt. [A, 67]

MICHAEL O'SHEA'S IRISH
AMBER PUB STYLE LAGER — amber, cooked malt aroma, vapid dull flavor like the nose, dull dry malt aftertaste; specific gravity 1.046, 3.7% abw. [B, 23]

MICHAEL SHEA'S BLACK &
TAN — deep red-brown, faint chocolate malt aroma, light smoky

malt flavor, medium body, very drinkable, light dry chocolate malt aftertaste, ends very dry. Can says it is a blend of top-fermented porter and their lager (see above) with some chocolate malt added; specific gravity 1.046, 3.7% abw. [B, 43]

GENNY ICE BEER — gold; nose is mostly hops but there is some malt in back; dull hop flavor, grainy background, dull dry finish, medium body, short dull dry aftertaste; specific gravity 1.049, 4.2% abw. [B, 32]

TWELVE HORSE CELEBRATED ALE — brilliant gold, faint malt nose, slightly off-dry malt flavor, medium body; light dry malt aftertaste is medium long; good hot weather chugging beer. [B, 39]

J.W. DUNDEE'S HONEY BROWN LAGER — deep gold, light off-dry malt aroma, thin honeyed sweet malt flavor, good body, finish and aftertaste like the flavor, medium long aftertaste, overall on the flabby side; 3.6% abw. [B, 20]

KOCH'S GOLDEN ANNIVERSARY ICE BEER — gold, big malty nose, fruity fresh malty flavor, good body; hops appear at the finish; short dry malt and hop aftertaste. [B, 44]

MICHAEL SHEA'S BLONDE LAGER — pale gold, light malty nose, light dry malt flavor, medium body, light dry malt aftertaste, not much there. [B, 20]

GENNY RED LAGER — deep gold, faint hop and lightly toasted malt nose, light dry malty flavor, weak body, light dry malt and hop aftertaste. [B, 30]

Gentle Ben's Brewing Co.
Brewpub in Tucson, AZ

BEAR DOWN BROWN — amber-brown, hop aroma, malt flavor with a noticeable lactic acid background, lactic impaired finish and aftertaste. Made with crystal, brown, wheat, pale, chocolate, and dextrin malt; gravity 10.5 P, 5.4% abw. [A, 42]

HARVEST MOON LIGHT — pale gold, bright spicy hop aroma, lemony malt flavor, dry malt finish and aftertaste. [A, 47]

CATALINA ALE — pale gold, light malt aroma, very bright and very dry hop flavor, refreshing, long dry hop aftertaste. [A, 67]

COPPERHEAD PALE ALE — deep gold, rich hop and malt aroma, complex and interesting; flavor is both rich malt and strong dry hops; a big flavor, big body, long, dry, and delicious. Brewed with crystal and Munich malt with a touch of wheat for head retention; specific gravity 1.054, 4.2% abw. [A, 80]

Notes

TAYLOR JANE RASPBERRY WHEAT — deep gold, sprightly raspberry aroma, very much a raspberry taste, dry berry finish and medium length aftertaste. I'm told it is made with wheat malt, whole raspberries, and natural concentrate; specific gravity 1.038, 3.2% abw. [W, 67]

RED CAT AMBER ALE — amber, hop aroma and big hop flavor; seems faintly soapy but it is not obtrusive; malt comes in at the finish; long dry malt and hop aftertaste. [A, 53]

DESERT BIGHORN OATMEAL STOUT — dark amber, spicy malt nose, ginger-malt flavor, good body, not heavy, long dry and spicy malt aftertaste; specific gravity 1.064, 4.5% abw. [S, 67]

Golden City Brewery
Microbrewery in Golden, CO

GOLDEN CITY RED ALE — amber; aroma and flavor is mostly malt, but there are plenty of good floral Hallertau and Chinook bittering hops that hang in there with the malt (IBU 18); medium body, dry malt and hop aftertaste; specific gravity 1.056. [A, 65]

GOLDEN CREAM ALE — amber-gold, malt aroma, rich malty flavor, medium body, rich medium dry malty aftertaste; made with an ale yeast but cold lagered, using two-row Klages, Vienna, light Munich, and Carapils malts, with an IBU of 20 from Chinook hops, and flavored

with Hallertau hops; specific gravity 1.048, 4.4% abw. [A, 63]

Golden Pacific Brewing Co.
Brewery in Emeryville, CA

CRYSTAL BAY RED ALE — deep amber, malt nose, light malty flavor, medium body, dry malt finish and aftertaste; made with two-row, 40 Lovibond, 75 Lovibond, chocolate malt; specific gravity 1.050, 4.2% abw, SRM 20, 24 IBU. Produced under contract for Lake Tahoe B.C. of Lake Tahoe, CA. [A, 64]

GOLDEN GATE ORIGINAL ALE — amber, toasted malt and Northwest hop aroma and flavor, appetizing and attractive, smooth and rich, medium body, crisp long complex malt and hop aftertaste, very drinkable and flavorful. [A, 75]

COPPERHEAD RED ALE — hazy copper-red, butter-toffee nose, toasted malt flavor; a bit scorched, burnt nature stays way into the aftertaste and is not helpful. Made for Copperhead Ale Co. [A, 35]

Golden Prairie Brewing Co.
Microbrewery in Chicago, IL

GOLDEN PRAIRIE ALE — deep gold, malty aroma and flavor, medium body; medium long dry malt aftertaste has a faint buttery

background; specific gravity 1.053, 4.6–4.8% abw. [A, 54]

Golden Valley Brewpub
Brewpub in McMinnville, OR

GOLDEN VALLEY PORTER — brown, malt nose, dry malty flavor, fairly low hopping (25 IBU), light body, dry malt aftertaste, medium length; made with two-row Klages and imported specialty malts; specific gravity 1.018, 4.2% abw. [P, 68]

RED THISTLE ALE — reddish amber (mahogany as the brew-master describes it); malty aroma; dry malt flavor has a good hop support and is very tasty; light body, dry malt finish; long dry malt aftertaste shows plenty of hops as well (40 IBU); specific gravity 1.014, 3.4% abw. [A, 75]

Goose Island Brewing Co. / Lincoln Park Brewery, Inc.
Brewpub in Chicago, IL

GOLDEN GOOSE PILSNER — gold, mild hop aroma, very dry hop palate, good balance, very dry hop finish, long dry hop aftertaste. Made from pale and Munich malts with Saaz hops and Weihen-stephan yeast. [B, 62]

TANZEN GANS KOLSCH — gold, light hop aroma, zesty hop flavor, medium body, dry hop finish and aftertaste. Very good brew made with pale and wheat malt, imported hops, and Weihenstephan Kölsch yeast. [K, 73]

HONKER'S ALE — amber-gold, faintly sour hop nose, big hop flavor, especially good in back and sides of tongue, real bittering hops used, dry hop finish; long very dry hop aftertaste showing good malt at the end. Another very good brew. [A, 70]

PMD MILD ALE — amber brown, malt nose, good dry malt flavor; finishes dry hops but the malt is still there; excellent with food. Made with chocolate, caramel, and pale malts. [A, 68]

OLD CLYBOURN PORTER — deep brown, dry malt aroma, very dry malt flavor, medium to long dry malt aftertaste. [P, 61]

DUNKELWEIZENBOCK — hazy amber, some malty sweetness in the nose, big malt lightly spiced flavor, long off-dry malt aftertaste, a lovely sipping beer. [WBK, 80]

VICE WEIZEN — hazy gold, malt nose, smooth refreshing malt flavor, lightly spiced; finish and aftertaste is dry malt. [W, 72]

RAF BETTER BITTER ALE — deep amber-gold, bright hop aroma; has plenty of malt in back; zesty hop flavor still with plenty of supporting malt, dry hop finish, long very dry hop aftertaste. [A, 60]

GOOSE ISLAND PORTER — deep brown, rich coffee-toffee nose, bright rich dry coffee-malt flavor, good body, very likable,

smooth, perky, long dry malt aftertaste. [P, 67]

ROBERT BURNS — brown; smoky malt aroma and flavor of rich smoked malt that truly makes you briefly think single malt Scotch whiskey; finishes dry and smoky, nicely done of the type. [A, 60]

WINTER WARMER BARLEY WINE — amber, big malt and hop nose and taste, big body, off-dry malt and hop finish and aftertaste. [BW, 56]

OATMEAL STOUT — brown, dry roasted barley and chocolate malt aroma; flavor like the nose but not strong, rather it is smooth and light; medium body, fairly short dry malt aftertaste. [S, 54]

RUSSIAN IMPERIAL STOUT — black, tan head, dry roasted barley nose, medium strength dry roast malt flavor, medium body, fairly short dry roast malt aftertaste. [S, 47]

DEMOLITION 18 ALE — hazy gold, big bright hop nose, big dry hop flavor, huge body, dry hop finish, long strong dry hop aftertaste, a very big and very good brew. [A, 72]

HOPSCOTCH PALE ALE — bright gold, complex dry hop and light malt aroma and flavor, medium body, tasty right through to the dry hop finish and aftertaste, good length. [A, 62]

Gordon Biersch Brewing Co.
Brewpubs in San Francisco, Palo Alto, Pasedena, and San Jose, CA and in Honolulu, HI

GORDON BIERSCH PILSENER — deep gold, smooth malt aroma, hops over the malt in the flavor, good body, dry hop finish, long dry hop aftertaste; gravity 12.5 P. Tasted in Palo Alto. [B, 68]

GORDON BIERSCH AMBER — medium amber, hop aroma, smooth malt flavor with laid back hops, good body, richly flavored, long malt aftertaste. Tasted in Palo Alto. [B, 67]

GORDON BIERSCH DOUBLE BOCK — deep amber, rich malt nose, smooth big malt flavor with hops faintly in back, long medium dry malt aftertaste. Tasted in Palo Alto. [BK, 79]

GORDON BIERSCH MAERZEN — golden amber, malt nose; malt flavor has good hop sup-port; very good balance, long dry hop aftertaste, an excellent maerzen. This is as tasted in Palo Alto. In Pasedena it had a complex malt aroma and flavor with a spicy background, good body, and a long slightly off-dry malt aftertaste. Made with Hallertau hops; gravity 13.5 P. [B, 68]

GORDON BIERSCH EXPORT — deep gold, malty nose; malt flavor starts out quite sweet, dries by mid-palate; medium body; dry malt aftertaste shows little hop character anywhere. Tasted in Pasedena. [B, 67]

GORDON BIERSCH DUNKLES — deep amber, slightly hazy, malt aroma; flavor has the same sweetness up front as the maerzen, medium body, very smooth and somewhat creamy, medium dry finish, fairly long medium off-dry malt aftertaste; goes down very easy. Tasted in Pasedena. [B, 72]

Gray Brewing Co.
Microbrewery in Janesville, WI

AMERICAN PALE ALE — pale copper, mealy malt and light hop aroma, mildly bitter dry hop flavor with a malty caramel background, medium body; pleasant dry hop aftertaste retains the caramel backing for balance; specific gravity 1.055, 4.5% abw. [A, 67]

AUTUMN ALE — amber, dry toasted malt aroma; dry roasted malt flavor has good hop support; good body, dry hop finish and aftertaste, good length; specific gravity 1.060, 4.3% abw. [A, 78]

GRAY HONEY ALE — pale gold, honeyed malt nose; honeyed malt flavor is lightly hopped (18 IBU); light body; finish and aftertaste are still honeyed but much drier; made with 7 lbs. of honey per barrel; specific gravity 1.002, 4% abw. [A, 86]

GRAY OATMEAL STOUT — brown, chocolate malt and roasted barley nose; flavor is like the nose but benefits from some caramel and oatmeal character; light to medium body, long dry malty finish and aftertaste, a very good tasting stout if not a big one; specific gravity 1.012, 4.3% abw. [S, 98]

Great Basin Brewing Co.
Microbrewery in Sparks, NV

CERVEZA CHILIBESO — gold, lovely jalapeño chile nose, good tasting jalapeño flavor with mild heat, dry peppery finish and aftertaste, medium body, good length; made with partially seeded chiles added at the end of the boil; specific gravity 1.050, 4% abw. [B, 51]

GREAT BASIN OKTOBERFEST — deep gold, malt nose with aromatic hops in back, big malt flavor, good body; long dry malty aftertaste has a distinctive European hop background; made with Belgian and

German malts, Saaz and Hallertau hops; specific gravity 1.056, 4.6% abw. [B, 68]

ICHTHYOSAUR PALE ALE — deep gold, big hop aroma, excellent palate with plenty of big hop character and lots of complex malt flavors, good body, long complex malt and hop aftertaste; a complex IPA made with Munich malts and Cascade hops; specific gravity 1.056, 5% abw. [A, 69]

JACKPOT PORTER — brown, pleasant roasted malt aroma and flavor, smooth and dry, good body, complex and creamy, long dry malt aftertaste; made from seven malt varieties; specific gravity 1.057, 4.2% abw. [P, 67]

NEVADA GOLD — gold, malty aroma and flavor, light but complex flavor from two-row barley and wheat malts and a hint of sweetness from a caramel malt from Belgium, light body; some of the Saaz hops show faintly in the dry malt aftertaste; specific gravity 1.047, 4% abw. [W, 56]

RUBY MOUNTAIN RASPBERRY — pink color, faint berry aroma, dry raspberry flavor, light body, dry raspberry aftertaste, medium length, an ale with raspberry and boysenberry added at the end of fermentation; specific gravity 1.044, 4% abw. [A, 49]

WHEELER PEAK WHEAT — hazy gold, light dry malt nose; slightly yeasty palate is still fairly clean and refreshing; light body, light dry malt aftertaste, an unfiltered hefe-weizen, but not a spicy one; specific gravity 1.045, 4% abw. [W, 50]

WILD HORSE ALE — amber-gold, complex malty nose, dry malt flavor, medium body, dry malt finish and aftertaste; a German-style ale (or altbier) made from a blend of five malts; specific gravity 1.050, 3.7% abw. [A, 57]

Great Divide Brewing Co.
Microbrewery in Denver, CO

ARAPAHOE AMBER ALE brilliant golden-amber, malty aroma with some aromatic hops in back; rich malt flavor is quite fruity, big body, very mouth-filling; extremely long and clean aftertaste has good malt and dry hops; 5.4% abw. [A, 67]

WHITEWATER WHEAT ALE — bright gold; fruity malty aroma has a touch of pineapple; soft flavor is similar to the nose and a bit off-dry; medium body, dry malty aftertaste; 4.5% abw. [W, 54]

ST. BRIGID'S PORTER — dark brown, chocolate malt and deep roasted barley aroma; big roasted malt flavor is nicely done; some sweetness in the finish, good body, nicely balanced, roasty character throughout; a little burnt at the end; very drinkable. [P, 83]

Notes

WILD RASPBERRY ALE —brilliant red, raspberry syrup and grape nose; dry raspberry flavor comes as a surprise after the nose; medium body, dry raspberry aftertaste, very drinkable, the dry raspberry a pleasant change from many of the others of the type. Made from crushed raspberries. [A, 59]

Great Falls Brewing Co. / No Tomatoes
Brewpub in Auburn, ME

GREAT FALLS AMBER — amber, light hop aroma and taste, medium body, dry hop finish, medium length dry hop aftertaste. Made with Cascade and Saaz hops; OG 1048. [A, 64]

GREAT FALLS PORTER — medium dark brown, roasted malt nose; roasted malt flavor has a hint of chocolate malt; medium body, finishes drier, long dry malt aftertaste. Made with Munich and chocolate malts with Fuggles and Kent-Goldings hops; OG 1070. [P, 62]

GREAT FALLS WHEAT — hazy gold, light wheaty malt nose; bright lightly spiced flavor ends dry; medium to light body, short dry aftertaste. [W, 55]

Great Lakes Brewing Co.
Brewpub in Cleveland, OH

DORTMUNDER GOLD — golden-amber; beautiful malt and hop aroma is almost ale-like; very pleasant big malt flavor with plenty of hop bite; dry hop finish still shows malt; long rich dry hop aftertaste well backed with malt; both the malt and hops stay from start to finish keeping balance throughout; rich and tangy, pleasant and satisfying. At the brewpub this is called Heisman and is brilliant gold, has a bright hop aroma and taste, with a dry malt finish and aftertaste. Made with two-row pale, caramel-20, and Carapils malts, Cascade and Hallertau hops, this Dortmunder logs in with 28 IBU; gravity 14 P, 4.3% abw. [B, 78]

THE ELIOT NESS — deep amber, very faint malt and hop aroma; rich but dry roasted malt flavor that could be called nutty; medium long dry malt aftertaste, medium body, excellent example of a Vienna-style lager. At the brewpub this brew is amber, has a malt nose, a very smooth and balanced malt-hop flavor, and a dry malt aftertaste. Earlier it was labeled Great Lakes Vienna Lager. [B, 71]

BURNING RIVER PALE ALE STYLE — brilliant deep amber, delicious fruity hop and malt aroma, big concentrated malt flavor, medium body, some alcohol noted, dry hop finish, long dry hop aftertaste. Made with Cascade hops; specific gravity 1.056, 4.8% abw, 40 IBU. [A, 98]

THE EDMUND FITZGERALD PORTER — dark mahogany, roasted black malt nose aroma well-balanced with hops; great hop and malt flavor shows chocolate, caramel, and black patent malts; excellent balance, good body, finishes dry malt, very long dry malt aftertaste, a classic porter. Made with English two-row, crystal, and chocolate malts, with a touch of roasted barley; specific gravity 1.060, 4.9% abw. [P, 93]

THE COMMODORE PERRY INDIA PALE ALE — deep gold, beautiful bright fruity hop nose, huge bright spicy complex hop flavor with plenty of malt and alcohol, excellent balance, big body, very nice transitions between the malt and the hops on the palate, a great beer with a long dry hop aftertaste. Made with 12 lbs. of five varieties of hops for each 7 bbl batch; specific gravity 1.064, 5.5% abw, 65 IBU. [A, 92]

THE COMMODORE PERRY INDIA PALE ALE — hazy amber, beautiful bright fruity malt and hop nose, huge bright strong and spicy complex hop flavor with plenty of malt and alcohol, excellent balance, big body, very nice transitions between the malt and the hops on the palate, a great beer with a long dry hop aftertaste. Made with 12 lbs. of five varieties of hops for each 7 bbl batch; specific gravity 1.064, 5.5% abw, 80 IBU. This is a new (mid-1995) recipe and it hasn't given up a thing. [A, 92]

MOON DOG ALE — amber, nice hop fruity ale-like aroma; smooth and balanced hop-malt flavor that is lightly tangy; finishes smoothly and very clean; long dry aftertaste shows both the hops and malt in harmony; a very pleasant brew; gravity 12.5 P, 4.1% abw, 40 IBU. [A, 77]

HOLY MOSES ALE — amber, very nice fruity hop aroma, creamy malt flavor, balanced, smooth, long dry malt and hop aftertaste; gravity 16.5 P, 5.6% abw, 58 IBU. [A, 67]

THE ROCKEFELLER BOCK — deep amber, toasted malt nose; complex malt flavor that is at first toasted, then complex and alcoholic in the middle, slightly burnt at the finish; long dry malt aftertaste shows less of the burnt nature; overall very good and it grows on you as you drink it; made with five malts; specific gravity 1.068, 5.3% abw. [B, 70]

GREAT LAKES OKTOBERFEST — amber, big beautiful strong malt nose with alcohol showing; appearance of big body but it coats your mouth rather than filling it; creamy, complex grape malt flavor with hops in back, long dry malt aftertaste, delicious; specific gravity 1.060, 5.2% abw. [B, 80]

GREAT LAKES CHRISTMAS ALE 93 — amber, fruity estery aroma with spices (honey, cinnamon and ginger); complex spicy malt flavor is mostly smooth ginger root; medium body; spicy complex finish still gives some malt and hops; dry faintly spicy aftertaste. [B, 64]

GREAT LAKES CHRISTMAS ALE 94 — amber; spicy malt nose has cinnamon, ginger, and honey; flavor shows the spices and little malt; a very pleasant taste, good body; spicy complex finish and aftertaste, but there is enough spice to overcome the malt and hops. [A, 62]

GREAT LAKES CHRISTMAS ALE 1995 — amber; pleasant spicy aroma shows some malt and hops in addition to the ginger and cinnamon; flavor is like the nose but shows the honey as well; starts out strong, doesn't sag but is mitigated in the middle; spices blend with roasted malt in the finish; very long interesting aftertaste picks up on the malt and hops underlying the spicy flavors. [A, 77]

LOCH ERIE SCOTCH ALE — amber, big malt aroma, huge rich malty flavor with lots of caramel tones, big bodied, long strong rich malt aftertaste, a huge malty brew; made with extended boiling of the wort; specific gravity 1.084, 6% abw. [A, 73]

WIT'S END — gold; malt aroma shows some spiciness and citrus; spicy-fruity flavor, medium body; complex spicy-fruity aftertaste has only medium duration; a traditional Witbier made using unmalted wheat, oats, malted barley, coriander, orange peel, and hops; specific gravity 1.052, 4.1% abw. [W, 60]

Notes

Hair of the Dog Brewing Co.
Microbrewery in Portland, OR

GOLDEN ROSE BELGIAN TRIPEL STYLE ALE — hazy cloudy amber, complex fruity-estery malt and hop aroma, highly carbonated, big strong complex lactic-spicy (cloves and nutmeg)-fruity ale-like taste, very noticeable alcohol, big body, off-dry finish, very strong and quite long; made with Belgian candy sugar, bottle-conditioned; OG 1072, FG 1.010, 7.5% abv, 12 IBU. [A, 95]

HAIR OF THE DOG ADAM — deep garnet (almost opaque), brown head; rich concentrated malt aroma has tones of chocolate malt, coffee and smoke; huge rich roasted-smoky malt flavor, low carbonation, very alcoholic, creamy, tangy hoppy-ale background, huge body; has roasted malt but the roasted character barely shows above the pure malty nature, also there are plenty of hops but they are masked by the malt; a real bruiser of a beer, long dry roasted malt aftertaste; 8% abw. [A, 99]

HAIR OF THE DOG EVE — take Adambier, freeze it and drawn off the ice crystals and you have Eve; deeper garnet, a more concentrated malt and alcohol nose, very very low carbonation (maybe none), humongous body; strong flavored, maybe a bit too strong as it loses balance. Adam is as strong as it needs be. [A, 72]

Hale's Ales
Microbrewery in Spokane, WA and Kirkland Roaster & Ale House brewpub in Kirkland, WA. The microbrewery opened in Colville, WA in 1983, moving to Spokane in 1991.

MOSS BAY AMBER ALE — amber, light dry spicy hop nose; flavor is faintly of raspberry behind the hops; medium body; raspberry continues into the long fairly dry hop aftertaste; specific gravity 1.040. [A, 53]

HALE'S HONEY WHEAT ALE — slightly hazy deep gold; lightly honeyed nose shows some malt and hops; flavor is like the nose but is drier; finishes a bit sweeter but still moderately dry; light and smooth, medium body, then a dry malt aftertaste with the honey barely discernible. [W, 53]

HALE'S PALE AMERICAN ALE — golden amber, excellent bright and zesty hop nose; flavor is dry hops and malt and doesn't live up to the promise of the nose; medium body, slightly off-dry finish and aftertaste, medium duration; specific gravity 1.044. [A, 53]

HALE'S IPA — amber, light hop nose, pleasant smooth dry light hop taste, medium body, very good balance, light dry hop aftertaste of medium duration; fermented in an open air vat; made with pale and Carastan malts; hopped with Centennial and Nugget hops; OG 1054, FG 1.016, 5% abv. [A, 66]

The Hangtown Brewery
Microbrewery in Placerville, CA

PLACERVILLE PALE ALE — pale copper-amber, big northwest hop nose, big hoppy flavor, good big body, dry hop finish and aftertaste, long with good malt support. [A, 76]

MAD DOG BREW HOWLIN' BROWN ALE — dark amber-brown; rich concentrated malt nose has an off-dry burnt malt background, burnt malt flavor; medium body; dry burnt malt aftertaste has a fruity-citrus backing, but overall lacks interest. [A, 38]

Harbor Lights
Brewpub in Dana Point, CA. Originally called Heritage Brewing Co. The Heritage Brewing Co. microbrewery moved to Lake Elsinore, CA.

LANTERN BAY BLONDE — gold, bright hop nose, very dry hop flavor, light body; very dry and fairly short aftertaste, but is refreshing while it is there. Made with pale and wheat malt, Cluster and Hallertau hops. The malt does not show well. [A, 53]

SAIL ALE — amber; faint hop nose that is very pleasant; good hop flavor, dry, creamy; has some ale-like character and a trace of nutty caramel that appears mostly in the finish; dry hop aftertaste has good length. Made with pale and caramel malts and Nugget and Cascade hops. [A, 73]

DANA PORTER — deep amber-brown; dry malt nose and taste shows a little chocolate malt; good body; chocolate malt flavor stays right through into a long aftertaste. Made with black, chocolate, caramel, and pale malts. [P, 67]

IMPERIAL STOUT — deep amber-brown, roasted barley and chocolate malt aroma and flavor, strongly flavored, but smooth, good body, very good balance, dry malt finish and aftertaste. [S, 67]

WHITE FOX — gold, light bright hop aroma and flavor, light malt backing, light body, light dry hop aftertaste; believed to be a new label for Lantern Bay Blonde; specific gravity 1.050, 4.5% abw. [A, 60]

RED FOX PALE ALE — copper-amber, smooth dry hop aroma, bright dry hop taste, medium body, dry hop finish, very long dry hop aftertaste. A very good American-style pale ale made with Nugget hops and dry hopped with Cascades and Willamette hops; specific gravity 1.054, 5.2% abw. [A, 74]

BLACK FOX — deep amber-brown, dry chocolate malt and roasted barley aroma; smooth nutty malt flavor shows some of the choclate malt; medium body, dry toasted malt finish and long aftertaste. Smooth and dry, this medium bodied and flavored stout has no harsh edges, and goes well with food; specific gravity 1.040, 3.8% abw. [S, 80]

Hart Brewing Co.
Brewery in Kalama, WA

PACIFIC CREST ALE — medium pale hazy amber, fruity toasted malt nose, big tangy ale flavor, lots of hops and toasted malt, good balance, fairly complex, big body, good dry hop finish and long hop and malt aftertaste; gravity 13.5 P, 4.1% abw. [A, 83]

PYRAMID WHEATEN ALE — amber-gold, pleasant malt and citrus hop aroma, light dry tangy flavor with a light citrus background, medium body, short dry hop aftertaste; what is there is good, but there just isn't enough of it. Brewed with wheat and barley malt, hopped with Cascade and Perles hops; gravity 10.5 P, 3.4% abw. [W, 40]

Notes

PYRAMID AMBER WHEATEN

amber, faint caramel nose, sort of spritzy dry hop flavor with caramel malt in back, finishes dry hops, malt and hop aftertaste. Made with 40% British specialty malts; gravity 9.75 P, 3.2% abw. [W, 60]

PYRAMID SPHINX STOUT

opaque brown, brown head; smoky slightly burnt roasted aroma shows some chocolate and black patent malts; medium body; big complex flavor shows plenty of roasted barley and other malts; dry smoky malt finish, very dry slightly smoky long malt aftertaste. Brewed with caramel, Munich, black, and roasted barley malts; hopped with Willamette and CFJ whole hops; gravity 15.0 P, 4.4% abw. [S, 72]

SNOW CAP ALE 1990

deep reddish amber, big complex malt and hop nose, huge flavor; malt dominates at first; the hops vie for the lead in mid-palate, they don't clash in the contest and it comes off very well; big body, long dry hop aftertaste with plenty of malt support. This is a winner. It is as good or better than any other seasonal winter beer offered. Flavored with Nugget and Liberty hops; specific gravity 1.072, 5.5% abw. [A, 93]

SNOW CAP ALE 1993

very deep hued red-brown, big roasted malt nose; very strong roasted malt flavor is sweet on front and well-hopped from the middle on to the finish where the malt resumes dominance; big body, great complexity; long dry malt aftertaste takes on some more late hops at the end. This brew has not lost its appeal in the years I missed tasting it. [A, 78]

SNOW CAP ALE 1994

deep amber; complex concentrated malt nose has a candy sweetness and roasted quality in back; huge complex malt flavor, big body, dry concentrated malt aftertaste, very long. This is a winner. It is as good as any other seasonal winter beer offered. Flavored with Nugget and Liberty hops; specific gravity 1.072, 5.5% abw. First tasted in early January 1995; retasted in March 1995 at which time the richness and balance among the hop and malt flavors appeared to be improved. This is a beer that improves with time in the bottle. [A, 89]

SNOW CAP ALE 1995

deep brilliant red-amber, lovely malt aroma and flavor; there is considerable alcohol present; big body, excellent balanced malty flavor, smooth despite its huge size, very long malty aftertaste, one of the best seasonal beers offered. [A, 91]

PYRAMID PALE ALE

amber, dry malt nose and taste, good body; malt gains strength as it goes to the finish, dry hop aftertaste still has good malt; lacks complexity. Made with roasted malts and Cascade hops; specific gravity 1.048, 3.82% abw, 40 IBU. [A, 73]

PYRAMID BEST BROWN ALE

hazy light orange-amber, pleasant fruity malt and northwest hops, complex big malt flavor with hops now in back, dry hop finish, long dry hop aftertaste, good body, tasty and very drinkable; made with Liberty and Nugget hops; specific gravity 1.052, 3.9% abw, 25 IBU. [A, 68]

PYRAMID WHEATEN BOCK ALE

orange-amber, complex malty fruity aroma, big flavor with dry toasted malt, light to medium body; faintly spicy and a bit honeyed at the finish, but aftertaste is dry. [BKA, 61]

ESPRESSO STOUT

deep brown, dark brown head, creamy, big chocolate malt and charcoal nose, concentrated smoked malt flavor, good body; dry roasted malt finish has a bit of the smokiness; long coffee-like aftertaste. [S, 64]

PYRAMID ANNIVERSARY BARLEY WINE STYLED ALE

hazy tawny-gold, complex rich malt and hop aroma, big rich malt, hop, and alcohol taste, very smooth and silky; big hop character balanced with high residual malt sugars from a concentration of malts; huge body, long rich malt and complex hop aftertaste; OG 1096, 9.75% abv. [BW, 97]

PYRAMID APRICOT ALE — amber-gold; malt aroma has a fruity apricot background; lightly hopped (17 IBU) flavor follows the nose; light body; long fruity malt aftertaste has medium length and revives the apricot character. This well-made beer is an unfiltered hefe-weizen flavored with apricots; specific gravity 1.045, 3.3% abw. [A, 51]

PYRAMID PORTER — brown, rich and dry toasted malt nose; clean rich malt flavor is a little sweet briefly at first but mostly dry and smooth; good body, very long dry malt aftertaste, a good classical porter; 4.4% abw. [P, 68]

PYRAMID SPECIAL BITTER — pale amber, hop aroma, big bitter hop flavor, bright and refreshing, good body, long dry hop aftertaste, good Cascade and Willamette hop character throughout, a very attractive ale. [A, 70]

PYRAMID KALSCH — gold, malty nose with hops in back, bright well-hopped flavor, light to medium body, dry hop finish and aftertaste; put forth as a kölsch type (with a pun intended — a Kölsch from Kalama is a kalsch), but it has much more substance than a kölsch. [K, 66]

PYRAMID HEFE-WEIZEN ALE — cloudy gold, light lambic-like fruity malt nose; bright malty

flavor starts out a little sour but sourness eases as you sip; faintly soapy with no spiciness or banana; there is a little fruit, but very little; light body, malty aftertaste borders on off-dry, never gets dry either. The bottled version seemed a bit dank and dull, but on draft it was bright, clean, and refreshing. [W, 66]

The Hartford Brewery Ltd.
Brewpub in Hartford, CT

PITTBULL GOLDEN — hazy gold; aroma is malt at first, then hops; hop flavor, long rich dry hop aftertaste; feels good in your mouth; OG 1042. [A, 77]

ARCH AMBER — hazy amber, hop aroma and flavor, very dry hop finish and aftertaste, almost too bitter. Made with pale, Munich, wheat, crystal, and chocolate malts; bittered with Chinook, Willamette, Tettnanger, Cascade, and Hallertau hops; and dry hopped with Cascade, Willamette, and Tettnanger; OG 1048. [A, 70]

MAD LUDWIG'S OKTOBERFEST ALE — deep hazy amber, hop nose, big body, complex hop and malt flavor, dry hop finish and aftertaste, smooth brew; OG 1058. [A, 68]

SINISTER SNEER — amber-brown, malty nose; malty flavor is both rich and dry; medium body, dry and smooth; finishes lighter than it starts but takes on a little roasted character, fades to light chocolate malt in the aftertaste. [A, 58]

HARTFORD RUSSIAN IMPERIAL STOUT — very deep brown; rich roasted malt aroma shows some alcohol; big rich complex flavor also shows its potency; big body; long strong and rich aftertaste stays fairly dry although it shows very little hop presence. Made with crystal and black patent malts, cedar aged; FG 1.090. [S, 68]

PRAYING MANTIS PORTER — brown; malty nose forecasts the complex malt flavor which is more or less British (but not entirely); good body; the chocolate malt shows well in the dry finish and into the long dry malty aftertaste; made with Chinook and Willamette hops; low temperature mash (148°F); OG 1055. [P, 59]

HARTFORD BROWN ALE — brown; aroma shows mostly the toffee-caramel nature of the crystal malt, but the hops are there too; very smooth flavor shows the malt and hops; dry malt finish, medium body; long malty aftertaste has some zestiness. The hops are Cascade and Willamette. Mashed at 151°F, mostly crystal malt is used; OG 1048–1050. [A, 64]

BACCHUS STRONG OLD ALE — deep brown, big dry malt aroma and taste, strong with noticeable alcohol and ample hops to balance the malt, big body, dry strong malt finish, very long dry malt aftertaste; has some horsepower and complexity; made with lots of chocolate malt and some (7–8%) wheat malt and heavily hopped; OG 1063, 6–6.5% abv. [A, 76]

HARTFORD SCOTCH ALE — amber; pleasant aroma shows more malt than hops; big bright malt and hop flavor gets more malty as you go; really good tasting, smooth dry malt finish, long complex aftertaste; specific gravity 1.054. [A, 78]

PITBULL DRY LITE ICE — deep gold; faint vegetal malt nose gets a little stinky as it warms; light malt flavor is slightly sour; dry light hop finish, medium length; specific gravity 1.037. [LO, 24]

CAVANAUGH'S IRISH RED — deep reddish-amber, faint malt aroma, dull malt and hop flavor, light medium dry finish, short aftertaste, not likable; specific gravity 1.047. [A, 31]

HORACE WELLS BROWN ALE — deep amber, malty nose, big pleasant malty flavor; not complex but very nice to sip; finish shows malt and the beginnings of some hops; smooth dry hop aftertaste; specific gravity 1.054. [A, 62]

John Harvard's Brew House
Brewpub in Cambridge, MA

JOHN HARVARD'S CRISTAL PILSNER — gold, light clean malt aroma, light dry hop flavor (Bouillon and U.S. Hallertau), medium body, dry hop finish and aftertaste, as tasted in 1993. [B, 80]

JOHN HARVARD'S CRISTAL PILSNER — golden-amber, light clean hop aroma, big dry Saaz hop flavor, big body, balanced and refreshing, some tannin from beechwood lagering apparent, dry hop finish and aftertaste. This is the 1994 recipe for this brew, giving it more of a Bohemian Pils character and raising the hop by about 10 IBU from the earlier formula. [B, 80]

JOHN HARVARD'S PALE ALE — amber-gold, light dry hop aroma and flavor done in an English style using Kent and Fuggles hops, medium body, dry hop finish and aftertaste. [A, 69]

JOHN HARVARD'S NUT BROWN ALE — amber, light malt aroma, complex malt and hop flavor (Bouillon and Hallertau hops and some chocolate malt), medium body, light dry malt finish and aftertaste. This description applies to the brew as presented in 1993. [A, 67]

JOHN HARVARD'S NUT BROWN ALE — amber, big hop and light malt aroma, complex hop and malt flavor (Brewer's Gold and Cascade hops and some chocolate malt), medium body, light dry malt and hop finish and aftertaste. This is the version found at the brewpub in 1994. [A, 67]

ALL AMERICAN LIGHT LAGER — gold, faint malt nose; bright but light malt flavor tends to dry hops at the finish; medium to light body, medium long dry hop aftertaste. [B, 65]

OLD WILLY INDIA PALE ALE — amber-gold, bright well-hopped

aroma, big bright hoppy taste, finishes strong hops but with plenty of malt in support, long malty aftertaste with dry hops at the end. Made with Brewer's Gold and Cascade hops, dry hopped with Cascades, this is a very well made IPA; gravity 14 P. [A, 80]

JOHN HARVARD'S EXPORT STOUT — dark brown, roasted barley aroma; chocolate malt and roasted barley dominate the palate; smooth and balanced, good body; chocolate malt stays right to the end in long roasted malt aftertaste; goes very dry at the very end. [S, 71]

Hazel Dell Brewpub
Brewpub in Vancouver, WA

HAZEL DELL BERRYWEIZEN — pinkish cloudy gold, fruity malty nose, flavor like the nose; fruit and non-fruit flavors weave in and out on the palate but don't quite come together; light bodied, medium length, decoction mashed, with raspberries folded in; OG 1044, FG 1.912, 4.2% abw. [W, 47]

Heavenly Daze Brewery & Grill
Brewpub in Steamboat Springs, CO

WAPITI WHEAT — pale gold, light floral hop and malt aroma, light malt flavor, light body; light fairly dry malt aftertaste shows a little wheaty grain. Top-fermented

with 40% wheat malt; specific gravity 1.044, 4% abw. [W, 58]

IGGY'S INDIA PALE ALE — pale amber, pleasant hop aroma and flavor, good body, smooth and balanced, long dry hop aftertaste; specific gravity 1.052, 4.8% abw, 49 IBU. [A, 67]

DOG'S BREATH BROWN ALE — brown, dry malt aroma and flavor, good body, smooth and balanced, dry hop and malt finish and aftertaste; specific gravity 1.050, 4.6% abw. [A, 65]

WOODCHUCK PORTER — dark brown; malt aroma has tones of coffee and chocolate; smooth dry tasty malt flavor, good body, bright dry hoppy finish and aftertaste. Top-fermented and dry hopped; specific gravity 1.050, 4.6% abw. [P, 60]

COW CREEK CREAM ALE — bright clear gold, malt aroma, smooth malty flavor, complex dry hop finish, good body; malty aftertaste is drier than the flavor; specific gravity 1.048, 4.5% abw. [A, 63]

HEAVENLY HEFE-WEIZEN — cloudy amber-gold, huge fruity malt aroma with all kinds of fruit and spices (cloves, citrus, smoke, banana, etc.); delicious flavor uncovers layer after layer of taste promised by the nose; medium body is big for the style; lingering delicious aftertaste; a big winner with great complexity; specific gravity 1.060, 5% abw. [W, 90]

Notes

HEAVENLY DAZE RASPBERRY WHEAT — deep gold, raspberry aroma, dry raspberry flavor, light to medium body; very dry long aftertaste retains raspberry in the corners of your mouth; specific gravity 1.044, 4.0% abw. [W, 53]

G. Heileman Brewing Co.

Breweries in La Crosse, WI; Seattle, WA; Baltimore, MD; Portland, OR; and San Antonio, TX.

HEILEMAN'S SPECIAL EXPORT BEER — tawny-gold, lusty hop aroma; flavor starts out hops but slightly off-dry, then gets bigger and more hoppy at mid-palate and into the finish; medium body, stays smooth; is complex and very much European in style; has plenty of character; finishes dry hops and has good length. The brew is kraeusened; gravity 11.2 P, 4% abw. [B, 72]

HEILEMAN'S SPECIAL EXPORT LIGHT BEER — pale bright gold, pleasant malt aroma, thin body, light malt flavor with some sour hop background in mid-palate, fleeting off-dry malt finish, very little aftertaste. Kraeusened; gravity 9.0 P, 3.40% abw. [LO, 53]

HEILEMAN'S SPECIAL EXPORT DARK — deep copper color, very little nose, only a faint sense of sweetness, faint hop flavor, low carbonation, light body,

dull and uninteresting; gravity 11.3 P, 3.85% abw. [B, 23]

OLD STYLE LIGHT LAGER BEER — gold color, fragrant malt and hop nose, bright hop flavor, balanced and fairly long. A kraeusened brew; gravity 11.2 P, 3.8% abw. [LO, 35]

OLD STYLE SPECIAL DRY — pale gold, sweet malt aroma, highly carbonated, off-dry malt front palate, dry middle and finish, faint brief malt aftertaste. [D, 31]

OLD STYLE PREMIUM DRY BEER — pale gold, apple-malt nose, fairly dry and smooth hop flavor, plenty of malt in support, finishes dry, not much aftertaste. [D, 34]

OLD STYLE CLASSIC DRAFT — gold, pleasant malt and hop aroma, high carbonation; flavor is malt, hops, and carbonation; light but clean, melony finish, dry aftertaste; gravity 10 P, 3.6% abw. [B, 38]

OLD STYLE CLASSIC DRAFT LIGHT — gold, light malt and faint hop aroma, high carbonation; light flavor like the nose but the carbonation is a major part; light bodied, light dry finish, little aftertaste; gravity 9 P, 3.3% abw. [B, 35]

OLD STYLE ROYAL AMBER NON-ALCOHOLIC MALT BEVERAGE — deep gold, light malt aroma and flavor, light body; dry malt aftertaste has little duration; 0.50% abw. [NA, 31]

OLD STYLE ICE BREWED ALE — gold, hop nose, big strong sour hop flavor, malt stays in back, big body, sour hop finish and aftertaste; 5.8% abw. [B, 39]

HEILEMAN'S LIGHT BEER — bright pale gold, faint malt aroma; light hop flavor that is less dry in front than it is in middle and finish; good balance and fairly long. [LO, 62]

WIEDEMANN BOHEMIAN SPECIAL FINE BEER — pale gold, fresh malt aroma with some hops, light malt flavor with a hop background, good fresh tasting pilsener-type beer, fairly long dry hop aftertaste. [B, 52]

WIEDEMANN LIGHT — gold, grainy aroma with a soapy background, light body, weak malt flavor, seltzer-like finish and aftertaste, clean but uninteresting. [LO, 24]

RED WHITE AND BLUE SPECIAL LAGER BEER — pale gold, light clean malt aroma and flavor, light body, dry malt finish and short aftertaste, quaffable hot weather beer. [B, 47]

BURGERMEISTER BEER — pale gold, pleasant light hop nose, light hop and malt flavor, dry hop finish and aftertaste, medium duration. [B, 38]

BLATZ BEER — pale yellow-gold, light malt nose, light malt flavor, light body; finishes dry and has a short malt aftertaste; what hops there are are well in back; another hot weather quaffing beer. [B, 48]

BLATZ LIGHT BEER — pale gold, lovely malt nose; malt flavor but you can taste the carbonation; hops come in with a bitter touch in the finish leading to a dry, brief, and slightly bitter hop aftertaste. [LO, 41]

BLATZ LIGHT CREAM ALE — medium yellow-gold color, off-dry fruity malt aroma, tangy hop flavor; some off flavors in the backtaste which take a more dominant position in the aftertaste. [A, 29]

BLATZ LA BEER — gold, pleasant fragrant aroma with both malt and hops, watery body, very little flavor; what is there is pleasant but it is too weak. [RA, 27]

BLATZ MILWAUKEE 1851 — bright gold, sweet malt nose, sort of a fruity-apple; palate is off-dry with a bite in the middle; quick finish, and little aftertaste. A bit too sweet up front, but improves across the palate as it gets drier. Overall reasonably drinkable. [B, 41]

BLATZ MILWAUKEE 1851 LIGHT — brilliant pale gold, lovely beery malt aroma, light body, pleasant malt flavor, some hops in aftertaste, pleasant but too watery and too brief. [LO, 36]

BLITZ-WEINHARD BEER — tawny-gold, malt and hop nose, high carbonation; malt flavor that has a salty component; dry malt finish with some hops in aftertaste. [B, 45]

HENRY WEINHARD PRIVATE RESERVE — light to medium gold, good hop aroma, very appetizing; a zesty flavor that features both malt and hops; good balance, medium to good body, light hop aftertaste with good length. Each bottling is numerically identified on the neck label. Made with Cascade hops; gravity 11.05 P, 3.75% abw. [B, 43]

HENRY WEINHARD'S PRIVATE RESERVE DARK BEER — medium tawny-brown, slightly smoky malt aroma, light body; flavor starts dry but becomes less so toward the middle; some complexity but not much, pleasant and refreshing. It is more like a colored light beer than a dark beer; gravity 11.5 P, 3.7% abw, SRM 25. [B, 32]

HENRY WEINHARD PRIVATE RESERVE LIGHT BEER — bright gold, dull hop nose, light malt and hop flavor, not interesting and not long. Made with Cascade hops; gravity 9.10 P, 3.00% abw. [LO, 30]

WEINHARD'S IRELAND STYLE PREMIUM LIGHT ALE — deep gold, tangy hop aroma, light hop flavor, light body, pleasant and drinkable, medium to long aftertaste; malt is there but well in back. This is a dry hopped (Cascades) lager-ale; gravity 9.1 P, 3.0% abw. [B, 41]

WEINHARD'S RED LAGER — red-amber; pleasant malty-fruity nose has some hops; palate is beautiful on the first sip but becomes dull by the finish, tails off fast and the light dry malt aftertaste is uninteresting; gravity 11.6 P, 3.65% abw. [B, 49]

WEINHARD'S BLUE BOAR
ICE ALE — amber-gold, vegetal
malt and hop nose; complex flavor
has plenty of malt and hops,
noticeable alcohol; mid-palate
goes off-dry, malty finish and
aftertaste is dry at the end; 5.8%
abv. [B, 49]

WEINHARD'S PALE ALE —
brilliant gold, spicy hop nose,
spicy hop flavor, light body,
perfumy hoppy aftertaste, ends dry
and spicy. [A, 34]

WEINHARD'S HONEY
HEFEWEIZEN — cloudy gold, dry
faint mead-like aroma; dry flavor is
slightly honeyed; ends sweeter than
it starts; aftertaste is sort of dull and
quite sweet. [W, 33]

EUREKA! ORIGINAL
LAGER — golden amber; fresh
malt and hop aroma has a touch of
apple in front; balanced malt and
hop flavor is quite tasty, smooth
with no warts; the malt comes at
you more as you sip; long medium
dry malty aftertaste. Made for
Eureka! B.C. [B, 66]

EUREKA! ALE — gold, malt
aroma, off-dry malty front palate,
malty sour from middle-on, ends a
bit "dirty," medium body, not likable and not long. [A, 30]

EUREKA! RED PREMIUM
ALE — deep amber; hop and malt
aroma is a bit stinky at first but
this quickly clears and cleans;
bright balanced hop and malt flavor is smooth and drinkable;
medium body, fairly dry and long
malt and hop aftertaste. [A, 59]

CHAMPALE MALT LIQUOR —
pale gold; grapelike aroma that
makes you think of champagne,
light body, good carbonation,
slightly sweet grape flavor. Certainly tries to be champagnelike
and does so fairly successfully.
[ML, 45]

GOLDEN CHAMPALE
FLAVORED MALT LIQUOR —
bright gold, fruit gum aroma,
flavor much like a Scottish soda
called Irn-Bru (Iron Brew in eastern Canada), fairly sweet and
clean tasting, interesting for a flavored malt liquor. [ML, 18]

PINK CHAMPALE FLAVORED
MALT LIQUOR — pale pink;
nose like Cold Duck which I presume it is intended to emulate;
mildly flavored sweet taste (possibly grenadine), very drinkable and
pleasant. [ML, 40]

BLACK HORSE ALE — tawny-
gold, bright hop aroma with plenty
of supporting malt, caramel-malt
flavor, good balance, long rich
malt aftertaste. [A, 72]

METBRAU NEAR BEER — pale
gold, faintly salty malt aroma,
highly carbonated; flavor is light
malt and CO_2; little finish and
aftertaste. [NA, 18]

HAUENSTEIN NEW ULM
BEER — pale gold, clean malt
aroma with some hops, clean
bright malt flavor, light body, light
hop finish and aftertaste. [B, 50]

GRAIN BELT BEER — pale
gold, off-dry malt nose, light malt
flavor, high carbonation, short
malt aftertaste. [B, 42]

GRAIN BELT PREMIUM — pale
gold, light malt aroma; malt flavor
is lightly hopped and off-dry; light
malt aftertaste shows a little more
hopping but not much. [B, 29]

SCHMIDT BEER — pale
gold, light fragrant hop aroma,
medium body, malt and hop
flavor on the light side, weak
bodied and brief. [B, 35]

SCHMIDT EXTRA SPECIAL
BEER — pale gold, fruity malt
aroma, off-dry malt flavor, only
lightly hopped, medium aftertaste
like the flavor. [B, 47]

SCHMIDT LIGHT BEER —
pale gold, pleasant light malt and
hop aroma, light but complex
hop flavor, dry hop finish and
aftertaste. [LO, 19]

SCHMIDT SELECT NEAR
BEER — pale gold, faint malt
aroma, weak watery body, dry
dusty malt flavor, brief aftertaste. [NA, 19]

KINGSBURY BREW NEAR BEER — very pale golden color, faint malt nose, watery body, grainy flavor; faint grainy aftertaste has little length. [NA, 24]

LONE STAR BEER — gold, light malt and hop aroma, flavor to match, light body, medium dry finish, little aftertaste; gravity 10.8 P, 3.5% abw. [B, 43]

LONE STAR LIGHT BEER — pale gold, light malt aroma, weak body, light malt flavor, fairly short light malt aftertaste; gravity 8.6 P, 3.15% abw. [LO, 36]

LONE STAR DRAFT BEER — pale yellow-gold, full malt aroma, good malt flavor, medium dry malt aftertaste with good duration. [B, 49]

LONE STAR NATURAL BOCK BEER — amber, thick head (showing what 100% barley malt can do); rich malt aroma and flavor is off-dry and a little alcoholic; finishes off-dry malt, medium long off-dry malt aftertaste, very little hop appearance; gravity 10.8 P, 3.65% abw. [BK, 30]

STAG LIGHT BEER — pale gold, light malt aroma and flavor, little finish and aftertaste save some faint hops. [LO, 19]

STAG BEER — gold, clean fresh malt aroma, good body; flavor starts off good malt and hops but does not sustain becoming more faint as it crosses the palate; light hop aftertaste. [B, 52]

RAINIER ALE — amber, good well-hopped nose, big body, tangy

hop and malt flavor; the malt is off-dry but the bite of the hops keeps it all in balance; good length; gravity 15.1 P, 5.6% abw, 21 IBU. [A, 54]

RAINIER MOUNTAIN FRESH BEER — pale gold; hoppy nose, but the flavor is more malt and even more carbonation; finish and aftertaste seem highly influenced by the CO_2 and ends brackish; gravity 10.8 P, 3.65% abw. [B, 30]

RAINIER LIGHT — pale gold, pleasant malt and hop nose, low carbonation, malt palate with very little hops, fairly brief; gravity 8.6 P, 3.15% abw. [LO, 15]

RAINIER DRY — pale amber, big hop nose, very little flavor, finish, or aftertaste; gravity 10.5 P, 3.85% abw, 14.5 IBU. [D, 20]

RAINIER DRAFT BEER — tawny-gold, hop and malt nose, dry malt flavor, not much flavor though, medium body, short dry malt aftertaste, gravity 10 P, 3,6% abw. [B, 17]

RAINIER DRAFT LIGHT — pale gold; very light pleasant aroma shows a little malt and less hops; malty flavor tends toward graininess; light body, brief aftertaste. [LO, 27]

CARLING'S BLACK LABEL BEER — pale yellow-gold; palate is off-dry malt at first, then some hops come in for the finish and aftertaste; medium body, fair length. [B, 63]

Notes

CARLING'S BLACK LABEL 11–11 EXTRA SPECIAL MALT LIQUOR — light gold, sweet malt aroma with a hop tang in back, highly carbonated, sweet malt flavor with a fruit background; complex, but it would be a matter of taste to like it. [LO, 23]

CARLING'S BLACK LABEL L.A. — yellow-gold; stinky hop nose that faded; watery body, slightly sweet malt flavor, little left at the finish, only a faint sweetness for an aftertaste. [RA, 23]

CARLING'S BLACK LABEL LIGHT BEER — gold, faint malt aroma, light and dry malt flavor with a trace of hops, little aftertaste. [LO, 54]

CARLING'S BLACK LABEL NA MALT BEVERAGE — deep gold, grainy nose, grainy watery palate, thin and short. [NA, 20]

CARLING'S ORIGINAL RED CAP ALE — tawny gold, big hop aroma, strong hop flavor, good body; long hop aftertaste that has too much malt to be called dry, but well-balanced. [A, 65]

COY INTERNATIONAL — pale yellow, good malt nose; off-dry malt flavor that continues into a long aftertaste. [B, 42]

HEIDELBERG BEER — pale gold, faint malt aroma, light malt and hop flavor, light body, little finish and aftertaste. [B, 43]

HEIDELBERG LIGHT — very pale gold, malt nose, light clean malt flavor, off-dry, medium body, dry malt aftertaste. [LO, 30]

NATIONAL BOHEMIAN LIGHT BEER — gold, good clean malt aroma, sprightly clean malt and hop flavor, off-dry at first then good balanced dry malt and hops; finishes well and has a long crisp aftertaste. [B, 63]

NATIONAL PREMIUM PALE DRY BEER — medium deep gold, good malt aroma, pleasant light hop flavor, good balance, smooth and long. [B, 50]

NATIONAL PREMIUM LIGHT BEER — pale yellow, pleasant light malt aroma, fresh light hop flavor, light body, touch of sour malt in the brief aftertaste. [LO, 39]

COLT .45 MALT LIQUOR — deep gold, lovely malt aroma, smooth and soft, off-dry malt flavor and long aftertaste; gravity 12 P, 4.4% abw. [ML, 63]

COLT .45 SILVER DELUXE MALT LIQUOR — pale yellow, malt nose, malt flavor, fairly heavy body, long malt aftertaste with some imbalance in back. [ML, 20]

COLT .45 DRY — bright gold, dry malt nose; dry malt palate with a sweetness in back that stays into a long long aftertaste. [D, 31]

COLT .45 POWERMASTER MALT LIQUOR — gold, light malt aroma, big alcoholic malt flavor, sweet and smooth with sweet hops in back of the malt, good balance, quite long. Very good of type. Reportedly 5.7% abw. [ML, 63]

COLT .45 PREMIUM MALT LIQUOR — deep gold, big malt

aroma with plenty of hops, big malt flavor; hops show at the finish; long off-dry malt and hop aftertaste, very good of type. [ML, 63]

COLT .45 PREMIUM BEER — gold, malt nose (you can really smell the barley); pleasant malt flavor is a bit off-dry and not big; medium body, no hop presence, low carbonation, finishes a bit drier, fairly short and on the dull side; 3.8% abw. [B, 34]

COLT .45 PREMIUM LIGHT BEER — gold, pleasant fruity-estery malt nose; highly carbonated such that most of the fruity malt flavor is masked; light body, brief light malt aftertaste, 3.3% abw. [LO, 27]

COOL COLT — gold, aroma of mint and menthol; flavor is minty like spearmint, mint finish and aftertaste, fairly long on the palate. [ML, 25]

COLT ICE — deep gold, hop nose, sour hop flavor, sweet malt finish, good body, long off-dry malt and hop aftertaste. Full name is Colt Ice, Ice Brewed Malt Liquor, 7.5% abv; specs given at GABF gravity 15.7 P, 5.9% abw. [B, 31]

TUBORG GOLD EXPORT QUALITY BEER — medium gold, well-hopped malt aroma; off-dry malt palate up front, but the hops soon come in for a clean complex and well-balanced flavor; long and pleasant throughout. [B, 62]

TUBORG DELUXE DARK EXPORT QUALITY BEER — copper-brown color, malty molasses nose, light body; mild malt flavor with the hops present but in back; malt finish and aftertaste. [B, 76]

FISCHER'S OLD STYLE GERMAN BEER — pale yellow-gold, pleasant off-dry malt and hop nose, light malt flavor, light body, pleasant, off-dry, and short aftertaste. [A, 42]

FISCHERS OLD STYLE ENGLISH ALE — pale yellow-gold, pleasant malt and hop aroma, dry malt flavor, faint hops in back, short dry aftertaste. [B, 43]

FISCHER'S LIGHT BEER — deep bright gold, fresh malt nose with a yeasty background, light body; light hop flavor that finishes dry and a bit sour; fairly short. [LO, 35]

SCHMIDT'S OF PHILADELPHIA — pale gold, pleasant hop and malt nose, off-dry malt flavor with hops in back, medium body, dry finish, pleasant but short aftertaste, good summer quaffing beer. [B, 51]

SCHMIDT'S BAVARIAN BEER — pale gold, faint malt aroma, slightly sour malt flavor, bitter hop finish, dry hop aftertaste. [B, 34]

READING LIGHT PREMIUM BEER — pale gold, light malt aroma, pleasant malt flavor with some light hop background, light bodied, clean, refreshing, light dry hop aftertaste. [B, 56]

KOEHLER QUALITY BEER — pale gold, good malt aroma, pleas-

ant light malt flavor, hop finish, long pleasant dry malt and hop aftertaste. [B, 43]

RHEINGOLD EXTRA DRY LAGER BEER — pale gold; fresh malt aroma with some hops in back, light body, light malt flavor with some bittering hops in back, these hops come forward in the finish and aftertaste, but more to make the effect of being dry rather than bitter. [B, 41]

RHEINGOLD EXTRA LIGHT — pale gold, light malt aroma; off-dry flavor takes on some sour malt character in the finish and aftertaste. [LO, 32]

RHEINGOLD PREMIUM BEER — pale gold, hop and corn aroma, light malt, corn, and hop flavor, light body, very faint at finish, short aftertaste, unusual to notice the smell and taste of corn to that extent. [B, 30]

RHEINGOLD PREMIUM LIGHT BEER — pale yellow, faint hop nose, faint malt flavor, light body, no aftertaste; offers even less than most light beers. [LO, 20]

KNICKERBOCKER NATURAL — pale gold, malt nose, smooth, soft malty flavor with good hop balance, light body, long dry aftertaste. [B, 36]

COQUI 900 MALT LIQUOR — bright deep gold, malt aroma, sweet malt flavor, clean malt finish and aftertaste. [ML, 27]

McSORLEY'S CREAM ALE —
tawny brown, tangy malt and hop
aroma, full flavored with plenty of
both malt and hops, good balance,
well-hopped but not overly bitter
for the malt, long aftertaste, very
good with food; gravity 14.1 P,
4.85% abw. [A, 49]

ABC BEER — gold, big head,
lovely hop and malt nose, very fragrant, clean malt flavor, light but
pleasant, medium length. [B, 47]

ABC ALE — gold, big head, dry
hop nose, dry hop flavor, pleasant,
medium body, brief aftertaste.
[B, 47]

ABC LIGHT — pale gold, pleasant malt and hop nose, almost
perfumy, light malt flavor, highly
carbonated, short malt finish and
aftertaste. [LO, 29]

MIDNIGHT DRAGON SPECIAL
RESERVE MALT LIQUOR —
gold, slightly stinky malt nose, high
carbonation, big malt and hop flavor, very drinkable and very good;
backs off a bit in the finish and
aftertaste, but still a big flavorful
brew. Contract brew for Ferolito &
Vultaggio & Sons of Brooklyn, NY,

along with the three following
brews. The three Midnight Dragon
brews were likely made at Pittsburgh prior to the split and, at
present, details of production
haven't been revealed. [ML, 52]

MIDNIGHT DRAGON ROYAL
RESERVE LAGER — gold, flowery hop aroma, light dry hop flavor
and finish, short aftertaste. [B, 26]

MIDNIGHT DRAGON GOLD
RESERVE ALE — golden amber,
slightly stinky malt nose, highly
carbonated, big malt and hop flavor, finishes strong with big hops
well-backed with malt, long, very
drinkable, and very good. [B, 63]

CRAZY HORSE MALT
LIQUOR — deep gold, slightly
sour malt nose, big malt palate,
noticeable alcohol, long off-dry
malt aftertaste. Made for Dakota
Hills Ltd. by Hornell Brewing
Co., Inc. of Baltimore, but
Ferolito & Vultaggio & Sons is
embossed on the shoulder of the
large painted bottle that makes
you think it is a whiskey. [ML, 45]

JAMES BOWIE PILSNER
BEER — deep gold; basically a
malt nose but there are some hops;
big malt flavor, big body, medium
long off-dry malt aftertaste.
Apparently a successor to Crazy
Horse as it is produced in a large
painted bottle that looks like a
whiskey bottle. Embossed on the
bottle is Ferolito & Vultaggio &
Sons. [B, 43]

ST. IDES PREMIUM MALT
LIQUOR — deep gold, malt nose,
off-dry malt flavor, smooth and

mellow, refreshing, finishes
medium dry, long malt aftertaste.
Made with long fermentation and
dry hopping. Made for the
McKenzie River Corp. of San
Francisco, CA. [ML, 43]

BREWSKI BREW PUB
LIGHT — pale gold, pleasant
flowery malt aroma with a carbon
dioxide tang, light body, light dry
malt and carbonation flavor, short
aftertaste. Contract beer made for
Brewski Brewing Co.; gravity 8 P
(1.003), 2.86% abw. [LO, 23]

BREWSKI BREW PUB CLAS-
SIC — gold, faint malt aroma,
light malt flavor, light body, short
dry malt aftertaste. Made for
Brewski Brewing Co.; gravity
11.5 P (1.010), 3.83% abw. [B, 27]

RHINO CHASERS LAGER
BEER — hazy gold, faint hop and
fruity malt aroma; flavor shows
both malt and hops; medium body,
smooth, balanced, and bright; finishes dry malt and hops, long dry
aftertaste. Made with two-row
malt and Saaz hops; 3.77% abw.
Contract beer made in San Antonio for William & Scott Co.
Culver City, CA, as found in California in early 1994. [B, 59]

MICKEY'S FINE MALT
LIQUOR — bright gold, malt
nose; fruity malt flavor that is on
the sweet side; finishes sweet but
the malt in the aftertaste dries a
bit; medium duration; gravity
12.2 P, 4.4% abw. [ML, 68]

McSORLEY'S CREAM ALE —
tawny brown, tangy malt and hop
aroma, full flavored with plenty of

both malt and hops, good balance, well-hopped but not overly bitter for the malt, long aftertaste, very good with food; recipe has been changed; gravity 13.6 P, 4.65% abw. New label says McSorley's Ale, see below. [A, 49]

MICKEY'S ICE ICE BREWED ALE — pale gold; malty aroma does have some hops in back; off-dry malt flavor, light body, quick finish; short malt aftertaste is drier than the flavor; gravity 12.2 P, 4.5% abw. [A, 32]

McSORLEY'S DOUBLE DARK — dark brown, malty nose, sweet malt flavor with a semi-dry finish, thin body, short dry malt aftertaste. [B, 40]

McSORLEY'S ALE — deep amber-gold, faint malt nose; tangy hop flavor has plenty of bite, especially at the finish; medium body, long dry hop aftertaste; could use more malt for balance. New 1994 recipe. [A, 38]

TYE DYE PREMIUM LAGER — orange-amber, very attractive fragrant dry light hop and malt aroma, dry hop flavor, very smooth and balanced, easy drinking beer, medium body, dry hop finish and aftertaste, good length; gravity 10.8 P, 3.6% abw. Made for Tye Dye Brewing Co. of Melbourne, FL. [B, 66]

EMERALD CITY ALE — amber, faint malt aroma; off-dry malt flavor is a bit flabby; light body, undercarbonated for the sweetness, short basic (vice acidic) malt aftertaste, no follow-through;

brewed to gravity 12.4 P, 4% abw, 25–30 IBU. [A, 43]

WINDY CITY AMBER ALE — hazy amber, toasted malt nose; malty flavor is a little sweet at first, dry in the middle, driest at the finish; good body, long dry malty aftertaste, hops at end. [A, 65]

BREWSKI BAR ROOM ALE — amber, very bright malt and hop nose; big zesty flavor of malt, hops, and carbonation; dry malt finish, long dry malt aftertaste, dry and refreshing; described as an American brown ale that is warm-fermented and cold-lagered; made with American grown hops of British origin; 4.1% abw. [A, 68]

BREWSKI HOLIDAY SALUTE 1994 — deep amber, faint roasted malt and alcohol nose, strange roasted malt and alcohol flavor, medium body, faintly burnt malt aftertaste, not likable because of the sharp burnt background, contract beer made for Brewski Brewing Co. [B, 44]

JET CITY PALE ALE — bright gold, faint hop malt aroma and light malt and hop taste, weak body; what there is of flavor is pleasant enough but the beer is just too watery; touch of oxidation, faint and brief aftertaste. This is how it was on draft. In bottle, it was similar except that the aroma was stronger and more hopped; the flavor was a slight bit bigger as was the body, with an off-dry malt finish and short dry hop aftertaste. The bottled sample was better than the draft. Made for the Jet City B.C. of Seattle, WA. [A, 45]

Notes

JET CITY ROCKET RED ALE — amber, light toasted malt nose, big toasted malt flavor, medium to light body, toasted malt finish and aftertaste; hops show well late in the palate and balance off the sweetness of the hops giving it a dry ending. Made for the Jet City B.C. of Seattle, WA. [A, 62]

WEINHARD'S BLUE BOAR COLD-FILTERED DRAFT — gold, hop nose; flavor is malty with a sour hop background; good body, dry hop finish, long dry hop aftertaste. [B, 44]

LONE STAR ICE ICE BREWED ALE — gold; aroma is at first sour hops then malt, off-dry malt flavor, big body, hop finish; off-dry malt aftertaste has hops in back, brief; 5.6% abw. [B, 46]

KINGSBURY RED NON-ALCOHOLIC BREW — amber-red, grainy malty nose, dry weak grainy flavor, weak body; short aftertaste tastes like grainy water that has run through a rusty iron pipe. [NA, 14]

OREGON IPA — pale amber-gold; very attractive fragrant hop nose shows some Cascades; big dry hop flavor is very assertive and not as pleasant as the aroma; medium body, very dry hop finish and aftertaste, very dry and very long; most of the points scored by this brew come from the glorious aroma. Made for Oregon Beer and Ale Co., Lake Oswego, OR. [A, 52]

OREGON NUT BROWN ALE — brown, roasted malt aroma and rich dry roasted malt palate, medium to good body, dry roasted malt finish and aftertaste, good length; made with pale, crystal, roasted, and Victory malts; gravity 13.5 P, 4.2% abw. Made for Oregon Beer and Ale Co., Lake Oswego, OR. [A, 56]

OREGON HEFEWEIZEN — hazy amber, aroma of beef and barley soup, dry malt palate, medium body, slightly vegetal malt aftertaste. Made for Oregon Beer and Ale Co., Lake Oswego, OR. [W, 24]

OREGON ESB — gold, hop aroma, dry hop flavor, light to medium body, dry hop finish and aftertaste, gravity 11.5 P, 3.2% abw. Made for Oregon Beer and Ale Co., Lake Oswego, OR. [A, 56]

OREGON HONEY RED — amber, nice Cascade hop nose, very clean and bright, pleasant bright hop and roasted malt flavor, medium body, lightly and finely carbonated, light and dry malt and hop aftertaste. Made for Oregon Beer and Ale Co., Lake Oswego, OR. [A, 49]

OREGON RASPBERRY WHEAT ALE — hazy gold; berry and wheat malt aroma has a ripened cheese background; tastes better than it smells but is still not attractive; fruity sour aftertaste. Made for Oregon Beer and Ale Co., Lake Oswego, OR. [W, 12]

POST ALLEY PALE ALE — copper-amber, lightly toasted malt aroma and flavor, medium body, medium dry toasted malt finish and aftertaste. Attributed to Emerald City B.C. [A, 52]

LA PAZ CERVEZA — bright amber-gold, creamy texture; aroma is good malt and fragrant hops; pleasant malty flavor is lightly hopped, medium body, light dry hop aftertaste. [B, 45]

Heritage Brewing Co.
Microbrewery in Lake Elsinore, CA previously in Dana Point, CA

IMPERIAL STOUT — deep amber-brown, roasted barley and chocolate malt aroma and flavor; strongly flavored, but smooth; good body, very good balance, dry malt finish and aftertaste. [S, 67]

FRUGATTI ALE — gold, bright hop nose, very dry hop flavor; aftertaste is long dry hops. Made for the Frugatti Restaurant of San Bernardino. [A, 53]

WHITE FOX — gold, light bright hop aroma and flavor, light malt backing, light body, light dry hop aftertaste, specific gravity 1.050, 4.5% abw. [A, 60]

RED FOX PALE ALE — copper-amber, smooth dry hop aroma, bright dry hop taste, medium body, dry hop finish, very long dry hop aftertaste. A very good American-style pale ale made with Nugget hops and dry hopped with Cascades and Willamette hops; specific gravity 1.054, 5.2% abw. [A, 74]

BLACK FOX — deep amber-brown, dry chocolate malt and roasted barley aroma; smooth nutty malt flavor shows some of the chocolate malt; medium body, dry toasted malt finish and long aftertaste. Smooth and dry, this medium-bodied and flavored stout has no harsh edges and goes well with food; specific gravity 1.040, 3.8% abw. [S, 80]

LEGENDS BLONDE ALE — brilliant gold, light malt nose with hops in back; palate starts out malty, but overly bitter hops come in at mid-palate and stay giving it a "jagged" effect that just won't balance; medium body, dry bitter hop finish and aftertaste, much too bitter at the end. Made for Legends Sports Bar and Restaurant of Los Angeles, CA. [A, 34]

MULLIGAN PREMIUM LAGER — gold, fruity litchi nose, sour fruity taste, dry sour aftertaste. [B, 13]

CATALINA GOLD ALE — hazy gold, big head, creamy texture, fruity malt aroma with some hops in back, fruity front palate, dry tart hops in middle and finish, tending to sour in the aftertaste. Made by Catalina/Mainland B.C., Lake Elsinore. [A, 42]

CATALINA RED ALE — hazy reddish gold, nice northwest hop nose, big complex and bitter northwest hop flavor, a very good sipping beer, with a malty sweet finish and an extremely long dry bitter northwest hop aftertaste; nicely made. [A, 73]

CALIFORNIA PROPHET RASP-BERRY ALE — bright fairly deep gold, big real raspberry aroma; flavor is raspberry with malt in back, fairly sweet; tries to dry a bit at the finish but can't lick the raspberry soda nature; made with real raspberries but there is too little else to balance off the sweetness. Made for Prophet B.C. of Los Angeles. [A, 46]

AIRSHIP ALE — hazy amber, big head, rising malt and northwest hop aroma; tangy hop flavor has a lactic acidic sour backtaste; the acidic bite intensifies at the finish and rides into the aftertaste marring the flavor; very long. Airship Beer Co., Lake Elsinore, CA. [A, 33]

OLDE 4.20 DEADHEAD DRAFT — hazy amber; big creamy head is long lasting; big hop palate has a hint of lactic acid in back, much like the Airship Ale but it hasn't developed enough to mar the flavor; tart hop finish and very long and hoppy aftertaste has a faint tart quality in back. Could be the same brew as the Airship Ale. Made by the Creston B.C. of Creston, CA and Lake Elsinore, CA. [A, 57]

Notes

High Country B.C.
*Microbrewery in
Boulder, CO*

RENEGADE RED — golden amber, big hop nose, huge hop flavor, big body, very mouth filling, extremely long hop aftertaste. An IPA made with English malt and yeast brewed with Chinook and Cascade hops; OG 1060, 6.25% abw. [A, 76]

Hill Country Brewing & Bottling
*Microbrewery in
Austin, TX*

BALCONES FAULT RED GRANITE EXTRA SPECIAL BREW — deep red-amber; clean malty-hop aroma has a faint background smokiness that could come from chocolate malt; flavor is complex and lightly spicy; English in style and reminds one of English yeast and Fuggles hops; medium body, good complexity; dry malt finish and aftertaste has a light smoky-hoppy background. [A, 51]

BALCONES FAULT PALE MALT EXTRA SPECIAL BREW — amber-gold, interesting bright hop nose, zesty spicy hop flavor, good body, creamy texture, very tasty, good mouthfeel, long dry hop aftertaste. [A, 75]

Hoboken Brewing Co.
*Microbrewery in
Hoboken, NJ*

MILE SQUARE GOLDEN ALE — deep gold, sweet fruity malt nose; off-dry malt palate has a touch of celery up front; medium body, some sourness and bitterness in the aftertaste clashes with the sweetness of the malt and harms the overall effect. [A, 33]

MILE SQUARE AMBER ALE — bright amber, dull dry malt nose, dull dry malt flavor finishes a bit sour, medium body, dry malt aftertaste. [A, 32]

HOLY COW! Casino, Cafe and Brewery
*Brewpub in
Las Vegas, NV*

HOLY COW! PALE ALE — deep gold, light hop aroma and flavor, good body, dry hop finish, medium to long dry hop aftertaste; made from two-row and caramel malts, an English-style pale ale; specific gravity 1.056, 4.2% abw. [A, 73]

HOLY COW! RED ALE — reddish-amber, dry malt aroma, medium body, dry malt flavor, finish, and aftertaste, not much duration on the palate; made from two-row and caramel malts, Fuggles hops; specific gravity 1.048, 4.5% abw. [A, 53]

HOLY COW! BROWN ALE — deep amber, dry hop and malt aroma, flavor like the nose, very smooth, good body, a drinkable brew with good length; made with caramel malts, Cascade and Mt. Hood hops; specific gravity 1.055, 4.5% abw. [A, 68]

HOLY COW! AMBER ALE — deep gold, dry hop aroma, light dry hop flavor, finish, and aftertaste, medium duration. [A, 54]

HOLY COW! CREAM ALE — gold, bright dry malt and hop aroma, very refreshing dry malty flavor, medium body; dry malt aftertaste has good length, very lightly hopped with Fuggles hops; made with 10% wheat malt; specific gravity 1.056, 4.5% abw. [A, 67]

HOLY COW! HEFE WEIZEN — hazy gold, bright spicy aroma, good classical hefe-weizen clove flavor, medium body, long spicy dry malt aftertaste; a good refreshing wheat beer made with 70% summer and winter wheat malts and 30% two-row barley malt; slowly fermented with Bavarian traditional weizen yeast, specific gravity 1.052, 4.2% abw. [W, 67]

HOLY COW! AMERICAN PALE ALE — deep gold, very pleasant fragrant Cascade hop nose, bright hop flavor, good body, dry hop finish and aftertaste, good length; specific gravity 1.056, 4.2% abw. [A, 68]

HOLY COW! STOUT — brown, chocolate malt and roasted barley aroma, bright dry roasted malt flavor, good body; long dry roasted malt aftertaste is long, a good classical stout; specific gravity 1.064, 5.5% abw. [S, 72]

HOLY COW! ALTBIER — amber, big dry complex hoppy aroma and flavor, plenty of supporting malt, medium body, complex dry hop finish and aftertaste; made with Tettnanger and Hallertau hops, dark malts, and traditional German alt yeast; specific gravity 1.048, 4% abw. [A, 71]

HOLY COW! WHEAT BEER — gold, light malt aroma and flavor, light body, refreshing, fairly short aftertaste. [W, 45]

Hops! Bistro and Brewery
Brewpubs in Scottsdale, AZ and La Jolla, CA

HOPS! PILSNER — gold, light malt and hop nose; flavor starts out initially as malt but the hops don't take long to arrive and dominate the taste thereafter; medium to good body, crisp and clean; dry finish and aftertaste stays hoppy but the malt also peeks through again; good length, a very different kind of pils, complex and tasty. Brewed from two-row and Carapils malts with Hallertau hops; gravity 11.5 P, 4.2% abw. From Scottsdale. [B, 53]

HOPS! AMBER ALE — amber, faint malt and dry English hop aroma, bright dry hop flavor, finish and aftertaste similar to the flavor but more dry, good body. Dry hopped with Centennial hops; gravity 14.5 P, 4.9% abw. From Scottsdale. [A, 62]

HOPS! HEFE-WEIZEN — gold, bright and spicy clove aroma, spicy clove and fruity malt flavor, plenty of both malt and cloves; aftertaste is long and shows more of the malt than the spice. Made from 50% malted wheat; unfiltered brew; gravity 14.5 P, 4.9% abw. From Scottsdale. [W, 64]

PETER'S PORTER — brown, dry malt aroma and flavor; could use even more malt; light body, dry malt aftertaste. Brewed from roasted barley, chocolate, black, and caramel malt; gravity 14.5 P, 5% abw. From Scottsdale. [P, 47]

HOPS! RASPBERRY — reddish-amber, raspberry aroma, dry berry flavor, brief dry malt aftertaste; gravity 10.5 P, 3.6% abw. From Scottsdale. [A, 52]

HOPS! BARLEY WINE — amber gold, huge malt aroma, hefty malt flavor, huge body, syrupy, long off-dry malt aftertaste. This winey brew is dry hopped and cask-conditioned and was made in 1991. This is it at age two and it just gets better and better; gravity 27.5 P, 9.5% abw. A subsequent version is dry hopped and cask-conditioned; gravity 19.4 P, 6.5% abw. This latter version has not yet been tasted. From Scottsdale. [BW, 67]

THE DICTATOR'S LITTLE SISTER BOCK — brown, very dry hop and malt aroma and taste, finishes even drier, too dry; it misses out on much of the flavor of the malt and hops. Made using black patent, roasted barley, dark crystal, and Munich malts; gravity 17 P, 6% abw. From Scottsdale. [BK, 47]

Notes

We Serve
Naturally Carbonated
FRESH BEER
❦ Fire Brewed On the Premises ❦
In Small Batches

HOSTER
BREWING CO.
COLUMBUS, OHIO

❦ In The Brewery District ❦
(614) 228-6066

HOPS! OCTOBERFEST — amber brown, big hop and malt aroma, dry hop and malt flavor, good body, long dry hop finish and aftertaste. Pale, Vienna, Munich, and three crystal malts, with Cascade and Saaz hops are used; gravity 15.5 P, 5.2% abw. From Scottsdale. [B, 67]

HOPS! CHRISTMAS ALE — deep amber, aroma of ginger, cinnamon, nutmeg, hops, and fruity malt, very complex, good flavor like the nose, good body, long dry spicy aftertaste, one of the better wassails. From Scottsdale. [A, 75]

HOPS! OATMEAL STOUT — opaque brown, toasted barley and caramel aroma, complex and aromatic; extremely complex flavor that is sometimes not dry (I can't really call it being sweet) and sometimes dry as it crosses your palate; when it is being not dry it takes on a candy caramel nature; when it is dry it still has the caramel but shows the hops and

grains; big body, good balance; the finish and aftertaste actually show oats. A unique and excellent brew made with 150 lbs. of oats; gravity 12.5 P, 4% abw. From Scottsdale. [S, 90]

HOPS! PILSNER — gold, hop aroma and light hop flavor; fairly zesty despite its lightness; medium body, dry hop aftertaste. From La Jolla. [B, 52]

HOPS! HEFE-WEIZEN — hazy gold, malt aroma with a little spice, clean lightly spiced flavor, bright and refreshing, medium body, dry faintly spicy aftertaste, made with 50% wheat. From La Jolla. [W, 68]

RASPBERRY LAGER — amber, raspberry aroma, off-dry red raspberry flavor, low carbonation, medium dry finish, dry aftertaste; retains the raspberry character throughout. From La Jolla. [B, 41]

HOPS! EXPORT LAGER — amber-gold, malt aroma and flavor, high alcohol, big body, long strong malt aftertaste; balance could be better. From La Jolla. [B, 65]

HOPS! OATMEAL STOUT — very deep brown, complex malt aroma, roasted barley and chocolate malt flavor; some oats show in the finish; noticeable alcohol, but good balance overall; medium body, pleasant and drinkable, long fairly dry aftertaste like the flavor. Made with 5% blackened malt and 20% oats. From La Jolla. [S, 79]

HOPS! EXTRA SPECIAL BITTER — amber, hop aroma;

bold hop flavor shows plenty of malt; medium to big body, certainly a big flavor and aftertaste with plenty of malt and hops; very long, but the balance could be better. From La Jolla. [A, 54]

HOPS! MAERZEN — deep amber, pleasant malt aroma; bright malty flavor is slightly off-dry; finishes strongly with a little tang in back; long off-dry malt aftertaste has strength as well as length. From La Jolla. [B, 63]

Note: All La Jolla brews tasted at the brewpub or other San Diego area pubs featuring local craft brews. Scottsdale brews tasted at the brewpub or at GABF.

Hops Grill & Bar
Chain of brewpubs with two locations in Tampa, FL and other Florida locations in Clearwater, Palm Harbor, Jacksonville, Orlando, Bradenton, and Lakeland

CLEARWATER LIGHT — gold, faint but pleasant hop aroma, dry hop flavor, light body, very drinkable, smooth, and refreshing, dry hop finish and aftertaste, little length. Tasted in Tampa. [LO, 62]

HOPS GOLDEN LAGER — gold, light flowery hop and malt aroma; dry hop flavor well balanced with the malt that shows well all across the palate; good body, smooth; long dry aftertaste shows both hops and malt and has some duration. Finishing with

Czechoslovakian Saaz hops gives it a European style. Tasted in Tampa. [B, 68]

HAMMERHEAD RED — amber, light dry hop aroma; big dry hop flavor is quite tangy and shows little of the pale, crystal, caramel, and chocolate malts which are evidenced by the ample body; big (and good) mouth feel, long dry hop aftertaste, stays dry and hoppy. Tasted in Tampa and Orlando. [B, 60]

LIGHTNING BOLD GOLD — gold, pleasant malt and hop nose; balanced malt and hop flavor stays dry and has a European flair; medium body, dry hop finish and aftertaste, refreshing and fairly long. [B, 64]

Hoster Brewing Co.
Brewpub in Columbus, OH

EAGLE LIGHT — pale gold, almost no discernable aroma, clean light and dry hop flavor, light body, dry hop finish and brief aftertaste. [LO, 42]

GOLD TOP — deep gold, hop nose, pleasant dry hop flavor, good body, long dry hop aftertaste. [B, 63]

AMBER — amber, light roasted malt aroma, flavor like the nose but with some hops, pleasant and tasty, good body, fairly long aftertaste much like the flavor, a Vienna-style lager, version on draft at the brewpub. [B, 65]

EAGLE DARK-SON OF BLACKTOP — dark brown, complex malt and hop aroma on the dry side, big body, dry stout-like flavor but not heavy like a stout, long dry malt aftertaste. [B, 52]

BUCKEYE BOCK — deep amber, big hop and malt aroma, big hop flavor, plenty of malt backing, long dry hop aftertaste. [BK, 69]

HOSTER'S AMBER LAGER — amber, roasted malt aroma and flavor, medium body; malt is sweetest at the finish; long dry malt aftertaste, very smooth and drinkable, bottled version. [B, 65]

Houston Brewery
Brewpub in Houston, TX

HOUSTON BREWERY WHITE ALE — hazy gold, fruity malt nose, fruity-estery malt flavor, medium to light body; dry malt aftertaste is a bit tart. [A, 55]

HOUSTON BREWERY LIGHT ALE — pale gold, grainy malt aroma and flavor; palate is fairly dry; medium to light body, dry malt finish and aftertaste. [A, 49]

HOUSTON BREWERY STEAM BEER — amber-gold, fruity malt nose; fruity-estery palate has a faint phenolic background and finish; medium body, ends dry and hoppy without any trace of the phenolic background. [S, 35]

HOUSTON BREWERY BEST BITTER — amber-gold, fruity aroma and flavor, good body; hops not that evident in the flavor but show well in the finish and aftertaste; ends dry but not hoppy. [A, 59]

HOUSTON BREWERY INDIA PALE ALE — amber-gold, pleasant malt and hop aroma, balanced malt and hop flavor, very malty for the style, good body, very drinkable; nicely done although an IPA should lean more toward the hops; smooth long dry malty aftertaste. [A, 66]

HOUSTON BREWERY STOUT — deep brown, chocolate malt and roasted barley aroma and flavor, medium body, good roasted malt aftertaste; long and delicious although a bit light bodied for a stout. [S, 58]

Hubcap Brewery & Kitchen

Brewpubs in Vail, CO and Dallas, TX

WHITE RIVER WHEAT — pale amber-gold, malt nose and taste, medium body, dry malt finish and aftertaste. Bottled samples were marred with a butterscotch nose and taste. Made from 35% malted wheat and 65% malted barley; specific gravity 1.044, 3.70% abw. From Vail. [W, 50]

CAMP HALE GOLDEN ALE — gold, dry malt and hop nose; malt flavor had a light hop background; dry hop finish and aftertaste. Bottled samples had a buttery background to the predominantly

malt flavor which tended to make the palate slightly dull. Made with Munich and Carapils malt; specific gravity 1.047, 3.70% abw. From Vail. [A, 49]

ACE AMBER ALE — gold, dry hop nose, smooth malt flavor, medium body, somewhat dry hop finish and aftertaste. Bottled samples had a buttery background to the flavor and a sourness in the aftertaste. Made with crystal malt, Cascade, and Willamette hops; specific gravity 1.045, 3.7% abw. From Vail. [A, 64]

BEAVER TAIL BROWN ALE — deep amber, malt aroma and flavor with solid hop support, medium body, well-balanced, but fairly short. Again, bottled versions were overlaid with a butterscotch flavor. Made with crystal malt and a touch of chocolate malt, and dry hopped with Cascades, this is an interesting dry stout-style brew; specific gravity 1.048, 3.7% abw. From Vail. [A, 54]

RAINBOW TROUT STOUT — deep brown, chocolate malt and roasted barley nose, medium body, big flavor like the nose; dry hop aftertaste is a little sour at the end. Another nice dry stout made from roasted barley, chocolate and crystal malts, and Cluster hops; specific gravity 1.050, 3.7% abw. From Vail. [S, 65]

SOLSTICE ALE — gold, hoppy aroma and flavor, good body, dry hop finish and aftertaste. Highly hopped with Centennial and Cascade hops and dry hopped; the

secondary fermentation extends to three weeks. From Vail. [A, 52]

BOCK N' ROLL — gold; dry aroma has both malt and hops; smooth flavor is good malt well supported by hops; well-balanced, good body, long dry malt and hop aftertaste. From Vail. [BK, 67]

ALLEY CAT ALE — gold; malt aroma has a bright hop background; smooth malt and hop flavor is bright and dry; medium body, dry hop and malt finish and aftertaste; made with two-row, Munich, and Carapils malts, with Saaz and Oregon Hallertau hops; specific gravity 1.056. 4% abw. From Dallas. [A, 68]

BLUE MOUNTAIN HEAVEN — amber, coffee bean aroma, dry coffee bean flavor, medium body, dry coffee finish and aftertaste; coffee beans are added to the secondary fermentation for five days; specific gravity 1.042, 3.2% abw. From Dallas. [B, 74]

DOWNTOWN BROWN — brown, malt nose, rich off-dry malty flavor, medium body, good complexity, long fairly sweet malt aftertaste; made from pale and crystal malts with a touch of chocolate malt, together with Cascade and Willamette hops; specific gravity 1.052, 4.4% abw. From Dallas. [A, 67]

PEGASUS PILSNER — gold, bright hop nose, spicy hop flavor, medium body, dry hop finish and aftertaste. From Dallas. [B, 59]

RANGER RED — reddish amber, bright hop aroma and flavor,

pleasant, tasty, refreshing, balanced, medium to light body, long dry hop finish and aftertaste; specific gravity 1.044, 3.3% abw. From Dallas. [A, 75]

TEXFEST — amber, hop nose, light hop flavor, good body, dry hop finish and aftertaste, a very good tasting beer; made with Munich malts with Hallertau and Tettnanger hops; specific gravity 1.060. From Dallas. [B, 84]

WEST END WHEAT — gold, malty aroma and flavor, light body, smooth and refreshing, dry malt finish and aftertaste, medium duration; made with 35% malted wheat and lightly hopped with Hallertau and Tettnanger hops; specific gravity 1.040, 3.2% abw. From Dallas. [W, 60]

VAIL PALE ALE — amber, Northwest hop nose, big bright hop flavor (90 IBU), good body, long dry hop aftertaste, very nice for hop-heads; made with pale ale and crystal malts bittered with Columbus hops, then dry hopped for three weeks with Cascades; OG 1058, FG 1.012, 6% abv. From Vail. [A, 77]

Huber-Berghoff Brewing Co.

Brewery in Monroe, WI. Several corporate names used on labels, including Jos. Huber B.C.

REGAL BRAU BAVARIAN STYLE BEER — gold, fresh clean malt aroma, good malt and hop balanced flavor, off-dry finish, sour malt aftertaste. [B, 40]

WISCONSIN CLUB PREMIUM BEER — medium gold, pleasant malt nose, malt palate, light body, off-dry malt finish and aftertaste. [B, 46]

HUBER PREMIUM BEER — bright gold, good hop and malt aroma, fresh and clean off-dry malt and hop flavor, nicely balanced, pleasant malt finish, long malt aftertaste. [B, 50]

HUBER PREMIUM BOCK BEER — deep amber-brown, malt nose; malt flavor up front becomes more and more hoppy as it proceeds to a dry, almost bitter hop finish and aftertaste. [BK, 47]

RHINELANDER EXPORT PREMIUM BEER — bright gold, clean malt aroma; off-dry malt flavor up front, but this dries toward the finish and ends in a fairly dry hop aftertaste of little length. It is good with food. [B, 39]

ED DEBEVIC'S BEER — tawny-gold, good big hop aroma; off-dry hop front palate, drier at the finish, and ends with a short dry hop aftertaste. Made for a Chicago restaurant, but available elsewhere. [B, 46]

ROUGHRIDER PREMIUM BEER — hazy pale gold, light malt nose, high carbonation, light malt flavor and finish, short dry hop aftertaste, light bodied. Contract brew for Dakota B.C. [B, 23]

BRAUMEISTER LIGHT BEER

Specially Brewed only in Wisconsin ...with the finest ingredients

OLD CHICAGO LAGER BEER — gold, sour hop nose; hop flavor that is a little sour in front, dry hop finish and aftertaste. [B, 14]

BERGHOFF BEER — bright amber, hop nose, bright hop and malt flavor, good body, tasty, light hop finish, long dry hop aftertaste, complex and likable brew; specific gravity 1.0543, 4.35% abw. [B, 73]

BERGHOFF DARK BEER — amber-brown, rich hop aroma, light body; fairly rich malt flavor that is a tad burnt; fairly pleasant, light body, long dry malt aftertaste, a little hop bitterness at the very end. You could drink a lot of it; specific gravity 1.0535, 4.3% abw. [B, 47]

BERGHOFF BOCK BEER — deep mahogany, dry slightly roasted malt nose, roasted malt flavor, medium body, medium dry malt aftertaste, straightforward dry and light beer with little complexity. [BK, 42]

BERGHOFF LIGHT BEER — deep gold, flowery malt aroma, light malt and hop flavor,

balanced but light, medium to short dry hop aftertaste. [LO, 43]

BERGHOFF FAMOUS BOCK BEER — deep amber-mahogany, medium rich malt and dry hop nose, fairly big malt and dry hop flavor, smooth and balanced, very quaffable, dry hop finish, medium long dry hop aftertaste. [BK, 65]

BERGHOFF GENUINE DARK BEER — brown; dry malty aroma has a little roasted character; big dry lightly roasted malt flavor, medium body, fairly long medium dry malt aftertaste. [B, 53]

BERGHOFF FAMOUS RED ALE — amber; pleasant malt and hop nose has a light roasted character; dry palate is mostly lightly roasted malt; medium to good body, long dry roasted malt aftertaste. [A, 67]

BERGHOFF ORIGINAL LAGER BEER — deep gold, big hop nose; big dry hop flavor has plenty of malt support; medium to good body, dry hop finish and aftertaste, very long on the palate. [B, 68]

A. FITGER & CO.'S EXPORT BEER — pale amber, light hop nose, good body, good dry hop and malt flavor, long dry hop aftertaste. [B, 49]

VIENNA LAGER BEER — amber, complex off-dry malt and hop aroma, bright hop flavor, finish, and long aftertaste, an interesting and appetizing beer. [B, 70]

AMBIER VIENNA STYLE BEER — brilliant amber, very light toasted malt aroma; front

palate is malt, dry hop middle and finish; complex long candy-malt aftertaste that slowly dries as it goes on. This brew is very much a Vienna-style lager. Made for Ambier (Vienna) B.C. of Milwaukee, WI. [B, 71]

LEMON & LAGER — light gold, lemon aroma; zesty lemony flavor but little resemblance to a beer as there is very little malt showing through the lemon except in the long aftertaste; it is supposed to be like a lemon shandy by the style. [B, 31]

VAN MERRITT LIGHT BEER — bright gold, light hop nose, very light hop flavor, almost nothing at the finish and there is no aftertaste. [B, 17]

DEMPSEY'S ALE — pale amber, beautifully balanced hop and lightly roasted malt nose, zesty ale taste with good hops and some toasted malt, high carbonation, light body, dry malt finish, medium length dry malt aftertaste; specific gravity 1.056, 4.7% abw. [A, 53]

HARLEY DAVIDSON HEAVY BEER 1988 — hazy-gold; malt nose is a touch sour; big malt and hop palate, heavy body, good balance, long malt aftertaste. Made annually for a Harley-Davidson motorcycle meet held each year in the vicinity. [B, 47]

HARLEY DAVIDSON HEAVY BEER 1989 — pale amber, malt aroma, good malt flavor, big body, long pleasant malt aftertaste. [B, 42]

HARLEY DAVIDSON HEAVY BEER 1990 — gold, clean fruity

malt nose and taste, big body, long dry malt aftertaste. [B, 53]

HARLEY DAVIDSON BEER DAYTONA 1993 — gold, sweet estery malt aroma, big sweet malt flavor, tinny finish, dull malt aftertaste. [B, 27]

BOXER PREMIUM MALT LIQUOR — deep gold, good fruity malt nose, pleasant straightforward malt flavor; finishes as it starts; long malt aftertaste. [ML, 64]

BRAUMEISTER LIGHT BEER — deep gold, pleasant malt and hop aroma, light malt-hop flavor, very thin, very short. [LO, 18]

TELLURIDE BEER — tawny-gold, pleasant soft malt aroma, pleasant off-dry malt front palate; dry hops come in the middle, finishes dry malt; long dry malt and hop aftertaste, medium body, overall dry and well-balanced and very drinkable; 4.25% abw. Made for Telluride B.C. Moab, UT, and Telluride, CO. [B, 60]

SNAKE BITE BEER — gold, faint melony malt nose, light malt flavor; carbonation bite pretty much overwhelms anything subtle; short dry malt aftertaste. Made for Snake Bite Beer Co., Muskego, WI. [B, 26]

FOECKING PREMIUM BEER — pale gold, light malt aroma, high carbonation, good malt flavor with the hops in back, balanced and very drinkable; dry aftertaste drops off very fast. Made for Foecking Alcohol Beverage Co. of Illinois, Rock Island, IL. [B, 42]

FOECKING PREMIUM LIGHT — gold, pleasant malt and hop nose, high carbonation, light dry malt and hop flavor, light body, short dry finish and aftertaste. Contract brew as above. [LO, 27]

CERVEZA VICTORIA — deep gold, good fragrant hop and malt nose, dry malt palate, good body, dry malt aftertaste with a hop background, touch of bitter hops at the end of the long aftertaste. Made under license of Compañhia Cerveceria de Nicaragua, a contract brew for distribution in Nicaragua. [B, 48]

CERVEZA VICTORIA LIGHT BEER — pale gold, flowery hop and malt aroma, big malt flavor, very refreshing, medium body, medium long dry hop aftertaste. Contract brew as above. [B, 53]

CERVEZA VICTORIA MORENA BEER — deep amber-brown, fragrant rich malt nose, good malt flavor, pleasant and straightforward, light body, long rich and dry malt aftertaste. Contract brew as above. [B, 43]

LIQUOR MART BOCK BEER — deep amber, buttery malt aroma, malt and butterscotch flavor, medium body, burnt buttery malt aftertaste. Made for Liquor Mart of Boulder, CO. [BK, 34]

NEWPORT CLASSIC LIGHT BEER — gold, pleasant malty nose; flavor is dry hops, slightly oxidized; light body, light dry hop aftertaste. Made for Old Newport B.C. of Newport Beach, CA. [B, 18]

Notes

TUN TAVERN FOUNDER'S LAGER — gold, pleasant malt and hop aroma, good body, light malt and hop flavor; decent balance, neither the malt nor the hops try to dominate; dry finish and aftertaste, faintly sour at the end; specific gravity 1.046. 3.8% abw. Made for the Tun Tavern of Philadelphia, PA. [B, 40]

ANDECHS SPEZIAL HELL LAGER — hazy gold, nice fresh malt aroma (like Grape-Nuts); big rich flavor is mostly malt, but there are hops as well; bitter hop finish, long malt and hop aftertaste with the bitter hops gaining at the end; specific gravity 1.050, 4.4% abw. Made under license and with the authority of Klosterbrauerei Andechs of Erling-Andechs, Germany. [B, 53]

STARKE'S ORIGINAL HEAD HOG PREMIUM BEER — gold, dull faintly buttery malt nose, dull malt flavor like the nose, finishes up the same way. Made for Head Hog Brewing Co. [B, 24]

HARLEY DAVIDSON BEER DAYTONA 1994 — deep gold; fragrant malt and hop aroma is very pleasant; big malty flavor with a hop background, good body; big finish has a malty sweetness and a long aftertaste. [B, 53]

TELLURIDE BEER — tawny-gold, pleasant soft malt aroma, pleasant off-dry malt front palate; dry hops come in the middle; finishes dry malt, long dry malt and hop aftertaste, medium body, overall dry, well balanced and very drinkable; specific gravity

1.057, 4.3% abw. Made for Telluride B.C., Moab, UT and Telluride, CO. [B, 60]

STEAMBOAT LAGER BEER — amber-gold, pleasant malt and hop aroma, good body; flavor is first light malt but hops come in better from mid-palate on; good balance; neither the malt nor the hops try to dominate; dry finish and aftertaste, driest at the end. Made for Steamboat B.C. of Clinton, IA. [B, 53]

Sudwerk Privatbrauerei Hubsch
Microbrewery and brewpub in Davis, CA

HÜBSCH BRÄU GERMAN STYLE BEER — gold, finely carbonated, pleasant fruity malt aroma, big hop flavor, big body, dry hop finish, long dry hop aftertaste. [B, 67]

HÜBSCH BRÄU LAGER — amber, low carbonation, pleasant malt nose, smooth slightly off-dry malt flavor, good balance, very drinkable, fairly long dry malt aftertaste. Cold-fermented and long aged; gravity 11.8 P, 3.8% abw. [B, 63]

HÜBSCH BRÄU PILS — gold, faint hop aroma, pleasant smooth light hop flavor, low carbonation, dry hop finish and aftertaste, medium duration. Made exclusively with two-row malt and no specialty malts; hopped with Hallertau and Tettnanger hops; gravity 12.5 P, 4% abw. [B, 62]

HÜBSCH BRÄU WEIZEN — gold, low carbonation, bright malt

and light lactic spice nose, bright wheat and malt flavor, very smooth; hops come in at the middle, faint spiciness stays in back behind the hops; nicely balanced, fairly complex, interesting, a nice beer somewhere between American and German styles. This is Hübsch's first top-fermented beer made with 60% wheat malt and 40% two-row malt; gravity 12 P, 3.8% abw. [W, 62]

HÜBSCH BRÄU MÄRZEN — amber, low carbonation, light roasted barley nose, dry malt flavor, light on the hops, smooth, dry malt aftertaste; gravity 13.5 P, 4.5% abw. [B, 63]

HÜBSCH BRÄU DARK — brown, roasted malt nose and taste, very smooth and balanced, dry malt finish and aftertaste, very drinkable; gravity 13 P, 4% abw. [B, 67]

HÜBSCH BRÄU OKTOBERFEST MÄRZEN — amber, beautiful malt nose with good complexity, extremely smooth and delicious malt flavor, a classic Märzen throughout, finishes dry, long complex medium dry malt aftertaste, very drinkable. Made with six different malts; gravity 13.5 P, 4.2% abw. [B, 63]

HÜBSCH DOPPEL BOCK — dark red-amber, dry very rich roasted malt nose, very dry yet rich slightly roasted malt flavor, big body, dry malty finish and aftertaste; flavor is not long but the dryness lingers. [BK, 67]

HÜBSCH HEFE-WEIZEN WHEAT BEER — hazy gold,

complex spicy-lactic weizen-style aroma, lightly spiced malt and hop flavor, bright, smooth, and delicious, just a tad yeasty, a bit drier at the end than in the middle, long and very refreshing, nicely made. [W, 67]

Hudepohl-Schoenling Brewing Co.

Company is result of the merger of the two Cincinnati, OH breweries

BOHEMIAN TAP LAGER BEER — bright gold, slightly sweet malt aroma, highly carbonated, light sweet malt flavor, off-dry malt finish and aftertaste. [B, 37]

HOFBRAU BIER — deep gold, clean malt and hop nose, light body, bright hop flavor up front; malt comes in middle and adds a little sweetness to the finish and aftertaste. [B, 54]

HUDEPOHL GOLD — bright gold, big fruity malt aroma, good dry malt flavor, light but pleasant, refreshing, well balanced. [B, 49]

HUDEPOHL 14K PREMIUM BEER — pale gold, vegetal malt nose, grainy off-dry malt flavor, somewhat straw-like in back and in the finish and aftertaste. [B, 27]

HUDY DELIGHT BEER — pale yellow-gold; faint roasted character to the malt but there is a little straw in back that seems to dull the taste; light body, light malt aftertaste with little length; specific gravity 1.030, 3.1% abw, 10 IBU. [LO, 16]

HUDEPOHL PURE GRAIN BEER — pale gold, light hop aroma followed by a hop palate well backed with malt, good body, lightly spicy hop and malt finish and aftertaste. [B, 20]

BURGER BEER — very pale gold, pleasant light malt aroma and taste; this continues into the medium length aftertaste. [B, 23]

LUDWIG HUDEPOHL ORIGINAL BOCK BEER — deep amber, lovely roasted malt nose, smooth dry roasted malt flavor, long malt aftertaste, medium body, very drinkable. [BK, 62]

LUDWIG HUDEPOHL SPECIAL OKTOBERFEST BEER — pale amber-orange, dry malt aroma, good dry malt flavor, good body, well-balanced, long refreshing malt aftertaste. [B, 65]

CHRISTIAN MOERLEIN CINCINNATI SELECT BEER — amber-gold, big malt aroma with plenty of hops in back, big malty flavor with good support from hops in back, hint of smokiness in the middle; finish cuts off quickly but there is a long dry malt aftertaste. An all-barley malt beer; specific gravity 1.048 (11.8 P), 3.91% abw, 16 IBU. [B, 43]

CHRISTIAN MOERLEIN DOPPEL DARK BEER — amber color, sweet rich malt nose, dry toasted malt flavor, medium body, off-dry malt at finish, slightly off-dry malt aftertaste of medium length; specific gravity 1.048, 3.91% abw, 22 IBU. [B, 67]

Notes

CHRISTIAN MOERLEIN BOCK
BEER — dark amber; malt nose
that is slightly smoky; malt flavor
with a touch of potato peel at the
finish, medium body, little finish
and aftertaste, overall on the dull
side. Made with two-row and caramel malt; specific gravity 1.049,
3.9% abw, 14 IBU. [BK, 28]

MOERLEIN'S CINCINNATI
BOCK BEER — deep amber,
toasted off-dry perfumy malt aroma;
dry malt flavor that fades away fast;
medium body; aftertaste is only a
roasted dry quality. [BK, 38]

LITTLE KINGS CREAM ALE
(SCHOENLING CREAM
ALE) — gold; fragrant aroma has
both hops and malt; flavor starts
out briskly with fresh bright hops,
it sweetens out a bit at the finish,
and ends that way; long aftertaste.
A bright good tasting little brew.
Bottom-fermented; specific gravity 1.0539 (12.55 P), 4.5% abw, 15
IBU. [B, 43]

TOP HAT BEER — pale gold, faint
malt aroma with even fainter hops

in back, very light malt and hop flavor, medium body, short dry malt
and hop aftertaste. [B, 46]

SCHOENLING DRAFT BEER —
gold, beautiful malt nose, high
carbonation, pleasant malt and
hop flavor, brief but clean and
refreshing. Also labeled Big Jug
Beer. [B, 48]

SCHOENLING OLD TIME
BOCK BEER — deep ruby-
amber, malt aroma, thin body,
high carbonation, malt and cherry
pit taste, off-dry malt finish and
medium aftertaste. [BK, 29]

WILLIAM PENN COLONIAL
LAGER — deep amber, rich malt
aroma, good body; a good malt
and hop flavor but it is quite light;
dry malt aftertaste, very drinkable.
Contract brew for Wm. Penn B.C.
of Langhorne, PA. [B, 56]

BRUCKS JUBILEE BEER —
pale gold, good malt aroma and
flavor, decent body, good long
malt aftertaste. Contract brew for
C.J. Brockman Brewery, Cincinnati, OH. [B, 47]

FEHR'S XL — bright gold, big
rich malt aroma, hops in back,
clean dry malt flavor, very dry
malt finish, fairly short dry ma
t aftertaste, a little charcoal/sm
ke in the background, very drinka
le; nice while it is in your mouth.
Made for Frank Fehr B.C., Cincinnati
OH. [B, 67]

MT. EVEREST MALT
LIQUOR — gold, soapy malt
nose like a perfumed apple scent
bath soap or shampoo, soapy

apple flavor, good body, dry malt
aftertaste; gravity 14.15 P, 4.85%
abw. [ML, 23]

BANKS BEER — gold, litchi nut
nose, dull fruity-vegetal malt flavor,
good body; vegetal malt aftertaste is
sour at the end. This is the U.S.
domestic version of the Banks beer
of the Bahamas. [B, 36]

BRUIN PALE ALE — amber,
highly carbonated; big aroma
shows plenty of hops; malt, and
carbonation, bright fresh dry hop
and sweet malt flavor, appetizing
and balanced, very drinkable, dry
hop finish, long dry hop aftertaste;
made with two-row Harrington,
chocolate, and caramel malts, with
Cascade, Mt. Hood, and Saaz
hops, and ale yeast. [A, 54]

WILD IRISH ROSE MALT
LIQUOR — gold, aroma of malt,
carbonation, and hops; malt flavor
is highly carbonated and lightly
hopped; off-dry approaching
sweet, ample alcohol for the type,
faint vegetal and corn background,
good body, light semi-dry malt
finish and aftertaste. Made for
Wild Irish Rose B.C. [ML, 32]

LITTLE KINGS ICE CREAM
ALE — gold, pleasant malty
aroma; palate is flowery malt up
front, hops come in the middle,
but the perfumy malt prevails;
medium body, long perfumy off-
dry malt aftertaste. [B, 52]

LITTLE KINGS RED ALE —
amber, lightly toasted fruity malt
aroma, toastiness fades on the palate (or at least doesn't develop);
medium body, dry malty finish

and aftertaste, medium length. Label assures us that it is top-fermented. [A, 47]

JACK DANIELS 1866 CLASSIC AMBER LAGER — amber, malty nose, dry malty flavor, medium body, drops off rapidly after you swallow; very brief. Made for Jack Daniels Brewery, Lynchburg, TN. [B, 33]

Humboldt Brewery
Brewpub in Arcata, CA

RED NECTAR ALE — hazy amber, strong hop nose, big smoky dry malt and hop flavor, medium body, strong and long dry malt after-taste with hops breaking through at the end. I have also tasted this brew where it is big dry hops throughout without much malt at all, and certainly no smoky malt. Several malts, four varieties of hops, and high mashing temperature combine to give this brew its character; gravity 12.5 P, 4.4% abw. [A, 87]

GOLD NECTAR ALE — pale gold, fruity malt nose, soft dry malt flavor, dry malt finish and aftertaste, dry malt all the way through. [A, 53]

GOLD RUSH EXTRA PALE ALE — gold, pleasant fruity-malt nose, dry hop and malt flavor with a citrus background, medium body; brief aftertaste is just a memory of the flavor. Made with Chinook, Cascade, and Hallertau hops; gravity 11 P, 4.4% abw. [A, 27]

STORMCELLAR PORTER — brown, rich malt nose and flavor, good body, dry malt finish and aftertaste. Made with crystal and chocolate malts with Chinook, Mt. Hood, and Cascade hops; gravity 14.25 P, 5% abw. [P, 70]

OATMEAL STOUT — deep brown, rich roasted cherry malt nose, dry roasted malt flavor, medium body, dry malt aftertaste. Brewed with oats and three different roasted grains, together with Chinook and Willamette hops; gravity 1.056, 4.9% abw. [S, 74]

CHESHIRE CAT — amber, complex big hop aroma and flavor, big body, dry hop finish and aftertaste, great length, a very good tasting English-style barleywine; made with Cascade hops; specific gravity 1.095, 9.5 abw. [BW, 80]

Humes Brewing Co.
Microbrewery in Glen Ellen, CA

CAVEDALE ALE — hazy deep gold, fruity phenolic nose; complex flavor follows the direction of the aroma, medium body, long sour bitter aftertaste; made with Canadian and Scottish two-row malt, and Tasmanian, California, and German hops; specific gravity 1.050, 4.2% abw. Tasted on draft at GABF. [A, 35]

CAVEDALE ALE — cloudy gold, light pleasant litchi nut fruity nose, spicy herbal, rich, and complex, unusual flavor, lots of hops, medium to good body, dry hop finish and aftertaste. Tasted in bottle found in Connecticut. [A, 43]

Notes

STEEP CANYON STOUT — opaque brown, brown head; burnt chocolate nose has a dank vegetal background, burnt malt palate, and very long aftertaste; medium body; not attractive or likable as the dankness is reflected into the flavor; very burnt at the end. Tasted in bottle. [S, 26]

STEEP CANYON STOUT — deep brown, chocolate malt aroma and taste, medium body; strong rich malty flavor is a bit off-dry; long aftertaste is dry Cluster hops; specific gravity 1.055, 4.7% abw. Tasted on draft at GABF. [S, 61]

JAIPUR PALE ALE — hazy deep gold, spicy aroma, lightly acidic malt flavor, medium body; taste stays spicy through the finish and aftertaste but gradually takes on a bit of malty sweetness; dry hopped; specific gravity 1.060, 5.3% abw. [A, 48]

Huntington Beach Beer Co.
Brewpub in Huntington Beach, CA. Affiliated with Manhattan Beach Brewing Co. brewpub in Manhattan Beach, CA.

BOLSA CHICA BITTER — deep amber-gold, tight head, complex hop nose, smooth bitter dry hop flavor, very long dry hop aftertaste, refreshing, especially good in the middle. Made with Tettnanger, Northern Brewers, and Fuggles hops. [A, 78]

PIER PALE ALE — pale amber; bright hop nose is a bit estery; tight head, very smooth, clean, and bright hop flavor, very drinkable, long dry hop aftertaste. [A, 68]

BRICHSHOT RED — reddish amber, fruity malt aroma and flavor, very smooth but light, long malt aftertaste. [A, 43]

AMBER DEXTROUS ALE — copper color, malty aroma and flavor, a richly flavored big bodied ale, assertively hopped with Northern Brewer and Liberty hops, balanced, refreshing taste, dry malty finish and aftertaste; specific gravity 1.056, 4.2% abw. [A, 69]

BLACK GOLD PORTER — brown, chocolate malt aroma and taste, richly flavored and a bit on the sweet side, medium body, dry malt finish and aftertaste; made with crystal, chocolate, and black malts; specific gravity 1.052, 3.7% abw. [P, 67]

CROWLEY'S CREAM ALE — golden amber, smooth light hop aroma and taste, medium body, dry hop finish and aftertaste, not much length; made with ale yeast, then cold-fermented and conditioned; specific gravity 1.052, 3.9% abw. [A, 64]

PIER PALE ALE — amber, big hop aroma and flavor, very bright and refreshing, medium body, dry hop finish and aftertaste, dry hopped with Cascades; specific gravity 1.056, 4.2% abw. [A, 68]

Independence Brewing Co.
Microbrewery in Philadelphia, PA

INDEPENDENCE ALE — dark amber, big dry hop aroma and flavor, medium body, dry hop finish and aftertaste; a good light pale ale made with Cascade, B.C. Kents, and Fuggles; 3.8% abv. [A, 60]

Indianapolis Brewing Co.
Brewery in Indianapolis, IN

MAIN STREET GOLDEN PILSENER — pale gold, hop aroma, hop flavor, dry hop finish and aftertaste. [B, 31]

DUESSELDORFER DRAFT ALE — hazy amber, melony malt nose, fruity malt flavor with the hops in back, dry hop finish and aftertaste. [A, 36]

DUESSELDORFER AMBER
ALE — golden amber, complex fruity malt nose, soft off-dry malt flavor, big body, finishes dry; hops are there but in back, medium long dry somewhat dull malt aftertaste. Made with two-row pale, caramel, and Munich malts, Perle and Mt. Hood hops; specific gravity 1.047, 4% abw, 29 IBU. [B, 63]

DUESSELDORFER PALE
ALE — medium deep gold, light dry hop nose, very dry lightly hopped flavor, medium body, light dry hop finish and aftertaste, good length; a good dry refreshing ale that goes very well with food; made with two-row and dextrin malts with Tettnanger hops (27 IBU); specific gravity 1.044, 3.4% abw. [A, 65]

PIKE PLACE PALE ALE — deep amber, northwest hop and fruity malt nose, big burnt malt flavor, too much so; burnt taste shoves every other flavor into the background and lasts and lasts. Made for the Pike Place Brewery and Merchant du Vin of Seattle, WA for national distribution. [A, 50]

SAN JUAN IPA — hazy golden-amber; fruity malt nose has a citrus-mandarin orange background; a big flavor with plenty of hops and malt with a sense of alcohol; gets dry as you go to the finish and aftertaste; big body, very tasty and alcoholic, good by itself or with food, long and very drinkable. Made for San Juan Brewing of Telluride, Colorado. [A, 84]

DUESSELDORFER DARK
ALE — deep amber, lightly spicy malt aroma, bright spicy hop flavor, good body; dry hop finish and aftertaste shows some malt; fairly dry with good length, touch of smoke in the aftertaste as well. [A, 67]

Ipswich Brewing Co.
Microbrewery in Ipswich, MA

IPSWICH ALE — hazy amber, big hop nose; big dry hop flavor could use more malt presence; fairly smooth, however, and it grows on you; dry hop finish and aftertaste, very good duration. [A, 54]

IPSWICH DARK ALE — deep amber; big malt nose has estery-fruity ale tones; big rich malt flavor is a bit chocolate-like, clean and creamy, good body; flavor finishes with a touch of sweetness but this is gone from the aftertaste, a long satisfying ale. [A, 73]

DORNBUSCH GOLD — gold, tight head, big European hop aroma; rich flavor has plenty of malt and bitter-dry hops; long dry aftertaste has a European style, very long. Offered in a painted ceramic top bottle for Dornbusch Inc. of Ipswich. [B, 75]

Irish Times Pub & Brewery
Brewpub in Palm Beach Gardens, FL

IRISH RED ALE — deep amber, light malt aroma with hops in back; both malt and hops work in the flavor where they take turns leading as the brew crosses the palate; good body; hops emerge a bit more at the finish making the aftertaste a bit more dry than the flavor, but the malt stays throughout. The brew stays balanced, interesting and complex and is very enjoyable. Made with five different malts, Nugget and Willamette hops, dry hopped; specific gravity 1.055, 4.6% abw. [A, 83]

IRISH PALE ALE — amber, light hop, chocolate malt and roasted barley aroma; smooth dry hop flavor shows some toasted malt faintly and a sourness that augments the complexity; good body, good balance, long dry hop and malt aftertaste, finely balanced, excellent with food. Made with roasted barley, chocolate and two-row pale malts, Nugget and Willamette hops; specific gravity 1.046, 3.9% abw. [A, 80]

Irons Brewing Co.
Microbrewery in Lakewood, CO

IRONS GREEN MOUNTAIN ALE — gold, malt nose, malt flavor with hops supporting, light body, short medium dry malt aftertaste. Made with two-row and dark caramels malts, Perle and Willamette hops; gravity 12 P, 4.4% abw. [A, 51]

IRONS AMBER LAGER — cloudy gold, hop aroma, tangy hop flavor, medium body; brief dry hop aftertaste cuts off abruptly. Brewed with Vienna and dark caramel malts, Perle and Tettnanger hops, gravity 12 P, 3.2% abw. [B, 50]

HIGH PLAINS PORTER — dark red-brown, dry malt aroma and flavor, medium body, dry malt finish, short dry malt aftertaste. Made with two-row and Vienna malts with some chocolate malt; specific gravity 1.049, 3.5% abw. [P, 43]

ALPINE PILSNER — deep gold, fresh malty aroma, good balanced malt and hop flavor, medium body, medium dry hop finish and aftertaste. Made with two-row, Munich, and dextrin malts, Perle and Hallertau hops; gravity 12.5 P, 3.7% abw. [B, 50]

ROCKY MOUNTAIN RED ALE — deep gold, moderately dry hop and lightly roasted malt aroma and flavor, medium body; dry malt aftertaste has good length. Made with roasted barley; specific gravity 1.044, 3.2% abw. [A, 50]

DARK IRON — reddish-brown color, off-dry malt aroma and flavor, medium body; malty finish and aftertaste are drier than the main palate, but not really dry; specific gravity 1.050, 4.2% abw. [A, 57]

HARVEST IRON — amber, off-dry malt aroma and flavor, medium to good body; finish and aftertaste are still malty but slightly drier than the main palate; a smooth Vienna Oktoberfest-style lager; 1.056 gravity, 4.2% abw. [B, 63]

LONG IRON BOHEMIAN STYLE PILSENER BEER — amber-gold, bright hop and fruity malt nose; flavor strongly sweet malt at first, then bright bitter hops with a good malt backing; medium body, dry hop finish and

aftertaste; specific gravity 1.050, 3.5% abw. [B, 67]

AMERICAN IRON AMBER ALE — amber-gold, pleasant malt and hop nose, flowery rich big well-hopped and off-dry malt taste, medium body; dry hop finish and aftertaste shows plenty of off-dry malt with an increasing hop presence as it goes, a straightforward amber ale; specific gravity 1.050, 3.6% abw. [A, 67]

DARK IRON CHOCOLATE BROWN ALE — reddish-brown color, off-dry roasted malt aroma and flavor, medium body, coffee-like malty finish and aftertaste are drier than the main palate, but not really dry; specific gravity 1.050, 4.2% abw. [A, 57]

IRON HEART RED ALE — reddish-amber, tight head, malt nose; soft smooth palate is mostly malt; a little dull with a sweetness in back, medium body, dry malty aftertaste; hops stay in back, there is a sense of hops throughout but they never emerge. [A, 50]

WINTER IRON — dark amber, malt aroma; dry flavor shows big malt and plenty of Tettnanger and Perle hops and some alcohol; good body, dry hop finish and aftertaste; specific gravity 1.066, 5.2% abw. [B, 72]

GRID IRON AUTUMN BREW — amber-gold, lovely hop and malt nose, big bright hop flavor, good body, well-hopped finish and aftertaste, long dry and hoppy, hearty and satisfying. [A, 79]

J & L Brewing Co.
Brewery in San Rafael, CA

SAN RAFAEL GOLDEN ALE — hazy gold, fruity malt aroma with an ale-like tang, faintly lemony, tangy dry hop and fruity malt flavor, dry finish and long dry malt aftertaste, good body. Made using 30% raw wheat and Cascade and Tettnanger hops; gravity 10 P, 2.8% abw. [A, 50]

SAN RAFAEL AMBER ALE — amber; pleasant fruity malt aroma that is citrus-orange; dry toasted malt flavor has the citrus nature as well; pleasant and dry; dry chocolate malt aftertaste is lightly hopped and still has the touch of orange; smooth and drinkable. Made using four crystal malts; gravity 12.5 P, 3.5% abw. [A, 79]

SAN RAFAEL TRADITIONAL ALE — gold, clean malty ale-like nose, tangy light citrus hop flavor, may be a faint trace of lactic acid developing in back, hop finish and aftertaste, refreshing but short. [A, 61]

SAN RAFAEL ALE — deep amber, zesty hop nose, bright malt background, sharp hop flavor, good body, long dry hop aftertaste. [A, 60]

Jaipur Restaurant & Brewpub
Brewpub in Omaha, NE

JAIPUR IPA — amber, hop nose and very dry hop taste, medium body, very dry hop finish and aftertaste, well hopped and very dry; specific gravity 1.052, 4.5% abw. [A, 63]

KATMANDU PORTER — dark brown, dry malt aroma and flavor; medium body, complex malt flavor shows the roasty character of the black, chocolate, and crystal malts; bittered with Northern Brewer hops; long dry aftertaste shows both malt and hops; specific gravity 1.050, 4.2% abw. [P, 65]

RAJ'S JALAPEÑO ALE — gold, faint peppery nose; very faint peppers on the palate so the malt can show through; light body, short faintly peppery aftertaste; specific gravity 1.042, 4% abw. [A, 45]

James Bay Restaurant & Brewery
Brewpub in Port Jefferson, NY

JAMES BAY PALE ALE — deep gold, light dry hop aroma and flavor, good body, ends drier and more strongly hopped, long aftertaste; made with East Kent-Goldings and Cascade hops; OG 1058, 50 IBU. [A, 66]

JAMES BAY PORTER — brown, brown head, big toasted malty aroma and flavor, full bodied, very dry on the palate with good strength of flavor, long dry roasted malt aftertaste; made with pale, caramel-20, black, and chocolate malt; OG 1060, 45 IBU. [P, 65]

Notes

J.D. Nick's Restaurant & Brewery / O'Fallon B.C.

Brewpub in O'Fallon, IL formerly called Wolfgang's Restaurant & Brewery

J.D. NICK'S PILSNER — gold, hops and malt both in the aroma; smooth dry hop and malt flavor continues into the long aftertaste; gravity 13.0 P (FG 2.3), 30 IBU. [B, 68]

J.D. NICK'S OKTOBERFEST-MÄRZEN — deep gold, bright hop aroma and flavor, good body, long dry hop aftertaste; gravity 14.0 P (FG 3.0), 25 IBU. [B, 64]

J.D. NICK'S NUMBSKULL AMBER LAGER — amber, hefty malt aroma, big strong malt flavor, good body, very long big malt aftertaste, a real mouthful of beer; gravity 14.0 P (FG 3.0), 23 IBU. [B, 61]

J.D. NICK'S DUNKEL LAGER — amber-brown, light malt aroma, smooth light dry malt flavor, very drinkable, medium to good body, long dry malt aftertaste; gravity 10.4 P (FG 2.3), 20 IBU. [B, 62]

J.D. NICK'S WHEAT BOCK — gold, light malty aroma, very smooth light dry malt flavor, medium body, light dry malt aftertaste; gravity 16.0 P (FG 3.0), 21 IBU. [BK, 68]

J.D. NICK'S HEFEWEIZEN — cloudy gold, off-dry malt aroma, bright hop and malt flavor, very short aftertaste with a slightly "dirty" component. [W, 45]

Joe & Joe's Brewing Co.

Brewpub and restaurant in Simi Valley, CA

JOE JOE'S GOLDEN ITALIAN ALE — hazy amber-gold, bright complex malt and hop aroma and flavor, medium body, dry malt and hop finish and aftertaste, long, very dry, and somewhat dull. [A, 47]

CARLEE'S SPECIAL LITE ALE — pale amber-gold, faint malt and hop aroma, dry hop flavor, light body, decent balance; flavor has some follow-through; long very dry aftertaste, dry yet has zest. [LO, 54]

HIP HOP WHEAT — hazy pale amber, dry wheaty-malt aroma, dry malt flavor, light body, no hops evident, light dry malt finish and aftertaste, brief. [W, 47]

Jones Brewing Co.

Brewery in Smithton, PA, subsidiary of Ft. Pitt B.C., Pittsburgh, PA

ESQUIRE PREMIUM PALE BEER — pale straw color, pleasant grainy hop nose, light hop flavor and finish, brief dry hop aftertaste. [B, 43]

ESQUIRE EXTRA DRY BEER — deep gold, rich malt aroma with plenty of hop backing, big malt flavor with hops well in back; fairly long malt aftertaste with hops arriving at very end; gravity 11.0 P, 3.85% abw. [B, 15]

ESQUIRE DRY LIGHT — pale gold, dry malt aroma, light malt flavor, light body; highly carbonated such that much of the flavor is masked; brief aftertaste of malt and faint hops. [LO, 13]

OLDE TOWNE OCEAN CITY BEER — bright gold, faint malt aroma, very light body, dry malt flavor, dry malt aftertaste with medium length. Made for Ocean City B.C. [B, 28]

BUBBA'S BREW — bright gold, malt aroma and flavor, light to medium body, dry malt aftertaste. Made for Alabama B.C. [B, 34]

PENNSYLVANIA PILSENER — deep bright amber, zesty off-dry malt and hop nose, plenty of both malt and hops on the palate, beautiful balance, good body, solid finish, long and lovely aftertaste. A contract brew for the Pennsylvania B.C./Allegheny Brewery & Pub of Pittsburgh, PA. [B, 65]

MANAYUNK'S MAIN STREET DRAFT BEER PILSNER — pale brilliant gold, dank malt nose, light body, light malt and carbonation flavor, slight vegetal taste; short, slightly dank dry hop finish and aftertaste. Made for Manayunk Malt & Hops Co., Manayunk, PA. [B, 25]

FOODS OF ALL NATIONS PREMIUM AMERICAN PILSNER — pale gold; malty nose has a touch of canned corn; dry malt flavor, thin and watery, short dry malt aftertaste. [B, 20]

STONEY'S LIGHT — bright golden color, pleasant fruity malt and hop aroma, highly carbonated, light and dry malt flavor, very lightly hopped, medium to light body, brief aftertaste. Long fermented without enzymes; gravity 8.9 P, 3.2% abw. [LO, 37]

STONEY'S PILSENER BEER — bright yellow gold, appetizing malt aroma, good malt and hop flavor with a salty nature, malt finish with hops returning in the aftertaste. Made with barley malt and brewer's grits; gravity 11.0 P, 3.55% abw. [B, 29]

HINKY DINK KENNA'S BEER — pale amber, good malt aroma with hops in back, good malt and hop flavor, fairly long aftertaste. Brewed for Alabama B.C. for distribution by Marshall Field's in Chicago. [B, 68]

NASHVILLE BEER — gold color, light malt aroma, dry malt palate and aftertaste, fairly short. Made for Alabama B.C. [B, 29]

FT. PITT SUPER PREMIUM BEER — hazy gold, pleasant malt aroma and flavor, more or less dry especially at the finish, short dry hop aftertaste. [B, 23]

BIRELL — gold, hop aroma, good hop and malt flavor, good body, fairly long dry hop and malt aftertaste, good for a non-alcoholic brew. Production of Birell by Jones was replaced by Evansville B.C. in 1993. [NA, 50]

AMBER STYLE NON-ALCOHOLIC BREW — gold, grainy malt nose and flavor, medium body, some hops in the finish and light malt aftertaste. Low alcohol brew (less than 0.5% abw) made for the Korean market. Made with pale, black, and crystal malts; specific gravity 1.0197. Also seen as Stoney's Non-Alcoholic Brew. [NA, 30]

HOG BREW — gold, malt nose, good dry malt flavor, light dry hop finish and aftertaste. [B, 35]

Jones Street Brewery
Brewpub in Omaha, NE

HARVESTER WHEAT BEER — pale gold, light wheaty malt nose, light dry malt flavor, light body, light dry malt aftertaste. Made from 50/50 wheat and two-row malts, and top-fermenting yeast; specific gravity 1.039, 3.2% abw. [W, 45]

BOLT, NUT & SCREW GOLDEN ALE — gold, light dry hop aroma and flavor, medium body, light dry hop and malt aftertaste. Dry hopped with Saaz hops; specific gravity 1.047, 4% abw. [A, 45]

PATCH PALE ALE — pale amber, big dry malt and hop aroma, big well-hopped palate, long dry malt aftertaste has plenty of hops. Dry hopped with Fuggles and Goldings; specific gravity is 1.045, 3.6% abw. [A, 50]

Notes

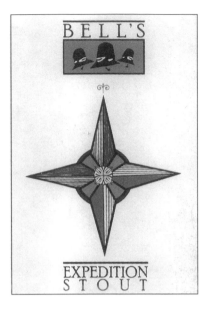

RYAN'S IRISH STOUT — brown; chocolate malt is the aroma; complex dry malt flavor comes from seven different malts; medium body; dry aftertaste continues to show the malt but features hops as well; a very drinkable dark light-bodied stout. Hopped with Cascades, Nugget, and Chinook hops; specific gravity 1.048, 4% abw. [S, 73]

MY OLD ALE — amber, malt aroma; smooth light malt flavor comes from chocolate and caramel malts; light body, light fairly dry malty aftertaste, not long or big; specific gravity 1.035, 2.7% abw. [A, 56]

PEACE PORTER — dark brown, chocolate malt aroma and flavor, smooth but lightly flavored with some nutty character, medium body, light dry hop aftertaste from Chinook hops; specific gravity 1.051, 4.1% abw. [P, 60]

HOPHEAD IPA — golden amber, hop aroma, very unusual complex hop flavor comes from ten different hop varieties; hops in boil and dry hopped both, medium to good body, long complex dry hop aftertaste; specific gravity 1.055, 4.5% abw. [A, 69]

GRAND SLAM AMBER — dark amber, smooth complex malty aroma and flavor, medium body, complex dry malt and hop aftertaste; made with seven different malts and hopped with Liberty hops; specific gravity 1.045, 4.1% abw. [A, 68]

BROWN STUDY ALE — amber-brown, complex hop aroma; equally complex smooth hop flavor has a roasty quality; medium body, light dry hop aftertaste; hopped with Chinook and Liberty hops; specific gravity 1.048, 4.1% abw. [A, 67]

Judge Baldwin's Brewing Co. / Kelly Brewing
Brewpub in Colorado Springs, CO

AMBER ALE — pale gold, malt aroma, smooth malt flavor, light body, fairly dry malt finish and aftertaste. [A, 47]

PORTER — brown, roasted barley nose; flavor is roasted malt with a chocolatey background; light body, smooth flavor, very pleasant, medium long malt aftertaste; gravity 15 P, 6% abw. [P, 50]

WHEAT — gold, nice malt nose, good malty flavor, light body, light medium dry malt aftertaste. [W, 47]

PALE ALE — pale gold, pleasant malt aroma, good malt flavor, very lightly hopped, finishes dry malt, light dry malt aftertaste; specific gravity 1.047, 4.5% abw. [A, 45]

RASPBERRY ALE — deep gold, delicate raspberry aroma and flavor, light body; seems to be dry malt under the raspberry at the finish and in the aftertaste; refreshing in hot weather; specific gravity 1.046, 4.5% abw. [A, 50]

Kalamazoo Brewing Co.
Brewery in Kalamazoo, MI

BELL'S BEER — hazy gold, faint malt nose with melon, pineapple, and kumquat in back; fruity malt flavor, dry hop finish and aftertaste, medium length, doubtful balance. [B, 67]

BELL'S AMBER ALE — golden amber, spicy malt and hop nose, big hop flavor well-backed with malt, complex, dry, tart; malt moves forward at the finish but still can't match the hops; long dry aftertaste has plenty of both malt and hops; a very good drinking beer. [A, 67]

THIRD COAST BEER — hazy amber; litchi nut aroma that takes on a citrus character in time; flat fruity malt palate, very dry malt aftertaste. [B, 20]

THIRD COAST OLD ALE — hazy deep amber, coconut chocolate malt nose, huge off-dry malt taste, complex and interesting, dried apple finish, heavy body; extremely tenacious complex dry aftertaste with candy, coconut, chocolate, malt, and hops. [A, 67]

GREAT LAKES AMBER ALE — hazy amber, light litchi nut nose, light citrus malt flavor, pleasant; fairly long hop aftertaste that is drier than the flavor; tastes a lot like a toned down Sierra Nevada Pale Ale. [A, 53]

BELL'S KALAMAZOO STOUT — opaque brown, coffee colored head, delightful appetizing malt aroma with plenty of smoky chocolate malt, strong but pleasant dry roasted malt flavor, dry malt finish and aftertaste; smoke enhances rather than diminishes; long and good. [S, 78]

GREAT LAKES CHERRY STOUT 1988 — opaque brown, coffee-colored head, fruity malt aroma, black cherry flavor with a tart artificial quality, medium body; medium long malt aftertaste that is dry on the tongue but sour in the corners of the mouth. [S, 30]

EXPEDITION STOUT — deep opaque brown; lovely sweet malt aroma is very strong at the outset, softens slightly with time; first seems to be off-dry malt on the palate but becomes more dry as it goes; high density, huge body, almost viscous, long strong complex off-dry malt aftertaste. [S, 70]

BELL'S SPECIAL DOUBLE CREAM STOUT — deep brown, pleasant light malt nose, very pleasant smooth and mellow big straightforward malt flavor, satisfying and very long. The brew is on the off-dry side, but can't be called overly sweet for the type. [S, 76]

BELL'S PORTER — deep amber, rich chocolate malt nose with a little fruitiness in back, straightforward dry malt taste, big body, touch of sourness behind the malt in the finish, long dry malt aftertaste, well-done drinkable brew. [P, 62]

Kennebunkport B.C.

Microbreweries in Kennebunkport and Portland, ME and brewpub in Kennebunkport, ME called Federal Jack's. Many bottled products cite both the Kennebunkport and Portland, ME facilities. The facility in Portland accounts for 73% of the combined capacity and is called The Shipyard.

GOAT ISLAND LIGHT ALE — gold, light malt nose, very dry malt palate, light body; hops reappear in the finish and bring the malt with them leading to an interesting and long aftertaste; 3.25% abv. Tasted on draft at Kennebunkport. [A, 62]

Notes

BROWN ALE — brown, faint malt and hop aroma, zesty malt flavor with plenty of good hop support, dry hop finish, very long dry hop aftertaste. Tasted on draft at Kennebunkport. [A, 63]

BEAR SNOUT STOUT — dark brown, brown head with great retention; dry malt nose has some roasted character; fairly complex, but not as much as the Bluefin; dry lightly hopped flavor, smooth and dry; long malt aftertaste is less coffeelike than the Bluefin. Tasted on draft at Kennebunkport. [S, 53]

TAINT TOWN PALE ALE — gold; big hop aroma has plenty of supporting malt; big bright hop flavor, dry hop finish, long dry hop aftertaste; 4.6% abv. Tasted on draft at Kennebunkport. [A, 61]

BLUEFIN STOUT — very deep brown, thick tan head; dry malt nose shows some roasted barley (and a little scorching); very complex dry roasted malt flavor is lightly hopped; plenty of roasted barley and chocolate malt in there with other malts, smooth and dry, balanced, good body; long malt aftertaste makes you think of roasted coffee beans; 5% abv. This tasted on draft at the brewery restaurant in Kennebunkport. Bottles labeled The Shipyard Bluefin Stout are similar but with a more concentrated malt flavor and the aftertaste has a faint sweetness at the end. This is an excellent smooth dry stout. [S, 67]

KENNEBUNKPORT INDIA PALE ALE — gold, light dry hop nose, faintly sweet malt palate up front; there are hops in mid-palate but they don't show much until the aftertaste and then they are more dry than bitter; good body, long aftertaste. Tasted on draft at Great Lost Bear in Portland. [A, 49]

PRELUDE ALE 1993 HOLIDAY CHEER — cloudy amber, rich alcoholic malt nose and flavor, sweet and rich, big hops balance the malt; alcohol gives it a liqueur quality and huge body; big toasted malt finish and aftertaste; alcohol shows strongly right through to the end. Found in bottle. [A, 86]

THE SHIPYARD GOAT ISLAND LIGHT ALE — hazy gold, faint hops in the nose, light malt taste, medium to light body, highly carbonated, faintly bitter finish, light dry malt aftertaste. Found in bottle. [A, 62]

MOOSE BROWN ALE — brown, faint malt and hop aroma, zesty malt flavor with plenty of good hop support, dry hop finish, very long dry hop aftertaste. Tasted on draft at the Great Lost Bear in Portland. In bottle it showed more of a creamy mouthfeel, more alcohol, and some good roasted malt that lasted quite well. [draft A, 53; bottle A, 73]

OLD THUMPER EXTRA SPECIAL ALE — amber-brown; great complex dry hop aroma shows all kinds of fruity hints; big extremely bright hop and malt flavor; good body, excellent balance, very tasty and refreshing, very long dry hop aftertaste; OG 1058. This brew is made with pale ale, crystal, and chocolate malts and hopped with Challenger, Goldings, and Progress hops. Its label bears the same logo as the Old Thumper of England, which is now made exclusively by Shipyard/Kennebunkport for the U.S.A. Found in bottle and on draft at The Old Bay in New Brunswick, NJ. [A, 79]

THE SHIPYARD EXPORT ALE — gold, pleasant hop and malt aroma, bright dry malt flavor, big body, long dry malt and hop aftertaste, a full-flavored brew; 5% abv. Canadian-style ale. Found in bottle. [A, 43]

MAGIC HAT ALE — amber, roasted malt aroma, big roasted malt and hop flavor, dry hop finish and aftertaste, interesting and complex, made for Magic Hat B.C. of Burlington, VT. Found in bottle. [A, 52]

PRELUDE ALE 1994 HOLIDAY CHEER — amber; rich fruity roasted malt and hop nose is very appetizing; excellent rich roasted malt and strong hop flavor, chewy and alcoholic, huge body, big toasted malt and bright hop finish and aftertaste; alcohol shows strongly right through to the end. Found in bottle. [A, 90]

MYSTIC SEAPORT PALE ALE — amber, pleasant light northwest hop aroma, slightly buttery bitter hop flavor, dry hop finish and nutty dry hop aftertaste; a flavor that grows on you; made for Mystic Seaport. Found in bottle. [A, 62]

LONGFELLOW WINTER ALE — deep ruby-amber; big roasted malt

nose shows some chocolate malt; roasted malt flavor shows alcohol as well, big body; finish is a bit harsh from the roasted malt, but there is great length, and you really know that you have had a mouthful of beer. [A, 68]

NOT QUITE PALE ALE — amber-gold, flowery herbal-green apple aroma, flowery fruity flavor like the nose, sweetest at the finish, dry hop aftertaste. Made for Magic Hat B.C. of Burlington, VT. [A, 53]

Montana Beverages, Ltd. / Kessler B.C.
Brewery in Helena, MT

KESSLER BEER — pale gold, complex malt nose with a lightly toasted nature, medium body, good complex rich malt flavor; feels good in your mouth; excellent balance; ever so slightly off-dry, but aftertaste is drier; full flavored long aftertaste. [B, 69]

KESSLER DOPPELBOCK — amber, big hop and malt nose, strong hop and malt flavor, big body, long and strong dry hop and malt aftertaste, well-balanced and bright throughout. Made with caramel malt and four different hops; 6.2% abw. [BK, 69]

KESSLER INDIA "PALLALIA" ALE — light amber, big hop nose; bright hoppy flavor has plenty of malt in support; good body and good balance, long dry hop and malt aftertaste; 4% abw, 37 IBU. [A, 67]

KESSLER BOCK BEER — deep copper-red, citrus hop aroma, big body, big sweet and sharp citrus flavor, a bit too sharp, long malt aftertaste on the sour side. [BK, 50]

KESSLER CENTENNIAL — golden amber, appetizing hop aroma; bright tasty flavor has a little malty sweetness that expertly balances the dry hops; good body, long bright dry hop aftertaste; very tasty well-hopped brew that is smooth and a pleasure to drink; 4.2% abw. [A, 78]

KESSLER WHEAT BEER — medium to deep copper-brown color; sweet fruity malt aroma that is quite attractive; there is a brief sweet foretaste, then it turns sort of burnt vegetal that tastes much better than it reads; a faint spicy-lactic touch appears at the end and in the brief aftertaste. Actually, it is a very good try at making a weizen. [W, 29]

BACH'S BOCK — deep brown, light malt aroma with a fruitiness; malt palate that is dry, well-balanced, and quite long. There certainly is plenty of alcohol, but otherwise it is not a big brew. It is very tasty and very drinkable. Made for Eugene City B.C. of Eugene, OR. [BK, 79]

SUN VALLEY WHITE CLOUD ALE — amber, complex aromatic malt and hop nose, a fruity citrus well-hopped flavor, medium body, dry hop aftertaste, pleasant, complex, and very drinkable. Made for Sun Valley B.C., Bellevue, ID. [B, 65]

Notes

SUN VALLEY SAWTOOTH GOLD LAGER — hazy amber-gold, big malt nose with a hop background, malt flavor, finish, and long aftertaste. Made for Sun Valley B.C. Latest label (Feb 1992) calls this brew Sun Valley Gold Lager. [B, 63]

SUN VALLEY OUR HOLIDAY ALE 1989 — amber, slightly toasted malt nose, big roasted rich malt flavor slightly on the sweet side, dry in the middle, good body, very tasty, finishes strongly, stays smooth, mostly malt but plenty of hops in back, very long malt aftertaste. Made for Sun Valley B.C. [A, 83]

SUN VALLEY OUR HOLIDAY ALE 1990 — bright amber, malt and pineapple juice aroma at first, then roasted malt, off-dry strong malt flavor with noticeable alcohol, complex, hops arrive at the finish and add dryness to the long aftertaste. Made for Sun Valley B.C. [A, 71]

SUN VALLEY OUR HOLIDAY ALE 1991 — deep amber, laid back malt aroma, strong malt flavor; finish and aftertaste even

strong as that is where the hops come in with a bang; very very long hop and malt aftertaste, a blockbuster brew. Made for Sun Valley B.C. [A, 93]

SUN VALLEY OUR HOLIDAY ALE 1992 — deep amber, finely carbonated, rich malt aroma, strong malt flavor with good hop backing, big body, finishes strongly, great balance; marvelous to sip; very long hop and malt aftertaste, another treasure. [A, 91]

EUGENE CELEBRATION LAGER — hazy gold, fruity apple and malt nose with some background hops; pleasant malt flavor has a light tangerine background; zesty citrus nature adds to the character of the long aftertaste which is more complex than the flavor. Made for Eugene City B.C. [B, 46]

EUGENE ALE — deep amber, lovely toasted malt (Ovaltine) nose, very tasty and drinkable complex malt front palate; the zest sags a bit in mid-palate, but finishes with that pleasant fruity-Ovaltine flavor, and ends dry. Made for Eugene City B.C. [A, 50]

EUGENER WEIZEN WHEAT BEER — slightly hazy-amber, delicious sweet malt aroma, light and bright clean fresh flavor, medium body, pleasant dry malt finish and aftertaste, very refreshing. Made for Eugene City B.C. [W, 68]

KESSLER LORELEI EXTRA PALE BEER — tawny-gold, big complex flowery hop and malt aroma, smooth rich malt flavor with good hop support, a little

molasses in back, medium body, good balance, dry hop finish and aftertaste, fairly short. [B, 65]

KESSLER WINTER BEER — amber, grainy roasted malt aroma; flavor like the nose but the hops appear in back; off-dry flavor starts to dry at finish; aftertaste is very long, very dry, and very grainy. The hops never come out of the background. [B, 64]

FRONTIER TOWN SELECT BEER — gold, lovely malt and hop aroma, refreshing off-dry malt flavor; finish shows a bit drier; aftertaste is dry hops and has good length; good tasting balanced brew. [B, 65]

PACIFIC COAST PREMIUM LAGER — hazy yellow-gold, canned corn nose, malt palate, medium body, dry malt finish and aftertaste. Made for Pacific Coast Beer Co., Newport Beach, CA. [B, 32]

PACIFIC COAST LAGER — gold, light fruity-lemony nose, dry malt flavor, medium body, pleasant creamy texture, feels good in your mouth, finishes dry with a trace of grapefruit in the long aftertaste. Contract brew as above. [B, 32]

OREGON STATE FAIR GOLDEN ALE — gold, appetizing malt-Ovaltine nose, pleasant very malty flavor, light to medium body, very drinkable, pleasant malt finish, fairly long dry malt aftertaste. [A, 59]

ST. NICK'S DARK ALE — deep amber, rich sweet slightly roasted malt aroma, rich smooth off-dry malt flavor benefits from some chocolate malt, very pleasant and very drinkable, quite long. Made for Eugene City B.C. [A, 80]

BONE DRY WET DRY BEER — gold, lovely malt aroma (lots of malt), very dry malt flavor, light body, light hops, dry right to the end. [D, 51]

IDAHO CENTENNIAL PILSNER BEER — hazy gold, toasted malt nose and taste, light body, dry malt finish, short dry malt aftertaste; seems to be an old sample. [B, 30]

Kidder's Brewery & Eatery
Brewpub in Ft. Myers, FL

KIDDER'S PALE ALE — amber, hop aroma, dry hop flavor, a bright hoppy brew, good body, dry hop finish and long aftertaste. Made from Brewer's Gold Briess malt extract and pale malt, Fuggles and Willamette hops, dry hopped, 90 minute boil; gravity 13.5 P, 5% abv, 45 IPU. [A, 63]

KIDDER'S SCOTTISH ALE — amber, hop nose, dry hop flavor, good balance and body, dry hop finish, long dry hop aftertaste. Made from northern Brewer Briess malt extract and caramel malt, Hallertau and Cascade hops, 90 minute boil; gravity 12.5 P, 4.5% abv, 20 IBU. [A, 65]

Kona Brewing Co.
Microbrewery in Kona, HI

FIRE ROCK PALE ALE — amber-gold, hop aroma, big complex well-hopped flavor, medium body, dry hop finish, long dry hop aftertaste; made with Munich, wheat, and honey malt, Galena, Cascade, and Mt. Hood hops; OG 1059, FG 1.015, 5.5% abv; SRM 10, 40 IBU; a very tasty likable beer. [A, 80]

La Jolla Brewing Co.
Brewpub in La Jolla, Ca

SEALANE STEAM BEER — very dark amber, malt nose, very dry smooth malt flavor, long dry malt aftertaste. [A, 56]

LITTLE POINT PALE ALE — gold, light malt and faint hop nose and flavor, brightly flavored, dry malt finish, long dry hop-ale aftertaste. [A, 49]

SEALANE AMBER — amber, dry malt aroma and taste, light body, dry malt finish and short dry malt aftertaste. [A, 45]

RED ROOST ALE — deep amber, dry malt aroma and flavor, light body, dry malt finish and aftertaste, some hops show, but not much. [A, 47]

PUMP HOUSE PORTER — deep brown, dry roast malt aroma and flavor, light body, dry roasted malt finish and aftertaste, very dry and very brief. [P, 49]

WIND 'N SEA WHEAT — pale gold, light malt aroma, dry malt flavor, light and refreshing American style, finishes dry, medium long dry malt aftertaste. [W, 56]

LA JOLLA RED ROCK — deep amber, finely carbonated, big malt aroma, strong malt and hop flavor, really big taste, good body and balance, complex; very long aftertaste continues to show plenty malt and hops both. [A, 83]

Note: All brews tasted on draft at the brewpub or in other San Diego area pubs.

Lafayette Brewing Co.
Brewpub in Lafayette, IN

ED'S ORIGINAL BATHTUB PALE ALE — hazy gold, zesty hop aroma, big bright dry hop flavor, medium to big body, dry hop finish, long dry hop aftertaste. Made with Munton and Fison malts and Cluster and Willamette hoops; gravity 13 P (1.054). [A, 64]

BLACK ANGUS OATMEAL STOUT — deep brown, strong chocolate malt and roasted barley nose, flavor to match the aroma, big and bold, dry chocolate malt finish and long aftertaste. Made with a small amount of oatmeal and northwest hops; a brawny brew; gravity 17.5 P (1.068). [S, 78]

BIG BORIS BARLEYWINE — amber, big malt nose; rich malt flavor shows some of the alcohol (8% abv); big body, off-dry malt finish and aftertaste; made with pale and crystal malts; specific gravity of 1.082. [BW, 73]

Laguna Beach Brewing Co.
Brewpub in Laguna Beach, CA

FESTIVAL LIGHT ALE — pale gold, very pleasant likable dry hop aroma and flavor, medium body, dry hop finish and aftertaste, good for hot weather refreshment, made with 100% two-row pale malt, bittered with Willamette hops, and finished with Yakima Hallertau hops; OG 1043, 3.5% abw. [A, 68]

RENAISSANCE RED ALE — red-amber, malt nose; big malty palate shows a little sweetness in the finish; big body, long malty aftertaste, made with Belgian specialty malt; OG 1064, ~6% abw. [A, 77]

GREETER PALE ALE — gold, lovely dry Cascade hop aroma; excellent hop and malt flavor is American-style (not British); very good mouthfeel, big body; a little sweetness appears in the finish and long aftertaste; made with pale and light crystal malts, bittered with Chinook hops, and dry hopped with Cascades; OG 1060, ~6% abw. [A, 79]

THOUSAND STEP STOUT — deep brown, brown head; faintly sweet malt aroma and there is a touch of sweetness in the flavor as well; medium body, smooth and drinkable, soft and dry, not long; some roasted/burnt character develops late in the aftertaste; made with 12% oatmeal, roasted barley, black patent, and chocolate malts, bittered with Cluster hops, and finished with American Fuggles; OG 1052, ~5% abw. [S, 55]

WINTER WASSAIL ALE — amber; smooth lightly spiced aroma shows some vanilla; lightly spiced palate shows lots of vanilla, some honey, and a touch of the nutmeg and cinnamon; medium body, very lightly spiced finish, dry lightly spiced aftertaste; very refreshing for a spiced winter ale, but in Laguna Beach the winter is not cold and many days you prefer a refreshing thirst-quenching brew; made with some dark malt and lots of honey; OG 1053, ~5% abw. [A, 59]

HEISLER HEFE-WEIZEN — bright gold, slightly hazy, big fruity nose, big flavor of banana fruit and light cloves, good body; a sweet graininess appears in the aftertaste; a classical unfiltered hefe-weizen. [W, 69]

HEISLER KRISTAL-WEIZEN — bright gold, fine malty-fruity banana aroma, great banana-clove palate, good to medium body, long dry fruity aftertaste, better balanced and more refreshing than the hefe-weizen above. [W, 78]

VICTORIA ESB — beautiful brilliant amber-gold, lovely complex fragrant hop nose; bright bitter hop flavor is very attractive; good body, long complex hop aftertaste, a very good ESB. [A, 87]

Note: Laguna Beach B.C. brewed beers for its sister pub, Newport Beach B.C., in the period between opening on April 1, 1995 and their own first brewing a month later.

Lake St. George Brewing Co.

Microbrewery in Liberty, ME

DIRIGO BROWN ALE — dark brown, malt nose, big smooth malt flavor, hops in back, good body, rich yet dry, dry malt aftertaste is not long. [A, 53]

LAKE ST. GEORGE ANNIBEARSARY ALE — amber-gold, light dry hop aroma, medium dry hop flavor, very dry hop finish and aftertaste, not long. Made for The Great Lost Bear pub in Portland, ME. [A, 49]

LAKE ST. GEORGE AMBER ALE — deep amber, light dry malt aroma, complex dry malt flavor; finish and aftertaste are dry malt and hops; good length, very good with food. [A, 63]

LAKE ST. GEORGE PALE ALE — pale amber; bright hop nose is very attractive; bright fresh well-hopped flavor, medium body, long crisp and dry hop aftertaste; a lot of Cascade hops give this brew its character and zest; OG 1046. [A, 88]

LAKE ST. GEORGE OATMEAL STOUT — brown, tan tight head, aroma of chocolate malt and roasted barley; smooth but bright flavor is like the aroma; medium body, long tasty aftertaste like the main palate. [S, 79]

Lakefront Brewery, Inc.

Microbrewery in Milwaukee, WI

EAST SIDE DARK — dark amber, fruity chocolate malt nose and flavor; shows some alcohol; medium body; aftertaste is a continuation of the flavor and it dries as it goes; fairly long and has good complexity. Made from roasted barley, caramel, chocolate, and black patent malts; unfiltered and flavored with Mt. Hood hops; gravity 18.75 P, 5.2% abw. [B, 72]

KLISCH LAGER BEER — gold, lightly sweet malt nose, off-dry malt flavor, very lightly hopped, light body, light dry malt aftertaste. Made with 10% wheat and Mt. Hood hops, Klisch is bottom-fermented at warm temperature (55°F); specific gravity 1.046, 4.1% abw. [K, 63]

CREAM CITY PALE ALE — amber; big complex hop aroma has hints of pine or spruce and citrus; big complex hop flavor is spicy and faintly citrus; medium body, long dry hop aftertaste. Top-fermented using 2-row malted barley, Carapils, and caramel specialty malts; specific gravity 1.055. 4.2% abw. [A, 67]

LAKEFRONT HOLIDAY SPICE — amber, big spicy aroma; flavor of cinnamon, nutmeg, clove, and ginger ride on a base of honey, malt, and hops; heavy body, very alcoholic (8.1% abw), long complex spiced aftertaste, a huge spiced brew; specific gravity 1.080. [A, 68]

Notes

RIVERWEST STEIN BEER — amber, northwest citrus hop aroma, good fruity malt and dry hop flavor, dry hop finish, medium body, complex long dry hop and fruity malt aftertaste, good balance, refreshing. [B, 63]

LAKEFRONT HOLIDAY SPICE 1992 — amber, big spicy aroma; flavor of cinnamon, nutmeg, clove, and ginger ride on a base of honey, malt, and hops; seems to be a touch of citrus/orange as well; heavy body, very alcoholic (8.1% abw), long complex spiced aftertaste; a brew that is so spicy it overwhelms the beer character; specific gravity 1.080. [A, 50]

LAKEFRONT HOLIDAY SPICE 1993 — deep amber, huge spicy aroma; spicy flavor is a bit less spicy than with the 1992 and makes for a less assertive brew; shows a bit more of the orange peel and more malty character; good body, plenty of alcohol for warming, long dry well-spiced aftertaste. [B, 47]

Lancaster Malt Brewing Co.
Brewpub in Lancaster, PA

LANCASTER AMBER ALE — amber, light malty nose, good malt flavor, medium body, smooth and fairly dry malt character, dry lightly hopped long aftertaste. [A, 66]

LANCASTER PORTER — deep brown, big toasted malt aroma and flavor, fairly dry with considerable richness, medium body, creamy mouthfeel; a sweetness stays in back but lasts well into the after-

taste; long and generally dry and malty. [P, 86]

Latrobe Brewing Co.
Brewery in Latrobe, PA owned and operated by Labatt's U.S.A., Darien, CT

ROLLING ROCK PREMIUM BEER — pale gold, very pleasant light malt aroma with light hops in back; fairly big malt flavor is strongest in front; bittering hops in back make for balance and a dry finish and aftertaste. A good beer for the bowling alley. [B, 56]

ROLLING ROCK LIGHT BEER — pale gold, faint malt aroma, light body, malt flavor with hops in back, dry faintly hopped finish and aftertaste. [LO, 32]

ROLLING ROCK BOCK BEER — amber, faint fruity-candy malty nose, dry malt flavor, finish, and light aftertaste, medium body, medium length; made from 100% pale and caramel malts with Cascade and Mt. Hood hops. [B, 47]

ROCK ICE AMBER LAGER — pale amber, malt nose, dry malt flavor, good body, dry malt finish and aftertaste, good serviceable malt beverage. [B, 53]

Leavenworth Brewery
Brewpub in Leavenworth, WA

WHISTLING PIG WHEAT — hazy gold, faintly fruity malt aroma, light body, dry malt flavor,

light dry medium long malt aftertaste. An American-style hefeweizen that contains pale, wheat, crystal, and Carapils malt, and Perle and Cascade hops; specific gravity 1.054, 4.5% abw. [W, 50]

FRIESIAN PILSNER — gold, hop aroma; flowery hop flavor that continues through the finish into the aftertaste which is drier hops; good body, good length. Made with pale, Carapils, crystal, and Munich malts, and Saaz hops; specific gravity 1.052, and has 4.4% abw, 40 IBU. [B, 67]

ESCAPE ALTBIER — bright amber, good appetizing aroma with both hops and malt; shows a faint roasted character; big well-hopped flavor is also quite malty; medium body; long aftertaste continues to show both the malt and hops very well. Made with pale, Munich, crystal, and special roast malts, Northern Brewer and Tettnang hops, and is aged at 33°F; specific gravity 1.052, 4.3% abw, 40 IBU. [A, 69]

HODGSON'S IPA — deep gold, bright hop aroma, big hop taste, very good body, long dry hop aftertaste. Made from pale and crystal malts, Galena, Cascade, and Kent-Goldings hops; specific gravity 1.062, 5.5% abw, 50 IBU. [A, 72]

BARKING DOG BITTER — gold, light dry hop aroma, light dry malty flavor, medium body, dry malt aftertaste with good length. Made with pale, crystal, and Carapils malts, Willamette and Kent-Goldings hops; specific gravity 1.048, 3.9% abw. [A, 63]

SNOW BLIND WARMER — amber; light malt and hop aroma, but a big dry complex flavor that reflects the nose and shows a little roasted malt; good body; long dry aftertaste shows both hops and malt as well as a sense of the alcohol (5.8% abw). Made with pale, crystal, special roast, wheat and chocolate malts, some roasted barley and Kent-Goldings hops; specific gravity 1.064. [A, 67]

BULL'S TOOTH PORTER — dark brown, big bright roasted malt aroma well backed with hops, equally forceful flavor shows plenty of hops with roasted malt; smooth, complex, well-balanced, delicious, long dry hop and good malt aftertaste. Made with pale, crystal, and chocolate malts, roasted barley, and Cascade and Northern Brewer hops; specific gravity 1.060, 5% abw, 45 IBU. [P, 75]

DIRTY FACE STOUT — deep brown; aroma is mostly roasted barley; flavor is dry roasted barley, very smooth, balanced, highly drinkable, medium body, long dry roasted malt aftertaste. Made with pale, crystal, and black malts, roasted barley, Chinook, Galena, and Cascade hops; specific gravity 1.064, 5.3% abw, 50 IBU. [S, 67]

BLIND PIG DUNKEL WEIZEN — brown, rich malt aroma and flavor, medium to good body, no spiciness, long mostly malty aftertaste; specific gravity 1.056, 4.7% abw, 25 IBU. [W, 62]

DORTMUNDER EDEL EXPORT — deep gold, dry hop flavor, finish, and aftertaste, smooth and balanced, medium body, medium hop character (26 IBU); specific gravity 1.056, 4.5% abw. [B, 53]

INGALL'S ESB — deep gold, hop aroma, light hop flavor, dry finish and aftertaste, little flavor or character, more dry than anything else, just light and dry; made with pale and crystal malts, bittered with Cascade and Centennial hops, flavored with Kent and Stryian Goldings; OG 1058, 5.9% abv, 35 IBU. [A, 52]

Left Hand Brewing Co.
Microbrewery in Longmont, CO

SAWTOOTH ALE — amber, beautiful hop aroma, big dry hop flavor; tastes very appetizing; smooth dry hop finish and aftertaste, great balance and flavor; specific gravity 1.054, 4.3% abw. [A, 86]

BLACK JACK PORTER — brown, complex hop and chocolate malt aroma, bright dry malt flavor, good body, tasty English style, long dry malt and hop aftertaste; specific gravity 1.060, 4.7% abw. [P, 67]

JUJU GINGER ALE — gold, hop and ginger aroma and light ginger and hop flavor, dry ginger and malt finish and aftertaste, tasty good beery flavor with the ginger added; specific gravity 1.046, 3.3% abw. [A, 53]

Notes

MOTHERLODE GOLDEN ALE — gold, big malty nose, rich malty flavor, big body, good balance, long rich malty aftertaste; specific gravity 1.057, 3.6% abw. This is the draft version. In bottle, it is hazy gold, has a very malty nose, big tasty malt flavor, light body, and long malty aftertaste. [A, 67]

LEFT HAND XXXMAS ALE — deep amber, malty nose, rich malty flavor; slightly candylike ginger background is very lightly done; medium body, light ginger-malt aftertaste. [A, 53]

Legend Brewing Co.
Microbrewery with a bar in Richmond, VA. A full-scale pub is planned for installation in the building.

LEGEND LAGER — hazy gold, gingery hop nose, bright dry hop flavor, medium body; finish is a little ginger-like from the Mt. Hood hops that are used for dry hopping the brew; long dry hop aftertaste. [B, 54]

LEGEND PILSNER BEER — bright deep golden color; hoppy nose again has that gingery background, finely carbonated; good hop flavor has plenty of malt in back; good body, dry hop finish, long dry hop aftertaste. [B, 65]

LEGEND BROWN ALE — very deep gold, malt aroma with a touch of the ginger in back, big body, big malt and hop flavor, finishes dry, long dry malt and hop aftertaste. [A, 63]

LEGEND PORTER — opaque brown, roasted malt aroma and flavor, smooth and dry, a good classical porter, medium body, ends dry malt with a long dry roasted malt aftertaste. [P, 73]

Jacob Leinenkugel Brewing Co.
Brewery in Chippewa Falls, WI is a subsidiary of the Miller B.C.

LEINENKUGEL'S BEER — pale gold, light malt aroma, slightly grainy malt flavor, very light hops well in the back, light body, light dry malt aftertaste. Made with malted barley, corn grits, hops, and bottom-fermenting yeast; gravity 12.1 P, 3.7% abw. [B, 46]

LEINENKUGEL'S GENUINE BOCK BEER — copper-amber, faint malt aroma, weak malt flavor, brief malt aftertaste. [BK, 32]

LEINENKUGEL'S LIMITED BEER — deep gold, light malt aroma and flavor, good body, pleasant malt finish and aftertaste, good tasting and very drinkable, slides down easily, a quality beer. An Oktoberfest style beer made with four malts and two domestic hop varieties, and long aged; gravity 12.71 P, 3.81% abw. [B, 53]

LEINIE'S LIGHT NATURAL LIGHT PREMIUM BEER — tawny-gold, appetizing malt and hop aroma, light body; light malt flavor with some hops in back and more toward the finish; medium long malt aftertaste; gravity 8.7 P, 3.36% abw. [LO, 30]

CHIPPEWA PRIDE LIGHT PREMIUM BEER — bright gold, clean malt aroma; flavor is more malt than hops but still has good character and balance; good long dry malt aftertaste. [B, 32]

TAHOE BEER — pale gold; malt aroma has a sour component; palate starts out off-dry malt and finishes dry hops; long dry hop aftertaste. Contract brew for Carson B.C., Carson City, NV. [B, 29]

BOSCH PREMIUM BEER — pale gold, fragrant malt aroma, malt flavor, dry malt finish and aftertaste of medium length. [B, 27]

LEINENKUGEL'S RED LAGER — deep red-amber, pleasant well-hopped nose shows some malt in back; good dry hop and malt flavor is interesting; medium body; flavor drops off sharply to dry hops at the finish; medium long light dry hop aftertaste. Good taste and intensity at the outset, but it fails to hold. Still, it is very good while it is in your mouth. Made with five different malts and two varieties of Yakima Valley hops; gravity 12.82 P, 3.91% abw. [B, 62]

LEINENKUGEL'S WINTER LAGER — very dark red-amber, big dense head, very smooth light dry nose; smooth dry malt flavor has roasted character; medium to big body; dry finish and long dry aftertaste shows mostly toasted malt but there are hops showing as well; stays smooth, very drinkable, and very good with food. [B, 75]

LEINIE'S ICE PREMIUM BEER — gold, sweet malt and sour hop nose, big refreshing hop flavor, sour hop aftertaste drops off quickly; 5.6% abv. [B, 34]

LEINENKUGEL HONEY WEISS BIER — clear gold, dusty faint malt nose; flavor is a little malt and a lot of carbonation; light body, a little sweetness on the end; dry malt aftertaste has little character. [W, 31]

LEINIE'S ICE LAGER — gold, very attractive flowery malt and hop aroma, off-dry malt and hop flavor and finish, fairly dry malt aftertaste, light to medium body; 5.6% abv. Found on east coast, the other ice beer was found on the west coast. [B, 47]

LEINENKUGEL'S AUTUMN GOLD LAGER — golden amber, hop nose, malt flavor, medium body, dry hop finish and aftertaste, very drinkable, dry and refreshing. [B, 49]

Liberty Brewing Co. / Saxer Brewing Co.
Microbrewery in Lake Oswego, OR

SAXER PILSNER — gold, lovely big malt and hop nose, big hop flavor; bitter like a German-style Pils should be; good body, smooth finish; dry hop aftertaste has the malt showing well. Made with two-row malt and Perle and Saaz hops; gravity 12.02 P, FG 2.04, 3.9% abv, 28 IBU. [B, 70]

SAXER AMBER LAGER — gold, very attractive and appetizing malt aroma, good tasting malt flavor, good mouthfeel, soft and a bit off-dry; medium dry malt aftertaste is fairly long. A very good German "export"-style beer. Made from Munich malt and Hersbrucker and Saaz hops; gravity 12.04 P, FG 2.04, 3.8% abw, 20 IBU. [B, 75]

SAXER THREE FINGER JACK STOUT — opaque brown; malt aroma and flavor is dry roasted malt and almost smoky; medium to good body, long dry smoky-roasted malt aftertaste, pleasant and very drinkable although not like a classical stout. Made with Munich and black malt with Cascade hops; gravity 13.2 P, 4.8% abw, 30 IBU. [S, 65]

SAXER LEMON LAGER — pale yellow-gold, clean fresh lemon nose, bright lemony beer flavor, light body, very refreshing; dry aftertaste is more beery as the lemon slides into the background. Made to taste like a lemon shandy of England, and well done as such; gravity 9.0 P, 2.8% abv. [B, 40]

SAXER LIBERATOR DOPPELBOCK — deep amber, complex malt nose, very rich complex malty flavor, concentrated malt, big body, long very rich concentrated malt aftertaste; brewed with two-row pale, Munich, and caramel malts using a two-step decoction mashing method along with 10 weeks of lagering; gravity 18.7 P, 6.2% abv. [BK, 84]

Notes

SAXER HEFEDUNKEL — deep amber; malt nose has a touch of caramel; fairly rich dry malt flavor, medium body, medium long dry malt aftertaste; an unfiltered dark lager brewed with two-row pale, Munich, and dark caramel malts, and lagered for 4 weeks; gravity 13.1 P, 4.1% abv. [B, 57]

SAXER THREE FINGER JACK ROASTED RED HEFE DUNKEL — amber, malt and hop aroma, dry hop and lightly roasted malt flavor, medium body; faintly roasted malt finish and aftertaste is more roasted than the main flavor, good length. [B, 59]

SAXER THREE FINGER JACK AMBER — pale amber; good malty aroma has a substantial hop background; flavor is more malt than hops and stays dry; dry malt finish, long dry malt and hop aftertaste, very good with food. [B, 56]

Lift Bridge Brewing Co.
Microbrewery in Ashtabula, OH

LIFT BRIDGE INDIA PALE ALE — gold, faint malt aroma, grainy malty taste, medium body, very dry nondescript aftertaste, medium length. [A, 45]

LIFT BRIDGE AMBER LAGER — amber-gold, off-dry malt aroma, dry lightly toasted malt flavor, medium body; decent balance between the malt and hops which show equally; light dry finish and aftertaste. [B, 67]

LIFT BRIDGE OKTOBERFEST BEER — deep amber; roasted malt aroma has a strawberry background; roasted malt and flavor with a background like chocolate milk, medium body, long light roasted malt aftertaste, not robust but pleasant. [B, 64]

LIFT BRIDGE WINTER GALE ALE — hazy amber; faint hoppy nose has a touch of acid; complex flavor is mostly hops but it seems to have an acidic background as though some lactic fermentation had occurred; complex, well bodied; finishes dry and there is a lot of hop bite at the end, even after you think it is over it sort of bounces back for another shot at your palate. [A, 79]

Lind Brewing Co.
Microbrewery in San Leandro, CA

DRAKE'S GOLD — gold, bitter hop and fruity malt aroma and flavor, good body, quite complex, very dry and well-hopped finish and aftertaste, good length. Made with 20% wheat malt and Oregon Cascade hops; specific gravity 1.050. [A, 50]

DRAKE'S ALE — amber; strange aroma is fruity yet hoppy; this strangeness is reflected on the palate; dry hop and malt aftertaste. Made with English crystal malt, Fuggles and Kent hops; specific gravity 1.056. I believe the "strangeness" to be from the Fuggles. [A, 43]

SIR FRANCIS STOUT — brown, faint roasted barley malt nose, very very dry roast malt flavor, finish, and aftertaste; made using pale, caramel, roasted barley, chocolate, and black malts, with Galena and Cascade hops; specific gravity 1.064. [S, 49]

LIND RASPBERRY WHEAT — pale gold, light raspberry aroma and taste, light body, dry malt aftertaste still dominated by the raspberries. There is little beyond the raspberries; specific gravity 1.046. [W, 62]

ZATEC ALE — deep gold, European style bright spicy hop aroma and flavor, medium body, dry hop finish, long dry hop aftertaste, hopped with Saaz, Cascade, Galena, and Hallertauer hops; OG 1053, FG 1.015, 5% abv. [A, 60]

The Lion, Inc.
Brewery in Wilkes-Barre, PA. A number of corporate names are used, e.g., Pocono Brewing Co.

GIBBONS FAMOUS LAGER BEER — gold, clean light malt nose, fresh malt flavor, medium dry finish, short dry malt and hop aftertaste. [B, 42]

LIEBOTSCHANER CREAM ALE — pale gold, fresh and clean slightly sweet malt aroma, off-dry malt flavor, light bodied, quick finish, little aftertaste, pleasant and refreshing, good hot weather beer, bottom-fermented; specific gravity 1.050, 4.15% abw. [A, 41]

LIEBOTSCHANER BOCK
BEER — copper colored, light
malt aroma, lightly scorched malt
flavor, light body, dry finish, brief
aftertaste. [BK, 23]

ESSLINGER PREMIUM
BEER — light yellow, light malt
aroma, pleasant malt and hop flavor, good balance, some character,
light body, dry finish, medium
length dry aftertaste. [B, 46]

LIONSHEAD DELUXE
PILSENER BEER — tawny-gold,
malt aroma, light body, high carbonation, good bright clean flavor
with both malt and hops, off-dry
malt finish and aftertaste. [B, 49]

STEGMAIER GOLD MEDAL
BEER — pale gold, light malt
aroma, light malt flavor, light
body; finish drops off to nothing,
little aftertaste. Made with 60%
two-row and six-row malts and
40% adjunct; hopped to 12 IBU
with Cascade, Willamette, Mt.
Hood, and Saaz hops; gravity
10.5 P, 3.6% abw. [B, 30]

STEGMAIER 1857 LAGER
BEER — pale amber, pleasant
malt nose; palate starts out malt,
finishes hops; just hop bitterness
for an aftertaste, medium body. It
is brewed from two-row malts,
Tettnanger, Saaz, Mt. Hood. and
Hallertau hops; specific gravity
1.047, 3.98% abw. [B, 39]

STEGMAIER PORTER — ruby-
toned brown color, fresh clean
malt aroma; dry malt flavor cuts
off abruptly; little or no aftertaste,
thin body. Brewed from pale, caramel, and chocolate malts; hopped

with Cascades and Willamette
hops; specific gravity 1.058,
4.43% abw. [P, 30]

STEGMAIER 1857 LIGHT
BEER — golden amber, malt
aroma, light hop flavor is mostly
CO_2, light body; aftertaste is hops
with a touch of malt but is not
long. [LO, 43]

STEGMAIER LIGHT BEER —
pale gold, light malt aroma and
very light malt flavor, little hops,
plenty of carbonation (maybe too
much), not much finish or aftertaste. [LO, 27]

STEGMAIER 1857 DRY
BEER — very deep gold, pleasant
malt and hop nose, bright malt
flavor, high carbonation, quick
finish, no aftertaste. It is good
while it is in your mouth. [D, 43]

MALTA INDIA — opaque brown,
big grainy malt nose, big malt flavor, light to medium body; long
malt aftertaste is not dry, but is
drier than the flavor. Made for
Cerveceria India, Mayaguez,
Puerto Rico. [M, 17]

MIDNIGHT DRAGON MALTA
ESPECIAL — deep brown, concentrated Ovaltine malt nose and
flavor with some hops for balance,
heavy body; short palate is sweet
but not cloying. [M, 34]

BARTELS PURE BEER —
medium gold, faint malt aroma
and flavor, some hops but not
much, malt finish, brief malt aftertaste. [B, 42]

Notes

NEUWEILER'S TRADITIONAL LAGER BEER — pale gold, malt nose; palate is mostly malt in front, hops come in middle and make their contribution at the finish and in the aftertaste; bright and refreshing, medium body, medium length; gravity 11.8 P, 4.1% abw, 22 IBU. Made for Neuweiler B.C. of Allentown, PA. [B, 38]

NEUWEILER'S BREWED PORTER — brown; malt nose is very complex with interesting sour tones; medium to light dry malt flavor with some hops that show best in the finish; somewhat light body; brief dry malt aftertaste shows a little hop tang; gravity 13 P, 4.5% abw, 26 IBU. Contract brew made for Neuweiler B.C. [P, 53]

NEUWEILER BLACK AND TAN — light brown, malt aroma and flavor, medium body; hops come in at mid-palate and help to balance malt which stays dominant; flavor is medium dry, finish and aftertaste are drier; medium length; gravity 12.2 P, 4.3% abw, 24 IBU. A blend of the Stegmaier Porter and 1857 Lager, and perhaps better than either. Made for Neuweiler B.C. [P, 43]

NEUWEILER STOCK ALE — gold, faint fruity malt nose, sour malt flavor, good body; has strength of flavor but it features the sourness which becomes the aftertaste; 5% abw, 30 IBU. Made for Neuweiler B.C. [B, 29]

CRYSTAL PREMIUM BEER — bright pale gold, light malt aroma and flavor, high carbon-ation, light body, fairly short; a refreshing hot weather beer that a beer drinker would like better than Perrier. [B, 41]

KAPPY'S PREMIUM QUALITY BEER — gold, pleasant malt and hop aroma, light dry malt flavor, fairly short dry malt aftertaste. Store label for Kappy's liquor stores in the Boston area. [B, 34]

TRUPERT AMERICAN PILSENER BEER — golden amber, toasted malt aroma and flavor, good balance, dry malt finish and aftertaste, not long but very drinkable. Contract brew made for Braumeister Ltd., Drexel Hill, PA. [B, 64]

BLUE HEN BEER — bright tawny gold, pleasant fruity-malty nose with some hops in back, off-dry malt front palate, hop middle, dry malt finish and aftertaste, medium long; flavors seem a bit separated. Contract brew for Blue Hen Brewery, Ltd. of Newark, DE. Made using two-row and six-row malts, Hallertau, Cascade, and Saaz hops; gravity 11.8 P, 3.9% abw. [B, 47]

JERSEY LAGER BEER — deep gold, beautiful malt and hop aroma, dull malt flavor, light body, little finish and no aftertaste; it's all in the nose. Contract brew for Jersey Lager Beer Co. of Bordentown, NJ. [B, 32]

SKIPJACK LAGER — pale amber, toasted malt aroma, pleasant roasted malt flavor, has zest, long toasted malt aftertaste. Con-tract brew for Skipjack B.C. of Secaucus, NJ. [B, 58]

HOPE LAGER BEER — golden amber, very pleasant dry malt aroma with a European hop background, finely carbonated, malt flavor, medium length malt aftertaste, medium body, pleasant and drinkable. Contract beer made for Hope B.C. of Providence, RI. [B, 51]

HOPE BOCK BEER — medium deep amber, light toasted malt nose, medium body, dry toasted malt flavor; has a touch of smoked malt in back; finish and aftertaste are more smoky; dry, refreshing, and very drinkable. Contract brew as above. [BK, 64]

HOPE LIGHT LAGER — gold, vegetal malt nose, off-dry but fruity malt flavor; finishes quite dry and has good length; excellent balance, a very good light beer. Contract brew as above. [LO, 50]

HOPE RED ROOSTER ALE — bright amber, faintly soapy hop aroma, complex bright and dry hop palate, very long dry hop aftertaste, excellent beer. Contract brew as above. [A, 77]

NATHAN HALE GOLDEN LAGER — deep gold, soapy malt and hop nose, fairly dry malt flavor, medium body, clean light dry malt aftertaste with medium duration. Contract brew for Connecticut B.C., Hartford, CT. [B, 47]

ATLANTIC CITY DIVING HORSE LAGER BEER — light amber, lovely hop aroma, dry hop flavor, very drinkable but brief on the palate. Made for Atlantic City B.C. of Atlantic City, NJ. [B, 65]

BUNKERHILL LAGER BEER — pale amber, hop nose, sour hop flavor; dull hop aftertaste that retains some of the sourness of the flavor. [B, 25]

STOUDT'S OKTOBERFEST DARK — deep amber, off-dry malt nose, big hop flavor, quite dry, medium to light body, dry hop aftertaste of medium duration. A contract beer for Stoudt B.C. of Adamstown, PA which allowed the release of the beer in 12-oz. bottles. [B, 47]

QUEEN CITY LAGER — gold, very pleasant clean malt nose, bright clean crisp off-dry malt flavor, very refreshing, good body, medium long dry malt aftertaste with good hop support. Contract brew for Queen City Brewing Co., Buffalo, NY. [B, 50]

GOLDFINCH AMBER BEER — deep amber, finely carbonated, clean mild hop aroma, medium body, pleasant light hop and malt flavor, good balance, long dry spicy hop and malt aftertaste, very drinkable. Contract brew for Goldfinch B.C., Mt. Laurel, NJ is made from two-row and six-row malted barley and crystal malt; brewed with Cascade, Mt. Hood, and Willamette hops; dry hopped with Cascades; gravity 12.5 P, 4.3% abw. [B, 63]

NEUWEILER STOCK ALE — gold, faint fruity malt nose, sour malt flavor, good body; has strength of flavor but it features

the sourness which becomes the aftertaste; gravity 12.8 P, 5% abw, 30 IBU. Made for Neuweiler B.C. [B, 29]

BOSTON BURTON ALE — amber, fruity malt and northwest hop aroma; flavor is big malt up front, citruslike northwest hops come in at the middle; fairly complex, big hop finish; dry hop aftertaste has good length. Made for Commonwealth B.C. of Boston. [A, 73]

RED BELL BLONDE ALE — brilliant gold; light but rich toasted malt nose has some fruitiness; pleasant toasted malt and caramel flavor, light body, light and smooth, dry light toasted malt finish and aftertaste, medium long; made with two-row barley with 10% wheat malt, Hallertau and Saaz hops; specific gravity 1.048, 5.1% abw. Made for Red Bell B.C., Philadelphia, PA. [B, 43]

BREWERY HILL BLACK & TAN — dark brown; malty nose has a richness; dry mostly malty flavor, some hops, very high carbonation, dry malt finish and aftertaste, medium body and medium length; specific gravity 1.051, 4.2% abw. Label attributes the beer to Brewery Hill B.C. of Wilkes-Barre and describes it as a blend of the 1857 lager and porter, which makes it the same as the Neuweiler Black & Tan. [B, 63]

IRON HORSE DARK ALE
1 PINT 6 FL. OZ. (650 ML)

BREWERY HILL HONEY AMBER ALE — amber, sweet malty nose; sweet malty flavor is mitigated only slightly by the high carbonation; good body; sweet aftertaste has some duration; overall it is sweetness vs. carbonation, and the sweetness wins. [A, 31]

RED BELL AMBER LAGER — amber, nice bright hoppy nose, well-hopped flavor, some soapy background, medium body, dry hop finish and aftertaste, good duration; made for Red Bell B.C. of Philadelphia, PA. [B, 60]

OLDE CAPE COD SMUGGLERS ALE — amber-gold, faint hop and fainter malt nose, dull malt and hop flavor, dry hop finish and aftertaste, an ordinary beer; shows a very faint sense of alcohol. Made for Olde Cape Cod B.C. of Sandwich, MA. [A, 30]

STOUDT'S FEST MÄRZEN STYLE — copper-amber, light hop aroma; flavor is mostly malt but there are some hops in back; bitter hop finish is not likable and clashes with the malt; aftertaste is more malty but not well balanced. Made for Stoudt B.C. of Adamstown, PA. [B, 32]

BREWERY HILL RASPBERRY RED ALE — hazy gold, fruity-berry aroma, clean light fruity-berry flavor and aftertaste, light body, very pleasant; made with raspberry juice and natural raspberry flavors. [A, 32]

Lone Tree Brewing Co.
Microbrewery in Denver, CO

SUNSET RED ALE — reddish amber, light malt aroma, smooth balanced flavor of malt and hops, light body; light long dry malt aftertaste has the hops showing at the very end; made with American six-row, caramel 10, 40, and 120 Lovibond malts, Northern Brewer, Tettnanger, and Hallertau hops; specific gravity 1.056, 4.54% abw. Original 1993 recipe. [A, 76]

SUNSET RED ALE — reddish amber, light malt aroma, smooth balanced flavor of malt and some fairly assertive hops; flavor goes hops-malt-hops; good body, complex; long dry malt aftertaste has the hops showing at the very end. This beer is made with Northern Brewer, Tettnanger, and Mt. Hood hops. 1994 recipe. [A, 76]

IRON HORSE DARK ALE — dark brown, pleasant chocolate malt and roasted barley aroma and flavor, much like a Porter in style, medium body, very smooth and tasty, long aftertaste, a good enjoyable brew. Made with chocolate malt, roasted barley, and Willamette and Northern Brewer hops; specific gravity 1.066, 5.5% abw. [A, 85]

COUNTRY CREAM ALE — gold with a little chill haze; fragrant hop aroma and a flavor that follows through from the nose; excellent mouthfeel, creamy, delicious, good body, long dry hop aftertaste, an excellent very drinkable brew, highly recommended. This beer is best when bottle-conditioned about eight weeks. It is made with six-row and caramel malts, some wheat and hopped with Northern Brewers, Mt. Hood, and Tettnanger hops; specific gravity 1.054, 4.62% abw, 22 IBU. [A, 83]

HIGH POINT ALE — deep gold, hoppy aroma and dry hop flavor, very dry hop finish and aftertaste, good body, good length, a full-bodied assertively hopped ESB; specific gravity 1.062. Made under contract for High Point Brewing Corp. of Denver. By 1995, this was being labeled High Point ESB. [A, 75]

HORIZON HONEY ALE — hazy gold, honeyed malt aroma; honey and malt flavor follows the nose but is a bit drier than expected; honeyed malt background but is mostly hops; medium body; off-dry malt finish, but goes dry malt in the aftertaste; OG 1050, FG 1.014. Made under contract for High Point Brewing Corp. [A, 71]

Long Island Brewing Co.
Microbrewery and Brewpub in Jericho, NY

LONG ISLAND OKTOBERFEST BEER — amber, bright hop nose with some good malt in back, dry malty flavor, fairly complex malt and hop finish, dry malt aftertaste; a bit drier than most of the genre, but still a good interesting brew. [B, 63]

Long Valley Pub & Brewery
Brewpub in Long Valley, NJ

GRIST MILL GOLDEN ALE — deep gold, pleasant malt and hop aroma; palate has a malt front and a dry hop middle and finish; long dry hop aftertaste, goes well with many foods; brewed primarily with pale two-row malt, with Willamette and East Kent-Goldings hops. [A, 72]

GERMAN VALLEY AMBER — amber, light malt and hop aroma, estery malt flavor; malt dominates; medium body, fairly long dry hop aftertaste; made with crystal malt and roasted barley; hopped with Nugget and Willamette hops. [B, 56]

BLACK RIVER BROWN — brown color, very faint malt aroma; dry malt finish and aftertaste has some hops in back; made with chocolate and crystal malts; hopped with East Kent-Goldings hops. [B, 60]

LAZY JAKE PORTER — dark brown, light dry malt aroma, roasted malt flavor, very smooth, medium body; hops kick in at the finish; ends with dry hops; made with five varieties of malt. [P, 66]

Los Gatos Brewing Co.
Brewpub in Los Gatos, CA

LOS GATOS HEFE-WEIZEN — hazy gold; wheat aroma shows some spice; classical smooth hefe-weizen flavor with plenty of cloves, medium body; spicy finish has a nice refreshing tang; good long spicy aftertaste continues to show some malt; nicely done in a German style. [W, 65]

LOS GATOS LAGER — gold, dry hop aroma, bright dry hop and malt flavor, medium body, very smooth, finishes nicely into a long dry hop aftertaste, well balanced. Saaz, Hallertau, and Tettnang hops all add to the European style and complexity; 3.8% abw. [B, 68]

LOS GATOS OKTOBERFEST — amber, malt aroma; palate starts out dry and malty, a little less dry malt in the middle, but it is dry again by the finish and into the aftertaste; hops stay in back throughout; a good German-style Oktoberfest lager; 3.9% abw. [B, 78]

LOS GATOS PILSNER — pale gold, big hoppy aroma, big bright hop flavor, very European in style, finishes quite bitter, long dry hop aftertaste. Made with Saaz and Hallertau hops; 4.2% abw. [B, 53]

Notes

LOS GATOS DUNKEL — dark brown; dry toasted malt aroma shows some chocolate malt; big complex malt flavor is on the dry side; good balance, medium body; hops show a bit in the finish, but the aftertaste is mostly dry malt. Made with roasted chocolate and Munich malt; 3.9% abw. [B, 62]

HELLES OCTANEATOR — pale gold, big assertive hop aroma and flavor, big body, plenty of alcohol showing (8% abw), long well-hopped aftertaste; made with liberal amounts of Hallertau and Tettnanger hops for a very German-style brew; specific gravity 1.850 (that's what they said, but they could possibly mean 1.085). [BK, 79]

LOS GATOS NUT BROWN ALE — brown, nutty roasted malt nose; big rich malt flavor is excellent with its roasty chocolate style; good body; off-dry rich complex malt finish continues into the long aftertaste where it dries slightly and retains its richness and complexity. A very very good tasting English-style ale. [A, 93]

LOS GATOS PORTER — brown, brown head; good malty flavor shows some chocolate character; good body, dry malt and hop finish and aftertaste, good length. [P, 80]

OKTOBERFEST — amber, attractive and appetizing malty nose, balanced bright malt and hop flavor, very tasty, long dry malt and hop aftertaste, a smooth bright and balanced lager in a true Oktoberfest style; made with two-row, Munich, and crystal malts;

hopped with Hallertau and Tettnanger hops; OG 1056, FG 1.013, 5.2% abv, 32 IBU. [B, 78]

Lost Coast Brewery & Cafe
Microbrewery and brewpub in Eureka, CA

LOST COAST BREWERY PALE ALE — hazy gold; fruity malt aroma has a pineapple background; fruity flavor (again the pineapple), pleasant tasting, good body, dry malt finish and aftertaste, nice but not much depth; hopped with Cascade hops (30 IBU), specific gravity 1.050, 3.6% abw. [A, 52]

LOST COAST BREWERY DOWNTOWN BROWN ALE — hazy amber, slightly toasted malt nose, mild chocolate roasted malt flavor, medium body, pleasant, very drinkable, light malt aftertaste, good with food. Made with roasted barley and caramel and chocolate malts, with Cascade and Chinook hops; specific gravity 1.049, 3.6% abw. Good in the bottle, smoother and even better on draft. [A, 73]

LOST COAST BREWERY AMBER ALE — hazy deep amber; big nose is rich roasted malt backed with citrus hops; bright and luscious hop and roasted malt flavor; good body, very flavorful, balanced; long dry and rich malt aftertaste shows some hops at the end. Feels very good in your mouth; an excellent amber ale type brew, hopped with Mt. Hood and Hallertau hops;

specific gravity 1.050, 3.6% abw, 30 IBU. Some production runs tend to be more hoppy; others decidedly feature the malt. It is always good. [A, 92]

LOST COAST BREWERY STOUT — opaque brown, brown head, light dry malt aroma, faintly roasted and faintly chocolate, smooth chocolate malt flavor with a slightly roasted barley background, fair body; hops show a bit at the finish; medium long dry malt aftertaste. Made with two-row roasted barley, dark crystal, chocolate, and caramel malts, with Cascade and Chinook hops; specific gravity 1.064, 4.5% abw. [S, 65]

LOST COAST SUMMERTIME WHEAT — hazy amber, big dry malt nose and very dry flavor, good body, finishes dry malt like it starts, a hefe-weizen but done American style. Done 50-50 wheat and barley, with Cluster and Hallertau hops; gravity 12.5 P, 5% abw. [W, 47]

WINTERBRAUN SPECIAL HOLIDAY ALE 93 — deep red-brown; zesty complex rich roasted malt aroma has a little bite to it; big complex rich malt flavor, very zesty and with a robust body, a strong flavor with a strong finish; what might be taken for sweetness in the long aftertaste is really a richness; a wonderful monster brew first appearing in late 1993. [A, 46]

WINTERBRAUN SPECIAL HOLIDAY ALE 94 — dark amber; faint malt nose has a touch of roasted malt and soapiness; soft light toasted malt flavor has a touch of hops but they are weak rather than subtle; soft and drinkable but a little too light, medium body, a pussycat compared to last year's beautiful brute. [A, 92]

CABO BLANCO MIST AMERICAN WHITE ALE — cloudy gold, fruity aroma, fruity-spicy palate, off-dry middle, dry finish and aftertaste, a wheat ale flavored with coriander and other spices; OG 1050, FG 1.014, 15 IBU. [A, 59]

ALLEY CAT AMBER ALE — amber, fruity roasted malt nose; excellent roasted malt flavor is smooth and has a good hop balance; very good carbonation level, good body, lemony feel on the roof of the mouth, long dry complex roasted malt and hop aftertaste, a very fine well-made ale. [A, 77]

Lowell Brewing Co.
Microbrewery in Lowell, MA

MILL CITY CLASSIC LAGER — gold; fruity malt aroma has a soapy component; big bitter hop flavor, tastes of the wort, finish is a little sour; dry hop aftertaste; made with two-row and six-row pale and Carapils malts, barley and Tettnanger, Perle, Mt. Hood, and Saaz hops. [B, 29]

MILL CITY AMBER ALE — brilliant deep amber-gold, fragrant complex malt and hop nose; big dry hop palate has a backing of caramel-toffee malt; good balance, good body, dry hop finish, long dry hop aftertaste, well-made

American pale ale. Made with six- and two-row malts, Cascade, Willamette, and Galena hops, infusion mashed; 4.2% abw. [A, 73]

MILL CITY OATMEAL STOUT — very deep brown (almost black), very nice mocha nose; not quite so attractive flavor is bitter coffee; medium to light body; long dry roasted chocolate and coffee aftertaste is a little burnt. [S, 51]

Lucky Labrador Brewing Co.
Brewpub in Portland, OR

QUALITY RYE — gold; rye nose (can't describe it any other way as rye has a distinct aroma and taste); light dry malty-rye flavor, medium to light body, dry malty-rye finish and aftertaste. [A, 66]

QUALITY RYE (CASK CONDITIONED) — gold, rye nose, light dry malty-rye flavor, very smooth, medium to light body, dry malty-rye finish and aftertaste; very much like the above except that it is smoother and less "gutsy." [A, 60]

UK IPA — brilliant gold, bright hop aroma and flavor, good body, dry hop finish and aftertaste, a big full-flavored hoppy brew right through, especially hoppy at the end. [A, 72]

HAWTHORNE'S BEST BITTER — amber-gold, dry malt and hop aroma and flavor, medium body, smooth but unexciting, dry malt finish and aftertaste. [A, 59]

Notes

STUMPTOWN PORTER — amber-brown, malty aroma, medium to light body, pleasant drinkable dry malt flavor, dry malt finish, long dry malt aftertaste, smooth and balanced. [P, 66]

BLACK LAB STOUT — dark brown, light roasted malt aroma and flavor, smooth and balanced, very likable, medium body, no chocolate or black patent malt evident; dry finish and aftertaste is lightly roasted malt; good length; a lovely stout made from pale malt, roasted barley and crystal malts (20L, 80L, and 165L); hopped with Northern Brewer, Fuggles, and Willamette hops; OG 1069. FG 1.020, 5% abv, 60 IBU. [S, 72]

M.J. Barleyhoppers, Brewery and Public House
Brewpub in Moscow, ID

PALOUSE WEIZEN — gold, malt aroma, uninteresting malt flavor, finish, and aftertaste, somewhat dull overall. Made with 30% wheat malt and top-fermenting yeast; gravity 11.5–12.5 P, 3.5% abw. [W, 27]

PARADISE PALE ALE — gold, hop aroma, good English-style pale ale hop palate, good body, dry hop finish and aftertaste, fairly long. Made with pale and carastan malts, with Willamette and Cluster hops; gravity 11.5–12.5 P, 3.7% abw. [A, 50]

BARLEYHOPPER BROWN — brown, malt and hop nose and taste, medium body, dry light hop finish and aftertaste. Made with pale, carastan, and chocolate malts; hopped with Willamette and Tettnanger hops; gravity 11.5–12.5 P, 3.7% abw. [A, 47]

MC GINTY'S OLD IRISH STOUT — deep brown, hop aroma, roasted malt flavor, dry roasted malt and hop finish and aftertaste. Made with pale and carastan malts, plus roasted and raw barley, and Willamette hops; gravity 13.5 P, 3.9% abw. [S, 47]

Mad River Brewing Co.
Brewery in Blue Lake, CA

STEELHEAD EXTRA PALE ALE — gold, beautiful appetizing fruity hop aroma, big delicious hop flavor, zesty and smooth, good body, extremely long dry hop aftertaste, marvelous. [B, 75]

STEELHEAD EXTRA STOUT — dark brown, brown thick head; aroma is complex roasted barley and chocolate malt; very complex flavor like the nose, finishes dry roasted malt, long roasted dry malt aftertaste. [S, 71]

JOHN BARLEYCORN BARLEYWINE STYLE ALE — amber, big ginger and coriander aroma, big complex citrus-ginger taste, very sweet (too sweet); ginger aftertaste is a bit drier; light body and fairly brief, not what I think of as a barleywine. This was the 1992 version. The 1993 version was similar but spiced with a lighter hand; OG 1101, 8.1% abw. [BW, 63]

ROCK BOCK — deep amber-brown, smoked malt nose; flavor is huge and like liquid smoke; smoked flavor, finish, and aftertaste, no room for anything else. [B, 20]

JAMAICA BRAND RED ALE — deep amber, grapefruit-pineapple-litchi nut aroma, bright refreshing very fruity flavor, complex, good body; plenty of hops that show best in the finish and aftertaste; very long. [A, 79]

Maine Coast Brewing Co.
Microbrewery in Portland, ME

MAINE COAST ALE — amber, faint malt aroma, light malt flavor with a hop background, hop finish, medium body, hop aftertaste, ends very very dry. [A, 44]

MAINE COAST REDNECK ALE — deep amber; hop nose, very dry hop flavor has a piney-resinous background which becomes more noticeable as you reach the finish and aftertaste; a strange and not a likable feature. [A, 44]

MAINE COAST GREAT HEAD ALE (PALE ALE) — amber, strange perfumy-caraway hop aroma and flavor, medium body; that unusual flavor persists through the finish and into the aftertaste. [A, 42]

Manhattan Brewing Co.
Brewpub in New York City, NY

MANHATTAN BRITISH AMBER ALE — amber, malt nose, lightly carbonated, light smooth grainy malt flavor, dry malt finish, light dry malt aftertaste, light body; what little hop character there is is mostly in the aroma; specific gravity 1.045, 3.6% abw. [A, 40]

MANHATTAN EXTRA STOUT — deep brown, dry chocolate malt and roasted barley aroma; flavor much like the nose, off-dry in front, dry in the middle, very dry in the finish and aftertaste; balanced, excellent length; really hangs on retaining the full character of the malts and roasted barley flavor; very nicely done. Brewed from a blend of six malts; specific gravity 1.058, 4.4% abw. [S, 79]

MANHATTAN INDIA PALE ALE — amber-gold, big dry well-hopped aroma, big bright hop and malt flavor, hefty body, smooth and balanced, very drinkable, finishes with strength, long complex dry hop and malt aftertaste, nicely

made; specific gravity 1.066, 5.4% abw. [A, 58]

MANHATTAN GOLD ALE — gold; big clean flowery hop aroma shows Cascade and Willamette hops; bright hoppy flavor, medium to light body, dry hop finish and aftertaste, fair length; specific gravity 1.040. 3.2% abw. [A, 60]

MANHATTAN BAVARIAN HEFE-WEIZEN — deep gold, bright spicy nose and taste, classical hefe-weizen with plenty of clove spice and fruity character; finishes clean and refreshing but very spicy (almost like spice had been added — which it was not, the spice being derived from the use of Weihenstephan yeast); long tangy aftertaste. Made using 55% wheat malt; specific gravity 1.042, 3.3% abw. Also seen at beer festivals as Bavarian Wheat Beer, being different only in how hazy it was (or was not) and the intensity of spice in the nose. [W, 68]

Manhattan Beach Brewing Co.
Brewpub in Manhattan Beach, CA

DOMINATOR WHEAT BEER — deep gold, bright malt and hop nose and taste, good body, dry light malt aftertaste, good length. A good American-style wheat beer. [W, 68]

SOUTH BAY BITTER — amber, faint dry hop aroma, dry bitter hop flavor, medium body, dry hop finish and aftertaste, good duration. [A, 43]

Notes

PACIFICA PALE ALE — gold, good malt and hop aroma, bright but light malt and hop flavor, dry malt finish, long dry malt aftertaste. [A, 54]

LIVE OAK GOLD — amber-gold; no aroma I could find, weak malt flavor; long dry malt aftertaste is a little grassy. [A, 42]

STRAND AMBER — amber, light malt nose, hop flavor, good body, long dry hop aftertaste. [A, 57]

MANHATTAN BEACH BLONDE — gold, fresh malt aroma, light malt flavor, medium body; has a slight soapy character but it is not troubling; dry malt finish and aftertaste. [A, 59]

VALENTINE HONEY ALE — gold, faint malt nose, honeyed malt flavor with an ale-like tang in back, good body, dry malt finish and aftertaste. [A, 57]

INDIA PALE ALE — deep gold, soapy hop nose; very bitter hop flavor shows a little of the soap as well; big hop finish, big body, long and strong dry bitter hop aftertaste. [A, 70]

EL PORTO PORTER — brown, tan head, faint chocolate malt aroma, dry chocolate malt and roasted barley flavor, good body, dry chocolate malt and roasted barley finish and aftertaste, very smooth, and it grows on you. Made with chocolate malt, roast barley malt, and oatmeal. The brewmaster says it is an oatmeal stout, but the manager wants to call it a porter. In style, it cer-

tainly is an oatmeal stout, and a very good one. [S, 78]

OLD PERPENDICULAR — deep amber-brown, very complex malt aroma, big balanced complex malt flavor; there is a sweetness but it is way in back; dry finish, big body, long dry malt aftertaste; the sweetness is not obvious and has to be sought out, but it is beneficial for the balance. This is the Christmas seasonal strong ale (7.5% abw), made with nine malts (pale, cara-Vienna, cara-Munich, biscuit, aromatic, dark English carastan, Belgian Munich, brown, and a touch of chocolate). Tasted when 3 months aged. [A, 94]

Marin Brewing Co.
Brewpub in Larkspur, CA

MT. TAM PALE ALE — cloudy amber-gold, citrus-hop and kumquat malt nose; flavor is a bit hoppy like the nose at first but subsequent sips develop the malt; kumquat and malt aftertaste with good length; interesting brew is not bad at all. Brewed with wheat, pale, Munich, and dextrin malts combined with Chinook, Cascade, and Centennial hops; specific gravity 1.055, 5% abw. [A, 50]

POINT REYES PORTER — deep brown, zesty hop nose, big bright roasted malt and hop flavor, long dry malt aftertaste, very drinkable; specific gravity 1.060, 6% abw. [P, 80]

SAN QUENTIN'S BREAKOUT STOUT — opaque almost black, smoky malt nose, high alcohol,

medium dry scorched dry barley malt and hop flavor; finishes drier than it starts; very long dry malt and hop aftertaste, good balance, very good; made from black malt and roasted barley; specific gravity 1.065, 6% abw. [S, 83]

RASPBERRY TRAIL ALE — tawny-gold, fruity raspberry nose, big bright raspberry-malt flavor; tart rapsberry is best at the finish and stays in a long dry tart raspberry malt aftertaste; very nicely done; specific gravity 1.050, 5% abw. [A, 65]

OLD DIPSEA BARLEY WINE — deep amber, very big malt and hop flavor, all kinds of malt and very hoppy (especially at the end), strong and long, a monster. Made with Chinook, Cascade, and Mt. Hood hops; flavored with licorice root and honey; OG 1090, 9.9% abw. [BW, 67]

BLUEBEERY ALE — gold, blueberry pie nose, tart blueberry flavor, balanced, very interesting and very good, the best blueberry effort I've tasted. Made with a small amount of wheat and blueberry flavoring; specific gravity 1.050. [A, 69]

STINSON BEACH PEACH — gold, clean fresh peach nose, fresh peach flavor, good body; peach and malt get a bit drier at the finish, even more dry and less peachy aftertaste; really captures the peach quality in a very nice way. Made with a small amount of wheat; specific gravity 1.050, 5% abw. [A, 70]

HOPPY HOLIDAZE ALE — golden amber, light vanilla and pumpkin pie spice nose, flavor like the nose but bigger, good body, finishes dry; aftertaste loses some of the malt and hops but retains the vanilla and spice like it started. Ingredients include cinnamon, nutmeg, vanilla, and orange-flower water; brewed with pale, wheat, and dextrin malts and Centennial and CJF4 hops; 7% abw. [A, 68]

MIWOK WEIZENBOCK — amber, alcoholic malt nose, dry malt palate; dry malt finish quickly fades to nothing. Made from pale, Munich, dextrin, and wheat malts. [W, 38]

ST. BRENDAN'S IRISH ALE — amber, faint malt nose and taste, no follow-through on the flavor. Brewed from lightly roasted malts; 6% abw. [A, 30]

Maritime Pacific Brewing Co.
Microbrewery in Seattle, WA

NIGHTWATCH DARK ALE — ruby-amber, pleasant malt nose with fruity hop background, big body, rich chewy malt flavor, plenty of malt in the long aftertaste. [A, 83]

SALMON BAY BITTER — amber, pleasant smooth Northwest hop nose, big well-hopped caramel malt flavor, lots of hops and malt, complex and smooth, long dry hop aftertaste; nicely made brew with pale malted barley, malted wheat, crystal malt and brown malt; hopped with Challenger, Progress, Northdown, and East Kent-Goldings hops; dry hopped with Centennial (no wonder it is complex);OG 1060, FG 1.013, 4.9% abv, 42 IBU. [A, 79]

ISLANDER PALE ALE — hazy gold; toasted malt aroma and flavor has a touch of honeyed sweetness in back; smooth and balanced, medium body; malty finish and aftertaste is drier than the flavor. [A, 43]

Market Street Pub & Brewery / Sunshine Brewing Inc.
Brewpub in Gainesville, FL

HONEY WHEAT BEER — amber, light malt aroma, clean refreshing off-dry malt flavor, finishes dry, medium length dry malt aftertaste. [W, 54]

GAINESVILLE GOLDEN ALE — hazy deep gold, mild hop nose, very dry hop front palate; malt shows at the finish and balances well with the dry hops that come to the fore in the aftertaste; overall, though, it is much like a good homebrew. [A, 47]

BULLGATOR ALE — pale amber, light malty hop nose, sour hop palate (like the hops were too old), dry and sour hop finish and aftertaste. Bullgator intends to be an IPA and might well be if fresher hops were used. [A, 32]

Notes

DOWNTOWN BROWN — deep amber, fairly rich malt aroma; dry and sour flavor that has plenty of malt but, like the Bullgator above, the sourness of the hops impairs the effect; light body, dry sour finish and aftertaste; 5% abv. [A, 45]

Martha's Exchange Restaurant & Brewing
Brewpub in Nashua, NH

MARTHA'S SCOTCH ALE — amber, malt aroma, big malty flavor, big body, very richly flavored; malt dominates right through the finish and into the long aftertaste, a good classical Scottish-style ale, hopped with Cascade hops; gravity 19 P, 7% abw, 25 IBU. Also seen named Untouchable Scotch Ale. [A, 64]

AL CAPONE INDIA PALE ALE — deep gold, bright hop nose, big dry hop flavor (40 IBU); big body, gets even drier at the finish leading into a very dry and very long hop aftertaste; hopped with Willamette hops; gravity 13.5 P, 5.7% abw. [A, 74]

INDIAN HEAD RED — deep amber, rising bright hop aroma, zesty big hop flavor, dry hop finish; long dry hop aftertaste has plenty of malt to back it and to balance; another big likable brew. [A, 75]

WHITE MOUNTAIN WHEAT — hazy gold, ample malt nose, bright wheat malt flavor, big body for an American wheat beer; finish is dry hops with a malt background; fairly brief, top-fermented, hopped with Hallertau hops; gravity 12 P, 4.5% abw, 16 IBU. [W, 46]

MARTHA'S STOUT — deep brown, chocolate malt and roasted barley aroma and flavor, good clean taste, light body, medium long aftertaste, stays light and dry throughout. [S, 60]

Marthasville Brewing Co.
Microbrewery in Atlanta, GA

MARTHA'S PALE ALE — gold, big bright dry hop aroma and flavor, smooth and dry, medium body, dry hop finish and aftertaste; specific gravity 1.047, 4.9% abw, 30 IBU. [A, 67]

Massachusetts Bay Brewing Co.
Brewery in Boston, MA has a capacity of about 6000 bbl. Bottled products are made by F.X. Matt of Utica, NY under contract. Very early and selected bottlings were made at the brewing facility in Boston. Also see F.X. Matt for other brews.

HARPOON WINTER WARMER (1988) — medium to deep amber; complex aroma of nutmeg, chocolate, peppermint, spices, malt, and rye bread; equally complex palate of chocolate, malt, alcohol, spices, and citrus; big body, long long complex aftertaste like the flavor. This one was produced in Boston. Subsequent WW's (1989–1992) were made in Utica and, although good, have never measured up to this one. [A, 71]

HARPOON WINTER WARMER 1993 — orange-amber, faint pumpkin pie spice; light spicy flavor seems mostly cinnamon; light body; spicy finish, disappears almost immediately on swallowing. [A, 26]

HARPOON WINTER WARMER 1994 — amber; aroma has nutmeg and cinnamon; spicy flavor is mostly cinnamon and shows little malt and hops; medium body, dry spicy finish and aftertaste. [A, 45]

HARPOON WINTER WARMER 1995 — amber; aroma is mostly nutmeg and cinnamon; flavor is mostly spicy; medium body, medium dry spicy finish and aftertaste; made with pale and caramel malts and spiced with cinnamon and nutmeg. [A, 44]

HARPOON STOUT — deep brown, roasted barley and chocolate malt nose with a sense of licorice; roast barley and chocolate malt flavor that is complex and dry; smooth and rich, good balance; a bit light for a stout, but very flavorful; smooth dry chocolate malt finish and aftertaste, fairly long. [S, 65]

HARPOON LIGHT — pale gold; faint malt aroma is lightly hopped; light but bright malt and hop flavor; malt is better than the hops; very little finish and aftertaste; 2.9% abw. [LO, 54]

HARPOON INDIA PALE ALE — deep gold, big rising fruity northwest hop aroma, bright complex refreshing balanced big ale flavor with lots of malt and hops both, hops biggest at first and malt dominating from the middle onward, good mouthfeel, plenty of alcohol; keeps its strength and complexity throughout; stays refreshing and satisfying; long flavorful aftertaste, an excellent beer. [A, 98]

HARPOON ALT — copper, roasted malt nose, dry lightly roasted malt flavor; hops come in at the finish; drinkable; has a refreshing quality; medium body, dry hop finish and aftertaste, much more pleasant than my experience with German altbier. [A, 69]

HARPOON PILSNER — medium deep gold, European hop and fruity malt (peachy) aroma; pleasant bright flavor is like the aroma but not so forthcoming; highly carbonated, medium body, fairly long dry hop aftertaste; well done but could use more malt for better balance. [B, 48]

F.X. Matt Brewing Co.
Brewery at Utica, NY. Several corporate names used including Old New York Beer Co. formerly of New York City, NY.

UTICA CLUB PILSENER BEER — gold, smooth malt and hop aroma a bit on the sweet perfumy side; flavor is mostly malt, soft and somewhat dull. [B, 47]

UTICA CLUB CREAM ALE — yellow-gold, zesty malt and hop aroma, highly carbonated, dry balanced malt flavor, fair length. [B, 34]

UTICA CLUB NON-ALCOHOLIC — deep gold; attractive off-dry aroma mostly malt but backed with good hops; off-dry malt flavor, medium body, good malt finish and medium dry malt aftertaste. [NA, 45]

UTICA CLUB LIGHT BEER — bright golden color; aroma is mainly malt but there are hops in back; flavor is like the nose; little finish and no aftertaste to speak of. [LO, 27]

MATT'S LIGHT PREMIUM BEER — pale gold, light dry malt and hop nose, pleasant malt flavor not quite so dry as the nose; finishes dry malt but the aftertaste is brief. [LO, 57]

MATT'S PREMIUM LAGER — golden color, aroma of malt with hops in back, malt flavor, light body, malt finish and aftertaste, medium length. Made with two-row and six-row malt, rice, and corn, and kraeusened. [B, 36]

Notes

MATT'S SPECIAL DRY — pale gold, melony off-dry malt aroma; flavor is off-dry malt at first, then is tart hops in the middle and finish, ending up in a long not-so-dry malt aftertaste. [D, 23]

F.X. MATT'S TRADITIONAL SEASON'S BEST PREMIUM AMBER BEER 1991 — amber, faint malt aroma, highly carbonated; flavor is malt with faint hops; medium length, overall light and not interesting for a Xmas brew. The 1990 was less carbonated and had a malt flavor with an apple-like background. It was only slightly more interesting. [B, 46]

F.X. MATT'S TRADITIONAL SEASON'S BEST PREMIUM AMBER BEER 1992 — golden amber, piney-waxy malt nose, odd spicy flavor sort of like bayberry, medium body, dry soapy hop finish and aftertaste. [B, 30]

SARANAC SEASON'S BEST 1993 HOLIDAY AMBER BEER — amber, spicy-piney malt and hop aroma, smooth spicy hop flavor with plenty of malt support, good body, good balance, dry hop finish and aftertaste, very drinkable. [B, 59]

SARANAC ADIRONDACK LAGER — golden amber, bright hop and malt aroma, zesty big hop flavor, dry hop finish and aftertaste, well balanced and very drinkable. Seems to be the new label for Saranac 1888 All Malt Lager. Made with all two-row malt, Cascade and German Hallertau hops, and kraeusened. [B, 60]

MAXIMUS SUPER MALT LIQUOR — golden amber, flowery malt nose, high carbonation; big flavor is mostly malt but there are some hops; off-dry malt finish and aftertaste, quite long and very good of the type. [ML, 58]

EL PASO LIGHT BEER — very pale golden color, faint malt aroma, very watery, faint and short malt palate. [LO, 14]

STALLION X EXTRA MALT LIQUOR — pale gold, dusty malt nose, big vegetal malt flavor, bittering hops in back, noticeable alcohol; doesn't quite come together. Made for Tighe, International. [ML, 38]

MONTAUK LIGHT — pale gold, pleasant but fleeting malt nose, light malt flavor, low calorie (105), short aftertaste. Made for Long Island Brewery Co., Huntington, NY. [LO, 28]

SPORTS LIGHT BEER — medium to deep gold color, malt and light hop aroma, light malt flavor, medium to light malt aftertaste with short duration. Made for Manhattan B.C. of NY. [LO, 30]

M.W. BRENNER'S AMBER LIGHT BEER — amber, tangy hop nose, dry lightly hopped malt palate, light body, short dry finish and aftertaste. Made for Monarch B.C. of Brooklyn, NY. [B, 43]

INDEPENDENCE ALE — deep amber, well-hopped ale-like aroma, strongly flavored with a good ale tang, zesty, tasty, and long. Made for Manhattan B.C. [A, 64]

OLDE HEURICH MAERZEN BIER — hazy amber, light malt and hop aroma, good bright malt and hop flavor, tasty, balanced, well-bodied, pleasant long mild hop aftertaste, very drinkable and refreshing. Made for Olde Heurich B.C., Washington, DC. [BK, 67]

PORTLAND LAGER — amber, good malt aroma, big balanced malt and hop flavor, good body, tasty and complex; aftertaste is long extension of the flavor. Made for Maine Coast B.C., Portland, ME. [B, 54]

HARPOON ALE — hazy tawny-amber, complex hop aroma, big hop flavor well backed with malt, good body, complex, balanced, and long; 4.2% abw, 21 IBU. Made for Massachusetts Bay B.C., Boston, MA. [A, 75]

HARPOON WINTER WARMER 1991 — amber, spicy malt nose much like a pumpkin pie, flavor like the nose but with the addition of hops, medium body, medium length. The 1990 was similar and also made by Matt for Mass Bay B.C. of Boston, MA. [B, 65]

HARPOON OCTOBERFEST BEER — amber, pleasant malt and hop nose, good hop flavor, but thin and brief. Made with pale two-row, crystal-80 malts, and cluster hops; carbonation 2.75, 5.3% abw, SRM 18, 30 IBU. Made for Mass Bay B.C. [B, 43]

GOLDEN HARPOON LAGER — deep gold, light fruity hop aroma; malt appears first on the palate then hops through the finish and into the long aftertaste; finely carbonated and well balanced. Made for Mass Bay B.C. [B, 76]

SPECIAL OLD ALE — hazy amber, fruity malt aroma, an off-dry malt flavor with strawberry tones, some chocolate malt as well, big body, dry hop aftertaste, pleasant, long, and interesting. Made with English pale malt and Kent-Goldings hops; gravity 11 P, 7.4% abw. It is made for Commonwealth B.C. of Boston, MA. [B, 52]

GOLDEN EXPORT SELECT BEER — deep gold, bright clean malt nose, finely carbonated, zesty fresh hop flavor, straightforward, tasty, well bodied, medium duration, very drinkable. Made for Commonwealth B.C. of Boston. [B, 63]

FAMOUS PORTER — nearly opaque ruby-brown, big head, fairly dry malt aroma, dry roasted malt flavor, medium body; bite in the aftertaste which is dry but not very long, very drinkable. This ale is comprised of pale, crystal, chocolate and black malts from Muton and Fison; boiled with Yakima Cluster hops; and finished with Kent Golding and Yakima Cascades. Made for Commonwealth B.C. [P, 43]

DOCK STREET AMBER BEER — amber, beautiful malt nose, bright flavor with good malt and hops, good body, long and delicious. Made for Dock Street B.C. of Bala Cynwyd, PA. [B, 83]

DOCK STREET BOHEMIAN PILSNER BEER — deep gold, vegetal malt aroma and flavor, dry

hop finish and aftertaste, big body, lots of flavors but not all of them likable. [B, 30]

D'AGOSTINO FRESH REAL PUB BEER — hazy tawny-gold, sweet malt nose, balanced hop and malt palate, low carbonation, good body, dry hop finish, long hop aftertaste, very tasty. Made for Manhattan B.C. of New York City for sale at D'Agostino Markets. [B, 63]

BROOKLYN BRAND LAGER — pale amber, pleasant malt and hop aroma, bright malt and hop flavor, well balanced, clean and pleasant, dry malt finish and aftertaste of medium length. Recipe calls for a blend of pale, crystal, and dextrin malts seasoned and dry hopped with Cascade and Hallertau hops. Made for Brooklyn Brewery, Brooklyn, NY. [B, 64]

BROOKLYN BROWN DARK ALE — amber-brown, lovely malt and hop aroma, pleasant balanced dry malt and hop flavor, not complex but very likable, medium to long dry malt aftertaste. It is a blend of pale, crystal, chocolate, black, and dextrin malts; hopped and dry hopped with Cascade and Northern Brewer hops; specific gravity 1.056, 4.6% abw. Made for Brooklyn Brewery. [B, 67]

NEW AMSTERDAM AMBER BEER — pale copper-amber, toasted malt aroma, bright well-hopped flavor with plenty of lightly toasted malt in support, good balance, long and very drinkable. Original brew of Old New York Beer Co., now part of Matt. [B, 64]

NEW AMSTERDAM NEW
YORK ALE — amber, ale-like
aroma; tangy citrus-hop flavor
that tails off into a dry hop aftertaste; medium body; starts out
strong, but doesn't develop. Old
New York Beer Co. brand that was
originally scheduled to be released
as Whyte's Pale Ale. [A, 52]

NEW AMSTERDAM WINTER
ANNIVERSARY NEW YORK
BEER 92–93 — deep amber, nice
roasted malt aroma, pleasant dry
roasted malt flavor, good body,
brief light dry roasted malt aftertaste. [B, 60]

NEW AMSTERDAM WINTER
ANNIVERSARY NEW YORK
BEER 93–94 — deep amber-
brown, very appetizing dry lightly
roasted malt and hop aroma, good
quite dry malt flavor with some
hop support, good balance, good
body, long dry malt and hop aftertaste, all hops at the very end, very
good with food. [B, 57]

NEW AMSTERDAM WINTER
ANNIVERSARY NEW YORK
DARK ALE 95–96 — brown, big
malty nose, big dry roasted malt
flavor, good body, long dry
roasted malt aftertaste, a good
very "roasty" tasting brew. [A, 64]

NEW AMSTERDAM LIGHT
AMBER BEER — gold, lightly
toasted malt aroma; light toasted
malt flavor with some Cascade
and Hallertau hops arriving late,
but becoming more pronounced as
you drink it; light body; flavor
fades before it fully develops; virtually no aftertaste. [LO, 36]

OLD BUCKEYE DRAFT
STYLE — gold color, malty
aroma with fruity hops in back,
high carbonation, light malt flavor,
dry malt finish, short malt aftertaste. Made for Old Buckeye B.C.,
Toledo, OH. [B, 48]

OLD BUCKEYE DRAFT STYLE
LIGHT — very pale gold, Concord grape aroma; light malt flavor that is faintly grape; dry
finish, short aftertaste, 89 calories.
Made for Olde Buckeye B.C.
[LO, 41]

PRIOR DOUBLE DARK — dark
amber-brown, good malt aroma,
medium body, pleasant bright hop
and malt flavor, long dry malt and
hop aftertaste. Not the old brew
from a decade back, but still
enjoyable to drink. It's on draft
only. [B, 61]

SHAN SUI YEN SUM BEER —
gold, bright hop nose with plenty
of malt in back; flowery malt and
light hop flavor lacks the sparkle
of the nose; light body; made with
ginseng extract which doesn't
show up until the finish and it is
blended with the hops since both
are bitter; long flowery dry hop
and ginseng aftertaste. The ginseng is the most remarkable thing
about it and that is barely noticeable; gravity 12 P, 3.75% abw.
Made for Shan Sui Brewing Co. of
Hong Kong. [B, 43]

MANHATTAN GOLD LAGER
BEER — hazy pale amber, pleasant fruity-malt aroma; complex
rich and dry malt flavor carries
into the long aftertaste where it is
joined by some hops; good body,
good tasting satisfying brew.
Made for Manhattan B.C. of New
York City, NY. [B, 72]

COLUMBUS 1492 LAGER —
amber-gold, big hop nose well
backed with malt, bright and zesty,
big hop and malt flavor; some
caramel comes through at the finish; good long dry hop aftertaste.
Made with Hallertau hops; gravity
12 P, 4.5% abw. Contract brew
made for the Columbus B.C., Columbus, OH. [B, 67]

FREEPORT USA — pale gold,
grainy cardboard nose and taste,
no aftertaste beyond the oxidation.
Matt's new nonalcoholic (0%)
brew; newly bottled and apparently quite fragile. [NA, 7]

SARANAC GOLDEN PILSENER
BEER — hazy gold, flowery hop
aroma, good malty flavor, light
body; malt is sweetest at the finish
leading into an off-dry malt aftertaste; starts better than it ends. Made
with two-row malt and Cascade and

Tettnanger hops, and dry hopped as well. [B, 40]

SARANAC BLACK & TAN — dark brown, chocolate malt and roasted barley nose also has fruity hops, dry malt flavor, medium body; dry malt aftertaste has some hops in back. Made from a specially made stout (not separately released by Matt) blended with Saranac Adirondack Lager. [B, 70]

RHINO CHASERS AMBER ALE — brilliant amber, bright hop nose, zesty hop and malt flavor, smooth, balanced, very drinkable, medium to good body, dry hop finish, long dry hop aftertaste, a well-made beer. Made for William & Scott, Culver City, CA. [A, 76]

SARANAC SEASON'S BEST 1994 HOLIDAY AMBER BEER — dark amber, excellent toasted malt and northwest hop nose, very dry light hop flavor, medium body, dry hop finish and aftertaste; flavor is a bit of a letdown after the very promising aroma, but still a decent brew. [B, 47]

SARANAC ADIRONDACK LAGER — golden amber, bright hop and malt aroma, zesty big hop flavor, dry hop finish and aftertaste, well balanced and very drinkable. Seems to be the new label for Saranac 1888 All Malt Lager. Made with all two-row malt, Cascade and German Hallertau hops, and kraeusened; specific gravity 1.049, 4% abw. Also called Saranac Adirondack Amber at GABF in 1994. [B, 48]

BROOKLYN BRAND LAGER — pale amber, pleasant malt and hop aroma, bright malt and hop flavor, well balanced, clean and pleasant, dry malt finish and aftertaste of medium length. Recipe calls for a blend of pale, crystal, and dextrin malts seasoned and dry hopped with Cascade and Hallertau hops; gravity 13.0 P, 5% abw. Made for Brooklyn Brewery, Brooklyn, NY. [B, 64]

BROOKLYN BROWN DARK ALE — amber-brown, lovely malt and hop aroma, pleasant balanced dry malt and hop flavor, not complex but very likable, medium to long dry malt aftertaste. It is a blend of pale, crystal, chocolate, black, and dextrin malts; hopped and dry hopped with Cascade and Northern Brewer hops; specific gravity 1.056 (15 P), 5.7% abw. Made for Brooklyn Brewery. [B, 67]

BROOKLYN BLACK CHOCOLATE STOUT — deep brown, rich malty aroma with chocolate and black patent malts, rich rather than sweet malt, very smooth, complex flavor, long rich malt aftertaste, a rich and soft sipping beer with great malt character, made with a six-grain recipe with the accent on chocolate malt; gravity 20.4 P, 8% abw. I hope this will be a regular item or at least an annual Christmas offering. Made for Brooklyn Brewery. [S, 92]

Notes

NEW AMSTERDAM WINTER ANNIVERSARY NEW YORK BEER 1994–1995 — amber, malt aroma; malt flavor has a touch of chocolate, medium body, dry hop finish and aftertaste; tasty but seems to lack the depth of the 1993–1994. [A, 47]

NEW AMSTERDAM WINTER ANNIVERSARY NEW YORK BEER 1995–1996 — the first dark ale in the winter anniversary release made from black, chocolate, and Victory malts with Northern Brewer and Willamette hops. [A, 64]

RHINO CHASERS AMBER ALE — brilliant amber, bright hop nose, zesty hop and malt flavor, smooth, balanced, very drinkable, medium to good body, dry hop finish, long dry hop aftertaste, a well-made beer; gravity 13.2 P, 4.4% abw. Made for William & Scott, Culver City, CA. [A, 76]

DOCK STREET ILLUMINA-TOR — deep amber; curious malt aroma has back notes of meat and cut potato; fairly rich bright malt flavor, medium body; dry malt finish has a little alcohol, but it drops off the palate almost immediately on swallowing; nice while it is in your mouth but disappears too rapidly. Perhaps one expects a double bock from the name, but it just isn't up to that standard or style. [BK, 84]

NANTUCKET ISLAND AMBER — golden amber, fruity malt and hop nose, big and good hop flavor, good body, balanced and complex, dry hop finish, long dry hop aftertaste. Made for Nantucket B.C., Nantucket, MA. [B, 60]

NEW AMSTERDAM BLACK & TAN — dark amber, light toasted malt aroma and flavor, lightly hopped, medium body, pleasant but not complex, dry malt finish and aftertaste, medium length. Made from a blend of stout and amber lager. The stout is specially brewed for the blend using black and caramel malts, Kent-Goldings and Willamette hops, and ale yeast. This then is added to New Amsterdam Amber Beer. [S, 57]

SARANAC TRADITIONAL PALE ALE — coppery gold, beautiful complex appetizing hop nose, big bright zesty hop flavor, excellent middle palate, dry hop finish and aftertaste; made with six specially roasted malts, East Kent-Goldings and Cascade hops, top-fermented; specific gravity 1.055, 4.4% abw. [A, 75]

OXFORD CLASS AMBER ALE — amber; malt aroma has some coffee, chocolate, and smoke; complex malt flavor has a little acrid bite on the end and is not at all like the aroma; medium body, malty long dry aftertaste. Made for Oxford B.C. of Linthicum, MD. [A, 48]

BROOKLYN EAST INDIA PALE ALE — amber, fruity-pine needle-herbal-spicy aroma, big malt and dry hop flavor, good body; dry hop aftertaste has plenty of supporting malt, but the flavors just don't come together. [A, 49]

BROOKLYN BROWN ALE — amber-brown; big dry complex malt nose seems to have a celery component in the background; strong malt

flavor, good intensity, good balance, good body, smooth and stays dry, roasted malt finish and aftertaste, not especially complex but a good taste. This is a reformulated version, made by Matt for the Brooklyn Brewery. [B, 67]

NEW AMSTERDAM BLONDE LAGER — gold, lovely fruity malt and hop aroma, very pleasant and appetizing, medium body, balanced hop and fruity malt flavor, dry malt and hop finish and aftertaste, medium length. Made with Belgian wheat and CaraVienna malts and hopped with Saaz and Tettnanger hops. [B, 55]

DOCK STREET ILLUMINATOR BOCK BEER — amber, roasted malt aroma, big roasted malt flavor, good body, dry roasted malt finish and aftertaste. Made for Dock Street Brewery, Philadelphia, PA. [BK, 53]

TENNESSEE RED WILD CHERRY MALT BEVERAGE — gold, skunky aroma, strange candy cherry and honey sweet flavor, way too sugary; reminds you of one of those old cherry cough syrups. Made for Tighe, Int'l. [ML, 11]

SARANAC MOUNTAIN BERRY ALE — orange-amber, aroma of honey and malt, tasty fruity malt and honey flavor; there are berry fruits, but they are not specifically identifiable; light fruity finish and aftertaste. [A, 37– 47]

SARANAC CHOCOLATE AMBER — dark amber, roasted malt and hop aroma; big complex roasted malt flavor is strong and bright, medium body, good chocolate character; a little burnt but still good; hops come in at the finish and stay through the long aftertaste, very good of type, a Munich-style beer; made with roasted chocolate, Munich, wheat, and caramel malts. [A, 75]

NEW AMSTERDAM BLONDE LAGER — gold, faint malt aroma, balanced malt and hop flavor, nothing sticks out, good body; dry finish and aftertaste has both malt and hops; made from Belgian wheat and CaraVienna malt with Saaz, Tettnanger, and U.S. Northwest hops. [B, 55]

SARANAC STOUT — deep brown, big attractive chocolate malt aroma; flavor very dry with little of the qualities promised by the nose; unmalted roasted barley flavor is mostly offered; not unpleasant but lacks character; short relatively uninteresting finish and dry malt aftertaste. [S, 59]

BLUE MOON HARVEST PUMPKIN — color of brilliant sherry, pleasant pumpkin pie spice nose, medium dry slightly tangy pumpkin pie spice flavor; very pleasant and quite tasty with some beery qualities appearing in the aftertaste; nicely done, perhaps the best pumpkin pie spiced beer I have tasted. Made for Blue Moon B.C., Denver, CO. [A, 38]

BLUE MOON BELGIAN WHITE BRAND — hazy gold, citrus (orange) and spice aroma, spicy flavor with an orange background, light and pleasant; the aroma is better than the flavor which is weak and more orange than spice; watery body, faint orange aftertaste. An ale made for Blue Moon B.C., Denver, CO. [A, 32]

BLUE MOON HONEY BLONDE — pale amber; faintly sweet aroma and flavor is slightly buttery and shows the honey; medium body, light sweet honey malt aftertaste. Made for Blue Moon B.C., Denver, CO. [A, 34]

BLUE MOON NUT BROWN ALE — brilliant deep amber, lightly toasted malt and hop nose, big roasted malt flavor, medium to light body, no follow-through, light dry malt aftertaste. Made for Blue Moon B.C., Denver, CO. [A, 34]

SARANAC SEASON'S BEST 1995 NUT BROWN LAGER — pretty brillant deep amber; fairly rich roasted malt nose is perfumy and shows some chocolate; pleasant deep roasted malt flavor; a touch of malty sweetness starts off an otherwise dry roasted malt finish and aftertaste; medium body, very smooth, a good tasting brew. [B, 80]

BROOKLYN CHOCOLATE STOUT 1995–96 — dark brown, complex roasted malt aroma, very complex roasted chocolatey malt flavor, good body, delicious, and long on the palate. Tasted together with the 1994–95 version (a year in bottle); the recipe is the same, the year old version being a little softer on the edges and showing more of the chocolate nature, and less of the roastiness. [S, 99]

HEURICH'S FOGGY BOTTOM ALE — hazy amber, lots of toasted malt and bright northwest hops in the nose; tastes like the aroma but not so flowery; medium body, dry hop and malt finish and aftertaste, a good tasting brew. Made for Old Heurich B.C. [A, 60]

Gritty McDuff's Brew Pub
Brewpub in Portland, ME

McDUFF'S BEST BITTER ALE — amber-gold, light fruity-spicy malt nose, medium body, bright hop flavor, dry bright spicy hop finish and aftertaste. Made with Goldings hops, cask-conditioned; OG 1049. [A, 26; A, 50]

SEBAGO LIGHT ALE — very pale gold, good malt aroma, light body, pleasant dry hop flavor and finish, long dry hop aftertaste. Hopped with Willamette and Cascade hops. [A, 43]

PORTLAND HEAD LIGHT PALE ALE — pale gold, light fruity-malt aroma, medium body, good hop flavor, dry hop finish and aftertaste, medium length. Hopped with Cascade and Willamette hops. [A, 45]

LION'S PRIDE — brown-amber, light caramel-malt nose, very light malt flavor, medium dry malt aftertaste, fair length. Made with Goldings and Willamette hops; OG 1043. [A, 52]

BLACK FLY STOUT — deep brown, very faint malt nose, dry hop flavor, soft, smooth, drinkable, dry hop finish and aftertaste. Made with smoked malt, Kent and Willamette hops; OG 1048. [S, 64]

GRITTY McDUFF'S PALE ALE — amber, light dry hop nose, very smooth dry hop flavor, good body; dry hop finish and long aftertaste stays smooth. Tasted in Portland, ME at The Great Lost Bear on draft. [A, 68]

GRITTY McDUFF'S INDIA PALE ALE — beautiful reddish-amber, light hop and malt nose, smooth soft malt and hop flavor, excellent balance, very drinkable, long dry hop aftertaste. Tasted at The Great Lost Bear on draft. [A, 72]

GRITTY McDUFF'S HALLOWEEN ALE — brilliant deep amber; smooth ale nose has more malt than hops; flavor is soft smooth malt on the off-dry side; aftertaste is dry malt, driest at the very end. No spices in this one, just a good autumn ale. Tasted on draft at The Great Lost Bear (1994 version). [A, 62]

McDUFF'S BEST BROWN ALE — dark amber-brown, light hop and malt aroma and flavor, very smooth and silky on the palate, light dry malt and hop finish and aftertaste, medium length; an English "mild" made with Yakima, Cascade, and Willamette hops; OG 1044. [A, 59]

GRITTY'S CASK CONDITIONED HALLOWEEN ALE — amber, faint malty nose, mild malt flavor, soft yet rich, very smooth, good body, long malt aftertaste. [A, 62]

McGuires Irish Pub & Brewery
Brewpub in Pensacola, FL

McGUIRES STOUT — deep opaque brown color, faint roasted barley aroma, light smooth malt flavor; pleasant dry malt aftertaste shows plenty of hop character which has stayed in back under the roasted barley all the way through. Brewed with black roasted barley and chocolate malt with Chinook hops; specific gravity 1.060, 4.1% abw. [S, 58]

McGUIRES LITE — gold, good malt aroma, pleasant bright brew with good fruity malt and hop character, long dry malt and Tettnanger hop aftertaste; a light ale that is more like a "regular" beer. Some malted wheat (10%) gives it the fruity character, but it is not like a weizen. Very nicely done. Brewed with Munich, Carapils, and flaked corn; gently hopped with Mt. Hood hops, and dry hopped with Tettnanger hops; gravity 10.42 P, 3.3% abw. [LO, 60]

McGUIRES IRISH RED ALE — amber, dry well-hopped aroma, smooth but tangy ale flavor, plenty of northwest (Willamette and Chinook) hops and good malt support, very good balance, plenty of character, long dry hop aftertaste. Made with two-row American and caramel malts; specific gravity 1.048, 3.6% abw. [A, 61]

McGUIRES PORTER — dark brown, chocolate malt aroma; flavor is complex malt from a mix of pale, chocolate, and caramel malts with roasted barley; big and bright, stays malty throughout and finishes off-dry. Chinook and Willamette hops provide a good balance; specific gravity 1.055, 4.2% abw. [P, 67]

McGUIRES IRISH STOUT — deep opaque brown color, faint roasted barley aroma, light smooth malt flavor; pleasant dry malt aftertaste shows plenty of hop character which has stayed in back under the roasted barley all the way through. Brewed with black roasted barley and chocolate malt with Chinook hops; specific gravity 1.060, 4.2% abw. [S, 54]

McGUIRES AUTUMN ALT — brownish amber; aroma shows more of the malt than hops but both are there; dry ale-like hop and malt flavor, medium body, smooth dry hop and malt aftertaste; made with caramel, toasted, and chocolate malts with Mt. Hood hops; specific gravity 1.046, 3.5% abw. [A, 59]

WHAT THE GENTLEMAN ON THE FLOOR... — deep amber, strong malt and alcohol aroma; big hop and alcoholic palate does have malt as well; big body, rich heavy and complex; very long malt and hop aftertaste, but the alcohol reigns; aged one full year; specific gravity 1.095, 8.3% abw (10.2% abv). [A, 86]

McNeill's Brewery
Brewpub in Brattleboro, VT

DUCK'S BREATH BITTER — golden amber, bright English-style malt and hop aroma, light but complex malt flavor, lightly hopped using Kent, Fuggles, and Goldings hops, medium body, light and dry hop finish and aftertaste; hops stay in back until the finish; overall nicely done; specific gravity 1.045, 4.7% abw. [A, 67]

MC NEILL'S SPECIAL BITTER — amber, big hop nose and taste, good complexity, fairly rich tasting, good body, good balance, big dry hop finish and aftertaste; a lot of flavor but it stays smooth. Heavily dry hopped with Cascade hops; specific gravity 1.050, 4.4% abw. [A, 67]

SLOPBUCKET BROWN — brownish amber, malt aroma, big dry malt flavor, dry hop finish, and long dry malt aftertaste, medium body, fair length, very drinkable; uses several different malts including crystal and chocolate; specific gravity 1.051, 4.8% abw. [A, 84]

Notes

DEAD HORSE IPA — deep amber-gold, bright complex malt and hop aroma, flavor like the nose, very good balance, medium body, smooth, very long dry malt and hop aftertaste, more malt than hops in this IPA. Complexity comes from use of Kent, Golding, and Fuggles hops with a late addition of Cascades. Cask-conditioned and unfiltered; specific gravity 1.055, 5.8% abw. [A, 63]

PALE BOCK — gold, hop aroma and taste, big body, balanced, dry hop finish, long dry hop aftertaste, good effort; gravity 16 P, 5% abw. [BK, 67]

MUDPUDDLE MILD ALE — amber-brown, light mild malt aroma and taste, light body, light dry malt finish and aftertaste. [A, 50]

MUNICH PILS — deep gold, big European style nose and taste (Saaz hops most notable but there is also Moravian), big body, bright finish, long very dry hop aftertaste. [B, 67]

BOHEMIAN PILSNER — hazy gold; big nose is a trifle soapy; bright hop (Saaz and Moravian) flavor well backed with malt, smooth, well-balanced, stays dry, dry malt finish and aftertaste; specific gravity 1.046, 3.25% abw. [B, 67]

McNEILL'S MAIBOCK — amber, light hop nose, strong and complex hop flavor, lots of alcohol (7–7.5%), huge body, dry hop finish; extremely long big hop aftertaste still shows alcohol; gravity 17.25 P. [BK, 56]

PAY DAY VIENNA STYLE — deep gold, big malt aroma and flavor, well hopped in back, smooth and dry, good body; finish is a bit off-dry; long malt aftertaste is drier. [B, 61]

BIG NOSE BLONDE — hazy gold; touch of sweetness at first in the nose, also in the flavor; finish is big dry and well hopped; nice transition from the sweet to the dry, very drinkable, long dry aftertaste; specific gravity 1.052, 3.25% abw. [B, 73]

BUCKSNORT BARLEYWINE — deep amber-brown, tan head, strong malt aroma and flavor, full bodied, big but not overwhelming, smooth, alcoholic (10.5% abw), very complex, strong and long; specific gravity 1.095–1.110 (23 P). [BW, 78]

PULLMAN'S PORTER — deep brown, big hop and malt aroma; hefty flavor matches the nose; plenty of everything, especially the hops; despite the hoppiness there is enough malt to balance and create complexity; big body, great taste, medium dry finish, very long and very drinkable despite the heft; specific gravity 1.052, 4.6% abw. [P, 80]

RAY'S HELL BOCK — deep gold, big hop aroma with plenty of malt showing, big complex hop flavor, big body, finishes strongly, very long quite dry hop aftertaste; very satisfying and it grows on you. [B, 67]

EXTERMINATOR DOPPELBOCK — brilliant amber, big hop aroma, strong hop flavor, big body, long dry hop aftertaste, a brute worth trying; specific gravity 1.075, 5.8% abw. [BK, 76]

FIREHOUSE AMBER ALE — amber-gold, big dry malt and hop aroma, very dry malt flavor, long very dry aftertaste; really grows on you; specific gravity 1.052, 5.2% abw. [A, 63]

McNEILL'S OATMEAL STOUT — deep brown, big rising complex malt aroma from roasted barley and eight different malts (includes black, Munich, pale, and oats, but only chocolate clearly discernible), rich yet dry complex malt flavor, full body, high alcohol (6% abw), dry malt finish and long complex dry malt aftertaste; OG 1058 (14 P). [S, 87]

DUESSELDORFER ALTBIER — brown, tight tan head, lovely malty nose, rich malty flavor, medium body, balanced, long fairly dry aftertaste, very smooth for an alt and very likable; made with crystal, black, roasted, chocolate, and Munich malts with some malted wheat; hopped with Northern Brewer in the kettle; finished with Hallertau and Tettnanger; OG 1048–1051, 4.2% abv. [A, 60]

PROFESSOR BREWHEAD'S OLD FASHION BROWN ALE — brown; big nose has plenty of hops and malt; big lightly toasted malt flavor with caramel and toffee notes, bright well-carbonated mouthfeel, not heavy, refreshing and drinkable, finishes dry malt and has good duration; specific gravity 1.045, 4.3% abw. [A, 73]

Melbourne Brewing Co.
Brewpub and Restaurant in Strongsville, OH

WOMBAT WHEAT BEER — deep gold, fresh fruity aroma, fresh clean pilsener style flavor, refreshing light and dry, dry hop finish and aftertaste. Uses mix of one-third wheat with two-row and Carapils malt; 3.8% abw, 20–28 IBU. [W, 46]

BONDI BEACH BLONDE — amber-gold, nice hop aroma, light hop flavor, good body, plenty of malt, dry hop finish and aftertaste. Made with two-row, Carapils, and Munich 10L malts; 4% abw, 20–26 IBU. [B, 64]

DOWN UNDER BEER — deep brown, clean malt nose, rich roasted chocolate malt flavor; stays dry despite richness; long dry malt aftertaste. Top-fermented with two-row, Munich 10L, caramel 90L, chocolate, and caramel malts; 4.5% abw, 28–36 IBU. [B, 68]

MELBOURNE'S IRISH RED ALE — amber, dusty hop nose, big malt and well-hopped flavor, balanced, long hop and malt aftertaste like the flavor, very drinkable. [A, 62]

Mendocino Brewing Co.
Brewery and brewpub in Hopland, CA

RED TAIL ALE — hazy copper; fruity citrus aroma that reminds you somewhat of a California Johannisberg Riesling wine; good body, dry hop finish and aftertaste. From a starting sugar of 13.5%, a blend of pale and caramel malts are balanced with Yakima Valley hops; 5.25% abw. [A, 72]

BLUE HERON PALE ALE — cloudy amber; pleasant aroma shows both hops and malt; flavor like the nose, good body and good balance; highly carbonated but the flavor is big enough to handle it; good long aftertaste, considerable complexity. Made with 100% pale malt, cluster and Cascade hops (for finishing) starting from a 13.55 sugar extract; gravity 13.5 P, 5.25% abw. [A, 75]

BLACK HAWK STOUT — opaque brown, rich off-dry malt aroma, dry palate with plenty of malt and hops, good body, good length. The brew is made with a 13.55 sugar extract, roasted black malt, pale and caramel malt; balanced with Cluster and Cascade hops; 4.5% abw. [S, 64]

YULETIDE PORTER — deep amber-brown, lovely fragrant malt aroma with a touch of citrus, big malt flavor; finishes quite dry but there is noticeable alcohol; long dry malt aftertaste. [P, 64]

EYE OF THE HAWK — amber, very big malt and hop nose, strong malt and hop flavor, alcoholic; long dry hop aftertaste has plenty of malt in support; a big lusty brew. Pale and caramel malts are combined to produce a 16.5% sugar malt extract which is blended with several varieties of hops. [A, 71]

Notes

EYE OF THE HAWK SPECIAL EDITION ALE (10TH ANNIVERSARY ALE) — brilliant amber, malt nose, concentrated malt and big hop flavor, highly alcoholic, big body; long malty aftertaste maintains the complexity of the flavor. This brew seems much more malty than previous editions. [A, 82]

FROLIC SHIPWRECK ALE — dark amber, rising Cascade hop aroma; you just don't get a better more appetizing nose than this; flavor like the nose but unfortunately not as big but has the Cascade character and plenty of malt, dry hop finish and aftertaste; long aftertaste is more dry than hops but at the end there is a resurgence of the Cascade character; the aroma is enough to garner many points of its rating. It is intended to represent a Scottish-style ale of the 1850s and, except for the northwest hops, does so quite well. [A, 69]

Miami Brewing Co.
Microbrewery in Miami, FL

HURRICANE REEF LAGER — bright medium deep gold, malt and hops both show well in the nose; big malt and hop flavor is more malty; big body, finishes with both malt and hops; continues to feature both the malt and hops in the aftertaste; balanced, dry, and long. [B, 56]

Middlesex B.C.
Microbrewery in Burlington, MA

MIDDLESEX GOLDEN ALE — gold, interesting complex aroma with Willamette and Cascade hops; bright tangy dry hop flavor has a spruce-like component; long dry hop aftertaste is complex and flavorful; cask-conditioned; OG 1046. [A, 60]

MIDDLESEX BROWN ALE — brown, pleasant malt aroma, interesting minty malt flavor, good body, good balance, quite zesty, fairly long dry malt aftertaste; made with Cascade, Chinook, and Willamette hops; cask-conditioned; OG 1044, 3.4% abw. [A, 63]

MIDDLESEX OATMEAL STOUT — very deep ruby-brown; nose shows roasted barley, oats, mint, and berries; flavor is much like the aroma; no chocolate malt, good body, dry and fairly long aftertaste; stays interesting throughout; cask-conditioned; made with Cascade, Chinook, and Willamette hops; OG 1050, 4% abw. [S, 59]

MIDDLESEX RASPBERRY WHEAT — cloudy gold with a rose tinge, beautiful raspberry nose; flavor is raspberry but it has an artificial quality about it and is a little "perfumy" on the palate; medium body; an unattractive bitterness comes in at the finish and stays through the aftertaste marring the pleasantness of the raspberry. [W, 43]

Milestown Brewing Co.
Microbrewery in Miles City, MT

OLD MILESTOWN — deep gold, light hop nose, bright hop flavor, medium body, light dry hop finish and medium long aftertaste, smooth and light, very drinkable. Beer is naturally kraeusened and unpasteurized; aged six weeks; specific gravity 1.048, 4.2% abw. [B, 73]

MILESTOWN COAL PORTER — dark brown; malt aroma and flavor is a bit nutty; tangy finish; bright malt aftertaste shows some of the nuttiness of the flavor. Made from dark crystal and chocolate malts with a touch of almond; Northern Brewer and Cascade hops; specific gravity 1.052, 4.9% abw. [P, 69]

PAUL'S LEMONGRASS — deep gold, spicy lemony aroma and flavor, light body; fruity aftertaste has the spicy lemony nature. Made with wheat malt and Asian lemon grass, both of which are quite evident; specific gravity 1.048, 4.2% abw. [W, 64]

The Mill / Whiskey Creek Brewing
Brewpub in Ft. Myers, FL

MILL SCOTCH ALE — golden amber, dry hop aroma and flavor, big body; big dry hop flavor has some complexity; long dry hop aftertaste. [A, 65]

Miller Brewing Co.

Breweries in Milwaukee, WI; Azusa and Irwindale, CA; Eden, NC; South Volney, NY; Trenton, OH; Albany, GA; and Fort Worth, TX

MILLER HIGH LIFE — bright gold, pleasant aromatic hop nose, clean flavorful malt and hop palate, refreshing and fairly complex, good body, long dry hop aftertaste. Made with barley malt and corn. [B, 64]

MILLER LITE PILSENER BEER — pale gold, good malt aroma, light body, pleasant malt flavor, dry finish and aftertaste; has good length. Made with pale malted barley; specific gravity 1.031, 3.3% abw. [LO, 48]

LITE ULTRA — gold, very pleasant malt and hop aroma; front palate is pleasant dry malt with a substantial CO_2 component; flavor cuts off suddenly without much finish and no aftertaste, but it is very good while it is there. This is a test brew for Miller in a very low-calorie beer (77 calories) and, for the type, is excellent. [LO, 36]

LOWENBRAU LIGHT SPECIAL — light gold, clean malt aroma; hops dominate the flavor; good balance, good body, long dry hop aftertaste; specific gravity 1.048, 3.85% abw. Since the introduction of the low-calorie Lowenbrau, this has been more simply called Lowenbrau Special. [B, 67]

LOWENBRAU DARK SPECIAL — deep amber; appetizing malt and hop aroma is very Bavarian; big hop flavor, surprisingly light body, very little aftertaste. Brewed with pale, crystal, and black malts; specific gravity 1.04917, 3.85% abw. [B, 53]

SHARP'S NA BEER — gold, off-dry malt aroma and flavor, light body, short aftertaste; 0.5% abw. [NA, 26]

MEISTER BRAU — bright gold, dry malt nose, off-dry malt and tangy hop flavor; hops develop nicely at finish and in aftertaste; the malt, however, doesn't and tends toward sour; long aftertaste. [B, 43]

MEISTER BRAU LIGHT — bright gold, pleasant malt and hop nose, light malt flavor, light body, good but brief. [LO, 29]

MAGNUM MALT LIQUOR — pale yellow, fruity sweet malt aroma, slightly sweet malt flavor, light bodied for a malt liquor, slightly sweet malt finish and aftertaste with medium duration. [ML, 20]

MILLER SPECIAL RESERVE BEER — bright deep gold, rich malt nose; smooth malt flavor has a richness but stays on the dry side; hops show only as a hint and that comes in the aftertaste. Made with American pale and caramel barley malt, Cascade and Mt. Hood hops; 3.9% abw. [B, 30]

Notes

MILLER SPECIAL RESERVE
LIGHT — gold, dusty light malt
nose, light dry malt flavor, light
body, only a brief malt faint aftertaste. Made from all barley malt.
[LO, 27]

MILWAUKEE'S BEST BEER —
pale gold, pleasant malt aroma,
highly carbonated, light body,
slightly sweet malt flavor, good
finish and long aftertaste feature
both malt and hops. [B, 29]

MILWAUKEE'S BEST ICE
BEER — deep gold, malty aroma,
malt flavor, medium to good body;
fruity malt aftertaste has good duration; hops are there but stay in the
background; 5.5% abv. [B, 46]

MILWAUKEE'S BEST LIGHT —
pale gold, malt aroma, light slightly
sweet malt flavor, high carbonation;
hops appear at the finish and carry
into the aftertaste which is light and
short. [LO, 23]

MILLER GENUINE DRAFT —
medium deep gold, faint malt
aroma, wonderfully dry malt flavor
without being bitter, dry finish and

aftertaste, good length; specific
gravity 1.044, 3.65% abw. [B, 29]

MILLER GENUINE DRAFT
LIGHT — very pale gold, very
faint malt aroma and flavor, very
little finish and almost no aftertaste; specific gravity 1.031, 3.3%
abw. [LO, 10]

DAKOTA WHEAT BREWED
BEER — pale gold, slightly off-
dry malt and hop aroma, pleasant
dry malt flavor, good body; ends
abruptly; very clean and refreshing, very good except for the lack
of an aftertaste. Miller has tried
this several times in test markets
and, despite it being one of the
best efforts in the genre, decides
not to follow through with regular
production. [W, 51]

COLDERS 29 LIGHT — pale
gold, light very pleasant off-dry
malt nose, light malt flavor, light
body, refreshing like a dry malty
club soda, short faint dry malt
aftertaste. [LO, 20]

COLDERS 29 — pale gold, light
fruity malt nose, smooth balanced
light malt and hop flavor, light body,
brief dry malt aftertaste. [B, 24]

MILLER RESERVE VELVET
STOUT — deep amber-brown,
faint dry malt nose; dry malt flavor has a richness but is not big;
medium body, smooth but lightly
flavored, a hint of sweetness at the
finish, dry malt aftertaste of average length. Made with pale, caramel, and black malts; Cascade and
Cluster hops; specific gravity
1.048, 4% abw. [S, 47]

MILLER CLEAR BEER — clear,
perfumy grapey nose, light body;
sweet malt flavor at first, doesn't
last to the finish; faint malt aftertaste; tastes a lot like a seltzer with
faint off-dry malt. Made with Cascade hops and specially filtered to
remove the color. [B, 20]

MILLER RESERVE AMBER
ALE — bright amber, fresh faint
hop-ale, fairly big bright hop flavor, medium body; fades and goes
a little sour in the finish which
hurts; dull aftertaste, good start,
poor finish. Made with pale and
caramel malts; Cascade and Mt.
Hood hops; specific gravity 1.049,
4% abw. [A, 47]

ICEHOUSE BEER — gold,
plenty of hops and malt in the
nose, off-dry malt flavor, light to
medium body, dry hop finish,
short dry hop aftertaste. Miller's
entry in the ice beer competition,
label says made by Plank Road
Brewery, Milwaukee, WI; specific
gravity 1.046, 5.5% abv (4.2%
abw) Shortly after release in New
Mexico, I saw table tents naming
this as Ice House Premium Ice
Brewed Ale; it is bottom-fermented
but, because of its alcohol it cannot
be called a beer and is labeled an ale
in California. [B, 43]

LITE ICE — gold; nose is first
hops then malt; flavor starts out
well hopped; malt comes out
briefly at the finish, drops off
quickly to nothing more than a
sense of dryness, which itself is
short-lived; light to medium body
(though better than most low-calorie brews). This is also labeled an

ale in California; specific gravity 1.040, 5% abv, 4.2% abw according to the brewery. [B, 34]

RED DOG — gold, hop nose with some malt in back, thin sour hop flavor, light body; dry hop aftertaste is a bit sour as well. Same logo as Molson Red Dog, but a different beer. [B, 37]

MILLER HIGH LIFE LIGHT BEER — gold, good hop and malt aroma; light dry hop and malt flavor is mostly carbonation; good tasting but the carbonation is a bit too dominant; medium to light body; dry hop finish and aftertaste retains the carbonic bite. [LO, 34]

MILLER GENUINE RED — brilliant reddish amber, faint malt aroma; malty flavor is lightly toasted but not appetizing; medium body, dull semi-sweet malty aftertaste; not bad but no raves, better than Red Dog. [B, 52]

MILLER HIGH LIFE ICE BEER — bright gold, perfumy malt nose, sweet malt palate, pleasant tasting, medium to good body, smooth, fairly long off-dry malt aftertaste. [B, 47]

Millstream B.C.
Brewery in Amana, IA

MILLSTREAM LAGER BEER — hazy gold, good malt and hop aroma; lots of both malt and hops for the palate but the balance is not as good as it could be; comes off as being off-dry malt and sour hops right into the aftertaste. It is naturally kraeusened and not pasteurized; specific gravity 1.048, 4.2% abw. [B, 49]

SCHILD BRAU AMBER — amber; beautiful roasted malt nose, has a fruity component as well; delicious complex roasted malt flavor, great balance, zesty hops in support, fresh fruity malt finish and long aftertaste, an excellent brew. Made with two types of Yakima and Cluster hops and six-row and roasted caramel malts; specific gravity 1.054, 4.6% abw. [B, 80]

MILLSTREAM WHEAT LAGER BEER — bright gold, perky malt aroma, low carbonation, even to the eye, light malt flavor, dull malt aftertaste of medium length. Made with 60% wheat and 40% barley malt; specific gravity 1.040, 3.4% abw. [W, 20]

MILLSTREAM OKTOBERFEST — amber-gold, big malt nose, big malt and hop flavor, good body, long dry malt aftertaste; specific gravity 1.052, 4.5% abw. [B, 54]

Minnesota Brewing Co.
Brewery in St. Paul, MN (the old Jacob Schmidt brewery)

PIGS EYE PILSNER — gold, hop and vegetal aroma, hop flavor with some sour malt in back, medium body, dry malt and hop finish and long aftertaste; gravity 10.8 P, 3.55% abw. [B, 45]

LEAN PIG'S EYE LIGHT BEER — pale gold, pleasant malt nose, light malt flavor, light body, a bit off-dry, little finish and aftertaste, a good quaffing beer well-chilled; gravity 9.1 P, 3.3% abw. [LO, 36]

LANDMARK LIGHT — gold, pleasant malt aroma and flavor; hops are in back; good tasting, good body, short dry hop finish and aftertaste. [LO, 41]

LANDMARK — gold, dry hop nose, dry hop flavor, thin body, light finish, short dry aftertaste; gravity 11.5 P, 3.8% abw. [B, 50]

LANDMARK OKTOBERFEST BEER — brilliant amber, lovely toasted malt nose, dry toasted malt flavor, good body, dry malt finish and long aftertaste. Uniform throughout and very good with food. An all-barley malt beer; gravity 13.2 P, 4.12% abw. [B, 67]

LANDMARK BOCK — amber; malt nose is faintly fruity; light mild spicy roasted dry malt flavor, some light hop character in the finish, medium body, fair to good balance; dry malt aftertaste has good duration; more like a märzen, very drinkable. An all-barley malt brew; gravity 13 P, 4% abw. [BK, 67]

GRAIN BELT BEER — gold, vegetal malt aroma, vegetal malt and light hop flavor, light body, short dry malt aftertaste. [B, 24]

GRAIN BELT LIGHT — pale gold, malt aroma; grainy fruity-grapey malt flavor at first, then goes a bit drier (but stays malty); medium body, dull malt finish and aftertaste. [LO, 31]

GRAIN BELT PREMIUM — gold, malt aroma, light dry malt and hop flavor, medium body, dry malt and hop aftertaste; gravity 11.3 P, 3.78% abw. [B, 42]

GRAIN BELT PREMIUM LIGHT — pale gold, malt nose, light dry hop and malt flavor, light body, light dry hop and malt after-taste, medium length; gravity 9.1 P, 3.3% abw. [LO, 47]

CERVEZA CALIENTE — gold, light honeyed malt nose; light malt at first (for an instant) on the tongue, then dry hot pepper for flavor; finish, and aftertaste. Made for Cerveza Caliente Ltd. [B, 9]

RHINO CHASER'S AMERICAN ALE — amber-gold, pleasant appetizing hop aroma; dry hop flavor is a little coarse at the finish; dry hop aftertaste; 4.15% abw. Made for William & Scott Co., Culver City, CA. [A, 61]

RHINO CHASER'S AMBER ALE — bright amber, big head, light citrus-ale aroma and flavor, good body, tasty and complex, medium dry hop finish, long dry hop aftertaste; 4.4% abw. Contract brew for William & Scott Co. as above. [A, 76]

RHINO CHASER'S LAGER BEER — hazy gold, fruity malt aroma, tangy malt flavor, medium body; hops are more for bittering than flavor; finishes dry malt, brief dry malt aftertaste. Made with two-row malt and Saaz hops; 3.77% abw. Contract beer as above. [B, 36]

RHINO CHASER'S DARK LAGER — amber, light toasted malt nose and taste, light body, light dry malt aftertaste; 3.92% abw. Contract beer as above. [B, 40]

RHINO CHASER'S WINTERFUL 1993 — amber, fruity malt nose and taste, pleasant but not very interesting; hops are up front but fade after the initial burst; dry malt finish and after-taste; 4.8% abw. Contract beer as above. [B, 40]

SHAMS PREMIUM BEER — gold, complex hop and malt aroma; flavor starts hoppy but ends musty; dry hop aftertaste. Made for Shams Beer Co. [B, 26]

WIT ORIGINAL 1444 RECIPE — cloudy whitish-yellow, faint citrus nose; palate is at first a burst of orange and a bit off-dry, it soon dries and picks up some spicy complexity; faint hops add to the finish, light to medium body, long faintly citrus aftertaste, very drinkable and very refresh-ing, top-fermented; made with or-ange peel, coriander, 50-50 wheat and malted barley, and Cluster and Tettnanger hops; very lightly hopped; gravity 12 P, 3.8% abw. Made for Spring Street B.C. of NY. [W, 56]

AMBER WIT — amber; orange peel-cardamom nose smells like

Indian cuisine; cardamom dominates the flavor; medium body cardamom finish and aftertaste; try this with your curries and tandoori chicken; made with witbier yeast and wheat malt with caramelized malt and a different mix of spices; gravity 12 P, 3.8% abw. [B, 18]

GILA MONSTER BEER — amber; light roasted malt aroma, flavor to match; light to medium body; light dry roasted malt aftertaste that is quite lengthy. [B, 68]

McMAHON'S IRISH STYLE POTATO ALE — gold, fruity aroma, dry hop flavor, thin body, ephemeral palate, very little aftertaste. Made with potato and specialty malts; gravity 12.4 P, 4.3% abw. [B, 32]

PIG'S EYE ICE BEER — gold, hop aroma; flavor is all-European hops at first then the malt rolls in and takes over; off-dry malt finish, medium long off-dry malt aftertaste, good body, decent beer; gravity 12.3 P, 4.4% abw. [B, 47]

BLUEBERRY LAGER — pale gold, very subtle blueberry-malt nose, a faint blueberry background to a light malt flavor, light body; blueberry is still subtle in the aftertaste but a bit more noticeable; specific gravity 1.012, 3.9% abw. [B, 43]

BEARTOOTH BLUEBERRY LAGER — deep gold, fruity-berry nose; fruity malt flavor could be blueberry; fruity-berry aftertaste is on the dry side and a bit tart; medium long. Made for Beartooth B.C. [B, 43]

CRANBERRY LAGER — pale gold, light cranberry aroma and flavor, light body; dry aftertaste gets bittering from hops and the cranberries; specific gravity 1.012, 3.8% abw. [B, 45]

BEARTOOTH CRANBERRY LAGER — deep gold, slightly tart cranberry nose; tart cranberry flavor is a bit candylike (but still tart); medium long cranberry aftertaste stays tart. Made for Beartooth B.C. [B, 33]

RASPBERRY LAGER — gold, big raspberry aroma, big fruity flavor, light body, dry raspberry malt aftertaste; specific gravity 1.012, 3.8% abw. [B, 47]

BEARTOOTH RASPBERRY LAGER — gold, very faint raspberry nose, only the faintest touch of raspberry on the palate, medium body; a very faint raspberry flavor shows in back of the aftertaste, so little it hardly seems appropriate to call it a raspberry lager. Made for Beartooth B.C. [B, 39]

BREWSKI'S BAR ROOM BLONDE LAGER — brilliant gold, tight head, dry malty flavor, good balance, medium body, dry malt finish and aftertaste, good duration; OG 1048, 25 IBU. Made for Brewski's of El Segundo, CA. [A, 56]

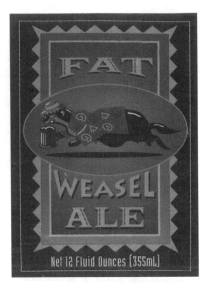

BREWSKI'S BAR ROOM ALE (BROWN ALE) — amber-brown, dry malty aroma and flavor, medium body; medium hop presence arrives at the finish; dry malt and hop finish and aftertaste, medium hoppy and very drinkable, good with food; OG 1045, 19 IBU. Made for Brewski's of El Segundo, CA. [A, 59]

BREWSKI'S BAR ROOM HONEY RED ALE — amber-gold, big head, smooth hop aroma; good hop flavor has plenty of supporting malt; well balanced, long dry hop and malt aftertaste; made with real honey; OG 1052, 20 IBU. Made for Brewski's of El Segundo, CA. [A, 56]

SLO GARDEN ALLEY AMBER ALE — medium deep amber, faint malt nose, big complex malt flavor, big body; strong hops come in at the finish and stay into the long strong dry hop and big malt aftertaste.

Made for SLO Brewing of San Luis Obispo, CA. [A, 65]

FAT WEASEL ALE — hazy amber-gold, faint malt and hop aroma; bitter hop flavor has plenty underlying malt; hoppy aftertaste but there is a sweetness that comes in late, but the very end is again dry hops. [A, 72]

BILLY GOAT BOCK BEER — amber-brown; malty nose has a faintly dank component; good roasted malt flavor, good body; dry malt finish has some background hop character and a long dry malt aftertaste; except for the offishness in the nose it is much like the Landmark Bock. Made for the Billy Goat B.C. [BK, 62]

ROAD RUNNER RED ALE — hazy amber, lightly roasted malt aroma, zesty flavor like the nose, plenty of roasted malt, medium body, a long roasty malt aftertaste; a bright brew that slides down easily. [A, 50]

HUMPBACK PREMIUM ALE — hazy amber-gold; lightly roasted malt aroma is like the Road Runner but is weaker; flavor like the aroma but lighter and drier than the Road Runner; medium body, good length, good taste. [A, 50]

BLACK TOAD DARK ALE — deep amber, roasted malt aroma and flavor; supporting hops are there but more in the nose than in the taste; smooth and balanced, medium body, good long malty aftertaste. [A, 73]

FRUGATTI'S BIG RED ALE — amber, lightly toasted malt aroma; very malty flavor shows a bit of alcohol; smooth, medium body; hops are there but never emerge from below the toasted malt; long dry malt aftertaste, very good with food. Made for a California restaurant. [A, 54]

PIGS EYE RED AMBER ALE — amber-gold, big sweet malt nose, pleasant malt flavor, medium body, fairly long malty aftertaste. [A, 57]

Miracle Brewing Co.
Microbrewery in Wichita, KS

MIRACLE MILD — deep gold, fruity malt nose, huge fruity ester flavor with lots of hops, very complex, more like a bitter than a mild, good body, long complex malt and hop aftertaste; specific gravity 1.041, 4.7% abw. [A, 73]

RED DEVIL ALE — amber, smooth off-dry roasted malt aroma and flavor, good body; stays dry into a long aftertaste; unidimensional but pleasant; specific gravity 1.042, 4.8% abw. [A, 61]

PURGATORY PORTER — deep ruby-brown, pleasant malt aroma; big smooth flavor is a bit chocolate-like; good body; somewhat dull malt aftertaste is a veneer of malt; specific gravity 1.044, 4.8% abw. [P, 49]

ARK ANGEL ALE — amber; smooth lightly toasted malty aroma and flavor has a little caraway in the background; medium to light body, off-dry malt and light hop finish and aftertaste, fairly long; specific gravity 1.040, 4.7% abw. [A, 49–62]

PICKERING'S OLD ENGLISH ALE — amber-gold, bright hop aroma; flavor is big hops and dry malt; medium body, medium long dry hop and malt aftertaste; specific gravity 1.044, 5% abw. Made for Pickering's Pub of Olathe, KS. [A, 59]

Mishawaka Brewing Co.
Microbrewery in Mishawaka, IN

SOUTH SHORE AMBER ALE — deep amber-gold, fruity malt nose with an ashy background; somewhat dull slightly sweet malt flavor with that same ashy background, though faintly so; medium body, toasty finish, slightly dry and slightly toasted malt aftertaste. Made with English pale ale malt, crystal 65, and dextrin malts; specific gravity 1.047, 3.8% abw, 28 IBU. [A, 43]

MISHAWAKA GOLD LAGER — gold, light dry malt aroma and taste, medium body, dry hop finish, light long dry hop and malt aftertaste. Made with Vienna and Munich malts balanced with Saaz and Hallertau hops. [B, 47]

LAKE EFFECT PALE ALE — pale gold, bright hop aroma and flavor, big body; some samples had a light toasted malt character in the finish; starts out faintly sweet but dries as it goes; extremely long dry hop aftertaste. Well hopped with Perle, Cascade, Mt. Hood, and Willamette hops; specific gravity 1.056, 4.4% abw. [A, 73]

FOUNDER'S STOUT — deep mahogany brown; roasted barley and chocolate malt nose that has definite dry coffee tones; flavor like the nose but shows the dry coffee even more; good body, long aftertaste like the flavor but drier. If you like the coffee touch (which I do), this is an excellent stout of the dry type; specific gravity 1.048, 4.2% abw, 42 IBU. [S, 80]

MISHAWAKA RASPBERRY WHEAT BEER — hazy pink, very nice raspberry nose; light pleasant somewhat dry raspberry flavor is not really as expected from the nose; very refreshing, light body, some complexity and length, very good of style. [W, 58]

Mountain Sun Pub & Brewery
Brewpub in Boulder, CO

COLORADO KIND ALE — deep amber; big dry aroma shows plenty of both malt and hops; hefty flavor follows the nose; medium body, plenty of Cascade hops, strong and long dry hop aftertaste, a brawny enough brew for any hop-head; specific gravity 1.053, 5.5% abw. [A, 89]

Notes

ISADORE JAVE PORTER — brown, coffee malt aroma and flavor, medium to good body, plenty of coffee taste in the aftertaste as well, 5 lbs. of coffee per every 7 bbl of beer produced; specific gravity 1.052, 5.5% abw. [P, 68]

RASPBERRY WHEAT — pinkish gold, dry raspberry aroma and slightly tart dry raspberry flavor, light body, dry raspberry aftertaste; made using 60 lbs. of Oregon raspberries; specific gravity 1.040, 3.9% abw. [W, 46]

THUNDERHEAD STOUT — dark brown, almost black; rich malt aroma has no chocolate malt or roasted barley in evidence; more like a porter than a stout, rich malt flavor is a bit more stout-like; big body; long aftertaste is an extension of the palate; Cascade and Chinook hops provide the bitterness to offset the richness of the malt; specific gravity 1.065, 6.5% abw. [S, 53]

Mountain Valley Brewing Co.
Brewpub in Suffern, NY

MOUNTAIN VALLEY CHRISTMAS ALE — brilliant copper-amber; light spicy nose of cinnamon and ginger, but you can smell the malt as well; very smooth, good body, excellent balance, long lightly spiced aftertaste, a very classy spiced ale. [A, 87]

MOUNTAIN VALLEY PALE — gold, malt nose and flavor; hops come in at the middle; medium body, light malt finish, dry malt aftertaste. [A, 34]

MOUNTAIN VALLEY COPPER LIGHT — amber, light malt nose, light malt flavor, some hops in middle and back, light body, light dry malt aftertaste with some hops faintly in back. [LO, 64]

MOUNTAIN VALLEY COPPER — deep amber, light hop and malt nose, good light subtle dry malt and hop flavor, bright and tasty, pleasant and balanced, medium to good body, malt and hop finish, light dry hop aftertaste, good duration; nicely made beer. [A, 73]

MOUNTAIN VALLEY PORTER — brown; light malt nose has tones of chocolate and coffee from black patent malt; pleasant dry malt flavor, medium body, very drinkable, light dry complex roasted malt finish and aftertaste, low carbonation, medium length. Made with four English malts including black and chocolate, balanced with Northern Brewer and East Kent-Goldings hops; gravity 14 P (1.055), 4.4% abw. [P, 78]

MOUNTAIN VALLEY NUT BROWN — amber-brown, light off-dry malt nose, slightly off-dry malt flavor, light body; malt shows best at the finish; pleasant light and dry malt aftertaste. [A, 67]

MOUNTAIN VALLEY BLOND DOUBLE BOCK — gold, big hop aroma, huge estery fruity hop and malt flavor, big body, alcohol showing, a big bold brew, heavily hopped, long dry hop and big malt aftertaste, huge and very good. Made with European two-row malts, Hersbrucker and Saaz hops; aged four months; specific gravity 1.080, 6.2% abw. [BK, 89]

MOUNTAIN VALLEY OKTOBERFEST — pale amber, light malt nose; off-dry malt flavor that stays into the long aftertaste; big body, seems to get sweeter as it goes; very much an Oktoberfest-style brew; made with pale and dark German malts and Hersbrucker hops; gravity 14.0 P, 4.7% abw. An earlier version was more golden in color and drier in flavor reflecting use of a different malt. [B, 68]

MOUNTAIN VALLEY RAUCHBIER — dark amber-brown, faint smoky nose and lightly smoked malt flavor; done very much like a fine Bamberger Rauchbier; good body, lightly smoked dry malt and bright hop aftertaste, good length, a fine effort. Made with German two-row barley malt; cold-smoked for 12 hours; balanced with Saaz and Hersbrucker hops; specific gravity 1.050, 4% abw. [B,70]

MOUNTAIN VALLEY INDIA PALE ALE — brilliant gold, light hop aroma, dry malt flavor up front, dry hop finish with good malt balance, good body, long complex dry hop and malt aftertaste. Dry hopped with Kent-Goldings hops; specific gravity 1.053, 4.2% abw. [A, 76]

MOUNTAIN VALLEY CHRISTMAS ALE 93 — brilliant copper-amber; light spicy nose of cinnamon and ginger, but you can smell the malt as well; very smooth, good body, excellent balance, long lightly spiced aftertaste, a very classy spiced ale. [A, 87]

RUFFIAN XMAS ALE 1994 — bright amber, light spicy ginger-cinnamon aroma; light spicy flavor lets the malt and hops shine through; very much like the above, but the spices are handled even more lightly. [A, 60]

MOUNTAIN VALLEY MAI-BOCK — deep tawny gold, finely carbonated, bright refreshing clean hop nose; malt in back is enough for balance; bright hop flavor is very refreshing; taste and mouthfeel is almost like a cream ale; medium to good body, a very nice malty background to the hop flavor all the way through, dry hop finish; long dry hop aftertaste has that good malt support; a nicely made good-tasting refreshing bock-style beer. [B, 70]

MOUNTAIN VALLEY IRISH RED ALE — reddish amber, malt aroma; dry malt flavor with hops coming in at mid-palate; tasty and smooth, excellent with food, dry malt finish and aftertaste, good duration. [A, 73]

MOUNTAIN VALLEY WEIZEN DOPPELBOCK — appearance like homemade cider (cloudy amber-gold); grainy nose like the smell you get in an operating brewery; malty flavor makes you think of Ovaltine, off-dry with a little acidic bite; aftertaste is sweeter, dry clean malt at the end; made with Guinness ale yeast; gravity 18–22 P, 9.5% abv. [BK, 90]

Mountain Brewers, Inc.
Brewery in Bridgewater, VT

LONG TRAIL ALE — amber, big toasted malt aroma, dry malt and bright hop flavor, very dry hop finish and aftertaste, top-fermented with a cold finishing temperature; specific gravity 1.046, 3.6% abw. [A, 67]

VERMONT BICENTENNIAL ALE — hazy gold, light citrus-ale aroma, bright hop flavor with a good ale character, good-tasting bitter hop finish, and long dry hop aftertaste, medium body, good balance. [A, 78]

LONG TRAIL LIGHT — gold, dry malt nose and taste, light body, short dry malt aftertaste; top-fermented cream ale; specific gravity 1.044, 3.4% abw. [LO, 26]

LONG TRAIL IPA — amber-gold, bright hoppy aroma and flavor, strong and complex, lots of ale bite; alcohol shows a bit; good body, extremely long dry hop aftertaste; specific gravity 1.055, 4.3% abw. [A, 75]

Notes

O'BRIEN'S LONG TRAIL STOUT — dark, roasted barley and chocolate malt aroma and taste, somewhat light on flavor and body, good aftertaste like the flavor, but again light and a bit short. Draft version. [S, 50]

LONG TRAIL STOUT — opaque brown, nose like ashes and roasted barley, smoky, burnt malt flavor, low carbonation, overhopped, un-balanced, rough to drink. Bottled version, made with roasted barley; specific gravity 1.043, 3.4% abw. [S, 24]

LONG TRAIL KÖLSCH ALE — deep gold; bright off-dry nose is a bit winelike and has a citrus back-ground; big bold dry hop flavor with noticeable alcohol, creamy; some malt showing in back; good body, dry hop finish and aftertaste, very long on the palate, a big bright refreshing winey ale with considerable complexity; specific gravity 1.044, 3.9% abw. [K, 79]

MULLIGAN'S BREW — gold, malt aroma, dry hop and malt fla-vor, smooth and balanced, long dry hop aftertaste. [A, 54]

BROWN BAG ALE — amber-brown; very nice roasted malt nose is a bit off-dry; light dry roasted malt flavor, light body, dry roasted malt finish and long aftertaste, a northern English-style brown ale with chocolate malt; specific gravity 1.042, 3.6% abw. [A, 42]

HARVEST ALE — pale hazy amber-gold, light malt nose, dry malt fla-vor, light body, dry malt finish and aftertaste, not interesting. [A, 33]

Mt. Hood Brewing Co.
Microbrewery in Government Camp, OR

CLOUDCAP AMBER ALE — coppery amber, dry hop aroma with a malt background; hop palate has a caramel and crystal malt backing; medium body, dry hop finish and aftertaste; specific gravity 1.048, 4% abw. [A, 67]

HOGSBACK OATMEAL STOUT — dark brown, big roasted malt aroma, rich complex roasted malt and hop flavor, big body; rich dry malt finish and aftertaste shows a bit of sweetness; specific gravity 1.064, 4.5% abw. [S, 71]

ICE AXE INDIA PALE ALE — gold, spicy hop aroma; complex hop palate also shows a spicy nature and has a background rich-ness of malt and some alcohol; hefty body; long fairly rich after-taste has plenty of hops and malt; made with two-row, carastan light, dark crystal, Munich, and wheat malts; hopped with East Kent-Goldings, Mt. Hood, and Willamette hops; specific gravity 1.062, FG 1.012, 5.9% abw. [A, 67]

PINNACLE ESB ALE — amber-brown, big bright hop aroma and flavor; complex and strong hop palate backed with an abundance of rich malt; good body, dry hop finish and aftertaste, a big bright good tasting balanced well-hopped and heavily malted brew; specific gravity 1.058, 4.6% abw. An excellent tasting ale. [A, 91]

Multnomah Brewing Co.
Microbrewery in Portland, OR

SAUVIE ISLAND PALE ALE — deep gold, beautiful Cascade aroma, bright well-hopped flavor, smooth, medium body; dry hop finish and aftertaste has good length; made with Gambrina's pale and wheat malt, flaked barley, and flaked corn; hopped with Galena, Mt. Hood, Hallertauer, and Kent Goldings; OG 1052, FG 1.009, 4.25% abv, 28 IBU. [A, 73]

Murphy's Creek Brewing Co.
Microbrewery in Murphy's, CA

MURPHY'S BLACK GOLD — dark brown, dry chocolate malt and roasted barley aroma and flavor, medium body, smooth and dry, fin-ish and aftertaste dry malt, very drinkable; made with 20% wheat balanced with chocolate malt and roasted wheat; hopped with Cascade and Tettnanger hops; specific grav-ity 14 P, 4.3% abw. [S, 65]

MURPHY'S RASPBERRY WHEAT — faintly pinkish gold, faint berry nose, raspberry flavor, light body, finish, and aftertaste; the cherry shows only in the end; made with raspberries and cherries; spe-cific gravity 1.051. [W, 46]

MURPHY'S RED BEER — hazy reddish amber-gold, creamy with small bubbles, fairly tight head, bright hop aroma, well-hopped malt flavor, long dry spicy hop aftertaste; very good with food. This is an ESB red ale brewed with British crystal malt and Cascade and Centennial hops; gravity 12.5 P, 4.8% abw. [A, 64]

MURPHY'S GOLDEN WHEAT BEER — hazy amber-gold, big tight head, zesty tangy hop and spice aroma; light spicy hop flavor has a little bite; light to medium body, dry hop aftertaste, refreshing but brief; made with 50% white winter wheat; hopped with Centennial hops; specific gravity 11.3, 3.1% abw. [W, 66]

RASPBERRY REDRUM — hazy copper-red; fruity-berry nose has a back tartness; tart lactic acid flavor has a berry-cherry backing; not complex; has an astringent aftertaste; there is a refreshing quality but it is not balanced and not attractive; made with wheat and barley malt, an ale top-fermented with raspberries and cherries. [W, 37]

Napa Valley Brewing Co.
Brewpub and restaurant in Calistoga, CA

CALISTOGA RED ALE — amber, dry malt nose, dry hop flavor, good balance, smooth, dry hop finish and aftertaste; made with crystal malt and three hop varieties; specific gravity 1.056, 4.1% abw. [A, 63]

CALISTOGA GOLDEN LAGER — gold, hop aroma, malt flavor, smooth, light but balanced, dry hop and malt finish and aftertaste, a bit short. Brewed and dry hopped with Tettnanger hops; specific gravity 1.049, 3.6% abw. [B, 62]

CALISTOGA WHEAT ALE — gold, malt nose, American-style malt and wheat flavor (no spiciness), brief aftertaste; specific gravity 1.050, 4% abw. [W, 42]

CALISTOGA PALE ALE — amber; big malt and hop nose that is a little soapy; bright hop and malt flavor, smooth and balanced, very drinkable; flavor finishes nicely leading into a long dry hop and malt aftertaste; made with caramel malt, five hops, and dry hopped with Cascades; specific gravity 1.056, 4.2% abw. [A, 67]

Napa Valley Ale Works
Microbrewery in Napa, CA

NAPA VALLEY ALE WORKS RED ALE — a really red amber color, very pretty, pleasant northwest hop and malt nose, very ale-like, good rich and complex well-hopped flavor, very drinkable and very good; finishes dry hops and has a long dry hop aftertaste; very big and rich and very well balanced. [A, 83]

Notes

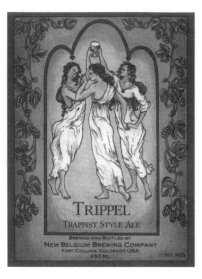

TRIPPEL
TRAPPIST STYLE ALE

BREWED AND BOTTLED BY
NEW BELGIUM BREWING COMPANY
FORT COLLINS, COLORADO USA
650 ML.

NAPA VALLEY ALE WORKS
WHEAT ALE — hazy gold,
foamy, big head, fine small bubble
carbonation; nice bright grainy
aroma has just the faintest trace of
lactic acid (which does not appear
in the taste); a very nice slightly
fruity palate is bright and tasty;
finishes off-dry malt, but as soon
as you swallow it is dry, and there
is a long dry aftertaste; nicely balanced and very good. [W, 70]

Neptune Brewery
*Microbrewery in
Manhattan's Chelsea
District, New York City*

NEPTUNE U PREMIUM ALE —
hazy amber, toasted malt and
flowery hop aroma; complex taste
shows a variety of hops including
some Fuggles up front, some
fruitiness in back; dry hop finish
and aftertaste. [A, 53]

NEPTUNE 66 PREMIUM ALE —
hazy amber-gold, northwest hop

aroma; flavor is just like the nose
with plenty of good northwest hops
and malt, a little chocolate character; hops fade a bit in the middle but
regain strength at the finish; medium body, very tasty, long, and
drinkable. [A, 79]

Nevada City Brewing Co.
*Brewery in
Nevada City, CA*

NEVADA CITY CALIFORNIA
LAGER GOLD — deep gold,
bright hop nose, big hop flavor with
plenty of malt backing, good body,
long dry hop aftertaste, smooth and
very well balanced. [B, 65]

NEVADA CITY CALIFORNIA
DARK LAGER — deep amber, big
malt nose, very big malt flavor, big
body, long aftertaste. [B, 61]

New Belgium Brewing Co.
*Microbrewery in
Fort Collins, CO*

SUNSHINE WHEAT BEER —
hazy gold; complex nose has ginger, orange, nutmeg, and spruce;
light body, very complex ginger-
allspice flavor, light body; long
dry spicy aftertaste retains the
complexity; not especially dry;
spiced with coriander and orange
peel; specific gravity 1.048. 4.2%
abw. [W, 58]

FAT TIRE AMBER ALE —
amber, lovely appetizing hop nose
(Cascade hops); flavor is nutty

malt but is very light, and it finishes weakly; specific gravity
1.049. 4.2% abw. [A, 53]

OLD CHERRY ALE — peachy-
amber; aroma is faintly of cherries; front of the palate is tart
cherries, middle is bright malt,
finish is again the cherry tartness
with a hint of cinnamon in there as
well; body is good, balance is
shaky. The cherry tartness builds
as you continue to sip. A very interesting beer; specific gravity
1.058, 5% abw. [A, 52]

ABBEY TRAPPISTE STYLE
ALE — brown, complex alcoholic
malt aroma, big rich alcoholic
malt flavor with a lactic background, huge mouth-filling brew;
hops jump out at the finish and
balance the malt in the long dry
aftertaste; a superior brew that is
absolutely true to style; specific
gravity 1.064, 5.5% abw. [A, 80]

TRIPPEL TRAPPISTE STYLE
ALE — pale amber-gold, big hop
nose and bigger hop flavor; smooth
despite the hoppiness because there
is more than enough malt for good
balance; dry finish and aftertaste;
made with Saaz hops; specific gravity 1.073, 6.8% abw. [A, 56]

FRAMBOZEN RASPBERRY
BROWN ALE — amber; fruity
raspberry nose is a bit tart;
refreshing dry and tart raspberry
flavor, medium body, brief dry
raspberry aftertaste. [A, 57]

New England Brewing Co.
Brewery in Norwalk, CT

NEW ENGLAND ATLANTIC AMBER ALE — amber, good hop aroma, complex hop palate with plenty of malt in back, medium dry hop finish, long dry hop aftertaste, lots of character and excellent balance. Brewed with English two-row and crystal malts, Cascade, and Northern Brewer hops; done with a lager yeast in the American "steam-style"; gravity 12 P, 4.8% abw. [A, 73]

NEW ENGLAND GOLD STOCK ALE — deep golden color, great complex hop and malt nose with faint citrus in the background, big body, big hops but also plenty of malt for a great balanced brew, noticeable tannin from the beechwood aging, complex and very long rich hop and malt aftertaste, a fine big brew worth trying. Made from domestic two-row pale malt and a combination of Perle, Tettnanger, Hallertau, Cascade and Hersbrucker hops; dry hopped and aged with beechwood chips; gravity 15 P, 6.2% abw. [A, 72]

NEW ENGLAND HOLIDAY ALE — deep amber, spicy gingerbread nose, big ginger and malt flavor, off-dry; the good ale flavor comes out from behind the spices at the finish and holds well through a long aftertaste; spiced with cinnamon, nutmeg, and ginger (vanilla bean, cardamom, and other spices have been used in earlier years); gravity 13.4 P, 5% abw. [1993 A, 46]

NEW ENGLAND OATMEAL STOUT — deep brown, beautiful nose of roasted barley, big dry roasted malt flavor, like a coffee, richly flavored, long smooth dry malt aftertaste, very drinkable. Eight malts and oatmeal are used; gravity 13.5 P, 5.2% abw. [S, 71]

NEW ENGLAND LIGHT LAGER — hazy gold, big malt aroma, hops are there as well but in back; big malty flavor, medium body, good tasting long dry malt aftertaste. Made in a Munich-style with American two-row malt and Hallertau hops; gravity 8.5 P, 3.3% abw. [LO, 49]

New Glarus Brewing Co.
Microbrewery in New Glarus, WI

NEW GLARUS EDEL PILS — gold, bright hop nose; good flavor shows hops and malt; medium body, dry hop finish and aftertaste; gravity 11.5 P, 3.75% abw. [B, 61]

NEW GLARUS SOLSTICE WEISS — hazy gold, spicy aroma, bright fruity malt and clove spice flavor, medium to good body; dry hop finish and aftertaste shows the spice; gravity 12.0 P, 4% abw. [W, 58]

Notes

STAGHORN OCTOBERFEST — amber, malt aroma, big bright malty flavor, big body, hefty complex spicy fruity malt aftertaste, a good classical Oktoberfest brew; gravity 14.0 P, 4.5% abw. [B, 72]

UFF-DA WISCONSIN BOCK BEER — amber-brown, big malty aroma; strong malty flavor shows coffee and chocolate tones and some alcohol; big body, off-dry rich malt finish and aftertaste, long and good; gravity 16.5 P. [B, 86]

NEW GLARUS ZWICKEL — gold, dry hop aroma and flavor, light body, dry hop finish and aftertaste; gravity 11.0 P, 4% abw. [B, 57]

New Haven Brewing Co.
Brewery in New Haven, CT

BLACKWELL STOUT — deep amber, rich chocolate malt nose, light toasted chocolate malt flavor, light body, very drinkable, malt finish, medium length malt aftertaste. [S, 67]

ELM CITY GOLDEN ALE — clear gold, pleasant malt and hop aroma; flavor is malt with hops in back; dry hop finish, long dry hop aftertaste. [A, 50]

ELM CITY CONNECTICUT ALE — pale amber, fragrant malt and hop aroma, light dry malt flavor with some caramel hiding in back, dry malt finish, medium long dry hop and malt aftertaste. [A, 62]

HOBOKEN SPECIAL RESERVE ALE — gold, clean and big malt nose, big malt flavor, good body; hops show well in the finish; long dry hop aftertaste, tasty brew. Made for Gold Coast Brewery of Hoboken, NJ. [A, 64]

MR. MIKE'S LIGHT ALE — gold, fresh malt nose, light body, light malt flavor; you can feel the high carbonation; brief malt aftertaste, very quaffable. [LO, 31]

BELLE DOCK BARLEYWINE STYLE ALE — amber, big perfumy English-style malt and hop nose, delicious clean toasted malt and northwest hop flavor, big mouthfeel, bold taste, hefty body, alcoholic, excellent balance, very long and complex; aftertaste gets drier as it goes; a marvelous brew. [BW, 94]

ELM CITY DRAUGHT CONNECTICUT ALE — pale hazy amber, rich malt aroma, dull malt flavor, medium body, dull dry malt finish and aftertaste, very long duration. [A, 45]

NEW HAVEN IMPERIAL STOUT — opaque brown, big aroma of complex roasted barley and chocolate malt and hops, huge rich roasted malt flavor; more rich than sweet but it is a bit off-dry; big body, very balanced, very long with a trend toward increasing dryness over that long long aftertaste. [S, 93]

Newport Beach Brewing Co.
Brewpub in Newport Beach, CA, an affiliate of Laguna Beach B.C.

NEWPORT BEACH BLONDE — very pale gold, highly carbonated, light malt and hop nose, bright dry hop flavor, medium body, very dry hop finish and aftertaste; Munich-style pilsener made with noble hops; OG 1046. Started at Laguna Beach B.C., finished at Newport Beach B.C. [A, 55]

BALBOA BROWN — fairly deep amber, light malt aroma, good big flavor with malt (possibly some crystal malt) and light hops (possibly Goldings), medium body; hops are not aggressive; dry hop finish and aftertaste. Started at Laguna Beach B.C., finished at Newport Beach B.C. [A, 55]

PELICAN PALE ALE — deep gold, malt and hop aroma, good balanced malt and hop flavor, good balance, good body, dry hop finish and aftertaste; bittered with Galena hops and finished with Cascades (but not obviously so since I could not detect them); made with Carastan malt; OG 1060. Started at Laguna Beach B.C., finished at Newport Beach B.C. [A, 72]

BISBEE'S ESB — amber-gold, complex hop nose identifiable as Kent Goldings (dry hopped), bright bitter dry hop flavor, good body, dry hop finish; long dry hop aftertaste shows plenty of the Goldings; OG 1052. Started at

Laguna Beach B.C., finished at Newport Beach B.C. [A, 69]

BREWHOUND RED ALE — amber, pleasant well-malted aroma, smooth big malty flavor, good body, long dry hop aftertaste, well-made balanced American red ale; OG 1064. Started at Laguna Beach B.C., finished at Newport Beach B.C. [A, 74]

BISBEE'S ESB II — amber, dry malt and hop aroma; dry malty flavor has a hop and fruity ester background; medium body, dry hop finish and aftertaste. Now completely brewed at the pub. [A, 59]

THE WEDGE WEIZEN — cloudy amber-gold; malt aroma shows a trace of clove and banana; light body, good cross between American and traditional German-style weizen; nicely done but a bit brief on the palate, still it is a nice taste and should be popular at the pub. Now completely brewed at the pub. [W, 70]

HOLIDAY BELGIAN TRIPLE ALE — cloudy deep amber-gold, light estery nose, big estery malt flavor, big body; alcohol shows but is not obtrusive; creamy mouthfeel, rich and long malty aftertaste, good rendition of the style. Now completely brewed at the pub. [A, 70]

NEWPORTFEST BIER — amber, malt aroma, big malty flavor, plenty of hops in back, medium body, good balance, good hop presence, long and tasty, made with altbier yeast and Hallertau hops; the brewmaster Julius Hum-mer intends to use Saaz hops next time to give it more of an east European style. Now completely brewed at the pub. [B, 63]

NEWPORT BEACH BLONDE — pale gold, bright malt and hop aroma; hefty malt flavor is smooth and delicious; medium body, fairly long dry malt and hop aftertaste. Now completely brewed at the pub. [B, 63]

NEWPORT BEACH IPA — amber; balanced hop and malt aroma has real character; very bright and tasty hop palate, medium body, dry hop finish and aftertaste; an absolutely delicious brew that is the best yet from this brewery, it is not to be missed, probably well within the top 100 American brews made today. Brewed at the pub. [A, 89]

North Coast Brewing Co.
Brewery and brewpub in Fort Bragg, CA

RUEDRICH'S RED SEAL ALE — hazy amber, good malt nose, lightly smoked zesty malt palate, medium body, dry hop finish, long dry hop aftertaste. Later samples were more highly hopped and had more of a citrus back taste. Made with two-row and caramel malts, Cluster and Centennial hops; gravity 13.75 P, 4.2% abw. [A, 61]

Notes

CHRISTMAS ALE 1989 — hazy deep amber, light toasted malt aroma, light toasted smoky malt flavor, dry finish and aftertaste like the flavor; seems like there is just too much toast and it masks the rest of the flavors. [A, 29]

CHRISTMAS ALE 1990 — hazy amber, lovely huge toasted malt nose, with a fruity-ale tang, big taste just like the nose, big malt finish; long aftertaste like you had been chewing on malt; very flavorful, subtle hop presence throughout. [A, 94]

CHRISTMAS ALE 1991 — deep amber, rich roasted chocolate malt nose, creamy dry chocolate malt flavor, good body, chewy, good complexity; long dry malt aftertaste has hops in back. [A, 80]

CHRISTMAS ALE 1992 — amber, light dry hop aroma with some faint chocolate malt background; dry hop flavor shows none of the malt promised by the aroma; lacks the mouthfeel of the 1991, some faint off-dry malt in back in the aftertaste. [A, 59]

CHRISTMAS ALE 1993 — amber, malt nose with a yeasty background, big malt flavor, strongly alcoholic, but not complex, finishes dry, long dry malt aftertaste. This wheat beer is just straightforward malt. [A, 52]

CHRISTMAS ALE 1994 — dark hazy amber, well-hopped northwest hop aroma, huge assertive hop palate, strong and rich with a citruslike style, huge body; powerful flavor is

balanced with plenty of malt; long, strong, and smooth; this is their best effort to date. [A, 93]

CHRISTMAS ALE 1995 — hazy amber, toasted malt aroma, complex and refreshing toasted malt flavor, touch of alcohol on the palate, tastes just like the nose, long nutty aftertaste; goes down very smoothly; seems a little softer than last year's. [A, 73]

SCRIMSHAW PILSENER STYLE BEER — hazy gold, complex aroma with malt, chocolate, tobacco, etc.; off-dry complex malt flavor with grapefruit, cherry pits, tobacco, and chocolate; smooth and mellow, good long dry malt aftertaste. Made of two-row and Munich malts, Hallertau and Tettnanger hops from Yakima; gravity 11.25 P, 3.6% abw. [B, 76]

SUMMER ALE 1990 — hazy amber-gold, fruity malt aroma, big hop and fruity-malt palate, very good balance, touch of sour hops at the finish, long malt aftertaste. [A, 73]

OKTOBERFEST ALE — hazy amber, complex fruity hop California ale nose, big toasted malt flavor, hop finish, long hop and malt aftertaste, complex, balanced, and drinkable; gravity 13.75 P, 4.4% abw. [A, 65]

OLD No. 38 STOUT — deep ruby color, chocolate malt nose; roasted chocolate malt flavor is slightly burnt; good body, long burnt malt/ smoky aftertaste, still very palatable despite the over roasting of the malt. Roasted malts, two-row,

and caramel malts are used with Cluster hops for bittering; gravity 14 P, 5% abw. [S, 67]

TRADITIONAL BOCK — hazy amber, big malt nose; flavor starts out big and malty, finishes with dry hops; long dry malt aftertaste; has complexity, balance, and body; an autumn beer; gravity 16.5 P, 5.3% abw. [BK, 92]

CENTENNIAL 100 ALE — amber-gold, chocolate-Ovaltine malt nose, big malt flavor, big body, smooth, dry malt finish and long dry malt aftertaste; gravity 16.5 P, 5.3% abw. [A, 76]

ALT NOUVEAU — deep gold, bright hop aroma, smooth and zesty hop and malt flavor, medium body; delicious long dry hop and malt aftertaste holds on to the character of the flavor for quite some time; 4% abw. [A, 74]

BLUE STAR WHEAT BEER — hazy gold, clean grainy malt nose; bright fruity palate has a tangy front; sour malt finish and aftertaste, medium body. [W, 43]

Nor'wester Brewery & Public House / Willamette Valley B.C.
Microbrewery and brewpub in Portland, OR, originally and still called Willamette Valley B.C. on some labels.

NOR'WESTER BEST BITTER ALE — pale gold, hop aroma, big complex dry hop flavor, medium body, dry hop finish and aftertaste; specific gravity 1.054, 3.9% abw. [A, 61]

NOR'WESTER DUNKEL WEIZEN ALE — hazy amber-brown, malt nose; dry roasted malt flavor has some chocolate malt but no spice; medium body; dry roasted malt finish and aftertaste is almost burnt; a dark hefe-weizen, top-fermented; made with two kinds of roasted malts added to the wheat malt grist; specific gravity 1.050, 3.8% abw. [W, 60]

NOR'WESTER HEFE-WEIZEN ALE — pale hazy gold; light bright hop aroma shows no spiciness; zesty hop and wheat malt flavor, light body, dry hop and malt finish and aftertaste, not long; made with 55% wheat malt grist; an American-style weizen with no spiciness, but plenty of bittering hops, pleasant and refreshing; specific gravity 1.048, 3.6% abw. [W, 67]

NOR'WESTER RASPBERRY WEIZEN — cloudy amber-gold, raspberry aroma; clean crisp raspberry flavor goes dry at mid-palate; light body, very dry wheat-malt finish and aftertaste shows no berry whatever; seems to be the hefe-weizen with added raspberries; specific gravity 1.048, 3.6% abw. [W, 60]

NOR'WESTER BLACKSMITH PORTER — dark brown, deep brown-colored head; roasted malt aroma has definitely coffee-like tones and shows northwest hops; bright well-hopped roasted malt flavor is a delightful creamy coffee

style and shows little hop character; medium body, balanced; long dry malty aftertaste shows roasty character and lots of tasty coffee; a delicious after dinner beer made with two-row pale, wheat, Munich, Carapils, brown, and chocolate malts; hopped exclusively with Willamette hops. Never mind the Espresso, try this! [P, 60]

Norman Brewing Co.
Brewpub in Norman, OK

NORMAN DOWNTOWN BROWN — deep amber, dry malty aroma and flavor, medium to good body, off-dry malt finish and aftertaste; made with Victory and roasted malts. [A, 59]

HARVESTER WHEAT — gold, light hop aroma, light crisp hop flavor, bright and refreshing, light bodied, light dry hop finish and aftertaste; made with 65% two-row domestic barley malt and 35% red winter wheat. [W, 53]

RAILYARD AMBER ALE — amber, malt aroma and taste, good body, dry hop finish and aftertaste shows Hallertau and Tettnanger hops giving a distinct European character. [A, 60]

SOONER STOUT — brown, roasted malt aroma, flavored like the nose, medium to good body; dry malt finish and aftertaste makes you think of coffee; made with roasted barley and black malts. [S, 57]

Notes

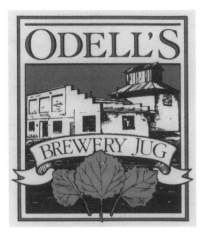

Northampton Brewery

Brewpub in Northampton, MA. Affiliated with and shares a brewmaster with The Portsmouth Brewery of New Hampshire.

GOLDEN — gold, malt aroma at first, then hops; palate is sweet malt in front, hop middle, dry malt and hop finish; off-dry hop aftertaste, complex, good body, good length interesting. [A, 61]

AMBER — amber, bright hop nose, hop palate with a hop background, medium dry hop finish and aftertaste. [A, 53]

DANIEL SHAY'S BEST BITTER — hazy amber, big hop nose, zesty spicy hop flavor, dry hop finish, long dry spicy hop aftertaste. [A, 62]

BROWN DOG — deep amber-brown, hop nose, dry hop flavor with plenty of malt in the middle, smooth dry hop finish, long dry aftertaste, a porter-style brew. [A, 65]

MAGGIE'S WEE HEAVY — deep amber, lovely bright hop and malt aroma, some alcohol showing, big flavor, big body, delicious, long complex malt and hop aftertaste, a very good Scotch ale. [BW, 78]

NORTHAMPTON SPRING BOCK — deep brown, aroma of malt and hops; good malty flavor has plenty of supporting hops, dry hop and malt finish; fairly long dry aftertaste retains all of the malt and hops of the flavor; specific gravity 1.067. [B, 58]

BLACK CAT STOUT — black, chocolate malt and roasted barley aroma and taste, light body for a stout; flavor is good classical stout but not big, still it is smooth and tasty; fairly long roasted malt aftertaste. [S, 59]

O'Fallon Brewing Co.

Brewpub in O'Fallon, IL

NUMBSKULL AMBER LAGER — golden amber, malt aroma; malt flavor has some faint lactic acid in back behind the hops; dry malt and hop finish and aftertaste; made with Hersbrucker hops; gravity 14 P, 4.3% abw. [B, 61]

HORST'S OKTOBERFEST — amber; hop nose and flavor has a lactic background; dry hop finish and aftertaste follow from the flavor; gravity 14 P, 4.7% abw. [B, 27]

Oaken Barrel Brewing Co.

Microbrewery in Greenwood, IN

SNAKE PIT PORTER — brown, very malty nose, nice dry malt palate, some vegetal character in the finish and aftertaste, medium body, long dry complex malt aftertaste. [P, 66]

RAZZ-WHEAT — pinkish amber, big raspberry aroma, smooth light raspberry flavor, light body, medium dry raspberry malt finish and aftertaste, quite short. [W, 47]

Oasis Brewery

Brewpub in Boulder, CO

OASIS OKTOBERFEST — deep amber, no discernible nose, touch of malty sweetness on the front and middle of the palate, finish is dry malt; lightly hopped dry malt aftertaste disappears abruptly. [B, 48]

TUT BROWN ALE — deep ruby amber-brown, beautiful northwest citrus-hop aroma; roasted malt flavor is somewhat nutty; smooth and refreshing; hops are there but stay in back; good body; great complexity appearing sometimes to be off-dry and other times to be crisp and dry, constantly changing on the palate; finish and aftertaste are a continuation of the big bright flavor but more dry; gravity 14 P, 4% abw. [A, 35]

ZOSER OATMEAL STOUT — black, roasted barley and rich malt and faintly chocolate malt nose, big body; hops start off the flavor but rich malt quickly joins in like the aroma; plenty of both malt and hops, quite zesty, good balance, dry malt finish and aftertaste, enjoyable stout; made with Centennial hops; gravity 14 P, 3.75% abw. [S, 90]

CAPSTONE ESB ALE — deep orange-amber, big complex northwestern hop nose; big hop flavor (there is plenty of malt but even more bittering hops); very assertive, big body, creamy texture, strong and complex; dry hop finish, and a dry hop aftertaste that has a sharply bitter ending; gravity 14 P, 4.5% abw. [A, 51–80]

OASIS PALE ALE — deep gold, light dry malt and hop aroma with a citrus and faint butterscotch background, rich roasted malt flavor, medium body, rich malt and dry hop aftertaste, quite long and good; gravity 12.5, 4% abw. [A, 73]

SCARAB RED ALE — cloudy amber-gold; toasted honeyed malt nose, some aromatic hops there as well; complex roasted malt flavor, slightly scorched and with some chocolate malt, good body, smooth on the palate, finish is very slightly sweet; flavor continues into a long, drier aftertaste. [A, 80]

OASIS BLUEBERRY ALE — hazy amber; malty aroma has a fruity tone but it is hard to tell it is blueberry until tasted; the flavor is strange but clearly blueberry (blueberry is not an easy fruit to brew); dry hop aftertaste has the blueberry flavor in back; gravity 13.3 P. [B, 45]

Ocean Avenue Brewery
Brewpub in Laguna Beach, CA

MUDDY WATER ALE — amber, bright malty aroma and flavor, medium body, assertive somewhat sweet flavor, stays off-dry into the finish and aftertaste; driest at the end but never is really dry. [A, 51]

HONEY WHEAT ALE — gold, faint barley-wheat malt aroma; medium dry barley-wheat malt flavor is honeyed, light and refreshing without complexity; medium long aftertaste is driest. [W, 62]

RED SUNSHINE ALE — red-amber, faint malt aroma, light dry malty flavor, medium body; malt finish and aftertaste is a bit sweet on the end, hops never really come to the fore; medium long, an Irish-style brew. [A, 51]

OCEAN AVE DOPPELBOCK — deep brown, faint malt nose; malty flavor has an off-dry caramel richness; little complexity, dry malt finish and aftertaste, not long, an unfiltered beer. [BK, 47]

O'Dell Brewing Co.
Microbrewery in Fort Collins, CO

90 SHILLING ALE — amber, bright complex hop aroma; big malt flavor stays dry and is well backed with hops; nicely

balanced, very pleasant drinkable beer, long dry malt and hop aftertaste, excellent with food; brewed with two-row English, crystal, and Vienna malts and Northern Brewer and Cascade hops; OG 1055, 4.2% abw. [A, 70]

HEARTLAND WHEAT — gold, bright fresh malt nose and flavor, lightly hopped, long dry malt aftertaste, an American-style wheat beer. This brew was called Wheatland Wheat at the brewery made with 50% wheat malt and finished with Saaz hops. [W, 50]

OLD TOWN ALE — amber, bright complex malt and hop nose, smooth balanced mostly malty flavor, good hop backing, long dry aftertaste. [A, 57]

O'DELL'S GOLDEN ALE — amber-gold, bright dry malt flavor, lightly hopped, medium to light body, cuts off quickly, dry malt finish and aftertaste; Willamette hops; gravity 12 P, 4% abw. [A, 43]

EASY STREET WHEAT — hazy gold, grainy nose, light grainy flavor, light body, a little banana in the light brief malt aftertaste; OG 1044, 3.8% abw. [W, 50]

ODELL'S SPECIAL BITTER — gold, hop aroma and dry hop flavor, medium body, short dry hop aftertaste. The malts are amber and crystal, the hops are British with Kent-Goldings for finishing. [A, 43]

CUTTHROAT PORTER — brown color, roasted malt aroma, big roasted malt flavor, full bodied, fairly rich tasting, dry hop

finish, short dry hop and malt aftertaste. Brewed with roasted malt and caramalt, finished with English Kent hops; OG 1053, 4.1% abw. [P, 68]

Old Baldy Brewing Co.
Brewpub in Upland, CA

OLD BALDY BLONDE ALE — deep gold, faint malt and hop nose, bright hoppy flavor, good taste, medium to good body, dry hop finish and aftertaste shows some malt; made with two-row pale, Munich, and wheat malt, with Northern Brewer and Cascade hops; OG 1048, 3.8% abw. [A, 61]

OLD BALDY BROWN ALE — deep amber, faint caramel and roasted malt nose; complex flavor shows caramel, roasted, and slightly burnt tones; good body, medium carbonation, smooth and malty although complex, balanced and likable, caramel malt finish and aftertaste; made from pale two-row, caramel, crystal (30–37 Lovibond and 70–80 Lovibond), and chocolate malt, with Northern Brewer and Liberty hops; OG 1060, 5% abw. [A, 70]

OLD BALDY DRY STOUT — deep brown, roasted and chocolate malt aroma with a slightly grassy background; dry smooth malt flavor has a touch of roasted character and no bitterness; dry and smooth, nothing mean about it, some residual sweetness in the long aftertaste; made with two-row pale, crystal 30–37 Lovibond, roasted barley, black patent, and English Carapils malt, Kent-

Goldings, Cascade and Fuggles hops; OG 1052, 4.2% abw. [S, 68]

OLD BALDY WINTER SPICE — amber, very complex spicy-gingery aroma, complex spicy flavor, medium body, dry spicy finish and aftertaste; made with 511 lbs. of two-row pale, 13–17 Lovibond crystal, 30–37 Lovibond crystal, 70–80 Lovibond crystal, and chocolate malt with added ginger, allspice, nutmeg, cinnamon, and vanilla bean, Northern Brewer, Willamette, and Cascade hops; made with a five-step hopping; unfiltered; OG 1065, 7% abw. [A, 40]

OLD BALDY PEACH ALE — gold, light peachy nose and taste, off-dry fruity and clean, peach aftertaste is a bit off-dry and fairly long; made with peach syrup added to the Blonde Ale as a base; specs like the Blonde Ale. [A, 43]

OLD BALDY RASPBERRY ALE — gold, raspberry nose and taste, clean and refreshing; made by adding raspberry fruit concentrate to the Blonde Ale base; specs like the Blonde Ale. [A, 59]

Old Dominion Brewing Co.
Microbrewery in Ashburn, VA

DOMINION LAGER — gold, pleasant malt and hop aroma and flavor; some esters give it a fruity quality balanced with flowery hops; highly carbonated, good body, dry malt finish and long dry malt aftertaste has good hop support in back; made with two-row pale, Munich, Carapils, and caramel malt with Cluster, Yakima, Hallertau, Czech Saaz, Tettnanger, and Hallertau Hersbrucker hops; gravity 13.7 P, 3.9% abw. [B, 47]

DOMINION STOUT — deep amber-brown, dry hop and chocolate malt aroma, dry chocolate malt flavor; there is very little roasted character; good body, smooth dry chocolate malt finish, tasty and drinkable, and medium long dry malt aftertaste. Made with two-row pale, Carapils, caramel, and chocolate malts, roasted barley, and wheat, using Cluster and Willamette hops; gravity 13.7 P, 3.9% abw. [S, 63]

DOMINION ALE — amber-gold, dry hop and fruity malt aroma; big bright flavor starts out with malt; hops emerge at mid-palate; good body, flowery-spicy hops at the finish and aftertaste, a good complex brew that tastes like "more." In general, samples tasted on draft have been much better than bottled versions, but this description is from a bottle. Made with two-row pale, Munich, Carapils, caramel, black patent malts, Cluster, Kent-Goldings, and Willamette hops; gravity 12.5 P, 3.8% abw. [A, 74]

DOMINION BLUE POINT ALE — amber, lovely bright hop aroma, big bright hop flavor, good body, dry hop finish, long dry hop aftertaste; feels very good in your mouth; good carbonation level enhances effect. [A, 62]

HARD TIMES SELECT — gold, malt nose and taste; has some complexity; the hops stay in the background but provide enough character for interest and balance; long fairly dry malt and hop aftertaste. Made with two-row pale, Munich, caramel-40, malts, and Cluster, Yakima Hallertau, and Hersbrucker hops; gravity 13.7 P, 4.7% abw. [B, 72]

ST. GEORGE BEER — pale gold, light fruity malt and hop aroma, highly carbonated, good body, good mouthfeel; big hop flavor fades a bit at the finish; long dry hop aftertaste. As it gets older, it takes on a toasted malt character. Made for ADK productions, Inc., Ethiopia. [B, 67]

DOMINION HOLIDAY ALE — brilliant amber, light citrus malt and hop aroma, big bright dry malt and hop flavor, good body; seems a bit spicy but it is only from the hops; strong dry bitter hop finish, long dry austere hop aftertaste. Made with increased malt quantity over their regular ale, using American two-row pale, Munich, and caramel malts, Washington State Perles and German Hallertau Hersbrucker hops in the brew kettle; dry hopped with Kent-Goldings and Cascade hops. [A, 64]

DOMINION SPRING BOCK — deep gold, tight European-style head, pleasant floral fruity malt aroma; flavor starts out big and sweet, goes to dry malt in the middle and finishes that way; medium to good body, long dry malt aftertaste, decoction; uses Perle, Mt. Hood, Hersbrucker, and Liberty hops; specific gravity 1.070, 7.4% abw. [BK, 47]

DOMINION OCTOBERFEST — deep gold, complex hop nose, big hop and malt flavor, buttery finish, dry malt aftertaste. Decoction brewed with two-row pale, U.S. Munich, Belgian Caravienna, and Munich malts and Hallertau Hersbrucker, Liberty and Czech Saaz hops; specific gravity 1.055, 5.8% abw. [B, 67]

AVIATOR LAGER BEER — bright gold; smooth hop aroma is a Dortmunder style; very smooth hop flavor with good malt backing, good body, very enjoyable, dry hop finish and long dry hop aftertaste. Made for McGarvey's in Annapolis, MD. [BK, 67]

TUPPERS HOP POCKET ALE — hazy amber-gold; light citrus hop nose shows the Cascade and Mt. Hood hops; big strong hop flavor; creamy texture and fine carbonation makes for a good mouthfeel; good body, dry hop finish, long dry hop aftertaste, a big attractive mouthful of a beer. Made for Tuppers restaurant. [A, 81]

DOMINION MILLENIUM — orange-amber; complex fruity-berry-hop nose also seems to show a touch of orange; big alcohol, hop, and concentrated malt flavor again with a trace of orange; huge body; big finish, winds down very gradually and lasts and lasts; great complexity; must be a barleywine although this is not stated on the label. [BW, 93]

Old Harbor Brewing Co.
Microbrewery in Ipswich, MA

PILGRIM ALE — deep amber, bright lightly roasted malt nose; big sprightly malt flavor has a richness; good mouthfeel, dry roasted malt finish and big rich aftertaste, balanced and complex, lots of malt, very good and very tasty, and very long on the palate. [A, 85]

HARBOR LIGHT ALE — hazy gold, fruity malt aroma, flavor of fruity malt, flowery hops, and yeast; sweetness at mid-palate, but it ends dry, not long; needs a little more bite for balance; also there is a little metallic flavor in the aftertaste. [A, 41]

PILGRIM CREAM ALE — hazy gold, grainy aroma, grainy malt flavor, medium body, dry malty finish and aftertaste, good length. [A, 50]

PILGRIM ESB — amber, dry hop aroma, dry hop flavor, finish, and aftertaste, quite long on the palate. [A, 49]

LARRY'S BEST BITTER FESTIVE ALE — hazy amber, bright complex malt and hop aroma; big complex hop flavor shows Chinook, Centennial, and Cascade hops; medium body (OG 1048), very tasty, long complex dry hop aftertaste. [A, 78]

TRAIL BOSS ESB — hazy amber, light hop aroma, light dry hop flavor, medium body, long dry hop finish and aftertaste, a pleasant drinkable brew with plenty of malt. Made for the Eagle Brook Saloon of Norfolk, MA. [A, 80]

DOG'S BREATH BITTER — hazy amber, hop aroma, assertive hop palate, medium body, dry hop finish and aftertaste; a bit too assertive such that it is harshly bitter. Made for the Eagle Brook Saloon of Norfolk, MA. Tasted at the Eagle Brook, but is also bottled. [A, 60]

DOG POUND PORTER — deep brown, no discernible aroma; chocolate and toasted malt flavor lacks complexity; medium body, dry malt finish and aftertaste; has the flavor of a stout with the body of a porter. Made for the Eagle Brook Saloon of Norfolk, MA. [P, 53]

LONE PINE LAGER — hazy amber-gold; pleasant malt and hop aroma is a bit sweet; off-dry malt flavor, good mouthfeel, medium body; finish and aftertaste continue the sweet malt character; good long aftertaste, doesn't even approach dryness until the end. Made for the Eagle Brook Saloon of Norfolk, MA. [B, 50]

BAGGY KNEE'S LIGHT — hazy gold, sweet malt aroma, flavor, and finish, light body, long dry hop finish and aftertaste; lacks complexity and depth. Made for the Eagle Brook Saloon of Norfolk, MA. [A, 43]

OLD BOOTS DARK — deep amber, light hop aroma and flavor, medium body, very dry hop finish and aftertaste, long dry and well hopped with plenty of supporting malt for balance. Made for the Eagle Brook Saloon of Norfolk, MA. [A, 53]

BLUEBERRY ALE — hazy gold, big blueberry aroma, off-dry malt and berry flavor, medium body; finish and aftertaste are distinctly dominated by the blueberry taste. Made for the Eagle Brook Saloon of Norfolk, MA. [A, 47]

PAINTED PONY PALE ALE — amber-gold, light hop aroma, delicious well-hopped flavor, medium to good body, dry hop finish and excellent dry hop aftertaste, very tasty and smooth right to the end. Made for the Eagle Brook Saloon of Norfolk, MA. [A, 82]

KING PHILIP AMERICAN ALE — dark amber, big rich malty nose, rich malt flavor, full body; hops appear at the finish; slightly dry malt and hop aftertaste; the dryness lasts and lasts; solid dark ale. Made for the Eagle Brook Saloon of Norfolk, MA. [A, 72]

FT. DEVENS BEER — gold, rotting vegetation and slightly skunky nose, hop and sweet veggie malt flavor, medium to light body, light slightly sweet vegetal malt aftertaste, probably a spoiled sample. [B, 24]

The Old Market Pub & Brewery
Brewpub in Portland, OR

MR. TOAD'S WILD RED ALE — cloudy amber (like homemade cider), rich malty nose, bright rich tangy malt flavor, tasty

and complex, very interesting; off-dry malt finish and aftertaste, keeps its tangy quality to the end; a little homebrew-like, but good; made from two-row pale and white wheat malts plus three types of roasted malts; hopped with Cascades for a northwest character; OG 1057, FG 1.012, and 5.8% abv. [A, 59]

Old West Brewery
Brewpub/Microbrewery in the Mesilla section of Las Cruces, NM

SANTA FE ALE — amber, lovely hop nose, big dry off-dry malt and hop flavor, pleasant and easy to drink, good body, long rich hop and off-dry malt aftertaste. [A, 60]

OLD WEST PALE ALE — pale gold, malt and Cascade hop nose, light malt and Cascade hop palate, light body; dry hop aftertaste gets drier as it goes. [A, 53]

AKELA ALE — gold; fruity estery aroma shows an applejack character; sweet fruity cidery palate; finishes a bit drier, but medium long aftertaste is off-dry hard apple cider. [A, 47]

IMPERIAL ALE — pinkish-gold, raspberry nose, raspberry taste, medium body; dry raspberry aftertaste shows some hops; fairly long. Fresh raspberries added during aging cause a secondary fermentation. [A, 47]

Notes

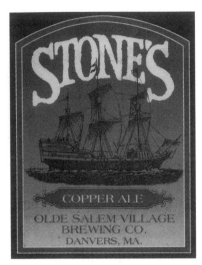

MESILLA GOLDEN ALE — amber-gold, fruity-estery nose hints at pineapple; fruity palate has a hop finish; medium body, aftertaste shows both fruity malt and dry hops. [A, 49]

OLD WEST MAIBOCK — deep amber, fruit and acetone nose; acetone dominates the flavor; some hops appear at the finish; in time the acetone fades from the long aftertaste but the dry hops linger. [B, 33]

OLD WEST PORTER — brown, soft malty nose, flavorful palate features dry rich lightly roasted malt, a bit of alcohol, and lusty hop bitterness, good body, long dry roasted malt aftertaste, a well-made very flavorful brew. [P, 60]

OLD WEST AMBER ALE — amber-gold, complex dry malt and hop nose, lightly fruity malt flavor, light to medium body, dry malt and hop aftertaste; 3.5% abw. [A, 53]

Olde Salem Village Brewing Co.
Microbrewery in Danvers, MA

STONE'S COPPER ALE — amber, malt and hop aroma, tangy ale-like flavor is bright and refreshing, stays complex, ends dry, long dry hop aftertaste, an altbier. [A, 59]

STONE'S CRIMSON ALE — pretty amber, lovely hop aroma; excellent bright hop flavor has good malt support; nicely balanced, dry hop finish and aftertaste, very pleasant drinking pale ale; made using a double decoction mash at 142°F and 158°F. [A, 71]

STONE'S BLONDE ALE — gold, malty aroma and flavor, fruity ester is in back; light body, dry malty finish and aftertaste is faintly sweet in back; intended to be a Belgian saison-style brew. [A, 51]

Note: These were tasted on draft. Several times I tasted these in bottles with bad results, the beers being spoiled and infected.

Oldenberg Brewing Co.
Brewery, restaurants, hotel, shops, entertainment and convention center in Ft. Mitchell, KY

OLDENBERG PREMIUM VERUM — tawny-gold, good dry hop and malt aroma; dry malt and hop flavor has some zest; good balance, some malty sweetness in the middle; has some complexity; pleasant malt finish with hops in back, medium dry long malt and hop aftertaste, a good beer by itself or with food. Brewed with two-row pale, black, and Munich malts; hopped with Cascade and Saaz hops; gravity 11.5 P (1046), 3.8% abw. [B, 57]

VAIL ALE — brilliant amber, citrus hop and malt aroma, good body, big malt flavor well backed with citrus and hop character; malt is first encountered with the hops coming in at the middle and staying on; smooth, good body, off-dry malt and hop finish and long aftertaste. Made with two-row pale and caramel malts; gravity 12.5 P, 4.2% abw. Made for Vail B.C., Vail, CO. [A, 47]

OLDENBERG BLONDE DRY LIGHT PILS — deep gold, bright malt aroma, complex dry malt flavor, off-dry malt in finish, medium length off-dry malt aftertaste; gravity 11 P, 3.5% abw. [B, 39]

OLDENBERG STOUT — opaque brown, dry roasted barley, chocolate malt, and hop aroma and flavor, lightly hopped, good body (but not big), dry almost coffee-like finish, long dry aftertaste like the flavor, satisfying substantial brew. [S, 59]

OLDENBERG WINTER ALE 1992 — amber-gold, tangy bright hop nose and taste, plenty of both hops and malt, zesty up front, smooth in the middle, big right to the end, long dry hop aftertaste. [A, 72]

OLDENBERG WINTER ALE 1993 — amber; light toasted malt nose seems to have some honeyed quality; flavor is light dry toasted malt, light to medium body; at the finish the flavor departs leaving only a dryness which lasts a long time. [A, 40]

McGUIRES IRISH OLD STYLE ALE — brilliant reddish-amber, pleasant light hop and malt aroma, light dry malt flavor with light hops in back, medium body, good balance, robust character, dry malt finish and medium length aftertaste. Made for McGuires B.C., Pensacola, FL, this brew uses two-row American malt with 10% caramel malt, hopped with Willamette hops; gravity 12 P, 3.6% abw. [A, 52]

LAS BRISAS CARIBBEAN STYLE BEER — hazy gold, sour malt aroma, light body, zesty hop and malt flavor; malt is a bit on the sour side but there is a balance of sorts achieved through the bitterness of the hops; good length. [B, 43]

OLDENBERG WEISS WHEAT BEER — gold, light but bright fruity wheat-malt nose with a very faint toastiness in back, pleasant light wheaty-malt flavor, light body, medium long malt aftertaste, pleasant but a bit too light flavored. Made with 60% malted wheat and six-row barley; Saaz and Cascade hops; OG 1042 (10 P), 3.0–3.2% abw. [W, 36]

PITTS ALL AMERICAN BEER — golden-amber, faint fruity malt nose, dry malt flavor, hop finish, long dry hop aftertaste. Made for Burbank's Bar-B-Q, a local restaurant. [B, 53]

IRONSIDE ALE — amber, appetizing hop and malt nose, some caramel in back, light tasty smooth malt palate, light body, even balanced, long dry malt aftertaste. On draft, it is even smoother. Made with two-row malted barley and English Kent-Goldings hops; gravity 12 P, 4.02% abw. Contract brew for Olde Time Brewers Inc., Boston, MA. [A, 65]

RAY'S CLASSIC LAGER — hazy pale amber, fresh malt and hop nose, good hop flavor, quite tasty, balanced and full bodied, some complexity, long dry hop aftertaste. [B, 60]

OLDENBERG CELEBRATION ALE — amber, bright hop nose and flavor, good dry malt and hop finish and aftertaste, good body, balanced, drinkable and fairly long. A top-fermented brew with two-row and caramel malts; gravity 12.5 P, 4.2% abw. [A, 60]

OLDENBERG BOCK — mahogany color, light malt aroma, dry light hop and malt flavor, very smooth and stays fairly dry throughout, good balance, long dry hop aftertaste. As found on draft at the brewpub. [B, 74]

OUTRAGEOUS BOCK BEER — deep amber, malt aroma, light malt flavor with some alcohol, medium to light body, light malt finish, short malt aftertaste. [B, 39]

Notes

HARRIGAN'S IRISH STYLE ALE — pale amber, big toasted malt nose and flavor, light body; burnt malt finish is harsh and affects the balance; long burnt malt aftertaste. Made for Harrigan's Tavern of Kettering, OH. [A, 48]

OLDENBERG OKTOBERFEST LAGER — deep amber-gold; malt aroma has good hops in back, dry malt flavor, finish, and aftertaste. There's a little bite at the end but it is only a mere annoyance and not a glitch. Made with two-row pale, Vienna, and caramel malts; specific gravity 1.054, 4% abw. [B, 88]

WILLIAM HENRY HARRISON ALE — slightly hazy pale amber, appetizing hop aroma; flavor comes as a surprise as it starts out with a light acidic bite, which backs off a bit at mid-palate as the hops come in to take precedence; dry hop finish borders on bitterness (which the background acidity does nothing to assuage); long aftertaste shows the bitterness and acidity to disadvantage. Made for Tippecanoe B.C., Lafayette, IN. [A, 21]

HARRY'S SAFARI BEER — golden-amber, malt and hop nose has some complexity; pleasant dry hop flavor is backed well with malt; good body; at first it seems malty, but is definitely hoppy from the middle-on; dry hop finish, long dry hop aftertaste still has enough malt support for balance. It is very much like Oldenberg Premium Verum. [B, 46]

HOLY GRAIL NUT BROWN ALE — brilliant amber, complex rich malt aroma is a bit toasty; finely carbonated, lovely complex rich roasted malt flavor; a little sweet but feels good in the mouth; long likable roasted malt aftertaste, a good very-easy-to-drink brew. [A, 67]

Oliver Breweries, Ltd.
Brewpub in Baltimore, MD (The Wharf Rat)

FARRELL IRISH STRONG — golden amber, northwest hop ale-like aroma, complex hop palate, good ale character, well bodied, well-made flavorful brew, good balance, dry hop finish, long dry hop aftertaste. [A, 65]

BLACKFRIARS STOUT — dark brown, chocolate malt and roasted barley nose, flavor like the aroma but surprisingly weak, light to medium body, light dry malt aftertaste, not very "stout." [S, 42]

OLIVER'S BEST BITTER — hazy golden amber, hoppy nose, soft dry hop palate, very low carbonation, light dry hop finish and aftertaste, good length, tasted cask-conditioned on draft. [A, 53]

Onalaska Brewing Co.
Microbrewery in Onalaska, WA

RED DAWG ALE — very hazy amber, very finely carbonated; northwest hop aroma seems to be Cascades; somewhat of a home-brew character to the malty flavor but it is very likable; bright, refreshing, and drinkable, good body, dry hop finish, long dry hop aftertaste, a very easy drinking beer. Made from four malts (63% pale two-row, 18% Baird's Munich, 18% caramel, and 1% black) and three hop varieties (40% Cascade, 20% Chinook, and 40% Hallertau); fermented at 76–80°F and coarse filtered to 0.8 micron; OG 1050, 4.5% abw, SRM 19.5, 22 IBU. [A, 65]

ONALASKA ALE — hazy amber, bright malt and northwest hop aroma; again the flavor is a bit homebrew-like, but still quite likable and easy to drink with a malty-nutty style; dry hop finish, long dry hop aftertaste; 4% abw. [A, 57]

HOWLIN' STOUT — deep brown, rich roasted malt nose, clean roasted malt flavor, medium body, medium long clean dry roasted malt aftertaste; nicely made easy drinking stout. [S, 76]

Orange County Brewery / McCormick & Schmick's Pilsner Room
Brewpub in restaurant in Irvine, CA

BAY HAWK AMBER ALE — amber, hop nose, light dry hop flavor, highly carbonated, light body, light dry hop finish and aftertaste, not very distinguished, smooth, light, dry, and not long. [A, 52]

BAY HAWK ORANGE ALE — hazy amber-gold, light hop nose, dry perky hop flavor, dry hop finish and aftertaste, not long and not distinguished. Tasted at The Goat Hill Tavern in Costa Mesa on draft since the brewpub was out of it. [A, 53]

BAYHAWK CHOCOLATE POR-TER — deep brown, roasty malt aroma, smooth and balanced flavor shows some chocolate malt; light body comes as a surprise; smooth dry roasted malt aftertaste is on the short side. [P, 53]

Oregon Trail Brewery

Microbrewery in Corvallis, OR that shares its site with The Old World Deli that serves as its brewpub.

OREGON TRAIL BROWN ALE — brown, roasted malt aroma and flavor, medium body, dry malty finish and aftertaste, good length; made with pale, brown, and chocolate malts; hopped with Perle and Willamette; OG 1048, FG 1.013, 3.8% abv. [A, 53]

Oregon Trader Brewing Co.

Microbrewery in Albany, OR

GREEN CHILI BEER — gold, chili pepper nose, hot chili flavor, dry hot chili aftertaste, nothing but chili heat and flavor; made with two-row and 50L crystal malts plus Nugget and Tettnanger hops. The chili peppers are Anaheim, Hungarian Wax, and Serano; OG 1052, FG 1.010, 4.4% abv. [B, 40]

O'Ryan's Tavern and Brewery

Microbrewery located in Ryan's Tavern in Las Cruces, NM. Originally was to have been named Organ Mountain Brewery.

DOG SPIT STOUT — deep brown, smoky nose, flavor of roasted barley and chocolate malt but none of the smokiness of the aroma, good body, finishes well with a long aftertaste like the flavor. Hopped with Cascade and Kent Goldings; specific gravity 1.082, 8% abw. [S, 65]

RED DOG ALE — golden amber, pronounced hop aroma, big bright hop flavor, good body, long dry hop aftertaste; made with pale and caramel malts and Fuggles and Cascade hops; specific gravity 1.050, 4.2% abw. [A, 65]

ORGAN MOUNTAIN WEIZEN — amber, malt aroma, pleasant malt flavor finishes with some hops, medium long dry wheat and hop aftertaste, pleasant. Made with 55% wheat together with pale and amber malts, Tettnanger, Saaz, and Hallertau hops; specific gravity 1.048, 4.2% abw. [W, 52]

BROWN DOG ALE — amber-brown, light dry malt aroma and flavor, light body, smooth and balanced, very drinkable, light dry malt aftertaste; hopped with Willamette, Goldings, and Cascades; specific gravity 1.040. 4.7% abw. [A, 62]

Notes

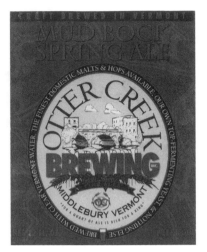

Otter Creek Brewing Co.
Microbrewery in Middlebury, VT

OTTER CREEK COPPER ALE — hazy copper-amber; nice malt and hop aroma is a little sweet; big malt taste has some good sharp hop flavors; dry hop finish and aftertaste, good body, good length; made with six malts, hopped with Chinook, Hallertau, and Tettnanger hops; warm fermentation and cold-conditioning; specific gravity 1.050, 4.2% abw, 21 IBU. [A, 63]

MUD BOCK SPRING ALE — deep amber, tight tan head, big tangy malt nose; big dry tangy ale-malt flavor makes you think German dark alt; good body, long dry tangy malt and hop finish and aftertaste, interesting and good as a dark alt-style beer. [A, 60]

STOVEPIPE PORTER — brown; coffeelike aroma that was at first chocolatey; very smooth complex dry malt flavor, good body; bal-anced throughout with hops staying just behind the malt; long dry malt aftertaste is just a little too much burnt, but otherwise a pleasant porter; hopped specific gravity 1.054, 4.3% abw, 30 IBU. [P, 65]

OTTER CREEK HELLES ALT BIER — pale gold, light malty aroma, dry malt flavor, very lightly hopped, dry hop finish and aftertaste, medium body, good duration; made with two-row pale, Munich, and dextrin malts, Hallertau and Tettnanger hops; specific gravity 1.043, 3.5% abw, 18 IBU. [A, 64]

OTTER CREEK SUMMER WHEAT ALE — pale gold, pleasant very light fruity malt flavor with a fresh hop background, pleasant bright refreshing flavor, very drinkable, light body, good carbonation, medium dry flavor, dry finish and aftertaste, dry rather than either malty or hoppy, a very slight bite at the end; made with 40% wheat malt, hopped to specific gravity 1.040, 3.2% abw, 17 IBU. [A, 57]

Otto Brothers' Brewing Co.
Microbrewery in Jackson, WY

TETON ALE — amber, English-style hop aroma, very dry and strong hop flavor, good body, very dry hop finish and long dry hop aftertaste, a lusty well-hopped brew. An ESB-style ale, this brew is made with roasted malts and triple hopped (in the boil, finishing, and dry hop-ping); specific gravity 1.048, 4.75% abw. [A, 61]

OLD FAITHFUL ALE — gold, dry hop aroma and flavor, good body, dry hop finish and aftertaste; hopped with Cascade and Willamette hops; specific gravity 1.043, 4.5% abw. [A, 50]

MOOSE JUICE STOUT — amber-brown, very big dry malt and hop aroma and flavor, not roasted or chocolate malt, just huge malt and hops, great complexity, big body, very dry finish, long dry malt and hop aftertaste; made with dark roasted and chocolate malts, balanced with Chinook and Cascade hops; specific gravity 1.065, 5.9% abw. [S, 57]

Ould Newbury Brewing Co.
Microbrewery in Newbury, MA

YANKEE PORTER — brown, dry malt aroma and flavor, quite tangy, very dry malt finish; long dry malt aftertaste has a slightly roasted nature; made with Perle and Cascade hops; OG 1050 (12.5 P). [P, 54]

YANKEE ALE — golden amber, big hop nose, bright hop flavor, good body, dry hop finish, long dry hop aftertaste; made with Cascade and Willamette hops; OG 1046 (11.5 P) [A, 53]

OULD NEWBURY PORTER — amber-brown, big tight head, big roasted malt nose, hefty dry roasted malt flavor, trifle burnt, medium body, lovely dry roasted malt aftertaste, smooth despite the burnt nature; a good porter made with Perle and Cascade hops; OG 1050 (12.5 P). Seems to be a new label for Yankee Porter. [P, 63]

OULD NEWBURY SPICED ALE — amber, complex spicy aroma; flavored like the nose, lots of nutmeg, cinnamon, cloves and orange peel; big body, bright and sweet, and very long on the palate; made with Perle and Tettnanger hops; OG 1070 (17 P). [A, 47]

OULD NEWBURY BELGIAN WHEAT ALE — hazy gold, finely carbonated and creamy; nose is clean brightly hopped wheat; clean fruity flavor follows the cue from the aroma and adds a little citrus and spiciness; medium to light body, ends dry and malty, long lightly spiced aftertaste, pleasant, smooth, and refreshing; made with Perle and Tettnanger hops; OG 1040 (10 P). [W, 84]

PLUM ISLAND EXTRA PALE ALE — gold, light dry hop aroma and flavor, light body, dry hop finish and aftertaste, a nice straightforward beer. [A, 36]

OULD NEWBURY RYE ALE — deep amber; malty rye aroma and flavor has a grainy sweetness in back, this sweetness emerges at the finish and is most noticeable in the long dull grainy aftertaste; light bodied, lacks complexity; gravity 11.5 P. [A, 36]

Oxford Brewing Co.

Microbrewer in Linthicum, MD. This brewery began as the British B.C. of Glen Burnie, MD.

OXFORD RED ALE — cask-conditioned, amber, big Cascade hop aroma and flavor, a big bright brew with lots of class, big body, long dry hop aftertaste, plenty of character and very well made. [A, 70]

OXFORD CHERRY PORTER — amber, big hop nose, dry hop flavor, good body, finishes dry hops as well with a long dry hop aftertaste. If there are cherries (which there are according to the brewer's stats), they are too subtle for me to detect, still it is a very good porter. [P, 60]

OXFORD SANTA CLASS — deep amber, light spicy-soapy hop nose, big malt flavor, complex dry hop finish and aftertaste. Although a Christmas ale, it is not spiced; the spicy nature comes from the hops; specific gravity 1.060. [A, 61]

OXFORD CLASS AMBER ALE — dark amber, fruity malt nose, big complex malt and hop flavor, pleasant bright and refreshing, medium body; finish is more malt than hops; medium long dry malt aftertaste; specific gravity 1.055, 5.4% abw. [A, 48]

OXFORD RASPBERRY WHEAT ALE — reddish amber, faint dry raspberry aroma, dry raspberry flavor, light body; dry malt finish and aftertaste is dominated by the raspberries; not particularly interesting; made with Belgian wheat and the addition of real raspberries during the secondary fermentation; specific gravity 11.5 P, 5% abw. [W, 66]

OXFORD CASK ALE — deep amber, rich malty well-aged nose, big very rich malty flavor, finishes dry and with a sense of alcohol; long dry aftertaste has some sweetness; a fairly strong flavorful brew. [A, 67]

OXFORD INDIA CLASS PALE ALE — amber; malt aroma has a sweetness in back; dry hop and English-style malt flavor is drier than the nose; dry hop finish and aftertaste shows plenty of malt support; good length; made with B.C. Goldings and two-row British malts. [A, 53]

Pacific Beach Brewhouse
Brewpub in Pacific Beach, CA

OVER THE LINE STOUT — deep amber, smooth dry malt nose and taste, light body, very drinkable; hops don't show until the aftertaste; more like a porter than a stout. [S, 56]

PACIFIC BEACH BLONDE — gold, light hop nose and taste; malt shows only in the finish; long dry hop aftertaste, refreshing with

good hop character all the way across the palate; made with 20% wheat malt. [B, 59]

SUNSET RED — amber-brown, faint malt nose, big complex malt flavor (made with pale, crystal, dextrin, and a touch of chocolate malts); some hops show in the finish and stay into the aftertaste; very drinkable; made with two-row Brewers and an assortment of caramel malts with Pacfic morthwest hops; specific gravity 1.060, 5.75% abw. [A, 73]

BITTER END ALE — deep amber-gold, light hop aroma and flavor, dry hop finish with a touch of malt in the back, light body; aftertaste is just dry hops; no length. [A, 47]

GHOSTLY PALE ALE — deep gold, light but complex hop aroma, light hop flavor, good body, light dry hop finish and aftertaste, good duration. [A, 48]

BLARNEY STONE STOUT — opaque brown, roasted malt aroma, pleasant dry roasted malt flavor, light to medium body, fairly long dry roasted malt aftertaste. [S, 35]

PACIFIC BEACH RED — dark red-amber, bright malt and hop aroma; very complex malt and hop flavor is a little sweet; malt finish shows some bitterness; long dry hop and off-dry malt aftertaste. This may be Sunset Red, found at the San Diego B.C. among their 50 taps. [A, 70]

Pacific Coast Brewing Co.
Brewpub in Oakland, CA

HOLIDAY ALE 1988 — hazy amber, huge head, effervescent citrus-soapy malt and hop nose, huge flavor of hops and malt, high alcohol, chewy body, hop finish, long hop aftertaste, another really good Xmas beer. [A, 87]

HOLIDAY BARLEYWINE ALE 1990 — cloudy amber, tangy citrus-ale nose, big spicy complex hop and malt flavor, both sweet and sharp at the same time; very complicated palate with all different kinds of malt showing; big body, huge and extremely long. This is another fine Christmas brew. [BW, 90]

HOLIDAY STRONG ALE 1991 — hazy amber, fruity kumquat-malt nose; interesting odd malt flavor that is fruity sweet and dry at the same time; very complex and very drinkable, long off-dry malt and hop aftertaste. [A, 64]

GRAY WHALE ALE — hazy amber, malt nose, dull malty flavor, good body, dry malt aftertaste; made with 40L caramel malt, Chinook, Nugget, Perle, and Willamette hops; specific gravity 1.050, 4.5% abw. [A, 42]

BLUE WHALE ALE — deep amber, fruity hop nose and taste, good body; dry hop aftertaste has length; a good tasting ale. Made from 120 L caramel malt, Nugget, Chinook, Perle, Centennial and Willamette hops, oak chips added to secondary; fined with isinglass; specific gravity 1.070, 7.0% abw. [A, 73]

KILLER WHALE STOUT — deep brown, pleasant roasted barley nose, very light roasted malt flavor, medium body, dry and light roasted malt aftertaste, not much length; made with black malt, 120L caramel malt, roasted barley, chocolate malt, Chinook, Nugget, and Willamette hops; fined with isinglass; specific gravity 1.054, 5% abw. [S, 47]

IMPERIAL STOUT — deep brown; alcohol in the nose dominates the roasted malt; big body, alcohol and roasted malt flavor, dry malt finish and aftertaste, considerable length. Made with honey, roasted barley, 120L caramel and black malt; Chinook and Nugget hops; fined with isinglass; specific gravity 1.080, 8% abw. [S, 43]

TRADITIONAL IPA — amber, hop nose and taste, good body, dry hop finish, long dry hop aftertaste. Dry hopped with Centennial hops and matured over oak chips; specific gravity 1.060, 4.7% abw. [A, 50]

PEARL WHEAT — hazy golden amber, faint malt and butterscotch nose and taste, brief buttery aftertaste; made with 60% wheat and Perle hops; gravity 12 P, 5% abw. [W, 35]

EMERALD ALE — amber, beautiful malt and hop nose, flavor to match, balanced, short dry hop aftertaste, except for the brevity of the aftertaste a very well-made brew; specific gravity 1.066, 5.2% abw. [A, 67]

HOLIDAY RUSSIAN IMPERIAL STOUT 1992 — deep brown, off-dry vinous complex malt aroma and flavor, good body; malt finish shows some burnt character; long malt aftertaste, specific gravity 1.080, 6.1% abw (8% abv). [S, 98]

ORCA PORTER — brown, dry malt aroma and flavor, light smooth and fairly dry throughout, medium body; dry finish and short dry hop aftertaste still shows the dry malt as well; made with roasted barley, 20 L caramel and chocolate malt; flavored with Nugget and Chinook hops; fined with isinglass; specific gravity 1.054, 5% abw. [P, 65]

AMETHYST ALE — amber, blackberry aroma and bigger blackberry taste, medium body, berry finish, long medium dry berry aftertaste. A pale wheat ale, with blackberries added to the primary; specific gravity 1.050, approx. 5% abw. [A, 43]

ACORN ALE — amber-gold, hop nose; bright spicy flavor is sort of odd; long somewhat strange spicy aftertaste, strangeness not readily identified; made with Chinook and Kent-Goldings hops; oak chips added to the secondary; mineral salts added to approximate English brewing water; some 20 L caramel malt used; fined with isinglass; specific gravity 1.054, 5% abw. [A, 45]

Notes

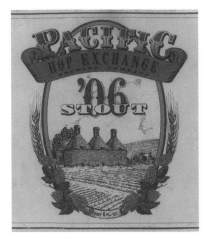

YELLOW JACKET ALE — gold, malt nose, honeyed malt flavor, off-dry malt finish and long aftertaste; made with honey, all pale malt, Nugget hops; fined with isinglass; specific gravity 1.048. 4.9% abw. [A, 50]

HOLIDAY BELGIAN TRIPLE 1993 — hazy amber, aroma of malt, fruit, citrus, and alcohol; very complex flavor is zesty malt and hops; marvelous creamy texture feels like there is a party going on in your mouth; lots of alcohol, huge body, strong malt finish; long tangy malt aftertaste goes dry at the end; triple fermented using a Belgian ale yeast; lightly hopped; specific gravity 1.080, 6.5% abw. [A, 84]

PACIFIC COAST HOLIDAY IPA 1994 — hazy red-amber, bright spicy hop and big malt aroma, a great bracing nose, huge malt and hop flavor, big body, balanced flavor, extremely long citrusy aftertaste, bottle-conditioned; made with plenty of Cascade hops (to a noticeable degree) and Columbus hops; rated at 15.8%, the highest alpha acid rated hop available. This is an excellent IPA. [A, 86]

Pacific Hop Exchange Brewing Co.
Microbrewery in Novato, CA

GASLIGHT PALE ALE — hazy amber, citruslike northwest hop aroma, finely carbonated, big bright hop flavor, some off-dry malt in back; has some trouble balancing; good body, dry complex finish and aftertaste, not long; made with crystal and pale malts and dry hopped; specific gravity 1.046, 3.25% abw. [A, 67]

'06 STOUT — opaque brown, fruity citrus, roasted barley and chocolate malt aroma, big and complex; big flavor of roasted barley, chocolate malt, and hops tends toward the dry side; heavy body, not really rich or satiating but is satisfying; balanced throughout though it is not hopped to the level of the malt; not bold at all despite its heft; malt finish and aftertaste has good duration. On draft it seems quite a bit lighter, but that may be an illusion caused by its smoothness. Made with crystal, chocolate and black patent malts; specific gravity is 1.058, 3.75% abw. [S, 68]

GRAINTRADER WHEAT ALE — hazy yellow, faint malt and hop aroma, bright slightly spicy palate, light body, medium long dry malt and hop aftertaste; made with 50% malted wheat and dry hopped; specific gravity 1.044, 3.25% abw. [W, 54]

HOLLY HOPS SPICED ALE — amber, light pumpkin pie spice (cloves, nutmeg, and cinnamon) aroma and flavor; taste bigger than nose has some chocolate malt showing; only lightly hopped, smooth and pleasant, light body, good length; specific gravity 1.050, 3.6% abw. At 1994 GABF, called Holly Hops Winter Ale. [A, 51]

Pacific Tap & Grill
Brewpub in San Rafael, CA

BOHEMIAN BLONDE — gold; dry hop aroma has a European style from the Tettnanger hops; dry hop flavor is very much a Pils; light and smooth, dry hop finish and aftertaste; specific gravity 1.045, 3.8% abw. [B, 54]

BOOTJACK AMBER — amber, dry malt aroma, malt flavor is in an English style with some coffee and caramel tones, light body; aftertaste is mostly dry English hops; 1.045 gravity, 3.85% abw. [A, 67]

BREWBERRY PALE — amber; blueberry aroma has a sort of artificial quality to it but is clearly blueberry; berry flavor, finish, and dry berry-like aftertaste; light body; specific gravity 1.037, 3.06% abw. [A, 43]

HIGH TIME BARLEYWINE — amber-gold, rich malty aroma and flavor with a roasted quality, good body, rich off-dry malt finish and aftertaste; made with crystal malt. [BW, 67]

MISSION GOLD — gold, dry hop nose; very highly hopped flavor that shows lots of Cascades; medium body, dry hop finish and aftertaste, fairly bright and refreshing; specific gravity 1.046, 3.9% abw. [A, 78]

NOAH'S DARK — amber-brown, dry malty aroma; complex dry nutty-chocolate flavor is a good tasting top-fermented porter; light to medium body, dry malt finish and aftertaste; specific gravity 1.047, 3.83% abw. [P, 67]

James Page Brewing Co.
Brewery in Minneapolis, MN

JAMES PAGE PRIVATE STOCK — amber, malty nose with a trace of fruit, good dry malt flavor with hops in back, medium body, dry malt finish, long dry malt aftertaste, pleasant dry beer. Vienna-style lager brewed with six-row pale, Munich, and caramel malts; specific gravity 1.050, 3.9% abw. [B, 67]

BOUNDARY WATERS BOCK — hazy amber, malt nose, dry malt flavor, briefly a touch of something metallic in the finish, dry malt aftertaste. I never would guess that it was made with wild rice. [BK, 42]

BOUNDARY WATERS BEER — hazy amber-gold, faint hop nose, dry hop flavor, mellow and smooth, light body, dry hop finish,

medium long dry hop aftertaste, a pleasant dry beer. [B, 53]

BOUNDARY WATERS WILD RICE BEER — deep gold, off-dry malt aroma and flavor, medium body; light off-dry malt aftertaste has medium length; quite refreshing while it is in your mouth. Made similar to the Private Stock amber beer, but with the addition of wild rice; specific gravity 1.046, 3.7% abw. [B, 43]

A. FITGER & CO. FLAGSHIP BEER — bright tawny-gold, light pleasant malt and hop aroma, light hop flavor well backed with malt, medium body, dry hop finish, very long dry hop aftertaste. [B, 65]

JAMES PAGE WILD RICE BEER — hazy amber, dull malt aroma and flavor, medium to light body, fairly dry malt finish and aftertaste, probably a new bottling of the Boundary Waters Wild Rice Beer, found in 1994. [B, 34]

Paso Robles Brewing Co.
Brewery in Paso Robles, CA

DRY LAND LAGER — hazy amber, big head, creamy texture all the way through to the end; fruity malt nose and taste reminds me of a spruce beer but is not spruce-like; extremely long malt aftertaste. [B, 48]

Notes

Potomac River Brewing Co.

Microbrewery in Chantilly, VA

PAWTOMACK ALE — light amber, fruity malt nose, dry hop flavor, finish, and aftertaste, medium body; mostly hoppy but the malt arrives at the finish for support and good balance; long interesting well-hopped aftertaste. [A, 64]

RAPPAHANNOCK RED ALE — deep amber, light toasted malt aroma; flavor follows the nose in style, as does the finish and aftertaste; smooth and very drinkable, good malty taste and feel, not complex, just straightforward toasted malt. [A, 60]

Pavichevich Brewing Co.

Brewery located in Elmhurst, IL

BADERBRÄU PILSENER BEER — amber, appetizing malt and hop aroma, somewhat smoky roasted malt flavor, good body, dry smoky finish, long roasted malt aftertaste; has a European style and is well made. [B, 64]

BADERBRÄU BOCK BEER — very deep amber, big burnt malt nose, burnt chocolate malt flavor, medium body, dry malt finish and aftertaste, medium length. [BK, 42]

Pennsylvania Brewing Co. / Allegheny Brewery & Pub

Microbrewery and brewpub in Pittsburgh, PA

PENN OKTOBERFEST — golden amber, slightly off-dry malt and hop aroma; big off-dry malt flavor is lightly toasted; light to medium body, medium dry malt finish and aftertaste; gravity 14.5 P, 4.5% abw. [B, 48]

PENN LIGHT LAGER — gold, light hop and malt aroma, pleasant light dry hop flavor, light body, very mild on the palate, long dry hop and malt aftertaste, very drinkable. This is a light in terms of color, not calories, and is hopped with Hallertau hops. [B, 47]

KAISER PILS — deep gold, big very dry hop pils nose and taste; feels good in your mouth; good texture, thick head, good body, smooth and dry on the palate, long dry hop aftertaste, very good with food; made with only Hallertau hops; gravity 11.9 P, 3.7% abw. [B, 67]

PENN MAERZEN — amber, almost no aroma at all, big rich and strong malt flavor, some alcohol, malt finish; long malt aftertaste lacks the richness of the flavor and is a bit more dry; very little hops. [B, 61]

PENN PILSNER — amber-gold, big hop aroma; light hop flavor has a faint citrus background; medium body, light dry hop aftertaste; made with two-row malt and Hallertau hops; gravity 12.8 P, 4% abw. [B, 47]

PENN DARK LAGER — deep amber; lovely malt aroma is slightly sweet; big fairly dry malt flavor; hops come in at the middle, flavor strongest at the finish; good body, smooth and soft, nicely balanced, dry malt and hop aftertaste only of medium duration; gravity 12.8 P. [B, 54]

HELLES GOLD — gold, dry malt and European hop aroma, dry malt and hop flavor, medium body, bright and refreshing, dry hop finish and aftertaste. [B, 34]

PENN MAI BOCK — deep golden amber, alcoholic malt and hop nose, flavor a bit sweet like the nose, medium to good body, very richly flavored, long malty aftertaste, noticeable alcohol, not very hoppy. [BK, 54–79]

ST. NIKOLAUS BOCK BIER — rosy brown color, dry malt aroma, big off-dry malt flavor, medium body, medium dry malt finish and aftertaste, good length. [BK, 52]

Pete's Brewing Co.

Contract brewer with offices in Palo Alto, CA. Originally the beer was made at Schell, then the St. Paul brewing facilities of Minnesota B.C. and, most recently in mid-1995, shifted to the Stroh brewery in St. Paul, MN.

PETE'S WICKED ALE — brilliant deep amber, slightly toasted malt and hop aroma, zesty malt flavor with hops rolling in from mid-palate on, a malt and hops balanced throughout, good hop and malt finish and a long dry aftertaste; an excellent, balanced, satisfying, drinkable brew; made with pale, chocolate, and caramel malts and Cascade and Brewer's Gold hops; gravity 13.1 P, 4.2% abw. [A, 62]

PETE'S WICKED LAGER — deep gold, citruslike northwest hop aroma, good balanced hop flavor, medium body, smooth and tasty, long dry hop aftertaste. This is a Bohemian-style pils made with pale and caramel malts, kraeusened, and brewed with Willamette, Tettnanger, Liberty, and Mt. Hood hops; gravity 12.2 P, 3.9% abw. [B, 60]

PETE'S GOLD COAST LAGER — hazy amber, bright hop aroma, big hop flavor, big body, complex, balanced, delicious, feels good in your mouth, long dry hop aftertaste. This is presently discontinued. [B, 64]

PETE'S WICKED WINTER BREW — amber, raspberry and faint nutmeg nose; raspberry clashes with the hops and spice in the flavor, simply does not balance; medium body, dry hop aftertaste with a hint of raspberry remaining in the rear; 4.1% abw. [B, 30]

PETE'S WICKED RED — brilliant copper-amber, lovely smooth hop aroma, rich complex drinkable hoppy flavor, good balance, good big rich flavor, no warts, finishes dry hops, long dry hop aftertaste; this should be a very popular

brew; made with pale, caramel, and Munich malts; hopped with Yakima Cluster and Cascade hops, with Tettnanger hops added late in the kettle; gravity 12.5 P, 3.85% abw. [A, 73]

PETE'S WICKED WINTER BREW '94 — pinkish amber, raspberry aroma; raspberry and spice flavor (we know it to be nutmeg, but you can't identify it from the taste); balance is not good between berry and spice; dry hop aftertaste has a raspberry background; gravity 13 P, 4.1% abw. [B, 51]

PETE'S WICKED SUMMER BREW — brilliant gold, bright tangy hop aroma, dry tangy hop flavor; label says there is natural lemon flavor added but I cannot detect it in either the nose or the palate; medium body, long dry hop aftertaste, a very dry and refreshing beer, a welcome addition to the summer beer scene. [B, 72]

PETE'S WICKED HONEY WHEAT — hazy amber, perfumy off-dry honey-fruity-estery malt aroma; sweet grainy malt flavor has a honey background; ends drier with plenty of hops, a bit short but fairly refreshing. [W, 49]

Notes

Phantom Canyon Brewing Co.
Microbrewery in Colorado Springs, CO

CASCADE AMBER ALE — amber, bright dry hop aroma and flavor, good tasting, good body, long complex dry hop aftertaste; made with Centennial and Cascade hops and American two-row and British crystal malts; specific gravity 1.052, 4.0% abw. [A, 85]

ERIK'S SPECIAL BITTER — amber, big bright hop aroma; lusty hop flavor has some complexity; big and bold, long complex dry hop finish and aftertaste; made with Chinook and Centennial hops with American two-row and British specialty malts; specific gravity 1.060, 4.5% abw. [A, 94]

QUEEN'S BLONDE ALE — gold, bright hop aroma and taste, good body, dry hop finish and aftertaste; nade with German hops, American two-row and British Munich malts; specific gravity 1.044, 3.4% abw. [A, 56]

THE PHANTOM INDIA PALE ALE — gold, hop aroma; big hop flavor is bright and complex; good body; long dry hop aftertaste retains much of the complexity of the flavor; made with Centennial and Cascade hops; dry hopped with Centennials, and uses British specialty and American two-row malts; specific gravity 1.060, 4.5% abw. [A, 67]

ZEBULON'S PEATED PORTER — deep brown; lovely complex aroma shows only faintly the smoky peat promised by the name but rather is roasted malt; beautiful roasted malt flavor repeats the smoky peat character but only as a faint background to good malt and complex hops; big body, dry roasted malt finish; long complex aftertaste has roasted malt and hops; made with Nugget, Cascade, and Centennial hops; dry hopped with Centennial, American two-row pale and British specialty malts; specific gravity 1.062, 4.6% abw. [P, 90]

Pike Place Brewery
Microbrewery in Seattle, WA

PIKE PLACE PALE ALE — amber, hop aroma; big hop flavor is balanced well with background malt; very tasty and drinkable, good body, dry hop finish and aftertaste; finished with Kent-Goldings hops; gravity 13 P, 4.5% abw. [A, 59]

EAST INDIA PALE ALE — amber, hop aroma, big hop flavor, good balance, good body, long dry hop aftertaste; cask-conditioned in oak; gravity 11.6 P, 5.5% abw. [A, 54]

PIKE PLACE XXXX STOUT — deep brown, roasted barley and chocolate malt aroma with some hops in there, big flavor like the nose, big body; excellent balance, smooth, dry, and long; gravity 19 P, 7% abw. [S, 68]

OLD BAWDY BARLEY WINE — gold, big hop and malt aroma; huge flavor is balanced hops and malt, very big and bold with high alcohol; long long complex hop and malt aftertaste; the hops tend to dry and the malt tends toward sweetness so they never get either place but the balance stays; very enjoyable. Brewed with peated distiller's malt, so there is a suggestion of smokiness, but it doesn't develop; gravity 26 P, 10% abw. [BW, 67]

PIKE PLACE BIRRA PERFECTO — amber; spicy nose overwhelms the malt, same for the flavor; too much spice and not the right kind for an attractive beer; made with oregano and other Italian spices, it just doesn't make it; 4% abw. [A, 43]

Pikes Peak Brewery
Microbrewery in Colorado Springs, CO

JACK RABBIT PALE ALE — gold, big hop nose; big dry hop flavor has some spicy character; medium body, finishes dry hops and there is a long dry hop aftertaste; made with two malts and northwest hops; specific gravity 1.052, 4.7% abw. [A, 67]

RED GRANITE AMBER ALE — amber, aromatic hop nose; dry complex flavor shows plenty of both the hops and malt; medium body, long aftertaste continues the flavor; made with three malts and northwest hops; specific gravity 1.058, 5% abw. [A, 62]

MOONLIGHT PORTER — dark brown, complex malt aroma; flavor is like the nose but starts out with a hop bite; big body, ends very smooth with a long complex and tasty aftertaste; overall impression is fairly big and bright; made with five malts and three northwestern hops; specific gravity 1.060, 5.5% abw. [P, 70]

Pittsburgh Brewing Co.

Brewery in Pittsburgh, PA. Until quite recently was owned by the Bond Corp. of Australia and, through that ownership, affiliated with G. Heileman producing many Heileman labels for distribution on the east coast. At time of this writing, there is no information available on what future affiliation might result.

IRON CITY PREMIUM BEER — gold, light malt aroma with a faint hop background, light malt and hop flavor, medium body, light malt finish, dry hop aftertaste of medium length; made with barley malt and corn; specific gravity 1.044, 3.6% abw, 14 IBU. [B, 51]

IRON CITY DARK — almost opaque brown, light smoky-toasted malt aroma, similar flavor but with hops in back, medium body, good coffee-like finish and aftertaste, good length. [B, 54]

IRON CITY DRAFT BEER — gold, light off-dry malt aroma, off-dry malt flavor; medium length aftertaste is still malty but is a little drier. [B, 46]

IRON CITY LIGHT — pale gold; malt aroma has a slight sour backing, light malt flavor has that sourness as well; dry malt finish and brief aftertaste; made with barley malt, corn, and domestic hops; specific gravity 1.031, 3.35% abw, 10 IBU. [LO, 13]

I.C. SPECIAL DRY BEER — bright gold, bright malt nose; light dry malt palate does have some zest; thin body, light malt aftertaste of medium duration. [D, 32]

I.C. GOLDEN LAGER — pale gold, off-dry malt aroma, soft malt flavor, low carbonation, only a faint hop background, medium length; made with corn, barley malt, roasted malt, and a combination of domestic and imported hops; specific gravity 1.047, 3.6% abw, 15 IBU. [B, 45]

I.C. ICE ICE FILTERED BEER — pale gold, pleasant malt aroma, weak malt flavor, weak body, weak malty finish, short dry malt aftertaste, overall fairly dull; specific gravity 1.040, 3.45% abw. [B, 25]

I.C. PREMIUM LAGER — pale gold, slightly sweet malt aroma, soft malt flavor with a light dry hop background, medium body; finishes drier than it starts; medium long dry hop aftertaste. [B, 47]

PITTSBURGH BREWING CO. CLASSIC DRAFT LIGHT — pale gold, fruity light malt nose, dull dry malt flavor, short malt aftertaste. [LO, 24]

PITTSBURGH BREWING CO. CLASSIC DRAFT — gold, herbal aroma, grapey malt flavor, soapy malt aftertaste. [B, 10]

OLD FROTHINGSLOSH PALE STALE ALE — gold, light grainy nose, light malt flavor, light body, short dry aftertaste. [B, 47]

AMERICAN BEER — gold, malt aroma with a very slight hop character; a lot of the flavor is CO_2; light body, off-dry malt finish, short off-dry malt aftertaste; made with barley and corn; specific gravity 1.041, 3.5% abw, 13 IBU. [B, 31]

AMERICAN LIGHT BEER — pale gold, malt nose, light body, off-dry malt finish and aftertaste, light and short; made with barley and corn; specific gravity 1.029, 3.3% abw, 9 IBU. [LO, 25]

TECH LIGHT BEER — gold, grainy malt nose, light body, light malt palate, brief malt aftertaste. [B, 34]

OLD EXPORT PREMIUM BEER — gold, malt aroma and flavor, faint hops in back, medium length malt aftertaste. [B, 7]

MUSTANG PREMIUM MALT LIQUOR — deep gold, light sweet malt aroma, big body, smooth malt flavor, finishes clean, long malt aftertaste; made with barley and corn; specific gravity 1.053, 5% abw, 16 IBU. [ML, 57]

ST. MICHAEL'S NON-ALCOHOLIC MALT BEVERAGE — pale gold; light hop aroma has some skunkiness hiding in back; low carbonation, light grainy malt flavor, very weak body, very brief. Made for St. Michaels B.C., Lancaster, PA. [NA, 14]

OLDE HEURICH AMBER LAGER — pale amber, pleasant malt and hop nose with a faint citruslike tang in back, big hop palate backed with sufficient malt for excellent balance, long dry hop aftertaste. A very good brew made under contract for Olde Heurich B.C. of Washington, DC; now believed to be replaced by Olde Heurich Maerzen Bier (See F.X. Matt). [B, 73]

ERIN BREW — amber, lightly toasted malt aroma, clean fresh off-dry malt flavor, dry hop middle and finish, long dry hop aftertaste, well made and well balanced, very drinkable. Made for Cleveland B.C., Cleveland, OH; now understood to be made by F.X. Matt, but this product has not yet been tasted. [B, 80]

HARD ROCK CAFE BEER — hazy gold, light grainy malt and CO_2 flavor, light dry hop finish and aftertaste; not much there but it is refreshing. [B, 30]

BILLARY BEER — bright gold, pleasant dry light malt and slightly soapy hop nose, light dry hop and malt flavor, light dry malt and hop finish, and medium length dry hop aftertaste; reminds me of Iron City. Made for Presidential Bottling Co., of Cleveland, OH. For every case sold, they promise to give 25¢ to the federal government to ease the national debt. [B, 47]

SIERRA LAGER — gold, light malt aroma with a faint hop background, light malt and hop flavor, medium body, light malt finish, dry hop aftertaste of medium length. [B, 43]

SIERRA LIGHT — pale gold; light malt aroma has a slight vegetal backing; pleasant malt flavor, light body, dry hop finish and brief aftertaste. [LO, 27]

J.J. WAINWRIGHT'S SELECT LAGER BEER — golden amber, pleasant sweet Cascade hop aroma, light pleasant malt and dry hop flavor, good body, dry hop finish and short aftertaste; specific gravity 1.051, 3.8% abw. [B, 46]

DRUM ROCK PREMIUM LAGER BEER — gold; big malty nose is off-dry; brightly carbonated, and this shows in the flavor helping the hops to balance the malt; off-dry malt finish and aftertaste are refreshing; brief, lawnmowing beer. Made for Drum Rock B.C. of Providence, RI and found in Providence. [B, 45]

J.J. WAINWRIGHT'S EVIL EYE ALE — golden amber; nose has malt and hops but is slightly dank; finely carbonated; flavor is sparkling grapey; medium body, light off-dry grapey finish and aftertaste with some sourness at the end. [A, 30]

J.J. WAINWRIGHT'S BLACK JACK BLACK & TAN — dark amber-brown; faint roasted malt aroma is slightly burnt; roasted malt flavor starts sweet, dries toward the finish; short dry malt aftertaste has an underlying sweetness. [B, 39]

NANTUCKET BRAND FINBACK LAGER — deep gold, light dry hop and faint grainy nose; light dry hop flavor is complex and balanced; well hopped but pleasant and not assertive, good mouthfeel; a touch of malt sweetness appears in the finish and aftertaste. Made for Brandt Point B.C. of Nantucket, MA. [B, 63]

Note: Pittsburgh B.C. has made contract brews for Boston Beer Co. for some time, but since these brews are not made exclusively by Pittsburgh, they are listed under Boston Beer Co. They include Boston Lightship, Samuel Adams Boston Lager, Samuel Adams Bock, Samuel Adams Double Bock, Samuel Adams Winter Lager, Samuel Adams Oktoberfest, Samuel Adams Boston Stock Ale, and Samuel Adams Wheat Beer.

Port City Brewery
Brewpub in Mobile, AL

ADMIRAL SEMMES' STOUT — brown, chocolate malt and roasted barley nose; big complex malt palate has some coffee-chocolate-licorice tones; medium to good body, dry malt finish and aftertaste, a very likable stout; gravity 13.5 P, 4% abw. [S, 91]

AZALEA CITY STEAMER — amber; dry hop aroma leads to a complex dry malt and hop flavor; medium body, dry malt and aftertaste; gravity 13 P, 3.85% abw. [A, 53]

GULF COAST GOLD — amber-gold, bright European hop aroma, Pils-style dry hop flavor, bright dry hop finish and aftertaste, medium body; gravity 12 P, 3.5% abw. [B, 67]

MIDDLE BAY LIGHT — gold, light dry hop aroma and flavor; Saaz hops give it a Bohemian pils style; light body, dry hop finish and aftertaste; gravity 10.5 P, 2.9% abw. [B, 52]

Portland Brewing Co.
Brewpub in Portland, OR

PORTLAND DRY HONEY BEER — deep gold, honeyed (really) malt aroma; off-dry malt flavor has a touch of honeyed sweetness; medium dry finish; long malt aftertaste is reasonably dry. Tasted on tap over a period of 3–4 years in various west coast pubs. [B, 72]

WINTER ALE WITH SPICES — deep ruby-brown; spice aroma, nutmeg, cinnamon, etc.; spice flavor with malt and alcohol showing; medium length spicy-malt aftertaste. [A, 21]

PORTLAND ALE — tawny-gold, big hop and malt nose, very smooth malt flavor, medium body, dry hop finish and aftertaste, fairly long, well hopped throughout; brewed with two-row malt with Galena and Cascade hops; specific gravity 1.048 (12 P), 3.8% abw. [A, 62]

PORTLAND PORTER — opaque brown, dry chocolate malt and roasted barley nose, sort of coffee-like, big soft chocolate malt and roasted barley flavor, very pleasant and drinkable, medium to light body, long medium dry malt aftertaste; hopped with Willamette and Nugget hops; specific gravity of 1.048 and 3.7% abw. [P, 48]

PORTLAND STOUT — deep brown, faint malt aroma, big rich chocolate malt and roasted barley nose like a classical stout, very creamy texture; very rich flavor delivers the promise of the nose, stays rich, no harshness whatever; long off-dry aftertaste continues to show the major flavor components; nicely done smooth stout. [S, 86]

MT. HOOD BEER — gold, faint off-dry malt nose, dry CO_2 and malt flavor; long dry malt aftertaste turns to hops at the very end; made with Mt. Hood and Galena hops, pale and Carapils malts; gravity 12 P, 3.9% abw. [B, 47]

DOWN AND OUT STOUT — dark brown, faint malt nose, dry roasted barley and chocolate malt flavor, medium body; weight is more like a porter than a stout; has bitterness but not much depth; not well knit, is even a bit a harsh. [S, 41]

McTARNAHAN'S ALE — amber, citrus-ale nose, bright hop flavor, good body, smooth and bright, finely carbonated, pleasant drinking, very dry hop aftertaste; made with pale and 40-Lovibond caramel malts, hopped to 40 IBU with Cascade hops; specific gravity 1.052 (13 P), 3.9% abw. [A, 56]

OREGON HONEY BEER — slightly hazy gold, honeyed malt nose and taste, good body; off-dry nature stays into the aftertaste but it goes dry at the end; made with honey, barley malt, Nugget and Willamette hops; gravity 11.2 P, 3.6% abw. Bottled version found in early 1994. [B, 38]

ICICLE CREEK WINTER ALE 1994 — deep amber, lovely rich malty aroma; dry rich smooth roasted malt flavor is quite good; in the middle is off-dry with chocolate tones, but goes very dry as you approach the finish; dry malt and hop aftertaste has good length, but the flavors seem to be partitioned and don't come together. [A, 64]

MALARKEY'S WILD IRISH ALE — brilliant amber; faintly smoky aroma is reflected in the flavor; peaty and not assertive, medium to good body, pleasant tasting; lightly dry faintly smoky aftertaste has good duration; made with British peated malt. [A, 73]

PORTLAND WHEAT BERRY BREW — deep gold, big very fruity nose; odd fruity flavor (relatively unfamiliar marionberry is dominant) that is overly sweet, faintly like a coconut-pineapple; tartness clashes with the berry taste, medium to light body; long fruity aftertaste tries to be dry; made with pale, Carapils, and wheat malts with Galena and Mt. Hood hops; marionberries are added to the brew kettle and again marionberry juice is added at filtration. [W, 59]

McTARNAHAN'S ALE (CASK CONDITIONED) — amber, faint malt and hop aroma, very smooth balanced malt and hop flavor, medium body, very drinkable, likable, smooth light dry malt and hop aftertaste, good length. Tasted on draft at the pub. [A, 70]

UNCLE OTTO'S OKTOBERFEST ALT — amber, malt aroma; "troubled" malty flavor has the alt character clashing with the hops; estery-phenolic background is not unlike many altbiers tasted in Germany so the beer may not be out of character for its intended style, but I don't find the acrid background as attractive; long fruity-sour aftertaste. [A, 37]

Portsmouth Brewery

Brewpub in Portsmouth, NH. It is affiliated with and shares the brewmaster of the Northampton Brewery of Massachusetts.

GOLDEN LAGER — gold, fruity malt and hop nose, mild fairly dry hop flavor, long dry hop aftertaste; finished with Saaz hops; OG 1048. [B, 51]

AMBER LAGER — amber, faint caramel and hop nose, complex hop and caramel malt flavor, fairly dry, smooth and refreshing, flavor tails off at the finish, light dry hop aftertaste. [B, 54]

BLONDE ALE — light gold, mild malt and hop nose, very light malt flavor, light dry hop finish, dry malt aftertaste, medium length. [A, 49]

PALE ALE — deep amber, clean light malt and hop aroma, zesty almost spicy hop-ale flavor, dry hop finish, long dry hop aftertaste; made with Cascade and Willamette hops; specific gravity 1.055. [A, 60]

OLD BROWN DOG — deep amber, faint hop nose, fairly rich but dry malt and hop flavor; malt shows well in mid-palate; dry hop finish, long dry hop aftertaste; OG 1060. [A, 61]

BLACK CAT STOUT — very deep brown, faint roasted barley and chocolate malt aroma, medium body, medium concentration, flavor like the nose, medium to long dry malt aftertaste; OG 1065. [S, 68]

MURPHY'S LAW RED ALE — deep amber, light hop aroma and flavor, medium to good body, dry hop finish, long dry hop aftertaste; made with Perle and Cascade hops, dry hopped with Cascades; OG 1048. [A, 56]

PORTSMOUTH WEIZENHEIMER — gold, big head, dry malty flavor, light body, no spiciness, brief aftertaste. [W, 45]

PORTSMOUTH 70 SHILLING SCOTCH ALE — dark amber, malt aroma, big malty flavor, big body, rich alcoholic long off-dry malt finish and aftertaste. [A, 60]

Prescott Brewing Co.
Brewpub in Prescott, AZ

LIQUID AMBER — amber; bright hoppy aroma shows some Cascade hops; tasty complex flavor has plenty of hops and malt showing; medium to good body, dry hop finish and aftertaste shows Cascades and Tettnanger hops; brewed with a blend of caramel malts; gravity 12.5 P, 4.2% abw. [A, 69]

LODGEPOLE LIGHT — gold, dry hop aroma and flavor, light body, dry hop finish and aftertaste; made with low amounts of Tettnanger and Willamette hops, and two-row barley; gravity 11.100 P, 3.8% abw. [A, 63]

PETRIFIED PORTER — brown, dry malt aroma and flavor, very ample body; finish and aftertaste are an extension of the main palate; quite a bit of complexity and hearty character, top-fermented; made with chocolate and caramel malts, Northern Brewer and Willamette hops; gravity 14.4 P, 5.6% abw. [P, 73]

PRESCOTT PALE ALE — amber-gold; dry hop aroma and palate has a medium level of malty background; medium body, very pleasant; dry hop finish and long dry hop aftertaste is derived from generous amounts of Northern Brewer, Liberty, Chinook, and Willamette hops; gravity 12.1 P, 4.1% abw. [A, 83]

Ragtime Tavern & Grill
Brewpub in Atlantic Beach (Jacksonville), FL. It was also identified as Ragtime Tavern & Taproom and Ragtime Tavern & Seafood Grill/Taproom Brewery at the GABF.

RED BRICK ALE — pale amber, light malt aroma, light dry malt flavor, medium body, fairly long dry malt aftertaste; made with two-row Munich caramel, and chocolate malt, Perle, East Kent-Goldings, Hallertau, and Willamette hops; specific gravity 1.050, 4% abw. [A, 60]

RAGTIME RASPBERRY WHEAT — gold, faint raspberry nose, dry raspberry and wheat flavor, light body, dry malt finish, long dry malt aftertaste. [W, 60]

WESTBURY WHEAT — gold, light malt aroma, good dry wheat beer flavor (American style—no spiciness), very refreshing, light body, medium long dry malt aftertaste; brewed with 30% wheat malt, two-row barley and Munich malt; hopped with Perle and Hallertau hops; specific gravity 1.046, 3.8% abw. [W, 54]

RAGTIME OKTOBERFEST — amber, light malt nose, medium dry malt flavor, good body; finishes as it starts; good tasting long dry malt aftertaste. [B, 56]

A STRANGE STOUT — deep amber-brown, faint malt nose, big body; light dry malt flavor shows a trace of chocolate malt; light and brief dry malt aftertaste. Recipe calls for a blend of seven malts (including chocolate, caramel, and roasted); Perle, Hallertau, and Willamette hops; specific gravity of 1.052, 4.4% abw. [S, 67]

Red Hook Ale Brewery, Inc.
Brewery and brewpub in Seattle, WA

RED HOOK ESB ALE — deep amber-gold, more malt than hops in the aroma; very flavorful big hop flavor has a light malt backing; big body, dry hop finish, long dry hop aftertaste complex and long; hopping gives more bitterness than dryness; a good tasting brew that is excellent with food; made with two-row Klages caramel 60 L malt, and Willamette and Tettnanger hops; OG 1054, 5.3% abw. [A, 70]

BLACKHOOK PORTER — deep ruby-amber, big bright and dry malt nose, dry malt palate, medium body, malt finish with a touch of fruity-citrus-spice-smoke, dry malt aftertaste, good length, pleasant, very drinkable. Top-fermented with two-row Klages caramel 40 L, Black Malt, and roasted barley with Eroica, Willamette, and Cascade hops; OG 1047, 4.9% abw. [P, 53]

BALLARD BITTER PALE ALE — deep gold, malt aroma, light body, malt flavor, dry hop aftertaste. Top-fermented with two-row Klages caramel 40 L and Eroica, Willamette, and Cascade hops; OG 1044, 4.8 % abv. [A, 53]

WHEAT HOOK WHEATEN
ALE — hazy gold, fruity complex
malt nose with a hint of butterscotch; very complex dry flavor that
shows some hops, malt, fruitiness,
butterscotch, and tartness; long dry
hop aftertaste. Uses two-row Klages
Malted Wheat and Tettnanger,
Hersbrucker, and German Hallertau
hops; OG 1034, 4.7% abv. [W, 39]

WINTERHOOK CHRISTMAS
ALE 1990 — hazy amber, light
malt aroma, good toasted malt flavor, good body, dry malt finish,
nicely balanced, long malt aftertaste, noticeable alcohol, very
drinkable. Recipe changes annually. [A, 78]

WINTERHOOK CHRISTMAS
ALE 1991 — amber color, malt
nose with a light citrus background, complex ale flavor, dry
hop finish and long dry hop aftertaste, very good brew. [A, 71]

WINTERHOOK CHRISTMAS
ALE 1992 — deep amber, fragrant
malt nose; strong malt flavor has a
faintly sour hop background; rich
malt finish, somewhat drier in the
aftertaste but keeps its strength; very
long on the palate, hops more noticeable at the end, and the last impression is slightly sour hops.
Several samples that were tasted on
the east coast had been mishandled.
[A, 43]

WINTERHOOK CHRISTMAS
ALE 1994 — amber, buttery malt
nose, dull malt and dry hop flavor,
medium body, tinny finish; aftertaste has a metallic component
that is not likable; long with a buttery background. [A, 31]

WINTERHOOK WINTER ALE
1995 — amber, toasted malt nose;
light toasted malt flavor is at once
scorched and sweet; the flavors
tend to clash and don't come
together. [A, 37]

RED HOOK HEFE-WEIZEN —
cloudy gold, slightly tangy dry malt
flavor, light to medium body, finishes like it starts; very dry malty
aftertaste has only a vestigial rem-
nant of the tangy backtaste; it fits a
category somewhere between an
American- and German-style hefe-
weizen. [W, 57]

REDHOOK RYE BEER — gold,
rye malt aroma and flavor, dry
grainy taste, dry malt finish and
aftertaste, light to medium body;
made with two-row Klages and
Munich malts plus flaked rye;
hopped with Mt. Hood and
Yakima Hersbrucker hops; OG
1052, 5% abv. [A, 66]

Redondo Beach Brewing Co.
Brewpub in Redondo Beach affiliated with Manhattan Beach B.C. and Huntington Beach B.C.

DOMINATOR WHEAT —
deep gold, dry malty-hop nose,
bright dry wheat and barley malt
flavor, very refreshing, good body,
dry malt finish and aftertaste,
some hops at the end. A good
American-style wheat (no spicy
estery quality), brighter and more
refreshing than most. [W, 67]

REDONDO BEACH
BLONDE — gold, fresh malt
aroma; light malt flavor is a little
grapey; medium body, dry malt
finish and aftertaste. [A, 59]

PIER PALE ALE — pale amber,
complex hop and malt nose, assertive very sweet hop flavor,
medium to big body; sweetness
stays through the finish into the
very long aftertaste, and it gets
sweeter as it goes. [A, 54]

SOUTH BAY BITTER — amber,
faint dry hop nose, dry and bitter
hop flavor, medium body, very dry
finish and aftertaste. [A, 65]

Richbrau Brewery &
Queen's Arms Pub

Brewpub in
Richmond, VA

GOLDEN GRIFFIN ALE — deep
gold, light fruity hop aroma,
bright dry hop flavor, medium to
good body, finishes very dry, long
dry hop aftertaste; made only with
two-row malt and hopped with

Tettnanger and Hallertau hops;
3.7–4% abw. [A, 52]

OLD NICK PALE ALE — amber,
very faint malty nose, big bright
flavor shows both big malt and
hops, good balance, good body,
smooth light dry hop finish and
aftertaste, quite long and satisfying.
Made with only two-row malt and
hopped with Cascade and Fuggles
hops; 3.7–4% abw. [A, 76]

BIG NASTY PORTER — brown,
faint malt aroma; tasty malt flavor
shows a bit of the chocolate malt,
smooth, medium body, toasted
malt finish; rich malt aftertaste has
good duration; made with two-row
pale, chocolate, and black malts;
brewed with Northern Brewer
hops; dry hopped with Tettnanger
and Cascade hops; specific gravity
1.058, 5.25% abw. [P, 79]

RICHBRAU SHANDY — amber-
gold, ginger aroma and flavor, malt
does show through the ginger, good
body, fairly long slightly off-dry
ginger-malt aftertaste. The ale used
to make the shandy was brewed
specially for the purpose and was
similar to the Golden Griffin, but a
more lightly hopped. [A, 49]

RICHBRAU BLACK & TAN —
This blend of the Golden Griffin
Ale and the Big Nasty Porter
shows more of the ale than the
porter; amber-brown, a light malty
nose (like the porter, but fainter);
smooth light malt flavor (like the
ale, but with the hop character
mitigated by the specialty malts in
the porter); light dry malt aftertaste. [A, 50]

Rikenjaks Brewing Co.
Microbrewery in
Jackson, LA

RIKENJAKS E.S.B. — amber-
gold, complex malt and hop aroma,
bright hop flavor, dry Goldings hop
finish; made with nine different
malts; medium body, single-
infusion mash; specific gravity
1.054, 5% abw, 36 IBU. [A, 61]

RIKENJAKS SELECT
AMERICAN ALE — hazy gold;
big fruity malt aroma has a touch
of litchi; flavor is like a light
fruity soda with some vegetal
background, but is ephemeral;
faint dry hop aftertaste is brief;
finished with Cascade hops;
single-infusion mash; specific
gravity 1.048, 4.5% abw, 27 IBU.
A second sample obtained from a
different batch was similar but did
not have the litchi, it was judged
to be a bit dull. [A, 59]

RIKENJAKS OLD HARDHEAD
SCOTTISH STYLE ALE — deep
amber; aroma has fruity esters,
roasted malt, alcohol, and something that makes you think of
pumpkin pulp; dry malty flavor
comes as a surprise but the pumpkin is still there in back; big body,
alcoholic; long dry roasted malt
aftertaste has some of the fruity
esters, one of them being pineapple; finished with Goldings
hops, single-infusion mash,
fermented under 60°F; specific
gravity 1.070, 6% abw, 28 IBU.
A second sample obtained from
another batch was like a sweet

Ovaltine malt and fairly dull. There was no pumpkin flavor in this one. [A, 60]

Rio Bravo Brew Pub

Brewpubs in Albuquerque, NM and Santa Barbara, CA. The California location is the site of the recently (1994) closed State Street Brewery and is named Rio Bravo #2.

CORONADO GOLD — gold, big bright hoppy nose; great highly hopped flavor is more appetizing than bitter; good body; good supporting malt level but this is basically a well-hopped pils; dry hop finish and aftertaste, good length; a very bright refreshing and drinkable beer made with Munich malt; specific gravity 1.048, 3.6% abw. Tasted in Albuquerque. [A, 90]

HIGH DESERT PALE ALE — amber, light hop aroma, dry hop flavor, plenty of malt to support, good body, dry hop finish and very long aftertaste shows Chinook and Cascade hops; specific gravity 1.056, 4.1% abw. Tasted in Albuquerque. [A, 73]

ESTEBAN DARK — deep amber-brown, light malt nose, dry yet rich malt palate, good body, finish like the flavor; aftertaste shows some chocolate malt and licorice; good length, a nicely done porter-style dark brew; specific gravity 1.056. 3.8% abw. Tasted in Albuquerque. [A, 68]

RIO BRAVO OLD ALE — amber; malt aroma has a hop background; complex malt flavor, smooth and delicious, good body, very drinkable; smoothness extends through the finish into the long malty aftertaste. Tasted in Albuquerque. [A, 74]

RIO BRAVO RUSSIAN IMPERIAL STOUT — deep amber-brown, faint dry malt aroma; complex very rich malt flavor has the sense of a sweetness in back but the finish and aftertaste are dry malt; a very good construction (a term rarely thought of in describing a beer, but this one has a most interesting structure); medium to long duration, one of the better imperial-style stouts. Tasted in Albuquerque. [S, 78]

RIO BRAVO BLONDE ALE — gold, bright hop aroma, dull dry hop flavor and grainy aftertaste, medium body, medium duration. Tasted at Santa Barbara. [A, 43]

RIO BRAVO INDIA PALE ALE — amber, faint nose has little hops or malt, light dry malt and hop flavor and aftertaste, too lightly flavored, undistinguished. Tasted at Santa Barbara. [A, 40]

RIO BRAVO STOUT — deep brown, light chocolate malt and roasted barley nose; equally light dry malt flavor shows a trace of chocolate malt and roasted barley; brief aftertaste barely reflects the main flavor components. Tasted at Santa Barbara. [S, 47]

Notes

Brewski's Gaslamp Pub, Inc. / San Diego's Riptide Brewery
Brewpub in San Diego, CA

RED SAILS ALE — amber, light malt aroma and flavor, medium body, long dry malt aftertaste, not much hops showing anywhere. Made using two-row American, British crystal, and a dash of British chocolate malts; specific gravity 1.050, 4% abw. [A, 52]

AZTEC AMBER ALE — golden amber, ale-like hop and fruity malt aroma, hop and fruity malt flavor, good body, nicely balanced, dry hop finish; long dry hop aftertaste has plenty of supporting malt, very drinkable. Made with two-row British and American crystal malts; dry hopped with Yakima Cascades; specific gravity 1.052, 4% abw. [A, 72]

PIONEER PORTER — brown, medium dry malt aroma and flavor, good body, decent balance, dry malt finish and aftertaste; hopped with Northern Brewer and Yakima Cascade hops; gravity 14 P, 4.5% abw. [P, 60]

CHARGER GOLD — golden amber, big hop aroma, very flavorful hop palate, good body, long slightly dry hop aftertaste; made with American two-row and a sprinkle of British crystal malts; hopped with Hallertau hops; specific gravity 1.050, 4% abw. [A, 65]

TOO BERRY ALE — a weizen with a blackberry/raspberry aroma, more berry flavor than weizen, on the sweet side, more like a cooler than a fruit-weizen, long off-dry berry aftertaste. [A, 40]

DOWNTOWN CHESTNUT BROWN — dark amber, mild malty ale aroma, light malt and hop flavor includes chocolate malt, medium body, long dry malt aftertaste, pleasant and refreshing. [A, 53]

DUNKELWEIZEN — dark amber, very little aroma, just some faint malt, mild malt flavor, light body, brief malt aftertaste. [A, 27]

WEIZEN ALE — gold, light hop aroma, lemony flavor, medium body, light lemony malt aftertaste with not much duration. [A, 30]

WHALE'S TALE HONEY ALE — gold, light malt aroma, light dry malt flavor, faint honey sweet background, medium body, dry finish and aftertaste, very pleasant and drinkable; made with American two-row malt and raw citrus honey; hopped with Tettnanger and Cascade hops; specific gravity 1.048, 3.8% abw. Also seen as Original Honey Ale. [A, 56]

OATMEAL STOUT — dark brown, chocolate malt and roasted barley aroma and flavor, good body, fairly rich, long and dry, a classic stout; made with oatmeal, roasted barley and Chinook hops; specific gravity 1.056, 4.8% abw. [S, 74]

RIPTIDE HONEY ALE — hazy gold, honeyed malt aroma, bright honey-malt flavor, refreshing and a bit off-dry, finishes dry, medium body; fairly long medium dry aftertaste keeps some of the honeyed quality. [A, 64]

River City Brewing Co.
Brewpub in Sacramento, CA

RIVER CITY DOPPELBOCK — deep amber, big malt aroma and flavor, huge body, off-dry malt finish and aftertaste, alcohol level (8% abw) shows all the way through; specific gravity 1.078. [B, 87]

RIVER CITY HEFE WEIZEN — hazy gold, light spicy aroma, spicy clove flavor, light body; made with 60% wheat malt, two-row pale and a dash of Munich malts; fermented with German weizen yeast; specific gravity 1.054, 4.2% abw. [W, 56]

RIVER CITY HELLES — gold; aroma is malt with hops in back; bright spicy hop flavor, dry Hallertau hop finish and aftertaste; made with Munich malts; specific gravity 1.050, 3.9% abw. [B, 67]

RIVER CITY VIENNA — amber-gold, complex malty aroma, dry hop and malt flavor, medium body, dry hop finish and aftertaste; made with Munich and Vienna malts and Hersbrucker, Spalt, and Hallertau hops, creating a very Germanic-style lager; specific gravity 1.056, 4.5% abw. [B, 72]

River City Brewing Co.
Brewpub in Jacksonville, FL

RED ROOSTER ALE — dark amber; smooth hop nose has some malt to balance; good hop flavor, medium to big body, dry hop finish, long dry hop aftertaste, excellent with food. [A, 75]

JAGUAR LIGHT — golden amber, light hop nose, light dry hop flavor, medium to light body, dry hop finish and aftertaste. It is named for a local college football team and was called Jag Light by most at the pub. [LO, 47]

JACKSON PALE ALE — amber-gold, bright hop aroma and flavor, very tasty and smooth, medium body, light dry hop finish and aftertaste, good length. [A, 76]

RIVER CITY AMERICAN ALE — deep gold, dry malt and hop aroma; very dry hop flavor has malt backing; medium body, very long and very dry hop aftertaste. [A, 59]

RIPTIDE PORTER — light brown, lightly toasted malt aroma and flavor, very attractive and likable, smooth and soft, medium body, smooth light dry finish and aftertaste; has some complexity; quite drinkable. [P, 63]

River City Brewing Co.
Brewpub in Wichita, KS

HOCKADAY PALE ALE — amber-gold, fragrant Cascade hop and malt aroma, dry malty flavor, medium body, dry hop finish and aftertaste; specific gravity 1.056, 4% abw. [A, 67]

OLD TOWN BROWN ALE — amber-brown, light malt nose; smooth dry light malt flavor has good character; slightly nutty English style, light to medium body, dry malt finish and aftertaste; specific gravity 1.048, 3.6% abw. [A, 75]

RASPBERRY AMBER ALE — amber, raspberry nose, dry raspberry flavor, medium body; dry finish and aftertaste shows less of the raspberries than the main palate; made with raspberries added to the amber ale; specific gravity 1.056, 3.8% abw. [A, 50]

RIVER CITY EYE ALE — amber, grainy malt nose, dry grainy malt flavor, light body, dry malt finish and herbal aftertaste; made with rye malt and Mt. Hood hops; specific gravity 1.048, 2.7% abw. [A, 53]

Riverside Brewing Co.
Brewpub in Riverside, CA

GOLDEN SPIKE PILSNER — gold, good hoppy aroma, big dry crisp Czech hop flavor, good body, very dry hop finish, very long dry hop aftertaste, very true to the classical Pils style and very well made. This lager is made with Saaz hops; dry hopped, specific gravity 1.045, 4.15% abw, 28 IBU. [B, 72]

RAINCROSS LAGER — medium deep gold, light malt aroma, light dry malty flavor, medium body, finishes dry, has a fairly long dry malt aftertaste; specific gravity 1.050, 4.3% abw. [B, 51]

RIVERSIDE EXTRA SPECIAL BITTER — amber, lovely bright hop and malt aroma, big malty flavor, big body, not sweet but not dry either, a malty beer with heft, more dry at the finish, long malty aftertaste. [A, 73]

PULLMAN PALE ALE — deep gold, pleasant hop and malt aroma; complex malt and hop flavor shows the Fuggles hops; good body, finishes dry hops; long dry malt and hop aftertaste retains the complexity and interest. The way this hop variety has been used in this recipe with pale and caramel malts has created a rather unique beer flavor that I have not previously experienced. Bittered with Centennial hops and dry hopped with English Fuggles; specific gravity 1.052, 4.64% abw, 28 IBU. [A, 60]

VICTORIA AVENUE AMBER ALE — deep amber, malt aroma; malt flavor has a sweetness in back that emerges at the finish; good body; medium dry malt aftertaste made with English Goldings hops; specific gravity 1.060, 4.6% abw. In bottle, there was a touch of apple in the nose

and a peaty-estery background to the flavor, as well as some homebrew flavors hidden in back and a little ashtray quality to the aftertaste. [A, 53]

SEVENTH STREET STOUT — deep brown, light chocolate malt and roasted barley aroma and flavor, medium to light body, smooth and pleasant, very quaffable for a stout, finishes dry roasted barley; dry roasted malt aftertaste has good duration; specific gravity 1.056, 4.7% abw. In bottle, the aroma was a bit more complex with a light taste of citrus orange and faint melon, the roasted malt in the flavor seemed stronger, and blended well with the chocolate malt; a complex and delicious brew that is very drinkable. As tasted at the brewpub. [S, 49]

RIVERSIDE CREAM ALE — beautiful gold, pleasant well-hopped aroma and bright hop flavor, good body, quite dry, long dry hop aftertaste, very good with food; specific gravity 1.050, 4.3% abw. [A, 64]

RIVERSIDE SAISON — gold; malty off-dry aroma has lots of fruity esters; the flavor is also very fruity and estery; medium body, very clean and refreshing; a very nice berry-fruity-honey taste while it is in your mouth; berry-like finish, off-dry fruity-berry aftertaste with no bitterness; made with an ale yeast augmented by sedimentary yeast from a bottle of Belgian pale ale; 6.5–7% abw. [A, 61]

RIVERSIDE HOLIDAY BOCK — red-amber, light dry

hop aroma; very dry hop flavor does not show much malt; medium body, long dry hop aftertaste; this is the 1994 Xmas offering. [BK, 68]

RIVERSIDE IRISH RED ALE — reddish-amber, big tight amber head (the first time Riverside has developed a brew with natural carbonation instead of injecting it and it comes off well); smooth aroma is a bit more malty but has both malt and hops; well-balanced malt and hop flavor, medium body, starts out medium dry, ends dry; long aftertaste shows both malt and hops and keeps the balance throughout. [A, 80]

SEVENTH STREET STOUT II — dark brown, light smooth chocolate malt and roasted barley nose and flavor, more mellow than hoppy, good roasted malt finish and aftertaste, light but long, good balance, quite drinkable. As found in 22-oz. bottles. [S, 71]

RAINCROSS CREAM ALE — cloudy amber, pear and applesauce nose, spicy clove flavor, creamy, crisp and tart, good summertime refreshment; has hops for balance and style, a wheat ale more in a Belgian than German style. [W, 55]

Rock Bottom Brewery

Brewpub in Denver, CO; Houston, TX; and Portland, OR. They are affiliated with the Rockies B.C. and the Walnut Brewery of Boulder, CO.

AZTEC ALE — very deep amber, faint malt nose, caramel malt flavor, dull malt finish and aftertaste; specific gravity 1.054. Tasted at Denver. [A, 41]

FALCON PALE ALE — deep amber, faint hop and malt aroma; flavor has plenty of both hops and malt but the balance is not good; medium body, dry hop finish and aftertaste. Brewed with crystal and Munich malts, Tettnanger and Mt. Hood hops; specific gravity 1.048, 3.4% abw. Tasted at Denver. [A, 42]

RED ROCKS RED — amber, light hop nose, bright medium dry hoppy flavor, quite zesty, good body; long dry hop aftertaste has plenty of malt for balance; made with English malt, and hopped with Mt. Hood and Tettnanger hops; specific gravity 1.054, 3.8% abw. Tasted at Denver. [A, 59]

ROCKIES PREMIUM DRAFT — pale gold, lovely hop aroma; bright hop and malt flavor is very tasty, excellent balance; light dry hop finish and aftertaste, a delicious and very drinkable brew; made with Tettnanger, Cascade, and Mt. Hood hops; specific gravity 1.042. Tasted at Denver. [B, 73]

ARAPAHOE AMBER — deep amber, faint malt nose, bright hop flavor, good body, plenty of malt; at the finish it abruptly and simply goes dry like the hops and malt disappear. Tasted at Denver. [A, 63]

RED HAWK ALE CASK CONDITIONED — gold, malt nose, weak malt flavor, slightly oxidized, dull malt finish and aftertaste. Tasted at Denver. [A, 37]

MOLLY'S TITANIC BROWN ALE — deep amber-brown, malt nose, big malt and hop flavor; just doesn't quite come together; made with dark crystal, Munich, and chocolate malts, Willamette and Mt. Hood hops; specific gravity 1.052, 3.6% abw. Tasted at Denver. [A, 47]

BLACK DIAMOND STOUT — deep ruby-brown, faint malt nose, bright malt and roasted barley flavor, good body, good carbonation level, very tasty, quite drinkable, and long; specific gravity 1.060. Tasted at Denver. [S, 67]

JAZZBERRY — amber, very fruity raspberry aroma, raspberry flavor, good body, medium dry raspberry aftertaste; made with fresh raspberries; specific gravity 1.054, 3.9% abw. Tasted at Denver. [A, 48]

LAGERHEAD — gold, malt and hop nose, slightly sour malt flavor with hops in back, dry hop aftertaste; brewed with Tettnanger and Hallertau hops; gravity 12.5 P, 3.45% abw. Tasted at Denver. [B, 45]

Notes

SCHWARZ HACKER — brown, big hop nose well backed with malt, flavor like the aroma, good body, light dry malt finish and aftertaste, good length; finished with Hallertau hops; specific gravity 1.056, 4% abw. Tasted at Denver. [B, 49]

ROBERT ALTMAN AMBER ALE — amber, pleasant light hop nose, light dry hop flavor, finishes very dry, medium body, long light dry hop aftertaste. Tasted at Denver. [A, 50]

OLD THUMPER BARLEYWINE — deep amber; slightly soapy nose has plenty of malt; big malty flavor has enough hops to balance the abundance of malt; alcohol shows strongly as well; finely carbonated, big but not huge, good balance, long medium dry hop aftertaste, very drinkable, but a bit austere. Tasted at Denver. [BW, 60]

PALOMINO PALE ALE — pale gold, light malt and hop aroma and flavor, light body, dry light hop and malt finish and aftertaste, medium long, not much character beyond being dry; made with

three varieties of northwest hops. Tasted at Houston. [A, 40]

CRYIN' COYOTE WHEAT ALE — hazy gold, light dry hop nose with a fruity background, complex hop and malt flavor, light and dry, light to medium body, stays light and dry in the long aftertaste. Tasted at Houston. [W, 66]

BUCKIN' ALE — deep gold, light hop and malt aroma, dry light hop palate, medium body, dry hop finish and aftertaste. Tasted at Houston. [A, 55]

ROCKET RED ALE — red-amber-gold, light malt aroma and flavor, medium body; dry malt finish and aftertaste has a fruitiness in back; very long. Tasted at Houston. [A, 58]

BIG HORN BROWN ALE — brownish-amber, dry roasted malt aroma, spicy hop and lightly roasted malt flavor, long dry roasted malt aftertaste. Tasted at Houston. [A, 57]

BLACK GOLD STOUT (CASK CONDITIONED) — deep brown, chocolate malt and roasted barley nose and taste, rich coffee and chocolate notes, medium body, long dry roasted malt aftertaste. Tasted at Houston. [S, 77]

BEAUMONT BITTER — amber-gold, dry well-hopped nose, dry bitter hop palate, medium body, dry hop finish and aftertaste, long and dry and bitter throughout. Tasted at Houston. [A, 55]

BIG HORN NUT BROWN ALE (CASK CONDITIONED) — deep

amber-brown, rich malt aroma and flavor, smooth like a fine English "mild," good body, dry mild finish and long dry malt aftertaste. Tasted at Portland. [A, 78]

BLACK SEAL STOUT — dark brown with a tan head, chocolate malt and roasted barley aroma, smooth slightly bitter roasted malt taste, good body; a little malty sweetness sneaks in at the finish and stays for the aftertaste. Tasted at Portland. [S, 73]

FALCON RED ALE — amber-gold, dry hop and malt aroma and flavor, medium body; becomes drier in the finish and aftertaste, ending very dry; made with Baird's pale ale and crystal malts, Willamette, Northern Brewer, Mt. Hood, and Liberty hops; OG 1053, FG 1.014, 5.25% abv, 28 IBU. Tasted at Portland. [A, 53]

CRYIN' COYOTE WESTERN ALE — gold, bright hop aroma and flavor, medium body; dry hop finish and aftertaste has a substantial malt component and seems to get sweeter as you sip it. Tasted at Portland. [A, 59]

WHITE PELICAN AMERICAN PALE ALE — amber, dry hop aroma and flavor, medium body, dry hop finish and aftertaste, has some complexity, medium body; there is a malty sweetness that pushes a bit more to the fore in the aftertaste but overall the palate stays dry. [A, 59]

Rockford Brewing Co.
Microbrewery in Wilmington, DE

ROCKFORD GOLDEN LAGER — hazy gold, faint slightly acidic nose; flavor is lightly acidic hops; good body, slightly sour dry hop aftertaste; seems to be a bit "off." [B, 27]

ROCKFORD RED ALE — pale reddish-amber, spoiled acidic aroma and flavor, sour and gone bad. [A, 2]

Rockies Brewing Co.
Brewery in Boulder, CO. Was named Boulder Brewing Co. until 1993.

BOULDER ENGLISH ALE — pale orange-amber, complex citrus-ale aroma, big well-hopped flavor, complex and full-bodied, very long and very good. [A, 36]

BOULDER EXTRA PALE ALE — pale orange-amber, big northwest hop aroma, strong hop flavor, big body, bold and balanced, long and delicious; made with crystal malt and Cascade hops; gravity 13.5 P, 3.8% abw. [A, 68]

BOULDER STOUT — deep amber-brown, big complex malt and tobacco nose, equally complex flavor of roasted (almost burnt) malt with hints of molasses and citrus, good balance, good body, smooth, mellow, and a long dry malt aftertaste with a trace of licorice; gravity 14 P, 4% abw. [S, 62]

BOULDER PORTER — deep copper, rich roasted malt aroma with a citrus nature and plenty of hops, fine balance, strong and rich off-dry hop and malt ale flavor, long dry hop aftertaste; gravity 13.0 P, 3.6% abw. [P, 53]

BOULDER BLACK CHERRY PORTER — opaque brown, attractive smoked cherry nose; smoked flavor is faintly fruity in the finish and aftertaste; light body, not a big number for Boulder. [P, 25]

BOULDER SPORT — bright gold, almost skunky hop aroma, big hop flavor with only a faint hint of malt, fairly brief. [B, 19]

BEST OF SHOW 1988 OKTOBERFEST BEER — bright amber, big toasted malt and hop aroma, smoky-malty dry flavor, medium body, very drinkable but not complex. [B, 52]

BEST OF SHOW 1989 INDIA PALE ALE — golden amber, bright tangy hop nose, big body, big clean and fresh hop flavor well backed with malt, complex dry hop finish, long malt aftertaste, drinkable and refreshing. [A, 79]

BOULDER LIGHT ALE — pale gold, lovely toasted malt nose, off-dry malt palate with hops in back, short watery aftertaste. [LO, 27]

TANKER ALE — hazy amber, appetizing delicious toasted malt aroma, almost smoky malt flavor, light body, bit of harshness from the burnt malt at the very end. [A, 37]

BUFFALO GOLD PREMIUM ALE — bright gold, toasted malt aroma, honeyed malt flavor, complex, fairly dry finish and aftertaste with some alcohol noticeable, very drinkable; gravity 13 P, 4% abw. Made under license from The Walnut Brewery. [A, 75]

BOULDER AMBER ALE — amber color, zesty hop aroma with plenty of malt, good body, well-hopped flavor; malt doesn't show until the finish and then stays through the aftertaste; very good balance; dry aftertaste has malt but is mostly hops; made with caramel malt and Hallertau hops; gravity 12.5 P, 3.6% abw. Bottled version described. [A, 69]

WRIGLEY RED — amber, weak dull malt nose, malt flavor, hop finish, a bit sudsy, dry hop aftertaste, very drinkable; brewed with two varieties of crystal malt with Nugget, Willamette, and Cascade hops; gravity 14 P, 4% abw. Made for affiliate Old Chicago Pasta & Pizza chain of restaurants in Colorado. [A, 40]

ROCKIES PREMIUM DRAFT — gold, malt aroma and flavor, light but balanced, dry hop finish and aftertaste; gravity 12 P, 3.4% abw. [A, 61]

BUFFALO GOLD PREMIUM ALE — tawny-gold, big hop aroma and palate, balanced off well with plenty of malt, big bodied, long dry hop finish and aftertaste, very satisfying brew in a well-hopped style; gravity 13 P, 4% abw. [A, 75]

BOULDER SUMMER ALE — amber, faint hop nose, fairly bright hop flavor, medium body, smooth, drinkable, slightly dry malt aftertaste. [A, 59]

BOULDER SUMMER ALE CASK CONDITIONED — amber, light hop nose, light dry hop flavor, light body, smooth, light dry hop finish and aftertaste. [A, 56]

BOULDER OKTOBERFEST — gold, hop nose with a faint grainy background, bright hop palate, good body, long aftertaste just like the flavor, a very good brew. [B, 67]

BOULDER OKTOBERFEST CASK CONDITIONED — gold, hop nose, very smooth hop flavor well backed with malt; very good and drinkable, but not quite as bright as above; long dry hop aftertaste. [B, 57]

BOULDER AMBER ALE — amber, hop and faint caramel aroma, flavor like the nose, good balance, good body, dry hop finish and aftertaste. This is the draft version served at the brewery. [A, 69]

BOULDER PORTER — brown, roasted malt nose and flavor, good body, dry malt finish and long dry malt aftertaste; draft version at brewery; gravity 13 P, 3.6% abw. [P, 53]

ASPEN SILVER CITY ALE — hazy gold, fruity malt aroma, interesting complex citrus fruit malt flavor; a little off-dry but there is plenty of hop bitterness in there as well; a hint of spiciness but not lactic; stays clean and has

great length. Made for Aspen Beer Co. in 1992, contract in 1993 was with Breckenridge. [A, 63]

ROCKIES PREMIUM ALE — gold, hop nose; fairly bright hop flavor has good balancing malt; medium body, long dry hop finish and aftertaste; gravity 12 P, 3.4% abw. [A, 61]

BOULDER FALL FEST — amber, dry northwest hop nose; bright bitter and dry hopped flavor has plenty of malt support for balance; medium body; long dry aftertaste shows some malty character in behind the hops; very drinkable, good duration on the palate; seems to soften as you continue to drink it; gravity 14 P, 5% abw. [A, 63]

BOULDER FLATIRONS ESB — gold; bright hop aroma has plenty of malt backing, starts out all hops, but the malt soon takes over; malty finish and aftertaste are not dry; it is likable but not a bitter; made with pale and caramel malts; hopped with Nugget, Tettnanger, and Cascade hops; OG 1056, FG 1.016. [A, 62]

BOULDER IGLOO ALE — dark amber, malty aroma, big dry malty flavor, medium body, dry malt finish and aftertaste. [A, 63]

Oregon Brewing Co. / Rogue Ales

Microbrewery formerly known as the Rogue Brewing Co. in Newport, OR. Serves the brewpub in Newport and wide distribution. It is affiliated with the Rogue River Brewing Co. brewpub in Ashland, OR, which does its own brewing.

ROGUE SPRINGBOCK — hazy amber, off-dry flowery malt nose, strong fruity malt flavor, medium body, very drinkable, long dry malt aftertaste, good brew. [BK, 62]

ROGUE WELCOMMEN RAUCH BIER — deep amber, smoked meat nose, smooth smoked malt flavor, medium body, extremely long dry smoked malt aftertaste, done with a delicate hand; made with Harrington, Munich, and crystal malts, smoked alder wood, and Perle and Mt. Hood hops; gravity 14 P, 4.6% abw. [B, 46]

ROGUE SMOKE — amber, beautiful smoked malt nose, sort of a meaty smoke with a touch of sweetness, flavor true to the aroma, lacks body, a bit harsh without being bold, fairly long; made from Northwest Harrington, crystal, carastan, and hand-smoked Munich malts, Perle and Saaz hops; gravity 14 P, 40 IBU. [B, 27]

MEXICALI ROGUE ALE — deep gold, light hop and spicy malt nose, light jalapeño and malt flavor; the pepper is more in the throat than on the tongue; good body; dry spicy finish and very long dry spicy-pepper aftertaste, very lightly done with the peppers and very pleasant; interesting and well balanced; the first one of the chili beers I actually enjoyed.

Brewed with smoked chipotle peppers, Harrington and Munich malts, and Willamette hops; gravity 13 P, 4.6% abw, 26 IBU. [A, 67]

ROGUE ALE — hazy amber, rich toasted malt aroma, flavor like the nose only lighter, medium body, light malt finish and aftertaste, faintly sour at the end; an ESB made with Harrington pale and crystal malts, Willamette and Kent-Golding hops; specific gravity 1.048, 3.9% abw, 35 IBU. [A, 43]

ROGUE-N-BERRY — cloudy brown, chocolate cherry nose, flavor like a Black Forest cake, sour berry finish and aftertaste, perhaps a bit salty as well; specific gravity 1.045, 4% abw; 20 IBU. [B, 34]

ROGUE GOLDEN ALE — hazy gold, bright flowery hop and malt nose, pleasant big hop flavor; lots of fruity malt balanced with big tangy hops; big hop finish, extremely long fruity malt and bright dry hop aftertaste, well-made brew; made from Northwest Harrington and Munich malts, Willamette hops; gravity 12.2 P, 26 IBU. This beer is marketed in Japan as White Crane Bitter Beer. [A, 74]

ROGUE NEW-PORTER — deep ruby-brown, brown head, smooth toasted malt nose, very dry malt flavor with a smoky-toasty character, rich yet dry, good malt finish, long dry toasted malt aftertaste; balanced, smooth, and flavorful; made with Northwest Harrington, crystal, chocolate, and Munich malts, Perle and Centennial hops; gravity 13.25 P, 4.3% abw, 35 IBU. [P, 75]

Notes

ROGUE SHAKESPEARE STOUT — near opaque ruby-brown, brown head, chocolate malt nose with a fruity background, also some faint smoke in back, fairly dry and faintly smoky malt palate, medium body, dry finish and long dry malt aftertaste, very drinkable; made from oats, roasted barley, Harrington, crystal, and Munich malts, roasted barley and rolled oats, with Cascade and Mt. Hood hops; gravity 15 P, 4.6% abw, 45 IBU. In Japan, this beer is labeled Brown Bear Black Beer. [S, 60]

ST. ROGUE RED — deep reddish-amber; fresh roasted malt and hop nose has a little citric tang in back that blends in nicely; big rich hop and roasted malt flavor is very well balanced; medium body, dry hop and malt finish, long dry hop aftertaste, a super brew with enough hops and malt for anyone; made with Northwest Harrington, crystal, and Munich malts, Chinook and Centennial hops; gravity 13.75 P, 4.6% abw, 42 IBU. In Japan, this beer can be found labeled Red Fox Red Beer. [A, 68]

ROGUE OLD CRUSTACEAN BARLEY WINE — hazy amber, strong good malt nose, lovely with a touch of citrus fruit, huge body, high alcohol, concentrated hop and malt flavor, big and strong, good fruity finish, very long malt aftertaste, excellent sipping beer; made from Harrington, crystal, and Munich malts with Chinook and Centennial hops; aged one year before release; OG 1095 (24 P), 8% abw, 80 IBU. [BW, 91]

ROGUE IMPERIAL STOUT — dark brown, huge nose of alcohol, Cascade hops, and malt that comes out almost like pineapple; enormous flavor loaded with both hops and malt almost overwhelms the senses; high octane brew, rich and syrupy, complex, chewy, very long and respectfully strong, a marvelous enticing brew; made with Harrington, Munich, crystal, chocolate, and black patent malts, Chinook, Cascade, and Willamette hops; gravity 24.5 P, 8% abw. Not generally available in bottles, this was bottled in a 375 ml size bottle. After one year in this size bottle, the Imperial Stout had improved showing more of the chocolate malt and less fruitiness, a strengthening of body, balance, and general cohesiveness of flavors, greater complexity, and a slight drying of the aftertaste. The year-old is better and truly makes your mouth happy. [S, 95]

ROGUE MOGUL ALE — deep amber, appetizing northwest hop aroma; complex flavor is first citrus hops, then dry hops with a good malt backing; medium to good body; long dry malt aftertaste seems to be a blend of chocolate and black patent malt; made with Perle, Saaz, Centennial, Chinook, Willamette, and Cascade hops with Northwest Harrington, Munich, crystal, and chocolate malts; specific gravity 1.065 (16.5 P), 5.2% abw, 45 IBU. I have seen it called Rogue Mogul Madness and it is Rogue's winter ale. [A, 72]

ROGUE MAIER BOCK — deep golden-amber, beautiful rich malt and big hop nose, great complexity; well-rounded malt flavor has a spicy hop bite in back on the palate; some alcohol noticeable, big body (17 P); tends toward malty sweetness at the finish and in the aftertaste; a complex very flavorful brew, a true Mai-bock. A later batch, about two years later, was much more hopped like a Heller Bock, but still had great balance and length. The later version is made with Northwest Harrington, Munich, and Carastan malts, with Perle and Saaz hops; gravity 16.5 P, 30 IBU. [B, 89]

ROGUE MO ALE — hazy yellow-gold, pleasant spicy malt and hop nose; brisk flavor has plenty of hops and malt up front, ginger and coriander (a lemony note) stay in back until it warms up; starts soft but you can feel it in your throat; long and very tasty. Label calls it a Belgium Style Unfiltered Ale and while it barely seems to qualify as that, it is good. This brew was developed at Rogue in Ashland as Snow White (as a witbier) with gravity 13 P, OG 1052, using Northwest Harrington and wheat malts, coriander, ginger, and Saaz hops to 25 IBU. [A, 59]

ROGUE DRY HOPPED RED — deep amber, bright strong northwest hop aroma, beautiful appetizing well-hopped flavor, big body, very dry and bitter with a real hop kick, extremely long and very delicious. [A, 84]

ROGUE DEAD GUY ALE — orange-amber, complex off-dry roasted malt nose and taste, a good flavor, crisp, clean, and complex, a very nice herbal finish and aftertaste; the Halloween offering from Rogue. [A, 78]

ROGUE WHALE ALE — orange-amber; fruity roasted malt nose is complex, weak fruity-estery palate; fruity finish and aftertaste has a "dirty" component; same recipe as Dead Guy Ale, but not at all the same in these samples. [A, 49]

ROGUE GRAND MOGUL ALE — deep amber, beautiful highly hopped nose and flavor, excellent balance despite its very hoppy style, big body, long dry hop aftertaste. The recipe calls for twice the malt of regular Mogul Ale; cask-conditioned; dry hopped; specific gravity 1.076, 6.11% abw, 74.5 IBU. [A, 81]

WILD IRISH ROGUE — deep brown-black, brown head, strong chocolate malt and roasted barley aroma, rich dry complex chocolate malt and roasted barley taste, fairly bitter, some earthy character, big body, long dry and bitter aftertaste, very good tasting bitter dry stout; made with two-row crystal and chocolate malt, roasted barley, rolled oats, and Cascade hops; gravity 15 P, 69 IBU. [S, 89]

ROGUE AMERICAN AMBER ALE — deep red-amber, zesty fragrant northwest hop (Cascade) nose; flavor is big dry citrus Cascade hops; good body, quite complex and delicious; very long dry hop aftertaste retains the northwest hop character. [A, 86]

ROGUE HAZELNUT BROWN NECTAR — deep dark amber-brown, chocolate malt and hazelnut nose, nutty chocolate flavor (not chocolate malt, real chocolate), medium to good body, long nutty chocolate-coffee aftertaste, delicious, balanced, made with Oregon hazelnut extract, two-row Harrington, brown, crystal and Munich malts, hopped with Perle and Saaz hops; gravity 14 P, 30 IBU, Seen labeled Rogue Hazelnut Nectar on tap handles. [A, 98]

ROGUE MOCHA PORTER — brown, malty nose has a coffee-chocolate background; very dry roasted malt flavor has a coffee-chocolate-smoky background; medium body; very long dry aftertaste is a continuation of the flavor; a well-made porter. [P, 60]

MAIERBOCK ALE — amber, big complex fruity malt and northwest hop aroma, creamy mouthfeel; balanced clean and interesting flavor is strong and malty; rich and tasty, very smooth but big and strong like a barleywine, very long. Made using Harrington and Klages, Carastan and Munich malts; top-fermented with Perle and Saaz hops. [A, 96]

McROGUE SCOTCH ALE — amber, oat aroma, big rich malty flavor, good body, long rich malty aftertaste, extremely well balanced; made from two-row pale, brown, and Cara Munich malts, with roasted barley, rolled oats, hopped with Willamette and Kent Goldings; top-fermented at 55°F; OG 1076 (17.5 P), FG 1.017, 8.2% abv, 45 IBU. [A, 86]

ROGUE CRAN-N-CHERRY ALE — red; strange fruity nose is very complex showing cranberries, cherry, honey, chocolate, and vegetal tones; dry sour fruit palate is not likable although tolerable, mercifully short. [A, 20]

ROGUE SANTA'S PRIVATE RESERVE ALE — hazy reddish amber, big northwest hop aroma, flavor to match the aroma, huge and delicious, well bodied, creamy, rich, and balanced, a real lip-smacker, extremely long. [A, 83]

Rogue River Brewing Co.
Brewpub in Ashland, OR. It is affiliated with the Oregon B.C. of Newport, OR and shares some common brands although it does its own brewing.

ROGUE GOLDEN ALE — deep gold, dry but rich malt nose, pleasant light malt flavor, light body, light dry hop aftertaste. Made with Northwest Klages, Harrington, and Munich malts

with Willamette hops; specific gravity 1.050, 4.2% abw. [A, 47]

ROGUE ASHLAND AMBER — deep amber, dry light malt aroma and flavor, medium body, dry light hop finish and aftertaste made with Northwest Klages, Harrington, and dark crystal malts and hopped with Cascades; specific gravity 1.050, 4.2% abw. [A, 47]

ROGUE SNOW WHITE — hazy gold, light spicy nose and taste, light body, finishes with spicy hop character, fairly long dry spicy aftertaste; wheat ale made with ginger root and coriander seeds dry hopped with Saaz hops; specific gravity 1.050, 4.2% abw. [W, 50]

Rohrbach Brewing Co.
Brewpub in Rochester, NY

GREGORY ST. LAGER — amber-gold, malt aroma; dry malt flavor with some hops showing; medium body, dry hop finish; aftertaste is long and dry showing plenty of both malt and hops; specific gravity 1.052. [B, 63]

SAM PATCH PORTER — brown; toasted malt nose is almost smoky; light toasted malt flavor, medium body, lightly hopped finish, medium long dry malt aftertaste; specific gravity 1.050. [P, 53]

HIGHLAND AMBER — copper colored, dry malt nose and flavor, medium body, finishes dry malt; fairly long dry malt aftertaste has little hop character; made with two-row pale and English crystal malt; specific gravity 1.048. [B, 47]

Rubicon Brewing Co.
Brewpub in Sacramento, CA

RUBICON INDIA PALE ALE — hazy gold, bright hop nose, light dry hop flavor; good balance provided by some malt in mid-palate; long dry hop aftertaste; made with two-row malted barley and Cascade and Chinook hops; gravity 14.2–14.8 P, 4.5% abw, 40 IBU. [A, 60]

RUBICON WHEAT — gold, malt nose, bright malt flavor, clean fresh malt aftertaste, no spiciness; made with 67% malted wheat and hopped to about 20 IBU with American Hallertau, Liberty, and Clusters; gravity 11.2–11.8 P, 3.8% abw. [W, 50]

RUBICON STOUT — dark brown, roasted barley nose, smooth roasted barley and chocolate malt flavor, good body, long dry aftertaste like the flavor. Recipe calls for two-row American malt and roasted barley hopped with Yakima Willamette, and Continental Hallertau, Northern Brewer, and Kent Goldings; gravity 13.2 P, 4.5% abw. [S, 57]

RUBICON HEFE WEIZEN — gold, mild malt aroma, smooth malt flavor, medium to good body, long clean malt aftertaste; made with wheat and two-row barley, hopped to 25 IBU with Saaz hops; gravity 13.2–13.6 P, 4.5% abw. [W, 54]

RUBICON AMBER ALE — amber, clean malt nose, smooth malt flavor, good balance with the hops of the background, long dry malt and hop aftertaste; made with two-row malted barley, caramel malt, Tettnanger, Hallertau, and Northern Brewers hops; gravity 12.4 P, 4% abw. [A, 58]

RUBICON BLOND BARLEYWINE — deep gold, very big malty aroma, even bigger flavor of concentrated malt; shows the Centennial hops strongly as well (100 IBU); big body, very long strong aftertaste with oodles of malt and hops, very tasty but it is a mouthful. Made with 100% two-row pale malted barley. [BW, 61]

The Russell Brewing Co.
Microbrewery in Santa Fe, NM

BLACK CLOUD PORTER — deep brown; light malt aroma shows some chocolate malt and citrus hops; complex light dry and very smooth malt flavor, some roasted barley, medium body, pleasant long light dry malt aftertaste, good complexity and very drinkable. [P, 63]

LA CANADA PALE ALE — hazy copper-gold, lovely appetizing citrus hop aroma, very finely carbonated, smooth dry citrus-hop flavor, medium body, long dry hop aftertaste, very refreshing and very easy to drink. [A, 67]

75th Street Brewery
Brewpub in Kansas City, MO

75TH STREET SUMMER ALE — deep gold, pleasant good off-dry malt aroma and flavor, good tasting, creamy textured, medium body, slightly drier malt aftertaste, not long; specific gravity 1.045, 3.8% abw, 13 IBU. [A, 67]

COW TOWN WHEAT — gold, faint wheat malt aroma, dull wheat flavor, light body, dull dry malt aftertaste; made from Kansas wheat and Munich malts; topped with Hallertau and Saaz hops; specific gravity 1.044, 4% abw, 12 IBU. [W, 45]

FOUNTAIN CITY AMBER ALE — copper-amber, hop nose, dry hop flavor with a faint roasty background, good body, long dry hop aftertaste; 28 IBU from Cluster and Cascade hops; specific gravity 1.058, 4.4% abw. [A, 68]

POSSUM TROT BROWN ALE — deep amber, malt nose, dry malt flavor, medium to good body, long dry malt aftertaste; made with Cluster and Cascade hops and a variety of barley malts; specific gravity 1.055, 4.7% abw. [A, 59]

ROYAL RASPBERRY ALE — pinkish-gold, subtle raspberry aroma and flavor of dry raspberry-malt, light body; lightly hopped (11 IBU) with Hallertau and Saaz hops; dry malt aftertaste retains the raspberry character; specific gravity 1.044, 4% abw. [A, 47]

YARDBIRD'S SAXY GOLDEN ALE — hazy gold, hop nose, light body, light smooth hop flavor featuring Cascade hops, dry hop aftertaste; made using Vienna and Munich malts; specific gravity 1.048, 4.2% abw, 23 IBU. [A, 47]

Notes

S & P Co.

Group of brewing companies including Falstaff, Pearl, General, and Pabst with brewing plants listed as being in Tumwater, WA (Olympia); Milwaukee, WI; San Antonio, TX; and Ft. Wayne, IN. There are additional corporate names used including San Antonio Beverage Co. Corporate headquarters are in Corte Madera, CA.

FALSTAFF BEER — pale yellow, rich malt nose; clean fresh flavor is mostly malt but there are hops in support; pleasant average American pilsener-style beer that sometimes is overcarbonated; specific gravity 1.0076, 3.55% abw. [B, 50]

FALSTAFF FINE LIGHT BEER — pale gold, light fresh malt nose, light malt aroma; flavor is light malt but the contribution of the carbonation is significant; light bodied, little aftertaste. [B, 30]

FALSTAFF LITE BEER — deep gold, very faint malt aroma, malt flavor decidedly on the sweet side, finishes a bit drier (but not much); neutral malt taste has little duration. [LO, 34]

FALSTAFF NA NON-ALCOHOLIC MALT BEVERAGE — deep gold, faint grainy nose and taste, light body, dull dry grainy finish and aftertaste, very short. [NA, 28]

LUCKY LAGER BEER — bright clear gold, interesting and somewhat complex malt and hop nose; off-dry flavor that doesn't dry out; still pleasant and refreshing, good length; specific gravity 1.009, 3.6% abw. [B, 49]

LUCKY BOCK BEER — dark brown but not deeply colored; sweet malt nose that doesn't really change across the palate; high carbonation tries to balance off the sweetness but the end result is a bit dull. [BK, 45]

LUCKY 50 EXTRA LIGHT BEER — bright pale gold, faint grainy aroma, light grainy palate, little aftertaste; the major flavor component is carbonation. [LO, 25]

LUCKY ORIGINAL DRAFT BEER — gold, big hop aroma, malt and hop flavor, good body, fair duration with both the malt and hops showing in the aftertaste. [B, 47]

LUCKY ORIGINAL DRAFT LIGHT BEER — pale yellow-gold, carbonation and hops for aroma; flavor is malt; light body; dry finish is mostly malt; brief dry malty aftertaste. [LO, 32]

BREW 102 PALE DRY BEER — pale yellow-gold, clean fresh malt aroma on the sweet side, pleasant slightly sweet malt flavor, good length; would be better if less sweet but still is pleasant and refreshing in hot weather. [B, 46]

HAMM'S SPECIAL LIGHT — medium to deep gold, light malt and hop aroma, weak and watery,

faint malt flavor, little finish and aftertaste; specific gravity 1.002, 3.3% abw. [LO, 36]

HAMM'S BEER — bright gold, pleasant malt nose, off-dry malt flavor, short malt aftertaste with some hops in back, pleasant hot weather quaffing beer; specific gravity 1.009, 3.95% abw. [B, 53]

HAMM'S ICE — pale gold; malt nose has a bright hop backing; dull off-dry malt flavor, sourness in back, dry hop aftertaste; 5.8% abv. [B, 35]

HAMM'S GENUINE DRAFT BEER — pale gold, faint malt nose, light off-dry malt flavor, very short on the palate; cold-filtered; specific gravity 1.009, 3.5% abw. [B, 43]

HAMM'S NON-ALCOHOLIC MALT BEVERAGE — gold, malt aroma, sour malt flavor, very weak and grainy, fairly brief; specific gravity 1.014, 0.15% abw. [NA, 9]

HAMM'S BIG BEAR MALT LIQUOR — pale gold, light malt nose, malt palate, sense of high alcohol, winey finish, long malt aftertaste. [ML, 36]

BALLANTINE PREMIUM LAGER BEER — light gold, clean fresh malt aroma; clean fresh light flavor is more malt than hops; medium body, pleasant and refreshing, medium length. [B, 53]

BALLANTINE XXX ALE — deep gold, big well-hopped and malt nose, big taste with plenty of hop bite, good body, good length, dry hopped; specific gravity 1.053, 4.3% abw. [A, 68]

BALLANTINE INDIA PALE ALE — tawny-gold, pungent hop aroma, big well-hopped nose, big hop flavor, good body, good balance, lingering full flavored aftertaste. It's not as big as it used to be, but it is still a mouthful; gravity 14.2 P, 5.10% abw. [A, 65]

NARRAGANSETT LAGER BEER — bright gold, off-dry malt nose, flavor mostly malt as the hops are very light, medium body, light dry aftertaste. [B, 50]

NARRAGANSETT PORTER — deep brown with a red-orange tinge, clean light malt nose, clean light malt flavor, slightly sweet at the finish, hops show only in the aftertaste. [P, 47]

PABST BLUE RIBBON BEER — pale gold, light malt and hop nose, clean malt and hop flavor, pleasant, light, and refreshing, light body, fairly dry, medium length; made from domestic malted barley and corn grits; specific gravity 1.044, 3.7% abw. [B, 50]

PABST BLUE RIBBON LIGHT BEER — pale bright gold, pleasant malt aroma, light dry mostly malt flavor, tasty, very drinkable, light and refreshing, good length. [LO, 50]

PABST BLUE RIBBON DRY BEER — pale yellow-gold, refreshing malt and hop nose, light body, good carbonation level, pleasant light off-dry malt flavor, refreshing, medium length. [B, 31]

PABST BLUE RIBBON DRAFT BEER — deep gold, malt nose, pleasant malt flavor, off-dry palate, medium dry finish and aftertaste; tastes better well chilled. [B, 31]

PABST GENUINE DRAFT — gold, fresh malt nose, faint off-dry malt and light hop flavor, medium body, smooth malt and hop aftertaste, medium to short in length; cold-filtered; specific gravity 1.044, 3.75% abw. [B, 39]

PABST GENUINE DRAFT LIGHT — gold, fresh malt nose, light hop flavor, light body; more aftertaste than flavor showing both malt and hops; medium to brief duration, also cold-filtered; specific gravity 1.034, 3.3% abw. [LO, 34]

PABST COLD FILTERED ICE DRAFT BEER — gold, malt nose and taste; flavor is a bit sweet; finishes off-dry malt; driest at the aftertaste but only slightly less sweet; specific gravity 1.050, 4.6% abw. Also called Pabst Ice Ale regionally, probably to meet local labeling laws regarding alcohol. [B, 40]

PABST PREMIUM QUALITY NON-ALCOHOLIC MALT BEVERAGE — pale gold, faint malt aroma, light grainy malt flavor, weak body; some hops show at the finish; fairly brief, probably a new label for the above. Can was white, now it is green (like O'Doul's). [NA, 26]

Notes

PABST LIGHT BEER — pale gold, faint hop and malt aroma, weak off-dry malt flavor, faint hops in back; short malt aftertaste is drier than the flavor; made using Styrian hops from Yugoslavia; gravity 8.7 P, 3.25% abw. [LO, 37]

PABST EXTRA LIGHT BEER — very pale gold, light hop nose, light body, weak malt flavor, little aftertaste, overall weak and watery; made with Cascade hops; specific gravity 1.001, 1.4% abw. [LO, 23]

PABST COLD FILTERED LIGHT BEER — brilliant deep gold, very nice flowery malt and hop aroma; light malt flavor resembles the nose but is very faint, finishes a bit better; light body, short dry aftertaste; would be pleasant if more were there. [LO, 37]

PABST NON-ALCOHOLIC MALT BEVERAGE — pale gold, faint malt aroma with hops in back, light malt flavor, very weak and grainy, fairly brief; specific gravity 1.0133, 0.19% abw. [NA, 26]

JACOB BEST PREMIUM LIGHT BEER — pale gold, appetizing malt aroma, clean crisp malt flavor, a little off-dry at the finish, pleasant malt aftertaste; made with Styrian hops; gravity 8.7 P, 3.35% abw. [LO, 36]

ANDEKER LAGER BEER — bright gold; hop aroma seems to off-dry but is more fragrant than it is sweet; pleasant hoppy flavor finishes off-dry, nicely balanced and fairly long; would be better if more dry; made with only two-row malt; gravity 11.5 P, 3.8% abw. [B, 47]

PEARL FINE LAGER BEER — bright gold, good malt nose, good flavor, plenty of hops to support the malt, clean and refreshing, good balance, good length; gravity 11.0 P, 3.7% abw. [B, 72]

PEARL XXX LIGHT LAGER BEER — pale gold, good malt and hop aroma, light body, light malt and hop flavor finishes off-dry, short aftertaste; specific gravity 1.022, 3.2% abw. [B, 30]

PEARL CREAM ALE — bright clear gold, off-dry malt nose; off-dry malt flavor but there are hops in back for balance; finishes clean; has a long pleasant dry aftertaste. [A, 58]

PEARL NA NON-ALCOHOLIC BEER — brilliant gold, grainy malt nose, light dull malt flavor, light body, little aftertaste. [NA, 18]

BUCKHORN BEER — pale gold, pleasant off-dry malt aroma; malt flavor has very little hop support until the finish; little aftertaste, pleasant but very light. [B, 42]

JAX BEER — yellow-gold; pleasant malt nose has to compete with high carbonation; pleasant mild flavor has a good hop and malt balance; off-dry aftertaste, refreshing for hot weather drinking. [B, 47]

OLYMPIA BEER — pale gold, light malt aroma, clean light flavor with the hops apparent only in the finish, medium dry hop aftertaste; a light pleasant tasting beer that is very drinkable. [B, 56]

OLYMPIA DARK BEER — deep amber, pleasant light malt and hop aroma with a metallic (tinny) background, dull malt flavor, dry malt finish and aftertaste; made with caramel and black malts with a touch of chocolate malt; specific gravity 1.044, 3.6% abw. [B, 30]

OLYMPIA GENUINE DRAFT BEER — pale gold, dusty dry malt nose; off-dry malt palate that is fairly pleasant; high carbonation, good balance, faint fruity malt and dry hop finish and aftertaste; cold-filtered; gravity 11.0 P, 3.7% abw. [B, 49]

OLYMPIA DRY BEER — pale gold, malt aroma, light dry grainy malt flavor, short; gravity 10.0 P, 3.95% abw. [D, 26]

OLYMPIA LIGHT — pale gold; good hop aroma that is a bit grainy; thin hop flavor that has sour malt tones; finishes dull and doesn't last. [LO, 32]

OLYMPIA GOLD LIGHT BEER — pale gold, light fresh malt aroma; light malt flavor that picks up quite a bit of hops in mid-palate; dry well-hopped finish and brief aftertaste. [LO, 38]

ST. BART'S NON-ALCOHOLIC MALT BEVERAGE — bright gold, pleasant grainy aroma with a touch of fruitiness; dry palate that is pleasant malt in front but there is little or no finish and aftertaste. [NA, 22]

COUNTRY CLUB MALT LIQUOR — tawny-gold, winey malt aroma, light malt flavor, off-dry finish; aftertaste is only malt; specific gravity 1.043, 3.8% abw. [ML, 23]

COUNTRY CLUB ALE — very pale gold; nose is stinky at first with a lemon oil background, this turns to a candy sweetness; dull malt flavor, faintly sweet dull malt aftertaste. [B, 26]

GOETZ PALE NEAR BEER — brilliant deep gold, light cereal grain aroma; flavor is grain and carbonation; light body, grainy malt aftertaste with little length. [NA, 26]

TEXAS PRIDE EXTRA LIGHT LAGER BEER — bright gold, light malt aroma, light malt flavor only faintly hopped, little finish and aftertaste. [LO, 45]

TEXAS PRIDE LIGHT LAGER BEER — gold, malt nose, light malt flavor, light body, weak malt finish, light and brief malt aftertaste. [LO, 39]

TEXAS SELECT — bright yellow, faint grainy nose, light grainy malt flavor, somewhat unbalanced hop and malt aftertaste. [NA, 17]

TEXAS LIGHT NON-ALCOHOLIC MALT BEVERAGE — bright yellow, light grainy malt nose and flavor, little finish and aftertaste. [NA, 29]

TEXAS LIGHT DARK NON-ALCOHOLIC MALT BEVERAGE — red-brown, light malt aroma; a watery malt flavor that has little depth; finish is even weaker and there is virtually no aftertaste. [NA, 19]

LODI BEER — bright gold, good rising malt and hop aroma, zesty malt and hop flavor; hop finish and aftertaste that has good length and hop balance. [B, 53]

JOLIE BLONDE BEER — hazy amber, big complex malt aroma, heavy body, a lot of malt extract, soft and winelike in style; faint hops in the finish, but this is a predominantly malty brew. Contract brew for Bayou Brew Bros. Inc of LA. [B, 51]

ORIGINAL CAJUN FLAVORED BEER — amber, fruity malt aroma; flavor starts out fruity malt but quickly there is hot Cajun spice that dominates by the finish and extends through the long long dry aftertaste. [B, 36]

SMITH & REILLY HONEST BEER — faintly hazy gold, good hop nose, bright zesty hop flavor, dry hop finish, hop aftertaste of medium duration, a refreshing all-malt (no adjuncts) beer. Contract brew for Smith & Reilly, Vancouver, WA. [B, 57]

CHEERS NON-ALCOHOLIC MALT BEVERAGE — tawny-gold, slightly dank malt and hop nose; flavor is thin malt and hops; light dry hop finish; brief aftertaste has faint hops. [NA, 21]

BEER — gold, light malt and hop aroma, light malt and hop flavor, medium body, short hop aftertaste. Generic supermarket beer on west coast. [B, 29]

LITE BEER — pale gold, light slightly grainy malt nose and taste, light body, little aftertaste. Generic brew for supermarkets on west coast. [LO, 33]

NA NON-ALCOHOLIC BEER — deep gold, malt nose, grainy malt flavor, weak body, light and short malt aftertaste. [NA, 17]

OLDE ENGLISH 800 MALT LIQUOR — gold, strong malt aroma, big aromatic malt flavor, big body; very long malt aftertaste that is quite sweet like the flavor; specific gravity 1.057, 5.6% abw. [ML, 29]

OLDE ENGLISH 800 GENUINE DRAFT MALT LIQUOR — gold, fruity malt aroma, dry sharp fruity malt flavor, not balanced; finish is malt but drier; short dull malt aftertaste. [ML, 29]

BEACH BREW NA MALT BEVERAGE — pale gold, grainy malt nose, slight hops in back, malty water flavor, sour finish, short, overall dank and weak. Contract brew for Beach Beer Brewing Co. of CA. [NA, 27]

ORIGINAL BEACH BEER — pale gold, hop aroma, sour malt and hop flavor, light and dry, somewhat sour finish and aftertaste. Contract brew as above. [B, 27]

STEAMER LANE LAGER BEER — tawny-gold, pleasant malt aroma; palate is slightly sour malt at first, then is dry toasted malt and hops; hops are bigger at finish leading into a long dry hop aftertaste. Contract brew as above. [B, 39]

BEACH BEER NATURAL DRAFT — gold; aroma starts out hops and then the malt comes in; the flavor is big malt but with the hops sufficient for balance; soft textured, big bodied, dry finish, short aftertaste. Contract brew as above. [B, 43]

BROWN DERBY LAGER BEER — pale gold, light hop nose, big malt flavor, medium dry malt aftertaste, not long. Made for Safeway markets. [B, 30]

MILWAUKEE GERMANFEST BIER — gold, faint hop nose, hop and malt flavor, dry hop finish and aftertaste, medium length; brewed with Styrian hops; gravity 12.9 P, 4.2% abw. Also made for Specialty B.C. [B, 47]

BURGEMEISTER (BURGIE) — gold, malt aroma with some hops in back, medium to light body, hops show better in the finish and aftertaste, lightly dry malt and hop ending. [B, 27]

BURGIE LIGHT GOLDEN — pale gold, light malt aroma with faint hops, light body, light malt flavor, some light malt and hops in a brief aftertaste. [LO, 23]

HAFFENREFFER PRIVATE STOCK MALT LIQUOR — medium deep gold color, malt aroma, light malt flavor; medium body is light for a malt liquor; soft light malt flavor, medium length aftertaste; specific gravity 1.045, 4.3% abw. [ML, 43]

OLD TANKARD ALE — amber, zesty malt nose, very ale-like, big

hop flavor, hops well balanced with malt, quite tangy, very long dry well-hopped aftertaste, a pleasant surprise; made with caramel malt; gravity 13.8 P, 4.7% abw. Made for Specialty B.C. of Milwaukee, WI, a wholly-owned subsidiary of Pabst. [ML, 43]

LASER SPECIALTY MALT LIQUOR — bright gold, malt aroma and flavor, light body, brief malt aftertaste; specific gravity 1.058, 5.55% abw. Made for Specialty B.C. [ML, 31]

ICE MAN MALT LIQUOR — gold, pleasant malt aroma with hops in back, off-dry malt flavor, stays sweet into fairly long aftertaste. Made for Specialty B.C. at Tampa, FL; Winston-Salem, NC; and Lehigh Valley, PA, all Stroh brewing plants. [ML, 50]

IZEN KLAR CRYSTAL CLEAR MALT — clear colorless, touch of citrus and berry in the nose, sweet lemon and lime flavor like soda pop, very sweet palate, sweet finish, short sweet aftertaste, S&P's answer to Zima. Made for Specialty B.C. [ML, 15]

PRIVATE SELECTION PREMIUM LIGHT BEER — gold, fragrant sweet malt nose, very light body, grainy malt and light hop flavor, light dry hop aftertaste of short to medium duration. Made for Lakeport B.C. of Hamilton (Ontario) for sale at Ralph's Grocery Co., Los Angeles, CA. [B, 56]

PRIVATE SELECTION PREMIUM DRAFT BEER — gold;

fragrant nose is similar to brew above but showing much more malt; flavor is more malty and sweeter; light to medium body, light off-dry malt finish, medium dry light malt aftertaste, short to medium duration. Also made for Lakeport B.C. for Ralph's Grocery Co. [B, 53]

800 ICE ICE BREWED MALT LIQUOR — gold; malt nose has a vegetal backing and also shows some hops; pleasant sweet malty flavor; some of the 8% abv shows on the palate; big body, medium long off-dry malt aftertaste. [ML, 30]

RED BONE RED LAGER — deep amber-gold; vegetal malty nose seems to show some corn; malt palate has a grainy background; medium body, medium long grainy aftertaste. This is the Pabst entry in the red beer sweeps. [B, 20]

BALLANTINE TWISTED RED ALE — deep amber; very complex fruity nose is sort of closed and unyielding; complex fruity malt flavor shows some alcohol; good balance from background hops, good body, smooth, low carbonation, ephemeral aftertaste; what is showing is good, but nothing sticks out; overall a good brew that reminds you slightly of Ballantine IPA as it is today. Falstaff's red entry. [A, 66]

TRADER JOE'S ALL BARLEY MALT BEER — deep gold, sweet grapey vegetal malt and hop nose; malty flavor shows no hops and is off-dry; medium dry malt finish and aftertaste, fairly dull. [B, 52]

PROSPECTOR JOE'S SPECIAL DARK GOLDEN BEER — beautiful orange-amber, dry malt nose, slightly roasty dry malt flavor, medium body, medium long dry roasted malt aftertaste. Made for Trader Joe's. [B, 59]

Note: Many of the S&P brews distributed on the east coast are made and packaged in Stroh breweries.

Saint Arnold Brewing Co.
Microbrewery in Houston, TX

SAINT ARNOLD WEIZEN — hazy gold, fruity wheaty malt nose, dry wheaty taste, light body, dry wheaty aftertaste, refreshing, stays dry, fairly long. [W, 61]

SAINT ARNOLD AMBER — amber-gold, light bright fruity hop nose (reminds me of a Keith's IPA from Nova Scotia); dry malt flavor has a hop finish with a bit of sweetness showing; medium body, medium long all dry aftertaste. [B, 61]

Salt Lake Brewing Co. / Squatter's Pub Brewery
Microbrewery and brewpub in Salt Lake City, UT.

EMIGRATION AMBER ALE — amber-gold, hop nose and taste, dry hop finish, short dry hop aftertaste, just hops. [A, 46]

PARLEY'S PORTER — brown, hop nose, dry hop flavor, finish, and short aftertaste. [P, 47]

ROCKY MOUNTAIN
WHEAT — gold, light hop nose,
light malt flavor, light body; what
little finish and aftertaste exists is
dry malt. [W, 49]

COLE'S SPECIAL BITTER —
gold, hop nose, light hop flavor,
medium body, dry hop finish and
aftertaste. [A, 63]

Samuel Adams Brewhouse / Philadelphia Brewing Co.

*Brew-pub in Philadel-
phia, PA. All beers are
made from extracts.*

BEN FRANKLIN'S GOLDEN —
gold, big hop nose, slightly soapy
malt palate, hops in finish, long
dry hop aftertaste; made with pale
malt, hopped with Hallertau and
Northern Brewer hops, dry
hopped with Hallertau; gravity 12
P, 3.5% abw. [B, 43]

POOR RICHARD'S AMBER —
golden amber, light smooth hop
nose, smooth very hoppy flavor,

long hop aftertaste; brewed with
pale and caramel malts, hopped
with Fuggles and Goldings, dry
hopped with Goldings; gravity
13.5 P, 3.8% abw. [B, 56]

GEORGE WASHINGTON'S
PORTER — deep amber, chocolate malt nose with some hops,
very dry hop and malt flavor, dry
hop finish and aftertaste; made
with pale, caramel, chocolate, and
black malts; hopped with Northern
Brewers, Hallertau, and Goldings,
honey added for balance; gravity
15 P, 4% abw. [P, 63]

BREWHOUSE NUT BROWN
ALE — brown, malt nose and
taste, light body, dry malt finish
and aftertaste; made from pale
malt and four roasted malts
(including caramel and chocolate),
Fuggles and East Kent-Goldings
hops, and top-fermented; gravity
12 P, 3.8% abw. [A, 45]

BREWHOUSE CRANBERRY
WHEAT — amber-gold, malt
nose; tart cranberry malt flavor
that is very tasty; long off-dry
fruity aftertaste; brewed with pale
and wheat malt; hopped with
Hallertau hops, with fresh cranberries added to the fermenter;
gravity 12 P, 3.8% abw. [W, 70]

SAMUEL ADAMS BROWN
ALE — pale brown, malt aroma
and flavor, medium body, dry
malt finish, long dry malt aftertaste; brewed with pale, caramel,
and chocolate malts; hopped
with Northern Brewers and
Goldings hops; gravity 12 P,
3.5% abw. [A, 53]

SAM ADAMS BREWHOUSE
SUMMER SPECIAL — gold,
light malt aroma; flavor is also
light malt but there is a good hop
balance; light body, very tasty and
refreshing, light dry hop finish and
aftertaste; made with Saaz and
Hallertau hops; 3% abw. [B, 47]

SAM ADAMS BREWHOUSE
SPICED BROWN ALE — brown,
spicy malt aroma; pleasant complex spicy flavor shows some malt
and citrus; light body; long dry
spicy aftertaste has a tart citrus
background; made with pale,
chocolate, and caramel malts; flavored with coriander and dried
tangerines; 4% abw. [A, 58]

San Andreas Brewing Co.

*Brewery and brewpub in
Hollister, CA*

KIT FOX AMBER RICHTER
SCALE ALE — hazy amber, zesty
tangy ale nose and flavor, bright
citrus character, sour cherries in
the finish, tangy dry malt aftertaste; made with crystal and
Munich malt; finished with
Chinook, Cluster, Goldings, and
Cascade hops. [A, 18]

EARTHQUAKE PALE ALE —
amber-gold, light hop aroma; big
very smooth dry hop flavor has a
citrus background; medium body,
dry hop finish, long dry hop aftertaste, very drinkable and very
good with food; brewed with a
touch of crystal malt; hopped with
Cascade and Chinook hops in the

brew kettle; dry hopped with Tettnanger hops; 3.5% abw. [A, 64]

EARTHQUAKE PORTER — deep brown, almost totally opaque, brown head, complex fruity roasted malt aroma, big smoky dry malt flavor, light body, dry malt finish; long dry malt aftertaste has a faint citrus component; brewed with crystal and chocolate malts, and malted barley, with Cascade, Chinook, and Goldings hops; 4% abw. [P, 62]

OKTOBER QUAKE ALE — hazy amber, big sharp hop nose, assertive hop flavor, light body, sharp hop finish, long harsh hop aftertaste, a bit too sharp; made with a high percentage of Munich malt and Tettnanger and Mt. Hood hops; 5.5% abw. [A, 13]

SEISMIC ALE — hazy amber, fruity malt nose, low carbonation, big malt flavor, not complex, ale-like hop bite at the finish, short to medium malt aftertaste, questionable balance; brewed with crystal and Munich malts; hopped with Cascade, Chinook, Cluster, and Goldings hops; 4% abw. [A, 37]

GREEN LEPRECHAUN ALE — lime green, malt aroma; flavor is mostly hops but there is malt in back; light bodied, dry bitter hop aftertaste, a very dry beer. [A, 53]

CRANBERRY NOEL (1991) — pinkish orange-amber, fruity-berry (cranberry) fruit flavor, not tart or sour or sweet, good malt background, good balance with the fruit and malt, long dry malt aftertaste. [A, 46]

CRANBERRY ALE (1992) — pinkish-orange, cranberry and grape aroma, cranberry flavor; hops show up in the middle and finish; medium body, a bit out of balance; bitterness of the cranberry clashes with the bitterness of the hops; dry long aftertaste; lightly hopped; 3.8% abw. [A, 42]

WOODRUFF ALE — amber, raspberry-woodruff nose, interesting spicy flavor, quite drinkable, very dry finish, spicy dry aftertaste; made with secondary addition of woodruff extract; 4.0% abw. [A, 47]

APRICOT ALE — gold, hop nose, dry malt flavor with faint apricot; dry fruity finish shows the apricot a little better, but the long dry aftertaste is just hops; light ale made lambic style with a secondary addition of one pound of fresh fruit per gallon and slow cold-fermented; 3.8% abw. [A, 63]

SURVIVOR STOUT — very deep brown color, tight brown head, big chocolate malt aroma; chocolate malt and roasted barley flavor is full but not overwhelming; good body, stays fairly dry; your palate gets used to it as you sip giving the effect of softening or lessening in strength; dry malt finish, long dry malt aftertaste. It is not unusual for a full flavored brew to appear to become reduced in strength as you continue to drink it, but the degree and speed of the transition on this stout is remarkable. Made with large amounts of crystal, roast, black, and chocolate malts with Chinook, Cluster, and Goldings hops; 4.1% abw. [S, 65]

San Diego Brewing Co.
Brewpub in
San Diego, CA

GRANTVILLE GOLD — gold, very bright hop aroma, big zesty hop flavor up front, very bold and quite tasty, dry hop middle and finish, long dry hop aftertaste really lasts. [A, 75]

SAN DIEGO AMBER — deep amber, light malt aroma, dry malt flavor with a hoppy finish, medium body; stays dry and malty into the aftertaste. [A, 59]

MISSION GEORGE PORTER — deep brown, chocolate malt and roasted barley aroma and flavor, dry, light taste, very drinkable, light to medium body, dry finish and aftertaste like the taste; aftertaste is brief; overall impression is that, although a good taste, it is too light for the style and doesn't get a chance to develop. [P, 60]

ADMIRAL BAKER BITTER — amber-gold, light hop nose, light dry hop and off-dry malt flavor, light to medium body; finishes dry and still shows hops and malt in the aftertaste which is not long. [A, 64]

OLD "395" — brown, faint malt aroma, good tasty malt flavor, fairly big body; alcohol is noted, but not found to be obtrusive; malty nature carries through the finish into a long slightly off-dry aftertaste; one of the lighter-flavored and bodied barleywines, but potent nonetheless; 8% abv. [BW, 67]

San Francisco Brewing Co.
Brewpub in
San Francisco, CA

ALBATROSS LAGER — deep tawny-gold, light hop nose, big hop flavor, medium body, very long dry hop aftertaste; specific gravity 1.047. [B, 63]

ALBATROSS LAGER — hazy gold, light malt and hop nose, bright hop flavor, but a bit austere, good body, long dry hop aftertaste. Tasted on draft at the pub. [B, 63]

EMPEROR NORTON LAGER — amber, malt aroma; hop and malt flavor has a sour background; hop finish, medium long dry hop aftertaste, specific gravity 1.056. [B, 65]

EMPEROR NORTON LAGER — hazy tawny-amber, good malt and hop nose; bright hop flavor is similar to Albatross but less austere having much more malt; very good body; long dry hop aftertaste has good malt in behind; very enjoyable. Tasted on draft at the pub. [B, 65]

GRIPMAN'S PORTER — cloudy-brown, citrus hop and malt nose, citrus overshadows the malt in the flavor, finishes like the flavor, medium long aftertaste; specific gravity 1.060. [P, 29]

BONZO'S BROWN ALE — dark brown, very light malt nose, light dry malt flavor with some roasted malt and celery seed in back, medium body, long dry malt aftertaste. Special Chinese New Year draft beer for Year of the Monkey. [A, 51]

San Francisco Bar & Grill
Brewpub in Tuscon, AZ

CACTUS LAGER — cloudy amber, dry hop aroma, extremely dry hop flavor, short dry hop aftertaste. Sometimes made by Electric Dave B.C. of Bisbee, AZ, when demand exceeds brewery capacity. [B, 53]

San Juan Brewing Co.
Brewpub in Telluride, CO

BLACK BEAR PORTER — brown, chocolate malt and roasted barley nose, taste like the aroma but very light, medium body, dry malt finish and aftertaste; made with black and chocolate malts with three varieties of hops; gravity 16 P, 6% abw. [P, 67]

BOOMERANG BROWN — brown, hop nose, hop flavor with good malt backing, good body, very drinkable, fairly complex as well, dry hop finish and aftertaste; gravity 16 P, 5.5% abw. [A, 69]

TOMBOY BITTER — amber, hop aroma and flavor, medium body, dry hop finish and aftertaste, somewhat unidimensional; gravity 14 P, 5% abw. [A, 47]

GALLOPING GOOSE GOLDEN ALE — gold, hop nose, balanced hop and malt flavor; a bright taste that is very drinkable; fairly dry finish and aftertaste, but short in length. Two-row and Munich malts are used with Cascade and Chinook hops; gravity 14 P, 4.5% abw. [A, 67]

LITTLE ROSE AMBER ALE —
amber, light dry hop aroma and
flavor, good body, dry hop finish
and aftertaste; specific gravity
1.058, 4.5% abw. [A, 47]

San Juan Brewing Co. / Front Street Ale House
Brewpub in Friday Harbor, WA

BROWN ISLAND BITTER —
amber, dry hop aroma with a faint
background of roasted malt, very
big dry bitter hop flavor, light to
medium body, dry and bitter hop
finish and long bitter dry hop
aftertaste; made with some black
malt, strongly bittered with Cluster hops; finished with Willamette
hops; specific gravity 1.042, 3.7%
abw. [A, 73]

EICHENBERGER HEFE-
WEIZEN — deep gold, spicy
fruity aroma, off-dry spicy clove
and malt flavor, medium to good
body; off-dry spicy aftertaste has
some length; made with 60%
wheat and a hint of Carastan malt;
hopped with Perles; specific gravity 1.057, 4.7% abw. [W, 72]

RAGING MAIN ALE — deep
amber, malt aroma; big malt flavor
is off-dry and a bit alcoholic
(5.8% abw); big bodied; long off-
dry malt aftertaste has hop support
and some complexity; a winter
warmer made with two-row pale,
Munich, crystal, and black malts;
hopped with Cluster and Willamette hops; specific gravity
1.072. [A, 80]

STARBOARD PORTER —
brown, slightly roasted malt
aroma, dry malt flavor, medium
body, dry malt finish and aftertaste; made with Carastan and
black malts; balanced with Cluster, Mt. Hood, and Willamette
hops; specific gravity 1.054, 4.3%
abw. [P, 60]

San Marcos Brewery & Grill
Brewpub in San Marcos, CA

SAN MARCOS PREMIUM —
gold, light dusty dry hop aroma, dry
hop flavor, medium body, very dry
finish, fairly long dry aftertaste
shows some malt; brewed with Mt.
Hood hops and finished with Saaz
hops to give it a distinct European
pils-style even though it is top-
fermented; gravity 13 P. [A, 67]

SAN MARCOS AMBER ALE —
amber, light hop aroma, big malt
flavor with the hops in back, good
body, complex malt and hop
finish, dry hop aftertaste; top-
fermented; made with Nugget and
Northern Brewer hops; specific
gravity 1.056, 4.25% abw. [A, 59]

SAN MARCOS
WINTERFEST — deep amber,
big spicy hop aroma and flavor,
plenty of malt in support, dry
spicy hop finish, good body,
medium long dry and spicy hop
aftertaste, overall more of a
malty Märzen-style beer; top-
fermented; brewed with Nugget
and Saaz hops; gravity 16 P.
[A, 67]

Notes

SAN MARCOS OATMEAL STOUT — opaque, dense brown head, light chocolate malt and roasted barley nose (more chocolate malt than roast barley), light smooth roasted barley flavor, medium body, dry malt finish and aftertaste, short but very drinkable; top-fermented stout; specific gravity 1.052, 4.25% abw. Also called Old Goat's Stout. [S, 76]

SAN MARCOS UNFILTERED WHEAT — hazy gold, no head, faint malt nose, lightly spiced clove flavor, dry malt finish and aftertaste; some European hops show in the aftertaste made with special German weizen yeast and 50% wheat malt; specific gravity 1.052, 4% abw. [W, 60]

Santa Clarita Brewing Co.
Brewpub in Santa Clarita, CA

TUMBLEWEED WHEAT — hazy deep gold, sweet honeyed berrylike nose, very honeyed palate, medium body, sweet finish, long fairly sweet aftertaste; goes down easily, a bit too sweet but still refreshing. [W, 53]

BEALE'S BITTER — dark amber, very faint malt aroma; front palate is off-dry malt; dry finish, medium body; long dry aftertaste shows little in the way of hops. Sampled two days earlier from the same cask, the brew was very hoppy and bitter, but appears to have softened out considerably as it lowered in volume. The brewer and bartenders had noticed this as well. [A, 47]

RAILROAD PORTER — deep amber-brown, smoky peated malt nose and flavor, with an off-dry malt background, good body; smoky taste stays through a long aftertaste. Earlier versions of this brew were made more smoky, but it has been toned down. The smoky nature still dominates, but it is no longer overwhelming. The present style is very likable. [P, 73]

Santa Cruz Brewing Co.
Brewery and brewpub located in Santa Cruz, CA

LIGHTHOUSE LAGER — gold, light citrus nose, refreshing and bright malt and citrus hop flavor, complex, good body, hop finish, long hop aftertaste, good balance; made with two-row pale malt and Cluster and Hallertau hops; specific gravity 1.046, 3.8% abw. [B, 63]

LIGHTHOUSE AMBER — hazy amber, faint grapefruit and malt aroma, very dry malt palate; so dry you are reminded of a tannic wine; complex dry hop finish, good body, short dry hop after-taste; made from two-row pale and caramel malt; specific gravity 1.048, 3.8% abw. [B, 63]

PACIFIC PORTER — deep almost opaque brown, off-dry malt nose, dry malt flavor, short dry malt aftertaste, medium body, little complexity; made using black barley; specific gravity 1.055, 4.6% abw. [P, 43]

HOPPY HOLIDAYS 1992 — amber, malt nose, big strong hop flavor, some alcohol noticeable but not overly so, good body, long strong hop aftertaste. [A, 62]

BEACON BARLEYWINE STYLE ALE — amber, good malt nose, huge malt flavor, big body, long and strong, a huge malt sipping beer, powerful stuff; brewed from two-row malt and Yakima hops; specific gravity 1.095, 8.5% abw. [BW, 67]

Santa Fe Brewing Co.
Brewery in Galisteo, NM

SANTA FE PALE ALE — hazy amber, luscious off-dry citrus hop and malt nose, very appetizing, big malt flavor with a light citrus background, dry hop finish and aftertaste, good length; made with pale and caramel malts, hopped with Cluster hops, and finished with Cascade and Willamette hops; single-step infusion mashed bottle-conditioned; OG 1052 (13 P), 4.2% abw, 36 IBU. [A, 62]

FIESTA INDIA PALE ALE — amber-gold, big Northwest hop nose and flavor (Cluster and Cascade), bright hop finish, long dry hop aftertaste, excellent balance; well put together thanks to three months bottle-conditioning; made with pale, light caramel and caramel malts, Cluster and Cascade hops for bittering; OG 1060 (15 P). [A, 63]

SANTA FE NUT BROWN ALE — pretty amber-brown, dry chocolate malt and hop aroma and taste; aroma is more chocolate malt than is the flavor; very complex with a fine balance, good body, smooth; dry aftertaste like the flavor is plenty long; brewed with pale, caramel, and chocolate malts, Willamette hops, single-step infusion mashed; bottle-conditioned; OG 1052, 4.2% abw, 25 IBU. [A, 73]

OLD POJOAQUE PORTER — deep amber-ruby brown, big complex nutty malt nose and taste, good body, excellent balance, dry malt finish and aftertaste, a classical porter; brewed with pale, caramel, and chocolate malts, Cluster hops for bittering, and Cascade and Willamette hops for finishing; single-step infusion mashed and bottle-conditioned; OG 1056 (14 P), 4.8% abw, 36 IBU. [P, 74]

GALISTEO WEISS — amber, malt nose and flavor, no spiciness, medium dry malt finish and aftertaste, pleasant American-style wheat beer; made from 50–50 pale and wheat malt; bittered with Cluster hops to 17 IBU with Cascade and Willamette hops for finishing; single-step infusion mashed, bottle-conditioned; gravity 12 P. [W, 47]

CHICKEN KILLER BARLEY WINE — deep amber, dry malt nose and taste, not big like most barleywines, but rather nicely smooth and deliciously malty, long malt aftertaste; made from pale and caramel malts, Cluster hops for bittering, Willamette and Cascades for finishing; single-step infusion mashed, and bottle-conditioned; specific gravity 1.096, 7.5% abw, 80 IBU. [BW, 67]

SANGRE DE FRAMBUESA — reddish gold, pink foam, raspberry nose; big tart raspberry flavor is fruity but not really sweet; good body, dry raspberry finish and aftertaste, quite pleasant and very nice of the style; made from pale and caramel malts with Willamette hops (17 IBU), no finishing hops, single-step infusion mashed; raspberries added to hot wort and added to primary (3 lbs. berries per gallon); bottle-conditioned; specific gravity 1.058, 4.5% abw. [A, 75]

SANTA FE IMPERIAL STOUT — deep brown; big malt aroma and flavor shows a touch of chocolate; big body, plenty of alcohol (OG 1080), hefty malt finish and long malt aftertaste shows alcohol. [S, 83]

Santa Rosa
Brewing Co.
Brewpub in Santa Rosa, CA, formerly known as Kelmer's Brewhouse.

KRYSTAL FRESH WHEAT BEER* — hazy gold, wheat nose, touch of lactic in back, creamy texture, dry slightly lactic grapefruit-like flavor, fairly short aftertaste like the flavor; made with 60% malted wheat. [W, 49]

KRIS KRINGLE SPECIAL CHRISTMAS ALE 1990* — amber, big head, zesty soapy hop nose, big hop flavor, big and alcoholic, finishes dry hops, long dry hop aftertaste, very good full-flavored brew. [A, 68]

KRIS KRINGLE VERY SPECIAL CHRISTMAS ALE* — amber, big pleasant malt nose, rich malt flavor, burnt malt backtaste, harsh at the finish; burnt nature stays to mar the aftertaste. [A, 17]

KELMER'S KLASSIC FINE ALE* — hazy amber, clean zesty hop nose much like a pils; complex flavor is smoky malt and hops; smoky finish, long very dry malt aftertaste without any smokiness whatever. [A, 65]

KELMER'S BREWMASTER'S SPECIAL ALE* — amber, grassy malt aroma, sharp hop and sour malt flavor, finish, and aftertaste. [A, 7]

* Brews produced by Kelmer's Brewhouse, closed in 1993, reopened that same year as Santa Rosa Brewing Co. at the same location. These beers were discontinued in late 1992/early 1993 so any samples found are likely to be too old.

TIMOTHY'S TIPPLE — deep amber, strong aroma features hops and malt; rich and powerful flavor has plenty of malt, hops, and alcohol; big body; very long aftertaste shows all of the complex flavor and richness; barleywine top-fermented and matured over Cascade hops for four months; specific gravity 1.097. [BW, 74]

CASCADES IPA — gold, a beautiful appetizing hop and malt nose, equally attractive flavor with plenty of both malt and hops, big body, smooth and balanced, delicious, long dry aftertaste; classical IPA that really shines; made with Cascade and Chinook hops; gravity 15 P. [A, 85]

ST. PADDY'S PORTER — brown, lovely malt aroma, big rich malt flavor, good body, dry malt finish, very long complex malt aftertaste; top-fermented; gravity 13 P. [P, 71]

EMPIRE AMBER — amber; pleasant malt aroma is lightly hopped with Fuggles hops; dry malt flavor, medium body, brief dry malt aftertaste; this light ale's best feature is the nose. [A, 52]

SANTA ROSA GOLDEN PALE ALE — gold with a touch of amber, hop aroma and flavor, good body, dry hop finish, fairly long dry hop aftertaste; top-fermented; gravity 14 P. [A, 65]

SANTA ROSA RASPBERRY ALE — deep gold, light raspberry aroma and flavor, fairly good body, light raspberry and dry malt finish, long light raspberry aftertaste; made with 60% malted barley and 40% wheat and 120 lbs. of fresh seedless pureed raspberries; specific gravity 1.060. [A, 43]

Santa Rosa Bay
Brewery &
Waterfront Cafe
Brewpub in Ft. Walton Beach, FL

PILSENER LION — pale gold, light dry hop aroma and flavor, light to medium body, short dry hop aftertaste. [B, 51]

RED LADY — amber, light malt nose, big malt flavor with good hops in back, good body, light dry malt and hop aftertaste, a very tasty brew. [A, 65]

THOMAS JEFFERSON BROWN ALE — brown, dusty malt nose; light malt flavor has some faint roasted barley character; medium body, medium length light dry malt aftertaste; specific gravity 1.056, 4.3% abw. [A, 50]

SANTA ROSA BAY INDIA PALE ALE — deep gold, malt aroma, big complex malt flavor, good body; malty finish and long malt aftertaste maintains the complexity of the flavor; delightful satisfying brew, the star of the Santa Rosa Bay lineup. [A, 79]

Sarasota Brewing Co.

Brewpub in Sarasota, FL (A Bradenton, FL location was closed in late 1993.)

SEQUOIA AMBER LAGER — amber, dusty dry malt nose, big dry hop and malt flavor; like the Cobra it is basically a highly hopped beer, but there is enough malt to show and to balance; good body; long dry aftertaste is mostly hops but with a good malt structure; hopped with Yakima Cascades; 4–5% abw. Tasted a second time, at GABF, the brew seemed less hoppy, rather more a light smooth malty beer with a dry malt finish and aftertaste. This latter version made with two-row pale malt, 16% Munich 20, 10% caramel 60, 0.6% chocolate malts, hopped with Cluster and Cascades to 16 IBU, lager yeast, 7-day ferment, 2-week lager, 1.5 micron filter, and forced carbonation, to spec at gravity 13.9 P, 4.5% abw. [A, 78]

HOP HARVEST PALE ALE — amber-gold, big fragrant hop nose, fairly strong hop palate, bitter enough for most hop-heads, big body, good complexity at the finish, long dry and bitter hop aftertaste, well made and good of type; hopped with Cascades; 5% abw. [A, 63]

QUEEN'S PORTER — brown, light roasted malt aroma; smooth roasted barley flavor shows a little chocolate malt; good body, dry malt finish and aftertaste, very good with food; made with pale two-row, 14% caramel 60 Lovibond, 3% Munich 20, 4% Carapils, 5% chocolate, and 1% black malts; hopped with Cluster and Fuggles to 22 IBU, with ale yeast; 4-day ferment, 7-day maturation; gravity 15.5 P, 5.5% abw (4.5–5% abw). [P, 73]

YA MILLS HONEYMEAD ALE — deep gold, honeyed malt aroma; front palate is honeyed malt like the nose, but it dries by mid-palate and is dry by the finish; big body, rich and complex malt flavor; well hopped which shows in the dry hoppy aftertaste; made with Florida honey, pale and roasted malts, and Cluster and Tettnanger hops; gravity 14.9 P, 5.0% abw. [A, 72]

SARA DE SOTO GOLDEN ALE — gold, light smooth dry malt aroma and flavor, medium body, lightly hopped dry finish and aftertaste; made with pale two-row, 4% Munich 20, 6% Carapils; hopped to 14 IBU with Perle and Fuggles hops, ale yeast, 3-day ferment, and 1-week maturation; gravity 12.9 P, 4% abw. [A, 74]

OKTOBERFEST — deep amber, light dry malt aroma; very dry palate shows both malt and hops (but more of the hops); medium body, dry malt finish and aftertaste, a bit short. [B, 52]

WEIZEN WHEAT — deep gold, faint malt nose; tangy malt flavor is more acidic than spicy; very refreshing, tangy finish, short dry tart aftertaste, a good hot weather beer. [W, 53]

COBRA LIGHT — gold, light hop aroma, bright very dry refreshing hop flavor; good supporting malt but this is basically a highly hopped beer; dry hop finish and aftertaste with hops definitely dominating at the end; excellent "light" beer; made using Wisconsin malt and Saaz hops and has 3.5–4% abw. Also seen at GABF as Cobra Lite. [LO, 63]

GLACIER BAY PILSNER — gold; bright hop aroma and flavor is very central European in style; medium body; finish is pleasantly bitter; long dry and slightly sour-bitter hop aftertaste completes the style; 3.8% abw. [B, 54]

BLACKBEARD'S DARK LAGER — amber-brown; toasted malt aroma shows a chocolate malt background; medium body, bright balanced flavor is mostly of the malts, but there is a good hop supporting to balance; fairly long dry malt aftertaste is like the flavor; made from Munich, high-kilned chocolate, and black patent malts, with Perle hops; 3.5% abw. [B, 68]

HONEY MAIBOCK — deep gold; honeyed malt nose has an aromatic hop background; palate favors the honeyed malt character, but the hops are there in back; big body, alcohol (6.5%) shows but doesn't interfere; malt finish; off-dry malt and dry hop aftertaste maintains the balance. [BK, 64]

Note: At the pub several combinations are offered including Black Diamond, a mix of Cobra and Porter; Black Gold, a mix of Sequoia and Porter; Black Satin,

Porter and "special investor's brew" (whatever that might be); and Black Velvet (Porter and champagne). They also offer Florida Rattlesnake-Cobra Lite with a jalapeño pepper.

August Schell Brewing Co.
Brewery at New Ulm, MN

AUGUST SCHELL PILS BEER — deep amber-gold, beautiful flowery hop nose, big hop flavor with plenty of malt, good body, long dry hop aftertaste; classic German-style pilsener, a great recipe and excellent execution; brewed with barley malt, Hallertau and Cascade hops, and a lager yeast; gravity 13.4 P, 4.55% abw. [B, 67]

AUGUST SCHELL EXPORT BEER — right gold, faint malt aroma, light malt flavor, light body, faintly sweet malt finish and brief malt aftertaste. [B, 27]

AUGUST SCHELL LIGHT BEER — pale gold, light malt aroma, light body, dry hop finish, short dry hop aftertaste. [LO, 42]

SCHELL DEER BRAND BEER — very pale gold, pleasant malt aroma with a faint trace of apple, high carbonation, off-dry malt flavor with some esters in back, dry malt finish, short aftertaste. [B, 20]

AUGUST SCHELL WEISS BEER — brilliant pale amber, grainy nose; spicy malt palate that stays throughout and into a long aftertaste. [W, 34]

AUGUST SCHELL WEIZEN BEER — bright gold; clean fresh fruity-malt nose is a bit on the sweet side; light body, tangy background to the malt flavor much like many German weizens, clean and refreshing, finishes dry, medium length aftertaste, refreshing hot weather beer; made with 60% wheat and 40% barley malt, using a German wheat beer yeast strain, Cascade and Mt. Hood hops; gravity 10.8 P, 3.5% abw. [W, 43]

AUGUST SCHELL OKTOBERFEST 1991 — rosy-amber, pleasant complex malt aroma, good body, big strong hop and malt flavor, complex and balanced, smooth and delicious, dry hop finish, long dry hop aftertaste. [B, 84]

AUGUST SCHELL OKTOBERFEST 1990 — amber, bright tangy hop aroma, big ale-like flavor with lots of hop bite and plenty of malt, good body, dry hop finish and aftertaste, an assertive brew. [B, 77]

SCHELL BOCK BEER — bright amber, dry caramel malt nose, dry caramel flavor, light body, could use more hops, light medium dry malt finish, off-dry short malt aftertaste. [BK, 39]

GEMEINDE BRAU — medium pale gold, malt nose, good body, good flavor with plenty of malt and light hops, off-dry malt finish and aftertaste. Contract brew for Gemeinde Brau, Inc., Amana, IA. [B, 45]

ULMER BRAUN BEER — deep amber-brown, dry malt nose and taste; almost soapy, but that feature doesn't develop enough to mar the flavor; dry malt finish and medium length aftertaste. Ulmer B.C., New Ulm, MN. [B, 45]

HELENBOCH BEER — clear deep gold, appetizing hop nose, dry hop flavor, long dry hop aftertaste; made with Hallertau and Saaz hops, pale lager, Munich, and Carapils malts; gravity 12.0 P, 4.1% abw. Contract brew for Friends B.C., Helen, GA. [B, 43]

HELENBOCH 1992 OKTOBERFEST — amber, zesty hop aroma, big flavor with lots of hop bite and plenty of malt, good body, dry hop finish and aftertaste; made with Hallertau and Saaz hops with Munich, pale, and specialty malts; gravity 12 P, 4.2% abw. Contract brew for Friends B.C., Helen, GA. The 1991 version had a higher gravity (13 P). [B, 69]

JEFFERSON BLUE RIDGE MOUNTAIN BRAND LAGER — sherry color, lovely toasted malt aroma, full rich malt flavor, good hop balance, malt and hop finish, long malt aftertaste. Contract brew for Federal Hill B.C., Forest, VA. [B, 81]

SUMMER PALE LAGER — bright gold, fresh clean bright malt nose, dry hop palate, highly carbonated; dry hop aftertaste is a bit dull. Contract brew for Saloon B.C., Sweeny's Saloon in St. Paul, MN. [B, 37]

SALOON LIGHT LAGER — brilliant pale gold, dry malt nose, very little flavor, just a hint of banana behind some malt, dull short malt aftertaste. Contract brew as above. [LO, 20]

AUBURN DARK LAGER — deep amber-brown, malt nose, thin malt flavor, light body; thin malt aftertaste that lasts a short time. Contract brew as above. [B, 46]

PECAN ST. LAGER — amber-gold, very pleasant toasted malt and hop nose; hefty toasted malt flavor with hops coming in well at the finish; long dry aftertaste, smooth, pleasant, and drinkable; brewed with pale and crystal malts, and flavored with Hallertau, Tettnanger, and Cascade hops; kraeusened. Made for The Old City B.C., Austin, TX. [B, 67]

ALIMONY ALE — amber, fruity malt and light hop nose, big bitter hop flavor with plenty of malt in back, bitter finish, long dry hop aftertaste, nicely done. Contract brew for Buffalo Bill Brewery of Hayward, CA. [A, 63]

GROWLIN GATOR LAGER — pale yellow-gold, pleasant malt nose; refreshing malt flavor is good while it lasts (which is not for long); light body, fine for hot weather drinking; brewed with pale malt and Yakima hops with Saaz dry hopping. Fermentation reaches a temperature of 56°F; gravity 11.2 P, 3.7% abw. Made for Florida Beer Brands of Orlando, FL. [B, 41]

OLD WEST FAMOUS AMBER BEER — deep amber, bright hop and malt aroma, smooth and well balanced, tasty dry malt flavor with good hop support, finishes like it starts, dry malt and hop aftertaste, good length; brewed with six-row malt with a touch of caramel, and Yakima Valley and Saaz hops; bottom-fermented to a maximum temperature of 58°F; gravity 11 P, 3.71% abw. Nothing stands out, but it is well made. Made for Florida Beer Brands of Orlando, FL. [B, 61]

FLYING ACES LIGHT LAGER BEER — gold; aroma is mostly hops but there is malt in back; light flavor shows a little malt and hops but not much of either; light body, dry finish, short dry aftertaste; made with six-row malt and Chinook and Cascade hops; slow-fermented at 58°F for 8 days; low-calorie; gravity 8.0 P, 3.25% abw. It is made for Florida Beer Brands of Orlando, FL. [LO, 47]

SPANISH PEAKS BLACK DOG ALE — amber, good fruity malt aroma; some samples were slightly buttery; bright well-hopped flavor, dry finish cuts off quickly, very slight dry hop aftertaste; made from pale malted barley, Munich and Carastan malts, a touch of chocolate malt, Pacific Northwest hops, and ale yeast; gravity 12.5 P, 3.8% abw. Made for Spanish Peaks B.C., Bozeman, MT; also made at Spanish Peaks. [A, 53]

SPANISH PEAKS BLACK DOG YELLOWSTONE PALE ALE — gold, bright but light hop nose; zesty hop flavor has plenty of good malt backing; bright and balanced, long dry and bitter hop aftertaste, attractive appetizing well-made beer; brewed from pale, crystal, and Carastan malts; specific gravity 1.054, 4.5% abw. Contract for Spanish Peaks as above. [A, 67]

SPANISH PEAKS BLACK DOG SWEETWATER WHEAT ALE — yellow-gold, clean light malt and hop aroma, light but bright hop flavor, light body, dry hop finish; dry hop aftertaste is on the brief side; American-style wheat ale; gravity 11 P, 3.8% abw. Contract for Spanish Peaks. [W, 61]

SCHMALTZ'S ALT — very deep dark reddish brown, pleasant light roasted malt aroma with a little sweetness and a faintly soapy background; rich roasted malt flavor is very tasty; good body, medium dry finish and long medium dry aftertaste; very pleasant using an altbier yeast, pale, caramel, chocolate, and Munich malts, with Chinook and Mt. Hood hops; gravity 14.5 P, 4.65% abw. [A, 73]

BEVERLY HILLS HARVEST ALE — amber, pumpkin pie spice (nutmeg, cinnamon, clove, allspice) aroma, carbonated pumpkin pie flavor, medium body, dry finish; flavor cuts off as soon as you swallow it; very little aftertaste. Made for Beverly Hills Beerhouse Co., Ltd., Los Angeles, CA. [B, 50]

AUGUST SCHELL OKTOBERFEST 1993 — amber, complex and rich malt aroma, delicious rich malt and bright hop flavor, good body, good balance, smooth and delicious, long malt and hop aftertaste; made with two-row pale, caramel, Munich, black and chocolate malts with domestic Cascade and Nugget hops; gravity 13.8 P, 4.4% abw. [B, 47]

HELENBOCH 1992 OKTOBERFEST — amber, zesty hop aroma, big flavor with lots of hop bite and plenty of malt, good body, dry hop finish and aftertaste; made with Hallertau and Saaz hops with Munich, pale, Carapils, caramel, and chocolate specialty malts; gravity 12 P, 4.2% abw. Contract brew for Friends B.C., Helen, GA. The 1991 version had a higher gravity (13 P) and won a gold medal at the GABF. The 1993 and 1994 versions are like the 1992. [B, 69]

HECKLER BRÄU FEST MÄRZEN — very pretty copper-amber color, pleasant hop and malt aroma, bright dry hop and malt flavor, good body, very pleasant to drink, dry malt finish and aftertaste, bottom-fermented; made with two-row barley, Saaz hops, and Bavarian yeast; gravity 13.5 P, 6.2% abw. Made for Heckler B.C. of Tahoe City, CA. [B, 63]

HECKLER BRÄU HELL LAGER — amber-gold, fruity apple malt nose, light malt flavor; dry malt aftertaste, hops come in at the end adding to the dryness; made using a graduated step infusion mash; gravity 12.5 P, 5.5% abw. Also made for Heckler B.C. [B, 64]

SLO GARDEN ALLEY AMBER ALE — amber, pleasant light citrus hop and malt aroma, bright complex hop flavor, very enjoyable drinking, finishes very nicely, long dry aftertaste; specific gravity 1.052, 4.2% abw. Made for SLO B.C., San Luis Obispo, CA. [A, 68]

EARTHQUAKE PALE — amber-gold, light hop nose, very smooth dry hop flavor, medium body, dry hop finish and aftertaste, good duration, very drinkable. Made for the San Andreas B.C. of Hollister, CA. See San Andreas B.C., for description of their effort. [A, 67]

JUMPING COW AMBER ALE — amber, fruity malt aroma, very fruity-estery malt flavor; carbonation provides some balance as the hops don't appear until the aftertaste; sweet malt up to the finish; aftertaste has some hops and toasted malt. Made by Schell for Steinhaus B.C. [A, 63]

RED ROOST ALE — deep reddish-amber, estery malt nose; big fruity flavor has hops in back and some alcohol shows; good body; bitter hops come in assertively at the finish and stay for the long dry hop aftertaste; made with chocolate and caramel malt with lots of Cascade hops. Made for La Jolla B.C. of La Jolla, CA. [A, 68]

SLO BRICKHOUSE EXTRA PALE ALE — hazy gold, malt aroma, big strong fruity malt and bitter hop flavor, nothing subtle about it, good body; dry hop finish has a real bite; long dry hop after-

taste. Made for SLO B.C. of San Luis Obispo, CA. [A, 64]

SLO COLE PORTER — brown, big malt nose, clean and complex, enormous roasted malt flavor, big body; dry toasted malt aftertaste is incredibly long; very complex and ever changing on the palate, a beauty. Made for SLO Brewing of San Luis Obispo, CA. A sample tasted in late 1995 had much more hop presence and was neither as good a porter nor as good tasting a brew. [P, 98]

GEORGIA PEACH WHEAT BEER — peachy color, peach nose, finely carbonated, light peach flavor, medium body, light clean peach flavored aftertaste, same all the way through. Made for Friends B.C. of Atlanta, GA. [W, 45]

SCHELL DOPPEL BOCK — dark amber, malt aroma, well-hopped brew with lots of malt support; not European hops, nor are there Cascades; big body, good flavor, lots of everything including alcohol; plenty of warmth indicating a high alcohol level, a very well done double bock. [BK, 89]

HECKLER BRAU DOPPELBOCK — dark brown-amber; beautiful rich malt and hop nose shows some chocolate malt; smooth rich malt flavor; has roasted malt and chocolate malt; good body, good carbonation level, dry but rich, excellent balance, long dry hop and rich malt aftertaste, a beauty. [BK, 86]

Notes

EARTHQUAKE PORTER —
Dark brown, choclate malt and
roasted barley aroma and taste,
medium to good body, long dry
roasted malt aftertaste. Made for
the San Andreas B.C. of Hollister,
CA. See San Andreas B.C., for
description of their effort. [P, 71]

AFTERSHOCK WHEAT — hazy
amber, bright spicy clove aroma,
dry spicy flavor, finish, and aftertaste, medium body, fairly long
and very refreshing. Made for
San Andreas B.C. of Hollister,
CA. [W, 67]

SLO HOLIDAZE ALE — hazy
amber; ginger hits you first and
only in the nose, palate, and aftertaste, there is a good body, but the
flavor is only ginger; made with
Hawaiian ginger root; specific
gravity 1.052, 4.4% abw. Made
for San Luis Obispo Brewing,
SLO, CA. [B, 31]

PECAN ST. TRUE BOCK —
deep amber-gold, malty nose, big
off-dry malt flavor with a hop
background, medium to good
body; dry malt and hop aftertaste

has length. Made for The Old
City B.C., Austin, TX. [BK, 63]

SPANISH PEAKS HONEY RASP-
BERRY ALE — deep amber-gold,
raspberry aroma; raspberry flavor
stays more or less dry; medium to
good body, clean dry raspberry finish; long dry raspberry aftertaste
shows some honey; made with
wildflower honey and natural raspberry extract. [A, 31]

LOUIE'S EVIL LAGER — amber,
Northwest hop and malt aroma,
highly carbonated, a little caramel
background to a dry hop flavor,
pleasant and tasty, a little dull in the
middle, caramel shows well in the
aftertaste, balanced and creamy,
good length. Saloon B.C. [B, 66]

PALIMONY BITTER — hazy
gold, very hoppy nose, big hop
flavor, medium to good body,
creamy mouthfeel, big dry hop
finish and aftertaste, long and
heavily hopped; really dries out
your mouth. Found on the east
coast. There is a Palimony ESB on
the west coast that may be the
same brew. [A, 62]

JOE'S WHEAT BEER — cloudy
amber-gold, pleasant malty-wheaty
hop nose, good complexity, big hop
and carbonation flavor, some
toastiness in the finish; flavor cuts
off quickly but a dryness stays for a
long aftertaste. [W, 40]

SLO BLUEBERRY ALE — hazy
amber, nice blueberry jam nose,
clean blueberry flavor, medium
body; finish and aftertaste show
the malt and hops of the beer and
the blueberry slides into the back-

ground; fermented with blueberry
juice and nicely done. Made for
San Luis Obispo B.C. of San Luis
Obispo, CA. [A, 39]

LA JOLLA WIND & SEA WHEAT
BEER — hazy pale gold, pleasant
malt nose, soft wheaty malt flavor,
light body, fairly dry malt aftertaste,
not interesting. [W, 28]

SCHELL MAIFEST BLONDE
DOUBLE BOCK BEER — deep
gold, big malt and alcohol aroma
and flavor, richly malted, good
bodied, reminds you of a Belgian
tripel; very smooth, very long;
stays malty and continues to show
alcohol. [BK, 86]

STONE MOUNTAIN SOUTH-
ERN LAGER — hazy gold, fruity
malt aroma and flavor, dry hop
finish, medium body; dry hop
aftertaste is quite bitter at the end.
Made for Stone Mountain Brewers, Inc. of Atlanta, GA. [B, 40]

GATOR LIGHT LAGER
BEER — gold, soft malty nose,
light malt flavor, light body, very
light dull malty aftertaste, a dull
taste thru and thru. Made for
Florida Beer Brands. [LO, 30]

HELENBOCH HOLIDAY ALE
1995 — dark amber, ginger nutmeg
and clove aroma; big spicy flavor is
mostly ginger; medium body, dry
spicy aftertaste. Made for Friends
B.C. of Atlanta, GA. [A, 60]

Schirf Brewing Co. / Wasatch Brewery
Brewery and brewpub located in Park City, UT

WASATCH CHRISTMAS ALE — deep gold, fragrant hop and malt aroma, flowery hops and good malt flavor, complex palate; dry hops in front, then it takes on a stronger hop-ale character with plenty of malt; excellent balance, dry hop finish; some dry hops at the end but the long aftertaste is mostly malt; a very good effort. [A, 73]

WASATCH SLICKROCK LAGER — hazy gold, fresh fruity malt aroma, big malt up front; hops join in at mid-palate and give the flavor some complexity; light body; finish is still malty and the aftertaste is faintly roasted malt; made with two-row and some crystal malt, Chinook, Perle, and Willamette hops; specific gravity 1.040, 3.2% abw, 28 IBU. [B, 56]

WASATCH PREMIUM ALE — medium deep amber, big toasted malt nose, roasted malt flavor, long off-dry malt aftertaste, very drinkable; made with two-row pale, crystal 70–80, and some roasted malt, Chinook and Cascade hops; specific gravity 1.040, 3.2% abw, 34 IBU. [A, 73]

WASATCH IRISH STOUT — deep brown, dry chocolate malt nose, roasted barley in back, creamy very dry roasted malt flavor, medium body, long dry malt aftertaste, nicely done and very drinkable. [S, 77]

WASATCH STOUT — opaque brown, dry chocolate malt aroma with some roasted barley in back, smooth and dry; seems to have less bite than the Irish stout, but they are very similar; medium length; made with two-row, crystal 70–80, roasted, black patent, and chocolate malts, Chinook and Cascade hops; specific gravity 1.040, 3.2% abw, 28 IBU. [S, 50]

WASATCH WEIZENBIER — hazy gold, dry slightly toasted malt nose, good dry malt flavor like the nose, medium body, very long malt aftertaste, not much hops to find. [W, 43]

WASATCH WHEAT BEER — hazy light amber, very fruity aroma, medium dry palate, finishes dry malt, short dry malt aftertaste. [W, 40]

SNOWBIRD TRAM ALE — amber, toasted malt nose, dry toasted malt flavor, low carbonation, medium body, finishes pleasantly malty; has a long dry malt aftertaste, not much hops evident. [A, 49]

WASATCH RASPBERRY WHEAT ALE — hazy gold, big fruity raspberry nose, clean light raspberry flavor, light body, dry faintly raspberry finish and aftertaste, medium long, pleasant and refreshing, very good of type; made with 50% wheat and raspberry essence; specific gravity 1.040, 3.2% abw. [A, 60]

Notes

Sea Dog Brewing Co.
Brewpub in Camden, ME

OLD EAST INDIA PALE ALE — amber, mild malt and hop aroma and flavor, low carbonation, very smooth and tasty, medium body, light and dry malt-hop finish and aftertaste; specific gravity 1.068, 6% abw. As tasted in Camden. [A, 82]

OLD GOLLY WOBBLER BROWN ALE — amber-brown, malt aroma, dry malt flavor, medium body, dry malt finish and aftertaste, very light flavor, short; specific gravity 1.045, 3.8% abw. As tasted in Camden. [A, 49]

WINDJAMMER MAINE ALE — golden amber, light hop nose, big bright hop flavor, tasty, dry, very drinkable, medium body, dry hop finish and aftertaste; purports to be a blonde ale; uses Cascade hops and British malt; specific gravity 1.050, 4% abw. Also called Windjammer Blond Ale. As tasted in Camden. [A, 72]

SEA DOG MAI BOCK — deep gold, malt nose, very huge malt flavor, dry malt finish, long dry malt aftertaste; specific gravity 1.068, 5.7% abw. As tasted in Camden. [B, 80]

JUBILATOR DOPPELBOCK — deep amber-brown, big dry toasted malt flavor, big body, lots of power, dry malt finish, and long dry malt aftertaste; specific gravity 1.074, 6.2% abw. As tasted in Camden. [BK, 74]

OLD BAGGYWRINKLE EXTRA SPECIAL BITTER — amber, malt and hop aroma and flavor, low carbonation, smooth dry malty flavor, dry hop finish and aftertaste, very drinkable. As tasted in Camden. [A, 53]

PENOBSCOT MAINE LAGER — gold, pleasant light hop aroma and flavor, very drinkable, medium body, dry hop finish, long dry hop aftertaste. Supposed to be a Bohemian Pilsener but uses British malt, still it works out. As tasted in Camden. [B, 67]

OWLS HEAD LIGHT — pale gold, light dry hop nose; malt flavor is bone dry; light body, dry malt finish and aftertaste, very drinkable. As tasted in Camden. [A, 64]

SEA DOG OATMEAL STOUT — deep brown, tan head, smoky malt nose, bitter smoky malt taste, lots of well-roasted malt here, good body, long roasted malt aftertaste; lots of roasted malt but it lacks complexity. As tasted in Camden. [S, 39]

SEA DOG RIVER DRIVER PORTER — dark brown, malty aroma and flavor, good body, long dry well-hopped aftertaste, good complexity; made with Cascade, Northern Brewer, and Willamette hops; OG 1058. Tasted at Boston Brewers Festival. [P, 66]

PENOBSCOT MAINE PILSENER — gold, pleasant light hop nose, very drinkable light hop flavor, medium body, long dry hop aftertaste. A good pils called Penobscot Maine Lager at Camden. Tasted at Bangor. [B, 67]

SEA DOG WEIZENBERRY — dark amber, berry aroma and flavor, medium body; not sweet as it has more of a berry tartness; ends dry; made with blackberries and red raspberries; cask-conditioned German-style wheat ale whose spicy nature is well hidden under the berries. Tasted at Bangor. [W, 58]

BLACK IRISH WINTER STOUT — black, low brown head, smooth roasted malt aroma; rich roasted malt flavor has an underlying sweetness; when served near room temperature (like at Bangor) all the flavor components are apparent; long slightly off-dry roasted malt aftertaste, very pleasant. As tasted in Bangor. [S, 66]

OLD EAST INDIA PALE ALE — reddish amber, smooth malt and hop aroma and flavor, very smooth and tasty, hoppy but more flavorful than bitter, medium body, light and dry malt-hop finish and very long well-hopped aftertaste, excellent brew; specific gravity 1.068, 6% abw. This is the Bangor bottled description. [A, 82]

OLD GOLLY WOBBLER BROWN ALE — amber-brown, bright hop aroma, dry and somewhat bitter hop flavor, medium body, dry malt finish and aftertaste, very light flavor, short, a little dull; specific gravity 1.045, 3.8% abw. This is the Bangor bottled description. [A, 47]

WINDJAMMER MAINE ALE — golden amber, beautiful floral hop nose, big bright and strong hop flavor, tasty, more flavorful than bitter, dry, very drinkable, medium body, dry hop finish and aftertaste; purports to be a blonde ale; uses Cascade hops and British malt; specific gravity 1.050, 4% abw. Also called Windjammer Blond Ale. This is the Bangor bottled description. [A, 72]

Seabright Brewery
Brewpub in Santa Cruz, CA

SEABRIGHT AMBER ALE — amber, beautiful light hop aroma, smooth and mellow malt flavor with light hops in back, dry malt finish, medium length dry malt aftertaste; brewed with two-row pale and caramel malts, Chinook, Cascade, and Willamette hops; gravity 13.25 P and 4.2% abw. [A, 67]

PELICAN PALE — gold, hop nose, delicious malt-hop flavor, excellent balance, dry hop finish and aftertaste with good length, a beautful brew — Seabright's best. [A, 94]

SEABRIGHT EXTRA SPECIAL BITTER — amber, zesty fresh malt and hop aroma and flavor, smooth, well balanced, plenty of good hop character, dry hop finish, long dry hop aftertaste, very drinkable; made with two-row pale and caramel malts, Chinook and Willamette hops, dry hopped; gravity 13 P, 4.2% abw. [A, 73]

BANTY ROOSTER IPA — gold, light hop nose and taste, good body, dry hop finish and aftertaste; hops light at first in the malt, but they come on strong in mid-palate; brewed with two-row pale and

caramel malts; hopped with Chinook, Cascade, and Centennial hops; specific gravity 1.056, 4.4% abw. [A, 59]

TRI-CENTURY PORTER — deep dark amber-brown, coffee-like malt aroma, smooth, dry malt flavor, finish, and aftertaste, very long and very drinkable. [P, 79]

CENTURY RED — amber, very attractive fresh and lively malt and hop aroma, bright hop flavor with good malt, very refreshing, long dry hop aftertaste. [A, 65]

ACE'S STRONG ALE — deep gold, big hop aroma; huge hop flavor also is well stocked with malt; big body; feels great in your mouth; high density (16), long dry hop aftertaste. [A, 83]

SEABRIGHT OATMEAL STOUT — deep brown, roasted barley and chocolate malt aroma, dry malt flavor, smooth, well balanced, good body, very drinkable; long dry malt aftertaste shows some of the roasted quality; made with two-row pale and a blend of specialty dark malts and rolled oats, Nugget, Fuggles and Willamette hops; specific gravity 1.062, 4.7% abw. [S, 80]

SEABRIGHT WEIZEN — hazy gold, 50–50 wheat and malt nose, very lightly hopped malt palate, good body, smooth and clean, refreshing, long off-dry malt aftertaste; made with 40% wheat malt and 60% two-row pale and dextrin malts; hopped with Hallertau, Liberty, and Tettnanger hops; gravity 12 P, 3.6% abw. [W, 60]

Notes

PLEASURE POINT PORTER — deep amber-brown, malt aroma, dry malt flavor, smooth and very drinkable; finish and aftertaste show some hops but mostly it is malt; very long and enjoyable; brewed with two-row pale, caramel, Munich, black, and chocolate malts; assertively hopped with Chinook, Cascade, and Willamette hops; specific gravity 1.056, 4.2% abw. [P, 80]

The Seven Barrel Brewery
Brewpub in Lebanon, NH

CHAMPION RESERVE IPA — hazy amber-gold, big hop nose, big dry hop flavor, medium to good body; has a tartness, big long dry hop finish and aftertaste; made with English Boot pale, caramel, and crystal malts, hard water; heavily hopped with Cascade and Perle hops. [A, 66]

R.I.P. STOUT — deep brown, deep brown head, chocolate nose; palate is coffee and chocolate; good body, big flavor, long chocolate-coffee aftertaste. R.I.P. stands for Russian Imperial Porter. [P, 62]

Sharky's Brewery & Grill
Brewpub in Omaha, NE

HARVEST MOON PUMPKIN ALE — gold, pumpkin pie spice aroma and flavor; a good tasty pumpkin pie beer with nutmeg, cinnamon, ginger, cloves, etc.;

medium body, dry spicy finish and aftertaste, fairly long and tasty throughout; specific gravity 1.055, 4.2% abw. [A, 68]

RED SHARK ALE — amber, big well-hopped malty nose and taste, fine balance, good body, dry finish, medium long dry hop and malt aftertaste; 4.2% abw. [A, 60]

GREAT WHITE PALE ALE — pale hazy gold, hop aroma and flavor, fairly light in body, very dry finish and aftertaste; 3.9% abw. [A, 52]

HAMMERHEAD ALE — deep amber, complex chocolate malt aroma, big malty flavor, good complexity, dry finish and aftertaste, very good length; 4.5% abw. [A, 65]

THE GREAT PUMPKIN ALE — gold, light spicy aroma and flavor; made with real pumpkin seed, nutmeg, ginger, cloves, and cinnamon; medium body, light dry aftertaste, medium duration. [A, 45]

The Shed Restaurant & Brewery Pub
Brewpub in Stowe, VT

SHED AMBER — amber, attractive dry malt and hop nose, dry hop flavor; grainy malt stays in back; medium body, dry hop and malt finish and aftertaste, good duration; made with Cascade, Willamette, and Tettnanger hops in the boil, finished with Cascades; OG 1052. [A, 70]

SHED WINTER — deep amber-brown, light hop aroma; big malty

flavor has a richness; medium to good body, long malty aftertaste; made with Fuggles, Mt. Hood, and Tettnanger hops in the boil; finished with Fuggles; OG 1065. [A, 73]

Sheepscot Valley Brewing Co.
Microbrewery in Whitefield, ME

SHEEPSCOT WHITE RABBIT — gold, fruity aroma, big fruity smoky spicy flavor, very complex and most delicious, big body; long dry tasty aftertaste follows the main flavors; a Belgian white ale that scores points on all fronts. [L, 83]

SHEEPSCOT BELGIAN ALE — amber, fruity light malt aroma; spicy malt flavor has a lactic finish; ends very dry and very spicy, a well-made ale with great complexity. [L, 62]

SHEEPSCOT MAD GOOSE ALE — gold; faint malt aroma has a touch of tangy lactic acid; very complex hop and spicy lactic palate, medium body; complexity continues into the long aftertaste which retains the spicy hoppy nature. [L, 60]

Shield's Brewing Co.
Brewpub in Ventura, CA

GOLD COAST BEER — hazy deep gold, malt aroma and flavor, good body, long malt aftertaste, very drinkable. [B, 62]

CHANNEL ISLANDS ALE — amber, light hop aroma with good malt in back; flavor is like the aroma but with more malt; good body, hops show more in the finish; the long aftertaste is dry hops; boiled with Cluster hops and finished with Cascades; specific gravity 1.050. [A, 53]

SHIELD'S STOUT — dark brown, light malt aroma, smooth off-dry malt flavor, dry malt finish, medium body, short dry malt aftertaste, good balance, but very brief. [S, 51]

CHANNEL ISLANDS WHEAT ALE — bright gold, light hop aroma, smooth malt and light hop flavor, good body and balance, a "soft" feel on the palate, fairly dry finish, medium long dry aftertaste; the softness tends to make it seem dull, but many would like the style and it would go well with many foods; made from a 50–50 wheat and barley malt mix; specific gravity 1.045. [W, 47]

The Ship Inn
Brewpub in Milford, NJ, the brewery is named the Milford Brewing Co.

MILFORD BEST BITTER — brilliant clear amber, very smooth hop nose; bright dry hop flavor has plenty of hops; medium to good body, complex dry hop aftertaste, long, definitely a bitter ale, English style, a big well-hopped beer. [A, 80]

MILFORD CELEBRATION ALE — deep amber, dry hop aroma; big balanced flavor has plenty of hops and malt; bright and refreshing, good body; dry hop aftertaste is long and tastes good; leaves a great feel in your mouth. [A, 92]

SHIP INN INDIA PALE ALE — amber, enormous Cascade hop nose, lusty Cascade hop flavor, low carbonation, medium body, very tasty bright hop finish and aftertaste, long and zesty. [A, 83]

SHIP INN OATMEAL STOUT — dark brown; complex roasted malt aroma shows some of the oatmeal; good flavor is soft and smooth, a bit fruity as well; plenty of roasted barley and oatmeal character; long aftertaste is a trifle burnt. [S, 66]

Sierra Nevada Brewing Co.
Brewery at Chico, CA

SIERRA NEVADA PALE ALE — deep amber; complex tangy Cascade hop and malt aroma that seems off-dry; smooth rich malt and hop flavor, hops strongest at the finish, very long hop aftertaste, a big delicious brew; gravity 13 P, 4.4% abw. [A, 64]

SIERRA NEVADA PORTER — deep red-brown, complex tangy off-dry malt and hop nose; smooth rich roasted malt flavor with strong hops coming in for the finish; very long and very delicious, a big satisfying brew; gravity 14.5 P, 4.7% abw. [P, 63]

SIERRA NEVADA STOUT —
opaque brown, big rich clean and
sweet nose, complex herbal flavor
in front, good hops and roasted malt
at the finish, very long off-dry and
roasted malt aftertaste, another big
bodied full-flavored brew; gravity
16 P, 4.8% abw. [S, 45]

SIERRA NEVADA PALE
BOCK — bright pale gold, great
nose with lots of hops and malt, big
body, big hop flavor, extremely long
bright hop aftertaste, a big and
beautiful brew with incredible balance; Maibock-style beer; gravity
16 P, 5.2% abw. [BK, 96]

BIG FOOT BARLEYWINE
STYLE ALE 1987 — hazy amber,
complex citrus and licorice nose,
huge citrus-ale flavor, enormous
body, great complexity; more malt
and hops than you've had in a
mouthful before, almost too powerful but it is balanced so you can
enjoy its quality; extremely long
on the palate; gravity 23 P, 10.1%
abw. [A, 75]

BIG FOOT BARLEYWINE
STYLE ALE 1988 — cloudy
amber, toasted malt nose, huge

almost overwhelming toasted
malt flavor with incredible duration. [A, 49]

BIG FOOT BARLEYWINE
STYLE ALE 1990 — deep amber,
complex malt aroma, strong alcoholic rich malt flavor, excellent
balance; richness stays right
through the long long toasted malt
aftertaste. Note that these Big
Foot brews can handle quite a bit
of bottle aging; try keeping them
for a year or so. [A, 84]

BIG FOOT BARLEYWINE
STYLE ALE 1991 — brilliant
deep amber, big head but not tight,
lovely rich well-malted and
hopped aroma, strong malt flavor,
big body, well balanced; alcohol
not as noticeable as some other
issues but after a bottle your face
feels warm indicating there is
plenty; clean rich malt finish, long
richly malted aftertaste. Seems a
bit easier to drink this year, but
this may be because it is so well
balanced. Still made with gravity
23 P, 10.1% abw. [BW, 91]

SIERRA NEVADA
CELEBRATION ALE 1987 —
brilliant deep amber, roasted malt
aroma, big strong beautifully balanced roasted malt and hop flavor,
delicious and very long. [A, 95]

SIERRA NEVADA
CELEBRATION ALE 1988 —
orange-amber, a citrus and pine
aroma, intense malt flavor with a
big hop finish and long hop aftertaste; big delicious brew. [A, 98]

SIERRA NEVADA
CELEBRATION ALE 1989 —

medium amber, complex tangy
citrus-ale nose, big zesty ale flavor, lots of both malt and hops;
complex sipping beer, not overwhelming, just big and good;
excellent balance, very long hop
aftertaste. [A, 86]

SIERRA NEVADA
CELEBRATION ALE 1989 —
batch made October 25, 1989;
golden amber, big fruity-citrus
nose, strong malt and hop flavor,
high alcohol, very dry finish and
aftertaste, huge and long. [A, 86]

SIERRA NEVADA
CELEBRATION ALE 1989 —
batch made November 27, 1989;
golden amber, faint malt aroma,
same flavor as above but lighter,
excellent balance, long dry malt and
hop aftertaste, much like brew above
but a more subtle version. [A, 86]

SIERRA NEVADA
CELEBRATION ALE 1990 —
medium to deep amber, huge citrus-
ale nose, enormous but smooth malt
and hop flavor, excellent balance,
extremely long aftertaste. [A, 93]

SIERRA NEVADA
CELEBRATION ALE 1991 — pale
amber, fruity citrus and apricot
aroma, big citrus-ale flavor, very
good balance, plenty of both malt
and hops, smooth, rich, and a great
tasting long long aftertaste. [A, 95]

SIERRA NEVADA
SUMMERFEST BEER 1991 —
gold, clean malt and hop aroma; big
flavor is mostly hops but there is
malt aplenty in support; malt kicks
in at the finish and it ends refresh-
ingly dry and quite long. [B, 58]

SIERRA NEVADA PALE BOCK 1992 — gold, big hop aroma, big rich malt and hop flavor, beautiful balance, great taste, big body, long and good. [BK, 73]

SIERRA NEVADA SUMMERFEST BEER 1992 — gold, hop and melon aroma; pleasant hop and malt flavor is both fruity and spicy; finishes dry, long fruity malt aftertaste with a dry hop background; gravity 11.5 P, 3.5% abw. [B, 51]

SIERRA NEVADA CELEBRATION ALE 1992 — golden amber, beautiful citrus hop nose, big and luscious flavor, simply wonderful, big and bold, bitter hop finish and long bitter hop aftertaste. [A, 94]

SIERRA NEVADA CELEBRATION ALE 1993 — amber, great malt and citrus hop aroma, huge concentrated flavor; hops tend to overwhelm the malt even though it is concentrated as well; big body, very long complex hop and malt aftertaste; needs some more time to come together, should be spectacular by Xmas '94. Note that this brew was made twice for the season. The second batch, made in November seems less highly hopped than the October batch. [A, 98]

SIERRA NEVADA PALE BOCK 1994 — deep gold, bright tangy citrus hop nose; big dry hoppy flavor doesn't seem quite as rich as earlier versions, good body, strong dry hop finish, long and strong dry hop aftertaste, very well balanced, very good tasting, delightful. [B, 83]

SIERRA NEVADA CELEBRATION ALE 1995 — copper color, magnificent northwest hop aroma and flavor, cascades of Cascades, smooth despite its size, extremely long complex hop aftertaste; this is the best of the seasonal offerings. [A, 97]

SIERRA NEVADA DOO DAH 10 BEER — hazy amber, great malt aroma, pleasant malt flavor, smooth and lovely, complex, delicious, long rich malt aftertaste. This was bottled in 1986 and tasted in 1993 — shows how well the Sierra Nevada beers hold up with time. [B, 84]

SIERRA NEVADA PASEDENA DOO DAH PARADE 11 PALE ALE — hazy amber, light malt aroma, delicious malt flavor, smooth and lovely on the tongue, complex and delicious, long rich malt aftertaste. Made in 1987 and tasted in 1993. [A, 98]

SIERRA NEVADA DARK OCTOBER LAGER — very deep amber, bright hop nose, lusty full-bodied flavor, lots of malt and sufficient hops for balance, very complex, long dry aftertaste; a sensational beer even if it is not a traditional Octoberfest style. [B, 91]

SIERRA NEVADA WHEAT BEER — pale gold, fruity-citrus aroma shows northwest hops, creamy mouthfeel, big fruity-citrus hop flavor like the nose, sort of a pils style but with a northwest slant, medium body, dry bitter finish, long dry hop aftertaste. [W, 63]

Notes

SIERRA NEVADA IPA — copper-amber, beautiful fresh hop aroma, huge northwest hop flavor, creamy mouthfeel, big body; big long dry hop aftertaste has plenty of supporting malt; very complex, delightful. [A, 83]

BIG FOOT BARLEYWINE STYLE ALE 1995 — dark amber; big well-hopped aroma is most hoppy I can recall in a long time; big rich flavor is well endowed with both hops and malt; huge body, excellent balance, plenty of alcoholic warmth, long rich malt and dry hop aftertaste, another beauty, great concentration; perhaps the best Big Foot ever offered; gravity 24 P, 11% abv. [BW, 99]

Signature Beer Co.
Microbrewery in St. Louis, MO. Bottled products brewed by Oldenberg.

THE SPIRIT OF ST. LOUIS ALE — gold, hop aroma, light malt and hop flavor, dry hop finish and aftertaste; made with Fuggles, Chinook, and Willamette hops; specific gravity 1.056, 4% abw. [A, 50]

Silo Brew Pub & Microbrewery
Brewpub in Louisville, KY

YULETIDE ALE — deep gold; spicy aroma shows ginger, nutmeg, cloves, and cinnamon; flavor starts off as slightly sweet, big and spicy, but finishes quite dry; good body, good length, very good of

type; specific gravity 1.062, 5% abw. [A, 61]

HERCULES WINTER WARMER — dark amber, dry malt nose, rich off-dry malty flavor, good body, off-dry malt finish and aftertaste; made with two-row caramel and chocolate malts; balanced with Galena and East Kent-Golding hops; specific gravity 1.068, 5.4% abv. [A, 75]

SILO OKTOBERFEST — gold; bright nose shows both malt and hops; tasty flavor is like the aroma, richly malted and nicely hopped, medium body, long dry hop finish and aftertaste; made with two-row, Munich, and caramel malts, Galena and Willamette hops; specific gravity 1.058, 4.8% abv. [B, 85]

RED ROCK ALE — gold, dry malt aroma and flavor, fairly well balanced, medium body; dry malt finish and aftertaste has good hop support; brewed with two-row, Munich, caramel, and chocolate malts; balanced with Galena and Willamette hops; specific gravity 1.050, 3.9% abw. [A, 47]

DERBY DAY DARK — deep gold with amber tinge, dry malt aroma and flavor from pale, caramel, and Munich malts; finish and aftertaste are dry malt as well; specific gravity 1.059, 4.1% abw. [B, 43]

SILO GOLDEN WHEAT — gold, light malt aroma, dry malty flavor, light body, clean and refreshing, fairly short dry malt aftertaste; made with 35% wheat and two-row pale and Munich malts; specific gravity 1.039 and 3% abw. [W, 53]

Silver Plume Brewing Co.
Microbrewery in Colorado

SILVER PLUME PILS — hazy gold, light hop aroma; good hoppy flavor has a grainy malt background; good body, dry hop finish and aftertaste. [B, 49]

BULL'S HEAD BLACK RASPBERRY PORTER — dark brown, faint berry fruit and malt aroma, malty black raspberry flavor, a bacon-like backtaste from the yeast and dark malts, medium body, brief berry-malt aftertaste. [P, 59]

Sisson's South Baltimore Brewing Co.
Brewpub in Baltimore, MD

MARBLE PILSENER — hazy gold, very faint hop aroma, austere dry hop flavor, medium body, long sour and dry hop aftertaste. [B, 50]

STOCKADE AMBER — hazy amber, very faint hop aroma, dry hop flavor, finish, and aftertaste; a bit more malt in the aftertaste, but the overall effect is very dry hops. Despite the austerity, the balance is good with a creamy texture to it, good body, good length, and complexity. [A, 60]

EDGAR ALLEN PORTER — amber-brown, light malty nose, good malty flavor, light body, light dry toasted malty finish and aftertaste. [P, 60]

SLO Brewing Co.
Brewpub in San Luis Obispo, CA

SLO PALE ALE — gold, nice hop nose, bright hop flavor, faint bite in back, bright and smooth, well balanced, long medium dry hop aftertaste; specific gravity 1.052, 4.1% abw. [A, 52]

SLO AMBER ALE — amber, light hop aroma; malt flavor is smooth; medium body; hops are light and in back; medium dry malt finish, long dry malt aftertaste. [A, 61]

SLO COLE PORTER — deep brown, light coffee-malt nose, light malt flavor, medium body, more dry than rich, dry malt finish, medium length, dry malt aftertaste; specific gravity 1.055, 4.5% abw. [P, 54]

SLO NUT BROWN ALE — deep amber, hop nose, smooth dry nutty flavor, very dry finish, long dry nutty aftertaste. [A, 67]

GARDEN ALLEY AMBER ALE — deep amber, quite dry malt nose and flavor, long dry malt aftertaste; specific gravity 1.052, 4.2% abw. [A, 68]

Smoky Mountain Brewery
Microbrewery in Waynesville, NC

INDIA RED PALE ALE — amber-gold, hop aroma with a toasted malt background, bright hoppy flavor, light body; long dry hop aftertaste has a faint off-dry malt background and a European character; made with mostly crystal malt; hopped with Saaz, Hallertau, and Cascade hops; unfiltered and cask- or bottle-conditioned; specific gravity 1.048, 3.36% abw. [A, 72]

LIONHEART STOUT — dark brown, deep brown head; big roasted malt aroma shows some chocolate and black patent malt; light body; the roasted character carries into the long malt aftertaste; specific gravity 1.048, 3.6% abw. [S, 67]

Smuttynose Brewing Co.
Microbrewery in Portsmouth, NH using the equipment formerly used by the defunct Frank Jones B.C. of Portsmouth (and which originally was operated by the Renegade Brewery of Thunder Bay, Ontario, Canada). Smuttynose is a joint venture of the owners of the Northampton and Portsmouth breweries and the owners of Ipswich B.C. and thereby are affiliated with those brewing operations.

SMUTTYNOSE SHOALS PALE ALE — hazy amber-gold, lightly sweet but very bright hop nose and assertive hop flavor, finishes mostly dry with a faint background sweetness, long dry hop aftertaste; hops override the malt and try to disrupt the balance; very good with food, an unfiltered ESB; made with English two-row pale, crystal, Carapils, and wheat malts; hopped with Chinook and Cascade hops; specific gravity 1.050, 5.3% abw. [A, 67]

OLD BROWN DOG — amber-brown; fruity malt aroma has a hint of butterscotch; malty-buttery flavor, medium body, dry malt finish and aftertaste. [B, 35]

Snake River Brewing Co. / Jackson Hole Pub & Brewery
Brewpub in Jackson, WY

SNAKE RIVER LAGER — amber-gold, dry malt and hop aroma and flavor, medium body, slightly tangy ale-like hop finish and aftertaste; made with two-row, Munich, and several caramel malts, Perle and Tettnanger hops; lager yeast fermented warm at 55°F, aged four weeks; specific gravity 1.052, 4.4% abw. [B, 62]

SNAKE RIVER PALE ALE — gold, hoppy nose, dry hop flavor, medium to light body, dry hop finish and aftertaste; Chinook and Cascade hops are used with two-row pale, Munich, and caramel malts; fermented with Sierra Nevada ale yeast; specific gravity 1.050, 4.2% abw. This was tasted on draft. In bottle, hazy gold, beautiful northwest citrus hop aroma, big northwest hop flavor is very assertive; highly carbonated such that it assails your tongue; tasty, refreshing, good for hop-heads, dry and long. [A, 71]

ZONKER STOUT — opaque brown, chocolate malt and roasted barley nose and taste, good body, long dry finish and aftertaste; mildly bittered with Chinook, Perle, and Willamette hops; made with lots of roasted barley and other dark malts; specific gravity 1.060, 4.5% abw. A nice classical stout. This as tasted on draft. In bottle, it seems less complicated, has less hop character, and no chocolate tones. [S, 67]

Southern California Brewery
Formerly known as the Alpine Village Brewery, Inc. Brewery in Torrance, CA. attached to a restaurant which gives effect of a brewpub. Part of the Alpine Village complex of shops, hotel, restaurant, etc. All bottling prior to 1994 was done at the Angeles B.C. in Chatsworth, CA.

ALPINE HOFBRAU SPECIAL RESERVE LAGER — deep gold, malt and hop aroma, smooth dry malt and hop flavor, good body, dry malt finish, long dry malt and hop aftertaste; made with two-row pale, Munich, and roasted malts; specific gravity 1.055, 4.5% abw. [B, 67]

ALPINE HOFBRAU SUPERIOR PILSNER — pale gold, bright pilsener-style hop and malt nose, bright dry hop flavor, good body, great balance, long dry hop aftertaste, good Eastern European style; made with Saaz hops from the Zatec region of the Czech Republic; fermented for 10 days and lagered for 4 weeks; specific gravity 1.048, 4% abw. [B, 67]

ALPINE VILLAGE HOFBRAU BOCK — copper-brown, big dry malt nose, big dry roasted chocolate malt flavor, smooth, dry and well hopped, long hop and malt aftertaste, big bodied and delicious; specific gravity 1.068, 5.7% abw. [BK, 73]

ALPINE VILLAGE HOFBRAU PREMIUM LIGHT — gold; light hop nose has a faint strawberry background; light dry hop flavor, dry hop finish and medium dry hop aftertaste with fair length; specific gravity 1.042, 3.5% abw. [LO, 51]

ALPINE VILLAGE HOFBRAU RED ALE — amber, light malt nose, bright hop flavor with great malt backing, off-dry malt finish, long dry malt aftertaste with a sense of nutmeg in there somewhere, a big bright delicious brew. [A, 64]

ALPINE VILLAGE HOFBRAU WHEAT BEER — gold, faint dry malt and wheat aroma, light wheat and malt flavor, faintly off-dry, dry finish, long dry malt aftertaste, refreshing and interesting. Malt mix contains 40% wheat. [W, 65]

ALPINE VILLAGE HOFBRAU HEFE-WEIZEN — hazy gold; a nice citrus background adds to the malt and wheat nose, also gives zest to the flavor, finish, and aftertaste; like the above but a little more bright, more refreshing, and more satisfying. [W, 68]

ALPINE VILLAGE HOFBRAU FESTBIER — bright amber, dry malt and hop nose; dry malt flavor well backed with hops; dry hop finish, smooth long dry hop aftertaste, a zesty highly malted and well-hopped brew. [B, 67]

3 CLUBS RED — amber, rich malt nose, dry malt and hop flavor, dry finish, short very dry aftertaste. Made for Steamroller Brewing Co. under contract. [B, 41]

RANCHO PALOS VERDES LAGER — bright gold, dense head, hop nose; flavor starts out hops, goes to malt in the middle, then finishes with dry hops; long dry hop aftertaste, good tasting dry satisfying brew. This sample was tank aged for 3.5 months and drawn from the secondary fermenter at that time. It had developed very nicely, coming together and mellowing out, showing how a well-made lager can really benefit by extra aging. Palos Verdes Lager is the new name for A.V. Special Reserve Lager. [B, 75]

ALPINE VILLAGE UNFILTERED WHEAT BEER — hazy gold; huge dense head is left in the bottom of the glass when you have consumed the beer; dry malt-wheat nose, refreshing dry wheat and malt flavor, medium body; dry malt aftertaste persists on the palate. [W, 68]

OLDE RED EYE — reddish amber, malt aroma, dry malt flavor, medium body; smooth and has a richness; dry finish and aftertaste shows both malt and hops; specific gravity 1.053, 4.2% abw. [A, 59]

SOUTHERN CALIFORNIA HONEY WHEAT ALE — deep gold, honeyed aroma, some malt but mostly honey, rich honey flavor; finish is also honey; honeyed aftertaste is off-dry and rich rather than sweet, long but never dry; too much honey to show malt, wheat, or ale character; top-fermented wheat beer with raw honey added during the fermentation; made with 40% wheat malt, pale and caramel malts, plus amber honey, with Perle and Willamette hops; OG 1046, FG 1.010, 3.8% abw, 15 IBU. Tasted in bottle and on draft and both were the same. [W, 61]

SOUTHERN CALIFORNIA BLONDE LAGER — brilliant pale gold, malty aroma has a hop background; flavor starts out dry hops and finishes more malty but hops stay in the foreground; medium body, dry hop aftertaste, dryness lingers. Tasted in bottle. [B, 47]

SCREAMING LOBSTER LAGER — orange-reddish amber, Bohemian hop nose (probably Saaz), big dry hop flavor, medium body, long dry hop aftertaste, dry and hoppy throughout, a good Bohemian-style pils. Tasted in bottle. [B, 60]

NATUKA OF AFRICA PREMIUM BEER — cloudy gold, spicy nose (possibly nutmeg, pepper, ginger), strange unbalanced flavor, light body, not at all pleasant. Made for Ngok Brewery, Torrance, CA. [B, 15]

Notes

Solana Beach Brewery / Pizza Port
Microbrewery and brewpub in Solana Beach, CA

PILBOX PALE ALE — gold, dry malt aroma and flavor, dry hop finish and aftertaste, great length, crisp, and refreshing; specific gravity 1.047, 4.76% abw. Called Pilbox at the brewpub, Pill Box at the GABF. Never mind which spelling, as long as the beer is good. [A, 60]

RIVERMOUTH RASPBERRY — amber, dry raspberry-malt aroma, dry hop flavor with raspberry faintly in back, dry hop finish; long dry hop aftertaste has a faint raspberry character; made with raspberries and caramel malt; specific gravity 1.050, 5% abw. [A, 56]

SHARKBITE RED ALE — deep amber, hop nose, big hop flavor, large bodied, nicely balanced, long hefty hop aftertaste; a big brawny beer that is very well made; made with 80 Lovibond caramel malt using Centennial and Cascade hops; specific gravity 1.054, 5.47% abw. [A, 72]

SWAMIS INDIA PALE ALE — deep amber, light hop nose, very very dry hop flavor, good body, very long dry hop aftertaste; cask-conditioned in oak at 55°F, unfiltered, and dry hopped; specific gravity 1.068, 6.8% abw. [A, 67]

PORT'S PORTER — brown; creamy tan head is tight and long lasting; malt aroma shows some chocolate malt; dry roasted malt flavor, very smooth and soft, fairly dry complex malt finish, good body, long dry roasted malt aftertaste; cask-conditioned and unfiltered; specific gravity 1.066, 5.57% abw. Tasted on draft at pub. [P, 69]

PIPE'S PALE ALE — hazy gold, bright dry hop aroma and flavor from Styrian Goldings hops, bright and refreshing, very drinkable, long dry hop aftertaste, a well-made tasty pale ale; OG 1045. Tasted on draft at pub. [A, 80]

OLD BONEYARDS BARLEYWINE — deep amber, malty nose, big very malty flavor; has alcohol but doesn't flaunt it; flavor is mostly roasted barley, good albeit a bit clumsy; long off-dry malty aftertaste; long aged (18–20 weeks in cask); OG 1102, 10.2% abv. Tasted on draft at pub. [BW, 66]

SOLANA BEACH NUT BROWN ALE — brown, lovely malty nose; complex malt flavor is rich, dry, and tangy; good body, great depth of flavor and considerable charac-ter including some nuttiness (and maybe even a touch of oatmeal), good English style; long malty aftertaste is a true continuation of the main palate. [A, 72]

BUBBA'S BREW — deep amber, bright hop aroma and flavor, big body, excellent balance, big hop finish and aftertaste, very long. Made for Bubba's Bar-B-Que Restaurant in Escondido, CA and probably is Sharkbite Red Ale. If not, it is just as good. [A, 81]

Spanish Peaks Brewing Co., Ltd.
Brewpub and cafe in Bozeman, MT

SPANISH PEAKS PORTER — brown, malt aroma, bright hop and malt flavor, good balance, good body, smooth, dry malt and hop finish and aftertaste, nicely done classical porter; ale brewed from pale, crystal, Munich, and choco-late malts, with Pacific Northwest hops; specific gravity 1.056, 4.75% abw. [P, 74]

YELLOWSTONE PALE ALE — bright gold, hop aroma, balanced hop flavor with good supporting malt, bright dry hop finish and aftertaste; brewed using pale, crystal and Carastan malts, Pacific Northwest hops; specific gravity 1.054, 4.5% abw. [A, 67]

BLACK DOG BITTER — gold, no nose, hoppy palate, long dry hop aftertaste; brewed from pale, Munich, Carastan, and chocolate malt with Pacific Northwest hops; gravity 12.5 P, 3.8% abw. [A, 50]

EYE OF THE ROCKIES WHEAT ALE — gold, malt nose and clean malt flavor, medium body, dry malt finish and brief dry malt aftertaste; brewed from wheat and pale malted barley; gravity 11.5 P, 3.8% abw. [W, 51]

AUTUMN FEST ALE — amber, hop aroma, balanced hop and malt flavor, smooth, light, light dry hop finish, short dry hop aftertaste; made from two-row malted barley, Vienna, Munich, Carapils, and crystal malts. [A, 67]

SPANISH PEAKS HONEY RASP-BERRY ALE — deep amber-gold, raspberry aroma; raspberry flavor stays more or less dry; medium body, dry raspberry finish, long dry raspberry aftertaste; made with wildflower honey and natural rasp-berry extract. [A, 31]

Schell has been making many of the Spanish Peaks brands under the name of the Black Dog Brewing Co.

Spenard Brewing Co.
Brewery in Seattle, WA

CHILKOOT CHARLIE'S SOUR-DOUGH WHEAT ALE — hazy golden-amber; dry malt and hop aroma has a sausage background (like bologna); light body, off-dry dull malt flavor, dry hop finish and aftertaste. [W, 16]

Spoetzl Brewing Co.
Brewery in Shiner, TX, offices in San Antonio, TX

SHINER PREMIUM BEER — pale gold, well-hopped malt aroma, well-balanced slightly hoppy flavor, hops better in the finish and aftertaste, pleasant and refreshing; made with three malts, Cascade and Cluster hops; specific gravity 1.008, 3.4% abw. [B, 43]

SHINER PREMIUM BOCK BEER — brilliant amber color, strong hop and roasted (almost burnt) malt aroma, weak body; pleasant malt flavor is sometimes too burned; finish has little zest; made with Blue, Excel, and Black malts; specific gravity 1.009, 3.5% abw. [BK, 47]

KOSMOS RESERVE LAGER — deep gold; grainy malt nose shows a little toastiness; good lightly toasted malty flavor, medium body; good clean dry malt after-taste has a slight vegetal nature developing in back. [B, 45]

RATTLESNAKE BEER — pale yellow, hop nose, pleasant malt flavor, little body, little aftertaste. [B, 41]

DEVIL BEER — pale gold, light grainy malt aroma; flavor domi-nated by the CO_2; faint malt finish and aftertaste. [B, 26]

Sprecher Brewing Co.
Brewery in Milwaukee, WI

SPRECHER MAI BOCK — hazy gold, great appetizing hop and malt aroma, big malty flavor, well backed with hops, long malt aftertaste with a hop bite in back, a real honest maibock. [BK, 75]

SPRECHER MILWAUKEE WEISS — hazy gold, lovely fresh malt nose with hints of grapefruit and lemon, tart citrus flavor, light body, tart malt finish, long dry and slightly tart malt aftertaste. [W, 17]

SPRECHER DUNKEL WEIZEN — deep amber, off-dry roasted malt nose, slightly burnt roasted malt flavor, light body, well made, long dry roasted malt aftertaste. [W, 53]

SPRECHER OKTOBERFEST — hazy amber, dusty malt aroma, lightly toasted malt flavor, light body, some complexity, dry malt finish and aftertaste. [B, 25]

SPRECHER SPECIAL AMBER — amber, malt and hop aroma, hop flavor with a citrus background, bright and crisp, low carbonation, clean refreshing hop aftertaste with a trace of yeast at the end, a zesty brew. [B, 64]

SPRECHER BLACK BAVARIAN STYLE — deep ruby-brown, rich malt aroma, faint licorice background, dry malt flavor, dry malt aftertaste, uniform flavor throughout. [B, 50]

SPRECHER WINTER BREW — ruby-brown, toasted malt aroma with a hop tang in back, slightly scorched malt flavor, off-dry malt finish; long aftertaste starts as off-dry malt and goes to dry malt at the end. [B, 51]

Squatters Pub & Brewery
Brewpub in Salt Lake City, UT

PARLEY'S PORTER — brown, light malt aroma, light dry malt and pleasant hop flavor, medium body, fairly dry finish, light dry malt and hop aftertaste of medium length; made with black malt and Cascade and Hallertau hops; 28 IBU. [P, 47]

MILLCREEK STOUT — dark brown, light malt nose, smooth fairly complex malt flavor with good roasted malt character, medium body, dry finish; light long dry aftertaste is mostly malt; made with pale, caramel, and chocolate malt, roasted barley, and Chinook hops. [S, 46]

THE HEAD RED — copper color, bright well-hopped aroma and flavor, medium body, finishes dry, long dry hop aftertaste. Recipe calls for a "ton" of Saaz and Bullion hops; specific gravity 11.5 P, 3.1% abw. Also called Hop Head Red with Bullion hops substituted for the Saaz. [A, 60]

ANNIVERSARY PILSNER — deep gold; complex appetizing aroma shows both the malt and hops; very complex flavor seems to have a faint roasted character; good body, finishes dry hops, long complex dry hop aftertaste, a very good pils; made with two-row biscuit and Munich malts with Northern Brewer and Mt. Hood hops. [B, 72]

St. Stan's Brewing Co.
Brewery in Modesto, CA. Previously known as the Stanislaus B.C.

ST. STAN'S AMBER ALT — hazy amber, big citrus hop aroma, zesty hop flavor with plenty of malt backing, fair balance, complex and flavorful, medium to long hop aftertaste; made with pale, caramel, and chocolate malts and four types of hops using an alt yeast that ferments at the top in the primary and then is cold stored for the secondary fermentation; specific gravity 1.048, 4.5% abw. [A, 51]

ST. STAN'S DARK ALT — deep amber-brown, very complex aroma with blueberries, raspberries, currants, and melon, dry but rich malt palate; finishes with roasted malt, there are strong hops in the aftertaste with the rich malt; good length. Seems to be more heavily hopped and less toasted than it was a few years ago. Using caramel and chocolate roasted malts and three varieties of hops, it is made like the Amber above; specific gravity 1.052, 5% abw. [A, 47]

ST. STAN'S GRAFFITI ALT 1990 — light hazy amber, complex fruity malt aroma with all kinds of interesting components, a regular fruit cocktail, smooth hop flavor, light body, fairly short aftertaste, but a good effort nonetheless; made with 50–50 pale and wheat malt with Hallertau and Willamette hops; specific gravity 1.050, 4.5% abw. Made annually, but available only briefly each time. [A, 36]

CHAU TIEN EMPEROR ALE — hazy gold, pleasant off-dry malt nose, pleasant clean malt flavor; hops appear in the finish; light body, long malt aftertaste, quite pleasant. [A, 50]

ST. STAN'S GRAFFITI ALT 1993 — hazy gold; malt aroma has a northwest hop citrus-like background; smoky malt flavor seems to clash a bit with the hops; dry hop finish and aftertaste. [A, 42]

BEERGUY GROOVY ALE — golden-amber, lovely hop nose; good well-hopped flavor has plenty of supporting malt; good body; dry finish and long dry aftertaste shows both the hops and malt to advantage. Made for American Beerguy, Inc. of Berkeley, California. [A, 64]

FOG AMBER MIST ALE — beautiful amber, attractive and appetizing hop aroma, lovely and balanced hop and malt flavor, good complexity, good body, very satisfying; long dry hop aftertaste has enough malt support to carry on the balance, satisfaction, and complexity throughout the experience. Made for San Francisco Fog Inc., of San Francisco, CA. [A, 78]

ST. STAN'S FEST ALT BIER — hazy amber-gold, complex zesty big citrus hop and fruity malt aroma; big malt flavor with plenty of hops to support the balance and to provide a bright zesty quality; medium to good body, high alcohol, good drinking beer, long alcoholic aftertaste, really good and really long; made with crystal malt hopped with Fuggles and Tettnanger hops; intended as an Oktoberfest brew; specific gravity 14 P, 4.6% abw. Improves with bottle aging — if you think it is good at Christmastime, try it again about May or June. [A, 87]

ST. STAN'S RED SKY ALE — amber, toasted malt nose, very smooth complex malt flavor, good body, dry malt finish and long dry hop aftertaste; very easy to drink; made with a blend of five malts; specific gravity 13.5 P, 4.3% abw. [A, 70]

CENTENNI-ALE — amber, hop aroma, light hop flavor, medium body, quite smooth and tasty, dry hop finish and aftertaste, dry hopped with Cascade hops; gravity 12.5 P, 4.3% abw. [A, 73]

ST. STAN'S WHEAT GRAFFITI 1994 — gold; hop aroma has some malt; big hop flavor, good body; long hoppy aftertaste has enough malt for balance. Best of the Graffitis to date. [W, 58]

ST. STAN'S FEST ALT 1995 — hazy gold; nose starts out dusty but soon goes to flowery malt; medium body, big malty flavor, finish, and long malty aftertaste. [A, 64]

Star Brewing Co.
Microbrewery in Portland, OR

PINEAPPLE ALE — deep gold, dry hoppy-fruity nose; flavor is briefly pineapple, then is very hoppy; hops are used to subdue the pineapple flavor and do so; tartness of pineapple and hops tend to clash; made with two-row pale, chocolate, Munich, crystal 50L, and wheat malts; hopped with Northern Brewer, Perle, and Tettnanger hops (according to Oregon Brewers Fest program) or Columbus and Liberty hops (according to a brewer from Star); OG 1052, FG 1.016, 4.5% abv, 26 IBU. [A, 47]

STAR INDIA PALE ALE — amber-gold, huge tight head; big and nice hoppy homebrew-style aroma has tones of citrus, pine resin, and soapiness; soapy-grapefruit-lemony flavor, dry northwest hop finish and aftertaste, quite long. [A, 65]

STAR BLACK CHERRY STOUT — dark brown, sour infected nose and taste, bad, bad, bad. [S, NR]

STAR HOP GOLD ALE — hazy gold; huge head made it difficult to get a glass of anything but foam; light fruity aroma, tangy sour acidic infected palate, sour fruity aftertaste, medium length. [A, 39]

ELFIN ALE — very deep amber, big and good malty nose, malty candy sugar palate, good body, a bit too sweet and loses interest, long off-dry candy-malt aftertaste, too sweet to be attractive. [A, 33]

Star Union Brewing Co.
Microbrewery in Hennepin, IL

STAR MODEL BEER — gold; aroma and flavor are mostly hops and are faintly phenolic; medium body, dry hop finish and aftertaste. [B, 34]

Stark Mill Brewery
Brewpub in Manchester, NH

TASHA'S RED TAIL ALE — reddish amber, light hop aroma and flavor; highly carbonated giving it a brighter character than it might otherwise attain; refreshing, medium body; dry hop finish and aftertaste shows the Willamette hops; OG 1052. [A, 61]

GENERAL STARK DARK PORTER — brown, tan head; light dry toasted malt aroma and taste is a bit chocolatey; medium body, dry malt and light hop finish and aftertaste; OG 1050. [P, 60]

MT. UCANOONUC LIGHT CREAM ALE — deep gold, light hop aroma, dry hop flavor, medium to light body, tasty and refreshing, dry hop finish and aftertaste, medium length. [A, 59]

Steamboat Brewery and Tavern
Brewpub in Steamboat Springs, CO

BRUIN BROWN ALE — light brown, dry hop aroma; smooth light dry hop flavor does have some malt but it stays behind the hops; medium body, fairly long dry hop aftertaste; specific gravity 1.048, 3.4% abw. [A, 52]

PINNACLE PALE ALE — amber-gold, hop aroma, smooth balanced hop flavor, medium body, dry hop finish, fairly brief dry hop aftertaste; specific gravity 1.048, 3.8% abw. [A, 57]

HAHN'S PEAK GOLD — pale gold, Cascade hop aroma, pleasant bright hop flavor, light body, medium to short dry hop aftertaste; specific gravity 1.042, 2.5% abw. [A, 53]

Steelhead Brewery and Cafe
Brewpub in Eugene, OR, Burlingame, and Irvine, CA

STEELHEAD AMBER — amber, malt and hop aroma, balanced malt and hop flavor, very smooth, drinkable, medium body, dry finish and aftertaste; made with Centennial, Perle, and Cascade hops; gravity 13.5 P, 4.7% abw, 33 IBU. From the Eugene Pub. [A, 60]

OATMEAL STOUT — brown, dry malt and hop aroma and flavor, heavy body, dry malt finish and aftertaste, good length; 10% oatmeal and 2.5% rye malt are used with Chinook and Willamette hops; gravity 17.7 P, 6.5% abw, 58 IBU. [S, 50]

STATION SQUARE STOUT — a black bitter imperial stout, this has a huge complex very bitter aroma and flavor, big body, long rich dry and bitter aftertaste; 65 IBU from Chinook and Perle hops; 5.8% abw. [S, 61]

FRENCH PETE'S PORTER — brown; big dry malt aroma shows some chocolate malt; big dry malty flavor just like the nose promised; hefty body, long dry malt aftertaste, Galena and Willamette hops; gravity 15 P, 5.2% abw, 40 IBU. [P, 67]

GINGER BELLS — amber, light gingery aroma like a gingersnap cookie, flavor the same, ditto the finish and aftertaste; not bad, but I'd like it better if it were less gingery and more beerlike. Hopped with Galena and Cascade hops to 27 IBU. [A, 50]

RILEY'S RYE — amber, hop nose, hop flavor, dry malt aftertaste (where's the rye?); 10% rye malt used balanced with crystal malt, together with Galena, Centennial, and Willamette hops; gravity 13.9 P, 5% abw. [A, 45]

TIME WARP WEIZENBOCK — amber, malt aroma, malt and hop flavor, fair balance, good body, medium dry malt finish and aftertaste with the hops in back; CFJ-4 and Tettnanger hops; gravity 15 P, 5.9% abw, 31 IBU. [W, 50]

STEELHEAD CREAM ALE — gold, hop nose, light hop and malt flavor, medium body, medium dry finish and aftertaste; only Galena hops used (22 IBU) with 20% flaked maize; gravity 13.5 P, 4.8% abw. [A, 50]

BOMBAY BOMBER IPA — deep gold, big well-hopped aroma; huge complex flavor shows plenty of malt; big body; long complex aftertaste is a continuation of the flavor and holds the complexity; brewed with Chinook and Mt. Hood hops; dry hopped with Chinook; excellent IPA; OG 1053 (15 P), FG 1.009, 4.8% abw (6%abv), 45 IBU. [A, 79]

EMERALD SPECIAL BITTER — deep gold; beautiful rising hop aroma is most attractive; big complex flavor with plenty of hops and malt, good body, great complexity, long crisp hop aftertaste, a superb beer; hopped with Chinook, Willamette, and Centennial hops; 4.4% abw, 36 IBU. [A, 93]

STEELHEAD AMBER — amber, malt and hop aroma, balanced malt and hop flavor, very smooth, drinkable, medium body, dry finish and aftertaste; made with Centennial, Perle, and Cascade hops; gravity 13.5 P, 4.7% abw, 33 IBU. From the Eugene Pub. [A, 50]

Notes

OATMEAL STOUT — brown, dry malt and hop aroma and flavor, heavy body, dry malt finish and aftertaste, good length; 10% oatmeal and 2.5% rye malt used with Chinook and Willamette hops; gravity 17,7 P, 6.5% abw, 58 IBU. From the Eugene Pub. [S, 50]

STATION SQUARE STOUT — a black bitter imperial stout, huge complex very bitter aroma and flavor, big body, long rich dry and bitter aftertaste; Chinook and Perle hops; 5.8% abw, 65 IBU. From the Eugene Pub. [S, 61]

FRENCH PETE'S PORTER — brown; big dry malt aroma shows some chocolate malt; big dry malty flavor just like the nose promised, hefty body, long dry malt aftertaste; Galena and Willamette hops; gravity 15 P, 5.2% abw, 40 IBU. From the Eugene Pub. [P, 79]

GINGER BELLS — amber, light gingery aroma like a gingersnap cookie, flavor the same, ditto the finish and aftertaste; hopped with Galena and Cascade hops to 27 IBU. Not bad, but I'd like it better if it were less gingery and more beerlike. From the Eugene Pub. [A, 50]

RILEY'S RYE — amber, hop nose, hop flavor, dry malt aftertaste (where's the rye?); 10% rye malt used balanced with crystal malt, together with Galena, Centennial, and Willamette hops; gravity 13.9 P, 5% abw. From the Eugene Pub. [A, 45]

TIME WARP WEIZENBOCK — amber, malt aroma, malt and hop flavor, fair balance, good body, medium dry malt finish and aftertaste with the hops in back; CFJ-4 and Tettnanger hops; gravity 15 P, 5.9% abw, 31 IBU. From the Eugene Pub. [W, 50]

STEELHEAD CREAM ALE — gold, hop nose, light hop and malt flavor, medium body, medium dry finish and aftertaste; only Galena hops used (22 IBU) with 20% flaked maize; gravity 13.5 P, 4.8% abw. From the Eugene Pub. [A, 50]

BOMBAY BOMBER IPA — deep gold, big well-hopped aroma; huge complex flavor shows plenty of malt; big body; long complex aftertaste is a continuation of the flavor and holds the complexity; brewed with Chinook and Mt. Hood hops and dry hopped with Chinook; excellent IPA; OG 1053 (15 P), FG 1.009, 4.8% abw (6% abv), 45 IBU. From the Eugene Pub. [A, 66]

EMERALD SPECIAL BITTER — deep gold; beautiful rising hop aroma is most attractive; big complex flavor with plenty of hops and malt, good body, great complexity, long crisp hop aftertaste, a superb beer; hopped with Chinook, Willamette, and Centennial hops; 4.4% abw, 36 IBU. From the Eugene Pub. [A, 93]

STEELHEAD HEFE-WEIZEN — hazy gold, light malty aroma and dry malt flavor, light body, dry malt and hop finish, medium long dry malt aftertaste, definitely an American-style Hefe. As found in Irvine, CA. [W, 47]

STEELHEAD AMBER — amber, malty aroma, off-dry malt flavor, very slightly toasty, medium body; off-dry malty aftertaste is a bit on the dull side. As found in Irvine, CA. [A, 50]

BOMBAY BOMBER IPA — amber, light hop nose, hop flavor supported with off-dry malt, medium body, good character, very tasty, likable, dry malt and hop aftertaste. As found in Irvine, CA. [A, 66]

SON OF BOMBAY PALE ALE — deep amber-gold, hop aroma and flavor, medium to good body, northwest hop taste; big hop aftertaste is long and has plenty of supporting malt. As found in Irvine, CA. [A, 70]

FRENCH PETE'S PORTER — deep dark brown, lovely roasted-chocolate malt, coffee-chocolate-style palate, complex and roasty, medium body, tasty and balanced, good long toasted/roasted malt aftertaste; very well made and likable. As found in Irvine, CA. [P, 67]

Stevens Point Beverage Co.
Brewery at Stevens Point, WI

POINT SPECIAL PREMIUM BEER — pale gold, light malt aroma with just a trace of hops, pleasant clean light malt flavor, light body, medium length dry malt aftertaste, smooth and very drinkable; made with a high malt ratio; hopped with Cluster and Galena hops; specific gravity 1.047, 3.75% abw, 14 IBU. [B, 53]

POINT LIGHT — gold, very pleasant fragrant malt and hop nose, medium body, good tasting dry malt flavor, light dry hop aftertaste, highly carbonated; specific gravity 1.0047, 2.62% abw. [LO, 39]

POINT GENUINE BOCK BEER — brilliant amber, big malt aroma, big dry malt flavor, very smooth, light body, long fairly dry malt aftertaste, very much like a Mai-bock; made with barley roasted to slightly caramelized, two-row and six-row caramel and dextrin malts; hopped with Cluster and Galena hops with a high malt ratio; specific gravity 1.055, 4% abw, 22 IBU. [BK, 57]

POINT SPECIAL EDITION — bright deep gold, good hop and malt nose, good body, satisfying malt flavor, balanced, dry hop finish and aftertaste, not long but good, all-malt beer; specific gravity 1.01173, 3.2% abw. [B, 47]

EAGLE PREMIUM PILSNER — pale yellow-gold, good malt and hop nose, bright hop flavor, medium body, good long aftertaste with both malt and hops, a good little beer. [B, 43]

CHIEF OSHKOSH RED LAGER BEER — amber, mostly malt in the aroma and on the front of the palate; hops come in at the finish and stay through the long dry aftertaste; despite the initial malty character, the overall impression is dry hops; made with Belgian Cara-Munich (two-row) Carapils and six-row blend malts, Northern Brewer, Hallertau, and Cascade hops; kraeusened, and lagered in cypress tanks; gravity 12.15 P, 4% abw, 22 IBU. Contract brew for Mid-Coast B.C. of Oshkosh, WI. [B, 41]

NEW YORK HARBOR ALE — bright deep gold, good malt and hop aroma; lusty hop flavor with some complexity stays fairly dry; good body and some complexity, long dry hop aftertaste; in general the malt stays in the background, but is at a good level; uses pale, Carapils, caramel, and Munich malts with Chinook, Cascade, and Hallertau hops; gravity 13 P (1052), 5% abw. Made for Old World Brewing Co., Staten Island, NY. [A, 59]

NEW YORK STYLE HARBOR DARK ALE — brown, dry malt nose and taste, dull malt finish; dry malt aftertaste has a touch of toasted malt at the end; made with crystal, chocolate, and black malts with Cascade and Fuggles hops; OG 1058. Made for Old World Brewing Co., Staten Island, NY. [A, 40]

SPUD PREMIUM BEER — gold, vegetal malt aroma, earthy dry malt palate, medium long dry malt aftertaste with some hops showing. [B, 23]

RJ'S GINSENG BEER — bright gold, intriguing spicy aroma, flavor is even more spicy; good body, dry but zesty spiced finish and aftertaste, good length; brewed using three malts, three varieties of hops, and three types of American ginseng root; starting gravity 12.2 P, 3.96% abw. The most interesting of the ginseng beers. Made for R.J.'s Ginseng Co. Inc. of Chicago, IL (R J Corr Natural Beverages, Posen, IL). [B, 50]

ARNOLD'S AMBER — amber; very pleasant malty nose has a slightly roasted character; good dry malt flavor has some hop support; medium body, dry malt finish and aftertaste. Made for Woodstock Brewing & Bottling. [B, 50]

LIONSTONE LAGER — brilliant deep gold; faint flowery malt nose is light and clean; flavor grows as you sip, stays malty bordering on sweet but never quite getting there; dry hops in the finish and aftertaste, medium body, and good length. [B, 58]

RUSTY'S ROAD KNIGHT AMBER — amber, soapy malt nose; soapiness fades quickly leaving a nice malt flavor; very little hops; hops evidenced only by the dryness in the aftertaste. [B, 36]

LAKE HIGHLAND AMBER — brilliant amber, bright hop aroma, big hop and malt flavor, decent balance, zesty dry aftertaste, very tasty with plenty of both malt and hops. Made for Full Moon Int'l of Orlando, FL. [B, 66]

Stewart's B.C.
Brewpub in Bear, DE

GOVERNOR'S GOLDEN ALE — deep gold, mild hop nose, dry hop flavor, very pleasant with food, tasty by itself, medium body, dry hop finish and aftertaste; nicely made well-balanced brew; made with Styrian hops; 4.2% abw. [A, 79]

STEWART'S PALE ALE — deep gold, light dry hop aroma and flavor, medium body, very dry finish and aftertaste, good length; made with Fuggles hops; 4.75% abw. [A, 60]

BIG BEAR AMBER ALE — amber, malt and hops about even in the nose and mouth, very flavorful and complex, dry hop finish and aftertaste, very dry and very long; made with five malts and four hops; 5.2% abw. [A, 59]

HIGHLANDER STOUT — dark brown, creamy brown head, smooth roasted malt aroma and flavor; hops barely show; smooth and soft, no harsh notes whatever, long soft dry roasted malt aftertaste; made with Cascade hops but they are not noticeable. [S, 66]

STEWART'S BLACK & TAN — brown, creamy tan head, light roasted malt aroma and flavor, medium body, smooth and balanced, end fairly dry; has good malty character; a blend of the Highlander Stout and Governor's Golden Ale. [A, 72]

RASPBERRY PORTER — dark brown, raspberry aroma; smooth raspberry flavor is fairly dry, especially at the end; medium body, dry raspberry aftertaste. [P, 69]

Stoddard's Brewhouse & Eatery
Brewpub in Sunnyvale, CA

STODDARD'S ESB — amber, Cascade hop aroma, good dry hop flavor, medium body, very tasty and likable, dry hop finish and aftertaste; made with English two-row specialty malts and Klages two-row pale malt; several varieties of hops are used but it is mostly Cascades; specific gravity 1.053, 4.9% abw. [A, 74]

STODDARD'S KÖLSCH — gold, malt nose, light bright malt flavor, medium body, dry malt finish and aftertaste; made with 5% wheat malt using a single temperature infusion mash and noble hops; specific gravity 1.054, 4.5% abw. [K, 70]

STODDARD'S KRISTALL WEIZEN — amber-gold; malty aroma shows no spice; big tasty dry malt palate, no spice whatever, dry malty-wheaty aftertaste, traditional filtered German-style wheat beer; made with 65% malted wheat and two-row Klages; top-fermented; brewed using a single-step infusion mashing process; specific gravity 1.052, 4.3% abw. [W, 74]

STODDARD'S PALE ALE — golden amber, dry highly hopped aroma and flavor, medium to light body, dry hop finish and aftertaste; brewed using single-temperature infusion mash, two-row Klages and British specialty malts, Bullion and Fuggles hops; specific gravity 1.050, 4.7% abw. [A, 67]

STODDARD'S PORTER — brown, light dry roasted malt aroma and flavor, medium to good body; dry malt and hop finish and aftertaste is more malt than hops; made with dark roasted malt and American hops; specific gravity 1.056, 4.6% abw. [P, 60]

Stone Mountain Brewers

Microbrewer in Marietta, GA.

STONE MOUNTAIN SOUTHERN LAGER — gold, faint malt nose, light thin malt flavor, light body, light grainy malt aftertaste; 3.3% abw. Tasted at the GABF in 1993. Since then, I have seen where the beer is being made at Schell as Stone Mountain Extra Special Southern Lager. [B, 34]

Boar's Head Pub & Grille

Brewpub in Austin, TX, originally named The Stonehouse Brewery.

CANTERBURY LAGER — gold; dry aroma shows both malt and hops; big rich but dry malt and hop flavor; hops are not those most commonly encountered being New Zealand high-alpha hops and have their own flavor; good body, long dry hop aftertaste. [B, 71]

B.J. SMITH PALE ALE — deep gold, dry hop aroma, austere dry hop flavor, good body, long dry hop aftertaste; again using the New Zealand hops but this time with a touch of Cascade hops to give a bit of a northwest slant. [A, 68]

UNCLE DOUG'S AMBER ALE — very deep tawny gold color; dry hop aroma and flavor again using the New Zealand hops which give these beers a common thread that could be likened to a house flavor; good body, dry hop finish and aftertaste. [A, 75]

BULLDOG DARK — amber-brown, dry roasted malt aroma and flavor, medium to good body, nutty dry hop finish and aftertaste; a very good dry hop and roasted malt brew again using the New Zealand hops. [B, 81]

FRANKIE STEIN — amber-brown, dry hop and malt aroma, flavor like the nose features the New Zealand hops, good body; dry hop finish and aftertaste shows some nuttiness from the roasted malts. This is a blend of the Canterbury Lager and the Bulldog Dark. [B, 72]

Stoudt Brewing Co.

Brewery, brewpub, restaurant, antique center in Adamstown, PA

STOUDT'S GOLDEN LAGER — gold, good malt nose, dry malt flavor with good hop support; touch of off-dry malt at the finish, then a long dry malt and hop aftertaste; very good balance, very drinkable; hopped with German Hallertau and Tettnanger hops; gravity 12.5 P, 4.5% abw. [B, 73]

STOUDT'S ADAMSTOWN AMBER — bright amber, hop nose, hop taste with plenty of malt in support, very good balance, good body; malt comes to the fore at the finish; long dry malt and hop aftertaste, another very drinkable brew. [B, 81]

STOUDT'S HOLIDAY BOCK — ruby-amber, light toasted malt aroma; toasted malt flavor that might have a little smokiness way way back; long dry malt aftertaste, good brew but somewhat unidimensional. [BK, 47]

STOUDT'S OKTOBERFEST DARK — see Lion, Inc.

STOUDT'S MARDI GRAS (FASCHING) — beautiful deep ruby-amber color, light malt aroma, dry malt and hop flavor, mild and smooth, long dry malt aftertaste. [BK, 32]

STOUDT'S OKTOBERFEST — deep amber, good roasted malt and hop nose, big hop and well-roasted malt flavor; finishes as it starts; extremely dry brief roasted malt aftertaste. [BK, 43]

STOUDT'S PILSENER STYLE — gold, lovely European (Saaz) hop nose, big dry hop flavor, big body, complex, dry hop finish and long aftertaste; gravity 12.5 P, 4.5% abw. [B, 56]

STOUDT'S BOCK BIER — deep mahogany color, toasted malt nose and taste, some complexity; creamy texture with a big solid head that lasts to the bottom of the glass; fairly dry malt finish and aftertaste, good length. [BK, 56]

STOUDT'S BOCK — mahogany color, light roasted malt nose and taste, some hops in the finish, medium length dry hop aftertaste; gravity 16 P, 6% abw. [BK, 56]

STOUDT'S BULL ALE — amber, faintly soapy malt nose; light malt flavor feels good in your mouth; off-dry malt finish and aftertaste, good length; gravity 12.3 P, 4.5% abw. [A, 41]

STOUDT'S SOUR MASH ALE — deep amber, slightly buttery malt nose, off-dry malt flavor, slightly sour finish, long dry aftertaste. [A, 12]

STOUDT'S RASPBERRY WEIZEN — reddish color; dry raspberry nose is a little sour; very dry malt and faint raspberry in the flavor; maintains a fruity malt character; finishes dry malt, fairly long dry malt aftertaste; gravity 11.5 P, 4.2% abw. [W, 58]

STOUDT'S OKTOBERFEST BOCK -— deep ruby-amber, very faint malt aroma, dry lightly scorched malt flavor, pleasant, long dry aftertaste like the flavor. [B, 72]

STOUDT'S OKTOBERFEST MAERZEN — medium deep amber, dry malt nose, thin body, odd sort of vegetal malt flavor, not appetizing, short malt aftertaste. [BK, 30]

STOUDT STOUT — opaque brown, light malt nose, dry malt palate; some malty sweetness appears at the finish; long dry malt aftertaste, very drinkable, medium body; gravity 13 P, 4.5% abw. [S, 62]

STOUDT'S HOLIDAY ALE — amber, big hop and big malt aroma; flavor starts out with big hops and plenty of bite, malt comes in the middle and stays; excellent balance, big body, luscious and long, a real lip-smacker. [A, 87]

STOUDT'S GOLD MEDAL HEFE-WEIZEN — cloudy gold, fresh clean lightly spiced malt nose, light dry spicy malt flavor, hops come in at the finish, moderately dry hop aftertaste with good duration. [W, 57]

STOUDT'S ANNIVERSARY ALE — amber, hop nose with some caramel, very big hop flavor, good body, big long dry hop aftertaste. [A, 52]

STOUDT'S BEERFEST BOCK — very deep amber, dry malt nose with a hint of caramel, very dry malt flavor, long dry malt aftertaste with hops faintly in back. [BK, 56]

STOUDT'S DOPPELBOCK — amber, buttery malt nose; malt and

hop flavor with the butter still there but far in back; dry malt finish and long aftertaste; finished with Hallertau and Tettnanger hops; gravity 18 P, 8% abw. Bottled version. [BK, 43]

STOUDT'S RED ALE — reddish-amber, faint hop-ale aroma, big tangy hop palate, good malt backing, good body, long dry hop aftertaste. [A, 47]

STOUDT'S WINTERFEST — amber, light malt and hop nose, off-dry malt and bitter hop palate, balanced, somewhat winey in nature, dry malt finish, medium length dry malt aftertaste, very nice drinkable brew. Labeled Oktoberfest, but released in January and, according to the Stoudts, it's their winterfest beer. [B, 67]

STOUDT'S DOUBLE BOCK — deep amber, big rich malt nose, bright malt flavor with an off-dry quality in back, big body, big flavor, some alcohol noted; long malt aftertaste is drier than the flavor; a big rich enjoyable brew; finished with Hallertau and Tettnanger hops; gravity 18 P, 8% abw. Version on draft at the brewery. [BK, 83]

STOUDT'S FESTIVAL RE-SERVE FEST BEER — amber, light malt nose, light dry malt and hop flavor, dry malt and hop aftertaste; hops dominate at the end; medium duration; gravity 12.5 P, 4.5% abw. [B, 20]

STOUDT'S HONEY DOUBLE BOCK — tawny-gold, mellow off-dry malt and hop aroma, big body, big bright malt flavor;

honey shows best in the middle, hops come in at the finish to stay for the aftertaste; aftertaste is balanced off-dry malt and dry hops; very complex and interesting brew. [BK, 65]

STOUDT'S FESTIVAL RESERVE EXPORT GOLD — deep gold, malt aroma with a faintly buttery background, big malt flavor, full body; finish and aftertaste are dry malt with a faint buttery background that tends to make it seem dull. Bottled at the brewery. [B, 52]

STOUDT'S RESERVE BOCK — deep amber, rich malt nose, pleasant rich malt flavor; some alcohol shows and it is slightly sweet in the middle; good body, smooth, chewy, very good balance, dry malt finish and aftertaste, lots of flavor and very drinkable. Bottled at the brewery. [BK, 71]

STOUDT'S MAI BOCK — very deep amber, rich flowery malt aroma, big malt taste and big body, plenty of alcohol showing, great mouth feel; long rich malt aftertaste shows some hops and is drier than the flavor; very long and very good; made with Munich and pale malts; gravity 18 P, 8% abw. Version on draft at the brewpub. [BK, 76]

STOUDT'S DOUBLE MAI BOCK — tawny-gold, aroma with plenty of both hops and malt, good body; big hop flavor overrides the malt, could use a better balance especially at the finish; long hop aftertaste; gravity 18 P, 8% abw. [BK, 60]

Notes

STOUDT'S HONEY DOUBLE MAI-BOCK — amber-gold, off-dry malty aroma; malty flavor is definitely on the sweet side, even sweeter than the regular Honey Double Bock; big body, finishes sweet leading into a long off-dry malt aftertaste, very smooth and drinkable. [BK, 65]

STOUDT'S HONEY DOUBLE MAI-BOCK RESERVE BEER — deep bright gold, very attractive malt nose, big rich malt flavor, good hops at finish, balanced; dry malt aftertaste with plenty of hops staying on for balance; big bodied with a great mouthfeel. [BK, 65]

STOUDT'S HONEY NUT OATMEAL STOUT — deep brown; dry malt aroma is nutty (Victory malt), faintly of mocha (Chocolate malt), and shows a trace of oats; flavor is at first roasted barley, light chocolate, and nuts, but this only lasts to mid-palate when it goes dry roasted malt alone; faint hops come in the middle and stay briefly; good body (but not big), dry malt finish and aftertaste. [S, 60]

OLD BAY AMBER — amber, pleasant bright malt aroma, dry malt flavor, good body, big dry malt finish, long dry malt aftertaste. Made for The Old Bay restaurant of New Brunswick, NJ. [B, 54]

STOUDT'S AUTUMN BOCK — amber; perfumy malt aroma is ale-like; big fairly dry malt flavor is off-dry at the finish; good body, long dry malt aftertaste. [BK, 49]

STOUDT'S APPLE CINNAMON ALE — cloudy orange, dry light cinnamon-apple aroma and taste, light to medium body, very dry throughout, long dry aftertaste like the flavor; all done with a light hand so you can taste the malt and hops under the headlined flavors. [A, 62]

STOUDT'S WEIZEN — hazy gold, sour lemony nose, lemony flavor with a slight clove background, lemony aftertaste, sort of unidimensional; top-fermented with 60% wheat malt; gravity 11.5 P, 4.2% abw. [W, 34]

STOUDT'S EXPORT GOLD — deep gold, light appetizing hop nose, smooth light hop flavor, light dry hop finish and aftertaste, quite long; Dortmunder-style Helles; gravity 13.5 P, 5.5% abw. [B, 52]

STOUDT'S FESTIVAL RESERVE EXPORT GOLD — deep gold, malt aroma with a faintly buttery background, big malt flavor, full body; finish and aftertaste are dry malt with a faint buttery background that tends to make it seem dull; made with five roasted malts; hopped with Hallertau and Tettnanger hops; gravity 13.5 P, 5.5% abw. Bottled at the brewery. [B, 21]

STOUDT'S FESTIVAL BOCK — light amber, big flowery malt nose, rich semi-dry malt flavor, driest of the Stoudt Maibocks, good body, long fairly dry malt finish and aftertaste; best bock to have with food. [B, 72]

STOUDT'S INDIA PALE ALE — amber, light spicy malt aroma, big burst of flavor at first, tangy hops and big malt; mid-palate is smooth and dry as the hops back off momentarily revealing some spiciness; big dry hop finish now with the malt retreating; long dry hop aftertaste shows little or no malt; gravity 13.5 P, 5% abw. [A, 62]

STOUDT'S TRIPLE BREW — a triple decoction lager, amber-brown, complex light dry malt nose, very dry malty flavor, medium body, not high in alcohol or in hops, dry malt finish and aftertaste; flavor doesn't deliver the complexity that is hinted at in the aroma, but it has good duration. [B, 53]

STOUDT'S ABBEY TRIPEL — deep amber, big sand-colored head, malty aroma, beautiful bright refreshing malt flavor with a good lactic acid bite, very smooth; very long flavor that ends dry; a very good Belgian abbey-style ale with excellent acid balance. [A, 86]

STOUDT'S SMALL ALE — dark ruby-brown, tangy malty altbier nose, flavor very much like the nose; very malty, quite rich, dry, but has an ale bite that detracts a little bit from the overall effect; long aftertaste is a continuation of the flavor. [A, 53]

Straub Brewery, Inc.
Brewery in St. Mary's, PA

STRAUB ALL GRAIN BEER — light tawny gold, big malt nose with plenty of hops, big body, full malt and hop flavor, a hefty mouthful of beer, long dry aftertaste with plenty of malt and hops. [B, 47]

STRAUB LIGHT BEER — pale gold; malty grainy nose shows a little corn; fairly bright malty flavor has good hop support; medium body; dry hop aftertaste has medium duration, not bad for a low-calorie beer. [B, 71]

PYMATUNING DAM BEER — orange-amber; grainy malt aroma shows a faint trace of corn; dull dry malt flavor, finish, and aftertaste. Label attributes the beer to Crooked Creek B.C. of St. Mary's, PA. [B, 22]

Karl Strauss' Old Columbia Brewery & Grill
Brewpub in San Diego, CA

KARL STRAUSS AMBER LAGER — amber-gold; big malt nose has a faint roasted background, big body; hefty malt flavor has hops for balance; lightly dry hop finish and aftertaste, smooth and long; gravity 12.5 P, 4% abw. [B, 71]

POINT LOMA LIGHTHOUSE — gold, malt aroma and palate; dry malt finish and aftertaste has some hops but they are faint; gravity 8.1 P, 3.1% abw. [LO, 41]

GASLAMP GOLD ALE — deep gold, faint malt and hop aroma, big malty flavor, some hops in back, good body, very dry malt and hop finish and aftertaste, good length and lots of depth; gravity 13.8, 3.8% abw. [A, 67]

HORTON'S HOOTCH — amber-gold, off-dry malt nose and flavor, drier at the finish; somewhat bitter and alcoholic as it crosses the palate and fairly dry hop aftertaste with the malt now in back; could be better balanced; advertised as a doublebock; gravity 17 P, 6% abw. [B, 45]

AMERICA'S FINEST PILSENER — gold, light hop aroma, well-balanced dry hop and malt flavor, lightly hopped finish, smooth but not crisp; dry hop and malt aftertaste has good length. [B, 49]

RED TROLLEY ALE — ruby-amber, faint roasted barley aroma and flavor; hops are in back; fair to good balance; you taste the malt and feel the hops; dry malt and hop aftertaste is quite long. [A, 57]

CYNIC'S ELECTION LAGER — golden amber, faint malt aroma, light malt flavor with just a hint of hops, brief malty aftertaste. [B, 34]

Notes

POINT LOMA LIGHTHOUSE LIGHT — gold, light hop nose; bright dry hop flavor is very good for a low-calorie beer; good body, dry hop finish and aftertaste, medium length, dryness lasts, nicely done. [LO, 61]

DRY HOPPED BROWN ALE — deep mahogany, faint malt nose, dry malt and hop flavor, sort of a roasted quality to it; at the end it is all dry hops, not much length; a final parting flavor is again the roasted malt. [A, 45]

BLACK'S BEACH EXTRA DARK — deep mahogany, faint malt nose, dry malt flavor, hop finish; dry malt and hop aftertaste is just dryness at the end. [A, 45]

OATMEAL STOUT — very deep mahogany, malt and oatmeal nose; sort of a medium dry sourish flavor (not unfamiliar in an oatmeal stout) that clashes with the barley malt; aftertaste starts out off-dry malt and ends dry. [S, 34]

JEFF & JER'S HOOTCH — amber, malt aroma and flavor, medium dry, alcoholic, finishes dry malt leading into a long dry malt aftertaste, good balance, a very good doublebock. [B, 65]

Stroh Brewing Co.
Headquarters in Detroit, MI; breweries in Lehigh Valley, PA; Longview, TX; St.Paul, MN; Los Angeles, CA; Memhis, TN; Winston-Salem, NC; and Tampa, FL.

STROH'S OWN BOCK BEER — copper-amber, good malt aroma and caramel-malt flavor, flavorful, smooth, balanced, and long. [BK, 70]

STROH'S PREMIUM QUALITY AMERICAN BEER — bright gold, fresh malt aroma, bright hop flavor with malt supporting and in balance, good hop-malt finish and aftertaste; specific gravity 1.043, 3.4% abw, 14 IBU. [B, 48]

STROH LIGHT BEER — pale gold, light malt aroma, refreshing light malt flavor, pleasant and with better than average length for a light beer; specific gravity 1.036, 3.3% abw, 12 IBU. [LO, 50]

STROH SIGNATURE — brilliant gold, very good hop aroma with complexity and character, dry well-balanced malt and hop flavor, good and long, a true super premium beer; hopped with Saaz and Styrian hops; specific gravity 1.048, 3.9% abw, 16 IBU. [B, 62]

GOEBEL GOLDEN LIGHT LAGER — pale gold, faint malt aroma, light but balanced and clean tasting, highly carbonated but refreshing. [B, 49]

SILVER THUNDER MALT LIQUOR — bright pale gold, pleasant malt aroma, sweetish malt flavor (but not flabby); has complexity and interest; fairly long and balanced; gravity 12 P, 4.6% abw. [ML, 56]

SCHLITZ BEER — pale gold, light malt aroma with hops faintly in back, light malt flavor lightly

hopped, pleasant and inoffensive and dry overall. Now brewed to its original formula and hopped with Yakima, Cascade, and Galena hops; gravity 11 P, 3.6% abw. [B, 43]

SCHLITZ LIGHT BEER — pale gold, light malty-vanilla nose and taste, pleasant, fairly dry and brief; made with Cascade hops; gravity 9.4 P, 3.4% abw. [LO, 28]

SCHLITZ MALT LIQUOR — deep gold, hearty malt aroma and flavor, medium body, off-dry malt finish and aftertaste; specific gravity 1.054, 4.6% abw, 12 IBU. [ML, 54]

SCHLITZ GENUINE DRAFT — pale gold, sour hop nose, light but brisk hop and malt flavor, good balance, medium dry malt finish, short malty aftertaste; specific gravity 1.044, 3.6% abw, 14 IBU. [B, 39]

SCHLITZ RED BULL MALT LIQUOR — pale gold, heady aromatic malt nose, off-dry and faintly salty malt flavor, heavy body, sweet malt finish and aftertaste; gravity 14.6 P, 5.5% abw. [ML, 23]

SCHLITZ ICE — pale gold, pleasant malt nose, likable light malt flavor, light body, very smooth on the palate, light off-dry malt aftertaste. Full name is Schlitz Ice, Ice Brewed Premium Beer. [B, 50]

SCHLITZ NA NON-ALCOHOLIC MALT BEVERAGE — gold, faint off-dry malt aroma, light off-dry malt flavor, light to medium body, not as grainy as most of the type, medium long off-dry malt aftertaste; fairly good of type; less than 0.5% abv. [NA, 39]

OLD MILWAUKEE BEER — bright pale gold, faint hop aroma with malt, good malt flavor; finishes pleasantly malted and has a good aftertaste; gravity 11 P, 3.6% abw. [B, 62]

OLD MILWAUKEE PREMIUM LIGHT BEER — pale yellow, faint but clean malt aroma; carbonation dominates the palate wiping out what malt there is; slight malt finish, little aftertaste; gravity 9.5 P, 3.4% abw. [LO, 23]

OLD MILWAUKEE NON-ALCOHOLIC — very pale gold, faint grainy aroma, very light grainy flavor, short. Stroh says that this is Old Milwaukee beer, brewed to completeness, then with the alcohol removed; gravity 5.2 P, 0.30% abw. [NA, 35]

OLD MILWAUKEE GENUINE DRAFT LIGHT — pale gold, light hop nose and flavor, high carbonation, light dry hop aftertaste, decent light-bodied summertime quaffing beer. [LO, 36]

OLD MILWAUKEE GENUINE DRAFT — gold, hop nose and flavor, high carbonation, medium body, fairly long dry hop aftertaste. [LO, 30]

OLD MILWAUKEE ICE — deep gold, pleasant hop nose, good body, good dry hop and malt flavor; dry malt aftertaste is long; 5.5% abw. [B, 52]

SCHAEFER BEER — bright gold, good malt and hop aroma, zesty hop flavor, good body, good balance, overall dry, well-hopped long aftertaste; gravity 10.5 P, 3.4% abw. [B, 53]

SCHAEFER LIGHT LAGER BEER — bright gold, faint malt aroma, faint hops and slightly sour malt palate, little flavor, less aftertaste; gravity 8.6 P, 3.1% abw. [LO, 20]

SCHAEFER LOW ALCOHOL BEER — medium deep gold, grainy off-dry malt aroma, dry sour malt flavor, watery, no follow-through. [RA, 23]

PIELS LIGHT BEER — pale gold, light malt aroma, light malt flavor, lightly hopped, long and pleasant aftertaste, thirst quenching. [LO, 50]

PIELS REAL DRAFT PREMIUM BEER — bright gold, clean malt aroma; high carbonation pretty well wipes out the light malt and hop flavor; gravity 10.3 P, 3.7% abw. [B, 36]

PRIMO BEER — pale yellow-gold, vegetal malt aroma and flavor, bit of sweet malt in front and in finish, light bodied; gravity 10.5 P, 3.4% abw. Primo Brewing & Malting Co., Ltd. made from wort brewed on mainland. [B, 34]

AUGSBURGER BEER — gold, very bright hop nose, zesty hop flavor, great character and excellent balance, bitter hop finish with a nice touch of malt underneath, long fairly dry hop aftertaste, one of America's best beers; gravity 12.6P, 3.9% abw. Also called Augsburger Golden. [B, 80]

AUGSBURGER DARK — reddish-brown, slightly off-dry roasted malt aroma, malt palate, finish, and aftertaste, very good balance, and quite satisfying; made with hi-dried and caramel malts; gravity 12.6 P, 3.9% abw, 22 IBU. [B, 62]

AUGSBURGER BOCK — deep amber-brown, faint malt aroma, big smooth dry malt palate; there are hops in there, but it is mostly malt; dry finish, good body, long dry malt and hop aftertaste; an excellent bock and probably one of the top ten nationally distributed dark domestic brews; gravity 12.6 P, 25 IBU, 3.9% abw. [BK, 75]

AUGSBURGER LIGHT — bright gold, clean appetizing hop aroma, medium body, bright crisp hop flavor, dry finish, and fairly long dry hop aftertaste. [LO, 49]

AUGSBURGER WEISS — brilliant gold; faint malt aroma has a hint of orange peel in back; light malt flavor dominated by carbonation but it is not fizzy; light body; wheat barely shows; light and refreshing, not long; made from a blend of pale and wheat malts; specific gravity 1.042, 3.7% abw. [W, 30]

AUGSBURGER DÖPPELBOCK — very dark ruby-brown, faint malt aroma, complex roasted malt flavor, medium body; flavor picks up strength at the finish with a little malty sweetness in back; good body, pleasant medium long dry malt aftertaste, very drinkable, an excellent beer with food;

specific gravity 1.058, 3.9% abw, 25 IBU. [BK, 72]

AUGSBURGER OKTOBERFEST BEER — pale amber, flowery fruity hop and malt aroma, good balanced hop and malt flavor, somewhat light but good and drinkable, medium long aftertaste; specific gravity 1.052, 3.9% abw. [B, 65]

AUGSBURGER ROT BEER LAGER — pale reddish-amber, very faint malt aroma, light malt flavor, light to medium body, dry hop and malt finish and aftertaste, smooth and dry, nothing stands out; OG 1048, 3.9% abw, 19 IBU. [B, 52]

RED RIVER VALLEY SELECT LAGER — deep gold, bright hop aroma, well-hopped zesty hop flavor, medium body, dry hop finish and aftertaste; made with pale and caramel malts, Saaz and Styrian hops; specific gravity 1.049, 3.9% abw, SRM 19, 16 IBU. Made under contract for Northern Plains Brewing Co. of St. Paul, MN. [B, 60]

LOST RIVER LIGHT — pale gold; very pleasant malt aroma has good balancing hops; smooth nicely balanced malt and hop flavor, light body, very drinkable and refreshing, little aftertaste; goes down easily. Attributed to Lost River B.C., Box 32875, Detroit. [LO, 56]

RED RIVER VALLEY SELECT RED LAGER — amber; toasted malt aroma and flavor, just a tad scorched and a little off-dry; medium body; dry toasted malt aftertaste has good duration.

Attributed to Northern Plains B.C., St. Paul, MN PO Box 64115, Zip 55164. [B, 55]

RED BULL STRONG BEER — deep amber, big alcoholic malt nose and taste, big body; long off-dry malt and alcohol aftertaste has some fruitiness; made for Canadian market; 7.1% abw. [ML, 58]

BULL ICE-ICE BREWED MALT LIQUOR — deep gold, big malt nose; strong malt flavor shows some alcohol; malty finish has a sweetness in back that comes out more in the aftertaste, medium long malty aftertaste; very good of type; 7.7% abv. [ML, 53]

SCHLITZ ICE — deep gold, fragrant malt and hop aroma; big malt and hop flavor is a bit off-dry; good body, big dry hop and sweet malt finish and aftertaste; some alcohol shows. [B, 50]

SCHLITZ ICE LIGHT — gold, fragrant hop and malt nose; flavor is also European hops and malt; medium body, dry hop finish and brief aftertaste, big for a light beer. [B, 22]

OLD MILWAUKEE RED — amber, faint malty aroma, highly carbonated, light malty flavor, light body, thin even, light dry malty aftertaste. [B, 33]

AUGSBURGER ALT — deep gold, laid back fruity nose, lightly toasted malty flavor, light body, ends dry malt, a bit dull. [A, 29]

PETE'S WICKED ALE — brilliant deep amber, slightly toasted malt and hop aroma; zesty malt flavor with hops rolling in from mid-palate on; malt and hops balanced throughout, good hop and malt finish and a long dry aftertaste; an excellent, balanced, satisfying, drinkable brew; made with pale, chocolate, and caramel malts and Cascade and Brewers Gold hops; gravity 13.1 P, 4.2% abw. Made for Pete's B.C. of Palo Alto, CA. [A, 62]

PETE'S WICKED LAGER — deep gold, citruslike northwest hop aroma, good balanced hop flavor, medium body, smooth and tasty, long dry hop aftertaste; Bohemian-style pils made with pale and caramel malts, kraeusened, and brewed with Willamette, Tettnanger, Liberty, and Mt. Hood hops; gravity 12.2 P, 3.9% abw. Made for Pete's B.C. of Palo Alto, CA. [B, 60]

PETE'S WICKED WINTER BREW — amber, raspberry and faint nutmeg nose; raspberry clashes with the hops and spice in the flavor, simply does not balance; medium body; dry hop aftertaste with a hint of raspberry remaining in the rear; 4.1% abw. Made for Pete's B.C. of Palo Alto, CA. [B, 30]

PETE'S WICKED RED — brilliant copper-amber, lovely smooth hop aroma, rich complex drinkable hoppy flavor, good balance, good big rich flavor, no warts, finishes dry hops, long dry hop aftertaste; this should be a very popular brew, made with pale, caramel, and Munich malts; hopped with Yakima Cluster and Cascade hops, with Tettnager hops added late in the kettle; gravity 12.5 P, 3.85% abw. Made for Pete's B.C. of Palo Alto, CA. [A, 73]

PETE'S WICKED SUMMER BREW — brilliant gold, bright tangy hop aroma, dry tangy hop flavor; label says there is natural lemon flavor added but I cannot detect it in either the nose or the palate; medium body, long dry hop aftertaste, a very dry and refreshing beer, a welcome addition to the summer beer scene. Made for Pete's B.C. of Palo Alto, CA. [B, 72]

PETE'S WICKED HONEY WHEAT — hazy amber, perfumy off-dry honey-fruity-estery malt aroma; sweet grainy malt flavor has a honey background, ends drier with plenty of hops; a bit short but fairly refreshing. Made for Pete's B.C. of Palo Alto, CA. [W, 49]

REDNECK PREMIUM BEER — bright gold, grapey-grainy nose, grapey flavor, a bit sweet and a bit short. Made for Fischer B.C., which may be for Wynn-Dixie supermarkets. [B, 30]

2-II STEEL RESERVE HIGH GRAVITY LAGER — pale gold, flowery off-dry malt aroma, taste like the nose; some of the 5.7% abv shows; medium body, soft malty finish and aftertaste, a bit on the dull side. [B, 32]

Note: Many of the S&P Co. brews are made in eastern Stroh breweries for distribution on the east coast. They are listed under S&P. Production of beer for Pete's B.C. contract beers was begun in mid-1995.

Sugarloaf Brewing Co. / Theo's Pub
Brewpub in Carrabassett Valley, ME

CARRABASSETT PALE ALE — amber, appetizing dry hop nose, very dry hop flavor, good body, very long dry hop aftertaste. Tasted on draft at Great Lost Bear in Portland, ME. [A, 47]

CARRABASSETT PALE ALE — amber, fruity hop and malt aroma, big estery hop and malt flavor, complex, medium body, dry finish, very long off-dry fruity aftertaste; doesn't quite come together. As tasted in bottle. [A, 71]

CARRABASSETT HONEY BROWN — dark amber, malty nose. off-dry honeyed malt flavor, medium to good body, medium long off-dry honeyed malt aftertaste, very pleasant. [A, 55]

CARRABASSETT KÖLSCH — gold, slightly fruity malt nose;

grainy malt flavor has a bite to it; medium to light body, finishes dry, medium long dry tart aftertaste. [K, 48]

CARRABASSETT INDIA PALE ALE — amber, big bright hop aroma, zesty hop palate, good body, dry hop finish and aftertaste, good length. [A, 66]

CARRABASSETT BLUEBERRY ALE — amber, faint berry nose, definitely a blueberry flavor, medium body, dry blueberry and hop aftertaste, fairly long, and very well made. [A, 61]

Summit Brewing Co.
Brewery in St, Paul, MN

SUMMIT EXTRA PALE ALE — pale amber, flowery hop and malt aroma, clean big hop flavor, medium body, dry malt finish and long dry hop aftertaste; made with two-row Harrington malt and caramel malt with Cascade, Eroica, and Fuggles hops; gravity 12 P, 3.9% abw. [A, 51]

SUMMIT SPARKLING ALE — deep gold, malt nose, off-dry malt flavor, dry hop finish, medium body, weak brief hop aftertaste. [A, 40]

SUMMIT WINTER ALE — deep brownish amber, big malt aroma, fruity and grape-like, thin smoked malt flavor, medium body, simple and drinkable, light long dry malt aftertaste. [A, 45]

SUMMIT GREAT NORTHERN PORTER — deep brown, sharp malt nose, lots of chocolate malt,

somewhat winelike malt flavor, medium body, long malt aftertaste; brewed with two-row Harrington pale, caramel, and black malt; gravity 13.4 P, 4.3% abw. [P, 45]

Sun Valley Brewing Co.
Microbrewery in Hailey, ID. Products are familiar in the west having been made under contract at Kessler for seven years.

SUN VALLEY OUR HOLIDAY ALE 1992 — deep amber, finely carbonated, rich malt aroma, strong malt flavor with good hop backing, big body, finishes strongly, great balance, marvelous to sip, very long hop and malt aftertaste, a treasure; Scotch-style ale made from four malts and four hop varieties; specific gravity 1.073, 5.3% abw. [A, 91]

SUN VALLEY WHITE CLOUD ALE — amber, complex aromatic malt and hop nose, a fruity citrus well-hopped flavor, medium body, dry hop aftertaste, pleasant, complex, and very drinkable; all-malt ale using Cascade and Hallertau hops; specific gravity 1.049, 3.4% abw. In 1994, the recipe substituted Liberty hops for the Hallertau, changed the alcohol to 4% abw, specific gravity 1.012, altered the aroma to a less aromatic style, and changed the flavor to less hoppy and more dry malty. [B, 65]

SUN VALLEY SAWTOOTH GOLD LAGER — hazy amber-gold, big malt nose with a hop background, malt flavor, finish, and long aftertaste; 15% wheat malt is used; specific gravity 1.046, 4% abw. In 1994, gravity 12.7 P, 4.2% abw, but beyond subtle differences, I could detect no change in taste. [B, 63]

SUN VALLEY BLONDE — gold, malty aroma, bright malt taste, light body, light and refreshing summertime brew, dry malt finish and aftertaste, medium length; gravity 11.6 P, 3.4% abw. [B, 57]

ROCKY MOUNTAIN OKTOBERFEST — amber, dry hop aroma and flavor with good supporting malt, medium to good body; dry hop finish and aftertaste shows some background malt; made with English malts; gravity 13.5 P, 4.5% abw. [B, 67]

Sunday River B.C.
Brewpub/Microbrewery in Bethel, ME. The brewpub is called The Moose's Tale Food & Ale.

MOLLYOCKETT IPA — amber, light malt and hop aroma; big malty flavor that is slightly on the sweet side; good body, dry hop finish, long dry hop aftertaste. [A, 60]

REDSTONE ALE — deep amber, interesting hop aroma, big bright complex hop flavor, good body, dry hop finish and long dry hop aftertaste, a marvelous brew with great balance and complexity; made with Chinook, Cascade, and Mt. Hood hops; specific gravity 1.052 (14 P), 3.7% abw. [A, 93]

BLACK BEAR PORTER — dark brown color, dry malt nose, rich roasted malt flavor, long dry roasted malt aftertaste, good body, a very likable porter; made from two-row domestic barley and dark specialty malts balanced with Chinook hops; specific gravity 1.056 (15 P), 5.5% abw. [P, 98]

SUNDAY RIVER BROWN ALE — dark amber-brown, malt aroma, big sweet malt flavor, dry malt finish; there are hops but they are well in back; flavor a bit yeasty; fairly short on the palate; specific gravity 1.048, 4.2% abw. [A, 53]

SUNDAY RIVER ALT — amber, aroma of malt, hops, and yeast, big complex flavor like the aroma, medium body, finishes dry, a bit unbalanced at the aftertaste; OG 12 P, 4.5% abw. [A, 53]

Sunset Beach Brewery & Fish House
Brewpub in Huntington Beach, CA (near Sunset Beach and Seal Beach)

SUNSET BEACH BLONDE LAGER — gold, light dry malt and hop aroma and flavor, medium body, dry hop finish and aftertaste, overall a very tasty and refreshing brew, very drinkable. In early March 1995 being made by So. California B.C. for Sunset Beach. [A, 73]

Notes

SCREAMING LOBSTER —
reddish amber, rich malt aroma,
dry malt and hop flavor, medium
body, dry malt and hop finish and
aftertaste; shows a European-
Bohemian character that would
appear to come from Saaz hops. In
early March 1995 being made by
So. California B.C. for Sunset
Beach. [A, 67]

PACIFIC PILSNER — gold, faint
dry malt aroma and flavor, medium
body, very dry malt and hop finish
and aftertaste; has little character.
In early March 1995 being made
by So. California B.C. for Sunset
Beach. [B, 50]

LIGHTHOUSE AMBER — amber,
light fairly smooth aroma and taste,
medium body, dry malt finish and
aftertaste, medium length. [A, 49]

CAPTAIN'S PALE ALE — amber,
bright dry malty aroma and flavor,
well balanced; malty aftertaste is
slightly sweet, fairly long. [A, 67]

SHARKBITE RED — red-amber,
malt aroma; malty flavor has a
touch of sweetness but stays
reasonably dry and has a good hop
balance; dry malt finish and aftertaste, medium body; complex
aftertaste has a good hop bite; a
good tasting brew. In early March
1995 being made by So. California B.C. for Sunset Beach. [A, 79]

WHALE STOUT — deep dark
brown; medium dry malty nose is
a bit roasted; big smooth roasted
malt flavor is more dry than
sweet; medium dry, dry malt finish and aftertaste, good length. In
early March 1995 being made by

Anderson Valley B.C. for Sunset
Beach. [S, 58]

DOCKMAN'S PORTER — deep
brown; aroma shows much roasted
quality and some chocolate malt;
big roasted and chocolate malt
flavor, good body, long pleasant
roasted malt aftertaste. [P, 67]

SUNSET HEFE-WEIZEN —
cloudy gold; spicy aroma and taste
shows a very nice clove and banana
nature; light to medium body, spicy
banana finish and aftertaste, pleasant and refreshing. [W, 67]

DECKHAND WHEAT — gold,
dry malt and wheat nose; light
wheat and barley malt flavor is
slightly off-dry; long dry malt finish; made with approximately
30% wheat malt. In early March
1995 being made by So. California B.C. for Sunset Beach. [W, 62]

Sweet Waters of Acadia Brewing Co.
Microbrewery in Bar Harbor, ME

SWEETWATER STOUT — dark
brown, complex malt aroma (pale,
chocolate, black patent 8:1:1);
light malt flavor shows almost
none of the chocolate malt; light
body, finishes dry, short light dry
malt aftertaste. [S, 48]

PRECIPICE PALE ALE — pale
gold, light malt and hop aroma;
light refreshing malt flavor shows
little of the 10% wheat but the
Golding and Cascade hops are a
pleasant background; medium

body, dry malt and hop finish and
aftertaste. [A, 49]

RUSTICATOR — light amber-
brown, complex malt aroma
(mostly pale, some crystal, and a
touch of black patent and chocolate malts), light body; good
Golding and American Hallertau
hop character shows in the finish
and aftertaste; stays fairly dry
throughout; fair duration. [BK, 53]

T. Roy Brewing Co.
Microbrewery in San Jose, CA

HOPPY FACE AMBER ALE —
deep gold, big hop aroma and flavor, good body, dry hop finish and
aftertaste; shows some alcohol,
good length; made with two-row
malted barley and Northwest
hops; specific gravity 1.062, 5.8%
abw. Tasted at GABF 1994.
Tasted in early 1995 packaged in a
12-oz. bottle, the brew was more
amber, had a complex fruity-litchi
nose, complex hoppy flavor, even
bitter, long very complx hop aftertaste, a very good brew if you like
hops. [A, 84]

Tabernash Brewing Co.
Microbrewery in Denver, CO

DENARGO LAGER — copper-
amber, dry light malt aroma and
flavor, low hop content, good
body, mild dry malt aftertaste,
medium length; gravity 12.5 P, 5%
abw. [B, 48]

GOLDEN SPIKE LAGER — gold, dry malt aroma, very dry malt flavor, medium body, dry malt finish and aftertaste; gravity 12.7 P, 5.5% abw. [B, 68]

TABERNASH WEISS — cloudy gold, classical spicy clove nose, big tasty spicy hefe-weizen style, refreshing smooth and creamy, long spicy-fruity malt aftertaste, very good of the style, unfiltered; gravity 12.5 P, 5.5% abw. [W, 61]

TABERNASH O'FEST — brilliant deep copper-amber, light hop and toasted malt aroma; good dry hop flavor has a malty sweetness in back; good body, very long dry hop aftertaste; gravity 13.5 P, 5.9% abw is noticeable but not obtrusive. [B, 67]

TABERNASH HEFE-WEIZEN — hazy gold, mild yeasty malt nose, big banana and light clove palate, medium body, creamy mouthfeel, refreshing; lightly dry finish, fades fast, though nicely done. [W, 68]

Texas Brewing Co.
Brewery in Dallas, TX, formerly named the Dallas Brewing Co.

WEST END LAGER — brilliant pale gold; pleasant fruity malt nose reminds me of litchi nuts; fruity malt and light sour hop flavor, medium body, hop finish, very short dry malt and hop aftertaste; made from American two-row and Belgian Viennese-style malt with American Hallertau hops; gravity 11 P, 3.6% abw. [B, 46]

OUTBACK LAGER — bright pale gold; malt aroma has a fruity nature like litchi nuts and citrus; dry malt and hop flavor, medium body, long dry malt and hop aftertaste; made from American two-row malt and Cascade hops from Washington and Ringwood hops from Australia; specific gravity 1.042, 3.7% abw. [B, 23]

DALLAS GOLD — gold; strong malt nose has a mandarin orange-litchi nut style; good body, big hop and malt flavor, dry hop aftertaste; made with American two-row and Belgian Viennese- and Munich-style malts with domestic Hallertau, Tettnanger, and Cascade hops; specific gravity 1.042, 3.7% abw. Now called Texas Gold. [B, 41]

COWBOY PREMIUM — amber; big fruity malt nose has a faintly vegetal background; bright malt flavor, medium body, dry malt aftertaste; Märzen-style beer made from American two-row and Belgian Munchener-style malts with Cascade hops; gravity 10.4 P, 3.5% abw. [B, 43]

TEXAS BLUEBONNET — pale gold, faintly vegetal malt aroma and taste, dry malt finish and aftertaste; made from American two-row malt and Tettnanger hops; specific gravity 1.038, 3.3% abw. [B, 41]

TEXAS BLUEBONNET LIGHT BEER — hazy gold; big malty nose has some faint hops in back; malty flavor, medium body, dry malt finish and aftertaste, short. [LO, 49]

Notes

TIED HOUSE
CAFE & BREWERY
MOUNTAIN VIEW
SAN JOSE
ALAMEDA

TEXAS GOLD SPECIAL
PILSENER — hazy amber-gold,
very malty nose and taste, medium
body; some hops appear in the finish and stay for the aftertaste, but
the beer is malty throughout and
never hoppy; made with American
two-row and Belgian Viennese and
Munich-style malts with domestic
Hallertau, Tettnanger, and Cascade
hops; specific gravity 1.042, 3.7%
abw. Previously named Dallas
Gold. [B, 47]

TEXAS COWBOY SPECIAL
AMBER — golden amber, big
toasted malt aroma with a syrupy
character, scorched malt flavor,
light body, long burnt aftertaste;
made with plenty of caramel malt,
specific gravity 1.042, 3.6% abw,
18.5 IBU. [B, 27]

*Note: The following brews were
labels of the Reinheitsgebot B.C.
of Plano, TX. Mary and Donald
Thompson owned and operated
Reinheitsgebot until it closed a
few years back. Mary is now
Brewery Manager of Texas B.C.
and Donald is the new
brewmaster. They plan to begin*

*production of the Collin County
brands, so I am including two of
them here.*

COLLIN COUNTY BLACK
GOLD BEER — deep amber,
perfumy and tangy malt aroma, a
touch of citrus in back, light body;
mild malt flavor has a slightly
burnt backtaste; malt finish;
medium long malt aftertaste is a
touch sour. [B, 36]

COLLIN COUNTY EMERALD
BEER — brilliant green, nice hop
aroma, bright hop flavor, clean
and refreshing, medium body,
long dry hop aftertaste. [B, 47]

Kemper Brewing Co.
*Brewery in Poulsbro, WA.
Purchased by Hart Brew-
ing in late 1995.*

THOMAS KEMPER ROLLING
BAY BOCK — hazy gold, malt
aroma, finely carbonated; malt and
hop flavor seems to have a citrus
background; long and strong dry
hop finish and aftertaste. [BK, 17]

THOMAS KEMPER PILSENER
BEER — hazy yellow-gold; hop
aroma has citrus tones; hop flavor
has a lemony background but
there is plenty of malt; good body,
medium dry hop aftertaste. [B, 38]

THOMAS KEMPER WINTER
BRÄU — deep amber, faint malt
nose, light pleasant slightly off-
dry toasted malt flavor, light
toasted malt finish and aftertaste,
smooth but very light. [B, 51]

TK WINTERBRÄU 1995 — deep
amber, big head, malty homebrew-
like nose, sour malty flavor,
medium body, sweet and sour
malty finish and aftertaste; long
but not good, must be spoiled
sample. [B, NR]

THOMAS KEMPER INTEGRALÉ
AMBER LAGER — reddish
amber, fruity caramel malt and
spicy hop aroma, big fruity malt
flavor up front, dry finish;
medium long dry hop aftertaste
shows the Saaz hops; medium to
good body; specific gravity 1.050,
4% abw. [B, 60]

THOMAS KEMPER WEIZEN
BERRY — gold; raspberry shows
in the aroma and front palate, this
fades in mid-palate to better show
the wheat malt which continues
into the finish and aftertaste; specific gravity 1.050, 4% Abw.
Tasted on draft. [W, 46]

THOMAS KEMPER WHITE —
pale gold, light fruity spicy aroma;
bright spicy flavor has a faintly
sweet fruity-citrus background;
medium to light body, light dry
hop finish and aftertaste, fair
length; made with curaçao orange
peel, coriander seed and other
spices added to pale malt; malted
and in malted wheat, and rolled
oats; hopped with Liberty hops;
OG 1048, FG 1.016, 4.4% abv,
14 IBU. [B, 73]

THOMAS KEMPER
HONEYWEIZEN — hazy gold,
distinct clover honey aroma and
flavor, a little sweet but also
very pleasant and refreshing,
light to medium body, medium

long off-dry honeyed aftertaste, nice summer refreshment. Tasted on draft. [W, 72]

THOMAS KEMPER WEIZENBERRY — hazy gold; berry fruit aroma and flavor shows a great deal of raspberries; medium to light body; tartness appears in the finish and aftertaste; good length, and fairly refreshing. Tasted in bottle. [W, 46]

THOMAS KEMPER AMBER LAGER — amber, fruity malt aroma and flavor, medium body; some hops show up in the finish and aftertaste, but mostly it is a malty brew. Tasted on draft. [B, 60]

THOMAS KEMPER DARK LAGER — amber, malty aroma and flavor, medium body, pleasant and satisfying, long malty aftertaste. Tasted in bottle. [B, 66]

Tied House Cafe & Brewery / Redwood Coast Brewing

Brewpubs in San Jose, Alameda (Tied House Pub & Pool), and Mountain View, CA. Microbrewery in Mountain View, CA (Redwood coast).

TIED HOUSE AMBER — deep tawny-gold, bright hop and malt nose and taste, very long dry complex aftertaste much like the flavor, a good lusty brew. [B, 67]

ALPINE PEARL PALE — gold, light malt nose and taste, medium body, light dry malt finish and after-taste; in 1993 gravity 13 P, 4.2% abw. From Alameda. [A, 83]

ALPINE PEARL ALE — brilliant amber-gold, big hoppy aroma and flavor, very tasty, medium to good body; bright dry hop finish and aftertaste is derived from Perle hops; a very pleasant hoppy blonde ale; specific gravity 1.052, 4.2% abw. This version was from Mountain View, tasted in 1994. [A, 83]

CASCADE AMBER — deep amber, faint Cascade hop aroma, good hop flavor, dry hop finish, not much aftertaste; gravity 12 P (1.048), 3.6% abw, 20 IBU. From Alameda. [A, 47]

WHEAT BOCK — brown, hoppy nose and taste, dry sharp hop finish, long dry hop aftertaste; gravity 16 P, 5% abw. From Alameda. [W, 60]

PASSION PALE — gold, fruity malt aroma, flavor like the nose, good body, off-dry malt finish and aftertaste; has length, blonde ale; made with addition of passion fruit; gravity 12 P (1.048), 4.0% abw. From Alameda. [A, 50]

IRONWOOD DARK — brown, lightly toasted malt nose, dry roasted malty flavor, light to medium body, dry roasted malt finish and aftertaste; made with crystal malt and English yeast; specific gravity 1.048, 3.5% abw. [A, 67]

PEACHY PALE — gold, faintly peachy aroma, smooth fruity flavor, medium body, slightly off-dry peachy-malt aftertaste; made with peaches; specific gravity 1.052, 4.2% abw. [A, 47]

Notes

YULE-TIED — dark amber; spicy aroma seems to be cinnamon and nutmeg, but could be ginger; the flavor is certainly ginger; light body, long dry spicy aftertaste; made by blending the Ironwood Dark with spices; specific gravity 1.048, 3.4% abw. [A, 52]

Traffic Jam & Snug Restaurant
Brewpub restaurant in Detroit, MI

TJ'S COAL PORTER — dark brown, roasted malt aroma and flavor, big nose and big taste, good body, excellent mouthfeel, finishes dry roasted malt, fairly long dry toasty aftertaste. [P, 73]

WEST CANFIELD WHEAT BEER — hazy gold, dry light malty nose and very light malty taste, light body, dry finish, short dry malt aftertaste; an American-style hefe-weizen but there is little hefe-weizen character. [W, 49]

Trinity Brewhouse
Brewpub in Providence, RI

TRINITY PALE ALE — bright gold, tight head, big bright hoppy aroma, strong assertive hop taste, medium to good body, long very highly hopped aftertaste; an assertively hopped pale ale. [A, 71]

TRINITY EXPORT DOPPELBOCK — amber, light hop and malt nose; dry hop flavor has plenty of supporting malt; medium to good body, good com-plexity, long dry hop aftertaste; drier than the pale ale but the strong hops are better balanced by the malt; very good with food. [B, 72]

TRINITY SCOTCH ALE — deep dark amber, malt aroma with good hop backing, creamy off-dry malt and hop flavor, full body, finishes sweeter than the main flavor, long roasted malt aftertaste; strong, sweet, and alcoholic; 8% abv. [A, 68]

TRINITY NUT BROWN ALE — brown-amber, roasted malt aroma and flavor, fairly rich and a bit off-dry, light to medium body, finishes a bit drier, long medium dry roasted malt aftertaste, not long. [A, 56]

TRINITY CHOCOLATE STOUT — deep brown, brown head, chocolate malt and roasted barley aroma; lightly flavored chocolatey-coffee taste is a bit ephemeral; medium body, soft and smooth textured; short aftertaste is a continuation of the palate. [S, 53]

Triple Rock Brewery & Alehouse
Brewpub in Berkeley, CA

SWHEATHEART HEFE-WEIZEN — cloudy gold, lovely big malt nose, bright malt flavor, long and dry; as nice a weizen as I've found in the U.S.A. [W, 74]

HOP OF THE ROCK IPA — deep gold, big hop aroma, big bright hop flavor, very long dry hop aftertaste, a very pleasant enjoyable beer; gravity 12.5 P, 4.5% abw. [A, 78]

RED ROCK STRONG ALE — amber, hop aroma, dull hop flavor, dull and short dry hop aftertaste; 4.3% abw. [A, 38]

TREE FROG STRONG ALT — dark amber, light hop nose, malt and dry hop palate, good body, very long dry hop aftertaste; gravity 14.5 P, 4.8% abw. [A, 47]

PINNACLE PALE — gold, hop and malt aroma, bright hop flavor, very tasty and interesting, good body, dry hop finish and aftertaste, quite long; gravity 11.5 P, 3.6% abw. [A, 74]

STONEHENGE STOUT — brown, smoky dry aroma, fairly big dry roasted malt flavor, no caramel or chocolate malt, big body, long dry malt aftertaste; 6.5% abv. [S, 73]

Triumph Brewing Co.
Brewpub in Princeton, NJ

TRIUMPH INDIA PALE ALE — amber-gold; very complex aroma shows a lot of both hops and malt; bright complex hoppy flavor has plenty of good malt support; medium body, a very long well-hopped dry aftertaste, a very well-made ale. [A, 83]

TRIUMPH PALE ALE — deep gold, aroma shows both hops and malt, an English-style brew; big hop flavor is not quite so big or as complex as the IPA; dry hop finish and aftertaste, very long. [A, 63]

TRIUMPH AMBER ALE — amber, hop nose, dry well-hopped flavor, good malt support; dry hop finish and aftertaste continues to show the malt. [A, 52]

TRIUMPH IRISH STOUT — dark brown, chocolate malt aroma, fairly dry roasted barley and chocolate malt flavor, medium body; long dry and bitter aftertaste continues the flavor; a good classical dry Irish stout. [S, 72]

TRIUMPH HONEY WHEAT — deep gold, faint malt nose, light medium dry malty flavor; dry faintly hopped finish and aftertaste; light body; shows more of the sense of honey than a presence; made with Tettnanger hops. [W, 56]

TRIUMPH PUMPKIN ALE — amber, light pumpkin pie spice aroma, off-dry and spicy flavor, medium to light body, very short on the palate. [A, 46]

TRIUMPH MÄRZEN — deep amber-gold, malty aroma, off-dry malty flavor, big body, off-dry malty finish and aftertaste, a well-made malty Märzen-style beer. [B, 62]

TRIUMPH HOP HARVEST — deep gold, creamy texture, well-hopped aroma and flavor, good balance, medium to good body, dry hop finish, long dry hop aftertaste; well hopped but not assertive or rough in its bitterness. [A, 71]

Truckee Brewing Co.
Microbrewery in Truckee, CA

BOCA BOCK LAGER — dark amber; faint malty nose is fruity and herbal; interesting and unusual taste is cherries, spice, herbs, and phenolic; finishes with a distinct black cherry character, fairly long. [BK, 53]

Tugboat Brewing Co.
Brewpub in Portland, OR

TUGBOAT IPA — amber-gold, hop nose, bitter hop flavor, bitter hop finish, long dry and bitter hop aftertaste; made with pale, dark Carastan, crystal, Carapils, and Munich malts; hopped with Nugget, Willamette, Northern Brewer hops; dry hopped with Cascades; OG 1.062, FG 1.011, 6.2% abv, 55 IBU. [A, 59]

Tulsa Brewing Co.
Brewpub in Tulsa, OK

SHAMROCK LAGER — amber, light hop aroma, well-hopped dry flavor, light body, very dry finish, long dry hop aftertaste. [B, 47]

OSAGE GOLDEN WHEAT ALE — very pale gold, faint malty aroma, very light body, very light flavor, very dry finish, brief dry malt aftertaste; made with 50% wheat and 50% barley malt and Northern Brewer and Mt. Hood hops. [W, 38]

HONEY BLONDE LIGHT PALE ALE — pale gold, light but complex malt and hop aroma, flavor like the nose, ends dry with a long dry malt aftertaste; made with honey, pale and Carapils malts; hopped at three different times with Saaz hops. [A, 67]

Notes

ROUTE 66 AMBER ALE —
fairly deep amber, dry hop and
malt flavor, good body, medium
dry malt and hop finish, medium
long dry malt and hop aftertaste,
very drinkable; made from five
different malts and three hop
varieties. [A, 54]

TORNADO ALLEY PORTER —
dark brown; chocolate malt nose
and taste has some hops in back,
but the chocolate malt outweighs
the hops all the way through even
though the hops rally at the finish;
dry malt aftertaste, some coffee-
like flavors surface every so often;
made with six malts. [P, 60]

*Other brews include Red Ranger
Ale, Santa Fe Green Chili Ale,
Uncle Red's Raspberry Ale. Mistle-
toe Oatmeal Stout, Pecan Nut
Brown Ale, Golden Driller Ale,
Spiced Pumpkin Ale, and an IPA.*

20 Tank Brewery
Brewpub in San Francisco

MARTIN'S MELLOW-GLOW
PALE ALE — pale gold, good
hop nose, bright hop flavor,
creamy, good body, long dry hop
aftertaste. [A, 56]

MOODY'S HI-TOP ALE — deep
gold, sweet malt nose, big off-dry
malt flavor, creamy, good body,
medium length dry hop aftertaste.
[A, 54]

DOUBLE BOCK
HEFEWEIZEN — light hazy
amber; off-dry malt aroma at first,
dries as it goes; flavor a lot like the
nose (first off-dry malt, dries toward

finish), good long dry malt aftertaste, 40% wheat not really noticeable, decent American-style
hefe-weizen (no clove spice).
[WBK, 62]

INDICATOR DOPPELBOCK —
deep amber, big malt nose, hefty
body, alcohol noticeable (6.5%),
big off-dry malt and hop flavor,
dry malt aftertaste, a good
doublebock. [BK, 69]

KINNIKINICK IMPERIAL
STOUT — opaque brown, fresh
malt nose, big strong and complex
malt flavor, big body; long aftertaste
is reasonably dry malt; alcohol is
present throughout (8%), good brew
for the strong of spirit. [S, 74]

Umpqua Brewing Co.
Brewpub in Roseburg, OR

NO DOUBT STOUT — dark
brown, roasted barley and chocolate
malt nose, flavor like the aroma but
very light, medium body, dry
roasted malt aftertaste, medium
length; cask-conditioned, single-
stage infusion mashed,
unfiltered; made with Chinook
hops; gravity 15 P, 5% abw. [S, 47]

DOWNTOWN BROWN —
brown, lactic malt aroma and
flavor, spoiled sample. Cask-
conditioned, single-stage infusion
mashed, hopped with Cascades,
unfiltered; gravity 12.5 P, 4.5%
abw. [A, 14]

SUMMER WHEAT — gold, veg-
etal malt nose, lightly lactic malt
flavor, light body; dry malt aftertaste still has the acid background,

not unexpected in a wheat beer,
but this comes off as being somewhere between a German style
and an American style and isn't
quite either. [W, 23]

ROSEGARDEN WHITE ALE —
amber, faint fruity nose, light spicy-
fruity palate, light body, dry hop
finish and aftertaste, good length;
made using coriander, orange peel,
Bulgar wheat, and flaked oats with
six-row pale malt hopped with
Goldings; 4.5% abv. [A, 40]

Union Station Brewery
*Brewpub in
Providence, RI*

UNION STATION GOLDEN
ALE — gold, lovely hop aroma,
bright dry hop flavor, good body;
finishes well leading into a very
dry long hop aftertaste; well made
and very well balanced; OG 1042.
Subsequently named Golden
Spike. [A, 62]

UNION STATION AMBER
ALE — amber, nose of malt and
hops, well-malted flavor with
good hop balance, good body, finishes fairly dry, dry hop aftertaste;
OG 1048. [A, 62]

UNION STATION PORTER —
dark brown, pleasant light malt
nose, fine dry malt and hop flavor,
fairly big, bright and balanced;
long dry malt aftertaste has hops
in back; OG 1060. Subsequently
named Blackstone Porter. [P, 67]

UNION STATION IRISH
ALE — medium pale amber,
faint malt nose; palate has hops

up front, but is mainly malt in the middle; hops close in from behind and emerge again at the finish; smooth and well balanced; dry hop aftertaste has considerable length; OG 1042. [A, 74]

UNION STATION SCOTTISH ALE — amber, malt aroma, big malt flavor with plenty of hop support, hefty body, richly flavored, malty finish, long dry malt aftertaste; OG 1042. [A, 71]

PEQUOT TRAIL PALE ALE — amber, hop aroma, bright hop flavor, good body, long hop aftertaste, good tasting and refreshing. [A, 61]

UNION STATION OKTOBERFEST — cloudy amber; big aroma has lots of both hops and malt but is more malty overall; big hoppy flavor, good body, very dry hop finish and aftertaste, a highly hopped unfiltered brew. [A, 60]

UNION STATION RASPBERRY ALE — amber-gold; raspberry aroma and taste seems to have a vanilla component; highly carbonated, medium body, medium dry raspberry finish and aftertaste. [A, 55]

UNION STATION VELVET STOUT — dark brown, roasted barley nose, chocolate malt and roasted barley flavor, soft and smooth, medium body; the chocolate malt component is faint; dry roasted malt finish and aftertaste, medium length. [S, 66]

UNION STATION SPRING WHEAT — amber; spicy nose and taste is cinnamon but you wouldn't recognize it as cinnamon unless told that it was; otherwise it is very malty and a bit sweet; medium body; dry spicy hop finish and aftertaste still shows quite a lot of the malt; made with cinnamon and maple syrup. [W, 54]

The Vermont Pub & Brewery
Brewpub in Burlington, VT

BLACK BEAR LAGER — amber, malt nose, rich malt flavor, long dry malt aftertaste, pleasant and drinkable; gravity 11 P, 3.7% abw. [B, 47]

AULD BARLEY BREE WEE HEAVY — very dark brown, fairly strong malt nose, big strong and rich malt flavor, noticeable alcohol, long rich medium dry malt aftertaste; gravity 13.5 P, 7.7% abw. I have seen this noted as Avid Barley Bree Wee Heavy as well and one may be a misprint, or whatever. It's good under either moniker. [BW, 78]

GLEN WALTER WEE HEAVY — amber, big malt nose, big rich caramel malt and molasses flavor, big body, long off-dry malt aftertaste; gravity 13.2 P, 6.4% abw. [BW, 72]

AVID TARTAN WEE HEAVY — deep amber, rich malt nose, very rich malt flavor, huge body, extremely long malty aftertaste; specific gravity 1.093, 6.2% abw. [BW, 78]

FARMALL WHEAT BEER — gold, clean malt aroma with a wheaty background, bright spicy flavor, finish, and aftertaste, very nice zesty European-style wheat beer. A hefe-weizen brewed from 50% red wheat and sour mashed to give it acidity; gravity 13.5 P, 3.6% abw. [W, 67]

ZATEC RED — gold, malt aroma, lactic backing to a malt palate, dry spicy finish and aftertaste; brewed with Saaz hops from Zatec, Czechoslovakia; gravity 12 P, 3.7% abw. [B, 38]

O'FEST — amber, malt aroma, dry malt flavor, no aftertaste; made with roasted malts; gravity 14 P, 4.2% abw. [B, 47]

VERMONT SMOKED PORTER — deep brown, marvelous lightly smoked dry malt aroma, light smoky dry malt flavor, good body; smoked malt aftertaste is very long, very likable, excellent of type. One of six malts are roasted over apple, maple, and hickory wood fire; gravity 11 P, 3.3% abw. [P, 65]

GRAND SLAM BASEBALL BEER — gold, winey fruity malt and light hop nose; fruity hop flavor, reminds one of a Riesling grape wine; off-dry malt aftertaste. Called Pilsener Grand Slam at the GABF in 1992 (vice the above name in 1993), this is a Canadian-style ale with 100% malt and Cascade bittering; gravity 11.25 P, 3.6% abw, 32 IBU. [B, 43]

VERMONT MAPLE ALE — gold, sweet maple aroma, smooth

maple flavor, off-dry maple finish, dry malt and maple aftertaste; 50% maple definitely shows and even dominates. [A, 47]

WILD THING — reddish-orange color, faintly sour cherry nose, light cherry flavor, light body, very faint aftertaste, 15% wheat and cherries. [W, 49]

BETELGUISE WEISS — hazy gold, good spicy hefe-weizen aroma; flavor is excellent spicy hefe-weizen up front; good balance, not overwhelming, very drinkable and likable, medium to light body, faintly dry malt aftertaste; Bavarian-style hefe-weizen; specific gravity 1.045, 3.6% abw. Called Beetlejuice at the GABF. [W, 47]

BOMBAY GRAB — deep gold, bright hoppy aroma and flavor, a very good classical IPA, medium to big body; long delicious aftertaste shows plenty of the hops and malt; a winner; specific gravity 1.051, 4% abw. [A, 72]

Village Brewery
Brewpub in Houston, TX

HOUSTON-WHEAT — pale gold, faint malt aroma, creamy mouthfeel, refreshing grainy quality to the flavor, light body, pleasant long and dry aftertaste. [W, 61]

VILLAGE PALE ALE — amber-gold, English-style hop aroma, big dry English hop flavor, some fruity esters in back, medium body, long dry hop aftertaste. [A, 59]

HAMPTON BROWN ALE — amber-brown, rich malty off-dry

nose and flavor; more dry but fades a bit at the finish; soft and smooth, medium long dry malt aftertaste. [A, 59]

ARMADILLO STOUT — deep brown, roasted malt nose, soft pleasant roasted malt flavor, smooth, medium body, very drinkable, no harsh edges, tastes "nourishing," no meanness, long roasted malt aftertaste. [S, 88]

RASPBERRY IMPERIAL STOUT — deep brown, brown head, hint of raspberry in the nose, big rich fresh raspberry and roasted malt flavor like a raspberry and chocolate dessert beer, very interesting and very well made, long raspberry and roasted malt aftertaste, great at the end of a meal. [S, 90]

AMBER OWL ALE — amber, malt aroma, off-dry malt flavor, some caramel tones, good body, smooth and rich caramel finish and aftertaste, long and rich, but a little too sweet; could use some more hopping to enhance balance. [A, 50]

Vino's Brewing Co.
Brewpub & Pizza Parlour in Little Rock, AR

SEVENTH STREET PALE ALE — cloudy brownish-gold, pleasant hop nose, big hop flavor, malt and lactic acid in back; infected but not to the point where it is undrinkable; more spicy than acidic, long spicy hop aftertaste. [A, 27]

BIG HOUSE BROWN ALE — amber, faint malt nose, pleasant hop

and malt flavor; spicy background which comes from a faint acid infection; good body, dry hop finish and long dry hop aftertaste. [A, 29]

LAZY BOY STOUT — deep brown, faint malt nose; spicy acidic flavor overrides some chocolate malt; medium body; dry malt finish is marred by the lactic acid; short dry acidic malt aftertaste. [S, 24]

Wachusett Brewing Co.
Microbrewery in Westminster, MA

WACHUSETT IPA — amber; nose briefly is malt vinegar but that disappeared shortly after being poured to become light and malty; highly hopped bitter palate, a bit harsh with metallic notes in the finish, long and assertively hopped. [A, 50]

WACHUSETT COUNTRY ALE — brilliant deep golden amber, dank sweat sock nose, malty flavor; has a burnt harsh component in the finish; dry malt aftertaste. [A, 43]

The Walnut Brewery
Brewpub in Boulder, CO affiliated with the Boulder B.C.

INDIAN PEAKS PALE ALE — pale gold, faint malt and hop nose; light malt flavor is slightly soapy and very little hops at all; light body; finishes dry and has a brief aftertaste; made with Cascade hops; gravity 11.5 P, 3.4% abw. [A, 42]

OLD ELK BROWN ALE — amber, malt aroma, flavor like a homebrew; not well knit, malt and hops are coming at you and not blending; dry finish and short dry aftertaste; made with Nugget and Willamette hops; 4.2% abw. [A, 38]

BIG HORN BITTER — amber, no nose; flavor is mostly hops with a caramel background; dry hop aftertaste; hopped with Chinook and Willamette hops; gravity is 13.P, 3.5% abw. [A, 48]

BUFFALO GOLD PREMIUM ALE — gold, no nose, faint butterscotch in behind light malt and hops on the palate, just some faint dry malt for an aftertaste; made with pale and crystal malts with Willamette and Cascade hops; gravity 12.5 P, 3.45% abw. [B, 30]

THE JAMES IRISH RED ALE — reddish-amber, soapy malt nose and taste, medium body, just a very faint malt aftertaste; gravity 13.5 P, 4.2% abw. [A, 37]

DEVIL'S THUMB STOUT — deep brown, light dry chocolate malt and coffee nose and taste; finished quite well and the aftertaste was good and like the flavor, dry but not overly so; best beer tasted at The Walnut; made with Nugget and B.C. Kent hops; gravity 16.5 P, 5.0% abw. [S, 65]

BLUE NOTE AMBER ALE — amber, light hop nose and taste, dry hop finish and aftertaste; gravity 14 P, 4.5% abw. [A, 50]

Notes

SWISS TRAIL WHEAT — hazy gold, malt and wheat nose; bright refreshing flavor, but not lactic or spicy in any way; light dry malt aftertaste. [W, 56]

Water Street Brewery
Brewpub in Milwaukee, WI

OLD WORLD OKTOBERFEST — deep gold, big malt and hop aroma and flavor, very alcoholic, big bodied, long dry malt and hop aftertaste, a hearty brew; specific gravity 1.056, 4.7% abw. [B, 67]

WATER STREET OKTOBERFEST — amber, dry malty aroma and flavor, medium body, dry malt finish and aftertaste brewed with Carapils, black, pale, and caramel malts; specific gravity 1.055, 4.95% abw. [B, 58]

WATER STREET WEISS — deep gold, light spicy nose, bright zesty lightly spiced flavor, light to medium body, long spicy malt aftertaste; gravity 6.75 P, 3.41% abw. [W, 48]

BAVARIAN WEISS — deep gold, cloudy like a hefe-weizen, clove nose, bright zesty well-spiced flavor, good body, long spicy malt aftertaste, well made in a Germanic style; made from 55% wheat malt; specific gravity 1.056, 5.9% abw. [W, 73]

CALLAN'S ENGLISH RED ALE — medium to deep amber, malt aroma, smooth hop flavor, good body, dry hop aftertaste;

made with Galena hops; specific gravity 1.048, 3.8% abw. [A, 67]

WATER STREET PALE ALE — amber, hop aroma, zesty hop flavor, good malt backing, complex, big body, dry malt finish and aftertaste, a very good ale; made with caramel malt and dry hopped for ten days; specific gravity 1.056, 4.3% abw. [A, 75]

Waterloo Brewing Co.
Brewpub in Austin, TX

CLARA'S CLARA — gold, dry malty aroma and flavor, light body, crisp dry hop finish and aftertaste; made with Saaz hops and two-row malt giving it a European character; specific gravity 1.047, 3.5% abw. [B, 67]

GUYTOWN IPA — deep gold, big dry hop aroma and taste, a very good taste, good body, very dry hop finish and aftertaste; made heavily hopped with East Kent-Goldings and Fuggles hops; specific gravity 1.059, 5% abw. [A, 82]

O. HENRY'S PORTER — brown, dry malt aroma and flavor, medium body; dry malty finish and aftertaste has good length; made with two-row, caramel, and chocolate malts; specific gravity 1.054, 4.75% abw. [P, 59]

ONE TON STOUT — dark brown, almost opaque; big malty nose seems dry, but the flavor is concentrated sweet malt and alcoholic (7.5% abw); huge body, long off-

dry malt and alcohol aftertaste; brewed with one ton of grain per 14 barrels; specific gravity 1.085. [S, 59]

SAMUEL HOUSTON'S AUSTIN LAGER — amber, malty aroma announces a Vienna-style amber lager; flavor is very dry and shows both the malt and Hallertau hops; medium body, long dry aftertaste; made with two-row and Munich malts; specific gravity 1.050, 3.9% abw. [B, 62]

WATERLOO WHEAT — hazy gold; classical hefe-weizen aroma shows lots of clove spice; fruity-spicy flavor, good body, long refreshing fruity-spicy-wheaty aftertaste; made with 55% wheat blended with two-row malt and top-fermented; specific gravity 1.049, 4% abw. [W, 67]

ED'S BEST BITTER — amber-gold, bright hop aroma and flavor, light body, dry hop finish and aftertaste; made with two-row and crystal malts hopped with Fuggles hops; specific gravity 1.042, 3.25% abw. [A, 69]

WATERLOO HEFE-WEIZEN — hazy gold, very pleasant American-style malty-wheaty nose, lightly spiced malt flavor, light body, long lightly spiced aftertaste. [W, 53]

BEN'S BROWN ALE — light brown color, malt aroma, light dry malt flavor, light body, dry malt finish and aftertaste. [A, 53]

Weeping Radish Restaurant & Brewery
Brewpub and restaurant in Manteo, NC

WEEPING RADISH HELLES BEER — hazy gold, fresh malt aroma, creamy, dry malt flavor with the hops far in back, light body, off-dry malt flavor, slides down easily; light dry malt aftertaste with some hops showing lightly; an easygoing brew; hopped with Hallertau and Saaz hops; specific gravity 1.048, 4.4% abw, 21 IBU. Also called Corolla Gold. [B, 51]

WEEPING RADISH FEST BEER — hazy amber, fruity-melony malt nose and taste, light body; dry hop flavor has malt close in behind; medium body; a little malty sweetness in the finish carries into the aftertaste; medium long, very drinkable; specific gravity 1.052, 4.6% abw, 23 IBU. [B, 53]

WEEPING RADISH BLACK LAGER — deep amber-brown, faintly sour malt aroma, flavor like the nose but with more hops, good body, dry hop aftertaste; specific gravity 1.054, 4.7% abw, 23 IBU. Also called Black Radish. [B, 41]

WEEPING RADISH MAI BOCK — amber, pleasant slightly off-dry malt aroma; complex malt flavor is a bit on the sweet side; finish is even more sweet than the earlier palate; sweet malt extends into the long aftertaste; questionable balance. [BK, 50]

WEEPING RADISH OKTOBERFEST — amber, big tight head, malty aroma and flavor; sweetness there throughout but it stays in back emerging its best at the finish and aftertaste which is decidedly off-dry malt and fairly long. [B, 50]

Weidmans Brew Pub
Brewpub in Ft. Smith, AR

WEIDMANS STOUT — dark brown, malt aroma, light smooth pleasant roasted malt palate, medium body, dry roasted malt finish, smooth malty and light hop aftertaste; specific gravity 1.018, 4.2% abw. [S, 61]

WEIDMANS SMOKED PORTER — brown, lightly smoked malt nose, smooth lightly smoked malt flavor, on the light side but very pleasant and easy to drink, dry smoky malt finish and aftertaste. [P, 61]

WEIDMANS PALE ALE — gold; sour bite in nose forecasts the spoiled acidic palate; specific gravity 1.044, 4% abw. Bad sample. [A, 32]

WEIDMANS MÜNCHNER — brownish amber, light hop aroma, dry lightly hopped flavor, finish, and aftertaste, medium body, medium length, a Düsseldorfer-style ale. [B, 47]

WEIDMANS PILSNER — gold, malty aroma and flavor; sample tasted was a bit off; made with all Saaz hops; specific gravity 1.045, 4% abw. [B, 34]

Notes

BIG WHEEL STOUT — brown, toasted malt aroma; dry toasted and caramel malt flavor shows no chocolate malt; medium body, dry malt finish and aftertaste; specific gravity 1.045, 4.2% abw. [S, 67]

FOUR SEASONS — amber-gold; pleasant very fruity aroma shows some honey and orange; equally pleasant malt flavor has a faint touch of honey and orange as well; light body, malty finish and aftertaste; made with addition of honey and orange peel; specific gravity 1.031, 3.5% abw. [B, 67]

FT. SMITH LIGHT — gold; crisp clean light and bright hop aroma and flavor has good malt support; specific gravity 1.047, 4% abw. [B, 67]

HELL ON THE BORDER PORTER — brown, light smoky malt aroma; smooth balanced dry malt flavor has a smoky background; very long dry malt aftertaste keeps some of the smokiness; pleasant and very drinkable. [P, 73]

RASPBERRY ALE — faintly pinkish gold, light raspberry aroma and flavor, both on the dry side, light body, short dry raspberry aftertaste; specific gravity 1.030, 3.5% abw. [A, 54]

ROPE SWING RED ALE — reddish-amber, pleasant malt aroma and flavor, light body, dry and smooth, medium long dry malt aftertaste. [A, 73]

Weinkeller Brewery
Brewpub in Berwyn, IL

ABERDEEN AMBER ALE — amber, dry coffee-like malt nose, dry malt flavor, light body, fairly smooth and balanced, short dry malt aftertaste with hops in back; brewed with two-row, Munich, caramel-60, and chocolate malt; hopped with Northern Brewer and Fuggles; specific gravity 1.055, 4.6% abw. [A, 43]

DÜSSELDORFER DOPPELBOCK — gold, malt aroma, off-dry malt flavor; finishes dry as some hops come in for the ending, but the hops are very light and don't stretch the aftertaste enough; brewed with two-row, Munich, caramel, and chocolate malts, Northern Brewer and Hallertau hops; specific gravity 1.075, 5.4% abw. [BK, 62]

DUBLIN STOUT — brown, roasted barley and chocolate malt nose and flavor; light flavored, but well-balanced; medium body; long good tasting aftertaste reflects the flavor; nicely made; made with two-row, Munich, caramel, chocolate malts, black barley, Northern Brewer, Fuggles, and Cascade hops; specific gravity 1.050, 5.9% abw. This has been called Doublin Stout, but that may be a misprint. [S, 67]

BAVARIAN WEISS — gold, very fruity off-dry malt-wheat nose, only the faintest suggestion of spice, medium body, light off-dry malt aftertaste; a hefe-weizen made with two-row, wheat, and Munich malt with Northern Brewer and Hallertau hops; specific gravity 1.048, 3.9% abw. [W, 53]

OKTOBERFEST — gold, malt aroma, off-dry malt flavor, finish, and aftertaste; made with two-row, Munich, caramel, and chocolate malts, Hallertau and Northern Brewer hops; specific gravity 1.054, 4.5% abw. [B, 50]

WEINKELLER ESB — copper color, light dry hop aroma, good body; good dry hop flavor has some complexity; dry hop finish and aftertaste, good duration; made with two-row, Munich, caramel, and chocolate malts, Northern Brewer, Tettnanger, Cascade, and Fuggles hops; specific gravity 1.050, 4.4% abw. [A, 46]

BERWYN BREW PILSNER — gold, malty aroma, European-style dry malt flavor, medium body, dry finish, medium long dry malt aftertaste; uses two-row, wheat, caramel, and Carapils malts, Hallertau and Saaz hops; specific gravity 1.048, 4% abw. [B, 45]

WESTMONT PALE ALE — gold, malt aroma, dry malt taste, medium to good body; finishes dry malt with some hops showing with the malt in the dry aftertaste; recipe calls for two-row, Carapils, and caramel-20 malts with Northern Brewer, Fuggles, and

Willamette hops; specific gravity 1.050, 4.3% abw. [A, 47]

West Seattle Brewing Co.
Brewpub in Seattle, WA

ADMIRAL ESB — amber, hop aroma, big hop flavor, medium body, long bright dry hop aftertaste; good balance enhanced by a fruity malt background; made with two-row pale and caramel malt hopped with Cluster, Nugget, Cascade, and Tettnanger hops; OG 1055, FG 1.012, 4% abv. [A, 79]

Westside Brewing Co.
Brewpub in New York City

WESTSIDE PALE ALE — deep golden amber, pleasant hop aroma, big hop flavor with plenty of malt support, good body, medium dry hops and malt at the finish; dry aftertaste shows both the malt and hops. [A, 60]

WESTSIDE WHEAT ALE — gold; big off-dry malty nose shows the wheat; light and medium dry wheat and barley malt flavor; medium dry finish shows a fading palate; short aftertaste. [A, 47]

WESTSIDE RED ALE — deep amber, hop aroma; dry hop flavor has some malt showing; good body, dry hop finish, long dry hop aftertaste; has some complexity. [A, 58]

WESTSIDE BITTER — deep golden amber, malty aroma; dry malt flavor has the hops in back;

medium to good body; dry hop finish has the malt in back; short aftertaste. [A, 49]

WESTSIDE BLONDE ALE — gold, pleasant light malt and hop aroma and flavor, light to medium body, dry hop finish and aftertaste, good balance throughout. [A, 56]

WESTSIDE COPPER ALE — amber, hop aroma, malt flavor, medium body, off-dry malt finish and aftertaste. [A, 52]

WESTSIDE NUT BROWN ALE — brown, malty aroma, bright malt flavor, highly carbonated, medium body, dry malt finish and aftertaste. [A, 60]

White Tail Brewing Co.
Microbrewery in York, PA

WHITE TAIL PALE ALE — amber, hop nose; nice hop flavor shows an English malt style and northwest hops; medium body, dry hop finish and aftertaste; made with several different British malts and Cascade, Tettnanger, and Mt. Hood hops. [A, 67]

Notes

Whitefish Brewing Co.
Microbrewery in Whitefish, MT

MONTANA NUT BROWN ALE — dark amber, clean fruity roasted malt aroma, clean malt flavor, straightforward roasty character; hops show well in the finish and aftertaste; well balanced, good length, very drinkable; made with two-row pale and dextrin malts, with some roasted barley; hopped with Willamette hops; OG 1048, FG 1.012, 5% abv. [A, 73]

Widmer Brewing Co.
Brewery in Portland, OR, situated adjacent to a restaurant giving the effect of a brewpub

WIDMER HEFE-WEIZEN — cloudy gold, malt and faint smoked sausage nose; malt flavor is neutral (neither dry nor sweet); long dry malt aftertaste; there are faint off flavors that get in the way of the goodness. [W, 41]

WIDMER OKTOBERFEST — deep amber, no discernible aroma; flavor starts out tangy hops, quickly turns to malt with some chocolate malt noticeable; stays malty thereafter, much like a porter. [B, 76]

WIDMER WILDBERRY WEIZEN — amber, tart berry aroma, light slightly tart berry taste, medium body, long light berry aftertaste. [W, 46]

WIDMER SPEZIAL AMBER — amber, big bright hoppy nose, big well-hopped flavor, very tasty and smooth, plenty of malt for balance; malt shows best in the long aftertaste; well-made brew; made from three malts and hopped with Centennial and Willamette hops; OG 1055, FG 1.015, 3.9% abv, 40 IBU. [A, 66]

Wild Goose Brewery
Brewery in Cambridge, MD

WILD GOOSE AMBER BEER — bright amber, very nice smooth hop aroma, big rich malt and hop flavor, aromatic and bitter hop finish and long aftertaste, a good English-style beer; made with British two-row pale ale, crystal, and chocolate malt; hopped with Cascade, Willamette, and Hallertau hops in the boil; finished with Tettnanger and Hallertau; gravity 12.75 P, 3.8% abv. [B, 67]

THOMAS POINT LIGHT GOLDEN ALE — hazy gold, appetizing malt aroma, good dry malt and hop flavor, light body, refreshing and drinkable, dry malt finish, medium length dry malt and hop aftertaste; brewed with pale malt and boil-turrified wheat; hopped with Hallertau and Willamette hops; finished with Tettnanger; specific gravity 1.037, 4.2% abv. [B, 76]

SAMUEL MIDDLETON'S PALE ALE — hazy tawny-gold, dull malt nose, slightly buttery; flavor is faintly sour malt, but dry and also faintly buttery; long dry malt

aftertaste; made with two-row British pale ale malt with some crystal malt, Cascade and Willamette bittering hops; finished with Hallertau and Tettnanger; gravity 12 P, 3.75% abw. [A, 25]

SNOW GOOSE WINTER ALE 1992 — reddish-orange-amber, beautiful dry toasted malt aroma, big hop and toasted malt flavor, long and complex, big bodied, really well-made brew, dry hop finish and aftertaste, excellent brew. [A, 88]

SNOW GOOSE WINTER ALE 1993 — amber, bright lightly hopped nose; good hop flavor has some fruity esters and is complex; big body, long dry hop aftertaste; could use a tad more malt. [A, 83]

SNOW GOOSE WINTER ALE 1995 — amber, roasted malt and soapy hop aroma; dry roasted malt flavor ends like it starts; light to medium body, long dry roasted malt aftertaste; good but doesn't seem as complex as in previous years. [A, 63]

WILD GOOSE SPRING WHEAT ALE — pale amber, tangy hop-ale nose, zesty and bright, big dry citrus-hop ale flavor, most complex at the beginning, finishes even drier, long dry hop aftertaste; uses 51% wheat and crystal and pale malts with Saaz and Hallertau hops; specific gravity 1.048, 4.4% abw. [W, 52]

FAGER'S ISLAND BLUE DOG ALE — deep gold, pleasant hop aroma, dry hop flavor, finely carbonated, dry hop finish and aftertaste, very drinkable. [A, 43]

PRIDE OF MARYLAND AMBER BEER — amber-gold; malt aroma is faintly of caramel; dull malt flavor, faintly sour at the finish, dull malt aftertaste. [B, 19]

OLIVER'S ALE — amber-gold, malt aroma, very dry malt flavor with a background of English hops, some complexity, good body, dry finish and aftertaste. One taster recognized Ringwood yeast. Made for Oliver's Breweries, Ltd. of Baltimore. [A, 51]

SNOW GOOSE WINTER ALE 1994 — amber; rich malt aroma has a trace of chocolate malt; big rich malty flavor, big body, rich long dry malt aftertaste; a pleasure to drink. [A, 78]

WILD GOOSE PORTER — deep ruby-brown, light malt and good hop aroma, big complex malt and hop flavor, good balance, good body, very dry aftertaste, pleasing and satisfying; made with pale, crystal, chocolate, and black patent malts; specific gravity 1.054, 5.2% abw. [P, 74]

WILD GOOSE GOLDEN ALE — fairly deep golden color, finely carbonated, creamy; big beautiful nose shows citrus, malt, and hops; bright refreshing ale-like palate with the hops in front, good body, smooth and very drinkable, light dry hop finish; malt stays in back and appears best in the aftertaste. [A, 71]

WILD GOOSE INDIA PALE ALE — pale amber; dry English-style nose shows both malt and hops; big dry well-hopped flavor; excellent balance with the hops and malt married as well as you could want; big, full, smooth, and very enjoyable; long dry hop aftertaste, a classic pale ale; a British pale ale style with Cascade, Willamette, Goldings, and Tettnanger hops; specific gravity 1.056, 5.25% abw. [A, 89]

Wild River Brewing Co.
Brewpubs in Cave Junction and Brookings Harbor, OR, originally Pizza Deli & Brewery.

HARBOR LIGHTS KÖLSCH — hazy gold, bright zesty clean fruity mango and Northwest hop aroma; dry hop flavor has an off-dry malt backing; light body, hop finish and long dry hop aftertaste, pleasant and easy to drink, very thirst quenching; hopped with Perle and Mt. Hood hops; gravity 11.25 P (1.045), 4% abw, 23 IBU. This was earlier called Steelhead Harbor Lights. [K, 75]

CAVE BEAR WHEAT WINE — hazy amber, big complex malt aroma, big body, high alcohol, off-dry malt flavor, low carbonation, long malt aftertaste; it really grows on you. [W, 53]

Notes

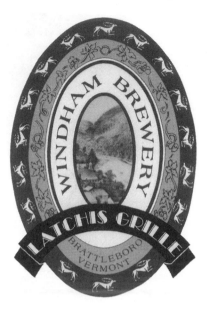

PIZZA DELI HEFE-WEIZEN — hazy pale amber, wheaty malt aroma, light malt flavor; hops appear softly in the finish; very drinkable, medium long dry malt aftertaste, very smooth and very Germanic. In 1994 the name of this brew was changed to Wild River Hefe-Weizen. [W, 59]

ENGLISH BROWN NUT BROWN ALE — hazy amber-brown, fruity malt aroma, smooth very good tasting roasted malt flavor; dry but not pushing it; medium body, strong malty finish and aftertaste, excellent with food, and very drinkable; specific gravity 1.042, 3.3% abw. Also seen named Steelhead Nut Brown Ale. In 1994, this brew was renamed Wild River Nut Brown Ale and specs revised to specific gravity 1.036, 2.5% abw. [A, 48]

PIZZA DELI EXTRA SPECIAL BITTER ALE — deep amber; lovely toasted malt aroma reminds you of fine rich English bacon; malt flavor is not as good as the nose; malt gradually fades and is replaced with hops, malt reappears at the finish and stays for the aftertaste with the hops in back; specific gravity 1.050, 4.2% abw. This was earlier called Steelhead ESB, and in 1994, was renamed Wild River ESB. A respecification at that time adjusted to 4% abw. [A, 60]

WILD RIVER IMPERIAL STOUT — reddish brown, roasted barley and chocolate malt aroma; very smooth roasted malt flavor shows a bit of the chocolate malt with plenty of hops in support; big body; long rich malt and hop aftertaste retains some of the roasty character; made with Fuggles and Chinook hops, using an 1880 Whitbread triple stout formulation; specific gravity 1.075, 5.8% abw, 55 IBU. [S, 83]

WILD RIVER BLACKBERRY PORTER — brown, brown head, complex toasted malt nose, big rich toasted malt flavor, good body, great balance, long malty aftertaste; brewed to a Whitbread formulation from 1750 with 8 lbs. per barrel of blackberries; specific gravity 1.060, 4.3% abw. [P, 78]

CAVE BEAR BARLEY WINE — brown, big rich malty aroma; huge complex palate starts out malty but soon shows heavy hopping and plenty of alcohol; the flavor is delicious, the body is enormous; long rich malt and bright hop af-

tertaste; made with 89% American pale malt, 10% British crystal malt, and 1% black patent malt; hopped with British and American hops; gravity 1.11 P, 9.4% abw, 80 IBU. [BW, 97]

Brewpubs in Cave Junction and Brookings Harbor, OR.

SNUG HARBOR OLD ALE — deep mahogany, big malt aroma, huge rich alcoholic malt flavor, straightforward malt, stays rich throughout, a long delicious sipping beer; warm-fermented; specific gravity 1.074, 6.7% abw. Latest specs (1994): specific gravity 1.070, 5.3% abw, 30 IBU. [A, 85]

Wild Wild West Gambling Hall & Brewery
Brewpub and casino in Cripple Creek, CO

WOMACK WHEAT — pale gold, light malt nose, light dry malty flavor, light body, finishes dry as well; made with 38% wheat malt; specific gravity 1.045, 3.6% abw. [W, 46]

FULL MOON LAGER — very pale gold, odd grainy nose and taste, medium body, lightly hopped malt finish and aftertaste; specific gravity 1.044, 3.6% abw. [B, 42]

CRIPPLE CREEK BEER — pale amber, odd grainy aroma, faint malt flavor, light to medium body, dry hop finish and aftertaste; specific gravity 1.050, 3.8% abw. [B, 34]

DONKEY BEER — deep gold, buttery malt aroma and flavor, dry

malt finish and aftertaste, medium body, medium length; specific gravity 1.068, 5.4% abw. [B, 32]

WEST FEST — amber; aroma is malt and faintly buttery; malt flavor lightly hopped with Cascade and Willamette hops; medium to good body, fairly long malt aftertaste; specific gravity 1.050, 3.5% abw. [B, 40]

MINE SHAFT STOUT — amber, dull malt nose, medium rich tasting roasted malt flavor, medium body, light dry malt finish; aftertaste has a slight bite from the roasted barley and hops; specific gravity 1.050, 3.4% abw. [S, 36]

Willamette Brewing Co.
Brewpub in Salem, OR

MARION BERRY ALE — amber, faint fruity-berry nose, berry and hop palate, fruit in front, hops in middle to end, dry hop finish, long dry hoppy aftertaste, only hops remaining at the end; made from two-row malted barley with mashed wheat, Mt. Hood and Willamette hops, with two parts marionberries to one part red raspberries; OG 1046, Fg 1.011, 3.8% abw. [A, 40]

Windham Brewery
Brewpub at Latchis Grille in Brattleboro, VT

MOONBEAM PALE ALE — golden amber, beautiful hop aroma, bright hop flavor, good malt back-ing, complex, good body, balanced, long medium dry hop aftertaste; made with Cascade and Chinook hops; OG 1125. [A, 60]

WHETSTONE GOLDEN LAGER — gold, honeyed malt and light hop aroma, smooth off-dry malt and hop palate, light body, low hops, medium dry long malt aftertaste; made with wheat malt and wildflower honey, mildly hopped with Cascades and Mt. Hood hops; OG 1175. [B, 57]

WINDHAM PORTER — brown, roasted barley and chocolate malt aroma, flavor like the nose, body on the light side, good long dry malt aftertaste; made with roasted barley, caramel and chocolate malts; lightly hopped with Cascades; OG 1150. This may also be named Old Guilford Porter. [P, 61]

WINDHAM MAIBOCK — amber, malt nose; dry malt flavor is complex; medium body, long dry malt aftertaste, very easy to drink. [BK, 62]

Woodstock Brewing and Bottling Co.
Brewery in Woodstock, IL

ARNOLD'S AMBER LAGER — light amber-gold, faint fruity malt nose; light malt flavor has some hops to balance; smooth and pleasant, crisp dry hop finish, light to medium body, medium long dry hop aftertaste; made with Cascade, Cluster, and Hallertau hops; gravity 12.2 P, 3.7% abw, 18 IBU. [B, 50]

Woodstock Brewing Co.
Microbrewery in Kingston, NY

HUDSON LAGER — deep gold, complex malt and hop aroma, dry hop flavor balanced very well with the supporting malt, good body, long medium dry hop aftertaste, a very smooth and drinkable beer; gravity 13 P, 4.22% abw. [B, 68]

BIG INDIAN PORTER — deep amber-brown, rich malt aroma; dry malt flavor is driest in mid-palate; tends toward sweeter malt at the finish; good body; dry malt flavor has a little hop bite for strength; long malty aftertaste is the sweetest part of the flavor; nicely done. [P, 86]

ST. JAMES ALE — gold, grainy malt nose, attractive dry malty flavor, light body, refreshing long dry malty aftertaste. [A, 47]

Wynkoop Brewing
Brewpub in Denver, CO

WILDERNESS WHEAT — pale gold, light malt nose, light fresh malt flavor, no spice; dry malt finish, sort of peters out right after the finish so there is little after-taste. [W, 47]

ELVIS BRAU — gold, faint hop nose, good hop flavor, malt finish, medium body, dry hop aftertaste, very long on the palate, a good brew; made with pale malts, Saaz hops, and ale yeast; gravity 12.5 P, 3.78% abw. [B, 63]

INDIA PALE ALE — pale amber, light hop nose, light fruity malt flavor, hop finish, medium dry hop aftertaste, a soft and smooth beer; aged in oak and dry hopped; gravity 13.5 P, 4.41% abw. [A, 47]

ST. CHARLES ESB — amber, hop nose and bitter hop flavor; some caramel comes in at the middle and mitigates the bitter-ness; caramel finish, fair to good balance, good body; after initial big hoppy character, the caramel balances it off and it becomes soft and smooth, unfortunately it is too much so and ends up rather bland; light dry hop aftertaste. [A, 45]

SAGEBRUSH STOUT — dark brown, roasted barley and choco-late malt nose and taste, light body, finishes medium dry malt; aftertaste is more dry and shows some hops. [S, 47]

MONTEZUMA CHILI BEER — gold, chili pepper nose; hot chili flavor especially gets you in the throat and wipes out everything else. [B, 35]

KYLE'S LIGHT BROWN ALE — amber-brown, faint malt aroma, very light hop and malt flavor, medium body, low carbon-ation, light dry hop aftertaste, sort of dull. [A, 43]

SPLATZ PORTER — dark brown; big malt nose followed by a big malt flavor with plenty of hops in back; good body, long dry malt aftertaste; gravity 14 P, 4.2% abw. (Splat was the infamous brewer's cat.) [P, 53]

IRISH CREAM STOUT — very dark brown, black malt nose, big malt flavor like the aroma, good body, long dry malt aftertaste; gravity 14 P, 4.2% abw. Also called Sagebrush Stout. [S, 47]

CHURCHYARD ALE — brown, big hop nose, sharp hop flavor; long dry hop aftertaste with some-thing faintly in back that may be lactic acid; gravity 16.25 P, 5.4% abw. [A, 46]

RAILYARD ALE — amber, light hop aroma; big flowery dry malt flavor is especially good up front; big body; finish is dry malt and there the hops appear; dry hop af-tertaste still shows the malt; made with English two-row pale, crystal caramalt, and Munich malts bal-anced with Hallertauer and Tettnanger hops; 4.2 abw. [A, 70]

LIL' RED RASPBERRY ALE — deep reddish amber, raspberry nose; raspberry and carbonation are the flavor; dry raspberry finish and long aftertaste of same. Fresh raspberries thrown into the fer-menter of a medium bodied ale; gravity 12 P, 3.5% abw. [A, 41]

PATTI'S CHILI BEER — gold, chili pepper nose, green chili pep-per taste, smooth enough but too much for the hops, very little malt shows through. [B, 39]

ALFALFA MEAD — pale gold, honeyed alfalfa nose; flavor is sweet and honeyed yet has a sharpness; finishes a bit drier but it is still sweet; long off-dry slightly grainy aftertaste; the alfalfa really shows. [M, 42]

Yakima Brewing & Malting Co.

Brewery and brewpub in Yakima, WA. First brewpub in U.S.A. in modern era.

GRANT'S IMPERIAL STOUT — deep brown color, toasted dry caramel malt aroma, big dry malt flavor with good hop backing, medium body, good balance, smooth, clean pleasant long dry finish and aftertaste; specific gravity 1.070, 5.8% abw, 70 IBU. [S, 69]

GRANT'S WEIS BEER — amber-gold, pleasant citrus-malt aroma, refreshing tangy palate like the nose, medium body, zesty; citrus tang balances the sweetness of the malt; likable and long. [W, 83]

GRANT'S INDIA PALE ALE — tawny-gold, complex citrus-ale aroma; big hop flavor well balanced with malt; malty sourness in middle, big body, long hop aftertaste; specific gravity 1.047, 3.9% abw, 55 IBU. [A, 67]

GRANT'S CELTIC ALE — very deep amber-rose, off-dry malt aroma and flavor, dry finish and aftertaste, delicate and brief. [LO, 43]

GRANT'S SPICED ALE — amber, spicy malt (pumpkin pie) aroma, strong pleasant spicy flavor, a wassail, light body; aftertaste is only the spice. [A, 49]

GRANT'S INDIA PALE ALE — tawny-gold, complex citrus-ale aroma; big hop flavor well balanced with malt; malty sourness in middle, big body, long hop aftertaste; specific gravity 1.047; 3.9% abw, 50 IBU. [A, 67]

GRANT'S SCOTTISH ALE — amber, mild malty-citrus aroma, big but well-mannered fruity malt and citrus-ale palate, very flavorful but smooth and balanced, long dry aftertaste; specific gravity 1.045, 3.6% abw, 40 IBU. [A, 73]

GRANT'S APPLE HONEY ALE — hazy gold; aroma is mostly honey with apple and malt far behind; palate is at first honey, then honeyed apple, and finally apple; faintly sweet but drying as it goes to the finish and into the aftertaste, where it is more or less dry, but brief; body is medium throughout. [A, 42]

GRANT'S PERFECT PORTER — very deep brown-black, brown head, dry rich roasted malt aroma, flavor like the nose with an added hint of smoke, medium body, medium intensity, smooth, bright, and refreshing, very long aftertaste; specific gravity 1.047, 3.9% abw, 30 IBU. [P, 62]

Notes

Yards Brewing Co.
Microbrewery in Philadelphia, PA

YARDS PORTER — deep brown, beautiful roasted malt aroma with some roasted barley and chocolate malt, very low carbonation, lovely tasty flavor like the aroma; could use more carbonation; dry malt finish, long dry roasted malt aftertaste; made from a blend of Yards Imperial Stout and Yards Mild Ale. [P, 72]

Ybor City Brewing Co.
Microbrewery in Tampa, FL

YBOR GOLD — pale gold, malt and hops both in the aroma; dry malt flavor has a good hop background but is basically a grainy malt taste; medium body, long dry malt and hop aftertaste, bright and refreshing. [B, 60]

GASPAR'S ALE — amber, lovely malt nose, big lusty malt flavor, good body, rich malty aftertaste; there is an off-dry malty component that comes out best in the aftertaste; a very pleasant English mild brown ale. [A, 71]

CALUSA WHEAT (WIT) — gold, big head, slightly fruity-phenolic aroma and flavor, complex, medium to big body; a little sweet showing some orange curaçao; very smooth, ends drier than it starts; made with Belgian witbier yeast, 40% malted wheat with orange curaçao added making for a very nice witbier style;

14 IBU. This is one of two recipes being considered for their summer wheat beer offering. The other is described below. [W, 66]

CALUSA WHEAT — pale gold, ample head, dry malty aroma; dry malty flavor has noticeable hop support; medium to light body; aftertaste is dry and quite well hopped; long dry and refreshing; made with 45% malted wheat, has substantially more hops on the palate than indicated by the bitterness rating (17 IBU); a good American-style wheat beer. [W, 60]

YBOR BROWN ALE — deep amber; pleasant light toasted malt aroma is toffee-like; soft roasted malt flavor is very tasty; long roasted malt aftertaste; made using kilned-dried crystal malt, a delicious appetizing English-style brown ale. [A, 76]

Yegua Creek Brewing Co.
Brewpub in Dallas, TX

BIG "D" ESB — deep gold, malt and hop aroma; big tasty flavor has plenty of malt and hops; fairly malty and lightly hopped (29 IBU) for an ESB; light to medium body; long aftertaste is a continuation of palate; specific gravity 1.050, 4% abw. [A, 67]

ICE HAUS PALE ALE — bright amber-gold; bright hop aroma shows Cascades; well-hopped (49 IBU) flavor, medium body, dry hop finish and long hoppy aftertaste; specific gravity 1.056, 4.6% abw. [A, 67]

O'BRIENS TEXAS STOUT — reddish-brown, light chocolate malt and roasted barley nose; big bright flavor like the nose is a classical stout style; medium body, very complex, good long complex malt aftertaste; made with roasted barley, black and chocolate malts and oats with Northern Brewer and Cascade hops; specific gravity 1.056, 4.3% abw, 46.6 IBU. [S, 68]

RED RIVER RED — red-amber, malty nose; big malty flavor stays dry and has good hop support; medium body, dry malt and hop finish and aftertaste; specific gravity 1.050, 4.3% abw, 36.5 IBU. [A, 61]

SARAS BROWN ALE — amber, light malt aroma and flavor, smooth, lightly hopped (22.2 IBU), light flavored, light to medium body; specific gravity 1.050, 5% abw. [A, 59]

TUCKERS GOLDEN WHEAT — gold; light bright fresh aroma is malty without spiciness; malt palate is also without spice even though this is an unfiltered wheat beer; light body, refreshing American style made with 30% wheat; lightly hopped (19.5 IBU); specific gravity 1.045, 3.5% abw. [W, 56]

YEGUA CREEK OKTOBERFEST — deep amber, malt aroma; slightly rich malt flavor is lightly hopped (28 IBU); good body, long malty aftertaste, aged ten months; specific gravity 1.060, 5% abw. [B, 70]

Yellow Rose Brewing Co.
Microbrewery in San Antonio, TX

YELLOW ROSE PALE ALE — deep gold; malty nose has a light hop backing; dry malt and hop flavor, medium body, dry hop finish and aftertaste, very long, pleasant. [A, 55]

BUBBA DOG WHEAT BEER — deep gold, beautiful northwest hop and light malt nose, refreshing dry hop and malt flavor, light to medium body, ends very dry; very long dry aftertaste has some hop bite; not at all like a conventional American wheat beer. [W, 64]

CACTUS QUEEN ALE — hazy amber-gold, perfumy malt and fruity hop nose, light dry malt and hop flavor, medium body, light dry medium long toasted malt and hop aftertaste. [A, 66]

HONCHO GRANDE BROWN ALE — amber-brown, toasted malt nose, dry toasted malt flavor, medium body; light dry roasted malt aftertaste is long. [A, 66]

VIGILANTE CREAMY DARK BEER — dark amber, fresh malt nose; fairly strong malt flavor shows some alcohol; fairly assertive, medium body; very long very malty aftertaste almost gets to be called sweet. [A, 69]

WILDCATTER'S CRUDE STOUT — dark brown, black patent and chocolate malt nose, big roasted malt flavor, stays smooth; stays dry although there is some sweetness lingering deep in the background; good body, light dry long malt aftertaste. [S, 79]

D.G. Yuengling & Son, Inc.
Brewery in Pottsville, PA

YUENGLING PREMIUM BEER — light gold, good malt aroma with subtle hop background, clean and bright hop flavor, fine malt finish and aftertaste. [B, 65]

YUENGLING'S PREMIUM LAGER — amber, balanced hop and malt aroma, medium body, smooth balanced hop and malt flavor, long fresh and clean aftertaste. [B, 65]

YUENGLING DARK BREW PORTER — deep red-brown; dry malt aroma has a richness; roasted malt flavor has a coffee-like background which you then notice in the aroma; good body; dry hops come in for the finish and fairly long aftertaste. [P, 47]

YUENGLING TRADITIONAL AMERICAN LAGER — amber color, complex malt aroma, good dry malt flavor; finish cuts off quickly. [B, 37]

YUENGLING PREMIUM LIGHT BEER — pale yellow-gold, bright malt and light hop aroma; flavor is carbonation and light malt; medium to light body, short light dry malt and hop finish and aftertaste. [LO, 27]

Notes

OLD GERMAN BRAND BEER — pale gold, malt nose and flavor, dry hop finish and aftertaste, medium length. [B, 47]

LORD CHESTERFIELD ALE — yellow-gold, good off-dry malt aroma, bright clean hop flavor, good body, good balance, lingering hop aftertaste. [A, 65]

BAVARIAN TYPE PREMIUM BEER — medium gold, off-dry malt aroma with some hops in back, hop flavor up front; malt comes in middle, but the finish and aftertaste are a forceful return of the bittering hops. [B, 28]

YUENGLING BLACK & TAN — dark brown, malt nose, dry malt flavor, very drinkable, fairly dry finish, lightly hopped, short dry malt aftertaste. [P, 49]

Zip City Brewing Co.
Brewpub in
New York City, NY

ZIP CITY CZECH STYLE PILSENER — hazy gold, aroma of hops and malt; big dry hop flavor well backed with malt; quite tasty and very well hopped; finishes like it starts; medium to long dry hop aftertaste; made with a double decoction mash process from two-row pale Briess malt and 100% Saaz hops; gravity 12.5 P, 4% abw, 40 IBU. [B, 72]

ZIP CITY HELLES — pale hazy gold, light malt aroma, light body, light malt flavor, some hops in back, light dry malt aftertaste. [B, 46]

ZIP CITY VIENNA AMBER — slightly hazy amber, rising hop aroma with a dry malt background, rich malt and hop flavor, good hop support; very long dry aftertaste shows both the malt and hops; good balance. [B, 74]

ZIP CITY DUNKEL — brown, fairly dry malt aroma and taste, very mild and smooth, soft dry malt finish and aftertaste; made from two-row pale, caramel-60, Carapils, and black Briess malts and Mt. Hood hops; gravity 13.5 P, 4.2% abw, 25 IBU. [B, 53]

ZIP CITY MÄRZEN — amber-gold; malt nose and flavor have a little lactic acid way in back; off-dry malt finish and aftertaste still have that faint acidity; made from two-row pale, Munich, caramel-60, and Carapils Briess malts and Mt. Hood hops; gravity 14.9 P, 4.8% abw, 22 IBU. [B, 36]

ZIP CITY OKTOBERFEST 1994 — hazy golden amber, light but rich malty aroma; rich malty flavor has a hop background; dry at finish, long dry malt aftertaste. [B, 64]

ZIP CITY OKTOBERFEST 1995 — hazy golden amber; light but rich malty aroma has a hop background; rich flavor has more hops than malt but plenty of supporting malt nonetheless; dry hop at finish, long dry hop and malt aftertaste. [B, 64]

ZIP CITY HEFE-WEIZEN — cloudy amber-gold, clean fresh lightly spiced nose, creamy texture, spicy clove-like flavor; fruity-sweet banana stays in back until the finish and then comes forward; dry spicy hop aftertaste has good fruity banana support; a nicely made hefe-weizen. [W, 66]

ZIP CITY MAIBOCK — hazy amber, mild malt aroma and flavor; hops are in back but do provide balance; dry malt finish and aftertaste; a light, smooth, pleasant tasting beer; very drinkable. [B, 61]

ZIP CITY BLOND DOPPELBOCK — hazy gold, fresh assertive malt nose with a sort of "meaty" character, big malt and light hop flavor, good body, smooth and balanced, complex and alcoholic; assertive malt character stays throughout becoming just a little sweet at the very end; long and good. [B, 77]

ZIP CITY ALT — hazy amber, malt aroma; malt flavor has a bitter middle but otherwise is complex with a caramel-coffee background; dry caramel-malt finish, long malty aftertaste. [A, 67]

ZIP CITY RAUCHBIER — amber, smoked malt nose, pleasant and appetizing; big smoked flavor (like smoked sausage) that is quite assertive up front; finishes a bit softer than it starts; long dry smoked malt aftertaste; brewed with beechwood smoked malt imported from Franconia in a double decoction Hallertau; specific gravity 1.052, 4.8% abw. [B, 60]

SOUTH AMERICA

Argentina

Cerveceria Bieckert, S.A.
Breweries in Buenos Aires, Rio Segundo, and Cochobamba

BIECKERT ETIQUETA AZUL PILSEN ESPECIAL CERVEZA BLANCA GENUINA — yellow-gold with a greenish cast; fruity-malt aroma that is almost winelike; heavy body, complex sour malt flavor with a touch of anise in back, long malt aftertaste, an interesting brew. [B, 41]

BIECKERT ESPECIAL LIVIANA — deep amber, toasted malt and prune aroma; scorched malt flavor that finishes a bit sour; long malt aftertaste, unusual brew, very interesting. [B, 36]

LEON de ORO CERVEZA GENUINA — deep gold, delicate malt and hop aroma, pleasant flavor like the nose only much bigger, lots of hops across the palate, good malt finish, complex, good body, long dry malt and hop aftertaste, a well-made, well-balanced, likable brew. [B, 64]

BIECKERT PREMIUM IMPORTED BEER — pale gold, sweet malt and cardboard nose, fruity malt flavor with a papery background, faint sweet malt aftertaste. [B, 75]

Notes

Cerveceria Cordoba, S.A.
Brewery in Cordoba

CORDOBA DORADA — brilliant pale gold, clean fruity malt nose, zesty hop and fruity malt palate with some melon and papaya; flattens out at the finish leading into a brief dull malt aftertaste. [B, 39]

Cerveceria Y Malteria Quilmes
Brewery in Buenos Aires

QUILMES EXPORT — very pale yellow; highly carbonated, so much so that it dominates the nose and taste; what isn't CO_2 is like fresh cut alfalfa, short dry aftertaste. [B, 29]

QUILMES IMPERIAL — pale yellow-gold, slightly papery malt nose, good body, pleasant light malt flavor, good balance; hops appear in the finish and stay through the long dry aftertaste. [B, 60]

Cerveceria Santa Fe, S.A.
Breweries in Santa Fe and Buenos Aires

SANTA FE PREMIUM LAGER BEER — tawny-gold; a touch of skunk started the nose, but this quickly yielded to green hay; the flavor was off-dry malt with a slightly oxidized finish; short dry malt aftertaste with tones of the oxidation. [B, 29]

Bolivia

Cerveceria Boliviana Nacional, S.A.
Brewery in La Paz

PACENA CENTENARIO BEER — slightly hazy gold; fruity malt nose, malt palate has a sour middle, sour-bitter finish, and a long dry hop aftertaste. [B, 29]

Cerveceria Taquiña, S.A.
Brewery in Cochabamba and Santa Cruz

TAQUINA EXPORT CERVEZA — pale yellow, pleasant off-dry malt aroma with good hop balance; flavor is pleasant off-dry malt up front; finish is slightly sour malt and hops, dry aftertaste similar to the flavor, very good when fresh. [B, 48]

Brazil

Companhia Antarctica Paulista, S.A.
Brewery in Sao Paulo

ANTARCTICA BRAZILIAN BEER — gold, faint sour malt nose, high carbonation; sour hop flavor has a papery finish; long dry hop aftertaste. [B, 31]

Companhia Cervejaria Brahma
Breweries in Rio de Janeiro, Sao Paulo, Porto Alegro, etc.

BRAHMA CHOPP EXPORT BEER — yellow-gold with a green cast, vanilla malt cookie dough nose and taste, sour malt finish, dry malt aftertaste with little length. [B, 30]

BRAHMA BRAZILIAN PILSENER BEER — gold, fruity malt nose; malt flavor has some roasted malt backing that appears a little bit stronger in the finish and aftertaste; medium dry malt flavor throughout. [B, 16]

BRAHMA BEER — medium gold, pleasant malt and hop aroma, medium body; pleasant hop flavor has decent off-dry malt backing and a little apple is in there too; long dry hop aftertaste. [B, 34]

Cervejaria Cacador, S.A.
Brewery in Cacador

XINGU BLACK BEER — opaque brown; dry malt aroma is faintly coffee-like; clean off-sweet roasted malt palate, a trifle less sweet would be better, but not bad; long medium dry malt aftertaste, very drinkable. [B, 50]

Cervejaria Mogiana, Ltda.
Brewery in Mogi Mirim

INGLESINHA STOUT — opaque brown; foam is deep brown; very faint roasted malt nose, very sweet roasted malt flavor, soapy treacle finish and aftertaste; very sweet and lacks balance. [S, 26]

Cervejaria Paraense, S.A.
Breweries in Belem and Cerpasa

TIJUCA EXTRA PREMIUM BEER — brilliant gold, faint malt nose, good body; malt flavor has some licorice and fruit; dry malt finish, brief dry malt aftertaste; flavor is good but ephemeral. [B, 26]

Cervejarias Reunidas Skol Caracu, S.A.
Breweries in Rio Clara, Nova Lima, Guarulhos, Bonsucesso, etc.

SKOL LAGER BEER — yellow-gold, faintly sweet malt nose, clean grainy malt flavor, austere finish and very little aftertaste. [B, 38]

CARACU CERVEJA FORTE STOUT — opaque brown, roasted malt nose, low carbonation, sweet palate with roasted/smoky malt, big body, almost too sweet, long clean off-dry malt aftertaste. [B, 37]

Chile

Cerveceria y Embotteladora Austral S.A.
Brewery in Punta Arenas

IMPERIAL POLAR BEER — gold, fruity malt nose, big dry malt flavor, bitter hop finish and long hop aftertaste; at the end it is very bitter and slightly sour. [B, 30]

AUSTRAL POLAR BEER — hazy gold, hop nose, big bitter hop flavor, thin body, very dry bitter hop finish, long bitter and dry hop aftertaste. [B, 24]

Compañia Cervecerias Unidas, S.A.
Brewery in Santiago

ESCUDO CHILEAN PILSENER — pale gold, fairly decent malt and hop nose, flavor like the nose except for a sour component, long very dry hop aftertaste. [B, 47]

CRISTAL PILSENER — gold, off-dry malt nose; palate is malt up front, hops in the middle; has a dry hop finish and a long dry hop aftertaste; good balance through-out. [B, 52]

ANDES CHILEAN PILSENER — gold, faintly skunky nose at first, thence good hops; flavor has a touch of barley at first, then hops; malt returns in the aftertaste, pretty good except for that skunk. [B, 47]

Colombia

Cerveceria Aguila, S.A.
Brewery in Barranquilla

CERVEZA AGUILA — gold, hop and malt aroma, flavor just like the nose, dry finish, and dry hop aftertaste. [B, 33]

Bavaria, S.A.
Breweries in Bogota and Santa Marta

CLUB COLOMBIA PILSENER-TYPE BEER — pale yellow-gold with a greenish cast, malty pine-apple aroma; malt flavor is sweet in front, dries to middle and finishes bitter hops; dry very bitter hop aftertaste, balance is off. [B, 35]

CERVEZA CLAUSEN EXPORT — medium yellow-gold, interesting appetizing hop aroma, big hop flavor; good balance up to the finish which gets too bitter; long dry and bitter hop aftertaste. [B, 44]

COLUMBIAN GOLD BEER — gold, malt nose, sour malt palate with a slightly sweeter finish, very little aftertaste. [B, 24]

Ecuador

Cerveceria Club, S.A.
Brewery in Quito

CERVEZA CLUB PREMIUM — pale tawny-gold, mushroom nose; palate is hops first, then sweet malt in the middle, and sour hops at the finish and aftertaste; poorly balanced. [B, 10]

Guyana

Banks DIH, Ltd.
Brewery in Georgetown

BANKS BEER — bright gold, fruity malt nose with a touch of oxidation; faint fruity malt flavor has a butterscotch background; weak body, very brief dry malt aftertaste. [B, 30]

Peru

Cerveceria Backus y Johnston, S.A.
Brewery in Lima

CRISTAL — pale gold, faint malt nose and flavor, clean, but weak and short. [B, 16]

CERVEZA MALTINA — deep brown, sweet smoky malt nose, sweet slightly smoked malt flavor, big long dry malt aftertaste. [M, 33]

Compañia Nacional de Cerveza, S.A.
Brewery in Callao

CALLAO PERUVIAN PILSEN BEER — pale yellow-gold, off-dry malt nose, good tasting hop flavor, well-balanced; has complexity and zest; very drinkable, long dry hop aftertaste. [B, 62]

CALLAO EXPORT DARK BEER — opaque brown, faint burnt toast and caramel nose, unusual chocolate-smoky-BBQ sauce flavor, heavy body, neither dry nor sweet, sort of in-between, complex and interesting, long dry malt aftertaste; flavors are sort of compartmentalized and don't come together; needs food to be at its best. [B, 38]

DURANGO IMPORTED BEER — pale yellow, slightly skunky hop nose, hop flavor, dry and sour hop aftertaste with considerable length. [B, 30]

Companhia Cerveceria del sur del Peru, S.A.
Brewery in Cuzco

CUZCO PREMIUM PERUVIAN BEER — brilliant gold, clean malt aroma, highly carbonated, bright zesty flavor, light body, clean and refreshing, long dry hop aftertaste. [B, 43]

Uruguay

Fabricas Nacionales de Cerveza, S.A.
Brewery in Montevideo

DOBLE URUGUAYA — bright pale amber, off-dry fruity malt nose with an estery background, smoked malt flavor with a sour backing, bitter hops with the malt in the finish, and a long dull smoky faintly chemical aftertaste. [B, 20]

PILSEN — hazy gold, malt aroma, watery body, faint fruity malt and butterscotch flavor and aftertaste, not likable. [B, 10]

Venezuela

Cerveceria Nacional
Brewery in Caracas

CERVEZA ANDES — pale gold, nice malt and hop nose, crisp malt flavor, dry and refreshing; touch of sour malt in the aftertaste does little to mar a nice effect. [B, 54]

CARDENAL TIPO MUNICH — medium pale gold; faint sour citrus nose, light off-dry malt flavor with that same citrus component, more noticeable in the finish and long aftertaste, but the beer remains quite drinkable despite the flaw. [B, 29]

Cerveceria Polar, S.A.
Brewery in Caracas

POLAR CERVEZA TIPO PILSEN — gold, light malt nose, smooth, well-balanced good flavor of hops and malt, long dry hop aftertaste. Domestic version. [B, 53]

POLAR BEER — gold, fresh malt nose, well-balanced hop and malt flavor, very tasty, long dry hop aftertaste. Export version. [B, 51]

POLAR DARK BEER — deep ruby-brown, faint sweet malt nose and flavor, long off-dry malt aftertaste, very malty much like a malta. [B, 49]

Notes

Appendix

U.S. Breweries Listed by State

Alaska
Alaskan Brewing & Bottling Co.
Bird Creek Brewery

Alabama
Birmingham Brewing Co.
Port City Brewery

Arizona
Bandersnatch Brewing Co.
Beaver Street Brewery & Whistle Stop Cafe
Black Mountain Brewing Co.
Coyote Springs Brewing Co. and Cafe
Gentle Ben's Brewing Co.
Hops! Bistro and Brewery
Prescott Brewing Co.
San Francisco Bar & Grill

Arkansas
Vino's Brewing Co.
Weidmans Brew Pub

California
20 Tank Brewery
American River Brewing Co.

Anchor Brewing Co.
Anderson Valley Brewing Co.
Anheuser-Busch, Inc.
Anheuser-Busch, Inc.
Belmont Brewing Co.
Bison Brewery
Blind Pig Brewing Co.
Bluewater Brewing Co.
Bootlegger's Brewing Co.
Brewmeisters Brewpub and Grill
Brewski's Gaslamp Pub, Inc. / San Diego's Riptide Brewery
Buffalo Bill's Brewpub
Butterfield Brewing Co.
Callahan's Pub & Brewery
Crown City Brewery
Dempsey's Sonoma Brewing Co.
Devil Mountain-Bay Brewing Co.
El Dorado Brewing Co.
El Toro Brewing Co.
Etna Brewing Co.
Fremont Brewing Co.
Fullerton Hofbrau / Whaler's Brew
Golden Pacific Brewing Co.
Gordon Biersch Brewing Co.
Harbor Lights
Heritage Brewing Co.
Hops! Bistro and Brewery

Humboldt Brewery
Humes Brewing Co.
Huntington Beach Beer Co.
J & L Brewing Co.
Joe & Joe's Brewing Co.
Karl Strauss' Old Columbia Brewery & Grill
Laguna Beach Brewing Co.
La Jolla Brewing Company
Lind Brewing Co.
Los Gatos Brewing Co.
Lost Coast Brewery & Cafe
Mad River Brewing Co.
Manhattan Beach Brewing Co.
Marin Brewing Co.
Mendocino Brewing Co.
Miller Brewing Co.
Murphy's Creek Brewing Co.
Napa Valley Ale Works
Napa Valley Brewing Co.
Nevada City Brewing Co.
Newport Beach Brewing Co.
North Coast Brewing Co.
Ocean Avenue Brewery
Old Baldy Brewing Co.
Orange County Brewery / McCormick & Schmick's Pilsner Room
Pacific Beach Brewhouse
Pacific Coast Brewing Co.

Pacific Hop Exchange
   Brewing Co.
Pacific Tap & Grill
Paso Robles Brewing Co.
Pete's Brewing Co.
Redondo Beach
   Brewing Co.
Rio Bravo Brew Pub
River City Brewing Co.
Riverside Brewing Co.
Rubicon Brewing Co.
San Andreas Brewing Co.
San Diego Brewing Co.
San Francisco
   Brewing Co.
San Marcos
   Brewery & Grill
Santa Clarita Brewing Co.
Santa Cruz Brewing Co.
Santa Rosa Brewing Co.
Seabright Brewery
Shield's Brewing Co.
Sierra Nevada
   Brewing Co.
SLO Brewing Co.
Solana Beach Brewery /
   Pizza Port
Southern California Brewery
St. Stan's Brewing Co.
Steelhead
   Brewery and Cafe
Stoddard's
   Brewhouse & Eatery
Stroh Brewing Co.
Sudwerk Privatbrauerei
   Hubsch
Sunset Beach Brewery &
   Fish House
T. Roy Brewing Co.
The Hangtown Brewery

Tied House Cafe &
   Brewery / Redwood Coast
   Brewing
Triple Rock
   Brewery & Alehouse
Truckee Brewing Co.

Colorado
Adolph Coors Co.
Anheuser-Busch, Inc.
Avery Brewing Co.
Big Nose Brewing Co.
Boulder Creek Brewing Co.
Breckenridge Brewery
Brewed and Baked in
   Telluride
Carver's Bakery Cafe
   Brewery
Champion Brewing Co.
CooperSmith's Pub &
   Brewing
Crested Butte Brewery &
   Pub, Idlespur, Inc.
Durango Brewing Co.
Flying Dog Brew Pub
Golden City Brewery
Great Divide Brewing Co.
H.C. Berger Brewing Co.
Heavenly Daze
   Brewery & Grill
High Country B.C.
Hubcap Brewery & Kitchen
Irons Brewing Co.
Judge Baldwin's Brewing
   Co. / Kelly Brewing
Left Hand Brewing Co.
Lone Tree Brewing Co.
Mountain Sun Pub &
   Brewery
New Belgium Brewing Co.

O'Dell Brewing Co.
Oasis Brewery
Phantom Canyon
   Brewing Co.
Pikes Peak Brewery
Rock Bottom Brewery
Rockies Brewing Co.
San Juan Brewing Co.
Silver Plume Brewing Co.
Steamboat Brewery and
   Tavern
Tabernash Brewing Co.
The Broadway Brewing Co.
The Walnut Brewery
Wild Wild West Gambling
   Hall & Brewery
Wynkoop Brewing

Connecticut
New England Brewing Co.
New Haven Brewing Co.
The Hartford Brewery Ltd.

Delaware
Rockford Brewing Co.
Stewart's B.C.

District of
Columbia
Capitol City Brewing Co.

Florida
A1A Ale Works
Anheuser-Busch, Inc.
Beach Brewing Co.
Brooker Creek Grille &
   Taproom
Buckhead Brewery

Hops Grill & Bar (several
locations)
Irish Times Pub & Brewery
Kidder's Brewery & Eatery
Market Street Pub &
Brewery / Sunshine
Brewing Inc.
McGuires Irish Pub &
Brewery
Miami Brewing Co.
Ragtime Tavern & Grill
River City Brewing Co. (in 2
locations)
Santa Rosa Bay Brewery &
Waterfront Cafe
Sarasota Brewing Co.
Stroh Brewing Co.
The Florida Brewery, Inc.
The Mill / Whiskey Creek
Brewing
Ybor City Brewing Co.

Georgia

Marthasville Brewing Co.
Miller Brewing Co.
Stone Mountain Brewers

Hawaii

Kona Brewing Co.

Iowa

Dallas County Brewing Co.
Dubuque Brewing &
Bottling Co.
Millstream B.C.

Idaho

Coeur D'Alene Brewing Co.
M.J. Barleyhoppers, Brewery
and Public House
Sun Valley Brewing Co.

Illinois

Berghoff Brewery &
Restaurant
Chicago Brewing Co.
Golden Prairie Brewing Co.
Goose Island Brewing Co. /
Lincoln Park Brewery,
Inc.
J.D. Nick's Restaurant &
Brewery / O'Fallon B.C.
O'Fallon Brewing Co.
Pavichevich Brewing Co.
Star Union Brewing Co.
Weinkeller Brewery
Woodstock Brewing and
Bottling Co.

Indiana

Broad Ripple Brewing Co.
Evansville Brewing Co.
Indianapolis Brewing Co.
Lafayette Brewing Co.
Mishawaka Brewing Co.
Oaken Barrel Brewing Co.
S & P Co.

Kansas

Free State Brewing Co.
Miracle Brewing Co.
River City Brewing Co.
Kentucky
Bluegrass Brewing Co.

Oldenberg Brewing Co.
Silo Brew Pub &
Microbrewery

Louisiana

Abita Brewing Co.
Crescent City Brewhouse
Dixie Brewing Co.
Rikenjaks Brewing Co.

Maine

Allagash Brewing Co.
Andrew's Brewing Co.
Atlantic Brewing Co.
Bar Harbor Brewing Co.
Casco Bay Brewing Co.
D.L. Geary Brewing Co.
Great Falls Brewing Co. / No
Tomatoes
Gritty McDuff's Brew Pub
Kennebunkport B.C.
Lake St. George Brewing
Co.
Maine Coast Brewing Co.
Sea Dog Brewing Co.
Sheepscot Valley
Brewing Co.
Sugarloaf Brewing Co. /
Theo's Pub
Sunday River B.C.
Sweet Waters of Acadia
Brewing Co.

Maryland

Baltimore Brewing Co.
Frederick Brewing Co.
G. Heileman Brewing Co.
Oliver Breweries, Ltd.
Oxford Brewing Co.

Sisson's South Baltimore
   Brewing Co.
Wild Goose Brewery

Massachusetts
Atlantic Coast Brewing, Ltd.
Berkshire Brewing Co.
Boston Beer Co.
Boston Beer Works
Brew Moon
Cambridge Brewing Co.
Commonwealth Brewing Co.
Ipswich Brewing Co.
John Harvard's Brew House
Lowell Brewing Co.
Massachusetts Bay
   Brewing Co.
Middlesex B.C.
Northampton Brewery
Old Harbor Brewing Co.
Olde Salem Village
   Brewing Co.
Ould Newbury Brewing Co.
The Brewery at 34 Depot St.
Wachusett Brewing Co.

Michigan
Detroit & Mackinac Brewery
Frankenmuth Brewery, Inc.
Kalamazoo Brewing Co.
Stroh Brewing Co.
Traffic Jam & Snug
   Restaurant

Minnesota
Cold Spring Brewing Co.
August Schell Brewing Co.
James Page Brewing Co.
Minnesota Brewing Co.

Stroh Brewing Co.
Summit Brewing Co.

Missouri
75th Street Brewery
Anheuser-Busch, Inc.
Boulevard Brewing Co.
Flat Branch Pub & Brewing
Signature Beer Co.

Montana
Bayern Brewing Co.
Bridger Brewing Co.
Milestown Brewing Co.
Montana Beverages, Ltd. /
   Kessler B.C.
Spanish Peaks
   Brewing Co., Ltd.
Whitefish Brewing Co.

Nebraska
Crane River Brew Pub
   and Cafe
Jaipur Restaurant &
   Brewpub
Jones Street Brewery
Sharky's Brewery & Grill

Nevada
Great Basin Brewing Co.
HOLY COW! Casino, Cafe
   and Brewery

New Hampshire
Anheuser-Busch, Inc.
Martha's Exchange
   Restaurant & Brewing
Portsmouth Brewery

Smuttynose Brewing Co.
Stark Mill Brewery
The Seven Barrel Brewery

New Jersey
Anheuser-Busch, Inc.
Hoboken Brewing Co.
Long Valley Pub & Brewery
The Ship Inn
Triumph Brewing Co.

New Mexico
Assets Grille and
   Brewing Co.
Eske's: A Brew Pub / Sangre
   de Cristo Brewery
O'Ryan's Tavern and
   Brewery
Old West Brewery
Rio Bravo Brew Pub
Santa Fe Brewing Co.
The Russell Brewing Co.

New York
Buffalo Brewing Co.
Buffalo Brewpub
Clement's Brewing Co.
F.X. Matt Brewing Co.
Genesee Brewing Co.
James Bay Restaurant &
   Brewery
Long Island Brewing Co.
Manhattan Brewing Co.
Miller Brewing Co.
Mountain Valley
   Brewing Co.
Neptune Brewery
Rohrbach Brewing Co.
Westside Brewing Co.

Woodstock Brewing Co.
Zip City Brewing Co.

North Carolina
Dilworth Brewing Co.
Miller Brewing Co.
Smoky Mountain Brewery
Stroh Brewing Co.
Weeping Radish Restaurant
  & Brewery

Ohio
Anheuser-Busch, Inc.
Barley's Brewing Co.
Burkhardt Brewing Co.
Columbus Brewing Co.
Crooked River Brewing Co.
Gambrinus Brewing Co.
Great Lakes Brewing Co.
Hoster Brewing Co.
Hudepohl-Schoenling
  Brewing Co.
Lift Bridge Brewing Co.
Melbourne Brewing Co.
Miller Brewing Co.

Oklahoma
Bricktown Brewery
Cherry Street Brewery
Norman Brewing Co.
Tulsa Brewing Co.

Oregon
Bend Brewing Co.
Brandon Brewing Co.
Bridgeport Brewing Co.
Cascade Lakes Brewing Co.
Deschutes Brewery &
  Public House

Edgefield Brewery
  (McMenamins)
Eugene City Brewery
Fields Restaurant &
  Brewpub
Full Sail Brewing Co. / Hood
  River Brewing Co. /
  McCormick & Schmick
  Restaurant
G. Heileman Brewing Co.
Golden Valley Brewpub
Hair of the Dog Brewing Co.
Liberty Brewing Co. / Saxer
  Brewing Co.
Lucky Labrador
  Brewing Co.
Mt. Hood Brewing Co.
Multnomah Brewing Co.
Nor'wester Brewery &
  Public House / Willamette
  Valley B.C.
Oregon Brewing Co. /
  Rogue Ales
Oregon Trader Brewing Co.
Oregon Trail Brewery
Portland Brewing Co.
Rock Bottom Brewery
Rogue River Brewing
  Company
Star Brewing Co.
Steelhead Brewery and Cafe
The Old Market Pub &
  Brewery
Tugboat Brewing Co.
Umpqua Brewing Co.
Widmer Brewing Co.
Wild River Brewing Co.
Willamette Brewing Co.

Pennsylvania
Arrowhead Brewing Co.
D.G. Yuengling & Son, Inc.
Dock Street Brewing Co.
Erie Brewing Co.
Independence Brewing Co.
Jones Brewing Co.
Lancaster Malt Brewing Co.
Latrobe Brewing Co.
Pennsylvania Brewing Co. /
  Allegheny Brewery & Pub
Pittsburgh Brewing Co.
Samuel Adams Brewhouse /
  Philadelphia Brewing Co.
Stoudt Brewing Co.
Straub Brewery, Inc.
Stroh Brewing Co.
The Lion, Inc.
White Tail Brewing Co.
Yards Brewing Co.

Rhode Island
Trinity Brewhouse
Union Station Brewery

South Dakota
Firehouse Brewing Co.

Tennessee
Adolph Coors Co.
Bohannon Brewing Co.
Boscos Pizza Kitchen &
  Brewery
Stroh Brewing Co.

Texas
Anheuser-Busch, Inc.
Boar's Head Pub & Grille

Brazos Brewing Co.
Brewpub / Café on the
　Square
Celis Brewery
Copper Tank Brewing Co.
Fredericksburg Brewing Co.
Frio Brewing Co.
G. Heileman Brewing Co.
Hill Country
　Brewing & Bottling
Houston Brewery
Hubcap Brewery & Kitchen
Miller Brewing Co.
Rock Bottom Brewery
S & P Co.
Saint Arnold Brewing Co.
Spoetzl Brewing Co.
Stroh Brewing Co.
Texas Brewing Co.
The Bitter End Bistro &
　Brewery
Village Brewery
Waterloo Brewing Co.
Yegua Creek Brewing Co.
Yellow Rose Brewing Co.

Utah

Eddie McStiff's
Salt Lake Brewing Co. /
　Squatter's Pub Brewery
Schirf Brewing Co. /
　Wasatch Brewery
Squatters Pub & Brewery

Vermont

Catamount Brewing Co.
McNeill's Brewery

Mountain Brewers, Inc.
Otter Creek Brewing Co.
The Shed Restaurant &
　Brewery Pub
The Vermont Pub & Brewery
Windham Brewery

Virginia

Anheuser-Busch, Inc.
Bardo Rodeo
Blue Ridge Brewing Co.
Legend Brewing Co.
Old Dominion Brewing Co.
Patomac River Brewing Co.
Richbrau Brewery &
　Queen's Arms Pub

Washington

Big Time Brewing Co.
Birkebeiner Brewing Co.
Fish Brewing Co.
G. Heileman Brewing Co.
Hale's Ales
Hart Brewing Co.
Hazel Dell Brewpub
Kemper Brewing Co.
Leavenworth Brewery
Maritime Pacific
　Brewing Co.
Onalaska Brewing Co.
Pike Place Brewery
Red Hook Ale Brewery, Inc.
S & P Co.
San Juan Brewing Co. /
　Front Street Ale House
Spenard Brewing Co.

West Seattle Brewing Co.
Yakima Brewing &
　Malting Co.

West Virginia

Cardinal Brewing Co.

Wisconsin

Appleton Brewing Co. /
　Adler Brau
Brewmasters Pub Restaurant
　& Brewery
Capital Brewing Co.
Cherryland Brewery
G. Heileman Brewing Co.
Gray Brewing Co.
Huber-Berghoff Brewing Co.
Jacob Leinenkugel
　Brewing Co.
Lakefront Brewery, Inc.
Miller Brewing Co.
New Glarus Brewing Co.
S & P Co.
Sprecher Brewing Co.
Stevens Point Beverage Co.
Water Street Brewery

Wyoming

Otto Brothers' Brewing Co.
Snake River Brewing Co. /
　Jackson Hole Pub &
　Brewery

Beer Index

(see also p. 592 Brewery Index)

O

Brewery Index